THE NEW
UNGER'S
BIBLE
HANDBOOK

MOODY
PUBLISHERS

THE NAME YOU CAN TRUST®

Revised and Updated edition:
© 1966, 1984, 1998, 2005 The Moody Bible Institute
of Chicago.

Except where noted otherwise, all Scripture
quotations in this book are from the Holy Bible: *New
International Version*, © 1973, 1978 by the
International Bible Society. Used by permission of
Zondervan Bible Publishers.

Library of Congress Cataloging in Publication Data

Unger, Merrill Frederick,
    The new Unger's Bible handbook.

    Rev. ed. of: Unger's Bible handbook. [1st ed.].
    1966
    Includes index
    1. Bibles—Handbooks, manuals, etc. I. Larson, Gary N. II. Unger, Merrill
Frederick, Bible handbook. III. Title.
BS417.U5 1984 220.7 84-1032
ISBN 0-8024

Designed and produced for Moody Press by
Three's Company and Lion Hudson plc

Cover design: Paetzold Associates
Photo: Getty Images

Worldwide co-edition produced by Lion Hudson plc,
Wilkinson House,
Jordan Hill Road,
Oxford OX2 8DR, England.
Telephone: +44 (0) 1865 302750.
Fax: +44 (0) 1865 302757.
Email: coed@lionhudson.com. www.lionhudson.com

Printed in Singapore
2 3 4 5 6 / 15 14 13 12 11 10

Since 1894, Moody Publishers has been dedicated to
equip and motivate people to advance the cause of
Christ by publishing evangelical Christian literature
and other media for all ages around the world.
Because we are a ministry of the Moody Bible
Institute of Chicago, a portion of the proceeds from
the sale of this book go to train the next generation
of Christian leaders.

If we may serve you in any way in your spiritual
journey toward understanding Christ and the
Christian life, please contact us at
www.moodypublishers.com.

Picture Acknowledgments
Photographs
Bible Scene: p. 561
Karen Demuth: pp. 70, 72
Tim Dowley: pp. 12, 13, 26, 30, 31, 32, 33, 57 bottom,
60, 81, 91/2, 92, 99, 117, 125, 136, 146, 147, 149, 155,
158, 159, 164, 166, 170, 172, 173, 176, 181, 188, 205,
221, 222, 228, 229, 230, 233, 235, 240, 243, 245, 248,
257, 261, 262, 265, 267, 269, 275, 284, 291, 296, 297,
298, 307, 320, 321, 327, 333, 335, 336, 339, 344, 348,
355, 356, 358, 368, 371, 374, 380, 381, 387, 389, 390,
392, 401, 402, 405 bottom, 407, 408, 411, 412, 413,
414, 427 bottom, 429, 431, 433, 439, 444, 447, 451,
454, 459 bottom, 464, 468, 473, 479, 482, 484, 485,
488, 492, 493, 498, 505, 513, 525, 529, 538, 544, 545,
546, 551, 563, 575, 585, 593, 599, 609, 615, 621, 629,
637, 643, 653, 655, 659, 673, 679, 685, 687, 693, 714,
716, 721
Hanan Isaachar: pp. 105, 107
Zev Radovan: p. 109
Jamie Simson: pp. 23, 36, 40, 47, 62, 215, 263, 305, 503,
517, 565, 567, 573
Peter Wyart: pp. 1, 27, 57 top, 63, 71, 73, 103, 111,
114, 128, 132, 144, 150, 162, 169, 185, 186, 191, 199,
200, 202, 204, 224, 227, 239, 241, 249, 250, 256, 277,
279, 281, 294, 299, 322, 324, 325, 327, 337, 342, 346,
353, 359, 373, 386, 391, 393, 395, 399, 405 top, 406,
415, 418, 423, 427 top, 428, 435, 443, 445, 446, 448,
452, 459 top, 463, 471, 480, 486, 490, 491, 500, 502,
504, 515, 516, 518, 521, 527, 531, 549, 571, 576, 579,
581, 611, 624, 525, 633, 651, 657, 669, 671, 675, 710

Illustrations
Frank Baber: pp. 93, 121
Brian Bartles: pp. 206/7, 416/17, 474/75
Peter Dennis: pp. 10, 14, 39, 369, 589, 691, 697, 698,
700, 717
Jeremy Gower: pp. 74/5, 456/57, 497
Alan Harris: p. 76
Mike Lacey: pp. 430/31
James Macdonald: pp. 55, 184, 208, 315, 332, 340, 353,
365, 366, 473
Alan Parry: pp. 285, 583, 617
Richard Scott: pp. 78, 100, 220, 244, 251, 301, 501,
578, 596, 619, 664, 695

Charts
Peter Wyart

Maps
Hardlines

Foreword

As a lover of the sacred Scriptures from childhood, I have always realized what a tremendous treasure the Word of God is and what an indescribable blessing to all who study and receive its great soul-transforming truths into heart and life. Thus, a keen desire has been aroused to stimulate others to read God's Word and to share in the vast benefits of Bible study.

To accomplish this purpose, for years I have had in mind a simple and concise Bible handbook that could appeal to all classes of people – the layman as well as the clergyman, the young convert as well as the seasoned saint, the non-Christian as well as the Christian believer.

The plan called for full array of the latest scientific information about the Bible, such as geography, chronology, history, archaeology and biblical criticism. Although this information is an important aspect of this book, and extremely essential in a day of vast strides in technical studies, yet this is not the principal feature. The chief emphasis is the message of the Bible itself. To achieve this feature a complete commentary on the entire sixty-six books is presented. Each verse is related to its chapter, each chapter to the book, each book to the entire Bible. Careful interpretation is striven for from the original Hebrew and Greek and related to the overall message and purpose of divine revelation.

An attempt is made to face difficulties. The aim is to place in the hands of the Bible student a ready reference tool in which he may at a glance relate chapter and verse to the immediate as well as the overall context in which they occur, and thus obtain light on the accurate interpretation of any passage that may be desired.

Acknowledgment is made to innumerable sources from which I have drawn – commentaries, learned journals, histories, Bible geographies, dictionaries, handbooks, travel in Bible lands, and personal study. But above all I have striven to be guided by the Holy Spirit in expounding the written Word and in exalting Christ the living Word.

It is my prayer that *Unger's Bible Handbook* will kindle love in the hearts of many for the precious oracles of God, revealing that 'they are more precious than gold, than much pure gold; they are sweeter than honey, than honey from the comb' (Ps 19:10).

Merrill F. Unger

Reviser's Preface

The grass withers, the flowers fall, But the word of our God stands forever.
Isa. 40:8

The truth of God's unchangeable Word becomes increasingly evident when attempts are made to revise the work of previous generations of devout Christian scholars. While theological opinions change, while archaeology and other sciences shed new light on the meaning and veracity of Scripture and human reasoning grasps at complex interpretive questions, the matchless truth of God's Word does indeed stand. This revision has as its goal to spotlight the eternal truth of God's revelation while endeavoring to update and make more accessible the cultural, historical, and theological insights that illuminate the text.

The task of revision is always a difficult one. That is particularly true when one attempts to revise or edit the work of someone who is as well-known and literate as the late Dr. Unger. This revision humbly attempts to do four things. First, recent discoveries in archaeology and advances in historical research that improve our understanding of the biblical text are noted, particularly in the Old Testament where great advances have been made. Second, the revision includes and critiques a broader range of interpretive positions on difficult texts. Sincere effort has been made to retain the theological distinctives of the book, while representing the broad scope of conservative evangelical scholarship. In most cases, the positions forwarded are those of Dr. Unger, without allowing the biases of the reviser to be interposed. Third, the revision adopts the *New International Version* as its working text. Unless otherwise noted, all quotations and allusions are from NIV. References marked '(Gr.)' or '(Heb.)' are translations by Dr. Unger himself, though they have been checked for accuracy. Finally, the language style of the first edition has been updated and made more accessible to the reader.

While we can have complete confidence in the Word of God, we are to be cautioned when we evaluate the works of men. No claim of infallibility is made for this handbook. God is to be praised for His infallible Word, which serves as the motivation for this work. As sinful men, we must take responsibility for its failings. Above all, we must all rely on the Holy Spirit to illuminate the text of God's Word so that it will be 'the power of God for the salvation of everyone who believes' (Rom 1:16).

Sola Fidei, Sola scriptura,
Gary N. Larson

Contents

Introduction 8

The Bible and archaeology 23

Old Testament

Genesis 36

Exodus 73

Leviticus 89

Numbers 99

Deuteronomy 114

Joshua 125

Judges 136

Ruth 146

1 Samuel 149

2 Samuel 162

1 Kings 172

2 Kings 184

1 Chronicles 200

2 Chronicles 204

Ezra 217

Nehemiah 221

Esther 224

Job 228

Psalms 232

Proverbs 244

Ecclesiastes 248

Song of Solomon 251

The Prophets 253

Isaiah 255

Jeremiah 281

Lamentations 294

Ezekiel 296

Daniel 309

The Minor Prophets 318

Hosea 320

Joel 324

Amos 327

Obadiah 332

Jonah 334

Micah 337

Nahum 340

Habakkuk 342

Zephaniah 344

Haggai 346

Zechariah 348

Malachi 358

Between the Testaments 364

New Testament

The Four Gospels 374

Matthew 380

Mark 401

Luke 420

John 444

Acts 464

The Epistles of Paul 501

Romans 502

1 Corinthians 515

2 Corinthians 528

Galatians 537

Ephesians 546

Philippians 554

Colossians 559

1 Thessalonians 565

2 Thessalonians 571

1 Timothy 575

2 Timothy 583

Titus 591

Philemon 596

The Jewish-Christian Epistles 599

Hebrews 600

James 624

1 Peter 632

2 Peter 640

1 John 646

2 John 655

3 John 657

Jude 659

Revelation 662

How the Bible came to us 690

Bible statistics 703

Outline of church history 704

Early church 705

Medieval church 711

Modern church 717

Principal Religions of the World 729

Index 737

Some ways into your Bible 744

Special Features

Historical Background of the Old Testament	16
Creation tablets	39
Creation stories	40
Contemporary Mesopotamian history	50
Tower of Babel	55
The World of Abram's day	56
Land of the patriarchs	62
Egypt	70
The Hebrew Calendar	118
Worship in Solomon's Temple	174
Chronology of the Dual Kingdoms	182
Assyria	197
Jerusalem in the time of David and Solomon	206
The Chaldean Empire	214
Contemporary Kings of Israel, Syria and Assyria	254
Great prophetic themes of Isaiah still unfulfilled	258
Kings of Judah	283
Contemporary kings	319
The Post-exilic Period	351
Bible Weights and Measures	362
Events of the Intertestamental Period	365
Political background of New Testament times	377
A peasant's house of Bible times	384
Matthew and Mark compared	400
Capernaum	405
Demonism	409
Miracles	410
The Sea of Galilee	412
Jericho	414
Jerusalem in the time of Jesus	416
Order of Events after the crucifixion	419
Incidents and events exclusive to Luke	422
Nazareth	427
Satan	428
The synagogues of Galilee	430
Passion week April A.D. 30	440
Trials of Jesus	441
The Dead Sea Scrolls	446
John and Isaiah	455
Herod's Temple	456
Jesus' Burial	459
The Resurrection authenticated	461
Chronological Chart of Acts	465
Speaking in tongues	472
Caesarea	473
Antioch-on-the-Orontes and archaeology	476
Antioch of Pisidia	479
Archaeology and Athens	484
Corinth of Paul's day	487
The city of Ephesus	490
Paul's life	496
Rome of Paul's day	498
Condemnation and Justification contrasted	507
Sanctification	509
God's glory lost and regained	514
Judgments mentioned in Scripture	523
Allegory: law vs. grace	543
Salvation in panorama	547
The covenants of Scripture	613

Abbreviations

Books of the Bible

OT	Old Testament
Gen	Genesis
Ex	Exodus
Lev	Leviticus
Num	Numbers
Deut	Deuteronomy
Josh	Joshua
Jud	Judges
Ruth	Ruth
1 Sam	1 Samuel
2 Sam	2 Samuel
1 Kgs	1 Kings
2 Kgs	2 Kings
1 Chr	1 Chronicles
2 Chr	2 Chronicles
Ezr	Ezra
Neh	Nehemiah
Est	Esther
Job	Job
Ps	Psalms
Prov	Proverbs
Eccl	Ecclesiastes
Song	Song of Solomon
Isa	Isaiah
Jer	Jeremiah
Lam	Lamentations
Ezk	Ezekiel
Dan	Daniel
Hos	Hosea
Joel	Joel
Amos	Amos
Ob	Obadiah
Jon	Jonah
Mic	Micah
Nah	Nahum
Hab	Habakkuk
Zeph	Zephaniah
Hag	Haggai
Zech	Zechariah
Mal	Malachi

NT	New Testament
Mt	Matthew
Mk	Mark
Lk	Luke
Jn	John
Acts	Acts
Rom	Romans
1 Cor	1 Corinthians
2 Cor	2 Corinthians
Gal	Galatians
Eph	Ephesians
Phil	Philippians
Col	Colossians
1 Thess	1 Thessalonians
2 Thess	2 Thessalonians
1 Tim	1 Timothy
2 Tim	2 Timothy
Tit	Titus
Phm	Philemon
Heb	Hebrews
Jas	James
1 Pet	1 Peter
2 Pet	2 Peter
1 Jn	1 John
2 Jn	2 John
3 Jn	3 John
Jude	Jude
Rev	Revelation

Apocrypha

1 Esd	1 Esdras
2 Esd	2 Esdras
Tob	Tobit
Wisd	Wisdom of Solomon
Sir	Wisdom of Jesus the son of Sirach, or Ecclesiasticus
Bar	Baruch
Bel	Bel and the Dragon
1 Macc	1 Maccabees
2 Macc	2 Maccabees

Others

A.D.	*anno domini* (in the year of our Lord)
ASV	American Standard Version
AV	Authorized Version (King James Version)
B.C.	before Christ
c.	*circa* (about)
cen.	century
cf.	confer (compare)
ch.	chapter
E	east
eg	*exempli gratia* (for example)
et al.	and others
f., ff.	following
Gr.	Greek
Heb.	Hebrew
i.e.	*id est* (that is)
Jos	Josephus *Antiquities*
KJV	King James Version
LXX	Septuagint (Greek translation of Old Testament)
marg.	Margin, marginal reading
MS., MSS.	manuscript, manuscripts
N	north
ORINST	Oriental Institute of the University of Chicago
p., pp.	page, pages
q.v.	*quod vide* (which see)
RSV	Revised Standard Version
S	south
UML	University of Michigan Library
v., vv.	verse, verses
W	west

Introduction

What the Bible is

The word 'Bible' designates the Scriptures of the Old and the New Testaments recognized and used by the Christian churches. Judaism recognizes only the Scriptures of the OT. Other religions such as Buddhism, Hinduism, Zoroastrianism and Islam, have their sacred writings.

But there is only *one* Bible – incomparable, unique as far as all other 'sacred' literature is concerned, because: (1) It is *the* revelation of God. (2) It is 'God-breathed' (2 Tim 3:16) and inspired in a different sense from all other literature. (3) It discloses God's plans and purposes for the ages of time and eternity. (4) It *centers in God incarnate in Jesus Christ,* the Saviour of mankind (Heb 1:1-2).

Meaning of the name 'Bible'

The word 'Bible' comes from the Greek word *biblia* ('books'), a diminutive from *biblos* ('book'), denoting the inner bark of the papyrus reed (ancient paper) from which ancient books (scrolls) were made. Daniel 9:2 refers to the OT prophetic writings as 'the scriptures' (*ta biblia* in the Gr.).

The prologue to Ecclesiasticus (an apocryphal book dating *c.* 130 B.C.) calls the OT writings outside the Law and the Prophets 'the rest of the books.' The writer of 1 Maccabees (another apocryphal book) designates them 'the holy books' (12:9). The usage passed over into Christian terminology (2 Clement 14:2) and by the 5th cen. A.D. came to be applied to the whole Scriptures. Jerome (*c.* A.D. 400) called the Bible *Bibliotheca Divina* ('the Divine Library').

By the 13th cen., ' . . . by a happy solecism, the neuter plural came to be regarded as a feminine singular, and "the Books" became by common consent "The Book" (*biblia,* sing.), in which form the word was passed into the languages of modern Europe' (Westcott, *Bible in the Church,* p.5). This evolution of the term 'the Bible' from the plural to the singular concept has proven to be providential, stressing the *unity* of the 39 books of the OT and the 27 of the NT.

A meadow of papyrus reeds on an Egyptian papyrus. The word 'Bible' is from a Greek word meaning the inner bark of papyrus reed.

Scriptural designations of the Bible

Our Lord customarily referred to the OT books as 'the Scriptures' (Mt 21:42; Mk 14:49; Jn 5:39). His followers did likewise (Lk 24:32; Acts 18:24; Rom 15:4). Paul referred to them as 'the sacred writings' (2 Tim 3:15, RSV), 'the Holy Scriptures' (Rom 1:2), 'the very words of God' (Rom 3:2).

Jesus once referred to them as 'the Law of Moses, and the Prophets and the Psalms' (Lk 24:44), echoing the formal arrangement in the Hebrew. The OT is more briefly termed 'the Law and the Prophets' (cf. Mt 5:17; 11:13; Acts 13:15). Even more briefly the term 'Law' comprehends the other divisions (Jn 10:34; 12:34; 15:25; 1 Cor 14:21).

There is no name in the Bible for the complete body of Scripture. The only Scriptures then known were those of the OT and the earliest NT books. In the latter category Peter refers to Paul's epistles as 'Scriptures' (2 Pet 3:16).

The terms 'Old Testament' and 'New Testament'

Since the close of the 2nd cen. the terms 'Old Testament' and 'New Testament' have been used to differentiate the Hebrew from the Christian Scriptures. The formal collection of Christian writings made after the middle of the 2nd cen. was called the New Testament. This collection was placed alongside the Hebrew canonical books as of equal inspiration and authority. The Hebrew Scriptures were then called the Old Testament. Tertullian, an early Latin father (c. 200), first employed the term *Novum Testamentum*. Thereafter it came into general use, and the concept of a Christian Bible was crystallized.

Applied to the Scriptures the terms Old Testament and New

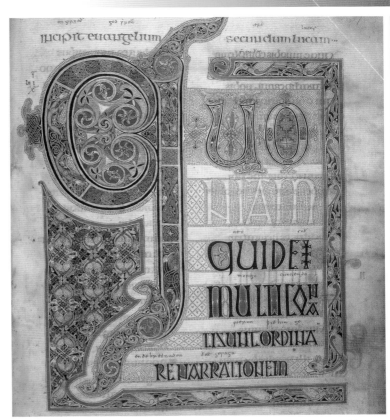

A richly ornamented page from the Lindisfarne Gospels, copied in Latin C. A.D. 700.

Testament mean strictly Old and New Covenant. The Covenant (Heb. *berith;* Gr. *diatheke*) is a continuation of the OT designation for the Mosaic law, the book of the covenant (2 Kgs 23:2). Paul in this sense speaks of reading 'the old covenant' (2 Cor 3:14).

Similarly, the NT use of *diatheke* is not testament or will (except in Heb 9:16, 17), as in classical Greek, but covenant. The older usage, however, is too firmly fixed to be changed. It is important to note that even within the New Testament, many of the events recorded (e.g. the majority of the four gospels) occurred under the Old Covenant. Not until Christ's death, attended by the tearing of the curtain which separated the holy place from the most holy place (Mt 27:51), did the legal age end, and the new testament (covenant) actually begin.

The languages of the Bible

The OT was written almost entirely in Hebrew, a Semitic dialect akin to Phoenician and Ugaritic. The only portions written in Aramaic, another Semitic language akin to Hebrew, were Ezr 4:8-6:18; 7:12-26; Dan 2:4-7:28, and Jer 10:11. The NT was written entirely in Greek. Archaeology has shown this to be the common everyday language *(Koine)* of the contemporary Graeco-Roman world.

Order of H

Th
pre
ber
thre
(Tor
and

referred to as 'the Psalms' (Lk 24:44). This division is old, being clearly implied in the prologue to the apocryphal book of Ecclesiasticus (c.180 B.C.), known by Philo and referred to by our Lord (Lk 24:44). The threefold division, however, experienced some evident shifting of books from the second to the third section in the early Christian centuries.

The form as it has come down to us from the Masoretic period (c. 600-900 A.D.) is as follows:

1. The Law (Torah), 5 books: Genesis, Exodus, Leviticus, Numbers, Deuteronomy

2. The Prophets (Nebiim), 8 books: Former Prophets, 4 books: Joshua, Judges, Samuel, Kings Latter Prophets, 4 books: Isaiah, Jeremiah, Ezekiel, the Twelve

3. The Writings, 11 books:

Poetical Books, 3 books: Psalms, Proverbs, Job The Scrolls (Megilloth), 5 books: Song of Solomon, Ruth, Lamentations, Ecclesiastes, Esther Prophetic-Historical Books, 3 books: Daniel, Ezra-Nehemiah, Chronicles

Josephus, expressing current Jewish opinion of the 1st cen. A.D., reckons 22 books (5 of the Law, 13 of the Prophets, 4 of the Writings), instead of the later 24. In the books of the Law he, of course, included Genesis, Exodus, Leviticus, Numbers and Deuteronomy. Josephus' 13 books of the Prophets included all the historical and prophetic Scriptures, counting as one book each Judges-Ruth, 1 and 2 Samuel, 1 and 2 Kings, 1 and 2 Chronicles, Ezra-Nehemiah, Jeremiah-Lamentations, and the Twelve Minor Prophets (total 7 books).

Josephus also included in the Prophets Joshua, Isaiah, Jeremiah, Ezekiel, Job and Esther. In the Writings he placed Psalms, Proverbs, Canticles and Ecclesiastes.

Josephus' 22 books were, therefore, those of the Hebrew canon only (no apocryphal books were included). His arrangement in 22 books (the number of letters in the Hebrew alphabet) apparently represented an earlier order than the rabbinic arrangement in 24 books which has come down to us in modern Hebrew Bibles.

Melito of Sardis (c. A.D. 170), Origen (c. 250) and Jerome (c. 400), following Jewish authorities, confirm Josephus' 22-book division with some variation of enumeration. Jerome was also acquainted with the rabbinic 24-book division, which was obtained by separating Ruth from Judges and Lamentations from Jeremiah.

Artist's impression of two Jewish rabbis studying the Hebrew Law on characteristic papyrus scrolls.

The inspiration of the Bible

Inspiration has reference to the influence God exerted over the human authors of Scripture so that the words and thoughts they recorded in the original autographs were without error (cf. 2 Tim 3:16; Jn 10:35; 2 Pet 1:19-21). This inspiration covers the original writings only, although a high degree of accuracy in the transmitted text is not only what is to be expected if God directed the process, but a fact demonstrated by textual criticism. Ferreting out any scribal errors which may have crept into the transmitted text is an activity belonging to the domain of lower criticism and the legitimate labors of consecrated scholars.

Divine inspiration makes the Bible uniquely the Word of God and not merely a book containing the Word of God, and as such is different from any other book sacred or secular. It is an inspired revelation of God's redemptive

The 66 Books of the Bible
(English order)

Historical
17 Books

Law of Moses
Genesis
Exodus
Leviticus
Numbers
Deuteronomy
Joshua
Judges
Ruth
1 Samuel
2 Samuel
1 Kings
2 Kings

1 Chronicles
2 Chronicles
Ezra
Nehemiah
Esther

Poetical
5 Books

Job
Psalms
Proverbs
Ecclesiastes
Song of Songs

Prophetic
17 Books

Isaiah
Jeremiah

Lamentations
Ezekiel
Daniel
Hosea
Joel

Amos
Obadiah
Jonah
Micah
Nahum
Habakkuk

Zephaniah
Haggai
Zechariah
Malachi

Note on the 39 Books of the Old Testament.
The content of the English OT is identical with that of the Hebrew. The only difference is in the arrangement of the material. The English translators followed the order of the books in the Septuagint (Greek) translation made about 280-150 B.C. Roman Catholics followed the Septuagint translation further by including 11 apocryphal books.

Note on the 27 Books of the New Testament.
The gospels, although composed later than many of the epistles, in completed collections were placed before Acts and the epistles for chronological reasons. Cataloging the earthly life and ministry of our Lord, they naturally precede the book of Acts, which describes the formation and history of the early church.

The 21 epistles consist of 13 by Paul, one (Hebrews) anonymous and addressed to Hebrew Christians, another (James) also addressed to the twelve tribes of the diaspora, with two by Peter, three by John and one by Jude. James, 1 and 2 Peter, 1, 2 and 3 John, and Jude are called the Catholic epistles.

Revelation, the capstone of biblical prophecy, completes the NT books.

Biographical
4 Books

Matthew
Mark
Luke
John

Historical
Acts

Pedagogical
21 Books

Romans
1 Corinthians
2 Corinthians
Galatians
Ephesians
Philippians
Colossians
1 Thessalonians
2 Thessalonians
1 Timothy
2 Timothy

Philemon
Hebrews
James
1 Peter
2 Peter
1 John
2 John
3 John
Jude

Prophetic
Revelation

plan and purposes in Christ on behalf of man, and not a revelation of natural science or a book of secular history. Alleged scientific discrepancies are due either to faulty scientific theories or inadequate interpretations of Bible thought forms. Alleged historical blunders may be due to such factors as a faulty textual tradition, or wrong interpretation of historical or archaeological evidence or of the biblical text itself.

The authority of the Bible

Authority resides in God's inspired Word (the Bible) interpreted by God's Spirit operating through Spirit-taught human agents. Orthodox Protestantism differs from Catholicism in claiming no other authority than canonical Scripture

as the voice of the Holy Spirit.

During the Middle Ages the Church of Rome concentrated in itself all authority through the episcopacy, assuming that the *magisterium* held the key for the interpretation of Scripture and God's divine laws. This movement culminated in the decree of Papal Infallibility of 1870, which holds that 'the Roman Pontiff, when he speaks *ex cathedra,* has that infallibility with which the Divine Redeemer endowed his church, in defining a doctrine of faith or morals.'

Neo-orthodox and liberal wings of Protestantism deny final authority to Scripture as inerrant and infallible, substituting some internal authority such as feeling, conscience, experience, 'Christ speaking through the Holy Spirit,' etc.

Christ the unifying theme of the Bible

Although the Bible consists of 66 books (39 in the OT and 27 in the NT) it is nevertheless *one* book. The unifying theme of Scripture is Christ. The OT prepares Him and predicts Him in both type and prophecy. The gospels present Him redemptively in divine-human manifestation. Acts portrays Him preached and His gospel propagated in the world. The epistles expound His redemptive work. The Revelation reveals Him as the consummation of all the plans and purposes of God. From the offspring of the woman (Gen 3:15) promised in paradise lost, to the 'Alpha and Omega' (Rev 22:13) realized in paradise regained, He is 'the Beginning and the End', 'the First and the

The roof and dome of St Peter's, Rome. During the Middle Ages the Church of Rome concentrated in itself all authority.

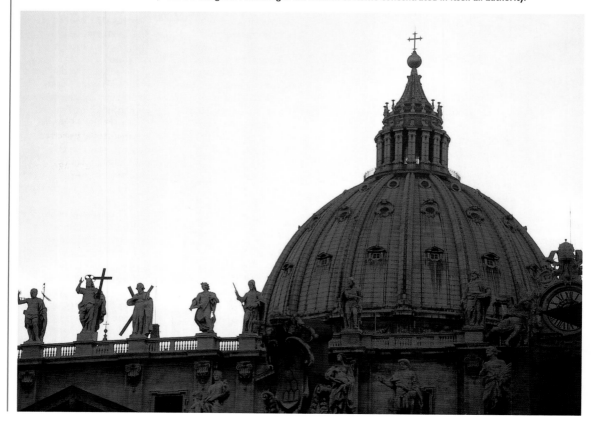

Last' in God's revealed ways with man.

The purpose of the Bible

The Bible was given to bear witness to one God, Creator and Sustainer of the universe, through Christ, Redeemer of sinful man. It presents one continuous story – that of human redemption. This story is a progressive unfolding of the central truth of the Bible that God in His eternal counsels was to become incarnate in Jesus Christ for the redemption of fallen man.

The unfolding of this central truth of redemption is set forth through history, prophecy, type and symbol. This revelation of human redemption through Christ orients man in the larger framework of God's plans for him in the ages of time, as well as the divine purpose for him in eternity.

Typology of the Bible

Definition. A type (from the Gr. *typos,* 'a blow or mark left by a blow; a pattern or impress') is a double representation in action, the literal being intended and planned to represent the spiritual. A type is thus the divine impress of spiritual truth upon a literal event, person or thing. Rightly understood and appreciated, typology offers a strong proof of divine inspiration. It is in reality the divine redemptive program of the ages deftly woven into the warp and woof of Scripture by God Himself.

Extent. All Scripture is not equally typical. Scripture offers its own clues as to which passages permit typical interpretation. The book of Hebrews is a NT witness to the concentrated typical quality of the Pentateuch and Joshua. First Corinthians 10:11 offers a NT

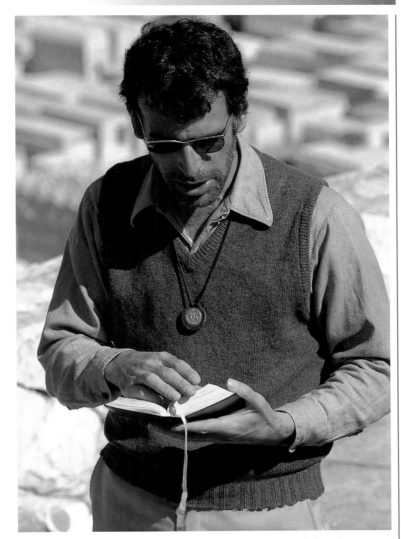

The Bible was given to witness to one God, Creator and Sustainer of the universe.

basis for the rich typology of the Pentateuch. 'These things happened to them [that is, Israel in the wilderness] as examples [Gr. *tupikos,* typically or as types] and were written down as warnings for us, on whom the fulfillment of the ages has come.' Modern interpreters should exercise caution in going beyond Scripture's own program of typology.

Purpose. Typology as the divine inworking of God's purposes in Scripture is a means of making the Word of

God relevant for every age and situation. Since Jesus Christ is the constant subject of all Scripture, His person and work are divinely impressed upon it in type, symbol and prophecy.

Varieties of types.

(1) Typical *persons,* such as Cain, a type of the natural man, destitute of any adequate sense of sin or atonement (Gen 4:3; 2 Pet 2:1-22; Jude 11). Abel, by contrast, is a type of the spiritual man whose sacrifice of blood (Gen 4:4; Heb 9:22) evidenced his guilt of sin and his reliance upon a substitute.

Writing in ancient times. Left to right: cuneiform writing on stone; scribing on a waxed tablet; cuneiform writing on soft clay; pictographs on papyrus; writing with pen on paper.

Similarly, numerous other OT saints are typical of some aspect of the Messiah or some phase of redemption.

(2) Typical *events* include the Flood, the Exodus, the desert sojourn, the giving of manna, the bronze snake, the conquest of Canaan.

(3) Typical *institutions* include the Levitical ritual where there is a concentration of typology. For example, the whole Levitical ritual in which lambs or other animals were slain to atone for sin (Lev 17:11) prefigured the Lamb of God (Jn 1:29; Heb 9:28; 1 Pet 1:19). The Passover (Lev 23) portrayed Christ our Redeemer (1 Cor 5:6-8).

(4) Typical *offices* include prophets, priests and kings. For example, Moses as a prophet was typical of Christ (Deut 18:15-18; Jn 6:14; 7:40).

(5) Typical *actions* include Jonah's experience with the great fish, a prophetic type of our Lord's burial and resurrection (Mt 12:39).

Type as a prophecy.
Typology has been called a species of prophecy. This is true, but the typical import may not be made known in the age in which the type appears. Much of the typology of the OT deals with events and truths concerning a period which was unrevealed to the OT seers (Mt 13:11-17), so that it may be stated that this period, known to us as the Church Age, although undisclosed to OT prophets, was nevertheless impressed upon OT institutions, persons and things through the omniscient authorship of the Holy Spirit. For this reason OT ritual, institutions and experiences have an interest and instructive value to NT saints. This fact, when properly understood and appreciated, is a wonderful evidence of the divine authorship of Scripture, making it practical and omnitemporal in its instruction and everyday relations.

Ancient writing

Writing in the time of Abraham. By Abraham's day (c. 2050 B.C.) writing already had a long and illustrious history. Cylinder seals were invented about 3400 B.C. in the Warkan culture at Uruk, biblical Erech (Gen 10:10), modern Warka on the lower Euphrates in Babylonia. Writing soon followed. In the Red Temple of Uruk a number of clay tablets were found inscribed in the earliest known crude pictographic script (c. 3300 B.C.), the direct ancestor of the cuneiform (wedge-shaped writing) of early Sumer (lower alluvial plain of the Tigris-Euphrates Valley). By Abraham's time Sumerian and later Babylonian cuneiform writing had become well-known and widespread. This fact is attested by finds at Kish, Larsa, Fara, Ur (Abraham's own town), Nippur, Eridu, Accad, Lagash.

Writing in the time of Moses.

By the time of Moses, 1526-1406 B.C. (early chronology), alphabetic writing had become common, as attested by the religious literature found at Ras Shamra (ancient Ugarit). The Ugaritic dialect (c. 1400 B.C.) is very close to Hebrew, so Moses could have written the Pentateuch in old Hebrew. Further parallels to old Hebrew are found in the Eblaite documents found at Tell Mardikh in northern Syria. Those date 900 years earlier to 2300 B.C.!

Since Moses was educated in Egypt, he could also have written in Egyptian hieroglyphics. The Rosetta Stone, discovered in 1799 at Rashid (Rosetta) at the westernmost mouth of the Nile, proved the key to deciphering ancient holy writing of Egypt called hieroglyphics.

Since Moses was elevated to prominence in Egypt, he could also have written the Pentateuch In Akkadian cuneiform. This fact is established by the discovery of the Tell-el-Amarna Tablets in 1886, at Amarna in Egypt halfway between Cairo and Luxor. Written in Akkadian cuneiform, the international diplomatic language of the era, the Amarna Tablets belong to about 1380-1360 B.C., just after Moses' death, when Israel was entering Palestine.

The discovery of a great cuneiform library at Boghaz-koy (1906) in the Hittite center there shows that Babylonian writing and literature were widely spread throughout the world around 1400 B.C. The Code of Hammurabi dates three centuries earlier, around 1700 B.C.

Authorship of the Pentateuch

Archaeology fully demonstrates that Moses could have written the Pentateuch either in early Hebrew, Akkadian cuneiform or Egyptian hieroglyphics, had he desired. The traditional view is that Moses did write it substantially as we have it today. It is, accordingly, authentic, historical and reliable, worthy of the name Holy Inspired Scripture.

The higher critical view is that Moses did *not* write it. It is a patchwork of discordant and conflicting oral traditions, written centuries after Moses. The J tradition (using the name YHWH) was written c. 850; the E tradition (using the name Elohim), c. 750; D tradition (Deuteronomy), c. 621 B.C.; and P, a priestly invention, c. 500 B.C. It is, on this supposition, unauthentic, unhistorical and unreliable, a fabrication of men, not the inspired work of God.

Reasons why Moses did write the Pentateuch.

1. He was well-qualified scholastically to do so (Acts 7:22), and there is no rational reason archaeologically, historically or culturally that he should not have done so. Would he have been so foolhardy as not to? Would he have been so unwise as to entrust his whole life's work and teaching to oral tradition, especially when he was the founder and father of the Hebrew nation?

2. The Pentateuch claims that Moses wrote it, at least in part (cf. Ex 17:14; 24:4; 34:27; Num 33.2; Deut 31:19, 24-26).

3. The rest of the Bible claims that Moses did so (Josh 1:7; 1 Kgs 2:3; Lk 24:44; 1 Cor 9:9).

4. Our Lord Himself claimed that Moses wrote of Him (Jn 5:46-47; cf. Gen 3:15; 49:10; Num 24:17; Deut 18:15-18, etc.).

5. The foundation of all revealed truth and of God's redemptive plan is based on the Pentateuch. If this foundation is unreliable, the whole Bible is unreliable.

6. Higher critical theories that partition the Pentateuch are methodologically unsound. Whether the division is made on the basis of divine names, rare words, Aramaisms or the 'evolution' of religion, modern scholarship has established that these divisions do not withstand close scrutiny.

Historical Background of the Old Testament

Biblical event	Contemporary scene
Undated past Universe created.	Various geologic eras. Pre-historic Stone Ages.
Probably 10,000-8000 B.C. or earlier Man created.	First farming and cattle raising. Beginnings of urban life. Crude arts.
Probably before 5000 Noahic Flood.	
5000 Noahic descendants (Shem, Ham, Japheth) develop into the first nations.	Earliest culture in Meso-potamia, Jarmo (6500-5000), Catal Huyuk (6000). Beginning of Chalcolithic (stone-copper) Age, first pottery. Badarian and Amratian cultures (Egypt).
4800 Tower of Babel. Earliest languages.	First large buildings in Babylonia. Earliest occupa-tional levels at Tepe Gawra, Nineveh, Tell ed-Judeideh, etc.
4500-3000 City-states in Baby-lonia. Urban civilization de-velops.	Halafian culture (4500), Ubaid culture (3600) at Tell El-'Ubaid near Ur. Warka (Erech, Uruk, 3200) flourishes, earliest writing, first cylinder seals; Jemdet Nasr culture (3000).
3000-2200 Noahic descendants develop in civilizing arts but lapse into polytheism. Knowledge of the one true God lost (Gen 11).	Rise of perverted tradition of creation and Flood, pre-served in Sumerian and Babylonian literature. Union of Lower and Upper Egypt (3100). Dynasties I and II (3100-2686). Old Kingdom (2686-2181). Pyramids. Early dynastic (Sumerian period) in Babylonia. First Semitic dynasty in Babylonia founded by Sargon I (2371-2316).
2225 Terah born.	First Intermediate Period (Dark Ages) in Egypt (2181-2040).

Biblical event Date	Contemporary scene
2166 **Abram** (Abraham) **born** (chronology of Hebrew Bible).	Gutian rule in Babylonia (2250-2120). Third Dynasty of Ur arises to power in Abraham's birth-place. (2113-2006).
2116 Abram migrates to Haran ('caravan city', prominent in Cappa-docian Tablets of 19th cen. B.C. and Mari Texts of 18th cen.)	Ur-Nammu, Dungi, Bur-Sin, Gimi-Sin and Ibi-Sin rule at Ur. Flourishing donkey caravan trade between Ur, the greatest commercial capital of the world to that time, and Haran, Damascus, Egypt.
2091 Abram enters Canaan.	Central highland ridge of Palestine, wooded and sparsely settled.
2080 Invasion of Transjordan by a coalition of Meso-potamian kings (Gen 14).	The *Apiru* (donkey cara-vaneers) carry on a flour-ishing trade on the Fertile Crescent between Ur in Mesopotamia and Egypt via Syria-Canaan. Abraham 'the Hebrew' (Gen 14:13), one of this class.
2056 **Sodom and Gomorrah destroyed.**	
2066 Isaac born.	2006-1859 Jacob.
	Ur destroyed by the Elamites. Elamite princes in Isin and Larsa in Lower Babylonia and Elamite city-states in other parts of Babylonia.
	Strong Middle Kingdom (Dynasty XII) in Egypt. Amenemhet I-IV, Senusert I-III (1991-1790).
Joseph viceroy in Egypt	

Biblical event Date	Contemporary scene
1750 Enslavement in Egypt (if Hyksos were pharaohs who did not know Joseph).	First Dynasty of Babylon (1894-1595) Hammurabi (c.1792-1750). Mari a powerful city-state on Middle Euphrates. Hyksos (Asiatic foreigners) invade and dominate Egypt (c.1684-1567).
1575 Enslavement (if New Kingdom pharaohs began oppression).	Dynasties XV-XVII.
	Dynasty XVIII (1567-1314); Ahmose, Thutmose I, II, Queen Hatshepsut (1570-1482).
1526 Moses born.	Thutmose III (1504-1450).
1446 Exodus from Egypt (early date; some advocate 1290 Exodus) Israel in the desert	Amenhotep II (1450-1425). Thutmose IV (1425-1412).
1406 Fall of Jericho.	Amenhotep III (1412-1375) and Amenhotep IV or Akhnaton (1375-1359). Period of the Amarna letters. Wane of Egyptian control over Palestine.
1406-1382 Conquest of Canaan Joshua and elders rule.	Invasion of Habiru (Hebrews?). Advance of Hittites. Greek world. Downfall of Crete (1400).
1375 Invasion of Cushan-Rishathaim.	Tutankhamn in Egypt (1359-1350).
1367 Othniel rescues Israel – 40-year period of peace.	Haremhab (1350-1319).
1327 Eglon of Moab oppresses the Israelite tribes.	Dynasty XIX in Egypt Seti I(1319-1299).
1309 Ehud's deliverance. – 80-year peace.	Ramses II (1299-1232), wars with Hittites at Kadesh (1286), and concludes a Hittite treaty. Merneptah stele alludes to Israel in Palestine (1224).

Biblical event Date	Contemporary scene
1229 Jabin of Hazor over-runs Israel.	Egyptian pharaohs (Amenmose, Siptah, etc.) weak
1209 Deborah's judgeship. 40-year peace.	Ramses III (1198-1167) repulses invasion of Philistines and other 'sea peoples'. Palestine.
1169 Midianites invade Canaan.	
1162 Gideon's judgeship. 40-year peace.	Weak successors of Ramses III (Ramses IV and V).
Abimelech is king at Shechem.	Increase of power of *Pelisti* (Philistines) in SW.
1096 Philistines begin to harass Israel.	
1078 Jephthah's judgeship.	
1075 Samson's exploits. Eli priest Hophni and Phinehas at Shiloh.	Decline of Hittite, Assyrian and Egyptian imperial power making possible David's conquests (c.1 010-970) and Solomon's empire (c.970-931).
1035 Philistines defeat Israel at Ebenezer. Ark captured.	
1050 Samuel judge and prophet	
1043 Saul and beginning of monarchy.	
1010	

David king. of Judah

Biblical event Date	Contemporary scene
1003 David reigns over Israel at Jerusalem.	
Solomon succeeds David.	

Division of the Kingdom 931

970 Solomon

Judah/Biblical event

Kings

Prophets

Rehoboam
931-13

Abijah
913-11

Asa
911-870

Jehoshaphat
873-48

Jehoram
853-41

Ahaziah
841

Athaliah
841-35

Joash
835-796

Amaziah
796-67

Azariah
792-40

Isaiah

Israel/Biblical event

Kings

Prophets

Contemporary scene

Jeroboam
931-10

Nadab
910-9

Baasha
909-886

Elah
886-85

Zimri
885

Tibni
885-80

Omri
885-74

Ahab
874-53

Elijah

Ahaziah
853-52

Jehoram
852-41

Elisha

Jehu
841-14

Jehoahaz
814-798

Jehoash
798-82

Jeroboam II
793-53

Amos

Rezon seizes power in Damascus. Ascendancy of Damascene state as foe of Israel.
Pharaoh Shishak's invasion (c.925).

Rise of Assyria. Ashurnasirpal II (833-859).
Conquest of Shalmaneser (859-824).

Battle of Qarqar (853). Palestine-Syrian coalition vs. Assyrian advance.

Judah/Biblical event

Kings

Prophets

Jotham
750-32

Ahaz
735-16

Hezekiah
716-687

Manasseh
697-43

Micah

Amon
643-1

Josiah
641-09

Jeremiah

Jehoahaz
609

Jehoiakim
609-598

Jehoiachin
598-97

Zedekiah
597-86

Ezekiel

Fall of Jerusalem
586

Israel/Biblical event

Kings

Prophets

Contemporary scene

Zechariah
753-52

Shallum
752 and
Menahem
752-42

Pekah
752-32

Isaiah

Hoshea
732-22

Pekahiah
742-40

Fall of Samaria
722

Micah

Syro-Ephraimite war
(734).Tiglath-pileser invades Israel
(733-732). Assyrians lay siege to
Samaria (724-722).

Sargon III takes Samaria (722).
Sennacherib invades
Judah (701).

For biblical events, the chronology underlying the
Hebrew Bible is followed; for the contemporary
scene *The Cambridge Ancient History* is generally
followed. Discrepancies between the years
assigned to a reign and the actual years computed
in the Bible are due to a number of factors, such
as overlapping coregencies reckoned in the actual
reign, antedating or non-accession year system, or
post-dating or accession year system of
computing the reign, corruption of numbers in
transmission, etc. No absolute chronology as yet
exists. Many of the dates used here are those of
Edwin R.Thiele, *The Mysterious Numbers of the
Hebrew Kings* (Chicago: University of Chicago
Press, 1951), p.283.

Josiah slain by Pharaoh Necho (608).

Nabopolassar's death;
first siege of Jerusalem (605).

Nebuchadnezzar's
second invasion (598-597).
His third invasion (588-586).

Judah/Biblical event

Kings

Prophets

Contemporary scene

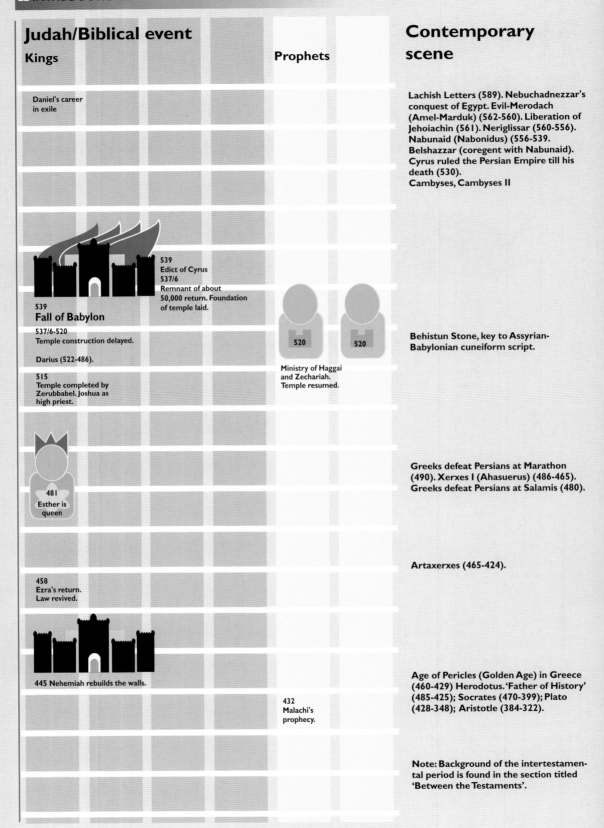

Daniel's career in exile

Lachish Letters (589). Nebuchadnezzar's conquest of Egypt. Evil-Merodach (Amel-Marduk) (562-560). Liberation of Jehoiachin (561). Neriglissar (560-556). Nabunaid (Nabonidus) (556-539). Belshazzar (coregent with Nabunaid). Cyrus ruled the Persian Empire till his death (530).
Cambyses, Cambyses II

539
Edict of Cyrus
537/6
Remnant of about 50,000 return. Foundation of temple laid.

539
Fall of Babylon

537/6-520
Temple construction delayed.

Darius (522-486).

515
Temple completed by Zerubbabel. Joshua as high priest.

520

520

Ministry of Haggai and Zechariah. Temple resumed.

Behistun Stone, key to Assyrian-Babylonian cuneiform script.

481
Esther is queen

Greeks defeat Persians at Marathon (490). Xerxes I (Ahasuerus) (486-465). Greeks defeat Persians at Salamis (480).

Artaxerxes (465-424).

458
Ezra's return. Law revived.

445 Nehemiah rebuilds the walls.

Age of Pericles (Golden Age) in Greece (460-429) Herodotus. 'Father of History' (485-425); Socrates (470-399); Plato (428-348); Aristotle (384-322).

432
Malachi's prophecy.

Note: Background of the intertestamental period is found in the section titled 'Between the Testaments'.

The Bible and archaeology

Biblical reference and archaeological illustration

Creation
Gen 1:1-2:25
The Creation Tablets (Enuma elish) record a perverted polytheistic version of creation in cuneiform writing on seven clay tablets. They were found at ancient Nineveh A.D 1848-1876 in the library of the Assyrian king Ashurbanipal (669-626 B.C.), but composed earlier in the reign of Hammurabi (1728-1686 B.C.). See Gen 1.

The Garden of Eden
Gen 2:8-14
Archaeology has established the lower Tigris-Euphrates Valley (the location of Eden) as the cradle of civilization. The *Hiddeqel* (Babylonian *Idigla, Diglat*) is the Tigris River. F. Delitzsch located Eden just N of Babylon; Sayce, near Eridu, anciently on the Persian Gulf.

The Fall
Gen 3.1-24
The Myth of Adapa was discovered on four cuneiform fragments, three from Ashurbanipal's famed library in Nineveh (7th cen. B.C.) and the fourth from the archives of Amenhotep III and IV at Amarna, Egypt, c. 1375 B.C. The myth is not a parallel to the biblical story of the Fall, but offers suggestive illustration to the fruit of the tree of life (Gen 3:3, 22) and other details.

Earliest civilization
Gen 4:1-26
Farming and cattle raising (Cain's and Abel's occupations) are shown by archaeology to be the beginning of man's civilization. Arts, crafts, music (Gen 4:16-24) and the rise of urban life are illustrated at Tell Hassuna, Nineveh, Tepe Gawra, Tell El-'Ubaid, Tell Chagar Bazar and other Mesopotamian mounds (lowest levels).

Metallurgy
Gen 4:22
Copper has been attested as early as 4500 B.C. By 3000 B.C. it had displaced stone for tools and weapons. Henri Frankfort attests an iron dagger handle at Tell Asmar c. 2700 B.C. From Ur has come an iron ax.

Pre-Flood longevity
Gen 5:1-32
The Weld-Blundell Prism preserves a very ancient Sumerian King List. It contains eight pre-Flood rulers said to have reigned a total of 241,200 years over the Lower Mesopotamian cities of Eridu, Badtibira, Larak, Sippar and Shuruppak. The shortest reign was 18,600 years, the longest 43,200. These apparently exaggerated figures put the comparatively modest biblical figures in a different light.

Sunset in the marshlands of southern Iraq, near biblical Ur of the Chaldees.

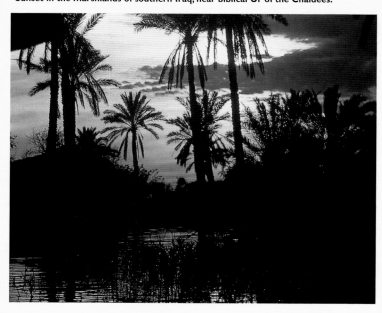

The Flood
Gen 6:1-9:29
Its historicity
C.L. Woolley's 8-foot flood stratum at Ur and S. Langdon's at Kish were the result of local Tigris-Euphrates inundations, not evidence of the universal Noahic deluge. Evidence of the latter must be sought in geology before 4000 B.C.

The Flood
Its reality
The Epic of Gilgamesh (both Sumerian and Babylonian) gives evidence that this event *did* occur. The oldest account is the Sumerian from Nippur, dating before 2000 B.C. The Babylonian is recorded in the 11th book of the Epic of Gilgamesh. The Flood Tablets were unearthed at Nineveh by H. Rassam (1835) from Ashurbanipal's library (669-626 B.C.) and furnish the most striking extrabiblical parallel to any biblical event, even including sending out of the birds from the ship by the Babylonian Noah (Ut-hapistim).

The table of the nations
Gen 10:1-32
The names and places of this marvelous ethnographical table have been largely illuminated and clarified by modern scientific archaeology. See notes on Gen 10.

The Tower of Babel
Gen 11:1-9
The location of more than two dozen ancient temple-towers of Mesopotamia, called ziggurats and possibly illustrative of the Tower of Babel, is now known. These towers were gigantic artificial mountains of sun-dried bricks. The oldest one recovered is that at Uruk (biblical Erech, Gen 10:10), from the fourth millennium B.C. Other famous ziggurat ruins remain at Ur, Borsippa and Babylon.

Abraham's birthplace
Gen 11:27-31
C.L. Woolley's excavations in 1922-34 have made Ur one of the best-known ancient sites of southern Babylonia. Under the

Main Archaeological Sites

K SEA

CASPIAN SEA

Alaca Huyuk
ogazkoy

Nimrud Dagh

Tigris R.

Haran   Tel Halaf

Carchemish   Euphrates R.

Nineveh

Nimrud
Asshur

Hatra

Nuzi

Bisitun   Hamadan
(Ecbatana)

Siyalk

nis   **SYRIA**   **I R A Q**

os
n   Palmyra
Damascus

Mari

I R A N

Tel Asmar

Aqar Ouf   Ctesiphon

Babylon   Jemdet Nasr

Kish   Nippur   Susa

Erech   Larsa

Eridu   Ur

Bishapur

Persepolis

Elath

PERSIAN GULF

S A U D I

A R A B I A

RED

SEA

Main archaeological sites

famous Third Dynasty (c. 2070-1960 B.C.), when Abraham left the city, it was at the height of its splendor as a commercial and cult center dedicated to the moon-god Nanna. The famous ziggurat, temple and sacred precincts of the moon-god have been uncovered.

Terah's religion
Gen 11:31-32
Terah was apparently a worshiper of Ur's god Nanna. Terah's stay at Haran is singular, since Nanna was also worshiped there (cf. Josh 24:2).

Abraham at Haran
Gen 11:31; 12:5
Cuneiform sources confirm the existence of Haran in the 19th and 18th cen. B.C. The city appears in Assyrian documents as Harranu ('road'), because it was on the great E-W trade route between Nineveh, Damascus and Carchemish.

Patriarchal sojourn in Mesopotamia
Paddan Aram
Gen 25:20; 26:6
Nahor, Rebekah's home (Gen 24:10), often occurs in the Mari Tablets, discovered in 1935 and dating from the 18th cen. B.C. Also attested as cities in this region are Terah, Peleg (Paligu) and Reu (cf. Gen 11:10-30).

The patriarchal era
Gen 12:1-50:26
A relatively recent treasure store of archaeological data was unearthed in 1975 by Italian scholars Pettinato and Matthiae in Ebla (Tell Mardikh) in northern Syria. Cuneiform documents from the site attest to a proto-Canaanite language closely related to Hebrew, dating from 2300 B.C. Close parallels to names such as Eber (Ebrum), Ishmael (Ishmail), and Israel (Ishrail) have been found. Moreover, the findings attest to the cultural situation reflected in the patriarchal narratives, even noting place names of cities such as Hazor, Megiddo, Jerusalem, Lachish, Dan, Gaza, and perhaps even Sodom and Gomorrah.

The sphinx, Cairo. Archaeology has resurrected ancient Egypt for the Bible student.

Patriarchal sojourn in Canaan
Gen 12:1-50:26
Archaeology has corroborated the semi-nomadic life of the patriarchs as pictured in Genesis in the Middle Bronze Age (2100-1550 B.C.). Shechem, Bethel, Dothan, Gerar and Jerusalem (Salem) are all known from excavations to have existed in Abraham's day. Canaan, the older native name of Palestine, seems derived from Hurrian, meaning 'belonging to the land of red purple,' and applied to traders in purple dye obtained from the murex shells on the Phoenician seacoast.

Abraham in Egypt
Gen 12:10-20
This visit occurred during the Middle Kingdom under Dynasty XII (c. 1989-1776 B.C.). Archaeology has resurrected ancient Egypt for the Bible student.

Abraham and the Mesopotamian kings
Gen 14:1-24
The antiquity and historicity of this chapter are supplied by including such ancient sites as Ashtaroth and Karnaim in Bashan, as well as Ham (Gen 14:5). It is quite possible that several of the places and perhaps even the kings are named in the

Ebla documents. The line of march over the later designated King's Highway is perfectly in accord with archaeological knowledge of this region of eastern Gilead and Moab, where the Early Middle Bronze Age city at Ader was discovered in 1924.

Sodom and Gomorrah
Gen 19:1-32
Valley of Siddim (Gen 14:3) is known to be the area now covered by the southern end of the Dead Sea. This region was populous c. 2065 B.C. The city of Bab ed-Dra, which belongs to this era, came to an abrupt end at this time, as Kyle and Albright have shown. An earthquake and explosion of the salt and free sulphur made the area a burnt-out region of oil and asphalt.

Patriarchal customs
Gen 15:1-50:26
The tablets from Nuzu (1925-41) near Kirkuk illustrate such patriarchal customs as adoption, marriage, rights of the firstborn, the teraphim (household gods) and many other details of local color. The Mari Letters from Tell el Hariri on the Middle Euphrates, discovered in 1933, also illustrate this period, as well as the Code of Hammurabi from 1700 B.C. discovered in 1901.

Israel's entrance into Egypt

Ex 1:1-6
A fine archaeological parallel is the sculpture on a tomb from about 1900 B.C. at Beni Hasan showing the entrance of a group of Semites into Egypt under 'Sheik of the highlands, Ibshe.'

Evidence of Israel's sojourn in Egypt

Ex 1:7-12:41
(1) Egyptian personal names of Levites (Moses, Assir, Pashhur, Merari, Hophni, Phinehas and Putiel). (Cf. 1 Sam 2:27.)
(2) Authentic Egyptian local color in accord with data from Egyptian monuments, such as titles 'chief cupbearer' and 'chief baker' (Gen 40:2).

The Exodus

Ex 12:1-14:31
Under early view Thutmose III (1490-1445) was the oppressor; Amenhotep II (1445-1425 B.C.), the pharaoh of the Exodus. Late views place the events under Raamses II after 1280 or under Merneptah, whose famous stele contains the first extrabiblical mention of Israel (c. 1224 B.C.).

Excavations at ancient Jericho.

Excavations at ancient Hazor.

Fall of Jericho

Josh 6:1-27
The ancient city is illustrated by Ernst Sellin's excavations in 1907-09, John Garstang's in 1930-36 and Kathleen Kenyon's in 1950's.

Laws of Moses

Ex, Lev, Deut
Illustrated by the Code of Hammurabi (c. 1750 B.C.) discovered at Susa in 1901; the laws of Lipit-Ishtar of Isin (c. 1875 B.C.), and the even earlier laws of Eshnunna.

The conquest

Josh 1:1-11:23
Illuminated by: (1) excavation at Jericho, Lachish, Debir and Hazor. (2) The Amarna Letters discovered in 1886 in Egypt which, apparently, describe the invasion of Palestine by the Habiru (Hebrews?). (3) The religious literature from Ras Shamra (Ugarit), 1929-37, which illuminates the culture, religion and morals of the Canaanites.

Period of the Judges

Jud 1:1-21:25
Archaeological resurrection of Egyptian, Hittite, Aramean, Assyrian, Phoenician and Hurrian history now furnishes background to this period. Also excavations at Megiddo and Bethshan.

Period of Samuel

1 Sam 1:1-8:22
Shiloh, as a religious center, is illustrated by great pagan central sanctuaries at Nippur in Babylonia, Nineveh in Assyria, at Haran (temple of Sin), at Qatna (temple of Belit-ekalli) and at Byblus (temple of Baaltis). Excavations at Shiloh show that the city fell to the Philistines c. 1050 and was destroyed (cf. Jer 7:10-15).

Saul's reign

1 Sam 9:1-31:13
Saul's rustic palace-fortress of Gibeah (Tell el-Ful) about four miles N of Jerusalem was identified by Edward Robinson, the pioneer Palestinian explorer (19th cen.) and excavated by W. F. Albright in 1922 and 1933, shedding much light on the king's reign. Saul's resort to occultism (1 Sam 28:7-25) is abundantly illustrated by Hittite, Assyrian, Hurrian texts and the Mari Letters.

David's conquests

2 Sam 1:1-24:25
Archaeology has shown that the Jebusite city David took (2 Sam 5:6-8) was the SE part of Jerusalem above the Gihon spring. Old Jebusite walls and the ancient water tunnel and shaft have been explored, dating from 2000 B.C., like similar water works found at Gezer and Megiddo.

Solomon's empire

1 Kgs 3:1-11:43
Archaeology has brilliantly illuminated Solomon's reign.
(1) Excavations at Hazor, Megiddo, Gezer have confirmed his army and chariotry (1 Kgs 9:15-19; 10:26).
(2) Excavations of Nelson Glueck at Ezion-geber (cf. 1 Kgs 7:46) have uncovered Solomon's copper furnaces. (3) Solomon's matrimonial alliances (1 Kgs 11:1-5, 33) are illustrated by royal records of Egypt, Mitanni, etc. (4) His 'fleet of Tarshish' (smeltery or refinery fleet) is illustrated by Phoenician inscriptions. (5) His horse and

chariot trade and commerce with Hiram I of Tyre (c. 969-936 B.C.) are illustrated by archaeology.

Jeroboam's calves

I Kgs 12:25-33
This was a dangerous religious innovation which apparently represented the invisible Deity (Yahweh) enthroned or as standing on the bulls, rather than Yahweh as bull-god (cf. Ex 32:4-6). Pagan deities, such as Baal, are pictured on seals, etc., in the form of a bolt of lightning on a bull's back.

Shishak's invasion

I Kgs 14:25-28
The gold-masked body of Shishak (Sheshonk I, Dynasty XXII, c. 945-924 B.C.) was discovered at Tanis in 1938-39. His Karnak inscription lists his conquests in Judah in the coastal plain at Megiddo, where a part of his stele was discovered, and his advance into Gilead.

Ben Hadad of Damascus

I Kgs 15:18
His stele discovered in northern Syria (1940) confirms the dynastic order of 'Ben Hadad, son of Tabrimmon, son of Hezion, king of Syria, who dwelt in Damascus.'

Omri and Mesha

I Kgs 16:21-27
2 Kgs 3:4-27
Famous stele of Mesha of Moab set up at Dibon c. 840 B.C., discovered in 1868, mentions Omri, Ahab, Mesha, Chemosh (Moab's god) and many place names.

Omri and Samaria

Excavations of G. A. Reisner, C. S. Fisher, D. G. Lyon (1908-10) and J. W. Crowfoot, K. Kenyon and E. L. Sukenik (The Buildings at Samaria, 1942) have traced the city of Omri, Ahab, Jeroboam II and later periods.

Omri and Assyria

I Kgs 16:23-27
From Omri's time on, Israel is mentioned in Assyrian records as Bit-Humri ('house of Omri'), and Israelite kings as mar-Humri ('son,' i.e., royal successor of Omri).

The Black Obelisk of Shalmaneser III. Jehu kneels before the Assyrian emperor.

Ahab and Assyria

I Kgs 17:1-22:39
'Ahab, the Israelite' is mentioned by name on the monolith Inscription of Shalmaneser III (859-824).

Jehu and Assyria

2 Kgs 9:1-10:36
Hazael of Damascus (2 Kgs 8: 7-15) is mentioned in a text from Ashur, and Jehu (or an emissary) is actually pictured on the Black Obelisk of Shalmaneser III (found 1846) kneeling in tribute before the Assyrian emperor – 'tribute of Iaua (Jehu), son of Omri.'

Ben Hadad II of Aram

2 Kgs 13.25
Mentioned in the stele of Zakir, king of Hamath, found in 1903 in northern Syria, published 1907 by H. Pognon.

Jeroboam II

2 Kgs 14:23-29
Jasper seal of 'Sheme, servant of Jeroboam,' was found at Megiddo by Schumacher. Jeroboam II's capital at Samaria is illuminated by excavations there (see 'Omri' above).

Menahem

2 Kgs 15:19
Menahem's tribute is mentioned in the annals of Pul (Tiglath-Pileser III, 745-727 B.C.).

Fall of Damascus

2 Kgs 16:9
Described in Tiglath-Pileser's Annals but lost. Mentioned in Assyrian records also are Azariah of Judah (2 Kgs 15:1-7), Rezin (Rasunna) of Aram, Ahaz of Judah (2 Kgs 16:7-8), Pekah and Hoshea (2 Kgs 15:30).

Fall of Samaria

2 Kgs 17:3-23
Siege begun by Shalmaneser V (726-722 B.C.) completed by Sargon II (722-705 B.C.); cf. Isa 20:1. In his Khorsabad Annals Sargon relates how he deported 27,290 Samerinai (people of Samaria). He does the same in the 'Display Inscription' at Khorsabad, his capital.

Hezekiah and Sennacherib

2 Kgs 18:13-19:37; Isa 36:1-37:38
In the Annals of Sennacherib (705-681) preserved on the Taylor Prism in the British Museum, the Assyrian monarch tells of his siege of Jerusalem (701 B.C.) in which he says he shut up Hezekiah 'like a caged bird.' Sennacherib's great capital, Nineveh, excavated by Austen Layard, yielded the royal palace (1849-51), besides many other archaeological treasures.

Hezekiah's tunnel

2 Kgs 20:20
The Siloam Inscription, discovered in 1880, was carved on the conduit

Excavation Sites
in Palestine

Tell Dan
Tell Anafa

Hazor

Acre **GALILEE**

W. el-Mughara

Tiberias *Sea of Galilee*

Tell Megadim Carmel Caves Ubeidiya

Athlit Beth-Shearim

Megiddo *Jezreel Valley*

Caesarea Beth Alpha

Wadi Ara Beth-Shean

Hadera *Mt. Gilboa* Gilead

Mt. Ebal Tell el-Fara'h

Shechem *Mt. Gerizim*

Tell Qasile

Jordan R.

Jaffa

W. Natuf Bethel

MEDITERRANEAN Ekron Gibeon Jericho

SEA Beth-Shemesh Gibeah Qumran

Tell Ashdod *Valley of Sorek* *W. Maraba'at*

Ashkelon Tell el-Hesi Beth-Haccherem

Gath Mareshah Beth-Zur *Dead Sea*

Gaza Lachish Hebron

Tell es-Safi En-Gedi

Mt. Casion

Arad Masada

Tell Beersheba

El-Arish *Judaean Desert*

Har Yeroham

NEGEV

Kadesh-barnea

Jebel Helal

A R A B A H

S I N A I

| 0 | 10 | 20 | 30 | 40 | 50 | 60 miles |

| 0 | 20 | 40 | 60 | 80 | 100 km |

Major excavations

Timna

Ezion-geber

Excavations at Qumran have filled in historical gaps of the period 150 B.C.-A.D. 70.

about 19 feet from the Siloam end of Hezekiah's aqueduct to mark the completion of the 1777-foot-long rock tunnel (c. 700 B.C.)

Manasseh's idolatry
2 Kgs 21:1-15
The Ras Shamra Epic literature from Ugarit has shed a great deal of light on Baal, Asherah, and Canaanite fertility cults. Manasseh's compulsory visit to Nineveh (cf. 2 Chr. 33:10-13) is mentioned in Assyrian monuments.

Isaiah's prophecy
Isa 1:1-66:24
The Isaiah Scroll, discovered with other Dead Sea Scrolls at Qumran (1947), is the entire prophecy, antedating other known texts by 1,000 years.

Jeremiah's age
Jer 1:1-52:34
The Lachish Letters discovered in 1935 and 1938 at Lachish (Tell el-Hesy) illustrate Jeremiah's age and Nebuchadnezzar's invasion of Judah 588-586 B.C.

Jehoiachin's exile
2 Kgs 25:27-30
This is confirmed by Babylonian records which list *Yaukin* of the land of Yahud ('Jehoiachin of Judah') as one of the recipients of royal rations in Babylon. This text was published in 1940.

Ezekiel's prophecy
Ezk 1:1-48:35
The genuineness of this prophecy is supported by archaeology in such details as dating by King Jehoiachin's captivity. Jar handles from Tell Beit Mirsim and Bethshemesh are stamped 'Eliakim steward of Yaukin.'

Nebuchadnezzar II
Cf. Jer, Ezk and Dan 2:1-4:37
The splendors of his capital city Babylon are now well known from R. Koldewey's excavations 1899 onward (cf. Dan 4:30). The Ishtar Gate, the palace, the ziggurat, Marduk's temple and the Hanging Gardens have been discovered. Bricks stamped with Nebuchadnezzar's name attest his building activities.

Jewish exile
2 Kgs 25:1-30; Ezk, Dan, Ezr
Three hundred cuneiform tablets found near the Ishtar Gate in Babylon, dating between 595-570 B.C., include the name of Jehoiachin of Judah among other captive princes, besides many Jewish names similar to those in the OT.

Belshazzar
Dan 5:1-31
Belshazzar is corroborated as the eldest son and coregent of Nabonidus by contemporary Babylonian records. Belshazzar reigned in Babylon (Dan 5:1-31; 7:1;

8:1) from 553 B.C. to the fall of Babylon 539 B.C., as the Nabunaid Chronicle indicates.

Fall of Babylon
The Nabunaid Chronicle relates how Cyrus and his general Gobryas took Babylon (539 B.C.).

Cyrus' edict
Ezr 1:2-3; 2 Chr 36:22-23
Cyrus' Cylinder, discovered by H. Rassam in the 19th cen., tells of Cyrus' restoration of people and their gods, and is in line with the spirit of the decree recorded in the Bible.

The return
Ezr 1:1-10:44
Prominent leaders, such as Sheshbazzar (Ezr 1:11) and Zerubbabel (Ezr 2:2) bear good Babylonian names illustrated by discoveries in this area. The 'daric' (Ezr 2:69, RSV) is the Greek drachma, and shown to be authentic for this date.

Ezra-Nehemiah
The Elephantine Papyri (discovered 1903) dating 500-400 B.C., written in Aramaic by Jews on the island of Elephantine at the First Cataract of the Nile, are the chief archaeological source for illustrating detail and the genuineness of the books of Ezra and Nehemiah.

Haggai, Zechariah
Illustrated by the trilingual (Babylonian, Elamite and Persian) Behistun Inscription set up by Darius I, the Great (522-486 B.C.). (Zech 1:1, 7.)

Xerxes and Esther
The book of Esther is illustrated by inscriptions from Persepolis, the Persian capital. Xerxes (486-465 B.C.) suffered defeat by the Greeks at Salamis and Plataea. 'Shushan' (Est 1:2) is Susa where Xerxes' palace was discovered by the French (1880-90). The casting of the lot (Pur, 3:7) is illustrated by archaeology as well as details of local color.

Between the Testaments
Illustrated by the Dead Sea Scrolls: two scrolls of Isaiah, Habakkuk Commentary, Manual of Discipline of the pre-Christian sect of the Essenes, War between the Children of Light and Darkness, and fragments of almost all OT books, aiding textual criticism. Excavations of the Essene Community at Qumran (1953- 56) have filled in historical gaps of the period 150 B.C.-A.D. 70.

Luke's census
Lk 2:1-5
Papyri suggest that Quirinius was twice governor of Syria, probably briefly before 4 B.C. as well as in A.D 6-7. Papyri also show that a Roman census was conducted every 14 years and that people were required to go to their ancestral homes for it. Archaeology supports Luke as far as available evidence goes, showing how invalid was the old liberal charge that Lk 2:1-5 was a medley of errors.

Pontius Pilate
Mt 27:11-25
Coins attest the procurator Pontius Pilate A.D 6-36, as well as other procurators from Coponius to Antonius Felix.

Synagogues
Mk 1:21; Lk 7:1, 5
The most famous and best preserved of these is the synagogue at Capernaum (late 3rd cen.), probably built on the site of the one Jesus ministered in. Other synagogues have been uncovered at Chorazin, Bethsaida Julias, and Beth Alpha.

Crucifixion
Mt 27:32-60
Two views of the site prevail: (1) one within the Church of the Holy Sepulchre, thought then to be outside the walls (Heb 13:12-13); (2) the other at Gordon's Calvary near the Damascus Gate, outside the present walls on the north side.

Burial of Jesus
Jn 19:41-42
One view favors the site of the

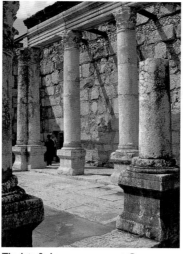

The late 3rd cen. synagogue at Capernaum.

Church of the Holy Sepulchre; the other the Garden Tomb unearthed by Gen. Christian Gordon (1881) near Gordon's Calvary.

Resurrection
The Nazareth Inscription is an imperial ordinance brought to Paris from Nazareth (1878) and now in the Bibliothèque Nationale. It concerns the crime of the violation of tombs with the death penalty. By those who assign it to Tiberius or Claudius it has been interpreted as evidence of Christ's resurrection. However, some connect it with later emperors, so the proof is not decisive.

NT Jericho
Lk 10:30-37
NT Jericho, excavated in 1950, was Herod the Great's and Archelaus' elegant winter capital. Ruins include a theater, palace, fortress and a hippodrome, like those at Jerash.

Herod's temple
Mt 24:2; Mk 13:2
Two signs from Herod's temple forbidding non-Jews to enter the court of the Jews have been found at Jerusalem, one in 1871 and another in 1935, near St. Stephen's Gate (see Acts 21:28-31). The stones read: 'No alien may enter within the balustrade and enclosure around the sanctuary. Whoever is caught will render himself liable to

the death penalty, which will inevitably follow.'

Bethlehem
Mt 2:1; Lk 2:4
A short distance SE of Bethlehem are the ruins of the Herodium, Herod the Great's fortress palace, and farther SE was his 'Mountain Stronghold' at Masada.

Nazareth
Mt 2:23; Lk 1:26
Site of Mary's Well. The important city of Sepphoris, just three miles N of Nazareth, was walled and embellished by Herod Antipas. Japha lay only one and a half miles SW.

Other cities
Tiberias (Jn 6:23), Magdala, Capernaum, Chorazin and Bethsaida were all on or not far from the Sea of Galilee and have been illuminated by archaeology. Caesarea Philippi near Hermon (Mk 8:27) and the Decapolis (Mt 4:25; Mk 5:20), the latter a ten-city confederation, are now much better known.

Samaria (Sebaste)
Cf. Acts 8:5
Excavations have resurrected the Hellenistic-Roman city, especially the fortifications of Herod the Great and his grandiose Temple to Augustus and stadium.

Caesarea Palestine
Acts 10:1, 24
This brilliant Hellenistic city built by Herod the Great was the scene in 1960 of undersea exploration of Herod's sea mole by the Link Expedition. Excavation of the city has uncovered a forum, theater, stadium, amphitheater, etc.

Antioch on the Orontes
Acts 13:1; 14:26-28
Extensive excavations since 1932 have shown the beauty and size of this third city of the empire and birthplace of Christian missions. Beautiful mosaics, the Chalice of Antioch, numerous Christian churches, etc., together with important diggings at Antioch's seaport Seleucia Pieria (Acts 13:4), are the result of these researches.

The Temple of Artemis, Sardis, where Christianity supplanted worship of Artemis.

Proconsul vs. Propraetor
Acts 13:7 (ASV)
Luke has been proved correct in calling Sergius Paulus 'proconsul,' *not* 'propraetor.' An inscription was found reading: 'under Paulus, the proconsul,' dated A.D 52-53.

Antioch of Pisidia
Acts 13:14-52
The site of this city was discovered in 1833. William Ramsay excavated the sanctuary of the god Men 1910-1913. Numbers of inscriptions were found. Later excavations by the University of Michigan have uncovered the Roman city.

Other Asiatic Cities
Iconium, Lystra and Derbe have also been identified and important inscriptions and other data gained.

Philippi
Acts 16:12-40
Excavated between 1914 and 1938, the site has revealed forum, porticoes, public temples, etc., of the Roman colony.

Thessalonica
Acts 17:6, 8
Accuracy of Luke's use of 'politarchs' (in original, for city officials) has been vindicated by some 17 inscriptions. The most famous from the Vardar Gate is now in the British Museum.

Athens
Acts 17:15-34
Since 1930 excavations of the American School of Classical Studies have uncovered the ancient agora.

Corinth
Acts 18:1-17
Extensive excavations since 1896 have resurrected the ruins of the ancient city. Gallio's proconsulship is attested.

Ephesus
Acts 19:1-41
Discovery of the Artemision, Dec. 31, 1869, was followed by the excavation of this most famous temple of antiquity, next to Solomon's. Later excavations uncovered the theater, stadium, Odeon, Arkadiane, forum (agora), etc.

Cities of the Lycus Valley
Colossae was identified and explored in 1835 and challenges further excavation. Laodicea, now Eski-Hissar (cf. Col 2:1; Rev 3:14), shows extensive remains for further excavation. Hierapolis (Col 4:13) also shows extensive Graeco-Roman ruins.

Pergamum
Rev 1:11; 2:2 (RSV)
Since 1878 this brilliant Hellenistic Roman city has yielded its exquisite works of art. Digging was done 1955-58.

Sardis
Rev 3:1-2
Excavations reveal how Christianity eventually supplanted the worship of Artemis. Campaigns began in 1958.

Rome
Acts 28:16-31
'The Eternal City' is an archaeological paradise. Excavations and researches have greatly illuminated and clarified temples, forums, theaters, circuses, palaces, inscriptions, arches, etc.

NT as literature
The papyri, ostraca and inscriptions discovered from the Graeco Roman period show that NT Greek was the common language of the period (Koine) with some literary element, not a special 'holy' tongue.

Text of the NT
The NT has been attested by 240 uncial mss., 2,533 minuscules, 1,678 lectionaries, 63 papyri and 25 ostraca. Particularly significant are the Chester Beatty papyri from the 3rd cen. A.D, edited by F. Kenyon 1933-37.

Old Testament

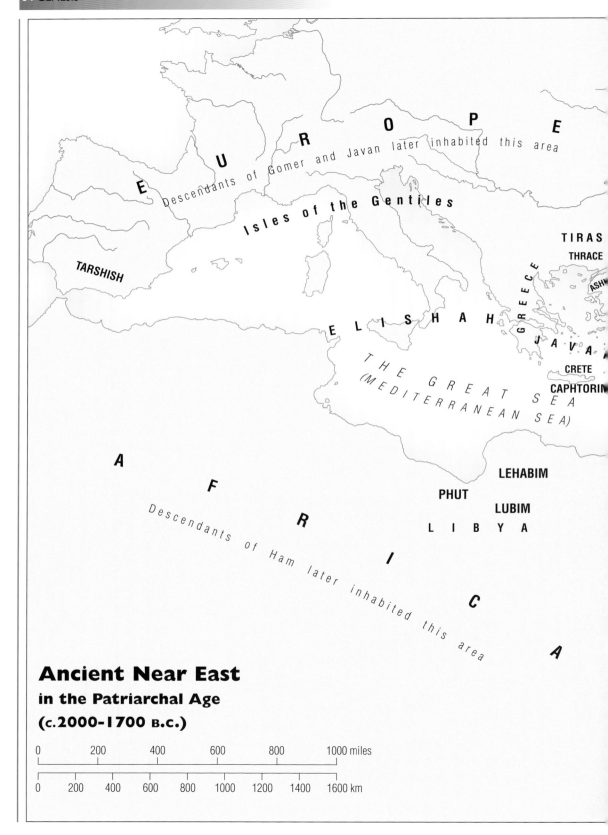

Ancient Near East
in the Patriarchal Age
(c.2000–1700 B.C.)

Descendants of Magog later inhabited this area

GENESIS

The book of creation

Nature of the book. Genesis, 'the Book of Beginnings,' is the indispensable introduction to the entire Bible, the foundation of all revealed truth. The book takes its name from the title given to it by the Septuagint (Greek) Version, derived from the heading of its ten parts *he biblos geneseos* (2:4; 5:1; 6:9; 10:1; 11:10; 11:27; 25:12; 25:19; 36:1; 37:2). The title of the book in the Hebrew is *beeresit* ('In the beginning').

Marshlands beside the Euphrates river, Iraq, the cradle of civilization.

Genesis records nine beginnings:

1.	1:1-2:3.	The beginning of the earth as man's habitation.
2.	2:4-25.	The beginning of the human race.
3.	3:1-7.	The beginning of human sin.
4.	3:8-24.	The beginning of redemptive revelation.
5.	4:1-15.	The beginning of the human family.
6.	4:16-9:29.	The beginning of the godless civilization.
7.	10:1-32.	The beginning of nations.
8.	11:1-9.	The beginning of human languages.
9.	11:10-50:26.	The beginning of the Hebrew race (covenant people).

Genesis records ten family histories:

1.	1:1-4:26.	The generations of the heavenly posterity and the earthly seed.
2.	5:1-6:8.	The generations of Adam.
3.	6:9-9:29.	The generations of Noah.
4.	10:1-11:9.	The generations of Noah's sons.
5.	11:10-26.	The generations of Shem.
6.	11:27-25:11.	The generations of Terah.
7.	25:12-18.	The generations of Ishmael.
8.	25:19-35:29.	The generations of Isaac.
9.	36:1-37:1.	The generations of Esau.
10.	37:2-50:26.	The generations of Jacob.

Outline

1-11 Primeval History of Humanity
1-2 Creation
3 The Fall
4-5 From the Fall to the Flood
6-9 The Flood
10-11 From the Flood to Abraham

12-50 Patriarchal History of Israel
12-25 Abraham
25-28 Isaac
28-36 Jacob
37-50 Joseph

Earth from space.

1. The beginning of the earth as man's habitation

God. In the first phrase of revelation occurs the declaration of the existence of God, whose eternal being is assumed and asserted, and in no sense argued and defined. He is presented here as the infinite First Cause, the Originator and Creator of all things.

'In the Beginning.' Evangelical scholars have taken a variety of positions concerning the significance of the creation account in Gen 1: 1-2:3. The opening words of Genesis have been commonly assumed to refer to the original creation of the universe. Some scholars prefer, however, to envision a relative beginning, allowing events such as Satan's fall (cf. Ezk 28:13-14; Isa 14:12) and the geological ages of the earth to precede 1:1 or 1:2 (the Gap Theory).

The issue of a relative beginning (re-creation) principally revolves around three considerations: 1. Is the phrase, 'in the beginning,' absolute or relative? 2. Does the word 'create' (Heb. *bara*) possibly mean 'fashion' or re-create'? 3. How do Gen 1:1 and 1:2 fit together grammatically and chronologically (i.e., is it possible that a gap intervenes)?

The phrase, 'in the beginning', is construed by most Hebrew scholars as absolute. It should be noted though that the phrase, 'in the beginning' of John 1:1 antedates the 'in the beginning' of Gen 1:1 in any case.

The Hebrew term *bara'* has the basic meaning 'create' in distinction from the word *yasar* (to fashion, form). In most of its OT usages *bara'* speaks of 'creating something new' or 'bringing into existence' (cf. Isa 41:20; 43:1; Ezk 21:30; 28:13, 15). As a result, most exegetes argue that *bara'* serves as testimony to God's *ex nihilo* (out of nothing) creation.

The phrase, 'Now the earth was formless and empty,' has been rendered, 'and the earth became . . .' to portray a chaotic visitation of divine judgment upon the original earth. To place a gap in 1:2 is untenable by the Hebrew text, which shows that all three clauses are circumstantial either to the main clause in 1:1 or that in 1:3. If a gap exists it must occur prior to 1:1 rather than after it. Gen 1:1-2 appear as a unit and serve as a summary introduction to the creative activity that follows. Although the gap theory framework seems to be declining in support, it does commend itself as a potential explanation for the fall of Satan and for the findings of modern science that suggest long geological ages in earth's prehistory.

Creation and the six days of Genesis

1. The six days of creation in Gen 1 can represent either (1) literal 24-hour days of creation,

(2) literal 24-hour days of divine *revelation* of creation, (3) extended geological ages or epochs preparatory for the eventual occupancy of man, or (4) a revelatory framework to summarize God's creative activity , asserting that 'by him all things were created: things in heaven and on earth . . .' (Col 1:16).

3-5. First day–light. The account of God's first creative acts contains several important affirmations. (1) God created *by his word* ('and God said'). The rest of Scripture echoes the power of God's creative word, culminating in the incarnate Word (Jn 1:1) who fulfills God's work of redemption. (2) The creation of light before the sun, moon, and stars (the agents of light) reminds us that light ultimately proceeds from God and only secondarily from His created 'lamps.' (3) The light also prefigures the 'light of God' come to earth in the person of Christ (Mt 4:16, Jn 1:3-9). (4) The state of Gen 1:3 is to be renewed in the New Jerusalem, where 'the city does not need of the sun or the moon to shine on it, for the glory of God gives it light, and the Lamb is its lamp' (Rev 21:23).

6-8. Second day–firmament. The second day involved the separation of the mixture of atmospheric waters from the terrestrial waters. The separation of the waters may well have resulted in vast amounts of subterranean and atmospheric waters (vapor) that remained in place until the cataclysm of the Flood.

9-13. Third day–land, sea, plants. After the separation from the atmospheric waters on the second day, the terrestrial waters were separated from the land to constitute the earth and to form the seas, making possible luxuriant plant and tree growth.

14-19. Fourth day–sun, moon, and stars. God now fills the universe He formed on the first day. These heavenly bodies (together with the vast galaxies in space) are now given responsibility as the source of light and heat on earth. Concerning the order of the creation that places *light* before the sun and stars, see the 'First Day'.

20-23. Fifth day–sea life and birds created. As God created the universe on the first day and filled it with the astral bodies on the fourth day, He filled the waters and atmosphere (created on the second day) on the fifth day, bringing forth fish and birds.

24-31. Sixth day–land life and man created. Man was created (not evolved) and appeared as the crown and goal of all God's creative activity with regard to the earth as man's special home. The expression 'Let us' (1:26) intimates the Triune God's counsel and activity in man's creation (cf. Jn 1:3; Col 1:16), as well as God's foreordained redemptive plan and purpose for man upon the earth (Eph 1:4-6). Man was given dominion over the earth.

2. Man in Eden

1-3. God's rest. God rested from His creative work of Gen 1 on the seventh day. This sabbath rest of God became the basis of the Mosaic Sabbath (Ex 20:11) and a type of the believer's rest in God's redemption to be realized in Christ. Elohim, the generic name of God, appears (1:1-2:3).

4-6. Edenic climate. The creative work of God is summarized and the prediluvian climate is described: 'but streams came up'. This passage may suggest that prior to the Flood the earth was watered by vapor from subterranean water (cf. Gen 7:11-12).

7. Man's creation. The creative act of 1:27 is here described in detail. YHWH (Yahweh, traditionally vocalized Jehovah, printed LORD), the redemptive name of Deity, is introduced in vv. 4, 7, when man filled the scene and assumed control of the earth recreated for him. In His Jehovah character, God is introduced in special revelatory and redemptive relationship to man.

8-14. The Garden of Eden. It was provided for unfallen man, 8-9. Its location, 10-14, was somewhere in the Tigris-Euphrates region, evidently in the easternmost end of the Fertile Crescent (the moonshaped rim of ancient civilization, with one point at Palestine-Syria and the other point in the lower Tigris-Euphrates Valley). The Hiddeqel is the ancient name of the Tigris River (Babylonian *Idigla, Diglat).* The Pishon and the Gihon were probably smaller channels that connected the Tigris and the Euphrates as ancient river beds. The accumulation of vast deposits of silt has changed the coastline of the Persian Gulf, pushing it farther out to sea.

A.H. Sayce and others located Eden near Eridu, anciently on the Persian Gulf *(Higher Criticism and the Verdict of the Monuments).* Friedrich Delitzsch (*Wo Lag das Paradies?)* placed it just N of Babylon where the Tigris and the Euphrates

Creation tablets

Illustration showing how a scribe wrote cuneiform on a clay tablet.

Creation tablets discovered. Between 1848 and 1876 the first tablets and fragments of tablets of the Babylonian creation epic called *Enuma elish* were found. Written in cuneiform characters the seven cantos of the epic were inscribed on seven tablets and were recovered from the library of the Assyrian emperor Ashurbanipal (669-626 B.C.) at his capital Nineveh. This version, though late, goes back in its political mold to the days of Hammurabi the Great. (1792-1750 B.C.), and beyond that to the Sumerians, the earlier inhabitants of Lower Babylonia.

Tablet 1. Tablet 1 presents the primitive scene when only living uncreated world matter existed, personified by two mythical beings. These two, Apsu (male) representing the primeval fresh water ocean and Tiamat (female) the primeval salt water ocean, gave birth to a brood of gods who were so ill-behaved that their father Apsu determined to slay them. But Ea, the father of Marduk, the city-god of Babylon, instead slays Apsu, thereby transforming Tiamat into a raging avenger of her slain husband.

Tablets 2-7. Tablets 2 and 3 recount how Marduk is selected to fight with the raging Tiamat. Tablet 4 tells how Marduk is chosen and how he defeats Tiamat (chaos) and brings about an ordered universe out of Tiamat's carcass. Tablet 5 describes Marduk's setting up the heavenly bodies for light. Tablet 6 sets forth the creation of man out of the blood of Kingu, Tiamat's commander-in-chief, who is slain. Tablet 7 describes Marduk's elevation as the chief of Babylon and head of the Babylonian pantheon because of his role in creation.

Similarities and differences with Genesis. The Babylonian account and that of the Bible are similar in that (1) both accounts speak of the primeval ocean, though the Heb. *tehom* (the deep) has been demonstrated not to be derived from the mythological Tiamat (cf. TWOT, pp. 2495-96). (2) Both accounts have a similar order of events — light, firmament, dry land, luminaries, man, and God or the gods of Babylon at rest. (3) Both accounts have a predilection for the number seven, seven days, seven cantos. But this similarity is superficial, and the differences between the gross polytheistic Babylonian version and the Genesis account are vast. The Babylonian account is a corrupted version of an original tradition, the truth of which was granted to Moses by inspiration and thus freed from its polytheistic incrustations.

Creation stories

The Temptation Seal portrays two persons sitting beside a fruitbearing tree, and behind one the upright figure of a serpent. But this is scarcely an accurate picture of the temptation scene, since both figures are fully clothed, contrary to the fact that both are explicitly said to be unclothed in Gen 2:25.

Adam and Eve Seal is from the fourth millennium B.C. level at Tepe Gawra near Nineveh, and now in the University Museum at Philadelphia. This small stone engraving found in 1932 shows a dejected naked man and woman followed by a serpent, and suggests to some the expulsion from Eden.

Worldwide traditions of the Fall are found among Chinese, Hindu, Greek, Persian, and other peoples and, like similar creation and Flood stories, go back to an actual event in history, being corrupted in transmission.

The Myth of Adapa. This account of creation was discovered on four cuneiform fragments, three from Ashurbanipal's library in Nineveh (7th cen. B.C.) and the fourth from the archives of the Egyptian kings Amenhotep III and IV at Amarna (14th cen. B.C.). This legendary tale, although not really parallel to the fall of Gen 3 as sometimes claimed, does contain striking similarities, such as 'the food of life' corresponding to the fruit of the tree of life (Gen 3:3, 22). The two accounts agree that eternal life could be obtained by eating a certain kind of food or fruit. Adam, however, forfeited immortality for himself because of a wrong desire to be like God. Adapa was already endowed with wisdom by the gods and failed to become immortal, not on account of disobedience or presumption, like Adam, but because of his obedience to his creator, Ea, who deceived him. Both accounts deal with the problem of why man must suffer and die, but are poles apart in the matter of an actual fall from a state of innocence, of which the Adapa myth knows nothing.

Shepherds at Qurna, Iraq, ancient Mesopotamia.

come close together. But changing topography renders any precise location now only a guess. It is significant, however, that both archaeology and the Bible concur that the Eastern Mediterranean Basin and the region immediately to the E of it (Breasted's Fertile Crescent) is indeed the cradle of civilization.

15-17. Man's testing in Eden. Created innocent, placed in a perfect environment, man was put under a simple test of obedience, to abstain from eating the fruit of 'the tree of the knowledge of good and evil.' The penalty for disobedience was death – *immediate* spiritual death (Mt 8:22; Eph 2:1-5), *eventual* physical death (Rom 5:12; 1 Cor 15:21-22). 'Altogether, Adam lived 930 years, and then he died' (Gen 5:5), and ever afterward death has 'reigned' in the fallen human family (Rom 5:14).

18-22. Man provided a companion. The Lord God declared that a sexless or unisexual race would not be good and enunciated His purpose to create 'a help suitable to man to be in his presence' (lit.), 'a helper suitable for him' (AV). Adam named the animals and birds; but these, although companions in a sense, were not suitable partners on the same physical, mental, moral and spiritual plane as he.

21-23. Woman created. (Cf. 1:27). The Lord God made woman from the man, and presented her to him. Only in this manner could man have 'a helper suitable for him.' Man is man by that spirit by which he *differs* from the beast. Gen 2:21-23 with 2:7 presents the details of man's creation in distinction to 1:26-27 which presents the general truth that man was created, not evolved, and that woman was created in man (*issâ*, because she was taken out of *is,* man).

24-25. Marriage instituted. The union of husband and wife prefigured the union of Christ and His church, the woman becoming a picture of the church as Christ's Bride (Eph 5:28-32; cf. Mt 19:5; 1 Cor 6:16; Eph 5:31).

3.The Fall Of Man

1. The Tempter. This verse introduces Satan, identified by subsequent Scripture (2 Cor 11:3, 14; Rev 12:9; 20:2), with his tool the Edenic serpent. Though the serpent (Satan) is presented here, many interpreters believe that he is introduced in Ezk 28:12-19 and Isa 14:12-14 where the king of Tyre and the nation of Babylon reflect the rise and fall of an exalted angelic being, Lucifer (Satan). The Edenic serpent (Satan's agent) was not a writhing serpent, which was the result of God's curse (Gen 3:14), but doubtless the most cunning and beautiful of God's animal creatures.

2-5. The woman tempted. Satan began by questioning God's word: 'Did God really say . . . ?' then he denied its teaching: 'You will not surely die.' Finally he substituted his own gospel, the immanence of God: 'You will be like Elohim,' 5. The woman's fall involved the basic ingredients of temptation; (1) the lust of the flesh, 'the woman saw that the fruit of the tree was good for food;' (2) the lust of the eyes, 'and pleasing to the eye;' (3) the pride of life, 'and also desirable for gaining wisdom' (cf. 1 Jn 2:16).

6-7. The Fall. The woman was deceived, but Adam sinned knowingly (1 Tim 2:14-15). Both lost their innocence, became conscious of sin and shame, and tried to cover this guilt and nakedness by some form of human effort (works).

8-13. The Lord God seeks fallen man. God's Sabbath rest of creation was broken by sin, 8, and He took the first steps in His new work of redemption to rescue fearful, ashamed, alienated, and confused fallen man. Adam hid from God, because of a change in him, not in God, His self-provided clothing seemed all right till God appeared and then it was found to be worthless. Similarly, sinners attempt to clothe themselves with their own righteousness.

14-15. The curse of sin in the serpent. Satan's tool, the serpent, was cursed and transformed from what probably was an upright, beautiful, intelligent animal to a revolting, crawling snake, 14. But in connection with the serpent not only was the deepest mystery of redemption-atonement hinted (typified by Moses' brazen serpent in Num 21:5-9; Jn 3:14-15; 2 Cor 5:21), but the first promise of a Redeemer was made, 15. This predicted that He would be of the human race, and would come through Abel, Seth, Noah (Gen 6:8-10), Shem (9:26-27), Abraham (12:1-3), Isaac (17:19-21), Jacob (28:10-14), Judah (49:10), David (2 Sam 7:5-17), culminating in Christ (Mt 1:1).

16. The curse and the woman. The status of woman in the fallen state is outlined and characterized by increased conception and childbearing attended with pain and sorrow, and the headship of the man, made necessary by the disorder brought in by sin (1 Cor 11:7-9; Eph 5:22-25; 1 Tim 2:11-14).

17-19. The curse and the man. The ground was cursed for fallen man's sake, for he could not wisely use too much leisure in his fallen condition, 17. Life was conditioned by inescapable sorrow, 17. Verse 18 may suggest that a vegetarian diet was prescribed. Light occupation of Eden (2:15) changed to heavy labor, 18-19. Physical death, 19, was pronounced (Rom 5:12-21), although man had already demonstrated spiritual death in his shame and fear in God's presence, 8-13 (cf. Eph 2.1-5; 4:18-19).

20-21. Unity of the race and typified redemption. Adam named his wife Eve ('living') 'because she would become the mother of all the living.' The unity of the human race in Adam is here declared.

22-24. Expulsion from Eden. As a result of disobedience man lost his innocence and experienced knowledge of evil. Through this knowledge conscience was awakened, and he entered a new time period in which God dealt with him not in innocence as in the garden but under conscience. He was responsible to do all known good and to avoid all known evil, and as a sinner to come before God through his prescribed means of redemption (the sacrificial system, though not explicitly commanded here, appears to now be operative, cf. Gen 4:3-5; 8:20; 12:7; etc.).

Man was accordingly expelled from Eden lest by eating of the tree of life he should perpetuate his misery. The cherubim at the gate of Eden vindicated God's holiness against the presumption of sinful man who, in spite of his sin, would 'reach out his hand and take also from the tree of life.' Later, in the Israelite tabernacle, cherubim hovered over the sprinkled blood in the holiest and portrayed the maintenance of the divine righteousness through sprinkled blood typifying the sacrifice of Christ (Ex. 25:17-20; Rom 3:24-26).

4. The first murder and civilization

1-5. Cain and Abel and their worship. Cain ('acquisition') was a type of a natural man of the earth. His religion was of works, destitute of saving faith, a sense of sin and need of atonement (cf. 'the way of Cain,' Jude 11). How mistaken Eve was concerning her first child,

when she said, 'With the help of the Lord, I have brought forth a man.' Eve may have thought that Cain was to be the fulfillment of the promise of Gen 3:15, but ironically, instead of getting the Saviour she got a murderer, illustrating the ignorance in which she was plunged because she trusted Satan for knowledge. When Eve gave birth to a second child, she named him Abel ('vanity'), perhaps in recognition of the seriousness of the curse. Cain and Abel stand as the prototypes of the division between the godly and ungodly that was to be perpetuated throughout man's history on earth. Though much has been made of the difference between the offerings, the principal reason God rejected Cain's offering was because it was not offered in faith (Heb 11:4). Even at that early period in God's redemptive program, true salvation is demonstrated to be by faith ('without faith it is impossible to please God,' Heb 11:6).

6-7. The Lord's plea with Cain. Just as God sought out Adam and Eve when they fell, God sought Cain. Cain, however, as a prototype of fallen man refused God's offer of reconciliation, preferring to pursue his own solution. Cain's actions reveal the plight of unregenerate man, compounding sin upon sin in his rebellion against God. Rejection produced rivalry, which produced hatred and finally murder. In Cain, sin ran its full gamut, beginning with alienation from God, and proceeding to alienation from other men, nature, and even oneself.

16-24. The first civilization. Cain left the place of God's manifested Shekinah presence above the cherubim eastward of Eden (3:24) and 'went out from the Lord's presence,' 16, taking up residence in the land of Nod ('wandering'). Departure from God's presence always involves the absence of divine guidance. Cain 'knew' (euphemism for having sexual relations with) his wife, one of his innumerable sisters since by this time Adam's progeny was numerous. Cain's son Enoch built a city (the first urban civilization). In the following verses the material growth and concomitant spiritual decline are portrayed. On one hand, we observe the growth of music (21), metallurgy (22), and poetry (23-24). At the same time, sin increased with the introduction of polygamy in apparent contradiction to God's monogamous standard of Gen 2:24, and Lamech presumptuously boasts about vengeance, a prerogative God claims as his own (cf. Deut 32:35; Heb 10:30).

Archaeological light

Beginnings of urban life. Excavations at Tell Hassuna, Nineveh and Tepe Gawra in northern Mesopotamia reach down to Neolithic times, 5000 B.C. or earlier, showing stone tools, beautiful pottery and architectural remains of skill. Around 4500 B.C. copper was introduced alongside stone. To the Copper-Stone Age, 4500-3000 B.C., belong such sites as Tell Halaf, Chagar Bazar and Tell Arpachiya in northern Mesopotamia. In southern Mesopotamia, the Tell Obeid culture about 3600 B.C. underlies Ur, Erech, Lagash and Eridu. Excavations here elucidate the succession of cultures in this prehistoric epoch, and bear out the biblical representations. Iron ore (cf. Gen 4:22) was occasionally smelted in Mesopotamia at an early date (or some suggest meteoric iron was used). At Tell Asmar (Eshnunna) Henri Frankfort found evidence of an iron blade dating about 2700 B.C. A small iron ax has been recovered from Ur. But iron smelting was not followed up on an industrial scale till after the Bronze Age, 3000-1200 B.C. The Iron Age extended from 1200 to 300 B.C.

25-26. Seth and the spiritual progeny.
The Lord raised up Seth and Enosh ('mortal') to be depositories of the messianic promise. Their birth closes the first section of Genesis (1:1-4:26), and sets the battle lines between the evil illustrated above and God's righteous remnant. This is reflected by the observation, 'At that time men began to call on the name of the Lord' (26).

5. From Adam to Noah

1-32. The messianic line from Adam to Noah. The second division of the book of Genesis is introduced by the words: 'This is the written account of Adam's line.' The next time the phrase appears is Mt 1:1, where the lineage of the new Adam is set forth. The godly race is marked by physical death, although long-lived.

The dirge 'and then he died' tolls like a funeral bell throughout this chapter. Alongside this sad litany comes the more pleasant refrain, 'and he lived . . .' Though death ruled from Adam until Christ, God preserved man long enough to bear children and preserve the messianic line. Enoch alone escaped death by translation, 24 (Heb 11:5) because he had 'walked with God.' Before the Fall God walked with man; after it, man walked with God.

The great age of the pre-Flood patriarchs was due probably to greater physical vitality and a more healthful pre-Flood climate.

6-8. The Flood

6:1-7. The moral cause of the Flood.
Several views have been advanced concerning this very difficult passage: (1) intermarriage of godly Sethites and ungodly Cainites; (2) polygamous marriage of ancient dynastic

Archaeological parallel

It has been customary for critics to treat the longevity of the pre-Flood patriarchs as obviously legendary or mythical. According to the Weld-Blundell Prism, eight antediluvian kings reigned over the lower Mesopotamian cities of Eridu, Badtibira, Larak, Sippar and Shuruppak; and the period of their combined rule totaled 241,200 years (the shortest reign being 18,600 years, the longest 43,200). Berossus, a Babylonian priest (3rd cen. B.C.), lists ten names in all (instead of eight) and further exaggerates the length of their reigns. Other nations too have traditions of primeval longevity.

Attempts to correlate Berossus' ten kings with the ten patriarchs from Adam to Noah have failed. However, the names as preserved by the Sumerian King List and Berossus evidently represent a corrupted tradition of the historical facts as preserved in Gen 5, besides giving extrabiblical indication of the greater length of human life before the Flood.

The ages of the patriarchs

Adam 930 years	Jared 962 years
Seth 912 years	Enoch 365 years
Enosh 905 years	Methuselah 969 years
Cainan 910 years	Lamech 777 years
Mahalaleel 895 years	Noah 950 years

Chronological light

It is highly improbable that the genealogical framework of Gen 5 was intended to be used, or can be used, for calculating the number of years (1656) between the creation of man and the Flood, thus dating man's creation 4004 B.C. (Ussher). There are several reasons: (1) The Hebrew terms 'begat,' 'son,' 'daughter' are used with great latitude and may involve a distant as well as an immediate descendant. (2) The ten generations from Adam to Noah and the ten from Noah to Abraham evidently aim at brevity and symmetry, rather than unbroken father-to-son relation. (3) Abbreviations due to symmetry are common features of Scripture genealogies (as in Mt 1). (4) In the recurring formula A lived — years and begat B, and A lived after he begat B — years and begat sons and daughters, B may not be the literal son of A. If so, the age of A may be his age when his descendant was born from whom B was descended. An indefinite time interval may therefore be intended between A and B. (5) Man is now scientifically known to have existed long before 4000 B.C., as both paleontology and archaeology show.

Archaeological light

The Babylonian flood story is preserved in the eleventh book of the famous Assyrian-Babylonian Epic of Gilgamesh, unearthed at Kuyunjik (Nineveh) in 1853. It describes a boat about five times larger than Noah's ark with a displacement of some 228,500 tons and cubical in structure. In both the Babylonian and the biblical accounts, bitumen or pitch to close up the seams of the vessel appears prominently. Both accounts hold that the catastrophe was divinely planned. But in striking contrast to the monotheistic Hebrew account, the Babylonian is polytheistic and has no adequate moral concept of the cause of the Flood. Both accounts assert that the hero of the deluge (Noah, Utnapishtim) was divinely instructed to build a huge boat to preserve life. Of all extrabiblical parallels that have come down to us from the vast cuneiform literature of the Tigris-Euphrates Valley of antiquity, the most striking remains the Babylonian account of the Flood.

rulers ('mighty men'); (3) intermarriages of the 'daughters of men,' i.e., women in the flesh, with the *bene Elohim,* 'sons of God,' i.e. angels. Of these three predominant views, the third is to be preferred because of the broad scope of the passage (i.e. cause for a cataclysmic flood); the origin of the *nephilim* (possibly related to races of giants that inhabited the earth, cf. LXX, 'gigantes'); parallels with Greek and Roman records that speak of Titans, mythological creatures that were part human and part divine; the OT's consistent use of *bene Elohim* as angels (cf. Job 1:6; 2:1; etc); and because the NT writers add their testimony in 2 Pet 2:4-4 and Jude 6.

6:8-12. The Lord's grace toward Noah. Noah found grace in the sight of God because of his faith in the promised Redeemer and the need of vicarious atonement (Heb 11:7). Therefore he

is said to have been 'righteous' and 'perfect' (possessed of spiritual integrity, *not* sinless). Like Enoch, he was an antediluvian of whom it was said, 'He walked with God' (Gen 5:24; 6:9). The ark Noah was told to construct was a type of Christ as the preserver of His people from judgment (Heb 11:7), specifically of the remnant of Israel who will turn to the Lord during the Great Tribulation (Isa 2:10-11; 26:20-21).

6:13-22. Instructions for building the Ark. 'Pitch,' 14, comes from a similar root as the Heb. word elsewhere translated, 'atonement' (Lev 17:11; etc.). As such its use may have a

The Ark dimensions

Three decks   Skylight   Roof   Length: 450 feet (137 meters)

typical significance with respect to Christ's atonement, which keeps out the waters of judgment. The ark was 300 cubits (450 feet) long, 50 cubits (75 feet) broad, and 30 cubits (45 feet) high with a displacement of 43,300 tons.

7:1-9. Instructions concerning the Flood.
Lev 11:1-31; Deut 14:3-20. Seven (or 'seven pairs' RSV) 'clean animals' (i.e., acceptable for sacrifice), are specified to be taken, in addition to male and female of each species for future increase (Gen 6:19). Such distinctions antedate the Mosaic law, which stipulates ten such animals fit for sacrifice.

7:10-24. The physical causes of the Flood.
The causes of the Noahic flood suggest a worldwide catastrophe, not simply a local flood (cf. 2 Pet 3:4-6). Several explanations have been offered for the source of the flood waters with the most popular suggested by Whitcomb and Morris in *The Genesis Flood.* They suggest that the Flood began with the displacement of vast quantities of subterranean water (Gen 7:11), certainly by earthquake, involving the sinking of land levels and raising of sea bottoms. This is mentioned first. The violent 40-day precipitation was only a secondary source of water and occasioned radical climatic changes. Up to that time the earth had evidently been watered by these subterranean fountains and an ascending mist (Gen 2:5-6), so that atmospheric conditions may not have existed to form a rainbow (Gen 9:13) as in the changed postdiluvian world.

8:1-6. The waters recede.
A wind dried up the water, 1; land and sea levels shifted back to normal positions, 2. Condensation of watery vapor which had surrounded the pre-Flood earth stopped, 2 (cf. Gen 1:6-8). The ark touched dry

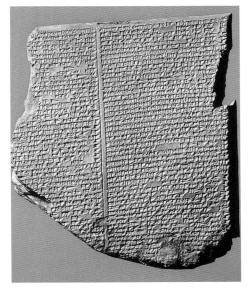

A flood account on tablet **XI** of the Assyrian version of the Epic of Gilgamesh.

ground on one of the mountains of Ararat, 4, not necessarily modern Mt. Ararat (Agri Dagh), the name being identical with Assyrian *Urartú*, signifying the general mountainous territory of Armenia (cf. 2 Kgs 19:37; Jer 51:27; Isa 37:38), W of the Caspian Sea and SE of the Black Sea.

8:7-14. The sending out of the birds.
A raven was sent out first, 6-7; then a dove was released on three occasions. The return of the second dove with a fresh-plucked olive twig showed that the valleys where the olive groves grew were almost dry .

8:15-22. Noah leaves the Ark and worships.
Noah offered burnt offerings on the altar which he built, 20, gratefully worshipping the Beloved One who had saved him and his family. Accepting Noah's act of worshipful gratitude, the lord 'smelled the pleasing aroma,' 21.

Great door

The ark was longer than a dozen big school buses or two dozen family cars, and taller than a four-storey school building.

Height: 45 feet (14 meters)

Width: 75 feet (23 meters)

Archaeological light

Both the Babylonian and the biblical accounts specify the duration of the Flood. The pre-Babylonian (Sumerian) account specifies seven days and seven nights, the Babylonian six days and nights. The Bible account indicates a little more than a year (371 days). The Bible also espouses supernatural catastrophism against the modern naturalistic theory of uniformity (2 Pet 3:56).

9. God's covenant with Noah

1-19. Elements of the Covenant.

(1) Promise that every living thing should never again be destroyed, 8:21. (2) Order of nature confirmed, 8:22. (3) Noah and his sons commanded to increase and subdue the earth, 9:1, 7. (4) Meat diet permitted but not with the blood, 3-4. (5) Human government (capital punishment) instituted, 5-6. (6) Rainbow appeared as the sign of the covenant, 8-19. Scripture does not specifically say whether the bow had previously existed and was now invested with the quality of a sign or whether it was a new phenomenon, indicating a changed climate after the Flood.

20-29. Noah's prophesy of the moral and spiritual history of the nations.

Noah in an unguarded moment dishonoured himself, demonstrating that salvation from the Flood did not ultimately change man's sinful nature, 20-21. His son Ham, exhibiting the lascivious bent of his character, shamefully dishonoured his father, 22-23. Noah by the spirit of prophecy foretold the inevitable outworking of this lascivious tendency in the curse that fell upon Ham's 'son' (descendant) Canaan, who represented the progenitor of that branch of the Hamitic peoples that later occupied Palestine before Israel's conquest (Gen 10:15-20).

The purpose of this prophecy was to indicate the origin of the Canaanites and to show the source of their moral pollution (cf. Gen 10:15-19; 19:5; Lev 18, 20; Deut 12:31). That Canaan's curse was fundamentally religious rather than racial is shown by the fact that Shem's contrasting blessing was religious, 9:26, with a knowledge of God and God's salvation coming through the Semitic line. Likewise Japheth's blessing was also religious, 27. He would dwell in the tents of Shem.

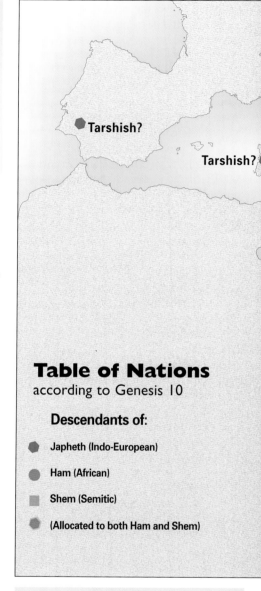

Table of Nations
according to Genesis 10

Descendants of:

- Japheth (Indo-European)
- Ham (African)
- Shem (Semitic)
- (Allocated to both Ham and Shem)

Archaeological light

In the Babylonian flood story, Utnapishtim offered sacrifice, poured out a libation, and burned 'sweet cane, cedar, and myrtle' after he left the boat, partly to appease the wrath of the angry deities who had decreed the complete extermination of mankind and partly to express his gratitude to the god Ea for sparing him. In both accounts the expression 'smell' occurs. Before he left the boat, like Noah, Utnapishtim sent out birds – a dove seven days after the boat landed on Mt. Nisir, followed by a swallow and finally a raven.

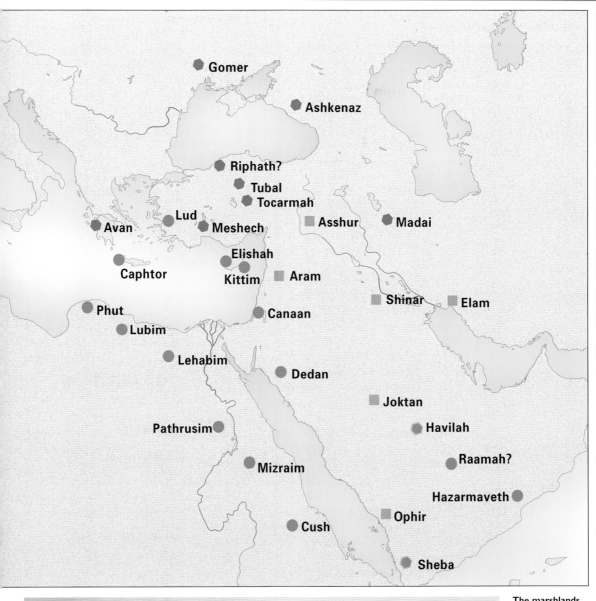

Gomer

Ashkenaz

Riphath?

Tubal

Tocarmah

Lud

Avan

Meshech

Asshur

Madai

Elishah

Caphtor

Kittim

Aram

Shinar

Elam

Phut

Canaan

Lubim

Lehabim

Dedan

Joktan

Pathrusim

Havilah

Raamah?

Mizraim

Hazarmaveth

Ophir

Cush

Sheba

The marshlands of southern Iraq–Mesopotamia – during a thunderstorm.

Archaeological light

The Canaanites were enslaved by one of the most terrible and degrading forms of idolatry, which encouraged their immorality. Discovered in 1929-37, Canaanite religious literature from Ras Shamra (ancient Ugarit in North Syria) reveals the worship of the immoral gods El and Baal and the sacred courtesans Anath, Asherah and Astarte. This literature fully corroborates the OT notices of the religious debauchery and moral degradation of the Canaanites. Cult objects, figurines and literature combine to show how sex-centered was Canaanite religion, with human sacrifice, cult of serpents, sacred courtesans and eunuch priests excessively common. The sordid depths of social degradation to which the erotic aspects of the Canaanite cults led can scarcely be imagined.

10. The Sons of Noah
Japhethites

Noah's panoramic prophecy of moral and spiritual history (cf. 9:24-27) forms an indispensible introduction to the principle that underlies the ethnographic table of Gen 10, viz., that in God's ways with men the moral character of a nation cannot be understood unless its source is known. The nation Israel, divinely elected to be the medium of redemptive blessing to the world, needed to know the source from which the various nations surrounding her sprang, that she might know how to act toward them. W.F. Albright writes concerning the table: 'It stands absolutely alone in ancient literature, without a remote parallel even among the Greeks, where we find the closest approach to a distribution of peoples in genealogical framework. But among the Greeks the framework is mythological and the peoples are all Greek and Aegean tribes . . . The table of Nations remains an astonishingly accurate document' (in Young's *Analytical Concordance to the Bible,* 22nd., p. 30). Although numerous names have been known from ancient Greek and Roman sources, modern archaeology of the past century and a half has elucidated many of them by its discoveries.

2-5. The descendants of Japheth. These formed the northern nations. *Gomer (Assyrian Gimir-raya),* Cimmerians of antiquity (Ezk 38:6), is mentioned in the annals of Assyrian emperors Esarhaddon and Ashurbanipal (7th cen. B.C.). Magog (Ezk 38:2; 39:6) were Scythians (according to Josephus), but probably this is a comprehensive term for northern barbarians. *Madai* are the well-known Medes (2 Kgs 17:6; 18:11; Isa 21:2) mentioned in the Assyrian

inscriptions. *Javan,* Ionian Greeks of Homer and particularly the Asiatic Ionians, was first mentioned by Sargon II (722-705 B.C.) and subsequently known in Jewish history (Ezk 27:13; Isa 66:19; Joel 3:6; Zech 9:13; Dan 8:21; 10:20). *Tubal and Meshech* (Ezk 27:13; 32:26; 38:2; 39:1; Isa 66:19) were the Tabali and Mushki of the Assyrian cuneiform records from the time of Tiglath-Pileser I (c. 1100 B.C.) onward. *Tiras* was probably the ancestor of the Tirsenoi, a pirate Aegean people.

Ashkenaz are the Scythians (Assyrian *Ashkuz*). *Riphath* were probably preserved in the Riphaean Mountains far to the N (Josephus calls them Paphlagonians).

Elishah is Kittim or Cyprus (Ezk 27:7), the Alashiya of the Amarna Tablets. *Tarshish* was the Phoenician copper smelting center at Tartessus, Spain, or one in Sardinia (Ezk 27:12). *Kittim* is Cyprus, connected with the ancient south coast city Kition (present-day Larnaka). *Dodanim* was perhaps the Dardana (Dardanians) of Asia Minor; also read *Rodanim* in 1 Chr 1:7 (RSV) and in the Greek and Samaritan texts of Gen 10:4, in which case the Aegean island of Rhodes is indicated.

Hamites

6-20. Descendants of Ham. These were southern nations. The earliest empire builders were in southern Babylonia and later in Egypt. *Cush* is connected with *Kish,* the ancient city-state in lower Babylonia. From Kish, where Babylonian emperors of the third millennium B.C. took their titles as kings of the world (cf. Nimrod, 8-12), the Cushites migrated to Africa (Kosh or Nubia). *Mizraim* is Egypt, whose civilization dates from about 5000 B.C. and includes the predynastic period to 3100 B.C. and 30 dynasties of splendid kings from 3100 B.C. to 322 B.C. *Put* is Cyrenaica in North Africa W of Egypt, as is now known from the inscriptions of Darius I of Persia (522-486 B.C.). *Canaan* represents the original Hamitic peoples settling in Palestine who yielded to racial amalgamation and became predominantly Semitic.

Seba is connected with South Arabia and is mentioned in the Assyrian inscriptions of the 8th cen. B.C. *Havilah* was ancestor to a people in central and southern Arabia partly Cushite and partly Semitic Joktanite (10:7-29). *Sabtah* is Shabwat, ancient capital of Hazarmaveth (10:26), modern Hadramaut. *Raamah, Sabteca,*

Sheba and *Dedan* are representative of Cushite tribes of Arabia.

8-10. Hamitic imperial power. This appeared in human history in Nimrod, founder of the kingdom of Babylon, plausibly explained as Sumerian (early non-Semitic Babylonian) Nin-Maradda ('Lord of Marad'), a town SW of Kish. The Sumerian King List names the dynasty of Kish with 23 kings first in the enumeration of Mesopotamian dynasties which reigned after the Flood. However, the name Nimrod suggested 'rebel' against God to the Hebrews, who took note of his character as a hunter, the opposite of the divine ideal of a king, that of a shepherd (2 Sam 5:2; 7:7).

Nimrod's Kingdom is mentioned in its inception in the land of Shinar (the entire alluvial plain of the Tigris-Euphrates River, the last 200 miles of their course to the Persian Gulf) with *Babel, Erech, Akkad* and *Calneh*, 10, all of which have been resurrected by archaeology. *Akkad (Agade)* and *Babel (Babylon)* were in the northern part of Shinar, called Akkad, and in the southern portion, called Sumer, was Erech (ancient Uruk), modern Warka, where the first ziggurat (temple tower) and cylinder seals were discovered. The name *Akkad* was given to the district of northern Babylonia from its chief city Agade; which Sargon made the capital of a Semitic empire 2371-2230 B.C. *Calneh* is still obscure, but is thought to be a shorter form of

Hursagkalama (Kalama), a twin city of Kish.

Asshur (Assyria), the capital and center of Assyrian power 60 miles S of Nineveh, now called Qalat Sharqat, was excavated 1903-14 and its occupation goes back to the early third millennium B.C.

Nineveh (modern Kuyunjik), about 60 miles N of Asshur, was the later capital of the Assyrian Empire. Resurrected by modern archaeology from the grave of its oblivion, it was anciently, like New York, the center of a complex of cities including Calah, 18 miles S; Resen, between Calah and Nineveh proper; and Rehoboth Ir (Rebit-Ninua), W of the capital.

13-14. Other Hamitic nations – descendants of Egypt are *Ludim* (thought by some to be for Lubim, Libyans, a tribe W of the Delta), the *Anamites, Lehabites, Naphtuhites* and *Casluhites* (all obscure). The *Pathrusites* are inhabitants of Ptores, Upper Egypt. *Caphtorites* are dwellers of *Kaptara* or Caphtor (Crete). The *Philistines* are abundantly illustrated by the monuments. They invaded SE Palestine en masse in the 12th cen. B.C., though small communities of Philistines may have been in Canaan from 2100 B.C. (cf. Gen 21:32-34; 26:1).

15-20. Other descendants of Canaan. *Sidon* (the oldest Phoenician city, 22 miles N of Tyre) represents the Phoenicians (Sidonians). The Hittites were an ancient imperial people of

The queen feasting with attendants, ancient Nineveh (modern Kuyunjik), about 60 miles N of Asshur, later capital of the Assyrian Empire.

Contemporary Mesopotamian history

Period (All dates B.C.)	Excavated site	Events
Neolithic Age 6500-5000	Earliest villages in northern Mesopotamia. Qal'at Jarmo, 30 miles E of Mosul, excavated 1948 by Univ. of Chicago.	Stone implements, simple houses, no pottery.
Hassuna Period	Tell Hassuna 25 miles S of Mosul. Excavated 1943-44 by Iraq Museum. Matarrah 25 miles S of Kirkuk. Excavated by Univ. of of Chicago 1948. Nineveh lowest levels. Samarra on Tigris N of Baghdad.	Crude pottery. Flint and obsidian artifacts. Development of agricultural implements, domestication of animals. Clay houses. No metal. Pottery improves. Painted pottery. Artistic height of Samarran Period.

Mesopotamia

TAURUS MOUNTAINS

AMANUS MOUNTAINS

IRAN

CYPRUS

SYRIA

MESOPOTAMIA

Tigris

Mt. Lebanon

LEBANON

Euphrates

MEDITERRANEAN SEA

IRAQ

ISRAEL

Jordan

DEAD SEA

JORDAN

SAUDI ARABIA

KUWAIT

LOWER SEA (THE GULF)

RED SEA

| 0 | | 250 | | 500 km |
| 0 | 100 | 200 | 300 miles |

Fertile land

Desert

IRAQ Modern state

Chalcolithic (Copper-Stone) Age. From 4500	Tell Halaf on the Habor River in northern Mesopotamia. Carchemish, 100 miles W of Tell Halaf, Tell Chagar Bazar 50 miles E of it and Tepe Gawra and Tell Arpachiya 175 miles to E of it.	Remarkable Halafian pottery. Wheeled vehicles. Copper begins to be used.
Halaf Period	Tell Abu Shahrain (Eridu) excavated 1946-47 by Iraq Dept. of Antiquities.	Settlement of southern Babylonia begun. Fine painted pottery. First prehistoric temples. Reed-clay dwellings.
Tell el-'Ubaid Period 4000	Tell el-'Ubaid on Lower Euphrates excavated 1923-24 by C. Leonard Woolley corresponds to lowest level of Susa in Iranian highlands.	Characteristic pale-green painted pottery, lapis lazuli jewelry, stone and copper implements and weapons.
Uruk 3500	Biblical Erech (Gen 10:10), modern Warka, 35 miles up the Euphrates Valley from Tell Obeid, excavated by Germans.	Oldest stone constructions, first ziggurat (temple tower); cf. Tower of Babel (Gen 11:1-4). Introduction of the cylinder seal and writing script. Arithmetic calculations.
Jemdet Nasr 3000	Jemdet Nasr in the Mesopotamian Valley near later Babylon. Q.E. Mackay and S. Langdon *Report on Excavations* at *Jemdet Nasr, Iraq, 1931.* Shuruppak (Fara), Eshnunna (Tell Asmar) and Kish founded.	Greater use of metal. Bronze introduced. Writing in crude pictographs. Sculptures of men and animals. Lower Mesopotamian cities of oldest flood traditions go back to this period. Sumerian King List.
Early Dynastic Period 2800-2371	Four dynasties in Kish. Two dynasties in Ur. Three dynasties in Uruk. Dynasties in Awan, Hamazi, Adab, Mari, Akshah and Lagash.	Pictograph writings, temples, statues, arts and sciences develop an elaborate idolatry by the Sumerians (pre-Semites in Babylonia).
Old Akkadian Period 2371-2180	Semites gain control. Sargon at Agade (Akkad) conquers Ur. Naram-Sin and his son Shar-kali-sharri rule a great empire.	Gasur (later Nuzi) important town. Efflorescence of art. Victory stele of Naram-Sin.
Third Dynasty of Ur 2113-2006	C.L. Woolley excavates Ur 1922-23.	Abram born 2161 B.C. Early life in Ur. Ur-Nammu was king. Famous ziggurat at Ur.
Isin-Larsa Period 2017-1763	Ur destroyed.	Patriarch period in Palestine.

Asia Minor with capital at Hattushash (Boghaz-köy) on the Halys River. The *Jebusites* settled in Jebus, the old name of Jerusalem (Josh 15:63; Jud 19:10-11; 1 Chr 11:4) before David's conquest (2 Sam 5:6-7).

The *Amorite* ('westerner') was applied by Babylonians in the sense of alien or foreigner to the inhabitants of Syria-Palestine. The *Girgashite* and *Hivite* were Canaanite tribes, which remain obscure archaeologically. The *Arkite* is represented by Tell Arka, 80 miles N of Sidon (Irkata in the Amarna Letters). The *Sinite* (Assyrian *Siannu)* is mentioned by Tiglath-Pileser III as a seacoast town.

The *Arvadite* denotes the inhabitants of Arvad, 25 miles N of Arka (Arwada in the Amarna Letters). The *Zemarite* alludes to the people of Simura (Simuros) six miles N of Arvad. The *Hamathite* represents the inhabitants of Hamath on the Orontes, excavated 1932-39.

Semites

21-31. Descendants of Shem. These made up the central nations. The special importance of the progeny of Shem in redemption is by their double introduction to that section of the table of the nations that deals with their genealogy and the solemn language employed; 21-22. Their languages were Eastern Semitic or Akkadian (Babylonian and Assyrian); North Semitic, Aramaic and Syriac; Northwest Semitic, Ugaritic, Phoenician, Hebrew, Moabite; South Semitic, Arabic, Sabaean, Minaean and Ethiopic.

Shem is designated 'the ancestor of all the sons of Eber,' 21. *Eber* includes all the Arabian tribes, 25-30, as well as Israelites (11:16-26), Ishmaelites, Midianites (25:2) and Edomites. The name Eber ('the other side, across') denotes either (1) those who came from 'beyond the River' (Euphrates), i.e., Haran (Josh 24:2-3, ASV), or (2) those connected with the Habiru (*'Apiru),* well known from archaeological records.

Elam is Susiana, capital Susa (Neh 1:1; Est 2:8), with excavated levels going back to 4000 B.C. *Asshur* is Assyria, founded by Hamites (Gen 10:11), but Semites overran the country. *Arpachshad* (ASV) is probably Arrapachitis NE of Nineveh. *Lud* (Lydians) with Semitic affinities was established by a dynasty of Akkadian princes of Asshur after 2000 B.C. *Aram* (Arameans) became an important people in Haran in the

Habur River region of Mesopotamia and later established states in Zobah, Maacah, Geshur, Beth-Rehob and Damascus. They were conquered by David. *Uz* (desert Arameans S of Damascus), *Hul, Gether* and *Mash* are Aramean desert tribes.

Descendants of Arpachshad were Shelah, Eber, Peleg and the thirteen Arabian tribes through Joktan (Arabia).

Descendants of Joktan were Arabian tribes. *Almodad* and *Sheleph* are uncertain. *Hazarmaveth* is present-day Hadramaut in southern Arabia, E of Aden. *Jerah, Hadoram, Uzal, Diklah, Obal* and *Abimael* are all archaic but unidentified. *Sheba* is a people of southwest Arabia, capital Mariaba (Saba), 200 miles N of modern Aden. *Ophir,* famous for its gold (Job 22:24; Ps 45:9; Isa 13:12) and Solomon's exotic trade (1 Kgs 9:28), is variously placed in India or coastal Africa. *Havilah* is perhaps different from that of 10:7. If the same, the Hamites held it previous to the Semitic Joktanites.

11. From Babel to Abraham
The Tower of Babel

1-4. The building of the tower. Noah's descendants spoke *one* language, 1. They journeyed eastward (that is, southeastward) from the mountains of Ararat (Urartu, Armenia; cf. Gen 8:4) to the garden spot of the very fertile alluvial plain of Babylonia (Shinar), between the Tigris and the Euphrates about the last 200 miles of their course before they enter the sea. The rich silt of these two great rivers built up this ideal location for the cradle of postdiluvian civilization and the Babel builders, 2. After a long period of sedentary occupation in southern Babylonia, and during the life span of Eber's son Peleg (Gen 10:25), which apparently occurred well before 4000 B.C., the human race had multiplied sufficiently and developed arts and crafts to build a city and 'a tower that reaches to the heavens.' This is not mere hyperbole, but an expression of pride ('make a name for ourselves') and rebellion against God and His explicit command to 'fill *the earth'* (Gen 9:1). Self-glory, instead of God's glory, and man-made unity to replace the unity forfeited by abandoning the fear of God were evidenced. Brick (sun-dried clay) and mortar (bitumen) were ready materials in the alluvial soil of the plain, 3.

5-9. The confusion of languages.

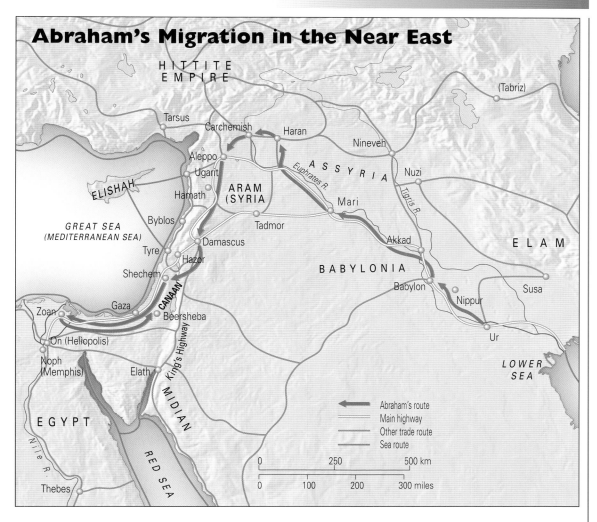

Abraham's Migration in the Near East

Babylon was undoubtedly one of the most polyglot cities in the ancient world, and the localization of the beginning of human languages there was effective. The confusion of languages was a divine judgment upon the pride and rebellion of the Babel-builders and effected their dissemination over the earth. But it was a divine act, and the precise way it was accomplished is not revealed. Gen 10 explaining the diversity of races is *much later* than the events of 11:1-9.

From the Flood to Abram

10-32. Genealogy from Shem to Abram. Ten names are recorded. These are apparently selective and the genealogy (like the ten names from Adam to Noah in Gen 5) is symmetrically and telescopically abbreviated because: (1) The apparent period of 427 years

covered (Hebrew), Septuagint 1307 years, is *much* too brief for known contemporary history in Egypt and Babylonia. (2) There is no evidence of a worldwide flood in excavated sites before at least 4500 or 5000 B.C. and to place the deluge at *c.* 2348 B.C. is archaeologically untenable. (3) Symmetry and abbreviation are characteristics of biblical genealogies. (4) The apparent intent of the narrative is to trace the messianic line with representative names.

12. The Call of Abram

1. The divine call in Haran. God initially called Abram in Ur (Acts 7:2-3; Gen 11:31) and renewed the call in Haran. He confirmed it at Shechem (12:7), again at Bethel (13:14-17), and twice at Hebron (15:5-18; 17:1-8), emphasizing how far-reaching in importance the call was. Heretofore the divine dealing had been with the whole Adamic race, now sunk into universal idolatry. God now selects a tiny stream from the great river of humanity through which He will eventually purify the river itself.

Haran, where Abram sojourned until the death of Terah, is still in existence on the Balikh River about 600 miles NW of Ur and some 400 miles NE of Palestine. It was a flourishing city in Abram's day, as is known from the frequent references to it in cuneiform sources. Its name *Harranu* ('road') in Assyrian sources points it out as located on the great commercial arteries between Nineveh, Damascus and Carchemish. Like Ur, it was a center of the worship of the moon-god Sin (Sumerian, Nanna).

Through Abram and the creation of the nation Israel, God established for Himself (1) a witness to the one true God in the midst of universal polytheism (Deut 6:4; Isa 43:10-12); (2) a recipient and a custodian of divine revelation (Rom 3:1-2; Deut 4:5-8); (3) a witness to the blessedness of serving the true God (Deut 33:26-29); (4) a people through whom Messiah the Redeemer would come (Gen 3:15; 12:3; 49:10; 2 Sam 7:16).

2-4. The Abrahamic Covenant given. The covenant, later confirmed (Gen 13:14-17; 15:1-7; 17:1-8), had seven parts: (1) *Abraham to be a great nation* – a natural progeny 'like the dust of the earth' (Gen 13:16), i.e., the Hebrew nation of the OT and the restored nation of the future kingdom; and a spiritual progeny including all men of faith, Jew or Gentile (Rom 4:16-17; 9:7-8; Gal 3:6-7). (2) *Abraham to be personally blessed* – 'I will bless you,' materially (Gen 13:14-17; 24:34-35) and spiritually (Gen 15:6; Jn 8:56). (3) *Abraham's name to become great* – 'And make your name great.' (4) *Abraham to be a personal blessing* – 'You will be a blessing' (Gal 3:13-14). (5) *Those who bless Abraham will be blessed* – 'I will bless those who bless you.' (6) *Those who curse Abraham will be cursed* – 'whoever curses you I will curse.' Antisemitism has always brought God's curse and will continue to do so (Zech 14:1-3). (7) *All earth's families to be blessed in Abraham through his posterity,* Christ (Gal 3:16; Jn 8:56-58).

5-9. Abram in Canaan. Abram's wife Sarai, his nephew Lot, and the persons (servants) he acquired in Haran migrated to the land of Canaan with him.

Shechem was Abram's first stopover in Canaan. This ancient city in the heart of Canaan is located in the pleasant valley between Mt. Ebal and Mt. Gerazim, the site of modem Nablus. Here Abram worshiped, some 30 miles N of Jerusalem (Jebus during the period of the Conquest-Judges).

Bethel, meaning 'house [dwelling place] of God,' was the second place at which Abram stopped. It commanded a magnificent view of Palestine, and was an ideal spot for Jacob's later vision of the ladder. The site, less than a dozen miles N of Jerusalem, has been excavated and its history in Bible times traced.

Canaan (from the Hurrian 'belonging to the land of the red purple'), at least as early as the 14th cen. B.C., became a geographical designation of the country in which the Canaanites or Phoenician traders trafficked in red-purple dye obtained from the murex shells on the Mediterranean coast. 'Palestine' is a later Greek term *(he Palaistine)* derived from the Philistines *(pelisti)* who settled along the SW coast (Philistia, Joel 3:4).

10-20. Abram in Egypt. Incidentally in connection with a famine in Canaan and Abram's trip to Egypt, the mighty empire on the Nile suddenly makes its debut in Bible history, but becomes common thereafter. Egyptian tomb monuments show bands of Semitic traders entering Egypt at early times, illustrating Abram's visit. Abram, leaving Canaan, got into difficulty over Sarai's beauty. It was common in antiquity for men of power to confiscate beautiful women. Abram's subterfuge of calling Sarai his sister was partly true. She was his half sister (20:12). Additionally, contemporary Hurrian records suggest that it was common for marriages to be formalized with an adoption so that the husband and wife also become adoptive brother and sister (cf. Jacob, Gen 29:14). Whether or not those practices affected Abram, the seriousness of his lie must not be underestimated.

13. Abram Separates from Lot

1-4. Abram and Lot return from Egypt. Abram's wealth is mentioned (cf. 12:2), and his return to Bethel (see note on 12:8) near Ai (see note on Josh 8).

5-13. Abram separates from Lot. Abram made the choice of faith and Lot made the choice of sight, resulting in spiritual progress for Abram and spiritual declension for Lot.

Tower of Babel

The Tower of Babel is illuminated by the gigantic artificial mountains of sun-dried bricks in southern Babylonia called *ziggurats* (Assyrian-Babylonian word *ziqquratu*, meaning 'pinnacle' or 'mountain top'). The oldest recovered ziggurat (one of more than two dozen known today) is at ancient Uruk (Erech, Gen 10:10; modern Warka). It was a vast pile of clay buttressed on the exterior with brick and asphalt (bitumen), like similar ziggurats at Borsippa, Ur and Babylon. Built in stages, three to seven stories high, they were varicolored. On the topmost stage, the shrine and image of the city's patron deity were housed. The tower of Gen 11 may well be one of the first such towers attempted, a symbol of man's revolt and rebellion against God. The polytheistic use of later towers, copies of the original, exemplified a complete apostasy into idolatry so characteristic of the Sumerians and the later Semitic Babylonians of the plain of Shinar.

The Nimrud ziggurat.

Artist's impression of a ziggurat similar to the Tower of Babel.

The World of Abram's day

Excavations at Ur. Until 1854 the site of Ur was unknown. In that year excavations yielded tablets stating that Nabonidus of Babylon (556-539 B.C.) had there restored the ziggurat of UrNammu. Excavations by H. R. Hall (1918) and C. L. Woolley (1922-34) made Ur one of the best known sites of Babylon.

The Ur Ziggurat was a solid mass of brickwork 200 by 150 by 70 feet high, called 'hill of heaven' or 'mountain of God.' On the top stage was the shrine of Nanna, the moon-god, patron of the city. The ziggurat stood in a *temenos* (sacred precinct) NW of the residential district, with the Euphrates skirting the city on the west and canals encircling and bisecting the town. Other temples and holy structures dominated the *temenos* of Nanna and his spouse Nin-Gal. Ur was a theocratic city-state where the moon-god deity was king as well as god, and the entire activity of the city, commercial, social as well as religious, revolved around the cult. Terah was very likely a devotee of the moon deity (cf. Josh 24:2). Abram left the city when it was at the height of its commercial prosperity.

Partial reconstruction of the ziggurat of Ur.

Abram in Northern Mesopotamia

Evidence of patriarch's sojourn. In spite of remarkable discoveries at Ur, especially the royal tombs (see Woolley's *Ur Excavations II: The Royal Cemetery,* 1934), no direct evidence has been found of Abram's residence there. Evidence of patriarchal sojournings

has come to light around Haran, however (see note on Gen 12:1-2). The Mari Tablets from the 18th cen. B.C., discovered in 1935, mention Nahor (Til-Nahiri, 'The Mound of Nahor'), Rebekah's home (Gen 24:10). Towns near Haran include Serug (Assyrian Serugi, Gen 11:20) and Til Turakhi, 'Mound of Terah.' Peleg recalls later Paliga on the Euphrates. Padan-aram (Gen 25:20) is Aramaic *paddana,* 'field' or 'plain' of Aram. Reu (Gen 11:20) also corresponds to later names of towns in the middle Euphrates Valley.

Contemporary Egyptian History

Biblical history is first laid in Babylonia, the 'cradle of civilization' (Gen 1-11). Not until Egypt was several thousands of years old in the time of Abraham (c. 2050 B.C.) did its history touch the Bible narrative (Gen 12 and onward).

Egypt was founded soon after the Flood by Mizraim, son of Ham. The Amarna Tablets indicate the Canaanites called it Mizri (Misraim being dual form, preserving the ancient divisions, Upper Egypt, above Memphis, and Lower Egypt, the Delta). Early and predynastic periods extend from c. 5000 to 3100 B.C.

Twelve of Egypt's thirty dynasties. In the 3rd cen. B.C. an Egyptian priest named Manetho arranged Egyptian history into 30 dynasties from Menes, alleged to be the first king of united Egypt (c. 3100 B.C.), to the conquest of Alexander the Great, 332 B.C.

The Pyramids. Abram may well have seen pyramids when he went into Egypt, for they were constructed in the Old Kingdom (Third to Sixth Dynasties, about 2700-2200 B.C.). The famous Imhotep under Zoser, first king of the Third Dynasty, built the famous 'step pyramid' at Saqqara, 190 feet high and the precursor of the other pyramids.

The Great Pyramid of Khufu of the Fourth Dynasty is the largest, consisting of 2,300,000 blocks of limestone with a base occupying thirteen acres, originally towering 492 feet, and each block weighing about two and a half tons. Khafre, a successor of Khufu, erected the Second Pyramid at Giza, which is almost as astonishing as the Great Pyramid. It towers 447.5 feet (its present height), being only slightly less than the present height of the Great Pyramid. East of the Second Pyramid is the great Sphinx. It has a lion's body and the head of King Khafre with customary headdress and cobra (uraeus), the royal symbol, coiled on his forehead ready to destroy the pharaoh's foes.

Pyramid texts. The pyramids prove the high degree of civilization of the Nile Valley and the strong centralized government. Fifth and Sixth Dynasty monarchs erected a number of smaller pyramids at Saqqara containing carved inscriptions known as Pyramid Texts, which describe the prospect of a happy life after death for the deceased ruler in the presence of the sun god. This was appropriate since the pyramids were tombs immortalizing the glory of the kings who built them.

First intermediate period. By Abram's time the glory of the Old Kingdom had passed, and the great pyramids were the mute monuments of its power. Dynasties VII-XI had no strong central government, Dynasties VII and VIII ruling at Memphis and Dynasties IX and X at Herakleopolis S of Cairo.

Above: The pyramids, Giza, Egypt. Below: The sphinx.

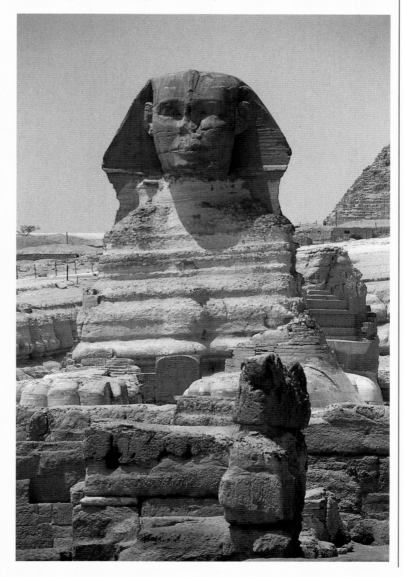

Archaeological light

In the Middle Bronze Age (2000-1500 B.C.) the highland ridge of Palestine was heavily forested with little arable land. Cisterns were not in general use. Consequently towns were located only by springs, so there was plenty of room for seminomadic herdsmen like Abram and Lot. Archaeology has shown that Shechem, Bethel, Gerar, Dothan, Jerusalem (Salem) and Beersheba were in existence in Abraham's day, as well as the Jordan Pentapolis – Sodom, Gomorrah, Admah, Zeboiim and Zoar (see note on Gen 19:1-38). Palestine was as yet thinly populated, with Canaanite towns located in the coastal plain and Esdraelon, and in the valley of the Jordan and of the Dead Sea.

14-18. Abrahamic Covenant confirmed.
See notes on Gen 12:2-4. The possession of Canaan and a natural posterity are stressed. Abram migrated to Mamre, near Hebron, and built an altar, 18. Hebron as a city was not yet in existence in Abram's day, not being founded till 'seven years before Zoan in Egypt' (Num 13:22), i.e., about 1700 B.C. Earlier the site was called Mamre and the mention of Hebron here, as in 23:19, is an explanatory note (prolepsis) to indicate where Mamre was located.

14. Abram the Hebrew warrior
1-12. Invasion of the Mesopotamian Kings. Four Mesopotamian kings fought against five kings of the Jordan Valley, 2, and were victorious, 3-12.

13-16. Victory of Abram the Hebrew. Abram is the first person in the Bible to be called the 'Hebrew,' 13. The occurrence of *Habiru* in the Mari Letters (18th cen. B.C.) and in the earlier Cappadocian Texts (19th cen. B.C.), as well as in later Nuzian, Hittite, Amarna and Ugaritic Texts (15th and 14th cen. B.C.), suggests the term is not an ethnic but a social designation describing 'wanderers' or 'those who pass from place to place.' Additionally, the Heb verbal root *'br* (possibly related to 'Hebrew') means 'to cross over,' further suggesting that the Hebrews were those who 'crossed over,' i.e., came across the river (either the Tigris-Euphrates or later the Jordan).

17-24. Melchizedek and Abram. Melchizedek, 'king of Salem' ('Uru-shalim' in the Amarna Letters, later Jerusalem), went out to meet Abram, who was returning from his victory over the confederated kings. Melchizedek, as a king-priest, prefigured Christ, who would arise as 'a priest forever, in the order of Melchizedek' and

thus fulfill the combined messianic offices of Prophet, Priest, and King (Ps 110:4; Heb 7:1-28). Abram glimpsed this messianic revelation of El Elyon (the most high God), possessor of heaven and earth (14:22), and paid tithes to Melchizedek in token of this recognition.

15. The Abrahamic Covenant confirmed
1. The divine promise. The Lord gave assurance of protection and reward for trusting Him.

2-3. The human predicament. Abram was childless. His steward Eliezer was his only heir. The adoption of a slave as a conditional heir is attested to in records dating from *c.* 1950 B.C. in Babylon and Sippar, and appears to have been common legal practice in Mesopotamia.

4-5. The promise of a son. This also included the promise of spiritual progeny as numerous as the stars: 'So [numerous] shall your [spiritual] descendants be' (RSV).

6. Abram's faith grasped God's promise, which ultimately centered in the greater Isaac (Messiah) and resulted in justification (Rom 4:3; Gal 3:6).

7-21. The covenant confirmed. God honored this justifying faith. The covenant announced (12:1-4), and confirmed (13:14-17; 15:1-7) was here ratified (15:18-21). The process by which the covenant is confirmed is illustrated in contemporary literature.

16. Ishmael and Abram's faltering faith
1-6. Temptation to unbelief. The stalwart warrior of faith in Gen 15 resorted to human means to help God out in the fulfillment of the promise. Unbelief manifested impatience in both Abram and Sarai, 2-3. Sarai pictures the covenant of grace, Hagar represents the covenant of the law that 'bears children who are to be slaves' (Gal 4:24-25).

7-16. Results of unbelief. The birth of Ishmael memorialized Abram's doubt and his tampering with the covenant given him by God. Hagar was given a promise that this son would father a prolific line, 10, and that Ishmael would be a wild, unruly, warlike man, 12. In this child of unbelief future generations were bequeathed a division, full of animosity, that is still a cause of international tension.

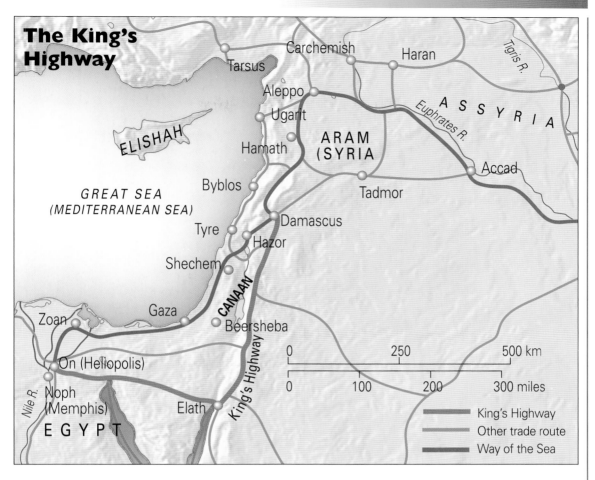

The King's Highway

Carchemish
Haran
Tigris R.
Tarsus
Aleppo
Ugarit
Euphrates R.
A S S Y R I A
ELISHAH
Hamath
ARAM (SYRIA)
Accad
Byblos
GREAT SEA (MEDITERRANEAN SEA)
Tadmor
Tyre
Damascus
Hazor
Shechem
CANAAN
Gaza
Zoan
Beersheba
On (Heliopolis)
King's Highway
Noph (Memphis)
Nile R.
Elath
E G Y P T

0   250   500 km
0   100   200   300 miles

King's Highway
Other trade route
Way of the Sea

17. The covenant reconfirmed

1-2. Covenant sealed by revelation.
God revealed Himself as El Shaddai (God Almighty), the All Powerful One, able to consummate the staggering promise of a coming Redeemer to Abram, to Isaac (Gen 28:3-4), to Jacob (35:11) and Joseph (48:3; 49:22-26; cf. Ex 6:2-4).

3-8. Covenant sealed by change of name. The name Abram ('eminent father') was changed to Abraham ('father of a multitude') as a token of what El Shaddai in His redemptive power would do. Sarai's name was also changed to Sarah ('princess'), 15.

9-27. Covenant sealed by circumcision. Circumcision was a sign or token of the covenant, 9-10, a seal of the righteousness wrought by faith (Rom 4:9-12). It suggested the putting away of evil (Deut 10:16; Jer 4:4), symbolizing the purification of life at its very source and thus saliently pointing to the

Archaeological light

Archaeology is attesting the high antiquity of Gen 14 as well as its accuracy. Examples of ancient archaic place names with scribal explanations, making them comprehensible to a later generation, are 'Bela (the same is Zoar),' 2; 'the vale of Siddim (the same is the Salt Sea),' 3; 'En-mishphat (the same is Kadesh),' 7; 'the vale of Shaveh (the same is the King's Vale),' 17, ASV .

The cities of Hauran (Bashan), Ashtaroth and Karnaim, were all occupied at this early period, as examination of their mounds has shown. The city of Ham has been found by A. Jirku and W. F. Albright to be identified with modern Ham and going back to the Middle Bronze Age (c. 2000 B.C.).

The route of the invading kings through Hauran, eastern Gilead and Moab to SE Palestine has been shown to be historically likely by a discovery of a line of Early and Middle Bronze Age mounds running along this route where the Early Middle Bronze city of Ader was found in 1924. Later this route, called the King's Highway, was famous, but does not appear to have been used after 1200 B.C. The asphalt of the Dead Sea, and the important copper and manganese deposits of Edom and Midian, appear to have been the purpose of the original invasion (twelve years prior to Gen 14, cf. 14:4).

The hills near Mamre and Hebron, where Abraham and his family settled.

Archaeological light

The five cities of the plain (rift) of the Jordan (Sodom, Gomorrah, Admah, Zeboiim, Zoar) were located in the Valley of Siddim (Gen 14:3) at the southern end of the Dead Sea. Now covered with water, this region in c. 2065 B.C. was fertile and populous. About 2056 B.C. the salt and free sulphur in this area, which is now a burnt-out region of oil and asphalt (Gen 14:10), were miraculously mingled, apparently by an earthquake common to this region. The violent explosion hurled the salt and sulphur into the air red-hot, so that it literally rained fire and brimstone over the whole plain (Gen 19:24, 28).

The great salt mass Jebel Usdum ('Mountain of Sodom'), a five-mile-long elevation at the SW end of the Dead Sea, recalls the episode of Lot's wife being turned into a pillar of salt. The Cities of the Plain are to be found under the slowly rising water of the southern part of the Salt Sea. Their ruins were still visible until the 1st cen. A.D.

messianic hope (through Isaac, 15-17, not Ishmael, 18-27). The greater Isaac, who Himself was to be born of woman, would be the Redeemer and Covenant-Fulfiller. He alone would exemplify all that circumcision pointed to.

18-19. Sodom and Gomorrah

18:1-16. The Lord's appearance at Mamre. An extraordinary interchange between God and Abraham climaxed the divine promises of posterity through Isaac to culminate in messianic redemption. The Lord in human form (theophany), apparently accompanied by two angels, appeared to the patriarch, 'the friend of God' (Isa 41:8, Jas 2:23) to assure the promise. The Almighty (El Shaddai) would demonstrate that nothing is too difficult for Him, 14.

17-33. Abraham's intercession for Sodom. The Lord reveals His secrets to His own. Abraham was therefore informed of the judgment of the wicked, that his posterity might know that what happened to them was divine judgment and not an accident. God's grace promised in the covenant to the believing is contrasted to His severity manifested toward the wicked and unrepentant. What boldness and humility combine in the patriarch's intercession for the sinners of Sodom 23-33!

19:1-38. Sodom's sin and destruction. The fearful degeneracy of the city and its overthrow serve as a warning to God's chosen people, especially in the case of the involvement of Lot and his family (cf. Lk 17:2; 2 Pet 2:6-9).

20. Abraham at Gerar

1-18. Abraham's lie. Abraham told Abimelech Sarah was his sister, repeating the same weakness of a former year (12:19-20) and demonstrating that the soon-to-be recipient of the fulfilled redemptive promise through Isaac was himself a needy subject for God's grace in view of his imperfections.

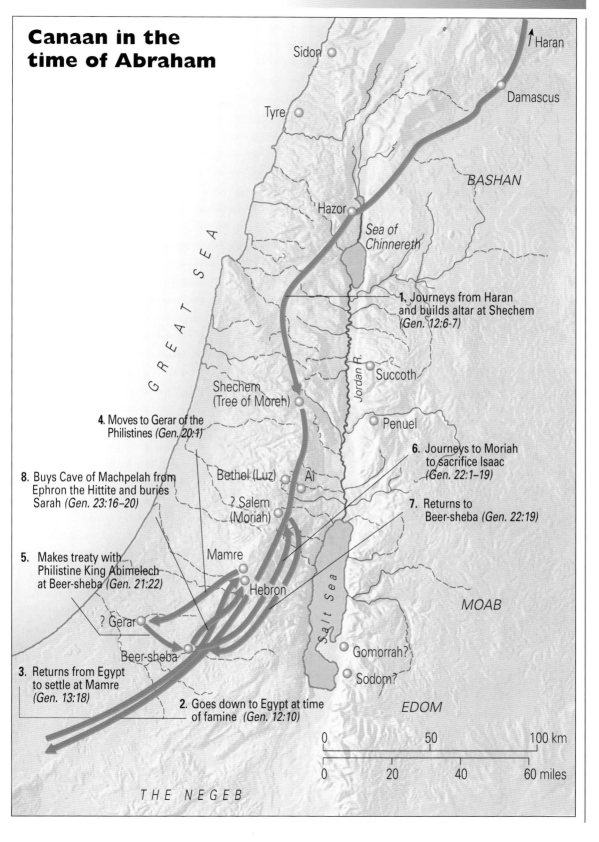

Canaan in the time of Abraham

Sidon

Tyre

BASHAN

Hazor

Sea of Chinnereth

GREAT SEA

1. Journeys from Haran and builds altar at Shechem *(Gen. 12:6-7)*

Jordan R.

Succoth

Shechem (Tree of Moreh)

Penuel

4. Moves to Gerar of the Philistines *(Gen. 20:1)*

6. Journeys to Moriah to sacrifice Isaac *(Gen. 22:1–19)*

Bethel (Luz)   Ai

8. Buys Cave of Machpelah from Ephron the Hittite and buries Sarah *(Gen. 23:16–20)*

? Salem (Moriah)

7. Returns to Beer-sheba *(Gen. 22:19)*

Mamre

5. Makes treaty with Philistine King Abimelech at Beer-sheba *(Gen. 21:22)*

Hebron

Salt Sea

MOAB

? Gerar

Beer-sheba

Gomorrah?

Sodom?

3. Returns from Egypt to settle at Mamre *(Gen. 13:18)*

2. Goes down to Egypt at time of famine *(Gen. 12:10)*

EDOM

0   50   100 km

0   20   40   60 miles

THE NEGEB

Haran

Damascus

Land of the patriarchs

Haran (see Gen 11-12) was about 400 miles NE of Canaan on the Balikh River, 60 miles above the spot where it flows into the Euphrates River. It was an important junction on the rich caravan route between Nineveh, Carchemish, Mesopotamia, the Hittite Empire and Egypt via Palestine. The town played a conspicuous role in Hebrew history.

Paddan Aram (Aramaic *paddana;* 'field or plain' of Aram; Gen 25:20; 28:2, 6), was the region in which Haran was located, and from which both Isaac and Jacob procured wives (Rebekah and Rachel) from among their relatives who had settled in Aram Naharaim ('Aram of the two rivers').

Nahor, Rebekah's home city (Gen 24:10), occurs often as Nakhur in the Mari Tablets, discovered in 1935 and belonging to the 18th cen. B.C.

Aram Naharaim, Gen 24:10, is sometimes translated Mesopotamia. It denotes the territory E of the Middle Euphrates, at least to the Habor River if not beyond. The actual term is Greek meaning 'in the midst of the rivers' (i.e., the Euphrates and Tigris) and reflects a much vaster territory than the early Hebrew term Aram Naharaim, which simply denoted the region of the Balikh and Habor Rivers which empty into the Euphrates within 200 miles of the river's course SE of Tiphsah.

Patriarchal customs

The discoveries at Nuzi SE of Nineveh near modern Kirkuk in 1925-41 have yielded several thousand cuneiform tablets illustrating such patriarchal customs as adoption (Gen 15:2, 4), the relationship between Jacob and Laban (Gen 29-31), marriage (Gen 16:1-16; 30:3, 9), rights of the firstborn (Gen 25:27-34), and the *teraphim* ('household gods' Gen 31:34), the possession of which implied family leadership. In the case of a married daughter, they assured the husband the right to the property of her father. Since Laban evidently had sons of his own when Jacob left for Canaan, they alone had the right to their father's gods. Accordingly, Rachel's stealing the *teraphim* was a serious offense (Gen 31:19, 30, 35) aimed at preserving for her husband the chief title to Laban's estate.

A shepherd with his flock in date palm groves in Mesopotamia, southern Iraq.

Archaeological light

The interaction among Abraham's servant, Laban, and Rebekah is illustrated in contemporary documents. The giving of gifts, the refusal to eat and Rebekah's choice all correspond to prevailing practices in Mesopotamian culture.

21. Isaac's birth

1-8. Birth of Isaac. The name Isaac ('laughter') suggests the joy the child of promise was to bring not only to his aged parents but to all the redeemed through the greater Isaac, Christ.

9-21. Expulsion of Ishmael. Ishmael mocked Isaac, perhaps as a result of his recognition that his hopes for inheriting Abraham's wealth had vanished. The text plays on Isaac's name, using an intensive form of the same verbal root to connote Ishmael's mocking. Paul says Ishmael persecuted Isaac (Gal 4:29). Abraham under divine direction sent Hagar and Ishmael away (cf. a similar event involving Ishmael's mother Hagar, 16:5-16).

22-34. Covenant with Abimelech. This incident shows what an influential and powerful man Abraham was as a result of God's blessing.

22. The sacrifice of Isaac

1-14. The supreme test. This event marked the highwater mark in Abraham's spiritual experience (cf. Heb 11:17-19). This, the greatest crisis of the patriarch's life, was made possible by three others which were foundational and preparatory to it: (1) His surrender of country and kindred (Gen 12:1). (2) His separation from Lot, a possible heir and fellow believer (Gen 13:5-18; 2 Pet 2:7-8). (3) His rejection of his own plan and hopes for Ishmael (Gen 17:17-18). Only with this previous spiritual commitment as a background was Abraham ready for the injunction, 'take your son, *your only son* Isaac, whom you love . . . Sacrifice him . . .' (22:2). The whole incident was filled with deep spiritual meaning. Abraham prefigures the Father who 'did not spare his own Son, but gave him up for us all' (Rom 8:32). Isaac pictures Christ 'obedient to death' (Phil 2:5-8). The ram sets forth substitutionary atonement through Christ offered as a burnt offering in our place (Heb 10:5-10).

15-24. The covenant repeated, dramatically and solemnly, in response to the patriarch's faith and obedience so clearly proved.

23. The death of Sarah

1-18. Sarah's death and burial. After the death of Sarah (from whom Isaac came), her grave was secured among the Hittites. Hittite documents illuminate the negotiations between Abraham and Ephron the Hittite. By purchasing the parcel of land along with the cave, Abraham became responsible for the feudal services connected with the land. Abraham demonstrates his faith by burying his wife in a land in which he was an 'alien and a stranger.'

24. A bride for Isaac

1-67. The servant seeks and secures the bride. The story of Abraham's servant and his search for a wife for Isaac stands as eloquent testimony of the life of faith. Obviously, Abraham's faith affected his household as his servant demonstrated great faith in his selection of Rebekah. Rebekah's willingness to follow the servant similarly reflects faith in the sovereign will of God. Scofield sees in the narrative a beautiful type of God's search for the 'bride of Christ' (the church), through the intermediary actions of the Holy Spirit.

25. Abraham's death

1-6. Abraham marries Keturah. With an account of this union and its offspring the story of the great patriarch ends.

7-11. Abraham's death and burial. The record of Abraham's death provides a fitting epitaph for the man of faith; 'Abraham breathed his last and died at a good old age, an old man and full of years . . .'

12-18. Ishmael's generations. When Israel is restored, Ishmael will not be forgotten (cf. Isa 60:7).

25:19-35:29. Isaac's generations. With the announcement, 'this is the account of Abraham's son Isaac,' the eighth division of Genesis begins, recording the perpetuation of the line through which the Promised One would come.

25:19-34. Esau and Jacob. Rebekah's sterility was cured by prayer, 21-22, and she gave birth to Esau and Jacob, 23-28 (cf. Rom 9:11-13). Esau sold his birthright, 29-34, which involved (1) paternal blessing and the place as head of the family; (2) the honor of being in the promised line out of which the Messiah should come (Shem-Abraham-Isaac); (3) the exercise of the family priesthood. Esau carnally despised all these blessings as a lover of pleasure more than a lover of God.

Archaeological light

Just as the table of nations (Gen 10) accurately portrays the tribal groups of the post-diluvian world, the genealogical notes in 25:2-4, 12-18 represent authentic records of the tribes descended from Abraham.

26. Isaac in Gerar

1-5. Abrahamic covenant confirmed.

6-11. Experience at Gerar. There Isaac failed as his father had done (cf. 20:1-18). Gerar was SE of Gaza in Philistia (Tell Jemmeh).

12-33. Isaac the well-digger. The Lord appeared to him at Beersheba ('well of the oath').

34-35. Esau's wives. These further showed the carnality of the despiser of the birthright.

27-33. The story of Jacob

Main periods of Jacob's life. (1) In Canaan, the stolen blessing, ch. 27; the flight and Bethel vision, ch. 28; (2) servitude in Paddan Aram, ch. 29-31; (3) return to Canaan, ch. 32-33. Jacob's life was a foreshadowing of the history of his descendants (Israelites). They were once in the land, now away from it, but will after spiritual renewal (Gen 32:30) return to it in fulfillment of the Abrahamic covenant so graphically confirmed to Jacob in the ladder vision at Bethel (ch. 28), as he was leaving the land.

34. Dinah avenged by Simeon and Levi

1-5. Jacob chastened. Although Jacob ('supplanter') had his name changed to Israel ('prince with God'), the patriarch's transformation in character was only gradual. He was still a man of guile and deceit. Reconciled to Esau, he told his brother he would follow him to Seir, but did no such thing. Instead he settled down at Succoth (Gen 33:18-20) among the Hivites for a sad experience.

6-31. Dinah's defilement. Jacob reaped what he had sown. The deceit of the father was to be reflected often in the deceit of his sons.

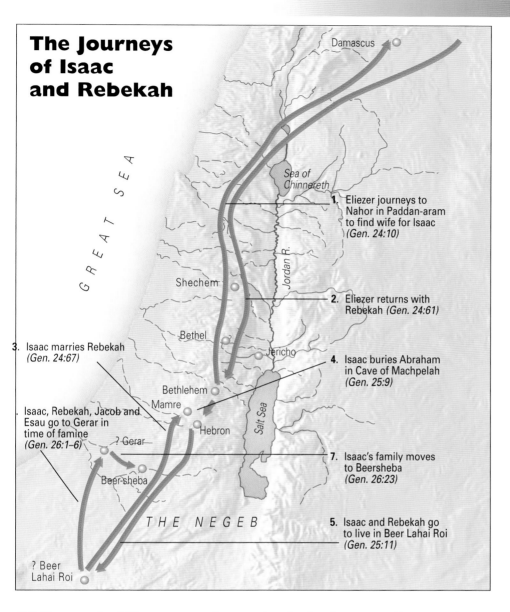

The Journeys of Isaac and Rebekah

Damascus

GREAT SEA

Sea of Chinnereth

Jordan R.

Shechem

Bethel

Jericho

3. Isaac marries Rebekah *(Gen. 24:67)*

Bethlehem

Mamre

. Isaac, Rebekah, Jacob and Esau go to Gerar in time of famine *(Gen. 26:1–6)*

Hebron

? Gerar

Salt Sea

Beer-sheba

THE NEGEB

? Beer Lahai Roi

1. Eliezer journeys to Nahor in Paddan-aram to find wife for Isaac *(Gen. 24:10)*

2. Eliezer returns with Rebekah *(Gen. 24:61)*

4. Isaac buries Abraham in Cave of Machpelah *(Gen. 25:9)*

7. Isaac's family moves to Beersheba *(Gen. 26:23)*

5. Isaac and Rebekah go to live in Beer Lahai Roi *(Gen. 25:11)*

35. Renewal of the covenant at Bethel

1-15. Jacob restored to fellowship at Bethel. The divine command, 1, was obeyed by destroying all idols that had contaminated them, 2-4. God protected on the journey, 5-6, and manifested Himself at Bethel, 7-15. Bethel ('house of God') is 12 miles N of Jerusalem and has been systematically excavated both as a Canaanite site and later prominent Hebrew town. In calling the place Bethel, Jacob (28:19; 35:15) reflected the impression the ladder vision made upon him there. Now in his deep spiritual renovation, it was the God of the place rather

than the place that captivated him, so Jacob called the hallowed spot El Bethel ('the God of the house of God').

16-26. Jacob's sons. Rachel died at the birth of Benjamin ('son of [my] right hand'), 16-21. Reuben, the oldest and heir to the birthright, sinned, 22, and lost the blessing (49:3-4). The other sons are named, 23-26.

27-29. Isaac's death.

36. Esau's line

1-19. Esau's country. Edom was the territory S of the Dead Sea reaching to the Gulf of Aqabah. Mountains and fertile plateaus on both

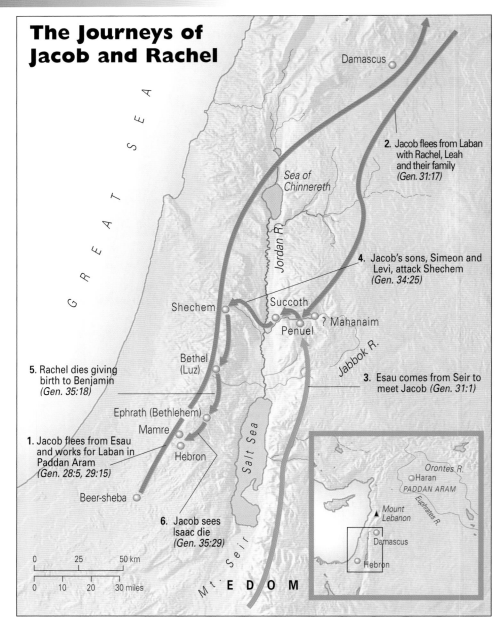

The Journeys of Jacob and Rachel

Damascus

2. Jacob flees from Laban with Rachel, Leah and their family *(Gen. 31:17)*

Sea of Chinnereth

GREAT SEA

Jordan R.

4. Jacob's sons, Simeon and Levi, attack Shechem *(Gen. 34:25)*

Shechem

Succoth

Penuel

? Mahanaim

Jabbok R.

Bethel (Luz)

5. Rachel dies giving birth to Benjamin *(Gen. 35:18)*

3. Esau comes from Seir to meet Jacob *(Gen. 31:1)*

Ephrath (Bethlehem)

Mamre

Salt Sea

1. Jacob flees from Esau and works for Laban in Paddan Aram *(Gen. 28:5, 29:15)*

Hebron

Beer-sheba

6. Jacob sees Isaac die *(Gen. 35:29)*

Mt. Seir

E D O M

0   25   50 km

0   10   20   30 miles

Orontes R.

Haran

PADDAN ARAM

Euphrates R.

Mount Lebanon

Damascus

Hebron

---

sides of the Arabah gave it about 100 square miles within its boundaries, which varied, however, with the fortunes of the kingdom. At the time of the Exodus the kingdom extended from the brook Zered S of Moab and the southern tip of the Dead Sea and skirted Judah in a southwesterly direction. Mt. Seir was a 5000-foot peak where Esau's descendants began their kingdom. Sela (later the Nabataean rose-coloured fortress of Petra) was the early capital of the country, which developed great wealth from agriculture, metal industry, cattle raising and caravan tolls from the

King's Highway which crossed its borders.

20-43. Horites. Hori or Horim were a tribe residing in Mt. Seir in Edom, 30, thought by many to be troglodytes (cave dwellers). Other scholars identify them with the Hurrians, non-Semitic people from Mesopotamia, known from cuneiform sources discovered within the last half century. The Hurrians were conquered by the Hittites in the 14th cen. B.C. and remnants of the latter also were scattered throughout Edom (cf. Gen 26:34-35) at an early date.

The Hittites (Heb. *Hitti, Heth*) were with

Biblical names

Biblical names help illuminate the Jacob narrative since many word plays are evident. Jacob (' deceiver') stole the birthright from his brother Esau ('red') with red pottage. He later manipulated the number of white sheep and goats to outwit his uncle Laban ('white').

Joseph the messianic patriarch

Why is so large a section of Genesis (ch. 37-48) devoted to Joseph? (1) He was the link between the family of Israel and the nation of Israel. Up to the time of Joseph the Israelites were a family. Joseph was connected with the Egyptian sojourn and the birth of the nation. (2) He is the Bible's most complete type of Christ – not that he was faultless, but his faults are not recorded. Numerous parallels between his life and that of Jesus may be enumerated, although it is nowhere actually stated that he was such a type. (a) Both were special objects of a father's love (Gen 37:3; Mt 3:17; Jn 3:35; 5:20). (b) Both were hated and rejected by their brothers (Gen 37:4; Jn 15:25). (c) In both cases brothers conspired to slay them (Gen 37:18; Mt 26:3-4). (d) Joseph was in intent and figure put to death by his brothers, as Christ actually was (Gen 37:24; Mt 27:35-37). (e) As Joseph reconciled his brothers to himself and afterward exalted them, so at His second advent Christ will be reconciled to converted Israel (Gen 45:1-15; Deut 30:1-10; Hos 2:14-18; Rom 11:1, 15, 25, 26).

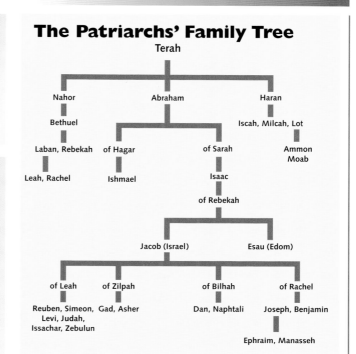

The Patriarchs' Family Tree

Egyptians, Mesopotamians and Hebrews one of the more influential peoples of early OT times. Their capital comprised the twin towns of Boghazkoy and Hattushash, not far from Ankara, capital of modern Turkey. They are mentioned 47 times in the OT.

37. Joseph introduced

1-11. The beloved son of Jacob. The varicoloured coat ('richly ornamented') his father gave Joseph was an indication of paternal favour and apparently of Jacob's intention to make him heir of the birthright. Reuben, the oldest, had forfeited the right by incest (35:22; 49:3-4; 1 Chr 5:1-2). Simeon and Levi, next in order, were ruled out because of their violence at Shechem (34:25-30; 49:5-7). Judah, the fourth son, was the next heir. Joseph, though eleventh in order, was Jacob's firstborn by his favourite wife Rachel and his father's favourite (37:3), and so apparently was Judah's rival.

12-27. The hatred of Joseph's brothers. They sold Joseph into slavery. (Cf. Judah's part, 26-27.) This rivalry between Judah and Joseph was to be perpetuated between Judah and Ephraim (Joseph's son). The division of the kingdom under Rehoboam saw Judah split from the ten tribes under Ephraim's leadership.

28-36. Joseph sold in Egypt.

38-41. Joseph's humiliation and exaltation in Egypt

Ch. 38. Parenthetical: Judah's shame. It is amazing the Spirit of God would recount this sordid story. But God's Word deals realistically with sin even in preserved family registers in the line of messianic succession.

Ch. 39. Joseph in prison. God's way up is often down, humiliation before exaltation. The Egyptian 'Tale of the Two Brothers' later in the reign of Seti II (c. 1300) bears resemblance to Joseph and Potiphar's wife.

Ch. 40-41. Joseph on the throne. He marries the daughter of the priest of On, a city of Lower Egypt, half a dozen miles from modern

Cairo. The Greeks called it Heliopolis ('city of the sun') since the sun god was the supreme deity of the Nile Valley. The worship of the sun at Heliopolis was the keynote of Egyptian ritual and the On priesthood was powerful and closely identified with the throne.

42-45. Joseph revealed to his brothers

This is one of the finest and most dramatic stories in all literature, filled with authentic Egyptian coloring. When Judah, who had years before engineered the selling of his brother into slavery (37:26), now climaxes the emotional throb of the story by offering himself a hostage for Benjamin (44:18-34), Joseph could no longer restrain himself (45:1-15) and made himself known.

46. Jacob and his family migrate to Egypt

1-4. The vision of God at Beersheba. In this last appearance to the patriarch, God assured him He would bring the Israelites again out of Egypt.

5-34. Arrival in Egypt. The descendants of Jacob are enumerated (8-26) as well as Joseph's sons who were born in Egypt, 27. Jacob met Joseph, 28-30, and Joseph gave directions concerning Pharaoh (31-34).

47. Settlement in Goshen

1-10. Jacob before Pharaoh. The mighty monarch of the Nile graciously received the

Archaeological light

It is noteworthy that so far no Egyptian records have been found of Israel's sojourn in Goshen. But since the pharaoh often allowed such groups to settle in Egypt, such an instance would scarcely be unusual. Besides the piece of sculpture depicting the entrance of the family of Ibshe into Egypt about 1900 B.C., another Egyptian inscription indicates that it was customary for frontier officials to allow people from Palestine and Sinai to enter this section of Egypt in periods of famine. This document (c. 1350 B.C.) tells of such a group 'who knew not how they should live, have come begging a home in the domain of Pharaoh ... after the manner of your [the Pharaoh's] fathers' fathers since the beginning ...'

Archaeological light

Ample evidence of famines in Egypt exists. At least two Egyptian officials list among their good deeds the dispensing of food to the needy 'in each year of want.' One inscription (c. 100 B.C.) actually describes a seven-year famine in the days of Zoser of the Third Dynasty (c. 2700 B.C.). The titles of 'chief of the butlers' and 'chief of the bakers' (40:2) were those of palace officials mentioned in Egyptian documents. The entire story of Joseph swarms with correct local and antiquarian details, as do the Egyptian narratives of Genesis and Exodus in general.

When Potiphar made Joseph 'in charge of his household' (39:4) the title employed was a direct translation of a position in the houses of Egyptian nobility. Pharaoh gave Joseph an office with a similar title in the administration of the realm (41:46) corresponding precisely to the office of vizier, the chief administrator of the country, second in power to Pharaoh himself. The Egyptian office of superintendent of the granaries was pivotal and apparently filled by Joseph in addition to his duties as prime minister (vizier). Pharaoh's giving gifts to Joseph (41:42-43) on the latter's induction into office was completely in accord with Egyptian customs.

patriarch. In turn the aged Jacob blessed the powerful potentate, an illustration of how Israel is yet to bless the nations.

11-31. Israel's settlement in Goshen. Goshen was the NE section of Egypt nearest Palestine. It was called 'the best of the land' and 'the land of Ramses,' which agrees with the character of this region, excellent for grazing and certain kinds of farming, but not particularly wanted by the pharaohs because it was distant from the Nile irrigation canals. This region is called Goshen only in the Bible. It was a valley some 35 miles long, centering in the Wadi Tumilat and stretching from Lake Timsah to the Nile.

48. Jacob's adoption of Ephraim and Manasseh

1-14. Joseph's sons presented. Since they were children of the Gentile wife Asenath, Jacob adopted Joseph's two sons to secure for them the family blessing and to ensure that they would remain true to Israel's God.

15-22. Jacob's blessing and last words

The Cave of Machpelah, Hebron, by tradition the burial place of the patriarchs Abraham, Isaac, Jacob, and Joseph.

to Joseph. Jacob's move was by faith (Heb 11:21), once again preferring the younger (Ephraim) before the elder (Manasseh).

49. Jacob's prophetic blessing of the 12 Tribes

1-2. Jacob's call. He assembled his 12 sons to prophesy their tribal future.

3-27. The prophecy. This covers in a remarkable manner the entire sweep of Israelite history – past, present, and future. The prophecy reflects the future roles of each of the tribes and may portray the entire scope of God's working with Israel from the conquest of Canaan to the restoration in Christ's millennial Kingdom.

50. Death of Jacob and Joseph

1-13. Jacob's decease and burial. Joseph grieved, 1-3, and had his father embalmed, 2, this being the only direct Bible reference to mummification by Hebrews. Spices were placed in certain body cavities and the body treated in an elaborate way to prevent decay. This highly developed science was practiced for 30 centuries in ancient Egypt. The Egyptians mourned for Jacob 70 days, which was the period required for mummification, while 40 days were specified for Jacob's embalming. Accompanied by a great company headed by Joseph and Egyptian officials, Jacob's body was taken to Canaan for burial, 4-13. Burial was in the cave of Machpelah.

14-21. The return to Egypt. Joseph's magnanimous treatment of his brothers is outlined.

22-26. Death of Joseph. Jacob was 147 years old (47:28) and Joseph 110 when they died. Joseph's faith is shown by the oath he made his brothers take to transport his bones to Canaan (cf. Ex 13:19; Josh 24:32; cf. Gen 33:19; Acts 7:15-16; Heb 11:22).

Egypt

Egypt: Its history and early contact with Israel

Early and Predynastic Periods, c. 5000-3100 B.C.

Neolithic and later cultures preceded the union of the kingdom by Menes. Manetho, a priest of the 3rd cen. B.C., wrote a history of Egypt dividing the historical period c. 2900-332 B.C. into 30 royal dynasties.

The land and the people

Egypt was a country 2 to 30 miles wide, situated along the course of the mighty Nile SW of Palestine, with no significant mountains or river separating, but only the small wadi El Arish, 'the river of Egypt' (Num 34:5; Josh 15:4, 47). Egypt was the Nile. The narrow ribbon of fertile alluvial land the river deposited was watered by an annual inundation, making it the bread-basket of the ancient world. Brisk land and sea traffic with Syria-Palestine and the rest of the Fertile Crescent poured a steady stream of wealth into Egypt. The result was fabulous affluence concentrated in the splendid courts at Thebes, Memphis and Akhetaton (Tell el-Amarna).

Store Cities. These towns were constructed to receive surplus grain in times of plenty. Hebrew forced labor was used to build a number of them, such as Pithom (Tell Retabeh) and Raamses (Tanis). These cities were also stocked with local and imported goods, and military equipment for campaigns in Syria-Palestine.

People and language. Ancient Egyptians were Hamitic (Gen 10:6), but later migrations, predominantly Semitic, left an imprint upon the language and culture. Earliest writing was a picture language (hieroglyphics), including representations of common objects and geometric symbols. Through the centuries this gradually gave way by the 8th cen. B.C. to a popular or 'demotic' cursive script.

In 1799 the Rosetta Stone was discovered written in Old Egyptian (hieroglyphics), demotic and Greek. The decipherment of the stone by the Frenchman Francois Champollion (1822) furnished the key to the language and the foundation of modern Egyptology.

Early Dynastic Period, c. 3100-2686 B.C. Menes reigned at

This below Thebes. Tombs of Thinite kings (Dynasties I and II) near Abydos have been excavated by Flinders Petrie.

Giant figure of a Pharaoh from Abu Simbel, southern Egypt.

Ancient Egypt

Joppa

Jerusalem

Gaza

On (Heliopolis)

Noph (Memphis)

Ezion-geber

RED SEA

Nile R.

Road

0   25   50   75 km

0   15   30   45 miles

The Step Pyramid, Saqqara.

Old Kingdom, c. 2686-2181 B.C., Dynasties III-VI. Dynasties III and IV were the age of the great pyramids and pyramid texts. Zoser (Third Dynasty) built the Step Pyramid at Saqqara. Khufu, founder of the Fourth Dynasty, built the greatest of the pyramids at Giza (492 feet high, 755 feet square at base, covering 13 acres, containing 2,300,000 limestone blocks each weighing two and a half tons). Khafre, Khufu's successor, constructed the Sphinx and the second great pyramid at Giza. Pyramid texts dealing with the future life of the deceased kings belong to the Fifth and Sixth Dynasties.

First Intermediate Period, c. 2181-1991 B.C., Dynasties VII-XI, ruled at Memphis and Herakleopolis, 77 miles S of Cairo. This was a period of comparative weakness. Abraham's visit to Egypt was during this time.

Middle Kingdom, c. 1991-1786 B.C., Dynasty XII, was ruled by native Thebans at Memphis and in the Fayum. It was coeval with the patriarchal period in Palestine. Probably during this period Joseph became prime minister. Jacob stood before one of the powerful rulers of this line, Amenemhet I-IV or Senusert I-III. An inscription on the tomb of Khnumhotep II, a powerful noble of Senusert II, depicts the visit of 37 Asiatics under 'sheik of the highlands, Ibshe,' recalling Abraham's Egyptian visit and Jacob's going down into the country.

Second Intermediate Period, c. 1786-1567, Dynasties XIII-XVII. The strong Middle Kingdom was succeeded by a period of turmoil under Dynasties XIII and XIV, in turn followed by Hyksos, 'rulers of the foreign lands.' These foreign princes reigned almost 150 years, Dynasties XV and XVI, at Avaris (Tanis) in the Delta. Horse and chariot and a spirit of war were introduced. Some scholars place Joseph's rule in this period.

New Empire, c. 1567-1150 B.C., Dynasties XVIII-XX. This was the period when Egypt ruled the East, the heyday of pharaonic glory. It was the time of enslavement of the Israelites. Great pharaohs of this era include Amenhotep I (c. 1546-1525), Thutmose I (c. 1525-1512, Thutmose II (c. 1512-1504), Queen

Hatshepsut (c. 1504-1482). It was the era of Moses' birth and youth. Thutmose III (c. 1490-1436) was a great builder, conqueror and enslaver of the Israelites. Amenhotep II (c. 1438-1425) was apparently the pharaoh of the Exodus. There was a decline under Thutmose IV. Amenhotep III reigned c. 1417-1379, called the Amarna period, followed by Amenhotep IV (Akhnaton), c. 1379-1362. The capital was at Akhetaton (Tell el Amarna). The Amarna Letters were discovered here in 1886. Tutankhamen's lavish tomb was unearthed in 1922. The Amarna period was perhaps coeval with Israel's wanderings and conquest of Palestine.

Many scholars place the Exodus and the Conquest under Dynasty XIX: Ramses I (c. 1319), Seti I (1318-1304), Ramses II (c. 1304-1237), Merneptah (c. 1236-1222). In the latter's famous stele, Israel is mentioned for the first time in Egyptian records: 'the people of Israel is desolate; it has no offspring.'

Dynasty XX (c. 1200-1085) had about ten rulers by the name of Ramses. Ramses III (c. 1198-1167) was the greatest. Dynasty XX was coeval with the period of the Judges in Israel. Dynasties XXI-XXX showed decline.

The ruins at Thebes

Thebes (Egyptian *Net*, biblical *No*, Greek *Thebai*) was the capital of the powerful Eighteenth Dynasty and possibly built by Israelite slave

The Karnak temple, Luxor, Egypt.

I	I	III	IV	V	VI	VII	VIII	IX	X	XI	XII
Dynasty											
Protodynastic c.3100-2686	Old Kingdom c.2686-2181					Intermediate Period c.2181-2040				Middle Kingdom c.2040-1786	
Menes c.3100 Egypt united	Colossal pyramids. Pyramid Texts.	Powerful centralized government on the Nile.				Period of confusion and weakness				Amenemhet I-IV Senusert I-III	

Egyptian events

Events in Genesis

Abram's birth 2166

Abram enters Canaan 2091

Joseph in Egypt

Sodom and Gomorrah destroyed c.2056 Isaac and Jacob

Summary of Egyptian History from the flood to the Patriarchs
(Dynasties I-XII)

labor. Its ruins are immensely impressive on the Nile 350 miles SE of Cairo, near the modern villages of Luxor and Karnak. The magnificent temple of Amun at Karnak is a world wonder, and approached by an avenue of sphinxes. Its great court measures 276 by 338 feet, traversed by a double line of colossal columns. The great hall or hypostyle, 1200 feet long and 350 feet wide, was supported by 134 columns in 16 rows, the central row being 78 feet high and 33 feet in circumference. Brilliantly painted and sculptured, it is a dazzling example of Egyptian architectural skill. Another temple of Amun, located at Luxor just S of

Karnak, was erected by Amenhotep III and his successors.

On the west bank of the Nile near the modern village of Medinet Habu is the palace of Amenhotep III, the two colossi of Memnon (64 feet high), the Raamaseum, a temple of Amun built by Ramses II, a temple of Thutmose III, and a number of other brilliant ruins. Amun (Amon Re) was the sun deity with a powerful priesthood centered in Thebes, against which Akhnaton rebelled when he built Amarna.

Raamses (Tell el-Dab'a) was called Pi-Ra'amese (the House of Ramses, c. 1300-1100 B.C.). The reference to this city in Ex 1:11 is to be construed as the modernization of an archaic place name. It stands for Zoan-Avaris, where the oppressed Israelites labored centuries earlier in the Hyksos capital built c. 1720 B.C.

EXODUS

The book of redemption

The book in general. Exodus takes its name from the Latin Vulgate through the Greek Septuagint, the word in both languages having the meaning of 'departure', 'a going' or 'way out' (cf. Ex 19:1; Heb 11:22). The Hebrew title, *se môt* is derived from the opening words of the book, 'These are the names of the sons of Israel …' The book focuses attention upon the great experience of redemption from Egypt as the type of all redemption and the constitution of the descendants of Jacob as a theocratic nation at Mt. Sinai. The Lord, heretofore connected with the Israelites only through His covenant with Abraham, Isaac and Jacob, now brings them to Himself nationally through redemption and puts them under the Mosaic covenant signified by the tabernacle, priesthood and the Shekinah glory of His presence. The entire book is typical of the person and work of Christ, especially the tabernacle, priesthood and sacrificial ritual as 1 Cor 10 and the book of Hebrews show.

Higher criticism of the book

makes it (along with Genesis) a late compilation of popular traditions (Jehovistic, *c.* 850 B.C.; Elohistic, *c.* 750 B.C.; and Priestly, *c.* 500 B.C.), these being combined with the original Mosaic tradition. So the book is adjudged non-Mosaic in authorship, unreliable historically, and the miracles in it traditional rather than factual.

The elements of the book are so intimately and closely welded together with such harmony with the other Pentateuchal books and the Bible as a whole, that the critical view appears at variance with clear lines of historical and scriptural evidence supporting the unity of the entire Pentateuch. The amazingly detailed typology and symbolism of the book, woven like a magnificent mosaic in God's great redemption plan from Genesis to Revelation, argues strongly against the naturalistic views of those who would partition the Pentateuch.

Outline

1–12 Israel in Egypt
1 Egyptian bondage
2-4 Deliverer
5-11 Struggle with Pharaoh
12 The Passover

13–18 Israel in the wilderness
13:1–15:21 The Exodus and pursuit
15:22-17:16 Journey to Sinai
18 Visit of Jethro

19–40 Israel at Sinai
19-20 Giving of the law
21-23 Social and ceremonial laws
24 Ratification of covenant
25-31 Tabernacle and priesthood instructions
32 Golden calf
33-34 Renewal of covenant
35-40 Erection of tabernacle and institution of priesthood

The pyramids, Giza, Egypt.

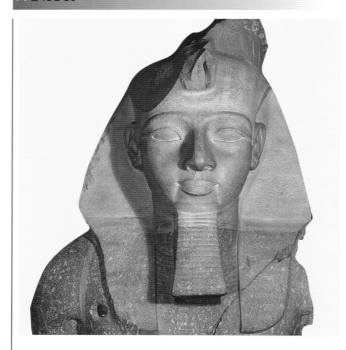

Head of Rameses II, Dynasty XIX, Egypt.

1. Israel enslaved in Egypt

1-14. Israel's increase. Joseph died and several centuries elapsed. A 'new king,' either from the Hyksos period or from the powerful Eighteenth Dynasty of Egypt, came to power. His oppression of the people is prefaced by an account of the expansion of the Israelites, 1-7. This picture of expansion precedes heartless oppression, 8-14. By forced labor, Pharaoh built Pithom Tell er-Retabeh or Tell el-Mask-huta and Raamses Pi-Ra'amesé in the Delta.

15-22 Planned extinction. Hebrew midwives were ordered to kill all male Israelite babies, but disobeyed their Pharaoh and were blessed by the Lord. Then the king ordered the populace to drown every male Hebrew baby in the Nile. Satan's attempt to destroy the promised seed and the Jewish people can be traced from Cain's murder of Abel to the time of Christ (cf. 2 Chr 21:4; 22:10; Est 3:13; Mt 2:16).

2. Moses the deliverer raised up

1-10. Birth of the deliverer. Moses' parents, Amram and Jochebed (6:20), were of the tribe of Levi, later designated as the priestly line. His ark was of woven papyrus plastered with bitumen. It has been often suggested that the daughter of Pharaoh here represented was Hatshepsut, who later became Pharaoh herself. The Bible, however, is silent concerning that point. The Hebrew *Mosheh* (Moses) is an active participle, 'the one drawing out,' because Pharaoh's daughter drew the infant out of the water. But this is the interpretation given by the sacred writer. Probably the name is Egyptian *Mose,* meaning 'the child.' Cf. Ahmose ('son of Ah, the god of light') and Thutmose ('son of Thoth').

11-23. Flight to Midian. At 40 (Acts 7:23), Moses cast his lot with his countrymen (Heb 11:24), in indignation killing the Egyptian taskmaster. Midian, 16-22, to which Moses fled, was a NW Arabian tribe descended from Abraham by Keturah (Gen 25:1-4; cf. 37:28 and Jud 6:2 ff.). Reuel or Jethro (he had two names as some Sebaean kings and priests) was head priest and secular head of his clan. The romantic story of how Moses won his wife Zipporah ('bird') is told. His son Gershom means 'a stranger here.'

24-25. God remembers the Covenant. The foundation of God's redemptive work on behalf of Israel is His covenant with Abraham. (cf. 6:4-5; 19:5-6; 34:10).

3-4. The call of Moses

3:1-3. The burning bush. As in Genesis, we see the introduction of God's divine purposes in a theophany ('the angel of the Lord appeared to him in flames of fire from within a bush,' Ex 3:2).

4-12. The call and commission. 'Moses, Moses' is an emphatic repetition (cf. Gen 22:11; 46:2). The divine presence necessitated removing one's sandals, still practiced by Muslims at their mosques and the Samaritans at their sanctuary at Gerizim. It was no new god who spoke, 6, but the God of Abraham, Isaac and Jacob.

13-14. The revelation of the name Jehovah (Yahweh). 'I am who I am,' the One who is, who was, who is to come (Rev 1:4), the eternal, unchanging living One, the name of our Lord who has redeemed us. 'Before Abraham was born, *I am*' (Jn 8:58). The divine name Yahweh most likely comes from the Heb. verb *haya* (to be). Most interpreters view it as an active verb, i.e., 'I am' or 'the self-existing one.' Some prefer to consider it to be causative, i.e., 'I cause to be.'

15-22. Directions for deliverance. The wilderness was et-Tih, the broad arid plateau extending from the NE border of Egypt to southern Palestine. Borrowing valuables from the Egyptians and despoiling them was not duplicity,

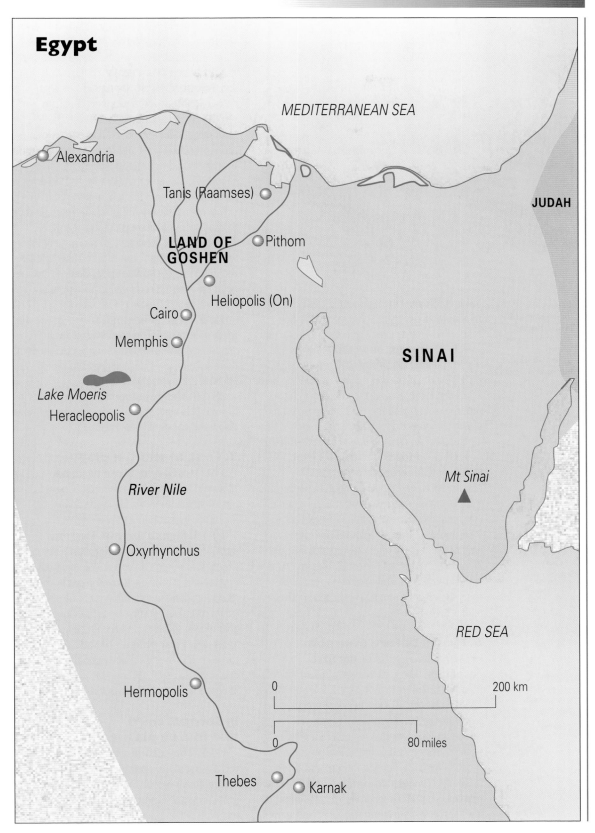

Egypt

MEDITERRANEAN SEA

Alexandria

Tanis (Raamses)

JUDAH

Pithom

LAND OF GOSHEN

Heliopolis (On)

Cairo

Memphis

SINAI

Lake Moeris

Heracleopolis

River Nile

Mt Sinai

Oxyrhynchus

RED SEA

0   200 km

0   80 miles

Hermopolis

Thebes   Karnak

Artist's impression of a locust. Locust invasions are well-known in Syria-Palestine, but rare in Egypt.

but according to Oriental social custom. Servants, in addition to a stipend, borrowed from their masters coveted articles which they called a 'gift.'

4:1-17. Moses' objections. Moses had already pleaded *no ability,* 3:11; *no message,* 3:13; now *no authority,* 4:1; *no eloquence,* 4:10; *no inclination,* 4:13. God countered with the promise of *His presence,* 3:12; the manifestation of *His omnipotence,* 4:2-9; *enablement,* 4: 11-12; and *His direction* and *instruction,* 4:14-16.

4:18-31. Moses' return to Egypt. Moses' wife, apparently objecting to her son's circumcision, had hindered Moses in performing a rite so closely connected with the Abrahamic covenant and the redemption of Israel back to Palestine. As deliverer, Moses was in immediate danger of being cut off for his sin. Accordingly, Zipporah circumcised her son. Moses' meeting with Aaron, 27-28, and their performance of signs signaled the progress of the redemptive plan.

5. Moses before Pharaoh

1-19. The results of the first encounter. The Lord made seven demands of Pharaoh (5:1; 7:16; 8:1; 8:20; 9:1; 9:13; 10:3). The king cruelly imposed heavier burdens, requiring the same number of bricks, yet compelling the Israelites to gather their own straw. Both straw-made bricks and pure clay variety have been found at Pithom and Tanis.

20-23. Israel's complaint and Moses' prayer. Though Israel professed belief that God had sent Moses and Aaron (4:31), when Pharaoh

increased their oppression, they blamed Moses who in turn blamed God.

6. The Lord's reply to Moses' first prayer

1-13. The Lord's answer. The Lord reminded Moses of His covenant with the patriarchs under the name *El Shaddai* ('God Almighty,' Gen 17: 1), but revealed the meaning of His personal redemptive name Jehovah *(Yahweh),* 2-3, now that He was about to deliver them from slavery, Pharaoh, and the land of Egypt, often typically linked to sin, Satan, and the world. The implication is not that the name *Yahweh* was not previously known in Genesis, where it occurs many times, but simply that its meaning had not yet become evident, as it would be in the redemption from Egypt (typical of redemption in Christ).

14-27. The genealogy. Divine grace called the people by name and was intimately acquainted with their burden and concerned with their deliverance. The genealogy is obviously selective and abbreviated.

28-30. Renewed commission. Moses' humanity is here emphasized, as he the deliverer also needs constant encouragement.

7. First of the ten plagues

1-9. Moses and Aaron assured. 'God to Pharaoh' means Moses' declarations were to have divine authority and Aaron was his appointed spokesman (cf. 4:16).

10-13. Sign of the rod. Magic was inextricably bound up with Egyptian religion, which was demon-controlled idolatry of the grossest sort. The miracles performed by the magicians were manifestations of evil supernaturalism, similar to demon powers operative in spiritism and occultism today.

14-25. First plague: blood. The Nile was turned to blood, a judgment upon the river deified on occasion as Hapi, 'the giver of life,' and at others as Osiris, the god of fertility.

8. Second, third and fourth plagues

1-15. The second plague: frogs. This was a miraculous intensification of a frequent natural phenomenon. After the low Nile in May-June comes the inundation in July. With the recession of the waters, leaving numerous pools

Egyptian wooden
model of a farm
laborer plowing
with oxen.

of stagnant water, come the frogs in August-September. This, too, was a judgment against the innumerable gods of Egypt, the frog being worshiped as a symbol of Hekt, a form of the goddess Hathor. Plagues of frogs in Egypt are referred to by ancient classical writers.

16-32. Third and fourth plagues: gnats and flies. Again divine miracles were performed, but based upon natural occurrences. The gnats (*kinnim*) were doubtless sand flies, these stinging insects of Egypt being notorious. The flies, literally swarms, were other common pesty insects which plague Egypt. These judgments were a blow against the prestige of Isis, wife of Osiris, and Hathor, Egypt's foremost goddess, represented by the cow.

9. Fifth, sixth and seventh plagues

1-12. Fifth and sixth plagues: murrain and boils. These plagues were directed against Ptah (Apis), the god of Memphis, represented as a bull, as well as other gods represented by the goat, the ram, the cow, etc. The sixth plague, described as a festering boil breaking forth (pustules) upon man and beast, was directed against both the idolaters and the idols they worshiped. The 'Nile scab' is a popular designation of a skin disease prevalent at the rising and falling of the Nile.

13-35. The seventh plague: hail. This plague from the sky would impress the Egyptians, who saw a deity behind every natural phenomenon, that Jehovah is Lord of heaven as well as of earth. Hail is rare in Egypt. This occurred in January, as indicated by the fact that the barley was in bloom, 31-32. Each of the plagues was seasonal, but miraculous.

10. Eighth and ninth plagues

1-20. The eighth plague: locusts. This was a grievous visitation. Locust invasions are well-known in Syria-Palestine, but rare in Egypt. The locusts were brought by the east wind and carried away by the west wind.

21-29. The ninth plague: darkness. This miracle is thought by some to have been caused by the west wind that carried away the locusts, bringing the dreaded *Khamsin* or blinding sandstorm from the desert that creates a darkness one can feel. The darkness of this visitation was so severe it paralyzed all ordinary activities for three days. This plague would have been particularly significant. The chief god in the Egyptian pantheon was Re, the sun god. Here, Jehovah demonstrates that He has power over sunlight as well.

Egyptian warrior.

and a new beginning. The Passover lamb slain spoke of Christ slain on Calvary. As the Israelites were shielded from the death angel, so the believer is shielded from the wrath of God (1 Cor 5:7). The unleavened bread (1 Cor 5:8) showed the clean-cut separation of the Israelites from Egypt and their hasty exit. The bitter herbs were apparently intended to recall their suffering in Egypt under Pharaoh's servitude.

14-28. The Feast of Unleavened Bread. The lamb slain on the fourteenth day at sunset was followed immediately by the putting away of all leaven for seven days. Leaven in Scripture is an illustration of sin, 'malice and wickedness' (1 Cor 5:8). The experience of being redeemed (the Passover) is to be followed by separation from sin and the living of a holy life.

29-51. Account of the tenth plague. The death of Pharaoh's oldest son and heir to the throne was effective. The Exodus took place at once, the sojourn of exactly 430 years, 40-42, abruptly ending. The Passover was made a perpetual commemorative celebration of redemption, 43-51.

13. Consecration of the firstborn

1-16. The firstborn given to the Lord. Since the firstborn had been most miraculously delivered, the Lord commanded that they be given to Him, 1-2. Holiness of life and redemption are inseparable. Those whom the Lord redeems, He claims for Himself (1 Cor 6:19-20). Basic to holiness, both positional and experiential, is redemption from bondage (penalty and power of sin). Salvation is unto a holy life.

Introductory to the dedication of the first-born and as a part of the separation. Moses emphasized the importance of the Feast of Unleavened Bread (see 12:15-20) as a perpetual ordinance stressing holy separation of the redeemed, 1-10, which was to be 'a sign' on their hand and a memorial on their foreheads, 9, 16 (cf. Deut 6:4-9). Upon these passages the Jews base their practice of phylacteries, using little boxes containing Scripture to fulfill by ritual what God meant to be performed by life. The requirement for the redemption of the firstborn is formally stated, 11-16.

17-22. Crossing the Red Sea. From Succoth God manifested His power. The pillar of

11. The tenth plague: death of the firstborn

1-10. The climaxing plague announced, and its effectiveness predicted, but its execution is not recorded until 12:26-39. The plague was either a direct judgment by God or a disease-like bubonic plague that killed the halest and best, as the firstborn was thought of in the East. Its miraculous intensity and sparing of those behind the blood-marked doors, made this wonder a fitting capstone to the other nine miracles.

12. The Passover and the Exodus

1-13. The Passover instituted. The birth of the nation and a change in the calendar were announced, 1-2. Redemption marks a new life

The Route of the Exodus

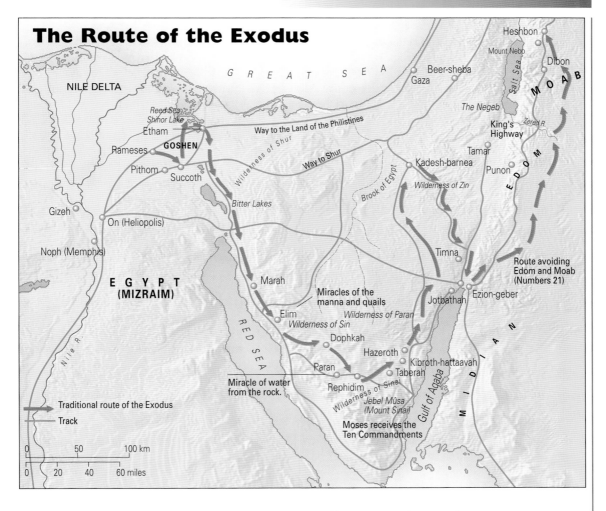

Heshbon
Mount Nebo
Dibon
M O A B
Salt Sea
G R E A T   S E A
Beer-sheba
Gaza
NILE DELTA
The Negeb
Reed Sea
Shihor Lake
Etham
Way to the Land of the Philistines
King's Highway
Zered R.
GOSHEN
Wilderness of Shur
Tamar
E D O M
Rameses
Way to Shur
Kadesh-barnea
Punon
Pithom
Succoth
Wilderness of Zin
Gizeh
Brook of Egypt
On (Heliopolis)
Bitter Lakes
Noph (Memphis)
Timna
E G Y P T
(MIZRAIM)
Marah
Miracles of the manna and quails
Jotbathan
Ezion-geber
Route avoiding Edom and Moab (Numbers 21)
Elim
Wilderness of Paran
Wilderness of Sin
M I D I A N
Dophkah
Nile R.
R E D   S E A
Hazeroth
Kibroth-hattaavah
Paran
Taberah
Rephidim
Wilderness of Sinai
Gulf of Aqaba
Miracle of water from the rock.
Jebel Mûsa (Mount Sinai)
Moses receives the Ten Commandments

→ Traditional route of the Exodus
— Track

0   50   100 km
0   20   40   60 miles

cloud and pillar of fire were given, 21-22, symbolizing divine guidance and protection.

14. The crossing of the Red Sea

1-12. Israel's predicament. Shut in, perplexed and confused by the wilderness, Israel was pursued by Pharaoh's light mobile chariotry, giving the Lord a chance to be glorified in the destruction of the pursuing Egyptians.

13-31. Redemption by power. The Red Sea is really Reed Sea (Heb. *yam suph,* the translation 'Red Sea' coming from the Septuagint). It apparently refers to the region of the Bitter Lakes N of the Gulf of Suez. These lakes were filled with sea water when the Suez Canal was built, having lain dry for centuries, but known as bodies of water in ancient Egyptian sources. The great miracle at the Reed Sea was the most dramatic and far-reaching manifestation of divine power in the OT and the most memorable event in Israel's national history.

15. The song of the redeemed

1-19. Israel celebrates deliverance. Filled with praise at their glorious rescue from the Egyptians, Israel sang ecstatically to the Lord. The great victory wrought was celebrated as the Lord's triumph, 1-10; His power, holiness and steadfast love were praised, 11-13. The terrifying effect of this great deliverance on Philistia, Edom, Moab and Canaan is described, 14-16, appended with a sure promise that the Redeemer would also bring them into Canaan, 17-18.

20-21. The women's chorus, under Miriam, joined the praise.

22-27. Israel tested. The bitter trial at Marah was the brackish water. In contrast, Elim provided a respite from testing with its 'twelve springs and seventy palm trees.' (15:27).

16. Manna from heaven

1-13. The redeemed tested by hunger. The wilderness of Sin, 1, is the wide Plain of Markha beyond Elim, where the desolation presented a genuine food problem. Sin and Sinai may be derived from the name of the moon-god of Ur and Haran, or from a Semitic root meaning, 'to shine.' In fertile Goshen, with two crops a year, there had never been any lack of food. Now bread from heaven and quails were to be providentially supplied.

14-22. Manna from heaven. When the people asked in Hebrew *man-hu'* ('What is it?'), 13-15, Moses explained it was bread from heaven. The manna foreshadows Christ, the food of God's people (cf. Jn 6:33-35).

23-30. Sabbath and manna. The sabbath, a type of Israel's kingdom blessing (Heb 4:8-9), was enjoined upon Israel in connection with the gathering of the manna. An omer (approx. 2.09 dry quarts) was the tenth part of an ephah, as distinguished from a homer (ten ephahs).

31-36. Manna kept for a memorial, in the golden pot (Heb 9:4), speaks of the true manna which we shall eat in God's own presence in glory – 'the hidden manna' (Rev 2:17), and concerning which our Lord said, 'He who feeds on this bread will live forever' (Jn 6:58).

17. Rephidim: water from the rock

1-4. The redeemed tested by thirst. At Rephidim (probably the Wadi Feiran, the natural route to Sinai), the Israelites, barred by the Amalekites from marching up the valley to natural springs, suffered thirst and rebelled against the Lord and Moses.

5-7. Water from the rock. This beautifully symbolizes Christ, the giver of life (Jn 7:37-39). The smitten rock illustrates the death of Christ resulting in an outpoured Spirit because of an accomplished redemption (Acts 2:1-4). Horeb here denotes the whole Sinaitic Peninsula. Massah ('test') and Meribah ('strife') were the names given to the place where Israel tempted the Lord and quarreled with Him.

8-16. Conflict with Amalek. This Bedouin tribe was a descendant of Esau (Gen 36:12), and Israel's implacable foe.

Jehovah-Nissi ('the Lord is my banner'), 15, assures the believer of victory .

18. Moses and Jethro

1-12. Jethro's visit. Moses rehearsed for Jethro the way the Lord had judged Egypt for Israel's sake, and the Lord's deliverance, 8. Thereupon all worshiped and fellowshiped together, 12. During the deliverance of Israel out of Egypt, Zipporah and her sons, Gershom ('a stranger') and Eliezer ('God my help'), were off the scene, 2-5. Now they appear again as Israel prepares for their divine appointment at Mt. Sinai, possibly a foreview of Israel's return to the 'mountain of God' in the coming Kingdom Age (Isa 2:1-5).

13-27. Government of the redeemed. Here God graciously supplied governmental administration, as He had graciously supplied redemption (12:37-13:18); guidance (13:19-22); deliverance (14:1-15:21); temporal provision (15:22-17:7); and victory in war (17:8-16).

19. Mt Sinai and the covenant of the law

1-2. Israel at Sinai. The site of Sinai is quite likely Jebel Musa in the Sinai Peninsula, marked by the monastery of St. Catherine. However, some scholars favor Jebel Serbal near the oasis of Wadi Feiran.

3-8. Free grace exchanged for law. Pointedly the Lord reminded the people that up to this time they had been objects of His free grace, 4. The 'if' of verse 5 indicates the legal method of divine dealing. Now a new economy was ushered in. The law was not set forth as a means of life, but as a medium by which Israel might become the Lord's 'treasured possession,' 'a kingdom of priests' and a 'holy nation,' 5-6, distinct from every other nation. This promise of priesthood is later extended to the church as well through the mediation of Christ (1 Pet 2:9; Rev 1:6). Moreover, the law was not *imposed* until it had been divinely proposed and accepted by Israel, 7-8. The Abrahamic covenant had ministered salvation and assurance because it imposed only one condition – faith. This the legal covenant could not do.

9-25. The legal age introduced. This was done by the terrifying appearance of the Lord on Sinai, 9-11; by distance, 12-13; by smoke, fire, threat of death. The law was designed to school the people in God's holiness, their own sinfulness, and by its austerity and severity be a 'tutor to bring [them] unto Christ' (Gal 3:24, ASV) to

whom it pointed in detail, that they might be saved by faith.

20. The Decalogue
1-12. The first table, duties to God. These guarded His unity and spirituality against idolatry, His holiness against profanity, and His worship on the seventh day against secularism.

13-17. The second table, duties to men. 'Honor your father and your mother' stands as the first command attended by a specific promise (20:12; Eph 6:2). 'You shall not murder,' 13, decrees the sanctity of life against murder. 'You shall not commit adultery,' 14, protects marriage and the home. 'You shall not steal,' 15, maintains the right of property against plunder. 'You shall not give false testimony,' 16, upholds the sanctity of character against slander. 'You shall not covet,' 17, protects the heart against wrong desires.

18-21. Israel asks for a mediator. Although God had called Israel to be a kingdom of priests (19:6), Israel fearfully asks Moses to be a mediator on their behalf.

20:22-23:33. The book of the covenant. So called in 24:7, this section outlines in greater detail the stipulations of God's covenant with Israel.

21-24. The social ordinances
21:1-36. Rights of persons. Laws were given concerning the regulations of slavery, 1-11; wrongs done to a fellowman, 12-27; injuries resulting from carelessness or neglect, 28-36.

22:1-15. Rights of property. Laws were given dealing with theft, 1-6, and dishonesty, 7-15.

22:16-23:19. Requirements of

personal integrity. Proper conduct, 22:16-31, was set forth; administration of common justice, 23:19, and observance of the festal seasons, 10-19.

23:20-33. Promise and prospect. Assurance of the divine presence with Israel, 20-23, was given and a blessed future predicted, if the people remained loyal to the Lord, 24-33. These injunctions of the book of the covenant were for the social and religious instruction of Israel.

24:18-31:18. Moses on the top of the mountain. The forty days and forty nights that Moses remained on the mountain was significant in its duration paralleling the length of Elijah's pilgrimage back to Mt. Horeb and Jesus' time of testing (also in the wilderness).

24:1-17. Acceptance of the legal covenant and worship. Again the voluntary acceptance of the law by Israel was stressed (cf. 19:78). The covenant was ratified.

25. The tabernacle: ark, table, candlestick
1-9. The materials were supplied by the people's offering, including three metals, coloured fabrics, animal skins, wood, oil and

Archaeological light
Discoveries of Near Eastern treaty texts have done much to explain the form and structure of God's covenant with Israel as recorded in Exodus, Leviticus, Deuteronomy, and Joshua. Mendenhall and Kline have observed a structural similarity between the Sinai covenant and Hittite suzerainty treaties; the correspondences argue for the authenticity of God's revelation to Moses on Mt. Sinai.

Plan of the tabernacle

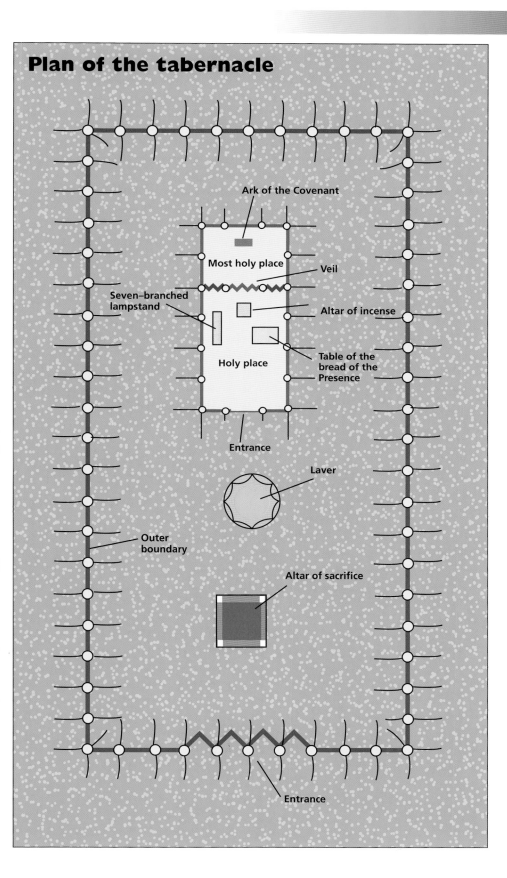

Ark of the Covenant

Most holy place

Veil

Seven–branched lampstand

Altar of incense

Holy place

Table of the bread of the Presence

Entrance

Laver

Outer boundary

Altar of sacrifice

Entrance

precious stones. All was by divine direction, 9.

10-22. The ark. This box, 3 3/4 feet long, 2 1/4 feet wide and 2 1/4 feet high, was made of acacia wood overlaid with pure gold. It held a pot of manna, the Ten Commandments and later Aaron's rod that budded. The mercy seat was the gold lid on top of the ark, illustrating how the divine throne is transformed from a throne of judgment to a throne of grace by atoning blood sprinkled upon it. The two cherubim represented guardianship of the holiness of God's throne, above which was enthroned the Shekinah glory presence of the Lord. The ark was the core of the tabernacle symbolism, God working outward in His outreach to man.

23-30. The table of shewbread. Made of acacia wood, it was 3 feet long, 2 1/4 feet high and 1 1/2 feet wide, and overlaid with pure gold. Upon it was placed the bread of the Presence made of fine wheat flour, baked in 12 loaves, renewed every sabbath to be eaten by the priests only. This bread looked forward to Christ, the Bread of life, nourisher of the believer as a priest (1 Pet 2:9; Rev 1:6; Jn 6:33-58).

31-40. The golden candlestick. This was of pure gold, seven-branched; a type of Christ our Light, shining in the plenitude of the Spirit, natural light being shut out of the tabernacle. Some link this lamp stand with the lamp stands of Rev 1:12-16, from the center of which shined the Son. The representation on the triumphal arch of Titus may give an accurate notion of its appearance.

26. The tabernacle: its general construction

1-6. The linen curtains. Ten in all, they were white linen with blue, purple and scarlet yarn embroidered into the shape of cherubim.

7-37. The tabernacle coverings, boards, veil and outer screen. The veil of the tabernacle separated the holy place from the holy of holies, the inner sanctuary where the ark of the covenant was located. Josephus reported that the veil was four inches thick and that the embroidered design had mystical significance. To the believer, the veil represents separation from the presence of God, a separation that was terminated when Christ was crucified, at which time the veil was 'torn in two from top to bottom' (Mt 27:51). Though the OT high priest could only go behind the veil once a year, Christ as our High Priest (Heb 9:11-12) provided access to the presence of God to all who would enter 'by a new and living way opened for us through the curtain, that is, his body' (Heb 10:20).

27. The tabernacle: bronze altar, court

1-8. The brazen (bronze) altar. This was the great altar for general sacrifice of animals, $7\frac{1}{2}$ feet square, $4\frac{1}{2}$ feet high, located at the threshold, signifying that the shedding of blood (atonement) is basic to man's approach to God. It is typical of the cross (death) of Christ, our whole burnt offering, who offered Himself without spot to God (Heb 9:14).

9-19. The court. The curtains of fine linen surrounding the court suggest that righteousness is required for true worship since they shut out all who will not enter by the gate. The gate, 16 (cf. Jn 10:9), suggests Christ. He is our access to God by virtue of His redemptive work.

20-21. The oil for light. The fine olive oil is symbolic of the Holy Spirit (Jn 3:34; Heb 1:9). In Christ the oil-fed light constantly burns.

28. The tabernacle priesthood

1-5. Priesthood in Aaron and his sons. Aaron, the high priest (Heb. 'great priest'), typifies Christ, who exercises His office after the Aaronic *pattern* (Heb 9), but being after the *order* of Melchizedek is an eternal, deathless High Priest. The holy garments for 'dignity and honor,' 2, represent the glory and beauty of Christ as our High Priest.

6-14. The ephod was an apronlike vestment worn under the high priest's breastplate, having shoulder straps, an embroidered girdle and worn over a robe. On top of each of the shoulder straps an onyx stone was encased in a filigree setting of gold and engraved with the names of six tribes of Israel. Christ bears His own on His shoulder (strength) by virtue of His present high priestly intercession.

15-29. The breastplate was gorgeously embellished with precious stones engraved with the names of Israel's tribes. It illustrates Christ bearing the names of His own upon His heart in God's presence as Aaron did when he went into the holy place, 29.

30. Urim and Thummim. The 'lights and perfections' were closely associated with the breastplate of judgment. They suggest the guiding ministry of the Holy Spirit, whether they were precious stones or oracular emblems.

31-35. Robe of the ephod. The bells on the hem of the robe spoke of God's acceptance of the priestly sacrifice. As long as the people heard the tinkling of the bells they knew that the high priest was still alive in the holy of holies and that God was satisfied with their atoning sacrifice, 35. In contrast, Christ, the better High Priest, *'always lives* to intercede for them' (Heb 7:25).

36-38. The gold headplate was inscribed with 'Holy to the Lord', a reminder of the unsullied purity of the priestly ministry of Christ (Heb 7:26).

39-43. Garments of the regular priests. The ordinary vestments of the high priest and the regular priests, over which the special high priestly regalia was placed, indicate that 'dignity and honor' that characterized Aaron (Christ) also characterized his sons (believer priests in this age). The linen trousers to cover their naked flesh, 42, portray the righteousness of Christ imputed to the believer, the absolute essential of access to God as a priest.

29. Consecration of the priesthood

1-4. The washing. This cleansing in water symbolizes regeneration (Jn 3:5; Tit 3:5), in which Aaron participated, because he was a sinner and needed it. Our Lord as the spotless Lamb of God (Heb 7:26-28), who did not need it, nevertheless yielded to John's baptism at Jordan to identify Himself with sinners and fulfill the Aaronic pattern (Mt 3:13-17).

5-25. The clothing and anointing. Clothed with his splendid garments, 5-6, and anointed, 7, symbolic of Christ's enduement with the Spirit (Mt 3:16; Acts 10:38), Aaron alone, it is to be noted, was anointed *before* the blood was shed (cf.21). The consecration of the priests required various offerings in which the shedding of animal blood took place, 8-25. This sets Aaron off as a striking picture of Christ, who was anointed with the Spirit by virtue of what He was in Himself in

Archaeological light

Comparisons have been made between the case law of the Mosaic covenant and earlier codes such as the Code of Hammurabi (c.1700 B.C.), the Lipit-Ishtar Code (c. 1875 B.C.) and the Ur Nammu Code (2050 B.C.). Sufficient similarity exists to affirm the antiquity of the Mosaic covenant – and yet even more striking differences attest to its uniqueness as a divine revelation.

His deity and sinless humanity, not by virtue of redemption, as is the case of all believers.

26-46. Special food for priests. This was fitting for those, 26-37, who represented the people before God in sacrifice and worship, 38-46.

30. The altar of incense and the worshipers

1-10. The altar of incense was of acacia wood overlaid with gold, 1½ feet square, 3 feet high. Equipped with inseparable horns and staves for transporting it, it was placed in the holy place in front of the veil. On it Aaron was to offer incense twice daily, 7-8. The incense fittingly symbolizes prayer, which like ascending sweet aromas, rises acceptably to heaven (Rev 5:8; 8 :3). The incense altar pictures Christ as the believer's intercessor (Jn 17:1-26; Heb 7:25), through whom the believer's prayer and praise rise up to God (Heb 13:15). No 'other incense,' 9, i.e., improperly compounded (cf. 30:34-38), was to be used. Cf. 'unauthorized fire' of Lev 10:1-3, which refers to fire kindled in some manner other than that divinely prescribed, and Jn 1:9). True worshipers must also be continually cleansed from daily defilement.

23-33. The anointing oil, a symbol of the Holy Spirit. The redeemed, those daily cleansed, and those empowered by the Spirit alone can worship God effectively (Jn 4:23; Eph 2:18; 5:18-19) in the beauty and fragrance of holiness.

34-38. The incense. The ingredients are also given, as in the case of the anointing oil. Only these redeemed, 11-16; cleansed, 7-21; and anointed, 34-38, can truly worship God with genuine prayer, praise and thanksgiving, 34-38, symbolized by the incense, which in turn was to be uniquely compounded and reserved for God's adoration alone, 37. T o imitate it was a crime punishable by death, showing that worship must be truly spiritual (Jn 4:23-24).

31. The workmen and the sabbath

1-11. The call of the workmen. Bezaleel ('in the shadow of God') and Aholiab ('tent of [my] Father') were filled with the Spirit of God, with ability and intelligence, with knowledge and all craftsmanship, 2-3, to execute all the skilled labor necessary .

12-17. The sabbath law restated. Cf. 16:23-29 for the first institution of the day of rest to be kept by Israel, in connection with the giving of the manna. Shortly afterward it was re-enacted in the fourth commandment (20:8-11), linking it with the creation rest of God (Gen 2:2). The sabbath is accordingly a Jewish institution, connected with the legal or Mosaic covenant, and its infraction punishable by death. Sunday is not a sabbath, but the first day of the week, and belongs to the new age of grace which followed the death and resurrection of Christ. Legalistic Sabbath keeping is to go back to the age previous to the rent veil (Mt 27:51).

18. Moses receives the tables of stone (cf. 32:16). It is significant that the tablets were written by 'the finger of God' rather than being entrusted to a human scribe. The extraordinary action testifies to the importance of God's law.

32. The broken covenant

1-14. The golden calf. The legal covenant, so glibly accepted, was here shamefully violated, showing the utter inability of the people to keep it in their own strength. Shortly after the people exclaimed that they would make no idols and worship no other gods, they fashioned a calf that either represented a return to the bull worship of Egypt (Apis), or the Canaanite practice of making a footstool or throne for God (Baal is often pictured on the back of a bull). Only the intercession of Moses rescued them from wholesale destruction, 11-14.

15-35. The broken tablets. A scene of terrible apostasy and debauchery met Moses, the man of God, coming down from the mountain of God with the law of God in his hands. The whole scene showed the inability of the law, itself good, to make men good. Depraved man is never saved by law-keeping, but by faith. Justification by faith is the way of salvation in every age. The law was a schoolmaster to reveal man's sin and his need of God's grace and redemption. Moses called for those who were on the Lord's side, and the Levites rallied to him, killing 3,000 of the worst offenders. Further confession and intercession by Moses, 30-35, presents a superlatively lofty scene of man's concern for the good of God's people, one of the most sublime pictures found anywhere in Holy Scripture.

33-34. Restoration of the law

33:1-23. Moses' new vision. The journey to Canaan was resumed, 16, and the 'tent of meeting' (not the tabernacle, which was later set up) was pitched outside the camp, 7-11. Moses prayed for a new vision, 12-17, and was promised it for a new task, 18-23.

34:1-4. Second tables of the law. Again, the inscription was by God. The second tablets were as authoritative as the first.

5-17. The new vision and commission. Moses saw the Lord pass by, 5-9, and his commission was renewed, 10-17. Here the patriarch saw the hidden nature of Jehovah.

18-35. The feasts and the sabbath again commanded. This is a reiteration concerning the Feast of Unleavened Bread, 18; redemption of firstborn, 19-20; sabbath, 21; Feast of Weeks and Ingathering, etc., 22-27. Moses' face shone after he descended from the 40-day session with God, 28-35 (cf. 2 Cor 3:6-18).

35-39. The tabernacle assembled

35:1-3. The sabbath. This basic tenet of Israel's worship was once more restated and emphasized (cf. 16:23-29; 20:8-11; 31:12-17; 34:21).

35:4-36:7. Gifts and workmen for the tabernacle. What was enjoined in Ex 25:1-8 concerning donations for the construction of the tabernacle was here carried out, as the people gave liberally. Bezaleel and Aholiab (cf. 31:1-11), the principal craftsmen, were again singled out and their God-given talents for the work again noted, 35:30-35. So liberally did the people give, they had to be restrained, 36:1-7.

36:8-39:43. The tabernacle made. These chapters record the material and furniture of the tabernacle collected and made according to the directions given in ch. 25-31, which are here repeated. Instructions are given concerning the linen curtains, 36:8-13 (cf. 26:1-6); curtains of goat's hair, 36:14-18 (cf. 26:7); covering of rams' skins, 36:19 (cf. 26:14); boards, 36:20-23 (cf. 26:15); silver sockets, 36:24-30 (cf. 26:19); the bars, 36:31-33 (cf. 26:26); gold overlay, 36:34 (cf. 26:29); the inner veil and outer veil, 36:35-38 (cf. 26:31, 36). Likewise the furniture is again detailed: the ark, 37:1-5 (cf. 25:10); the mercy seat, 37:6-9 (cf. 25:17); the table, 37:10-16 (cf. 25:23); candlestick, 37:17-24 (cf. 25:31); altar of incense, 37:25-28 (cf. 30:1); anointing oil, 37:29 (cf. 30:23-38); altar of burnt offering, 38:1-7 (cf. 27:1); basin, 38:8 (cf. 30:18); courts, 38:9-31 (cf. 27:9, 16); Aaron's high priestly garments, 39:1-43 (cf. 31:10).

40. The tabernacle set up

1-19. Built, according to God's direction, 1-15, in perfect obedience, 16-19.

20-33. Furnished. The ark was brought in, 20-21. The furniture was placed, 22-26. The prescribed offerings and ritual were performed, 27-33.

34-38. Divinely accepted. God blessed Moses and the people with His presence as the tent was filled with God's glory. So great was the splendor, Moses was not able to minister. A mob of miserable slaves in Egypt marks the beginning of Exodus. An emancipated nation in fellowship with God and on its way to Canaan ends it. This is truly 'the book of redemption.'

LEVITICUS

The book of atonement

Nature of the book. Genesis is the book of beginnings, Exodus the book of redemption, and Leviticus the book of atonement and a holy walk. In Genesis we see man ruined; in Exodus, man redeemed; in Leviticus, man cleansed, worshiping and serving. Leviticus says, *'Get right with God'* (the message of the five offerings: burnt offering, meal offering, peace offering, sin offering, trespass offering, ch. 1-7). Leviticus also says, *'Keep right with God'* (the message of the seven feasts: Passover, Unleavened Bread, First Fruits, Pentecost, Trumpets, Atonement, Tabernacles, ch. 23).

Leviticus is the book of *holiness*. (This keynote idea occurs 87 times.) God says to the redeemed, 'Be holy, because I am holy' (11:44-45; 19:2; 20:7, 26), and this book stresses the necessity of keeping the body holy as well as the soul. The redeemed must be holy, for their Redeemer is holy. A walk with God is on the basis of holiness which is by *sacrifice* and *separation*. As an illustration to NT believers, Leviticus pictures the holiness that comes not through the rituals of the law but through faith in Christ who fulfils the law.

Names of the book. The name *Leviticus* describes the contents of the book, as the law of the priests, the sons of Levi, and is adopted from the Septuagint (*Leuetikon*) and the Latin Vulgate (*Leviticus*), characterizing it as a handbook for the ritual of the old covenant, principally associated with what in the NT is called the Levitical priesthood (Heb 7:11).

Bronze statue of the sacred bull of Apis, found at Memphis.

The sacrificial system

Origin of the sacrifices.

Although the divine origin of sacrifices is not explicitly declared, the fact is everywhere implicit in the Bible. The way sinful man was to approach God was revealed to Adam and Eve immediately after the Fall. God's preparation of garments of skin for Adam and Eve may intimate His revelation that the guilt of sin must be paid for with the blood of an innocent victim (Gen 3:21).

Accordingly, divinely revealed and divinely ordered sacrifice is recorded in the case of Cain and Abel. Cain repudiated God's way of approach in worship. Abel accepted it and was received into God's presence on the basis of God's stipulated means of access to Himself (Gen 4:1-7; Heb 11:4). Likewise Noah (Gen 8:20), Jacob

(Gen 31:54), Job (Job 1:5; 42:8) and God's people down to the eve of the Exodus knew the way of access to God and practiced it (Ex 10:25).

When Moses led Israel out of Egypt, the sacrifical system that had at least in part existed from the beginning of the race was now expanded, given fresh meaning in the light of experienced redemption, organized, codified and written down by inspiration in the sacrificial codes of Exodus and Leviticus.

The witness of archaeology.

Archaeology and history have demonstrated the universality of some kind of sacrifice in human religions from earliest times. Hebrew sacrifices showed both likeness and significant differences to the sacrifical ritual of the Canaanites, Babylonians, Egyptians, Greeks and Arabs.

Sufficient similarity existed to demonstrate a *common origin* in a God-given revelation to the human race just after the Fall. This original source was corrupted and perverted as mankind lapsed more and more into paganism, and was reflected in the systems of sacrifice prevailing among the polytheistic neighbors of Israel. While ancient Sumerian, Babylonian, Hittite, Egyptian and Amorite records describe sacrifices similar to those of the Hebrews in the OT, the Ras Shamra religious tablets discovered at the site of ancient Ugarit in N Syria (1929-37 and later) have been most important in showing the similarities and differences in sacrificial terms and ritual between Israelite and Canaanite sacrifices.

The witness of theology.

The findings of archaeology concur with the reasoning of theology and the intimations of Scripture that the sacrifices were divinely ordained at the Fall. This is true because of the character of God – infinitely holy, yet gracious in His redemptive love

A camel train in Sinai.

(Gen 3:15). It is also true because of the character of man – a fallen creature, totally unable to approach God in his own merits, or to invent a way of approach by his own ingenuity.

Meaning of the sacrifices for the OT worshiper

Basic meaning.
While many elements entered into the religious and spiritual value of the sacrifices, the fundamental idea to the Hebrew worshiper was that they were a *means of approach to God*. This is evident from the underlying connotation of the broadest Hebrew term for 'sacrifice' (*qorban* from the root *qrb*, 'to draw near or approach'). This was the term used for a sacrifical offering either with or without blood, vegetable or animal, entirely or partially burnt (Lev 1:2-3, 10, 14; 2:1, 4; 3:1-2; 7:13; Num 5:15; 7:17; etc.; cf. Mk 7:11). Sinful, guilty man needed some way to draw near to the infinitely holy God with assurance of acceptance.

This was divinely provided in a sacrificial system presided over by the Levitical priesthood.

Further significance.
Besides the basic idea of the sacrifices as a means of his approach to God, the OT believer had other important aspects of worship in mind as he presented prescribed sacrifices. These included: (1) *Self-dedication to God,* in the burnt offering (Lev 1; cf. Rom 12:1-2). In this offering the idea of a gift prevailed, because none of it was returned to the worshiper. All was consumed as the Lord's property. (2) *Generosity in giving,* in the cereal offering (Lev 2). This offering closely followed the burnt offering and featured the donation of material substance in the fruit of one's labor as the natural result of dedication of oneself to God. (3) *Thanksgiving, praise, fellowship* and *communion* of the worshiper because God had accepted his offering of gratitude, devotion or vow, in the peace offering (Lev 3), or granted some personal or national deliverance.

(4) *Expiation by substitution,* in the sin offering (Lev 4), when there was sin against God with no restitution involved. (5) *Expiation and restitution,* in the guilt offering (Lev 5), where there were sin and injury involving restitution.

Classification of the sacrifices.

A twofold division is possible: (1) sacrifices used to approach God for the purpose of restoring broken fellowship – the sin offering (Lev 4) and the restitution offering (Lev 5); (2) sacrifices used to approach God for the purpose of maintaining fellowship – the burnt offering (Lev 1), the meal offering (Lev 2), and the peace offering (Lev 3).

Pagan ideas of sacrifice.

Perverted ideas of sacrifice prevailing among Israel's heathen neighbors included the following: (1) *The food idea.* The sacrifice was thought to feed the good who needed food. (2) *The totemistic idea.* The worshiper thought he fed upon the god himself in such offerings in which the offerer partook of the sacred meal. (3) *Life-liberation notion.* Union was considered to be effected between th offerer and his god as the slain animal's life was taken. The blood was received by the god and the flesh eaten by the offerer. (4) *The magic idea.* The sacrifice was a magical rite which acted as a lever to force the god to grant what was sought.

The typological meaning of the sacrifices.

For the NT believer the OT sacrificial system is particularly instructive through its illustrations of NT redemption. Many of the Levitical prescriptions are typical, i.e., they were symbolically *predictive,* expressing a need that they could not satisfy, but which the coming promised Redeemer would fulfill (Eph 5:2; 1 Cor 10:11; Heb 9:14). Others serve as principles that can be applied to the NT dispensation, while yet others illustrate the facets of God's interaction with man that are timeless in their application. This is the normal application of the OT sacrifices for the NT believer, although not their basic or practical meaning for the OT saint.

Outline

1–16 The way to God
1–7 By sacrifice
8–9 By priestly consecration
10 By avoiding priestly violation
11–15 By observing purification laws
16 By annual atonement
17–27 The way of fellowship with God
17–22 By separation from sin
23 By observing religious festivals
24 By obedience in worship and true reverence
25–26 By observing the sabbatical year and jubilee
26 By heeding God's promises and warnings
27 By keeping vows and paying tithes.

1. The burnt offering

1-9. The young bull. The first utterance of the Lord concerns the sweet-savor (smelling) offerings – the burnt offering, the meal offering and the peace offering. They prefigure Christ in His perfections and complete devotion to the Father's will. The nonsweet savor offerings – the sin offering and the trespass offering – set forth Christ as bearing the whole demerit of the sinner. The burnt offering pictures Christ offering Himself spotless to God (Heb 9:11-14; 10:5-7); the young bull or ox sets forth Christ as the patient, obedient Servant, 'obedient to death' (Phil 2:5-8). The offerer's putting his hand upon the head of the burnt offering illustrates the identification of the believer with his offerings. The antitype is the believer's faith in identifying himself with Christ (Rom 4:5; 6:3- 11) who died as his sin offering (2 Cor 5:21; 1 Pet 2:24).

10-13. The sheep or goat. The sheep (lamb) portrays our Lord in willing yieldedness to the death of the cross (Isa 53:7; Jn 1:29).

14-17. The turtledove or pigeon speaks of sorrowing innocence (Isa 38:14; 59:11; Heb 7:26), and is connected with poverty (5:7). It portrays Him who became poor that we through His poverty might become wealthy (2 Cor 8:9).

An altar with four 'horns' from Megiddo.

2. The meal offering

1-3. General meaning. In this nonblood offering Christ is prefigured in His sinless humanity, the perfect Man. The material of the meal offering was fine flour, evenly milled, portraying the perfection which was blended in every part of Christ's humanity. The fire may prefigure Christ's human sufferings unto death. Aaron and his sons shared this offering, 3, symbolizing our feeding upon Christ (Jn 6:51-54).

4-11. The meal offering baked. The unleavened bread, which is first baked and then broken into small pieces, pictures the scene of the Last Supper where Christ broke the unleavened bread as a symbol of His own death on Calvary (cf. Mt 26:26; Mk 14:22; Lk 22:19).

12-16. The offering of the first fruits. In connection with the first fruits, salt is mentioned with 'the covenant of your God.' As such it speaks of fellowship and friendship with God. Also salt is a preservative and refers to the continuance of that fellowship in contrast to the leaven of sin (Num 18:19; Mk 9:49-50; Col 4:6). The offering of the first fruits evidently connects Christ's sinless humanity with resurrection (cf. Lev 23:9-14; 1 Cor 15:20-23).

3. The peace offering

1-5. Offering from the herd. This offering presents Christ's work on the cross in the aspect of procuring peace for the sinner, God being propitiated and the sinner being reconciled. He who *made* peace (Col 1:20), *proclaimed* peace (Eph 2:17) and *is* our peace (Eph 2:14) is here typified as providing this 'peace with God' (Rom 5:1) as well as 'the peace of God' at the terrible cost of fire (suffering and testings) and blood (atoning death). Peace *with* God (justification) is thus the basis of the peace *of God* expressed in thanksgiving and fellowship. This makes the peace offering above all a thank offering (Lev 7:11-12).

6-17. Offering of the flock. This offering cannot be separated from the burnt offering, since it was offered on the altar *upon* the burnt sacrifice. Peace with God is inseparable from the death of Christ.

4:1-5:13. The sin offering

4:1-2. The Lord's second utterance. The first utterance (1:1-2) out of the glory that filled the completed tabernacle gave the divine direction for the sweet-savor offerings – the burnt, meal and peace offerings – setting forth the divinely appointed way of Israel's approach to God in the sanctuary (ch. 1-3). The last two offerings are the subject of the second utterance – the sin and the trespass offerings – which deal more specifically with the forgiveness of Israel's sins and restoration of fellowship with God.

3-12. The sin offering for the high priest. The sin offering pictures our Lord as the bearer of the sins of His people, 'made him who had no sin to be sin for us' (2 Cor 5:21). It is expiatory and substitutionary (Lev 4:12, 29, 35) and vindicates the claims of the law through substitutionary atonement. When the high priest sinned, it was as if the whole congregation sinned.

13-21. The sin offering. Regardless of who sinned among the Israelites, the sin could be atoned for by offering the specified sacrifice.

22-26. The sin offering for a prince (ruler). Sacrifices varied according to the person who sinned, but all, irrespective of position, were sinners and needed the prescribed sin offering.

27-35. The sin offering for a common person. He too was accountable to God.

5:1-13. For special offenses. Cf. Heb 13:10-13 for light on the sin offering.

5:14-6:7. The trespass offering
5:14-19. Trespass against the Lord. This offering portrays Christ atoning for the harmful effects of sin, that is, injury done. This offering was always an unblemished ram (15, 18; 6:6).

6:1-7. Trespass against man. In injury done either to God or man restitution had to be made along with an additional fifth (20 percent or a double tithe). In the case of wrong done to the Lord, the fifth part was given to the priest; in the case of wrong done to man, to the man defrauded.

6:8-7:38. The laws of the offerings
6:8-13. Law of the burnt offering (cf. ch. 1). This continual burnt offering with the fire that never went out portrays Christ constantly offering Himself in God's presence on our behalf as the One in whom all believers have a guarantee of their full acceptance. His presence in the heavenly sanctuary is ceaseless and

Artist's impression of high priest in his ceremonial costume.

infinitely efficacious. Our response to the burnt offering aspect of Christ's redemptive work is full surrender in devotion to God.

14-23. Law of the meal offering (cf. ch.2). The part of this offering eaten by the Aaronic priests (type of believers) shows the privilege of feeding upon Christ (Jn 6:53). 'It is to be eaten without yeast in a holy place,' 16. Such eating of the heavenly Bread is enjoyed only in separation (unleavened) in the *holy* place. This was a special meal offering of the high priest (19-23).

24-30. Law of the sin offering (cf. ch.4). The sin offering had to be killed in the place where the burnt offering was killed, showing the inseparable connection between substitutionary atonement and the sinless perfections of the Substitute. The holiness of the sin offering was carefully guarded. It was called 'most holy,' showing that although our Lord was 'made sin' (2 Cor 5:21) as the sin offering, He nevertheless was Himself sinless.

7:1-10. Law of the trespass offering
(cf. ch. 5). The trespass offering was also 'most holy,' like the sin offering, and depended upon shed blood.

11-38. Law of the fellowship offering
(cf. ch.3). Here the third of the sweet-savor offerings is put last in the laws of the offerings, perhaps because it represents the final result of Christ's atoning work – peace with God for the justified believer – with communion and thanksgiving preeminent. All the details of this blessed offering center in Christ.

8. The consecration of the priesthood

1-13. The consecration. The basis of holiness was the five offerings of ch. 1-7. The result was the priesthood of ch. 8-10, Aaron foreshadowing Christ, and his sons speaking of individual believers of this age. Their priesthood was dependent on their relation to Aaron, as the believers' priesthood is based on their relation to Christ. Three things were done to the priests. First, they were *washed,* 6, symbolizing regeneration (Jn 13:2-11; Tit 3:5; Heb 10:22). For the reason see Ex 29:1-4. Second, they were *clothed* (see Ex 28:1-43). Third, they were *anointed* (see Ex 29:5-25).

Two important features distinguish the high priest as a prefiguration of Christ from the ordinary priests' prefiguration of believers. First, he was anointed *before* the consecration sacrifices were slain in contrast to the priests, in whose case the application of the blood preceded the anointing. As the Sinless One, Christ required no preparation for the anointing oil (Holy Spirit). Second, only upon the high priest was the anointing oil *poured,* typifying Christ's immeasurable fullness of the Spirit (Jn 3:34; Heb 1:9).

14-30. The offerings of consecration.
The sin offering, 14-17; the burnt offering, 18-21; the ram of consecration, 22; the blood applied, 23-26, all minutely stressed the fact that priestly function depended upon a finished redemption. The blood sanctified the body (ear, finger, toe).

31-36. The sacrificial feast. The eating of the sacrifices and the bread, so frequently seen in the Levitical ritual, illustrates the necessity of believers feeding on Christ (Jn 6:50-55).

9. The priests minister

1-22. Inaugurating the ministry. The week of priestly ordination (ch. 8), symbolic of the priestly position of believers of this age, was followed on the eighth day by a series of new offerings of the priests in which the future priesthood of converted Israel, as a high priestly nation, may be portrayed. The eighth day could represent the millennial age when Christ as King-Priest will appear in glory to His people Israel and they will become indeed 'a kingdom of priests and a holy nation' (Ex 19:6; Zech 3:10; Isa 61:6). The sin offering, burnt offering and meal offering demonstrate that this future restoration of the kingdom of Israel (Acts 1:6) will be on the basis of Christ's sacrificial atoning work at His first advent.

23-24. The manifested glory. Aaron had blessed the people, 22, and then he retired into the tabernacle with Moses, 23. After he and Moses reappeared (possibly foreshadowing the return of Christ from His heavenly sanctuary in the dual role of King-Priest, Zech 6:9-15), the glory of the Lord fell and consumed the sacrifice.

10. Unauthorized fire of Nadab and Abihu

1-11. Sacrilege disciplined. By offering the 'unauthorized fire' to the Lord, Nadab and Abihu acted either ignorantly or presumptuously. The sin apparently derived from the fact that the incense was compounded improperly, they failed to take the coals from the brazen altar (cf. 6:12-13), or because it was not the time prescribed for such an offering (cf. Ex 30:7-8). In any case, they burned it in self-will without seeking or obeying God's directive in the matter. Their sin was official, hence serious. The seriousness of the sin is emphasized not only by the sudden death of the guilty, but by the command not to mourn for them, 6-7. The appended command against intoxicating liquor, 8-11, may give the reason for Nadab and Abihu's failure.

12-15. New instructions were given the priests concerning eating the sacrifices.

16-20. Failure forgiven. Eleazar and Ithamar failed to eat the sin offering, but this was excusable evidently because of the judgment that fell upon Aaron's other two sons, Nadab and Abihu. This indicated that Aaron and his two living sons were not sufficiently free of sin to deserve to eat the sin offering.

11. A holy people – their food

1-23. Clean and unclean food. Leviticus as a manual of holiness now sets forth the truth that *holiness is required* of God's redeemed people (ch. 11-15). The reason is, 'Be holy, because I am holy' (1 Pet 1:16; cf. Lev 11:44-45). 'Offer your bodies as living sacrifices, holy and pleasing to God' (Rom 12:1). 'Do you not know that your body is a temple of the Holy Spirit?' (1 Cor 6: 19). The pre-Flood distinction between clean and unclean animals (Gen 7:2) included in the Mosaic law was based partly on reasons of physical health and religious scruples, and was designed to mark Israel's separation from other peoples. Under the Christian dispensation such distinctions have fulfilled their symbolic significance and have been abrogated, as in the case of Peter's vision when the gospel was released to Gentiles (Acts 10:9-15).

24-47. Defilement by a dead body. Death, illustrative of that which is purely in the natural realm and has no place in the experience of one who serves a *living* God (cf. Heb 9:14), defiled on touch and required cleansing.

12. A holy people – childbirth

1-8. Childbirth and uncleanness. The uncleanness associated with giving birth may serve as a reminder of mankind's innate, congenital depravity (Gen 5:3; Ps 51:5; Rom 5:18; Eph 2:3). The primary function of the restrictions seems to be linked to the uncleanness of the postpartum (afterbirth) secretions since the situation is compared to menstruation (cf. 12:2). The declaration of uncleanness thus fulfills a religious, symbolic, and hygienic role for Israel. Circumcision of the male (cf. Gen 17:9-14) on the eighth day had hygienic as well as spiritual significance (Col 2:11-12). The Virgin Mary complied with the law and brought the sacrifice of the poor (Lk 2:22-24).

13-14. A holy people – leprosy

13:1-59. Leprosy. Leprosy refers not only to Hansen's Disease (modem leprosy) but also to various skin diseases (e.g., psoriases, vitiligo, scabies, etc.). Some have even linked the condition to various venereal diseases. Leprosy (Heb. *nagà,* 'to strike') illustrates the results of sin. The leper was excluded from the camp, 45-46. The believer who permits indwelling sin to work in him is similarly unfit for fellowship with God or His people.

14:1-32. Its purification. This ritual assumed that the leper had been healed. The actual healing, like the forgiveness of sin, could be effected by God alone. The priest examined the leper without the camp, and if he was persuaded

Sunset over Mount Sinai.

the sufferer was cured, he proceeded to purify him ceremonially by the two-bird ritual. The bird killed, and the live bird dipped in blood and let go, present our Lord in two aspects – ' delivered over to death for our sins and was raised to life for our justification' (Rom 4:25). It was the blood that purified from the leprosy of sin. The living bird in its upward flight bore upon its wings the blood, the badge of a finished redemptive work So the risen and ascended Christ bore the evidences of His atonement. The other details of the ceremony, the offerings, washings, etc., all speak of the sinfulness of sin and the efficacy of the person and work of Christ to cleanse it away.

33-57. Mildew in the house. This refers to various molds, mildews, or rots that may affect the moist plaster inside a house. It illustrates how sin may contaminate a home.

15. A holy people
– personal defilement

1-18. Man's uncleanness. Human nature is hopelessly defiled and defiling. This book holds up a faithful mirror to proud humanity and leaves 'the flesh' nothing to glory in before a holy God. The bodily secretions mentioned, both voluntary and involuntary, normal as well as pathological, give evidence of the deep-seated sin inherent in human nature and the curse upon it, revealing the need of continual cleansing by water (the Word) on the basis of the shed blood, 14-15 (Jn 13:3-10; Eph 5:25-27; 1 Jn 1:9).

19-33. Woman's uncleanness. Cf. the woman with a hemorrhage (Mt 9:20-22). Fallen human nature is defiled even in its secret involuntary operations. Holiness is demanded by a holy God on the basis of Christ's redemption.

16. In the holiest
– national atonement

1-28. The ritual portraying the Lord's objective redemption. *Yom Kippurîm,* the Day of Atonement, the fast (Acts 27:9), on the tenth day of the seventh month (Sept.-Oct.), marked the climax of access to God under the old covenant. It was the most solemn day of the entire year, when the high priest (a figure of Christ) entered the holy of holies to make annual atonement for the sins of the nation, 1-5 (cf. Ex 30:10; Heb 9:7-8; 10:19). The expiation for sin was for only one year, but it looked forward to the once-for-all removal of sin by Christ's death (Heb

9:12), illustrated by the various offerings, 6-10, and the blood of the sacrificed goat being carried into the holiest, 11-19.

The offering of the high priest for himself, 6, has no parallel in the sinless Christ (Heb 7:26-27). Illustrative significance focuses on the high priest and two goats selected from the congregation for the ritual. All was done by the high priest, the Israelites supplying only the animals. ('[Christ] provided purification for sins,' Heb 1:3.) Aaron cast lots on the two goats. The goat on which the lot fell for the Lord, 8-10, 15-17, depicts that aspect of our Lord's death which vindicates the divine holiness expressed in the law (Rom 3:24-26). The live goat, which was dispatched for the scapegoat (Heb. 'to Azazel') in the wilderness, 20-22, presents that aspect of Christ's atonement which expiates our sin from before God's presence (Rom 8:33-34; Heb 9:26). Azazel may simply signify 'dismissal,' or complete removal of sin from the camp of God's people. The high priest's entrance into the holiest pictures Christ entering heaven itself (Heb 9:24) to present the infinite merits of His shed blood before God's throne of judgment, which is thereby transformed to a throne of grace or mercy seat.

29-34. The ritual picturing man's subjective response for receiving the redemption. The command that 'you must deny yourselves,' 31, later came to include fasting (Acts 27:9). The rigid rest prefigures the rest of redemption and Israel's national enjoyment of a finished atonement. As believer priests of the new covenant we enjoy a permanently 'rent veil' and immediate access into the holiest place, that which Israel never knew (Heb 4:14-16; 10:19-22).

17. Reverence for blood

1-16. Concerning slain animals and the eating of blood. The blood was to possess sanctity because it represented life which God the Creator made. It was likewise the means of atonement, pointing to Him as Redeemer.

18. Unholy practices
forbidden

1-5. A holy life demanded. About 30 times in ch. 18-22 occur the solemn words: 'I am the Lord' and 'Be holy, because I, the Lord your God, am holy.' The holiness of the Redeemer is the all compelling reason for the holiness of the redeemed.

6-23. Unholiness specified. Various unholy relationships, 6-18, render a believer unfit for worship. This catalog of the degrees of consanguinity has provided the basis for common law and is still generally followed. The vile and abominable practices of the Canaanites and other idolaters are spelled out, 19-23.

24-30. Judgment threatened. The panorama of history has shown God's warning consummated in judgment, both for the Canaanites and for Israel.

19-20. Other prescriptions for holiness

19:1-37. Social regulations. These include honoring God and parents, 1-8; care of the poor, 9-10; commands against falsehood and theft, 11-12; oppression, 13-14; unjust judgment, 15-16; injunctions toward the love of neighbors, 17-18; and various other regulations, 19-37.

20:1-27. Special sins. Molech worship and demonism, 1-8; cursing parents, 9; and criminal arid vile relations, 10-21, are warned against. Exhortations are given for obedience and separation, 22-27. Worship of Molech (from *melek*, 'king'), a detestable deity adored by the Ammonites with sacrifice of the firstborn, offers a particularly cruel and revolting aspect of ancient Semitic paganism.

21-22. Prescriptions for priestly holiness

21:1-16. Holiness of the priests. The preceding laws concerned the holy nation. These special laws regulated the holiness of the priests, guaranteeing a ministry beyond reproach. Since the priesthood is illustrative of believers of this age, the various injunctions concerning ceremonial cleanliness, marriage, etc., show the importance of separation from sin on the part of Christians (2 Tim 3:16-17). The high priest's sanctity was particularly guarded.

17-24. Physical disqualifications of a priest. Disabilities, such as lameness (defective walk), blindness (defective sight) and arrested growth (immaturity), barred one from priestly function but not from priestly position. These illustrated defects in a believer's life do not abrogate his position 'in Christ' or his reception of grace ('He may eat the most holy food of his God,' 22), but they curtail his usefulness in ministry.

22:1-16. Personal purity of a priest. He must regulate his own personal life discreetly, and that of his family.

17-33. Priestly sacrifices must be unblemished and physically perfect. They are emblematic of the moral perfections of Christ (Heb 9:14).

23. The holy feasts

1-3. The weekly sabbath. This is not one of the seven annual feasts enumerated in 4-44, but is basic to the entire festal cycle and Israel's religion, and so introduces the description of these sacred seasons or 'appointed feasts.'

4-5. The Passover. (Heb. *pesah*. 'a passing over'). This memorialized redemption from Egypt, when the Lord passed over the blood-covered dwellings of Israel. This was the first feast, basic to all the rest, as all spiritual blessing rests on sinful man's redemption by Christ (1 Cor 5:7; 1 Pet 1:19) 'our Passover lamb, [who] has been sacrificed.'

6-8. Unleavened bread. Redemption is to be followed by a holy life and walk (1 Cor 5:7-8; 2 Cor 7:1; Gal 5:7-9). Communion with Christ, the unleavened Bread, will result in separation from evil (leaven, or yeast) .

9-14. Firstfruits. These typify Christ in resurrection (the first fruits) and those who are saved at Christ's appearing (1 Cor 15:23; 1 Thess 4:13-18).

15-22. Pentecost. This occurred 50 days after the Feast of First fruits, 15-16. The new meal offering, 16, looks forward to the church. The two wave loaves (a loaf, not a sheaf of separate grains) 'baked with yeast,' 17, anticipate that aspect of it in which Jew (Acts 2) and Gentile (Acts 10) are united in a genuine spiritual union (1 Cor 12:13) by the advent of the Spirit at Pentecost (Acts 1:1-4).

23-25. Trumpets. The blowing of trumpets after the church's ingathering furnishes a picture of Israel's age-end regathering from her long worldwide dispersion (Mt 24:31; Isa 18:3, 7; 27:12; 58:1-14; Ezk 37:12-14).

26-32. Day of Atonement. This solemn occasion prefigures the repentant sorrow of Israel at the time of her conversion at the second advent of Christ. This is the same day described in Lev 16 (cf. Zech 12:10-13:1). This was and is the spiritual highlight of the Jewish calendar year.

33-44. Tabernacles. This is the last and

great harvest home festival of the Jewish year. It foreshadows Israel's kingdom rest after regathering and spiritual conversion. It is commemorative of redemption out of Egypt, 43, and prophetic of the restoration of the kingdom over Israel.

24. Priestly duties; blasphemy

1-4. Oil for the tabernacle light (cf. Ex 25:6).

5-9. The bread (cf. Ex 25:23-30). Priests were to follow God's commands to Moses concerning these elements of the tabernacle worship.

10-23. Blasphemy dealt with. This is a fleeting narrative section describing the execution of a part-Danite, part-Egyptian (evidently part of the 'mixed multitude' [KJV] of Ex 12:38) for blaspheming the name of Jehovah *(Yahweh),* a name which signifies 'He *is present'* (redemptively, as in Ex 3:12-14). Traditional Judaism superstitiously refuses to pronounce the holy name Jehovah *(Yahweh)*, substituting *Adonai* on the strength of this passage.

25. Sabbatical year and jubilee

1-7. The sabbatical year. The sabbath of days was extended to a sabbath of years. Every seventh year was to be a year of rest for the land, 5. This was to restore the soil and provide for the poor from what grew from the untilled fields, 6, or as a humanitarian institution economically in the cancellation of debts (cf. 35-38). Primarily, however, it was a recognition of God's sovereignty over the land which He was to give them, 2 (see Lev 26:32-35). Failure to accept the Lord's supremacy resulted in captivity in a foreign land. The institution pictured the coming kingdom rest and prosperity, 20-23.

8-55. The year of jubilee. The cycle of seven sabbatical years was followed by the fiftieth year, 8, ushered in by the blowing of the jubilee trumpet on the Day of Atonement, 9. This portrays Israel's entrance into the blessings of the messianic reign, with the Lord in the midst of His people. But it means much more than the promised blessings to Israel. It foreshadows the blessings of Rom 8:19-23 for the entire earth. It will include a great outpouring of the Spirit, the complete fulfillment of Joel's prophecy (Joel 2:28-32).

26. Conditions of blessing in the land

1-13. The blessings for obedience. To receive blessing God's people had to be holy and maintain a holy reverence for Him according to the first table of the law given at Sinai, 1-2 (Ex 20:3-11). (Cf. Deut 28-30 for the conditions of the Palestinian covenant.)

14-39. The curse of disobedience. This culminated in captivity and dispersion among the nations. This prediction and its fulfillment in Jewish history contain powerful evidence for the divine inspiration of the Bible.

40-46. The restoration. Despite disobedience to the Mosaic and Palestinian covenants, the unconditional Abrahamic covenant remains, and through grace a remnant will be restored to kingdom blessing.

27. Appendix: vows

1-25. Persons and things dedicated. These were voluntary obligations assumed before God, often on condition of some desired blessing, as Jacob's vow (Gen 28:20-22).

26-34. Things intrinsically the Lord's. These included the firstborn of animals, 26-27; other things dedicated, 28-29; and all the tithe of the land, 30-34.

NUMBERS

Walk and service of God's people

Nature of the book. Genesis is the book of beginnings, Exodus the book of redemption, and Leviticus the book of atonement and worship. Numbers, on the other hand, is the book of testing. Number (L. *numeri*, Gr. *arithmoi*) is so named because the Israelites were twice numbered (ch. 1 and 26), the first time at the beginning of their journey, the second time at the close of the 28 years of wandering in the desert. Numbers is a wilderness book covering the time span from the second month of the second year after the exodus from Egypt to the tenth month of the fortieth year. But the years of unbelief and wandering are mostly passed over in silence.

Authorship. See 'Authorship of the Pentateuch,' p. 15.

Spiritual significance. The NT repeatedly alludes to or quotes the book of Numbers (cf. Jn 3:14 and Num 21:9). Balaam (Num 22-24) is referred to by Jude (11), Peter (2 Pet 2:15-16), and John (Rev 2:14). Jude also refers to Korah's rebellion (11; cf. Num 16; 27:3). Its spiritually illustrative contents are given deep meaning (1 Cor 10:1-11) and are inseparably connected with the rest of the Pentateuch, particularly with Exodus and Leviticus.

•Outline

1-10 Leaving Sinai
11-20 Wandering in the Desert
21-36 Journeying to the Land

After leaving Sinai, the Israelites spent many years wandering in the desert.

1. The people numbered

1-46. The numbering. The command to number, 1-4, was given one month after the erection of the tabernacle (cf. Ex 40:17). This numbering was apparently distinct from the atonement-money census (Ex 38:25-26), although the total number is the same (603,550; see Num 1:46). The count was for military purposes, 3, according to family lineage.

47-54. The Levites excluded, and separated to tabernacle service.

2. The tribes arranged

1-2. The command. The camp of God's people was divinely arranged and ordered, with the tabernacle in the center (showing that God's worship and service were to be central). In the NT every believer has his appointed place in the body (1 Cor 12), with Christ as the Head.

3-34. The ordered camp. On the east side were Judah, Issachar, and Zebulun, 3-9. On the south side were Reuben, Simeon, and Gad, 10- 16. The central position of the Levites was given, 17. On the west side were placed Ephraim, Manasseh, and Benjamin, 18-24. On the north side were Dan, Asher, and Naphtali, 25-34.

3-4. The Levites assigned their work

3:1-4. The priests. They are mentioned first, since the worship of God (sacrifice and intercession) was centered in them as representatives of the nation.

3:5-39. The Levites. Sovereign grace was exemplified in the choice of this tribe for holy tabernacle ministry (cf. Gen 34:25-31; 49:5-7). Leviticus gives a description of the work of Aaron and his sons. Here the work of the Levites in general is specified, the care of the tabernacle itself and its transportation, 5-10. Levi ('joined') was united to the Lord in holy service instead of the firstborn, 11-13. This tribe was numbered, 14-20; and the specific duties of Gershon, 21-26, Kohath, 27-32, and Merari, 33-37, are set forth. Again the sanctity of the Levites as substitutes for the firstborn is stressed, 40-51, being therefore numbered from infancy, 22, instead of 20 years of age and upward as in the case of the other tribes.

4:1-20. The Kohathites. The priests illustrate believers in their priestly capacity. Likewise the Levites, mustered from thirty years old and upward to fifty years, whose responsibility was to guard and transport the holy things of the Lord through the wilderness, picture believers guarding and keeping the precious things of 'the faith which was once for all entrusted to the saints' (Jude 3), in their pilgrimage through the desert of this world.

4:21-28. The Gershonites. Each Levite was divinely assigned his work according to his *birth* by tribe and maturity in *age.* Usefulness in ministry in holy things is on the basis not only of spiritual regeneration, but Christian maturity. In ch. 3 Gershon, the eldest, stands first. Here he

Artist's impression of the Ark of the Covenant.

takes a secondary place to Kohath, showing that divine grace appoints service and minutely outlines it for the believer in the will of God.

4:29-49. The Merarites. All the Levites, in being occupied with the holy things of the tabernacle, illustrate our being occupied with Christ in fellowship with God and holy service (cf. Num 8:10).

5. Separation from defilement

1-4. Separation from those unclean. The unclean included the leper (see Lev 13-14) and the one defiled by a physical secretion (see Lev 15) or by contact with physical death. This condition incapacitated one to serve the *living* God (cf. Heb 9:14), and illustrates the necessity of judging and putting away sin as a barrier to divine fellowship and service.

5-10. Restitution. This was for wrong committed in the camp. Unconfessed sin cannot be condoned among the Lord's people. The grace of God which grants unlimited forgiveness would be tragic if it did not discipline the believer to 'say "No" to ungodliness and worldly passions' and to 'live self-controlled, upright and godly lives in this present age' (Titus 2:12). Could anything be more calamitous than for those professedly brought near to God to have a weakening sense of the exceeding sinfulness of sin (1 Jn 1:7-9)?

11-31. Separation from adultery. This was scarcely a trial by ordeal, so common among ancient people and surviving in Europe till the Middle Ages, since the Mosaic law condemned popular heathen superstitions of the day. It was a

Diagram showing the position of the tribes in camp, with the Tabernacle sited symbolically and for security in the center of the encampment.

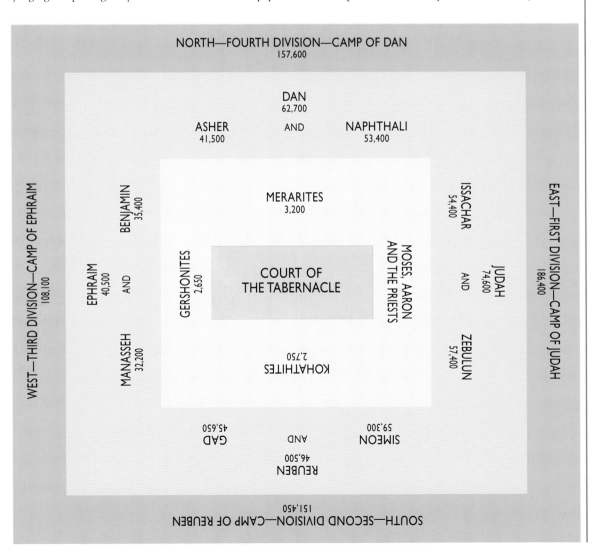

NORTH—FOURTH DIVISION—CAMP OF DAN
157,600

DAN
62,700

ASHER
41,500

AND

NAPHTHALI
53,400

MERARITES
3,200

BENJAMIN
35,400

GERSHONITES
2,650

COURT OF THE TABERNACLE

MOSES, AARON AND THE PRIESTS

ISSACHAR
54,400

EPHRAIM
40,500

AND

JUDAH
74,600

AND

EAST—FIRST DIVISION—CAMP OF JUDAH
186,400

WEST—THIRD DIVISION—CAMP OF EPHRAIM
108,100

MANASSEH
32,200

KOHATHITES
2,750

ZEBULUN
57,400

GAD
45,650

AND

REUBEN
46,500

SIMEON
59,300

SOUTH—SECOND DIVISION—CAMP OF REUBEN
151,450

simple ritual in which the Lord was to manifest His power in exposing the adulteress and punishing this serious sin in order to purge it out from among God's people.

6. The Nazirite

1-8. The vow. This was a voluntary dedication of a person to the Lord, 2. It involved abstinence from wine, 3, symbolic of the natural pleasures of life (Ps 104:15), and even from grapes in any form, 4, representing earthly joys harmless in themselves but which cannot give the believer the delight in the Lord which his heart craves. This feature is therefore the outward symbol of a yieldedness which finds all its joy in the Lord. The Nazirite vow also involved long hair, 5, the outward badge that the separated one was willing to identify himself as belonging to the Lord. The vow also entailed rigid separation from ceremonial uncleanness contracted by contact with a dead body, even that of a close loved one, 6-8. Samson, Samuel, and John the Baptist stand as premier illustrations of the Nazirite vow. Since it was a voluntary vow, Samson was able to break it, though he did so at great loss.

9-21. The cleansing of the Nazirite from defilement. Various sacrificial rituals were prescribed, all pointing to the finished redemptive work of Christ. Defilement of a dedicated saint is cleansed only by confession and forgiveness (1 Jn 1:7-9) based on the efficacious advocacy of Christ.

22-27. Priestly blessing of a cleansed and consecrated people. This is a beautiful threefold invocation of the Lord's providence, grace, and favor.

7. The gifts of the princes

1-88. The princes and their gifts. The chiefs of the tribes contributed wagons and oxen for transporting the tabernacle. Although the gifts are identified for each tribe, they are recorded in detail, not only because repetition was characteristic of ancient oriental lists, but because the Lord takes special note of the gifts of His people, and giving in His sight is an individual matter. The Gershonites and Merarites alone received wagons and oxen according to their needs. The Kohathites were appointed to carry on their own shoulders the particularly sacred furnishings, and therefore received no oxen or wagons. Verses 84-88 give the total

offering as 2400 silver shekels, 120 gold, and 240 sacrificial animals.

89. The voice from the mercy seat manifested the Lord's pleasure in the princes' offerings at the dedication of the altar, the promise of Ex 25:22 being fulfilled.

8. The Levites consecrated

1-4. The lampstand lighted (cf. Ex 25:31-40). The lighting of the seven-branched lampstand at the beginning of the wilderness journey focused attention upon the need of the Lord's people for the Holy Spirit (the oil in the seven branches) to shed His light upon them, 2, 4.

5-22. Purification of the Levites. First they were sprinkled with water, symbolizing their cleansing from sin (Eph 5:26; Jn 15:3; 17:17). Next, they were to shave off the hair of their bodies, symbolizing putting off what belongs to the old nature. Then they were to wash their clothes, signifying the water of the Word cleansing their habits and ways of life. The sacrifices, 8, show that consecration is on the basis of atonement for sin, 8. The laying on of hands upon the Levites by the Israelites points to the latter's identification with the Levites, who represented them and served in their place, 9-10, as well as in place of their firstborn, 11-22.

23-26. Levitical charge repeated. The period of service was from 25-50 years of age, which is not in contradiction to Num 4:3 where 30-50 years is specified. Apparently the Levites served a five-year apprenticeship before they were given full responsibility for the care of the tabernacle.

9. Guidance for the redeemed

1-14. The observance of the Passover (see Lev 23:4-5). The first Passover was held in Egypt. This second observance, held in the desert at Sinai as they journeyed toward Canaan, shows how necessary the feast of redemption with its atoning blood is to all in a walk for God. A gracious promise was made for the ceremonially unclean and the traveler, 6-14.

15-23. Supernatural guidance provided. The pillar of cloud by day and the pillar of fire by night were provided to lead the people. In the trackless desert of this world of sin God's people need the guidance of the Spirit by day and by night (Ps 23:2-3).

Modern sculpture from Jerusalem modelled on the ancient Jewish menorah, or seven-branched lampstand.

10. The silver trumpets; the camp moves

1-10. The silver trumpets. These were two in number and made of silver. Like the cloud and fiery pillar which were given for visible guidance, they made known the mind of the Lord in an audible way, 1-7. Aaron and the priests being in fellowship with God were to blow the trumpets and thus make known God's will to the people, 8. It was blowing the trumpets in faith in their status as a redeemed people that would assure victory, 9. In peace, the trumpets were to be blown at solemn feasts, over atoning sacrifices, at the beginning of months, to signify faith in the redemptive guidance of the Lord on behalf of His redeemed people, 10 (cf. Lev 23:24; Num 29:1; Ps 81:3; 89:15; Isa 27:13).

11-36. Departure from Sinai. The cloud moved, 11-13, and the camp went forward, the standard of the camp of Judah in the vanguard, 14-17, followed by that of Reuben, 18-21, of Ephraim, 22-24, and of Dan, 25-28. How beautiful and orderly the start according to the instructions of Num 1-10. Though God promised to lead Israel through the wilderness by the pillar of cloud and fire, Moses asked Hobab, his brother-in-law, to serve as a guide. The principle of divine guidance does not exclude human agencies.

11. Failure at Taberah and Kibroth Hattaavah

1-3. Murmuring at Taberah. This first recorded complaint of God's people so well-ordered, provided for, and led on to Canaan, is inexplicable except on the ground of the wickedness of the human heart. The chastisement was consuming fire. Therefore, the place was memorialized Taberah ('a burning').

4-9. Rejection of the manna. 'The mixed multitude' was doubtless composed of non-Israelite slaves attached to Israel, who had escaped with them from Egypt but who knew nothing of God's redemption. They illustrate those who are unable to appropriate or appreciate Christ as the Bread of God (cf. Ex 16:14-22), who lust for things pleasurable to the flesh and contrary to the Word in matters of worship and practice.

10-30. Moses' complaint and the appointment of the 70 elders. The situation was enough to tax any leader's courage. Accordingly, God directed in the appointment of 70 helpers for Moses in civil administration (cf. Ex 18:17-23), and put a portion of the Spirit that rested upon Moses upon them, so that Eldad and Medad prophesied in the camp, 26-27. Moses' humility is shown in 28-30.

31-35. Quails and the plague. There was abundance of quails 'about three feet above the ground,' meaning within easy reach of the people to catch. The lusting of the Israelites was punished by a great plague, 33, the place being called Kibroth-hattaavah ('graves of lust'), 34-35.

12. Miriam's and Aaron's criticism of Moses

1-10. The mutiny of Miriam and Aaron. The general cause for this mutiny was jealousy of Moses' prominence and the immediate occasion the marriage of Moses to an Ethiopian woman. Miriam the prophetess (Ex 15:20) was the leader. She was punished with leprosy, showing the seriousness of her sin of speaking against a servant of the Lord to whom the Lord revealed Himself in a uniquely intimate manner, 6-8, and yet who was at the same time so surpassingly meek, 3, a notation necessary to the narrative and not inconsistent with Mosaic authorship.

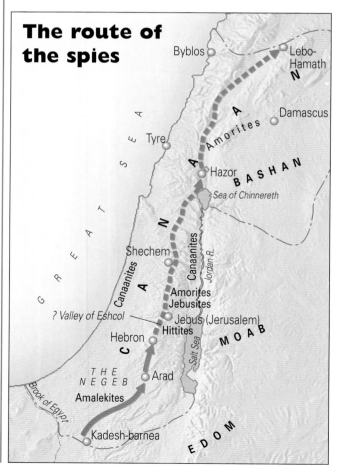

The route of the spies

Byblos
Lebo-Hamath
Damascus
Tyre
Amorites
Hazor
BASHAN
Sea of Chinnereth
Shechem
Canaanites
Jordan R.
Canaanites
Amorites
Jebusites
? Valley of Eshcol
Jebus (Jerusalem)
Hittites
Hebron
MOAB
THE NEGEB
Arad
Amalekites
Brook of Egypt
Kadesh-barnea
EDOM
Salt Sea
G R E A T
S E A
Canaanites

11-16. Aaron's repentance and Moses' intercession. Miriam was restored to fellowship with the nation through the intercession of her brothers.

13. Kadesh-Barnea: The evil report of the spies

1-25. The scouts sent out. Spies were sent out to explore the Promised Land by divine command, 1-3, which was an approval of the request of the people themselves (Deut 1:19-25). Of the twelve names given, 4-15, only Joshua and Caleb appear elsewhere in the Bible. At this time Moses changed Hoshea's name ('saviour') to Joshua, *Jehoshua* ('the Lord is Saviour, Deliverer'), 16. First the scouts were to go to the Negev, the southern steppe land, and then on to the mountain or the central highland ridge, 17, in late July or early August, the time of the first-ripe grapes, 20. At Eshcol ('cluster') they procured a huge bunch of grapes, 23. The Hebron region is famous for its grapes, and clusters weighing from 12 to almost 20 pounds are found there, often carried on a pole to keep the grapes from being bruised.

26-33. The report of unbelief. The land was truly all God said it was, 26-27. Note, however, the 'nevertheless' of unbelief, 28. High walled cities were characteristic of ancient Palestine as archaeological excavations have shown, 28, and it was 'a land that devours those living in it,' because of the intercity warfare of this era that tended to reduce its population, 32. Caleb was vocal in his faith, 30, but general unbelief drowned out his advice, 31.

14. Kadesh: The tragedy of unbelief

1-10. The rebellion of the people. The unbelief of the spies sowed a terrible harvest of despair and open rebellion against Moses and the Lord, 1-5. Joshua's and Caleb's exhortations enraged the people to the point of murder, 6-10.

11-25. Moses' intercession. What an eloquent selfless prayer for God's glory and for mercy upon the rebellious people, 13-19! God heard, spared the people, and announced eventual kingdom blessing, 21. The people's ten temptings of the Lord are mentioned, 22 (cf. Ex 14:11-12; 15:23-24; 16:2; 16:20; 16:27; 17:1-3; 32:1-10; Num 11:1; 11:4; 14:2). Their punishment is hinted at in 23-25.

26-39. The divine sentence. Death in the wilderness wanderings, a year for every day they spied out the land, was the penalty. Although the wilderness with its experiences of the Red Sea, Marah, Elim, and Sinai was part of God's essential discipline for His people, and has spiritual realities in a believer's experiences, Israel's *wanderings in the wilderness were not!* The Red (Reed) Sea speaks of the cross separating us from Egypt, the world (Gal 6:14). Marah tells of God's grace to turn testings into blessings. Elim tells of God's power to grant rest and refreshment in God's way. Sinai reveals God's

infinite holiness and our depravity (Rom 7:7- 24). But from Israel's failure at Kadesh to their entrance into Canaan, all is for warning (1 Cor 10:1-11; Heb 3:1-4:16), not for imitation.

40-45. A new sin – presumption. The sin of unbelieving despair in refusing to enter the conflict for the Promised Land in the strength of the promise of God was now capped with an additional sin of presumptuous confidence. They refused to believe in the severity of God's judgment by resolving to engage in conflict without God's help and purely in their own power. Their disgraceful defeat was inevitable.

Photograph of replicas of the contents of the Ark of the Covenant – Aaron's rod that budded, the Ten Commandments and a pot of manna.

Spiritual significance of Kadesh

The people had faith to apply the redemption blood (Ex 12:28) and to leave Egypt (the world), but lacked faith to enter their Canaan rest, enjoy conquest over enemies, and victorious possession of a land flowing with milk and honey (Heb 3:1-4:16). In other words, they failed to enter into spiritual conquest and victory.

15. Various laws

1-31. Concerning offerings in the land. Two divine communications concerning offering, 1, 17, are remarkable in that they were apparently given precisely when the people were turning in unbelief from the land of promise. What a comforting assurance of God's faithfulness in eventually bringing them into their inheritance despite their unbelief and unfaithfulness. While the great mass of people would die in the wilderness, God would bring a remnant in. They would offer these sacrifices, already described in Leviticus.

32-36. The Sabbath breaker. This was a case of presumptuous sin mentioned in 30-31, giving an example of the severity of the Mosaic law.

37-41. The tassel of blue. On the corners of the garments was to be a memento to Israel that they were to be a holy, separated people and that they were to keep God's commandments. Hasidic Jews are still distinguished by their tassels.

16. Korah's rebellion

1-19. The rebellion. This rebellion marks another step downward in unbelief and apostasy (cf. Jude 3-11). Korah's sin was the rejection of the authority of Moses as God's mouthpiece and flagrant intrusion into the priest's office, the honor of which no one was to take to himself, because 'he must be called by God, just as Aaron was' (Heb 5:4). Korah and the 250 insurgents who followed him attempted to create a priestly order without divine sanction (Heb 5:10).

20-50. The punishment. The glory of the Lord appearing, 19, dealt with this matter. Korah and the insurgents, 27-33, were swallowed by an earthquake and went down alive into Sheol. Fire from heaven devoured the 250 men who offered incense, 35, but the sons of Korah did not perish (cf. 26: 11), showing God's sovereign grace (cf. 1 Chr 6:54-67; 9:19-32; 26:1-20; 2 Chr 23:3-4, 19; 31:14-18). Provision was made for a memorial of this event as a permanent warning by hammering out a covering for the altar from the bronze censers the rebels had used, 36-40. The checking of the plague against the murmuring Israelites by Aaron, 41-50, shows the necessity of the priesthood of Him who had made atonement in the presence of God to keep His people.

17. Aaron's rod that budded

1-6. The divine command. This directive for each tribal head to bring an almond rod inscribed with the name of the tribe, with the rod of Levi bearing the name of Aaron as its representative, was meant to furnish further proof of the Lord's irrevocable choice of the Levites as ministers and the Aaronites as priests.

7-13. The sign. Standing among the dying 'to make an atonement' (16:46-48), Aaron reminds us of Christ in His redemptive work. All the tribal heads presented dead rods. The Lord

caused life to spring up in Aaron's rod alone, which became a picture of Christ in resurrection, acknowledged by God as High Priest. All the great founders of ethnic faiths have died, and are dead. Only Christ was raised from the dead and exalted to be a High Priest (Heb 4:14; 5:4-10). Aaron's priesthood, so blatantly denied in Korah's uprising, was here given the permanent divine sanction, 10, silencing the rebels as Aaron's rod was laid up as a memorial in the tabernacle (Heb 9:4). The rebellion of Korah thus yielded two things for the tabernacle – the plates from the censers for the altar covering (16:38) and Aaron's fruitful rod.

18. The importance of the Levitical priesthood

1- 7. It was to bear iniquity. The Levitical priests were to execute every divine regulation meticulously and make atonement for the sinfulness pertaining to the tabernacle and its priesthood. This was indispensable 'so that wrath will not fall on the Israelites again,' 5. Korah's rebellion was so wicked because it was directed against that which was meant to be Israel's very security. Except for the priestly service, all Israel would have been destroyed by the wrath of God. So Christ, our great High Priest, ever lives to make intercession for us, to keep us saved (Heb 7:25).

8-32. It was to be properly recompensed. Neither the priests nor the Levites were to have any land inheritance in Israel, thus avoiding a wealthy priestly caste such as existed in Egypt and other ancient nations. The priests, however, were to receive a large part of the offerings, such as meal, sin, and trespass offerings, 8-11; gifts of the first fruits, 12-13; things devoted, 14; and money from the redemption of the firstborn, 15-19. Aaron was to have no land inheritance because the Lord was his inheritance, 20. The Levites were to get a tithe, 21-24, and to give proportionately of what they received, 25-32.

19. The red heifer ordinance

1-10. The ordinance. This ordinance is unique to Numbers and to the wilderness wandering. It was instituted because of wholesale contact with the death of so many Israelites who perished during the 40-year period in the desert (cf. 1 Cor 10:5, 8-9). The use of the ashes of an

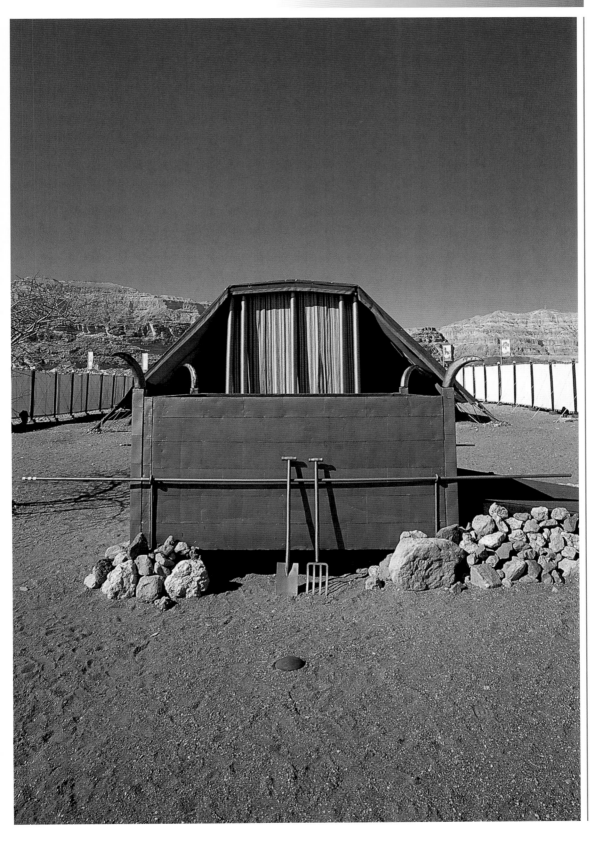

animal in water for purification purposes is a well-known ancient religious custom outside the Bible, here invested with unique significance as it is introduced to Israel's faith.

11-22. The meaning. The red heifer beautifully illustrates the sacrifice of Christ as *the basis* of the cleansing of a believer from sinful defilement contracted in his pilgrim walk (1 Jn 1:7-2:2; cf. Jn 13:3-10). The choice of the red animal is due, perhaps, to an association of that color with sin (Isa 1:18). Its spotless, unblemished character, 2, speaks of the sinlessness of Christ (cf. Heb 9:13-14). It was to be an animal on which no yoke had been placed, 2, the yoke being used to restrain an animal. Christ was completely yielded to the Father's will (Ps 40: 7-8; Heb 10:5-9) and needed no coercion. The heifer was killed 'outside the camp,' 3 (Heb 13:12). The sprinkling of the blood seven times toward the tabernacle speaks of full atonement, 4. The ashes of the heifer were the memorial of an already accepted sacrifice. *Death* here typifies the polluting effects of sin in making the saint with defiled conscience unworthy to 'serve the living God' (Heb 9:14).

20. Moses' sin; death of Aaron

1-13. Moses' sin. This chapter opens with death (Miriam's) and closes with death (Aaron's) and between recounts the failure of Moses. The long years of wandering were filled with failure and death (cf. Amos 5:25-26; Acts 7:42-43; 1 Cor 10:1-10). Yet God's grace never forsook His sinning people (Deut 2:7; 29:5). Even Moses was contaminated with failure as he was tried by the impatient murmuring people at Meribah, 2-6, again afflicted with thirst as in Ex 17:1-7 (cf. Deut 32:51). Moses' sin was twofold: (1) *Presumptuous disobedience.* He should have spoken to the rock, not struck it once, much less twice, 10-11. (2) *Self-exaltation.* assuming authority which was not his. He should not have said, 'Must *we* bring you water?' presumptuously putting himself in God's place, 10.

14-22. Futile negotiations with Edom. The descendants of Esau, the brother of Israel (Jacob), denied passage to the Israelites, thus aggravating the heartless cruelty in their kinship and racial tie with Jacob's descendants.

23-29. Death of Aaron. Aaron died on Mt. Hor. His son Eleazar succeeded him. Mt. Hor (Jebel Harun) is some 50 miles S of the Dead Sea.

21. The bronze serpent

1-3. Victory over the Canaanites. King Arad in the Negev, the waterless district S of Beersheba extending S and SW beyond Kadesh, was defeated and his towns placed under the ban of complete destruction.

4-9. The bronze serpent. Murmuring again broke out, 4-5, and was punished by fiery serpents, 6-7. The brass serpent which Moses was instructed to make and hang on a pole, to which the people bitten were to look, prefigures Christ 'made . . . sin for us' (Jn 3:14-15; 2 Cor 5:21), bearing on the tree the judgment of our sin (Rom 8:3). The serpent (Gen 3:14), as Satan's tool in the Fall, became God's illustration in nature of the effects of sin – from a beautiful, doubtless upright creature to a loathsome snake. The bronze serpent portrays sin – judged in the cross of Christ. Looking at the serpent of brass for healing of the snake bite speaks of faith in the cross of Christ for spiritual healing from the venom of sin, 8-9. That the serpent became an object of idolatrous worship demonstrates how a means of grace can be misused (cf. 2 Kgs 18:4). King Hezekiah destroyed it about 700 B.C.

10-35. Joyful journey to Transjordan. After healing, joyful singing is heard, 17. There is a beautiful spiritual sequence: (1) *redemption,* 8-9 (Jn 3:14-15); (2) *water,* speaking of the giving of the Spirit, 16 (Jn 7:37-39); (3) *joy,* 17-18 (Rom 14:17); (4) *power,* 21-35, seen in victory over Sihon, king of the Amorites, and Og, king of Bashan.

22. Balaam the mercenary prophet

1-20. Balak calls Balaam. Balak, king of Moab, fearful of Israel passing by on the way to Canaan, sent for Balaam, originally a pagan diviner from Pethor, a city of Mesopotamia (Deut 23:4). Balaam was asked to curse Israel with his demonic magical powers as the Israelites were encamped in the Plain of Moab (*c.* 1401 B.C.). Balaam, 'devourer,' was doubtless attracted to the Lord, as Jethro (Ex 18) and Rahab (Josh 2), by the fame of Israel's deliverance from Egypt (Ex 15:14; Josh 5:1), and he determined to practice his oracular gifts in the name of Israel's God.

21-35. Balaam goes to Balak. The directive will of God had been known to Balaam, 12, though he did not follow it. This left him to follow his own selfish inclination, as he preferred

Replica of the Table of Shewbread from the Tabernacle.

the permissive will of God, 20. The case of the speaking ass is an instance of the omnipotence of God, and is not to be explained away by unbelief (cf. the confirmation of the miracle, 2 Pet 2:15-16). That the dumb animal saw the Angel of the Lord first is in line with the frequently keener instinctive presentiments of impending danger possessed by animals over man.

36-41. Balaam with Balak. Balaam is the type of a mercenary prophet, ambitious to exploit his gift financially. This is 'the *way* of Balaam' (2 Pet 2:15). 'Balaam's *error*' (Jude 11) is the diviner-prophet's blunder in reasoning that God of *necessity* must curse the nation Israel because of its sin. The *'teaching* of Balaam' (Rev 2:14) was the teaching of the money-mad seer to abandon a separated pilgrimage for worldly conformity (Num 31:15-16; Jas 4:4).

23. Balaam's first two prophetic parables

1-12. The first parable and sequel.
Presented first is the sacrificial preparation, 1-6, for the prophecy itself, 7-10. It was impossible for Balaam to curse or denounce Israel whom God had blessed, 8-9. The reason is that Israel's *standing* as a redeemed people was immutable. Israel's *state* was morally reprehensible, but this called for the Lord's disciplinary action against the people, not His judgment or curse upon them (Rom 11:19). As a result of God's electing grace they were a *chosen nation,* different from the other nations, 9, destined for ultimate unforfeitable blessing, 10, a people set apart for a particular destiny.

13-30. The second parable and sequel.
The sacrificial preparation and conversation with Balak, 13-17, are introductory to the second oracle itself, 18-24. God's immutable national election of Israel and fidelity to His Word are stressed, 18-19. God's decreed blessing could not be revoked by Balaam, 20, nor indeed by all the sinister power of heathen occultism, 23. The oracles are to be construed as literal to Israel and illustrative to Christians. Israel's *standing* as a result of redemption, 22, was secure and perfect, 21, although her actual *state* required the divine discipline. Likewise the believer is saved and secure through Christ lifted up on Calvary (Jn 3:14), but he may need the Father's disciplinary dealing (1 Cor 11:30-32; 2 Cor 1:4-9). All the while, however, God was *for* Israel and against Balak and all enemies, 23, as well as *'for us'* (Rom 8:31). Eventually, when the kingdom is restored to Israel and she is saved, the universal testimony will be, 'What God has done!'

23 (cf. Rom 11: 26-36). Because Messiah-King will one day rule over the restored nation, Balaam said, 'The shout of the *King* is among them,' 21.

24. Balaam's last two prophetic parables

1-14. The third parable and sequel.
Introductory to the third parable, 2-9, was the account of Balaam's forsaking omens and the Spirit of God coming upon him in a vision, 4, to prophesy in beautiful figures concerning Israel's future kingdom glory, 5-7. 'Their king,' ultimately realized in the Messiah, 'will be greater than Agag,' 7, the traditional name for the king of Amalek (1 Sam 15:8), Israel's inveterate enemy, and suggestive of the Antichrist and all anti-Semitic forces. King-Messiah's kingdom will be exalted and victorious as a lion over his prey, 8-9. Balaam's allusion to blessing upon those who bless Israel and cursing upon those who curse her recalls the Abrahamic covenant (Gen 12:3), the fulfillment of which is certain. Balak's angry reaction, 10, and Balaam's reply are given, 10-14.

15-25. The last parable and sequel.
This is the most remarkable of the four parables, containing a magnificent messianic prophecy of 'a star . . . out of Jacob' and a 'Scepter . . . out of Israel,' which 'shall crush the foreheads of Moab' and destroy 'all the sons of Sheth.' Although the royal symbols 'star' and 'scepter' prefigure the Davidic dynasty, whose empire encompassed the Promised Land (Gen 49:10), yet they find their ultimate fulfillment only in the greater David when at the second advent the kingdom is restored to Israel (Acts 1:6). Then Israel's foes Moab, Edom, Amalek, Asshur, Eber, and Kittim, that portray the latter-day Gentile world powers, will be judged (Mt 25:31-46), before Israel's kingdom is set up.

25. Israel's sin with Baal of Peor

1-3. The sin.
This grievous sin of fornication and idolatry was the result of Balaam's teaching (Num 31:16; Rev 2:14; Jas 4:4). Although Balaam as an instrument of Satan could not turn the Lord against Israel, he could turn Israel from the Lord. Baal of Peor ('lord of the opening'), worshiped near Mt. Pisgah, 3 (cf. Deut 4:3; Ps 106:28; 2 Sam 5:20), was a farm and fertility god responsible for fecundity of family, flock, and field. This god was worshiped in high places or hilltops with licentious rites and ritualistic feasting.

4-9. The punishment.
There was a great slaughter of 24,000 (the 23,000 of 1 Cor 10:8 numbering only the common people who perished, not counting 1000 leaders of the people who were apparently executed earlier, 4).

10-18. Phinehas' action and reward.
Phinehas' zeal saved the people from further judgment, 11, and was rewarded by a covenant of peace and an everlasting priesthood, 12-13. He reminds us of Christ in His righteous burning zeal for God's glory. The Midianites were to be exterminated, 16-18, showing that snares to compromise and apostasy must be destroyed by God's people.

26. The second numbering

1-51. The command and its execution.
The new census was taken after the plague and the events of the wilderness, the grand total, 51, being slightly smaller than the previous census (Num 1:46 with Ex 38:25-26).

52-65. A fair method of dividing the land.
The new revision of the military lists provided figures for a more equitable division of the land by lot-drawing. Notice the fulfillment of God's judgment, 64-65; but compare Josh 14:1 and 22:13, showing that both Eleazar and Phinehas entered Canaan. Evidently the sentence of execution applied only to the tribes which had been numbered twice previously. Levi, not having been so numbered, not having sent a scout like the others to spy out Canaan (Num 13:4-15), and apparently not having concurred in the unbelief the adverse report occasioned, was not subject to this judgment.

27. Zelophehad's daughters; Moses' death announced

1-11. A question of inheritance.
The case of a man dying and having no male heirs, only daughters, became the occasion for a further elaboration of Hebrew inheritance laws. Daughters were to receive the right of inheritance, but were to marry only within their own tribe (cf. Num 36:8).

12-23. Appointment of Moses' successor.
Moses' death being announced, and the reason for it, 12-14, the great leader

demonstrated his humility and meek selflessness in thinking only of the interests of God's people, 15-17. Joshua was divinely chosen, 18, and ordained by Moses.

28-29. The offerings for festal seasons

28:1-29:11. The portion the Lord was to receive. This was to be taken from the daily offerings, 28:1-8; the weekly offerings, 9-10; the monthly offerings, 11-15; the Passover, 16-25; the Feast of First fruits, 26-31; the Feast of Trumpets, 29:1-6; and the Day of Atonement, 7-11. The key is 28:2: 'Give this command to the Israelites and say to them: "See that you present to me at the appointed time the food for *my* offerings made by fire, as an aroma pleasing to *me*." Cf. Lev 23 for the meaning of these set feasts.

29:12-40. Prominence given to the Feast of Tabernacles and its offerings. Cf. the 12 verses devoted to this feast in Lev. 23:33-44 with the 28 verses here. The seven days of this feast look forward to Israel's Kingdom Age and its worship, commemorating a finished redemption, while the eighth day of solemn rest, 35, points to the eternal state.

30. Laws regulating vows

1-2. Vows of a man. The man who keeps his word, who performs all he vowed, illustrates the sanctity and importance of the vow in ancient Israel.

3-16. Vows of a woman. These injunctions involved vows or pledges made by women in which men were involved as the heads of households, and were exceptions to the general rule that anyone who made a vow must perform it. The vow of an unmarried daughter living at home, 3-5, might be annulled by her father, or that of a married woman by her husband, but only if the objection to it was stated at the time the vow was made, 6-8. If the woman did not fulfill it, the man had to do so. The law also applied to widows and divorcees, 9-16. On vows see Lev 27.

31. War against Midian

1-12. The divine command. Vengeance upon Midian was the last official act of Moses' leadership. This was previously enjoined (Num 25:16-18), but delayed until now. The 'holy war' was to be conducted by Phinehas. It was designed to show how uncompromising God's servants must always be against idolatrous apostasy and

After forty years in the Wilderness the Israelites were preparing to enter the Promised Land.

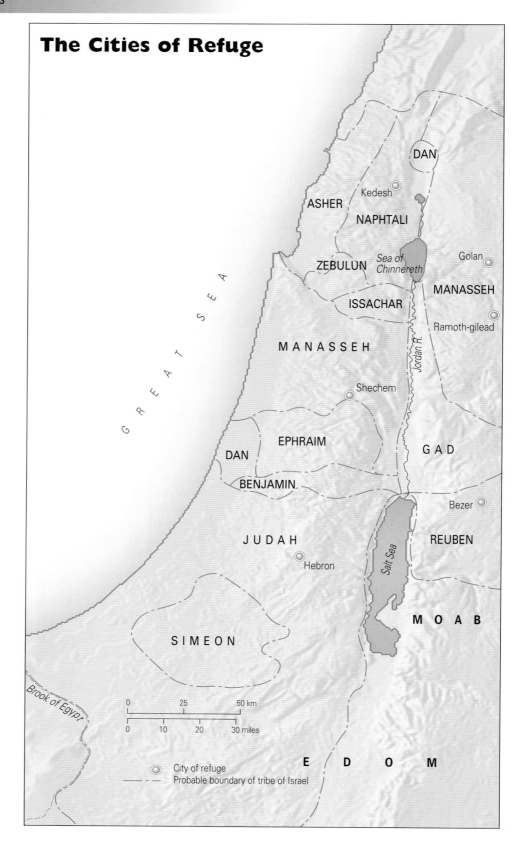

The Cities of Refuge

DAN

Kedesh

ASHER

NAPHTALI

Golan

ZEBULUN

Sea of Chinnereth

MANASSEH

ISSACHAR

Ramoth-gilead

MANASSEH

Jordan R.

Shechem

EPHRAIM

GAD

DAN

BENJAMIN

Bezer

JUDAH

REUBEN

Salt Sea

Hebron

MOAB

SIMEON

G R E A T   S E A

Brook of Egypt

0   25   50 km

0   10   20   30 miles

E   D   O   M

City of refuge
Probable boundary of tribe of Israel

apostate prophets like Balaam, 8. The war was to execute the vengeance of the Lord upon Midian, 3, as God will do to all apostates and especially to Israel's last-day enemies (cf, Isa 63:1-6; 2 Thess 1:7-9).

13-54. Cleansing, spoil gathering, and offerings. God gave complete victory Israel was enriched by rooting out the danger of apostasy and thankfully offered to God the spoils of conquest.

32. The portion of Reuben, Gad, and Manasseh

1-24. Their request and dispute with Moses. The request was a selfish one, characterized by worldly convenience, 1-5. The territory they chose, moreover, was outside the Promised Land and they thereby showed unbelief and a willingness to shun war. Moses' rebuke, 6-15, warned them of the fruits of unbelief at Kadesh when the spies were sent out. Their compromise to join their brothers in fighting in Canaan before settling down, 16-19, was accepted, 20-24.

25-42. The final arrangement. The tribes of Reuben and Gad and the half tribe of Manasseh, 33, obtained the rich grazing lands of Transjordan, but their choice was comparable to Lot's selfish decision (Gen 13:5-11), and manifested similar results of unbelief and worldly conformity (2 Kgs 15:29; 1 Chr 5:25-26).

33. Summary of the journey from Egypt

1-17. The first and second stages. This chapter shows God's concern for His people. The first stage was from Egypt to Sinai, 1-15. The second was from Sinai to Kadesh, 16-17.

18-49. The third and fourth stages. The third stage was from Rithmah to Kadesh, 18-36, the 38 years of wilderness wandering. The fourth stage was from Kadesh to the Plain of Moab in the fortieth year, 37-49. Most of the 21 places mentioned are yet unidentified in the travelog set down by Moses.

50-56. Directions to exterminate the Canaanites. Idolaters and every trace of their idolatry were to be rooted out. The reason is given in verse 55 (cf. Josh 23:13).

34. Directions for the conquest and allotment of Canaan

See 33:50-56. Canaanites to be exterminated.

1-29. The land divided. The boundaries of the land are given, 1-12, and the names of the men who would apportion it, 13-29.

35. Levitical cities and cities of refuge

1-8. The Levitical cities. These were 48 in all. They included six cities of refuge, which are specified (cf. Gen 49:5-7). The cities were set apart because the Levites were not entitled to a tribal inheritance (Lev 25:32-34; Josh. 21; 1 Chr 6:54-81).

9-34. The cities of refuge. The six cities of asylum are described (Deut 4:41-43; 19:1-13). They restrained the tribal law of blood revenge so that a suspected murderer might receive a trial, 12. Murder and manslaughter are distinguished, 16-34. Murder is a terrible crime because blood pollutes the land (Gen 4:10-11) in which the Lord dwells. Therefore, the murderer's blood alone can expiate the crime (Deut 19:10-13). The cities of refuge furnish illustration of Christ sheltering the sinner from judgment (Ex 21:13; Deut 19:2-9; Ps 46:1; 142:5; Rom 8:1; Phil 3:9).

36. Laws of female inheritance

1-4. The request of the tribe of Manasseh. This plea asked that tribal inheritance involving women be kept in the tribe (cf. Num 27).

5-12. Moses' response. Moses approved the request. Verse 13 refers to all statutes or amendments published by Moses in the plains of Moab (ch.27-36).

DEUTERONOMY

The book of obedience

Name of the book.

Deuteronomy is called by the Jews the 'five-fifths of the law,' since it completes the five books of Moses. It is logical both in its place in the canon and in the content of its message. Numbers brings the history of Israel up to the events in the Plains of Moab. Deuteronomy rehearses the law to the new generation that had come out of the wilderness and was looking toward the conquest of Canaan. The name Deuteronomy ('second law,' the inexact rendering in Greek of 17:18) should be rendered, 'This is the copy [or repetition] of the law.' The book, therefore, does not contain a 'second law' distinct from the Sinaitic legislation, but is simply a partial restatement and explanation of previous laws of Israel to the new generation which had grown up in the wilderness. Hence in the Masorah (Heb. tradition) it is styled *Mishneh Torah*, meaning 'repetition [or copy] of the law,' 17:18.

Nature of the book. This is

distinctly a book of *obedience*. Doing the commandments was the emphasis of Moses' sermon to the people. Everything depended on this – life itself, possession of the Promised Land, victory over foes, prosperity, and happiness. Blessing is the reward of obedience; the curse, the result of disobedience. It is a book of *remembrance* and *retrospect*. It looks back to redemption out of Egypt and discipline and punishment in the wilderness, beholding both the goodness and severity of God. It is also a book of *hope* and *prospect*, looking to the future in Canaan and the prophetic forecast of Israel's future. Deuteronomy was our Lord's favorite book, as the book of obedience reflecting his own perfect obedience to the Father. Significantly, he quoted from this great book in repelling the disobedience suggested by the tempter (Mt 4:1-11; Lk 4:1-13; cf. Deut 8:3; 6:16; 6:13; and 10:20).

Higher criticism of the

book. Despite the fact that the Mosaic authorship of the book is emphatically asserted (Deut. 31:9, 24-26), and our Lord validated its authenticity by prominent quotations, higher critics reject its Mosaic claims and relegate it to the time of Josiah, making its publication the basis of that king's great reformation (2 Kgs 22 and 23). This claim is to be rejected, because it makes the book a pious fraud, and explains away clear evidence of the early existence of the book by arbitrary assumptions that these were later additions.

Outline

1-4 Moses' first discourse –
historical
5-26 His second discourse –
legal
27-30 His third discourse –
prophetic
31-34 Historical appendixes

The Mountains of Moab reflected in the Dead Sea, viewed from the West side of the valley.

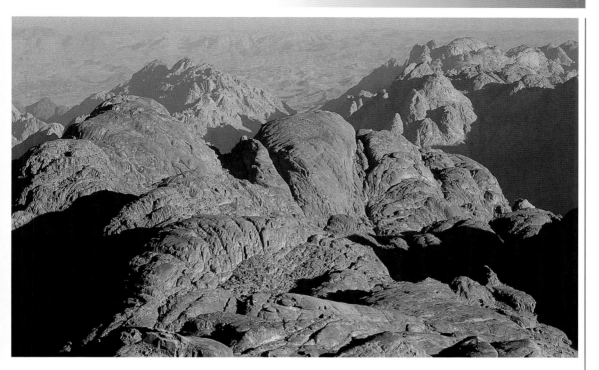

The view from Mount Sinai.

1-4. Historical review: Summary of events in the wilderness

1:1-5. Introduction. The synopsis of Israel's unbelief is given, 2-3. An 11 days' journey by faith was changed to 40 years' wandering by unbelief. Moses expounds (Heb. *be'er,* 'explains' or 'elucidates') the law to the new generation preparatory to entrance into the land (cf. 1 Cor 15:3; Heb 3:5).

1:6-46. Review of the journey from Sinai to Kadesh. A recapitulation of the wilderness wanderings is given. This is vital to clarify to the new generation the moral judgment of God upon Israel's unbelief and failure in these events. The command to go in to possess the land, 6-8, and the appointment of judges, 9-18, are summarized, as well as the failure of the people to possess the land, and the consequent visitation of divine judgment upon them, 34-46.

2:1-15. Thirty-eight years of wandering are merely glimpsed and stress is laid on not offending the Edomites or the Moabites.

2:16-3:29. New period of faith and advance. Israel marched on to the land of the Amorites, 2: 16-23. The command to possess the land was given, 24-25 , resulting in the conquest of Sihon, 26-37, and Og, 3:1-11, and the possession of Transjordan, 12-20, Joshua taking his place as Moses' successor, 21-29.

4:1-40. Moses' earnest exhortation to obedience. This speech strikes the keynote of the book (cf. 11:26-28).

4:41-43. Transitional statement. Cities of refuge were set apart, 41-43 (cf. Num 35, especially v. 14). There were to be six of these in all. Moses obediently set up three of them, Bezer ('defense'), Ramoth ('heights') and Golan ('their joy'), in the land already conquered. For their illustrative significance, see Num 35.

4:44-49. Introduction to Moses' second discourse. The summary of the first discourse, 44-45, declares Mosaic authorship of this material and divides the law into

Archaeological light

Recent study of Near Eastern treaty texts by Mendenhall, Kline, and others has suggested that God's covenant with Israel (Ex 20; Deut 1-28; Josh 24:1-26) bears remarkable similarity to contemporary suzerainty treaties from the 13th through 15th centuries B.C. The similarity in form argues convincingly for early (Mosaic) authorship of Deuteronomy as well as for the essential structural unity of the text.

testimonies, declaring the Lord's will; *statutes,* expressing moral and spiritual duties; *judgments,* indicating measures designed to secure social justice. The territory conquered, 48, is within modern Jordan, extending from the middle of the Dead Sea to Mt. Hermon and from the Jordan to the desert. All was set for conquest of the Promised Land itself.

5. Reiteration of the Ten Commandments

Introduction to Moses' second discourse. See 4:44-49.

1-21. The Decalogue repeated. Moses now recapitulated the Ten Commandments (see Ex 20:1-17). These were basic to the Mosaic covenant given to Israel and expressed man's duties to God and to his fellowmen. These, together with the 'judgments,' governing the social life of Israel (Ex 21:1-24:11), and the 'ordinances,' regulating the religious life (Ex 24:12-31:18), form 'the law' (Mt 5:17-18), or Mosaic covenant. Moses purposely varied the statement of the commandments; e.g., the supernatural redemption out of Egypt is presented as the basic reason for keeping the Sabbath in contrast to God's creation rest in Ex 20:11.

22-33. The meaning of the events at Sinai stressed. The aged Moses, soon to depart this life, solemnly impressed his hearers with the deep significance of the giving of the law at Sinai. He recalled the fire, cloud, and darkness, 22, and notably God's voice, 23. The people were deeply moved, 27-29, and Moses' role of mediator was indicated, 31.

6. Exposition of the First Commandment

1-3. Summary and exhortation to obedience. This section relates to the content of ch. 5.

4. The first commandment. This is the most significant verse for orthodox Jews, who call it *Shema* after the first word, 'Hear!' 'The Lord [*YHWH*] our God, the Lord is *one,*' the one, *'e-had,* expressing *compound unity* not *yahid,* meaning a *single* one, thus not supporting Jewish and Unitarian denial of the Trinity. The meaning is 'the Eternally Existing One is our God and He is the unique and *only* Eternally Existing One.'

5-25. Duties resulting from the first commandment. Since He is the unique and *only* Lord God, Israel is to love Him, obey, and serve Him supremely, 5-25 (cf. Mt 22:37; Mk 12:29-30). The basis for this is gratitude for redemption out of Egypt, 21-22, and safe passage into the Promised Land, 23. Likewise the NT believer is to love the Lord as his Redeemer (1 Cor 6:20; 1 Jn 4:19; 5:3). Jews have literally carried out verses 6-9, writing these words on parchment and binding them in little boxes on their forehead and hand. These were later called phylacteries (Mt 23:5; cf. Deut 11-8; Josephus *Antiquities* IV, 8, 13). But the command was not meant to be a ritual requirement, but a spiritual reality.

7. Possession of the land and separation from sin

1-11. Command to destroy idolatry. The Canaanites were to be exterminated, 1-4, because their immorality was infectious and their iniquity full (cf. Gen 15:16; 1 Cor 10:14). It was a question of destroying or being destroyed, being separated or polluted and ruined. Therefore both idolaters and their idolatry were to be wiped out, 5-11. The Ugaritic religious texts discovered in 1929-37 at Ras Shamra (ancient Ugarit) on the N. Syrian coast fully attest the moral depravity of Canaanite cults around 1400 B.C., and support the biblical notices and the justice of the divine severity in ordering their destruction.

12-26. Promise of blessed assistance. Victory, numerical increase, and general prosperity would attend godly separation from idolatrous contamination. The same principle holds good for God's people in every age.

8-10. Warnings to obedience

8:1-20. Remember the past, anticipate the future. God commanded the people through Moses to recall His gracious care over the last 40 years. They were to look forward to the gracious provision in the Promised Land, 7-10, and be very careful not to forget the Lord, 11-20.

9:1-10:11. Warning in the light of former failure. The warning, 9:1-6, was in view of past unbelief, 7-24. Moses' intercession on behalf of the people was recounted, 25-29, and the results of former disobedience, 10:1-11, presented to the new generation.

10:12-22. The Lord's love for His

An acacia tree in the Negev near Timna. Acacia wood was widely used in the construction of the Tabernacle and its furniture.

people and their responsibility. His love is set forth, 12-15, as well as His people's duty to fear and serve Him, 16-22.

11-12. The blessing of obedience; the curse of disobedience

11:1-21. Israel's supreme duty was to love the Lord and to show that love by keeping the commandments.

22-32. The blessing and the curse. The key word 'obedience' in Deuteronomy is further elucidated. The blessings were to be placed upon Mt. Gerizim and the curse upon Mt. Ebal, 29 (cf. Deut 27:12-13; Josh 8:33).

12:1-32. Conditions of blessing in the promised land. False worship had to be overthrown, 1-4; true worship of the Lord had to be maintained in a central sanctuary which the Lord would choose, 5-14. Further warning against idolatrous abominations was given, 15-32.

13. False prophets and their doom

1-5. Punishment of the false prophet. The penalty was death, because these charlatans would lead people into idolatrous apostasy. Their signs and wonders were wrought by evil supernaturalism to delude and distort the truth.

6-11. Punishment of blood relatives who tempt to idolatry. So terrible is the snare of idolatry that even the nearest of kin found guilty were not to be spared. One is ever to exercise discernment when religious teachers claim special miraculous powers.

12-18. Punishment of an apostate city. If it defected to idolatry, the city would be wholly destroyed and burned.

14. Separation of God's people

1-2. Basis of separation. They were 'children of the Lord your God . . . a people holy to the Lord your God . . . The Lord has chosen you to be his treasured possession' (cf. Ex 19:5-7). To them 'the adoption' still belongs (Rom 9:4). God called Israel His firstborn son among the nations (Hos 11:1), and hence they have a national election in which they will be reinstated. Relationship to God is to be the basis of separation from the sinful customs to the heathen, 1-2, notably mourning customs involving self-mutilation or cutting of hair in token of a covenant or propitiatory gift for the

The Hebrew Calendar

Month	Name (name before Exile)	Modern equivalent	Weather
1	**Nisan** (Abib)	March/April	Rain ('latter rain')
2	**Iyyar** (Ziv)	April/May	Dry
3	**Sivan**	May/June	Warm and dry
4	**Tammuz**	June/July	Hot and dry
5	**Abu** (Ab)	July/August	Very hot and dry
6	**Elul**	August/September	Very hot and dry
7	**Tishri** (Ethanim)	September/October	Rain begins
8	**Heshvan** (Bul) = Marcheshvan	October/November	Rainy ('former rain') Ploughing
9	**Chislev**	November/December	Cool and rainy
10	**Tebeth**	December/January	Cold, hail and snow
11	**Shebat**	January/February	Warmer and rain
12	**Adar**	February/March	Thunder and hail

The Jewish year is strictly lunar, with lunar months averaging 29.5 days, giving 354 days in a year. A thirteenth month, Veader, was added about every three years to align the calendar with the solar year.

dead (cf. Jer 16:6; 41:5 with Lev 21:5 and 1 Thess 4:13).

3-21. Separation and distinctions in food. These were principally religious, no doubt in part hygienic, and some had association with pagan rites. Boiling a kid in its mother's milk was a pagan custom, the milk later being poured out as a charm to guarantee fertility of the soil.

22-29. Separation and pure religion. The negative commands are followed by the positive requirements of the tithe. The tithe gave expression to the principle of the Lord's proprietorship of the people and the land they were to possess (cf. Num 18:21-32, which deals with Levites' use of the offerings). Once in three years the householder's tithe went not to the sanctuary and its established priests, but to the Levites who were in the outlying villages (Deut 18:6-8), the poor, foreigners in Israelite employ, and orphans and widows, 28-29, showing that charity toward one's fellowmen is linked with love and loyalty to God.

15-16. Sabbatical year and principal feasts

15:1-11. The Sabbatical year. The seventh year brought rest to the land and release from debts and obligations. An enlarged exposition of the previously given law is here noted (cf. Ex 23:10-11; Lev 25:2-7). Obedience to this humanitarian regulation would result in national blessing, 4-6.

Harvests/Agriculture	Festivals/Holy Days
Flax harvest	● 14th Passover ● 15th-21st Unleavened Bread ● 16th Firstfruits
Barley harvest	● 14th Second Passover
Wheat harvest	● 6th Pentecost (= Harvest, Firstfruits, Shavuot, Weeks)
Date harvest Grape harvest Summer fig harvest	
Olive harvest Grape harvest	● 1st Trumpets (= Rosh Hashanah) ● 10th Day of Atonement (= Yom Kippur) ● 15th-21st Tabernacles (= Ingathering, Succoth, Booths) ● 22nd Simhath Torah (= Solemn Assembly)
Olive harvest	
Winter fig harvest Sowing	● 25th-2nd Tebeth Dedication (= Hanukkah, Lights)
Sowing	
Almond blossoms, Sowing	
Citrus fruit harvest Sowing	● 14th-15th Purim (= Lots)

12-18. Liberation of Hebrew slaves (cf. Ex 21:1-11). God's merciful love was to permeate all phases of His people's living – care of poor, treatment of slaves, etc.

19-23. Sanctification of the firstling of the flock. This is supplementary to the law of the firstborn in Ex 13:1-16; Num 18:15-19. The eating of the unblemished sacrifice at the central sanctuary prefigures the believer's feeding upon the spotless Lamb of God in the presence of God the Father.

16:1-17. Principal annual feasts. These feasts were Passover, 18; Feast of Weeks, 9-12; and Feast of Tabernacles, 13-17 (cf. Lev 2 for the full number). Moses stressed the Passover and Tabernacles as marking the beginning and consummation of God's dealing with Israel – redemption for kingdom blessing. Special gifts of the males were specified to be brought at the three great festivals, 16-17.

18-22. Justice assured, by legal provisions.

17. Civil government in the land
16:18-17:13. Appointment of judges. Judges were to administer civil justice, idolaters being condemned to death by the testimony of at least two witnesses, who would be the first to throw stones (cf. Jn 8:7). The priests and Levites were also appealed to in difficult cases, 8-13.

14-20. Anticipation of a king. The Spirit of God in Moses foresaw the eventual rejection of the theocracy and the choice of a king in the time of Samuel. Solomon disregarded the Deuteronomic law and thus invited apostasy, 16-17 (cf. 1 Kgs 9-11).

18. Prophecy of the great prophet

1-8. The Levites' and the priests' portion. How the people were to minister to those who were dependent upon the Lord and closely identified with them is revealed.

9-14. Interdict against idolatry, divination, and the occult. That demonism is the source and dynamic of pagan idolatry is here revealed (cf. 1 Cor 10:19-20; 1 Tim 4:1-2; 1 Jn 4:1-6; Rev 16:13-16).

15-22. The great prophet to come. This is a wonderful prediction of our Lord as *the Prophet* (cf. Jn 1:21-45; 7:16; 8:28; 12:49-50; Acts 3:22-23; 7:37), to be immeasurably filled with the Spirit of truth as the True Prophet in contrast to the false prophets under demon inspiration (1 Jn 4:12). The test of false and true prophets is given, 20-22.

19-20. Laws for the nation in Palestine

19:1-13. The cities of refuge. See comments on Num 35:1-34; Deut 4:41-49. Mercy was prescribed for the accidental manslayer but none for the willful killer.

14-21. Other laws. Punishments for moving a boundary stone and perjury are specified.

20:1-20. Future wars of the nation. Since the Israelites were the Lord's people they were to be fearless, 1-4. The fearful and fainthearted are unfit for the battle, 5-9. The law of sieges is given,10-20.

21. Various laws and instructions

1-9. The expiation of an unknown murder. Bloodguiltiness of this sort had to be atoned for by killing a heifer in a deserted valley, and by the elders and Levites washing their hands over the dead animal. An illustration of Israel's blood-guiltiness in putting the Messiah to death at His first advent seems suggested here together with the nation's expiation on the basis of Christ's death (the slain heifer), effected at the second advent when they accept Him.

10-21. Family regulations. These include a woman taken in war to be a wife, 10-14, and the right of the firstborn when he was the son of an unfavored wife, 15-17, polygamy being taken for granted. The case of a rebellious and unrepentant son and his punishment is given, 18-21.

22-23. The burial of a criminal. That this case foreshadows the ignominious death on the cross suffered by our Lord in His being accounted a criminal is shown by the quotation of verse 23 in Gal 3:13 (cf. Jn 19:31). For Joshua's observance of this law in the burial of the king of Ai, see Josh 8:29.

22. Exposition of laws from the second table

1-8. Duty of neighborliness and humanity. Love for one's neighbor is shown by guarding and preserving his property, 1-4. The law forbidding one sex to wear the clothes of the other sex was not directed principally at licentiousness or idolatrous practice, but to preserve the sanctity of the divine distinction of the sexes established at creation. Ignoring the distinctive place of male and female as intended by God is an abomination, i.e., an act characterized by shameful flouting of God's established order.

Further laws of humanity and mercy govern a bird's nest, 6-7 (cf. Lev 22:28), and proper safety precautions to be taken on one's premises, 8.

9-12. Laws emphasizing separation. Common distinctions in everyday life are presented to impress the need for separation from evil and devotion to the Lord (2 Cor 6:11-7:1).

13-30. Laws against adultery, incest, and fornication. These were given to protect the home and family.

23. The holiness of the congregation of the Lord

1-8. Constitution of the congregation of the Lord. The congregation (*qahal*) 'assembly of the Lord' (YHWH), like the NT church (*ekklesia*), was to be separated from everyone and everything unclean or defiling (2 Cor 6: 11-7:1), because it was the Lord's assembly. Only those truly regenerated and hence *positionally* clean (cf. Jn 13:10 with Jn 13:3-15) actually belong to it, and only those experientially clean by continued cleansing by the Word (Eph 5:26) enjoy the fellowship and privileges of it. The assembly of Israel in the wilderness portrays this truth by excluding the profane, the maimed or those of blemished birth, 12 (cf. Zech 9:6), the Ammonite and the Moabite, 3-6, prefiguring those who are at enmity with the full truth of God and oppose God's spiritual children.

9-14. Cleanness of the camp in war. Especially necessary was separation from sin and defilement in time of war, illustrating the truth that spiritual conquest and victory (Eph 6: 10-18) are possible only in separation from complicity with evil, 14 (cf. Heb 12:1-4; 1 Cor 6:19-20).

15-18. The law of the escaped slave and harlot. How gracious that the poor escaped slave found a refuge in the assembly of the Lord, 15, and was not to be oppressed, 16. The harlot (Heb. *gedesâ,* 'female religious prostitute') and the homosexual (*gades,* 'male religious prostitute') had a polluted role in Canaanite degraded worship. Such ones separated to sexual sin, as in the fertility cults of the heathen, and thinking to honor their god with such license, as the Canaanites did, was an abomination to the Lord. Sexual perversions under the garb of religion are abominable in the extreme.

19-25. Other regulations of the congregation of the Lord. Usury or taking of interest was not to be practiced between brothers in the Lord's congregation, only among foreigners, 19-20. Vows, 21-23, were to be kept by God's people (cf. Lev 27:1-25; Num 30:1-16; Mt 5:33-37). The law of eating grapes and plucking corn, 24-25, demonstrated the Lord's essential ownership of the land, and He invited the hungry, as it were, to be His guests (cf. Mt 12:1; Lk 6:1). The Lord also graciously protected the rights of the tenant, however.

24. Divorce and other laws of mercy

1-4. Mosaic concession on divorce. This was *not a commandment,* as the Pharisees who encountered Jesus erroneously concluded (Mt 19:7-8), but merely a concession. That is, it was something which Moses allowed because of the hardness of the Israelites' hearts. (Cf. with Mt 5:31-32; 19:3-12; Mk 10:1-12; Lk 16:18; 1 Cor 7:10-15).

5-22. Other regulations. A newly wed man was free from war or business for one year to

Artist's impression of women grinding flour with a millstone. Mosaic law laid down that nothing necessary to people's existence, such as a millstone for grinding daily food, was to be taken as security for a debt.

make his wife happy, 5. Nothing necessary to a man's very existence, such as a millstone for grinding his daily food, was to be taken as security for a debt, 6. Kidnapping, 7 (cf. Ex 21:16), was punishable by death. Laws concerning leprosy, 8-9, were to be diligently observed, as well as those concerning the taking of a pledged garment, 10-13; treatment of servants, 14-15; punishment of sins, 16; justice, 17; and gleanings to be left for the poor, 18-22.

25. Various laws continued

1-3. Corporal punishment. Such discipline was to be administered, but a merciful provision limiting it to 40 lashes was given. Rabbinical instructions put the maximum at 39, and Paul was punished five times in this manner (2 Cor 11:24).

4. The ox. As the ox, reminding one of a slave, was to be allowed to eat when treading out the grain (cf. 1 Cor 9:9; 1 Tim 5:18), so the toiling servant of the Lord is worthy of his remuneration.

5-10. The brother-in-law's marriage. This custom of levirate marriage was pre-Mosaic (Gen 38:8-11) and finds its outworking in the kinsman-redeemer theme in the book of Ruth. Taking off the shoe, 9 (cf. Ruth 4:7), arose from the custom of walking on the soil as a symbol of declaring one's right of acquired possession.

11-16. Other laws. Prescriptions against foul play, 11-12, and dishonest weights are mentioned, 13-16.

17-19. Doom upon Amalek. See comments on Ex 17: 8-16. Amalek, the opposer of the people of God, was to perish forever (Num 24:20). When Israel possessed the land and their enemies were defeated, then the memory of Amalek was to be blotted out.

26. Offering of firstfruits and prayer

1-11. The basket of firstfruits. Possession of the land is anticipated. This beautiful ceremony anticipated presentation of its first fruits to the Lord at the central sanctuary (cf. Ex 23: 16-19), a token of praise, worship and thanksgiving to the Lord for His faithfulness and blessing. The lovely confession, 'My father was a wandering Aramean,' 5, is a reference to Jacob's seminomadic life in contrast to Israel's anticipated settlement in the land.

12-19. Obedience and prayer result in blessing.

27. Laws on stone: blessings and curses

1-26. Dramatization of Israel's covenant responsibilities. This ceremony was to be inaugurated on Mt. Ebal and Mt. Gerizim overlooking the city of Shechem, in the heart of the land. On Mt. Ebal the memorial stones were to be set up and the curses of the law pronounced. On Gerizim there were no stones engraved with the law, or curses pronounced, but only blessings. Gerizim speaks of the grace of God. Ebal speaks of the curse of the law (Gal 3:10). But upon Ebal, in addition to the stones plastered with the law engraved upon them, was also an altar to the Lord for burnt offerings and peace offerings for rejoicing before the Lord, 5-7. This looked forward to Christ's redeeming us from the curse of the law.

28. Blessings and curses prophesied

1-14. The blessing promised. These benefits were for obedience to the Lord in the Promised Land.

15-68. The prophesied curses. A prophetic glimpse of the history of Israel's tragic career of unbelief and sin is here outlined. The Spirit of prophecy through Moses foresaw the sufferings, tribulations, and worldwide dispersion of God's ancient elect nation. Reflected in these panoramic prophecies were the siege by the Babylonians and later the siege by the Romans, 49-50. The horror of the siege of Jerusalem by the Romans was foreseen, 54-57, and Israel's present worldwide diaspora, 64-68.

29. The Palestinian covenant and the curse

1-15. The covenant introduced. This was the 'Palestinian' covenant governing Israel's tenure of the Promised Land distinct from the Mosaic covenant given at Horeb, 1. Redemption was the basis of the covenant, 1-3, but the people were characterized by spiritual insensitivity, 4 (cf. Isa 6:9-10; Mt 13:14-15; Jn 12:40; Acts 7:51-52; 28:26-27), despite the Lord's wonderful care of them, 5-8. He therefore had a claim on their loyalty and love, 9-15.

6-29. The curse reiterated. Warning against apostasy was again given, 16-21. All the nations would know these punishments were because Israel forsook her covenant, 22-29.

30. The Palestinian covenant defined.

1-10. The terms of the covenant. Deut 28 and 29 introduce the Palestinian covenant (see 29:1), and are an integral part of it. This covenant, similar yet distinct from the Mosaic covenant, and governing the nation's life in Palestine, is here defined in seven prophetic declarations: (1) *Dispersion of Israel for disobedience and apostasy,* 1 (described in Deut 28:63-68). (2) *Israel's future conversion while in the dispersion,* 2. (3) *The second advent of Christ,* 3 (cf. Amos 9:9-14; Acts 15:14-17). (4) *Restoration of the land,* 5 (cf. Isa 11:11-12; 35:1-2; Jer 23:3-8; Ezek 37:21-25). (5) *Israel's future national conversion,* 6 (cf. Hos 2:14-16; Rom 11:26-27). (6) *The judgment of the nations,* Israel's oppressors, 7 (cf. Isa 14:1-2; Joel 3:1-8; Mt 25:31-46). (7) *National prosperity of the millennial nation,* 9 (cf. Amos 9:11-14). The unconditional Abrahamic covenant (Gen 15:1-18) guarantees the land on the basis of divine sovereign grace. This covenant is not to be confused with either of the conditional covenants, the Mosaic or the Palestinian.

11-20. Final ominous warning against violation of the covenant. This is one of the most eloquent statements in the Scripture that sets forth the choice between obedience and disobedience and the resultant blessings and curses that God promises to those who choose good or evil.

31. Moses' final charge and a solemn prophecy

1-8. Moses' final charge. He gave encouragement and tender loving exhortation to 'all Israel,' 1-6, and specifically to the new leader, Joshua, 7-8.

9-13. The law written and delivered to the priests for safekeeping. Instructions were set down for its reading every seventh year at the Feast of Tabernacles.

14-23. The Lord's prophetic disclosure. Israel would apostatize, 15-21. Therefore Joshua was solemnly ordained to leadership, 14, and Moses was given a prophetic song, 19-23, as a warning and witness against the sinning people.

24-30. Moses instructs the Levites. The law written by Moses and delivered to the Levites was to be deposited in the ark.

32. The Song of Moses

1-3. Introductory appeal (cf. Isa 1:2; Mic 1:2). This magnificent prophetic ode spans the entire history of Israel – past, present, and future. It is a great mountain peak of prophetic poetry like Balaam's oracles (Num 22-24; cf. with Rom 9-11).

4-6. Integrity of the Lord's ways vs. Israel's perversity. The Lord is 'the Rock,' 4, an ancient appellation for God, 15, 18, speaking of stability and dependability. God's Word is perfect. He is a God of truth, just and right. His people, 5-6, are perverse, crooked, foolish, and senseless.

7-14. The Lord's love for Israel. God set the bounds of the nations with Israel as the center of interest, 7-9. The divine name 'Most High' is the millennial title of deity, which He will assume when the Son receives the kingdom over Israel (cf. Gen 14:19) and this prophecy is fully realized. The Lord found Israel. He encircled, cared for, prospered, and blessed her, 10-14.

15-18. Israel's apostasy. Like a well-fed

Mount Gerizim and Mount Ebal. In a dramatization of Israel's covenant responsibilities, a ceremony was inaugurated on these hills overlooking Shechem. On Mt. Ebal memorial stones were set up and the curses of the law pronounced. On Gerizim there were only blessings.

animal, Israel rebelled against her master. Jeshurun ('the upright one') is an appellative applied ironically to Israel (35:5, 26). Israel took five steps downward: she forsook God, 15; scoffed at the Rock of her salvation, Messiah; served strange gods, 16; sacrificed to demons, 17; was unmindful of the Rock, 18. The term 'demons' refers to the gods of Canaan, since demonism is the dynamic of idolatry (1 Cor 10:19-20).

19-33. Results of Israel's apostasy. Again history is pre-written. The sufferings of the Babylonian captivity 587 B.C. and the worldwide woes from A.D. 70 to the second advent are reflected here.

34-42. The Lord's final dealing with Israel. The sudden change, 36, when Israel is reduced to the direst extremity and the Lord arises to deliver her from complete destruction by her enemies, is a prophecy of the Great Tribulation (Jer 30:5-7; Rev 8-17). The judgment, 40-42, is that which will fall upon the nations at the second advent of the Lord.

43. The final consummation. The nations will rejoice with and praise Israel, because the Lord has avenged her enemies. This envisions the full establishment of the kingdom over Israel when the nation will be the head and not the tail. Moses' song is a résumé of biblical prophecy.

44-47. The song of Moses taught to Israel.

48-52. Moses' death announced.

33. The blessing of Moses

1-5. The Lord's manifestation in glory. This, the basis of all blessing to Israel and the earth, is a prophetic picture of the second advent.

6-25. The tribes blessed. Moses' prophetic blessing envisioned the benefit Israel will enjoy when the Lord will be manifested in glory. The blessing of Reuben, Judah, and Levi, 6-11, reveals the salvation and deliverance Israel will enjoy at the second advent. The blessing of Benjamin and Joseph, 12-17, pictures the protection and prosperity of Israel in the Kingdom Age. The blessing of Zebulun and Issachar, 18-19, tells of the joy and spiritual worship Israel will have in that day. The blessing of Gad, Dan, Naphtali, and Asher, 20-25, prophesies the enlargement, victory, and strength of Israel in the kingdom.

26-29. The future joy of Israel. Jeshurun (see Deut 32:15-18) is happy in millennial restoration because of her incomparable, 26, eternal God. He is her dwelling place, 27; Deliverer, 28, and Saviour, 29, and He has conquered all the enemies of Israel, who now is really Jeshurun, 'the upright one,' restored and blessed by divine favor.

34. The death of Moses

1-7. Moses dies and is buried. Mt. Pisgah (Num 21:20; Deut 3:27) is a headland of the rocky Abarim range in Moab (modern Jordan) jutting toward the NE end of the Dead Sea opposite Jericho. Pisgah is closely associated with its neighboring elevation Mt. Nebo, slightly NW of the latter. From Pisgah and Nebo Moses saw the Promised Land. In the valley near Beth Peor he was buried by the Lord Himself, 6. Moses' body apparently became the subject of dispute between Satan and Michael, the archangel and protector of the people of Israel (Jude 9; Dan 12:1). While Moses did not enter the Promised Land prior to his death, the next time he is seen is on the Mount of Transfiguration with Jesus and Elijah (Mt 17:3; Lk 9:31), inside the Promised Land.

8. Israel mourns, and weeps for 30 days.

9. Joshua takes over (cf. Num 27:18-23).

10-12. Moses as a prophet. The greatest of Israel's prophets (Num 12:6-8; Deut 18:15-22, Hos 12: 13) had a touching homegoing and was honored by being the only man the Lord buried.

JOSHUA

The book of conflict and conquest

Place and nature of the book.
Joshua is the first book in the second part of the Hebrew canon called the Prophets, the Law (Pentateuch) constituting the first part, and the Writings the third part. Among the Prophets, Joshua heads up the Former Prophets, usually referred to in English Bibles as the historical books. This book takes its name from the great religious and military leader whose exploits it recites. The name Joshua, or Jehoshua, means 'the Lord [YWHW] saves or delivers.' Critics often make it a late composite work, one in literary composition with the Pentateuch, employing the term 'Hexateuch.' The idea of a Hexateuch, however, is lacking any traditional or historical corroboration, and is erected on the premise of unbelief in the miraculous and the prophetic. The conservative view would date the book early, probably in the time of Joshua or soon after, so that the book serves as an accurate historical record.

Spiritual meaning of the book.
Anticipation marks the book of Deuteronomy, *realization* the book of Joshua. Redemption *out of Egypt* under Moses gave the Israelites a redeemed *position*. Redemption *into the Promised Land* under Joshua gave them a redemption *experience* of victory and conquest in possessing their possessions. Two factors, *position* and *experience*, are inseparable in salvation. Salvation is basically a position or status, but it is also an experience of the blessings involved in possessing that position. In a

Part of the excavations of the ancient city of Jericho.

spiritual sense the book of Joshua is the Ephesians of the OT. 'The heavenly realms' of Eph 1:3; 6:12 are illustrated by the land of Canaan, which is a picture of the *experience* of victory and conquest belonging to those positionally redeemed. Those who had been redeemed out of Egypt by the Passover blood now claimed the blessing of that redemption by possessing the land.

The book of Joshua and New Testament truth.
This handbook includes illustrations of NT truth found in Joshua because that book, along with the redemptive narratives in the Pentateuch, forms a connective thread in the history of redemption. The NT references to this thread present interpretive leads which cannot be limited to historical features specifically mentioned, but must logically include illustrations of spiritual truth the reality of which is found in the NT. Christians are

more than students of ancient history, they are the learners of the spiritual principles of life. Therefore the illustrative nature of Joshua is given a rightful place in this study. Such a study must proceed carefully, however, so that the student gleans from (exegesis) rather than reads into (eisegesis) the text its spiritual applications.

Outline

1-12 Entrance into Canaan and the conflicts
13-22 Division and settlement of the land
23-24 Joshua's final words and death

1. Joshua assumes command

1-9. Joshua's commission. Moses' successor was commanded to lead God's people into their inheritance. He was given assurance of divine presence and success, conditioned on obedience. Joshua ('Jehovah is Saviour') prefigures Christ as the Captain of our salvation (Heb 2:10-11), leading His people in the power of His Spirit. Joshua succeeded Moses, who pictures Christ as the obedient Servant (Heb 3:5).

10-18. Joshua takes charge. He addressed the people, 10-15, who replied, 16-18, promising obedience. The energy of faith would be necessary to possess the land. This would lead to warfare, as active advance leads to spiritual conflict in the case of every believer (Eph 6:10-20).

2. The spies and Rahab's faith

1. The spies and Jericho. Joshua, who himself had been a spy, acted wisely in sending out the spies to learn the strategy of the enemy.

2-14. Rahab's faith. The harlot is an apt illustration of the power of the gospel of grace to save a sinner. '*By faith* the prostitute Rahab, because she welcomed the spies, was not killed with those who were disobedient' (Heb 11:31). She attested her saving faith by works. 'In the same way, was not even Rahab the prostitute considered righteous for what she did when she gave lodging to the spies and sent them off in a different direction?' (Jas 2:25). She gave a well-grounded reason for her faith, 10-11, and prayed for the salvation of her loved ones in Jericho, 13. Full assurance was given her, 14.

15-24. The scarlet line. Bound by Rahab to the window, this line by which she let the spies escape becomes a beautiful symbol of salvation.

3. The Jordan crossed

1-6. The ark of the Lord leads the way. The ark (Ex 25:1-22), one of the most inclusive object lessons of Christ, led on and made a way through Jordan. Beautifully pictured is our Lord going through the deep waters of death to make a way for His people to advance victoriously and possess their heavenly possessions in Him. Having accomplished redemption, He takes all His people through death into resurrection life and glory by 'a new and living way' (cf. v. 4; Heb 10:20).

7-8. Joshua begins to be magnified. When the Lord's people enter into the *experience* of their position in Christ, portrayed by Israel crossing Jordan, they begin to exalt and obey the divine Joshua, the Captain of their salvation.

9-13. Joshua directs the crossing. Joshua's message to the people assured them that 'the living God' would prove His presence among them, by driving out the Canaanites, 10. The ark of the covenant is that 'of the *Lord of all the earth,*' 11, 13, a title which Zechariah employs of the time when Israel is established in the kingdom (Zech 4:14) after all her enemies have been judged (Zech 6:5), and Messiah by right of creation, redemption, and conquest is King of kings and Lord of lords. How aptly was this used when Israel was entering her possession, held by formidable and wicked enemies. The mighty miracle of the parted waters was wrought by 'the living God,' that is, Deity in manifested omnipotence, not a creation of naturalistic religion 14-17. The crossing is made. It is wholly the result of a miracle, whether or not an earthquake dammed up the stream above the crossing at Adam, a town eight miles N of Succoth overlooking the Jordan. This has been identified by Nelson Glueck with Tell Damieh. Glueck also maintains that the dozen miles between Adam and Zarethan is the only stretch in the Jordan Valley where such a damming up and going over on dry ground could have taken place.

4. The memorial stones

1-18. The two memorials. Far from being the result of conflicting traditions, as critics hold, these monuments were two separate memorials, each expressive of an aspect of Christ's death. The twelve stones taken out of Jordan and erected as a monument at Gilgal, 1-8, 20, speak of redemption for Israel into the land and into a sphere and experience of victory and conquest. The stones left in the swirling Jordan to be overwhelmed by its waters are mementoes of Christ's death under judgment in the believer's place (Ps 22:1-18; 42:7; 88:7; Jn 12:31-33). This was the basis of victory and conquest in the land.

19-24. What mean these stones? The mighty God had provided redemption and had brought His people into their inheritance. The stones in Jordan mean: We *died* in Christ (Rom 6:1-10). The stones at Gilgal mean: Let us reckon on that death and enjoy life and conquest in the land (Rom 6:11).

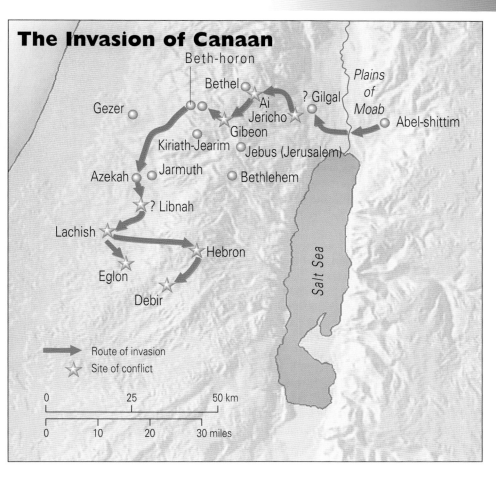

The Invasion of Canaan

Beth-horon
Bethel
Gezer
? Gilgal
Plains of Moab
Ai
Jericho
Abel-shittim
Gibeon
Kiriath-Jearim
Jebus (Jerusalem)
Azekah
Jarmuth
Bethlehem
? Libnah
Lachish
Hebron
Eglon
Debir
Salt Sea

→ Route of invasion
☆ Site of conflict

0   25   50 km
0   10   20   30 miles

5. Israel at Gilgal

1. Israel's terror-stricken enemies. All the surrounding kings of the Canaanites, who had so terrified the unbelieving people of God a generation previously, now were terrified as Israel took territory in the land at Gilgal. A redeemed and victorious people always disheartens the enemy.

2-8. The new generation circumcised. This sign of the Abrahamic covenant (see Gen 17; Ex 4:24-26), evidently in abeyance in the wilderness until the unbelieving generation should die, now again became meaningful, and the males of the new generation were circumcised at *Gibeah Haaraloth* ('the hill of foreskins'), 5, 7. Henceforth they bore the visible token of belonging to the Lord and the Lord, in turn, being in gracious covenant relation with them. Circumcision speaks of the execution of the sentence of death upon the flesh, Christ's death being a spiritual circumcision for His people (Col 2:11). But the fact that believers are

dead to sin by the circumcision of Christ, and thus have a death-to-sin *position,* must by appropriating faith be carried out in a death-to-sin *experience.* The sharp knife must be applied to the flesh and its lusts.

9-10. Reproach of Egypt rolled away. 'The reproach of Egypt,' which Joshua said he rolled away at Gilgal (Gilgal means 'a rolling') when he circumcised the people, was their bondage to Pharaoh in Egypt. In their uncircumcised state the people were without the sign and seal of the Abrahamic covenant and were in the same condition as they were in Egypt under no covenant relationship. Having been circumcised, they were ready to keep the Passover, the feast commemorating deliverance from Egypt, 10 (see comments on Ex 12:1-28; Lev 23:4-5).

11-12. Manna and the produce of the land. After circumcision and the keeping of the Passover, the Israelites ate 'the produce of the land.' The harvest of barley was then in progress so that the people of God could begin to enjoy the fruits of redemption. They appropriated the blessings of their privileged possession.

13-15. Joshua's vision of the divine captain of the Lord's army. The man with the drawn sword before Jericho was the Lord, the preincarnate Christ in visible form, who appeared as a man of war to undergird Joshua and to show him that He who marshals the armies of heaven was fighting for Israel. The ground was thus made holy for Joshua as it had been for Moses when the same preincarnate Christ appeared to him (see Ex 3:1-12).

6. Jericho taken

1-19. Divine instructions followed. The formidable walled city of Jericho, now known from archaeology to be one of the oldest occupied sites in the world, offered a real obstacle to Israel in the conquest of the land. It is analogous spiritually to the world which the believer must conquer if a life of victory is to be his. The city was to be taken in faith and obedience to God's word, and not by human wisdom. The miracle of its tumbling walls was the miracle of faith (cf. Heb 11:30). 'This is the victory that has overcome the world, even our faith' (1 Jn 5:4). Joshua did not reckon with the high walls or the human impossibilities, but counted solely on the power of God. Although a military general, he was foremost a spiritual leader. Nor was he offended by the divine direction to circle the city once each day for six days and seven times on the seventh day, with seven priests blowing seven horns, and then on the seventh day the people shouting. From a military point of view this was ridiculous, if not fantastic. But walking by faith and not by sight (2 Cor 5:7) is never sensible to the worldly-minded.

20-21. The fall of the city. Remains of the massive walls and the city that fell to Joshua (c. 1400 B.C.) have largely eroded, since Jericho was constructed of mud brick. The excavations of Kathleen Kenyon since 1952 reveal that most of the extant mound is 16th cen. B.C. or earlier. Joshua's Jericho has thus largely been washed away. It was apparently not a large city. So crowded were the living conditions that the houses, such as Rahab's, were built on the walls.

22-25. Rahab remembered. The scarlet line, doubtless an object of ridicule, saved Rahab and her house, while the entire city was devoted

The site of ancient Hazor, which was captured and burned by Joshua.

to destruction (Heb. *herem),* 17, 24. The expression *herem* refers to that which is irrevocably given over to destruction (cf. Deut 13:16) or devoted wholly to the Lord, not being used for secular purposes.

26-27. Curse upon Jericho. As an illustration of the world system, the fall of Jericho may well prefigure its destruction at the end of the age (Rev. 6:1-19:16). Jericho was put under the ban, *herem.* It was never to be rebuilt, except under the penalty of a curse, 26 (cf. 1 Kgs 16:34).

7. Achan's sin

1-15. Defeat of Israel and the reason. The unity and solidarity of God's people are here stressed. The sin of one involves all. Cf. the analogous case of Ananias and Sapphira (Acts 5: 1-11). The specific sin of Achan was disobedience to the command of separation from the 'devoted things,' *herem* (Josh 6:17-18), that is, from Jericho (the world), ripe for and under the sentence of judgment, 1,11 (cf. Jas 4:4; 1 Jn 2:15-17). This sin of complicity with evil was responsible for the defeat of God's people. Instant confession and self-judgment are necessary, 13-15. Severity is necessary in a 'sin that leads to death' (1 Cor 5:5; 11:20-32; 1 Jn 5:16) because the time, place, and nature of the sin tolerated bring slander upon the Lord and peculiarly jeopardize His people, 15 (cf. 8-9, 12). Joshua here demonstrates his typical character as the Captain of our salvation by being an advocate when his people suffered defeat, 5-9 (cf. 1 Jn 2:1).

16-26. The sin judged. It was an extremely serious offense and entailed physical death (see comment on 1-15). 'I saw . . . I coveted . . . and took,' 21, is the story of temptation and fall.

8. Ai taken

1-17. Joshua's strategy. The divine assurance of victory always follows self-judgment and confession of sin, 1. Divine directions can then clearly be given, understood, and obeyed, 2. The ruse of the ambush was by divine direction, not Joshua's brilliance, 3-8. Implicitly obeyed, it brought the desired result, 9-18. The believer's strategy is always to be secured from the Lord and based upon the strength of his position in Him (Eph 6:10-12).

18-27. The capture of Ai. The Lord's command to Joshua to stretch out his spear toward the city continuously until he completely destroyed all the residents, 18, 26, demonstrated the presence of the Lord to effect complete victory. Joshua's faith is thus emphasized. Cf. the uplifted hands of Moses (Ex 17:11-13) in the victory over Amalek. Spiritual victory is always by faith in the Word and the Spirit of God.

28-29. The destruction of the city. 'Joshua burned Ai and made it a permanent heap,' 28. Ai means 'the ruin' and has been identified with et-Tell, excavated in 1933-35. It shows no traces of occupation between 2200 and 1200 B.C., but there is no indubitable proof that et-Tell is really Ai. L.H. Vincent's suggestion that Ai was merely an outpost of Bethel, and so small (cf. Josh 7:3) that it has left no traceable remains, is likely the case. It is also possible that the residents of Bethel used the ruins (et-Tell) as an outpost to defend their city from the inevitable attack.

30-35. The altar at Ebal was erected in the scenic Shechem area in the heart of the land as a commemoration of victories at Jericho and Ai, and as an act of obedience to the command of Moses (Deut 27:2-8). The law copied on stones may have been the Ten Commandments and other laws, or the blessings and cursings of

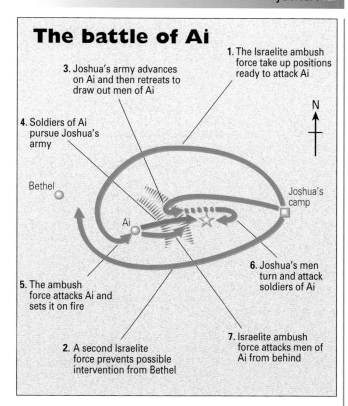

The battle of Ai

1. The Israelite ambush force take up positions ready to attack Ai

3. Joshua's army advances on Ai and then retreats to draw out men of Ai

4. Soldiers of Ai pursue Joshua's army

N

Bethel

Ai

Joshua's camp

6. Joshua's men turn and attack soldiers of Ai

5. The ambush force attacks Ai and sets it on fire

2. A second Israelite force prevents possible intervention from Bethel

7. Israelite ambush force attacks men of Ai from behind

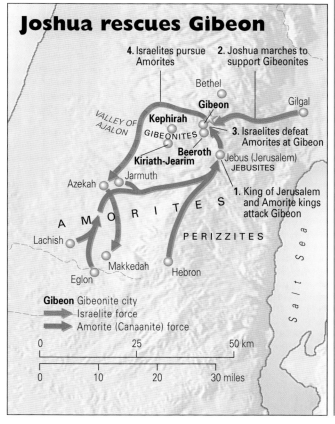

Joshua rescues Gibeon

4. Israelites pursue Amorites
2. Joshua marches to support Gibeonites

Bethel

Gibeon

Gilgal

VALLEY OF AJALON

Kephirah

GIBEONITES

3. Israelites defeat Amorites at Gibeon

Beeroth

Kiriath-Jearim

Jebus (Jerusalem)
JEBUSITES

Azekah

Jarmuth

1. King of Jerusalem and Amorite kings attack Gibeon

A M O R I T E S

Lachish

PERIZZITES

Salt Sea

Makkedah

Hebron

Eglon

Gibeon Gibeonite city
Israelite force
Amorite (Canaanite) force

0   25   50 km

0   10   20   30 miles

Deuteronomy, or the summary of the laws of the Pentateuch. The custom of inscribing law codes on stone had antiquity behind it, for such a practice prevailed in Sumerian and Babylonian times (cf. the Code of Hammurabi, *c.* 1700 B.C., with prologue, 282 sections, and epilogue).

9. The deception of the Gibeonites

1-2. The confederacy of the enemy. The kings of the hill country, the central highland ridge including Jerusalem and Hebron, of the low hills receding to the plain, and of 'the entire coast of the Great Sea' (Mediterranean) or Maritime Plain, united to fight Israel.

3-15. The ruse of the Gibeonites. However, a group of Hivites, 7, a little-known ethnic group of Palestine, perhaps a subsection of the Horites or Hurrians which were a well-known people of the ancient Middle East, determined on a course of diplomacy rather than war. Their capital city was Gibeon (ej-Jib), located five miles NW of Jerusalem on the road to Joppa. They pretended to be friends. Their lie, that their wineskins had become old and worn on the long journey, their bread moldy, and their sandals worn, completely deceived the Israelites, who made a treaty with the enemy. The reason was the Israelites took some of their provisions, and did not ask for the counsel of the Lord, 14, allowing them to live under peaceful treaty, 15.

16-27. The mistake discovered. The Gibeonites were found to be neighbors and enemies, among those who should have been eradicated, 16-17. The result was Israel's disobedience to the Lord in allowing enemies to be numbered among them. Though the Gibeonites were given menial tasks, being made woodcutters and water carriers, the fact that they were enemies remained. They are analogous to the spiritual forces that beguile us – 'the wiles' or stratagems of Satan, who often comes as 'an angel of light' to deceive us (2 Cor 11:14), rather than attack us openly.

10. Southern Canaan taken

1-6. Adoni-Zedek and his alliance. The name of this enemy king, meaning 'my lord is righteousness,' occurs in connection with the first mention of Jerusalem in the Bible. He was the head of an evil coalition, which was formed against Gibeon and Israel.

7-15. The war and the miracle. From Gilgal, Israel's first encampment, the place of self-judgment and the memorials of God's power, Israel issued forth to victory against the southern confederacy. This, the most remarkable battle in the history of Israel, is a foreshadowing of the coming day of the Lord (Hab 3:11). Following the victory, a poetic quotation from the ancient collection called the book of Jasher is preserved, 13 (cf. 2 Sam 1:18). The tremendous miracle, 12-14, the Lord performed to aid Joshua in the victory over the southern confederacy may have been the result of refraction of sunlight, producing intense cold and hailstones in a normally hot climate. Others have suggested that the phrase, 'stood still,' should be translated, 'be still' or 'cease,' thus connoting a continuation of semidarkness that would aid the surprise attack of the Israelites. The hailstorm provided this darkness and additionally neutralized the effectiveness of the Canaanite chariots (Josh 17:18) , the hailstones causing more deaths than the Israelite army. Whatever the explanation, Joshua's long day involved the setting aside of the normal laws of nature's operation. The utter uniqueness of the miracle is stressed, 14, and hence may be considered scientifically inexplicable.

16-43. A great victory and subsequent conquests. The five kings were executed, 22-27, and further conquests brought about the subjugation of all southern Palestine. Israel then returned to Gilgal (see Josh 5).

11-12. Further conquests of Canaan

11:1-15. Conquest of northern Canaan. Jabin, king of Hazor, formed a northern confederacy. Hazor (Tel el Waqqas, Qedah) was a site strategically located SW of Lake Huleh, near the headwaters of the Jordan. Joshua was divinely directed to hamstring the horses and burn the chariots, 6, 9, so that he might trust in the Lord and not in these means of warfare. Hazor was burned, but the smaller cities 'built on their mounds' (RSV, 'tells') Joshua did not destroy, 13. These could be useful to the Israelites later.

11:16-2:24. Résumé of the conquest. A general statement of the conquest is given in 11: 16-23. Conquests in Transjordan are reviewed, 12:1-6, and conquests in Canaan, with a roster of the kings conquered, presented in 12:7-24.

13. Joshua instructed to apportion the land

1-7. The Lord's message to Joshua. 'There are still very large areas of land to be taken over,' 1, is the sad story of Israel, and of many believers who fail to claim their full spiritual possessions. The unpossessed land is outlined, 2-7. In the foreground of undispossessed enemies were the Philistines, non-Canaanites, representing those who hinder God's people from possessing the land and thus enjoying their full inheritance.

8-33. The inheritance of Reuben, Gad, and half tribe of Manasseh, is restated and confirmed.

14. Caleb's request and inheritance

1-5. Summary of the apportionment of the land. Eleazar, Joshua and the tribal chieftains distributed the inheritance by lot (Num 26:55; 33:54; 34:13).

6-15. Caleb's request. Judah's portion was first, and Caleb stepped forward at Gilgal to present his testimony of the Lord's faithfulness, 6-12, and to receive Hebron, 13-15 (cf. Num 13:6; 14:24, 30).

15-16. Judah's and Ephraim's portions

15:1-63. The portion of Judah. Judah's inheritance was specified as to the southern border, 1-4, eastern and northern borders, 5-11, and the western border, 12. It is notable that Caleb specifically requested the land controlled by the Anakim, the same giants that discouraged the spies from taking the land at the beginning of the wilderness experience! Hebron was also called Kirjath-sepher ('city of [a] book').

16:1-10. The portion of Ephraim. Joseph's progeny was given a wonderful part of the land, 1-4. Ephraim ('doubly fruitful') received its territory, 5-9, but failed to possess it wholly, not expelling the Canaanites from Gezer, 10, a very ancient city on the low hills above the Maritime plain, 18 miles NW of Jerusalem and 17 miles SE of Joppa. Joshua smote the king of Gezer (12:12), yet the Canaanites somehow regained control of their city with its 14-foot-thick walls. The city remained under Canaanite control until Solomon's time (1 Kgs 9:16).

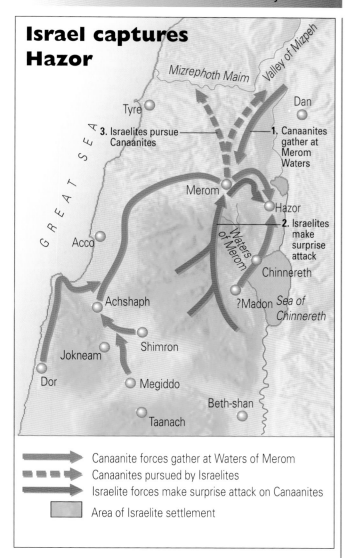

Israel captures Hazor

- 1, Canaanites gather at Merom Waters
- 2. Israelites make surprise attack
- 3. Israelites pursue Canaanites

Mizrephoth Maim · Valley of Mizpeh · Tyre · Dan · Merom · Hazor · Acco · Chinnereth · Achshaph · ?Madon · Sea of Chinnereth · Waters of Merom · Jokneam · Shimron · Dor · Megiddo · Beth-shan · Taanach · GREAT SEA

➡ Canaanite forces gather at Waters of Merom
▪▪▪▶ Canaanites pursued by Israelites
➡ Israelite forces make surprise attack on Canaanites
▯ Area of Israelite settlement

17. Manasseh's portion

1-13. The names and boundaries. The descendants of Joseph's firstborn were given portions both in Transjordan and in Palestine, 1-6, and their boundaries specified, 7-13.

14-18. Manasseh's complaint and Joshua's reply. The complaint showed selfish dissatisfaction. Joshua's courageous answer, 15, demonstrated faith and prudence and showed his faith in the promise of God (cf. Josh 1:3). Manasseh's plea of weakness, 16, revealed unbelief in looking at the iron chariots of the Canaanites in the valley of Esdraelon instead of the power of the Lord. These complainers offered a striking contrast to Caleb's faithful courage, yet Joshua encouraged them, 17-18.

The site of ancient Shiloh, which became the focal point of the 12 tribes till the destruction of the city by the Philistines and the capture of the ark.

18-19. The portion of the other tribes

18:1. Tabernacle erected at Shiloh. Shiloh became the focal point (Deut 12) of the 12 tribes till the destruction of the city by the Philistines (1 Sam 4:11; c. 1050 B.C.) and the capture of the ark.

2-10. Failure of the seven tribes to claim their possession. Evidently lacking faith and courage, seven tribes were urged on by Joshua to explore the land and claim their possessions by lot at Shiloh.

11-28. Portion of Benjamin. This was a small but influential tribe located in mountainous terrain.

19:1-51. Portion of the remaining tribes. The portions of Simeon, 1-9; of Zebulun, 10-16; of Issachar, 17-23; of Asher, 24-31; of Naphtali, 32-39; of Dan, 40-48; and of Joshua, 49-51, are described.

20. The cities of refuge

1-6. Repetition of the provision. This provision was according to the law of Deut 19:1-13 (see also Num 35:1-34). 'The avenger of blood' (or *go'el*), 3, 5, was the deceased man's nearest relative, upon whom the responsibility fell of avenging his death (cf. Ruth 3:9; in Prov 23:11 meaning 'kinsman-redeemer'). The gate of the city, 4, was the place where the council of elders convened and where town business was normally transacted. It was not merely an entrance in the city wall, but an enclosed building built into the wall, with several chambers and several stories. Unintentional homicide cases were protected by the institution of the cities of asylum.

7-9. The cities specified. The Pentateuch enumerates only the three cities outside the land. Here the three cities in the land are also specified as Kedesh ('sanctuary'), Shechem ('shoulder'), Hebron ('communion'), together with Bezer ('defense'), Ramoth ('heights'), and Golan ('their rejoicing') located outside the land. This may well illustrate our Lord's role as the sinner's place of refuge.

21. The Levites' portion

1-42. The portion of the Levites. Because of its religious functions, the tribe of Levi did not receive a territorial assignment like the other tribes. Although true in a sense of all the tribes, the Lord was the particular inheritance of the tribe of Levi (cf. Num 18:30; Deut 10:9; Josh 13:14, 33; 14:3-4). The Kohathites, 9-26; the Gershonites, 27-33; and the Merarites, 34-40, were distributed throughout the entire Israelite territory to exert an influence for pure worship against idolatry.

The land allocated to the tribes of Israel

DAN

Kedesh

ASHER

NAPHTALI

Golan

ZEBULUN

Sea of Chinnereth

MANASSEH

ISSACHAR

Ramoth-gilead

G R E A T   S E A

M A N A S S E H

Jordan R.

Shechem

EPHRAIM

G A D

DAN

BENJAMIN

Bezer

JUDAH

REUBEN

Salt Sea

Hebron

M O A B

SIMEON

Brook of Egypt

| 0 | 25 | 50 km |

| 0 | 10 | 20 | 30 miles |

E   D   O   M

City of refuge
— · — Probable boundary of tribe of Israel

43-45. The Lord's fidelity was renewed. He gave them 'all the land,' 43; 'rest' and victory, 44. Nothing He promised did He fail to keep (Num 23:19; 1 Kgs 8:56).

22. Return of the Transjordan tribes

1-9. Joshua sends the tribes home. Joshua commended the Reubenites, Gadites, and the half tribe of Manasseh for their faithful participation in the conquest of Palestine, 1-4, and with kindly exhortation, 5-6, sent them to their own lands E of the Jordan (1:12-18). So they departed with wealth and spoil, 7-9.

10-29. The great altar and the controversy. The departing tribes built an altar in the Jordan region on the frontier of Canaan, that is, on the west side of the river, since Canaan is strictly speaking the territory W of Jordan, 10-11. The people gathered at Shiloh to make war against them, 12, assuming a blatant violation of the law of the central sanctuary (Deut 12:13-14). The altar was interpreted as an act of rebellion against Israel and the Lord. A delegation headed by Phinehas was sent to examine the matter, 13-20, exhorting them and warning of the result of Israel's sin at Peor, 17-18 (Num 25:3-5), and the case of Achan, 10 (Josh 7:1). The explanation given was that the monument was not a real altar, but merely a memorial, a 'witness,' 21-29.

30-32. The controversy settled. It was a testimony that the 12 tribes, though separated by Jordan, were *one* people.

23. Joshua's farewell admonitions

1-13. Exhortations of fidelity to the Lord. Israel's great spiritual leader and military general, advanced in age, 1, assembled all Israel, 2, to review the goodness and faithfulness of the Lord, 3-5, and to exhort obedience to the Mosaic law, 6-11. Failure to keep clear of idolatrous unions would spell ruin, 12-13.

14-16. Concluding appeal. Warnings were sounded against the woes that would replace the blessings in case of disobedience and apostasy.

24. Covenant at Shechem; Joshua's death

1-15. Historical retrospect and Joshua's eloquent challenge. All Israel at Shechem heard the review of the Lord's dealings from Abraham to the conquest, 1-13, as a basis for the challenge to serve the Lord only, 14-15. Joshua in turn indicated his own irrevocable choice.

16-28. Covenant accepted. Israel accepted Joshua's challenge, 16-18, and asserted her loyalty to the Lord and the covenant. The generation which conquered the land now subscribed to the Covenant at Shechem, between Ebal and Gerizim in the heart of Canaan, as Joshua outlined the conditions of serving the Lord, 19-23, and set up memorials, 25-28.

29-33. Joshua's death. The great leader died and was buried, 29-31. Joseph's bones brought up from Egypt were buried in Shechem (cf. Gen 50:25; Ex 13:19; Heb 11:22). Record of the death of Eleazar, the priest, is also given, 33.

Israel in Canaan

AMURRU

Byblos
Aphekah
Lebo-hamath

Sidon

Damascus

Dan

Achzib
Kadesh
Hazor
Acco
Ramah
Rehob
Chinnereth
Nahalol
Aphek
Sea of Chinnereth
Ashtaroth
Kitron

Megiddo
Dor
Jezreel
Taanach
Beth-shan
Ibleam
Ramoth-gilead
Jabesh-gilead

Mount Ebal
Shechem
Mount Gerizim
Succoth
AMMON
Shiloh

G R E A T   S E A

Jordan

Aphek
Bethel Gilgal
Gezer
Gibeon
Heshbon
Ashdod
Ekron
Aijalon
Jebus
(Jerusalem)
Ashkelon
PHILISTIA
Beth-
Gath shemesh
Bethlehem
Medeba

Gaza
Lachish
Hebron
Dibon
Debir
Aroer

Salt Sea

Beersheba

M O A B

0   25   50 km

0   10   20   30 miles

Mount Halak
Zoar

Border of Canaan

Philistine city

Area controlled by Israelites

Tamar

Kadesh-barnea
E D O M

Egypt

JUDGES

The monotony and misery of sin

The name of the book.
Judges takes its name from the 12 Spirit-anointed military and civil leaders the Lord raised up to deliver the nation. As a loose confederacy (amphictyony) around the central shrine at Shiloh, the young nation had no stable central government, and forsaking the Lord, it became an easy prey for enemy invasion. The judges first delivered the people, then ruled over them. In their ruling role they corresponded to the *shufetim* of Phoenicia and the *sufetes* of Carthage (Heb. sopetîm).

The nature of the book.
Judges is a record of the dark ages of the declension and apostasy of Israel in the land. The people forsook the Lord (2:13); the Lord forsook the people (2:23). The key verse is: 'In those days Israel had no king; everyone did as he saw fit,' 17:6; 21:25. The record of Israel's failure in the land covers about 350 years – from Joshua to Saul. Seven

The book of Judges vs. the book of Joshua

Joshua	Judges
Victory	Defeat
Freedom	Servitude
Faith	Unbelief
Progress	Declension
Spiritual vision	Earthly emphasis
Fidelity to the Lord	Apostasy from the Lord
Joy	Sorrow
Strength	Weakness
Sense of unity	Declension, anarchy
Sin judged	Sin lightly regarded

apostasies, seven servitudes, and seven deliverances may be traced. The book of Judges begins in compromise and ends in anarchy and confusion.

The plain of Jezreel, biblical Esdraelon, from the stronghold of Megiddo. Manasseh failed to drive out the Canaanites of the valley of Esdraelon.

Date. Internal evidence and tradition suggest an origin for the book of Judges during the early years of the monarchy. The era of Saul (c. 1025) is a possible time. Samuel, as a member of the prophetic school, well have been the author-compiler.

Outline

1:1–2:5 Introduction to period of the Judges
1:1–36 Political conditions (from Joshua to the Judges)
2:1–5 Israel weeps in failure
2:6–16:31 The period of the Judges
2:6–3:6 Religious character of the period
3:7–16:31 List of the Judges
17:1–21:25 The double appendix
17:1–18:31 Idolatry of Micah and the Danites
19:1–21:25 The crime of Gibeah and its punishment

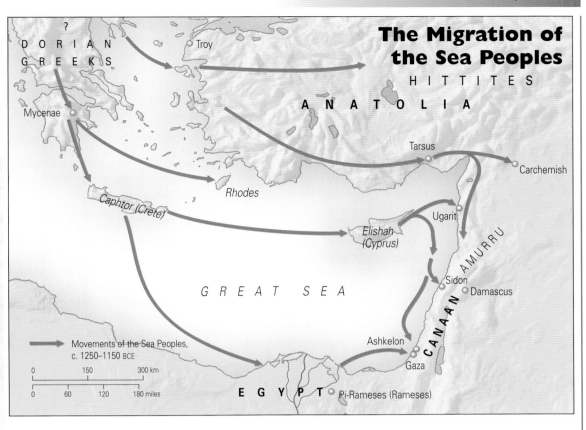

The Migration of the Sea Peoples

DORIAN GREEKS

Troy

HITTITES

ANATOLIA

Mycenae

Tarsus

Carchemish

Rhodes

Caphtor (Crete)

Ugarit

Elishah (Cyprus)

AMURRU

GREAT SEA

Sidon

Damascus

CANAAN

Ashkelon

Movements of the Sea Peoples, c. 1250–1150 BCE

Gaza

0   150   300 km

0   60   120   180 miles

EGYPT   Pi-Rameses (Rameses)

I. Israel's failure to drive out the Canaanites

1-4. The question of confronting the tribes. The Israelites 'asked the Lord' by consulting the sacred lots, 1: 'Who will be the first to go up and fight for us against the Canaanites?' The Lord directed Judah, 2, who apparently did not fully trust the Lord but relied on Simeon for help, 3-4.

5-20. Incomplete victory of Judah. Judah enjoyed some conquests, including Adoni-Bezek (uncertain), 5-7, and Jerusalem, which was either not actually captured, 8, or later recaptured by its inhabitants (cf.1:21), for it was not taken completely (i.e., the Jebusite fortress remained) until the time of David (2 Sam 5:6-7). Other conquests included the Negev and the western foothills, 9; Hebron, 10; Debir, identified as Khirbet Rabud, SW of Hebron, Caleb, 20 (cf. Josh 14:13-15), was given Hebron, the most important town of southern Palestine.

21. Incomplete victory of Benjamin. The Jebusites were not dislodged from the fortress of Jerusalem (cf. 1:8 with 2 Sam 5:67).

22-36. Failures of the other tribes. The house of Joseph, 22-26, took Bethel (Luz), 12 miles N of Jerusalem on the Shechem road (cf. Gen 12:8; 28: 11-17). Manasseh failed to drive out the Canaanites of the valley of Esdraelon; they had iron chariots. Israel disobeyed by enslaving rather than driving out the Canaanites, 28; Ephraim's failure at Gezer, 29; the failure of Zebulun, 30; Asher, 31-32; Naphtali, 33; Dan 34. Joseph, 35-36, did gain control, but did not drive out the Amorites. The Ugaritic religious literature from Ras Shamra (Ugarit, 1929-37) reveals the moral depravity and degrading character of Canaanite religion. Failure to exterminate this immoral people was Israel's grand act of disobedience that led to her apostasies and defeats in the era of the judges (1400-1040 B.C.).

2:1-3:4. Results of Israel's failure

1-5. The angel of Bokim. This was the Lord Himself who redeemed the Israelites from Egypt and brought them into the land, 1. He required complete separation from the Canaanites, 2, but the nation disobeyed. Consequently Israel was told the Lord would not

The cycle of the Judges

The book of Judges is organized around the rise and fall of Israel's spiritual fortunes. Israel prospered, became lax in its security, sinned, suffered judgment through foreign domination, turned to the Lord in repentance, the Lord sent a deliverer, and a period of peace and prosperity ensued. This recurrent cycle is instructive to the NT believer who may be lulled into following the same spiritual pattern.

drive out her foes but they would be a thorn in her side and their religion a corrupting snare. Israel wept, 4, but did not repent, calling the place Bokim, i.e., 'weepers,' 5, and so forfeited national prosperity and blessing.

6-15. Israel's earlier obedience contrasted to present apostasy. The nation had been obedient to the Lord under Joshua and the elders who outlived him, 6-9. Now the apostasy of the new generation aroused the Lord's anger, 10-15. Baals and Ashterahs were images of the male and female gods of the Canaanites, 11, 13, well known for their immoral license as seen in Ugaritic epics from Ras Shamra.

16-19. Résumé of Israelite history under the Judges. The Lord raised up 'judges,' i.e., military heroes, who by virtue of their successes were entrusted with government administration during their lifetime, 16. But as soon as the Spirit-anointed (charismatic) leader died, the people apostatised and again sank into political servitude to an invader, 17-19.

2:20-3:4. Nations left to prove Israel. The nations left in the land had a twofold divine purpose: (1) to punish Israel for disobedience, 2:20-21; (2) to test and prove the faithful and instruct them in warfare, 2:22-3:4.

3:5-31. Judgeships of Othniel, Ehud, and Shamgar

5-11. First apostasy, servitude, and judge (Othniel). The story of declension is told, 5-7: compromise, intermarriage with idolaters, finally idolatry itself, serving the gods and goddesses of the Canaanites – Baals and Asherahs – worshiping the various images of these deities. Punishment was meted out in Israel's being sold to Cushan-Rishathaim, a kinglet of northern Mesopotamia, for eight years. Othniel (1:13; Josh 15:18) of Judah was raised up to deliver the Lord's people.

12-30. Second apostasy, servitude,

and judge (Ehud). Eglon, king of Moab, the country E of the Dead Sea, was the oppressor, 12-14. He captured 'the City of Palms,' i.e., Jericho. A Benjamite hero named Ehud slew Eglon by a ruse. Ehud's deliverance from Moab was followed by an 80-year period of peace, 30.

31. Shamgar slew 600 Philistines with an ox goad.

4-5. Deborah and her exploits

4:1-3. Third apostasy, servitude, and judge (Deborah). The apostasy, 1, was followed by oppression under Jabin, king of Hazor, one of the most important Canaanite cities of Galilee, whose excavations have confirmed its capture in this era, 2-3. 'Iron chariots' put the Canaanites ahead of the Hebrews, who as yet did not have chariots nor were familiar with the art of iron smelting (Josh 17:16; 1 Sam 13:19-22). Jabin may here refer to a descendant of the Jabin defeated by Joshua in Josh 11:1, or may be a hereditary title adopted by the rulers of Hazor (cf. Pharaoh, Hiram).

4-24. Deborah and Barak and their victory. Deborah summoned Barak to muster an army at Mt. Tabor, 14, in Galilee N of the Plain of Esdraelon. The scene of Barak's victory was the river Kishon, a small stream flowing westward through Esdraelon N of Carmel. Zebulun and Naphtali were tribes of Galilee. Women continue to be prominent in the story as Sisera was killed by Jael, who drove a tent spike through his temple while he was sleeping. This episode shows the rough morality of the period.

5:1-31. The song of Deborah. This is a spirited poetic version of ch. 4. Graphically it ascribes praise to the Lord, 1-5; describes the condition of the people and their deliverance, 6-11; celebrates the victory and the victors, 12-22; and hails the destruction of the enemy, 23-31.

6. Gideon and the Midianite oppression

1-24. Fourth apostasy, servitude, and judge (Gideon). The Midianites, the Amalekites, and other peoples of the east, 3, were Bedouin raiders. These desert people overran the territory of Israel for seven years. Their use of camels enabled them to take waterless journeys of several days, which earlier nomads using donkeys were unable to do. Israel's distress, 1-5, and repentance, 6, brought a gracious answer

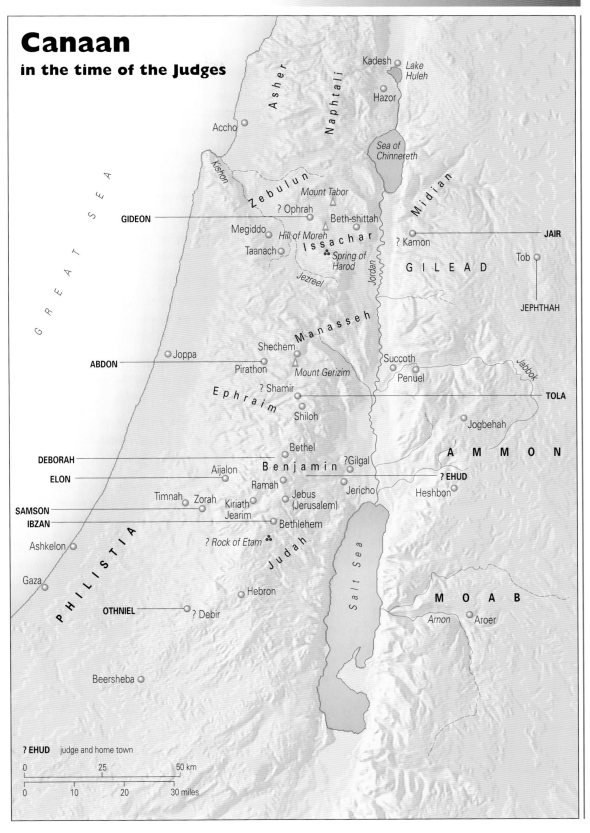

Canaan
in the time of the Judges

Kadesh ○ · *Lake Huleh*

Asher

Naphtali

Hazor ○

Accho ○

Sea of Chinnereth

Kishon

Zebulun

Midian

Mount Tabor △

? Ophrah ○

Beth-shittah ○

GIDEON ────────

Megiddo ○

Hill of Moreh

Issachar

? Kamon ○ ──────── JAIR

Taanach ○

Spring of Harod ♣

GILEAD

Tob ○

Jezreel

Jordan

JEPHTHAH

G R E A T   S E A

Manasseh

Shechem ○

Succoth ○

Jabbok

ABDON ──────── ○ Joppa

Pirathon ○

Mount Gerizim △

Penuel ○

? Shamir ○ ──────── TOLA

Ephraim

Shiloh ○

Jogbebah ○

Bethel ○

A M M O N

DEBORAH ────────

? Gilgal ○

Aijalon ○

B e n j a m i n

ELON ────────

Ramah ○

? EHUD ────

Timnah ○ Zorah

Jebus (Jerusalem) ○

Jericho ○

Heshbon ○

SAMSON ────────

Kiriath Jearim ○

IBZAN ────────

Bethlehem ○

Ashkelon ○

? Rock of Etam ♣

Judah

Gaza ○

P H I L I S T I A

S a l t   S e a

Hebron ○

M O A B

OTHNIEL ──────── ○ ? Debir

Arnon

Aroer ○

Beersheba ○

? EHUD   judge and home town

0 ─── 25 ─── 50 km

0 ── 10 ── 20 ── 30 miles

from the Lord through 'a prophet' of the tribe of Manasseh, a member of the small clan of Abiezer, 11, 15. Gideon was called to be a deliverer as he was beating out the wheat in the wine press, instead of the usual place on the hilltop, to hide from the marauding invaders, 11-24.

25-40. Gideon's initial exploits. The Lord directed Gideon to destroy the altar of Baal, the chief Canaanite deity, and the Asherah, a representation of one of the chief goddesses of Canaan, 25. An altar of the Lord was to be erected in its place, 25-26. Gideon obeyed, 27-32. The invaders pitched camp in the valley of Jezreel, 33, i.e., the eastern part of the great Plain of Esdraelon. Gideon, charismatically anointed (as were all the judges), mustered an army, 34-35, and was given the assurance of the sign of the fleece of wool, 36-40.

7. The victory of Gideon's three hundred

1-8. The reduction of the army. Gideon ('hewer down'), now called also Jerub-Baal ('let

Gideon and the Midianites

Zebulun
Naphtali
Asher
Endor
?Ophrah
Jezreel
Hill of Moreh
Beth-shittah
Spring of Harod
Beth-shan
Mount Gilboa
Tabbath
Abel-meholah
Succoth
Shechem
Penuel
Shiloh
Jordan R.
Rabbath-ammon

0   25   50 km

0   10   20   30 miles

→ Israelites gather
→ Midianites gather
⇢ Midianites flee

Baal contend') because he tore down Baal's altar, found his faith refined and valor strengthened by the sign of the fleece. He sifted his army of 32,000 to 10,000, and finally to 300. Spiritual quality and not numbers is important if God is to work and be glorified, 2-3. The test, 4-7, of lapping water in the hand like a dog instead of drinking the natural way, separated the vigilant and watchful from the more careless, who were more concerned about natural comforts and less fired by faith to spot the enemy and press on in victory. The Lord chose the 300 who lapped water, 7, to deliver Israel.

9-14. The Midianite's dream. The loaf of barley bread, 13, represented the Israelite farmers and homesteaders, and the tent which the barley loaf struck and flattened, the nomadic Midianite and Amalekite invaders.

15-25. The victory of faith. The trumpet was the sign of the battle advance against the enemy, the harbinger of faith's victory .

8. Gideon's failure

1-3. Jealousy of the Ephraimites. The victory over Midian and Amalek soon brought internal strife. Gideon's gracious reply (cf. Phil 2:1-5) to the jealous and selfish Ephraimites illustrated his strength of character. 'The gleanings of Ephraim's grapes,' i.e., the taking of Midianite chieftains Oreb and Zeeb by the Ephraimites, was 'better than the full grape harvest of Abiezer,' 2, i.e., the defeat of the whole invading horde in the valley of Jezreel. A soft, humble answer turns away wrath (Prov 15:1).

4-21. Complete victory over the invader. A greater test and victory followed the overcoming of internal strife. The people of Succoth and Peniel, 5-8, taunted Gideon and refused him aid, demonstrating that they were really secret allies of Midian, and treated as such by Gideon after his return.

22-32. Gideon's failure. Although Gideon refused the offer of hereditary kingship, 22-23, he fell into another snare in making an ephod (probably some kind of image or memorial), 24-27, and placed it in his hometown of Ophrah. This became an evil to Israel and Gideon, a violation of the sanctity of the priesthood.

33-35. The fifth apostasy. After Gideon's death, Israel served Baal-Berith (lord of the covenant). This was a perversion of Jehovah's covenant relationship with Israel.

9. Abimelech and his wickedness

1-5. The murder of Gideon's sons. Abimelech ('my father was king') claimed what his father had rejected. As a product of a Canaanite union, he showed the evils of compromise and disobedience to the word of God in his foul crime of the wholesale murder of Gideon's sons, except Jotham, the youngest, who escaped.

6-57. Abimelech's pretensions and end. Jotham's parable, 7-21, from Mt. Gerizim, the mountain S of Shechem (Deut 11:29), incisively shows the base worthlessness of Abimelech (a worthless 'thornbush,' 14). Abimelech's three-year reign marked a quarrel between himself and the men of Shechem, 26-49, climaxed by Gaal's rebellion, 26-41, which was put down. Abimelech died ignobly, as he had lived, besieging Thebez, about a dozen miles NE of Shechem, 50-57.

10. Tola, Jair, and the sixth apostasy

1-5. Tola and Jair. No record of achievement is given for Tola and little for Jair ('enlightener'). The latter had 30 sons, heads of 30 villages, called Havoth Jair ('the tent villages of Jair'). Riding on asses' colts, 4, indicated their high social status.

6-18. The sixth apostasy and servitude. A very serious departure, 6, brought the Philistine and Ammonite scourge, 7-9; then Israel's cry of distress, 10, and repentance, 15-16, but continual chastening,17-18.

11. Jephthah delivers from the Ammonites

1-11. Jephthah rejected but called to be leader. Jephthah was a man of great valor but of blemished birth, 1. Thrust out by his family, he went to Tob, a district of Syria, N of Gilead in Transjordan. There he became a roving outlaw. When war broke out with Ammon, a central Transjordanian people whose capital was at Rabbath-Ammon (modern Amman), Jephthah was called back by the elders of Gilead and made commander.

12-28. Jephthah's negotiations with Ammon. This showed tact, wisdom, and diplomatic skill, but was unsuccessful in averting war.

29-40. Jephthah's vow and its fulfillment. On the eve of the battle, 29, Jephthah (meaning 'he opens') made a vow that whoever came forth from his house first to meet him on his victorious return, 30, would be the Lord's and he would 'sacrifice it as a burnt offering,' 31 (Heb *'olah,* 'an offering that ascends'; cf. Lev 1). Opinion is divided whether or not this involved an actual human sacrifice, as Jephthah's only child, a young unmarried daughter, was the first to greet the returning hero at his home in Mizpah, 34-35. Those who believe this was an actual sacrifice argue: (1) the express terms of the narrative, 31; (2) the half pagan background of Jephthah, who in resorting to this extreme step of vowing a human sacrifice (cf. 2 Kgs 3:27) would follow a pagan custom and not be cognizant of or deterred by the Mosaic law forbidding such a practice (Lev 20:2-3), especially since his daughter concurred, 36. Moreover, Jephthah's excessive grief, 35, and the fact that there is nothing in the narrative to show that his conduct was sanctioned by the Lord argue that it was a real sacrifice. Jephthah's daughter asked for time to 'weep,' 37, because no greater disgrace could befall a Hebrew woman than to die childless. Some suggest that her perpetual virginity was a fulfillment of the vow, but the text seems to indicate that she died at the hands of her father.

12. Jephthah's war with Ephraim

1-7. The quarrelsome Ephraimites punished. This tribe, situated W of the Jordan, illustrates a spirit of divisive, sectarian strife. The people showed a similar contentious attitude toward Gideon (Jud 8:1). But in striking contrast to Gideon, Jephthah exhibited the selfish, proud, 'I-centered' attitude of sectarianism and provincialism. 'I and my people,' 2; 'I called,' 2; 'I saw,' 3; 'I took my life in my hands,' 3. The result was strife and war among brothers, death and long-lasting bitter feuds, so characteristic of believers who have lost the sense of the oneness of the Body of Christ (1 Cor 12: 13; Eph 4:1-6). In the great strife that followed, when the Ephraimites tried to slip back to their own country across the Jordan fords controlled by the Gileadites, those who pronounced *shibboleth* (meaning 'an ear or head of grain') *Sibboleth* ('s' for 'sh') were easily recognized and slain. The

Ephraimites spoke a slightly different dialect of Hebrew and could instantly be detected by their inability to make the 'sh' sound.

8-15. The Judges Ibzon, Elan, and Abdon. These were so-called minor judges (cf. 10:1-5), who perhaps were administrative and judicial but evidently never performed military exploits like the other judges.

13. Philistine domination; birth of Samson

1. The seventh apostasy. Israel was delivered into the power of the Philistines for 40 years. There was no cry to the Lord or record of repentance. This was the last and evidently the deepest apostasy. Also the deliverance was only partial and imperfect, 5, as was the career of Samson. The Philistines were intensely religious, celebrating their victories in the house of their idols (1 Sam 31:9), often carrying their gods into battle (2 Sam 5:21). Dagon ('grain') was a god of vegetation worshiped also in Ugarit and among the early Amorites. They also worshiped Ashtareth (1 Sam 31:10), corresponding to the ancient Assyrian goddess of propagation, Ishtar, as well as Baal-Zebub ('lord of flies'), a mocking distortion of Baal-zebul ('lord of the divine abode,' 2 Kgs 1:2). Beelzebub in Jewish theology became 'the prince of the demons' (Mt 12:24). Philistinism, therefore, represents religion intermixed with paganism, a syncretism totally unacceptable in the worship of the true God.

2-23. Philistinism vs. Naziritism. Who was to be the deliverer, 7, from the Philistines? A Nazirite, or 'separated one.' See the comments on the Nazirite's vow and his cleansing from defilement in Num 6:1-21. Not only was the deliverer to maintain Nazirite separation from birth, his parents were likewise to be separated, 2-14, and as a result of the vision of God were to trust in the power of God. The angel of the Lord, 3-23, was the preincarnate Christ, the same as appeared to Moses in the bush (Ex 3:1-8) and Joshua outside Jericho (Josh 5:13-15).

24-25. Samson's birth. Samson (Heb. *Shim-shon,* 'little sun') was born when his tribe Dan, 2 (cf. Mahaneh-dan, 'camp of Dan,' RSV), was located in the southwest near Philistia. Later the expanding Philistines forced the tribe to migrate northward (Jud 18).

14. Samson's early exploits

1-7. Samson kills the lion. Samson took the first step to compromise his Nazirite vow, 1. He went down to a Philistine city, where he fell into temptation, 1-2, as a result of his lust for a Timnite woman. Yet the Lord overruled Samson's mistake to show His power, 4. By virtue of Samson's Nazirite status, the Spirit of God came upon him mightily, as He always operates through a holy vessel set apart for God. Samson tore the lion to death with his bare hands, 6. But while the Nazirite did exploits and conquered Satan, as it were, on one front, he was falling a prey to the wiles of Satan on another front in becoming infatuated with the Timnite woman, 7-8.

8-9. Honey in the lion's skeleton. On his trip to take the woman as his wife, Samson, the Nazirite, turned aside to see the lion's carcass. He found therein bees and honey, and he scraped the honey into his hands. This was a direct violation of the Nazirite oath, which forbade contact with a carcass.

10-20. Exploits despite compromise. This first venture into alliance with the Philistines, although it furnished an occasion for the exhibition of Samson's strength, nevertheless was fraught with failure and frustration. His betrothed wife nagged and deceived him, and the Philistines outwitted him.

15. Samson in conflict with the Philistines

1-8. Samson's revenge. The marriage, which Samson believed himself to have contracted, was of the ancient type in which the husband came only periodically to visit his wife, who continued to reside at her parents' home. The kid apparently was a customary gift for sexual intimacy (Gen 38:17). The 300 foxes (jackals) with torches tied to their tails let loose in the grain and vineyards of the Philistines were apparently pure revenge, not led of the Spirit of God. Samson's trouble was of his own making, as contamination by Philistinism *always* is.

9-13. Bound by his own. His own Israelite brothers, out of fear, bound Samson to deliver him to the Philistines. Lehi, 9, 14, means a 'jaw-bone'.

14-17. The exploit with the ass's jawbone. At Ramath Lehi ('the hill of the jawbone'), 17, Samson killed 1,000 Philistines. But he wisely discarded the jawbone when it had

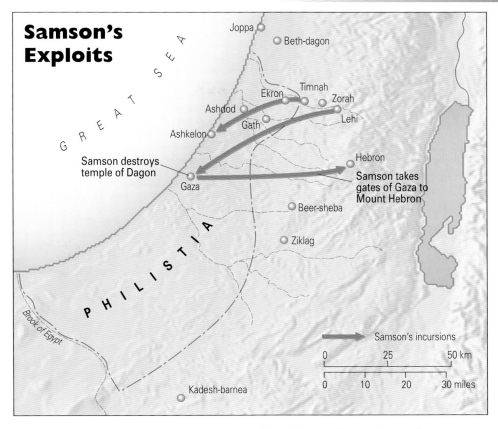

Samson's Exploits

Joppa
Beth-dagon

GREAT SEA

Timnah
Ekron
Zorah
Ashdod
Lehi
Gath
Ashkelon

Samson destroys
temple of Dagon

Hebron

Samson takes
gates of Gaza to
Mount Hebron

Gaza

Beer-sheba

PHILISTIA

Ziklag

Brook of Egypt

→ Samson's incursions

0   25   50 km

0   10   20   30 miles

Kadesh-barnea

---

accomplished its purpose, lest like Gideon's ephod (Jud 8:27) it should become a snare. Often the instrument of God's blessing is praised instead of God who uses the instrument.

18-20. Samson's prayer and its answer. Samson's thirst and the Lord's splitting open the hollow place at Lehi so that water flowed out at En Hakkore ('the spring of him who called'), illustrates the provision of God for His servant who called on Him in his need. Thus, he was strengthened in facing the vengeance of the other Philistines.

16. Samson and Delilah; his death

1-3. Samson at Gaza. Three Philistine women plagued the Nazirite Samson, stripped him of spiritual power, and finally accomplished his ruin – the Timnite woman, 14:1-4, the harlot at Gaza, 16:1-3, and Delilah, 16:4-20. Each one silhouetted the power of the Nazirite against the dark background of the compromising sin that was destroying him.

4-19. Samson and Delilah. Delilah, the instrument of Samson's downfall, is analogous to the world in its religious, pleasure loving aspects, which, like this wily woman, is bent on stripping the true Nazirite of his separation to God, the secret of power in the believer's life. Multifarious were Delilah's cunning subtleties, illustrated here, as she finally cajoled her victim into telling her the secret of his strength, 4-17. The secret *was Samson's Nazirite separation to God.* And when his locks, the badge of his Nazirite separation, were shaved off, his strength departed.

20-25. Results of Samson's violation of his separation. (1) Ignorance of his spiritual powerlessness. He *did not know* that his strength had left him, 20. (2) He was taken captive by the Philistines. (3) Lost his eyesight. (4) He was enslaved by the Philistines, 21. (5) Became a scandal and a means of glorifying a pagan god instead of the Lord, 23-25. (6) Became the object of Philistine ridicule and a religious clown, 25. On Dagon, see comments on Jud 13:1.

26-31. Samson's death. In a tragic irony, Samson's story ends with his heroic death, when in answer to his final prayer, God restored his strength so that he could kill 'many more when he died than while he lived,' 30.

Site of the shrine at Dan. The Danites, in their removal to the north, stole Micah's shrine.

17-18. Idolatry of Micah and the Danites

17:1-13. Micah and the Levite. The story of the relocation of the Danites is prefaced by the story of Micah and his idolatry. On receiving money Micah had stolen from her, 2-3, his mother appropriated 200 pieces of it to make several images under pretense of devotion to the Lord, 4. Micah also had an idolatrous shrine, and had made an ephod (an image) and 'some idols', and in the spirit of that lawless age installed one of his sons as priest, 5-6. When a Levitical priest arrived from Bethlehem in Judah, some seven miles S of Jerusalem, Micah persuaded him to act as chaplain in his shrine. This lawless man-made religious arrangement, showing the spiritual apostasy of the day, was ignorantly claimed by Micah as a basis of divine blessing.

18:1-31. The Danite migration. The Danites in their removal to the north (cf. Josh 19:40-47; Jud 1:34; 13:2) under Philistine pressure, stole Micah's shrine, including the Levite priest, 16-20. This is another evidence of the lawless apostasy and political confusion of the period (cf. Jud 17:6; 18:1; 19:1; 21:25). Moreover, the aim of the entire appendix of the book of Judges (ch. 17-21) is to show Israel's deep internal corruption. The Levite did not object to this flagrant injustice to Micah because it meant advantage to him personally. Micah's objections against this outrage were made in the name of religion. His efforts to recover his losses came to naught, 26. Ch. 17 and 18 show Israel's religious corruption. Ch. 19-21 show the moral and political lawlessness of the period.

Archaeological light

The Philistine Pentapolis. During the period of the Judges, the Philistines were ruled by a confederation of their five major cities: Gaza, Ekron, Ashkelon, Gath, and Ashdod. The ruling body was made up of five 'lords' (seranîm) who possessed complete military and civil authority.

Archaeological light

Samson's long hair and his accompanying strength is a common motif in ancient literature. The mighty Achaean warriors were known as 'long-haired' in the Iliad. The strength of Phoebus, a god in the Iliad, is associated with his uncut hair. Enkidu, in the Epic of Gilgamesh, similarly had 'long hair like a woman.' Samson stands unique, however, since the Bible makes it clear that his strength came from 'the Spirit of the Lord upon him' and not his long hair.

19-21. Gibeah's crime and its punishment

19:1-30. The deed of lust and violence. This chapter faithfully catalogs the horrible results of departure from God (cf. Rom 1:26-32; 2 Tim 3:1-5). Adopting Canaanite ways, Israel sank into the cesspool of Canaanite violence and immorality. Similar lawlessness attends present worldwide apostasy (Lk 17:28-30). The crime of the Benjamites of Gibeah shows that the city had sunk to the level of Sodom (Gen 19:1-14).

20:1-48. The harvest of war and bloodshed. Israelite chiefs gathered at Mizpah, a town on the northern boundary of Benjamin, to decide on a course of action, 1-7. They determined to punish the guilty persons by death, 12-13. Because the Benjamites refused to surrender the criminals, a horrible civil war ensued in which thousands perished. A tragic harvest was reaped (cf. Gal 6:7). The guilty tribe was almost wiped out.

21:1-25. Repentance concerning Benjamin. The inhabitants of Jabesh Gilead were smitten and the remaining virgins were given as wives to the remnant of Benjamin, 1-15, Benjamin was restored as a tribe and additional wives were supplied from the dancers at the annual festival at Shiloh, 16-22. Judges ends with the notation of the lawlessness of the era, 25.

RUTH

The rendezvous of romance and redemption

Place in the canon. This beautiful love story of redemption is closely associated with the book of Judges. Its events transpired during that period, c. 1400-1050 B.C. (Ruth 1:1). Therefore Ruth is correctly placed after Judges. Its place in the Hebrew Bible is in the third division of the threefold canon among the five shorter books called Megilloth or Scrolls (Song, Ruth, Lamentations, Ecclesiastes, Esther). It was apparently transferred from the second to the third division for liturgical reasons, its scenery of the harvest field adapting it for the harvest festival.

Author and date. The author is unknown, but since the genealogy is brought up to David (4:17, 22), it would appear it was written by an inspired writer during David's reign (c. 1010 B.C.). To place it later, particularly after the Exile, is based upon unsound critical criteria.

Typology. The rich underlying typology of this idyll makes the book of Ruth more than a pastoral story of love. It is an important link in the unfolding account of redemption, presenting in figure our Lord as the great Kinsman-Redeemer in general, but particularly as that aspect of His glorious character *will affect Israel,* His covenant people, in their future restoration. It presents an important link in the messianic family, from which our Lord came some 1,100 years later.

Outline

1. Ruth deciding by faith
2. Ruth gleaning under grace
3. Ruth communing in fellowship

Terraced hillside near Bethlehem.

1. Ruth deciding by faith

1-5. Naomi and her misfortunes. This book is a lovely story teaching moral lessons. But it is more than that, since it deals with redemption. As the romance of redemption it prefigures in a blessed sense the dispensational ways of God with the nation Israel, and from this aspect its message will be set forth, thus connecting it as a phase of God's redemptive love for the world. Naomi ('pleasant one') reflects Israel, the chosen people. Her happiness in Bethlehem ('house of bread') married to Elimelech ('my god is king') pictures Israel's prosperity in the land, married to the Lord, faithful to Him, and enjoying His favor and blessing. The sorrows that came upon Naomi as a result of the famine speak of spiritual failure and chastisement in the land. The enforced migration to Moab, a pagan nation, sets forth Israel's worldwide dispersion. The death of Naomi's husband in a foreign land illustrates Israel's national rejection during the centuries of her absence from the land, her widowhood and separation from her husband the Lord (cf. Isa 50:1-3). The death of Mahlon ('sick') and Chilion ('pining') in the foreign country shadow forth the trouble and calamities that have engulfed Israel (Naomi) among the Gentiles, where her condition is hopeless. Ruth and Orpah, Moabite wives of Mahlon and Chilion, were left widows.

6-18. Ruth and her decision. Naomi's hearing that 'the Lord had come to the aid of his people by providing food for them,' 6, and her plan to return to the land suggest the time when dispersed Israel sets her face homeward, 7. Orpah, who remained in Moab, speaks of the unbelieving mass of the nation that will elect to remain among the nations in the day of Israel's return to her homeland. Ruth, however, clinging to Naomi, beautifully portrays the believing remnant of the nation, which will trust in God's provision and ultimately come into touch with the mighty Kinsman-Redeemer, through whom they will inherit the promised blessings. Both Orpah and Ruth signify the nation in dispersion and unbelief. In such a condition of national rejection they have fallen into the same situation as the Gentiles – *Loammi* ('not my people') (Hos 1:9). The difference is that Orpah remained in that condition, while Ruth took the step of faith that eventuated in her not only being

'Boaz' Fields' near Bethlehem.

incorporated among the Lord's people, *Ammi* ('my people'), but actually becoming an ancestress of Christ.

19-22. Naomi and Ruth in the land. Arriving back in Bethlehem, Naomi ('pleasant one,' what she should have been in faith) called herself Marah ('bitter one,' what she would be in her return to the land in unbelief). The time indicated is 'as the barley harvest was beginning,' 22, which signifies the end of the age (Mt 13:30, 39). When that end comes, after the church has been glorified, Israel, like Naomi, with a believing remnant cleaving to her represented in Ruth, will return to the land (cf. Isa 6:13; 10:21-22; Mic 4:7; Zeph 3:7; etc.).

2. Ruth gleaning under grace

1-17. Ruth gleaning in the field of Boaz. Boaz ('in him is strength'), a relative of Naomi, was introduced as 'a man of standing,' 1. He is typical of the Lord Jesus Christ, the wealthy one. As Him 'in whom there is strength,' Boaz portrays the Kinsman-Redeemer. Ruth's desire to glean in the field of Boaz to find grace in his sight, 2-3, represents the longing of the remnant at the end time to seek after the Lord, the Kinsman-Redeemer, and to search the Scriptures to find Him in grace. Boaz' advent from Bethlehem, 4; his notice of and kindness to Ruth, 5-9; his words of grace to her, 11-12; and provision for her, 13-17, show the concern of Israel's Kinsman-Redeemer for the believing remnant of the nation.

18-23. Ruth learns about Boaz. Returning to Naomi with her gleanings, Ruth was told something about Boaz. She only knew him, however, as 'one of our kinsman redeemers,' not as *the* Kinsman-Redeemer, 20. This latter revelation Ruth would learn only from Boaz himself. So Israel will not know the full story of the divine Boaz until He reveals Himself in grace and power to the remnant of His people at His second advent (cf. Zech 12:10-13:1; Isa 60:1-22; Hos 6:1-11; 14:4-9; Rom 11:26-36).

3. Ruth communing in fellowship

1-13. Boaz guarantees Ruth's redemption. Naomi instructed Ruth in the custom of kinsman redemption, 1-5, according to the regulations of Lev 25:25-28 and the marriage of a brother-in-law (Deut 25:5-12). Ruth accepted Naomi's directions, 5, and obeyed them, 6. The object was 'rest' (KJV), 1. Boaz' discovery of Ruth resulted in Ruth's resting at his feet, 1, 8, experiencing the truth that rest can be found only at the feet of the Redeemer, both for the individual believer (Lk 10:38-42), and the converted nation Israel (Isa 59:20; Rom 11:23-29) when that nation experiences the redemption of the Kinsman-Redeemer and enters into its kingdom rest. Boaz' occupation of winnowing barley at the threshing floor, 2, when Ruth sought him to claim her blessing, foretells the work of the divine Boaz (Mt 3: 12) when at His second advent He separates among His people, and the believing remnant, like Ruth, seeks the place of rest at the feet of its Redeemer.

14-18. Ruth reported to Naomi, and looked for the promised redemption.

4. Ruth resting in redemption

1-8. The nearer kinsman renounces his right. At the gate, 1 (Gen 23:10, 18), the normal place for transacting business, Boaz told the nearer kinsman that he could not legally redeem the property without also marrying Ruth.

This the kinsman was unable to do, probably because he was already married. To raise up a son in the name of another would confuse the whole question of the inheritance of the estate. The unnamed redeemer could redeem the land but could do nothing for the poor foreigner. The symbolic act of removing the shoe, 8, was not connected with the regulation in Deut 25:8-10, where the action served to humiliate one who refused to accept the levirate marriage. Here the shoe symbolized the right of the owner to set foot upon the land (Ps 60:8) and the removal symbolized the act of ceding the rights of possession to another.

9-17. Boaz' redemption and the marriage of Ruth. Ruth the Moabitess, as a result of Boaz' action, 9-10, was officially accepted in Israel by the representatives of the city, and God sanctioned the act of redemption in the fertility of Ruth, 13-17. The marriage represents the consummation of the redemption of both the land and the people, when the redeemed remnant enters into the blessings of kingdom rest (cf. Isa 4:1-6; 11:1-16; Zech 8:6-8).

18-22. Messianic genealogy. The abbreviated list is given from Perez, the forefather of the royal family of Judah (Gen 38:29) who was also born of a levirate marriage, to David. The latter points to the true theocratic king, Messiah (cf. 1 Chr 2:5; 9:4; Mt 1:3-6). Thus through a simple story is interwoven God's plan for the redemption of the world and the restoration of His people Israel.

1 SAMUEL

From the judges to the kings

Nature of the book.

Treated as one book in the Hebrew, 1 and 2 Samuel constitute some of the finest historical writing in all literature. Written largely as historical biography, these narratives differ from contemporary documents (Assyrian, Egyptian, Hittite) in not being the mere pegging out of events on the line of time. The events themselves are stressed, and the moral and spiritual repercussions of these books have eminent ethical and didactic value. From a prophetic viewpoint they are also important in that they tell of the founding of Israel's kingdom under David. These events foreshadow the coming of Israel's kingdom under David. They also foreshadow the coming of Israel's true King (cf. Num 24:17-19 and 1 Sam 2:10) and the establishment of the kingdom under Messiah (Acts 1:6).

Authorship and authenticity.

While Samuel is not said to be the author, he may have been joint author with Nathan and Gad (cf. 1 Chr 29:29). The higher critical contention that 1 and 2 Samuel consist of various discordant traditions is not sustained by careful analysis and spiritually discerning exegesis of the books.

Outline

1–7 Samuel's judgeship
1–3 Samuel's childhood and call
4–6 The capture and return of the ark
7 Israel's demand for a king

8–31 Saul's reign
8–15 The rise of Saul
16–31 The rise of David and the decline of Saul

Nabi Samwil, by tradition identified as Ramah, and the burial place of the prophet Samuel.

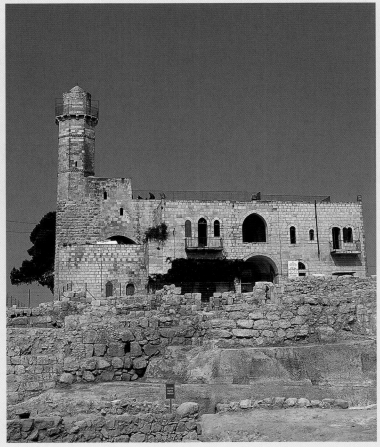

1. Samuel's birth and boyhood

1-18. Hannah's prayer and vow. The ancestry of Samuel is given, 1-2. God's sovereign working is seen in the child's birth. For similar unusual offspring of barren women cf. Sarah (Gen 17:16-19), Rebekah (Gen 25:21-26), Rachel (Gen 29:31; 30:22-24), Samson's mother (Jud 13:2-5), and Elizabeth (Lk 1:5-17). Hannah's prayer and consecration were answered.

19-28. Samuel born and given to God. The name Samuel ('requested of God') was given to the child as a token of the Lord's faithfulness in answering Hannah's prayer. The child was weaned and presented to Eli, the priest, at the central shrine at Shiloh (Seilun) in Ephraim, E of the main road from Shechem to Jerusalem.

2. The failure of Eli's house

1-11. Hannah's ode. This is an inspired song of praise to the Lord, 1-3, celebrating His power and grace in deliverance, 4-8, with a prophetic glimpse into the future day of the Lord preceding Israel's true King and the establishment of His kingdom, 9-10.

12-36. Failure of Eli's house. The moral decline and lawlessness of the period of the judges were reflected in the disciplinary weakness of Eli and the flagrant wickedness of his sons, Hophni and Phinehas, 12-17. While judgment was ripening for Eli's house, God's grace was manifested in the boy Samuel ministering at Shiloh, 18-26, amid the increasing laxity of Eli and the immorality of his sons, 22-25. God sent a prophet to pronounce doom upon the priestly sinners, 26-36.

3. Samuel's call

1-18. The call. Because of sin among God's people, 'the word of the Lord was rare; there were not many visions', 1. Samuel's call, 1-9, followed by the message from the Lord, 10-18, manifested the divine grace in supplying the need for a human instrument through whom the word of God might come.

19-21. Samuel's prophetic ministry. From Dan on the northern boundary of Israel to Beersheba on the southern border, all Israel became aware of God's chosen human instrument of revelation.

4. Judgment of Eli's house

1-22. The death of Eli and his sons. The Philistines (see Jud 13) were the human agents to fulfill the predicted judgment upon Eli and his sons (1 Sam 2:26-36). Israel trusted in the ark (see comments on Ex 25:10-22) rather than in Him of whom the ark spoke. Substitution of ritualism for spiritual reality always leads to domination by the 'Philistines' with its dire results – (1) spiritual death, here illustrated by the physical death of the priests Eli, Hophni, and Phinehas; (2) and loss of the spiritual presence of the Lord, the Shekinah, with Ichabod ('no glory'

Representation of the Ark of the Covenant from Capernaum.

Capture of the Ark

Yarkon

Eben-ezer

Aphek

Capture of the ark

Shiloh

Jordan R.

P H I L I S T I A

Mizpeh

Ark recaptured

Ekron

Kirjath-Jearim

Jebus

| 0 | | 10 | | 20 km |
| 0 | 4 | | 8 | 12 miles |

Ashdod

Beth-shemesh

Ark kept at the temple of Dagon

Gath

Ark in possession of Israelites
Ark in possession of Philistines

---

or 'alas for the glory') the result (cf. Ps 78:60-61). This is indicated by the name the widow of Phinehas gave to her newborn son.

5-6. The ark among the Philistines and its return
5:1-5. The ark in Dagon's temple.
Dagon (cf. Heb. *dagan,* grain) was venerated in Palestine as god of the harvest. His worship is abundantly attested by the religious tablets found at Ugarit in N. Syria. Numerous places were named after him (Josh 15:41). Ashdod was one of the principal towns of the Philistine pentapolis, composed also of Gaza, Gath, Ekron, and Ashkelon. The spiritual blindness of the

Philistines is seen in their superstitious veneration of Dagon.

5:6-6:21. The Lord's punishment of the Philistines. Malignant tumors and a plague of field mice (cf. 6:4, 11, 18) were the judgments visited upon the enemies of the Lord and His people. The plague may well have been bubonic plague, which is often transmitted through mice.

7. Samuel as judge
1-8. Samuel's message. The judge-prophet issued a general call to genuine repentance in turning away from Canaanite idolatry. The Baals were images of the great northwest semitic fertility deity Baal ('lord'), and the Ashtareth were replicas of Astarte, goddess of sexual love and fertility, 3-4. The water libation, 6, usually of wine, shows the preciousness of water to a people in a dry climate.

9-14. Victory at Ebenezer. For the significance of the whole burnt offering which Samuel offered, 9-10, see comments on Lev 1. Repentance and faith in the Lord's redemption always bring a manifestation of the Lord as Ebenezer ('the stone of help') .

15-17. Summary of the ministry of Samuel, the circuit-riding prophet-judge.

8. Israel's demand for a king

1-3. Failure of the judgeship. Samuel made the mistake of appointing his sons as judges. Though they possessed a godly heritage they were unworthy, guilty of taking bribes and perverting justice. This turn of events is tragically ironic since Samuel was chosen by God as a result of Eli's sons' failure to follow in their father's footsteps.

4-22. Demand for the kingship. Samuel's age, the unfitness of his sons, and the desire to be like other nations were the reasons given for demanding a king, 5. The evils of the kingship were pointed out by Samuel, 7-18. Unbelief and self-will were the basis of the rejection of the theocracy, 19-22.

9-11. Saul and his anointing

9:1-10:16. Saul's anointing. Saul's search for the lost asses of his father Kish, 1-10, furnished the occasion for his meeting with Samuel, 11-25, and his being anointed king by the prophet, 10:1-16.

10:17-27. Saul's fair beginning. Samuel again warned the people at Mizpah concerning their fault in rejecting the theocracy, 17-19. Saul was selected by lot, 20-22. His initial humility, 21-22, imposing appearance, and commanding physique made him a promising choice, 23-24. Though God's kingship was being rejected by the people, He was careful to choose their king. Samuel established the kingdom, 25, and Saul returned to Gibeah, 26-27.

11:1-15. Saul's initial victories. The gross insult of Nahash ('serpent') the Ammonite, 1-3, to the inhabitants of Jabesh, a town of Gilead in Transjordan, was told to Saul at Gibeah (modern Tel el-Ful, excavated by W.F. Albright), 4-5. Saul was anointed by the Spirit to deliver Israel in the manner of the earlier judges, 6. He mustered Israel to arms, 7, and won both a great victory over Ammon and public acclaim in the kingship as well, 8-15. The kingdom was consequently renewed at Gilgal, symbolic of self-judgment in Israel (see comments on Josh 5:2-10). This event may also have served as a covenant

The Rescue of Jabesh-Gilead

2. Israelites assemble

3. Saul attacks Ammonites

1. King of Ammon attacks Jabesh-gilead

Jabesh-gilead

Bezek

Tirzah

Shechem

Shiloh

Jordan R.

Rabbath-ammon

Israelites
Ammonites

Gibeah

0 — 15 — 30 km

0 — 6 — 12 — 18 miles

Salt Sea

The Kingdom of Saul

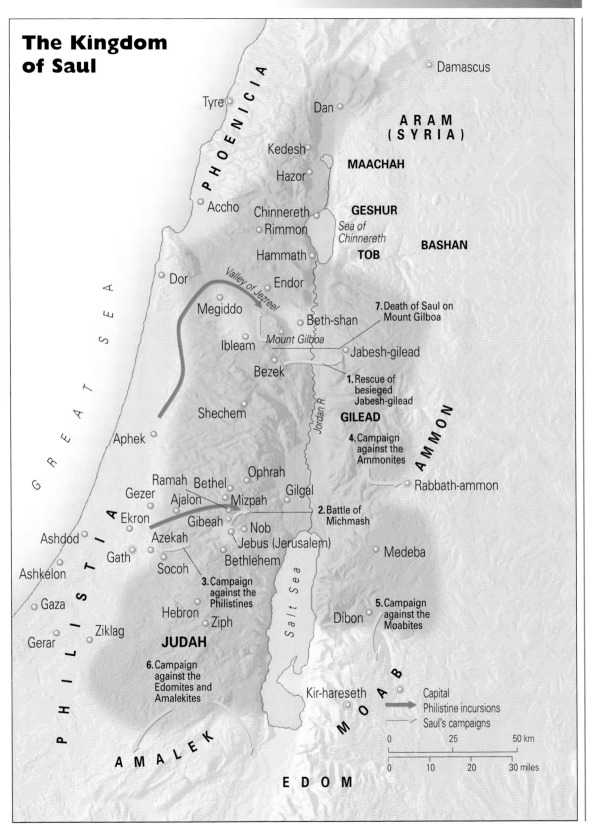

Damascus

Tyre

Dan

**ARAM
(SYRIA)**

Kedesh

MAACHAH

Hazor

Accho

Chinnereth

GESHUR

Rimmon

*Sea of
Chinnereth*

BASHAN

Hammath

TOB

Dor

Valley of Jezreel

Endor

Megiddo

Beth-shan

7. Death of Saul on
Mount Gilboa

Mount Gilboa

Ibleam

Jabesh-gilead

Bezek

1. Rescue of
besieged
Jabesh-gilead

Shechem

Jordan R.

GILEAD

Aphek

4. Campaign
against the
Ammonites

Ophrah

AMMON

Ramah Bethel

Gezer

Gilgal

Ajalon Mizpah

Rabbath-ammon

Ekron

Gibeah

2. Battle of
Michmash

Ashdod

Nob

Azekah

Jebus (Jerusalem)

Gath

Medeba

Ashkelon

Socoh

Bethlehem

Salt Sea

3. Campaign
against the
Philistines

Gaza

Hebron

Ziph

5. Campaign
against the
Moabites

Ziklag

Dibon

Gerar

JUDAH

6. Campaign
against the
Edomites and
Amalekites

Kir-hareseth

**M
O
A
B**

◎ Capital

➤ Philistine incursions

─ Saul's campaigns

0   25   50 km

0   10   20   30 miles

**P
H
I
L
I
S
T
I
A**

A M A L E K

E D O M

**G
R
E
A
T

S
E
A**

**P
H
O
E
N
I
C
I
A**

renewal ceremony as Joshua had done in Josh 24 and Moses in Deut. Saul was making a good start.

12. Samuel's farewell address
1-15. Samuel officially proclaims the kingdom.
Samuel declared his integrity as prophet-judge. This took place at Gilgal before the assembly of all Israel, 1-4. He affirmed the Lord and His anointed (Saul) were witnesses to the fact that he (Samuel) had given the people no cause to be weary with government by judges, 5. He implied that the blame for desiring the kingship rested with them. The aged prophet-judge thereupon reproved Israel for ingratitude, 6-15, as he rehearsed 'the righteous acts performed by the Lord,' 7. 'Samson,' 11, should possibly be read for 'Samuel.' The people's reasons for choosing a king were wrong, 12. The kingship would expose them to many dangerous temptations. Obedience to the theocratic ideal alone could save them from the consequences, 13-15.

16-25. The Lord's sign of Israel's sin in asking for a king.
Thunder and rain in the wheat harvest (last of June and early July) were so rare as to be miraculous, especially without any prior indications and wholly by the word of the Lord through the prophet. The people regarded the event as such, and asked Samuel to pray for them as they confessed their wrong motives in asking for a king.

13. Saul's first great failure
1-10. Saul's self-will.
In Saul's first year, 1, the events of ch. 9, 10, and 11 took place. In his second year he was severely tested regarding his fitness to be king by a formidable invasion of the Philistines, 2-7. Would he trust God and obey His word through Samuel? Jonathan, Saul's son, 3, a striking contrast to his father, did so. But Saul showed flagrant unbelief and disobedience in intruding into the priest's office at Gilgal (of all places! See notes on Josh 5). He, a Benjamite, offered the sacrifices which only a priestly Levite might offer (Num 16:1-3, 32-40). The act was a direct violation of God's law, a proof of the unbelief of his heart and his essential unfitness to be king over the Lord's people.

11-23. The Lord's rejection of Saul announced.
Saul's excuse to Samuel, 11-12, revealed his unbelief and disobedience. So the prophet announced Saul's unfitness and rejection

Archaeological light
The Philistines had a monopoly on iron (1 Sam 13:19-22) which gave them military advantage. They apparently obtained the secret of smelting from the Hittites. Saul and David by their conquests broke this monopoly. Verse 21 should read with the RSV: 'And the charge was a pim [two-thirds of a shekel, approx. one-quarter oz.] for the plowshares and for the mattocks, and a third of a shekel for sharpening axes and setting the goads.' The iron age extended from 1200 to 300 B.C.

as king, 13-14. The unworthy monarch's subsequent career demonstrated the futility of trying to discharge work for God without God's electing grace and blessing.

14. Jonathan's heroism
1-23. Jonathan's great victory.
He is one of the finest characters in sacred history, a glowing contrast to his father, a picture of genuine victorious faith, 6. King Saul was surrounded by a large company, among whom were relatives of Eli, but manifested unbelief. The Lord miraculously worked through an earthquake, sending confusion and destruction among the Philistines, 15-23.

24-45. Saul's foolish impetuosity.
Fearful of losing this advantage over the Philistines, Saul pronounced a curse on anyone tasting food till the evening. He was remiss as well as rash in failing to notify Jonathan. This episode shows how unreliable he was to be king over the Lord's people. Saul built an altar but his request was unanswered by the Lord, 35-37. Jonathan's condemnation by his own father, 38-44, and his rescue by the people, 45, again demonstrated the weak and unkingly character of Saul.

46-52. Saul's successes and his family.
Despite the king's unworthiness, God nevertheless graciously granted victories for the sake of His people, 46-48. Saul's pedigree and family are given in 49-52.

15. Saul's second great failure
1-8. Saul's commission to exterminate Amalek.
Samuel presented Saul with the Lord's plain command, 1, and the clear reason for the total blotting out of Amalek, 2-3. Saul's incomplete obedience was highlighted, 4-8, his

stubborn self-will again becoming evident. (For Amalek see notes on Ex 17.) Saul was, therefore, disqualified to lead God's people.

9-31. Saul's disobedience and rejection. He spared 'the best' and 'everything that was good,' forgetting that *nothing* of the flesh is good or can please God (Rom 8:8), but must be utterly wiped out, put under the ban, destroyed in the name of religion, i.e., exterminated by God's command (Deut 20:16-18). Little wonder the Lord's word of rejection was once more (1 Sam 13:14) enunciated, 10-11. Samuel's tearful intercession for the king could not avail. Saul's conduct in erecting a monument to himself, 12, and the evidences of his leniency with Amalek under the pretense of piety, 13-15, proved his guilt and called for divine rejection, despite his self-defense, 16-23. Saul's superficial repentance, 24-25, only brought a dramatic episode, 26-28, emphasizing Saul's loss of the kingdom so far as God's blessing him was concerned. Saul's pride appeared uncorrected, 29-31.

32-33. Destruction of Agag. Death alone must be pronounced upon the flesh and all that pertains to it, if the Word of God is to be obeyed (Rom 8:13; Col 3:5) and spiritual victory enjoyed.

34-35. Samuel separates from Saul. Samuel did not visit Saul again in any official capacity (cf. 1 Sam 19:24 and 28:11). The rejected king turned to his rustic palace at Gibeah (excavated by W.F. Albright and dating about 1015 B.C.).

16. David anointed king

1-13. David's anointing. The rejection of the king after the people's heart was followed by the choice of the king after God's own heart, 1-2, whose exile and sufferings are told in ch. 16-31. Like Jonathan, David was a man of faith, kingly in spirit, and in complete subjection to the Lord. He who was to be the type of the true King from Bethlehem of Judah ('praise'), the royal tribe (Gen 49:10). Samuel called Jesse and his sons to a sacrificial feast, 3-5, examined each prospect, 6-10, and finally chose David and anointed him, 11-13. It is instructive that while Samuel looked at the outward appearance God looked on the inside and chose accordingly.

14-23. Saul's decline. The Spirit of God departed from Saul and an evil spirit from the

Lord, 14, i.e., by the Lord's permission, began to torment him. Divine sovereignty controls evil forces for God's purposes. Believers who stubbornly reject God's Word expose themselves to demonic influence to a greater or lesser degree (1 Tim 4:1; 1 Jn 4:1-4; cf. Mt 12:43-45). David's skill in performing on the harp, that is, the lyre, 16-23, was called upon to refresh the harassed king. After the young shepherd-king had soothed the troubled monarch and was no longer needed, he returned to his father's sheep. (Cf. 16:19-23 with 17:55-58, where a discrepancy has been imagined. The preoccupied Saul did not bother to ascertain the lineage of this young musician until the latter was about to become his son-in-law.)

17. David and Goliath

1-11. Defiance of Goliath. The Philistines advanced, 1-3. Introduced is Goliath of Gath and his impious defiance of the Lord's people, and hence of the Lord Himself, 4-11. This Philistine giant furnishes an illustration of Satan as he defied and terrified God's people through Philistine doctrines and practices. Note the prominence of the number six, 5-7, the number of man under Satanic sway in opposition to God. Cf. also another giant (2 Sam 21:20), Nebuchadnezzar's image (Dan 3:1), and the number of the Antichrist, a triple six (Rev 13:18).

12-30. David appears on the scene. In the deeper spiritual sense David, whose name means 'beloved' as well as 'leader' (as archaeological evidence from the Mari Letters discovered at Tell el Hariri on the Middle Euphrates in 1933 shows), points to the Lord Jesus. David's being sent by his father Jesse, 12-19; his obedience, 20-27; his being misunderstood and unfairly accused by his own brothers, 28-30, tell of Him whom the Father sent into the world and of His treatment by His own.

31-54. David's victory. David went out to fight the giant with the confidence of faith and the shrewdness of wise preparation (see below).

55-58. Saul's question. See notes on 16:14-23 for the alleged discrepancy .

18-20. David's flight from Saul

18:1-30. Jonathan's love for David. This noble friendship, 1-4, was beautifully silhouetted against the dark background of Saul's demonic jealousy, 5-16, and his base treachery toward David with regard to his daughter Merab, 17-19, and his other daughter, Michal, 20-30. The latter, however, became David's wife, in spite of the trap Saul set for David.

19: 1-24. Saul's renewed attempt to kill David. So unprincipled had Saul become that he even tried to get Jonathan to kill David, in the face of the tender love that existed between the two, 1-6 (cf.1 Sam 18:1). The deranged king, in spite of his oath to Jonathan, 6, was overwhelmed by his mania and tried to pin David to the wall with his javelin, 7-10. Michal by a ruse, 11-17, saved David's life, and David fled to Samuel, 18-19. The grace of God dealt with Saul, 20-24, but his disobedience was his ruin.

20:1-42. Jonathan protects David. What a story of selfless love! The heir to the throne, far from being jealous or envious of David, who in a sense was a throne rival, loved him as himself (1 Sam 18:1). He himself was a hero, as his valorous triumph over the Philistines proved (ch. 14). He also possessed a sterling character worthy of being a king. But he had mastered the lesson that God's will is best and that God had ordained David to be king. To this he bowed with admirable self-effacement. Jonathan's devotion to his rival is a superbly noble story and one of the finest in history.

David's flight

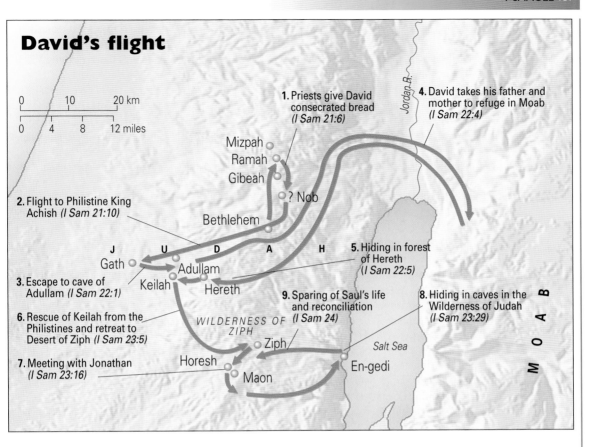

0   10   20 km
0   4   8   12 miles

1. Priests give David consecrated bread (I Sam 21:6)

4. David takes his father and mother to refuge in Moab (I Sam 22:4)

Jordan R.

Mizpah
Ramah
Gibeah
? Nob
Bethlehem

2. Flight to Philistine King Achish (I Sam 21:10)

J   U   D   A   H

Gath

3. Escape to cave of Adullam (I Sam 22:1)

Adullam
Keilah
Hereth

5. Hiding in forest of Hereth (I Sam 22:5)

6. Rescue of Keilah from the Philistines and retreat to Desert of Ziph (I Sam 23:5)

9. Sparing of Saul's life and reconciliation (I Sam 24)

8. Hiding in caves in the Wilderness of Judah (I Sam 23:29)

WILDERNESS OF ZIPH

7. Meeting with Jonathan (I Sam 23:16)

Horesh
Maon
Ziph

En-gedi

Salt Sea

M O A B

21. David's flight to Noh and to Gath

1-9. David at Noh. After leaving Jonathan, David fled to Noh not far N of Jerusalem, where Ahimelech, son of Ahitub (1 Sam 22:9), great grandson of Eli, was high priest. Hungry and unarmed, David arrived on the Sabbath and asked for food. The Bible's fidelity in showing the seamy side of a person's character is here illustrated in David's lapse in faith and his deception, 2. What a contrast to the Greater David (1 Pet 2:22). Then David and the men who were with him ate the consecrated bread, bread of presence (cf. Mt 12:1-8; Mk 2:23-28; Lk 6: 1-5). Using this incident in David's life, our Lord justified the conduct of His disciples in plucking and eating grain on the Sabbath. He was willing to set aside Jewish legal ordinances to give His own the true Bread of life of which the bread of presence speaks. (See Ps 34.)

10-15. David at Gath. Again a lapse in David's faith was seen. Once more his seamy side appeared, as he feigned insanity among the enemies of God's people.

22. David at Adullam; Saul's vengeance

1-5. David gains followers. David's headquarters at Adullam SW of Bethlehem became a stronghold, 4. He committed his parents to the king of Moab for protection. Read Ps 62 and 142.

6-23. Saul's desperate violence. Doeg, an unscrupulous foreigner, acted as an informer (see 21:7). Saul cruelly wiped out the entire priestly community at Nob, Abiathar alone escaping to inform David, 11-19. David therefore felt a sense of obligation to protect Abiathar, 20-23.

23. David delivers Keilah

1-15. David delivers Keilah. Abiathar had brought an ephod (a priestly garment containing the sacred lots) with him. By its use David was assured of divine help in rescuing Keilah, a few miles S of Adullam (1 Sam 22:1), from the Philistines. Also by the use of the ephod, 6-12, David was warned to flee Keilah, as Saul planned to besiege the town and kill David, 13-14.

16-29. David is hunted by Saul. David was a fugitive in Ziph, a rocky, remote terrain S of

Hebron, 15, where he was nobly visited by Jonathan, 16-17. The two made a covenant, 18. The traitorous Ziphites informed Saul of David's whereabouts, 19-24. Saul sought David at Maon, somewhat S of Ziph, Hakilah, and Jeshimoll (Josh 15:55) in the Arabah, here meaning simply 'desert' or 'wilderness,' not the Jordan-Dead Sea depression, 24-26. Tidings of a Philistine raid distracted Saul, 26-27. David had a moment of respite in the strongholds of En Gedi, 29, on the west shore of the Dead Sea, SE of Hebron. The rocky terrain here with its numerous caves offered natural fortresses.

24. David spares Saul's life

1-15. David spares Saul in the wilderness of En Gedi. After relief from the Philistine raid, Saul again took up his relentless pursuit of David in 'Crags of the Wild Goats,' 2, a graphic description of the wilderness around En Gedi. In this region Saul entered the same cave where David and his men were hiding. David refused to kill 'the Lord's anointed,' 4-7, merely cutting off the skirt of Saul's robe, 4. He acted on faith, allowing God to deal with his enemy. David's magnanimous conduct was reflected in his words to Saul, 8-15. ' A dead dog,' 14, was less than nothing since a live dog was little thought of in those days.

16-22. Saul's reply to David. Saul was broken, but essentially unrepentant, 16-19. He knew David was God's choice to be king, 20, and begged that his descendants be spared, 21-22.

25. David, Nabal, and Abigail

1. Samuel's obituary. It is brief but comprehensive and shows the great love of all Israel for this faithful man of God.

2-42. David obtains Abigail as his wife. David made a peaceful gesture to a wealthy Calebite whose wife was named Abigail, 2-8. Nabal ('fool') was shearing sheep in Carmel (Josh 15:55) between Ziph and Maon, SE of Hebron (not to be confused with Mt. Carmel N of the Plain of Sharon on the Mediterranean seacoast). Nabal senselessly repulsed David's men, 9-11, and played 'the fool.' Abigail acted wisely, 14-22, and went to meet David with provisions for him and his men, beseeching mercy in a nobly sagacious speech, 23-31. David replied just as nobly, 32-35. Nabal was struck by God and died, 36-38. Abigail became David's wife, 39-42.

> David had some respite in the strongholds of En Gedi on the west shore of the Dead Sea, SE of Hebron, where the rocky terrain with its numerous caves offered natural fortresses.

43-44. David also takes Ahinoam as his wife. She was from Jezreel, the Valley of Esdraelon. Explanatory note concerning Michal's relation to David is given in verse 44.

26. David spares Saul a second time

1-4. The Ziphites again inform against David (cf. 24:1-8). Critics make these events conflicting accounts of the same event. But numerous details show they are genuinely reliable accounts of two separate events. The Ziphites, having betrayed David once, knew the only thing that could save them from David's wrath was his death, so they were doggedly persistent in trying to deliver him to Saul.

5-16. Second reprieve of Saul's life. The whole *dramatis personae* of this incident is different from 24:1-22. Abner, Joab, and Abishai appear. All of these persons were destined to play an important role in David's reign, recorded in 2 Samuel. Ahimelech the Hittite is, of course, not to be confounded with Ahimelech the priest (ch. 21). Hittites who remained in the country from earlier times (Gen 23:7; Josh 1:4) adopted Hebrew names, as Uriah the Hittite (2 Sam 11:3). The details of Saul's being spared, 7-12, are diametrically different from 24:4-5. David amusingly taunted Abner, 13-16. Even at present the Bedouins shout across great distances in this way.

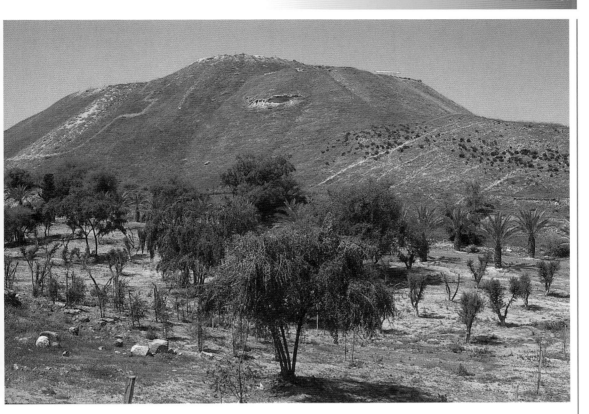

The ancient occupation mound at Beth Shan. After Saul's defeat and death at Gilboa, the Philistines took his body to this city.

17-25. Meeting between David and
Saul. David again challenged Saul concerning the wrong of his coming out to seek his life 'as one hunts a partridge in the mountains,' 17-20. Saul's confession, 21, and David's gracious reply, 22-24, are recorded. Saul's declaration to David, 25, was prophetic, 'May you be blessed, my son David; you will do great things and surely triumph.' So the enemies of the Greater David, the Lord Jesus, must confess His integrity and success (cf. Mt 27:24; Phil 2:10).

27. David's lapse of faith
1-7. Unbelief and discouragement. David's complaint, 1, is understandable on the human plane in the light of his long and grueling hounding by Saul. The discouragement of unbelief caused the Lord's anointed to go over to the enemies of the Lord's people, live with them, and settle down in the very city Goliath, the giant David slew by faith, came from. David was given Ziklag, located somewhere on the Judah-Philistine border, 5-7.

8-12. Deceit and deception. Unbelief produced other evil fruits. To court Achish's trust, David lied about the object of his military raids, 10.

28. Saul and the spiritistic medium
1-7. Saul's desperate straits. The Philistines advanced, 1, into the Valley of Jezreel, eastern end of the Plain of Megiddo (Esdraelon), and encamped at Shunem, opposite Mt. Gilboa near the fortress Bethshan, 4-5. Samuel had died, so there was no word from the Lord through him, 3, nor through dreams, Urim, or by prophets, 6. Heaven was closed, so to speak, to the rejected, disobedient monarch. So he resorted, as it were, to hell, 7. To make matters worse, the monarch himself in his better days had outlawed pagan occultism, 9.

8-19. Saul resorts to spiritism. Saul sought out a medium, 7. Disguised so as not to be recognized as the king, 8, he required the woman to call up the spirit of Samuel, that he might inquire what to do about the Philistine pressure. Samuel's spirit was brought back, but this was accomplished by God, not by the medium. The medium's fright proves this. This was not a case of a medium communicating with the spirit of a deceased person; it was God actually calling back Samuel in spirit form to pronounce impending doom upon Saul, 15-19. It is thus a once-for-all

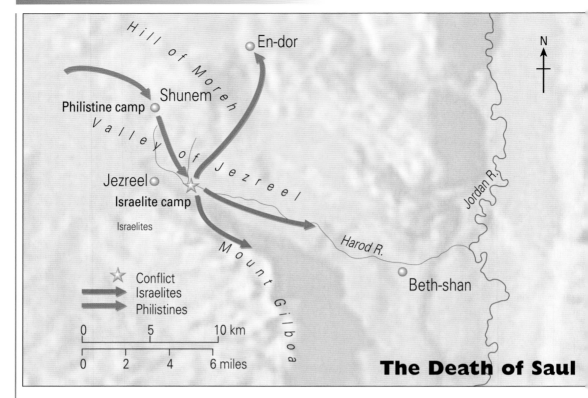

N

The Death of Saul

- ☆ Conflict
- → Israelites
- → Philistines

0 ——— 5 ——— 10 km

0 —— 2 —— 4 —— 6 miles

exposé of the fraud and wickedness of necromancy and all occultism.

20-25. Saul takes food. Saul received strength to go on to his last battle on Mt. Gilboa. He serves as an illustration of the believer who sins the sin to death, i.e., physical death (cf. 1 Cor 5:5; 11:30-32; 1 Jn 5:16).

29. David's defection to the Philistines

1-5. Results of David's lapse of faith. See ch. 27, which is here resumed. David not only found himself among the enemies of the Lord's people, but put in the deplorable situation of fighting against the Lord's people. Unbelief makes a sad spectacle of any believer. So much so in this case that David, as a result, became *persona non grata* as far as the Philistine lords were concerned. They still remembered the former exploits of a hero of faith, 5, and feared treachery.

6-11. Achish dismisses David. Achish showed his great respect for David, 6, by swearing by David's God and pronouncing him blameless in his sight 'as an angel of God,' 9. Nevertheless he bowed to the will of his colleagues, the Philistine lords, 7. David's reply, 8, asserting his

willingness to stay with the Philistines and fight against the Lord's people, showed how deeply unbelief can plunge a believer into inconsistency and spiritual treason. Only God's grace kept David from plummeting deeper into the ignominy unbelief always brings. The Philistines quickly marched on the Israelites at Jezreel (cf. 1), the Plain of Esdraelon (the Gr. form of Jezreel), from Aphek (modern Ras el-'Ain in the Plain of Sharon), from which rallying point they had captured the ark of the covenant years before (1 Sam 4:1).

30. David's chastening and restoration

1-6. The plundering of Ziklag. Achish had given David Ziklag as his residence (1 Sam 27:6). The town was about 80 miles S of Aphek, a strenuous two-day march, 1. When David with his men arrived on the third day, the plundered city was a token that the chastening hand of the Lord rested heavily upon him, 1-5. David was hard pressed and the embittered people were ready to stone him, 6. But the backslider was restored by discipline and 'found strength in the Lord his God,' 6.

7-20. The enemy defeated. David

consulted Abiathar's ephod (containing the sacred oracles), and received the go-sign to pursue the Amalekites, 8. With 600 men he crossed the Besor Ravine, S of Ziklag, 9. Four hundred were able to advance. Through the help of an Egyptian, 11-15, an abandoned servant of an Amalekite, who acted as a spy, the Amalekites (see Ex 17) were slaughtered and all David's family and possessions were retrieved, with great spoil, 16-20.

21-31. The spoil divided equitably. Thus David's fairmindedness and political sagacity were displayed especially in sending a gift to the elders of Judah, 26-31. All the places named, 27-31, were in Judah. It is no surprise David was soon to be made king of Judah (2 Sam 2:6).

31. Saul's death

1-7. Saul's suicide. In the battle with the Philistines on Mt. Gilboa, S of the eastern part of the Plain of Jezreel (Esdraelon), Israel was routed, 1. Saul's older sons, Jonathan, Abinadab and Malki-Shua, were killed, 2, and Saul was wounded, 3. He pressed his armor bearer to kill him, but committed suicide when the armor bearer refused, 4-6. This climactic tragedy followed his visit to the spiritistic medium at Endor, Saul's last step toward ruin (28:1-25). He died unrepentant, in rebellion against the Lord, as he had lived, the first suicide recorded in the Bible. Cf. also Ahithophel (2 Sam 17:23), Zimri (1 Kgs 16:18), and Judas Iscariot (Mt 27:5).

8-10. Saul's body dishonoured. The completely victorious Philistines beheaded Saul's corpse, put his armor in the temple of the Ashtareths and hung up his body and those of his sons in ignominy on the walls of Beth Shan, the fortress town which guarded the eastern approach to the Valley of Jezreel.

11-13. The men of Jabesh Gilead recover the bodies. They had now the chance to show their thanks to Saul for what he had done for them (1 Sam 11). They not only recovered the bodies of Saul and his sons, but gave them honourable burial and proper mourning.

2 SAMUEL

David king over Judah and all Israel

Theme of the book. Continuing the narrative (see introduction to 1 Samuel), 2 Samuel presents the biographical story of David. In 1 Samuel the failure of man is stressed as seen in Eli and Saul. In 2 Samuel the restoration of order follows the enthroning of God's king with the establishment of Jerusalem as the nation's political center (2 Sam 5:6-12) and Zion (2 Sam 5:7; 6:1-17) as the religious center. Following this arrangement the great Davidic covenant was established by the Lord (2 Sam 7:8-17), the basis of all revealed truth concerning the kingdom yet to be established over Israel (Acts 1:6). David prophetically sang of that kingdom (2 Sam 23-1-7).

Outline

1-4 David, King of Judah
5-10 David, King of Israel
11-20 David's sin and chastisement
21-24 Historical appendix

The market, Hebron. This city was David's capital until he captured Jerusalem.

Cross-section through the Gihon Spring, Jerusalem

Entrance to water tunnel

Jebusite wall

Gihon Spring

possible route taken by David's men

1. David's lament for Saul and Jonathan

1-16. The Amalekite's report of Saul's death. This is not contradictory to the account in 1 Sam 31: 1-6, as critics commonly claim, but supplementary. The Amalekite, noting Saul's suicide, apparently fabricated his story, thus hoping to gain David's favor and material reward. It is ironic that after Saul spared the Amalekites (15:7-9), an Amalekite wished to profit from his death. David's respect for God's anointed prevented him from honoring the ruse, however, so he had the Amalekite executed. His allegiance to Saul showed his magnanimity of character and noble statesmanship.

17-27. David's lament. This superb elegy shows the deep feeling of David. It is great lyric poetry from a skilled musician (1 Sam 16:23) and talented poet (cf. the many Davidic psalms), who was a man of God and a steadfast friend even in the face of such treatment as Saul gave him (cf. David's lament for Absalom, 2 Sam 18:33).

2. David made king of Judah; Abner's revolt

1-7. David anointed king over Judah. God's king at once showed faith in and dependence upon the Lord, 1-3. The answer was

plain. He was to go up to the cities of Judah, where he was made king. Judah was evidently living a separate existence from the other tribes. (Cf. 2 Sam 3:10; 5:5; 19:8-15, 40-43; 20:1-3 for other indications of separateness.) David's first official royal act in thanking the men of Jabesh Gilead for their service rendered in burying Saul was a foretaste of David's brilliant diplomacy and political sagacity, 5-7.

8-11. Abner sets up Ish-Bosheth as king. An attempt was made by Saul's army commander to perpetuate the Saul dynasty, 8-11. Ish-Bosheth ('man of shame') had the original name of Esh-Baal ('man of Baal') (1 Chr 8:33; 9:39). The Hebrew word for 'shame' bòsét was substituted for the hated name of the Canaanite fertility god (cf. Jerub-baal to Jereb-besheth, Merib-baal to Mephibosheth). Mahanaim was the principal town in Transjordan. The Philistines were in control W of the Jordan River. The servants of Ish-Bosheth under Abner and the servants of David under Joab clashed at the pool in Gibeon (Josh 9), an important city some five miles NW of Jerusalem, 12-17. Abner's killing of Asahel precipitated a blood feud between Joab and Abner, 22-23. David's forces were victorious, 29-32. This initial victory presaged further victories.

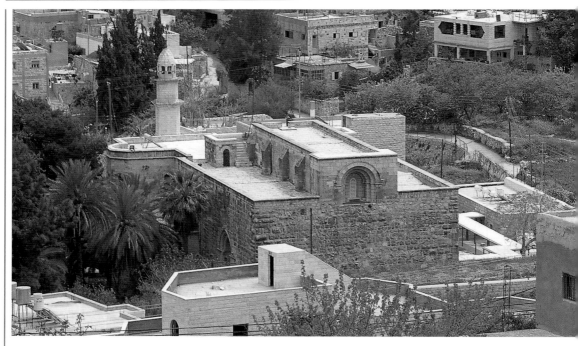

3. Abner's defection to David and his death

1-11. Quarrel with Ish-Bosheth. Summary statement of the war, 1, is followed by a description of David's family, 2-5, and the episode of Abner's break with Saul's house, 6-11. Ish-Bosheth's charge was serious, since in a harem a concubine was royal property and must be kept in the royal household. To seek to procure such a concubine was tantamount to treason (2 Sam 16:21-22; 1 Kgs 2:22).

12-30. Abner goes over to David. His negotiations with David, 12, were answered affirmatively with only the condition that Michal, Saul's daughter and David's first wife, be returned, 13 (cf. 1 Sam 18:20-27). This had a political purpose in bolstering David's claim to Saul's throne as the king's son-in-law. Abner's reception by David, 20-21, motivated him to campaign for David's kingship over all Israel. However, he was murdered by Joab in the blood feud occasioned by Abner's killing of Asahel, 23-30.

31-39. David's lament over Abner. The public mourning and wise conduct of David presaged his success in the kingship.

4. Ish-Bosheth's death

1-7. Ish-Bosheth's assassination. The hopeless prospect of Saul's house produced by Abner's defection, 1, occasioned other disloyalty. Baanah and Recab, two army officers, murdered Ish-Bosheth, 2-7. Mephibosheth, Jonathan's son, is introduced rather abruptly, 4, perhaps to show the sorry plight of Saul's house in general. David's later kindness towards Mephibosheth fulfilled his covenant with Jonathan (1 Sam 20:42).

8-12. David's punishment of the murderers. Bringing the head of the murdered king to David, these violent criminals tried to justify their crime by pious reference to the Lord's avenging David, 8; but David continued to honor Saul's house and to punish anyone who would harm it (cf. 2 Sam 1:14-16; 3:28-39).

5. David made king over Israel; captures Zion

1-5. God's king comes into his own. It was a magnificent occasion when all Israel came to Hebron to turn the kingdom of Saul over to David (cf. 1 Chr 12:23-40). The united nation was gripped by a tremendous enthusiasm after Ish-Bosheth's death. David's stirring coronation foreshadows that day when Israel's long-rejected King, the Messiah, son of David (Mt 1:1), returns in glory to be the Shepherd-King of Israel. The great feast of rejoicing mentioned in 1 Chr 12:39-40 offers a faint foregleam of Israel's joy when her true King is enthroned (cf. Isa 25:6-9).

6-25. David's conquest of Zion and other victories. The town of Jerusalem had been taken in the time of the judges (Jud 1:8), but not the stronghold of the Jebusites. This was the southeast hill, later called the city of David or Zion. Zion is closely connected with David's being made king over all Israel. Its capture was politically important because it rooted out the last vestige of Canaanite power in the region, and provided the kingdom with a neutral capital situated between Judah and Israel, but belonging to neither. Hiram I of Tyre (c. 969-936 B.C.) showed friendship to David, 11-12. He appears in Phoenician records both as a conqueror and builder. These ties of friendship continued through Solomon's reign (1 Kgs 9:10-14). David's expanding family in Jerusalem is described, 13-16, as well as his two victories over the Philistines, 17-25.

6. The ark brought to Zion

1-11. The sin of Uzzah. Since the Philistines had captured the ark and destroyed Shiloh, the ark had had no permanent resting place (1 Sam 4-7). The Levites alone were commissioned to transport (i.e. 'touch') the ark (Num 4:15; 1 Chr 13:9). Uzzah's sin was an infraction of this divine regulation. David apparently failed to inquire of the Lord, transporting the ark in a Philistine expedient and not according to the divinely prescribed manner. Obed-Edom, 10-11, was a Levite (1 Chr 26:1-5), and blessing upon his house encouraged David to bring the ark to Jerusalem.

12-19. The ark brought to David's city. This was done in the Mosaically prescribed manner (1 Chr 15:1-28), and blessing followed.

20-23. Michal's mockery. She is called not 'wife of the king' but 'daughter of Saul' and displayed the pride of her father, upon which the curse of God fell. David manifested singular humility and self-abasement in contrast.

7. The Davidic covenant

1-3. David desires to build the temple. This worthy ambition to build the Lord a house furnished the revelation through Nathan the prophet that the Lord would build David a house.

4-17. The Davidic covenant (cf. 1 Chr 17:4-15). This great covenant of kingship centering in Christ provided: (1) a Davidic

Archaeological light

The eastern hill where the Jebusite fortress was located was practically impregnable (2 Sam 5:6). It was located above the Gihon spring. Some scholars still maintain David's men gained access through the water shaft which was dug by the Jebusites to get water inside the city (cf. 5:8, RSV). Early searches of the Palestine Exploration Fund under the direction of Sir Charles Warren yielded important discoveries concerning this Jebusite water system. W. F. Albright, however, maintains the wall was scaled by a grappling hook and that this is the meaning of the word (as shown by Aramaic and Arabic) instead of water shaft. A third possibility is that David's men blocked up the water shaft, thus denying the besieged city its only water supply.

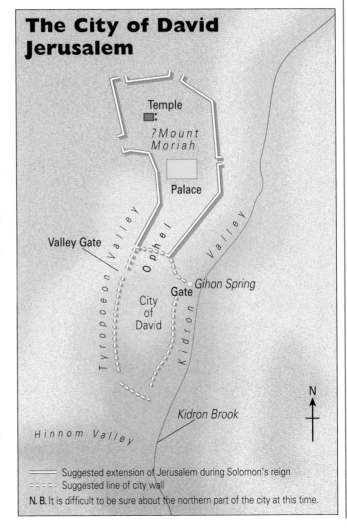

The City of David Jerusalem

Temple

?Mount Moriah

Palace

Valley Gate

Tyropoeon Valley

Ophel Valley

Valley

City of David

Gate

Gihon Spring

Kidron

Kidron Brook

Hinnom Valley

N

━━━ Suggested extension of Jerusalem during Solomon's reign
----- Suggested line of city wall

N.B. It is difficult to be sure about the northern part of the city at this time.

City of David
Archaeological
Garden, Jerusalem,
site of David's
citadel and center
of the city in his
time.

'house,' 11, or family through which Messiah would be born (Mt 1:1, 16; Lk 3:23); (2) a perpetual kingdom, 12, and a throne, 13. This regal covenant had only one condition – chastisement for disobedience in the kingly Davidic line. The covenant, however, was not to be abrogated, 15, but was to 'endure forever,' 16. It was renewed to Mary by the angel Gabriel (Lk 1:31-33; Acts 2:29-32; 15:14-17). Although since the Babylonian captivity only one king of the Davidic house has been crowned at Jerusalem, and He with thorns, He will yet be given the throne of His father David and sit on His own throne, as He now sits with the Father on His Father's throne (Rev 3:21). This throne will be millennial and merge into the everlasting kingdom of the eternal state (Rev 21:1-8).

18-19. David worshiped, in holy humility and awe.

8. David's kingdom established

1-14. David's conquests. The kingly covenant in ch. 7 is followed by the account of David's great conquests. These include victories over the Philistines and Moabites, 1-2; over Hadadezer of Zobah, 3-8; over the Edomites, 12-13; as well as diplomatic victory of Tou of Hamath, 9-11.

15-18. David's reign. His rule of justice and equity, 15, prefigures Messiah's administration of righteousness. David's sons were not priests but administrators (cf. 2 Sam 20-26; 1 Chr 18:17). The Kerethites and Pelethites were foreign mercenaries (2 Sam 15:18; 20:7, 23; 1 Kgs 1:38, 44), probably Cretans and Philistines.

9. David's kindness to Mephibosheth

1-6. Mephibosheth brought to David. Lame in his feet (cf. 2 Sam 4:$), a helpless cripple who was carried into the king's presence, Mephibosheth is a beautiful illustration of the sinner made helpless and worthless by the Fall, but a candidate for God's grace, 3. Hearing what kindness was to be shown him, Mephibosheth confessed his shame and nothingness, calling himself a 'dead dog' (cf. 1 Sam 24:14), less even than a live dog, little enough esteemed in those days.

Campaigns of David

Damascus

A R A M (S Y R I A)

Tyre
Dan
Beth-rehob

8. Conquest of the Arameans *(2 Sam. 8:5–6)*

P H O E N I C I A

Acco

Sea of Chinnereth

Helam

Edrei

Megiddo

Valley of Jezreel

Beth-shan

4. Conquest of the Plain of Sharon and Valley of Jezreel

I S R A E L

Shechem

3. Conquest of the Philistines *(2 Sam. 5 & 8)*

Yarkon

Jordan

A M M O

Gath (Metheg-ammah)

Geba
Jericho
Rabbah

7. War against Ammon *(2 Sam. 8:12)*

Gezer

Jerusalem

Ashdod
Jarmuth

Kidron
Bethlehem

Heshbon

Medeba

J U D A H

Keilah

2. Capture of Jerusalem *(2 Sam. 5)*

5. War against Moab *(2 Sam. 8:12)*

Gaza

Hebron

Salt Sea

M O A B

Ziklag
Gath
Beersheba

Kir-hareseth

THE NEGEB

1. Conquest of the Negeb *(1 Sam. 30)*

6. War against Edom *(2 Sam. 8:13–14)*

Besor

P H I L I S T I A

E D O M

Kadesh-barnea

Brook of Egypt

? Sela

T H E A R A B A H

→ Campaign of David
→ Campaign of the Philistines
→ Coalition forces of Aram and Ammom

| 0 | | 25 | | 50 | | 75 km |
| 0 | 15 | | 30 | | 45 miles |

Ezion-geber

G R E A T   S E A

7-13. David's mercy to Mephibosheth.
David, for Jonathan's sake (cf. 1 Sam 18:1-4), lifted the poor cripple to a place at the king's table as one of the king's sons. Similarly the gospel of Christ lifts us out of our shame, constituting us sons and giving us an inheritance (Rom 8: 16-17).

10-11. David's great sin
10:1-19. Prelude to the sin.
The Ammonite-Aramean War triggered by Hanun's insult to David, 1-5, furnished the background of David's sin. Mutilation of the beard, a badge of masculine honor, and enforced shameful exposure were heinous insults.

11:1-27. The terrible sin itself.
While Joab and the army were besieging Rabbah (modern Amman), David committed adultery with Bathsheba, wife of one of his army officers, Uriah the Hittite, 1-5. Thereupon David sent for Uriah, 6-13, and when subterfuge failed to hide his sin, he had Uriah murdered, 14-25, and then took Bathsheba as his wife, 26-27.

12. David's confession
1-13. The confession elicited.
The Lord's rebuke came through the message of the prophet Nathan, 1-4, showing the king's hypocrisy and guilt, 5-6, and bringing the denunciation, 'You are the man!' 7-9. The announced chastisement upon the Lord's disobedient servant, 10-12, brought a full confession, 13.

14-31. The chastisement begins,
in the death of the child and David's grief, 14-23. Solomon's birth, 24-25 , and the capture of Rabbah, 26-31, were mercies mingled with disciplinary dealing. Sin in the Lord's servant always brings divine discipline (1 Cor 5:1-5; 11:30-32; Heb 12:3-11). The Lord's grace spared David physical death (13; cf. 1 Jn 5:16) but not severe chastening.

13-14. Amnon murdered by Absalom
13:1-22. Amnon's sin against Tamar.
As the eldest son of David (2 Sam 3:2), Amnon was in line for the throne. Tamar was his half sister and any union was forbidden by Mosaic law (Lev 18:9). Lust and lawlessness ruled, however, and Amnon violated Tamar, full sister of Absalom.

23-29. Absalom murders Amnon and flees.
Incest and violence in his own family were the beginning of David's chastisements for his own twin sin of adultery and murder. Absalom not only avenged the wrong done his sister, but doubtless knew he was removing the heir apparent to the throne at the same time, 23-26. He fled to Geshur (1 Sam 27:8), the country of his maternal grandfather (2 Sam 3:3). This was an Aramean principality under David's control (2 Sam 8:3-8; 10:6-19).

14:1-33. Absalom's recall by Joab's craftiness.
Joab was powerful as well as subtle, and secured Absalom's return through the ruse of the woman of Tekoa, a town just S of Bethlehem, in the home country of David and Joab, 1-20. Absalom was partially forgiven, 21-24, and finally fully reinstated to the king's favor, 25-33.

15. Absalom's revolt
1-12. Absalom's conspiracy.
By flattery and David's failure to establish an adequate system, Absalom won the hearts of the Israelites, 1-6. It took him four years (Gr. and Syriac versions, not the 'forty years' of the Heb.) to plan his uprising, 7. He probably chose Hebron, for he had discovered disaffection there over its loss of prestige when David moved the capital to Jerusalem, 8-12.

13-27. David flees from Jerusalem.
David apparently decided that a showdown as to the loyalty of his professed followers would be better accomplished by this move and that his spies could operate better under this arrangement. The king left part of his harem, 16. He was accompanied by his servants, the Kerethites and Pelethites (see note on 2 Sam 8:18) and 600 Gittites, i.e., Gathites, Philistines from Gath, 18. The sad trek over Kidron, 23, the eastern extremity of the city, was made. The ark of the Lord was sent back to Jerusalem, 24-30, as well as Hushai the Arkite, 'David's friend,' 37, i.e., royal counselor, an official title (1 Kgs 4:5).

16. David in flight; Absalom in Jerusalem
1-14. David meets Ziba and Shimei.
Strangely, David believed the wily falsehood of Ziba concerning Mephibosheth, 1-4 (cf. 19:24-30), but acted with wisdom and restraint in the case of the cursing Shimei, 5-14. The latter represented an element of disaffection in Israel over the loss of the ruling house, 8. Cf.19:16-23 for the outcome.

15-23. Absalom follows Ahithophel's wicked counsel. Absalom's shameful public violation of his father's harem (royal property) was the final and irrevocable step in assuming the kingship (cf. 15:16; 1 Kgs 2:17-25).

17. Ahitophel and Hushai
1-26. Ahitophel's counsel vs. Hushai's. Ahitophel's advice was to aim only at the life of David, 1-4, while Hushai advocated a prepared attack taking time, 5-13. The result was that Ahitophel's good counsel, which spelled David's death, was set aside by the Lord who, though He was chastening His servant David, would not destroy him, 14, but rather Absalom. David was informed of the decision, 15-22. Ahitophel committed suicide, 23. Absalom pitched his camp in Gilead, 24-26, and David crossed the Jordan.

27-29. David's friends minister to him. Shobi, brother of Hanun, of Rabbah ('Amman), Makir of Lo Debar (cf. 9:4) and Barzillai, an Aramean by name and likely a non-Israelite, took care of David.

18. Absalom's death
1-8. The battle in the woods of Ephraim. Absalom's hastily recruited troops were no match for David's veteran army. David wisely kept out of the battle (cf. 12:28-29; also 21:17).

9-18. Absalom's death. His head not his hair (cf. 14:26) is said to have been caught in the oak, 9. The tradition that Absalom's hair was caught comes from Josephus (Antiq. 7.10.2). The pile of stones (cairn) signifies the grave of a criminal and has no connection with the present-day Absalom's Tomb in the Kidron Valley, dating from late Hellenistic times. 'No son,' 18, must mean his three sons (14:27) had died.

19-33. David's lament. A touching scene of paternal love for his son, though he probably deserved his fate.

19. David returns as king
1-15. Judah calls David back as king. Joab jolted David out of his excessive grief, 1-8. Movement in all Israel to call David back, 9-10, was followed by the king's successful overtures for Judah's initiative in the matter, 11-15.

16-40. Shimei, Mephibosheth, and Barzillai. David showed mercy to Shimei, 16-23. Mephibosheth's genuine joy, 24-30, at David's return was proof enough of Ziba's treachery. David apparently was not totally convinced, or else he was afraid of alienating Ziba, for he divided Mephibosheth's inheritance with him, 29. Barzillai's parting with David is beautiful, 31-39. Kimham was no doubt Barzillai's son (cf. 1 Kgs 2:7).

41-43. Antagonism between Judah

The hilltop platform on which the Dome of the Rock now stands in Jerusalem was probably the site of Araunah's threshing floor, which David purchased as the place where the Temple was to be constructed.

When David fled Jerusalem because of the rebellion of Absalom, he left via the Kidron Valley.

and Israel again broke out. This deep cleavage was to come to the fore in the final disruption after Solomon's death (1 Kgs 12:16-20).

20. Sheba revolts; Joab murders Amasa

1-22. Joab regains his position. Sheba, from the most disaffected tribe of Benjamin (16:5, 8), organized a final revolt. Israel sided with him (cf. 19:41-43). Amasa, having succeeded Joab as commander of the army (19:13), incurred the latter's implacable jealousy. His failure to subdue the revolt was a further reason for Joab's murdering him (1 Kgs 2:31-32). Joab again proved his cruel thoroughness by hunting down the rebel and using the woman of Abel Beth Maacah to accomplish Sheba's death. A mother city, 19, is one with dependent villages or 'daughters' (Num 21:25; Josh 15:45; Jud 11:26).

23-26. A list of David's officials. (Cf. a similar list in 8:16-18.) On Kerethites and Pelethites, 23, see note on 8:15-18.

21. Famine and Philistine wars

The last four chapters of 2 Samuel are an appendix.

1-14. The famine and the Gibeonites. A three-year severe famine is traced to

bloodguiltiness upon the land for Saul's murder of the Gibeonites, who were under a covenant of protection (Josh 9:25-27) in the Lord's name, which Saul had violated. David allowed the Gibeonites to execute seven of Saul's descendants as retribution. After the bodies had been disgraced by leaving them exposed in a field, David was moved by Rizpah's mourning, 10-11, to inter in their ancestral tomb, 12-14, the bones of Saul, Jonathan, and all the descendants who had been killed.

15-22. Memoirs of the Philistine wars. (Cf. 1 Sam 17:4; 1 Chr 20:5.)

22. David's great prophetic psalm

1-28. Praise to the Lord for His intervention. This great ode of deliverance was placed here and also as Psalm 18 in the Psalter. It is prophetic and looks beyond the sufferings and triumphs of David to David's son and Lord, Jesus Christ. The occasion of praise, 1-4, is followed by David's sufferings as a fugitive from Saul, 5-7, presaging Christ's rejection. God's intervention, 8-20, reflects our Lord's deliverance from death 'into a spacious place,' 20. The divine approval and reward, 21-28, go far beyond the earthly David to the heavenly.

29-51. Praise to the Lord for exaltation over foes. The judgment of enemies, 29-43, and exaltation over adversaries, 44-49, will be realized only by Him into whose hands is committed all judgment (Jn 5:22). In coming kingdom glory he will be 'head of nations,' 44, and in fulfillment of the Davidic covenant (ch. 7) verses 44-51 will become a reality.

23. David's last words; his heroes

1-7. His last words. This inspired prophecy, 1-2, celebrated again the theme of the perpetuity of the house (dynasty) of David, 5, to be realized in the righteous rule of David's Lord in the kingdom, fulfilling the royal covenant (see ch. 7). Verses 3 and 4 picture the clear morning of the Kingdom Age.

8-39. Roster of David's heroes. Cf. 2 Sam 21:15-22 and 1 Chr 11:11-47 for interesting points of variation in the lists.

24. David's failure in the census

1-17. The sin and its punishment. The Lord allowed Satan to move in David's heart (1 Chr 21:1) through pride (1 Tim 3:6), 1-9. David's confession, 10-14, was followed by the plague, 15-17.

18-25. The altar and atonement. David's negotiations for the threshing floor are instructive as he declines taking it, saying, 'I will not sacrifice to the Lord my God burnt offerings that cost me nothing,' 24. Araunah's threshing floor, where Abraham had offered Isaac and where the temple was to be set, was a fitting spot for mercy upon Israel.

1 KINGS

Solomon's reign and the divided kingdom

Name and purpose: 1 and 2 Kings are called the third and fourth books of the Kingdoms in the Greek version and the third and fourth books of Kings in the Hebrew and the Latin. Originally one book, they catalog the history of the undivided kingdom from David's death through Solomon's and Rehoboam's reigns and the divided kingdom till Israel's fall in 722 B.C. and Judah's captivity in 586 B.C.

Author: The author (or authors) was inspired to write these narratives from sources at his disposal. The result under the Holy Spirit's guidance is a historically reliable account. Although only conjecture, Jeremiah may have written all but the last chapter of Kings.

Outline

1:1–2:11 David's decease
2:12–11:43 Solomon's reign
12:1–16:34 The kingdom divided
17:1–22:53 Elijah's ministry

Part of the site of the fortress of Megiddo, one of king Solomon's regional capitals.

1-2. David's decease

1:1-27. Adonijah's bid to be king.
David's premature physical decline, 1-2, due to his great sin and chastenings, gave Adonijah, David's oldest living son, a chance to assert his claim of primogeniture, 5-9. Abishag, 3, was from Shunem (1 Sam 28:4) near Mt. Gilboa in the Esdraelon plain. Nathan's and Bathsheba's plot, 10-14, succeeded in David's proclaiming Solomon king, 15-27.

28-53. Solomon crowned. Gihon, 33, now Mary's Spring (2 Chr 32:30), like En Rogel, Job's Well, 9, was a sacred place suitable for affairs of this type (2 Sam 17:17). Solomon's anointing, 28-40, resulted in Adonijah's fear and submission, 41-53.

2:1-11. David's charge and death. He charged Solomon to follow the law of Moses (cf. Deut 4:40; 5:1; 11:1-12:32; 17:14-20). Elimination of Joab (2 Sam 3:27; 20:10) and Shimei (2 Sam 16:5-14; 19:18-23) was ordered.

12-46. Solomon eliminates his enemies. Benaiah was appointed leader of the army and Zadok priest in Abiathar's place, 35; Shimei was put to death.

3. Solomon's prayer for wisdom

1-3. Solomon marries an Egyptian princess. Undoubtedly she was a daughter of one of the pharaohs of the Twenty-first Dynasty, since Sheshonk (Shishak), founder of the Twenty-second Dynasty, did all in his power to weaken Solomon.

4-28. Solomon prays for wisdom. His reign began in wisdom and ended in folly. The 'high places' was a hilltop shrine. Gibeon (cf. Josh 9) was one of the most famous of these shrines (2 Chr 1:2-6). Worship at such places in itself was not evil (Gen 12:7; 22:2-4; 31:54; Jud 6:25), but was in conflict with the anticipatory provisions of Deuteronomy after the temple was established on Moriah (Deut 12:11-14).

4. Solomon's government

1-34. His administration. Solomon's high officials are listed, 16. His new administration ignored the old tribal divisions. The system of taxation supported the king's grand style of living.

5-8. Solomon's temple

5:1-18. Preparations to build. Hiram I

Tel Gezer. Gezer, along with a group of other fortress cities, was rebuilt and fortified by King Solomon

of Tyre (*c.* 969-936 B.C.) bore the title of 'King of the Sidonians.' His was a common Phoenician royal name as attested by the inscriptions, such as the sarcophagus of Ahiram at Byblos, biblical Gebal, discovered in 1923-24.

6:1-8:66. Description of the temple.
The temple was begun, 6:1, in Ziv (April-May) about 962 B.C. The specifications, pre-Greek and authentic for the 10th cen. B.C., displayed Phoenician influence, as a temple at Tell Tainat discovered in 1936 shows. Besides the temple, Solomon built his palace and administrative complexes, 7:1-51. The function of the two pillars, Jakin and Boaz, 7:21, is uncertain, but W.F. Albright suggested that they were huge incense stands with oil bowls at the top, which served to illuminate the facade of the temple.

9. Solomon's second vision and splendor

1-9. Solomon's warning against apostasy. He was admonished in a second vision.

10-28. Solomon's splendor. His foreign diplomacy and intermarriage designed to produce peaceful neighbors are described (3:1-3; 11:1-8). His building operations at Gezer, Hazor, are known, especially at the latter, which was the headquarters of Solomon's fifth administrative district. His navy, 26-28, was a refinery fleet which brought smelted copper from the colonial mines of the Phoenicians in Sardinia and Spain, Tarshish denoting a copper-refining port. Excavation of the copper refinery at Tell

Worship in Solomon's Temple

The Temple, like the Tabernacle, symbolized God's presence in the midst of his people (Ex 25:21-22). Because it was God's house, worshipers could not enter the holy place, reserved only for priests, still less the holiest place (Holy of Holies), which was entered only by the high priest only once a year (Lev 16). Worshipers gathered for prayer and sacrifice in the Temple courtyards, where they sang psalms as they watched their offerings presented to God on the great altar.

Although there is little evidence about Temple worship during the period of the monarchy, it probably followed the pattern laid down for the Tabernacle. The great festivals were observed annually, as well as the daily and monthly routine of sacrifices and the presentation of tithes and first-fruits.

Every year there was one official day of fasting – the Day of Atonement – and three great annual feasts – Passover, the Feast of Weeks (Pentecost) and the Feast of Tabernacles (or Booths). These times of joyful celebration are often called 'pilgrim feasts' because all adult males were supposed to travel up to the Temple to take part (Deuteronomy 16:16).

Pillars of Jachin and Boaz

The 'Molten Sea'

Steps leading up to the porch

Altar of Sacrifice

Ark of the Covenant

Holy of Holies

Storerooms

Gilded cedar panelling

Holy Place

Lampstands

Five Lavers (north and south side of the Temple)

Archaeological light

Solomon's stables. Early excavations at Megiddo unearthed ruins of what appeared to be a large stable complex for horses and chariots that was assigned to the period of Solomon (cf. 9:19; 10:26). Recent study has forced a more cautious conclusion. Some have argued that the complex dates to the time of Ahab (cf.1 Kgs 20; 22:39), while others have argued persuasively that it served as a storehouse rather than a stable (cf. 9:19). In any case, the excavations offer abundant testimony to the historical accuracy of the OT.

el-Kheleifeh (ancient Ezion Geber) disclosed Solomon's copper-smelting station on the Gulf of Aqaba.

10. Solomon and the Queen of Sheba

1-13. The queen's visit. Sheba is probably Saba in SW Arabia, modern Yemen, mentioned in cuneiform sources from the 8th and 7th cen. B.C. Although queens played little part in the later history of S. Arabia, they ruled large tribal confederacies in N. Arabia from the 9th to the 7th cen. B.C. Some identify this queen with a colony of Sheba in N. Arabia.

14-29. Solomon's revenues. His great wealth, 14-15, his famous targets and shields, 16-17, his ivory throne, 18-20, his opulence in gold

and silver, 21-22, and his horse and chariot trade, 27-29, are mentioned. The horse and chariot trade was one of the sources of Solomon's vast wealth. His annual income amounted to 666 talents of gold (1 Kgs 10:14), a talent of gold equaling about 75 pounds. He imported horses from Kue (Cilicia) and Egypt, acting as middleman in the horse and chariot trade between Egypt and Asia Minor. At the same time he built up his army of chariotry.

11. Solomon's failure

1-43. Solomon's sin and chastisement. His sin was apostasy and idolatry because of his numerous pagan marriages for the purpose of carnal security, 1-13. Raised up by God to chastise him were Hadad the Edomite, 14-22, Rezoh, founder of the Aramean kingdom of Damascus, 23-25, and Jeroboam, who later became head of the northern kingdom, 26-40. At his death, Solomon was succeeded by his son Rehoboam, 41-43.

12. Rehoboam and the revolt

1-24. The secession of the northern tribes. The folly of Rehoboam is almost unimaginable. But sin makes fools of its victims. The harm of this division of the Lord's covenant people was never healed.

25-33. Jeroboam's evil plans. He built two shrines to the Lord, one at Bethel in the S part of his country , a bare dozen miles N of

'King Solomon's Mines' at Timna, near the Gulf of Aqaba. Solomon had a copper-smelting station on the Gulf of Aqaba.

Palestine under David and Solomon

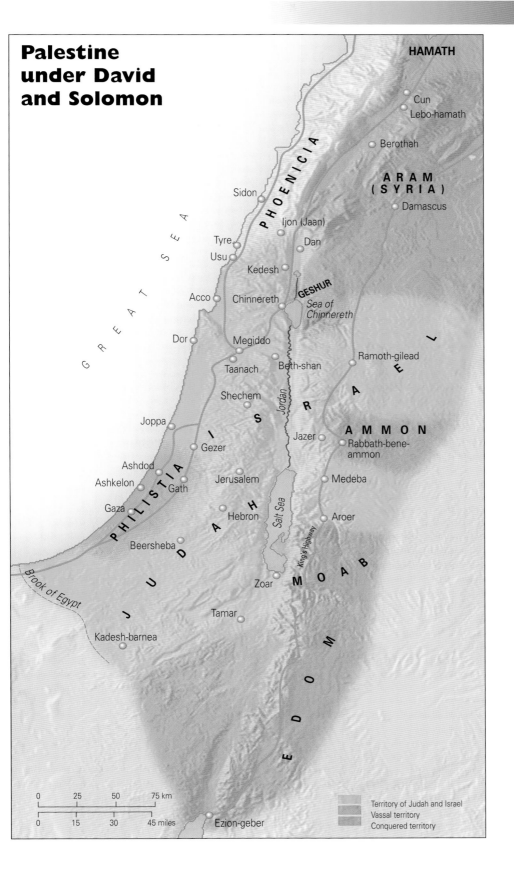

HAMATH

Cun
Lebo-hamath

Berothah

PHOENICIA

ARAM
(SYRIA)

Sidon

Damascus

Ijon (Jaan)

Tyre
Usu
Dan

Kedesh

Acco
Chinnereth
GESHUR
Sea of
Chinnereth

GREAT SEA

Dor
Megiddo
Ramoth-gilead

Taanach
Beth-shan

I
S
R
A
E
L

Shechem

Jordan

Joppa

Jazer
AMMON
Rabbath-bene-
ammon

Gezer

Ashdod
Jerusalem
Medeba

Ashkelon
Gath

Gaza
Hebron
Aroer

PHILISTIA

Salt Sea

Beersheba

King's Highway

J
U
D
A
H

Brook of Egypt

Zoar
MOAB

Tamar

Kadesh-barnea

E
D
O
M

0	25	50	75 km
0	15	30	45 miles

Ezion-geber

Territory of Judah and Israel
Vassal territory
Conquered territory

Archaeological light

In Rehoboam's fifth year Shishak (cf. 2 Chr 12:2-4) invaded Judah, and Israel as well. Archaeology shows Shishak is Sheshonk I of Egypt (c. 945-924 B.C.), founder of the Twenty-second Dynasty, whose gold-masked body was discovered at Tanis in 1938-39. His triumphal Karnak (Thebes) inscription lists towns taken in Judah as well as in Israel and Gilead. Part of his stele was excavated at Megiddo, showing that he actually took this city, as the Karnak relief shows.

Dynasties of Israel: Nine dynasties with 19 kings. Total reign 201 years, with average reign slightly over 10 years. All these kings were bad, with Ahab and his queen, Jezebel, the worst.

Dynasty of Judah: 20 kings, but only one dynasty, the Davidic, interrupted only by Athaliah, the usurper, who invaded the Davidic line by marriage for five years. Total reigns 335 years, with 16 average years per reign. The good kings included Asa, Jehoshaphat, Amaziah, Uzziah, Jotham, Hezekiah, and Josiah.

Jerusalem, and the other at Dan in the north, both ancient cultic centers. His two bull calves of gold were scarcely representations of Jehovah as a bull-god (though it is reminiscent of the golden calf of Aaron; see note on Ex 32:1-14), but like Israel's pagan neighbors, the deity was represented as standing on the back of an animal or on a throne borne by animals. The Lord was to be thought of as invisibly enthroned above the animal (cf. 1 Sam 4:4; 2 Kgs 19:15). The bull affiliations of Baal made this purely political plan dangerous and wicked.

13-14. Jeroboam's and Rehoboam's reigns

13:1-34. God sends a prophet to condemn Jeroboam's plan. The remarkable prophecy, 1-3, uttered by an unknown prophet, that Josiah would burn the bones of the priests on Jeroboam's false altar was fulfilled in 621 B.C. (2 Kgs 23:16-17). It served as a stinging rebuke to Jeroboam and his household, and incurred his subsequent vengeful displeasure, 4. The prophet resisted the king's attempt to get him to

Archaeological light

'Ben-Hadad son of Tabrimmon, the son of Hezion, king of Aram [Damascus],' 18, is attested on the inscribed stele of Ben-Hadad I discovered in N. Syria in 1940 (cf. *Bulletin of the American Schools* 87, October, 1942, pp. 23-29, 90; April, 1943, pp. 32-34).

compromise his directive from God, 5-10. But what the king could not do in dissuading the man of God from doing God's will an old prophet from Bethel accomplished by lying and deceit, 11-22. Disobedience brought immediate judgment on the prophet, 24, and bitter remorse to the one who had been used to tempt the Lord's messenger, 29-32. Jeroboam's impenitence sealed his doom, 33-34.

14:1-20. Jeroboam's punishment. God's disciplining hand of judgment fell on the king's son, his most precious possession. The boy's sickness led to a deceptive scheme to ascertain the future from Ahijah the prophet, 2-6. Ahijah learned of the plot and told the wife of Jeroboam that the king's house would be utterly destroyed because of adulterous disobedience and Israel would be sent into captivity, 7-16. The child died as the prophet foretold, 17-18.

14:21-31. Rehoboam's reign over Judah. This son of Solomon was a fool, driving the ten tribes to secede. He further showed his folly in his 17- year reign, which catapulted Judah from the glory it had enjoyed.

15:1-24. Abijah's and Asa's reigns

1-8. Abijah (cf. 2 Chr 13:1-12), had an unworthy reign of three years.

9-24. Asa's rule. He was a good king (c. 911- 870 B.C.), who bribed Ben-Hadad I of Syria to attack Israel to relieve him of Baasha's fortification of Ramah, a southern frontier fortress threatening Jerusalem's security. Asa cleansed the land of idolatry – pagan pillars, sun images, Asherah and male cult prostitutes.

15:25-16:28. Kings of Israel: Baasha to Omri

15:25-31. Nadab's reign over Israel. His was a short-lived, unworthy rule of two years.

15:32-16:7. Baasha warred with Asa and was cursed because of his idolatry and sin. He was buried in Tirzah, royal capital of Israel before Samaria was founded by Omri.

8-14. Elah was a drunkard. He reigned only two years.

15-20. Zimri was burned to death in his own house after a seven-day reign. Coup d'etats were common in this unsettled time in Israel. A rapid succession of kings struggled for dominance, with Omri finally consolidating his control over the kingdom.

21-28. Tibni and Omri. After the tragic death of Zimri, the people were divided, half following Tibni and half Omri. At the death of

Archaeological light

Omri's reign (c. 880-874 B.C.) ushered in a new era of Israelite power. He was an astute politician, cementing ties with Phoenicia to offset the Aramean commercial monopoly. The result was the marriage of his son to Jezebel, daughter of Ethbaal, king of the Sidonians (18:18). The Moabite Stone from Dibon discloses that it was Omri who conquered N. Moab. Omri's brilliant capital, Samaria, has been excavated. Periods 1 and 2 belong to Omri and Ahab. The foundations of his palace and other evidences attest he was the founder of the city (cf. *The Harvard Excavations at Samaria 1908-10*, 2 vols., 1924, and *The Buildings at Samaria*, 1942).

Omri's fame in the world of his day is attested by the Assyrians' reference to him on the Black Obelisk of Shalmaneser III over a century later in connection with King Jehu of Israel, who is styled 'son of [i.e., royal successor of] Omri,' although Jehu belonged to an entirely different dynasty. After Omri, Israel moreover is styled Bit-Humri ('house of Omri') in Assyrian cuneiform texts.

Tibni, Omri reigned over the entire nation. He was industrious, capable, energetic, and yet evil, founding the Omride dynasty (Ahab, Ahaziah and Joram). He built the new capital of Samaria, 24.

16:29-34. Ahab, king of Israel

29-34. Ahab was wise and effective as a ruler, but wicked and idolatrous. Ahab reigned 22 years at Samaria, the new capital of the Omride dynasty. He outstripped his predecessors in wickedness and shrewdness, erecting an altar to Baal, the great NW Semitic fertility god, in the Baal temple which he dared to build in Samaria, 32. He also made an Asherah, 33, a wooden pole symbolic of the Canaanite fertility goddess Asherah, known from the Ugaritic tablets discovered at Ras Shamra in N. Syria, 1929-37. This Canaanite goddess, mentioned some 40 times in the OT, was a snare to the Israelites, for her cult was viciously depraved. Ahab married Jezebel, a pagan princess and daughter of Ethbaal, 'king of the Sidonians,' 31, i.e., of the Phoenicians. This title reflects the earlier supremacy of Sidon following Tyre's assumption of commercial and political importance of the 11th cen. B.C. (cf. 1 Kgs 5:1, 5). On 34, cf. Josh 6:26. A detailed account of Ahab's reign is given in 17:1-22:40 because of the tremendous religious crisis it precipitated in Israel.

Omri's fame is attested by the Assyrians' reference to him on the Black Obelisk of Shalmaneser III in connection with King Jehu of Israel, who is styled 'son of Omri.'

Archaeological light

The Ugaritic texts from Ras Shamra (Ugarit), dating from the 14th cen. B.C., show Baal as the son of El, and the reigning king of the Canaanite pantheon, the god of the rain and the storm, whose voice thundered in the tempest. At Ugarit, Baal's consort was his sister Anath, but at Samaria in the 9th cen. B.C. Asherah appears as such (18:19). Like Anath, she was the patroness of sex and war. Snake worship, both male and female prostitution, child murder and sacrifice, and every conceivable vice were associated with Canaanite religion. Priests and prophets of Baal were official murderers of little children, and hence deserved death themselves (18:40).

The rebuilding of Jericho (16:34) is confirmed by archaeological diggings. Recent excavations trace the city's occupation from dim antiquity. Despite confusion in interpreting the evidence of Garstang's excavations of the fall of the city around 1400 B.C., the Bible stands confirmed on this point, with no occupational levels from Joshua's time to Ahab's era, when small ruins from the century point to Riel's rebuilding the site. It is noteworthy that at the rebuilding of Jericho, Joshua's prophecy was literally fulfilled as both the youngest and oldest children of Riel the Bethelite died.

17. Elijah before Ahab

1-7. Elijah's message to Ahab. Baal, the Phoenician storm god, was held by Ahab, Jezebel, and his other devotees to control the rain. Elijah ('my God is the Lord') abruptly announced to Ahab that Jehovah would be proved to be the one who does so. Elijah, of the town of Tishbe in Gilead, disappeared, directed by the Lord to a small stream E of the Jordan.

8-24. Elijah and the widow. After the brook dried up, Elijah was guided to the widow of Zarephath (Assyrian, *Sareptu,* 9, on the Phoenician coast, S of Sidon, N of Tyre) beyond Ahab's jurisdiction. Here the God-chosen destroyer of Baalism, whose God had power to shut the heavens for three and a half years, was miraculously fed by the ravens and then by the widow (cf. Jas 5:17). The widow's son was restored to life, 17-24. Unselfish devotion to God brings blessings of the choicest variety.

18. Elijah on Carmel

1-19. The question. The terrible three-and-one-half-year drought was about to end. Who withheld and would send the rain? 'Baal of the heavens' or the Lord? Obadiah ('servant of the Lord') showed his faith by saving the prophets of Jehovah whom Jezebel had designed for death, 3-16. Elijah met Ahab and called for the contest on Carmel, 17-19. The Baals were the local representatives of the great sky-god, 19. Asherah, Baal's consort, had 400 prophets and Baal 450, demonstrating the tremendous gain of Canaanite paganism under Ahab.

20-46. The contest. Elijah's faith was superb. He staked everything on Jehovah's answering by fire and rain, and both came. Jezebel, the wicked Phoenician queen, was unpersuaded and sought only to kill Elijah. Elijah uttered a masterful satire on idolatry, 27. Ritualistic gashing of the body, 28, was common (Deut 14:1; Lev 19:28; Jer 16:6; Hos 7:14). The struggle proved Jehovah's power. Elijah ran 17 miles to Jezreel, 46, Ahab's secondary capital (21:1), to herald complete victory of the worship of Jehovah over Baalism (cf. Isa 40:30-31).

19. Elijah at Horeb

1-14. Elijah's flight and despondency. Here the man of God demonstrated his fallibility by fleeing the wrath of Jezebel to Beersheba, 130 miles S of Jezreel, well into the territory of Judah and out of Jezebel's jurisdiction, 1-3. By divine assistance he reached Horeb, 4-8, also called Sinai, some 200 miles farther S, where the law had been revealed to Moses. There God also spoke to the distraught prophet, 9-18 (cf. Ex 33:17-23), rebuking him for being where he should not have been, 9, 13. What a contrast! Elijah the hero of faith on Carmel victorious over Baalism. Elijah the coward of unbelief at Horeb, self-occupied, utterly discouraged, wishing to die (cf. Rom 11:2-4).

15-21. The Lord's message. The Lord was not in the earthquake, wind, or fire but in the 'gentle whisper' of His revealed will, which probed the prophet's failure and directed him to finish his ministry.

Archaeological light

The Monolith Inscription of Shalmaneser III (859-824 B.C.), now in the British Museum, records Assyria's clash with a Syrian-Palestinian coalition at Qarqar, N of Hamath in the Orontes Valley, in 853 B.C. 'I crossed the Euphrates; at Qarqar I destroyed 1,200 chariots, 1,200 horsemen, and 20,000 men of Benhadad, and 2,000 chariots and 10,000 men of Ahab, the Israelite . . .'

20. Ahab's wars with Damascus

1-34. The siege of Samaria. The long-threatened attack from Syria came about five years before the end of Ahab's reign. Ben-Hadad suddenly besieged Samaria with a coalition of kings. Ahab's brilliant strategy won this battle and a later more decisive battle at Aphek, 22-34, E of the Sea of Galilee on the Bethshan-Damascus road.

35-43. The prophet's warning was focused upon Ahab's foolish release of his enemy (with whom he later allied himself to fight an advancing Assyria). The prophet's strategy of inducing Ahab to pronounce his own judgment is reminiscent of Nathan's interview with David after his sin with Bathsheba (2 Sam 12:1-15).

21. Ahab and Naboth's vineyard

1-16. Ahab murders Naboth. Naboth was religiously and legally right in keeping his ancestral property (cf. Lev 25:10-17, 23-24, 34). Ahab realized this. However, his wicked covetousness overpowered him. Jezebel scorned Israelite religious regulations, 5-7, and devised a diabolical plan to murder Naboth and take his vineyard, 8-14. Ahab was led to ruin by a wicked wife, 15-16.

17-29. Elijah's pronouncement of judgment. The dogs licked Ahab's blood at the place he had Naboth murdered, 19 (cf. 22:38), and dogs devoured Jezebel's body by the wall at Jezreel (2 Kgs 9:30-37). Jehoram, Ahab's son, also reaped the consequence of this curse, being murdered by Jehu at the same place (2 Kgs 9:25-26).

22. Ahab's death

1-28. Ahab and Jehoshaphat go up to Ramoth Gilead. They disregarded Micaiah's prophecy and listened to the 'lying spirit' of the false prophets, 23.

29-40. Ahab's death.

41-53. Jehoshaphat and Ahaziah. Cf. 2 Chr 17-20 and 2 Kgs 1:1-18.

The site of ancient Jericho. With no occupational levels from Joshua's time to Ahab's era, when small ruins from the century point to Riel's rebuilding, the Bible stands confirmed that the city was in ruins after Joshua's victory.

Chronology of the Dual Kingdoms

JUDAH

ISRAEL

Rehoboam
931-13

Jeroboam
931-10

Abijah
913-11

Asa
911-870

Nadab
910-9

Baasha
909-886

Jehoshaphat
873-48

Elah
886-85

Zimri
885

Tibni
885-80

Omri
885-74

Ahab
874-53

Jehoram
853-41

Ahaziah
841

Athaliah
841-35

Joash
835-796

Ahaziah
853-52

Jehoram
852-41

Jehu
841-14

Amaziah
796-67

Azariah
792-40

Jehoahaz
814-798

Jehoash
798-82

Jeoboam II
793-53

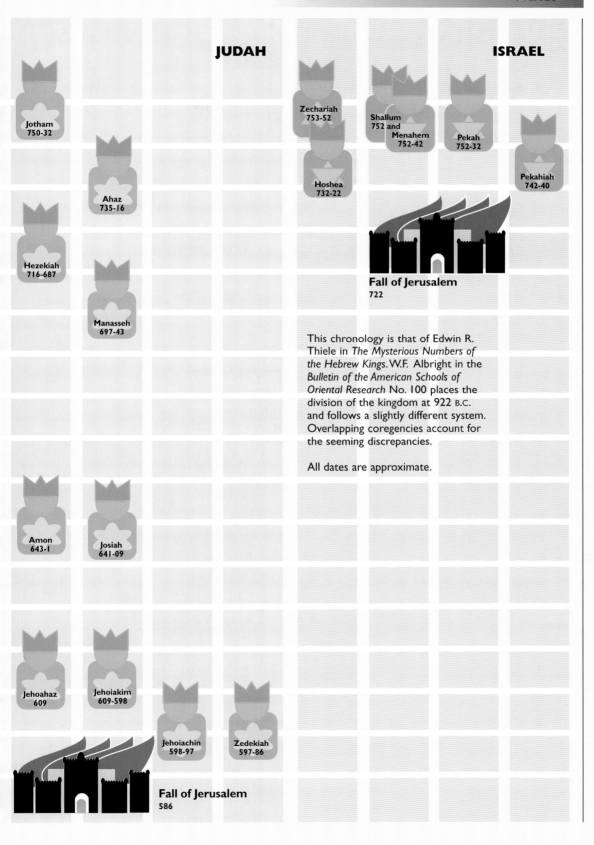

JUDAH

ISRAEL

Jotham
750-32

Zechariah
753-52

Shallum
752 and
Menahem
752-42

Pekah
752-32

Ahaz
735-16

Pekahiah
742-40

Hoshea
732-22

Hezekiah
716-687

Fall of Jerusalem
722

Manasseh
697-43

This chronology is that of Edwin R. Thiele in *The Mysterious Numbers of the Hebrew Kings*. W.F. Albright in the *Bulletin of the American Schools of Oriental Research* No. 100 places the division of the kingdom at 922 B.C. and follows a slightly different system. Overlapping coregencies account for the seeming discrepancies.

All dates are approximate.

Amon
643-1

Josiah
641-09

Jehoahaz
609

Jehoiakim
609-598

Jehoiachin
598-97

Zedekiah
597-86

Fall of Jerusalem
586

2 KINGS

The kingdom to the exiles

1 and 2 Kings in contrast

1 Kings	2 Kings
Begins with King David	Ends with the king of Babylon
Opens with Solomon's glory	Closes with Jehoiachin's shame
Begins with the blessings of obedience	Ends with the curse of disobedience
Opens with the building of the temple	Closes with the burning of the temple
Traces the progress of apostasy	Describes the consequences of apostasy
How kings failed to rule God's people	Consequences of that failure
Prophet Elijah introduced	Prophet Elisha presented
The long-suffering of the Lord	The Lord's sure punishment of sin

Outline

1:1-2:11 Elijah's final ministry
2:12-9:10 Elisha's ministry
9:11-17:41 From Jehu to Samaria's fall in 722 B.C.
18:1-25:30 Judah from 722 B.C. to the Exile

Ministries of the prophets. During this period Hosea and Amos prophesied in Israel. Joel, Micah, Isaiah, Obadiah, Nahum, Habakkuk, Zephaniah and Jeremiah prophesied in Judah.
Period covered. About the middle of the 9th to nearly the middle of the 6th cen. B.C.

Assyrian spearmen

1. Elijah and Ahaziah

1-18. Ahaziah's sickness and death.
Coregent with his father, a Baal devotee, Ahaziah preferred Baal to the Lord. Baal-zebub ('lord of flies') was a manifestation of the great Canaanite Baal, as worshiped at Philistine Ekron. It was an intentional distortion of Baal-zebul ('lord of the divine abode'), the epithet later being associated with Satan in Jewish theology (Mt 10:25; 12:24; Mk 3:22; Lk 11:15-19). Elijah's appearance, 3-8; the fate of Ahaziah's messengers, 9-15; and Elijah's word of doom to the Baal-worshiping king for consulting the pagan priests of the Philistines rather than the God of Israel, 16, are recorded.

17-18. Jehoram's accession. This last king of the Omride dynasty must not be confused with Jehoram, the son of Jehoshaphat, king of Judah (8:16-18, 25-27).

2. Elisha and the translation of Elijah

1-11. Translation of Elijah. The prophet of fire (1 Kgs 18:38; 2 Kgs 1:10, 12) was translated to heaven by a 'chariot of fire and horses of fire,' 11-12. Enoch (Gen 5:24; Heb 11:5) and Elijah (Mt 17:3-4) were the only two men ever to be translated without dying. This Gilgal, 1, was N of Bethel. The term 'company of the prophets,' 3, 5, 7, 15, means members of the prophetic order. 'Father' was an ancient title of a man of God, 12.

A 'double portion of your spirit,' 9, indicates the role of spiritual heir. In Deut 21:17 the firstborn was granted a double portion of the inheritance (i.e., if there are four sons, the property is divided into five parts and the firstborn receives two-fifths). The double portion does not mean Elisha had or did twice as much, though it has been noted that Scripture records approximately twice as many miracles in Elisha's ministry. This request was granted as Elijah's mantle fell on Elisha, 12-15.

12-25. Double portion upon Elisha.
The waters of the Jordan were divided, 14. The spring at Jericho was healed, 22. The idolatrous children at Bethel were killed by bears, 24, which God sent to punish the taunting of Elisha's God, not Elisha. Today the name of Elisha is attached to the finest spring in Jericho, Elisha's Fountain.

3. Elisha and Jehoram

1-20. Revolt of Moab. In Jehoram's (Joram's) reign (852-841 B.C.) Moab revolted and refused to pay tribute in lambs and wool, 1-8. The famous Moabite Stone, a Louvre treasure, discovered in 1868, gives a remarkable account of the war from the viewpoint of the Moabite king Mesha. Jehoram's plan required Judah's aid and that of its vassal Edom (1 Kgs 22:47), as the plan was to attack Moab from the rear. Elisha, who 'used to pour water on the hands of Elijah' when he washed, 11, denoting

Olive groves and distant hills viewed from the site of ancient Samaria. In the time of Elisha, Syria besieged the city.

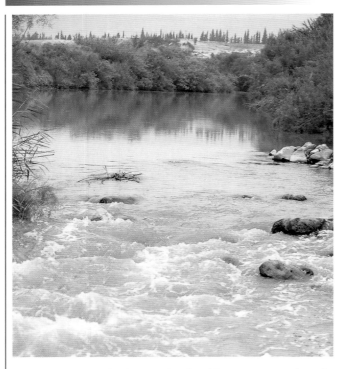

4. Four miracles of Elisha

1-7. The widow's oil increased. The section 4:1-8:6 breaks the synchronized story of the reigns of the Judahite and Israelite kings and constitutes an interlude dealing with Elisha's miracle-working ministry. In Israel a child could be sold into servitude for debt (Ex 21:7; Deut 15:12-18; Lev 25:9-34; cf. Jer 34:8-16; cf. Elijah's miracle, 1 Kgs 17:14-16).

8-37. The Shunammite woman's son raised from death. The woman lived in Shunem, about five miles N of Jezreel. Not only did she conceive a son late in life, according to God's word through Elisha, 8-17, but the lad was raised from death, 18-37. (Cf. Elijah's parallel miracle, 1 Kgs 17:17-24. Cf. also Heb 11:35.)

38-41. The poisonous stew healed. The meal, cast into the stew to counteract the poisonous wild gourds (probably colocynths, a strong laxative that is poisonous in large quantities), portrays God's power to remove evil. Through our faith He is able to remove the evil in us.

42-44. Bread multiplied, finds its striking parallel in our Lord's ministry (Mt 14:13-21; 15:32-38).

5. Elisha and Naaman

1-19. Naaman's healing. Naaman ('pleasant') is a picture of the natural man, enjoying the highest and best but unregenerate. 'But he had leprosy,' 1; leprosy vividly illustrates sin. The testimony of the captive Israelite maid was effective and Naaman went to the king of Israel for healing with 'ten talents of silver, six thousand shekels of gold,' 2-7. Naaman appears as a proud man, hurt by Elisha's curt directions to wash seven times in muddy Jordan, 8-12. His compliance is parallel to the proud sinner who accepts God's self-humbling way of salvation by grace and is cleansed of sin, 13-14, and saved, 15-19. Naaman's desire to take home 'as much earth as a pair of mules can carry' from Israel, 17, was due to his wrong idea that a god could not be worshiped apart from his own land. His official position required him to give lip service to Rimmon, the chief god of Syria, called also Hadad, but Naaman was really healed and saved. (Cf. Lk 4:25-27.)

20-27. Gehazi's sin and punishment. Covetousness earned Gehazi the leprosy from which grace had delivered the Syrian Gentile. The

that he waited on him like a servant, prophesied a divine supply of water and victory of the coalition over Moab, 10-20.

21-27. Defeat of Moab. The dry stream bed, 16, likely the brook of Zered (Deut 2:13), separating Edom from Moab, filled with pools and reflecting the rising sun and the red sandstone of Edom (Gen 25:30), was taken for blood. Mesha's sacrifice of his eldest son to Chemosh on the wall in plain sight of Israel, 26-27, filled the attackers with such horror that they returned to their own land without exploiting to the full their victory. This again was unbelief on their part. Human sacrifice was outlawed in Israel (Ex 22:29-30; 34:20; Deut 18:10), but was wickedly resorted to at times (2 Kgs 16:3; 21:6).

Archaeological light

The Moabite Stone, set up by King Mesha of Moab at Dibon, N of the Arnon, about 840 B.C., discloses the prominence of Chemosh, the national god of Moab. 'I am Mesha, son of Chemosh ... king of Moab, the Dibonite ... Omri, king of Israel ... oppressed Moab many days because Chemosh was angry with his land. And his son succeeded him, and he said, I will oppress Moab ...'

THE FLIGHT OF ELIJAH

Mount Carmel

Jezreel

Beersheba

Salt Sea

Elijah hears a whisper in a cave in Sinai
(1 Kings 19:4–18)

To Damascus

Mount Horeb

RED SEA

Sidon

Zarephath

Elijah raises the widow's son
(1 Kings 17:9)

Damascus

Elisha anoints Hazael king of Syria
(2 Kings 8:7–15)

Tyre

PHOENICIA

ARAM

G R E A T   S E A

Elisha raises child of the Shunammite woman
(2 Kings 4)

Aphek

Sea of Chinnereth

Mount Carmel

Kishon

Shunem

Elijah defeats prophets of Baal
(1 Kings 18:30–40)

Jezreel

Birthplace of Elijah (1 Kings

Ramoth-gilead (853 BCE)

Elijah flees from Jezebel
(1 Kings 18:41–46)

Dothan

Cherith

Abel-meholah

Tishbe

Elijah is fed by ravens
(1 Kings 17:3–5)

Samaria

Elisha prophesies lifting of the siege of Samaria (2 Kings 6–7)

ISRAEL

Jordan R.

Elisha cures Naaman of leprosy (2 Kings 5:8–14)

Elisha purifies poisoned food
(2 Kings 4:38–41)

AMMON

Bethel

Gilgal

Jericho

Elisha picks up mantle of Elijah
(2 Kings 2:1–9)

Jerusalem

Elijah ascends to heaven
(2 Kings 2:1–11)

Elisha purifies water
(2 Kings 2:23)

PHILISTIA

JUDAH

Beer-sheba

Salt Sea

MOAB

NEGEB

E D O M

Elijah and Elisha

Ezion-geber

Borders of Israel and Judah during the reigns of Omri and Jehoshaphat

conflict

0   25   50   75 km

0   15   30   45 miles

Above: Israelite remains at Samaria, capital of Jeroboam II.

Opposite: Several panels from the Black Obelisk of Shalmaneser III, which Layard found in the palace at Nimrod.

salvation that is greater than Elisha's has been accepted by the Gentiles, while those so closely connected with the Saviour (Israel) have hardened their hearts (Rom 11:1-25).

6-7. Elisha and other miracles

6:1-7. The floating ax head. Elisha recovered the iron ax head.

6:8-23. The Syrian army blinded and captured by Elisha's prayers. Dothan, some ten miles N of Samaria, has been excavated by J.P. Free of Wheaton College in Illinois.

6:24-7:20. Repulse of the Syrian siege of Samaria by Elisha's prophecy was fulfilled by the Lord's intervention.

8. Elisha and Hazael

1-6. Elisha again aids the woman of Shunem. Her story is continued from 4:8-37. Elisha predicted famine, 1-2, and sent her into Philistia (cf. Gen 26:1), where Isaac too had gone for the same reason. Elisha's influence restored her homestead in Shunem.

7-15. Elisha's prediction of Ben-Hadad's death and Hazael's usurpation. Hazael was divinely chosen to punish Israel for her sins, so Elisha wept, 11. Hazael became king of Syria as predicted (cf. 1 Kgs 19:15-16; Hos 13-16).

16-29. Jehoram's and Ahaziab's reigns in Judah. Athaliah was Jehoram's wife. The 'lamp' was symbolic of the permanence of the Davidic dynasty, 19 (cf. 2 Sam 21:17; 1 Kgs 11:36; 15:4). Jehoram (Joram) was followed by his son Ahaziah, whose mother was Athaliab. Jehoram reigned 852-841 B.C., Ahaziah in 841.

9-10. Jehu's reign

9:1-37. Elisha has Jehu anointed. Jehu had a long reign, *c.* 841-814 B.C. He was anointed (cf. 1 Kgs 19:15-16) as the rough instrument for the bloody task of exterminating the house of Ahab and Baalism. The latter was so unspeakably and viciously cruel that a person of Jehu's relentless thoroughness was necessary. Joram, Ahaziah and Jezebel were liquidated. Zimri, 31, was a brutal murderer (1 Kgs 16:8-12).

10:1-36. Jehu's purge continued. By cleverness and ruthlessness Jehu wiped out the entire house of Ahab, 'seventy sons,' 1, no doubt including grandsons, as well as the worshipers of Baal, 11. Jehonadab, the Rechabite ('Son of Recab'), 15-17, joined the purge. The Rechabites were a simple-living people who strictly maintained the desert life-style, avoiding the corruption of urban living (1 Chr 2:55; Jer 35). Jehu in his extermination of the priests and worshipers of Baal, 18-27, was similar to Elijah in zeal but a contrast to him in subtlety. Hazael's cruel career begins, 32-33.

11. Athaliah's reign in Judah

1-16. Athaliah's usurpation and death. Ironically Jehu's attempted eradication of the house of Ahab in Israel resulted in the temporary

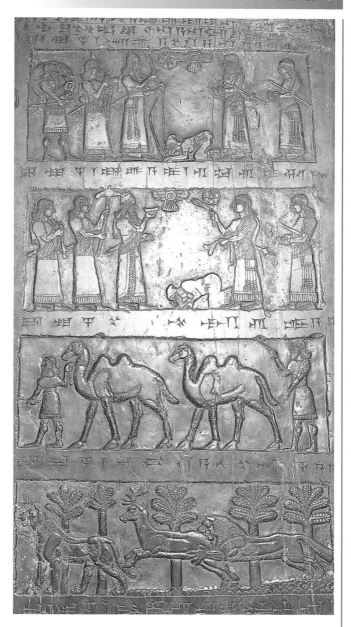

seizure of the throne of Judah by one who was not
only a member of Ahab's family but a Baal
devotee, 18. Jehosheba who saved Joash, the son
of Ahaziah, was not Athaliah's daughter, and
hence only a half sister of Ahaziah. She was wife
of the high priest Jehoiada (2 Chr 22:11), and
taught the young royal heir the Word of the Lord.
Jehoiada led the revolt, crowning Joash king, 4-
12, and ordering Athaliah killed, 13-16. The
'Carites,' 4, 19, perhaps a variant for Kerethites
(cf. 1 Sam 30:14; 2 Sam 8:18), were foreign
mercenaries.

17-21. Jehoiada's revival. The common
people, loyal to Jehovah, destroyed the temple of
Baal, 17-18.

12. Joash king of Judah

1-16. Repair of the temple. Joash (*c.*
835-796 B.C.) had a controversy with the priests
over the repair of the temple, 4-8. The new system
of collection, 9-16, secured the funds for repairs,
but not for replacements (cf. 2 Chr 24:7).

17-21. Joash's declension and death.
Joash bought off Hazael by despoiling the temple,
17-18. For his further spiritual decline and his
killing of Jehoiada's son, see 2 Chr 24:17-22.
Joash's own servants conspired against him and
slew him, 19-21.

13. Jehoahaz and Jehoash, kings of Israel

1-9. Jehoahaz' reign. Jehoahaz (*c.* 814-
798 B.C.), son of Jehu, was weak, and Israel was
brought very low by Hazael of Syria. He followed
the bull worship at Dan and Bethel. The Asherah,
6, was a replica of the Canaanite fertility goddess.

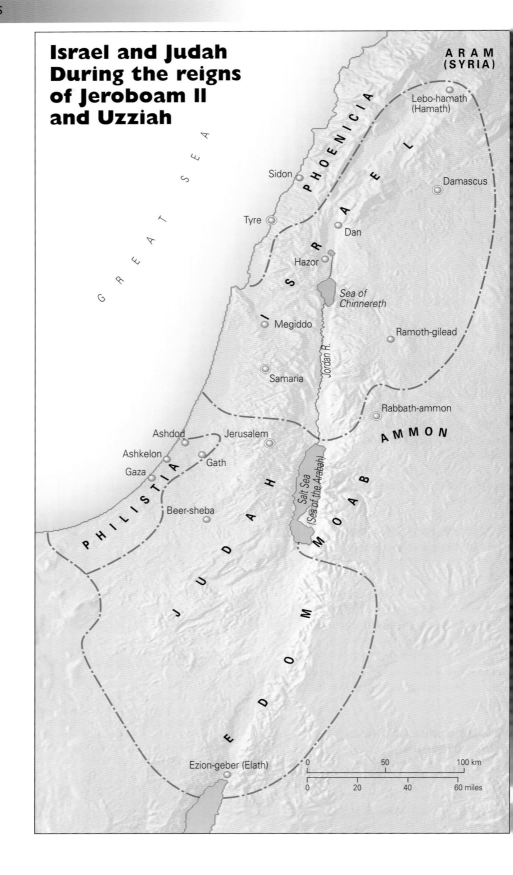

Israel and Judah During the reigns of Jeroboam II and Uzziah

ARAM (SYRIA)

GREAT SEA

PHOENICIA

ISRAEL

Lebo-hamath (Hamath)

Sidon

Damascus

Tyre

Dan

Hazor

Sea of Chinnereth

Megiddo

Ramoth-gilead

Jordan R.

Samaria

Rabbath-ammon

AMMON

Ashdod

Jerusalem

Ashkelon

Gath

Gaza

PHILISTIA

Salt Sea (Sea of the Arabah)

MOAB

Beer-sheba

JUDAH

EDOM

Ezion-geber (Elath)

0		50		100 km
0	20		40	60 miles

Relief of Tiglath-pileser III, the Assyrian king who invaded Israel, from Calah, Assyria.

10-25. Jehoash's reign. Jehoash, also called Joash (*c.* 798-782 B.C.), warred successfully both against Syria and Judah and reestablished Israel as a real power for his son Jeroboam II (*c.* 793-753 B.C.). The death of Elisha is recounted, 20-21.

14. Amaziah of Judah and Jeroboam II

1-22. Reign of Amaziah of Judah. Amaziah put to death the assassins of his father, 5-6 (cf. Ex 20:5, Deut 5:9-10; 24:16); subdued Edom, 7; and was defeated by Jehoash of Israel, 8-14. He reigned *c.* 796-767 B.C.

23-29. Jeroboam II of Israel reigned *c.* 793-753 B.C. and advanced the power of Israel against Damascus, lifting the northern kingdom to the height of its strength and prosperity. This conquest of Syria, 28, was possible because of the comparative weakness of Assyria.

15. Uzziah and Jotham; Zachariah to Pekah

1-7. Azariah (Uzziah) of Judah, like Jeroboam II of Israel, had a long and prosperous reign, *c.* 792-740 B.C. (see 2 Chr 26:6-15). When the king became a leper because of his intrusion into the priesthood, his son Jotham became

regent, 5. An inscription on limestone found at Jerusalem from the 1st cen. A.D. reads: 'Hither were brought the bones of Uzziah, king of Judah: not to be opened.' Jotham ruled *c.* 750-732 B.C. Tiglath-pileser III refers in his Annals to *Azriyau of Yaudu* (Azariah of Judah) in connection with a western coalition of kings.

8-22. Zachariah, Shallum and Menahem in Israel (about 753-742 B.C.). Jeroboam II's son Zachariah reigned only six months in *Samaria* (753/752 B.C.) and was assassinated by Shallum, thus ending the Jehu dynasty, 8-12 (cf. 10:30). Shallum, the usurper, reigned only a month, and in turn was murdered by Menahem, 13-22, who reigned *c.* 752-742 B.C. The horrible practice of disembowelling pregnant women (8:12; Hos 13:16; Amos 1:13) shows the bestiality of ancient warfare and Menahem's character.

23-26. Pekahiah's reign lasted only two years (742-740 B.C.).

27-31. Pekah's reign (*c.* 740-733; coregent 752-740). The '20 years' of 27 evidently indicate a coregency. Tiglath-pileser, who overran northern Galilee, refers to Pekah, Israel's king, in his records.

32-38. Jotham's reign. Rezin of Syria became a menace.

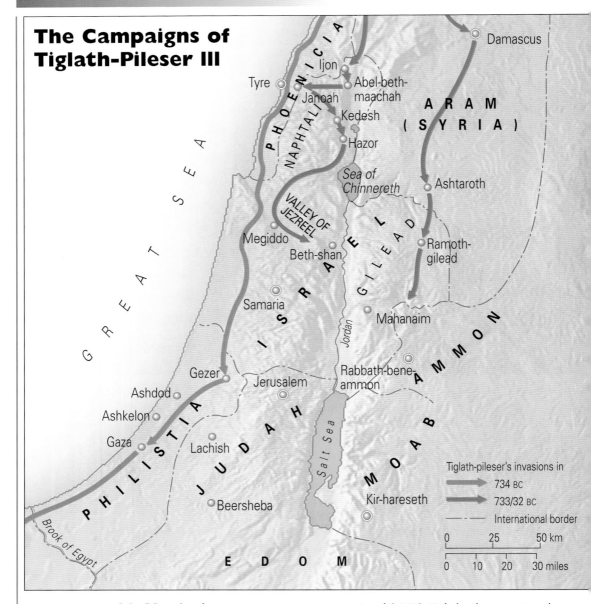

The Campaigns of Tiglath-Pileser III

Tiglath-pileser's invasions in
→ 734 BC
→ 733/32 BC
- - - International border

0   25   50 km

0   10   20   30 miles

16. Ahaz' reign

1-4. Ahaz' idolatries. Reigning c. 735-716, Ahaz revived Canaanite idolatry, including the horrible practice of child sacrifice (see 3:27; cf. Ex 34:20; Deut 18:10). For Ahaz' apostasy, see 2 Chr 28.

5-8. His appeal to Assyria. The Syro-Ephraimite war (2 Chr 28:5-8) displayed Ahaz' idolatrous perfidy when he appealed to Assyria for help (2 Chr 28:16-21) despite God's promise of assistance (Isa 7: 1-17). The king of Assyria, happy to be magnanimously compensated by the foolish Ahaz for what he planned to do anyhow, destroyed Damascus 732 B.C., and devastated

Israel (15:29). Tiglath-pileser mentions these events in his Annals.

9-20. His trip to Damascus, to pay homage to Tiglath-pileser III, further demonstrated his idolatrous folly.

17. Fall of the Northern Kingdom

1-23. Hoshea's reign. The last king of Israel (732-722 B.C.), Hoshea was dominated and heavily taxed by Assyria. He was imprisoned for conspiracy with Egypt, his capital Samaria was besieged, and its citizens carried captive 722 B.C. The 200-year old northern kingdom collapsed,

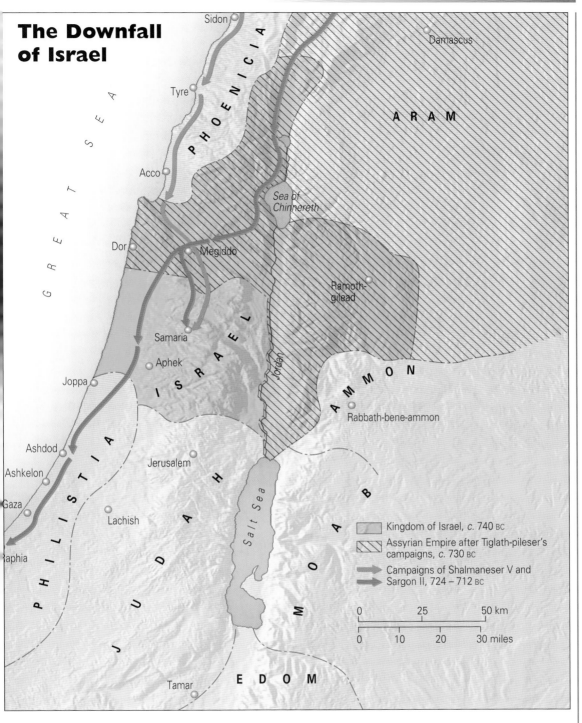

The Downfall of Israel

Sidon

Damascus

Tyre

PHOENICIA

ARAM

GREAT SEA

Acco

Sea of Chinnereth

Dor

Megiddo

Ramoth-gilead

Samaria

ISRAEL

Aphek

Joppa

Jordan

AMMON

Rabbath-bene-ammon

Ashdod

Jerusalem

Ashkelon

H

Salt Sea

B

Gaza

PHILISTIA

Lachish

J U D A H

A

O

Raphia

M

Kingdom of Israel, c. 740 BC

Assyrian Empire after Tiglath-pileser's campaigns, c. 730 BC

Campaigns of Shalmaneser V and Sargon II, 724 – 712 BC

0		25		50 km

0	10	20	30 miles

Tamar

E D O M

the result of its incurable apostasies, 7-23.

24-41. Assyria repopulates Israel.
Sargon's own records substantiate v. 24. '[The cities] I set up again and made more populous than before. People from lands which I had taken I settled there.' The country became known as Samaria (not Israel), its mixed population Samaritans, 29. Its worship became a syncretism of foreign cults, 34-40. Cf. the Jewish attitude originating here which continued into NT times (Ezr 4:1-4; Lk 10:33; 17:16-18; Jn 4:9; 8:48).

18.Hezekiah and Sennacherib's invasion

1-12. Hezekiah's reforms. His actual reign, not including coregency, was *c.* 716-687 B.C. Events listed here are doubtless to be placed in the coregency with Ahaz, such as Samaria's fall, 9-12. Hezekiah destroyed the Asherim or wooden poles symbolic of the Canaanite fertility goddess Asherah and the bronze serpent (Num 21:6-9). Because Baal religion had the serpent symbol, the bronze serpent (Nehushtan) had pagan associations and was abused.

13-37. Sennacherib's attack. See Isa 36. Aramaic was the language of Syria, 26, which in Palestine largely superseded Hebrew after the Exile.

19-20. Hezekiah and Isaiah

19:1-37. Hezekiah consults Isaiah. See Isa 37. Sennacherib was finally assassinated by his sons.

20:1-21. Hezekiah's sickness. See Isa 38-39.

21. Manasseh's and Amon's reigns

1-18. Manasseh's idolatrous orgy. Hezekiah's son Manasseh (696-642 B.C.), in stark contrast to his father, bent every effort to pervert the Hebrew faith by complete idolatrous contamination (cf. 2 Chr 33:1-20). The Baal cult included wildly licentious dances on wooded hilltops called 'high places,' 3. Baal's consort Asherah was the goddess of fertility. Snake worship, male and female prostitutes, planetary worship, human sacrifices and all kinds of demon-inspired pagan occultism constituted features of this horrible apostasy.

Archaeological light

It was customary in ancient times to deposit documents in foundations of buildings. Nabonidus, a Babylonian king of the 6th cen. B.C., delighted to dig into foundations of buildings to recover early documents, doing so at the temple of Shamash in Lower Mesopotamia. Doubtless masonry in the Solomonic temple had so cracked that this stone had to be replaced, and the books of Moses, which had been deposited there for three and one-half centuries, came to light.

Archaeological light

Piles of ashes and infant skeletons in cemeteries around heathen altars attest child murder in the name of religion. Archaeology has uncovered incantation tablets, exorcistic rituals, and abundant evidence of demon-inspired occultism in antiquity. For Manasseh and references to him in Assyrian inscriptions see 2 Chr 33.

19-26. Amon's reign. Wicked like his father, Amon was murdered.

22-23. Josiah's reign

22:1-20. Repairing the temple and finding the book of the law. Josiah's long and godly reign lasted *c.* 640-608 B.C. Unminted metal (money) was collected to repair the temple (cf. 2 Kgs 12:4-16). This was 621 B.C. The outstanding event of Josiah's reign was the discovery of the book of the law, 8-10, precipitating great reformation and revival, 22:11-23:37. It is consonant with the evidence to believe this scroll was 'the law of Moses,' i.e., the Pentateuch, copies of which during Manasseh's idolatrous reign had been destroyed. This recovery of the Pentateuch, placed in the cornerstone when Solomon's temple was erected (*c.* 966 B.C.), was due to the extensive repairs of workmen. Critical scholarship links this discovery with the book of Deuteronomy, which they allege had recently been written as a 'pious fraud' by members of the prophetic school. Little textual or historical support is now available for this cornerstone of the Documentary Hypothesis.

23:1-30. Reforms and death of Josiah. Historians used to wonder why Josiah advanced against Neco, 29, when the Pharaoh was evidently on his way to attack Assyria. The Babylonian Chronicle has put the whole matter in a new light and shows that Neco went to the Assyrian's aid, so that v. 29 should be translated: '. . . Neco . . . went up *to* [not *against*] the king of Assyria to the river Euphrates.'

23:31-37. Jehoahaz and Jehoiakim. Both were evil and were dominated by Pharaoh Neco of Egypt (609 B.C.). Jehoiakim reigned 609-598 B.C.

24. Jehoiachin and Zedekiah

1-17. Fall of Jerusalem and the first deportation. Egyptian control of Judah was lost at the battle of Carchemish (605 B.C.) when the Neo-Babylonians (Chaldeans) defeated both the Assyrians and Egyptians, 1-7. Jehoiachin thus rebelled against Nebuchadnezzar of Neo-Babylonia. Jehoiakim, the father, had died in 598 B.C. and his young son Jehoiachin assumed the shaky throne. On March 16, 597 B.C., in Nebuchadnezzar's seventh year (Jer 52:28), Jehoiachin surrendered to the Babylonian monarch, as told in cuneiform sources, 10-17 (see 25:27-30).

18-20. Zedekiah made king, ruling 597-586 B.C. He was Jehoiachin's uncle Mattaniah; later called Zedekiah in token of his servitude.

25. Jerusalem's destruction and the Babylonian exile

1-21. Zedekiah's rebellion. Despite his oath of allegiance (2 Chr 36:13), Zedekiah began to plot with Egypt and other nations. The result was that Jerusalem was laid under terrible siege and fell in 586 B.C. after frightful famine. The city was burned and the inhabitants deported or slain (cf. Jer 52:29). Temple equipment of any value was carried to Babylon, 13-17. Jeremiah gives many other details, but surprisingly the prophet is not mentioned in 2 Kings.

22-26. Gedaliah's governorship. His murder brought chaos and ruin (cf. Jer 40-42).

27-30. Jehoiachin's release. After being a political prisoner for 37 years in Babylon, Jehoiachin was set free by Nebuchadnezzar II's successor, Evil-Merodach (Amel-Marduk, Akkadian, 'man of Marduk'), 562-560 B.C. A vase from Susa corroborates this king and reads: 'Palace of Amel-Marduk, king of Babylon, son of Nebuchadnezzar, king of Babylon.' Babylonian records list 'Yaukin king of the land of Yahud,' i.e., Jehoiachin of Judah, as one of the recipients of royal rations. He was still considered king of Judah, even by the Babylonians themselves. Jar handles from Tell Beit Mirsim and Bethshemesh found in 1928-36 are stamped 'Eliakim steward of Yaukin' (Jehoiachin), evidencing the fact that the exiled king was recognized as rightful sovereign by the people of Judah also.

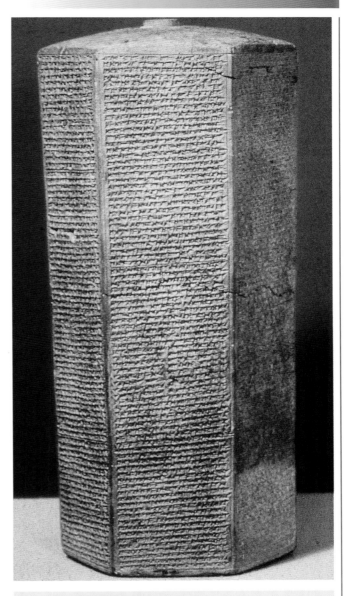

Archaeological light

The Taylor Prism in the British Museum describes Sennacherib's attack on Hezekiah's realm: 'As for Hezekiah, the Jew, who did not submit to my yoke, 46 of his strong walled cities ... I besieged and took ... Himself, like a caged bird, I shut up in Jerusalem, his royal city ... As for Hezekiah, the terrifying splendor of my majesty overcame him ...' It is noteworthy Sennacherib did not claim to have captured the city, and made as good a story out of the siege.

The destruction of the Assyrian army, 35, has been connected by some with a plague carried by field mice. Herodotus mentions such an onslaught in which the Assyrians suffered defeat on the borders of Egypt because the mice chewed up their bowstrings and leather equipment. Tirhakah, 9, was then a general, who later became king (690 B.C.).

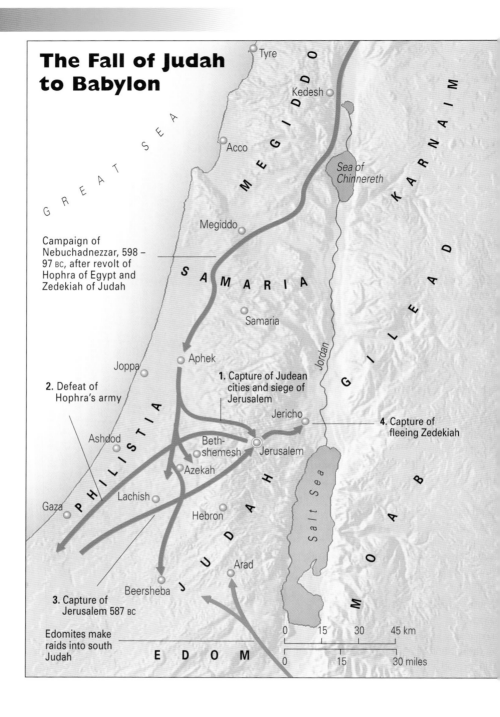

The Fall of Judah to Babylon

Tyre

Kedesh

G R E A T   S E A

M E G I D D O

Acco

Sea of Chinnereth

K A R N A I M

Megiddo

Campaign of Nebuchadnezzar, 598 – 97 BC, after revolt of Hophra of Egypt and Zedekiah of Judah

S A M A R I A

Samaria

G I L E A D

Jordan

Joppa

Aphek

1. Capture of Judean cities and siege of Jerusalem

Jericho

2. Defeat of Hophra's army

4. Capture of fleeing Zedekiah

Ashdod

P H I L I S T I A

Beth-shemesh

Jerusalem

H

Azekah

Salt Sea

Lachish

Gaza

J U D A H

Hebron

M O A B

Arad

3. Capture of Jerusalem 587 BC

Beersheba

Edomites make raids into south Judah

E D O M

| 0 | 15 | 30 | 45 km |

| 0 | 15 | 30 miles |

Assyria

Pekah and Hoshea. Tiglath-pileser on an inscription says: 'Pekah, their king, they had overthrown. I placed Hoshea over them. From him I received 10 talents of gold and 1,000 talents of silver.' Cf. 15:30; 17:3.

Shalmaneser V (726-722 B.C.) was the Assyrian emperor who began the siege of Samaria (cf. 17:3), being the son and successor of Tiglath-pileser III. Apart from Scripture he is known from a single inscription that memorializes his restoration of Nabu's temple at Borsippa in Babylonia '. . . its damage I repaired and strengthened the structure.' He imprisoned Hoshea for conspiracy with So (Sibe), a petty king of the east Delta of Egypt, 17:3-6. It is noteworthy that neither 2 Kgs 18:9-11 nor 2 Kgs 17:3-6 states that Shalmaneser himself actually took Samaria. 'And at the end of three years they [the Assyrians, i.e. under Sargon II] took it [the city].'

Sargon II (722-705 B.C.) actually took Samaria in the opening months of 722 B.C. after Shalmaneser's death. 'At the beginning of my rule, in my first year of reign . . . Samerinai [the people of Samaria] . . . 27,290 . . . who lived therein, I carried away . . .' In Sargon's 'Display Inscription' at Khorsabad, where Sargon's royal palace was discovered by Paul Emil Botta in 1843, the emperor says: 'I besieged and captured Samaria, carrying off 27,290 of the people who dwelt therein . . . I caused others to take their [the deported inhabitants'] portion. I set my officers over them and imposed upon them the tribute of the former king.' Before modern archaeology, Sargon's name in extant literature appeared only in the Bible and that only once (Isa 20:1). Now critics who impugned the Bible on this point are not only silenced, but must confess him one of the greatest and most powerful rulers of antiquity. Another Sargon inscription actually says: 'Azuri, king of Ashdod, planned in his heart not to pay tribute. In my anger I conquered Ashdod, Gath. I settled in them people from the lands of the east. I received tribute from Philistia, Judah, Edom, and Moab.'

Below: Assyrian queen feasting with attendants, from Nineveh, capital of Assyria.

The Assyrian Empire

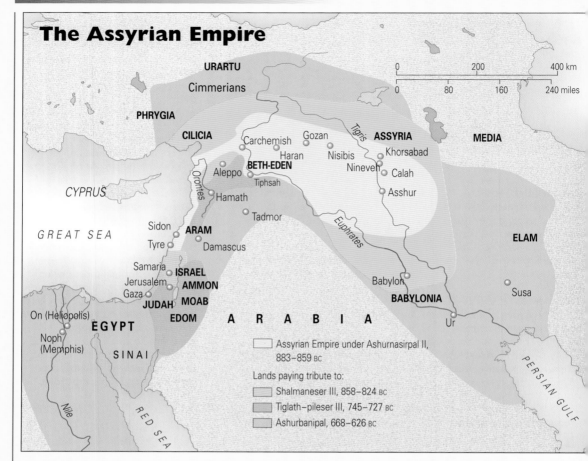

URARTU

Cimmerians

PHRYGIA

CILICIA

Carchemish Gozan ASSYRIA MEDIA
Haran Nisibis Khorsabad
Aleppo BETH-EDEN Nineveh Calah
Tiphsah
Hamath Asshur

CYPRUS

Orontes

Tadmor

GREAT SEA Sidon ARAM ELAM
Tyre Damascus

Samaria ISRAEL
Jerusalem AMMON Babylon Susa
Gaza MOAB BABYLONIA
JUDAH EDOM A R A B I A Ur

On (Heliopolis) EGYPT

Noph SINAI
(Memphis)

Nile

RED SEA

PERSIAN GULF

Tigris

Euphrates

0   200   400 km
0   80   160   240 miles

☐ Assyrian Empire under Ashurnasirpal II,
883–859 BC

Lands paying tribute to:
☐ Shalmaneser III, 858–824 BC
☐ Tiglath–pileser III, 745–727 BC
☐ Ashurbanipal, 668–626 BC

The Assyrian people
Asshur and Assyria's beginning. Located 60 miles S of Nineveh on the west bank of the Tigris River, this site (present-day Qalat Sharqat) was the original center of Assyrian power (c. 3000 B.C.). Named after Asshur, the national god of Assyria, the capital became the hub of the later Assyrian Empire and gave its name to the 'giant among the Semites.' Assyria was founded by colonists from Babylonia and periodically dominated the Tigris-Euphrates Valley. Tiglath-pileser I (c. 1115 B.C.) made it a great nation, but it declined during the Davidic-Solomonic era, 1010-931 B.C., making possible their empire.

The mighty Assyrian Empire (885-612 B.C.). Its capital was Nineveh. See the book of Nahum.

Ashurnasipal II (885-860 B.C.). His formidable fighting machine extended Assyrian might to the Mediterranean.

Shalmaneser III (859-824 B.C.) was the first Assyrian king to clash with Israel. Ahab fought against him with Ben-Hadad at Qarqar (853 B.C.). Jehu paid tribute to him.

Shamsi-Adad V (924-811 B.C.), Adadnirari III (810-783 B.C.) and several weak emperors till 747 B.C. enabled Uzziah of Judah and Jeroboam II of Israel to rule long and prosperously.

Tiglath-pileser III (745-727 B.C.), 'Pul,' carried northern Israel into exile, 734 B.C. Shalmaneser V (727-722 B.C.) besieged Samaria.

Sargon II (722-705 B.C.) took Samaria in 722 B.C.

Sennacherib (705-681 B.C.) was a great conqueror, but failed to take Jerusalem.

Esarhaddon (681-669 B.C.) rebuilt Babylonia and conquered Egypt.

Ashurbanipal (669-c.626 B.C.), Asnapper (Ezr 4:10), was the last great emperor. The period 626-607 B.C. witnessed the disintegration and fall of this cruel empire.

Assyrian annals mention contacts with some nine Hebrew kings: Omri, Ahab, Jehu, Menahem, Pekah, Uzziah, Ahaz, Hezekiah and Manasseh. Assyrian cruelty was proverbial and the Hebrews suffered severely at the hands of the Assyrian kings.

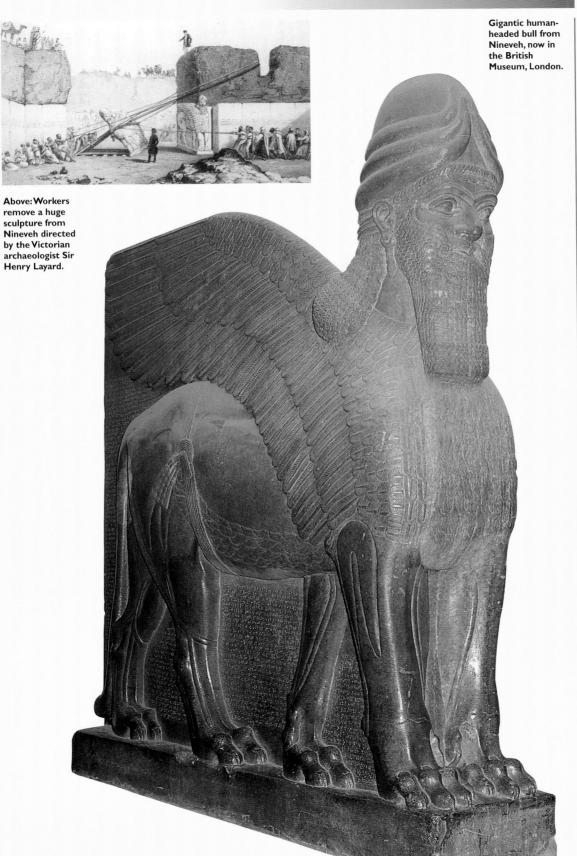

Gigantic human-headed bull from Nineveh, now in the British Museum, London.

Above: Workers remove a huge sculpture from Nineveh directed by the Victorian archaeologist Sir Henry Layard.

I CHRONICLES

The reign of David

Name and author. The name 'Chronicles' is from the Vulgate *Liber Chronicorum* ('book of Chronicles'). The Hebrew title is *Dibrî Hayyammîm* ('events of the times'). The Greek *Paraleipomena* signifies 'things left over', i.e., from the books of Kings. The author is unknown, but may have been Ezra. The date is post-Exilic, and the books appear at the end of the third part of the Hebrew canon, in the place where Malachi is found in the English order.

Chronicles and Kings compared. The books of Kings were written before the Captivity, the books of Chronicles after that event (1 Chr 6:15). Kings traces the history from the prophetic viewpoint, Chronicles from the *priestly* approach, emphasizing the temple ritual. The blessing and grace of God toward David, as the establisher of the temple worship, and his successors on the throne of Judah are set forth in Chronicles down to the Exile. The kings of Israel are ignored and treated only as necessity dictates, in contrast to 1 and 2 Kings, which interweave the history of the dual kingdom.

Outline

1:1–9:44 The genealogies
10:1–14 Saul's end
11:1–21:30 David's kingdom
22:1–29:30 David's temple ritual

Some musical instruments of Bible times. David was renowned as a harpist.

1-9. The genealogies

1:1-54. From Adam to the Edomites. (Cf. Gen 5, 10, 11, 25 for these names.) The genealogies of ch. 1-9 are given to show that the Chronicles are dealing with the true Chosen People, descended through Abraham, and destined to be the line through whom the Messiah was to come.

2:1-4:23. Genealogies of Judah. Judah is first because from this tribe Messiah was to come (Gen 49:8-12). David's line to Zedekiah is traced, 3:1-24, with additional genealogies of Judah given in 4:1-23.

4:24-5:26. Simeon, Reuben, Gad, and half of Manasseh. Listed are the sons of Simeon, 4:24-43; the sons of Reuben, 5:1-10; the sons of Gad and the half tribe of Manasseh, 5:11-26.

6:1-81. Levi. Mentioned are the high priestly line, 1-15, 49-53; Levitical lists, 16-30; chief musicians of David, 31-48; and territories assigned, 54-81.

7:1-40. Issachar, Naphtali, half of Manasseh, Ephraim, Asher.

8:1-40. Benjamin. Sons of Benjamin are mentioned, 1-28, as well as house of Saul, 29-40.

9:1-44. Jerusalemites after the return. Genealogical records were carefully kept in Israel. Those in ch. 1-9 are condensed.

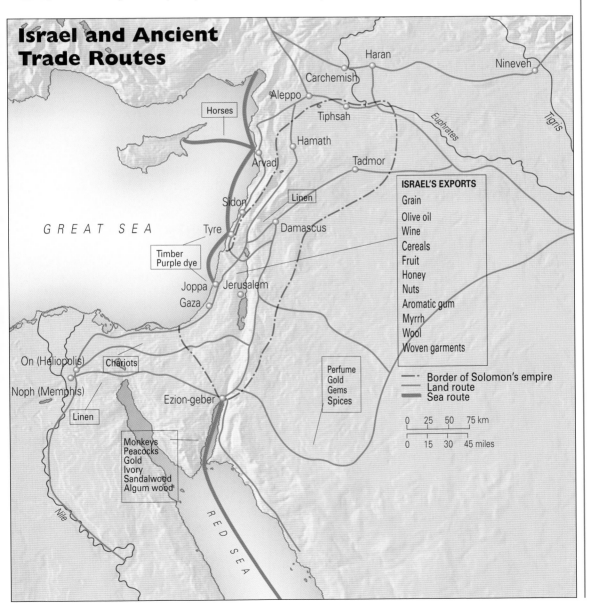

Israel and Ancient Trade Routes

ISRAEL'S EXPORTS

Grain
Olive oil
Wine
Cereals
Fruit
Honey
Nuts
Aromatic gum
Myrrh
Wool
Woven garments

Horses
Linen
Timber Purple dye
Chariots
Linen
Perfume Gold Gems Spices
Monkeys Peacocks Gold Ivory Sandalwood Algum wood

Haran
Nineveh
Carchemish
Aleppo
Tiphsah
Hamath
Arvad
Tadmor
Sidon
Damascus
Tyre
GREAT SEA
Joppa
Jerusalem
Gaza
On (Heliopolis)
Noph (Memphis)
Ezion-geber
Euphrates
Tigris
Nile
RED SEA

- - - Border of Solomon's empire
—— Land route
━━ Sea route

0 25 50 75 km
0 15 30 45 miles

Ancient musicians depicted on an Assyrian relief from Nimrud playing the lyre, vertical harp and double pipes.

10. Saul's overthrow and death

1-12. Death and burial of Saul (cf. 1 Sam 31). The Chronicler uses the downfall of Saul and his sons as the springboard to introduce the Lord's true king, David.

13-14. The reason for Saul's failure. His disobedience and unfaithfulness to the Lord are brought into final focus by his recourse to occultism (1 Sam 28).

11. David's accession as king

1-9. The king and his capital. David was anointed king at Hebron, 1-3 (cf. 2 Sam 5:1-3). He conquered Jebus (Jud 1:21; 19:10-11) and made it the capital, 4-9 (cf. 2 Sam 5:6-12).

10-47. List of David's warriors (cf. 2 Sam 23:8-39). Note additional names.

12. David's warriors

1-22. The Benjamite warriors at Ziklag and others. David's rejection and acceptance prefigure our Lord, of whom David is a prototype.

23-40. Those who came to crown him king. How much greater the joy and the feast when our Lord is made King over all nations.

13. David brings the ark from Kirjath-jearim

1-8. A praiseworthy thing performed wrongly. The ark, mentioned 46 times in 1 and 2 Chronicles, was to be carried on the shoulders of the Levites (Num 4:5, 15), not in a Philistine expedient, a cart. Kirjath-jearim is now called Tell el-Azhar, about seven miles NW of Jerusalem. The Shihor of Egypt, 5, was the east branch of the Nile delta. The entrance of Hamath was far to the N in Syria. The cherubim, 6, were guardians of sacred areas, like the sphinx of Egypt, and similarly may have been represented as winged lions with human heads (Ezk 41:18-19; Gen 3:24). In Phoenicia the king often appeared sitting on a cherubim-supported throne.

9-14. The punishment. Only Levites were to touch the ark (cf. 2 Sam 6:1-10). Uzzah's error, though well-meaning, was serious, punishable by death.

14. David's increase and success

1-7. His family. David's relation to Hiram of Tyre, 1-2, and his family are mentioned, 3-7 (cf. 2 Sam 5:11-25).

8-17. His victories over the Philistines. The Chronicler's summary is given in 17.

15-16. David brings the ark to Jerusalem

15:1-29. The right way of doing it (cf. 1 Chr 13 with Num 4:5, 15 and 2 Sam 6:1-10).

16:1-43. The service of dedication. Described are David's sacrifices, 1-3; his choir, 4-6; his great psalm of thanksgiving, 7-36; and his appointment of the tabernacle ritual and music, 37-43. Part of the tabernacle ritual being at Gibeon indicates the confusion of the times prior to the centralization of worship in Jerusalem, 39.

17. The Davidic Covenant

1-6. David's desire to build the temple (cf. 2 Sam 7:1-3).

7-15. The Davidic Covenant. Only in Christ, David's son and Lord (Ps. 110:1), will this great covenant be fulfilled, when our Lord returns at His second advent. Then 'the Lord God will give unto him the throne of his father David' (Lk 1:32; see 2 Sam 7:4-17).

16-27. David's praise and prayer (cf. 2 Sam 7:18-29).

18-20. David's wars

18:1-17. Full establishment of his kingdom (cf. 2 Sam 8:1-18).

19:1-19. Defeat of Ammonites and Aramean allies (cf. 2 Sam 10:1-19).

20:1-8. Other military successes. David and Joab took Rabbah, 1-3 (cf. 2 Sam 12:26-31) and defeated the Philistines, 4-8 (cf. 2 Sam 21:15-22).

21. David's sin in the census

1-7. Joab's protest (cf. 2 Sam 24:1-9). David's pride was apparently the cause.

21:8-22:1. The plague and the purchase of a site for the sanctuary. The Chronicler highlights David in his ecclesiastical and ritualistic activities in accordance with the purpose of 1 and 2 Chronicles.

22-27. David's temple ritual

22:1-19. Preparation and charge to Solomon. David chose the temple site, 1; gathered building materials, 2-5; instructed Solomon to build, 6-16; and ordered all the chiefs of Israel to help Solomon in the task, 17-19.

23:1-24:31. Preparation of the Levites and priests. The priests were divided into 24 orders, 24:1-19; see the division of Abijah (Lk 1:5).

25:1-31. Preparation of singers and musicians. The sons of Asaph, Jeduthun and Heman, 1-7, are described. They were divided into 24 divisions, like the priests.

26:1-27:34. Preparation of other temple officers. Gatekeepers, treasurers, and other functionaries were organized, 26:1-32, including officers over military and civil affairs, 27:1-34.

28-29. Last acts of David and his death

28:1-21. David's address to the assembly and to Solomon. The address, 1-10, was followed by the temple plans being given to Solomon, 11-19, with encouraging counsel, 20-21.

29:1-30. David's final words and death. He reviewed his plans and preparations for building the temple, 1-19, and invested Solomon as king, 20-25. David's death is recounted, 26-30.

2 CHRONICLES

Judah's history to the exile

Scope of 2 Chronicles.

Solomon is presented second only to David in importance in connection with the temple and its service, ch. 1-9. The bulk of the book, ch. 10-36, concerns the period of the dual monarchy, but centers in the Lord's gracious dealing with the Davidic house. The northern kingdom is referred to as summarily as possible. It was regarded as not representing true Israel and hence not important. Judah's apostasy from the Deuteronomic law is given as the reason for the disaster that overtook Jerusalem.

Outline

1:1-9:31 Solomon's reign
10:1-19 The division of the kingdom
11:1-36:14 History of Judah to the exile
36:15-23 Captivity and epilogue

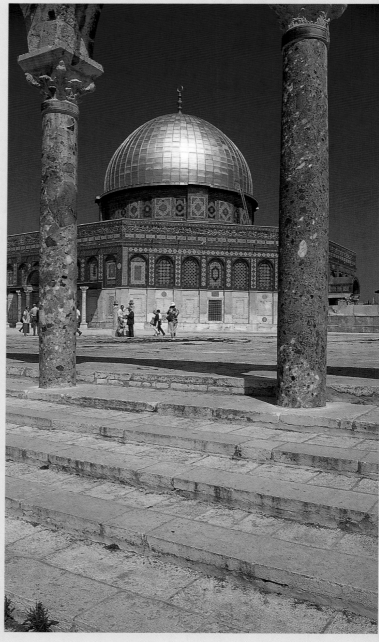

The Islamic Dome of the Rock stands over the same site as Solomon's Temple.

I. Beginning of Solomon's reign

1-13. His vision at Gibeon (cf. 1 Kgs 3:5-15). Gibeon el-Jib, about six miles NW of Jerusalem, was the place the tabernacle had been set up after Saul had destroyed Nob. It remained there until Solomon built the temple (1 Kgs 3:4; 1 Chr 16:39). Gibeon was excavated in 1956, walls and parts of the city water system being uncovered.

14-17. Résumé of Solomon's splendor and wealth (see 1 Kgs 10:26-29; 2 Chr 9:25-28). Solomon imported horses 'from Egypt and Kue [Cilicia], and the king's traders received them from Kue for a price,' 16 (RSV). Cilicia, in Asia Minor, was famous for its steeds.

2-4. Solomon's building of the temple

2:1-18. Solomon prepares to build (cf. 1 Kgs 5:1-6, 11). The king of Tyre is here called Huram instead of Hiram. 'Lebanon,' 8, 16, was famous in antiquity for its cedars. 'Huram-Abi', 13, was the artisan Hiram of Tyre, and not to be confused with the king of that name. The timber from Lebanon was to be floated in rafts by sea to Joppa, 16, ancient seaport of Palestine, about 30 miles NW of Jerusalem. Aliens were conscripted for forced labor, 17-18 (cf. 1 Kgs 5:13-18; 9:22).

3:1-17. Details of the building operation. Mt. Moriah, 1, appears only here and in Gen 22:2. Araunah is also mentioned in 2 Sam 24:16. Cubits 'of the old standard,' 3, were larger, about 20.9 inches in length. 'Gold of Parvaim,' 6, is obscure (cf. 1 Kgs 9:28). The location of Ophir (8:18) is also uncertain, probably in S. Arabia. The cherubim, 10-13, were human-headed winged lions. Jachin and Boaz, 15-17, may have been huge fire cressets with oil containers for flares to illuminate the temple façade (see 1 Kgs 7:15-22).

4:1-22. The temple furnishings (cf. 1 Kgs 7:23-51). The altar of bronze, 1, appears in 1 Kgs 8:64 and 2 Kgs 16:14. The sea was a huge basin built on 12 oxen, with capacity of 2,000 baths (a bath equals six gal.) and was for ritual washings, 2-6 (cf. 1 Kgs 7:23-26).

5-7. Solomon dedicates the temple

5:1-14. The ark brought in (cf. 1 Kgs 8:1-11). The Chronicler adds the account of the priests and singers, 11-13.

6:1-42. Solomon's prayer of dedication, taken from 1 Kgs 8:12-52. The address, 4-11, is followed by the prayer, 12-42.

7:1-22. The Lord's presence consecrates the temple.

8. Solomon's prosperity

1-11. His building activities. His campaign, 3, is otherwise unknown. Tadmor, 4, is Palmyra, the metropolis of the Syrian desert (cf. 1 Kgs 9:18).

Jerusalem in time of David and Solomon

Irrigation channels

David's City

Water gate

City walls

Stepped stone structure
The Millo?

Citadel of Zion

Royal palace

Solomon's Temple

Diagram of the city water system at Gibeon.

1. Spring
2. Feeder tunnel
3. Cistern chamber
4. Door
5. Tunnel of 93 steps

12-18. His religious activities. The expression 'in front of the portico,' 12 (cf. 1 Kgs 9:25), is employed because only the priests could go inside. For 17-18 see notes on 1 Kgs 9:26-28. Solomon's copper smelting establishment has been excavated at Ezion Geber (Tell el Khalifa).

9. The Queen of Sheba and Solomon's death

1-12. The queen's visit duplicates 1 Kgs 10:1-13 (see notes there). The Chronicler presents Solomon's good traits, as he did with David.

13-28. Solomon's wealth and splendor. Taken from 1 Kgs 10:14-29.

29-31. Solomon's death. Cf. 1 Kgs 11:41-43, omitting unfavorable details.

10. Secession of the ten tribes

1-15. Rehoboam's folly. This chapter closely follows 1 Kgs 12:1-19.

16-19. The sad result. Rehoboam's leadership was rejected by the northern tribes of Israel. The kingdom was divided. He reigned over Judah c. 931-913 B.C.

11-12. Rehoboam's reign

11:1-23. Beginning of Rehoboam's reign. Rehoboam was forbidden to fight against Jeroboam I, 1-4. He greatly fortified his kingdom, 5-12, and protected the priests and Levites, 13-17. His family is given, 18-23. He was obedient to the Lord for three years.

12:1-16. Rehoboam's sin and its punishment. Declension and apostasy resulted in Shishak's invasion (note 1 Kgs 14:21-31). Shishak was Sheshonk I (c. 945-924 B.C.), whose invasion of Palestine-Syria at that time is well known to archaeologists. Repentance averted complete destruction, 5-12. Rehoboam's acts and death are mentioned, 13-16.

Solomon's United Kingdom

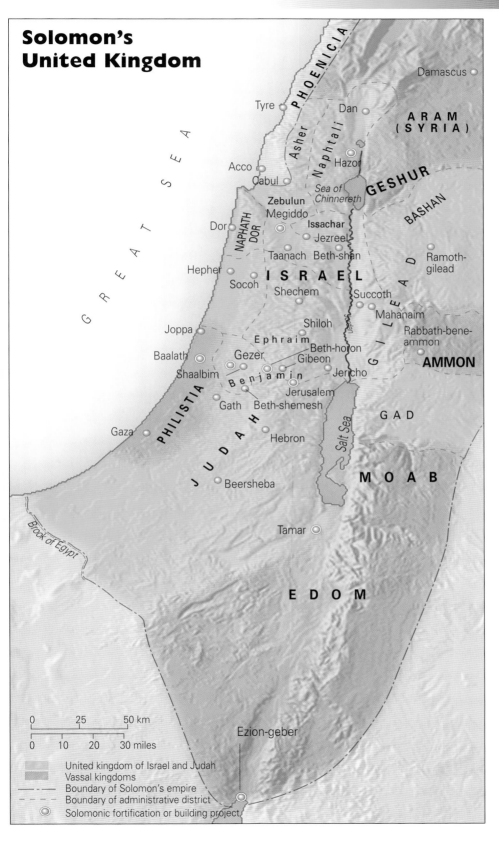

Damascus

Tyre

Dan

ARAM (SYRIA)

PHOENICIA

Asker

Naphtali

Acco

Hazor

GESHUR

Cabul

Sea of Chinnereth

BASHAN

Zebulun

Megiddo

GREAT SEA

Dor

Issachar

NAPHATH DOR

Jezreel

Taanach Beth-shan

Ramoth-gilead

Hepher

ISRAEL

Socoh

Shechem

Succoth

Mahanaim

Jordan

GILEAD

Joppa

Shiloh

Rabbath-bene-ammon

Ephraim

Beth-horon

AMMON

Baalath

Gezer

Gibeon

Shaalbim

Jericho

Benjamin

Jerusalem

Gath Beth-shemesh

GAD

Gaza

PHILISTIA

JUDAH

Hebron

Salt Sea

Beersheba

MOAB

Tamar

Brook of Egypt

EDOM

| 0 | 25 | 50 km |
| 0 | 10 | 20 | 30 miles |

Ezion-geber

United kingdom of Israel and Judah
Vassal kingdoms
— · — Boundary of Solomon's empire
— · · — Boundary of administrative district
⊚ Solomonic fortification or building project

The Kingdoms of Israel and Judah

Sidon

Zarephath

Damascus

Tyre

Dan

PHOENICIA

ARAM (SYRIA)

Hazor

GESHUR

Accho

Cabul

Hammath

Sea of Chinnereth

Dor

Megiddo

Shunem

Jezreel

BASHAN

Taanach

Beth-shan

Socoh

Ramoth-gilead

Samaria

Shechem

ISRAEL

Shiloh

Penuel

GILEAD

Joppa

AMMON

Aijalon

Bethel

Jordan R.

Rabbath-ammon

Gezer

Gibeon

Gath

Jerusalem

GREAT SEA

Hebron

Salt Sea

Gaza

Aroer

Arad Rabbah

Raphia

Kir-moab

Beer-sheba

PHILISTIA

MOAB

JUDAH

Tamar

Kadesh-barnea

EDOM

EGYPT

◎ Capital

☆ Sanctuary city

—·— International border

| 0 | 25 | 50 | 75 km |
| 0 | 15 | 30 | 45 miles |

13-16. Abijah and Asa

13:1-22. Reign of Abijah (c. 913-911 B.C.). The Chronicler shows that the true worship of the Lord was conducted in the Jerusalem temple, 1-12. Abijah's great victory over Jeroboam is described, 13-22.

14:1-16:14. Asa's reign (c. 911-870 B.C.). His reforms are noted, 14:2-8, as well as his great victory over Zerah, the Ethiopian. Asa's prayer, 11, breathed the freshness of faith and resulted in triumph, 12-15. Victorious Asa was warned by the prophet Azariah, 15:1-7, and as a result he conducted a religious reformation, 8-19. Asherah was an image of the Canaanite fertility goddess, 16. Asa's war with Baasha, his apostasy and death are mentioned in 16:1-14. Verse 9 is famous and often quoted. Asa's foot disease, 12, was severe. His funeral was elaborate, 14.

17-20. Jehoshaphat's reformation

17:1-19. Godliness and prosperity of his early reign. The 'Book of the Law of the Lord,' 9, which Jehoshaphat had taught in Judah was the law of Moses, critically alleged to have been a later fabrication of Josiah's day (see note on 2 Kgs 22:8-13; Deut 17:18-20).

18:1-19:11. His mistake. Jehoshaphat's alliance with Ahab (1 Kgs 22:1-40) was a serious compromise and blunder, deserving the stinging rebuke of the prophet Jehu, son of Hanani, 19:1-3. This was effective and Jehoshaphat restored judicial justice and priestly order in Judah, 19:4-11.

20:1-37. His deliverance from an invasion. The Moab-Ammon invasion, 1-2, in answer to Jehoshaphat's prayer, 3-13, was repulsed, 14-25. Great booty was taken and Jehoshaphat returned in triumph, 26-34. His compromising trading adventure with Ahaziah (1 Kgs 22:47-49) ended in disaster. Ezion Geber is modern Tell el Khalifa where a copper smeltery has been uncovered belonging to Solomon.

21-22. Jehoram, Ahaziah, Athaliah

21:1-20. Jehoram's wicked reign. Jehoshaphat's eldest son murdered his brothers and worked evil, 1-7. Edom and Libnah (Tell es Safi, some 22 miles SW of Jerusalem) rebelled, 8-10. Jehoram ordained high places, 11. His doom was pronounced by a letter which had been written by Elijah, 12-15, doubtless delivered by Elisha. His end was diasatrous, 16-20.

22:1-9. Ahaziah's wicked reign (cf. 2 Kgs 8:24-29). He was slain by Jehu.

22:10-12. Athaliah's usurpation (cf. 2 Kgs 11:1-3). Jehosheba hid Joash, Ahaziah's son.

23-24. Joash's reform and eventual apostasy

23:1-11. Joash becomes king, c. 835-796 B.C. (cf. 2 Kgs 11:4-12).

23:12-15. Athaliah executed, c. 841-835 B.C. (cf. 2 Kgs 11:13-16).

23:16-21. Revival through Jehoiada (cf. 2 Kgs 11:17-20).

24:1-27. Joash's reign. A synopsis of his rule is given, 1-2. The repair of the temple, 4-14; the death of Jehoiada, 15-16; and the apostasy of the princes and king, 17-19, are mentioned, climaxing in the stoning of Jehoiada's son, Zechariah, 20-22, and the invasion of the Arameans of Damascus, 23-24. At Joash's assassination, his son Amaziah succeeded him, 25-27.

25-26. Amaziah and Uzziah

25:1-28. Amaziah's reign, c. 796-767 B.C. (cf. 2 Kgs 14:1-2). His campaign against Edom, 5-13, and his idolatry, 14, resulted in divine wrath against him, 15-16. His mistake in hiring soldiers from Israel, 7, led to a disastrous war with Joash of the northern kingdom, 17-25, and a violent death, 26-28 (2 Kgs 14:8-20).

26:1-23. Uzziah's reign. The reign of Uzziah (also called Azariah) was long and prosperous (c. 791-740 B.C.). He intruded into the priest's office by offering incense and was struck with leprosy (see note on 2 Kgs 15:1-7).

27-28. Jotham and Ahaz

27:1-9. Jotham's reign. A good and prosperous king, 1-2, he built on 'the wall at the hill of Ophel,' 3, a fortified eminence in the eastern part of the city. He also subdued Ammon. Jotham reigned c. 750-732.

28:1-27. Ahaz' great wickedness. He reigned c. 735-716 B.C. His idolatries, 1-4, brought chastisement at the hands of Rezin, king of Syria, and Pekah, king of Israel, 5-8 (2 Kgs 16:5-6). The prophet Oded reproved the Israelite invaders, 9-15. Ahaz' dealings with Tiglath-pileser, 16-21, and his further acts of wickedness are told, 22-27.

29-32. Hezekiah's reformation

29:1-30:27. Hezekiah's reign, c. 716-687 B.C. (cf. 2 Kgs 18:1-20:1; Isa 36-39). He

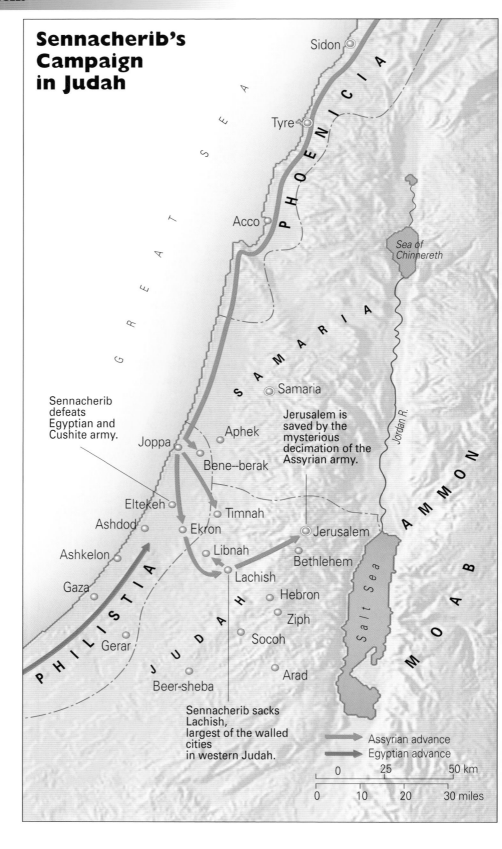

Sennacherib's Campaign in Judah

Sidon

Tyre

PHOENICIA

Acco

GREAT SEA

Sea of Chinnereth

SAMARIA

Samaria

Sennacherib defeats Egyptian and Cushite army.

Joppa

Aphek

Jerusalem is saved by the mysterious decimation of the Assyrian army.

Jordan R.

Bene–berak

AMMON

Eltekeh

Timnah

Ashdod

Ekron

Jerusalem

Ashkelon

Libnah

Bethlehem

PHILISTIA

Gaza

Lachish

Salt Sea

Hebron

Ziph

MOAB

Gerar

JUDAH

Socoh

Beer-sheba

Arad

Sennacherib sacks Lachish, largest of the walled cities in western Judah.

Assyrian advance
Egyptian advance

| 0 | 25 | 50 km |
| 0 | 10 | 20 | 30 miles |

effected a great revival, 29:1-19, restoring the temple worship, 20-36, and celebrating the Passover, 30:1-27.

31: 1-21. Other reforms. He rooted out idolatry and restored the temple ritual.

32: 1-23. Sennacherib's invasion. (See notes on 2 Kgs 18:13-19:37, and Isa 36:1-22.)

32:24-33. Hezekiah's sickness, recovery and embassy from Babylon. (See note on Isa 38-39.)

33. Manasseh's and Amon's idolatry

1-10. Manasseh's orgy of wickedness. (See notes on 2 Kgs 21:2-9.)

11-13. His captivity and restoration. The Babylonian Captivity of Manasseh was historically possible since his name appears in Assyrian annals as a vassal of Esarhaddon, 681-668 B.C., and Ashurbanipal, 669-626 B.C.

14-20. His reforms and death. Manasseh reigned *c*. 697-643 B.C.

21-25. Amon's rule (*c*. 643-641 B.C.). He was evil like his father.

34-35. Josiah's great reformation

34:1-7. Early reforms. Josiah reigned 640-609 B.C., as one of Judah's best kings. He fought against Canaanite Baal cults.

34:8-35:19. Great revival. This was the result of finding the Mosaic law lost in Manasseh's reign of terror. (See notes 2 Kgs 22:1-23:30.)

35:20-27. Josiah's death. (See notes on 2 Kgs 23:28-30.)

36:1-14. Jehoahaz to Zedekiah: the end

1-3. Jehoahaz deposed (cf. 2 Kgs 23:31-33; 609 B.C.).

4-8. Jehoiakim's reign (cf. 2 Kgs 23:34-24:6; 609-598 B.C.).

9-10. Jehoiachin's reign (cf. 2 Kgs 24:8-16; 598-597 B.C.).

11-14. Zedekiah (cf. 2 Kgs 24:17-25:7). He reigned 597-586 B.C. till the fall of Jerusalem.

36:15-23. Captivity and Cyrus' decree

15-21. Fall of Jerusalem and the exile (587-539 B.C.). The Chronicler reviews the Lord's grace and patience and gives the reason for the Exile. This is the only reference to Jeremiah the prophet in Kings and Chronicles (see 21). Cf. his prophecies in Jer 25:11-12; 29:10.

22-23. Decree of Cyrus (538 B.C.). See Ezra 1:1-4 in fulfillment of Jer 29:10, under divine direction (Isa 44:28-45:3).

The Chaldean Empire

Nebuchadnezzar II (605-562 B.C.). His first deportation of Judah (Dan 1:2) came in 605 B.C., the second in 597 B.C., and the third in 586 B.C., when he destroyed Jerusalem. He besieged Tyre (585-573 B.C.) and also invaded and desolated Moab, Ammon, Edom and Lebanon. He invaded Egypt in 572 and 568 B.C., and died in 562 B.C., one of the most autocratic and splendid rulers of the ancient world, with his capital city at Babylon (see notes on Jer 50) immortalized for its magnificence (cf. Dan 4:30).

Old Babylonian period (1830-1550 B.C.). Babylon dates from prehistoric times but did not itself become the capital of a great empire until this period. Hammurabi (1728-1686 B.C.), of the first dynasty of Babylon, lifted it to the height of power. Babylon and Assyria struggled till Assyrian supremacy (885-626 B.C.).

The Chaldean Empire (605-539 B.C.). This Neo-Babylonian Empire was coterminous with Judah's captivity.

Nabopolassar (625-605 B.C.), governor of Babylon, threw off the Assyrian yoke and destroyed Nineveh, 612 B.C. He was the father of Nebuchadnezzar II.

Evil-Merodach, Amel Marduk ('man of Marduk') (562-560 B.C.), son of Nebuchadnezzar, was slain by his brother-in-law Nergal-shar-usur.

Neriglissar, Nergal-shar-usur (560-556 B.C.), reigned only four

Babylonian Empire

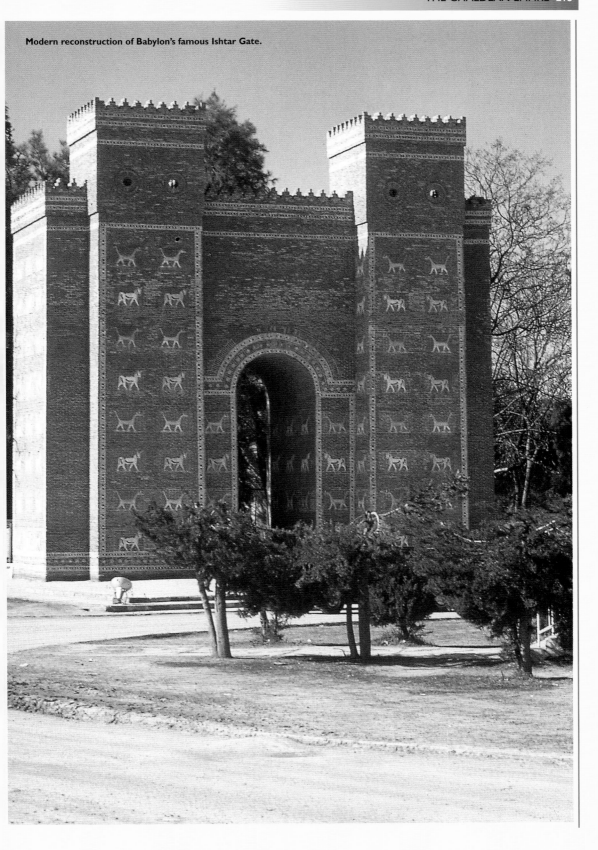

Modern reconstruction of Babylon's famous Ishtar Gate.

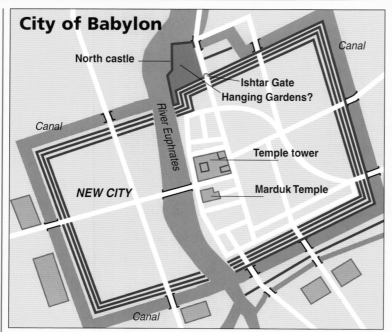

City of Babylon

North castle

Ishtar Gate
Hanging Gardens?

River Euphrates

Canal

Canal

NEW CITY

Temple tower

Marduk Temple

Canal

Inscriptions. Most of the bricks found carry Nebuchadnezzar's stamp, 'Nebuchadnezzar; king of Babylon . . .' One inscription recalls his boast in Dan 4:30: 'The fortifications of Esagila [Marduk's temple] and Babylon I strengthened and established the name of my reign forever.'

Fall of the city. Both Isaiah (13:17-22) and Jeremiah (51:37-43) prophesied Babylon's fall. Inscriptions of Cyrus the Persian and the royal records of Babylon describe the fall of the city in 539 B.C.

Extent. Babylon's wall is said by Herodotus to have been 60 miles in length, 15 miles on each side; 300 feet high, and 80 feet thick. It was protected by moats or canals, and its 250 towers were manned by soldiers. The city had 100 gates of brass, and the Euphrates flowed through the city.

years. His son *Labashi-Marduk* was murdered after reigning only a few months.

Nabonidus (556-539 B.C.) was one of the nobles who usurped the throne. He was called also Nabuniad ('the god Nabu [Nebu] is exalted'). His eldest son Belshazzar, *Bel-shar-usur* ('Bel protect the king'), was coregent when Babylon fell to the Persians (Dan 5) in October, 539 B.C.

The city of Babylon

Excavations. The splendors of Nebuchadnezzar's Babylon (Dan 4:30) are now well known. From 1899 to 1914 the Germans uncovered remains of vast building projects which the king's own inscriptions describe. The Ishtar Gate led through a massive double wall of fortification decorated with bull dragon motifs done in enameled colored bricks. The Great Processional Street fed from the Ishtar Gate. A dominating building was the royal ziggurat or temple tower rising to eight stages. Marduk's temple stood nearby. The famous hanging gardens were constructed in terraces and constituted one of the seven wonders of the world. Nebuchadnezzar was an avid builder and Babylon a dazzling capital (Isa 14:4).

Ruins. Although Herodotus may have exaggerated slightly, excavations have largely attested the almost fabulous ancient accounts of the city. Present-day mounds are mostly found E of the river, and consist of Kasr, the central ruin, and Amran, the southern mound which contains the ruins of Esagila, the vast Temple of Marduk, the city's patron deity. The Amran mound contains the ruins of the great Tower of Babylon. Babil was the fortress guarding the northern entrance to the city and is almost a dozen miles from Kasr. These sprawling ruins attest the great size of the ancient metropolis of the world (see Jer 50-51).

EZRA

Return from Babylon

Chronology of the return

605-536 B.C.	General period of captivity
605, 597, 586 B.C.	Leading Judean citizens deported including Daniel and Ezekiel
538 B.C.	Edict of Cyrus permitting the return
536 B.C.	Return of 49,897 from Babylon to Jerusalem
536 B.C.	Altar rebuilt, sacrifice offered in seventh month
535 B.C.	Temple begun, but stopped
535-520 B.C.	Economic and political struggle
520 B.C.	Ministry of Haggai
520-515 B.C.	Ministry of Zechariah
515 B.C.	Temple completed
458 B.C.	Ezra returned
445 B.C.	Nehemiah rebuilt the walls

World events during the return

557-447 B.C.	Buddha (in India)
551-478 B.C.	Confucius (in China)
549 B.C.	Cyrus united Persia and Media
546 B.C.	Cyrus conquered Lydia
539 B.C.	Cyrus conquered Babylon
530 B.C.	Cyrus died
539-331 B.C.	Persian Empire
530-522 B.C.	Cambyses ruled
522-486 B.C.	Darius I
490 B.C.	Darius defeated at Marathon
486-465 B.C.	Xerxes I (Ahasuerus)
485-425 B.C.	Herodotus
480 B.C.	Persians defeated at Thermopylae and Salamis
470-399 B.C.	Socrates
460-429 B.C.	Golden age of Pericles
428-322 B.C.	Plato and Aristotle

Outline

1-6 Return under Zerubbabel
Temple rebuilt
7-10 Return under Ezra
His reformation

1. The edict of Cyrus

1-4. The proclamation. Cyrus' first year at Babylon, 1, was 539 B.C. Prophecies by Isaiah (Isa 44:28-45:3) and Jeremiah (Jer 29:10) were divinely fulfilled in Cyrus, by means of the Persian monarch's decree, 2-4. Archaeology has shown that Cyrus' concession to the Jewish exiles was not an isolated act of kindness but the general policy of a humane ruler. His cylinder found by H. Rassam in the 19th cen. shows he reversed the inhuman deportation policy practiced by Assyrian and Babylonian conquerors and restored displaced peoples and their deities to their homelands.

5-11. Gifts provided. These included the holy vessels appropriated by Nebuchadnezzar (2 Kgs 25:13-16). Mithredath, 8, was the temple treasurer and Sheshbazzar was the Babylonian name of a Jewish official in the Persian court.

2. The returning exiles

1-65. Register of those who returned. Enumerated are the people in general, 1-35; the priests, 36-39; the Levites, 40-54; the descendants of Solomon's servants, 55-60; other priests, 61-63. The total number was 49,897, see 64-65. Apparently others were included, and all the tribes of Israel were represented (Cf. Lk 22:30; Acts 26:7; Jas 1:1; Ezr 2:70; 6:17; 8:35). Notions of the 'ten lost tribes' are dispelled here as elsewhere in post-exilic Jewish history.

66-70. The property and gifts of those who returned. The drachma (daric) was a Persian coin equivalent to approximately $8.50.

3. The temple begun

1-7. The altar erected. In the seventh month, Tishri (Sept.-Oct.), the altar of burnt offering was set up, the first step in rebuilding the temple and reestablishing the nation. The Feast of Tabernacles was kept, 4-6, and materials to build the temple were assembled, 7. Sheshbazzar (Ezr 5:14-16) was governor.

Carchemish

Aleppo

Hamath

Tad

Byblos

Sidon

Tyre

Damascus

Ezra and Nehemiah return with exiles, c. 458–428 B.C.)

Samaria

Jerusalem

Archaeological light

Esarhaddon's annals on a cuneiform cylinder now in the British Museum recount the deportation of the Israelites and the settlement of colonists in their place.

8-13. Foundation of the temple laid in the second month (May) 535 B.C. Zerubbabel, 2, grandson of King Jehoiachin (1 Chr 3:17-19), later appointed governor by Cyrus, and Jeshua (Joshua), the high priests (Hag 1:1; Zech 3:1), were leaders in the undertaking. Great rejoicing and also weeping, 12-13 (cf. Hag 2:3) accompanied the ceremony.

4. Work on the temple stopped

1-5. Enemies endeavor to hinder the building of the temple. These were the Samaritans, the result of foreigners from Assyria (676 B.C.) being settled in the territory of the former northern kingdom by Esarhaddon (681-668 B.C.), 2, and by 'noble Osnappar' (RSV), i.e., Ashurbanipal (669-626 B.C.), 10. The offer of help was a snare because it entailed a compromising union with semi-idolaters, 3 (cf. 2 Kgs 17:32).

6-24. Recital of continued opposition (parenthetical). Despite attempts to harmonize this section with the reigns of Cambyses (530-522) and Darius (522-486), and critics who suggest that the section is misplaced, this recital of later opposition in the reigns of Ahasuerus (Xerxes I, 486-465) and Artaxerxes (465-424) serves an important function. It emphasizes the constant difficulties that beset the post-exilic community. Just as Rehum and Shimshai would succeed in stopping the building of the walls during the reign of the Artaxerxes (c. 486 B.C.), Tattenai and Shethar-bozenai succeeded in delaying the building of the temple until Darius's second year (520 B.C.).

5-6. The temple work resumed and completed

5:1-17. Haggai's and Zechariah's ministry. Darius (522-486 B.C.) ascended the throne of Persia, and through his kindness and the prophetic ministry of Haggai and Zechariah (Hag 1:1-4; 2:1-4; Zech 4:9; 6:15) the work was

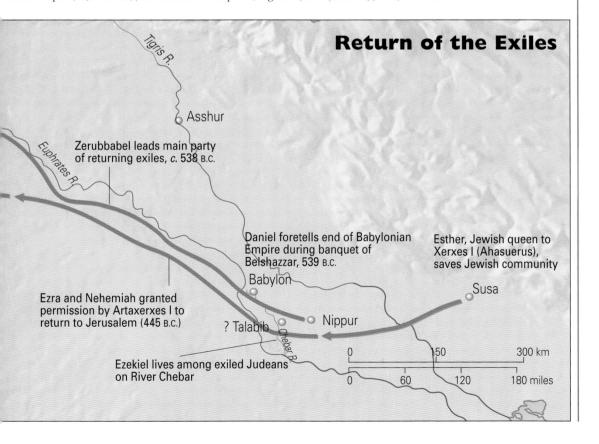

Return of the Exiles

Tigris R.

Euphrates R.

Asshur

Zerubbabel leads main party of returning exiles, c. 538 B.C.

Daniel foretells end of Babylonian Empire during banquet of Belshazzar, 539 B.C.

Babylon

Esther, Jewish queen to Xerxes I (Ahasuerus), saves Jewish community

Susa

Ezra and Nehemiah granted permission by Artaxerxes I to return to Jerusalem (445 B.C.)

? Talabib

Nippur

Chebar R.

Ezekiel lives among exiled Judeans on River Chebar

| 0 | | 150 | | 300 km |

| 0 | 60 | | 120 | 180 miles |

Artist's impression of the rebuilding of Jerusalem under Ezra and Nehemiah.

resumed. Cuneiform tablets mention Tattenai, 3, governor of the province Trans-Euphrates.

6:1-22. The temple finished. Darius found the decree of Cyrus at his summer capital in Ecbatana, 1-5, and ordered the completion of the temple, 6-13. The house was finished, 14-15; dedicated, 16-18; and the Passover and Feast of Unleavened Bread were kept, 19-22.

Note on 'king of Assyria,' 22. The ruler was probably so designated because Persia then ruled the former Assyria.

7-8. The arrival of Ezra

7:1-28. Ezra went to Jerusalem in the reign of Artaxerxes I (465-424 B.C.) to teach the law of God, 6, 10. The royal decree was made on Ezra's behalf, 11-26, who gave thanks to God, 27-28.

8:1-36. Ezra's mission. Ezra's companions are named, 1-14. Ahava Canal is unidentified, 21, but it is probably a tributary of the Euphrates. Casiphia is also unknown, 17. The treasure was committed to 12 priests, 24-30, and delivered to the temple storehouses ('chambers'), 29.

9-10. Ezra's reform

9:1-15. Loss of separation. Mixed marriages with semi-idolaters caused Ezra great pain, 1-4. His intercession and confession are recorded, 5-15.

10:1-44. Separation restored. The people repented and put away foreign wives, 1-17. The register is given of those who had married foreign women, 18-44. Kislev is the ninth month (Nov.-Dec.), 9, when heavy rains are common. Tebet is the tenth month (Dec.-Jan.), when the work started. It was finished in Nisan (the first month, Mar.-Apr.).

NEHEMIAH

Rebuilding Jerusalem's walls

Name and purpose of the book. Nehemiah takes its name from its principal character and traditional author (1:1). The rebuilding of Jerusalem as a fortified city, the establishment of civil authority under Nehemiah, and his governorship are recounted. More civil and secular than the book of Ezra, it is nevertheless also written from the priestly viewpoint. Ezra-Nehemiah, until 1448 one book called the book of Ezra, demonstrates God's fidelity in restoring His exiled people. The divine working is seen through great Gentile monarchs – Cyrus, Darius and Artaxerxes, and the Jews' own anointed leaders – Haggai, Zechariah, Zerubbabel, Jeshua, Ezra and Nehemiah.

The Persian Empire (539-331 B.C.). The Persian kings constituted a humane line of world rulers who permitted the Jews to return and rebuild their temple and city. Persia reversed the cruel policy of Assyria and Chaldea by repatriating displaced peoples. Under the two-century beneficent Persian regime, Judah was a tiny province in the Fifth Persian Satrapy. Its southern frontier fortress Lachish, well-known from archaeological investigation, was controlled from the palace of the Persian administrator.

Cyrus (539-530 B.C.) united Media and Persia (549 B.C.), conquered Lydia (546 B.C.), and Babylon (539 B.C.), which was ruled by Nabonidus and the crown prince Belshazzar. His decree (Ezr 1:1-4; 2 Chr 36:22-23) permitted the return of the Jews to Palestine.

Cambyses (530-522 B.C.) conquered Egypt. His death was by suicide.

Smerdis (522 B.C.) was a Magian usurper who precipitated civil war.

Darius I the Great (522-486 B.C.) put down the insurrection under Smerdis and saved the Empire. He erected the famous Behistun Inscription on the road from Babylon to Ecbatana which furnished the key to Babylonian-Akkadian cuneiform, as the Rosetta Stone in Egypt proved to be the key to Egyptian hieroglyphics. The temple at Jerusalem was completed in 520-515 B.C. (Ezr 6:15).

Xerxes I (486-465 B,C.) was Ahasuerus, the husband of Esther; Mordecai was one of his prime ministers. Ahasuerus warred against Greece.

Artaxerxes I Longimanus (465-424 B.C.) was favorable to Jerusalem. Ezra returned in 458 B.C.; Nehemiah became governor (Ezr 7:1, 8; Neh 2:1) in April/May, 445 B.C. The famous Elephantine Papyri from the Jewish military colony at the First Cataract of the Nile, discovered in 1903, confirm this period and mention Sanballat (Neh 2:19) and Johanan (Neh 3:1; 12:23).

Xerxes II (424 B.C.) was followed by *Darius II* (423-404 B.C.), *Artaxerxes II* (404-358 B.C.), *Artaxerxes III* (358-338 B.C.), *Arses* (338-336 B.C.), and *Darius III* (336-332 B.C.).

Outline

1-7 Nehemiah's restoration of the walls
8-13 Ezra's and Nehemiah's reforms

The Dung Gate of the Old City of Jerusalem today.

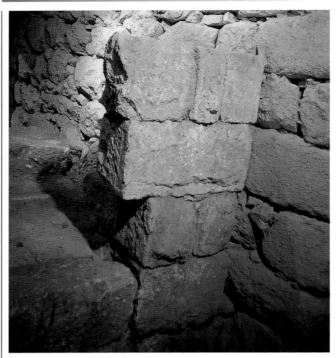

Remains of an
Israelite tower in
the defensive
walls of Jerusalem
probably dating
to the 7th
century B.C.

who worked with Zerubbabel, and grandfather of the later high priest Jonathan (12:11). Through the Sheep Gate sacrificial animals were led to the altar.

3-32. Builders of the other gates are mentioned along with the builders of the walls between. *The Jeshanah,* 6-12, was perhaps the Corner Gate (Jer 31:38). *The Dung Gate.* 14, was that from which refuse was removed from the city. *The East Gate,* 29-32 (cf. Ezk 43:1-2), was that from which the Shekinah glory left and by which it will return. *The Inspection Gate* (Heb. *mipqàd* 'an appointed place'), 31, may speak of the gate of judgment.

4-5.Opposition to the work

4:1-9. Opposition by ridicule and anger. Ridicule, 1-3, was answered by prayer, 4-6. Anger, 7-8, was likewise met successfully by further intercession to God and vigilance, 9.

4:10-23. Opposition by discouragement. The spirit of defeatism, 10-13, was met by faith, 14, 20, and hard work, 15-23.

5: 1-19. Opposition by selfishness. The internal greed (Deut 23:20) and covetousness, 1-5, had a remedy in restitution, 6-13, reinforced by Nehemiah' s personal example of unselfishness during his 12-year term as governor, 14-19.

6. The walls completed

1-14. Opposition by craftiness. For Sanballat, Tobiah and Geshem, see note in Neh 2:1-20. These wily Satanic foes tried to lure Nehemiah to Ono near Lydda, some six miles SE of Joppa, 2. Unsuccessful, they once again tried intimidation by threatening to report him to the king, mentioning 'prophets,' since these were often fomenters of rebellion (Jer 28: 1-4). The hireling Shemaiah, 10-14, tried his strategy (cf. Zech 13:2-6).

15-19. Wall completed. This event was consummated on the 25th day of Elul, the sixth month (Aug.-Sept.), despite every conceivable type of evil opposition.

7. Register
of Zerubbabel's return

1-4. Provisions for the defense of the city. At last Jerusalem was a fortified city once again. Nehemiah set up laws for its safety.

5-73. The census of the first return

1-2. Nehemiah' s call

1:1-11. Nehemiah's concern for Jerusalem. In Kislev (Nov.-Dec.) in Artaxerxes' twentieth year (445-444 B.C.; cf. 2:1), Nehemiah ('the Lord comforts') heard of the sorry state of Jerusalem, 1-3. The men from Judah, 2, were visitors to the Persian winter capital at Susa in Elam (Est 1:2.5; Dan 8:2). Nehemiah's great sorrow and prayer appear in 4-11 (cf. Deut 30:1-5). 'This man,' 11, was Artaxerxes. The cupbearer was a royal butler who tasted the king's wine, etc., to see it was not poisoned. This office was one of high honor (Herodotus 3.34).

2:1-20. Nehemiah's mission. The king sent Nehemiah to build Jerusalem, 1-8. Sanballat, mentioned in the Elephantine Papyri, the governor of Samaria, and Tobiah, an Ammonite official in the hire of Persia, planned resistance, 9-10. Nehemiah inspected the walls of Jerusalem by night, 11-16, and urged immediate rebuilding, 17-18. Geshem, an Arab, 19, joined the opposition. Non-Jews had no portion, property, right, authority, or memorial, i.e., remembrance, in the Jewish community, 20.

3. Jerusalem's gates
and walls repaired

1-2. Builders of the sheep gate. Eliashib (12:22; 13:4) was the grandson of Jeshua (12:10), (see Ezr 2:1-70). The genealogy is recorded, 5-65; the whole number given, 66-69; and gifts for the work described, 70-73.

8. Public reading of the law

1-8. The law read before the Water Gate. First day of the seventh month Tishri (Sept.-Oct.) was a day of convocation (Num 29:1). The Water Gate became the place of cleansing by the refreshing power of God's Word. Here the law of Moses written in Hebrew was interpreted in the common Aramaic, 7-8.

9-12. Effect of the word. Revival and keeping of the Feast of Tabernacles, 13-18 (cf. Lev 23:33-44), were the results.

9. Spiritual revival

1-5. The public confession. Reading, hearing, believing, obeying the Word always brings spiritual revival with humiliation, self-judgment, confession and true worship.

6-38. The great confession and prayer. Ezra's prayer is one of the longest recorded prayers in the Bible, 6-37. For the covenant that was made, 38, see ch. 10.

10. The covenant renewed

9:38-10:28. The commitment to support God's house. Those who signed the covenant are named, 9:18-10:28. Talmudic tradition makes these signers 'the Great Synagogue.'

29-39. The obligations of the covenant. These included the duty not to intermarry with Gentiles, 28-30; to observe the sabbath, 31; to support the temple ritual, 32-36; to pay tithes and priestly dues, 37-39 (see Lev 27:30; Num 18:25-32). 'The storerooms,' 39, were part of the temple (cf. Neh 13:12; Ezr 8:29; 10:6).

11-12. The dedication of the walls

11:1-36. Faithful workers. Those who lived in Jerusalem, then a place of danger and death, are specified, 1-2. Registers of Judahites, Benjamites, priests, temple officials, Levites, Nethinim, etc., are given, 11:3-24. Registers of those who lived outside Jerusalem are also indicated, 11:25-36.

12:1-26. Other faithful people. Named are priests and Levites of the first return, 1-9;

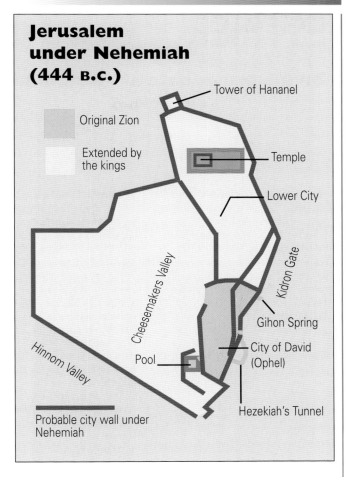

Jerusalem under Nehemiah (444 B.C.)

- Original Zion
- Extended by the kings
- Tower of Hananel
- Temple
- Lower City
- Cheesemakers Valley
- Kidron Gate
- Gihon Spring
- City of David (Ophel)
- Hinnom Valley
- Pool
- Hezekiah's Tunnel

Probable city wall under Nehemiah

descendants of Jeshua the high priest, 10-11; heads of priestly houses, 12-21; and of Levitical houses, 22-26.

12:27-43. Dedication of the walls.

12:44-47. Provisions for temple personnel.

13. Evils corrected

1-9. Separation enforced from a mixed crowd, 1-3, and from unholy alliances, 4-9. Eliashib was the high priest of 3:1, 20; 12:22; Ezr 10:6, who was related to Sanballat by marriage, 28.

10-29. Nehemiah corrects other evils.

30-31. His testimony concerning his work was characterized by modesty and piety.

ESTHER

Divine providence at work in history

Nature of the book and author.
Esther is the last of the five scrolls (*Megillôt*) found in the third section of the Hebrew Bible called *Ketûbîm* or 'Writings.' The book describes the origin of the festival of Purim ('lots'). This solemnity was celebrated on the 14th or 15th of Adar (Feb.-Mar.). Thus Esther is the Purim scroll (roll). Its author is unknown. Ezra, Mordecai, Joiakim or men of the Great Synagogue are possible authors.

History.
Despite the common critical contention that the story is legendary fiction, its historicity is supported (1) by its being entrenched in history and its being specifically dated (1:1, 15; 2:1, 10, 20) in the reign of Ahasuerus, i.e. Xerxes I (486-465 B.C.); (2) by the author's familiarity with Persian life – the architectural plan of the palace and court (1:5; 2:11, 21; 7:8), court etiquette (4:11; 8:11-18), palace intrigues (2:21-23; 7:9), banquet customs (1:6-8; 5:5); (3) by external evidence from excavations at Susa, etc., and cuneiform texts referring to a certain Marduka (cf. Mordecai), an official at Susa under Xerxes.

Outline
1. Vashti deposed
2. Esther made queen
3. Haman's plot
4-7. Esther's courage
8. Vengeance executed
9. Purim kept
10. Epilogue

Relief head of Darius, King of Persia, who ruled from Persepolis.

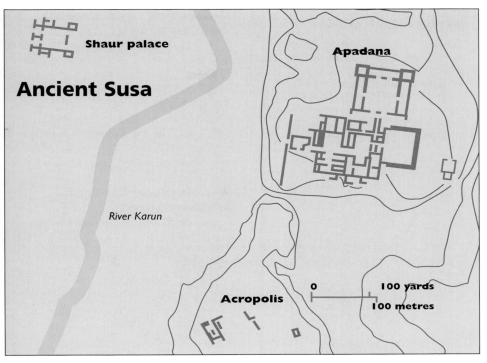

Shaur palace

Apadana

Ancient Susa

River Karun

Acropolis

0   **100 yards**

100 metres

1. Vashti deposed

1-9. Ahasuerus' feast. Ahasuerus was probably Xerxes I (486-465 B.C.), though the LXX equates him with Artaxerxes II. The third year of his reign was 483 B.C., 3. He fought the Greeks at Salamis and Thermopylae in 480 B.C. His empire, 1, extended from India (Indus Valley) to Ethiopia (modern Nubia) and included 20 satrapies (cf. Herodotus *History* III, 89), which were divided into numerous provinces. Fabulous Persian feasts are described by Greek writers, and excavations at Susa, 5, capital in Elam, have uncovered such a court. Herodotus says Amestris was Xerxes' queen *(History* VII, 61). Vashti apparently was one of the royal concubines.

1-22. Vashti's deposition. Her name was Elamite.

2. Esther made queen

1-4. Search for Vashti's successor. Between Vashti's demotion and Xerxes' marriage to Esther (478 B.C.), the monarch was absent on his ill-fated campaign against the Greek states.

5-23. Mordecai and Esther. Mordecai was Esther's foster father (having adopted her in her childhood), as well as her cousin, 7. He, like Saul, was a Benjamite, 5. His office was apparently that of a eunuch gatekeeper, since he was closely connected with the harem, 11, 19, 21 (cf. 6:10). Esther was chosen queen in the month

Tebeth (Dec.-Jan.) in the seventh year (478 B.C.) of Xerxes, 16. The conspiracy of the eunuchs, 21-23, who guarded the royal bedchamber, 21, was of the type Xerxes finally fell victim to in 465 B.C.

3. Haman's plot

1-6. Haman's promotion. He was made grand vizier. All lesser officials were required to do obeisance to him. The reference to 'Haman, son of Hammedatha, the Agagite,' 1, may refer to the region of Agazi, adjacent to Media, or suggest that Haman was a descendant of Agag, the Amalekite king that Saul spared (cf. 1 Sam 15:7-9). In any case, Mordecai's faith prevented him from paying homage to any but the true God. Haman was enraged.

7-15. Haman's plot to exterminate the Jews. Casting the lot (*pur,* an Akkadian word), 7, was for the purpose of determining a suitable time for the pogrom. Haman offered 10,000 talents to the king to bribe him to massacre the Jews. The royal signet ring, 10, 12, stamped the order of annihilation with authority (cf. 8:2, 8; Gen 41:42), although the king refused the bribe. The edict of extermination, 12, was published by couriers, 13, i.e., the renowned post service of fleet horses which Cyrus had instituted throughout the Persian Empire. The apocryphal additions to the book of Esther give the text of the edict.

Archaeological light

Shushan (Susa), 2, was the winter capital of
Persia; Ecbatana, the summer residence. Susa
shows ruins dating from c. 4000 B.C.
through A.D. 1200. Excavated ruins reveal
remains from the palace begun by Darius
the Great and enlarged by subsequent kings.
The palace had three courts with
multitudinous rooms decorated with
warriors, winged bulls and griffins. The
famous Code of Hammurabi was found here
in the excavated area (1901). Other finds
from Susa include inscriptions of Artaxerxes
II (404-358 B.C.)

4-5. Esther's intercession before the king

**4:1-17. Esther's decision to go before
the king.** Mordecai's mourning in sackcloth
made him ritually unclean, since it was a badge
of mourning for the dead among the Persians,
1-3. Esther was informed of the edict, and
volunteered to go before the king, 4-17.

5:1-14. The king received Esther and
indicated he would grant her petition, 1-8.
Haman determined to liquidate Mordecai, 9-14.

6-7. Mordecai honored; Haman hanged

6:1-14. Mordecai honored by the

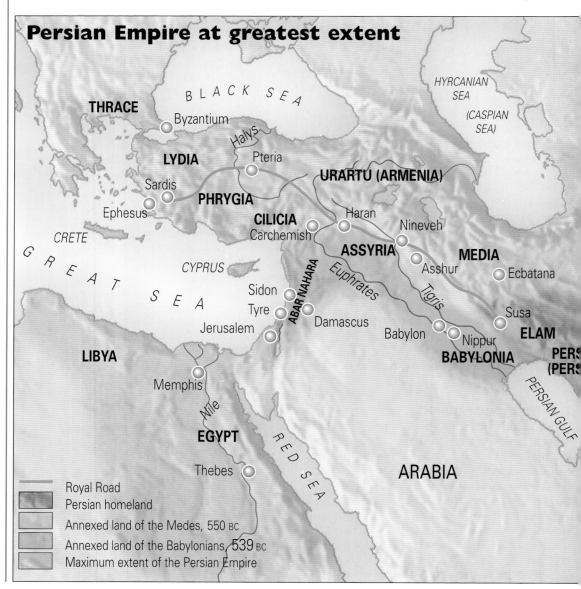

Persian Empire at greatest extent

THRACE

BLACK SEA

Byzantium

Halys

HYRCANIAN SEA

(CASPIAN SEA)

LYDIA

Pteria

Sardis

PHRYGIA

URARTU (ARMENIA)

Ephesus

CRETE

Haran

Nineveh

CILICIA

Carchemish

ASSYRIA

MEDIA

Asshur

Ecbatana

CYPRUS

Euphrates

Tigris

Sidon

ABAR NAHARA

Tyre

Damascus

Susa

Jerusalem

Babylon

Nippur

ELAM

LIBYA

BABYLONIA

PERS
(PERS

Memphis

PERSIAN GULF

Nile

EGYPT

RED SEA

ARABIA

Thebes

Royal Road
Persian homeland
Annexed land of the Medes, 550 BC
Annexed land of the Babylonians, 539 BC
Maximum extent of the Persian Empire

king. The king, sleepless, had 'the book of the chronicles,' 1, read, in which Mordecai's exposé of a plot against the king's life was told, 1-3. Haman was forced to honor Mordecai, 4-11.

7:1-10. Haman hanged. He was charged with his wickedness by Esther before the king and incriminated by an unforeseen circumstance.

8. The edict of deliverance

1-2. Mordecai's exaltation. It was customary for convicted criminals to have their property confiscated (Herodotus III, 29). The signet ring given to Mordecai signified his exaltation to Haman's prime ministership.

3-17. Revocation of the edict. Esther's

Head of King Hammurabi of Babylon, the monarch responsible for the famous Law Code found at Susa in 1901.

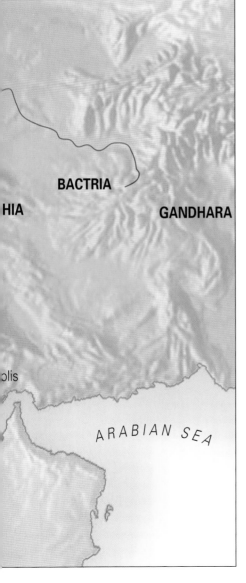

ability to handle the monarch was enviable. Mordecai was authorized to make a decree that the Jews defend themselves.

9. Origin of the Feast of Purim

1-16. Vindication of the Jews' enemies including Haman's sons.

17-32. Institution of Purim. It was held on the 14th or 15th day of Adar, the twelfth month (Feb.-Mar.). In later times the book of Esther was read on these festal days, while the congregation interrupted with shoutings of curses on Haman and praises on Esther and Mordecai.

10. Epilogue: Mordecai's greatness

The continual greatness of Xerxes and the power of Mordecai are recounted. The names of both Mordecai (Marduka) and Esther (*Ishtar*; Heb. *Hadassah,* 'myrtle') are Babylonian. It was customary for native names to be given foreigners (cf. Dan 1:7).

JOB

Why the righteous suffer

The book of Job as literature.
This poem is widely recognized, even in secular circles, as one of the world's most magnificent dramatic poems. The sublimity of its theme, the majesty of its thought patterns, the grandeur of its literary sweep are unexcelled in any piece of literature.

The book of Job and its order in the canon.
This great dramatic poem heads the so-called poetical books of the OT in the English order, coming before Psalms, Proverbs, Ecclesiastes, and the Song of Solomon. In the Hebrew it is placed in the third section of the canon, the *ketûbîm* or Writings, third in the order – Psalms, Proverbs, *Job,* Canticles (Song of Songs), and then Ecclesiastes. It is also part of the OT Wisdom Literature which presents the simple, pious philosophizings of the Hebrew mind on practical godly living.

The book of Job and Hebrew poetry.
Hebrew poetry, unlike Occidental verse, does not possess meter or rhyme. Its basic structure is *parallelism* or thought arrangements rather than word arrangements. Common types of such *parallelism* are (1) *synonymous parallelism,* where the second line or stich reiterates the first, giving a distich or couplet (cf. Job 3:11-12; 4:17; Ps 2:4); (2) *antithetic parallelism,* in which the second line presents a contrasting thought to emphasize the first (Job 42:5; Ps 34:10); (3) *synthetic parallelism,* in which the second and succeeding lines add a progressive flow of thought to develop the first (Job 4:19-21; Ps 1:3). Other variations of these basic forms of thought rhythm occur. In addition to parallelism Hebrew poetry possesses rhythm or pulsating beats: (1) 3+3 is *epic* or *didactic,* as in Job and Proverbs; (2) *lyric* is 2+2, as in Canticles; (3) *dirge* or *qinah* is 3+2, as in Lamentations. Hebrew poetry is also highly figurative, rich in imagery, simile, metaphor, metonymy, synechdoche, hyperbole, personification, and alliteration.

The theme of the book.
It treats a perplexing, profound subject. Why do righteous people suffer? How can their sufferings be consonant with a holy, loving God? Job's three friends offered essentially the same answer, ch. 3-31. Suffering, they intimated, is the outcome of sin. In desperation Job was driven to the dilemma that God must be dealing unfairly with him. However, he struggled with the confidence that he would eventually be vindicated. At this point Elihu appeared and declared the truth that afflictions are often a means of purifying the righteous, the testings or chastenings of a loving father, in no sense the vindictive anger of an implacable God, ch. 32-37. By God's speech out of the whirlwind, ch. 38-41, Job was humbly led to detest himself in relation to the divine majesty of God, 42:1-6. His self-renunciation and spiritual refining were the entrée to his restoration and blessing, 42:7-17.

Outline

1:1-2:13 Prologue. Job's test
3:1-31:40 False comfort of his three friends
32:1-37:24 Elihu's speeches
38:1-42:6 God's discourses
42:7-17 Epilogue: Job's restoration.

Why do righteous people suffer? Can their sufferings be consonant with a loving God?

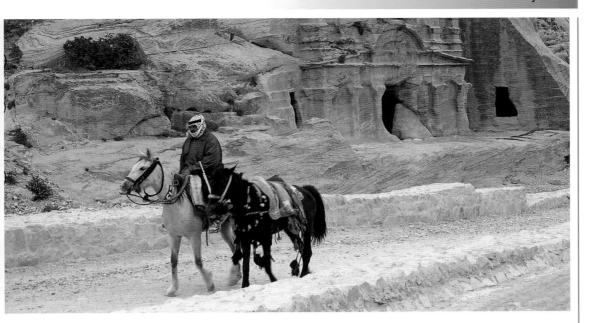

1-2. Prologue: Job's testing

1:1-5. Job's resting and integrity. The land of Uz was likely Edom (cf. Gen 36:28; Lam 4:21). Job was blameless, not sinless or perfect, 1. He was a historical character (Ezk 14:14, 20; Jas 5:11). The date is unknown. The name 'Job' (*'iyyôb*) occurs extrabiblically in the Berlin Execration Texts as the name of a prince of the land of Damascus 19th cen. B.C., and later around 1400 B.C. as a prince of Pella (modern Fahil).

1:6-12. Satan's accusation. The *benê ha'elohîm* (Heb.) were angels. Satan ('the Adversary') was Lucifer, 'son of the dawn' (Isa 14:12-14; Ezk 28:11-19), the tempter of Gen 3. Here he appears, as often in Scripture, as the 'accuser of our brothers' (Rev 12:10).

1:13-2:13. Job's affliction. Severe testing came. Possessions and family were taken away, 2:18. His wife turned against him, 9-10. His three friends came to comfort, 11-13. The Sabeans (1:15) were Arab nomads. The Chaldeans (1:17) were Semitic Arameans who finally invaded Mesopotamia.

3-14. The first cycle of speeches

Ch. 3. Job's first speech. He cursed the day of his birth, 1-9, and longed for death, 10-26. In the controversy that followed, Job spoke nine times, Elpihaz three, Bildad three, Elihu one, God one.

Ch. 4-5. Eliphaz' first speech. He rebuked Job, 4:1-6, and insisted the righteous are not cut off, 7-11. His awe-inspiring vision, 12-21, fitted him for exhortation, he thought, 5:1-16. The man is fortunate whom God corrects, 17-27.

Ch. 6-7. Job's reply. He justified his despair by the magnitude of his affliction, 6:1-7, requesting to be cut off, 8-13, at the same time reproaching his friends, 14-30. The misery of life, 7:1-7, involved two questions: Why does God deal with me in this manner? Why does He not pardon? 8-21.

Ch. 8. Bildad's first speech. He followed the general logic of the other of Job's comforters. God was punishing Job for his sins, 1-7, appealing to the traditions of the past, 8-10, namely, the wicked cannot really prosper and God will not cast off the righteous, 11-22.

Ch. 9-10. Job answers Bildad. God is so supremely powerful, 9:1-10, how can Job meet Him? 11-24. Job confessed his weakness and longed for an umpire 'to lay his hand upon us both,' 25-35. He bitterly complained, 10:1-17, welcoming death, 18-22.

Ch. 11. Zophar's first speech. Job's wordiness was rebuked, 1-6, and God's greatness and omnipotence were lauded, 7-12, with exhortation that Job repent to be restored and blessed, 13-20.

Ch. 12-14. Job's reply to Zophar. He was vexed into biting sarcasm, 12:1-6, and dwelt

Job's servants brought him terrible news. His donkeys had been stolen; his sheep killed; and his camels stolen by Chaldean raiders.

upon God's power, 7-25. Denouncing his 'friends,' 13:1-13, he appealed to God, 14-28, dwelling upon the brevity and trouble of life, 14:1-6, relieved only by a faint hope of immortality, 7-22.

15-21. Second cycle of speeches

Ch. 15. Eliphaz' second speech. The controversy grew more heated. Eliphaz assumed Job's guilt, charged that Job stood self-condemned, 1-6, in his conceit and pride, 7-16, and described the wicked and their end, 17-35.

Ch. 16-17. Job's reply to Eliphaz. Job branded his 'friends' as 'miserable comforters,' 2. 'Will your long-minded speeches never end?' 3. Suppose you were in my place? 4-5. God had afflicted him, 6-22. Trouble upon trouble overwhelmed him, 17:1-12. Where was his hope? 13-16.

Ch. 18. Bildad's second speech. Harshly he reproached Job, 1-4, and attempted to frighten him by describing the doom of the wicked, 5-21.

Ch. 19. Job's reply to Bildad. Unhumbled and acutely disturbed by Bildad's words, 1-6, Job stumbled in confusion, blaming God, 7-12, and falling into a doleful lament at his pitiable condition, 13-24. But there was a flash of faith and light! The Spirit of God enlightened him and lifted him out of the doldrums of despair, 25-27, to utter one of the most superlative statements of faith in all the OT: 'I know that my Redeemer lives, and that in the end he will stand upon the earth. And after my skin has been destroyed, yet in my flesh I will see God; I myself will see him, . . . and not another.' The *Goel,* Kinsman-Redeemer (Ruth 3:12-13; 4:4-6; Isa 59:20) is the Lord Jesus Christ, risen, coming again, Victor over death and the grave. What a witness to the blessed hope of the Lord's coming, the resurrection of the body, and the glorification of the saints (1 Thess 4:13-18; 1 Cor 15:52; Ps 17:15).

Ch. 20. Zophar's second speech. His hasty reply, 1-3, followed proverb and tradition, and he mistakenly classified Job with the wicked and their fate, 4-29.

Ch. 21. Job's reply. He looked to God for help and showed how the wicked often prosper in this life, 1-26, branding the conclusions of his friends as pure falsehoods, 27-34.

The book of Job is a story of Patriarchal days. Job's wealth was measured in sheep, cattle and camels.

22-31. Third cycle of speeches

Ch. 22. Eliphaz' third speech. Eliphaz of Teman (apparently SW of Sela in Edom at Tawilan) concluded Job was a great sinner, 1-5, charging him with greed and cruelty, 6-11, and hypocritically dwelling upon God's omniscience and man's wickedness, 12-20, urging Job to get right with God, 21-30.

Ch. 23-24. Job's reply. He groped for God, proving he was not defiantly wicked, 23:1-9, meanwhile wavering between faith and unbelief, 10-17. Had God failed? 24:1-12. Job gave further testimony of the frequent prosperity of the wicked, 13-25.

Ch. 25. Bildad's third speech. Although his arguments were exhausted, he presented a forceful description of what God is, 13, and what man is, 4-6.

Ch. 26. Job's reply. He sarcastically dismissed Bildad's arguments, 1-4, and knowingly and with great feeling described God's greatness, 5-14.

Ch. 27-31. Job's closing words of self-vindication. He clung to his righteousness, 27:1-6, contrasting himself with wicked people, 7-23. He described the treasures of earth, 28:1-6, and the higher wealth of wisdom, 7-22, which is known by God, 23-28. Job outlined his past blessings and honors,

29:1-10, and the good deeds he had wrought, 11-25, contrasting his present shameful humiliation, 30:1-19, with God's silence, 20-31. He ended confidently maintaining his chastity and righteousness, 31:1-12; his philanthropy, 13-23; and his integrity and hospitality, 24-34. He challenged God and man to disprove his claim, 35-40. He concluded by saying in a word: '*I am clean!*' The next time he spoke, he declared in essence, '*Behold I am vile*' (42:6). The reason for the change is recorded in the rest of the book.

32-37. Elihu's speeches

Ch. 32-33. Elihu's first speech. God instructs man through affliction. Elihu ('my God is He') is introduced, 32:1-6. He was a Buzite, living near Edom, for Buz (Gen 22:21) was a brother of Uz (Job 1:1) and an Aramean (Gen 11:26-32). Buz in Jer 25:23 was a place name in Edom. Elihu was a true moderator, in a sense the answer to Job's desire for such an umpire. Elihu's speeches thus served to prepare the way for the interposition of God Himself, ch. 38-41.

Ch. 34. Elihu's second speech. God's justice was vindicated against Job's insinuations, 1-30. Job had not yet learned the purpose of suffering, 31-37.

Ch. 35. Elihu's third speech. The advantages of piety were set forth as a refutation to Job's wrong reasoning, 1-8, showing that it does matter with God whether a man is righteous or wicked, 9-16.

Ch. 36-37. Elihu's fourth speech. God has a purpose in afflicting the godly, 36:1-7. He does so to wean man from pride and to show His disciplining grace and love, 8-18. Job was to take note of this, 19-21, and to acknowledge God's power and presence in nature, 22-33; in the thunderstorm, 37: 1-5 ; and in snow and rain, 6-16. Elihu's concluding remarks stressed man's sinful frailty before God, 17-24, clearing the way for the Almighty to speak.

38:1-42:6.God's discourses to Job

38:1-40:5. God's first discourse to Job. Creation proclaims God's omnipotence. The Lord spoke 'out of the storm,' 38:1, a frequent setting for theophanies (Nah 1:3; Zech 9:14; Ps 18:7-15; Ezk 1:4; Hab 3). God is Creator of the sea, 8-11; of time, 12-15; He is Master of the deep, light, darkness, snow, hail, lightning, constellations, clouds, and mist, 16-38; God is the Creator and Protector of animals, 38:39-39:30. Job made a confession, 40:1-5.

40:6-42:6. God's second discourse to Job. God's power and man's frailty are contrasted. Job was silenced as a contender and faultfinder with God, but not as a sinner. So the divine controversy was renewed. 'Would you condemn me to justify yourself?' 40:6-8, asks the Lord in His appeal to Job, 9-14. 'Behemoth,' 15-24, apparently is a plural of intensity of Hebrew *be- hemâ* ('beast') and refers probably to the hippopotamus (Egyptian *p-ehe-mou)* or water buffalo. Figures of this huge amphibian have been found on amulets and in Palestinian temples. 'Leviathan,' 41:1-11, is the crocodile, but is generally interpreted elsewhere to refer to a mythical chaos-monster (Ps 74: 14; 104:26; Isa 27:1). Description of Leviathan, 12-24, and his remarkable strength, 25-34, is given.

Job's reply to God *solves the problem* of suffering, 42:1-6. Affliction is God-permitted to refine man so that he may see God, 5, in all His greatness and splendor, and see himself in his despicableness and sin to the intent that man may repent of his pride 'in dust and ashes.'

42:7-17. God rebukes Job's friends and restores Job

7-9. The Lord's vindication of Job against his friends. God's grace forgave Job's sin, and Job prayed for his erring friends.

10-17. Job's fortunes restored. His end was peace.

PSALMS

Prayer book and hymnal of God's people.

Nature and number.
The Hebrew title for the Psalter is 'Book of Praises' (*seper Tehillim*). Praise, worship, confession and the outpouring of prayer characterize the Psalms. The Psalter was the hymnal of the Jewish people and is the prayer and praise manual of the Christian church. Martin Luther called the Psalter 'a Bible in miniature.' Our English word 'Psalms,' from the Septuagint *Psalmoi*, means 'songs' accompanied by string instruments. In the Hebrew Bible, Psalms head the third division, called the *ketûbîm* or Writings (cf. Lk 24:44). The Hebrew Bible contains 150 psalms.

The Psalms and Hebrew poetry.
See introduction to Job on the nature of Heb. poetry.

Themes of the Psalms
1. The spiritual conflicts and triumphs of saints under the old dispensation constitute the basic theme, but these reflect the conflicts of God's people in every age.
2. Great prophetic themes run through the book, as NT quotations prove. These are: (a) The far-reaching predictions concerning Messiah (cf. Lk 24:44), including His first advent in humiliation; His death, resurrection and exaltation; and His second advent in glory and triumph, Ps 2, 8, 16, 22, 45, 69, 72, 89, 110, 118, 132. (b) Sorrows, trials and sufferings of a godly portion of Israel in the nation's coming time of trouble eventuating in deliverance, restoration and glory, Ps 52, 58, 59, 69, 109, 140. (c) Future glories for

redeemed Israel, the earth and all creation, Ps 72, 110.

Note: In the necessarily brief comments that follow, the focus is upon the more difficult prophetic themes, since the devotional meanings are more obvious to the reader and thus need less comment.

Authorship as indicated by the titles
David 73 (Book 1, 37; Book 2, 18; Book 3, 1; Book 4, 2; Book 5, 15)
Asaph 12 (Ps 50, 73-83)
Korahites 12 (Ps 42-49; 84, 85, 87, 88) Solomon 2 (Ps 72, 127)
Moses 1 (Ps 90)
Ethan 1 (Ps 89)

Classification
Five books: Book 1, Ps 1-41; Book 2, Ps 42-72; Book 3, Ps 73-89; Book 4, Ps 90-106; Book 5, Ps 107-150.

Royal Psalms. 2, 18, 20, 21, 45, 72, 89, 101, 110, 144. They anticipate Christ as King.

Alphabetic Psalms. 9, 10, 25, 34, 37, 111, 112, 119, 145. They employ some arrangement based on the Hebrew alphabet.

Penitential Psalms. 6, 25, 32, 38, 39, 40, 51, 102, 130. These psalms breathe deep contrition for sin committed.

Messianic Psalms. 2, 8, 16, 22, 45, 69, 72, 89, 110, 118, 132. They preview the person and work of the coming Messiah.

Imprecatory Psalms. 52, 58, 59, 109, 140. All of these implore God's vindication of His own against godless persecutors.

Hallelujah Psalms. 111, 113, 115-117, 146-150. These psalms employ the term Hallelujah, meaning 'Praise Jah (Jehovah).'

Elohistic Psalms. 42-83. They employ the name *Elohim* for God. Others use the name of Jehovah.

Ascent Psalms. 120-134. They were recited or sung as the pilgrims went up to Jerusalem to celebrate the feasts.

A kinnor, or ancient harp, from Megiddo.

1. The godly man vs. the ungodly

The godly man is happy, 1-3, because he is separated from sin, 1; Bible-centered, 2; and prosperous, 3. The ungodly, 4-6, in contrast, is unlike the godly, 4, and is doomed to judgment, 5-6. A wisdom psalm introductory to the entire Psalter.

2. Messiah's kingship and kingdom

This previews Christ's present rejection, 1-3 (cf. Acts 4:25-28), which continues throughout this age and culminates in the abysmal apostasy of the Great Tribulation. Messiah's attitude of disdain toward His enemies and His future throne are foretold, 4-6. The future incarnate and risen Lord (cf. Acts 13:33-34) vindicates His sonship at His second advent and assumes the kingdom, 7-9. He exhorts kings and warns rebels in view of the establishment of His kingdom, 10-12.

3-7. Trials of the godly

Psalm 3. Peaceful trust in God. In time of deep anguish when Absalom rebelled against him, 1-2, David found God his glory, as his shield (protector) and encourager, 2-3; as the One who answered his prayers, 4; and as the One who gave him peace and deliverance, 5-8.

Psalm 4. Evening prayer sustaining faith results in enlargement of heart, 1; assurance of God's help, 2-3; faith, 4-5; divine approval 6; joy, 7; peace and security, 8.

Psalm 5. Morning prayer giving courage, 1-3, bestows a sense of God's goodness and justice, 4-6; secures God's guidance, 7-8; His protection and punishment of enemies, 9-10; and His blessing upon the righteous, 11-12.

Psalm 6. Heart cry of one distressed. Sorely chastened, 1-3; beset by death, 4-5; and stricken with grief, 6-7, the psalmist expresses faith in God's deliverance, 8-10.

Psalm 7. Cry for protection against cruel enemies, 1-2. Personal innocence is protested, 3-5, and punishment upon evildoers is requested, 6-16. Praise is accorded the Lord, 17.

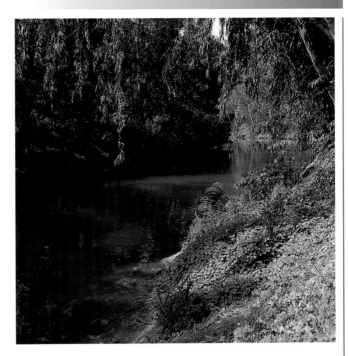

A tree planted beside water does not dry up – Psalm 1. A view of the Jordan river south of the Sea of Galilee.

8. The sovereignty of the Son of Man (Messianic)

As Son of Man, Christ appears in humiliation, a little lower than angels (Mt 21:16; 1 Cor 15:27; Heb 2:6-9), to taste death for every man, and is now crowned with glory and honor, 1-5. Man (the first Adam being a figure of the Second Man or the last Adam) was given dominion over creation, which was lost by sin, and which is to be restored only by the Second Adam (Christ), 6-9. This achievement of the Creator-Redeemer will redound to God's glory, 1, 9.

9-15. The godly and the Wicked One

Psalm 9. The godly praise the most high, 1-2, for His kingdom blessings and glories, 3-12, with prayer for the Lord's intervention in the judgments preceding the establishment of the kingdom, 13-20.

Psalm 10. Supplication of the godly for divine intervention continued, 1-2, directed against the Wicked One, 3-18.

Psalm 11. Faith's resources are for the day of trouble ('Jacob's trouble,' cf. Jer 30:5-7), when 'the foundations are destroyed' in that dark hour of universal apostasy, 1-3. But the Lord will judge sinners and reward the righteous, 4-7.

Psalm 12. The arrogance of sinners, 1-3, is described. But God is about to judge them, 4-6, as their iniquity comes to the full, 8.

Psalm 13. The faith of the godly, 1-4, eventuates in victory, 56.

Psalm 14. Human apostasy and depravity are described, 1-3, especially the period preceding Christ's second advent when Israel will suffer violent persecution, 4-6. Messiah's advent, bringing salvation for Israel and joyful restoration, is prayed for, 7 (cf. Rom 11:26-27; Ps 53).

Psalm 15. The character of the godly. Such a saint has fellowship with God in worship, 1, and his life conforms to his profession, 2-5.

16-24. Prophetic vistas of Christ

These nine psalms reflect the character of the godly but find their *ultimate* fulfillment in Christ, starting in Psalm 16 with our Lord in His obedience on earth, climaxing in His second advent manifestation as 'the King of glory' (Ps 24).

Psalm 16. Christ obedient is resurrected. He is the Obedient One, 1-3, whose path was one of complete devotion to God, 4-8, which led Him to death and resurrection, 9-11 (cf. Acts 13:35).

Psalm 17. Christ the Intercessor (cf. Jn 17). He only fits the righteous Intercessor, 1-5. His prayer for His own, 6-12, and the deliverance, 13-15, will find fruition only in the Greater David, David's Lord.

Psalm 18. God's power preserved Christ. David as a prophet (Acts 2:30) here predicts Christ's experience of death, 1-6, and God's manifest power and glory in Christ's behalf, 7-18. He speaks not only of raising Him from the dead but giving Him glory, 19-27, subduing His enemies, 28-42, and making Him 'Head of the nations,' 45-50.

Psalm 19. Christ in creation and revelation. He appears first in creation, 1-6; then in revelation (His written Word), 7-11. Man's response follows, 12-14.

Psalm 20. Christ and His salvation. Prayer for the earthly king's victory, 1-2, foreshadows the greater victory of Christ's salvation, the whole burnt offering, 3, typifying the death of Christ. Celebration of Christ's glorious salvation, 4-8, is climaxed by a cry of the godly in the time of trouble, 9.

Psalm 21. Christ's kingly glory is anticipated, 1-7, and His victory over His foes celebrated, 8-12. Then redeemed Israel will sing the anthem of 13.

Psalm 22. Christ's sufferings and coming glory. The sufferings, 1-21, are a graphic portrayal of crucifixion (cf. Mt 27:27-50), and are followed by the glory, 22-31.

Psalm 23. Christ the Great Shepherd. The *Good* Shepherd of Ps 22, giving His life for the sheep (Jn 10:11), appears in Ps 23 as the *Great* Shepherd brought up from the dead 'through the blood of the eternal covenant' (Heb 13:20), caring for the sheep, giving them assurance, 1-3, and comfort, 4-6.

Psalm 24. Christ the Chief Shepherd. The *Good* Shepherd of Ps 22 and the *Great* Shepherd of Ps 23 now is revealed as the *Chief* Shepherd, the 'King of glory,' appearing to acknowledge and reward His sheep (1 Pet 5:4). Who shall dwell with Him in His kingdom advent, 1-6? What suitable welcome shall be accorded Him at His coming, 7-10?

25-39. Soul exercise of the godly

Psalm 25. Petition for deliverance. This is an acrostic (cf. Ps 9, 10) in which an arrangement of the letters of the Heb. alphabet is used to provide poetic unity.

Psalm 26. Prayer for vindication against an unjust charge is presented, 1-3, with protestations of innocence, 4-7, dramatized by a liturgical ceremony, 6 (cf. Deut 21:6-8; Ps 51:7). A prayer for aid is uttered, 8-12.

Psalm 27. Prayer for spiritual orientation, toward God, 1-3; toward life, 4-6; toward self, 7-14.

Psalm 28. Prayer for deliverance. The prayer, 1-5, is followed by thanksgiving for the answer, 6-9.

Psalm 29. The storm of judgment. Ascription of praise to the Lord, 1-2, because the day of the Lord shall come as a great tempest, 3-9, to clear the air for the calm of the Messianic Age when the Lord is King, 10-11.

Psalm 30. Praise for healing. The recovery is noted, 1-3, and praise is offered, 4-12.

Psalm 31. Victory over enemies.

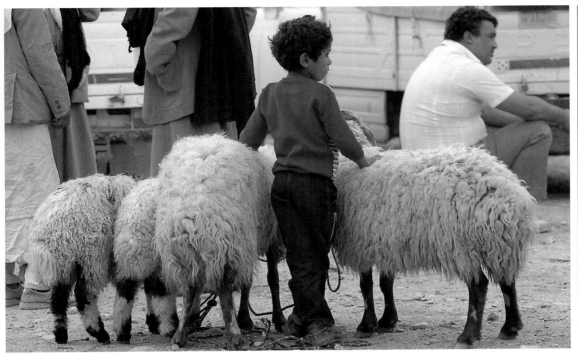

Prayer of the saint is for deliverance, 1-18, and the answer points to victory, 19-24. Jesus quoted verse 5 as He expired on the cross (Lk 23:46).

Psalm 32. The blessing of being justified. This is the first of 13 Maskil psalms, i.e., psalms of spiritual instruction. The justifier, 1-5, is also a hiding place, 6-7; a Guide and a Preserver, 8-10, in whom the saint is to rejoice, 11.

Psalm 33. Praise to the Lord is rendered to Him as Creator, 1-9; as Governor, 10-17; and as Keeper and Deliverer of the righteous, 18-22.

Psalm 34. Full praise of God's redeemed is sung for deliverance, 1-10; for instruction, 11-14; for redemption, 15-22. Verse 20 was fulfilled in Jn 19:36.

Psalm 35. Cry for help in distress. This is an imprecatory psalm like 52, 58, 59, 69, 109 and 137. These must be understood as the prayers of the godly in a day of abysmal apostasy and violence. The Spirit of God prays through them for the destruction of the wicked, whose cup is full and whose judgment is executed in the day of the Lord. To see a conflict here with Jesus' teaching of love and forgiveness is to misunderstand God's holiness, which demands judgment when grace is rejected. It is also important to remember that these psalms accurately reflect human attitudes that may not

be fully understood (cf. Job, Ecclesiastes).

Psalm 36. Contrast of the wicked and the Lord. What the wicked man is and does, 1-4, is contrasted with what the Lord is and does, 5-9. The Lord is to be petitioned and trusted, 10-12.

Psalm 37. The righteous and wicked in contrast (cf. Ps 1). The wicked will most surely be punished. Let the righteous who have been wronged not be discouraged.

Psalm 38. The suffering saint and sin. When the suffering saint, 1-8, looks to the Lord, 9-15, confession of sin and prayer result, 16-22.

Psalm 39. Human frailty. The emptiness of life, 1-6, should lead to self-judgment and prayer, 7-13.

40-41. David's experiences foreshadow Christ's

Psalm 40. The obedient Christ (cf. Heb 10:5-7). His path of obedience, 1-12, is prefaced by the Redeemer's resurrection song, 1-3. The phrase, 'My ears you have pierced,' 6, indicates total obedience, referring either to the piercing of a servant's ears (Ex 21:6) or an openness to hear and obey God's Word (Isa 50:45). The fruit of the Redeemer's work is outlined, 13-17, as He prays as the Sin-Bearer of His people.

The Good Shepherd of Ps 22 and the Great Shepherd of Ps 23 is revealed in Ps 24 as the Chief Shepherd appearing to acknowledge and reward His sheep.

Psalm 41. Messiah betrayed. David's experience, 9, foreshadows Christ's (Jn 13:18-19). Verse 13 will be redeemed Israel's shout as a result of Messiah's redemption.

42-49. Through tribulation to kingdom blessing

These psalms open Book 2 of the Psalter, which begins with the oppression of the godly Heb. remnant of the last days and ends with Ps 72, the great Kingdom Psalm of the Psalter. The first group (42-49) presents aspects of this troubled scene and final deliverance.

Psalm 42. Longing for God in deep distress, 1-6, is described with the tonic of faith and the comfort of hope, 7-11. This is a Maskil (instruction) psalm for the godly remnant of that terrible time of trouble (Dan 12:1).

Psalm 43. Cry to God against enemies, namely, the lawless one, 2, and his wicked nation. Ps 43 is one with Ps 42 (cf. the Septuagint which makes them one psalm).

Psalm 44. Increased cry for help. The psalmist pleads with God to command deliverance, 1-8. A period of great national peril effects the lament, 9-21, possibly prefiguring the Great Tribulation. (cf. Rev 4:1-19:16). This anguish calls for help, 22-26.

Psalm 45. The answer: King Messiah's advent in glory. His majesty and power, 1-5. His dominion and glory, 6-8, and those who share His kingdom, 9-17, are foreseen (cf. Heb 1:8-9 and Isa 11:1-2).

Psalm 46. Deliverance from tribulation and the sequel. The great time of trouble, 1-3, is followed by Messiah's advent in power and glory, 4-7, and the establishment of the kingdom, 8-11. 'Selah' is a liturgical direction of some sort, the meaning of which is now uncertain.

Psalm 47. Messiah King in His kingdom is seen among His redeemed, 1-5, the object of the praise of His ransomed people, 6-9.

Psalm 48. Nations judged, the kingdom established. Jerusalem is seen as the capital of the earth in the Kingdom Age, 1-3 (cf. Isa 2:1-5). The nations are judged, 4-7, and the kingdom set up, 8-14 (cf. Mic 4:1-10; Zech 14:9-21).

Psalm 49. Transiency of the wicked

and their wealth. Contrast is made to the lot of the righteous who trust in the Lord.

50-51. The righteous God and His penitent people

Psalm 50. God's demands for holiness. God comes to Israel in His revealed righteousness and demands righteousness of His people, 1-6; not mere ritualism, 7-15, but spiritual reality, 16-22, which will in turn result in the revelation of the salvation of God, 23.

Psalm 51. The sinner in deep penitence. This is the greatest of penitential psalms. David's great sin of adultery and murder is confessed before God and forgiven. The sinner, 1-2, becomes the penitent, 3-11, and the forgiven, 12-17, who in turn becomes the intercessor for Zion, 18-19.

52-55. Israel's time of trouble

These four psalms are Maskil (instruction) odes reflecting experience of affliction of the Psalmist himself (David). They may also be prophetic of Israel's last-day troubles under the false messiah (Zech 11:15-17; 2 Thess 2:7-12).

Psalm 52. The wicked tyrant and his destruction. The wicked one's character (Doeg, the Edomite), 1-7, contrasting vividly with the character of the godly psalmist, 8-9, furnishes the historical occasion for a description of an arrogant tyrant who will experience the retribution of God (1 Sam 21:7; 22:9, 18, 22).

Psalm 53. An age of apostasy. The last day of denial of God, 1; wickedness, depravity, 2-3, and persecution of God's people are foreseen, 4. Judgment then falls on the apostates, 5. The godly remnant prays for the advent of Messiah and the restoration of Israel, 6. Ps 53 is almost identical with Ps 14, but uses *Elohim* instead of *Jehovah*.

Psalm 54. Petitions of the godly. David's betrayal by the Ziphites (1 Sam 23:19-27) furnishes the historical occasion for this psalm and offers a prophetic parallel to the prayers, 1-3, of the Jewish saints previous to the advent of Messiah, 4-7.

Psalm 55. In the vortex of great distress. The base defection of Ahithophel, David's trusted counselor, to the traitor Absalom (2 Sam 15:12-17:23) furnished the occasion for the psalmist's deep distress, 3, and anguish to escape the plot, 4-8. Jerusalem had become a city of violence and strife, 9-11, because of the treason of Ahithophel, 12-15. David's assurance of God's help, 16-19, was uttered while suffering from this classic treachery, 20-21. Comfort for the righteous and judgment for the wicked are indicated,22-23 (cf. 2 Sam 17:23).

56-60. Trials of the saints before blessing

Psalm 56. Praise for anticipated deliverance. David was hemmed in by two enemies, his own people and the Philistines while living with the latter in Gath (1 Sam 27: 1-28:22). His trust and comfort, 1-9, produced assurance of deliverance, 10-13.

Psalm 57. Deliverance in distress. David cries to God, 1-5, amid enemies and dangers when he found deliverance from Saul in a cave at Adullam (1 Sam 22:1; 24:3). When his attention shifted from present circumstances his heart became fixed on the God of mercy and truth, and triumph followed, 6-11.

Psalm 58. Judgment upon the wicked. They must suffer punishment, 1-5. The execution of punishment is described, 6-11.

Psalm 59. The hatred of the wicked for the righteous. This cruel animosity is reflected in David's lament when Saul tried to

trap him in his home (1 Sam 19:10-17). It was then the psalmist experienced the hatred from sinners which all God's saints have periodically known.

Psalm 60. A national lament. A temporary reverse of David in the war with the Syrians and Edomites (2 Sam 8:13-14) furnished a lament, 1-5, to be echoed by the Israelite remnant of the end time, 6-12.

61-68. Through sufferings to kingdom blessing

This series, through the experiences of the psalmist, reflects not only the heart cries of suffering saints in general, but of the godly in Israel in the period of trouble before the Kingdom Age.

Psalm 61. Prayer for the king. The personal lament of David, 1-5, perhaps penned on a distant expedition or at the time of Absalom's rebellion, expresses the heart cry of the godly in the nation who look for Messiah's advent to establish the kingdom. The petition for the king, 6-8, goes beyond King David and embraces King-Messiah, as the Targum, the ancient Jewish commentary, correctly interprets.

Psalm 62. The saints' waiting and trusting for deliverance. David's waiting in faith, 1-4, has its expectation in God alone, 5-8, not in the vanity of man, 9-12.

Psalm 63. The saints' thirst for God.
David's burning desire for fellowship with God
despite his trials in the wilderness, 1-8,
prefigures the heart exercise of every true saint
in trouble. The coming judgment of the godless
gives encouragement in tribulation, 9-11.

Psalm 64. The fate of the wicked.
Their bold wickedness, 1-6, will be judged, 7-9,
and the godly remnant will rejoice in the Lord,
10.

**Psalm 65. Millennial restitution of
the earth.** Spiritual blessings are realized, 1-5,
as well as temporal and material benefits, 6-13.
Psalms 65-68 describe 'the time . . . for God to
restore everything, as he promised long ago
through his holy prophets' (Acts 3:21).

**Psalm 66. Worship and praise in the
kingdom.** God's mighty deliverances are
rehearsed, 1-7, with Israel's adoration and
worship resulting, 8-20.

**Psalm 67. Full kingdom joy and
blessing.** The nations know and praise God, 1-
4, and worldwide prosperity ensues, 5-6.

**Psalm 68. Consummation of
redemption.** Israel's joy in the kingdom is the
outcome of the Lord's mighty deliverances, 1-20.
Verse 18 is quoted in Eph 4:7-16 of Christ's
ascension ministry. Israel is regathered and her
last-day enemies are destroyed, 21-23. Full and
universal kingdom blessing is celebrated, 24-35.

69-72. Christ rejected
and exalted

**Psalm 69. The sufferings of the
rejected Messiah.** He is hated without cause,
1-6; bears reproach, 7-12; and prays, 13-21. The
retribution upon His enemies is described, 22-28.
His exaltation and glory follow, 29-36. On 14-20,
cf. Christ's experiences in Gethsemane (Mt
26:36-45). Verse 21 connects with the cross (Mt
27:48; Mk 15:36; Lk 23:36; Jn 19:28-29). Acts
1:20 recalls verse 25. This remarkable psalm
illustrates the deep prophetic strain running
through the Psalms (cf. Lk 24:44).

**Psalm 70. Israel's prayer for
deliverance** recalls and repeats Ps 40:13-17,
David's prayer in time of great stress.

Psalm 71. Israel's paean of hope. The
psalmist declares his faith, 1-18, resulting in
spiritual reviving and victory, 19-24.

Psalm 72. The great kingdom psalm.

The king is invested, 1-4. The extent of the
kingdom, 5-11, and its blessings are viewed, 12-
20. All David's prayers, 20, will find their
fulfillment in the kingdom (cf. 2 Sam 23:1-4).

73-83. Psalms of Asaph
concerning the sanctuary

Book 3 of the Psalter, Psalms 73-89, deals
with the holiness of the Lord's sanctuary. This
portion has been compared to the book of
Leviticus. Eleven psalms are by Asaph, leader of
David's choir (1 Chr 6:39) and composer
(2 Chr 29:30).

**Psalm 73. Problem of the prosperity
of the wicked.** The perplexing question is
the same as in the book of Job, Why do the
wicked flourish, 1-9, and the righteous suffer,
10-14? God's justice and the holiness of the
sanctuary provide an answer to the psalmist,
15-28.

**Psalm 74. Desecration of the
sanctuary by the enemy.** The sight of the
enemy in the sanctuary, 1-9, goes beyond the
historical background of the psalm in the
Babylonian destruction in 586 B.C., or the
desecration by Antiochus Epiphanes. It will be
realized in the Antichrist of the end-time (Mt
24:15). Prayer is made for divine intervention,
10-23.

**Psalm 75. Divine intervention on
behalf of the sanctuary.** Messiah, the
righteous Judge, 1-7, executes His judgment at
His second advent, 8-10.

Psalm 76. Divine government set up.
The Lord reigns in Zion, 1-3, as a result of the
judgments upon the wicked, 4-12.

Psalm 77. The troubled saint, 1-10, finds
his comfort recalling past deliverances, 11-20.

**Psalm 78. God in Israel's history is
seen,** 1-55, despite continued provocation by His
people, 56-64. Grace appears to David, 65-72.

**Psalm 79. Prayer for judgment upon
Jerusalem's enemies.** This lament points to
some great national calamity, such as Shishak's
invasion, the fall of the city to the Babylonians
or to Antiochus Epiphanes. But the prophetic
meaning will find ultimate fulfillment in
Jerusalem under the false messiah when the
cruelties of Antiochus Epiphanes will be repeated
(cf. Rev 11:3-12).

**Psalm 80. Cry for restoration of the
nation Israel.** The Lord, the Shepherd of

Israel (Gen 49:24), is invoked, 1-2, to restore, 3, 7, the chastened and scattered nation, 4-6. Using the figure of a vine (cf. Isa 5:1-7), the psalmist describes the redemption of the nation out of Egypt, 8-13, which is made the basis of the appeal for final pre-kingdom restoration, 14-16, through Messiah, 'the man at your right hand,' 17, who will seek His scattered sheep, 18-19, to restore them, 19. (Cf. 3, 7, 19 with Ezk 35:11-31).

Psalm 81. Israel's regathering. The blowing of trumpets foreshadows Israel's age-end regathering, 1-5, the answer to the prayer of Ps 80:3, 7, 19. The restoration is focused against the background of deliverance out of Egypt, 6-10, and the nation's subsequent disobedience and chastisement, 11-16.

Psalm 82. Pre-kingdom judgment. God takes His place as the supreme and righteous Judge, 1*a*, to judge the nations and to administer justice in contrast to unjust judges, 1*b*-7. His right to judge is in the fact that all the nations belong to Him as He takes possession of the kingdom, 8.

Psalm 83. Israel's enemies overthrown. The nation's foes of the writer's day, 1-8, foreshadow the final coalition and its complete overthrow, 9-18 (cf. Isa 10:28-34; Joel 2:1-11; Dan 11:36- 42; Zech 12:2).

84-89. Prayer issuing in kingdom glory

Psalm 84. Spiritual vitality of the kingdom. Revitalized worship, 1-4; faith, 5-8; and service, 9-12, are realized by the manifestation of the Lord in the person of God's Anointed, 9, Israel's sun (cf. Ps 80:3, 7, 19) and shield, 11.

Psalm 85. Promised blessing in the kingdom. The benefits, 1-3, realized by prayer, 4-9, include righteousness and millennial peace, 10-13.

Psalm 86. A prayer, 1-9, and praise, 10-17, find full realization in the Kingdom Age, as 9 shows (cf. Isa 2:1-5).

Psalm 87. Zion attains glory in the kingdom. Zion (Jerusalem) is honored, 1-6, above all cities and celebrated as a fountain of blessing, 7.

Psalm 88. Soul cry of distress, 1-7, with no apparent answer, 8-18, pictures the dark experiences of the godly in Israel.

Psalm 89. God's fidelity, 1-18, is manifested in the fulfillment of the Davidic covenant, 19-37 (cf. 2 Sam 7:9-14, 27), which can refer only to Immanuel (Isa 7:13-15; 9:6-7; Mic 5:2). The plea of the godly remnant (cf. Isa 1:9; Rom 11:5) goes forth for the cessation of the chastening visited upon the Davidic house, 38-52.

A group of young pilgrim Jews march to the sanctuary of the Western Wall in Jerusalem, singing praises to God, in the same way as their ancestors did centuries earlier.

90-93. From sinful wandering to redemption rest

Book 4 of the Psalter, Psalms 90-106, is compared by some to Numbers, the book of wilderness wandering (cf. Ps 90). It contains numerous psalms describing the time when the wilderness experiences of God's people end with glory for Israel and the nations.

Psalm 90. Man's fallen condition. Moses meditates upon man's frailty and death because of sin, 1-10. He prays for God's intervention on behalf of sinful man, 11-17.

Psalm 91. Redeemed man in fellowship with God. His dependence upon God, 1-2, as He walks among men 'in the shelter of the Most High' under 'the shadow of the Almighty,' results in his security, 3-8, triumph and exaltation, 9-16. Satan realized the application of this psalm to Jesus, 11-12 (cf. Mt 4:6).

Psalm 92. Song of praise for ultimate rest (Song for the Sabbath Day) as a result of God's 'work' of redemption, 4; His conquest of the enemies of His people, 5-9; and His favor to His own, 10-15. The application of the psalm is perennial. Its fulfillment, however, is millennial.

Psalm 93. The Lord's millennial reign (cf. Rev 11:15-18). The Lord begins His reign over the earth in holiness, 5.

94-100. Judgment and the glories of the coming age

Psalm 94. Judgment of the wicked. Prayer is made for divine vengeance upon the wicked, 1-13. The righteous are comforted, 14-23, as their enemies and God's enemies are destroyed.

Psalm 95. Worship and joy in prospect of the advent of Israel's Saviour-King. His right to rule is by virtue of His ownership of the earth, 1-5, and man as a result of creation and redemption, 6-7a. Let those who are about to enter kingdom rest take warning against disobedience from those who forfeited the rest of Canaan, 7b-11 (cf. Heb 3:7-11).

Psalm 96. The second advent. The Lord is supreme, 1-6. Creation celebrates, 7-13. The 'new song' is based on a finished redemption and its realized benefits for man and the earth (cf. Ps 98:1-3).

Psalm 97. The King reigns, 1-5. The results of His reign are indicated, 6-12.

Psalm 98. The new song of triumph. All creation is summoned to celebrate the establishment of the Lord's kingship in the earth with a new song, 1-9.

Psalm 99. The Lord's earthly kingship. He is the ruler of the earth, 1-3. 'He is holy!' is the refrain, 5, 9. His rule will be just, 4:5; His dealings faithful, 6-9.

Psalm 100. Israel's kingdom praise. The call to worship is on the basis of the deity of the King and the redemption wrought by Him for His own, 2, and the fact of His goodness and His covenant mercy, 5.

101-106. The righteous king in humiliation and glory

Psalm 101. The righteous King and His rule. David speaks as a prophet of the true King's character, 1-3, and His righteous kingdom rule, 4-8.

Psalm 102. Christ the King in His rejection. The reference to verses 25-27 in Heb 1:10-12 demonstrates that this ode predicts the sorrow and anguish of the God-Man.

Psalm 103. Israel's kingdom praise is rendered for blessings of full salvation, 1-7; for the Lord's gracious character, 8-18; and for His established kingdom, 19-22.

Psalm 104. Creation's praise to the creator, Messiah-Christ, 1-9 (cf. 4 with Heb 1:7),

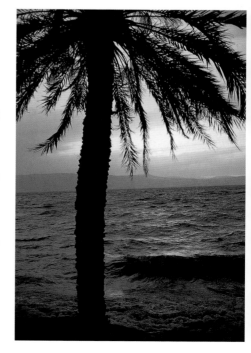

for His creation works manifesting His kindness and greatness, 10-35.

Psalm 105. Historical retrospect. The wonders of the exodus from Egypt are celebrated.

Psalm 106. Historical retrospect. The goodness and patience of God in the desert wanderings are recalled.

107 -108. Israel's deliverances and praise to God

Book 5 of the Psalter, Psalms 107-150, is compared by some to Deuteronomy. It sets forth the divine dealing with Israel eventuating in deliverance for them, the nation, and all creation. The book ends with a Hallelujah Chorus of redemption.

Psalm 107. God's mercies to Israel. Their final regathering and restoration, 1-9 (cf. Deut 30:1-10); their liberation from bondage, 10-16, despite their folly, 17-22, and unrest, 23-32, are reviewed. Their praise of God for His deliverances is recorded, 33-43.

Psalm 108. Israel's praise, 1-4, for her inheritance, 5-9, through the Lord, 10-13, is offered.

109-113. Christ in rejection, exaltation and coming glory

Psalm 109. Prediction of Christ's rejection. David as prophet sees the despised and rejected One, 1-5, His accusers and their doom, 6-20 (cf. 8 and Acts 1:20). The voice of the rejected One echoes in 21-25, and merges into the voice of the final remnant, 26-31, identified with Him.

Psalm 110. Christ as King-Priest. Christ, David's son and Lord (His deity), is exalted in resurrection and ascension, 1 (cf. Jn 20:17; Acts 7:56), and waiting till His enemies are put down. His second advent, 2-3, to accomplish this and reign as King-Priest according to His eternal priesthood, is described, 4 (Heb 5:6; 6:20; 7:21). His judgments and victories prior to His kingdom glory are predicted, 5-7 (cf. Joel 3:9-17; Zech 14:1-4; Rev 19:11-21).

Psalm 111. Hallelujah! The King-Priest on his throne (cf. Ps 110). First of the hallelujah ('Praise the Lord') psalms. His work of redemption is praised (Lk 1:68).

Psalm 112. Hallelujah! The righteous

Jews at Jerusalem's Western Wall surround the revered Torah scrolls. Psalm 119 celebrates the Law of God.

are rewarded by the King-Priest on his throne.

Psalm 113. Hallelujah! Praise the Lord for what He is, 1-6, and what He does, 7-9.

114-117. Past deliverances and future praise

Psalm 114. The Egyptian deliverance in retrospect. Future deliverance is implicit in prospect (cf. Jer 16:14-15).

Psalm 115. Israel's God. Who He is, 1-3, is contrasted with what idols are, 4-8. The exalted One can be implicitly trusted, 9-18.

Psalm 116. Israel's praise of God for deliverance from death, 19. This centers in the dark experiences of unparalleled suffering and martyrdom, 15. The godly who escape thank God, 10-19.

Psalm 117. Universal praise in the kingdom. The praise, 1, is followed by the reason for it, 2.

118-119. Messiah and the Word of God exalted

Psalm 118. Messiah exalted as the Chief Cornerstone. This great hallelujah psalm was sung along with Psalms 114-117 and 136 by our Lord and His disciples in observing the Passover the night He was betrayed (Mt 26:30; Mk 14:26). He applied verses 22-23 to Himself (Mt 21:42). The psalm looks beyond the rejection of the Stone (Christ) to His ultimate exaltation in the kingdom.

Psalm 119. The word of God exalted. Although applicable to all generations this magnificent alphabetic acrostic (each of the 22 letters of the Heb. alphabet occurs eight times in the 22 sections) will be finally fulfilled when Israel, under the new covenant, will have the law written 'on their hearts' (Jer 31:31-33).

120-134. The psalms of ascent

Apparently these psalms were sung as pilgrims went up to Jerusalem to the sacred feasts.

Psalm 120. Suffering of the godly. David's prayer for deliverance from enemies and persecutors breathes the same spirit as the cry of the distressed godly of all ages.

Psalm 121. Israel's keeper and preserver. He never fails His own, 1-8.

Psalm 122. Prayer for Jerusalem's peace. This is a song praising Zion as the pilgrims' goal. A group of pilgrims arrives for a feast and admires the city, 1-5, and prays for its peace and prosperity, 6-9.

Psalm 123. Cry for mercy in distress. Humble dependence upon God, 1-2, and a plea for mercy is made, 3-4, in the face of contempt from the proud and the worldly.

Psalm 124. Answer of prayer for mercy. This psalm is the answer to the cry of Ps 123.

Psalm 125. Reward of the righteous and punishment of the wicked. Expression of confident faith, 1-3, and prayer for help, 4-5, will be fulfilled in Israel's future blessings.

Psalm 126. Song of the returned captives. The joy of past favors, 1-3, inspires prayer for final restoration, 4-6.

Psalm 127. Praise God from whom all blessings flow. Faith in God is basic to all real prosperity, 1-2. The gift of many male children is a blessing to an Oriental father, 3-5.

Psalm 128. Blessings out of Zion are to be fully realized when the Lord reigns.

Psalm 129. The Lord, Israel's preserver, has protected His people in the past, 1-4. Prayer is offered that Israel's enemies may not triumph over her, 5-8.

Psalm 130. The Lord, Israel's faithful redeemer. The personal experience of a believer, 1-6, is a pattern for the nation, 7-8.

Psalm 131. The Lord, Israel's hope. The psalmist's experience of quiet submission, 1-2, is an example for the nation, 3.

Psalm 132. Messiah, David's son, enthroned. David's concern for God's house, 1-10, is rewarded by the Davidic covenant, 11-12. It will be realized in King-Messiah at His second advent, 13-18.

Psalm 133. The blessings of fraternal harmony. Such brotherhood is good and pleasant, 1, like Aaron's anointing, 2, and refreshing dew on Mt. Hermon, 3. It is the atmosphere in which God commands spiritual blessing.

Psalm 134. Blessed worship. The priests are called to render praise to the Lord, 1, and to bless the congregation, 2-3.

135-136. Restored Israel in praiseful worship

Psalm 135. The cleansed nation worships (cf. Ex 19:4-5; Zech 3:17). The call is to worship, 1-4, and adore Him who controls nature, 5-7; who redeemed the nation and set it in Palestine, 8-18; who is above all gods and is therefore worthy of all worship, 19-21.

Psalm 136. The redeemed nation's praise of God's mercy. His mercy is revealed in creation, 1-9; in Israel's redemption, 10-15; in the wilderness wanderings, 16; and in the conquest of Canaan, 17-22. A summary of His mercy follows, 23-26. This psalm is called the 'Great Hallel' (cf. Ps 114-118) in Jewish Passover liturgy and may have been sung by Christ and His disciples after the Last Supper (Mt 26:30; Mk 14:26).

137-139. The experiences of God's people in the light of their God

Psalm 137. The experience of the exile looks through the Babylonian Captivity to the final age-end restoration when Israel's foes are punished, 8-9 (cf. Isa 13:16; 47:6).

Psalm 138. Praise to the Lord, 1-3, culminates in full kingdom blessing, 4-6, but brings immediate blessing to the worshiper, 78.

Psalm 139. Israel's Creator-Redeemer is omniscient, 1-6; omnipresent, 7-12; worthy of all praise, 13-18; righteous and holy to punish sin and sinners, 19-24.

140-143. Trials and troubles of God's people

Psalms 140-143. Prayer for deliverance from enemies. These reflect David's various experiences of suffering. He cries for vindication in his distress, and prays for deliverance and restoration to spiritual prosperity.

144-145. David's experiences a mirror of Israel's future

Psalm 144. Prayer for manifestation of the Lord's power. God is praised, 1-2, and His help invoked in the light of man's weakness, 3-4. Let the Lord come to deliver from enemies, 5-8. Israel's 'new song' of redemption, 9-11, will be sung in kingdom blessing, 12-15 (cf. Ps 96:1; Rev 5:9; 14:3; 15:3).

Psalm 145. The glory of King-Messiah and His kingdom. This is an alphabetic acrostic of personal praise, 1-3; of the Lord's

wonderful works, 4-7; of His love, 8-9; of His millennial kingdom, 10-13 ; and His providential care for His creatures, 14-21.

146-150. The grand hallelujah finale

Each of these five psalms opens and closes with Hallelujah, 'Praise the Lord.'

Psalm 146. Hallelujah! The God of Jacob, 1-2. This is the designation of Him who loves the helpless sinner in redemptive compassion, 3-4; yet who is the mighty Creator, faithful, righteous, provident, 5-7; the glorious Saviour and Protector, 89,and the eternal King, 10.

Psalm 147. Hallelujah! For His power and providential care, 1-11, especially toward Israel, 12-20.

Psalm 148. Hallelujah! Let all creatures praise Him in heaven, 16, and on earth, 7-14.

Psalm 149. Hallelujah! Sing the new song of redemption. Redeemed Israel leads the Hallelujah Chorus, 1-3, because the Lord has given victory, vindicating His own, 4-9.

Psalm 150. Hallelujah! Climactic crescendo of universal praise. The ultimate purpose of creation is the praise of the Creator. God alone is worthy. Hallelujah!

Jerusalem viewed from the slopes of the Mount of Olives. The psalms of ascent were sung as pilgrims went up to Jerusalem for the sacred feasts.

PROVERBS

Compendium of moral and spiritual instruction

Nature of the book. Among the OT books, Proverbs is most typical of ancient Near Eastern wisdom literature. It is a library of moral and spiritual instruction for the young to ensure a godly, happy life here and reward in the life to come. A proverb (Heb. *masal*, possibly related to the identical root, *msl*, meaning 'to reign, rule.' It has the basic meaning, 'to be like, represent') is a short precept *regulating or governing* conduct and life, often taking the form of a resemblance or parable. Many proverbs are condensed parables.

Authorship. Many of the proverbs stem from Solomon (1:1; 10:1; 25:1; cf. 1 Kgs 4:32; 2 Chr 1:10; Eccl 12:9); some from Agur (30:1) and Lemuel (31:1), who are unknown persons.

Recipients. The writer's son (1:8; 2:1, etc.) is presumably Rehoboam. But the precepts are for all youth (4:1), and in broadest scope for all men (8:1-5).

Proverbs and Near Eastern literature. The section 22:17-24:34 bears special similarity to the proverbs of an Egyptian writer by the name of Amenemope (dated between 1000-600 B.C.), showing the prevalence of this type of wisdom literature outside the Bible. Proverbial literature is very ancient, going back in written form to about 2700 B.C. in Egypt.

'The fear of the LORD is the beginning of wisdom' (Proverbs 1:7).

Outline

1:1-9:18 Book 1. Proverbs of Solomon
10:1-22:16 Book 2. Various sayings of Solomon
22:17-24:34 Book 3. Words of the wise
25:1-29:27 Book 4. Proverbs copied by Hezekiah's Scribes
30:1-33 Agur's words
31:1-9 Queen mother's counsel to her son
31:10-31 The virtuous wife

1. Purpose of the book of Proverbs

1-7. To promote wisdom and godly living. Verse 7 strikes the theme of the entire book. Reverence toward God is the essential prelude to all wisdom and successful living.

8-19. Home discipline is a moral safeguard against a life of crime.

20-33. Wisdom personified as a prophetess and teacher. She shows the folly of those who reject moral instruction and discipline.

2-3. Results of the pursuit of wisdom

2:1-22. The promise of wisdom. The pursuit of wisdom brings a knowledge of God, 5; produces moral safeguards, 6-15; delivers from the loose woman, 16-19; and gives prosperity, 20-22.

3:1-35. The precepts of wisdom make for physical and spiritual well-being, 1-10. Even adversity becomes the discipline of a loving father, 11-12, and inculcates a true sense of values, 13-18, understanding of God's creation, 19-20, and practical righteousness, 21-35.

4. The primacy of wisdom

1-19. In both teacher and student. The teacher had been taught wisdom by his parents, 1-9, and the pupil is admonished

likewise to receive wisdom and profit by it, 10-19, as the principal acquirement of life.

20-27. Wisdom practiced is productive of life, health and personal integrity.

5-7. Moral restraint of wisdom

5:1-14. Restraint against sexual sins is urged and marital infidelity is warned against, 15-23.

6:1-35. Restraint against various sins. Mentioned are debt, providing surety (cosigning loans), 1-5; laziness, 6-11; irresponsible gossip, 12-15; wickedness in general, 16-19; and adultery, 20-35.

7:1-27. Restraint against the loose woman. Wisdom is personified, 4 (cf. 1:20-33).

8. Remarkable revelation of wisdom's identity

1-21. Personified wisdom. Her call, 1-5, is followed by announcement of her worth, 6-11; her authority, 12-16; her rewards, 17-21.

22-31. Revelation of personified wisdom's identity. Wisdom as a person is revealed to be the preincarnate Christ (although some scholars have denied this). Here wisdom is revealed to be coeval and coexistent with God. 'The Lord *possessed* [not created] me at the beginning of his work, *before* his deeds of old,' 22. This beginning, like John 1: 1: 'In the

Women at work in fields near ancient Samaria. Proverbs always commends hard work.

beginning was the Word,' is an absolute timeless beginning. This magnificent passage anticipates 1 Cor. 1:30; Jn 1:1-3; Heb 1:1-3.

32-36. Renewed appeal. How true it is that he who finds God is 'happy,' 32, 34, because he finds life in Christ the true wisdom of God.

9. Contrast between wisdom and folly

1-12. Wisdom's invitation. Personified wisdom (revealed to be Christ) issues an invitation (Mt 11:28-29; cf. Lk 14:15-24).

13-18. Folly's enticement. Folly, too, is personified as a foolish woman, and those who choose her instead of our Lord court death and hell.

10:1-22:16. The godly and ungodly in contrast and other maxims

10:1-11:31. Contrast in life and conduct is made in matters of work, diligence, ambition, speech, truth, stability, honesty, integrity, fidelity , guidance, graciousness, kindness, etc.

12: 1-28. Contrast is made in relation to various conditions, in thought, words, in domestic relationships, etc.

13:1-25. Contrast in relation to advantage and disadvantage.

14:1-35. Contrast between the wise and foolish, the rich and poor.

15:1-33. The better course of wisdom and serving God.

16:1-33. The better way of life through serving the Lord.

17:1-18:24. Various maxims regulating good conduct.

19:1-22:16. Various proverbs regulating personal conduct.

22:17-24:34. The words of the wise

This section, Book 3, shows affinity to the Wisdom of Amenemope (see above). This portion is a teacher's instructions to his student ('son') who is being educated for a place of responsibility.

22:17-21. Introduction. The Egyptian Wisdom of Amenemope also has 30 sections, of which ten have parallels here.

23:1-35. Various admonitions are given. These concern being a guest, 1-8; speaking, 9; removing a boundary stone, 10-11 ; parental discipline, 12-14, etc.

24:1-34. Various admonitions are added. These concern envy, 1-2; wisdom, etc.

25-29. Proverbs copied by Hezekiah's scribes

These constitute Book 4 and consist of separate proverbs guiding moral conduct. They were collected in Hezekiah's time (716-687 b.c.).

25.1-28. Wise conduct is enjoined before a king, 1-7; in court, 8-10; in speech, 11-18; in dealing with enemies, 19-22, etc.

26: 1-28. Other sins. Singled out are the fool, 1-12; the sluggard, 13-16; the meddler, the tale-bearer, 17-20, 22-23; the contentious, 21; the hater, 24-26; and the liar, 28.

27:1-29:27. Various other maxims. These cover different phases of conduct.

30. Agur's words

1-10. God's power, truth and centrality so overwhelm Agur (otherwise unknown) of Massa (cf. Gen 25:14) that he abases himself and owns his ignorance, 1-3. (Cf. Job 42:1-6 as a sequel to God's might as revealed to Job, ch. 40-41.) Such a God must have first place in Agur's life against the dangers of wealth with its pride or poverty, 7-9, with its desperation, 10.

11-17. Exposé of rogues and extortioners is made by their counterparts in nature of things 'never satisfied' – the leech, 15; the grave, the barren womb, thirsty land, and fire, 16.

18-20. Exposé of the shameless adulteress, by four wonders in nature: the eagle in flight, a gliding snake, a sailing ship, and a man and a maiden (cf. 2:16-20; 5:1-23; 23:27, etc.).

21-23. Exposé of the arrogant, foolish.

24-33. Exposé of the indolent, disorderly, cowardly, by the industrious ant, humble badgers, orderly locusts and puny lizard; by the fearless lion, strutting rooster, he-goat, and king. Warning against strife is given, 32-33.

Numerical Proverbs. Hebrew poetic literature often contains the formula, x, x+1 (e.g., for three . . . for four). This parallel structure signifies totality or completion (cf. Job 33: 14; Amos 1:3-2:16).

31:1-9. A queen mother's counsel to her son

1. Words of Lemuel are a twofold lesson taught him by his mother. His name is unidentifiable, and Massa could be a place name (cf. Gen 25:14), or simply 'King Lemuel – an oracle.'

2-9. The maternal warning is given negatively to avoid lust, 3, and strong drink, 4-7; and positively to rule righteously and impartially, 8-9.

31:10-31. The virtues of an ideal wife

This noble acrostic poem (each verse beginning with a letter of the Heb. alphabet) is a choice gem of wisdom literature. It may be a part of the queen mother's counsel to her son, 31:1-9, or a separate poem.

10-28. The character of the ideal wife. She is priceless, 10; trustworthy, 11; industrious, 12-19; charitable and unselfish, 20-22; a boon to her husband, 23; possessing business acumen, 24; strong, dignified, 25; wise, provident, 26-27; and respected and loved by her children, 28.

29-31. Writer's appraisal of her. She is superlative, 29. Two appended proverbs on the godly woman are deduced, 30-31.

The value of women. Contrary to critics who claim that the Bible has a demeaning view of women, this description is highly exalting, as it views women performing many economic roles in the family.

According to Proverbs 31, the ideal wife is priceless, trustworthy, industrious, charitable and unselfish, strong, dignified, wise, provident, and respected and loved by her children.

ECCLESIASTES

The futile thinking and living of the natural man

Place in canon. In the Hebrew Bible to book is placed in the third division with the books of the *Megillôt* (Song, Ruth, Lamentations, Esther) used at special feasts. Ecclesiastes was read at the Feast of Tabernacles in the fall. In the English order, it is placed as wisdom literature after Proverbs. Because its meaning has been frequently misunderstood, its legitimate place in the canon has sometimes been disputed.

Difficulty of the book. Ecclesiastes is perhaps the most perplexing and confusing book of the Bible to the average reader. Reasons: (1) Its spirit of hopeless despair, depicting the emptiness and disappointment of life. (2) Its lack of a note of praise or peace, in contrast to other wisdom literature of Scripture. (3) Its seeming sanction of conduct at variance with the rest of Scripture.

Nature and purpose of the book. The difficulties can be resolved only by a correct view of the nature and purpose of the book. (1) It must first be understood as the *book of the natural man* – his reasonings and actions apart from the Spirit of God and divine revelation (cf. 1 Cor 2:14). This is the meaning of the characteristic phrase 'under the sun,' occurring 29 times. This is why the covenant name 'Lord' (Jehovah) is not used, only Elohim as Creator. Hence throughout most of his musings, the writer is limited to natural revelation (the light which nature gives) and human reason (cf. the clause 'I thought to myself,' occurring seven times). (2) The

purpose of the book must be seen to demonstrate to the natural man the complete emptiness of that which is 'under the sun' apart from that which is *above* the sun, i.e., God's revelation and salvation.

Outline

1:1-3 The theme. The supreme emptiness of godless living

1:4-3:22 The theme proved
4:1-12:8 The theme expanded
12:9-14 The conclusion reached

Tombs on the Mount of Olives, Jerusalem. The purpose of this book is to demonstrate to the natural man the complete emptiness of that which is 'under the sun'.

Remember your creator while you are still young.

1:1-3. The theme of the book

See 'The Nature and Purpose of the Book' above. 'Meaningless! Meaningless!' is a Heb. expression meaning the supreme or consummate 'vanity' or 'emptiness' ('breath'). 'Teacher' (Heb. *qohelet; Gr. Ecclesiastes)* suggests one who addresses or teaches an assembly (Heb. *qahal*). The feminine signifies an office or title. Koheleth (a pen name?) is intimated to be Solomon, 1, 12.

1:4-3:22. The theme of the emptiness of life proved

1:4-11. By the transitoriness of things. Generations pass on, nature continues in the same round, but nothing new results.

1:12-18. By the futility of human endeavor.

2:1-26. By the emptiness of pleasure, wealth and work. Man's sole good is present enjoyment, argues the natural man, as later Gr. philosophers concluded by natural reason.

3:1-22. By the certainty of death. Mortality robs man of the fruits of his labor (cf. 2:12-26). Man is helpless to understand or alter the predetermined pattern of his life, 1-15. Is his end not like that of the beasts, 16-22?

4:1-12:8. The theme of the emptiness of life expanded

4:1-16. In view of the inequalities of life. The folly of wasting life through envy or avarice is noted, 1-6, a miser's wealth being a cheap substitute for human fellowship, 7-12. Even royal fame and power are evanescent, 13-16.

5: 1-7; 8:20. In view of religious insincerity and wealth.

6:1-12. In view of man's end. Both his life and his death are uncertain. The natural man without divine illumination is baffled by both.

7:1-29. In view of man's sin. The man 'under the sun,' the natural mind unilluminated by God's Spirit, sees no advantage in being righteous, 13-21, and is

Theological note

In a study of this book one must carefully distinguish between what is revealed truth and what is merely the inspired record of man's unaided reasonings. Erroneous teachings, such as annihilation, 3:16-22, and soul sleep, 9:5, 10, cannot be said to be taught by God's Word when they are recorded by inspiration as merely natural man's reasonings.

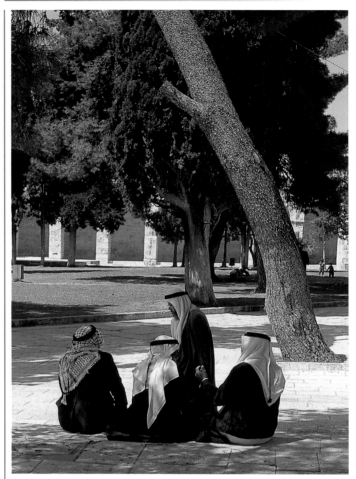

'What profit can we show for all our toil under the sun?'

need of salvation in Christ. The meaning of youth, 9-10, is vague to Koheleth in his natur[al] reasonings.

12:1-8. In view of old age. Koheleth does rise to see the creatorship of God and urg[es] remembrance of God as such in youth. But th[e] natural man needs more than the knowledge [of] God as Creator if he is to be lifted out of his natural blindness. He needs God as *Saviour.* Symbols of old age are set forth, 2-6: 'grinder[s]' (teeth?), 3; 'those looking through the windo[w]' (eyes?), 3; 'almond tree blossoms,' 5, are whi[te] suggesting the silver-white hair of the aged; 't[he] grasshopper drags himself along,' 5, the stiff-legged gait of the aged.

12:9-14. Conclusion reached – practical piety in view of judgment

'Fear [reverence] God and keep his commandments.' This is the whole duty of *redeemed* man. But Koheleth does not tell h[ow] man is to be redeemed.

hazy with regard to spiritual things and the meaning of earthly existence and its end.

8:1-9:18. In view of life's uncertainties. The natural mind flounders in obscurity. It vaguely bows to wisdom, 8:1, and to the king because he is absolute, 2-4. But life itself is a riddle and nothing absolute can be known about the future, 5-9, nor anything of life in general. Death is a conundrum, 9:1-16, to the spiritually unrenewed man.

10:1-20. In view of life's disorders. Only divine revelation can give symmetry and meaning to life. The man 'under the sun' here gives further proof of his lack of spiritual illumination.

11:1-10. In view of youth. Various proverbs are set forth, 1-7. The natural man needs a supernatural birth to enable him to discern spiritual meaning in life and death. Ecclesiastes proves it. The book mirrors the heart of the unregenerate man and points to his

SONG OF SOLOMON

Sanctity of wedded love

A Jewish bride.

The book and its author.

The author was likely Solomon as 1:1 states, and as the local color and internal evidence sustain. However, this verse may be rendered: 'The song of songs which is *about or concerning* Solomon' (cf. 1:4; 3:7-11; 8:11). 'Song of songs' is a Heb. idiom for 'chiefest' or 'most superlative song' of the monarch's 1005 songs (cf. 1 Kgs 4:32). The date is about 965 B.C. It is the first of the five scrolls in the third part of the Heb. canon, and was sung at Passover in the spring. It is a magnificent literary gem, considered eminently chaste among Orientals. What a pity that such a masterpiece should sometimes be perverted.

The purpose.

Critics quibble over the question of whether it is a homogenous poem, or just a collection of love lyrics to celebrate an Eastern wedding. We believe it is a homogenous poem and its purposes are:

1. In a general sense to honor marriage and the joys of wedded love. The key word is 'lover' (32 times), and the theme is the love of the bridegroom for the bride.
2. Additionally, the poem allows application as an allegory, proclaiming the Lord's love for Israel (Hos 2:10-20), and Christ's love for the church (2 Cor 11:2; Eph 5:25-33; Rev 19:79).

The characters.

Song of Solomon has been interpreted variously as having two or three principal actors. Traditionally, the poem has been set with two characters, the Shulammite maiden and the beloved (Solomon). Others prefer to see three characters; the maiden, the beloved (a shepherd lover to whom the maiden is betrothed), and Solomon, who tries unsuccessfully to win the maiden away from her lover. Those who take the second view typically deny Solomonic authorship, so this discussion will follow the traditional view

The background of the story.

H.A. Ironside's presentation of the setting of the poem is meaningful. King Solomon had a vineyard in the hill country of Ephraim, about 50 miles N of Jerusalem, 8:11. He let it out to keepers, 8:11, consisting of a mother, two sons, 16, and two daughters – the Shulammite, 6:13, and a little sister, 8:8. The Shulammite was 'the Cinderella' of the family, 15, naturally beautiful but unnoticed. Her brothers were likely half brothers, 16. They made her work very hard tending the vineyards, so that she had little opportunity to care for her personal appearance, 16. She pruned the vines and set traps for the little foxes, 2:15. She also kept the flocks, 18. Being out in the open so much, she became sunburned, 1:5.

One day a handsome stranger came to the vineyard. It was Solomon disguised. He showed an interest in her, and she became embarrassed concerning her personal appearance, 1:6. She took him for a shepherd and asked about his flocks, 1:7. He answered evasively, 1:8, but also spoke loving words to her, 1:8-10, and promised rich gifts for the future, 1:11. He won her heart and left with the promise that some day he would return. She dreamed of him at night and sometimes thought he was near, 3:1. Finally he did return in all his kingly splendor to make her his bride, 3:6-7. This prefigures Christ, who came first as Shepherd and won His Bride. Later He will return as King, and then will be consummated the marriage of the Lamb.

Outline

1:1-3:5 Bride muses in the bridegroom's palace
3:6-5:1 Bride accepts the bridegroom's invitation
5:2-6:3 Bride dreams of separation from the bridegroom
6:4-8:14 Bride and bridegroom express ardent love for each other

1:1–3:5. Musings of the bride in the bridegroom's palace

1:1-17. She muses on her first love for Solomon. On that title, 1:1, see introduction. The Song begins with the bride's recollection of her first intense longings for her beloved, 2-3, and how she had first voiced her love for him, 4. She explains her dark beauty to the palace women as due to sunburn and hard work in her brothers' vineyard before Solomon's visit, 5-6, when they fell in love (see background of the story in the introduction). She reminisces on her lover (Solomon) when he first appeared at the vineyard disguised as a shepherd, 7. Verse 8 is apparently the reply of the bride's companions. She vividly recalls the king's rapturous praise of her beauty, 9-11; her praising him as her beloved, 12-14; his assuring her of his delight in her beauty, 15; and her own response to his love, 16-17.

2:1-3:5. The bride's musings on the blossoming romance. She recalls Solomon's comparing himself and her to lovely flowers, 2:1-2, and her intense satisfaction in his companionship, 3-6. The refrain, 7 (cf. 3:5; 8:4), which the bride addresses to 'the daughters of Jerusalem,' i.e., the women of the king's harem in Jerusalem, is that Solomon and the maid are not to be disturbed 'until it so desires,' i.e., until love has run its full course. Continuing to turn leaves in her book of memory, she recalls rapturously Solomon's visit to her and his invitation to be his bride and come with him to Jerusalem, 8-17. The bride's first dream, 3:1-4 (cf. 5:2-8), is recalled in which she envisioned herself separated from her beloved at Jerusalem. After finding him, she dreamed she had led him to her humble home in the north.

3:6–5:1. The bride accepts the bridegroom's invitation

3 :6-11. Solomon brings his bride to Jerusalem. Her dream, 1-4, is closely connected with ch. 2 as well as 3:5 (cf. 2:7). Solomon comes for his bride and takes her from her rural home to Jerusalem, 6-11.

4:1-15. The bridegroom praises the bride. The beauty of marital love is here emphasized. Similarly, the Lord will proclaim His delight in His Bride on the day of His appearance.

4:16-5:1. Anticipation of the joys of married love, signifying the blessings of the Lord's redeemed in manifested union and glory with Him (1 Jn 3:3; Rev 19:5-7; 20:6).

5:2–6:3. The bride dreams of separation from the bridegroom but finds him

5:2-8. The bride's second dream (cf. 3:1-4). The bridegroom knocks at her door, but he is not there when she opens it. She wanders about the city in search for him. This experience is evidently a dream (see 6:2).

5:9-6:3. In praising him to others, she claims him as her own. Her dream shows how much she loves him and misses him.

6:4–8:14. The bride and bridegroom express their ardent love for one another

6:4-10. He praises her loveliness. His praise of her beauty recalls his ardent praise in 4:1-15. Tirzah, 4, was a city of northern Israel, which became the capital of the northern kingdom till Omri founded Samaria.

6:11-13. Her experience in the nut orchard. This experience was an emotional elation in connection with which she is called the 'Shulammite,' 13, i.e., 'a maid of Shunem,' a small town in northern Palestine (the *n* often inter-changes with *l* in Semitic languages). Others suggest that 'Shulammite' should read *Shelomith,* a feminine form of Solomon (Heb. *Selomo*), hence 'Solomoness' (i.e., 'queen or princess of Solomon').

7:1-8:14. Mutual praise and devotion. They both express their praise of and devotion to each other, 7:1-8:4, asserting their unquenchable love, 8:5-14.

The prophets

The prophets' messages.
These were primarily moral and spiritual in their purpose. Israel's prophets were rugged reformers, divinely raised up to call the nation from sin and idolatry in its periods of decline. They thundered forth warnings of impending doom in the centuries preceding the fall of Israel in 722 B.C. and the fall of Judah in 586 B.C. Their weighty messages of woe, however, were frequently the vehicle for far-reaching messianic prophecies.

Daniel and Ezekiel ministered hope and comfort to the exiles. Haggai and Zechariah encouraged the weak remnant that returned. Malachi sounded a somber note of warning and repentance illuminated by brilliant messianic flashes.

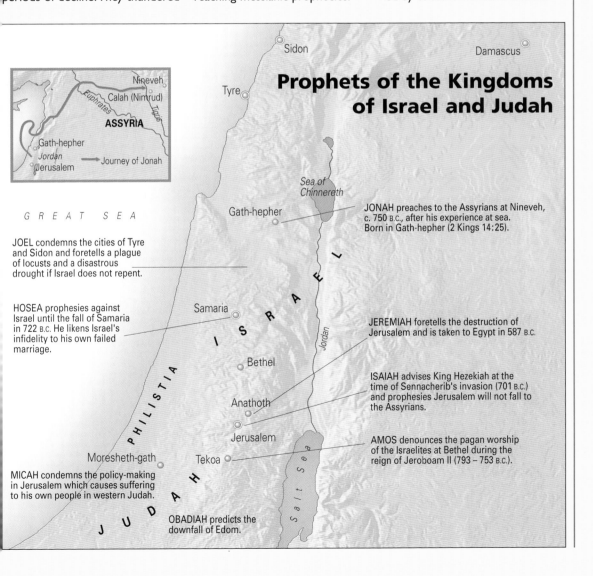

Prophets of the Kingdoms of Israel and Judah

Sidon

Damascus

Tyre

Nineveh
Calah (Nimrud)
ASSYRIA
Euphrates
Tigris
Gath-hepher
Jordan
Jerusalem
→ Journey of Jonah

Sea of Chinnereth

GREAT SEA

Gath-hepher

JONAH preaches to the Assyrians at Nineveh, c. 750 B.C., after his experience at sea. Born in Gath-hepher (2 Kings 14:25).

JOEL condemns the cities of Tyre and Sidon and foretells a plague of locusts and a disastrous drought if Israel does not repent.

I S R A E L

HOSEA prophesies against Israel until the fall of Samaria in 722 B.C. He likens Israel's infidelity to his own failed marriage.

Samaria

JEREMIAH foretells the destruction of Jerusalem and is taken to Egypt in 587 B.C.

Jordan

Bethel

ISAIAH advises King Hezekiah at the time of Sennacherib's invasion (701 B.C.) and prophesies Jerusalem will not fall to the Assyrians.

P H I L I S T I A

Anathoth

Jerusalem

AMOS denounces the pagan worship of the Israelites at Bethel during the reign of Jeroboam II (793 – 753 B.C.).

Moresheth-gath

Tekoa

Salt Sea

MICAH condemns the policy-making in Jerusalem which causes suffering to his own people in western Judah.

J U D A H

OBADIAH predicts the downfall of Edom.

Contemporary Kings of Israel, Syria and Assyria

Jeroboam II
793-53

Ben-hadad III
c.806-770

And a
successor?

Ashurdan III
773-55

Assyria weak

Zechariah
753-52

Shallum
752

Menahem
752-42

Pekah
752-32

Pekahiah
742-40

Ashur-nirari V
755-45

Assyria weak

**Tiglath-
Pileser III**
745-27

Pul of 2 Kgs 15:19
to whom Ahaz
appealed for
aid against Rezin
and Pekah,
and who invaded
and carried
captive northern
Israel (733). In
732 he captured
Damascus and
killed Rezin, and
put all northern
Palestine and
Syria under
tribute

Rezin
c.740-32

**722
Fall of Samaria**

Sargon II
722-05

Took Samaria in
722, when
27,290 chief
citizens were
carried into
captivity. This
was the end of
the northern
kingdom of
Israel

Shalmaneser V
727-22
(2 Kgs 17:3;18:9)

Conquered the
Phoenician coast,
received tribute
from Hoshea,
and laid siege
to Samaria when
Hoshea allied
himself with So
(2 Kgs 17:4),
an otherwise
unknown
Egyptian ruler

Hoshea
732-22

KEY

Syria

Israel

Assyria

Sennacherib
705-681

Great statesman,
conqueror,
aqueduct builder
invaded Judah in
701 B.C.
He mentions
Hezekiah in his
annals inscribed
in cuneiform on
clay prism in the
British Museum
(a copy is also in the
Oriental Institute
of the University
of Chicago).
(Cf. Isa 36-37;
2 Kgs 18-19).

ISAIAH

Prophecy of the coming Saviour and Israel's King

Writer

Isaiah ('Jehovah is salvation') is the great messianic prophet and prince of OT prophets. For splendor of diction, brilliance of imagery, versatility and beauty of style, profundity and breadth of prophetic vision, he is without peer. He was the son of Amoz (1:1) and traditionally said to be of royal extraction – the brother of King Amaziah, grandson of King Joash. The traditional dates for his ministry are c. 750-680 B.C.

Unity of the book

Since the days of J.C. Doederlein (1775) the Isaianic authorship of ch. 40-66 has been commonly denied. Critics have attributed this section to an unknown 'Deutero-Isaiah' of the period 550-539 B.C. and other have imagined a third author (Trito-Isaiah) for ch. 55-66, dating them around 450 B.C.

Three main arguments are advanced against the unity of the book: (a) *The literary style,* (b) *the theological ideas,* and (c) *the theme and subject matter* are supposedly different in the two (or three) main sections of the book. It is stated that these differences can be accounted for only by a difference in authorship. However, careful study reveals that *similarities in style* between the sections are more significant that the supposed differences, and even those differences are explained by the change in Isaiah's situation during the later years. The most notable similarity is the use of the title, 'The Holy One of Israel,' which occurs 12 times in 1-39, 14 times in 40-66, and only 6 other times in the entire Bible. As to the alleged theological

differences, the germinal doctrines of ch. 40-66 can be traced in the earlier section. *No theological contradictions* between the sections can be found. The changed political conditions under the wicked Manasseh in the later years account for the new emphases which appear.

The argument that the theme and subject matter of the later chapters require another author is more serious. Ch. 1-39 are contemporary in setting, while ch. 40-66 are future to Isaiah's time. Critics argue that it is rationally untenable to hold that the prophets ever projected themselves (by divine revelation) into an ideal standpoint in the future. Since in these later chapters Isaiah sees events distinctly related to the

Babylonian Captivity and the return therefrom, which have since been historically fulfilled, this material must have been added later by a 'Second Isaiah' who was contemporary with the return from the Captivity. However, *futuristic prophecy has an important role* in the first section as well as in the second. In addition, the decadent age of Manasseh demanded a series of prophecies which would reveal the future glory for Israel as the light of her testimony burned low. There is nothing unnatural about the themes of ch. 40-66 when compared with ch. 1-39.

Messianic character of the book

Of all the prophetic books of the

Outline

1-35 Prophecies from the standpoint of Isaiah's day.

1:1-6:13 Vol. I Book of reproof and promise
7:1-12:6 Vol. II Book of Immanuel
13:1-23:18 Vol. III God's oracle of judgment upon the nations
24:1-27:13 Vol. IV Book of judgment and promise
28:1-35:10 Vol. V Book of woes preceding restoration glories

36-39 Historical interlude

36:1-39:8 Vol. VI Historical parenthesis

40-66 Prophecies from the standpoint of the exile

40:1-66:24 Vol. VII Book of comfort
40 Comfort in the message of redemption
41 Comfort in the Lord's vindication
42 Comfort in the Lord's servant
43-45 Comfort In the national restoration
46-48 Comfort in the downfall of idolatry
49-57 Comfort in the prophecy of Messiah-Redeemer
58-66 Comfort in the prospect of Israel's future glory

Parallels between Isaiah 1-39 and Isaiah 40-66

1:2	66:24
1:5-6	53:4-5
5:27	40:30
6:1	52:13
6:11-12	62:4
11:11	53:2
11:6-9	65:25
11:12	49:22
12:6	54:1
35:10	51:11

Kings of Judah contemporary with Isaiah

Uzziah 792-740 B.C.*	**Good**		2 Kgs 15:1-5; 2 Chr 26:1-23
Jotham 750-732 B.C.*	**Good**		2 Kgs 15:32-38; 2 Chr 27:1-9
Ahaz 735-716 B.C.*	**Wicked**		2 Kgs 16:1-20; 2 Chr 28:1-27
Hezekiah 716-687 B.C.	**Good**		2 Kgs 18:1-20:21; 2 Chr 29:1-32:33
Manasseh 697-643 B.C.*	**Wicked**		2Kgs 21:1-18; 2 Chr 33:1-20

*Overlapping reigns indicate coregencies.

OT Isaiah is the most messianic, even more so than the book of Zechariah. Only the Psalms contain a larger number of messianic predictions. Every glory of our Lord and every aspect of His life on the earth are set forth in this great evangelical prophecy. His deity, eternity, preexistence, creatorship, omnipotence, omnipresence, omniscience, incomparableness (40:12-18; 51:13); His incarnation (9:6; 7:14, cf. Mt 1:23); His lowliness and youth in Nazareth (7:15; 9:1-2; 11:1; 53:2); His appearance as the Servant of the Lord, anointed as such (11:2), and chosen and delighted in as such (42:1); His tender ministering kindness (42:3; Mt 12:18-20); His obedience (50:5); His message (61:1-2); His miracles (35:5-6); His sufferings (50:6); His sufferings as the gateway to His exaltation (52:13-15); His rejection by the Jewish nation (53:13); His shame – struck, wounded, bruised (53:4-6); His vicarious death (53:7) and burial (53:9); His resurrection (53:10); His spiritual progeny (53:10) and present high priestly ministry (53:12); His future glory (53:12; 52:13; cf. Phil 2:9-11). After ch. 53 Messiah is not mentioned again as the Servant of the Lord, and His coming glory moves more into focus (59:20; 63:1-6; 66:15-19).

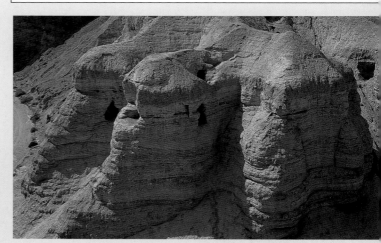

The caves where the Dead Sea Scrolls were discovered in 1947.

The Dead Sea scrolls of Isaiah

The two Isaiah scrolls from Cave 1 at Qumran in the original discovery of 1947 constitute the most famous finds of the Dead Sea Scrolls. The first scroll (St. Mark's Monastery Scroll, 1QIsa) contains the complete Heb. text of Isaiah. The second (Hebrew University Scroll, 1QIsb) contains about one-third of it.

The first Isaiah scroll dates from the 2nd cen. B.C. It consists of 17 sheets, 24 feet in length and 10.2 inches high. It is amazingly similar to the standard (Masoretic) Heb. text, the earliest extant manuscripts of which date almost a millennium later. This scroll constitutes one of the great manuscript discoveries of all time and authenticates the high accuracy of Heb. textual tradition.

VOL. I.
BOOK OF REPROOF AND PROMISE, 1:1–6:13

The Lord's case against Judah (first discourse)

1. Isaiah's preface. The prophet gives his name; the nature of the prophecy ('a vision,' implying supernatural revelation); the time, *c.* 750-680 B.C., and the subject, concerning Judah and Jerusalem, since Isaiah was a prophet of the southern kingdom.

2-6. The Lord's accusation. The charge takes the form of a courtroom scene in which the whole universe, 2, is called upon to witness the twofold accusation of base ingratitude, 2-3, and rebellious apostasy, 4, illustrated by the figure of a diseased body, 5-6.

7-9. The Lord's chastisement. Because of God's punishment the kingdom faced ruin, 7. Jerusalem's suburbs were overrun and forsaken, 8. A faithful remnant was the only hope against complete annihilation, 9.

10-15. The Lord's rejection of their religious externalism. They rejected the Lord, 10. He rejected their empty worship, 11-15, as being purposeless and nauseating, iniquitous, hateful, and devoid of spiritual power, 15.

16-20. The Lord's call to repentance and reformation is issued in a summons to cleanse themselves, 16-17, and then to reason with God, 18-20, in order to discover the equity of His way both to pardon, 18-19, and to punish, 20.

21-23. The Lord's challenge to contrast Jerusalem, past and present. What the city had been, 21: faithful, full of justice, the dwelling place of righteousness. What the city had become, 21-23: a faithless harlot, full of unpunished murderers and dishonest judges (illustrated by the figures of debased money and diluted wine).

24-31. The Lord's promised restoration of Jerusalem. Though a foretaste of the fulfillment is seen in the return from exile, the force of the prophecy indicates that the total fulfillment is yet future.

2. Jerusalem and the Day of the Lord (second discourse)

1-5. Jerusalem the center of the earth in the kingdom age. The subject of the prophecy is Judah and Jerusalem, 1; the time indicated is the futurity of the days of Israel, referring to her ultimate blessing at Messiah's second advent. This vision refers to the time when Israel is converted and restored to Palestine. It envisions Jerusalem's exaltation as the religious center, 2-3, with the site of the millennial temple established. This results in the spontaneous inflow of the nations, 2, for

The Old City of Jerusalem, with the Temple Mount in the middle distance and Mount of Olives on the horizon. Isaiah's vision refers to when Israel is restored to Palestine and Jerusalem is its religious center.

Great prophetic themes of Isaiah still unfulfilled

The Day of the Lord
Some 45 times Isaiah uses the term 'in that day' to describe this period of apocalyptic judgment 2:10-22; 4:1; 13:9-13; 24:1-23; 32:1-20; 63:1-6

Blessing upon restored Israel
2:1-5; 4:2-6; 9:7; 11:4-16; 12:1-6; 14:1-3; 25:1-12; 32:15-20; 35:1-10; 52:1-12; 59:20-21; 60:1-12; 61:3-62:12; 65:17-66:24

Restoration of Israel to Palestine
11:10-12; 14:1-2; 27:12-13; 35:10; 43:5-6; 49:10-12; 66:20

Restoration of Palestine itself
30:23-26; 35:1-10; 49:19; 60:13; 61:4; 62:4-5; 65:21-25

Jerusalem as capital of the earth
1:26; 2:3; 4:2-6; 12:6; 24:23; 26:1; 40:2; 52:1-12; 60:1-22; 62:1-7

Blessing upon the remnant
12:1-6; 25:1-12; 26:1-19; 33:24; 35:10; 43:25; 44:22; 46:13; 54:6-10; 61:6; 62:12; 66:8

Blessing upon the nations
2:1-4; 11:3-4, 9-10; 25:6-9; 60:1-12

Blessing to entire creation
Isaiah had a fleeting glimpse beyond the Kingdom Age to the new heaven and earth of the eternal state (65:17; 66:22). But like John in the Revelation (Rev 21-22) he saw a blended view of millennial and eternal conditions (cf. 11:6-8 with 65:25; 66:22)

---

worship and instruction, 3, because in that day Jerusalem shall be the place where the law and the Word of God go forth, 3. Jerusalem's exaltation as the governmental center will be made possible by Messiah as the ruling King-Judge. The result will be universal peace, with armaments of war converted to implements of peace and the science of war abandoned, 4. Converted and restored, Israel encourages her people to walk in the light of the Lord, 5.

6-22. The Day of the Lord. This is the time when the Lord visibly judges sinners in the earth (Rev 4:1-19:16), preparatory to the kingdom as outlined in 1-5. It is here described as the period when the Lord 'rises to shake the earth,' 19, 21, and reveals His glorious majesty in judgment upon sinners.

3. Judah's sin and the Day of the Lord (second discourse)
2:1-4:6. Isaiah's second discourse, of which this chapter is a part, shows how chastisement for the nation's sin in the future Day of the Lord can alone cleanse and equip the nation for her kingdom mission (2:1-4; 4:1-6). All classes of Judah's society are to be punished for their sin – the rulers, professional men, and others, 1-15, as well as the vain, wicked, worldly women, 3:16-4:1. The sins of the prophet's day demand the judgments of the Day of the Lord before national blessing can come.

4. The glory awaiting the redeemed remnant (second discourse)
1. The remnant survives the judgment of the Day of the Lord. Only one man in seven will survive, so that seven women (cf. 3:16-26) will court one man.

2. The remnant accepts Messiah the branch of the Lord. Compare Jer 23:5; 33:15; Zech 3:8; 6:12. The messianic idea is developed further in Isa 11:1-3, where 'a shoot will come up from the stem of Jesse; from his roots a Branch will bear fruit.'

3-4. The remnant is cleansed and converted, and hence is called 'holy.' This is accomplished by the decimating judgments of the Day of the Lord, 4, when the Lord cleanses Israel nationally (cf. Rom 11:16-27).

5-6. The remnant is sheltered and protected, by a pillar of cloud by day and a pillar of fire by night, recalling Israel's wilderness experience (Ex 13:21-22), and by a canopy over 'all the glory.' This will be the manifested glory of Messiah in the midst of His people. This chapter concludes Isaiah's second sermon begun at 2:1.

5. God's people shown their sin and its result (third discourse)

1-7. By a parable. The nation Israel is represented under the figure of the vineyard of the Lord, 7. The Lord's tender care of Israel is shown by His favorable location of the vineyard 'on a fertile hillside' (Palestine), 1; by intensive cultivation, choice of the finest vine, and by building a tower in it, 2. His normal expectation was of a good yield, 2; but its yield of wild grapes and the owner's complaint, 3-4, and threatened judgment upon His vineyard, 5-6, necessitated the removal of its protection (hedge) and wall (overrun by enemies) and the temporary setting aside of the vineyard.

8-23. By an enumeration of their sins. Covetousness and greed would be punished by famine, 8-10; rioting and drunken revelry, 11-12, 22, by the miseries of the Captivity, 13-17. God further revealed their presumption in sinning, 18-19; their self-indulgence and injustice, 23.

24-30. By a threat of captivity, with general desolation, 24-25, and foreign invasion, 26-30.

6. Isaiah's call and commission (fourth discourse)

1-4. The prophet sees God, i.e., 'Jesus' glory' (Jn 12:41), about 70 B.C. in the year of Uzziah's death, 1. It may have been an initial vision to launch him on his prophetic career, or to confirm him in a career already underway. It was, in any case, of Christ's glory – the Lord upon His throne, with the cherubim choir.

5. The prophet sees himself. He thus abhors himself and acknowledges his sin. This is always the divine order in a call to service – a vision of God, then of self.

6-7. The prophet is cleansed, fire being the symbol of cleansing.

8-10. The prophet is commissioned. The Triune God (note the plural, 'us') counsels concerning the commission and the prophet accepts it, 8, whereupon God communicates the commission, 9-10. This involved a hardening and blinding judgment upon the nation (Mt 13:14-15; Jn 12:39-41; Acts 28:25-27).

11-13. The prophet is given the outcome of the commission. How long would this spiritual deterioration go on? To the

complete blotting out of Israel's testimony to the one true God? No, came the divine answer. Only until the complete devastation of the land and the removal of its inhabitants to Babylon were accomplished. Thence a *remnant* would return to Palestine. Even this tenth part would be further reduced, yet a holy posterity would survive in whom the ultimate hope of Israel would rest and in whom the covenants and promises would be realized.

VOL. II.
BOOK OF IMMANUEL, 7:1-12:6

7. The great messianic sign concerning Immanuel (first discourse)

1-2. Historical circumstances calling forth the sign. About 735 B.C. Ahaz faced the coalition of Rezin, king of Syria (c. 740-732 B.C.), and Pekah (c. 740-732 B.C.), king of Israel. They advanced against Jerusalem to punish Ahaz for not aligning himself with them to check the growing power of Assyria who, under Tiglath-pileser III (745-727 B.C.), was relentlessly pressing toward the Mediterranean, 1. Ahaz and his people were fearful and hard pressed, 2. The issue? Where should help be found, in Assyria itself or in God?

3-9. A message of encouragement. The prophet was sent to the faithless monarch with his son Shear-Jashub ('a remnant shall return') to attempt to persuade Ahaz to trust in God instead of Assyria, since the Lord had already decreed the destruction of these ungodly allies and the frustration of their plan to set their puppet over Jerusalem. For a time the status quo would prevail both in Damascus (Syria), 8, and in Israel, 9, and Judah would not be conquered. Fulfillment came within 65 years, during Esarhaddon's reign (681-668) when foreigners were introduced and took possession of both Syria and Israel, that it might be forever said Ephraim was broken so as no longer to be a people, 8.

10-13. God's sign to confirm the prophet's message. The sign or miracle was unlimited and unrestricted, 11, but Ahaz in mock piety alluded to Deut 6:16 to cover his unbelief, already displayed in stripping the temple of treasure to bribe the king of Assyria. Thereupon the prophet reproved Ahaz as a member of the house of David, 13.

14-16. The great messianic sign itself. This passage presents one of the most difficult interpretive problems in the entire OT. The NT plainly testifies that the ultimate fulfillment of the sign is in the virgin birth of Christ (Mt 1:22-23). With this conclusion almost all commentators agree. Disagreement appears, however, concerning the possibility that the sign had an additional, contemporary significance. Two principal schools of thought dominate current evangelical thinking.

One suggests that the context of Isa 7 demands a miracle far more significant than the timely birth of a baby (7:11), and notes further that the sign extended beyond Ahaz to the whole house of David ('to you,' plural). The child's name, 'Immanuel' ('God with us'), refers preeminently to Christ. Others suggest that the sign can refer to a baby born in Isaiah's day as well as to the ultimate fulfillment in Christ. The term used for virgin (*'alma*) appears in Gen 24:43; Ex 2:8; Ps 68:25; Prov 30:19; Song 1:3; 6:8, referring generally to an unmarried woman who is chaste. Isaiah may well have been referring to the prophetess of 8:3, whom he married after the prophecy (Isa 8:1-12, cf. Herbert Wolf, *JBL,* 1972). Isaiah's son, Maher-Shalal-Hash-Baz, served as a miraculous chronometer for the first Assyrian invasion of Aram and Israel that took place in 732 B.C., just three years after the prophecy (7:15-16; 8:4). It is remarkable that both Pekah and Rezin were killed within three years of the prophecy .

17-25. Threatened punishment of Ahaz. The severity of the punishment is told, 17. The instrument of punishment was to be the king of Assyria, who was trusted instead of the Lord, and he therefore would desolate the land, 17-25.

8: 1-9:7. Present deliverance a precursor to future deliverer (second discourse)

8:1-4. The fall of Damascus and Samaria prefigured. Three children are mentioned in connection with the Syrian-Israelite invasion of Judah: (1) Shear-Jashub 7:3 ('a remnant shall return'), (2) Maher-Shalal-Hash-Baz, 8:1-4 ('quick to the plunder swift to the spoil'), both Isaiah's sons; and (3) Immanuel ('God with us'), David's son and

Lord (7:13-14). All three of these children portray emphases in Isaiah's daily preaching: (1) 'A remnant will return' (cf. Isa 10:21, 22), initially from Babylon and ultimately from end-time worldwide Diaspora (1:9; 4:1-4; 6:13, etc.). (2) 'Quick to the plunder, swift to the spoil' refers to present deliverance from Rezin and Pekah. Damascus was taken in 732 B.C. and Rezin was slain. The northern kingdom had to cede its northern provinces to Assyria (2 Kgs 15:29), and not many years later the capital city fell (722 B.C.). (3) The virgin-born Child is the future glory of the nation.

8:5-8. The choice of unbelief and its results. The people followed Ahaz and chose Assyria rather than God's guidance and help, which was symbolized by the gentle waters of the pool of Shiloah (the Siloam of Jn 9:7, 11; Lk 13:4). In unbelief and worldly wisdom rejecting these quiet waters, the disobedient nation was to be inundated by the floodwaters of the Euphrates, symbolizing invading Assyrian armies. Yet the fact that Palestine was called 'your land, O Immanuel' 8, brought assurance that in the light of the virgin-born Immanuel Israel would not be obliterated by this terrible flood.

8:9-15. The challenge of God's grace. The Lord challenged the enemies of Judah to do their worst to destroy her, 9-10. They would be smashed against the rock of divine judgment. The reason – His grace was to be manifested in Immanuel, 10, to His true elect people in Judah. The Lord encouraged and instructed Isaiah and His faithful adherents not to be frightened by the popular charge of conspiracy or treason, 12, hurled against them because of their opposition to an Assyrian alliance against the northern coalition. He promised to become a sanctuary for them, but a stumbling stone (1 Pet 2:7-8) and a snare to remove from Israel all the unfaithful and the rebellious, like Ahaz, who reject Immanuel (Christ), 14-15.

8:16-20. The challenge to trust God's grace alone. The testimony of the great tablet inscribed with the name Maher-Shalal-Hash-Baz, 1, was to be sealed up, that its fulfillment might be objectively verified by the Lord of history, 16. The believing remnant will take its stand upon the sure Word of God and confidently await its fulfillment. The faithful prophet declared his own steadfast testimony, 18-19, and warned that those who claim inspiration or authority contrary to the Word of God in demon-controlled religion will be deprived of spiritual light, 19-20. Spiritism and general cultism were condemned.

8:21-22. The alternative to trust in God, would be the indescribable anguish and distress of Assyrian invasion and deportation.

9:1-2. Prophecy of Immanuel as the great light. Prediction was made that He would providentially appear in dark, despised Galilee, 1. This was the very territory of Zebulun and Naphtali which was first plunged into gloom by the ravaging armies of Tiglath-pileser (732 B.C.). Here the radiant light of the Messiah, who made His headquarters in Galilee (Mt 4:13-17), shone.

9:3-5. Prophecy of Immanuel as the great liberator. He would multiply the nation and increase its joy, 3. He would liberate the nation from all its oppressors and foes, supernaturally (cf. Zech 12:1-8; 14:1-15), but in terrible final conflict, 5. This prophecy had application to the increase of the nation after the Babylonian Captivity and its victories in Maccabean times; but it will find its final fulfillment in Armageddon and the restoration of the kingdom over Israel (Acts 1-6).

9:6-7. Prophecy of Immanuel as the great Lord. The humanity ('a child is born') as well as the deity ('Mighty God') of Immanuel are foretold. His government is described as prosperous, peaceful, Davidic, righteous, eternal, and sure, 6-7. His messianic titles are given: (1) *Wonderful Counselor,* giving counsel which alone can save man from sin; (2) *Mighty God,* Deity in the special character of a champion in battle; (3) *Everlasting Father,* both as the possessor of eternity and the author of eternal life (Heb. 'father of eternity'); (4) *Prince of Peace,* the ruler who will bring about a warless world in the coming kingdom. The Davidic covenant (2 Sam 7:8-17) will be executed in the Kingdom Age, which in turn will merge into the eternal state by authority of the Lord's zeal; for He will perform these wondrous promises of ultimate blessing for Israel and the world.

9:8-10:4. Proud Samaria is doomed (third discourse)

9:8-10. Israel's pride and presumption would be punished by Syrian

Israelite remains at Samaria. Isaiah prophesied that captivity was imminent for the ruling class in Samaria who exploited their subjects.

and Philistine invasion, 11-12; her incorrigibility under chastisement, 13, would be punished by the destructive, pitiless wrath of the Lord, 14-19, civil war, and starvation, 20-21. The Lord's hand 'is still upraised' in wrathful chastisement and not withdrawn because of refusal to reform (cf. the doleful refrain in 9:12, 17, 21; 10:4; cf. 5:25). Captivity was imminent for the ruthless ruling class in Samaria who heartlessly exploited their subjects, 10:1-4.

10:5-34. The Assyrian invades Immanuel's land (fourth discourse)

5-19. Assyria, God's instrument for judging His people, shall in turn be judged. Assyria was the divine tool for chastening God's people, 5-6. In spite of her presumptuous pride, 7-14, she would be irretrievably destroyed by the Lord who employed her as His scourge, 15-19.

20-23. The return of a faithful remnant. The time: 'in that day,' the Day of the Lord (2:10-22), after Israel's *final* enemies have been destroyed. Although this had a historical fulfillment, the destruction of the Assyrian envisions a similar invasion of Palestine by 'the king of the North' (Dan 11:40) in the end-time (Isa 14:24-25; 30:31-33; Mic 5:4-7; Dan 8:23-26; 11:40-45). The remnant will, like Isaiah and his followers, reject this false ruler and 'truly rely on the Lord, the Holy One of Israel,' 20.

An oasis in the parched Jordan valley. A spring is a symbol of hope in a dry land.

24-34. Therefore Assyria is not to be feared by those who trust in the Lord, 24-27, even in her fearful advance on Immanuel's land, 28-32, for the Lord will make a sudden end of the Assyrian, 33-34.

11. Immanuel-King and His kingdom (fourth discourse)

1. Immanuel-King's Davidic descent. He is here prefigured as 'a shoot' from the truncated 'stump of Jesse,' showing His obscurity and lowliness, the house of David being poor and unknown at the time of Christ's nativity. He is also symbolized as a 'branch' (*neser*; cf. Mt 2:23: 'and [he] went and lived in a town called Nazareth. So was fulfilled what was said through the prophets: "He will be called a Nazarene"').

2. Immanuel-King's enduement. The Holy Spirit in His sevenfold measureless fullness (Jn 3:34) is to rest or remain upon Him an 1:32-34; cf. 'the seven spirits,' the one Spirit in all His plenitude, Rev 1:4; 4:5). The general enduement is 'the Spirit of the Lord,' which is the necessary qualification for righteous government. Its result is that Immanuel finds His delight in reverence for the Lord, 3.

3-5. Immanuel-King's equitable government. He will not arbitrate by mere external appearance, 3 (cf. 1 Sam 16:7), but judge equitably and govern forcefully, 4, ruling with an 'iron scepter' (Ps 2:9; Rev 2:27; 12:5; 19:15). He will vindicate God's holy law as the last Adam against Satan-dominated mankind's pride and rebellion, which will contaminate the earth till He destroys the Satanic world system at His advent and kingdom. He will be girded with righteousness and faithfulness, 5.

6-9. Immanuel-King's peaceful kingdom. Aggression will not be found in Immanuel's holy kingdom. So complete will be the change even the animal creation will be affected, sharing in the glorious liberation from the vanity and evil brought in by the Fall (Rom 8:19-22). Edenic conditions will be at least partly restored, predatory beasts and poisonous serpents no longer preying upon one another or upon man. The reason is that all men everywhere will know God and be completely dedicated to His will, 9.

10. Immanuel-King will bring the Gentiles into the kingdom. As a military standard or ensign, Messiah will appear 'that the nations will rally to him' (Rev 5:5; 22:16).

11-16. Immanuel-King will regather the Jews when His kingdom is set up, 11. This will be a second (final) regathering of a remnant from a worldwide dispersion, 11-12, consummated by divine power. The old animosity between Judah and Ephraim (southern and northern kingdoms) will be abolished, and security and dominion over any adversaries assured, 13-14. Every obstacle to the final regathering of Israel will be removed – here symbolized by great geographical barriers. The tongue (bay) of the Egyptian sea is the barrier they miraculously passed through when they came out of Egypt. The river is the Euphrates (8:7).

12. The remnant's song of redemption (fourth discourse)

1-3. The believer's song of redemption. It is a triumphant chorus of praise to Immanuel-Redeemer because the divine anger is turned away and comfort abounds, 1; because God is the singer's salvation, 2; and because He is his strength and song, 3. The song will be sung 'in that day,' 1, i.e., the day of regathering from the nations and Israel's final deliverance from the Egypt of the world, re-echoing the song of Moses and Israel after deliverance at the Red Sea (Ex 15:1-21).

4-6. The remnant's united song of redemption. This section changes from the singular to the plural 'you' as each of the redeemed joins the choir of all Israel's redeemed about to enter the kingdom. As a continued and amplified song of praise to God, it contains an exhortation to prayer and witnessing, 4; joyful singing, 5; and to holy exultation and joy, 6. What an ode expressing the boundless joy of Immanuel's redeemed when He comes again to rule over Zion and reign supreme over all the earth.

VOL. III.
GOD'S ORACLES OF JUDGMENT UPON THE NATIONS, 13:1–23:18

13. The judgment of Babylon

1-16. The confusion of the nations preparatory to destruction. Babel ('confusion') here appears symbolically to portray the political and governmental disorder which characterizes the earth during the times of the Gentiles (Lk 21:24). This is in contrast to the divine order (Isa 11) with Israel in her own land, the center of spiritual blessing and divine world government (Isa 2:1-5). Anything other than the nations blessed in association with Israel is politically Babel ('confusion'). The judgment of Babylon here refers both to the Persian conquest (539 B.C.) and ultimately to God's final judgment of the world system, of which Babylon is a type (Rev 17:5). Verses 12-16 focus upon the apocalyptic judgments of the

Restored tiled depiction of a mythical beast at the ancient Ishtar Gate, Babylon. Isaiah prophesied Israel's restoration and Babylon's fall.

Day of the Lord (Rev 6-16) which eventuate in the destruction of both religious (Rev 17) and political (Rev 18) Babylon.

17-22. Prophecy of Babylon's destruction in Isaiah's day. The Babylon of Nebuchadnezzar II (605-562 B.C.), which became mistress of the world and which fell to Cyrus the Persian (539 B.C.), is here in view. This Babylon with the Jew in captivity is a type of the political Babylon which will prevail until it is destroyed at the second advent of Christ.

14. Babylon's fall and Israel's restoration

1-3. Prophecy of Israel's restoration anticipates Babylon's fall. Israel's exaltation to her God-ordained place as a witness to the nations, and her rest from her worldwide woe, cannot be realized until political Babylon is destroyed.

4-11. Israel's song of triumph over Babylon's last king. This is not simply Nebuchadnezzar II nor Belshazzar, but the last-day political head of the restored Roman Empire (Rev 13:1-18), 'the man of lawlessness, the man doomed to destruction' (2 Thess 2:34), 'the little horn' (Dan 7:8, 24-27; 11:36-45). He is seen in Sheol (cf. Rev 19:20 where he is cast into Gehenna).

12-17. Satan addressed as energizer of Babylon's last king. Satan, organizer and head of the world's systems governmentally, is so intimately associated with its last and most diabolical ruler (2 Thess 2:9) that the occasion of the king of Babylon's fall furnishes the picture of Satan's original fall and the entrance of sin into the universe. The revelation also serves to show the role of Satan in human government, especially since Israel has been outside the focus of the divine order since her captivity.

18-27. Future destruction of the Satanic world system. This passage goes beyond the destruction of literal Babylon, 18-24, and of the Assyrian of that day, 25, and encompasses 'the whole world,' 26, in preparation for God's order in the kingdom which is guaranteed by God's immutable purpose, 27.

28-32. Oracle upon Philistia. Philistia would be crushed by Assyrian might under Sargon and Sennacherib, but the Lord would protect His people.

15-16. Judgment upon Moab

Moab was to be pitilessly desolated (15:1-16:9). Her arrogance and pride would be humbled by terrible devastation from Assyria, 16:10-14. Events in the Day of the Lord are foreshadowed (cf. 16:5).

17. Judgment upon Damascus and Samaria

Damascus and Ephraim (the northern kingdom) would be desolated, 1-3, but eventually Samaria would yield a remnant of true believers who would disavow idolatry, 3-8. Chastening must, however, precede blessing, 9-11, with the horrible atrocities of the approaching Assyrian invasion predicted, 12-14. Verse 14 may speak of the time the angel of the Lord struck down 185,000 Assyrians (37:16).

18. The judgment upon Ethiopia

The prophet apprises Ethiopian ambassadors that the birds of prey would feed upon their corpses rotting on the battlefield, 1-6. Yet 'gifts will be brought to the Lord Almighty . . . to Mount Zion, the place of the Name of Lord Almighty,' by Ethiopia in the millennial day, 7.

19-20. The judgment of Egypt

Civil war, drought, devastation plague Egypt as a result of Assyrian invasion, 19:1-10. Egypt's wisdom and pride turn to foolishness, 11-15. Egypt will yet be terrified by the land of Judah because of God's purpose through it against Egypt, 16-18, and Egypt will be converted and delivered to participate with Israel in God's favor, 19-25.

Yet impending conquest and captivity by Assyria (Esar-haddon) faced Egypt, 20:1-6. Isaiah walked naked and barefoot, 1-2, as a sign that the king of Assyria would lead away captive Egyptians and Ethiopians, 3-6, demonstrating to a strong party in Jerusalem who looked for help from Egypt how foolish such expectation was.

21. The judgment of Babylon, Edom, Arabia

1-10. The judgment of the desert by the sea. The 'Desert by the Sea' was Babylon (cf. 9). Media is mentioned as the instrument of judgment, 2. This event was some two centuries in the future, but the prophet envisioned the

Persian conquerors advancing. Such is the accuracy of the prophetic word, history rewritten.

11-12. The judgment of Edom. The Heb. reads Dumah ('silence'), which is evidently an anagram (a transposition of letters) for Edom. This land S of the Dead Sea, minerally rich, is also called Seir (Gen 32:3; Num 24:18; Jud 5:4), the home of Esau's ancestors, rivals of the tribes of Jacob. The wealth of Edom was shown by the heavy tribute it paid Esar-haddon. Copper and iron made Edom wealthy, as well as the tolls over the ancient king's highway which ran to Ezion-geber. The cry of the watchman and his cryptic reply were to be heard, 11-12.

13-17. The judgment of Arabia. The north-western tribes along the Red Sea (Gen 25:3; Ezk 27:20; 38:13) called Dedanites, who shipped goods to Phoenician Tyre (Ezk 27:15), and the Kedarites E of Palestine and Syria, noted for their flocks (Isa 60:7) and their black tents, were to be driven into flight by conquering Assyrians and Chaldeans.

22. Judgment upon Jerusalem

The joyous, world-renowned city, 1-4, invaded by armies, 5-7, was to suffer siege and calamity, 8-14. It is called the 'Valley of Vision,' 1, 5, for God revealed Himself on the hill of Zion, which was surrounded by valleys with higher hills beyond. Notice is made of the careless indulgence of its inhabitants, 13, in the face of Assyrian invasion. Shebna, the steward, 15-19, the proud materialistic usurper, was to be thrust out of office and to be replaced by the faithful Eliakim, 20-25.

Eliakim, serving as a type of Christ, would be given 'the key to the house of David,' 22 (Rev 3:7). But it is ultimately Christ who possesses the right to reign, 20, as the Holy and True One. 'I will drive him like a peg into a firm place; he will be a seat of honor for the house of his father,' 23-24 (cf. Zech 10:4).

23. The judgment of Tyre

Tyre is a type of the pomp and pride of the satanic world system (cf. Ezk 28:12-15) in its commercial aspects. Tyre was an opulent trading emporium on the Phoenician coast which all conquerors prized. Its dazzling splendor, proud self-sufficiency, and worldly wisdom had behind them the inspiration of

The ancient Treasury, Petra, part of the Nabataean kingdom of Edom. This land S of the Dead Sea is also called Seir. Isaiah foretold its downfall.

Satan. Nebuchadnezzar, after a 12-year siege, failed to take the island city which, however, Alexander accomplished in 332 B.C. (cf. Zech 9:2-4). Isaiah foresaw the downfall of this commercial center of the world, 1-7. God had decreed this calamity because of pride, 8-12. The 70 years during which Tyre would be forgotten, 17, perhaps refers to the time between Nebuchadnezzar's conquest in 571 B.C. and the fall of Babylon, at which time Tyre regained a measure of prominence.

VOL. IV.
BOOK OF JUDGMENT AND PROMISE, 24:1-27:13

These chapters form a continuous prophecy on the subject of judgment in the Day of the Lord with blessing afterward. They are sometimes styled Isaiah's Apocalypse.

24. The Day of the Lord and millennial blessing

1-13. The judgments of the Day of the Lord. The Lord will judge the earth and earth dwellers, 1. All classes of the Christ-rejecting society of the end-time will be affected, 2. The apocalyptic desolations are described, 3-13, and the reason for them specified, 5. This is the period described in 2 Thess 1:7-10; Mt 24-25; Rev 4:1-19:16; Isa 2:6-22; Zeph 1:1-18; Zech 12:1-14:15.

14-16. Interlude: the preservation and song of the remnant. Singing begins 'in that day' and is heard because of the experience of God's marvelous deliverance through the Great Tribulation (Rev 7:1-8; 14:1-5).

17-22. The judgment of the Day of the Lord continued. It will concentrate on the earth and wicked earth dwellers, and upon Satan and demons, 21. The latter indwell and energize wicked men (Eph 6:10-12; Rev 9:1-12, 20-21; 12:7-10), and particularly 'the kings of the whole world' (Rev 16:13-16) for the final phase of God-defying wickedness crushed at Armageddon. The fulfillment: Satan and the demons will be confined to the bottomless pit, 22 (cf. Rev 20:1-3), and the Beast and the False Prophet will be cast alive into Gehenna (Rev 19:20; 20:10). Wicked earth dwellers will be swept away by the seal, trumpet, and bowl judgments (Rev 6:1-19:16), or destroyed at the advent of Messiah (Rev 19:11-19).

23. The millennial reign of Christ. So glorious will it be that the sun and moon will be confounded when Messiah 'will reign on Mount Zion' in Jerusalem.

25. Israel's praise for kingdom blessing

1-5. The delivered nation praises the Lord. Israel praises her Lord for His miraculous deliverances, 1; His punishment of her enemies, 2-3 ; and His help of the poor and needy, 4-5 (cf. Isa 12:1-6).

6-8. Blessings for all nations described. A feast of fat things 'on this mountain,' i.e., Zion (cf. Isa 2:1-5), is promised; spiritual blindness will be removed, 7. Death will be swallowed up in victory (Hos 13:14; 1 Cor 15:54; Rev 20:14; 21:4). The Lord will remove the reproach of His people from all the earth, 8. The eternal state blends with this millennial scene.

9. Israel's reward for waiting. Salvation and attendant joy in the Lord are promised.

10-12. Israel's enemies judged, including Moab.

26. Judah's millennial song

1-6. Praise for the Lord's faithfulne and mercies. Jerusalem is celebrated as a saved city opening its gates to welcome the righteous, 1-2. The Lord's blessing upon those who trust Him, 3-4, and His humbling of the proud, 5-6, are stressed.

7-11. Experiences of waiting during the night.

12-18. Assurances of peace and deliverance. Israel restored and converted, enjoying the blessing of the land, expresses he worship of the Lord in glad praise and testimo

19. Assurance of the bodily resurrection of righteous OT saints. 'Your dead will live; their bodies will rise.' Although the restoration of Israel as a nation symbolized by the figure of resurrection (Ezk 37:1-11), like Dan 12:1-2, this passage eviden has in mind physical resurrection, since the fi resurrection involves participation in the kingdom (Rev 20:4-6).

20-21. Glimpse of the divine indignation in the Day of the Lord. A call is issued to the remnant to hide. Verse 21 graphically summarizes the judgment events c Rev 6:1-19:21.

27. Punishment of Israel's enemies and kingdom triumph

1. Destruction of Israel's enemies. These are symbolized by leviathan (Ps 74:14), the sea monster and the dragon, doubtless with implication of Satanic forces behind them as i the case of the king of Babylon (14:1-14) and Tyre (Ezk 28:12-14). (Cf. the seven-headed Lotan of the Ugaritic literature, Rev 11:7; 12:3; 13:1).

2-9. The Lord's care for his own even in chastening, is indicated under the figure o a vineyard (cf. Isa 5:1-7), with Israel hereafter flourishing, 6, after the chastenings are over, 8-9

10-11. Israel's enemies are destroye – totally and finally.

12-13. The return of the remnant. This last word of this Volume of Judgment and

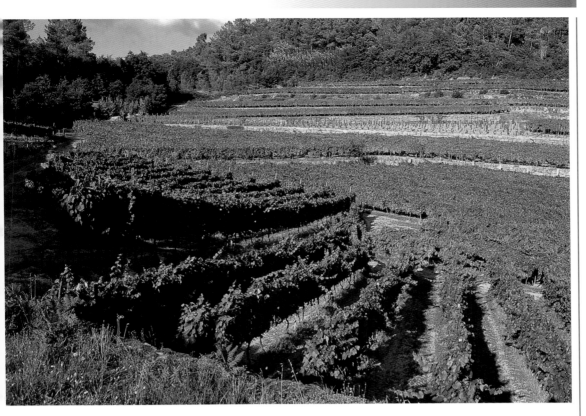

Ripening vines on the hillside. The Jewish prophets repeatedly compare the people of God with a vine or vineyard.

Promise tells of Israel's final regathering under the blowing of the trumpet (cf. Mt 24:31) and future worship in Jerusalem (cf. 2:1-45). The brook of Egypt (Gen 15:18; Ezk 47:19) is the Wadi el-Arish separating SW Palestine from Egypt.

VOL. V.
BOOK OF WOES PRECEDING RESTORATION GLORIES, 28:1–35:10

28. Woe against Ephraim

1-13. Judgment upon the ten tribes. Their pride and drunkenness are noted, 1, 3, 7-8. Their threatened punishment by Assyrian invasion is foretold, 2-4. The testimony of God's Word goes out to these sinners, 9-12, but they reject its warning, sealing their doom, 13. Nevertheless, a remnant shall be preserved to confess the Lord as 'glorious crown' and 'beautiful wreath' in the kingdom, 5.

14-29. Fate of Ephraim a warning to Judah. The scoffing rulers of Jerusalem have made 'a covenant with death' and 'the grave' (probably an alliance with Egypt) to escape the Assyrian invasion, 14-15, but the messianic reference to the 'tested stone' (Dan 2:34; 1 Pet 2:8) projects the prophecy to the end time and the covenant foreshadowing the time when the apostate nation enters into an agreement with the Antichrist (Dan 9:27). But all who trust in the false covenant rather than in God's deliverance through the Stone (Messiah) shall be swept away in judgment, 17-29.

29. Woe against Ariel (Jerusalem)

1-4. Jerusalem's last siege. Despite her sacred character as Ariel ('the lion of God'), associated with David, 1, a type of Jerusalem's great Deliverer ('the Lion of the tribe of Judah,' Rev 5:5), the Lord Himself through His instruments of chastening (Israel's last-day enemies) will encamp against her. He 'will besiege her, 2-3, till the city is brought to the dust, 4-5 (cf. Zech 12:1-14; 15; Mic 4:11; 5:4-15; Dan 11:40-45).

5-10. The Lord will then deal with Jerusalem's enemies. When the tools of His chastening anger have accomplished His purpose concerning His people, the Lord will turn against them and destroy 'the hordes of all the nations . . . that fight against Mount Zion,' 7-8, blinding and intoxicating them for their destruction, 9-10 (cf. Zech 14:3,12-15).

11-12. This prophecy is for the end time. It is to be sealed because neither Sennacherib's siege nor the siege by the Romans fully accomplished it. Its fulfillment is still in the future.

13-16. The condition of the people is one of religious blindness and empty formalism (cf. Mt 15:8-9; Mk 7:6-7). Woe is pronounced upon those who think their dark deeds are hidden from the Lord, 15-16.

17-24. Blessing for a redeemed remnant. The 'humble will rejoice' and the 'needy will rejoice in the Holy One of Israel,' 17-19. The wicked will be purged out, 20, and the house of Jacob blessed, 22-24.

30-31. Warning against alliance with Egypt

30:1-14. The wickedness of the pro-Egypt party. They fostered a foolish cause, 1-7, by resisting God's word, 8-11, and calamity was to result from following their advice, 12-14.

30:15-33. Advice to trust in the Lord. Blessing foreshadowing kingdom deliverance and joy is promised those who believe God, woe foreshadowing the judgments of the Day of the Lord for those who rebel.

31:1-9. The woe of trusting Egypt again outlined. A repeated condemnation of the Egyptian alliance is indicated, 1-3. The Lord promises to rescue Jerusalem, 4-9. The people of Israel are exhorted to turn in faith to Him from whom they have deeply revolted, 6-7, for the Assyrian of the end-time, 8, shall be supernaturally routed, 9, by Israel's messianic King.

32. Messiah-King and His kingdom

1-8. Israel's ultimate deliverance by Messiah-King. This chapter is part of the discourse begun in 31:1. Deliverance through God's gracious interposition, 31:1-32:20, will ultimately be by Israel's Messiah-King, 32:1-8 (not by trusting in Egypt, 31:1-9). The King (Jesus Christ) is seen as 'a shelter from the wind and a refuge from the storm,' 1-2, and His earthly rule is described, 3-8.

9-14. Israel's interim sins and sufferings outlined. Sins of the careless women (cf. Isa 3:16-4:1, 4) are specially mentioned. The spiritual state of its women is a sensitive barometer of the moral state of any nation.

15-20. Hope for the future – the outpoured spirit and the result. Israel's sorrow and judgment are not permanent – 'till the Spirit is poured upon us from on high,' 15, fulfilling Joel 2:28-32. Results of the outpouring of the Spirit are blessing on the land, 15; prevalence of justice and righteousness, 16; peace and security, 17-20.

33. Punishment of the Assyrian, triumph of Christ

1-12. The destruction of the Assyrian declared. Treacherous deceivers like Sennacherib are to be divinely destroyed, 1, as a result of God's favor to His people and His answer to their prayers, 2-6. The horror of the Assyrian's cruelty and perfidy as he invades the land is described, 7-9. The Lord announces the Assyrian's destruction, 10-12.

13-16. The plight of the godless in the face of the Assyrian menace. Their fearful trembling is the result of their sin and unbelief.

17-24. Salvation by seeing Messiah-King in His beauty. This vision of the coming Deliverer will dissipate the terror of the Assyrian menace and an alien invader, 17-19. Instead, Jerusalem will be seen as a secure city, filled with the Lord's majesty and deliverance, 20-22, and the remnant will divide the spoil, 23-24.

34. Armageddon and the destruction of Gentile world power

1-7. The battle of Armageddon. All nations are to be gathered to battle, 1-3. Frightful carnage results as the Lord wreaks vengeance upon the armies of the Satanic world system, centering in Edom, 4-6 (cf. Rev 19:11-21; Isa 63:1-6).

8-15. Desolation following this disaster. The indignation of the Lord is then revealed upon all nations and their demon-driven armies, who are bent on destroying Israel and taking possession of the earth (cf. Rev 16:13-16).

16-17. Divine guarantee that Israel will possess and inhabit the land. God's promise to Israel is to be fulfilled in securing the land and causing them to inhabit it perpetually, 16-17.

35. The glory of the kingdom

1-2. The restoration of the land and the manifestation of the Lord. Isaiah 34 is one of the darkest chapters in the Bible. Chapter 35 is one of the brightest and most joyful. It is a grand climax to the Volume of Woes Preceding Restoration Glories, which began at 28:1. Palestine, physically and climatically changed to welcome its Redeemer and the redeemed at the second advent, is poetically personified. With lilting joy the desert, Arabah, Lebanon, Carmel, and Sharon see 'the glory of the Lord, the splendor of our God.'

3-7. Retrospect upon the tribulation preceding blessing. The command is given to encourage the weak and fearful, 3-4, to tide them through the darkness preceding the dawn. They are to be encouraged because Messiah-King is coming to punish Israel's enemies; to reward and deliver His own, 4; to work miracles in men's bodies and souls, 5-6; and to effect wonders in nature, 6-7.

8-10. Return of the redeemed remnant to Zion. This will be by an appointed way, a highway, a holy way, a plainly marked way, 8, a safe way, 9. The redeemed will return joyfully to Zion, with everlasting exultation, at last obtaining gladness, with sorrow and sighing (so long plaguing them) fleeing away, 10.

VOL. VI. HISTORICAL PARENTHESIS, 36:1-39:8

36-37. Overthrow of the Assyrian army

Chapters 36-39 form a historical parenthesis connecting the first part of the book (ch. 1-35), consisting of predictions of judgment and blessings springing out of the Assyrian period, with the second part of the book, composed of prophecies of comfort emanating from the Babylonian period. Hezekiah's name is mentioned some 35 times in this section, and it is sometimes called the Volume of Hezekiah. This section is almost identical to the text of

1 Kgs 18:13-20:19. It is likely that Isaiah wrote the material that was later incorporated into the court history of Judah and ultimately into the Book of the Kings.

36:1-22. The Assyrian blatantly challenges the Lord. The arrogant conqueror Sennacherib in 701 B.C. sent his Assyrian commander-in-chief from Lachish (the Judean fortress commanding the road to Egypt) to demand the unconditional surrender of Judah. The commander met with Hezekiah's delegation, 1-3, and in its presence taunted Judah for trust in Egypt, 4-6, and in Hezekiah's God, 7-10. He continued his blasphemous taunts before all the people of Jerusalem, 11-22.

37:1-38. The Lord's reply to the challenge. Hezekiah laid the matter before the Lord in the temple, 1, and sent a delegation to Isaiah for counsel and prayer, 2-5. He received from the prophet the first assurance of deliverance, 6-7. Meanwhile, the commander returned to find Sennacherib besieging Libnah (another fortified city of Judah N of Lachish). Hearing that prince Tirhakah (Taharka in the Egyptian king lists, who later became third king in Egyptian Dynasty XXV) was preparing to attack, 8, Sennacherib dispatched another intimidating threat to Hezekiah, 9-13. The king spread it before the Lord in the temple and prayed, 14-20. The Lord granted a second assurance through Isaiah. The God-defying monarch would be crushed, 21-35.

38-39. Hezekiah's sickness and sin

38:1-22. Hezekiah's deliverance from serious illness. Isaiah announced that Hezekiah's sickness would be fatal, 1. The monarch's prayer, 2-3, was answered and God added 15 years to the king's life and confirmed His promise by the 'sign,' 4-8 (explainable only as a miracle). Hezekiah's psalm of thanksgiving and praise is recorded, 9-20. The remedy used for the recovery is specified, 21.

39:1-8. Hezekiah's foolish pride. Merodach-Baladan (Marduk-apil-iddina), pretending to congratulate Hezekiah on his recovery from illness, tried with an embassy and lavish presents to draw the Jews into a league against Assyria, 1. Hezekiah's egotistical folly in displaying all his wealth and power, 2, drew a scathing rebuke from Isaiah and a warning of

Historical note

Merodach-Baladan was twice ruler of Babylon (722-710 and 703-701 B.C.). He initiated the policy of strengthening Chaldea and set the stage for the rise of Nabopolassar and Nebuchadnezzar II, and Judah's subsequent captivity.

the Babylonian Captivity, 37. The king repentantly accepted God's sentence, 8.

VOL. VII.
BOOK OF COMFORT,
40: 1-66:244.

40. Comfort for delivered Israel

1-11. The call and circumstances of the promised comfort. A call is given to comfort Jerusalem, 1, because her suffering is foreseen as ended with her disobedience fully chastened and her sin forgiven, 2. The precursor to the promised comfort (John the Baptist and his message), 3-8, is seen preparing the way for Messiah, Israel's only true Comforter (Mt 3:3; Lk 3:4-6; Jn 1:23). The occasion for the comfort is the revelation of God in Christ, 9-11, as the personal God, Deliverer and King, 10, a Rewarder, 10, and a Shepherd, 11.

12-26. The character of the Comforter. His power is limitless to comfort, 12. His wisdom is unsearchable, 13-14. His Being is incomparable, 15-17. His worship must be spiritual, 18-26. Hence idolatry is utter folly and wickedly reprehensible, 18-20, in light of the infinite greatness of Deity, 21-26, witnessed to by God's creation, 21-22, 25-26, and declared by His works among men, 23-24.

27-31. The prescription for present comfort. The prophet reproves their discomfort, 27. He then prescribes for their comfort, 28-31, by reviewing God's character, 28-29, and by recalling God's faithfulness, 29-31, especially in helping the helpless, 29, and faithfully answering their prayers, 30-31.

41. The Lord's case against idolatry

1-7. Idolaters are arraigned. God's court is convened and His challenge presented,

1. His case against idolaters is proved by His raising up Cyrus, founder of the Persian Empire and liberator of the Jews from Babylon, 2-4. The folly of idolaters is exposed, 5-7. (For Cyrus, cf. 41:25-26; 44:24-28; 45:1-6, 13; 46:11; 48:14.)

8-20. God's people are encouraged. The basis of this encouragement, 8-9, is the fact that they are God's servants, His elect people, Abraham's progeny, 8, and objects of former deliverance, 9. As such they are the objects of special encouragement, 10-20. God promises His personal presence and protection, 10; deliverance from their enemies, 11-14; conquest over their foes, 15-16; and physical blessing for the land, 17-20.

Sennacherib watches the march-past. This arrogant conqueror in 701 B.C. sent his commander from Lachish to demand the unconditional surrender of Judah.

21-24. The idols themselves are challenged, to present proofs of their knowledge of the past or future, 21-23, and of their power to do anything – good or bad, 23. Failing to do either, they are condemned as nonentities and their worshipers as abominations, 24.

25-29. The Lord Himself produces proof of His sole deity. He alone has irresistible power to effect Cyrus's rise, and infallible foresight to foretell it over a century and a half in advance. He therefore pronounces the verdict upon both the idols and their worshipers. They are vanity, their works nonexistent, their representations are wind and confusion, 29.

42. The Messiah-Servant of the Lord

1-4. God (the Father) presents the Servant in relation to Himself as His Servant, His elect, and His delight, 1. He mentions the qualifications for His work, specifies His task, and describes His Servant's character, 2-4. This is the first 'Servant Song,' 1-6 (see 49:1-6; 50:4-11; 52:13-53:12).

5-9. The prophecy of the Servant's ministry. The description of the One who commissions the Servant to the ministry shows Him to be God (the Father), Creator of the universe, Sustainer of men upon the earth, 5. His assurances to the Servant guarantee success, 6. The description of the Servant's ministry itself sets Him forth as the Mediator of the covenant of grace, 6; as a Light to the Gentiles, 6-7; and as a Liberator of prisoners, 7. The ratification of the commission is assured, 8-9, by the deity and authority of the Commissioner, 8, and the integrity of His word, 9.

10-12. Expression of praise and worship to God for the coming Servant. This blessing requires a 'new song' from humanity everywhere to the ends of the earth.

13-17. Prediction of the Servant's vengeance. He will triumph as a warrior over His foes, 13. He will terminate His silence at His enemies' insults, 14-15. He will treat His friends with mercy, 16; but will thoroughly discomfit idolaters, 17.

18-25. Exposure and reproof of Israel the unfaithful servant. The Lord calls His people, 18, and faithfully appraises their sad condition, 19-20. Protecting His character and His word, 20, He must of necessity chasten His people's sinfulness and unfaithfulness as a servant, 22. However, He graciously provides for their relief by counseling them to acknowledge His hand in their affliction, 23-24, and confess their provocation in His punishment of them, 25.

43:1-44:5. Assurance for the restored nation

43:1-7. Promise of comfort for the remnant. The basis of the promise is twofold: (1) the Lord is the Creator, and (2) He is the Redeemer of the yet-to-be-restored nation. The promise to be with Israel through the water and the fire recalls the wilderness experience where the Lord took them through the sea and led them by a pillar of fire (cf. 1 Cor 10:1-2). The future efficacy of the promise is secured by the fact He will be with them personally, 5, and gather them from their captivity, 5-6. He will thus vindicate His purpose in calling the nation into existence, molding it, perfecting it to glorify Himself in it, and be glorified by it, 7 (cf. Rom 11:29).

43:8-13. Purpose of God in the nation. It was to be a witness to the pagan nations blinded by idolatry, 8-9, of the one true God and His Servant, 10-13.

43:14-21. God's sovereign power will be demonstrated by crushing the Chaldeans and restoring their captives. This will bring glory to God.

43:22-28. The nation's chastisements are the result of its ingratitude. This is manifested in its prayerlessness, 22; its religious indifference, 23; and its sin, 24, all in the face of God's ready grace to forgive, 25, and to plead and reason with it, 26-28.

44:1-5. God's saving grace will be manifested in the conversion of the servant nation. As His servant and His elect nation, 1, the Lord promises to pour out His Holy Spirit upon the converted nation (Isa 32:15; Joel 2:28-32), symbolically styled Jeshurun ('upright'), 2 (see Deut 32:15; 33:5-6).

44:6-28. Israel a witness to the one true God

6-8. God's declaration of His sole deity. As the Lord, the King of Israel, Israel's Redeemer, the Lord of armies, 6, He declares He is the only Deity, the Incomparable One, the Omniscient One, the Rock, 7-8.

9-20. Satire on the sheer folly of idolatry. It darkens the mind and blinds the eyes to spiritual truth.

21-23. God's nation Israel is to be a witness against idolatry. This is her servant role, 21, being redeemed, 22, so that God might be glorified in the nation, 23.

24-28. The Lord decrees the restoration of His people through Cyrus. He calls Cyrus 'my shepherd' who shall 'accomplish all that I please,' 28 (cf. 41:2-4; 44:24-28; 46:11; 48:14).

45. Cyrus a type of Messiah

See 44:24-28 above.

1-6. The Lord promises irresistible conquest to Cyrus as a type of Messiah. The Lord calls him 'his anointed,' which is the only case in which this descriptive title is applied to a Gentile. This, with the designation 'my shepherd' (Isa 44:28), likewise a messianic title, marks Cyrus an extraordinary exception, a Gentile type of Messiah. Both are restorers of Jerusalem (Isa 44:28; Zech 14:1-11). Both are irresistible conquerors of Israel's foes (Isa 45:1; Rev 19:19-21; Ps 2:9). Both are used to glorify the

name of the one true God (Isa 45:6; 1 Cor 15:28).

7-25. The Lord's sovereignty is vindicated against human critics. His lordship is vindicated by what He has done, 7-12; by His raising up Cyrus as His servant, 13; by the prediction that Gentiles are to be converted as well as Israel, 14-19; and by His open invitation to the 'ends of the earth' to believe and be saved, 20-25.

46-47. Deliverance from Babylon and its lessons

46:1-13. The helplessness of idols in contrast to the Lord's omnipotence. Bel (Marduk, Jer 50:2, the patron god of Babylon) and Nebo (an influential Babylonian deity, patron of culture and learning) will be a burden to the beasts who cart them into humiliating captivity, 1-2. In contrast, God bears and carries His people from birth till old age, creating and redeeming them, 3-4. He is moreover incomparable, 5, so unlike a wrought idol which is lifeless and must be carried by the worshiper instead of the worshiper being carried by his God, 6-7. It is dumb in contrast to the omniscient God who knows the future, 8-10, and demonstrates His purpose by raising up Cyrus, 11, and calling men to accept His

The site of the ancient stronghold of Lachish, captured by Sennacherib the Assyrian.

deliverance, 12-13.

47: 1- 7. Chastisement beyond that which God ordains punishable by enslavement in Babylon's case. Shame and enslavement shall be visited upon the proud city of the Chaldeans for excessive cruelty to God's people.

8-15. The godless culture, philosophy, and religion of this world are doomed. Babylon's carnal pleasure and self-security, 8-9; her pride, wisdom, and knowledge, 10-11; and her demonized occult religion, 12-13, shall be her undoing, 14-15. Her doom symbolizes the destruction of the Satanic world system at the advent of Israel's King and kingdom.

48. The Lord's dealing with disobedient Israel

1-8. The Lord presents the evidence of fulfilled prophecy. Idolatrous, hypocritical Jews, 1-2, are confronted with the truth of fulfilled prophecy as a manifestation of the omniscient power of God against any claim they might make for their idol.

9-11. God upholds His glory by means of Israel's chastening. For His name's sake, on the one hand, He restrains His anger that His people Israel might not be utterly destroyed, 9; yet, on the other hand, He must purify them in the furnace of affliction so that His name is unprofaned and His glory guarded, 10-11.

12-16. He will raise up a Gentile deliverer to liberate His people from Babylon. As the Eternal One, the Creator, 12-13, He assembles His erring people to foretell to them that He will raise up one beloved (Cyrus) who will do His will against Babylon, 14-16.

17-19. He laments the tragedy of their disobedience. The purpose of His chastening is to teach them 'what is best' and to lead them 'in the way [they] should go,' 17. Had they obeyed, numerous blessings should have been theirs, 18-19.

20-22. They are to advertise His redemption from Babylon. His goodness is to be witnessed both in deliverance from Babylon, 20, and in His gracious interposition in their deliverance from Egypt. They are to remember always: 'There is no peace . . . for the wicked,' 22.

49. The Messiah-Servant and His mission

1-4. The Servant's arresting exclamation. Dramatically the Lord summoned the Gentiles and announced to them that His call is divine, 1. Then He described His qualifications for the ministry (equipped with a powerful message and protected by the divine majesty), 2, and indicates its divine attestation, 3. Nevertheless, from the purely human standpoint (for He became a man!) the Messiah-Servant laments the apparent initial failure of His task, but quickly conquers the temptation to discouragement with the conviction that He did God's will, expecting God's reward, 4.

5-13. The Lord's assurance of the unqualified success of His Servant. The Lord's character and purpose, 5, as well as the Servant's specific ministry to the Jew first, 5-6, and to the Gentile, guarantee the worldwide extent of His blessing. This follows upon His sufferings and rejection, 7. He is granted not only a blessed ministry of redemption, 8-9, but His redeemed enjoy His full-scale blessings, 10-13.

14-26. The Lord encourages disheartened Israel. He has not forgotten His people; they are inscribed on the palms of His hands, 14-18. He will restore and bless them in their land, 19-23, punishing their enemies, 24-26.

50. Disobedient Israel versus the obedient Servant

1-3. The disobedient people presented. They are dramatically challenged by the Lord Himself to prove Him unfaithful as a husband and as a father, 1. They are charged with responsibility for their captivity and their divorce from the Lord, and decisively condemned because of their unbelief, disobedience, and disregard for God's power, 2-3.

4-9. The obedient Servant-Saviour prophesied. The coming of the Servant is foretold. He will come as the taught one, the docile one, the one obedient to suffering, rejection, and death, 4-6 (cf. Phil 2:6-8). The Servant will conquer as a courageous champion, depending upon God, doing His will, boldly confident in its success, and defying all opposition, 7-9.

10-11. His promise of salvation and threat of doom. The way of salvation is through faith and obedience, 10. The way of destruction is through unbelief and disobedience, 11.

51. Encouragement for the faithful

1-3. The faithful given promise of Zion's future. They are described in their present conduct, 1; reminded of their past descent, 2; and condoled with the promise of future deliverance for Zion, 3.

4-8. The faithful are assured of the fulfillment of the promise to Zion. The promise will be fulfilled by Messiah's personal administration, 4-5, and perpetual salvation, 6, with the prediction of the destruction of their persecutors explicit in the promise, 7-8.

9-16. The faithful petition for a demonstration of the promise by deliverance. The prayer is presented, 9, and enforced by a recital of the wonders of past deliverance from Egypt, 9-11. It is answered, 12-16, with regard to the fearful, 12; the fettered, 14-15; and the faithful, 16.

17-20. Predicament of Jerusalem portrayed. She is in a drunken stupor, 17; destitute of helpers, 18; decimated by desolation, 19-20.

21-23. Prediction of Jerusalem's future redemption. The Lord assures her that He is her God and will speedily end her affliction, 22. He will make her persecuting foes drink the same cup as she had to drink, 23.

52. Jerusalem aroused to glory

The dark background behind this bright scene is contained in 51:17-23.

1-2. Appeal to Jerusalem to prepare herself for glory. She is to arouse herself from the humiliation of her captivities, put on her high priestly apparel (cf. Zech 3:1-8), separate herself from defilement, and assume her regal position, 2.

3-6. The case the Lord presents for His people's liberation. Their oppressors paid nothing for God's property, nor acknowledged His power, and so have no claim on His people, nor are to be paid any price, 3. His people have been similarly delivered before, 4. Moreover, their captors depreciated God's glory by their excessive cruelty to His people, 5, so that God's glory will be promoted by their emancipation, 6.

7-10. Praise of prophet and people at Zion's liberation. The messenger of such an emancipation is very honored, 7. His message is theocratic, 'Your God reigns!' (cf. Zech 6:8-14, with Christ the King-Priest installed

The barren Judean Wilderness. Isaiah writes of a voice crying 'Prepare in the wilderness a road for our God.'

upon the throne). The recipients of the message are expectant, exultant, and specially illuminated, 8. The desolated city is commanded to rejoice, 9. The Lord is glorified and His worldwide salvation published, 10.

11-12. The importance of their repatriation demands speed and thorough separation from Babylon, 11, with an orderly return in dependence upon God, 12.

13-15. The preeminence of the Servant epitomized. He is exalted because the Lord God views the Servant as divinely commissioned and qualified, 13. The compass of His exaltation is given, from the depths of humiliation to a position 'highly exalted' (Eph 1:20-23; Phil 2:6-9). The precursors of exaltation were His abysmal degradation and sufferings, 14. He startles many nations and awes kings into silence as a consequence of His exaltation, 15.

53. Prophecy of the Messiah-Servant as sinbearer

52:13-15 Introduction: the preeminence of the Servant epitomized. (See above.)

1-3. The person of the Servant despised. Presented first is the incredible unbelief of the Jews concerning His person, 1 (cf. Jn 1:11). They despised His person because of His quiet, unobtrusive entrance among men, His poverty and obscurity, and His lack of worldly pomp and appeal, 2; but mostly because of their own blindness and sin, 3.

4-6. The passion of the Servant summarized. Although He died for mankind in general, this is the penitential confession of the future repentant nation. She will glimpse His vicarious bearing of her (and the world's) sins, as well as see His shame and misrepresentation, stripes and wounds.

7-10. The perseverance of the Servant particularized. He suffered silently, 7, unjustly, for our good and in our stead, vicariously, 8, ignominiously, 9, and under the frowns of heaven, 10.

10-12. The recompense of the Servant is realized. He acquires a glorious spiritual progeny ('he will see his offspring'), enjoys a splendid victorious resurrection ('he will . . . prolong his days'), and fully accomplishes the divine will ('the will of the

Lord will prosper in his hand'), 10. He is rewarded with abundant satisfaction, 11; justifies many, 11; obtains incontestable victory and universal domination, 12; and is given an efficacious high priestly ministry, 12.

54. The radiant joy of restored Israel

1-10. The blessings of the converted nation. Subsequent to the cross of Christ is the singing of the redeemed. When Israel looks unto Him whom they have pierced (53:1-8), what radiant joy, spiritual fruitfulness, and expansion will be theirs, 1-3. She who during her sin and faithlessness was put away as the wife of the Lord is now restored, 4-6. Her restoration will be permanent and God's covenant of peace shall not depart from her, 7-10.

11-17. The radiant beauty of the restored nation. She is likened to a beautiful city, 11-12. Her citizens shall be spiritually taught; will become spiritually prosperous, 13-14; and be victorious and secure, 15-17.

55. Worldwide evangelical invitation

1. The invitation offered. It is universal, to everyone; qualified only by a sense of need, 'all you who are thirsty.' They will find wine to revive and milk to nourish (1 Pet 2:2) their souls. Everyone is invited to 'come, buy and eat.' They are assured of a free, gracious communication because the salvation offered is priceless, having already been purchased by Christ's own blood (Isa 53:1-8; 1 Pet 1:19).

2-4. The invitation enforced. The appeal is strengthened by a consideration of the wrong to oneself in rejecting the invitation, 2, and the benefit by accepting it, 2-4.

5-7. The invitation extended and defined. It is extended by the calling of the Gentiles; 5 (Acts 15:14-15; Rom 1:16), and unknown nations, 5. It is defined as a call to 'seek the Lord,' 6; to repentance and faith, 7; and to obtain pardon, 7.

8-13. The invitation authorized and accepted. It is not authorized by man, because of the utter disparity between God's thought and man's, 8-9, but by God Himself, 9-10, and this by reason of the certain fulfillment of His word, 10-11. The invitation is accepted, 12-13, resulting in Israel's heart being regenerated, 12, and her land revived, 13, with creation being delivered from the bondage of corruption (Rom 8:19-23).

56:1-8. Gentiles included in kingdom blessing

1-2. Latter-day Israel admonished to maintain a godly witness. She is to preserve justice, do righteousness, keep the sabbath, and refrain from doing evil. Reason: the Lord's salvation is about to be revealed, 1-2.

3-8. Blessing is promised to non-Israelites. The foreigner and the eunuch who keep the Lord's sabbath and join themselves to God's covenant people, 3-5, will share the benefits of millennial worship in the temple at Jerusalem, 2:1-5, called 'a house of prayer for all nations,' 6-8.

56:9-57:21. Condemnation of the wicked in Israel

56:9-12. The sins of wicked rulers in Israel denounced. The sins of Israel's prophets are denounced – their spiritual blindness, covetousness, gluttony, false optimism.

57:1-13. The sins of the wicked populace in Israel denounced. They pay no attention to the death of a righteous man, 1-2.

They give themselves to idolatry, 3-10, but find no benefit, 11-13.

57:14-21. Mercy for the repentant, but judgment for the wicked. The contrite and humble are chastened and revived, 14-20, but the wicked have no peace, 21.

58. False worship versus the true

1- 5. Hypocritical worship and Israel's sins. The prophet's preaching commission, 1, is followed by a description of the sins exposed. As the first advent of our Lord was heralded by a message of repentance from John the Baptist (Mt 3:1-11), so the second advent will be similarly preceded by such a call (Mal 4:56).

6-7. True worship outlined. Repentance will result in true fasting and humiliation.

8-14. The promises for the repentant remnant. Here all the great future blessings of the converted remnant of Israel are set forth. It is the focus of the entire closing section of the book.

59. The coming of the Redeemer to Zion

1-8. Israel's unbelief and sin of the last days. The terrible catalog of the nation's depravity (cf. Rom 3:10-18) shows what has

Painting of Jesus being mocked before his crucifixion. Isaiah prophesies of the Messiah-Servant as sinbearer who suffered silently, unjustly, for our good and in our stead.

separated her from God.

9-15. Israel's last-day confession. They confess their spiritual darkness, 9; their desolation and deadness, 10; their unsaved condition, 11; their sinfulness, 12, and their wickedness, 13-15.

16-19. The Lord's gracious intervention. He personally interposes in their behalf, 16, judging and punishing the wicked, 17-18. His Spirit raises up a standard against the flood of iniquity of the Tribulation when it reaches its full, 19.

20-21. The second advent of the Redeemer. Christ appears in person for the salvation of them who turn from sin (Rom 11:26-27).

60. Jerusalem's glory in the kingdom age

1-2. Israel enlightened in the kingdom age. Messiah the Light shines on Jerusalem, Jerusalem shines on the earth, 1. Observe the close connection with ch. 58 and 59. First the call to repentance; then the uncovering of Jacob's sin; Israel's confession; and the answer of the Lord by His personal advent, dealing with His enemies and appearing as Redeemer in Zion. Then the glorious light of ch. 60 breaks forth. It is the glorious day preceded by the night of universal corruption and apostasy, 2.

3-14. Israel enlarged in the kingdom age. Gentiles are drawn to the Light, 3, and Jews return to the Light, 4. They bring in their wealth, and world conversion ensues, 5-9. Rich pastoral and commercial nations shall vie with one another in building Jerusalem, 10, and enriching Zion, 11. Rebels will be cut off, 12; the temple will be rebuilt (cf. 56:7) and beautified, 13; and enemies and revilers will humbly submit, 14.

15-22. Israel exalted in the kingdom age. Her humiliation gives way to exaltation, 15; her weakness to strength, 16; her poverty to wealth, 17; her troubles to salvation and safety, 18; her darkness to perpetual light, 19-20; her sin to righteousness, 21; and her insignificance to importance, 22.

61. Messiah's ministry for Israel and the world

1-2. Messiah's ministry in His first advent detailed. In its spiritual character, His ministry was anointed by the Holy Spirit of God, 1 (cf. 42:1). In its specific character, it was a ministry of gospel preaching, 1, of spiritual healing, and of gracious favor to believers at His first advent (cf. Lk 4:18-20 where Jesus stops at this point).

2-3. Messiah's ministry in his second advent. In this connection He announces the 'day of vengeance of our God,' 2, and comfort for all who mourn, especially in Zion, 3.

4-9. Results of Messiah's ministry at His second advent. Waste places are rebuilt, 4. Israel, lately enslaved, will be served, 5; lately abased, will be exalted as a priestly, wealthy, and honored nation, 6. Lately afflicted, she will be enriched and comforted, 7; lately scattered, will be divinely gathered and guided, 8; lately reproached, will be fully vindicated before the nations, 9.

10-11. The joy of Messiah's ministry is depicted. He personally exults that God has clothed Him with 'garments of salvation,' 10, because of what God will do before the nations.

62. Jerusalem a praise in the earth

1. The divine concern for Zion. The Lord Himself is the speaker and He resolves He will not keep silent nor rest till Jerusalem is made a praise in the earth, till her vindication goes forth as brightness, and her salvation as a burning torch. The Lord Himself is eager to see the millennial city blessed and made a blessing, 1.

2-5. The results of the divine concern for Zion. Zion shall be honored and admired by the nations, 2. She shall be called by a new name — a God-given, royal name. It will no longer be Deserted or Desolate, but Hephzibah ('my delight is in her') and Beulah ('married'), 3-4. The name will be given because the Lord's delight will be in her and she shall be married, as illustrated in the simile in 5.

6-12. The concrete expression of the divine concern for Zion. This is set forth in the Lord's actions ('I have posted watchmen on your walls'), 6; in the prophet's exhortation to intercession for the city, 6-7; in the Lord's oath that He will protect Jerusalem from ever again being overrun by enemies, 8-9; in the call to return from Babylon, 10; in the final end-time deliverance, 11, and in the final end-time blessing. This is expressed in a fourfold name for the Lord's own – 'The Holy People,' 'The Redeemed of the Lord,' 'Sought After,' 'The City no longer deserted,' 12.

63:1-6. The Messiah-Avenger and the day of vengeance

1-2. Messiah the Avenger interrogated, 1-2. 'The year of the Lord's favor' is ended and fearful judgment sweeps the earth (Rev 19:11-21). Two rhetorical questions are asked: 'Who is this coming from Edom?' and 'Why are your garments red?'

1-6. Messiah the Avenger's answer. Conquering, the figure (Christ in His second advent glory) replies, 'It is I, speaking in righteousness, mighty to save.' He moves up through Edom to the valley of Jehoshaphat (Joel 3) for the great slaughter at Armageddon. The brilliant red of His garments (Rev 14:18-19) is explained as the result of treading the winepress of wrath against His enemies, whom He vanquishes solely by His own power and zeal, in complete fulfillment of the prophetic word, 3-4. Despite the failure of His own people, 5, He accomplishes the complete overthrow of His foes, 6.

63:7-64:12 The remnant's great prayer of intercession

63:7-19. The remnant remembers past deliverances. Isaiah, as the representative of the godly remnant, utters one of the greatest prayers in the Bible, to be prayed by the godly remnant in the Tribulation preceding the kingdom. The steadfast love of the Lord in general is set forth, 7-9. Specific deliverance out of Egypt is cited, 10-14. The prayer is for the Lord's help in distress, 15-19.

64:1-4. The remnant beseeches the Lord to assert His power over the nations. In the dark night of the Tribulation when enemies of Israel close in, 1-2, divine intervention is pleaded for.

64:5-7. The penitent confession of the believing remnant. They are confident that the Lord will meet them, 5, in their confession of sin, 6-7.

64:8-12. The appeal for pardon and restoration. The touching plea is from a chastened and yielded people, 8-9, reviewing their punishments, 10-11, and interceding for help, 12.

65. The Lord's answer – His mercy reserved for the remnant

1-7. The sins of latter-day apostate Israel. The stern rebuke of the Lord goes forth because of their rebellion in the face of open opportunity, 1, and abundant divine revelation, 2, which they scouted for idolatry, 3-4, and self-righteousness, 5. The warning of punishment concerns the day of vengeance, 6-7.

8-10. The election and blessing of the righteous remnant. God will not destroy the remnant, because there is blessing in it, 8. He will restore it and the land for it to dwell in, 9-10.

11-12. The judgment of latter-day apostate Israel. Idolatry, covetousness, rebellion, and disobedience destine the apostates for slaughter.

13-16. The blessings of the remnant vs. the curses of apostate Israel. The state of God's servants is in sharp contrast to that of those who reject Him.

17-25. The glories and blessings in store for God's own. The prophet glimpses the eternal sinless state, 17. In the kingdom he sees Jerusalem blessed, 18-19; longevity restored, 20; security and happiness prevailing, 21-23; prayer answered, 24; and the curse lifted, 25 (cf. 11:6-9).

Jerusalem's Damascus Gate by night. Isaiah says that in the kingdom age, Messiah shines on Jerusalem, and Jerusalem shines on the earth.

66. Synoptic finale; the entire prophecy in retrospect

1-4. Wicked worship of age-end apostate Israel. This final chapter restates the leading prophetic themes of the book. The apostate mass of the Jewish nation (Israel) restored in unbelief erects a temple in Jerusalem and resumes its ancient worship. This is a worship of unbelief and is an abomination to the Lord, 1-4 (cf. 2 Thess 2:4; Dan 9:27; Mt 24:15; Rev 11:1-2). The true worshiper is contrasted with the apostate worshiper, 2-4.

5. The remnant persecuted and encouraged. The remnant trembles at God's Word and is hated and mocked by apostate brethren, who shall be put to shame, 5. In derision they taunt, 'Let the Lord be glorified.'

6. The coming of the Lord. Suddenly He comes to His temple (Mal 3:1). He appears rendering recompense to His enemies.

7-9. Israel's national rebirth. A people and a land are born in a day! A nation is regenerated in a moment (Rom 11:26-27).

10-14. Jerusalem' s millennial glory and exaltation. The city is likened to a mother who nurses her children, 10-11. Her kingdom, prosperity, and wealth are communicated to her children, 12-14 (cf. 60:1-7).

15-17. Messiah the avenger and the day of vengeance. The Lord will come with fire to render His anger in fury (cf. 61:2; 63:34) against His foes among the nations, 15-16, and against the apostate mass of Israel, 17.

18-21. Gentiles brought into the kingdom. All nations and languages will be brought in to see God's glory, 18. Those gathered are to evangelize and bring others in, 19. Jews also will be brought in, 20-21.

22. The perpetuity of Israel and the eternal state. The truth of the eternal state is used as a simile for the fact of Israel' s perpetual existence.

23. Blessings for the righteous. All mankind will worship the Lord.

24. The destiny of the wicked. Eternal perdition is their portion – 'their worm will not die, nor will their fire be quenched' (cf. the Lord's warning concerning Gehenna, Mk 9:44-48; Rev 20:14-15).

JEREMIAH

Death of a decadent nation

The world of Jeremiah.
Isaiah lived and prophesied under the Assyrian period. Jeremiah ministered when Assyria was tottering on the brink of ruin, and Babylon and Egypt were struggling to take over world control. He warned of Babylon's victory, but Judah failed to repent of her sin and accept his warnings. As a result Judah suffered destruction, but the prophet announced that she would one day be restored, and through Messiah would come into worldwide blessing. Babylon, however, would be destroyed, never to rise again.

Arrangement of book. The
messages that are dated show that the book was not arranged in chronological order. For instance, messages in *Josiah's* reign are found in 1:2 and 3:6, while those in *Jehoiakim's* reign are in 22:18; 25:1; 26:1; 35:1; 36:1; 45:1. Those in *Zedekiah's* reign are in 21:1, 8; 27:2, 3, 12; 28:1; 29:3; 32:1; 34:2; 37:1-2; 38:5; 39:1; 49:34; 51:59. Two were written late in Egypt, 43:7-7; 44:1. Most of the messages were obviously given in Jehoiakim's and Zedekiah's reigns. The lack of chronological order is evidently intentional. Probably the order is to be found in the arrangement of the subject matter by contrast, not by date of composition.

Message of Jeremiah. His
was principally a message of stern warning against the inevitable doom of the Babylonian Captivity (25:1-14), if the people did not repent of idolatry and sin. The menacing gloom of an iconoclastic message (1: 10) was highlighted, however, by bright messianic flashes (23:5-8; 30:4-11; 31:31-34; 33:15-18). Final restoration of Israel was to be accomplished after a period of unparalleled suffering (30:10), through the manifestation of David's righteous Branch, the Lord (23:6; 33:15).

Outline

1-45 Prophecies against Judah and Jerusalem
1-20 Under Josiah and Jehoiakim
21-39 At various periods till Jerusalem's fall
40-45 After Jerusalem's fall
46-51 Prophecies against the nations
52 Historical appendix

Assyrian bowman.

Relief of an Assyrian assault. Israel had lost her freedom and had become a slave of Assyria and Egypt.

I. Introduction; Jeremiah's call

1-3. Superscription. Jeremiah ('the Lord exalts') was a descendant of the priest Abiathar, who was banished by Solomon to Anathoth (Ras Karrubeh) about two miles NE of Jerusalem in Benjamin. Jeremiah's ministry, 2, extended from Josiah's thirteenth year (627 B.C.) to Zedekiah's eleventh year (586 B.C.).

4-19. Jeremiah's call. God's electing grace, 5, and the prophet's humility, 6, resulted in a definite commission to preach the unpopular message, 'to uproot and tear down, to destroy and overthrow'; as well as the positive ministry, 'to build and to plant,' 7-10. Jeremiah's encounter with God and His commission were buttressed by three visions, 11. The almond tree (Heb. *saqed*) is the first harbinger of spring and was a sign that God was *watching, awaking early* (Heb. *soqed*) to empower His word, 12. The boiling pot fanned by the north wind pictures God's judgment boiling over from the north on Judah for her sin and idolatry. God's Word is effective (1 Pet 4:17; Heb 4:12).

2:1-3:5. Sermon I – Sin of the nation

2:1-19. A faithful Lord vs. an unfaithful people. The review of the Lord's goodness, 1-3, is followed by an expose of the apostasy of the nation, 4-13. The people had committed two evils, forsaking the Lord, 'the spring of living water' (cf. Jn 4:10-15; 7:38), and by their idolatry were drinking the polluted water at the bottom of a cracked and contaminated man-made cistern, 13. As a result, Israel had lost her freedom and had become a slave of Assyria ('Lions') and of Egypt (Memphis, capital of N. Egypt), 14-19.

2:20-37. The divine impeachment and expostulation. Israel had become like a stubborn ox, 20; a wild vine, 21; a lustful prostitute, 22-25; a disgraced thief, 26; a foolish idolater, 27-28; a thoughtless, thankless people, 29-32; an impudent transgressor, 33; a blinded nation, 34-37.

3:1-5. The results of Israel's infidelity. Her callousness made her punishment inevitable.

3:6-6:30. Sermon 2 – Devastation from the north

3:6-25. Judah's apostasy greater than Israel's. The northern kingdom's punishment in captivity and eventual destruction did not properly impress Judah, 6-11. She was a harlot, made unclean by participation in idolatrous Canaanite religion, divorced from the Lord. Similar chastisement as that which befell Israel (2 Kgs 17:1-18) threatened Judah; but true repentance, 10-14, would be followed by blessing, 15-25.

4:1-31. The foe from the north. Jeremiah is apparently speaking of the imminent Babylonian invasion. Though Babylon was east of Jerusalem, the intervening desert made it necessary for the invading army to follow the Euphrates River to Carchemish and then attack Palestine from the north. Some believe Jeremiah is here referring to the Scythian invasion of Assyria (653-630 B.C.) or Cappadocia (c. 595 B.C.). This is unlikely, however, since there is no mention of Palestinian involvement.

5:1-31. Judgment and impending disaster. The weeping prophet of Anathoth bewailed the sins of Jerusalem, his moral

Kings of Judah
in the time of Jeremiah

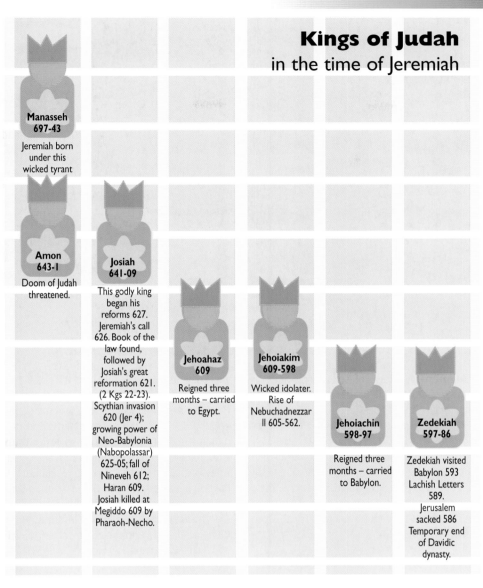

Manasseh 697-43

Jeremiah born under this wicked tyrant

Amon 643-1

Doom of Judah threatened.

Josiah 641-09

This godly king began his reforms 627. Jeremiah's call 626. Book of the law found, followed by Josiah's great reformation 621. (2 Kgs 22-23). Scythian invasion 620 (Jer 4); growing power of Neo-Babylonia (Nabopolassar) 625-05; fall of Nineveh 612; Haran 609. Josiah killed at Megiddo 609 by Pharaoh-Necho.

Jehoahaz 609

Reigned three months – carried to Egypt.

Jehoiakim 609-598

Wicked idolater. Rise of Nebuchadnezzar II 605-562.

Jehoiachin 598-97

Reigned three months – carried to Babylon.

Zedekiah 597-86

Zedekiah visited Babylon 593 Lachish Letters 589. Jerusalem sacked 586 Temporary end of Davidic dynasty.

---

sensitivity pained.

6:1-30. Continued warning. A great destruction was coming on Jerusalem, 1-26. Let its inhabitants flee to the wilderness of Tekoa (Amos' home), some dozen miles S of Jerusalem, the prophet urges, 1-2. Jeremiah appeared as the Lord's tester or assayer to try the Lord's people, 27-30 (cf. Job 23:10).

7-10. Sermon 3
– Threat of exile

This temple message, like the two preceding sermons, was a stern rebuke, warning and exhortation, but centered in the religious conditions in Judah.

7:1-34. Rebuke of apostate religionism. Would these empty ritualists of Jerusalem make God's house 'a den of robbers,' 1-11? The destruction of Shiloh (18 miles N of Jerusalem, destroyed about 1050 B.C.) should have been a lesson, 12-14 (cf. Jer 26:6; 1 Sam 4:10; Ps 78:60). The Lord's anger burned at Jerusalem's idolatry, 15-19, and apostasy, 20-34. The 'Queen of Heaven,' 18, was an ancient Semitic deity, Babylonian Ishtar (Venus) (cf. 44:17-19, 25). 'Topheth,' 32, was a high place in the Valley of Hinnom, SW of Jerusalem, where in the Isaiah-Jeremiah era people sacrificed children to Molech, a deity of Ammon.

8:1-22. Further warnings of

A pagan
Canaanite shrine
at Megiddo in the
Plain of
Esdraelon. Such
shrines were
often known as
'high places', and
were denounced
by Jeremiah.

judgment. All classes of God's people were corrupted, prophets as well as priests, 10; sinners were brazenly shameless, 12.

9:1-26. Jeremiah weeps over sinners. The prophet was torn between pity for sinners and revulsion at their sin, 1, which could not be condoned, 2-26.

10:1-25. The Lord and idolatry. The folly of worshiping idols is outlined, 1-16, and the judgment to be visited upon it, 17-22. A prayer is offered, 23-25.

11-13. Sermon 4 – The broken covenant; sign of the linen belt

11:1-12:17. The broken covenant. The rebukes, warnings and exhortations of this sermon were based upon the violation of the Palestinian covenant (Deut 28:1-30:9). Jeremiah championed the covenant, 11:1-8. The reformation under Josiah had been forgotten, 9-17, and the prophet's own countrymen at Anathoth planned to kill him, 11:18-23. This underhanded action and the prosperity of the wicked bothered the prophet, 12:1-6, and the Lord pronounced a lamentation for Judah through him, 12:7-17.

13:1-27. The parable of the linen belt. This parabolic sign was acted out by the prophet, 1-11. The pure white linen garment

worn next to the skin symbolized the pristine purity of the nation in fellowship with the Lord. Put off and exposed to dampness and soil at the Euphrates, 4, 6, 7, it showed the ruin of the nation away from God and in predicted captivity beyond the Euphrates in Babylon. The wineskins, 12-14, filled to the top, symbolized the people's drunkenness and their ruin under divine judgment. The warning against pride, 15-17, was followed by the dirge for the king (Jehoiachin) and queen mother, both of whom were taken captive to Babylon (597 B.C.), 18-19. Woes were pronounced upon Jerusalem, 20-27.

14-17. Sermon 5 – The drought; sign of the unmarried prophet

14:1-22. Drought and the nation's doom. This terrible calamity, 1-6; the empty ritualistic prayers of the nation, 7-9; and their rejection by the Lord, 10-12, are described. The false prophets, 13, who had no divine credentials, were to blame, 14-16. Jeremiah lamented for the nation, 17-22.

15:1-21. The Lord's answer to Jeremiah. Intercession was rejected and the nation's fate was sealed, 1-9. The prophet's grief was followed by the Lord's reply, 10-21.

16:1-21. The approaching disaster,

the wages of sin. The inexorable fulfillment of God's word is shown by the Lord's denying marriage to the prophet, 1-4, and even observance of funerals and festivities, 5-9, seen as signs of impending ordeals because of Judah's apostasies, 10-13. Ultimate blessing would result after judgment, 14-21.

17:1-27. Judah's terrible sin. A description of it, 1-4, with the curse and the blessing, was set before the people, 5-11. Jeremiah worshiped and prayed, 12-18. Sabbath desecration, an index of their disloyalty to the Lord, was warned against, 19-27.

18-20. Sermon 6
– Sign of the potter's house

18:1-23. The prophet's visit to the potter. This episode furnished a lesson in God's sovereign molding of his people (Rom 9:20-24). He dealt sovereignly with them; design for evil could be substituted for design for good if His people repented, 1-11. But their brazen unrepentance was noted by the Lord, 12-17; demonstrated by the wicked plots of the people against Jeremiah, 18; and lamented by the prophet's imprecatory prayer, 19-23.

19:1-15. The broken clay jar was another sign that the Lord would smash the idolatry-ridden people. Topheth (see 7:31) was the center of the cruel Molech cult. The Potsherd Gate (later the Dung Gate, Neh 2:13) led to Hinnom, the location of the idol Molech, where children were offered.

20:1-18. Public punishment of Jeremiah. Pashhur, chief temple policeman, imprisoned Jeremiah for his message on the broken flask, 1-6. Pashhur's doom was announced, 6, and his name changed to 'Terror,' 3 (cf. 6:25; 25:8-11; Ps 31:13). Jeremiah's severe testing produced momentary perplexity and complaint, but faith triumphed over unbelief in the prophet, 7-18.

21-24. Oracles concerning reigning kings

21:1-14. Jeremiah's message to Zedekiah. The inquiry of Zedekiah, 1-2 (597-586 B.C.), was made concerning Nebuchadnezzar (Akkadian *Nabu-kuddurriusur,* 'Nabu protect my boundary stone,' 605-562 B.C.). This Pashhur was different from the Pashhur of 20:1. Zephaniah, the priest,

Artist's impression of a biblical potter. The prophet visited the potter, an episode that furnished a lesson in God's sovereign molding of his people.

was later executed at Riblah (52:24-27). Jeremiah's reply to Zedekiah, 3-7; the people, 8-10; and the court, 12-14, was realistic and must have cut his sinful hearers to the quick.

22:1-30. Jeremiah's message concerning other kings of Judah. This was an introductory oracle warning the Davidic court, 1-9, and comforting Shallum (Jehoahaz), who reigned only three months and was carried to Egypt (608 B.C.), 11-12. An oracle concerning Jehoiakim (608-597), 13-19, a wicked idolater and foe of Jeremiah, was presented (cf. 2 Kgs 23:24-24:7). Judgment was pronounced upon Jehoiachin, 20-30, who was deported to Babylon. (In the Hebrew be is called Coniah here and 37:1; Jeconiah in 24:1; 27:20; cf. 2 Kgs 24:8-16; 25:27-30.)

23:1-40. Great messianic prophecy. The false shepherds (unworthy rulers) of Judah,

1-2, furnished the somber background for the bright prophecy of kingdom regathering and restoration, 3-4, under Messiah, the 'righteous Branch,' 5, 'The Lord Our Righteousness,' 6. This will be fulfilled in the end-time and will embrace the final exodus and redemption from worldwide bondage into kingdom status, 7-8, under the Messiah (Rom 11:25-27). Jeremiah's lament, 9-14, and condemnation of the false prophets, 15-32, followed the glorious messianic flash. The recalcitrant sinners of that day were given up to shame, 33-40.

24:1-10. Vision of the two baskets of figs directed against Zedekiah. The good figs symbolized the best of the people carried to Babylon with Jehoiachin (597 B.C.). The bad figs stood for the apostates who remained in Jerusalem to support the wicked Zedekiah, and who were of a mind to resist Babylon with Egypt's help (2 Kgs 24:10-20).

25. Prediction of the 70-year captivity

1-11. The exile declared. In the fourth year of Jehoiakim (604 B.C.), with the supremacy of Babylon assured by Nebuchadnezzar's defeat of Egypt at Carchemish, Jeremiah reviewed his previous 23-year ministry, 1-7. Then he announced the 70-year captivity, 8-11 (cf. Lev 26:33-35; 2 Chr 36:21; Dan 9:2).

12-38. Judgment of the nations and the Day of the Lord. Babylon with its king was to be punished, 12-14, as well as 'all the nations,' 15-29 (cf. Isa 51:17; Rev 14:10). This will usher in the Day of the Lord and the wrath of God, 30-38. This is the future period of judgment upon apostate Israel and the nations, culminating in the glorious second advent of Christ (Mt 24:30; Rev 4-19).

26. Jeremiah faces threat of death

1-11. His prediction of the destruction of the temple. It would be destroyed like Shiloh (cf. 7:12, 14 with 1 Sam 4:10-11). All classes rejected the truth and persecuted the prophet.

12-24. Jeremiah's deliverance. His brave defense and deliverance are described, 12-19, with reference made to Micah's similar ministry, 18-19 (cf. Mic 1:1), and Uriah's martyrdom under Jehoiakim, 20-24.

27-28. The sign of the yokes

27:1-22. The divinely imposed yoke of Babylon. Jeremiah saddled himself with an ox yoke to symbolize how Babylon would put a yoke on the neck of Jerusalem and Judah. This truth was distasteful to the people.

28:1-17. Opposition by false prophets. Hananiah, one of the false prophets, impudently broke Jeremiah's yoke, 10. He was punished by death.

29. Jeremiah comforts the exiles

1-23. His letter sent to Babylon. He urged the people to be law-abiding, peaceful exiles and to multiply, 1-9, against the day of restoration after 70 years, 10 (cf. 25:11; 27:7). The Lord had good plans for them, 10-14. They had a future and a hope, 11, but they must refuse the false prophets among them, namely, Ahab and Zedekiah, 21, whose doom was sealed, 22-23.

24-32. Shemaiah's attack and Jeremiah's second letter. Another prophet uttering lies and rebellion against the Lord sent a scathing letter to the new temple overseer, Zephaniah, attacking Jeremiah. Zephaniah showed the letter to Jeremiah, who then sent another letter to the exiles, condemning Shemaiah and prophesying that neither this false prophet nor his descendants would see the day of the return from exile (cf. 20:6).

30-31. Restoration and messianic promises

30:1-17. The time of trouble for Jacob. Jeremiah's dark warnings of judgment were relieved by a prophecy of the glorious future of the nation, ch. 30-31. But this great regathering and end-time restoration, 30:1-3, is to be preceded by the Great Tribulation, 4-11, the height of the nation's age-long sufferings, here called 'the time of trouble for Jacob' because it will center in latter-day Israel, 7 (cf. Mt 24; Mk 13; Rev 7). The return of Christ, 9 (cf Rev 19:11-16), will establish the kingdom after the sinful people have been purged, 12-17.

30:18-24. Israel's restoration to

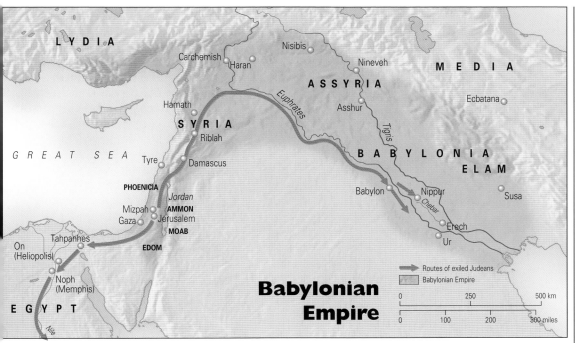

Babylonian Empire

Routes of exiled Judeans
Babylonian Empire

0   250   500 km

0   100   200   300 miles

kingdom glory. They will be restored as the Lord's people, 22.

31:1-26. The nation's homegoing and salvation. The restored nation, 1-6, will sing songs of redemption, 7-14, with the preceding tribulation (as in 30:1-17, 23-24) producing genuine repentance and preparing the nation for blessing, 15-20, and assurance, 21-26.

31:27-40. The new covenant and the everlasting nation. This restoration to the Lord's blessing is based on the new covenant, 31-34. The old covenant was the law covenant grounded in legal observance. The new covenant (Heb 8:8-12) will be entirely on the basis of grace and the sacrificed blood of Christ, which will be the foundation of Israel's future inward regeneration and restoration to God's favor. Israel's entering into the blessings of the new covenant will ensure her being an everlasting nation, 35-36 (cf. Rom 11:1-26).

32. Jeremiah's faith in the restoration

1-25. The sign of the prophet's faith. He purchased land in Anathoth, early in 586 B.C., before the fall of Jerusalem. Hanameel, Jeremiah's cousin, was eager to sell his land to the prophet to prevent loss of the family inheritance (Lev 25:25-28). Storage of deeds, written on papyrus, in earthen jars is known

from Elephantine in Egypt, 14. Jeremiah's faith in the hour of his imprisonment, 3, became vocal in prayer, 16-25. Baruch, 12, was Jeremiah's faithful secretary.

26-44. The Lord's answer. The fate of the doomed city was announced, 28-35, and the future final regathering, of which the restoration from Babylon was a foreshadowing, was declared, 36-44.

33. The great prophecy of the Davidic kingdom

1-5. Jerusalem's imminent overthrow. A call to prayer was issued, 1-3, as the siege of Jerusalem was begun. This picture of impending disaster furnished the dark background against which was flashed the future glory of the nation.

6-14. Future blessing and glory. Cleansing is to be effected after the return, 6-8 (cf. Ezk 36:25; Zech 13:1; Heb 9:13-14; Rom 11:25-27). The joy of salvation is echoed, 9-11, and kingdom peace and prosperity are described, 12-14.

15-26. The Davidic king and his kingdom. 'In those days' is the time of the second advent of Christ when He, the 'righteous Branch' will come to sit on the throne of His father David (Lk 1:31-33; cf. 2 Sam 7:8-16). Then the Lord in redemptive power will be manifested toward Israel as 'The Lord Our

Archaelogical light

The Lachish Ostraca discovered at Lachish (Tel ed-Duweir) in 1935 belong to this very time. Letter No. IV says, 'We are watching for the fire signals of Lachish ... for we no longer can see the signals of Azekah.' The names, places and circumstances of these 21 Heb. inscribed tablets closely resemble the times of Jeremiah just before the fall of Lachish, Azekah and Jerusalem, 589-586 B.C.

[Israel's] Righteousness,' 16 (cf. 33:6-8). Temple worship (see Ezk 40-44) will be restored, 18. The inviolability of the Davidic covenant was declared, 20-22, as well as God's faithfulness to perform all the covenants and promises made to Israel, 23-26 (cf. Rom 9:4-5; 11:29).

34. Jeremiah's warning to Zedekiah

1-7. The warning. The siege of the city (Jan., 588 B.C.) impending, Jeremiah warned Zedekiah of its fall. Lachish, the fortress city 23 miles SW of Jerusalem, and Azekah, 11 miles N of Lachish, are well known from the Lachish Letters.

8-22. Zedekiah's treachery. Zedekiah announced the release of all Hebrew slaves in fulfillment of the Sabbatical legislation of Ex 21:2. His intention, however, was to 'buy' God's favor and to provide more available fighting men. When the siege was temporarily lifted, Zedekiah's reversal exposed his true intentions. Jeremiah strongly condemned this base conduct 12-22, and declared punishment similar to the fate of the victim in the covenant ceremony, 18 (cf. Gen 15:9-17).

35. The loyalty of the Rechabites

1-11. The command concerning them. A religious order inculcating the simplicity and purity of bedouin life, the Rechabites were founded by Jonadab, son of Rechab, during Jehu's reign (841-814 B.C.). They assisted in the eradication of Baalism from Israel. City life with its corrupting influences was avoided, and they lived simply in tents as shepherds, drinking no wine (cf. the similar Nazirites, Num 6:1-21).

12-19. The lesson for the Jews. The Rechabites refused to drink wine and were obedient to their ancestor Rechab, 6, while the Jews were utterly disobedient to the Lord's command. This vivid illustration furnished a contrast and an occasion for pronouncing doom upon the Jews and blessings upon the Rechabites.

Assyrian relief of the advance on the stronghold of Lachish.

36. Jehoiakim's opposition to the Word of God

1-20. The reading of the scroll. The writing of the scroll was commanded in the fourth year of Jehoiakim (604 B.C.), 1-4. The purpose was to set before the people the evil coming upon them, so they might turn from their sin. The reading of the scroll, 510, was enjoined upon Baruch by Jeremiah. The occasion was the fast ordered by the king because of Nebuchadnezzar's advance against Ashkelon (Nov., 604 B.C.).

21-26. Jehoiakim cuts and burns the roll. The same Satanic spirit energizes unbelieving critics and opposers of God's Word in every age.

27-32. Indestructibility of God's Word. The Word moves on, but it pronounces doom upon its rejecters and would-be destroyers.

37-38. Jeremiah's experiences during the siege

37:1-10. Jeremiah's response to Zedekiah's inquiry. In the spring of 587 B.C., an army of Pharaoh-Hophra (Apries) appeared to relieve Jerusalem, and the Chaldeans withdrew, 5. Jeremiah answered Zedekiah's delegation, warning that the Chaldeans would shortly return and burn the city, 6-10.

37:11-38:13. Jeremiah's arrest. He was charged with desertion as he attempted to go to Anathoth 'to get his share of the property among the people there' (cf. Jer 32:8), and was imprisoned in the dungeon, 38:1-13. He was accused of treason and of 'discouraging ['weakening,' KJV] the soldiers who are left in this city, as well as all the people,' 4. This idiom occurs in Lachish Letter VI: 'And behold the words of the princes are not good, but to weaken our hands' (see Archaeological light, ch. 34).

38:14-28. Jeremiah's final appeal to Zedekiah. The prophet's wise advice to surrender to Nebuchadnezzar, so long made, was again finally rejected.

39. The fall of Jerusalem

1-10. The burning of the city and fate of Zedekiah. (See also 2 Kgs 25; Jer 52; 2 Chr 36.) The Word of God through Jeremiah was vindicated. The city was destroyed, Zedekiah's sons were killed, his eyes put out, and he was carried in chains to Babylon. The Rab-saris and the Rab-mag were titles of Babylonian officers (cf. 3, 13).

11-18. Kind treatment of Jeremiah. He was given a choice to go to Babylon or stay in Palestine. He chose the latter, 11-14, and cast his lot with Gedaliah, the governor. His oracle to

Assyrian relief of the capture of a town. As Jeremiah had warned, Jerusalem was captured and destroyed.

Ebedmelech, 15-18, and his deliverance (continued from 38:13) are presented here to show the truth that the faithful are rewarded when judgment falls.

40-41. Murder of Gedaliah

40: 1-8. Jeremiah chooses to cast his lot with Gedaliah. The governor appointed by the Babylonians had his headquarters at Mizpah (Tell en-Nasbeh or Nebi Samwil), seven miles N of Jerusalem. In 1935 a seal inscribed, 'Belonging to Gedaliah, who is over the house,' was found in ashes left by Nebuchadnezzar's fires at Lachish.

40:9-16. Plot against Gedaliah. His wise regime prospered, 9-12, but Ishmael, a member of the royal family, was sent by Baalis of Ammon to assassinate Gedaliah, 13-16.

41:1-18. The crime perpetrated. Ishmael with a company of ten men slew Gedaliah, 1-3, and a sorrowing band on the way to Jerusalem was also murdered en masse, 4-10. Ishmael fled to Ammon, 11-18.

42-43. The remnant's flight in to Egypt

42:1-22. Jeremiah the intercessor. The remnant in dire perplexity appealed to Jeremiah to pray for them, 1-6, but when the answer came from the Lord ten days later that they should remain in the land, they refused God's word and decided to go down to Egypt anyway, 7-22.

43:1-7. Rebellion against Jeremiah and the trip to Egypt. The people took Jeremiah along to Egypt and settled in Tahpanhes, 7, the Egyptian border fortress, also called Baal-Zephon (Gr. Daphne, modern Tell Defneh).

43:8-13. Jeremiah's prediction of Nebuchadnezzar's conquest of Egypt. This came true in 568 B.C. when Nebuchadnezzar, 'my servant' (25:9; 27:6; cf. 43:10), invaded Egypt against Amasis (Ahmosis II) (cf. 46:13-20). Verse 13 mentions Heliopolis (called On in Gen 41:45), 'city of the sun,' the center of the worship of the sun god Re. The famous obelisks found here were characteristic Egyptian monuments, slightly tapered granite shafts, capped by a prymidion which symbolized a shaft or ray of sunlight.

44. Jeremiah's final plea in Egypt

1-19. His expostulation with the Jews in Egypt. Jeremiah's message went to 'all the Jews,' 1, in Memphis (the capital of N. Egypt, 14 miles S of Cairo), Migdol (Tell el-Her, E of Tahpanhes, see 43:7), and 'Upper Egypt,' i.e., southern Egypt, where a Jewish colony at Elephantine (now well known from Aramaic papyri from the 5th cen. B.C.) was already doubtless in existence. The prophet's plea, 1-10, was followed by a prediction of punishment, 11-14. The diaspora at Pathros impudently defied Jeremiah, 15-16, stoutly declaring they would continue adoration of the 'Queen of Heaven,' 17-19 (the Assyrian Ishtar, Canaanite Astarte, Gr Aphrodite, Rom. Venus), a polluted cult. Offerings included cakes that were apparently shaped in the form of the goddess.

20-30. The Lord's answer and sign. Judgment was pronounced upon these impudent idolaters, 20-28. The sign given to confirm God's word through Jeremiah was Pharaoh-Hophra (Apries, 588-569 B.C.; cf. 37:5), who was to be given 'over to his enemies' and slain. He was assassinated by Ahmosis II (Amasis, 569-526 B.C.), a former court official, founder of Dynasty XXVII (Libyan).

45. Jeremiah's message to Baruch recalled

1-3. Baruch's initial complaint. This was made and Jeremiah's message given in 604 B.C., Jehoiakim's fourth year, 1. Baruch, as Jeremiah's secretary and associate, was told at the beginning of his ministry of the difficulties ahead (cf. 1:10; 36:1-4).

4-5. The Lord's sustaining promise. Now as Baruch concluded his ministry with Jeremiah and his memoirs, he recalled God's promise of physical preservation through all his trials (cf. 39:15-18).

46. Prophecy against Egypt

This section of prophecies against foreign nations, ch. 46-51, compares with Isa 13-23 and Ezk 25-32.

1-12. Prediction concerning Pharaoh-Necho. Necho II of Egypt, in June, 604 B.C., was routed at Carchemish at the great bend of the Euphrates 60 miles W of Haran (cf. Gen 11:31). Victorious Chaldean crown prince

Nebuchadnezzar pursued his defeated foe to Egypt, 2-6. Egypt, represented by the Nile River, 7-8, was poised to flood the north country. She was humiliated. Put is Somalia, and Lydia is in Asia Minor.

13-26. Nebuchadnezzar's invasion of Egypt. In 601 B.C. Nebuchadnezzar fought an indecisive battle on the Egyptian border, according to the Babylonian Chronicle, but in 568 B.C. this prophecy was fulfilled (see note on 43:8-13). Thebes, 25, was the great metropolis of Upper Egypt, and Amon, the great sun deity adored there.

27-28. Promise of future blessing to Israel. Future comfort for God's people was given.

47. Prophecy against the Philistines

1-4. The advance of Nebuchadnezzar. This prediction is probably connected with the destruction of Ashkelon, 5, 7. Apparently Tyre and Sidon, 4, were in league with the Philistines (cf. 27:3).

5-7. Results of Nebuchadnezzar's invasion. The Philistines (Pelisti) were Indo-Europeans from Caphtor (Crete) (cf. Amos 9:7), the main wave of them settling in SW Palestine, 'the land of the Peleste,' in the 12th cen. B.C.

48. Prophecy against Moab

1-19. The overthrow of Moab. The advance of the enemy, probably Nebuchadnezzar, is described. Chemosh was the national deity, 7. Although protected because of her isolation from main trade or invasion routes, Moab would not escape, 11-17.

20-47. Reason for the overthrow. She was to reap the harvest she had sown, 20-28, and was to be punished for her pride, 29-42. After terrible devastation, Moab would be restored, 43-47.

49. Prophecy against various nations

1-6. Against Ammon. Ammon was the northern 'brother' nation of Moab (Gen 19:30-38). Molech (Malcam), 1, was the national god (1 Kgs 11:5, 33). Rabbah, present-day Amman in the kingdom of Jordan, was the capital city, 2-3.

7-22. Against Edom. Cf. Ob 1-9 for another prophecy of Edom's punishment for cruelties inflicted and for encroachment on Judah's frontier due to Arab tribal expansion. Teman, 7, is modem Tawilan, some three miles E of Sela (Petra), the rock-cut city. Bozrah, 13, is a N. Edom fortress city.

23-27. Against Damascus. Arpad in N.

The pyramids, Egypt. Jeremiah prophesied that Egypt, too, would be invaded by Assyria, and was vindicated.

Tablet of the Babylonian Chronicle describing the fall of Nineveh to Babylon.

Syria, about 23 miles N of Aleppo, is commonly mentioned in Scripture with Hamath, a well-known city-state on the Orontes River N of Damascus. The power of these city-states was broken by Assyria and further reduced by Babylon.

28-33. Against Kedar and Hazor. Hazor (not Tell el Qedah; five miles SW of Lake Huleh, dominating the ancient trade route via Maris) is a still-unknown place in the Arabian Desert E of Palestine which Nebuchadnezzar sacked in 598 B.C. Kedar (Gen 25:13) was an Arab tribe of desert bedouins descended from Ishmael. Nebuchadnezzar conducted a successful campaign against these desert dwellers (9:26; 25:23-24).

34-39. Against Elam. Elam, E of the Tigris- Euphrates country of Babylonia, with its capital at Susa, was overrun by Nebuchadnezzar in the winter of 596 B.C. Zedekiah ascended the throne in March, 597 B.C. with the deposition of Jehoiachin. 'The bow of Elam' refers to the skill of Elamite archers, 35.

50. Prophecy against Babylon

1-3. Fall to Persia. Two themes interlace, the fall of the historical Babylon of that day and the fall of the future Babylon (Rev 17-18). The gods of Babylon were confounded by the prophecy of Babylon's fall – Bel (Baal) and Marduk, the two chief deities. The disaster came out of the 'north,' a reference to Cyrus the Persian who took Babylon in October, 539 B.C. (cf. Dan 7:4-5).

4-7. Return of the exiles. This prediction included but went beyond the return from Babylon in 536 B.C. and embraced the final pre-kingdom regathering.

8-16. Fall of Babylon resumed. The vast ancient city of Babylon on a branch of the Euphrates near the modern town of Hilla, SW of Baghdad, was excavated by the Germans under Robert Koldewey (1899-1914) and later by Heinrich Lenzen. Its brilliant palaces, hanging gardens, temple tower, Ishtar Gate, walls and fortifications, are now well known. Archaeology fully confirms the splendor of the city. (See notes on 2 Kgs 25.)

17-20. Israel's restoration. Babylon, as Assyria in an earlier epoch, would be destroyed. Israel will be regenerated and regathered in the last day.

21-32. Divine judgment upon Babylon. Merathaim ('double rebellion'), 21, was a pun on *mat marrati* ('land of lagoons'), an epithet of S. Babylonia. 'Pekod' ('punishment'), 21, was a play on *Puqudu,* a tribe of E. Babylonia (Ezk 23:23).

33-34. Israel's deliverance repeated. Her 'Redeemer' would be strong to save her.

35-46. Babylon's downfall repeated. No nation can defy God with impunity.

51. Prophecy against Babylon continued

1-5. Divine judgment upon Babylon. Babylon would be mowed down and winnowed like grain, a common threshing figure indicating judgment (Isa 21:10). She was guilty of sin against 'the Holy One of Israel,' 5.

6-10. Address to the remnant.

Command was issued to God's people to flee from Babylon. (Cf. the fall of ecclesiastical Babylon, Rev 17, and the destruction of commercial Babylon, Rev 18.) Babylon was the 'gold cup,' 7 (Rev 17:4). The whole chapter is a forecast of the destruction of the Satanic world system at the end-time previous to the kingdom-advent of Messiah.

11-19. Attack by the Medes. Media lay NE of Babylonia. 'Many waters,' 13, refers to the Euphrates and the interlacing canals in S. Babylonia (cf. Rev 17:1, 15). Idolatry is satirized, 16-19, before Israel's true God, 15-16.

20-33. Babylon's utter ruin. As a hammer ('war club'), 20-23, Babylon was God's instrument to punish His disobedient people. But Babylon would fall like Assyria, 24-26. As Babylon conquered nations, 27-33, so nations would attack her. Ararat, 27, is Armenia, ancient Urartu, N of Lake Van. Minni embraced Mannaeans S of Lake Urmia. Ashkenaz included the Scythians.

34-40. Israel's deliverance was again reviewed.

41-64. Babylon's fall continued. Sheshach, 41-43, was Babylon, which would be inundated by attackers.

52. Fall and captivity of Judah; Jehoiachin's liberation

1-30. The fall of the city. This final chapter is a historical appendix, largely a repetition of 2 Kgs 24:18-25:30 (cf. also Jer 39:1-10; 40:7-43:7). Described are Zedekiah's reign, 1-3, and rebellion, 4-11. The siege lasted more than 18 months. Riblah, 9, was in the central valley NE of Byblos. Jerusalem was burned, 12-16, August, 586 B.C. Nebuzaradan was Nebuchadnezzar's field general. The booty taken from the temple is described, 17-23, together with the death of some temple priests at Riblah, 24-27. Three deportations are enumerated, 28-30, apparently connected with Jehoiachin's exile in 597 B.C. (2 Kgs 24:12-16); the suppression of Zedekiah's revolt in 586 B.C.; and the punishment for Gedaliah's assassination (40:7-41:18).

31-34. Jehoiachin's liberation. See 2 Kgs 25:27-30.

LAMENTATIONS

Lament over Jerusalem's desolation

Jews at Jerusalem's Western Wall, formerly known as the 'Wailing Wall', often read from the Book of Lamentations, weeping over the destruction of the Temple.

Place in the canon. In the English Bible, following the Septuagint tradition, Lamentations comes after Jeremiah. In the Hebrew Bible it is found in the third division, the *Ketûbîm* or Hagiographa, among the scrolls (*Megillôt*) – Song, Ruth, Lamentations, Ecclesiastes, and Esther. Like the others, it was read on special occasions, in this case during the fast on the ninth of Ab (Aug.) to commemorate the destruction of Jerusalem and the burning of the temple in 586 B.C.

Author. There is little doubt Jeremiah was the author. The Septuagint opens with a declaration of this fact in the words: 'And it came to pass that, after Israel was taken captive and Jerusalem was made desolate, Jeremiah sat weep-

ing and lamented with this lamentation, and said . . .' The Vulgate follows this very ancient tradition.

Literary form. Of the five poems, the first four are alphabetic acrostics. Poems (ch.) 1, 2 and 4 have 22 verses apiece, each beginning with one of the 22 letters of the Heb. alphabet. Poem (ch.) 3 has three verses to each letter, totaling 66. Poem (ch.) 5 has 22 verses, but is not in alphabetic order. Dirge (*qinah*) meter, 3+2, prevails, with a lively three beat trailing away in a sad two beat.

Message. 'The Lord is afflicted when His people die (Ex 3:7), He suffers when they suffer,' is the theme of this book. It is because of his loving-kindness that His own are not 'consumed' (3:22-23). Tradition

has the suffering prophet weeping in a grotto outside Jerusalem's north wall under the knoll called Golgotha where the suffering Saviour was to die. However that may be, the Spirit of Christ in the prophet made him in a real sense a prefiguration of our Lord (Jer 13:17), as the Master likewise wept over the erring city (Mt 23:36-38).

Outline

1 Desolated Jerusalem cries for pity
2 The Lord's chastening and its results
3 Heart cry of a chastened people
4 The horrors of the siege and fall of the city
5 Lament and petition for restoration

1. Desolated Jerusalem cries for pity

1-11. Her desolation is described. Only twice does the voice of the city, personified as a widow, speak in this section, 9*b*, 11*b*. The rest of the verses describe the misery of the ruined city. When she speaks, she breathes a prayer.

12-22. The personified city bewails her destruction. This whole passage, except 17, is a lament in the first person. Jerusalem declares her woe, 11-13; professes her penitence and just punishment for her iniquity, 14-16; asserts God's equity in punishing her, 18-20; and utters a prayer for vindication against her enemies, 21-22.

2. The Lord's chastening and its results

1-8. The Lord's punishment of the city. Jerusalem's woe was not a piece of bad luck or a mere accident. 'The Lord' occurs more than seven times in this section as the author of her calamity.

9-17. The results of the Lord's punishment. The city is desolated and spiritual darkness befalls its prophets and people, 9-10. The prophet Jeremiah weeps and laments because of these disasters, 11-14. Jerusalem's enemies rail, 15-16. But God's word and warning have been fulfilled, 17.

18-19. The prophet's exhortation to true repentance.

20-22. His prayer as identified with the chastened people.

3. Heart cry of a chastened people

1-24. A psalm of personal faith in God. This chapter is an acrostic in three parts with three verses allotted to each of the 22 letters of the Heb. alphabet. The prophet Jeremiah identifies himself with the chastened people, and in agony and distress pours out his heart to the Lord in faith. His laments recall Job's exercise of soul before the Lord: verse 1 (Job 9:34); 2 (Job 19:8); 3 (Job 7:18); 4 (Job 7:5); 5 (Job 19:6, 12); 6 (Job 23:16-17); 7, 9 (Job 19:8); 8 (Job 30:20); 10-11 (Job 16:9); 12-13 (Job 16:12-13); 14 (Job 30:9); 15 (Job 9:18); 16-18 (Job 19:10; 30:19).

25-51. Jeremiah enjoins repentance and submission to God. The prophet wisely counsels submission and penitential confession in view of God's righteous judgment.

52-66. Prayer for vindication against the enemy. Jeremiah recalls the Lord's faithful blessing in times past, and pleads for the punishment of Jerusalem's destroyers.

4. Horrors of the siege and fall of the city

1-20. Jerusalem's disaster described. The gold and stones of the temple had been desecrated, 1. Sons of Zion (Zionites), worth more than gold, were now reckoned as common clay, 2. Terrible famine stalked the city, 3-9, accompanied by horrible cannibalism, 10. Divine wrath was outpoured, 11-12, in bloody carnage and defilement, 13-15; captivity, 16; death, 17-19; and violence to the king (Zedekiah; 2 Kgs 25:4-6).

21-22. Prediction of disaster on Edom. Edom, too, would be punished (cf. Ob 8-14).

5. Lament and petition for restoration

1-18. Lament over Judah's misery under Babylon's heel. The people suffered agony and hardship, 1-14. The Davidic dynasty no longer reigned, the temple was destroyed, 15-18.

19-22. Intercession for divine mercy. These verses echo Ps 74:12; 79:5-8; 80:1-7, and capture the plea of the faithful remnant for the establishment of the kingdom.

EZEKIEL

Role of divine discipline

The prophet. Ezekiel (*Yehezqe'l*, 'God strengthens') was the son of a Zadokite priest. He was deported to Babylon in 597 B.C. with King Jehoiachin. The prophet's wife died the day the siege of Jerusalem began, 588 B.C. (24:1, 15-18). The prophet resided at Tel-abib, a town on the Chebar, a canal known from Babylonian sources which flowed from the Euphrates fork above Babylon through Nippur, winding back into the Euphrates near Erech.

Date. In the fifth year of Jehoiachin's exile Ezekiel began his prophetic ministry (1:1-2), i.e., 593 B.C., continuing till at least April, 571 B.C. (29:17), his last dated utterance.

Purpose. While Jeremiah in Palestine was prophesying the destruction of Jerusalem, Ezekiel, his younger contemporary in Babylon, was declaring the same fate for the apostate city (ch. 1-24). Unlike Jeremiah, however, Ezekiel, ministering prophetically to the exiles, had a large note of consolation in his messages. He showed his suffering colleagues that the Lord was justified in sending His people into captivity (cf. 18:25, 29; 33:17, 20). His ministry centered in showing the preventive and corrective nature of God's chastenings that His people might 'know that I am the Lord' (an expression occurring more than 30 times in the book, from 6:7 to 39:28). To this end Ezekiel showed

that the Lord's people had been at fault, not the Lord (18:25). The Lord would punish the nations jubilant over Israel's fall (ch. 25-32), and eventually restore Israel to kingdom blessing.

Ezekiel and the revelation. Ezekiel's visions bear striking resemblance to the book of the Revelation (cf. Ezk 1 with Rev 4-5; Ezk 3:3 with Rev 10.9-10; Ezk 9 with Rev 7; Ezk 10 with Rev 8:1-5). The prophet Daniel was already famous in Babylon when Ezekiel prophesied (Ezk 14:14, 20; 28:3).

Outline

1-3 The prophet's call
4-24 Prophecies against Jerusalem
25-32 Prophecies against the nations
33-48 Prophecies of the final restoration of Israel

Sculpture spelling 'love' in Hebrew, Jerusalem. Ezekiel showed that eventually the Lord would restore Israel to kingdom blessing.

Jerusalem's Kidron Valley. Ezekiel warned that the Gihon stream would dry up in this valley during the siege of Jerusalem.

1. Ezekiel's vision of God's glory

1-3. Introduction. 'The thirtieth year,' 1, probably means when Ezekiel was 30 years old. For Tel-abib (Babylonian *til abubi,* 'mound of the flood,' a Jewish settlement near Nippur on the Chebar canal), see 3: 15 and introduction. The fifth year of Jehoiachin's exile would be 593 B.C., fifth day, fourth month, July 31. 'The hand of the Lord was upon him' shows Ezekiel's contact with God, 3 (3:14, 22; 8:1; 33:22; 37:1; 40:1).

4-28. The vision of God's glory. This revelation of the Shekinah glory of God prepared Ezekiel for his great ministry, as in the case of Moses (Ex 3:1-10), Isaiah (Isa 6:1-10), Daniel (Dan 10:5-14), and John (Rev 1:12-19). Theophanic manifestations of God in wind (1 Kgs 19:11), cloud (Ex 19:16), and fire (1 Kgs 19:11-12) were usual. This vision is mentioned repeatedly in this book (10:1-22; 11:22-25; 43:1-7). It came 'out of the north,' 4, not because Ezekiel borrowed a literary figure from Canaanite (Ugaritic) mythology, according to which the gods lived in the north, but because a storm cloud of divine wrath from the north (Babylon) was about to burst over Judah. Though Babylon is due east of Jerusalem, the intervening desert forced travelers to follow the rivers of the Fertile Crescent. As a result, the invading armies from the east attacked from the north. The Holy One of Israel was revealed in His glory ready to deal in judgment with his apostate people. The 'living creatures,' 5, were cherubim (Rev 4:7) who were guardians of the holiness of God's throne (Ex 25:10-22; 1 Kgs 6:23-28, cf. Gen 3:22-24). They were winged creatures, distinct from the seraphim (Isa 6:2). Both are actual beings of the celestial realm, not merely artistic creations. The four wheels symbolize mobility in all directions. The Lord enthroned above His creatures, 26-28, compares with the Lord enthroned above the cherubim on the ark (Ex 37:9; 1 Sam 4:4).

2-3. Ezekiel's fivefold commission

2:1-20. His commission as a prophet. Whatever the reception of Ezekiel's ministry, the 'rebellious house,' a designation of apostate Judah in exile (Jer 2:29; 3:13), 'will know that a prophet has been among them,' 2:5. More than 90 times the nonmessianic expression 'son of man' (2:1) occurs in Ezekiel. This points not only to man's finite limitation and need before the vision of God's infinite glory, but also signals that although captive Israel was an evidence that the chosen nation had forgotten her distinctive ministry to the nations (Ezk 5:5-8; Rom 9:4-5), yet the Lord had not forgotten her. It would remind her that she is but a small part of the entire race of mankind for whom He is solicitous.

3:1-9. As a fearless denunciator. Ezekiel was to feed upon and digest the Word of God, symbolized by eating a papyrus scroll inscribed with divine judgments, 1-3 (cf. Zech 5:1-4; Rev 10: 8-11) .The fact that the scroll was inscribed on both sides, an unusual practice, may indicate God's concern that Ezekiel not add anything to it. God's Word was sufficient. The Word was 'sweet' (Ps 19:10) when obeyed, but bitter when given to unrepentant sinners ripe for judgment, 4-9.

3:10-15. As God's mouthpiece to the exiles. For Tel-Abib, Chebar, see 1:1.

3:16-21. As a watchman. A watchman (Heb. *sopheh*) is 'one who keeps on guard or on the lookout,' 17 (Isa 21:6; Mic 7:4), not only against the enemy but expectantly and in hope for the fulfillment of God's promise. Ezekiel's doctrine of personal responsibility (cf. 18:1-32) is here applied to his prophetic ministry (33:7-16).

3:22-27. As a faithful herald. 'The plain' (valley) was the flat alluvial southern Tigris-Euphrates country (Gen 11:2; Ezk 37:1). The prophet's protracted dumbness was a sign he was to be mute when God wanted him to be silent.

4-5. Symbolic prophecies of Jerusalem's siege

4:1-3. The sign of the brick. Jerusalem was outlined on a soft mud brick with the clay dried in the sun, so common in S. Babylonia. The 'iron pan' was evidently a griddle, showing how the Lord would fight against the city, not for it (cf. Jer 21:5). The captives were hoping for a speedy return to Jerusalem, but the prophet foretells Jerusalem's awful siege and fall.

4:4-8. Sign of the prophet's physical position. His discomfort for 390 days on his left side and 40 days on his right side (total 430 years, symbolically a year for a day) recalled the Egyptian servitude (Ex 12:40-41). A similar captivity would engulf both Israel and Judah. The captivity of the northern kingdom was to be longer.

An Assyrian winged protective spirit. Possibly the winged creatures of Ezekiel's vision were similar in appearance.

4:9-17. Sign of famine. Hunger and cannibalism were to stalk besieged Jerusalem. Mixing of grains, 9, indicates scarcity. Dried cow dung is still a common fuel in the East, but human excrement was unclean (Deut 23:12-14). Dearth of water, 16, would add to the horror. En-Rogel on the south and Gihon in the Kidron Valley would fail and the cisterns would be dry.

5:1-17. Sign of the shaved head and beard. Hair of the head and face cut with a sword, 1, spoke of the shameful military defeat of Jerusalem. The reason for this disgrace was Israel's abysmal failure in her favored position 'at the center of the nations' as a light and witness of the one true God, 5-6. The woes described were to come upon her for failure in her trust, 7-17.

6. Judgment against the mountains of Israel

1-7. Judgment upon the idolatry of the high places. Figuratively, 'the mountains of Israel,' 2, stood for the high places, used as outdoor pagan sanctuaries, while the sword, 3, spoke of their destruction, with their cultic personnel and devotees. Idols, 5, were part of the cultic equipment, being images of Baal and such fertility goddesses as Anath and Asherah, corrupt deities now so well known from Ugaritic mythology. Cf. Lev 26:27-33, which is here repeated by Ezekiel.

8-14. The surviving remnant. The remnant (Rom 11:5) would survive and learn the purpose of these terrible chastisements, 10, 14 (cf. Isa 6:10-13).

7. The end imminent

1-9. The doom of the city. The day of judgment upon Jerusalem prefigured the coming great Day of the Lord when wrath will be outpoured before Israel's restoration (Ps 2:5; Rev 6-19; cf. Joel 1:15; Mal 4:1; see Amos 5:18-20; Isa 2:11-17).

10-27. Horror in the city. The confusion and brutality in the fallen city are portrayed.

8-9. Vision of Jerusalem's sin

8:1-18. Vision of idolatry. The date, 1, was September 17, 592 B.C. For 'hand of the Sovereign Lord,' see 1:1-3. The renewed vision of God, 2-4, was a proper background for the judgment of false gods. 'The entrance to the north gate of the inner court,' 3, was the third gate leading N from the palace complex into the Temple area. 'The idol that provokes to jealousy' was perhaps that of Astarte. The worship of Egyptian Osiris, who was thought of as guaranteeing a happy life after death, is apparently referred to, 7-13. Tammuz worship, 14-15, was the adoration of the Sumero-Akkadian god of vegetation, whose descent into the nether world signaled the seasonal fading of life. Tammuz (Adonis) or the worship of Re, the Egyptian sun-god, is suggested, 16-18.

9:1-11. Vision of punishment for idolatry. A divine call went forth for destruction, 1-2. On the 'north,' see 1:4 note, from which direction the executioners came. For the mark or seal, 4-5, see Rev 7:3; 9:4; 13:16-17; 20:4; on a godly remnant, cf. Isa 1:9; Rom 11:5.

The Lord's linen-clothed scribe, signifying ritual cleanness, undoubtedly represented Deity. Cf. Nabu, the god of wisdom, among the Babylonian gods.

10-11. Departure of the Lord from His Temple

10:1-22. The renewed vision of God's glory (cf. Ezk 1, 11, 43). The manifested glory of Israel's God was the background for the judgment of Israel's idolatry and horrible profanation of the temple. The linen-clothed personage, 9:2-4; 10:2-4, who scattered coals from the fire between the cherubim (1:13) over the idolatry-ridden city, in the light of Rev 5:1; 8:3-5 was apparently the preincarnate Christ, the Angel of the Presence, who appeared to Abraham, Isaac, Jacob, Moses, Joshua, Gideon and Daniel (Dan 10:5-6). Judgment is committed to His hands (Jn 5:22). 'The glory of the Lord' (cf. Ex 16:10; Num 10:34) is the revealed holiness and power of God (Lev 9:23; Num 20:6).

11:1-25. Ichabod, the glory departs. A glimpse into the wicked political leaders is given, 1-13. A message of mercy follows, 14-21, predictions yet to be fulfilled for Israel. These include a spared remnant, 14-16, and the promise of restoration to the land and spiritual conversion, 17-21. The departure of the Shekinah glory from the wicked city now follows, 22-25. The departure was gradual (cf. 9:3; 10:4) from the temple outward and from the city to the Mount of Olives, 23. (Cf. 1 Kgs 8:5-11; Ezr 3:12; and its return to the millennial temple, Ezk 43:2-5.) It was from the Mount of Olives that Christ ascended (Acts 1:10-12) and to which He will return in glory (Zech 14:4).

12. The exile portrayed in symbol

1-20. Signs given through Ezekiel. On the 'rebellious people,' 2, see note on 2:5 and on Isa 6:10-13. Ezekiel was to enact the exiles' fate, 1-7. Zedekiah was the prince, 10, alluded to in 17:20, who was taken to Riblah and whose eyes were put out (Jer 39:1-10; 52:10-11; 2 Kgs 25:1-7).

21-28. Message of impending judgment. Unbelief in God's true prophets was the cause of judgment. God's word through His prophet could not be ignored (Hos 12:10).

13-14. Condemnation of false prophetism

13:1-23. Divine denunciation of false prophets. They spoke of falsehoods and were contaminated with pagan divination, 1-9. Those who proclaim, "'Peace,'" when there is no peace,' are as useless as whitewash on a mud brick wall to protect it against a storm, 10-16. Prophetesses (sorceresses and spiritistic mediums, 1 Sam 28:7-25) were also denounced, 17-23.

14:1-23. Depravity of the idol-loving elders. They revealed the extent of their depravity by daring to inquire of the Lord, 1-11, and rendered judgment imperative, 12-23.

15. Allegory of the vine

1-5. The allegory. The vine branch is no good for wood. It is used only to produce fruit. Even as fuel it is practically useless.

6-8. The meaning. The vine typified Israel (Jerusalem; cf. Ps 80:8-12; Isa 5:1-7; Hos 10:1). Jerusalem, an unproductive vine, was no longer good for anything but burning. This is the first of three parables in ch. 16 and 17 showing the empty hope of deliverance for the sinful city.

16. The allegory of the faithless wife

1-52. Israel's idolatry described figuratively as a homeless orphan, 1-7; as a maiden, 8-14; as a degenerate, 15-34; as a prostitute, 35-52. As a foundling, unrelated to God's covenant, Israel had a pagan origin, 3. The Canaanites were the Semitic-speaking residents of Palestine before Israel arrived on the scene. The Hittites, a well-known non-Semitic people (Josh 3:10; 2 Sam 11 :3), who established a significant empire encompassing northern Palestine and Asia Minor. As a foundling Israel was to be exposed to death as female babies often were in ancient paganism. As a young maiden, betrothed by covenant and married to the Lord, 8-14, she attained a regal status, but lapsed into harlotries (cult prostitution and general infidelity and degeneracy), 15:34. She became a shameless harlot, 35-52, and was to be stoned (Deut 22:21, 24). She was worse than 'Sodom' and her 'younger sister' Samaria (Jer 3:6-11).

53-63. Promise of gracious restoration. Even in this lurid setting the Lord pledged future blessing under the Palestinian covenant (Deut 30: 1-10) and the new covenant (Jer 31:31-34; Heb 8:8-12).

17. The allegory of the eagles and the cedar

1-2. The allegory of the eagles. The 'great eagle,' 3-6, was Nebuchadnezzar (Jer 48:22). 'The top of a cedar,' 3, was the house of David (Jer 22:5, 6, 23). The 'topmost shoot,' 4, was Jehoiachin; the 'city of traders,' Babylonia; 'the seed of your land,' 5, Zedekiah. 'Another great eagle,' 7, was Psammetichus II (594-588 B.C.), who enrolled Zedekiah and other western powers in a coalition against Babylon (Jer 27). 'The east wind,' 10, was Nebuchadnezzar before whom Zedekiah, 13-21, was doomed to fall (Jer 52).

22-24. The allegory of the cedar. Israel's hope for the future once again comes into view. The Lord will take a 'shoot' (Messiah) from 'the very top of the cedar' (Davidic house) and 'a tender sprig' (Messiah), and plant it 'on a high and lofty mountain' (Mt Zion, Mic 4:1,

Artist's impression of a Babylonian infantryman.

cf. Isa 11:1; 53:2; Jer 23:5-6; Zech 3:8). 'The tall tree' brought down and 'the green tree' dried up, 24, symbolize Gentile world power. 'The low tree' exalted and 'the dry tree' revived portray the restoration of the kingdom to Israel (Acts 1:6) when the Son of David returns. Gentile world power will be broken and Israel will be restored to governmental and spiritual glory under Messiah.

18. Divine judgment and individual responsibility

1-13. False accusation against God and the divine answer. Sinners in their plight incline to blame God and their forbears for their troubles. The exiles in Babylon and the sinners in Jerusalem were doing this, 1-2. The Lord rebuked this shifting of blame, 3-4, and through Ezekiel stressed God's justice and individual responsibility for wrongdoing. The way of life, 5-9, was stressed (not conditions of eternal life, but proof of justifying righteousness to escape physical death in the impending judgment). The conditions of death were set forth, 10-13.

14-32. Ezekiel's doctrine of individual responsibility. Eating upon the mountains, 6, 15, refers to partaking of sacred meals in pagan high places (6:1-14). The good or evil of one generation is transferable to the next, 19-20. To deny this truth is to fail to comprehend God's justice, 25-29. Israel must repent in the light of God's justice. This was the only escape from terrible judgment, 30-32.

19. Lament for the princes of Israel

1-9. Lamentation for the princes. The princes were Jehoahaz, the first cub, 3-4, who was taken to Egypt (Jer 22:10-12; 2 Kgs 23:30-34). The second cub, 5-9, was Jehoiachin, who was exiled to Babylon (Jer 22:24-30; 2 Kgs 24:8-16). The 'lioness,' 2, was Judah. This symbol is found on Israelite seals (cf. Gen 49:9; 1 Kgs 10:18-20).

10-14. Lament for the land. The vine portrays Judah (Isa 5:1-7; Jer 2:21). 'The branches were strong,' 11, stands for Zedekiah (17:13), who was stripped by 'the east wind,' 12, Nebuchadnezzar, and transplanted, 13, to Babylon (Jer 52:1-11).

20. Rehearsal of divine mercy to Israel

1-8. Israel's sins in Egypt. Dated August 14, 591 B.C., this message was occasioned by the inquiry of the elders of the Exile, 1-4 (14:1-11). The nation's idolatry in Egypt, 5-8, is described (cf. Ps 106). Yet God's gracious revelations are given.

9-26. Israel's sins in the wilderness. A review is made of wonderful redemption wrought for God's name's sake, 9, 10, 14, with the sabbath given, 11-13, and grace shown, 14-26.

27-49. Israel's sins in the land. Judgment and a future restoration are outlined.

21. Judgment by the sword

1-17. The Lord unsheaths His sword. The sword was a common symbol of divine judgment (14:21; Isa 34:5; Jer 14:12; Rev 6:8). It is seen sharpened, indicating judgment was imminent, 8-17 (cf. Jer 50:35-37). Striking upon the breast, 12, was an indication of mourning (Jer 31:19).

18-32. The sword of Nebuchadnezzar. His sword would actually be God's means of judgment, 18-19. His occultism, 21, would guide him to Jerusalem and slaughter. Divination was the pagan counterpart of prophecy. Belomancy, the tossing of arrows with names of enemies on them, and hepatoscopy, examining the liver of animals for omens, were highly developed in Babylonia. The household idols (teraphim) were small oracular deities. The sword would cut down Zedekiah, 25-27, and strike against Ammon, 28-32 (cf. 20).

22. Jerusalem's indictment

1-16. Jerusalem's violence and abomination. Before the retributive sword of justice fell, Jerusalem's horrible corruption was laid bare. Her iniquities included idolatry, violence, deceit, injustice, slander, sexual promiscuity (d. 6:2-14; 14:3-5; 18:6).

17-31. The smelting furnace of God's wrath refined all classes of corrupt Jewish society. The purpose of the smelting, 17-22, and the dross, 23-31, are indicated.

23. Oholah and Oholibah

1-4. The allegory. Oholah is Samaria (the northern kingdom) and her sister

Oholibah is Jerusalem (representing by metonymy the southern kingdom). The ungodly relations, politically and religiously, of these two sisters with the surrounding nations are inveighed against. There is a pun in the names: 'Oholah,' 'she who possesses a tent' (sanctuary), i.e., Samaria, and 'Oholibah,' 'my tent (tabernacle) is in her' (Jerusalem). The word play intimates that although Samaria had a place of worship, *the true sanctuary* was in Jerusalem. This fact was the crucial consideration in accentuating the enormity of Jerusalem's sin.

5-49. The meaning. Oholah, 5-10, politically and spiritually contaminated herself with Assyria by alliances and religious syncretism. Oholibah, 11-21, likewise sinned. Their political and religious sin had to be punished, 22-35. Judgment of the lewd sisters was forecast, 36-49.

24. The cooking pot and the end

1-14. The allegory of the pot was symbolic of the imminent destruction of Jerusalem. In the pot (Jerusalem) all would be boiled, as the besiegers heaped fuel (siege apparatus) about it (cf. Jer 1:13-19). After thorough boiling, the pot would be emptied after the siege, and the bones burned (city sacked). The encrusted deposits and impurities, 6, 11, refer to the city's sin and degeneration, 12-13. The date, 1, of the beginning of the siege is given, January, 588 B.C. (cf. 2 Kgs 25:1).

15-27. Death of Ezekiel's wife. He was not to mourn over his wife, who died the day the siege of Jerusalem began. As death dissolved the union between the prophet and his beloved wife, so the relationship between the Lord and Jerusalem was to be dissolved so that destruction would follow. This was an object lesson to the exiles, 19-24. The day the news of Jerusalem's destruction arrived, Ezekiel's tongue would be loosed for a new message, 25-27.

25. Prophecies against various nations

Ezekiel 25-32 corresponds to Isaiah 13-23 and Jeremiah 46-51. These nations were to be judged before Israel was restored (36:5-7).

1-14. Predictions against Ammon, Moab and Edom. The nations of this chapter were immediate neighbors of Judah. The Ammonites, 17, and the Moabites, 8-11, were racially connected with Israel (Gen 19:37-38) and constant enemies (cf. Isa 15:1-16:14; Jer 48:1-49:6). Edom, 12-14, also would know God's vengeance (Jer 49:7-22; cf. Deut 23:7; Amos 1:11).

15-17. Predictions against Philistia (cf. Jer 47). The Kerethites, 16 (Cretans), lived in Philistia.

26. Prophecy of Tyre's destruction

1-6. Judgment announced. Nebuchadnezzar besieged Tyre for 13 years (585-572 B.C.), 1. Its judgment was because of its refusal to help its ally Jerusalem (Jer 27:3) and its pride as the chief Phoenician sea mart (cf. 28:2-10).

7-21. Judgment executed. Tyre consisted of a main coastal city and an insular city on an island just off the coast. Nebuchadnezzar conquered the mainland city in 572 B.C. but failed to capture the island city. Alexander the Great completed the fulfillment of the prophecy (26:4) by taking the island in 332 B.C. after a six-month siege in which he built a causeway from the debris of the already destroyed mainland city. The lament would be made by Tyre's commercial neighbors, 'the princes of the seacoast,' 15-18. The city would sink into the pit (Sheol), the realm of the dead, 19-21 (cf. Isa 14:15; Zech 9:3-4).

27. Lament over Tyre

1-24. Tyre symbolized as a ship. The Tyrian commercial empire is fittingly described as a goodly merchant vessel, 3, 'perfect in beauty.' The ship was made of fir trees from Senir, i.e., Mt. Hermon (Deut 3:9). Lebanon ('the [snow] white') is the mountain mass composed of two parallel ranges, Lebanon and Antilebanon, famous in antiquity for its cedars, 5. The oaks of Bashan, 6, were the famous forests E of the Sea of Galilee. Elishah (Cyprus) and Gebal (Byblos) together with Arvad (an island coastal mart like Tyre) and Sidon, 20 miles N of Tyre, were the hub of Tyre's commercial center. The prose section, 10-25, describes many names elucidated by the Table of Nations (see notes on Gen 10).

25-36. Destruction of the ship. 'The east wind,' 26, is Nebuchadnezzar (cf. 19:12; Jer 18:17).

28. Lament over the king of Tyre

1-10. The king of Tyre. The 'prince' or ruler of the city at that time, Ittobaal II, headed up in himself the arrogance and pride of the city, claiming to be divine, 2, and 'wiser than Daniel,' 3. This was not the Danel of the Ugaritic tablets, the judge of the helpless orphan and widow, as the critics hold, but the historical contemporary Daniel, then of great fame in Nebuchadnezzar's court (cf.14:12-23).

11-19. The spiritual power behind the Tyrian king. This vast panoramic revelation, like Isa 14:12, reached beyond the human ruler to the spiritual power energizing him in the realm of human government. Satan and demons have a notable role in this sphere, as Dan 10:13 and Eph 6:12, 'the powers of this dark world,' show. As the inspirer, energizer and the invisible dynamic behind such godless, proud rule of the world governmental systems, Satan is portrayed in his unfallen state, and this passage together with Isa 14:12-14 gives the entrance of sin into a sinless universe and Satan's fall. The vision, however, is not of Satan in his own person, but as he is connected with the governmental administration of the present evil world system. The pride, pomp and arrogation of deity which belongs to God alone stamp the king of Tyre and the king of Babylon (Isa 14:12-14) as illustrations of the coming Antichrist, the last God-defying ruler of the Satanic world system before its destruction at the second advent of Christ (Rev 18:1-19:16). For a comment on Satan's pristine, unfallen glory see note on Jude 8-10.

20-26. Judgment of Sidon. Some 20 miles N of Tyre, Sidon (modern Saida in the Republic of Lebanon, 20 miles S of Berytus [Beirut]), was perhaps the oldest of the Sidonian (Phoenician) coast cities. After 1200 B.C. Tyre assumed ascendancy. Jeremiah also predicted Sidon's subjugation by Nebuchadnezzar (Jer 27:3, 6), which occurred when Tyre was defeated. The Sidonian worship of Baal served as 'painful briers and sharp thorns' for Israel, as it led them into many apostasies (cf. 1 Kgs 16:31-33; 18:17-40). Promise of restoration is made to Israel, 25-26 (cf. 11:17; 20:41; 34:13; 37:21; Isa 11:12), to be fulfilled after her enemies have been judged.

29-32. Judgment against Egypt

Egypt was to be reduced to a second-rate kingdom. This judgment was fulfilled after Nebuchadnezzar's invasion in 572 B.C. and 568 B.C.

29:1-16. Against Pharaoh-Hophra. This prophecy is dated 586 B.C., a half year before Jerusalem fell. Hophra's advance against Nebuchadnezzar in 588 B.C. had not relieved Jerusalem. Egypt is pictured as a great monster (crocodile), 3 (Isa 27:1). 'From Migdol to Aswan,' 10, is an expression indicating the northern limits (Aswan, at the fist Nile cataract).

29:17-21. Conquest of Egypt. This is Ezekiel's last dated orcale, April, 571 B.C. Since Nebuchadnezzar's long siege of Tyre proved to be an economic failure, the conquest of Egypt provided compensation so Nebuchadnezzar could pay his army. The 'horn,' 21, is Davidic and doubtless messianic.

30:1-26. Egypt's doom. This prefigures the day of the Lord in an eschatological sense (Isa 2:12; Jer 30:5-7), the time of the judgment of the nations, previous to kingdom blessing. Nebuchadnezzar's Egyptian successes furnish the background.

31:1-18. Lament over Pharaoh as a cedar dated in 586 B.C., just prior to the fall of Jerusalem.

32:1-32. Lament over Pharaoh as a lion dated March, 585 B.C. The proud Egyptian ruler considered himself a kingly lion, but he was only a sea monster to be caught in a net. The lament over Egypt, dated April, 586 B.C., shows that nation in Sheol with other governments of this evil world system, 17-32.

33. Ezekiel's responsibility as watchman

Chapters 33-39 portray events preceding the restoration of the kingdom to Israel (cf. Acts 1:6), and ch. 40-48 give the description of the restoration.

1-20. A watchman and his responsibility. The prophet's commission included his being a 'watchman' (see note on 3:16-21). Here Ezekiel applies his teaching of God's justice and individual responsibility developed in ch. 18 to his own ministry (see notes on ch. 18). In his discussion of individual responsibility, 10-20, the prophet reinforces what he had already taught in 14:12-23; 18:1-32.

A shepherd leads his flock in the desert. The shepherds of Israel had abused their position.

21-33. News of Jerusalem's fall.
Ezekiel's enforced silence (3:24-27) was lifted by news of Jerusalem's fall. The message he received thereupon is given, 23-29, and the assurance of the fulfillment of the Lord's word through the prophet declared, no matter what the people's reaction to it might be, 30-33.

34. False shepherd and the true

1-19. Indictment of the faithless shepherds (rulers). The law of individual responsibility (3:16-21; ch. 18 and 33) is applied to the nation's leaders, metaphorically called 'shepherds,' who were responsible for misusing God's flock (Jer 23:13-17) and scattering them (Jer 10:21; 23:1-4). The Lord is the Good Shepherd (Isa 40:11; Jer 31:10) who will regather the flock, 11-16, and judge between the sheep (the saved Israelite remnant) and the rams and he-goats (nations who have abused Israel, 17-19; cf. Mt 25:31-46; Joel 3:11-16). This is the judgment of the nations preceding the restoration of the kingdom to Israel.

20-31. Restoration of Israel under Messiah, the true shepherd. This prophecy goes beyond Zerubbabel, the civil head of Judah at the restoration from Babylon in 536 B.C. and refers to Messiah, David's son and Lord,

David's name being used typically (Jer 23:5-6; Hos 3:5; Isa 9:6-7; 55:3-4). 'The covenant of peace,' 25 (cf. Jer 31:31-34; Heb 13:20), is the new covenant. The 'wild beasts' are the nations, particularly Babylon, that have wronged Israel. The 'showers of blessing,' 26, are for Israel in her restoration (Acts 3:19-20), with a description of the kingdom given in verses 26-27 (cf. Isa 11:6-9; Rom 8:19-22).

35. The judgment of Edom

1-10. Edom's evil design. Mt. Seir, 3, 7, 15, is the plateau E of the Arabah in which Sela (Petra), the Edomite capital, was located (cf. 25:12-14; Isa 34; Jer 49:7-22). Edom's encroachment on southern Judah and the hatred engendered were reflected. With Israel and Judah in exile, Edom purposed to possess their land, 10 (cf. Obadiah).

11-15. Edom's ruin. Chapter 35 is inserted here as a background for ch. 36-37, dealing with Israel's restoration to her land.

36. Restoration to the land

Ezekiel 36-48 is yet unfulfilled and envisions the future restoration of the land and the people of Israel.

1-7. Future judgment of Israel's enemies. The 'mountains of Israel' form the central highland ridge and stand for all Israel (Deut 3:25; cf. 1, 4). The judgment of enemy nations (Mt 25:31-46) must precede Israel's restoration (Joel 3:11-16; Rev 16:12-16).

8-38. Promised return to the land. The sovereign 'I wills' of Israel's hope and glory are spoken by the Lord 18 times in this section. The land is to be restored to its former fertility, 11. Formerly desecrated by idolatry and pagan hilltop sanctuaries with fertility cults and human sacrifice, 14, the land shall 'no longer devour men' (cf. Deut 12:1-3, 29-31). Israel's past sins and chastisements are reviewed, 16-21, followed by the great promise of future restoration and gracious blessing, 22-38. The regathering, 22-24, goes far beyond the small return from Babylon. Spiritual regeneration follows, 25-29. The sprinkling with clean water, 25, refers to the water mixed with the ashes of a red heifer (Num 19; Heb 9:13-14; 10:22; cf. Zech 12:10; 13:1). The new covenant is here outlined, mandating that the new ('cleansing . . . new spirit . . . heart of flesh') be a prerequisite for kingdom entrance (cf. Jn 3:1-12).

37. Vision of the dry bones

1-14. Scope of the vision. The most satisfactory view of this passage sees it as setting forth the national and spiritual reinstatement of God's chosen people Israel in kingdom blessing. The method of the restoration will be by divine power, 3; by the divine Word, 4-6 (cf. Mt 24:32-35; Mk 13:27-31; Jer 16:14-15); and by the divine life, 7-10. The purpose of the vision is to fulfill God's word, 14; to revive Israel's lost hope, 11, 22; to settle Israel in her own land, 12-13; and to demonstrate Israel's status as an elect nation, 12-13. The 'bones' are the exiles; the valley, their dispersion; the graves, the death of their national life.

15-28. The extent of Israel's restoration. It embraces the entire house of Israel (the 12 tribes), comprising the union of both Judah and Israel into one nation, 15-17. The results of the restoration will be a land forever, 25; a king forever, 24-25; a covenant of peace forever, 26; a sanctuary forever, 26-27.

38-39. Destruction of Israel's last foes

38:1-6. The great last-day northern confederacy. Gog is the leader of the coali-

tion, 2; Magog his land. He is said to be 'chief prince' of Meshech (Assyrian 'Mushku') S of Gomer (Assyrian 'Gimirrai') or Cimmerians in central Asia Minor (Gen 10:2-3). Some make Gog 'prince of Rosh,' and identify it with Russia; but this identification is exceedingly tenuous, although the general area was that now occupied by Russia ('the remote parts of the north,' 6 RSV) and Turkey. Tubal, 3 (Assyrian 'Tabali'), is W of Togarmah (Tilgarimmu) near the Halys River, SE of Gomer. Allied with this great northern power are Persia (Iran), Cush (probably connected with ancient Kish in Mesopotamia) and Put (Libya?). (Cf. notes on Gen 10:6.)

38:7-23. Attack on Israel. The time is 'in future years,' 8, when Israel is restored and the Lord has resumed His relationship with the nation. The Lord personally undertakes and gives triumph, 14-23.

39: 1-24. Overthrow of Gog. His complete defeat, 1-10, is followed by a massive burial of his army, 11-20, resounding to God's glory, 21-24.

39:25-29. Vision of restored and converted Israel.

40. Description of the temple

Chapters 40-48 constitute Ezekiel's remarkable vision of restored Israel in the land during the Kingdom Age. Envisioned are the millennial temple, ch. 40-42; the millennial worship, ch. 43-46; and the millennial land, ch. 47-49.

1-4. The introduction. The date, 1, was April 28, 573 B.C., on the occasion of the twenty-fifth anniversary of the prophet's exile. Ezekiel was supernaturally transported in vision to Israel, 2, and prophesied from a future idealistic standpoint 'on a very high mountain' (Mic 4:1; Isa 2:2-3).

5-49. The vision of the temple. What was this temple? Various views are: (1) a somewhat idealized replica of Solomon's temple destroyed in 586 B.C. and which should have been built upon the return from Babylon; (2) a description of the kingdom of God in its final form; (3) the Christian church in its earthly glory and blessing; (4) the view which seems to fit the context in Ezekiel, however, and the testimony of other Scripture, is that Ezekiel's temple is a literal future sanctuary to be constructed in Palestine during the coming Kingdom Age.

The measuring rod, 5, was about 10 feet 4

inches (the small cubit about 17.5 inches, the large cubit about 20.4 inches). The East or Processional Gate, 6, may be compared to Solomonic gateways (excavated at Gezer, Hazor and Megiddo). The outer court is described, 17-27; then the inner Court, 28-37; and the tables for the offerings and chambers for the inner court, 38-47. The porch is also described, 48-49 (cf. 1 Kgs 7:15-22).

41. The arrangement of the temple

1-14. The house itself will be the dwelling place of the visible presence of the Lord in the kingdom. The holy place, 1-2, and the most holy place, 3-4, are described. There is no allusion to the ark, mercy seat, high priest, or tables of the law. All these will be superseded by the manifested divine glory. The chambers around the house, 5-11, are probably for the temple personnel.

15-26. Interior details. Paneled with wood, the temple was embellished with two-faced cherubim (cf. 1:6-12) and palms, symbols of victory. The face of a lion (kingly majesty) and that of a man looking on a palm tree describe the kingly role of the glorified Son of Man, the Lion of the tribe of Judah, ruling in regal splendor on David's throne. The doors of the sanctuary are also decorated with the palm-cherubim motif.

42-43. The purpose of Ezekiel's temple

42:1-20. To demonstrate God's holiness. This is the pervading theme of the entire book (see introduction) and especially so in the purpose and details of the kingdom temple (cf. 43:10). The holiness of the Lord is further emphasized by the principle of *separation*. At the very outset the wall separating the courts and temple from all that is defiling is introduced (40:5). The cell buildings, 42:1-14, are called holy and have a similar function of separation. The established separation of the whole enclosure is set forth, 15-20.

43:1-17. To provide a dwelling place for the divine glory. Ezekiel sees the return of the glory to take up residence in the temple's holy of holies during the Kingdom Age, as he had seen its departure before the fall of the city in 586 B.C. (cf. 9:3; 10:4; 11:23-24). The Lord promises to 'live among the Israelites forever,' 7.

43:7. To provide a center for the divine government. 'This is the place of my throne' (cf. Isa 2:2-3; Mic 4:2). The theocratic administration throughout the vision is stressed.

43:18-27. To perpetuate the memorial of sacrifice. This sacrifice, of course, is not rendered with a view of obtaining salvation, but it is commemorative of an accomplished redemption maintained in the presence of the revealed glory of God.

44-46. Worship in the Kingdom Age

44:1-31. Concerning the priests and the prince. The outward Eastern Gate for the Prince is described, 1-3, and the charge concerning aliens and rebellious tribes is set forth, 4-14. Matters concerning the priesthood (Zadokites) are given, 15-27, with a statement of the priests' inheritance, 28-31.

45:1-25. Portions of other groups. The portions of the priests, Levites, the whole house of Israel, and the Prince are specified, 1-8. The Prince is discussed, 9-17, as well as the feasts (Passover and Tabernacles), 18-25.

46:1-18. The worship of the prince. His personal worship, 1-8, and other institutions for worship are given, 9-15. The Prince's sons and servants are noted, 16-18.

46:19-24. A final description of places in the temple.

47-48. The millennial land

47:1-12. The river of the sanctuary (cf. Zech 14:8-9; Rev 22:1). The reality of this river is of one piece with the vision of the temple, the land and the people of Israel. It must be a literal river, as well as the blessed healing it accomplishes. It constitutes part of the topographical changes in Palestine when the covenants and promises made to Israel are fulfilled and the curse is lifted.

47:13-23. The boundaries of the land. The north boundary is traced from 'the Great Sea' (Mediterranean), the way of Hethlon (Heitala) E of Tripolis in Lebanon, 15, and Hamath (present-day Nahr el-'Asi) on the Orontes in Syria N of Damascus. The general borders are to be compared to the promise to Abraham in Gen 15:18-21 and instructions to Joshua in Josh 13:1-19:51.

48:1-29. The apportionment of the land. The name Lebo Hamath (cf. Num 34:8) is used in relation to the ideal limits of the Promised Land. Solomon's kingdom extended from 'Lebo Hamath to the Wadi of Egypt' (Wadi el-' Arish) (1 Kgs 8:65; cf. 2 Kgs 14:25; Amos 6:14). 'Lebo Hamath' is likely the name of a town (modern Lebweh) on the Orontes below Riblah. The general assignment by tribes, 1-9, is followed by the allotment for the priests and Levites, 10-20, and for the Prince, 21-29.

48:30-35. Jerusalem in the Kingdom Age (cf. Rev 21:10-27). Ezekiel sees the city as it will exist in the coming age, while the apostle John in Revelation has in view the eternal state, which will follow the final age of time. Since the kingdom will be eternal, the temporal kingdom merges into the eternal. Jerusalem's kingdom name is *YHWH-sàmmâ,* 'the Lord is there,' 35.

DANIEL

Prophecies of the times of the Gentiles

Relief of a lion released from its cage.

Outline

1-6 Daniel's prophetic careers in Babylon from Nebuchadnezzar's reign to Cyrus
7-12 Daniel's great visions under Belshazzar, Darius and Cyrus

Daniel the prophet. Daniel is called a prophet by our Lord (Mt 24:15), and His predictions are of immense importance, constituting the indispensable introduction to NT prophecy. Daniel was of princely extraction (1:3), a circumstance itself remarkably foretold by Isaiah (Isa 39:7; cf. 2 Kgs 20:18). He was contemporaneous with Jeremiah, Ezekiel a fellow exile (Ezk 14:20), and Joshua and Zerubbabel of the restoration. His long career extended from Nebuchadnezzar (605 B.C.) to Cyrus (530 B.C.).

Authenticity of the book. From the days of Porphyry, a neo-Platonic philosopher of the 3rd cen. A.D., to the present, the authenticity of the book of Daniel has been denied. Many have made it a pious forgery of the Maccabean era (167 B.C.). Two principal reasons exist why Danielic authorship is denied: (1) the minutely accurate picture of the Seleucid-Ptolemaic wars and the career of Antiochus Epiphanes (ch. 11), which are unthinkable as genuine prophecies to the rationalistic critic; and (2) alleged historical inaccuracies in the book.

The first objection rests on a denial of divine revelation, and the second rests on arguments from silence, plausible but erroneous presuppositions, insufficient data or untenable interpretations. Many alleged difficulties have been cleared up by archaeological and historical advance, but the book seems designed as a battleground between faith and unbelief.

The message of the book. The book is the key to all biblical prophecy. Apart from an understanding of the great eschatological disclosures of this book, the entire prophetic program of the Word of God remains sealed. Jesus' great Olivet Discourse (Mt 24-25; Mk 13; Lk 21), as well as 2 Thess 2 and the entire book of Revelation, can be unlocked only through an understanding of the prophecies of Daniel. The great themes of NT prophecy, the manifestation of the Antichrist (the man of sin), the Great Tribulation, the second advent of Messiah, the times of the Gentiles, and the resurrections and judgments are all treated in Daniel.

1. Daniel the man and his character

1-2. Beginning of Judah's exile. The third year of Jehoiakim was 605 B.C., but Jeremiah makes the fourth year of Jehoiakim Nebuchadnezzar's *first* year (Jer 25:1). He was evidently using the Palestinian system, not reckoning the year of accession as the first year as in the Babylonian scheme, which Daniel apparently used. This early subjugation of Jerusalem by 'King' Nebuchadnezzar (Daniel uses the term 'king' proleptically since Nebuchadnezzar did not ascend the throne until later), although not authenticated by positive extrabiblical evidence, nevertheless stands absolutely unimpugned by any negative evidence.

This date, 605 B.C., marks the beginning of the times of the Gentiles (Lk 21:24), the prophetic period when Jerusalem is under Gentile control. It is plain from 2 Kgs 24:1-4 and 2 Chr 36:6 that Judah from this moment on was subservient to Gentile rule. The Jew has remained so, even to a degree in the heyday of Maccabean power, and will remain so to the second advent. Nebuchadnezzar's god, 2, was Marduk (Bel, the head of the Babylonian pantheon). Shinar is Babylonia (Gen 10:10; Zech 5:11).

3-21. Daniel's great moral decision. In this deportation Nebuchadnezzar (sometimes spelled Nebuchadrezzar; Akkadian *Nabukudurri-usur,* 'Nabu protect my boundary') took only the most noble and promising. Daniel was of royal birth, highly gifted and showed great promise. His moral faith and spiritual courage were proved in his decision for godly separation from the defilement of Babylon. The name Daniel ('God judges') occurs with Noah and Job (Ezk 14:14, 20; 28:3). Higher critics connect Ezekiel's references to Daniel with the legendary judge of the widow and orphan in the religious texts from Ras Shamra (Ugarit) named Daniel. But Daniel had ample time to establish his truly great reputation in Babylon by the time of Ezekiel, who did not begin his ministry until some 13 or 14 years after Daniel's deportation. For Daniel's companions, also see note on 2:46-49. On Daniel's Babylonian name 'Belteshazzar,' see 10:1.

2. Nebuchadnezzar's colossus vision

1-28. The forgotten dream. The dream came to the king in his 'second year,' commonly considered to conflict with 1:5, 6, 17, 20. The solution is probably that the three years of training were not three full years, but parts of three years, and that the first year of training was the accession year of the king, the second year his first year, and the third year of training 'the second year' in which the dream occurred. The Chaldeans were a caste of wise men, associated with others in a category of diviners and occultists, 2-5. The crux was that the king claimed he forgot the dream. If the dream could be recalled, dream and omen lists could be consulted, as extant cuneiform divinatory tablets attest, 6-9. But to recall a forgotten dream was a matter beyond human or demonic ability, 10-16. Daniel and his friends prayed and received help from 'the God of heaven,' 17-23, and Daniel stood before the king, 24-28.

29-45. The revelation and interpretation of the dream. By divine help in answer to prayer, Nebuchadnezzar's forgotten dream was revealed by Daniel, 31-35, and interpreted to the king, 36-45. The large statue or colossus, as interpreted by Daniel, symbolizes the entire period known in prophecy as the times of the Gentiles (Lk 21:24, see note on 1:1). This is the long era when Jerusalem is politically subservient to the nations, among whom the chosen people are not to be reckoned (Num 23:9). It began with Judah's initial captivity to Babylon in 605 B.C., and will extend

The language of Daniel

The book of Daniel is unique in that it contains sections written in Hebrew and others in Aramaic. Aramaic, a Semitic language similar to Hebrew, was the *lingua franca* of the Assyrian, Neo-Babylonian, and Persian empires, and during this period became the common language of the Jews. Dan 2:1–7:28, a section relating to the Gentiles, quite naturally appears in Aramaic, though it is not known whether Daniel wrote the section in Aramaic or whether it was later translated.

Limestone relief of King Darius seated on the throne. Persepolis ca. fifth century B.C.

to the second advent of Messiah, the Smiting Stone, 34-35, who will destroy the Gentile world system catastrophically.

Then, and not till then, will the Stone (Christ) become a mountain (the millennial kingdom, Isa 2:2, since a mountain symbolizes a kingdom, Rev 13:1; 17:9-11) and fills 'the whole earth,' 35. This is the 'kingdom that will never be destroyed . . . and will itself endure forever,' 44; for after it has run its temporal course (Rev 20:4-5) it will merge into the eternal kingdom of the eternal state (1 Cor 15:24-28).

The four metals symbolize four empires – Babylon, Media-Persia, Macedonian Greece and Rome, 37-40. The fourth kingdom (Rome), 4044 (cf. 7:7), is envisioned panoramically, as it would exist in its ancient imperial glory, as divided into Eastern and Western empires in A.D. 364 (the two legs). Many believe that these two divisions will enjoy a last-day political revival in a ten-kingdom confederation of dictatorships (iron) and democracies (clay), 43. Then the supernatural Stone will strike and destroy Gentile world power and restore the kingdom to Israel (Acts 1:6).

46-49. Daniel's promotion (cf. Ezk 14:14, 20; 28:3). Shadrach is perhaps *Shudur-Aku* ('command of Aku,' Sumerian moon-god) or just a corruption of Marduk. Meshach is perhaps Akkadian *Mishaaku* ('Who is what Aku is?'). Abednego is for *Abednebo, Abdi-Nabu* ('servant of Nabu,' god of wisdom). It was customary to give Babylonian names to conquered peoples who served in the civil administration.

3. The fiery furnace
1-7. The image of gold.

Nebuchadnezzar's pride manifested in this act of idolatry and deification of man marks the spirit that prevails in the times of the Gentiles (see notes 1:1-2; 2:36-45). The image was 60 cubits (90 feet) high and six cubits (nine feet) wide, either a human form or the more customary obelisk. 'The plain of Dura' (Akkadian *dûru,* 'wall,' circuit') is perhaps Tulul *Dura,* a few miles S of Babylon. The music, 5-6, was to stir up the religious emotions to aid in the idolatrous worship.

8-25. The faithful three and their deliverance. Shadrach, Meshach and

Abednego were saved through the furnace of tribulation. The fourth person walking unscathed in the fiery furnace 'like a son of the gods,' 25, was evidently the preincarnate Christ, not a mere angel as the king thought, 28. In the presence of tribulation the Lord's own are assured of His presence and deliverance.

26-30. The king's confession and decree. Though the king perhaps never personally worshiped Jehovah, he gradually apprehends God's sovereign power (cf. 2:47; 3:28; 4:34-35).

4. Nebuchadnezzar's insanity

1-3. The king's salutation. He fully comprehended the universality of his rule, 1 (cf. 3:29).

4-27. The tree vision and its interpretation. Nebuchadnezzar sees a great tree, 4-18, a symbol of his pride and imperial self-exaltation (cf. 3:1-25; Ezk 17:22-24; 31:3-9; Mt 13:31-32). Daniel, whose Babylonian name was Belteshazzar (Akkadian *balusu-usur*, 'may he [Bel] protect his life'), interprets the true vision, 19-27.

28-37. The vision fulfilled. The king was punished for his pride by temporary mental derangement (lycanthropy), in which the victim imagined himself to be a wild beast. Berossus, a Babylonian priest of the 3rd cen. B.C., notes that Nebuchadnezzar after he had reigned 43 years 'was suddenly invaded by sickness' (*Contra Apionem* 1:20), obviously referring to some unusual malady. Eusebius in his *Praeparatio Evangelica* (9:41) quotes from Abydenus concerning Nebuchadnezzar in his last days 'being possessed by some god [demon] or other' and who having uttered a prophecy concerning the coming of the Persian conqueror 'immediately disappeared.' Critics disregard these allusions and maintain that Nebuchadnezzar's madness is a fictitious element of Daniel. But if history were silent, that in itself would not be sufficient evidence to reject the historicity of this chapter. The 'seven times,' 16, are likely 'seven years.' A Dead Sea Scroll text identifies such a mental malady with Nabonidus. Why then would it be impossible for Nebuchadnezzar? The king was restored, 34, and abased himself and praised 'the Most High,' 34, confessing Him King of heaven, 37.

5. Belshazzar's feast

1-9. Belshazzar's licentious and blasphemous celebration. The moral decline of the nation is evident. The holy vessels from the Jerusalem temple were desecrated by drunkenness, debauchery and idolatry. Babylon's iniquity, like the Amorites' (Gen 15:16), was full and judgment struck. Belshazzar (Akkadian *Bel-shar-usur*, 'Bel protect the king'), as is now well known from modern archaeology, was the son of, and coregent with, the king Nabonidus. What is unique in cuneiform literature is that Belshazzar is so recognized as coregent. Two legal documents dated to the twelfth and thirteenth years of Nabonidus record oaths sworn by the life of the king and of *Bel-shar-usur,* the crown prince. Nabonidus (Nabunaid, Akkadian *Nabu-na' id,* 'Nabu is inspiring') was the last king of Babylon, 556-539 B.C. In the Persian Verse Account it is stated that in his third year Nabonidus entrusted the kingship to his son Belshazzar, and he himself took up residence at Tema (in Arabia). The mysterious writing on the wall, 5-9, turned the feast into a nightmare of terror.

10-28. The forgotten Daniel and his message of doom. At this juncture the queen (probably the aged widow of Nebuchadnezzar) recalled Daniel, who had played so great a role in her husband's regime, 10-16. Daniel, the aged saint, was called in. Belshazzar confessed that in Daniel dwelt 'the spirit of the gods' or 'holy deity.' Daniel, knowing the impending doom, refused the empty honor of 'third highest ruler,' 16, 29, in the realm. Why *third* ruler? Because Belshazzar as coregent was himself the second.

Daniel became more than an interpreter of the handwriting. He was God's messenger of judgment and disaster upon Belshazzar and the Chaldean Empire. The writing, 'Mene, Mene, Tekel, Parsin,' 25, means literally: *mene,* 'numbered, numbered' i.e., 'thoroughly numbered,' where the repetition emphasizes the thought; *tekel,* 'weighed,' *parsin,* 'and divided.' *Peres,* past participle of 'divided,' is a word play on *Parus* ('Persia') or *perasin* ('Persians'). The import of the riddle is that the Chaldean Empire was completely numbered, weighed, and divided among the Medes and Persians. For the figure of weighing in a balance, see Job 31:6; Ps 62:9; Prov 16:2.

Relief of musicians. When the music played, the people were all to bow to the statue of King Nebuchadnezzar.

Archaeological light

Nebuchadnezzar was a great builder. For comment on his boast recorded in 30, see notes on 2 Kgs 25, where the excavations of his capital city, Babylon, are mentioned; also notes on Jer 50-51. The king's inscriptions closely parallel Dan 4:30.

29-31. The reward of Daniel and Belshazzar's death. Critics attack the historicity of the narrative on the basis that Belshazzar was so unconcerned as to reward Daniel at once. But the king was merely keeping his word and showing that he believed Daniel's prophecy. Moreover, there was no reason Daniel at this juncture should refuse the honors, since he had proved his disinterestedness. Critics also object that the fall of Babylon and Belshazzar's death are unauthentic. But there is nothing in the Gr. sources – Herodotus, Xenophon, Berossus, or the cuneiform records – the Nabonidus Chronicle or the Cyrus Cylinder – that indicates this would not be in keeping with the statement of the murder of Belshazzar. For the problem of Darius the Mede, see 6:1, 9, 25; 9:1.

6. Daniel in the den of lions
1-28. Darius the Mede and Daniel.
Daniel was now an old man, certainly well over 80 years of age. Darius himself was in his

sixties. It is maintained that Darius is to be identified with Gubaru who took charge of Babylon immediately after the death of Belshazzar, and who appointed satraps and presidents, including Daniel, to assist him in governing the extensive territory. He probably ruled about two years, until Cyrus was free to take over (6:28; 9:1; 11:1). That the Bible should record another name for the interim ruler Gubaru (or Cyaxares, the Median father-in-law of Cyrus, if Josephus' contention is correct) is not surprising. It was customary to have a Babylonian name in addition to one's native name (cf. Daniel and his three Jewish colleagues, 1:6-7).

Daniel's long diplomatic career and his prediction of a Medo-Persian victory were doubtless reasons that Darius placed him over the government. Daniel's faith and courage, 10-15, were the prelude to a mighty miracle, accentuated by the climactic struggle with pagan idolatry. This signal demonstration that the Lord of the captive Hebrews was really God had a great effect upon Darius, as is seen in his decree, 25-28, and doubtless also affected Cyrus favorably to issue his decree a few years later to permit the Jews to return to Jerusalem.

7. Daniel's four-beast vision
1-8. The vision of the beasts. The date was evidently 553 B.C. when Belshazzar began to act as coregent for his father, 1. The four winds

stirring up the 'great sea' (the nations, Rev 17:15) speak of evil celestial (demonic) powers (Dan 10:13; Eph 6:12), who have a conspicuous role in the government of the fallen man. The four beasts trace the same four world empires as in the image of 2:37-45, with this difference, that the colossus presents the outward dazzling brilliance of world governments in their political, economic, social aspects, while ch. 7 gives their intrinsic selfish and beastlike character.

These four empires, as in ch. 2, are Babylon, Medo-Persia (not a separate Median kingdom as higher critics posit), Greece and Rome. The lion prefigures Babylon, the bear Medo-Persia, the leopard Greece, and the nondescript iron beast admirably portrays Rome. The ten horns of ironlike Rome are ten kings, 7-8 (cf. 24), and correspond to the ten toes of 2:40-44.The little horn, 8, prefigured by Antiochus Epiphanes (8:23-25), is the latter day Antichrist, 'the man of lawlessness' in 2 Thess 2:3-8, 'the king' of Dan 11:36-45, 'the beast' of Rev 13:4-10, the last terrible ruler of the times of the Gentiles, who will be destroyed by Messiah at His second advent (Rev 19:20).

9-14. The vision of Messiah's second advent. This is the OT counterpart of Rev 19:11-16. 'The Ancient of Days,' 9, 13, is God. 'One like a son of man,' 13, is Christ invested with the kingdom and returning to earth as King of kings and Lord of lords (Rev 19:16). He will bring to an end the times of the Gentiles and Gentile world dominion, setting up His righteous rule over Israel and the nations. The Messiah's investiture with the kingdom in heaven, 13-14, is presented. This will take place *before* His coming portrayed in 9-12, and is identical with Rev 5:6-10. Daniel describes the judgment of the nations and the setting up of the kingdom, 10, 26-27 (cf. Mt 25:31-46; Rev 20:16). The vision of the destruction of the little horn, 11 (cf. 8) is fulfilled at the second advent (Rev 19:20; 20:10).

15-28. The interpretation of the vision. 'The saints of the Most High' who 'receive the kingdom,' 18, 22, 25, 27, are the saved Jewish remnant who pass through the Great Tribulation and inherit the kingdom and the covenants and promises made to Israel in connection with it. Note that the kingdom will be *eternal,* 18. The *mediatorial* and *temporal*

aspects of it, i.e., the thousand-year reign of Christ (Rev 20:4, 7), merge into the eternal state when Christ, after His reign on the earth, 'hands over the kingdom to God the Father . . . that God may be all in all' (1 Cor 15:24-28). It is important that the designation of God as the Most High, possessor of heaven and earth (Gen 14:18-22), is used when the Messiah comes to make good that title in His kingdom rule, 27. It is essential to see that the 'fourth beast,' 23, and the ten-kingdom confederation growing out of it, 24, are *not* Macedonian Greece and Antiochus Epiphanes, 25-26, as critics commonly assert, but last-day revived Rome, since the whole context involves the *second* advent of Messiah and His subsequent rule.

8. The ram, the goat and the small horn

1-14. The vision. Dated two years later than the beast vision (7:1), the time would be 551 B.C.. and the place Shushan (Susa), which became the winter capital of the Persian kings. The Ulai River is the Eulaeus of classical writers, 2,16, an artificial canal (Akkadian *U-la-a)* that flowed close by Susa on the N and NE, and connected the Kerkha and Abdizful Rivers. The Assyrian emperor Ashurbanipal claims to have reddened it with his enemies' blood when he invaded the province of Elam, E of Babylonia.

The ram, 3-4, with two horns (Media and Persia) is the Medo-Persian Empire, 539-331 B.C. The goat is Macedonian Greece in its lightninglike conquests under Alexander the Great, 'the prominent horn' of the goat, 5. Alexander's conquest of the Persian Empire is prophetically symbolized, 6-7, in the decisive battles of Granicus (334 B.C.), Issus (333 B.C.) and Gaugamela (331 B.C.). His untimely death in Babylon (323 B.C.) and the division of his world empire among his four generals are prefigured, 8. This resulted in three great Hellenistic empires by 275 B.C.: Macedonia, Egypt (Ptolemies) and Syria (Seleucids).

The career of Antiochus Epiphanes (175-163 B.C.) is prophetically outlined, 9-14. In 167 B.C. he conquered Palestine, defIled the sanctuary and dedicated it to Zeus Olympus. In 164 B.C. the temple was purified. This is the period of the '2300 evenings and mornings,' 14 (RSV). As 'another horn, which started small,' 9, he must not be confused with the little horn of Dan 7:8,

24-26, who is the Antichrist of the end time, although Antiochus Epiphanes foreshadowed him, 24-25. Both are similar in their idolatry and desecration of the temple (cf. 2 Thess 2:3-4; Rev 13:1-18), but are distinct as the context proves and as the book of the Revelation attests.

15-27. The interpretation of the vision. The angel Gabriel's interpretation shows clearly that the vision of Antiochus Epiphanes is a foreshadowing of the future tribulation, called 'the time of the end,' 17, 'the time of wrath,' 19, 'when rebels have become completely wicked,' 23.

9. The prophecy of the seventy weeks

1-19. Daniel's prayer. The date of the prophecy, given as a result of Daniel's deep penitential prayer, is 'the first year of Darius' (538 B.C.), 'son of Xerxes.' Daniel was stirred to intercession for the restoration of his people by reading Jeremiah's prophecies of the 70 years (Jer 25: 11-12; 29:10).

20-27. The answer – the prophecy of the seventy weeks. Jeremiah's prophecy of the 70-year Babylonian captivity is made the basis of a newly revealed panoramic prediction of the entire history of Daniel's people, the Jews, from the rebuilding of Jerusalem's walls until the ultimate establishment of Messiah's earthly kingdom.

The figure of 70 weeks is employed. The weeks (Heb. *sabûa,* Gr. *Heptads,* 'sevens') are *heptads* of years. The total given is 70 *heptads* or 490 years. It is a *historically complete* answer to Daniel's prayer (1-19), when Israel's national chastisement will be ended, prophetic vision sealed (closed) because it will be fulfilled (cf. Acts 3:21), and everlasting righteousness brought to Israel when she accepts her Messiah at His second advent, 24.

The total of 70 weeks ('sevens') is first divided into *seven weeks* or 49 years, 25. At the beginning of this time 'the decree to restore and rebuild Jerusalem' was issued in the decree of Artaxerxes I to rebuild Jerusalem's walls (Nisan, Mar.-Apr., 445 B.C., Neh 2). During this period (445-396 B.C.) it will be rebuilt with streets and a trench, but in times of trouble.'

The next division is 62 *weeks* or 434 years, 26. After this period (plus the first seven weeks, cf. v. 25) 'the Anointed one will be cut off' (396

Darius.

B.C. to Mar.-Apr., A.D. 30). The 62-week period ended and Christ was cut off in death and had nothing, i.e., nothing which was rightly His, no kingdom.

Following the 62 weeks an *unreckoned period* is prophesied, a time of Israel's national rejection, during which 'the people of the ruler who will come [the Beast, world ruler of the Gentile end-time, cf. 7:8; Rev 19:20] will destroy the city and the sanctuary,' 26*b.* The Romans under Titus destroyed Jerusalem in A.D. 70, the city has since been trodden down by the Gentiles (Lk 21:24), the Jews have been scattered, and wars and desolations have characterized the age.

The *final week* of seven years constitutes the climax of Jewish history prior to the establishment of the messianic kingdom, 27. It is divided into two half periods (three and a half years each). During the *first half* the 'prince' (world ruler, 'little horn' of 7:8, 24-25) will make a covenant with the Jews, who are restored in Palestine with a resumption of temple worship. In the *middle of the week* the

Verse 1 should be translated: ' . . . and the thing [revealed] was true [truth], and it was a conflict [involved a spiritual struggle or warfare].' The battle involved a spiritual tussle with demon powers operating in the government of the world system, 13. Daniel's three-week prayer and fasting, 2-3, challenged these 'spiritual forces of evil in the heavenly realms' (cf. Eph 6:12), i.e., evil spirits connected with governmental administration operating through Cyrus, 13. 'The prince of the Persian kingdom' was the evil spirit of government working in and through Cyrus (not Cyrus himself), to hinder him in his good intention to repatriate the Jews. Michael, 12-13, the archangel and patron of Daniel's people the Jews, 12: 1, came to Daniel's assistance in the conflict precipitated by believing prayer.

15-21. The meaning of the vision. The world governments of the times of the Gentiles (Lk 21:24) are operated by unseen evil spirits or demons in the Satanic world system. These tried to hinder Daniel's prayer for His people, whose ultimate restoration in the kingdom will be preceded by the end of the times of the Gentiles and the imprisonment of Satan and his demons (Rev 20:13) to make possible the perfect government of Messiah in the Kingdom Age.

11. Kings of the north and south

1-35. The wars of the Ptolemies and Seleucids. This marvelous prewriting of history by the Spirit of prophecy through Daniel of the 6th cen. B.C. seems impossible to rationalistic critics and is a chief reason for the rejection of the genuineness of the book of Daniel. History has minutely verified these prophecies fulfilled by Persian kings, 2; Alexander the Great, 3-4; the Ptolemies of Egypt, 5; 'the king of the South' and the Seleucids of Syria, 'the king of the North,' 6-35. Even the Romans, 30, in 'ships of the western coast' (Cyprus), mentioned in the description of Antiochus IV (Epiphanes), 21-45, and the 'abomination that causes desolation,' 31, which he set up when he profaned the Jerusalem temple, exactly fulfilled these prophecies (cf. notes on 8:1-14).

36-45. The end-time and the man of sin. Between 35 and 36 spans an unreckoned period of time, from the historical fulfillment of

A Babylonian boundary stone, carved with symbols of various deities, from which the modern signs of the zodiac are derived.

covenant is broken, worship for the Jews ceases (2 Thess 2:3-4), and the time of Great Tribulation ensues. The *advent of Christ* the Messiah consummates this period of desolation, bringing everlasting righteousness to Israel, 24, and judgment upon the 'one who causes desolation,' the ruler, and his hosts (Rev 19:20).

10. The role of demonic powers in governments

1-14. The vision. This chapter is the prologue for the vision of ch. 11, while ch. 12 is the epilogue. 'The third year of Cyrus' was 535 B.C. 'Belteshazzar,' Daniel's Babylonian name, was apparently an abbreviated form of the Akkadian *Bel-balasu-usur* ('may Bel [i.e., Baal] protect his life') .

these prophecies in Antiochus Epiphanes and the victorious Maccabees to the still future fulfillment of 36-45, fulfilling 10:14. The willful king of these verses is the Antichrist of the last days, the man of lawlessness of 2 Thess. 2:3-4, the lawless one of Rev 13:1-10, foreshadowed by Antiochus Epiphanes. 'He will be successful until the time of wrath is complete,' 36 (12:1), i.e., God's wrath outpoured (Mt 24:21; Rev. 6-19). His lawless, God-defying character, 36-39, is unfolded. His latter-day activity preceding his doom is outlined, 40-45 (cf. Rev 19:20; 20:10), and described in 2 Thess 2:3-10. The last day attack by the king of the North and of the South shall not destroy him. Only the direct judgment of God upon him by the returning victorious Christ shall seal his doom. While he reigns, he is invincible.

12. The great tribulation and Israel's deliverance

1. The great end-time period of trouble. 'At that time' (twice in v. 1) is the time of the end, the last half of Daniel's seventieth week (see notes on 9:27), the terrible period of 'trouble for Jacob' (Jer 30:5-7) preceding the return of Christ. This time is outlined in Rev 12:7-17, culminating in the terrible bowl judgments of Rev 15-16, and the destruction of the Satanic religions and political world system (Rev 17-18). It climaxes in the appearing Messiah (Rev 19:11-16). This 'end' time is referred to in Dan 8:17-19; 9:26; 11:35, 40; 12:4, 6, 9. 'Your people,' 1, are Daniel's people the Jews. Those 'found written in the book' are those delivered from physical death (Isa 4:2-3) and regenerated to enjoy kingdom blessing. For Michael's ministry on behalf of Israel in the end-time, cf. Rev 12:7-12 and Dan 10:21 (delivering the remnant of Israel from the wrath of Satan, who has been cast down to the earth).

2-3. Israel's resurrection. That this resurrection is predicated of Israel, and the idea of a general resurrection of all the dead is excluded, is shown by the following: (1) The context, which concerns Daniel's people, the Jews, 1. (2) The term 'multitudes,' not all. (3) The partitive preposition 'out from,' 'from among' a category 'who sleep' (the sleep of physical death) 'in the dust of the earth,' a figurative term for the grave (cf. Job 20:11; Gen 3:19). (4) The verb 'awake' to denote physical resurrection (Isa 26:19) from the sleep of death (2 Kgs 4:31; Jer 51:39, 57; Job 14:12). (5) The phrase 'to everlasting life,' showing that it is physical resurrection to eternal life. (6) The fact that Daniel himself (with all the OT saved) will participate in it, 12:13. (7) Fulfillment of such statements of our Lord as Mt 8:11; 19:28. (8) The phrase, 'some to everlasting life, others to shame and everlasting contempt,' does not mean the righteous and the unrighteous will be raised (cf. similar thought in Jn 5:28-29). The first category refers to all saved Israelites raised at that time, while the second embraces those left for the second resurrection (Rev 20:11-15). (9) Verse 3 refers to rewards of the resurrected OT saints.

4-13. The final consummation. The character of the intervening period, especially its latter part, 4, 9, was revealed to Daniel by the Lord, 5-8. But the prophecy was to be sealed up (not understood) to the end-time, 4. Verses 11 and 12 give the time of the setting up of Antichrist's image (9:27) in the Jerusalem temple (2 Thess 2:3-4), and the duration of the great time of wrath.

THE MINOR PROPHETS

The 12 so-called Minor Prophets are distinguished from the Major Prophets – Isaiah, Jeremiah, Ezekiel and Daniel. In the Heb. canon they are grouped together as *one* book called the Twelve, and with the first three major prophets make *four* books, known as the Latter Prophets. The Former Prophets are also reckoned four in number – Joshua, Judges, Samuel, Kings. The Heb. Bible then has eight prophets in its second section, called the Prophets (*Nebî'îm*). Daniel was placed in the third section among the Writings (*Ketûbîm*). From Augustine's time (late 4th cen.), the Latin church has employed the term Minor Prophets because of their brevity (not their unimportance) as compared with the Major Prophets.

The Minor Prophets and Their Message

Hosea
The Lord loves Israel despite her sin.
755-15

Joel
Judgment precedes Israel's future spiritual revival.
835-796*

Amos
God is just and must judge sin.
765-50

Obadiah
Sure retribution must overtake merciless pride.
848*

Jonah
Divine grace is universal in its sweep.
780-50

Micah
Bethlehem-born Messiah will be mankind's Deliverer.
740-690

Nahum
Doom is to descend on wicked Nineveh.
630-12

Habakkuk
Justification by faith is God's way of salvation.
625 or earlier

Zephaniah
The Day of the Lord must precede kingdom blessing.
625-10

Haggai
The Lord's temple and interests deserve top priority.
520

Zechariah
The Lord will remember His people Israel.
520-15; Ch. 9-14 after 500

Malachi
Let the wicked be warned by the certainty of judgment.
433-400

All dates are approximate.

*The text does not specifically date these prophets. As a result differences of opinion exist concerning the time of their ministries.

Contemporary Kings

Israel

Judah

Prophet

Jerboam II*
793-53

Azariah*
792-40

Hosea
begins

Zechariah
753-52

Shallum
752

Menahem
752-42

Pekah*
752-32

Jotham*
750–32

Anarchy and
civil war
Hosea 1:4

Pekahiah
742-40

Hoshea
732-22

Ahaz*
735-16

Fall of Samaria
722

Hezekiah
716-687

* Coregencies included

HOSEA

The love of God for His erring people

The prophet and his times.
Hosea began his ministry toward the latter part of the prosperous and morally declining era of Jeroboam II of Israel (782-753 B.C.) and continued on after the fall of Samaria (722 B.C.) into the troubled reigns of Jotham, Ahaz and Hezekiah (1:1). His ministry followed closely upon that of Amos. The latter thundered forth his scathing prophecies as a southerner to a prosperous, dissolute Israel, while Hosea spoke with the heart passion of a native son. Jonah was the northern kingdom's foreign missionary, while Hosea was its home missionary. With the brokenness and passion of Jeremiah, Hosea had a sensitivity of heart that made him the apostle of love in the OT. Although the theme of judgment for apostasy runs through the book, it is interwoven by the golden strand of mercy and love.

And Hosea's exposure of sin and impending judgment is not the fiery denunciations of Amos, but a mournful, solemn elegy that breathes the deep love of the Lord for His sinning people.

Outline

1-3 Israel's rejection as an unfaithful wife; her future reception and restoration
4-14 Messages of judgment mingled with pleadings of love and mercy

Beitin, biblical Bethel, called by Hosea 'Beth Aven' – house of wickedness.

A threshing floor in modern Israel. Hosea taught that the nation would reap what it sowed.

1. The prophet's marriage illustrates Israel's sin

1. Introduction. Hosea means 'salvation' or 'deliverance.' The fundamental conviction of Heb. prophecy is here expressed in the divine inspiration of the human agent and the consequent authority of the message.

2-9. Hosea divinely commanded to marry a harlot. Hosea took the prostitute Gomer, and she bore him children. He gave them names, 2-9, which were historically and prophetically meaningful. Jezreel, the son, means 'the Lord sows,' 3-5, and pointed back to the blood of Jezreel shed by Jehu (1 Kgs 19:15-17; 2 Kgs 10:1-14) and the approaching punishment of the Jehu dynasty of which the then reigning and prosperous Jeroboam II was a member. Jezreel also pointed forward to Israel's future restoration, 2:21-23. The birth of a daughter, Lo-Ruhamah ('unpitied') is announced, 6-7. The little girl would be a living reminder that because of her harlotry Israel would no longer be pitied. The name of the third child (another boy) Lo-Ammi ('not my people') made him a living reminder why the Lord would no longer pity. As a result of Israel's abandonment of God's law, the covenant relationship was broken. 'My people' refers to Israel as God's elect nation in the OT, while 'not my people' has reference to the temporary setting aside of this national election (cf. Rom 11:1-5). The 'Lo-Ammi' period of Israel would end with the nation's conversion and her reunion with Judah.

10-11. Future restoration of Israel. Cf. Rom 9:23-26 for the divine commentary on God's sovereignty and Israel's reinstatement. Verse 11 is still unfulfilled. 'The [great] day of Jezreel' will be Armageddon's slaughter, a prelude to the destruction of Israel's last-day enemies, and restoration, 11.

Moral problem

(1) Did the Lord command Hosea to marry a harlot, or

(2) did she become a harlot after his marriage, or

(3) is the incident only an allegory? Since Israel, the Lord's adulterous wife, was not always unchaste, number two is possible. But the text apparently supports the first option, which does not, as some claim, impinge upon the holiness of a sovereign God.

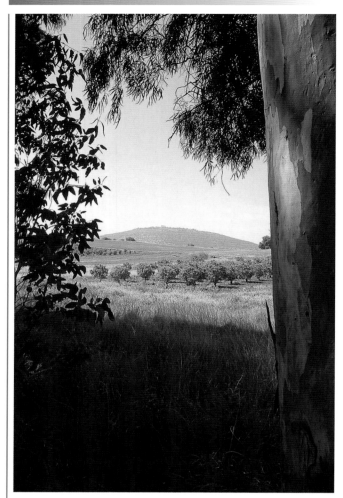

Mount Tabor seems to have harbored a pagan shrine on its heights.

3. Israel's future restoration

1-3. Israel's past symbolized. Hosea bought back his unfaithful wife, disciplined her as the Lord has done for Israel, and affirmed his undying love for her. ' As the lord loves the Israelites, though they turn to other gods,' 1, expresses the central theme of Hosea's prophecy – God's undying love for His covenant people. 'Raisin-cakes' were used in pagan festal worship (Isa 16:7; Jer 7:18). Although Hosea bought his wife back (implying Christ's ransom price paid at Calvary), she was not to live with him as his wife, but must sit as a widow in sorrow and discipline until he would one day take her to himself, after her cleansing.

4. Israel's present described. During this period of disciplinary dealing in a virtual state of widowhood, Israel would be deprived of her ceremonial and civil institutions, as has been the case.

5. Israel's future indicated. This is unfulfilled and will take place in the latter days of Israel, before kingdom restoration (Acts 1:6), when the adulterous wife is cleansed (Zech 12:10; 13:1) and restored.

4. Ephraim's attachment to idolatry

1-11. Fruits of idolatry. A general category of sins, 1-5, is augmented by the willful ignorance of the Lord's people, 6-11.

12-19. Description of Ephraim's idolatry. What an indictment of the foolishness and foulness of Canaanite cults! Beth Aven ('house of wickedness or vanity'), 15, is apparently a derogatory name for Bethel (5:8; cf. 10:8), a center of Canaanite idolatrous pollution (cf. 10:5, 'calf-idol of Beth Aven'). 'Ephraim,' 17, became the designation of Israel after the Syro-Ephraimite war (734-732 B.C.) when the northern kingdom lost its peripheral territories to Assyria and was reduced to its central core. Ephraim's pathetic occupation with idols, 17, resulted in inevitable judgment, 19, the wind having caught the people in its power to scatter them in exile.

5-6. Message of rebuke and future mercy

5:1-14. The favor of the Lord withdrawn. Israel's leaders (priests and civil rulers), 1, had been a trap to the people and

2. Israel's suffering for her harlotry

1-13. Appeal and warning. The godly remnant is addressed, 1, and urged to plead with faithless Israel (their mother), 2, who is disowned by the Lord as His wife because of infidelity. The Lord Himself dramatically threatens His unfaithful spouse with grievous punishments, 3-13.

14-23. Israel to be restored. The Valley of Achor ('trouble'; Josh 7:26; Isa 65:10) is SW of Jericho (modem el-Buqe'ah). Israel, the disowned, will be restored. She who has immorally taken Baal as her husband and engaged in the foul fertility rites of the Canaanites, 6-7, shall return to the Lord (*Ishi*, 'my husband') and no longer call Baal that detestable designation *Baali* ('my Baal,' Lord) 16. These verses present a glorious future for Israel (For v. 23, cf. Rom 9:25-26).

judgment was due. Tabor seems to have harbored a pagan shrine on its heights as well as Mizpah, N of Jerusalem (1 Sam 7:5). Ephraim (see note on 4:12-19) was so addicted to idolatry (4:17) she was unable to return to the Lord. 'Illegitimate children,' 7, were offspring unfaithful to the Lord.

5:15-6:3. Future return and blessing. The Lord withdrew from Israel. Her interim affliction resulted and will continue until He returns at His second advent, 5:15. The heart cry of the believing remnant of the last days is expressed, 6:1-3 (cf. Isa 1:9; Rom 11:5), their cry just before the return of the Lord declared in 5: 15. The 'two days,' 2, prefigure the long period of Israel's affliction (5:15). 'The third day,' 2, is her day of spiritual resurrection (regeneration) and consequent spiritual blessings (Joel 2:28-29).

6:4-11. The Lord's reply. He mourned over Ephraim and Judah, 4-6, exposing their sin, 7-11, which has caused their calamities.

7-13. The Lord's indictment of Israel

7:1-16. Her moral depravity. The horrible harvest of her idolatry, 1-7, in mixing with the polluted paganism of the surrounding nations, 8-16, is denounced.

8:1-9:9. Judgment upon her apostasy. The judgment announced, 8:1-7, upon her apostasy, 8-14, is followed by warnings against a spirit of self-security, 9:1-9.

9:10-11:11. Retrospect of the nation's sin and woe. How Israel requited the Lord's love, 9: 10-17, incurring awful guilt, 10:1-11, is told. Exhortations and rebuke were administered, 10:12-15. God's mercy is set forth, 11:1-11.

11:12-13:13. Ephraim's indictment. She is brought face to face with her polluting, idolatrous contamination, 11:12-12:2. Past mercies are recalled, 12:3-6, in view of Israel's present plight, 7-14. Her former greatness is contrasted with her shame and spiritual death, contaminated by impure Baal worship, 13:1-6. The Lord has had to turn against her as a leopard, 7, as a lion, 7, and as a bear robbed of her cubs, 8. Israel's ruin is in the fact that she is against the Lord, who is her help, 9-11, Could her kings save her from the destruction she had incurred by turning against the Lord? Israel's

kings could not save her from the Lord's destruction. God established the kings and He took them away in judgment.

13:14-16. Israel's future resurrection. This is a glorious promise of physical resurrection (1 Cor 15:55) for saved Israelites preceding for the kingdom (Dan 12:2). Physical resurrection for the faithful is an unchangeable fact of divine certainty.

14. Kingdom restoration of Israel

1-3. Call to return. God's Spirit through the prophet calls apostate Ephraim to come back to the Lord in repentance and faith. 'Fruit' is used in the sense of young oxen as thank offerings. 4-8. The Lord's gracious response. Sovereign love expresses itself in two 'I wills,' 4- 5. In kingdom glory Israel, the 'lily' and 'the olive tree' (cf. Rom 11:16-24) will flourish. The olive is a symbol of Israel in her spiritual blessing.

9. Concluding statement. The spiritually wise will understand these things, but not sinners.

JOEL

The great day of the Lord

Author and date. Joel means 'the Lord (*Yahweh*) is God.' The name of his father is given, but merely to distinguish him from others of the same name. He leaves even the time he prophesied to be guessed at. Although modern critics date him late (post-Exilic) conservative scholars place him as perhaps the earliest of the minor prophets, during the reign of Joash (*c.* 800 B.C.).

Outline

1:1-20 The locust plague – the Day of the Lord
2:1-32 Events of the Day of the Lord
3:1-16 The judgment of the nations
3:17-21 Kingdom blessing

Jewish rabbi with a *shofar* (sopar, a carved horn). Joel writes that, before Armageddon, the trumpet will warn of invading forces

1. The locust plague
– the Day of the Lord

1-7. The desolation of the land. The prophet is presented, 1. Description is given of an unprecedented locust plague, which was to be unforgettable in the future, 3. The plague was utterly destructive in its results. Four names are given to the locusts portraying their decimating destruction. 'The leavings of the *gnawer* the *multiplier* ate, and the leavings of the *licker* the *devourer* ate' (Keil and Delitzsch), 4. The nation's drunkards are called to bewail the calamity, 5. The locusts point to something still more terrible and form a prophetic picture of a greater disaster. They prefigure an invading army, 6-7 (cf. 2:25) and its desolation of the land. Both the vine (Ps 80:8, 14; Hos 10:1; Isa 5:1-7) and the fig tree symbolize Israel in her spiritual privilege and national election (Hos 9:10; Mt 24:32-33; Lk 13:67; Rom 11:17-24).

8-13. Appeal to lament the plague. All people, 8-10, especially the farmer and vinegrowers, 11-12, the priests and all spiritual leaders of the nation, 13, are called to mourn.

14. Call to self-humiliation and repentance. Fasting and prayer must give evidence of genuine repentance.

15-20. The plague a prophetic symbol of the Day of the Lord. Just as the Spirit of prophecy frequently uses some local circumstance as the occasion of a far-reaching prophecy (cf. Isa 7:1-14 in the case of the virgin birth prediction) so the locust plague is made a symbol of the yet-future Day of the Lord (Isa 2:12-22; 4:1-6; Ezk 30:3; Rev 19:11-21). In this apocalyptic period (Rev 6-19) the Lord will manifest His power in putting down His enemies actively and publicly in order to set up His millennial kingdom over Israel. It is the period described graphically in Ps 2.

2. Events of
the Day of the Lord

1-10. The invading army from the north. Joel 2 conducts us at once to the closing times of the Gentiles and the historical enactment of the Day of the Lord, 1. It is still future, as is ch. 3. The invading army is preparatory to Armageddon (Rev 16:13-16). Blowing the trumpet (*sopar*, a carved horn) signaled the danger of invading forces (Hos 8:1; Jer 4:5; 6:1). 'My holy hill' (Ps 2:6) is Moriah, the temple hill. The Day of the Lord and the terrible destructiveness of the army are described, 2-10, the locust (army) plague being in the background of the imagery .

11. The Lord's army appears. This involves the second advent of Christ and is a phase of the titanic struggle at Armageddon

The place of judgment is called 'the Valley of Jehoshaphat,' usually taken as a symbolic name. However, Joel and Zechariah regarded it as the Kidron Valley and the widening mountain basin to the S of the city beyond Hinnom. Kidron is now also known as the valley of Jehoshaphat, called so as early as Eusebius.

(3:9-13; Rev 16:14). The saints and angels will constitute the Lord's 'army.'

12-17. The repentant remnant. The Lord calls upon the remnant in the land genuinely to repent, 12-13, and to receive the Lord's blessing, 14. All classes, 15-17, are included. None is excused, not even the newlywed bridegroom (cf. Deut 24:5).

18-27. The Lord's response to the repentant Jews in the land. Instead of His fiery wrath burning against them, the Lord's fiery jealousy will flame for them and His mercy go out toward them, 18. He promises temporal prosperity, 19; military deliverance, 20; joy and gladness, 21-23; restored rainfall and abundant harvests, 24-26; restored fellowship, 27. Scholars have variously translated 23 as 'the early rain for your vindication' [NASB] or, 'the teacher of righteousness' [NIV], giving it a messianic connotation.

28-32. The promise of the outpoured Spirit. Keil takes the outpouring of the Spirit as a second and later result of the gift of 'a teacher for righteousness' (cf. 23). 'And afterward,' 28 (Acts 2:16), refers to the days of Israel's exaltation and blessing in the opening era of the kingdom (Isa 2:2-4; Mic 4:17). The term 'pour out' signifies a rich abundance of divine communication (cf. Isa 32:15; Ezk 39:29). Peter's use of this prophecy at Pentecost (Acts 2:15:21) was illustrative of what the Spirit of God can do. Its final fulfillment awaits the introduction of the Kingdom Age. The kingdom outpouring is to be universal, 28-29, and is to be connected with the climactic phase of the 'Day of the Lord,' 30-31, with preceding signs announcing the dispossession of wicked men at the setting up of Christ's kingdom on the earth, 32.

3. The judgment of the nations

1. Israel's end-time restoration. 'In those days and at that time' denotes that phase of the Day of the Lord which will witness Israel's restoration (Isa 11:10-12; Jer 23:5-8; Ezk 37:21-28; Acts 15:15-17). This passage is introductory to the primary theme of the judgment of the nations, 2-8, inasmuch as that event is a necessary prerequisite to Israel's reinstatement.

The nations that have persecuted Israel must be judged before Israel can be brought into safety and blessing (cf. Mt 25:31-46; Rom 11:25-27; Zech 6:1-8; Rev 16:14).

2-16. The nations judged. The Lord Himself is the speaker, 2-8. He announces what He will do to Israel's enemies when He restores His people (note 'my people,' 3). The place of the judgment is said to be 'the Valley of Jehoshaphat,' 2, 12. This is usually taken as a symbolic rather than a geographical name, as inferred from the etymology, '*Yahweh* shall judge' and from 14, where the same valley is called the 'valley of decision,' in the sense of a judicial sentence or verdict (rendered against the wicked nations judged there). However, both Joel and Zechariah (cf. Zech 14:4) evidently regarded this theater of judgment as the Kidron Valley and the widening mountain basin to the S of the city beyond Hinnom. Kidron is now also known as the valley of Jehoshaphat, called so as early as Eusebius, but evidently on the basis of the Joel and Zechariah passages.

The basis of the judgment will be 'concerning my inheritance, my people Israel,' 2. The sin of the nations has been their mistreatment of the Jew (cf. Ps 79:1-13; 83:1-18; Isa 29:1-8; 34:1-3; Jer 25:13-17; Zech 1:14-15; 12:2-3; Mt 25:31-46). Joel 3:2-3 indicates the crime of the nations, with special condemnation resting upon the Phoenicians and Philistines, 4-8. The Sabaeans, 8, were traders of SW Arabia. This initial judgment of the nations foreshadows Armageddon, 9-14 (Rev 16:13-16; 19:11-21), and 15-16 parallels 2:30-32. Verses 9-16 summarize 2:9-32.

17-21. Full kingdom blessing. At last unbelieving Israel receives the Messiah, the true basis of their holiness, 17 (cf. Zech 14:20-21).

'My holy hill' is Moriah, the temple hill (cf. Ps 2:6; Dan 11:45; Ob 16; Zech 8:3). The kingdom prosperity of Palestine, 18, is a common prophetic theme toward which all the prophets gravitate (cf. Isa 35:1-3). The related themes of the destruction of Israel's enemies, Egypt and Edom, 19 (cf. Zech 14:18-19), and the restoration of Judah, 20-21, are also prominent.

AMOS

Impending judgment

The times of Amos.

Amos' ministry occurred in the latter part of the reign of Jeroboam II (c. 793-753 B.C.) when this prosperous and idolatrous sovereign ruled contemporaneously with Azariah (Uzziah) of Judah (c. 792-740 B.C.). Therefore 765-750 B.C. would be approximately the time of Amos. It was an age of economic prosperity with luxurious living, moral corruption and rampant idolatry. Amos directed his fiery oratory against these sins.

The prophet.

Amos ('burden') was a simple shepherd and dresser of sycamore fruit (7:14) from Tekoa, a hill country town about 10 miles S of Jerusalem. He was called to be prophet to the whole house of Jacob (3:1, 13) but chiefly to the northern kingdom (7:14-15) at the main sanctuary at Bethel (7:10). He met the opposition of the high priest Amaziah, who reported the fearless preacher to Jeroboam II. Amos doubtless reduced his prophecies to writing shortly after his return to Tekoa.

Outline

1:1-2:16 Judgment on Israel, Judah and surrounding nations

3:1-9:10 The Lord's indictment of the whole house of Jacob

3:1-6:14 Four condemnatory sermons

7:1-9:10 Five symbolic predictions of punishment

9:11-15 Kingdom blessing for restored Israel

Amos the prophet was working as a shepherd when he received the call to warn God's people.

1:1-2:3 Judgment upon surrounding nations

1:1-2. Superscription. The earthquake is mentioned again in Zech 14:5. The Lord 'roars' as a lion in mounting wrath against increasing sin. Carmel ('the garden or orchard') a prominent headland jutting into the Mediterranean, was famous for its luxuriant growth of plants in antiquity.

1:3-2:3. Judgment upon six nations *Judgment upon Damascus,* 3-5. Damascus was the capital of a powerful Aramean city-state that harassed Israel (*c.* 900-780 B.C.) especially under Ben-Ha-dad I (*c.* 880-842) and Hazael (*c.* 842-806). 'For three sins . . . even for four,' 3, 9, 11, 13; 2:1; 2:4, 6, means sin multiplied on sin, more than enough. The numerical sequence *x*, *x+1* is a common device in Hebrew poetry (cf. Prov 3:18, 21, 29; Job 33:14), here designating fullness or completion. It was Hazael, the usurper, 3-4, who threshed Gilead in Transjordan 'with sledges having iron teeth' (2 Kgs 10:32-33; 13:7). 'The gate of Damascus,' 5, was the bar of its gates (Jer 51:30). 'The fortresses of Ben-Ha-dad,' 4, were the fortresses of Ben-Hadad II, son of Hazael (2 Kgs 13:3). The Valley of Aven, 5, is either the Valley of On (Ezek 30:17) or Baalbek, not far from Damascus. Beth Eden (Bit-idini of the Assyrian tablets) was situated by the Euphrates River, called Eden (Ezk 27:23).

2:4-16 Judgment upon Judah and Israel

4-5. Judgment upon Judah. Judah and Israel were as guilty as the nations around them and would be punished.

6-16. Judgment upon Israel. Israel's judgment was put in the same literary form and was more detailed because she enjoyed greater light and was more privileged.

3. Israel's greater privilege and guilt

1-11. Because of her greater privilege. She was a nationally elect nation, redeemed out of Egypt and under covenant responsibility (Ex 19:4-6; Deut 6:7; Lk 12:48). Her failure would therefore be severely judged, 1-2. Let Israel make an appointment to walk with the Lord, 3, to hear His warnings of judgment through His prophets and

Archaeological light

On Hazael, see comments on 2 Kgs 8. Kir is in Mesopotamia and is the place from which the Arameans migrated (9:7), and to which they were exiled (2 Kgs 16:9).

Judgment upon Philistia, 6-8. Gaza, Ashdod, Ashkelon and Ekron were judged because they sold the Israelites into slavery to Edom (2 Chr 21:16-17; Joel 3:4-8).

Judgment upon Tyre, 9-10. Cf. Joel 3:4-8 for its inhuman cruelty against Israel. 'Treaty of brotherhood' refers to the covenant David and Solomon made with Tyre (cf. 1 Kgs 9:13).

Judgment upon Edom, 11-12. Though closely related to Israel ('his brother'), 11, yet he was pitiless in his hatred and cruelty (cf. Mal 1:2; Ob 1-21). Teman is doubtless Tawilan SE of Sela (Petra), and Bozrah is in north central Edom. Judgment upon Ammon, 13-15 (cf. Zeph 2:8-11). The Ammonites, N of Moab, with capital at Rabbah (modern Amman) ravaged neighboring Gilead.

Judgment upon Moab, 2: 1-3. So fierce was their hatred they desecrated the body of the Edomite king by cremation (cf. 2 Kgs 3:26-27).

approaching calamity, 4-8, because as the Lord's elect nation she had been such a poor example to her pagan neighbors, 9-11.

12-15. The thoroughness of the divine judgment. This is vividly set forth, 12. The calamity would center upon the paganized altars at Bethel, 14, and the polluted wealth of the prosperous sinners of Jeroboam II's reign. 'Houses adorned with ivory,' 15 (cf. 1 Kgs 22:39), were so called because they were lavishly decorated with ivory inlays. Numerous fragments of such inlay have come to light in the archaeological diggings at ancient Samaria in the 'Samaritan ivories.'

4. Prepare to meet your God, O Israel

1-3. Indictment of the wealthy women of Samaria. These greedy, vain women (cf. Isa 3:16-26) were called 'cows of Bashan,' 1 (cf. Ps 22:12). This was rebuke for

Arrangement of the oracles

The arrangement of the text dramatizes the announcement of impending judgment upon Israel. Geographically, the judgments surround Israel in an ever-tightening noose that focuses God's wrath upon His sinful people. The order also provides focus by generally moving from distant ethnic relations (Aram, cf. Gen 25:20; Deut 26:5) to Israel's brother Judah.

their responsibility in making unnecessary demands upon the men for the luxuries of life. Bashan was a fertile area E of the Sea of Galilee known for its sleek, fat cattle.

4-5. Israel's abominable ritualism. They loved empty idolatrous ceremonialism in the name of religion. Bethel was the idol-ridden royal sanctuary and Gilgal was another polluted shrine.

6-13. Israel must face God's judgment. Failing to respond to God's chastening love, 6-11, Israel must now get ready to face God's justice and wrath, 12, and realize how great He is in His power, wisdom and justice, 13.

5. Seek the Lord and live

1-3. A lament for the fallen and forsaken nation. She who had once been a virgin, separated to the Lord, was now fallen into harlotries and abominations, unable to help herself, and was due for impoverishment by enemy invasion and death.

4-17. Seek the Lord. The only way Israel could be spared from national death was to seek the Lord rather than the idols of Bethel, Gilgal and Beersheba. Idolatry was a criminal abomination in the light of who the Lord was, 8-9, and its practice productive of every kind of immorality, 10-13. Therefore, they were to forsake it and seek the Lord, 14-17.

18-20. Be warned of the Day of the Lord. How wrong they were to think of it piously as a day of vindication against their foes. It would engulf them in its gloom.

21-27. The Lord's hatred of their empty religionism. To avert disaster, justice must 'roll on like a river, righteousness like a never-failing stream,' 24 – the essence of Amos'

message. Sikkuth and Kiyyun, 26, were Assyrian gods (Acts 7:42-43), designations of Saturn, here called 'your idols . . . your god.'

6. Calamity upon the self-secure

1-7. Warning to self-indulgent sinners. Let the secure in Zion (Jerusalem's temple hill, i.e., Judah) and in the mountain of Samaria (the hill of Shemer, upon which Samaria was built, i.e., by metonymy, the northern kingdom) take warning, 1, from the fate of Calneh in N. Syria and Hamath on the Orontes in Syria (the latter now well known from the Danish excavations there conducted by H. Ingholt). The dissipating indulgence, 4-5, and spiritual unconcern, 6, of the carnal rich in Samaria would result in early captivity to Assyria, as happened to Calneh and Hamath. 'Beds inlaid with ivory' (cf. 3:12-15 note) speak of the prosperity of Israel.

8-14. Punishment is inevitable. The solemn certainty was emphasized by the Lord's oath sworn by Himself, 8 (cf. Gen 22:16-17). Pride and injustice could not go unpunished. Entrance of Hamath, 14 (cf. 1 Kgs 8:65; 2 Kgs 14:28), marked Israel's ideal N boundary, while

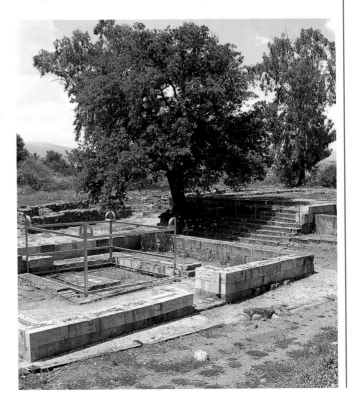

Site of the pagan shrine at Dan.

the 'valley of Arabah' probably the brook Zered (Wadi el-Hesa, which flows into the SE end of the Dead Sea), marked its extreme S border.

7. The locust plague, the drought and the plumb line

Amos presents five symbolic predictions of punishment, 7:1-9:10.

1-3. The locust plague. Impending judgment was prophesied by the Lord's 'preparing swarms of locusts after the king's share had been harvested and just as the second crop was coming up,' 1. So terrible was it, the Lord relented (cf. Joel 1-2).

4-6. The drought. This is evidently the meaning of this judgment by 'fire' (cf. Joel 1:19). Amos' plea for mercy stayed this plague also.

7-9. The plumb line. The Lord, however, declared the irrevocable sentence of destruction, after having measured His people with a plumb line (2 Kgs 21:13-15), and finding them so irremediably warped by sin as to be past correction.

10-17. Amos and Amaziah. Amos' bold prediction against the house of Jeroboam of the Jehu dynasty, 9, aroused the official priest of the royal sanctuary at Bethel to report Amos to the king. This weak religious conformist urged Amos to flee to Judah. Amos' reply showed his magnificent spiritual stature in that decadent syncretistic age, 16-17. There was one brave soul at least who would buck the tide of iniquity and easy conformity.

8. The fruit basket

1-3. The basket of ripe produce. The basket of perishable produce of the land symbolized the immediacy of Israel's end.

4-14. The reason for the end. Israel's terrible sin called forth scathing indictment. Crooked businessmen chafed at the sacred festal seasons and at the sabbath, because those days caused a lull in the dishonest money-making activities, 4-5, and their oppression of the poor, 6 (cf. Isa 1:13-17; Lev 19:35-36; Deut 25:13-16). The judgment detailed for 'Pride of Jacob,' 7, embraced mourning, 8-10, and famine of the word of the Lord, 11-14. Idolatry and pride put out the light God gave through His word.

Dan and Beersheba were pagan shrines in the farthest northern and southern limits of the land, 14. The patron deities of these idolatrous centers would be powerless to help in the coming calamity. 'The shame [*ashimah*] of Samaria,' 14, is rendered 'Ashimah of Samaria' in RSV, representing a deliberate Heb. distortion of the name of Asherah, the Canaanite mother goddess, to conform to the Heb. word for 'guilt' (*'asham*).

9:1-10. The Lord at the altar

1-6. The Lord at the altar. The Lord standing 'by' (rather than 'upon') the altar pronounced judgment. Properly symbolizing mercy because of judgment executed upon an interposed sacrifice, the altar, desecrated by idolatry and despised, became a place of poured-out judgment (Jn 12:31). This was the reason for the relentless pursuit of these sinners by the justice of God, 2-4. Because the Lord is the mighty God He is, 5-6, He must punish those who reject His mercy.

7-10. The Lord and sinful Israel. The Lord would destroy every sinful kingdom, Israel not excepted. His chosen nation had no special privilege in the moral sphere. The prophet tempered his teaching on election (3:2) with his doctrine of universalism (ch. 1-2). Caphtor, 7, was Crete. Kir was somewhere in Mesopotamia (Isa 22:6).

9:11-15. Future kingdom blessing

11-15. Messiah's return and reign. David's tent is the Davidic dynasty the Lord will raise up in the Person of the Christ returning in glory at His second advent to establish the kingdom over Israel (Acts 1:6). James quoted this great prophecy at the first church council (Acts 15:15-17). The Holy Spirit on that momentous occasion employed it to unfold the divine program for the future; that is, in this present age God is calling out a people for His name. After that the Lord will return and reestablish the Davidic dynasty in Christ, 11-12; and millennial prosperity, 13, will result in a restored Israel, 14-15.

The Provinces
of Assyria

in the time
of Tiglath-pileser III

SIDONIANS

MANSUATE

Damascus

DAMASCUS

Tyre

KARNAIM

DOR

Megiddo

GILEAD

HAURAN

ISRAEL

AMMON

Rabbath-bene-ammon

Jerusalem

PHILISTINES

JUDAH

MOAB

Gaza

EDOM

0   10   20   30

Scale in miles

OBADIAH

God's retributive justice

Nature of book. This is the shortest prophecy and the smallest book of the OT. Its author was Obadiah, whose name means 'the servant of the Lord.' The prophecy is wholly taken up with the condemnation of Edom for its treachery toward Judah, with a prophecy of its utter destruction and Judah's salvation in the Day of the Lord.

Date. Although numerous critics deny the unity of the prophecy, placing it in the Chaldean period after Jerusalem's fall in 586 B.C. or later, it is best to hold to the authenticity of the book and date it during the reign of Jehoram (c. 853-841 B.C.). At that time the Philistines and Arabians invaded Judah and plundered Jerusalem (2 Chr 21:16-17; Joel 3:3-6; Amos 1:6). The Edomites were also bitter enemies of Judah in that period (2 Kgs 8:20-22; 2 Chr 21:8-10). Thus, the requirements of Obadiah's having written this prophecy are satisfied in the historical context.

Obadiah and Amos. Amos (c. 760 B.C.) shows acquaintance with Obadiah (cf. 4 with Amos 9:2; vv. 9, 10, 18 with Amos 1:11-12; v. 14 with Amos 1:6, 9; v. 19 with Amos 9:14). Jeremiah apparently used this prophecy also (cf. Jer 49:7-22 with Ob 1-6). This gives additional support for an early date for the prophecy.

Outline

1-9 Edom's destruction foretold
10-14 Cause of Edom's fall
15-21 The Day of the Lord

Depiction of a Philistine priest, based on an ancient carving.

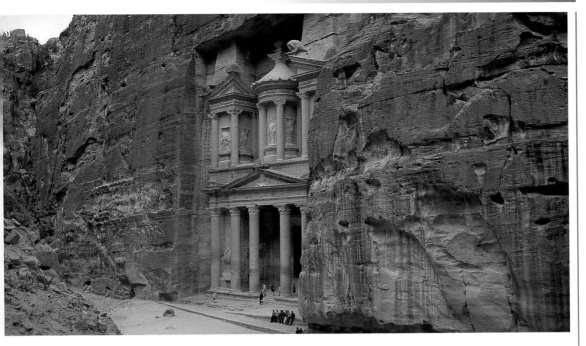

1-9. Edom's destruction foretold

1-4. Dislodged from her mountain fortress.
Obadiah ('servant of the Lord') is unknown, identifiable with none of the dozen or so men in the OT who bore the same name. Edom ('the red region') was Israel's neighbor on the SE, S of Moab and the Dead Sea. Its copper and iron rich territory extended S to the Gulf of Aqaba. Its entire boundary was dotted with a series of fortresses. North Edom ranges from 5,000 to 5,300 feet above sea level with one of its chief forts at Bozrah (modern Buseireh). Southern Edom with its mountains and plateaus rises from 5,300 to 5,700 feet above sea level, its chief fortress being Teman (Tawilan). Edom's pride, 3, was to be humbled. The expressions, 'the clefts of the rocks' (Sela, Gr. *Petra*), 3, and 'nest among the stars,' 4, admirably fit the country and the people.

5-9. Plundered and deserted completely.
Esau, 6 (Gen 25:30; 36:1), was the progenitor of the Edomites. Since he was Jacob's twin brother, there was close kinship between the Edomites and the Israelites (cf. 'brother Jacob,' 10). Esau's treasure was enormous wealth from iron and copper mines, and caravan trade, 6. Edom was famous for her wise men (Jer 49:7).

10-14. Cause of Edom's fall
'For the violence done to your brother Jacob,' 10 (RSV), describes Edom's failure to help his brother in distress. Edom became as culpable as those who attacked Jerusalem, 12; in fact, it did share in the attack, 13-14 (cf. Num 20:14-21; Ps 137:7; Ezk 35:5).

15-21. The Day of the Lord
In verse 15 the prophet links the future with the past in a prediction still unfulfilled, 'The Day of the Lord is near for all nations.' All nations will be judged as to their treatment of Israel, as Edom was (cf. Mt 25:31-46; Rev 16:13-16; with Joel 3:1-14). Jacob's deliverance and salvation, 17-20, are described (cf. Joel 2:32). The Negev, 19, the semi-desert region S of Judah. The inhabitants of the Judean foothills (Heb. 'falling off [region]' of 'Shephelah') shall inherit the Philistine plain, 19. Gilead was in Transjordan. 'Halah,' 20 (RSV), referring to 'the captivity of this host,' is in Mesopotamia (cf. 2 Kgs 17:6). Sepharad, 20, is uncertain; it may be Sardis in Asia Minor. Zarephath was a Phoenician town between Sidon and Tyre. Israelite 'deliverers' in the Kingdom Age shall administrate Edom. The Lord Himself in kingdom power shall rule over all (Ps 22:28; 103:19).

The rose-red city of Petra, ancient Sela, capital of Edom. Obadiah foretold Edom's destruction.

JONAH

Israel's mission to the nations

Jonah the man. Jonah ('dove') was the son of Amittai who came from Gath-hepher (Khirbet ez-Zurra') some three miles NE of Nazareth. A short distance to the N of this site is located the traditional tomb of Jonah at a village called Meshhed. Jonah's ministry shortly preceded that of Amos under Jeroboam II (782-753 B.C.) and predicted victory over the Syrians and the largest extension of Israelite border control (2 Kgs 14:25).

The book. The book is more than biographical history. It is *predictive typical history*, written by a prophet and possessing a prophetic motif. As such it prefigures Christ as the Sent One, suffering death, being buried, and after being raised, ministering salvation to the Gentiles (Mt 12:39-41, Lk 11:29-32).

Outline

1-2 Jonah's commission and disobedience
3-4 Jonah's renewed commission and its result

Contemporary illustration of a Phoenician warship.

1. Jonah's call and disobedience

1-3. The divine call and attempted escape. 'The great city of Nineveh' is aptly designated. At this period it was the capital of the Assyrian Empire at its height, and until its fall in 612 B.C. was the greatest city of the time. Its excavated ruins are marked primarily by two large mounds, Quyunjiq and Nebi Yunus (Prophet Jonah), enclosed by walls almost eight miles in circumference sprawling on the east bank of the Tigris across the river from modern Mosul. Nineveh's wickedness is amplified by Nahum (Nah 3).

Jonah's proposed flight to Tarshish, 3, in open rebellion against the Lord, 3-4, represents the most distant point the disobedient prophet could go. It was probably Tartessus in S. Spain near Gibraltar, a trading station visited by Tarshish or smelting fleets that traded in smelted copper. Joppa (modern Jaffa) was Palestine's ancient seaport 34 miles NW of Jerusalem, then the only harbor between Mt Carmel and Egypt.

4-7. The storm at sea. The Lord violently 'sent a great wind on the sea,' 4, to retrieve the recalcitrant prophet. The heathen sailors (Heb. 'salts'), 5, were well-seasoned mariners and rebuked the snoring Jonah, insensible of his peril, 6. Disobedience to God's word always brings spiritual torpor and frequently results in rebuke from the unsaved.

8-17. Jonah's witness and fate. In identifying himself he confessed his own sin, but even this furnished a witness to the pagan seamen. They realized the gulf between his creed and his conduct. The calmed sea evidently was a means of their conversion. Five 'greats'

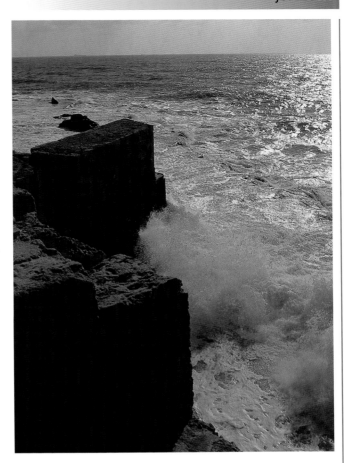

occur in the book: the *great* refusal, 3; the *great* fish, 17; a *great* city, 2; a *great* jealousy, 4:1; and a *great* God, 4:2b. Jonah, however, was not 'a *great* prophet.'

Turbulent sea off Acre, ancient Akko. The Jews feared the sea, and believed it to be inhabited by mythical monsters.

2. Jonah's prayer and deliverance

1-9. His prayer of thanksgiving. Remarkably this prayer is not petition of desperate entreaty but thankful praise for escape from physical death. His severe chastening to the point of physical death (cf. 1 Cor 5:5; 11:31-32; 1 Jn 5:16-17; Heb 12:4-11) resulted in renewed spiritual life. Jonah's praise is reminiscent of the Psalms. (Cf. 2:2 with Ps 120:1; 2:3 with Ps 42:7 ; 2:4 with Ps 31:22; 2:7 with Ps 143:4; 2:8 with Ps 31:6; 2:9 with Ps 3:8).

10. His deliverance. When he had learned his lesson, he was delivered to do God's will. The course of disobedience Jonah took proved to be the roughest distance between the two points involved in God's will.

Archaeological light

Critical scholarship has long denied Jonah's historicity, preferring to interpret the book as mythology, allegory, or midrash. Recent discoveries have added credence to the historicity of the book. Excavations have revealed that 'greater' Nineveh was a district 30-60 miles across, agreeing well with the text of Jonah. The details of the story also agree with the historical situation in Nineveh at that time (see note on 3:5-10).

Joppa (modern Jaffa) was Palestine's ancient seaport 34 miles NW of Jerusalem, then the only harbor between Mt Carmel and Egypt.

3. Jonah's renewed commission

1-4. Jonah's obedience. Verse 3 should read, 'Now Nineveh was an extremely large city requiring three days' travel.' That is, to go around the complex of suburbs that made up the great metropolis required three days (cf. notes on 1:2 and Gen 10:11-12). The long buried and forgotten city has amazed the archaeologist in its resurrection from dust since 1843. It was a complex of cities like modern New York, including Calah to the south, Resen between Calah and Nineveh proper, and Rehoboth-Ir (Rebit-Ninua) W of the capital. Other suburbs included Tarbisu and Dur-sharrukin. The latter swelled the size but was not yet built when Jonah preached to the Ninevites.

5-10. Nineveh repents. Under Adad-nirari III (810-782 B.C.) there was an approach to monotheism in the worship of the god Nabu (Nebo). Either in the closing years of this reign or early in that of Ashur-dan III (772-755 B.C.) Jonah appeared in Nineveh. Whether the total eclipse in 763 B.C., regarded as a divine portent, or the plagues of 765 and 759 B.C., recorded in Assyrian history, prepared the Ninevites for their repentance cannot be known. Sackcloth, 5, rough goat's hair worn over the naked body, was a garb of mourning. Nineveh was spared, 10 (cf. Amos 1-2).

4. Jonah's reaction to the revival

1-5. Jonah is angered. The pagan emperor of Assyria (3:7-9) sets a better example than the selfish, narrow-minded prophet.

6-11. The prophet rebuked. He must be shown that God loves all His creatures, not only sinful Ninevites but even dumb cattle.

MICAH

Personal and social righteousness

Micah the poet and Isaiah.
Micah's prophecy is a beautiful and moving example of classical Heb. poetry. Like his contemporary, Isaiah, Micah possessed great literary power. While Isaiah was a court poet, Micah was a rustic from an obscure village. Isaiah was a statesman; Micah, an evangelist and social reformer. Isaiah was a voice to kings; Micah, a herald for God to the common people. Isaiah addressed himself to political questions; Micah dealt almost entirely with personal religion and social morality.

Great emphases of Micah.
(1) Back to Bethlehem (5:2) back to David, back to Messiah, David's son and Lord. (2) Back to ethical righteousness (6:8), the practice of justice, kindness, compassion, mercy and humility. (3) Back to the coming Prince of Peace (4:3), the man who shall be 'their peace' (5:5), the world's only hope of permanent peace.

Outline

1-3 General prediction of judgment
4-5 The coming messianic Kingdom
6-7 The Lord's controversy with His people and final mercy

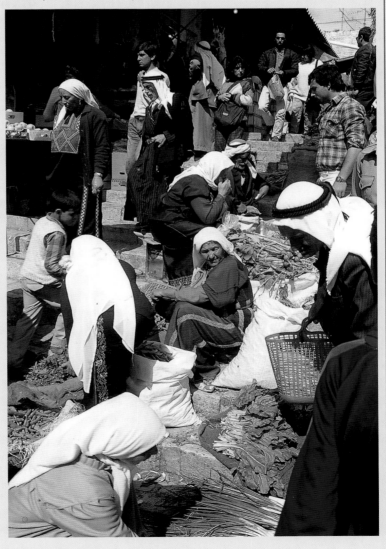

A busy scene in Bethlehem market. Micah takes the reader back to Bethlehem, back to David, and back to Messiah, David's son and Lord.

1. Judgment upon Samaria and Judah

Introduction. 1. The name Micah is apparently a shortened form of *Mîkayahû,* 'who is like the Lord' (cf. 7:18; Jer 26:18). He was a native of Moresheth, a small village, identified with Tell ej-Judeideh, about 20 miles SW of Jerusalem near Gath in N. Philistia (cf. 14 where it is called Moresheth Gath). Micah was contemporary with Isaiah (see Isa 1:1), prophesying in the days of Jotham (750-732 B.C.), Ahaz (735-716 B.C.), and Hezekiah (716-687 B.C.).

2-7. Judgment upon Samaria. The city of Samaria was founded by Omri (1 Kgs 16:24) about 857 B.C. So prosperous did this new city become it soon gave its name to the entire northern kingdom, of which it was the capital. This splendid city, whose brilliance has been revealed by archaeology, became a heap of rubble and her stones rolled down the hill of Shemer upon which it was built. This happened in 722 B.C., when Sargon of Assyria took the city. In his Khorsabad annals Sargon (722-705 B.C.) says, 'At the beginning of my rule in my first year of reign . . . Samerinai [the people of Samaria] . . . 27,290 . . . who lived therein, I carried away . . .'

8-16. Lamentation over Samaria and Judah. As a sign of the impending Assyrian invasion, Micah went naked, predicting the judgment of enemy invasion up to the very gates of Jerusalem, 8-9. In 701 B.C. Sennacherib's army took all the walled cities of Palestine and laid siege to Jerusalem itself. Micah, the poet, graphically predicted the terrors of the coming invasion by a series of lively puns, 10-14. Moffat freely translates this: 'Weep *tears* at *Tear*town [Bochim] grovel in the *dust* at *Dust*town [Bethophrah],' 10. '*Fare* forth stripped, O *Fair*town' (*Shaphir,* 'fair'). '*Stir*town [Zaanan] dare not stir,' 11. 'Harness your steed and away, O *Horse*town [Lachish] . . .' 13. 'Israel's kings are ever *balked* at Balktown [Achzib].'

2-3. Judgment upon various classes

2:1-11. The leaders of Samaria and Jerusalem mislead. They devised wickedness at night and performed it by day, 1-5. Seer and prophet preached lies, 6-11. Social and moral sins of the nation cried for judgment.

2:12-13. Mercy upon a remnant. The Lord would gather out His own.

3:1-12. Denunciation of various classes. The oppressors of the poor are indicated, 1-4. Their terrible greed is forcefully pictured by the figures of wild beasts tearing their victims, and a butcher cutting up meat for boiling. The mercenary prophets and seers, who peddled their solemn office to please sinners, were to be cut off from God, the true source of revelation, 5-7. Micah, by contrast, was filled with the Spirit and faithful in the deliverance of his message, 8. Mercenary priests were also upbraided and judgment was focused on Jerusalem, 9-12, fulfilled in the fall of the city in 586 B.C.

4. The establishment of Messiah's kingdom

1-5. Character of the kingdom. Ch. 4 and 5 present Israel's glorious future and the restoration of the Davidic kingdom. Verses 1-3 are duplicated by Isaiah (2:2-4). Both prophets received this message by divine inspiration, as they were contemporary. The mountain is Zion, 1, and the house is the millennial temple (Ezk 40-42). The prediction is that Jerusalem will be exalted in the kingdom to be the religious and governmental center of the earth, 2. The people are the nations which will 'stream' into Jerusalem spontaneously like a river, 1. The character of the restored Davidic kingdom, 3-4, its justice and peace, 3, and its security, 4, are presented. Verse 5 should read: 'For all the peoples walk [i.e., now are walking] each in the name of his god, but *we* will walk in the name of the Lord our God [i.e., free from idolatry] perpetually.' The verse predicates that Israel will be free from idolatry in the kingdom, but does not say or even imply that the nations will not be free also.

6-13. Establishment of the kingdom. Israel is to be regathered into the kingdom, 6-8 (Isa 11:11-16), the Babylonian Captivity, 9-10, intervening and typifying the final regathering. The manner of the setting up of the kingdom after the end-time assault of the nations upon Jerusalem is set forth, 11-13, eventuating in the battle of Armageddon. Jerusalem's victory, 11-13, is outlined as she threshes the sheaves (the hostile nations) gathered against her. 'The Lord of all the earth' is a kingdom appellative of

Christ when He returns as King of kings and Lord of lords (Rev. 19:16) to take possession of the earth, *His* by virtue of creation and redemption (cf. Gen 14:19, 22; Josh 3:11, 13; Zech 4:14; 6:5; Rev 11:4).

5. The first and second advents of Messiah

1. Prospect and retrospect. The future siege of Jerusalem by the end-time northern invader is in prospect in 1*a* (cf. Joel 1), connecting with the preceding context. The smitten ruler is spoken of in retrospect in 1*b* (cf. Mt 26:67; 27:30), presenting in the rejected Messiah the reason for Israel's long history of woe, culminating in the event prophesied in 1*a*. Smiting upon the cheek was the epitome of insult (1 Kgs 22:24; Job 16:10).

2. His first advent and rejection. Verse 2 tells who the 'smitten ruler' of 1 is. He is the Bethlehem-born preexistent, eternal One (cf. Isa 9:6-7). The Davidic family is significantly denoted as Ephrathites (Ruth 1:2; 1 Sam 17:12), that is, residents of Ephrath, a suburb of Bethlehem, which later became incorporated into the town. The double designation here not only connects Messiah with the Davidic line, but both Bethlehem ('house of bread') and Ephratah ('productivity') are reminiscent of the fertility of the region.

3. Interval between the advents. Verse 2 is parenthetical, 'therefore' of 3 connecting with the rejection of Israel's ruler, 1*b*. 'Therefore, Israel will be abandoned' refers to Israel's woes – because of her rejection of Messiah. 'She who is in labor' does not have reference to Israel as bringing forth the Messiah but to her last-day tribulation travail in bringing forth a believing remnant, here called 'the rest of his brothers,' as in Mt 25:31-46.

4-6. The second advent. The rejected One now becomes the Shepherd of Israel, standing and feeding in 'the strength of the Lord,' 4, for He is the Lord. Therefore 'they' (the saved remnant) shall dwell securely as He extends His kingdom sway over the redeemed earth. 'And he will be their peace,' 5 (cf. Isa 9:6-7; Zech 9:10), who made peace by the blood of His cross, and is our peace (Eph 2:14-15), as well as Israel's (Isa 9:7). The reference here is to the peace He has purchased and dispenses to His restored people Israel, the peace attained by

striking down the northern invader of the end-time, 6, the last-day Assyrian from 'the land of Nimrod' (Assyria, Gen 10:9-11).

7-15. The blessed remnant and the kingdom. The twofold character of the remnant is given as: (1) a spiritual witness and blessing, 7, and (2) an avenger of wrongs and destroyer of enemies, 8-9. Instruments of war shall be done away with, 10-11; and all demonic cults and idolatry, such as Asherim (pagan cult objects of Asherah, fertility goddess), shall be rooted out, 12-15.

6-7. Final controversy and mercy

6:1-7:6. The people's ingratitude and sin. The Lord's controversy was with His people, 6:1-8, because they had forgotten His mercies of old and the practice of common piety. The Lord must judge them, 6:9-16. Micah exposed their sin, 7:1-6.

7:7-20. Confession, petition and thanksgiving. This echoes the voice of the remnant in the endtime through the prophet who identified himself with Israel (cf. Dan 9:3-19). Those in Israel who kept faith, like himself, had an unquenchable trust in the Lord's faithfulness to restore the nation eventually in fulfillment of all His promises.

Israelite remains at Samaria. Sargon (722-705 B.C.) says, 'At the beginning of my rule in my first year of reign ... I carried away 27,290 people of Samaria.'

NAHUM

God's holiness vindicated in judgment

Nahum's theme. The prophet has one theme, judgment upon Nineveh, the capital of the mighty Assyrian Empire (see notes on Jon 3:14), and hence on Assyria, the 'giant among the Semites.' Its tyrannical cruelty scourged the ancient world periodically from 850 B.C. Nahum's ministry was exercised between the conquest of No-amon (Thebes) in Egypt (3:8) in 661 B.C. and Nineveh's fall in 612 B.C. The book is a classic of Heb. poetry, exceedingly fine and vivid in its descriptions. Critical attempts to deny part of the poem to Nahum have not been very successful.

Outline

1 A psalm of God's majesty
2-3 Prophecy of Nineveh's fall

An Assyrian siege-engine in action.

Assyrian relief showing the scene after battle. In 612 B.C. Nineveh collapsed, ending Assyrian hegemony.

1. God's majestic holiness

1. Superscription. Nahum ('consoler' or 'comforter') was a native of Elkosh (unknown). His prophecy of judgment upon wicked Nineveh and his indication of God's mercy to His own constitute him a 'consoler' to those who do good. A 'burden' is a prophecy full of weighty judgment.

2-11. Character of God in judgment. On one hand God is jealous, the source of His passion being in His love for His people, 2. Yet on the other hand He is also infinitely holy and must manifest His vengeance against those who wrong His people. He must punish the wicked, 3. His manifestation of His character in judgment is revealed, 4-6. The Lord is also good to those who trust in Him, 7, but severe in His dealings with His enemies, 8. Let none of His people vainly imagine He will not punish His enemies thoroughly, 9. The judgment of the Assyrian was assured, 10, from whom a wicked counsellor (cf. 2 Kgs 18:13-37) came, 11.

12-15. The fall of Nineveh announced. The Lord (through the prophet) announced Nineveh's coming doom, 12, 14, and deliverance for Israel, 12*b*, 13. Israel's glad proclamation of the good news of Nineveh's fall is a prefiguration of the fall of Israel's enemies in the last days and the joyous announcement of the final deliverance of Israel for kingdom blessing and worship, 15 (cf. Isa 52:7; Rom 10:15).

2. Siege and destruction of Nineveh

1-12. The overthrow of Nineveh predicted and described. In superb poetry Nahum dramatically portrays the city's siege. Under the combined attacks of the Medes of the north and the Chaldeans from southern Babylonia, Asshur, the ancient capital of the empire, fell in 614 B.C. In 612 B.C. Nineveh collapsed, ending Assyrian sway. Some scholars believe Nineveh's patron goddess Ishtar is referred to in 7.

13. The reason for Nineveh's destruction. The Lord was *against* her.

3. Nineveh an example of God's judgment

1-17. Her sins reap their harvest. Her violence, 1-3, her deceptions and false dealings with other nations are outlined, 17. The case of No-Amon (Thebes), the great Egyptian city, was a warning when it fell in 661 B.C., 8-10. Nineveh's fortifications and armaments would be useless, 11-13, her efforts to ward off disaster would come to nought, 14-17. She was doomed.

18-19. Lament over the king of Assyria. Dramatically he was addressed directly. His destruction was declared, 18, and the joy it would cause is outlined, 19. (See note on Jon 3:1-3.)

HABAKKUK

The just shall live by faith

The prophet and his message. Practically nothing is known of the prophet Habakkuk. It can be inferred, however, that he lived in the period of the rise of the neo-Babylonian empire (c. 625 B.C.), for the Chaldean invasion of Judah was threatening (1:5-6) and the iniquity of Judah was mounting. Habakkuk's theme centers in the theological question of how God's patience with evil can square with His holiness. The answer the prophet received is valid for all time. A sovereign God has the incontestable prerogative of dealing with the wicked in His own time and way. 'But the righteous will live by his faith' (2:4).

Literary beauty. Habakkuk, like Nahum and Isaiah, is couched in sublime poetry, reflecting the classical era of Heb. prophecy. The magnificent lyric ode of ch. 3 contains one of the greatest descriptions of the theophany in relation to the coming of the Lord which has been given by the Holy Spirit, awaiting fulfillment in the Day of the Lord (cf. 2 Thess 1:7-10).

Outline

1 Judah's judgment through the Chaldeans announced
2 Ultimate judgment upon the Chaldeans predicted
3 The prophet's vision of the coming king

Habbakuk says that he will climb up into his watch-tower and wait upon the Lord.

1. Judah's judgment by the Chaldeans

1-4. Problem: why the Lord had not judged Judah's sin. Habakkuk ('embrace') encounters the Lord and raises the question of the Lord's just government of the world. How can a holy God tolerate the sin of His own people Judah, 1-4?

5-11. The divine solution. The Chaldeans would judge Judah. According to Acts 13:37-41, verse 5 anticipates the redemptive work of Christ. The Chaldeans, or neo-Babylonians, ruled the ancient Near East 612-539 B.C., tyrannically administering a justice all their own and worshiping their own might (cf. 11, 'whose own strength is their god'). The Chaldeans were aggressive Semitic-Aramean nomads who gradually settled in southern Babylonia (Chaldea from Akkadian *Kaldu*). Nabopolassar (625-605 B.C.) was the founder of the Chaldean Empire, inherited by his son Nebuchadnezzar II (605-562 B.C.). Verse 10 accurately portrays the military practice of the Chaldeans in throwing up earthen ramparts to take fortresses.

12-17. Problem: why the wicked Chaldeans were used to punish Judah. How could the Lord employ people more wicked than His own sinning people as a rod of punishment? The question of God's holy character is discussed in the light of His silence in this matter, 12-13. The ruthless savagery of the Chaldean is pictured. Like a fisherman with rod and net, the Babylonian sat beside a pond which God had abundantly stocked with human fish, 14-15. Pulling up fish after fish, and eating to heart's content, he dumped out the surplus on the bank to die, 17. How long would this outrage of waste of human life go on and this brutality go unchecked by God's righteous intervention, 17?

2. The Lord's solution – judgment of the Chaldeans

1-5. A righteous remnant to be preserved. The prophet takes his stand to watch and stations himself on 'the ramparts,' waiting to see how God will answer his perplexities, 1. The Lord's answer: 'Write down the revelation and make it plain on tablets so that a herald may run with it,' i.e., as a messenger of the vision (cf. Zech 2:4-5). Those not upright in soul, 4, shall fall, 'but the righteous will live by his faith' (the godly remnant).

6-19. The Chaldeans themselves shall be punished. The five woes of this indictment fall upon the nation that plunders 'nations,' 6-8; obtains gain by violence, 9-11; 'builds a city with bloodshed,' 12-14; disgraces its neighbors, 15-17; and trusts in idols, 18-19. Noteworthy is the fact that in the midst of these woes the prophet catches a glimpse of the future Kingdom Age, 14, when all these evils will be eradicated (cf. Isa 11:9, which fixes the fulfillment of this prophecy when David's righteous Branch [Christ] has set up the kingdom). The transfiguration in Lk 9:26-29 was a preview of this happy event. 'The glory of the Lord,' 14, will be Christ revealed in kingly splendor (Mt 24:30; 25:31).

20. The sovereign Lord is ruling. This is part of the Lord's answer to the prophet. The Lord has not abandoned His holy temple (cf. Zeph 1:7 ; Zech 2:13), nor does His habitation cease to be holy. God's presence demands that the entire globe be silent before Him because His sovereign power and righteousness are operative in *all* the earth.

3. Vision of the Lord's coming and kingdom

1-2. The prophet's prayer. The prophet is thankful for the revelation of God's work and stands in awe of it. In anticipating the final consummation in the Day of the Lord, he pleads for mercy in the midst of wrath. 'Shigionoth,' 1, is unknown.

3-15. The coming of the Lord as judge and warrior (cf. Deut 33:2; Ps 18:8-19; 68:8; 77:17-20; Isa 63:1-6; Rev 6:1-19:16). Paran lay SE of Edom, and Mt. Paran is a prominent peak of the Sinai wilderness highlands, 3. Teman is in south central Edom near Sela (Petra), 3. Cushan, 7, is in Midian, S of Edom and E of the Gulf of Aqabah. 'Selah' is a pause for a musical interlude.

16-19. The effect of the theophany upon the prophet. His reaction and quiet trust reflect the attitude of the future godly remnant during the Great Tribulation, 16. He professes his deep faith in God, despite outward sufferings to be endured,17-19.

ZEPHANIAH

A warning of judgment

Date. Zephaniah, a contemporary of Jeremiah, exercised his ministry during the reign of Josiah (641-609 B.C.). He was doubtless instrumental in Josiah's revival (2 Kgs 22-23; 2 Chr 34-35), but the spiritual movement proved superficial considering the impending captivity (cf. Jer 2:11-13). Zephaniah had access to the royal court and had an influence on King Josiah's policies.

Outline

1:1-18 Judah's coming doom
2:1-3:8 Judgment upon surrounding nations
3:9-20 Israel in kingdom blessing

Jerusalem's Jaffa Gate. Zephaniah pronounces judgment upon Jerusalem for her disobedience, opposition to correction, unbelief, and godlessness.

1. Judah's doom and the Day of the Lord

1-3. Judgment of the whole earth. Zephaniah ('the Lord hides or protects') was perhaps a great grandson of Hezekiah. The scope of these verses embraces a worldwide judgment of the Day of the Lord (cf.1:17; 2:11, 14, 15).

4-13. Judgment of Judah and Jerusalem. The Lord will destroy Judah's ungodly religious syncretism. Molech, 5, was the chief Ammonite deity. The Assyrians adored 'the starry host.'

14-18. The Day of the Lord. The imminent invasion of the Chaldeans under Nebuchadnezzar is treated as a prefigurement of the apocalyptic Day of the Lord in which all earth judgments culminate (cf. Isa 2: 10-22; Joel 1-2; Rev 19:11-21).

2:1-3:8. The judgment of the nations

2:1-3. The call to repentance. The 'shameful nation,' i.e., apostate Israel, 1, is called upon to repent (cf. Jer 3:13). This section is a call to the Jewish remnant of the end-time just preceding the judgment of the nations. 'Be sheltered,' 3, is a play upon Zephaniah's name (see 1:1) and constitutes a promise to the faithful remnant.

4-7. Judgment upon the Philistines. The chief cities of Philistia in SW Palestine are named (cf. Joel 3:4-8). Kerethites, 5, were evidently Cretans living in Philistia (1 Sam 30:14; 2 Sam 8:18; Ezk 25:16). 'Canaan' (meaning traffic in red purple dye obtained from the shells of a murex mollusk of coastal Palestine) is the older name for Palestine. The later term Palestine is a Gr. corruption of the land of the Philistines (Gr. *Palaistine).*

8-10. Judgment upon Moab and Ammon. They shall be destroyed because they jeered at the Lord's people and boasted against the Lord (Isa 15-16; 25:10-12; Jer 48:1-49:6; Ezk 25:8-11; Amos 1:13-2:3).

11-15. Judgment upon other nations. The Cushites (Ethiopians) will be slain, and the proud Assyrians brought low. Nineveh's fall is predicted (cf. Nah 3; see note on Nineveh, Jon 3:1-3).

3:1-8. Judgment upon Jerusalem. Four charges are made against the city: disobedience, opposition to correction, unbelief, and godlessness. Threatened punishment is indicated by the Lord, 6-8.

3:9-20. Israel in kingdom blessing

9-13. Salvation and deliverance in the kingdom. The gift of a pure speech removes the curse of Babel (Gen 11:1-9) and anticipates the great outpouring of the Spirit (Joel 2:28-32), of which Pentecost (Acts 2:1-11) was the firstfruits. The redeemed remnant is graphically described, 12-13 (cf. Ezk 34:13-16; Zech 8:3, 16).

14-20. Praise in the kingdom. Israel's renown and praise of God fulfills the promise of the Abrahamic covenant (Gen 12:1-3).

HAGGAI

Call to complete the unfinished temple

Historical background.
Cyrus' decree (538 B.C.) permitted the Jews to return home and rebuild their temple at Jerusalem (Ezr 1:1-4). The monuments give clear evidence of this noble spirit of Cyrus. The remnant laid the foundation (Ezr 3:1-3, 8-10), but from c. 535 B.C. to 520 B.C. failed to go on to complete the edifice. Through Haggai's and Zechariah's combined ministry (520 B.C.), the temple was completed (520-515 B.C.). The circumstances of the construction of the temple gave rise to panoramic messianic predictions by the two prophets, especially Zechariah.

Outline

1:1-15 Call to rebuild the temple
2:1-19 Prophecy of the millennial temple
2:20-23 Prophecy of the destruction of Gentile world power

Model of Herod's Temple. Through Haggai's and Zechariah's ministry, the temple was completed. The construction of the temple gave rise to panoramic messianic predictions by both prophets, especially Zechariah.

I. Call to rebuild the temple

1-6. Call to face sinful neglect. The date was August-September, 520 B.C., the second year of Darius I the Great (522-486 B.C.), the monarch who is known through his famous Behistun Inscription. Haggai means 'festal.' Zerubbabel had succeeded Sheshbazzar as the governor under Persian overlordship (Ezr 1:8-11). Joshua ('the Lord is salvation') was the high priest (Ezr 2:2; 3:1-13). The rulers and the people at large were faced with their failure, 1-6.

7-11. Declaration of the Lord's judgment. Economic stress, drought, and unemployment (cf. Zech 8:9-13) were directly traceable to neglect in building the temple, 9.

12-15. The people's response. Rulers fell in line first, and then the people gladly responded, 12. Haggai gave a word of encouragement from the Lord, 13, and the people resumed construction on the twenty-fourth day of the same month Haggai began his ministry, 15 (cf. 1).

2:1-19. Prophecy of the millennial temple

1-9. The prediction of the temple. This, the second prophetic oracle, was delivered September-October, 520 B.C. Human disparagement of the modest plans for the second temple engendered pessimism and discouragement, 1-3. Haggai gave assurance of the divine presence and success of the venture, 4-5 (cf. Ex 29:45-46; Isa 43:1-7). The restoration temple, under construction at that time, furnished the background for the far-reaching prophecy of the kingdom temple, 7-9. The shaking of all nations refers to the end-time Tribulation, 7 (cf. Heb 12:26; Dan 12:1; Rev 16:18-20). The translation of the phrase, 'the desired of all nations,' 7, usually follows the Septuagint: 'The desirable things (*hilmudot*) of all nations shall come,' i.e., their costly treasures brought to beautify the millennial temple. But the Masoretic Heb. text has 'desire' (*hemdat*) feminine singular with a plural verb. Thus the text may be translated as 'the Desire of all nations will come,' construing the passage as messianic.

10-19. Promise of present blessing. This, Haggai's third discourse, is dated November-December, 520 B.C. By a ritual comparison, 10-14, the prophet demonstrated that the ruined and neglected temple, as an insult to God, had rendered all their worship and giving unclean. While one holy thing does not sanctify others, that which is unclean contagiously corrupts everything it touches. So it was with the people. Becoming clean would bring the Lord's favor and a solution to pressing economic problems among them, 15-19.

2:20-23. Destruction of Gentile world power

20-22. The shaking of the nations. This, the fourth and final sermon excerpt, is dated November-December, 520 B.C., and is still unfulfilled and prophetic. The shaking of heavens and the earth, 21, and the destruction of the kingdoms of the nations, refer to the future Tribulation, as does 2:7-9. This shaking will destroy the throne of kingdoms, so that the kingdom of Messiah may be set up. He is the 'stone' (Dan 2:44-45) that smites the image and destroys it.

23. The promised ruler. Zerubbabel, a son of David (Shealtiel was of the posterity of David, Mt 1:12; Lk 3:27), typifies Christ, the son of David. In that day Christ will receive His Davidic throne and be made a signet ring – a mark of honor, a badge of royal authority possessed by kings and conferred on their administrative agents.

ZECHARIAH

Israel, the nation God remembers

Nature of the prophecy.
This book is unique in its messianic
emphasis among the minor
prophets and in its unfolding of
events connected with the first and
second advents of Christ. It has
been called the most messianic, the
most truly apocalyptic and
eschatological of all the writings of
the OT.

**Important messianic
predictions.** These predictions
include: the Lord's Servant, the
Branch (3:8); the Man, the Branch
(6:12); the King-Priest (6:13); the
True Shepherd (11:4-11); the True

Shepherd vs. the false shepherd –
the Antichrist (11:15-17; 13:7); the
betrayal of the Good Shepherd
(11:12-13); His crucifixion (12:10);
His sufferings (13:7); His second
advent in glory (14:4).

Outline

Part one
1:1-6 Introduction
1:7-6:8 Eight night visions
6:9-15 Crowning the high priest
7:1-8:23 Question of facts

Part two
Oracle 1:
9:1-11 :17 Messiah's first advent
and rejection
Oracle 2:
12:1-14:21 Messiah's second
advent and acceptance

A shepherd leads his flock in the Jordan Valley. Zechariah predicts the coming of the True Shepherd and his betrayal.

1:1-17. Vision of the man among the myrtles

1. Preface. The time was October-November, 520 B.C., the second year of Darius I the Great (522-486 B.C.). Zechariah means 'whom the Lord remembers,' and appropriately this book is a testimony of that fact to the prophet and his (and the Lord's) people. He was the son of the priest Iddo (Ezr 5:1; 6:14; Neh 12:16).

2-6. The call to repentance. This is the spiritual keynote sounded so that the remnant of less than 50,000 might be spiritually prepared for the great visions given to them through the prophet. Zechariah enunciates divine wrath, 2, and also divine grace, 3, citing a warning from Heb. history, 4-6. 'The earlier prophets' had continually stressed repentance (Isa 1:16-20; 30:15; 55:6-9; Jer 3:12; Joel 2:12-13; Hos 7:10). Zechariah was imbued with knowledge of these prophets and their messages.

7-17. The man among the myrtle trees. This vision signifies hope for scattered and down-trodden Israel. The date of this and the other seven visions, all given the same night, was Shebat (Feb.) 24, 519 B.C. The red horse rider is the Lord in theophanic form, 8 (cf. 13), the color red speaking of Him who wrought redemption at His first advent and will come to judge and make war at His second advent (Rev 19:11). The patrol scouts are angelic agents who ascertain the condition of the earth 11-12 (cf. Hag 2:21-22). The myrtle trees symbolize Israel as the covenant people and the object of God's covenants and promises of restoration. The meaning of the vision, 9-12, is that the worldwide trouble which is to be a precursor to Israel's restoration is not in prospect (cf. Hag 2:21-22); but 'good and comforting words,' 13, are given through the prophet, assuring the people of God's great love for them, 14; His great indignation at the persecuting nations, 15; and the future final restoration in the kingdom, 16-17.

1:18-21. Vision of the four horns and four craftsmen

1:18-21. Israel triumphant over her foes. The prophet first sees four horns, 18-19. These represent hostile nations, i.e., the four great world powers of the times of the Gentiles (cf. Dan 2:37-45; 7:2-8, 17-28), namely, Babylon, Medo-Persia, Greece, and Rome (the latter to be revived at the end time, Dan 2:42-44; 7:7-8, 20; Rev 13:1).

The Lord then shows the prophet four craftsmen, 20-21. These artisans symbolize kingdoms which the Lord used to cast down the persecutors of His people Israel. Three of these craftsmen (Medo-Persia, Greece, and Rome) were horns, which *in turn* became craftsmen. The fourth craftsman is the kingdom set up by the returning King of kings and Lord of lords (Rev 19:16) who destroys the ten-kingdom confederation of the end time (Dan 2:44). Both the Babylonian (Jer 25:9; 27:6; 43:10) and Persian (Isa 44:28-45:1) as well as the Macedonian Greek power (Zech 9:34) were controlled by the Most High ruling in the kingdom of men. He used them first as a horn to chasten His people, and later as a craftsman to destroy the horn when its divine purpose had been accomplished.

2. Vision of the surveyor

1-3. The measuring line. This vision presents Jerusalem in millennial glory. The surveyor is probably the same divine Person as the red-horse rider of the first vision. His surveying activities intimate the growth and prosperity of Jerusalem, not only at that time, but ultimately to be fulfilled in the Kingdom Age, as 4-13 demonstrates.

4-13. Promises proceeding from the vision. Jerusalem is promised prosperous expansion, 4; divine protection and glory, 5; restoration, 6-7; vindication against her enemies, 8-9, in an earth prepared for full blessing, 10-13, when Palestine will be called 'the Holy Land.' Verse 13 is a grand synopsis of Rev 6-19.

3. Vision of Joshua's cleansing

This vision sets forth the restoration of Israel as a high-priestly nation.

1-3. Israel as defiled and condemned is pictured under the representative figure of Joshua, the high priest. As such she is accused as a criminal, 1-2, because she attempted to minister before the angel of the Lord (the Lord Himself), and because her sinful condition gave place to the devil (cf. Eph 4:27) who resisted her. Her 'filthy' (excrement-covered) garments represent her self-righteousness in not submitting to the righteousness of God (cf. Rom

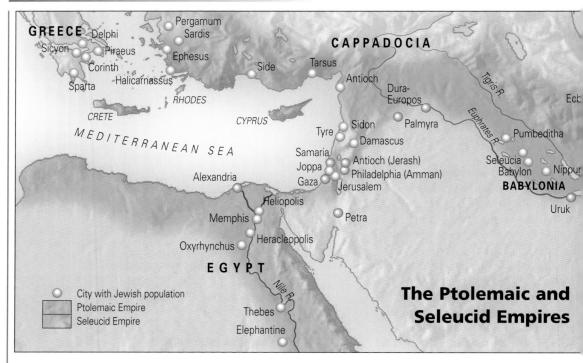

The Ptolemaic and Seleucid Empires

City with Jewish population
Ptolemaic Empire
Seleucid Empire

10:1-4). Satan, however, is reprimanded by the angel (the Lord) on the basis of God's sovereign electing grace, 2, despite Israel's sin, 3.

4-5. Israel as pardoned and repositioned. This portrays the conversion of the nation at Messiah's second advent. First comes the negative aspect of salvation, 4, the forgiveness of sin (cf. Rom 3:25; Eph 1:7). Then the positive bestowal of divine righteousness and reinstatement into full priestly function are given, 4-5 (cf. Ex 19:5-7; Rom 1:16-17; 3:22, 26; Zech 12:10-13:1). Ex. 28 shows how the high priest was clothed when he ministered.

6-7. Covenant of priesthood renewed with Joshua.

8-10. Prediction of restored Israel under the figure of Messiah, the Branch. Joshua and his colleagues were 'symbolic', i.e., men who personally signified future events for Israel, 8. 'My servant, the Branch' portrays Christ in the redemptive aspects of His first advent, 8 (cf. Isa 53:1-10; Phil 2:6-8), the basis of Israel's cleansing and restoration at His second advent. The omniscient 'stone,' a precious carved gem, portrays the Messiah in His glorious second advent when Israel will be converted, 12:10. The vision ends in full kingdom blessing, 10 (cf. Mic 4:4 with 1 Kgs 4:24-25).

4. Vision of the golden lampstand

This vision portrays Israel as the light of the world under Messiah King-Priest.

1-5. The symbolism of the vision. The prophet prepared, 1, is presented with the vision, 2-3. The lampstand of pure gold (Ex 25:31-40) typifies Christ our Light (Jn 8:12; Mt 5:14). He is manifested in His deity (pure gold) in the plenitude of the power of the sevenfold Spirit (Heb 1:9; Rev 1:4), prefigured by the seven lights (fullness of testimony). Israel was the *one* nation so chosen by God to be a witness to the one true God. The seven-branched lampstand *in the midst* of her therefore symbolizes the realization of Israel's divine vocation to be a witness and a testimony of God's salvation in Christ to the unbelieving pagan nations around her. Thus Israel is prefigured in full fellowship with God as she was meant to be, and as she will actually be in her millennial restoration.

6-10. The purpose of the vision. The prophet's inquiry, 4-5, elicits the angel's reply concerning the purpose, 6-10. The temple was to be completed by divine power, 6, with every obstacle removed, 7. Zerubbabel was to accomplish this, 7, 9. The word of God would be fulfilled, 9; critics would be silenced, 10; well-wishers would rejoice, 10; and God would be magnified, 10.

PARTHIA

BACTRIA

GEDROSIA

11-14. The prophet favored with a full explanation. The prophet's double question, 11-12, brings the angel's definite answer, 13-14. The two olive trees portray the civil (kingly) and priestly office. The two olive branches represent the present incumbents, Zerubbabel and Joshua. The two golden pipes symbolize these two offices united in Christ as King-Priest. The gold (oil) is the exquisite operation of the Holy Spirit through the medium of the King-Priest to the restored nation as lightbearer. 'The Lord of all the earth' (Josh 3:11, 13; Mic 4:13; Zech 6:5; Rev 11:3-4) is Messiah's kingdom appellative when He returns as King of kings and Lord of lords (Rev. 19:16). He will destroy His enemies and assume absolute ownership and control of the earth, now potentially His by virtue of creation and redemption (Eph 1:13-14). Regeneration, ch.3, is followed by witness, ch.4.

The Post-exilic Period

Palestine	Greece	Persian Empire
		549 Cyrus the Great united Persia and Media
538 Edict of Cyrus		
536 Jews return		546 Lydia conquered
536-34 Altar laid Economic and spiritual poverty		539 Crown Prince Belshazzar ruled Babylon
520 **Haggai Zechariah**		530-22 Cambyses
535-15 Temple rebuilt		525 Egypt conquered
	490 Greek ascendancy Defeated Persians under Darius I	522-486 Darius I
		490 Defeated by Greeks at Marathon
	485-25 Herodotus, Father of History	486-65 Xerxes I (Ahasuerus) Esther's husband
480 Zechariah's later ministry (Zech 9-14)	480 Defeated Persians under Xerxes I	480 Defeated by Greeks at Thermopylae and Salamis
458 Ezra's return	470-399 Socrates	465-24 Artaxerxes I
445 Nehemiah rebuilt walls	460-29 Golden Age of Pericles	424-23 Xerxes II
435 **Malachi**	428-348 Plato	423-04 Darius II
	384-22 Aristotle	404-358 Artaxerxes II
		358-38 Artaxerxes III
	336-23 Rise of Alexander	338-36 Arses
		336-31 Darius III
Dates (B.C.)		336-23 Kingdom fell to Alexander

5. Visions of the flying scroll and the measuring basket

1-4. The flying scroll. The sixth vision, 1-2, portrays a flying roll or scroll 30 feet long and 15 feet wide, illustrating the rod-of-iron rule of the kingdom. The meaning of the vision, 3-4, is that the scroll symbolizes the curse of God against sinners. The scroll involves both tables of the law and can only curse (Deut 27-28; Gal 3:10-14). The flying motion denotes the worldwide extent of the curse, 3, and the subjects mentioned are representative of all sinners, 3. Enforcement of the curse portrays Messiah's iron rule at His second advent and in His subsequent reign (Ps 2:9; Rev 2:27; 12:5; 19:15).

5-11. The measuring basket. This seventh vision portrays the removal of commercial and ecclesiastical wickedness from the earth. The ephah (Heb.), 6, is a Heb. dry measure (.67 bushels) and speaks of commerce, godless business, and inordinate gain. It is symbolic of commercial Babylon (Rev 18). The ephah (commerce; cf. Jas 5:1-3) is associated with a talent (also a commercial figure) of lead (heavy metal), 7. The woman introduced as sitting contentedly in the basket, 7, is personified wickedness (cf. Mt 13:33; Rev 2:20; 17:3-7). The woman symbolizes ecclesiastical Babylon (the religious aspects of the Satanic world system), i.e., religionism settled down in and nurtured by ungodly commercialism (cf. the harlot of Rev 17, which represents her in a more developed stage of iniquity). The reason the woman suddenly desires to get out of the ephah is because she wishes to escape its fate, 10-11, but her complicity in evil commercialism (the talent of lead) imprisons her and her sin becomes her undoing (cf. Prov 5:22). Shinar, 11, is Babylonia (Gen 10:10; 11:1-9; Dan 1:2).

6:1-8. Vision of the four chariots

This vision presents the judgment of the nations preparatory to Messiah's reign. The findings of the scouts in vision one are now executed.

1-3. The vision presented. The 'two mountains' (Olivet and Zion) are 'mountains of bronze' (i.e., mountains from which divine judgment issues), since bronze is typical of manifested divine judgment. (Cf. the bronze

altar, Ex 27:2; Jn 12:31-33; Jn 3:14 with Num 21:9.) The four chariots are pictured with their horses, 2-3. The *red* horses portray war and bloodshed (Rev 6:4); the *black* horses, famine and starvation (Rev 6:5-6); the *white* horses, victory and conquest (Rev 6:2); the *dappled* horses ('hail-spotted' and 'strong' horses) portray death (Rev 6:8).

4-8. The vision explained. Attention focuses on the horsed *chariots,* not the horses. The interpretive key is given in 5. These horsed chariots represent 'the four spirits' (angelic ministers, not 'winds'; cf. Dan 7:10; 1 Kgs 22:19; Ps 103:20-21; 104:4; Heb 1:7; Lk 1:19) who are the celestial agents executing judgment against the nations. The *horses* portray the judgments: the chariots, the *angelic* executors administering these judgments (as in Rev 8:2, 7-8, 10, 12; 9:1, 13; 11:15; 15:1; 16:1-3) to dispossess wicked earth squatters for possession by 'the Lord of the whole earth,' 5 (see comments on Zech 4:14). The message concludes with a note of hope for the prophet's own day, 8. The word 'spirit' (KJV) in 8 has the specialized meaning of anger (NAS, cf. Jud 8:3; Isa 33:11; Eccl 10:4).

6:9-15. Crowning the high priest

The eight visions have ended. Now follows an actual historical event – Joshua's coronation – for which the eight visions were preparatory. This symbolic occurrence constituted the summation and climax of these visions.

9-11. The historical event and the prophetic symbolism. The arrival of the deputies from Babylon with gifts for the temple constituted an event with symbolic and prophetic significance. Zechariah, prepared by the visions, was instructed to receive as a gift for the temple the gold and silver brought by the returned exiles, namely, Heldai ('[the Lord's] world'), Tobijah ('the Lord is good'), Jedaiah ('the Lord knows'), at Josiah's ('the Lord supports') house. In 14 Josiah is nicknamed 'Hen' ('graciousness'), perhaps because of his hospitality. Zechariah was enjoined to make a 'crown' (singular, the preferred reading rather than 'crowns' plural). The singular significance of the whole episode was that the crown was to be placed upon the head of the high priest Joshua, *not* Zerubbabel, despite the rigid separation of the priestly and kingly offices in Israel (cf. 2 Chr 26:16-21). The reason was that all eight night visions pointed to the kingdom restored to Israel under Messiah King-Priest (Heb 7:1-3; Ps 110:4).

12-13, 15. Messianic import of the prophetic symbolism. Messiah the Branch (see notes on 3:8) will appear as Joshua's antitype, 12a (cf. Jn 19:5; cf.Isa 53:2; Jer 33:15; Ps 2:6). This is Messiah in His humanity. Messiah the Branch shall build the millennial temple, 12-13 (Ezk 40-42; cf. Isa 2:2-4; Mic 4:1-2). He Himself (and no other) shall bear the glory (*hod*), which is used almost exclusively of the divine splendor, Ps 8:1; Isa 45:3; Ps 148:13; Hab 3:3; Rev 19:16). He will be a King-Priest, the Son of Man, the 'last Adam,' the second Man (1 Cor 15:45-47), with regained dominion over the earth lost by the first Adam. Messiah will combine in one Person the two offices in perfect harmony, 13, binding together in unity both Jew and Gentile, 15, vindicating the word of God and demanding unflinching obedience, 15.

14. Provision for a permanent memorial. The crown, as a prophetic symbolism, is to be kept as a memorial.

7. The question of the fasts

1-3. The question raised. The date is Chislev (Dec), 518 B.C. (cf. 1:1). The city of Bethel, 12 miles N of Jerusalem, sent a delegation to Jerusalem 'to entreat the Lord,' 2, and to inquire concerning observing certain fasts (cf. Lev 23:27; Joel 1:13-14). The question betrayed an attitude of ritualism rather than of spiritual reality. The fast of the fifth month

The prophet is presented with the vision of a lampstand of pure gold, typifying Christ our Light, manifested in His deity (pure gold), in the power of the sevenfold Spirit, prefigured by the seven lights.

The Mount of Olives, viewed from the city walls of Jerusalem. 'Two mountains' (this one and Zion) are 'mountains of bronze' – mountains from which divine judgment issues.

mourned the destruction of Jerusalem (2 Kgs 25:8-9; Jer 25:13; cf. Zech 8:19); that of the seventh month marked the murder of Gedaliah (Jer 41:1-2); the fourth month (Tammuz) recalled the breaching of Jerusalem's walls (2 Kgs 25:3; Jer 39:2-4); the tenth month (Tebeth) marked the beginning of the siege (2 Kgs 25:1).

4-7. The motive of selfishness exposed. The prophet rebuked meaningless ritualism, 4-6 (cf. Isa 1:10-15), and urged obedience to the word of God, 7, spoken by 'the earlier prophets,' Isaiah and Jeremiah in particular, but also including Joel, Amos, Hosea, Micah.

8-14. Call to repentance proclaimed. The divine command was to put the word of the Lord into practice, 8-10, and to take warning of the refusal of the pre-Exilic nation to obey that word, 11-12, with the dire results that followed, 13-14.

8. When the fasts become joyful feasts

1-8. Present partial restoration harbinger of an eventual full restoration of Israel. This full restoration is guaranteed by God's word and God's electing love, 1-2, the latter truth vehemently declared. The results of this future restoration will be: (1) *the Lord's return,* 3 (cf. 1:16; Hos 5:15; 6:3; Mt 23:39); (2) *the permanent divine presence,* 3 (cf. Ezk 11:22-25; 43:2-5); (3) *the exaltation of Jerusalem,* 3 (cf. Isa 1:26; 60:14; 62:12); (4) *her increase in size and security,* 4-5; (5) *the manifestation of God's power,* 6. In 7-8 the promise of future regathering and restoration, 1-6, is repeated.

9-17. Encouragement amid the hardships of the present partial restoration. Added to the subjects of encouragement, 9, are listed the reasons for their discouragement, 10, with details given for their hope, 11-15, and the practical use they were to make of it, 16-17.

18-23. Prediction of full millennial restoration. Fasts will one day give way to feasts, 18-19. The nations of the kingdom will eagerly seek the Lord, 20-22. The Jew will enjoy special divine favor, 23. Such an emphatic assertion of the reinstatement of the Lord's covenant nation summarizes and effectively climaxes the scope of the eight night visions

(1:7-6:8) and that of the symbolic crowning of the high priest (6:9-15), as well as giving a satisfactory answer to the question of the fasts in ch. 7-8.

9:1-10:1. Human world ruler vs. divine prince of peace

9: 1-8. Sudden rise of Alexander the Great. The oracle is here cast as an admonition or threat. The land of Hadrach, 1, is the region of Hatarika mentioned in the Assyrian annals. It is an Aramean country against which Assyria campaigned in the 8th cen. B.C. The well-attested city and region were in the hinterland of Phoenicia beyond the Antilebanon Mountains in the vicinity of Hamath on the Orontes and Damascus about 100 miles to the S. Tyre (the leader) and Sidon, 20 miles N on the coast about the same latitude as Damascus, were the prominent Phoenician cities taken in the whirlwind conquests of Alexander (333 B.C.), 2-3. Tyre's siege and fall to the conqueror are graphically predicted, 3-4, and dramatically fulfilled in Alexander's conquest of the insular city (located on an island) after an eight-month siege. Prophecy against the Philistine strongholds 5-7 , in SW Palestine indicates the conqueror's victorious sweep in Egypt. Of the Pentapolis, only Gath is omitted. The fate of Gaza is fully recorded in Alexander's annals after its five-month siege. Like Tyre, it dared to resist because of its strength, but suffered a violent destruction. Verse 8 is a prophecy, wonderfully fulfilled, of Jerusalem's escape from Alexander's destruction, 8a (cf. Josephus *Antiq* XI. 8.3). At the same time it is a harbinger of a complete future deliverance under Messiah at His second advent, 8b.

9:9. First advent of Israel's humble king and saviour. The joyful announcement of His coming, 9a, is followed by a featured account of His character and condition, 9b. He is to be righteous, showing Himself a saviour; and 'lowly,' shown by His riding a humble beast which no king at that period would ever ride.

9:10-10:1. Second advent of Israel's glorious king. He establishes peace, 9:10. Suffering Israel is encouraged in the light of the nation's future hope, 11-12. The Maccabean conflict with godless paganism (175-130 B.C.) was an illustration of Israel's final conflict, 13-15, with the nation's end-time deliverance and blessing predicted, 9:16-10:1.

10:2-12. Divine prince of peace and deliverer

2-4. The second advent and the cure of the nation's deception. The types of Israel's deception are outlined, 2, 5. The dire result of that deception is that the people have strayed like sheep, being severely afflicted, 2. However, the nation's oppressors will be punished and eventual national restoration and victory over enemies are assured, 3. The cure of the nation's deception, 4, is in Messiah's coming as (1) Cornerstone (Isa 28:15-16); (2) Tent Peg (Isa 22:15-25); (3) Battle Bow (cf. Ps 45:5; Rev 19:11).

5-12. The second advent and the nation's triumph over its foes. The Lord promises His presence with His people, the remnant, 5, and guarantees their empowering and repatriation, 6-7. He will gather Israel out of her present worldwide dispersion, 8-9, unto her own land, 10; remove every impediment, 11, and effect Israel's complete renovation, 12.

11. Israel's rejection of the good shepherd

1-3. Impending devastation of the land. This destruction due to the predicted rejection of Messiah at His first advent begins in the Lebanon region in the north, 1-2, and sweeps on into Bashan in Transjordan, noted for its splendid forests of oak (Isa 2:13). The devastation proceeds from the plateau of Bashan to the plain and on into the lower Jordan Valley, 3, whose pride is a luxuriant growth of tamarisks, willows, grasses, and cane; a favorite haunt of lions in antiquity (2 Kgs 17:25; Jer 49:19; 50:44).

4-14. Prediction of the rejection of the good shepherd. This is accomplished by the prophet's commission to perform an actual prophetic symbolic act before his contemporaries, 4. It would portray the ruin of 'the flock marked for slaughter,' because of their scurrilous treatment of him as representing their future treatment of Messiah Himself, 4-6. The two rods 'Favor' and 'Union' symbolize the Lord's final efforts to reclaim apostate Christ-rejecting Israel, 7-8. The breaking of these rods symbolizes the cessation of the Lord's gracious and patient dealing with the nation, and the loss of internal brotherhood and unity after the betrayal and rejection of the Lord, 9-10. This prediction marvelously envisioned the pitiable state of internal dissension and hatred which characterized the Jews from the crucifixion to the fall of Jerusalem in A.D. 70. 'Thirty pieces of

Shepherd near Bethlehem. Zechariah 11 tells of two shepherds.

The Mount of Olives at dusk. Messiah's personal advent will be on the Mount of Olives and result in a gigantic earthquake, effecting topographical changes.

silver,' 12, was the price of a common slave (cf. Ex 21:32; Mt 27:3-10). In fulfillment of this prophecy and a related prophecy by Jeremiah (Jer 18:1-4; 19:1-3), the chief priest purchased the Potter's Field with money that Judas was to receive for betraying Christ.

15-17. Prediction of the acceptance of the bad shepherd. Zechariah's commission to enact a second symbolic act, 15, looks forward to Israel's acceptance of the Antichrist, whose wicked character is outlined, 16, and whose doom is indicated, 17. The rejection of the good shepherd is connected with the first advent, as the acceptance of the evil shepherd is with the second advent an 5:43; Rev 19:20; 20:10).

12. Israel's deliverance and national conversion

1-9. Future siege of Jerusalem. The authentication of the second prophetic oracle (ch. 12-14) is given, 1. The nations attack Jerusalem, 2-3, and are confounded, 4. This is 'on that day,' i.e., the Day of the Lord, denoting that future period when the Lord will openly and publicly manifest His power in delivering Israel from her enemies and establishing her in peace and prosperity. Judah's signal faith in the Lord, 5, and His response to that faith, 6-7, result in

her triumph, 8, and the doom of her enemies, 9.

10-14. Vision of the crucified Messiah and the result. The appearance of the Pierced One (cf. Rev 19:13) will produce a great outpouring of the Spirit, 10 (cf. Joel 2:28-32; Ezk 39:29), and a sweeping national conversion, 11-14, that thoroughly purges out idolatry and sin, 13:1-5. Peter's quotation in Acts 2:16-21 was an illustration of the Spirit's effusion which is here fulfilled.

7. Provision for Israel's national conversion. This is Messiah, who was introduced with such dramatic abruptness in 6. He is now described by the Lord (the Father) in His *death*, 7a, and in His *deity, 7b,* 'the man who is close to me,' i.e., 'the man *My equal,* a human being closely conjoined or united to Me.' Here appears the divine-human person of our Lord in the OT – deity united to humanity in one unique Person.

13. Israel's national cleansing

1-6. Prophecy of Israel's national cleansing. The prophecy was fulfilled in the fountain of cleansing, 1, opened at Calvary for sin and uncleanness (cf. Rom 10:3). The prophecy of Israel's national cleansing is illustrated in the extermination of idolatry and its concomitant false prophecy, 2-5 (cf. Deut

18:20-22; Jer 14:14-15). In 6 the Cleanser from idolatry (Christ) is revealed, resuming the subject broached in 12:10 after the parenthesis of 12:11-13:5.

7-9. Prelude to Israel's national conversion. The sheep are to be scattered, and the faithful warned of persecution and death, 7, with the predicted Great Tribulation eventuating in the deliverance of a remnant, 8-9.

9. The appropriation of the provisions for cleansing. The remnant calls on the Lord, is delivered, and testifies to salvation, 9.

14. Messiah's second advent in glory

1-3. Last enemy siege against Jerusalem. The time is the Day of the Lord, 1 (see note on 12:1-9). The enemy apparently is triumphant, 2, and the imminent destruction of the city and the remnant threatened. But the Lord intervenes in deliverance, 3.

4-7. Personal advent of Messiah. The *place* is the Mount of Olives; the *result,* a gigantic earthquake, effecting topographical changes, 4. The *purpose* is to deliver His people and destroy their foes, 5. The *manner* is with His saints, 5 (Acts 3:21; 1 Thess 3:13; Jude 14; 1 Jn 3:2), including both angels and glorified men. The *time* is the second advent, 6-7.

8-21. Messianic kingdom established over Israel. The temporal and spiritual blessing of the kingdom, 8, and the absolute lordship of the King, 9, center in Jerusalem as the capital of the millennial earth, 10-11. Retrospectively the destruction of Israel's enemies is described, 12-15 (cf. Ezk 38-39). Millennial worship and government, with Jerusalem as the religious and political capital of the earth, 16-19, are predicted. The prophecy closes with Israel's holiness as a high-priestly nation (cf. ch. 3-4) set forth, 20-21.

MALACHI

The Lord's love for His sinning people

Opposite: The Golden Gate, Jerusalem, by tradition the entrance for the returning Messiah at the Last Judgment.

Name of the prophet and date.

The title of the book is often considered to be a title, 'my messenger' (cf. 3:1), rather than a personal name. It is more likely, however, that Malachi is the name of the prophet, considering that all other OT books are so named. Malachi is later than Haggai and Zechariah. The temple had long ago been completed and the priesthood and worship had been in operation for a number of years. The question is, how long? Evidently some time after Ezra's and Nehemiah's correction of current abuses, for decline had set in again. A date about 433-425 B.C. is perhaps not far afield.

Message of Malachi.

The last prophetic voice of the OT rings out over the years intervening till the coming of the forerunner, John the Baptist, and the King at His first advent. But Malachi's prophetic emphasis is on the Day of the Lord with its judgment of the wicked and the deliverance of a righteous remnant. These vast themes connect Malachi with the great stream of Heb. prophecy. His immediate message deals with the sins of the priests and the people of his day. These sins form the background for his prophecies of judgment certain to fall in the future.

Outline

1:1-5 Preamble: the Lord's love for Israel
1:6-2:9 Oracle against the priests
2:10-4:3 Oracles against Jewish laymen
4:4-6 Concluding warning

Below: The Jordan leaves the Sea of Galilee near Kinneret. Malachi, the last prophetic voice of the Old Testament, rings out over the years till the coming of Messiah's forerunner, John the Baptist.

1:1-5. The Lord's love for Israel

1-2. Declaration of that love. The message to Israel, God's ancient chosen nation, is 'I have loved you,' 2 (cf. Deut 10:15; 33:3; Hos 2:18-20; Amos 3:2). The record of this love is inscribed on every page of the OT. Their brazen questioning of this love, 2, shows their apostasy and ingratitude in the face of their deliverance from Egypt, restoration from Babylon, and many other tokens of divine care.

3-5. Contrast to Esau (Edomites). The descendants of Esau, Jacob's twin brother, had fully merited the divine hatred, while Jacob's posterity, on the other hand, had *not* fully merited the divine love. It was a gracious electing love in one case, but not an ungracious electing hate in the other, since it is not said in the book of Genesis, where Esau's career is described, 'Esau I have hated.' Only in the book of Malachi is the declaration made and then only after Edom's wicked character had been fully manifested (cf. Rom 9:13).

1:6-2:16. Oracle against the priests and people

1:6-14. The impenitence of the priests. The Lord as a father and a master rightly expected honor and obedience, 6. Yet the priests despised Him and denied their sin, 6, brazenly offering polluted food and blind or lame animals, 7-8, which were unacceptable for sacrifice (Lev 22:17-25; Deut 15:21); an insult to man, much more to God, 9. They were lazy and mercenary, 10-13. Verse 11 will yet be fulfilled, as it would have been if Israel had been true to her God in OT times. The conduct of the priests was utterly reprehensible in the light of who the Lord is and His reputation among the nations, 14.

2:1-9. Their impenitence to be punished. If they would not repent, 1, their blessings would be cursed, 2 (Deut 27:26; 28:15). The curse is spelled out, 3. The command to repent, 1, was to protect the covenant with Levi, 4-5 (cf.Num 25:12-13) and to restore the historical Levitical character of the priesthood with faithfulness of speech, uprightness of walk, and usefulness of service, 6-7. Repentance would preserve the true Levitical ideal of knowledge and authority, and expose their present shameful conduct, 8-9.

2:10-16. First oracle against the

people involved their treachery against men, 10, and God, 11. They would be chastened, 12. The results of this treachery were seen in divorce, infidelity, and violence, 13-16.

2:17-4:6. Prophecy of Messiah's advent

2:17. The occasion of the prophecy. This is the second oracle against the people, 2:17-3:6. The occasion of the prophecy was the prophet's rebuke of the people's insincere religious profession and unbelief, particularly their unbelief in divine judgment, 2:17.

3:1-6. The prophecy itself. 'My messenger' is a prediction of the forerunner of the Messiah, John the Baptist (cf. Mt 11:10). 'The Lord you are seeking,' 'the messenger of the covenant,' is Messiah envisioned particularly in His second advent in judgment, 2-5, in

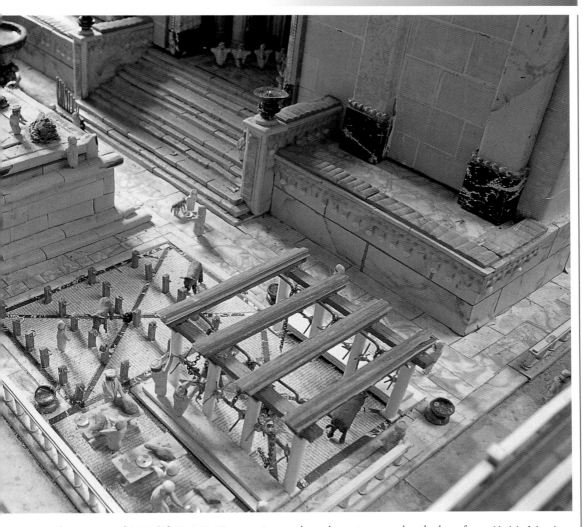

answer to the question of 2:17. (Cf. Mt 3:10-12; Isa 4:4; Mal 4:1; Rev 6:17.)

3:7-12. The people's sin of robbing God. This is the third oracle against the people, upbraiding them for withholding the Lord's tithe (cf. Neh 13:10, 12; Lev 27:30-32; Num 18:21, 24).

3:13-4:3. The people's sin of criticizing the Lord. This is the fourth oracle against the people. The charge is that they had said it doesn't pay to serve God; wickedness is the way to prosperity, 3:14-15. The answer to this calumny draws from the prophet the prediction of the godly remnant and its reward, 16-18, and the judgment to come in the Day of the Lord, 4:1. This will culminate in the second advent of Christ, 4:2-3, when the wicked will be punished.

4:4-6. Concluding warning. The wicked priests and people are to remember the law of Moses, 4, and to expect the coming judgments of the great and dreadful Day of the Lord as a punishment of sinners, 5. Elijah (cf. Mt 17:11; Rev 11:3-6) is promised to appear before that time and call out a righteous remnant from the apostate mass. Thus Malachi, in remonstrating with the priests and people of his day concerning their sins, has a message for us in our day when similar sins prevail. His messianic flashes (3:16; 4:2) prepare us for the NT revelation and focus our attention on Him who alone is the world's hope.

Model of the altar of the Temple. Malachi warns the wicked priests to remember the law of Moses, and to expect the coming judgments of the great Day of the Lord.

Bible Weights and Measures

finger

handbreadth

cubit

3 handbreadth =

span

fathom

cubit

furlong/stadion

Ezekiel's cubit

Measures of length OT

Finger	0.72 in.
Handbreadth = 4 *fingers*	2.91 in.
Span = *3 handbreadths*	8.74 in.
Cubit = *2 spans*	17.49 in.
Ezekiel's cubit = *7 handbreadths*	20.37 in.

Measures of length NT

Cubit *pechus*	about 1.5 ft.
Fathom *orguia*	about 72.4 in.
Furlong *stadion*	about 606 ft.
Mile *milion*	about 4,879 ft.
Sabbath day's journey	about 3/5 mile

Measures of capacity OT

Dry measures

Kab	1.159 qts.
Omar = 1 4/5 kabs	2.087 qts.
Seah = 3 1/3 omers	6.959 qts.
Ephah = 3 seahs	20.878 qts.
Lethech = 5 ephahs	3.262 bu.
Kor/homer = 2 lethechs	6.524 bu.

Measures of capacity NT

Dry measures

Choinex	0.98 qts.
Modios Lat. *modius*	7.68 qts.
Saton Heb. *Seah*	12.18 qts.
Koros Heb. *Kor*	6.52 bu.

Weights OT

Gerah 8.81 grains.
Bekah 10 gerahs = 88.10 grains.
Shekel 2 Bekahs = 176.20 grains.
Maneh = 50 shekels = 20.148 oz.
Talent = 60 manehs = 75.558 lbs.

Weights NT

Shekel (silver) = 4 Rom. denarii 4 Gr. drachma.
Shekel (gold) = 15 silver shekels.
Minah (silver) = 50 silver shekels.
Mina (gold) = 50 gold shekels.
Talent (gold) = 3,000 shekels.
Litra (Jn 12:3; 19:39) a Rom. pound (12 oz).

gerah	bekah
silver shekel	= 4 denarii
2 bekahs	I shekel
gold shekel	= 15 silver shekels
maneh	= 50 shekels
silver mina	= 50 silver shekels
talent	= 60 manehs
gold mina	= 50 gold shekels
	gold talent = 3000 gold shekels

Measures of capacity OT

Liquid measures

Log	0.674 pts.
Kab = 4 logs	1.349 qts.
Hin = 3 kabs	1.012 qts.
Bath = 6 hins	6.073 gals.
Kor = 10 baths	60.73 gals.

Measures of capacity NT

Liquid measures

Xestes (Lat. sextarius)	1.12 pts.
Batos (Heb. bath)	6.07 gals.
Metretes (Jn 2:6)	10.3 gals.
Koros (Heb. kor)	60.73 gals.

litra = Roman pound

Between the Testaments

The four hundred silent years

From Malachi (*c*. 400 B.C.), the last prophetic voice of the OT, to the advent of Jesus, divine revelation as it developed in the production of canonical Scripture was in abeyance. The result was the completion and delimitation of the Hebrew canon. According to Josephus, Jewish historian of the second half of the 1st cen. A.D., this took place in the reign of Artaxerxes I Longimanus, 465-424 B.C.

Importance of intertestamental period

Among many other important events of this 400 year period was the translation of the OT into the Greek language. The version was produced c. 280-150 B.C. and was called the Septuagint. It released the great truths of OT Scripture from the restricted influence of the Hebrew language and people, and gave them to the Graeco-Roman world in the common speech of the day.

The Apocrypha

The Apocrypha is the name given to 14 books which originated in the period between the OT and the NT *after* the OT canon had closed (see 'How the Bible came to us' in the appendix to this handbook). These apocryphal books were *never* in the OT Hebrew canon. They were included in the Septuagint and the Latin Vulgate, being placed between the OT and NT. The Roman Catholic church accepts 11 of the 14 as so-called deutero-canonical books, declaring them to be an equal part of Scripture by the Council of Trent in A.D. 1546. Protestants deny the canonical status of these books on the basis both of internal and external evidence. They were never recognized as Scripture by the Jews, nor by Jesus, nor by the apostolic community, nor by any of the church Fathers who objectively examined the evidence. The books in the Apocrypha are listed below and described.

1 Esdras

This book essentially covers the same historical material found in canonical Ezra, Nehemiah, and 2 Chronicles. However, it contains

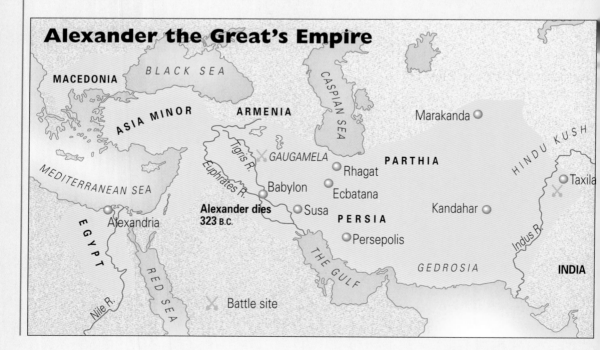

Alexander the Great's Empire

MACEDONIA

BLACK SEA

ASIA MINOR

ARMENIA

CASPIAN SEA

Marakanda

MEDITERRANEAN SEA

Tigris R.

Euphrates R.

GAUGAMELA

Rhagat

PARTHIA

HINDU KUSH

Babylon

Ecbatana

Taxila

Alexander dies 323 B.C.

Susa

PERSIA

Kandahar

Alexandria

Persepolis

Indus R.

E G Y P T

THE GULF

GEDROSIA

INDIA

RED SEA

Nile R.

✕ Battle site

Events of the Intertestamental Period

Jewish History

424-331 Malachi, last OT prophet.
Palestine a tiny province (satrapy) under under rule of Persian governor (satrap).

Palestine fell within the bounds of the Fifth Persian satrapy with the capital at Damascus or Samaria.

359-32 Jews enjoyed comparative peace and prosperity under their Persian overlords.

338-23 Jews were torn between allegiance to Persian overlords and threat of Alexander's conquests.

Alexander swept into Syria taking Palestine, Tyre (332), Gaza. Jews submitted to Alexander and were treated well. Alexander conquered Egypt (332).

Alexandria was founded.

323-277 Dissemination of Greek language, culture and philosophy by Alexander's conquests.

Contemporary Scene

Persian Empire
Xerxes II (424-23)
Darius II (423-404)
Artaxerxes II (404-358)
Artaxerxes III (358-38)
Arses (338-36)
Darius III (336-31)

Macedonian Empire
Philip (359-36) gained control of Greek states. Victory at Chaeronea (338). Power of Greek city-states broken.

Alexander the Great
(336-23) conquered Persian Empire in three decisive battles: Granicus (334), Issus (333), Gaugamela (331); reached India (327); died in Babylon (323).

Alexander's generals struggled for power.

Alexander the Great.

Jewish History

Contemporary Scene

Palestine under the Ptolemies (323-198)

Ptolemic and Seleucid Empires

Ptolemy I favored Jews and settled many in Alexandria, which he raised to economic and cultural heights.

Ptolemy II favored Jews. Began translation of OT into Greek (Septuagint).

Letter of Aristeas.

Hellenization of Alexandrian Jews continued. Palestinian Jews rigidly traditional.

Painted tombs of Marisa.

Palestine under Seleucids (198-65)

198 Antiochus III the Great expelled Egyptians from Palestine and annexed it to the Seleucid Empire.

Book of Ecclesiasticus written (c. 180). Septuagint completed (c. 150).

167-65 Enforced Hellenization of Jews.

Antiochus IV sacked Jerusalem, profaned the temple, offered sacrifices to Olympian Zeus on altar of burnt offering.

Maccabean revolt led by aged priest Mattathias and his five sons.

166-34 Palestine under the Hasmonaeans (166-63)

Judas (166-60) defeated Syrian armies, cleansed and rededicated the temple (166-65).

Jonathan (160-43) diplomatically and militarily made great strides towards Jewish independence.

Simon (143-35) inaugurated period of Jewish independence (143-63). Expelled Syrian garrison from Jerusalem, conquered Gezer and Joppa. Books of 1 Maccabees, Tobit, Judith.

Ptolemaic and Seleucid Empires

Ptolemy I
(323-282)

Ptolemy II
(284-46)

Ptolemy III
(246-22)

Ptolemy IV
(222-205)

Ptolemy V
(205-180)

Ptolemaic line continued under Roman domination until

Seleucus I
(312-280)

Antiochus I
(280-62)

Antiochus II
(261-46)

Seleucus II
(246-26)

Seleucus III
(226-23)

Antiochus III
(223-187)

Seleucus IV
(187-75)

**Antiochus IV
Epiphanes**
(175-63)

Egypt was incorporated into Roman Empire as a province (30).

Antiochus V
(163-62)

Demetrius I
(162-50)

Struggle between Demetrius II and Alexander Balas for throne.

Alexander Balas
(150-45)

Demetrius II
(145-39)
recognized Simon as high priest and granted Jews practically full independence (143).

Jewish History	Contemporary Scene

Jewish History

134-104
John Hyrcanus (135-104), son of Simon, embarked on a career of conquest in Transjordan, in Samaria (destroyed rival temple on Gerizim) and in Edom, ruling over a small empire from Lower Galilee to Negeb and from the Mediterranean to Nabatea.

Rise of the two great parties in Judaism—Pharisees and Sadducees – as well as the Essenes known from Philo, Josephus, Pliny and the Dead Sea Scrolls.

104-69
Aristobulus I (104-3) a son of John Hyrcanus, seized control, but died shortly after.

Alexander Jannaeus (103-76), ruthless conqueror, sealed fate of Hasmonaean dynasty by alienating the Pharisees.

Alexandra (76-67), Alexander Jannaeus' wife. Golden Age of Pharisaism. Probable date of Book of the Wisdom of Solomon, Sibylline Oracles, Book of Enoch, Book of Jubilees, 2 Maccabees.

Aristobulus II (67-3) Aristobulus II deposed and carried to Rome to grace Pompey's triumph.

63-41
Pompey brought Palestine under Roman control and organized the Decapolis league in Transjordan to balance the power of Judea, which was reduced to its former smallness.

40-4
Palestine under the Romans (63 B.C.–A.D. 135)
Antipater the Idumaean ruled Palestine under Roman grant (55–43). Herod and Phasael, Antipater's sons, were tetrarchs (41).

Antigonus, Aristobulus' son, was high priest and king by aid of the Parthians (40-37).

Herod the Great was king of Judea by Roman senatorial grant (37–4).

Birth of John the Baptist and Jesus (c. 6 or 5).

Contemporary Scene

Antiochus VII (139-29) invaded Judea, took Jerusalem, imposed heavy tribute, but his death (129) marked the virtual end of the Seleucid power over Palestine.

The weak uninfluential kingdom of Syria continued until Pompey took over area and made it a Roman province (64).

Khirbet Qumran, headquarters of the Essenes on the NW shores of the Dead Sea, founded c. 110 and flourished until about 37. Many of Dead Sea Scrolls date from this period and later (c. 100 B.C. to A.D. 70).

Hyrcanus, elder son of Alexandra, was high priest. At her death Antipater, governor of Idumaea, persuaded Hyrcanus to flee to Petra and engage the aid of the Nabatean prince Aretas to win the throne of Judea for him against the rival claims of his brother Aristobulus. In the ensuing struggle Rome was appealed to and took over, ending the Hasmonaean monarchy. Catiline's conspiracy, Cicero's career, Catiline slain (62).

Pompey, Caesar and Crassus formed Caesar's First Triumvirate (60). Caesar's Gallic Wars (58-1). Civil war (Caesar vs. Pompey) ended in Caesar's assassination (44).

Second Triumvirate: **Antony, Octavian, Lepidus** (43). Battles at Philippi (42) and Actium (31) left Octavian (Augustus) sole ruler.

Augustus emperor (27 B.C.–A.D. 14) Revival of Khirbet Qumran, Essenic headquarters near the Dead Sea, which flourished during the ministry of John the Baptist, Jesus and Paul.

an extended portion (3:1-5:6) that has no parallel in the Hebrew Bible. This portion consists mainly of a legendary story of a competition between three Jewish pages at Darius' court to ascertain the meaning of true wisdom. Zerubbabel was the winner and claimed as his prize the royal permission for the Jews to return and rebuild Jerusalem. The book is dated c. 100 B.C.

2 Esdras

This is an apocalyptic work of composite authorship that was completed c. A.D. 100. Ch. 1-2 are an anti-Jewish addition to the original Jewish Ezra Apocalypse, ch. 3-14. This latter consists of (1) the Salathiel Apocalypse, ch. 3-10, dealing with the problem of evil and its solution in the life to come; (2) the eagle vision, ch. 11-12, dealing with the Roman Empire and Messiah's coming; (3) the vision of the man (Messiah) rising from the sea, ch. 13; and a legend relating how Ezra rewrote the sacred literature, ch. 14. The last two chapters, 15-16, contain verbal echoes of the NT and were written later, probably as late as A.D. 270.

Tobit

This story, dated c. 150 B.C., is religious fiction. It is a didactic romance concerning a pious Jew of the Assyrian dispersion named Tobit, who is blinded accidentally in the course of giving decent burial to his fellow countrymen killed under Assyrian kings. In his distress Tobit prays for divine help and sends his son Tobias to recover a large sum of money he had deposited with a relative named Gabael. The angel Raphael, disguised as a dependable kinsman, accompanies Tobias, not only in answer to blind Tobit's prayer but also to help Sarah, the daughter of Raguel and Edna, in Ecbatana. Her seven husbands had been successively slain on the bridal night by the jealous demon Asmodaeus. Encamped on the Tigris, Tobias catches a fish. At Raphael's instruction he burns its heart and liver, exorcises the demon, and marries Sarah. Raphael, meanwhile, goes on to Raguel, gets the money,

and returns to conduct Tobias and his new wife back to Tobit and his spouse Hannah at Nineveh. Their great distress at Tobias' long absence gives way to joy as they greet their beloved son and his bride. Their poverty is relieved by the money, and Tobit's blindness is cured as Tobias, at Raphael's direction, places the fish's gall on his aged father's eyes and his sight is restored. The angel Raphael reveals his identity and vanishes.

Judith

This is another fictional narrative with didactic value dating from the 2nd cen. B.C. Judith is a beautiful and devout Jewish widow of Bethulia (a pseudonym for Shechem), who by her valor saves her city from Nebuchadnezzar's invading army under Holophernes (unknown in contemporary Babylonian literature). When the city's elders decide to surrender if no help is forthcoming within five days, the noble Judith leaves the city and goes into the camp of Holophernes, beguiling him by her beauty and promises, until she returns to Bethulia with the general's head in her handbag. The result is that the defenders of the city sally forth and the vast army of Holophernes is routed and destroyed in the ensuing confusion. The high priest, Joakim, and the elders of Jerusalem come to Bethulia to do honor to the heroine, Judith.

Solomon's Pools, near Jerusalem.

The remainder of Esther

These are passages composed in Greek that were inserted in the canonical book of Esther in the Septuagint version to show the hand of God in the narrative by putting the word 'God' into the text. These additions consist of:
(1) A dream by Mordecai and an account of his foiling a conspiracy against the king – a chapter of 17 verses preceding ch. 1 of the Hebrew canonical book. (2) A royal letter ordering the destruction of all Jews in the kingdom. This follows 3:13 of the Hebrew text. (3) Prayers of Mordecai and Esther, following ch. 4 of the Hebrew. (4) Esther's dramatic audience before Ahasuerus, adding 14 verses to ch. 5. (5) A royal letter telling of Haman's death, praising the Jews, and permitting them to defend themselves, following 8:12 of the Hebrew. (6) Interpretation of Mordecai's dream and a final word on the meaning of the feast of Purim. These follow the last chapter of the Hebrew Esther.

The Wisdom of Solomon

This is one of the most attractive and interesting of the apocryphal books, dating from about 50 B.C. The first section, 1:1-6:8, has been called 'the book of eschatology' and sets forth the truth of immortality by contrasting the destiny of the righteous and the unrighteous. The

A Jewish scribe.

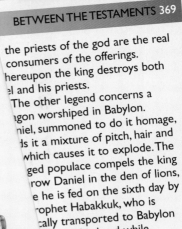

the priests of the god are the real consumers of the offerings. ...hereupon the king destroys both ...el and his priests.

The other legend concerns a ...agon worshiped in Babylon. ...niel, summoned to do it homage, ...ds it a mixture of pitch, hair and ...which causes it to explode. The ...ged populace compels the king ...row Daniel in the den of lions, ...e he is fed on the sixth day by ...rophet Habakkuk, who is ...cally transported to Babylon ...hair of his head while ...g food and drink to the ...in Judea. On the seventh day ...rescues Daniel and throws ...ld-be destroyers to the ...ions.

...ayer of Manasseh
...purported penitential ...Manasseh, the wicked king ...hen he was carried away ...Babylon by the ...was inserted after 2 ...and dates probably ...cen. B.C.

second section, 6:9-11:1, is a panegyric of wisdom, eloquent and beautiful, put upon the lips of Solomon. The third section, 11:2-19:22, is inferior to the first two sections. It presents a historical retrospect of Israel in Egypt and in the wilderness, interrupted by a discussion of the origin and evils of idolatry, ch. 13-15. The book is considered composite and anonymous.

Ecclesiasticus

This book of 51 chapters belongs to the *Hokmah* or wisdom literature of the Hebrews. This is the only book of the apocryphal literature whose author is known. He was Jesus the son of Sirach of Jerusalem (50:27), and he wrote about 175 B.C. His grandson translated the Hebrew original into Greek in 132 B.C., as is known from the Prologue. The traditional Latin name, Ecclesiasticus, designates it as *the* 'church book' par excellence among the apocryphal books, attesting the high moral and spiritual character of its aphorisms or 'wise sayings' and its general popularity among Christians from early times.

The Song of the Three Children

This apocryphal addition to canonical Daniel was inserted after the story of the fiery furnace (Dan 3:23). It contains an eloquent prayer of Azariah, an account of miraculous deliverance, and a psalm of praise in which all three join.

Story of Susanna

This is another apocryphal addition to the canonical Daniel, telling how Susanna, a chaste Babylonian matron, was cleared of the trumped-up charges of adultery by the wisdom of the young man Daniel. It appears before ch. 1 in the Greek version and as ch. 13 in the Latin Vulgate.

Bel and the Dragon

These legends were designed to ridicule idolatry. They constitute the third apocryphal addition to Daniel. It was claimed that the statue of the idol Bel was a living deity because it supposedly devoured large amounts of food placed beside it each night. By scattering ashes on the temple floor, Daniel proves to the king that

The ...idepigrapha

In add...the Apocrypha there are wr...lled the Pseude...('false writings'). These a...ious compositions penned ...false claim of authorshi...g the period 200 B.C.-A.D. 2...ng attributed to such notab...characters as Adam, Eno...ah, Moses, Zephaniah, ...etc. Unlike the Apocrypha (...the 14 of which are accepted...nonical by the Roman churc...Pseudepigraphal literature has ...been considered canonical. Thes...ks are mainly apocalyptic, did...and legendary. A word of desc...n of some of the most import...books follows.

Assumption ...Moses

This consists of all...d predictions of the great lawgive...oken and entrusted to Joshua...ortly before Moses' death. The b...was written by a Pharisee about A...15 as a protest against the gr...ing secularization of the P...risaic party of his day.

Judaism at the time of Christ

Ascension of Is:
This work consists parts – the Martyrdom of I[sai] Vision of Isaiah, and the Te[sta] of Hezekiah. The long[.] tament of Hezekiah (2:13-[gi]ves a useful insight into [spir]itual condition of the C[hristian] church at the close of the a[postoli]c period. The Vision of Isaia[h ([6]:9:40) gives valuable insight in[to 1]cen. beliefs on the Trinity, th[e incar]nation, the resurrection, and [secon]d. The Martyrdom of Is[aiah is] fragmentary (1:1-2, 6-13; 2:1[-] 3:12; 5:1-14). It recounts the [death] of Isaiah at the hands of wi[cked] Manasseh by being sawed to[piec]es.

Book of En[och]
This is a fragm[enta]ry work consisting of [rev]ations reputedly given to Noa[h] and Enoch concerning C[hris]t's coming and future judgm[ent.] It is by unknown authors and [wa]s written in the first two centurie[s B.]C.

Book of [Ju]bilees
Dividing the [h]istory of the world into jubilee[p]eriods of 50-year cycles (Lev. 5:8-12), the Pharisee

author of this work (153-105 B.C.) wrote to save Judaism from the demoralizing effects of Hellenism by extolling the law and presenting the Hebrew patriarchs in an irreproachable light.

Sibylline Oracles
These oracles originated in the Maccabean era. Dealing with the downfall of empires and the advent of the messianic age, they are modeled after the prophetic saying of the Greek Sibyls. The original Sibyl of Cumae is first alluded to by Heraclitus of Ephesus (500 B.C.).

Psalms of Solomon
These consist of 18 psalms stemming from the middle of the 1st cen. B.C. Apparently penned by an anonymous Pharisee, they tell of the coming Messiah.

Testaments of the Twelve Patriarchs
These 12 testaments allege to record the dying speeches of Jacob's twelve sons, being inspired by Gen 49. In its final form the book dates perhaps as late as A.D. 250, though it includes material composed as early as the 2nd cen. B.C.

The Targums
The Targums are free renderings of the Hebrew Scriptures into Aramaic after the latter had become the common language of Palestine in the post-Exilic period. They were first oral, the Hebrew Scriptures being read and the Aramaic rendering given (cf. Ezra 8:4-8). The earliest written Targums, such as Onkelos on the Pentateuch and Jonathan on the Prophets, date from Christian times.

The Talmud
This is a body of Hebrew civil and canon laws based on the Torah of Moses. It is the condensation of the thinking of rabbis from c. 300 B.C. to A.D. 500. The Talmud ('teaching') consists of the Mishnah, or traditional oral law deduced from the written law of Moses itself, and the Gemara, a commentary on these legal traditions. The Aramaic language is used in the Gemara. Closely connected with the Talmud is the Midrash, the earliest synagogue sermons in Hebrew and Aramaic, expounding the Hebrew OT Scriptures. The Midrash flourished 100 B.C.-A.D. 300.

Site of the Essene community at Qumran, with the cliffs where the Dead Sea Scrolls were discovered in the background.

Jewish interpretation in the Midrash

The Midrash often involved a rather loose interpretive procedure that considered the current practical application of the text to be more important than its contextual significance. Critics have frequently criticized NT writers (particularly Matthew and the author of Hebrews) for midrashic techniques in their use of OT Scriptures. The interpretive methods of the NT writers are quite defensible, however, particularly in light of their inspiration by the Holy Spirit

The synagogue

The synagogue (from the Gr. *synagoge,* 'a gathering' or 'assembly') had its origin evidently first in homes in Babylon (cf. Ezk 8:1; 20:1-3). The 'house synagogue,' like the first Christian churches which met in homes, after the Exile gradually developed into formal assemblies for instruction, public worship and prayer. They replaced the temple worship, which was now no longer possible for the Jews who were scattered far beyond Palestine.

Every town harboring a large number of Jews in the Graeco-Roman world of 300 B.C.- A.D. 300 had its synagogue for worship and instruction in the law and the prophets (cf. Lk 4:16-30). These were the repositories of the Hebrew Scriptures and were among the first places the Christian gospel was proclaimed (Acts 13:5, 14; 14:1). Since the dispersion was widespread, the synagogue was a common institution in the Roman world.

The Sanhedrin

The Sanhedrin was an aristocratic body possessing judicial powers, doubtless going back in principle to King Jehoshaphat's time (cf. 2 Chr 19:5-11). It developed into the supreme court of the Jews by Jesus' day and functioned in both civil and religious realms till the fall of Jerusalem (A.D. 70). A council in the Ezra-Nehemiah era (450-400 B.C.) known as the Great Synagogue is echoed in popular tradition and is thought to have given way about 250 B.C. to the 70-member Sanhedrin (Aramaized form of Gr. *synedrion,* 'a sitting together' or 'assembly') presided over by the high priests.

The Pharisees

During the Maccabean period in the reign of John Hyrcanus (134-104 B.C.), the conflicting parties in Judaism, the Pharisees, Sadducees, and Essenes, came into existence. The Pharisees were apparently successors to the Hasidim ('the pious'), who stood true to the law under Antiochus Epiphanes' proscription of Judaism in 168 B.C. They were rigid legalistic separatists, with watchwords of prayer, repentance, and charitable giving. From an admirable beginning in the fires of Maccabean suffering, they gradually degenerated into empty, unprincipled religionists in Jesus' day.

The Sadducees

Probably Zadokites, partisans of Solomon's priest Zadok (1 Kgs 2:35), the Sadducees were chiefly aristocratic, worldly-minded priests, who obeyed the letter of the law but denied resurrection and future retribution. They welcomed

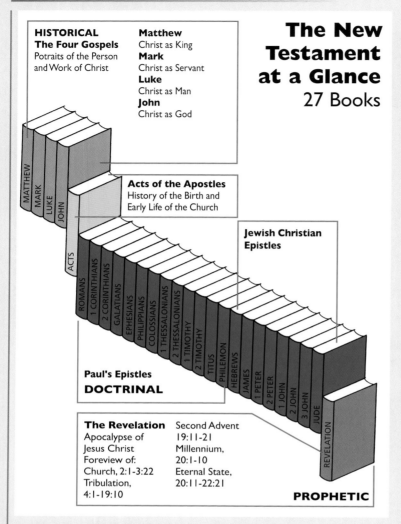

HISTORICAL
The Four Gospels
Potraits of the Person
and Work of Christ

Matthew
Christ as King
Mark
Christ as Servant
Luke
Christ as Man
John
Christ as God

MATTHEW
MARK
LUKE
JOHN

Acts of the Apostles
History of the Birth and
Early Life of the Church

Jewish Christian Epistles

ACTS

ROMANS
1 CORINTHIANS
2 CORINTHIANS
GALATIANS
EPHESIANS
PHILIPPIANS
COLOSSIANS
1 THESSALONIANS
2 THESSALONIANS
1 TIMOTHY
2 TIMOTHY
TITUS
PHILEMON
HEBREWS
JAMES
1 PETER
2 PETER
1 JOHN
2 JOHN
3 JOHN
JUDE

REVELATION

Paul's Epistles
DOCTRINAL

The Revelation
Apocalypse of
Jesus Christ
Foreview of:
Church, 2:1-3:22
Tribulation,
4:1-19:10

Second Advent
19:11-21
Millennium,
20:1-10
Eternal State,
20:11-22:21

PROPHETIC

The New Testament at a Glance
27 Books

conquests of Alexander the Great. This universal language affected vitally the Jews of the diaspora and eventuated in the translation of the OT into Greek (the Septuagint). This translation became an important factor in the formation of the NT, and with it constituted the Bible of early Christianity.

Moreover, Greek learning and culture, Roman law and Roman roads, Jewish monotheism and Jewish synagogues (the latter widespread as a result of the Jewish diaspora), and Jewish apocalyptic and messianic hopes prepared the world for the coming of Christ and Christianity. Divine providence can be traced everywhere in the long interval between the Testaments. The goal was the incarnation and birth of the long-awaited Messiah and Saviour of the world, prophesied so often in the OT. To this great event all preceding centuries of world history, especially Jewish history, pointed (cf. Gal 4:4).

Introducing the New Testament

The OT constitutes the *preparation* for Christ and contains prophecies of His divine person and redemptive work. The NT is the account of the realization of these predictions in the *appearance* of the Redeemer and the provisions of His glorious gospel.

In the gospels Christ is *manifested* to the world and His gospel *provided* in the death, resurrection, and ascension of the Redeemer. In the Acts Christ is *proclaimed* and His gospel *propagated* in the world. In the epistles His gospel is *expounded* in its doctrinal and practical meaning. In the Apocalypse all the redemptive purposes of God in and through the Redeemer are *consummated* for time and eternity. The NT is thus the capstone and fulfillment of the prophetic and redemptive truths contained in the OT, the OT forming the foundation for the completed edifice of revealed truth found in the NT.

Hellenistic culture and were willing to gain earthly advantage through military strategy or adroit diplomacy. Their deep cleavage with the Pharisees continued until Jesus' day, after their differences had wrecked the Hasmonaean kingdom years before.

The scribes and Essenes

The scribes were copyists of Holy Scripture, intimately conversant with the Mosaic law, hence also called lawyers. During the interbiblical period they became influential and appear prominently in Jesus' day.

The Essenes were a monastic sect rather than a political religious party such as the Pharisees and

Sadducees. Until the discovery in 1947 of the Dead Sea Scrolls, Philo, Josephus, and Pliny were the only sources of information on this communal monastic order. A similar if not identical group is now well known as a result of the excavation of its headquarters at Qumran on the NW shore of the Dead Sea. The recovery of their book of rules and order has corroborated ancient sources and added to our knowledge of sectarian Judaism from about 200 B.C. to A.D. 70.

Preparation for the Greek New Testament

The interbiblical period witnessed the development of the various Greek dialects into a *lingua franca* of the Hellenistic world through the

New Testament

The four gospels

What the gospels are

The four gospels are neither histories of the life of Christ nor biographies. They are rather portraits of the person and work of the long-promised Messiah, Israel's King and the world's Saviour. As portraits they present four different poses of one unique personality. Matthew by the Holy Spirit presents Christ as King, Mark as Servant, Luke as Man, and John as God.

While each of the gospel writers focuses on one specific role in his portrait of the Messiah, they all recognize and allude to each of the other facets of the Messiah's personality and ministry. Thus all four writers present the one and same unique Person, the God-Man, Servant of the Lord, King of Israel, humanity's Redeemer.

The purpose of the gospels

In their fourfold portraiture of Christ's person as King, Servant, Man, and God, the gospels center in Messiah's threefold ministry of Prophet, Priest, and King. As Prophet, fulfilling Moses' great prediction (Deut 18:15-19), He was the Prophet par excellence by virtue of the uniqueness of His person, He not merely spoke for God as other prophets who preceded Him, but God spoke through Him as Son (Heb 1:1-2). In contrast to the OT prophet who was a voice for God, the Son, being God, was the voice of God Himself. As a Priest Christ became both the Sacrifice and the Sacrificer as He died on the cross to save sinners (Heb 9:14), and through His

The Four Gospels and the Old Testament

	Quotations from OT	Allusions to OT
Matthew	53	76
Mark	36	27
Luke	25	42
John	20	105

Of the 3779 verses (AV), 1934, or more than 50%, were spoken by our Lord.

resurrection lives eternally to make intercession for them (Heb 7:25). As Israel's King He was rejected at His first advent, but will reign in that office at His second advent, fulfilling the Davidic covenant (2 Sam 7:8-16; Lk 1:30-33; Acts 2:29-36; 15:14-17).

The meaning of the word 'gospel'

As applied to the four portraitures of Christ, the term 'gospel' (cf. Mk 1:1) is used in the sense of the good news of salvation provided by the death, burial, and resurrection of Christ (cf. 1 Cor 15:1-3). The gospels, strictly speaking, are not an exposition of the gospel, although occasional expository notations occur, as in John. They are an account of the provision of the gospel for needy sinners in the person and work of Christ. For the historical outworking of the divinely provided gospel we must go to Acts. For a doctrinal exposition of the gospel we must go to the epistles, notably the 13 Pauline letters.

What the gospels accomplish

Describing the eternal preexistence, human birth, death,

Representation of the gospel-writer Luke from Church of the Annunciation, Nazareth.

Comparison of the Four Gospels

Matthew	Mark	Luke	John
The prophesied	The obedient	The perfect	The divine
King	Servant	Man	Son
Lionlike	Oxlike	Manlike	Eaglelike
Prophetic	Practical	Historical	Spiritual
To the Jew	To the Roman	To the Greek	To the church
The Davidic King	The Servant of the Lord	The Son of Man	The Word of God
David's righteous-branch *Jer 23:5-6*	My Servant the branch *Zech 3:8*	The Man the branch *Zech 6:12*	The branch of the Lord *Isa 4:2*

OFFICIAL			PERSONAL
King	Servant	Son of Man	Son of God
Synoptic			Supplementary
Outward, public, Galilean, earthly			Inward, private Judean heavenly

Christ's words in the Four Gospels

	Matthew	Mark	Luke	John
Verses, AV	1071	678	1151	879
Verses, RSV	1068	661	1149	866
Verses of Christ's words	644	285	586	419
Approx. percentage	60%	42%	50%	50%

resurrection, and ascension of Jesus the Christ, as well as His life and teachings, the four gospels present a living, dynamic, unique personality, God become man, to work out man's redemption from sin. These four portraits present Him as Lord and Saviour, rather than describing all He did and in the precise order in which He did it. They introduce us to Him, rather than to His life as a whole.

The gospels are designedly incomplete as a story, but marvelously complete and purposeful as a divine revelation of the Son of God our Saviour! And this is faith's need. It is also unbelief's stumbling block.

The key to the correct interpretation of the gospels

It is necessary to realize that the period described is culminative of the OT age, preparatory to and predictive of the new age, but not the new age itself. Not until the ascension of Christ and the consequent advent of the Spirit at Pentecost (Acts 2) did the new age of the church begin.

The Jewish background of the gospels

The fabric of the gospels is woven out of OT type, allusion, and quotation (cf. Mt 1:1; Lk 24:27, 44, 45). Our Lord was 'born under the law' (Gal 4:4), ministered primarily to the Jews in the legal age (Mt 10:5-6; 15:23-25), and was 'a servant of the Jews on behalf of God's truth, to confirm the promises made to the patriarchs' (Rom 15:8). As King and Messiah He was announced by John the Baptist, offered the kingdom to Israel, and was rejected by them (Mt 1-12). As Prophet He predicted the new age

(Mt 13), and His second advent (Mt 24-25). As Priest He died and rose again, fulfilling the law and bringing in grace (Jn 1:17).

Until the event of the cross the gospels are an extension of the OT dispensation seen in their strong Jewish colouring, which did not end till the veil of the Temple was torn supernaturally at Christ's death (Mt 27:51).

The gospels and humanity

The four gospels are directed toward the various classes of society which existed in the 1st cen. A.D. — Matthew toward the Jews, Mark toward the Romans, Luke toward the Greeks, and John toward those neither Jews nor Gentiles (cf. 1 Cor 10:32) but believers on the Lord Jesus Christ.

Political background of New Testament times

Roman Emperors

Caesar Augustus
27 B.C.–A.D. 14

Birth of Jesus boyhood at Nazareth.

Public ministry, death, resurrection of Jesus.

Tiberius Caesar
14–37

Caligula
37–41

Growth of church, conversion of Paul.

Claudius
41–54

Early missionary labors of Paul

Nero
54–68

Paul's later labors: martyrdom at Rome.

Otho

Vitellius
68–69

Vespasian
69–79

Jewish Roman war in Palestine

us
81

Domitian
81–96

John's probable exile to Patmos. The revelation.

Herodian Rulers

Herod the Great
37–4 B.C
King of the Jews, great builder, Hellenizer.

Archelaus
4 B.C.–A.D. 6
Son of Herod ethnarch of Judea, cruel.

Herod Antipas
4 B.C.–A.D. 39
Tetrarch of Galilee and Perea. Killed John the Baptist.

Philip
4 B.C.–A.D. 34
Tetrarch of Iturea and Trachonitis.

Herod Agrippa I
37–44
Ruled tetrarchy of Philip, Judea. Perea and Gailee. (41–44)

Herod Agrippa II
50–100
Ruled former tetrarchy of Philip and Lysanias and parts of Galilee and Perea.

Procurators of Judea and Palestine

Judea
A.D. 6–41

Coponius
6–10

M. Ambivius
9–13

Annius Rufus
12–15

Valerius Gratus
15–26

Pontius Pilate
26–36

Crucifixion

Marcellus
38

Marullus
37–41

Cuspius Fadus
44–c. 46

Tiberius Alexander
46–48

Ventidius Cumanus
48–52

Antonius Felix
52–59

Porcius Festus
59–61

Palestine
A.D. 44–66

Clodius Albinus
61–65

Gessius Florus
65–70

Fall and destruction of Jerusalem and the Jewish state. Jews scattered.

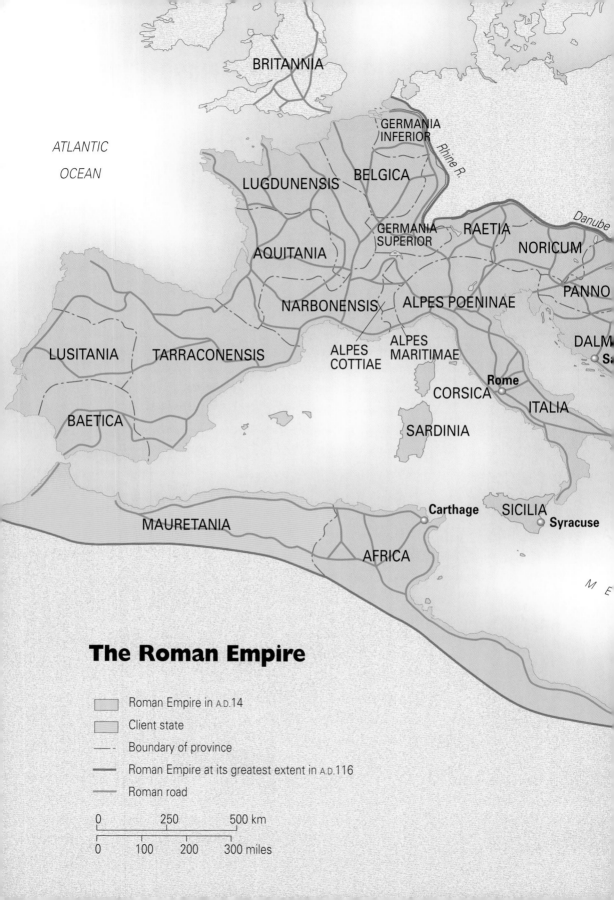

ATLANTIC

OCEAN

BRITANNIA

GERMANIA
INFERIOR

Rhine R.

LUGDUNENSIS

BELGICA

GERMANIA
SUPERIOR

RAETIA

Danube

NORICUM

AQUITANIA

PANNO

NARBONENSIS

ALPES POENINAE

LUSITANIA

TARRACONENSIS

ALPES
COTTIAE

ALPES
MARITIMAE

DALM

Sa

CORSICA

Rome

BAETICA

SARDINIA

ITALIA

Carthage

SICILIA

MAURETANIA

Syracuse

AFRICA

M E

The Roman Empire

Roman Empire in A.D.14

Client state

--- Boundary of province

Roman Empire at its greatest extent in A.D.116

Roman road

0	250	500 km

0	100	200	300 miles

CASPIAN SEA

DACIA

BLACK SEA

SIA

THRACIA

ARMENIA

BITHYNIA
AND PONTUS

CEDONIA

Nicomedia

CAPPADOCIA

Thessalonica

ASSYRIA

EPIRUS

MESOPOTAMIA

Tigris R.

ASIA

GALATIA

orinth

CILICIA

Ephesus

Euphrates R.

Athens

Antioch
SYRIA

ACHAIA

LYCIA AND
PAMPHYLIA

CRETE

CYPRUS

RANEAN SEA

JUDAEA

Jerusalem

ene

Alexandria

(ARABIA/
NABATAEA)

YRENAICA

AEGYPTUS

Nile R.

RED SEA

MATTHEW

The gospel of the Son of David

The author. The writer of this gospel is anonymous, but from a very early period he has been identified as Matthew or Levi, the publican, a Galilean Jew who became one of Jesus' disciples. Modern criticism disfavors authorship by Matthew and a traditional early date, generally positing an unknown Christian as the writer sometime after A.D. 66. It is held that the anonymous author used a collection of sayings compiled by Matthew, to which Papias refers (c. A.D. 140), and so the name of Matthew came to identify this gospel. This position, however, lacks proof. It seems best to hold to the traditional authorship by Matthew and date the book around the middle of the 1st cen.

Symbolic depiction of Matthew, the gospel-writer, from the Church of the Annunciation, Nazareth.

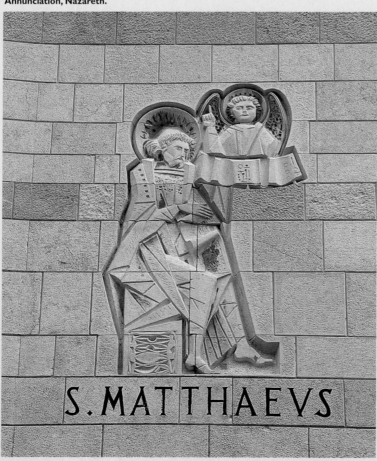

S. MATTHAEVS

The scope and theme. Matthew is a Jewish gospel, rooted in OT prophecy relating to the coming of Messiah-King and His kingdom. It sets forth the King in His lineage from David, His birth, and His royal infancy. Introduced by His herald, the King is presented in His public ministry. His rejection as King is followed by His death as the son of Abraham and His resurrection as the Son of God.

Since this gospel is Jewish, the key to the interpretation of Matthew is an understanding of God's program for Israel and her Messiah. This involves the great focal prophecy of Israel's future earthly kingdom under Messiah. It was rejected at the first advent but is to be established (Acts 1:6) at the second advent. The theme of Matthew is the Saviour-King and His kingdom.

Outline

1-12 The King manifested and His kingdom rejected
13-25 The rejected King, His teaching and ministry
26-27 The King's passion and death
28 The King's resurrection and commission

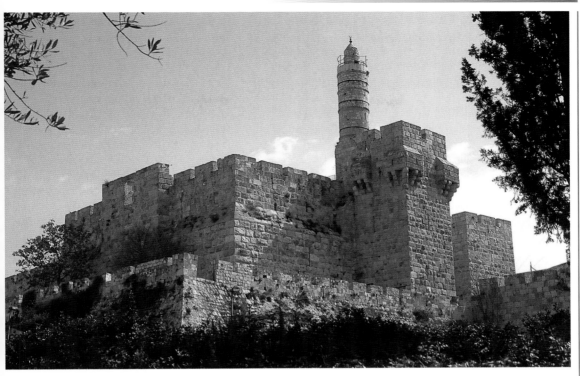

1. The genealogy and birth of the King

1-17. His royal descent. The King is *first* named 'son of David' in the kingly line, true heir to David's throne, 1; then 'son of Abraham,' the seed through whom the whole earth will be blessed. The order is significant because to the Jew (and this gospel is directed toward the Jew) the Lord was first to present Himself as *King*, after that as Saviour (cf. Jn 1:11-12). The genealogy, 2-17, is selective, having three divisions of 14 generations each, David alone being designated explicitly as king, 6 (cf. 2 Sam 7:8-16). Matthew's genealogy shows Jesus' *legal*

The Star of Bethlehem

Several explanations have been given for the appearance of the star, each with its own difficulties. Otherwise plausible suggestions that the star was a supernova or a comet that made a timely appearance, or that it was the triple conjunction of Saturn and Jupiter that occurred in 6 B.C., should not obscure the fact that the star served as a supernatural sign of the birth of the King of kings and Saviour of mankind.

right to the Davidic throne through the line of Solomon and Joseph, the latter being the supposed father of Jesus (Lk 3:23; 4:22). If Jesus had been the son of Mary without her being legally the wife of Joseph, a son of Solomon, His royal claim would have been rejected from the outset. Luke's genealogy presents Jesus as the Son of Man, and a descendant of David by Mary, but through the house of Nathan (not Solomon). As the virgin-born son of Mary, however, He had no legal right to the throne. This had to come through Joseph.

18-25. His virgin birth. The genealogy, 1-17, proves that Jesus was born with legal right to be King of the Jews since He was the son of David, the son of Abraham. The account of His conception by the Holy Spirit in the womb of a virgin, 18-25, shows Him also to be the Son of God, the Eternal Word, who was with God and was God (Jn 1:1-2) yet became man (Lk 1:26-35; 2:1-7; Jn 1:14), fulfilling Isa 7:14 (cf. Mt 1:22-23). The God-Man alone could be 'Jesus' (Gr. form of Heb. 'Jehoshua,' the Lord-Saviour). Verses 18-25 indicate Jesus was conceived by the Holy Spirit, and hence had a sinless human nature joined to deity. Thus Jesus is able to 'save his people from their sins,' 21.

The Citadel, Old City of Jerusalem, site of Herod the Great's palace, probably where the magi visited the notorious monarch in their search for the newborn King.

2. The infancy of the King

1-12. The visit of the magi. This visit of believing Gentiles to worship the newborn King particularly fits this gospel of the King and hence is recorded only here. It occurred perhaps months after the nativity, while the holy family, however, was still residing in Bethlehem. The magi were a learned class in Persia, either linked as priests of the religion of Zoroastrianism or to the practice of astrology. Herod the Great, an able and cruel Idumaean, ruled Judea as king by grant of the Roman senate from 37 to 4 B.C. At this time he was an aged, failing tyrant, notoriously jealous and unprincipled, a stark contrast to the true 'king of the Jews,' 2. The glimpse given here of the wicked wretch, insanely insecure, accords perfectly with what is known of him from history and archaeology. He who even murdered some of his own family appears as the murderer of the innocent children of Bethlehem and as the would-be murderer of Messiah. The Gentiles (cf. Lk 2:32) brought gold, bespeaking the King's deity; incense, indicating the fragrance of His life; and myrrh, used in embalming the dead, hinting of His mission to die.

13-23. Flight into Egypt. Demonic powers acting through Herod, and later through the leaders of His own nation, resisted the King. Satan centered His attack against God's plans in Christ for the earth. Egypt, the site of Israel's great enslavement, now became the refuge of Israel's Deliverer and the world's Redeemer in the form of a helpless baby.

3. The King's herald and baptism

1-12. The King's herald. John the Baptist, predicted in the OT, 3 (cf. Isa. 40:3-5; Mal 3:1), now appears as the King's forerunner. John's birth and mission are described by Luke (Lk 1:5-80). His message, 'Repent, for the kingdom of heaven is near,' 2, was an announcement of the messianic kingdom as foretold by OT prophets to be set upon the earth over which David's son and Lord is to reign. It was 'near' from the commencement of John's announcement here to the rejection of the King (Mt 12:1-45; cf. notes on Mt 4:17), and the announcement of a new brotherhood (Mt 12:46-50). It is the 'kingdom of heaven' because it is the administration of the heavens upon the

earth (Mt 6:10), being a term derived from Daniel (cf. Dan 2:34-35, 44; 7:23-27).

John's baptism was not Christian baptism (cf. Acts 19:1-7), but an outward act signifying the repentance of the candidate and identification with John's message, 11. In 11 and 12 the two advents blend. As a result of the first advent and Christ's finished redemption, He baptized with the Holy Spirit, in the sense that Pentecost (the initial occurrence of the baptism, Acts 2:1-4) was a result of Christ's atoning work. The baptism with fire (judgment) awaits the second advent.

13-17. The King's baptism. Why should the sinless One insist on a ceremony that signified confession of sin and repentance, 13-14? The answer was, 'to fulfill all righteousness,' 15, i.e., the righteous requirements of the Mosaic law. Since Jesus was here being consecrated to His public ministry of King, Prophet, and Priest, the essence of which was to center in His priestly work of redemption, it is His setting apart to His work as Priest that here comes into clearest focus. The levitical law required that all priests be consecrated when they were 'about thirty years old' (Lk 3:23; cf. Num 4:3) by washing, then anointing (Ex 29:47; Lev 8:6-36). Aaron shared in the washing, being a sinner and needing it, and thus furnishes the type of the baptism of Christ, who not being a sinner Himself and not needing it nevertheless identified Himself with sinners and fulfilled the Aaronic type. Jesus' baptism (washing), 14-15, was followed by His anointing, when the heavens were opened and the Holy Spirit came upon Him, 16, the Father's voice sealing His threefold ministry, 17. This was the priestly anointing (cf. Ex 29:5-7, where the anointing followed the washing) of Him who was thus divinely consecrated for the work of redemption (Acts 4:27; 10:38), as well as that of King and Prophet.

4. The testing of the King

1-11. The testing by the devil. This testing of the 'last Adam' (1 Cor 15:45) in the wilderness was in striking contrast to that of the first Adam in paradise. The first Adam, as lord of the first creation, acting in disobedience to God, fell and lost all. But the last Adam, as Servant in submission to the Father, acted wholly in dependence upon the Father, and in thus

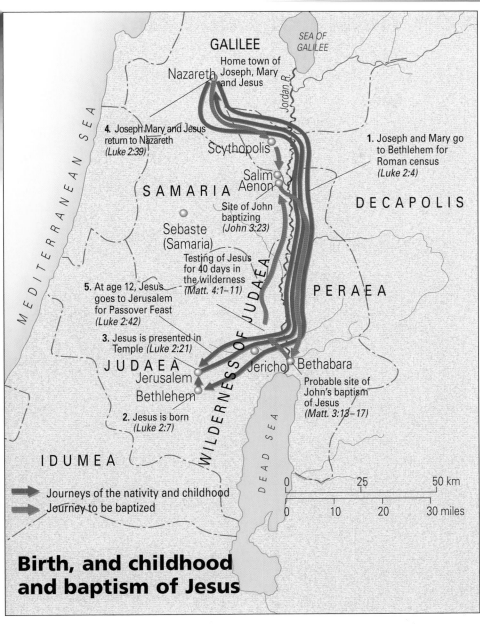

GALILEE

Home town of
Joseph, Mary
and Jesus

Nazareth

Jordan R.

SEA OF
GALILEE

4. Joseph Mary and Jesus
return to Nazareth
(Luke 2:39)

Scythopolis

1. Joseph and Mary go
to Bethlehem for
Roman census
(Luke 2:4)

Salim
Aenon

S A M A R I A

Site of John
baptizing
(John 3:23)

D E C A P O L I S

Sebaste
(Samaria)

Testing of Jesus
for 40 days in
the wilderness
(Matt. 4:1–11)

W I L D E R N E S S   O F   J U D A E A

P E R A E A

5. At age 12, Jesus
goes to Jerusalem
for Passover Feast
(Luke 2:42)

3. Jesus is presented in
Temple *(Luke 2:21)*

J U D A E A
Jerusalem

Jericho

Bethabara

Bethlehem

Probable site of
John's baptism
of Jesus
(Matt. 3:13–17)

2. Jesus is born
(Luke 2:7)

I D U M E A

DEAD SEA

0   25   50 km

0   10   20   30 miles

➡ Journeys of the nativity and childhood
➡ Journey to be baptized

MEDITERRANEAN SEA

Birth, and childhood and baptism of Jesus

resisting the threefold temptation of the devil
regained all. He thus proved His worthiness and
ability as the Sinless One to redeem sinners as
Priest; as the True One, rejecting Satan's lies, to
declare truth as the Prophet; and rejecting
Satan's false kingship, to be the true King of
kings and Ruler of the redeemed earth. The
Man of obedience conquered Satan by the Word
of God in Deuteronomy, the book of obedience
(cf. Deut 8:3; 6:16; 10:20).

**12-25. The King begins His public
ministry.** Jesus resided in Capernaum, 12-13

(Tell Hum), a populous, bustling fishing port on
the NW shore of the Lake of Galilee. His
incipient ministry fulfilled Isa 9:1-2. The King's
message (also that of His forerunner) was,
'Repent, for the kingdom of heaven is near,' 17
(cf. notes on Mt 3:2). This expression 'near' or
'has drawn near' meant that the King was then
present and that a bona fide offer of the
kingdom was being made to Israel on the *one
condition* of her repentance. The nation's
failure to repent even with its true King in its
midst, and the consequent rejection of both the

A peasant house of Bible times

Water jar

Oil lamp in alcove

Parapet stipulated
for safety in Jewish law

Grapes drying in sun

External stairs
to roof

Kindling for fire

Animals' section of house

Manger

Goats kept for milk

Platform for human habitation

Bed mat stowed during the day

Roller to smooth roof

Wattle and daub

Roof surface of hardened clay

Wooden roof support beams

Potage

Hand grinding grain to make flour

Bread oven

A peaceful stretch of the Jordan river south of the Sea of Galilee, one of the traditional sites for Jesus' baptism by John.

King and the kingdom were part of the divine plan to demonstrate the nation's inveterate sinfulness and the necessity of the King's atoning death as a prerequisite for the future establishment of the kingdom. The call of the disciples Peter and Andrew, 18-20 (cf. (Mk 1:16-20; Lk 5:2-11), and James and John, 21-22, is recorded. On Decapolis, 25, see note on Mk 7.

5-7. Kingdom proclamations of the King

5:1-16. Character of the citizens of the kingdom. Ch. 5-7 present the Sermon on the Mount, uttered by the King when 'the kingdom of heaven' was being announced. The beatitudes, 1-12, give the character of those who inherit the kingdom. Such who really 'repent' become also 'the salt of the earth,' 13, as well as 'the light of the world,' 14-16.

5:17-48. The King and the Mosaic law. The King fulfilled the law, confirming and emphasizing its deeper spiritual meaning. By so doing, He condemned every natural, spiritually unrenewed man, and showed that the kingdom of heaven will be established only through a King who must also become the Saviour of those who will be His citizens. Only then will they enjoy such righteousness, love, and perfection as the King here describes. That day will be fully realized at His second advent when the kingdom

will come and His will will be done on earth as it is in heaven (Mt 6:10).

6:1-18. Heirs of the kingdom and prayer. Heirs of the kingdom are to be motivated by true inner righteousness, which they are to possess and practice. This righteousness brings them into fellowship with God as their Father (used 12 times in this chapter). Such fellowship and consequent righteousness anticipate the cross where their possession was made possible. The Lord's Prayer, often more accurately termed 'The Disciple's Prayer,' is a timeless masterpiece that serves as a model for all prayer, containing all the essential elements of an effective prayer.

6:19-34. Heirs of the kingdom and the world. How those who have the true motive of righteousness, who move in the sphere of the Father's presence, are to act toward worldly wealth and cares is here outlined.

7:1-14. Heirs of the kingdom and censorious judging. Judgment of motives is here forbidden (cf. 1 Cor 4:5; 5:12-13). On verse 6 cf. 2 Pet 2:22, where 'dog' and 'sow' symbolize unregenerated externalists. Prayer is the cure for judgmentalism, 7-11, and the 'golden rule,' 12, summarizes proper human motives. The two ways, 13-14, recall Ps 1.

7:15-29. Heirs of the kingdom warned against false teachers. The fruits of false teachers attest them, 15-20, not their empty profession, 21-23, which is illustrated by those who build upon a rock and upon sand, 24-29.

8-9. The manifestation of the King

8:1-17. The King's power over sickness. Miraculous signs demonstrated to Israel that the kingdom was at hand. A leper was healed, 1-4; as well as the centurion's slave, 5-13; Peter's mother-in-law, 14-15, and many others, 16-17. Matthew arranges these miracles in a topical rather than a chronological arrangement (cf. Mark and Luke) to emphasize the Jewish character of his gospel.

8:18-34. The King's power over nature and demons showed Him Lord of creation and controller of the demon world. (Cf. note on Sea of Galilee in Mk 6.)

9:1-38. The King's power to forgive sin and other signs. The palsied man's healing showed the King's power to forgive sin, 1-8. Matthew's call, 9, and the King's eating with publicans, 10-13, demonstrated His mission to call sinners to repentance. The new cloth and new wine skins, 16-17, prefigure the better righteousness of grace contrasted with the old cloth and wine skins of legal ordinances (cf. Mk 2:21-22; Lk 5:36-39). Unfortunately, His

kingdom proclamation was being rejected, 27-34, despite the miracles accompanying it, 35-38.

10. The King's ambassadors

1-15. The Twelve and their commission. The King sent forth His 12 disciples, endued with miraculous powers, to proclaim the kingdom to Israelites only, 1-6. Their message was identical with that of John, the King's forerunner, 7 (cf. Mt 3:2 and comment), and of the King Himself (Mt 4:17 and comment). Their commission was to confirm the gospel of the kingdom with miraculous powers.

16-42. Resumption of the commission. The scope of 16-23 goes beyond the kingdom ministry of the 12 and is prophetic of the preaching of the Jewish remnant in the dark persecution-ridden days of the Great Tribulation preceding the second advent, when the gospel of the kingdom will again be proclaimed. Verse 23 will be fulfilled then. Verses 24-42 give encouragement to true disciples of the King.

11. Rejection of the kingdom message

1-19. John the Baptist rejected. Jesus' kingdom ministry prompted an inquiry from the forerunner, 1-6. John's imprisonment may

In the twentieth century a basilica was built on the Mount of Beatitudes, north of the Sea of Galilee, to mark the traditional location of Jesus' Sermon on the Mount.

have given rise to his doubts, but the miraculous evidences of Jesus' miracles were intended to calm his fears. The King's praise of John was gracious and eloquent, 7-19. He that is least in the kingdom of heaven, 11, when it is established on earth, will be greater in position (not in moral grandeur) than John, who did not enter the kingdom but merely announced that which was then rejected. Verse 12 emphasizes the violence the kingdom suffered from opposers and sinners.

20-24. The King rejected. The kingdom of heaven, announced by John, preached and authenticated by the King and His ambassadors by miraculous signs, was morally rejected, so the King announced judgment. Korazin (Kerazeh) was located scarcely two miles N of Capernaum(Tell Hum) in the area on the NW shore of the Lake of Galilee, where extensive ruins remain, including a synagogue known for two centuries. Bethsaida was the fishing quarter of Capernaum, the name meaning 'houses of fishing.' It evidently spread on both sides of the Jordan as the river entered the lake. Capernaum was the thriving populous metropolis of the region on the NW shores of Galilee.

25-30. The new message of the King. This was a crisis in the King's ministry. He turned from the rejecting, unrepentant nation, and offered rest and service to individuals in the nation who were repentant and conscious of need.

12. Rejection of the King consummated

1-21. The King in rejection. The events of this chapter focus upon the full rejection of the kingdom and mark the great turning point in Matthew's gospel. No longer was the kingdom preached to Israel. Rejection of the kingdom messengers was seen in the accusation of the Pharisees concerning breaking the Sabbath, 1-8. As the rejected *King,* our Lord aptly referred to what David did in rejection (1 Sam 21:6). He declared Himself Lord of the Sabbath, and healed the man with the atrophied hand on the Sabbath, 9-14. In demonic hate the leaders planned to murder Him, 14. The rejected King of Israel intimated a future turning to the Gentiles, 15-21 (cf. Mt 10:5-6; Isa 42:1-4). This would await His official rejection manifested in His crucifixion (Mt 26-27) and the final

rejection of the resurrected Christ (Lk 24:46-47; Acts 9:15; 13:46; 28:25-28).

22-45. The King and the unpardonable sin. The healing of the demoniac, 22-23, precipitated the blasphemy of the Pharisees, 24, who committed the unpardonable sin of attributing the mighty works of the incarnate King to Satanic (demonic) power, rather than to the Holy Spirit, 25-32. Announcing judgment once more, 33-42 (cf. 11:20-24), the King uttered a panoramic prophecy of the nation Israel under the figure of a demoniac, 43-45. That generation in its Pharisaic externalism was like a demoniac in the undemonized state – empty, swept, and put in order. The entrance of seven worse demons predicted the demon control of the nation in the last days, when it will fall under Antichrist's sway (Dan 9:27; Rev 9:1-12; cf.2 Thess 2:8-10; Jn 5:43).

46-50. The King's new relationship. King and kingdom message rejected, the King refused to see even His own, symbolizing the fact that His relationship to His own nation, to which He had come as promised King, was now abrogated. A new message and relationship was outlined (ch. 13).

13. The rejected King tells of the interim kingdom

1-2. The King at the seaside. The King began to teach in parables. These parables, reported in full only in Matthew, portray the mysteries of the kingdom of heaven. This was now no longer the kingdom so clearly promised to Israel by OT prophets, preached as at hand by the forerunner, the King Himself, and His heralds (ch. 3-12), and rejected (ch. 11-12). It was the kingdom of the heavens in its mystery form, setting forth spiritual conditions that will prevail on the earth between Israel's rejection of the King and His kingdom and her future acceptance of it. These mysteries were not revealed in the OT (cf. Mt 13:11, 34-35), in contrast to that kingdom which had just been rejected by the nation and was well known from full OT revelation (e.g., Isa 9, 11, 35; Mic 4, etc.).

3-52. The seven parables (mysteries) of the kingdom. They are called 'mysteries' because they contain truth previously not revealed. The seven parables deal with the

Herod the Great had John the Baptist executed after he had denounced the king's incestuous marriage. At this luxurious winter palace that Herod the Great built for himself near Jericho the tyrant died miserably.

present age when Israel, the vineyard, is untended (Isa 5:1-7). *Parable 1* reveals that our Lord sows the seed of the Word in the field (the world), 3-23. *Parable 2*, the good seed and the tares, 24-30, interpreted in 36-43, shows Satan's activity and deception during this age in counterfeiting the wheat, the true children of the kingdom, with false professors (Mt 7:21-23). *Parable 3*, the mustard seed, 31-32, symbolizes the rapid growth of the mystery form of the kingdom. *Parable 4*, the leaven hidden in three measures of meal, 35, warns of the permeation of the truth of the Word with the error of leaven by false teaching during this age (cf. Mt 16:11-12; Mk 8:15; 1 Cor 5:6; Gal 5:9). *Parable 5* portrays our Lord who gave all He had to possess the treasure (Israel) hid in the field, 44 (cf. Isa 53:4-10; Ps 22:1; 2 Cor 8:9). He will reinstate this treasure on the basis of His atoning death. *Parable 6* shows our Lord as a merchant, who found 'one [pearl] of great value' (the church, Eph 5:25-27) and sold all at Calvary to purchase it, 45-46. *Parable 7* presents the net gathering both good and bad, 47-52, which will remain together during this age until separated at its consummation.

53-58. Further evidences of the King's rejection, as He returned to Nazareth.

14. The martyrdom of the King's herald

1-14.John's martyrdom. Herod Antipas, a son of Herod the Great by a Samaritan woman, Malthace, therefore non-Jewish by birth, was tetrarch of Galilee (Lk 3:1) and Perea (4 B.C.- A.D. 39). He alienated himself from his

Jewish subjects by his incestuous marriage to his niece Herodias, former wife of his half-brother Herod Philip. This wickedness was denounced by John the Baptist and resulted in his beheading.

15-36. Jesus' ministry of mercy. He fed the 5,000, 15-21 (Mk 6:30-44; Lk 9:10-17; Jn 6:1-14), and stilled the raging sea, 22-36 (Mk 6:45-56).

15. Further ministry of the rejected King

1-20. His denunciation of the scribes and Pharisees. They accused Jesus of violating man-made traditions, 1-2. Jesus responded by condemning their sin of setting aside the Word of God by their traditions, 3-6. He further exposed their hypocrisy and corruption by quoting Isa 29:13, and denounced their wicked externalism, 7-20.

21-28. He ministers to a Gentile. After having been rejected by His own, Christ had hinted of His wider ministry to Gentiles (Mt 12:18; cf.Isa 42:1-4). Now began a precursive fulfillment. As the rejected son of David, He ministered to a non-Israelite of Phoenicia, here called 'the region of Tyre and Sidon' after its two principal seaports. The 'dogs' were Gentiles, outside the sphere of Jewish spiritual privilege denoted by 'the children's bread.' When the Canaanite woman addressed Him as 'Lord,' and took the place of humble faith, as it were, among 'the *little* dogs,' she obtained her request. This episode prefigured Gentile salvation in this age.

29-39. He ministers to the multitudes. The healing of the multitudes, 29-31, represented the blessings of Israel's God on all who come to Him by faith. Feeding the 4,000 further showed the compassion of the King for the multitudes, 32-39 (cf. Mk 8:19).

16. The rejected King predicts His death

1-12. The leaven of the scribes and Pharisees. Another exposé of the wickedness of the Jewish leaders was given, 1-4, as they tempted Jesus, asking for a sign after they had disbelieved and rejected all His previous miraculous works. The sign of the prophet Jonah concerning His resurrection, 4, was the only one He gave them (cf. Mt 12:39-41; Lk 11:29-32). This served to aggravate their guilt.

Jesus proceeded to interpret the symbol of leaven as evil doctrine, 6-12 (cf. Mt 13:33; 1 Cor 5:6). The leaven of the Pharisees was hypocritical externalism, that of the Sadducees rationalistic unbelief. Both rejected the King and His kingdom.

13-19. Peter's confession. On Caesarea Philippi, 13, see note on Mk 8:27. The confession of Peter involved the full deity of Jesus, 'Christ, the Son of the living God,' 16. This revelation to Peter, or anyone else, is not by human wisdom or ability but through God the Father, 17. Moreover, this truth of the deity of Christ ('the Son of the living God,' not 'the son of David') was to be the foundation of the church, 18, and not Peter himself. 'You are Peter (*petros,* a stone), and on this rock (*petra,* great ledge of rock) I will build my church' (cf. 1 Pet 2:4-6, where the apostle made it clear he was never to be thought of as 'the rock'). 'The keys of the kingdom of heaven,' 19, are to be thought of in the sense of Mt 13 (see note on Mt 13:1-2). Peter used these keys in opening gospel opportunity to Israel at Pentecost (Acts 2:38-42), to the racially mongrel Samaritans (Acts 8:14-17), and to Gentiles at Caesarea (Acts 10:34-44).

This was the limit of their use by Peter.

20-28. Christ foretells His death, resurrection, and return. The King enjoined His disciples not to tell anyone 'that he was the Christ,' 20, because they had been preaching Christ as the King of a covenanted kingdom promised to Israel. The church, on the other hand, must be built upon the proclamation of Him as the crucified, risen, and ascended Lord (Eph 1:20-23). Although the former testimony had ended, the new message was not yet ready, inasmuch as the blood of the new covenant had not yet been shed. Therefore, our Lord at this turning point of vast importance predicted His death, resurrection, 21, and second advent, 28. Little wonder Peter and the other disciples, hitherto preaching about and looking for the King to come into His kingdom, could not understand Christ's sudden prediction of His sufferings and death, 22-23. They thus had to be instructed in the rigors of true discipleship, 24-26, and rewards at the second advent when the King and His kingdom would be accepted by Israel, 27-28. Some of them saw this future kingdom presented in an audio-visual demonstration in ch. 17.

At Caesarea Philippi, in the far north of Palestine, in the foothills of Mount Hermon, Peter made his great confession that Jesus was the Messiah.

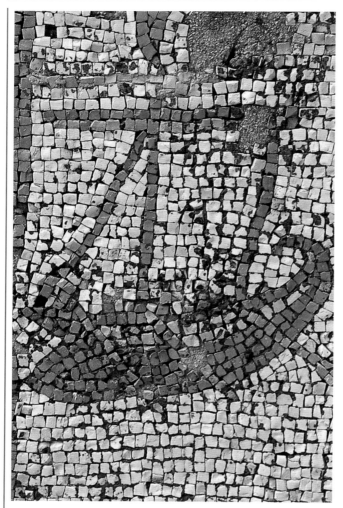

Mosaic of an ancient fishing vessel on the Sea of Galilee, discovered at the site of Capernaum, where Jesus miraculously found coins in a fish's mouth.

17. The rejected King and His coming glory

1-21. The transfiguration. See also comments on Lk 9:18-62. In 16:28, which belongs to this chapter, Christ had announced His second advent in glory (cf. 16:27) to establish the kingdom so lately rejected (Mt 3-12). He predicted that some who were with Him then (Peter, James, and John, 1) would not die until they saw 'the Son of Man coming in his kingdom' (16:28). This prediction was fulfilled a week later in Christ's transfiguration, which was a portrayal of this glorious future event in miniature (2 Pet 1:16-21). All the essential details of the picture are present: (1) Christ as Son of Man, not in the humiliation of His sinless humanity but in glory; (2) Moses glorified, representing the redeemed who have entered the kingdom via death; (3) Elijah, likewise glorified, but representing the redeemed who have entered the kingdom by translation (1 Thess 4:14-17; 1 Cor 15:50-53); (4) Peter, James, and John, unglorified, representing in the vision the Jewish remnant at the end who will enter the kingdom in unglorified bodies; (5) the crowd in its need at the foot of the mountain, 14-21, portraying the nations to be brought into the blessings of the kingdom after its restoration to Israel (Acts 1:6; Isa 11:10-12), with manifestation in deliverance from Satan and demon powers (Rev 20:1-3).

22-23. Jesus' repetition of His approaching death (cf. Mt 16:21; Mk 9:30-32; Lk 9:43-45). This was necessary because it was a prerequisite to His second advent and the kingdom. See also notes on Mk 9:1-13.

24-27. The tribute money. This miracle of the tax money retrieved from the fish's mouth at the busy lakeside metropolis of Capernaum demonstrates the humility and subjection of the omnipotent and omniscient Lord of the universe who had so recently revealed His glory in His coming kingdom. The tax in question was an ecclesiastical one, for the support of the Temple (Ex 30:13; 2 Chr 24:6, 9). Our Lord was actually saying, 'This is a tax for supporting My Father's house. As His Son, then, this tax is not incumbent upon Me. I am free.'

18. Instructions of the rejected King – forgiveness

1-14. Character of citizens of the kingdom. The disciples were interested in holding office in the kingdom, 1. Jesus stressed the importance rather of being a citizen of the kingdom by being converted, 2-3, and by showing the humility of a child, 4-5. Jesus then discussed offenses (actions and attitudes that harm others or cause others to sin), 6-10. These offenses must be dealt with severely, as denoted by Jesus' hyperbolic use of the figure of self-mutilation, which of course is not meant to be taken with bold literalness. Citizens of the kingdom have guardian angels, 10, and are the recipients of the saving shepherd ministry of the Son of Man, 11-14.

15-20. Discipline and prayer in the kingdom. It is the mystery aspect of the kingdom which is in view in this passage (see note on Mt 13:1-2). Since this form of the kingdom is largely, though not entirely, coterminous with the church, the church is here anticipated as in Mt 16:18. The complete concept of the church is not given until it is revealed through Paul (cf. Eph 3:1-10). Discipline in the church is to take a certain pattern so that the injured member will know how to respond. This is the procedure of love and patience, bathed in prayer.

21-35. Forgiveness in the kingdom. Seventy times seven is 490, implying that genuine forgiveness is beyond record-keeping or limitation. The parable of the kingdom (cf. the seven of Mt 13) teaches the importance of forgiveness (cf. Eph 4:32).

19. Instructions of the rejected King – divorce

1-15. Concerning divorce. Jesus left Galilee to begin His Perean ministry, 1-2 (ch. 19-20). A question by the Pharisees gave occasion for His teaching about divorce, 3-12 (cf. Mt 5:31-32; Mk 10:2-12; Lk 16:18; and Paul's discussion in 1 Cor 7). Monogamy is God's standard, 4-6, but certain accommodations to human frailty were permitted by the Mosaic law, 7-8 (Deut 24:1-4). Christ seems to allow only fornication as a ground for divorce, 9, but also takes into consideration men's weakness, 10-12. He had in mind the interest of little children, the sufferers

from divorce, 13-15.

16-26. The rich young man. Religious and moral but unsaved, lacking spiritual reality, this young man pictures the case of many in Christendom. They think it is necessary to *do* something (works) in order to be saved, rather than to *believe* the gospel that Christ has done something for them. The Lord did not promise the young man eternal life by doing, but told him to perform an act which would prove to him his lack of saving faith and the spuriousness of his claim of keeping the law (Mk 10:17-30; Lk 18:18-30).

27-30. Rewards in the renewal. This renewal (re-creation) refers to the renewal of the earth in the mediatorial Davidic kingdom offered and rejected (Mt 3-12), but restored at the second advent (Mt 25:31).

20. Instructions of the rejected King – the laborers

1-16. Parable of the laborers. This parable illustrates the truth Jesus declared in 19:30 and repeated in 20:16, to correct Peter's self-occupation and bargaining spirit (19:27). God does not evaluate man's service as man evaluates it. Some who are prominent and apparently successful in Christian work, whom we look upon as greatly used by God, will appear near the bottom of the Lord's list of

A shepherd leads his flock through the streets of Jericho, the ancient city where Jesus healed two blind men on his final journey to Jerusalem.

faithful servants, while humble, self-effacing servants, little recognized by men, will appear at the top. Moreover, we are to be interested in the Lord's service primarily, not in the reward; in the quality, not the length of our service.

17-28. Jesus again predicts His death and resurrection. This is the fourth prediction of these events (Mt 12:38-42; 16:21-28; 17:22-23). In the light of the foretelling of Jesus' suffering and death, 17-19, the selfishness of the request of the mother of James and John appears. She desired eminence for her sons in the promised kingdom, misunderstanding its character.

29-34. Two blind men healed. These called upon Jesus as 'Son of David,' 30-31, and were healed outside Jericho (Tulûl Abû el-'Alâyiq on the Wadi Qelt, 17 miles from Jerusalem). They recognized His messianic authority and may foreshadow the future conversion of the Jewish remnant who will accept the Messiah at His second advent. (Cf. Mk 10:46-52; see note there on Jericho.)

21. The rejected King enters Jerusalem

1-11. The royal entry into Jerusalem. He came to Jerusalem as King to fulfill the prophecy uttered by Zechariah (Zech 9:9). Although acclaimed superficially by excited mobs, He was still the rejected King, for the official representatives of the nation gave Him no welcome in this His final and official offer of Himself to them. Moreover, even the Hosanna-shouting (Ps 118:26), garland-waving throngs answered in terms of rejection to the question of who He really was, 11. Instead of the promised King-Messiah, Jehovah-Jesus, God-Saviour, they replied, 'Jesus, the prophet from Nazareth of Galilee.' But since the King and the kingdom (Mt 3-12) were rejected in the region of Galilee, it was necessary that Jerusalem, the royal city, be given an opportunity to accept Him.

12-32. Second cleansing of the temple and the fig tree cursed. The first cleansing of the temple was at the beginning of His ministry (Jn 2:13-17); this was at the end, 12-13. There it was His zeal for God's house, here He acted with kingly prerogative and miraculously ministered to the needy in the cleansed precincts, 14 (cf. Isa 56:7; Jer 7:11; Lk 14:21). The cursing of the barren fig tree, 18-22,

is a type of Israel (Joel 1:7), here symbolized in national rejection. Lk 13:6-9 is contrasted with Mt 24:32-33, where symbolic prophecy indicates that Israel shall again bud (be brought back to her national election, Rom 11:1-26). The questioning of Jesus' authority by the nation's leaders, 23-27 (cf. Mk 11:27-33; Lk 20:1-8), as well as the parable of the two sons, 28-32, demonstrates further their hatred and rejection of the King.

33-46. Parable of the landowner. The landowner (God) planted a vineyard (Israel, Isa 5:1-7). The servants were the prophets, who were ill-treated. Finally God sent His Son (Messiah) and they put Him to death, 37-39. The events of the Roman-Jewish war, A.D. 67-70, were prophesied, 40-41. Jesus aptly quoted prophecies referring to Himself as the Stone rejected (Ps 118:22-23), and showed that the kingdom of God in the larger sense of spiritual light and salvation would be taken away from Israel nationally and given to the Gentiles (Rom 9:30-33; 11:1-24). In verse 44 our Lord referred to Himself in judgment as the Smiting Stone of destruction (Dan 2:34).

22-23. The rejected King clashes with the leaders

22:1-14. Parable of the marriage feast. This parable portrays how the King and the kingdom were offered to the nation, 1-2, but were refused, 3. Verses 4-6 represent the repeated offer and its further rejection, the statement 'everything is ready' hinting at the death of Christ and its salvation benefits. After Christ's atoning death the nation had a chance to repent (Acts 1-8), but refused. The worldwide offer to Gentiles was predicted, 8-10, after the events of A.D. 67-70 were described, 6-7. The wedding garment, 11-14, is the righteousness of Christ. Many have the invitation to salvation extended to them, comparatively few accept, 14 (cf. Rom 8:30).

22:15-46. The nation further shows its rejection. The Herodians were Jews in external religious forms, but a bitter offense to the nation as a whole in their devotion to easygoing, world-conforming Hellenism, so avidly espoused by the Herods, 15-22. In hatred of Jesus they made common cause against Him with the Sadducees, 23-33, the religious rationalists, and the Pharisees, 34-40, empty externalists. Jesus confounded the blind Pharisees by asking them about Ps 110:1, which has reference to His own divine-human person, 41-46. All three parties, representative of all Israel, being silenced, were unrepentant. No further message was left them but one of impending doom.

23:1-39. The doom pronounced and lament made over Jerusalem. The thunderous 'woes' of the righteous wrath of the rejected son of David melted in tears as He announced blessing and hope for the repentant remnant who will greet Him at His second advent with the messianic welcome of Ps 118:26: 'Blessed is he who comes in the name of the Lord.'

24-25. The rejected King's Olivet discourse

24:1-3. Prophecy of the destruction of the temple. The rejected King as Prophet predicted, in this discourse, the events of that still future time when He will resume dealing with Israel (cf. 23:39) just before His return to earth in glory. The gorgeous edifice, 1-2, which provoked this great prophetic discourse was the Herodian temple. It was so superlatively beautiful that even the Romans, out of regard for its magnificence, were anxious to spare it

when the city fell in A.D. 70. It was in clear view from the superior height of the Mount of Olives as the Prophet par excellence foretold its doom and the doom of the Jewish state that would occur in A.D. 70. The disciples asked three questions, 3. 'When will this (destruction of the city and temple) happen?' The answer is found in Lk 21:20-24. 'What will be the sign of your coming and of the end of the age?' The answer is in Mt 24:4-34.

24:4-26. Events of the Tribulation. These prophecies deal with Israel in the period of Tribulation just prior to the return of Messiah-King to establish His earthly kingdom, although the end of the present age will be characterized by the general conditions mentioned in 24:4-8. A comparison of 4-8 with Rev 6 gives evidence that these verses have particular reference to the first half of the Tribulation period when Israel herself will dwell in relative safety because of the covenant made with 'the ruler who will come,' Antichrist (Dan 9:26).

Verses 9-26 describe the events of the last half of the Tribulation after the world leader (Antichrist) has broken his covenant with Israel and forces idolatrous worship of himself (Dan 9:27b; 2 Thess 2:4; Rev 13:15-18). This period will be characterized by great persecution, 9-10,

17ff. (Rev 12:12-17), desolation of the Temple and its worship, 15 (Dan 9:27), unbelieving Israel being deceived by false prophets, 11-12 (Rev 13:11-18), and believing Israel witnessing to the good news of Messiah's kingdom, 14. The advent of Messiah will terminate these events, 27.

24:27-30. Second coming of Messiah. The chronology of events is furthered by a description of the second advent. It follows immediately after the Tribulation, 29, preceded by a particular sign, 30. The coming will be sudden, 27, and evident to all, 30.

24:31. Regathering of Israel. The event following the second advent will be the national regathering of Israel's elect through special angelic ministries.

24:32-36. The certainty of Messiah's coming. The parable of the fig tree illustrates the certainty of the second advent, for the fulfillment of the signs that are to be given in the Tribulation will announce Messiah's coming as certainly as new shoots on the fig tree announce the approach of summer.

24:37-51. Exhortations to watchfulness. All three illustrations emphasize the unexpectedness of the Lord's coming by showing that the individuals concerned were occupied with the usual cares of life without giving thought to Messiah's return. Believing Israel is exhorted thereby to be prepared for that day.

25:1-30. The judgment of Israel. 'At that time,' 1, prepares for the next event following Israel's regathering, her judgment just prior to the establishment of Messiah's kingdom. This judgment is illustrated in the parables of the ten virgins, 1-13, and of the talents, 14-30. The ten virgins represent Israel at the end of the Tribulation. The five wise symbolize the believing remnant, the five foolish the unbelieving segment who only profess to look for Messiah's advent, 1-5. They will be without oil (a symbol of the Holy Spirit) and will be shut out of the messianic kingdom which is about to be set up, 6-10.

In the parable of the talents, 14-30, the man traveling in a far country represents Christ during His absence from the earth. He entrusted gifts to His servants. The servants with five and two talents are believers who enter into the 'master's happiness' (kingdom blessing), 21, 23.

The servant with one talent is excluded from the kingdom ('the darkness') and swept away in judgment with the ungodly, 24-30.

25:31-46. The judgment of the nations. The rejected King in concluding His great prophetic discourse presented a picture of that for which Israel had been looking in His first advent, Messiah sitting upon the Davidic throne of glory, 31. The time of this event is certain from the context, viz., at His coming in *glory.* The occasion is the judgment of the nations, 32-33, consisting of sheep and goats. The sheep are individuals who receive the gospel of the kingdom (Mt 24:14) and treat kindly 'these brothers of mine,' the believing remnant of Jews, 34-40. The goats are the wicked who reject the gospel of the kingdom and persecute the Jewish remnant, 41-46, thus showing their league with Satan, 41, the Beast, and the False Prophet (Rev 13:1-18). Those who thus align themselves against the 144,000 preachers of the coming kingdom (Rev 7:1-8; 14:1-5) will share Satan's fate, 41 (Rev 20:10).

26. Betrayal and arrest of the rejected King

1-16. His anointing for death. The King for the last time predicted His death, 1-2 (cf. Mt 12:38-42; 16:21-28; 17:22-23; 20:18-19). This prediction formed a prelude to the wicked counsel of the chief priests and scribes to kill Him, 3-5, and to His anointing by Mary of Bethany, 6-13 (cf. Mk 14:3-9; Jn 12:1-8). She alone seemed to have understood the meaning of His death. Matthew, recording the gospel of the King, relates that Mary anointed His head, as Samuel anointed the head of David (1 Sam 16:13), while John, recording the gospel of the Son of God, mentions only the anointing of Jesus' feet, the only suitable approach of the finite to the Infinite. This worshipful scene reveals Judas' base character (Jn 12:4-5) and is an introduction to his selling the Lord, 14-19 (cf. Mk 14:10-11; Lk 22:3-6). The price he received was 30 pieces of silver, the price of a common slave (cf. Zech 11:12-13; Ex 21:32).

17-35. The Passover and the Lord's supper. The Passover, commemorative of Israel's deliverance out of Egypt by the blood of the slain lamb (Ex. 12), was to be fulfilled in Christ's death, as the true Paschal Lamb. At the last Passover, 17-25, the King therefore

Jerusalem in the time of Jesus

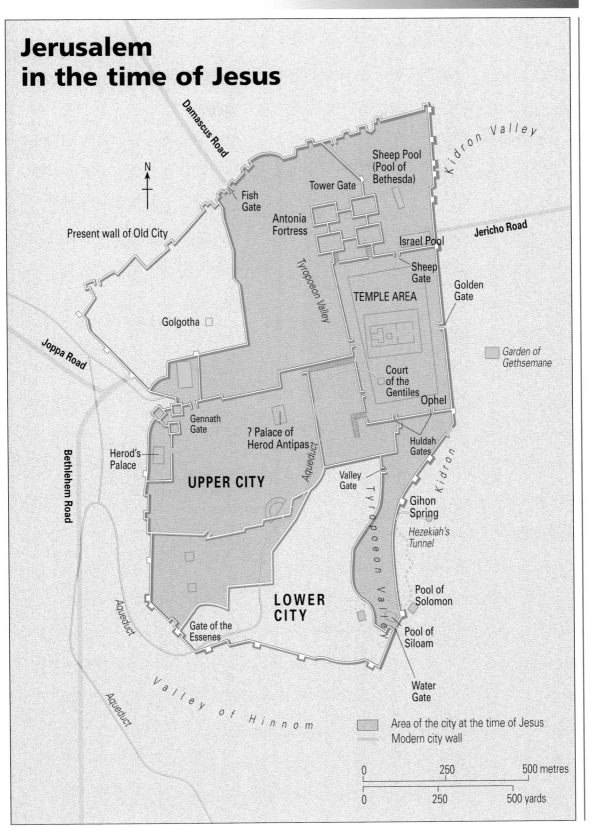

N

Damascus Road

Jericho Road

Joppa Road

Bethlehem Road

Present wall of Old City

Fish Gate

Tower Gate

Sheep Pool (Pool of Bethesda)

Kidron Valley

Antonia Fortress

Israel Pool

Sheep Gate

Golden Gate

TEMPLE AREA

Tyropoeon Valley

Golgotha

Garden of Gethsemane

Court of the Gentiles

Ophel

Gennath Gate

? Palace of Herod Antipas

Aqueduct

Huldah Gates

Herod's Palace

Kidron

UPPER CITY

Valley Gate

Tyropoeon Valley

Gihon Spring

Hezekiah's Tunnel

Pool of Solomon

LOWER CITY

Gate of the Essenes

Aqueduct

Pool of Siloam

Water Gate

Valley of Hinnom

Aqueduct

Area of the city at the time of Jesus

Modern city wall

| 0 | 250 | 500 metres |
| 0 | 250 | 500 yards |

introduced the new memorial, the Lord's Supper, with the new meaning, 26-30, 'Do this in remembrance *of me*' (1 Cor 11:24-25). The dividing line between the OT and NT is not the blank page between Malachi and Matthew, but Jesus' 'blood of the covenant, which is poured out for many [those who receive Him] for the forgiveness of sins,' 28. The King promised He would not drink the wine of this supper again with His disciples till the kingdom is established at His second advent. Thereupon Jesus foretold Peter's denial and His own resurrection, 31-35.

36-56. Christ's agony at Gethsemane. This involved no fear of death, but the contact of His sinless soul with the sin of the whole world as its vicarious bearer and expiator through the death on the cross (Isa 53:10; 2 Cor 5:21). This was the cup He prayed might pass from Him, 39, but *only* in the Father's will. His was an infinite anguish, as His infinitely holy soul faced the ordeal of 'being made sin' and knowing the prospect of the hiding of the Father's face (Ps 22:1; Mt 27:46). The betrayal and arrest of Jesus followed the great spiritual struggle in the garden, but the victory was won there and Calvary was a spontaneous outcome.

57-68. The King before Caiaphas and the Sanhedrin. In the trial the rejected King claimed to be the Son of God, 64 (cf. Dan 7:13-14). He was accused, accordingly, of blasphemy an 10:31-36). The conduct of the leaders in the nation's supreme court demonstrated their folly as they were forced to violate several of their own laws in order to condemn Christ (cf. *Mishnah,* Sanhedrin 4:1; 5:24).

69-75. Peter's denial displayed the infirmity even of one who knew the Lord yet failed to see his own weakness.

27. The trial and death of the rejected King

1-32. Jesus before Pilate. The Sanhedrin handed over Jesus to Pontius Pilate, the Roman procurator of Judea (A.D. 26-36), since Rome was the final authority. Pilate's headquarters were at coastal Caesarea, but he came to Jerusalem on Jewish feasts because of the danger of uprisings. His praetorium or palace was apparently part of the Tower of Antonia near the present Via Dolorosa. Meanwhile, Judas had repented of his foul deed, and taking the 30 pieces of silver (cf. Zech

11:12-13; Jer 18:1-14; 19:1-3) cast them into the Temple, and then committed suicide, 3-10. Pilate's weakness and his unavailing attempt to get out of crucifying Jesus were pathetic. The choice of Barabbas, a notorious criminal, 15-23, further accentuated Pilate's cowardice, as well as his washing his hands as a token of his innocence, 24. Flogging, 26, was pitiless lashing with a whip of leather thongs imbedded with pieces of metal. It usually preceded capital punishment. Evidently Pilate hoped that this severe punishment would satisfy the crowd and they would not further insist on crucifixion. Mocking the King, 27-31, shows the height of impious wickedness and the moral insensitivity of that brutal age. Simon, pressed into carrying Jesus' cross, 32, was probably a Jew since many Jews lived in Cyrene, the capital city of the N. African district of Cyrenaica.

33-44. The crucifixion of the King. 'Golgotha' is the Aramaic for 'skull' (L. *Calvaria,* 'Calvary'; Gr. *kranion,* Lk23:33). Since 1842, when Otto Thenius of Dresden located Calvary on a rocky hill 250 yards NE of the Damascus Gate, this spot has been popularly identified as the location of the crucifixion. Gall was a bitter and poisonous herb, offered to Jesus as a painkiller, but it was refused. Crucifixion had been practiced by Phoenicians and Persians and was taken over from them by Rome, where it could be inflicted only on slaves and non-Romans. In Palestine this shameful and slow torturous form of death served as a public reminder of the Jews' servitude to Rome, and was inflicted for robbery, tumult and sedition. The gambling soldiers fulfilled Ps 22:18. The complete accusation or charge from the combined gospel narratives was: 'This is (Matthew and Luke) Jesus (Matthew and John) of Nazareth (John) the King of the Jews (all).' Over the head of every victim of crucifixion was inscribed his crime. In the King's case it was meant to be mockery. How little did His blind crucifiers realize He *really was* Jesus the King of the Jews. Even their taunts were truer than they knew. 'He saved others, but he *can't* save himself!' 42. If He was to be the world's Saviour He could not save Himself. (See notes on 'Passion Week' and 'Trials of Jesus,' Lk 23.)

45-50. The death of the King. The three-hour darkness was a supernatural phenomenon when the Father hid His face from

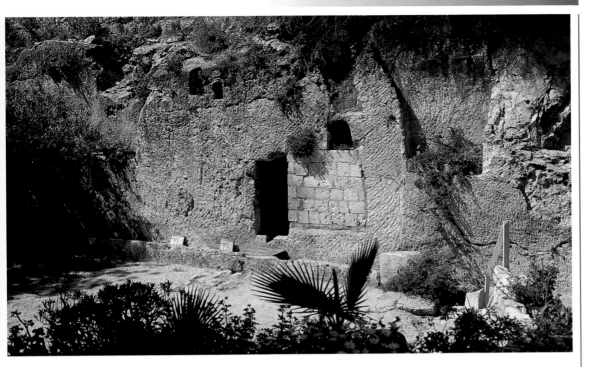

The Garden
Tomb, just outside
the Old City of
Jerusalem, gives a
clear idea of a
rock-cut tomb,
and is much loved
as a place of
tranquil
meditation amidst
the surrounding
noise and
busyness.

the Son as He became sin for us and cried out, 46, the pitiable words of Ps 22:1. The slow agony of physical torture was the least of our Lord's suffering as He became the Sin-bearer, for the Father turned His face from Him as His sinless soul felt the crushing load of the world's sin. The King willingly 'gave up his spirit,' 50 (cf. Jn 10:18). His death, as an act of His own will, made it different from the physical death of any other man.

51-56. The end of the legal age. The supernatural tearing of the curtain (Josephus reported that the curtain was four inches thick) that separated the holy place, into which the priests might enter, from the most holy place, which only the high priest could enter once a year on the day of atonement (Ex 26:31; Lev 16:1-34), signified that a 'new and living way' had been opened for all believers into the very presence of God by Christ's death (cf. Heb 9:1-8; 10:19-22). A new age was dawning in which bloody sacrifices, a temple, and a special Aaronic priesthood were no longer needed. The resurrection mentioned in 52-53 was after Christ's resurrection (cf. Lev 23:10-12), since He is the firstfruits (1 Cor 15:20). The Roman centurion recognized the crucified King as 'the Son of God,' 54 (cf. Mk 15:39-41; Lk 23:47-49).

57-66. The burial of the King.

Tenderly and lovingly was He buried in a new tomb provided by a rich man (Isa 53:9). Joseph was from Arimathea, about ten miles SE of Antipatris. The precautions His enemies took to secure the grave by sealing it and stationing a guard, 62-66, only resulted in God's overruling the plans of the wicked and offering indisputable proof of the King's resurrection.

28 The resurrection of the rejected King

1-10. The resurrection. The Sabbath (Saturday) ended at 6.00 p.m., and just before daybreak on Sunday, the first Easter (cf. Jn 20:1), the women came to the tomb to anoint Jesus' body. They thus showed much love but little faith in His resurrection (Mk 16:1, 11), being last at the cross and first at the tomb. The power and majesty of God were manifested in the earthquake, the angel who rolled back the stone and the stunned guards, 2-4. The stone, it is to be noted, was rolled away *after* the King was raised that the disciples might *look in, not* that the Lord of glory might come *out*. He had already risen in a body of glory (cf. Phil 3:20-21), which was no longer subject to natural laws. The sturdy Roman guards were not seeing a hallucination when they 'shook' before this manifestation of God's power 'and became like

Matthew and Mark compared

Matthew	Mark
Jesus as King	Jesus as Servant
Jews in mind	Gentiles in mind
Jesus predicted miracle-working King	Jesus the miracle-working Servant
Rooted in OT prophecy	Much fewer OT prophetic references
Key in God's purposes for Israel	Key in God's purposes for the world
Deity of the King by birth, fulfilled prophecy, works	Deity of the Servant by mighty works
Events recorded concerning the king – His genealogy, birth in Bethlehem, visit of wise men, childhood in Nazareth	All these omitted as not appropriate to the Servant portrait
Sermon on Mount, spoken as King, giving the principles of the kingdom	Omitted
Many parables included which belong to this gospel of the King but not appropriate to the gospel of the servant	Omits many of the parables – five of those in Mt 13; numerous others, and notably those of Mt 25
Presents the King of the Jews rejected, the mystery form of the kingdom from His rejection to His second advent to restore the kingdom to Israel	Presents the Servant of the Lord in life, death, resurrection bringing salvation to mankind

dead men.' The angel announced the Easter message of joy: 'He is not here; he has risen, just as he said,' and then the further proof of the reality of the event. 'Come and see the place where he lay,' 6. Slain because He claimed to be King of the Jews, He was now raised because He was King of kings and Lord of lords (Acts 2:20-36). Rejected by Israel at His first advent, He will be accepted as King at His second advent (Zech 12:10-13:1; Isa 9:1-7; 11:1-16; 52:13-53:12). After the angelic message, the risen King Himself appeared to the disciples, 8-10. For order of events see Mk 16. See note on Jn 20 for 'The Resurrection Authenticated.'

11-15. The false report of the Jews. The last crowning act of treachery by Israel's Christ-rejecting leaders displayed their terrible wickedness. They had first-hand proof of the resurrection, 11, but rejected it, 12, bribing the soldiers to lie about the whole matter. But God overruled and used the instance to give further proof of the resurrection. If the Roman soldiers fell asleep, 13, they were liable to death. And if they did fall asleep, their testimony concerning

the alleged theft would be worthless.

16-20. The great commission. The risen King gave the 11 disciples the great commission, couched in terms applicable to the present form of the kingdom (cf. note on Mt 13:1-2). His authority, which extends to every realm, supported His commission, which involved enlisting men under His lordship ('make disciples'), identifying them with Himself and His followers in the rite of baptism, and teaching them the truths of His Word, 18-20. The gospel ends with the promise of the Lord's continued presence with His own, 20b.

MARK

The gospel of the Servant of the Lord

Author. The early church ascribed the second gospel to John Mark, the son of a certain Mary of Jerusalem (Acts 12:12). He accompanied Paul and Barnabas on the first missionary tour (Acts 13:5), but for some reason left them at Perga (Acts 13:13). Later Paul and Barnabas separated because Paul refused to have Mark on the second tour. Mark accordingly went with Barnabas. Later Paul and Mark were reconciled (Col. 4:10-11). That Mark is the author of this gospel is mentioned by Papias about A.D. 135, Justin Martyr, about A.D. 150, as well as by Clement of Alexandria and Irenaeus somewhat later. Like Luke, Mark was not an apostle, as were Matthew and John.

Nature and purpose of Mark's gospel. This is the briefest of the four gospels. It is a narrative of dynamic movement and action, 'straightway' and 'immediately' being used more that 40 times in the KJV. It presents Jesus acting rather than speaking. It is directed not to the Jew as is Matthew, but to the Roman world, giving a portrait of Jesus as the powerful Son of God whose word was law in the natural as well as the supernatural realm. The paradox is that this strong Son of God is Servant of man, Savior, and Ransomer (Mk 10:45).

Place and date. Early church writers declare that Mark wrote his gospel while in Rome, as a disciple of Peter. It is to be dated, therefore, between A.D. 64 and 68. It is critically regarded as the earliest of the gospels. It has been calculated that it contains about 93 percent of the material the three synoptic gospels (Matthew, Mark and Luke) have in common. But dependence of the other synoptic gospels upon Mark is not a necessary conclusion. The Spirit of God inspired each writer independently, so that Matthew gospel may actually be earlier (c. A.D. 50) than Mark's, as well as Luke's (c. A.D. 58). See 'Synoptic gospels,' introduction to Luke.

Outline

1:1-13 The Servant's coming
1:14-13:37 The Servant's work
14:1-15:47 The Servant's death
16:1-20 The Servant's resurrection

Relief depicting Mark the gospel-writer from the Church of the Annunciation, which dominates the modern town of Nazareth.

S.MARCVS

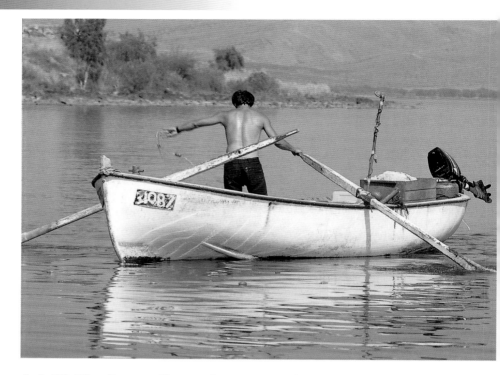

Laying down fishing nets on the Sea of Galilee. As a humble servant Himself, Jesus called lowly fishermen, to make them 'fishers of men.'

1:1-13. The Servant's coming

1. The Servant's identity. He is 'Jesus (see note on Mt 1:18-25) Christ [Messiah the Anointed One], the Son of God,' i.e., Deity incarnate. The deity of the Servant is first stressed. This is 'the gospel,' the good news. Apart from the fact of His being the Son of God He could not have been the perfectly obedient Servant, nor the triumphant miracle worker and the world's Saviour; His sonship and service are closely related.

2-8. The Servant's coming promised and announced. Malachi foretold His advent, 2 (Mal 3:1), as well as Isaiah, 3 (Isa 40:3); and John the Baptist, His forerunner, announced His coming (see notes on Mt 3:1-12). John's ministry, it must be remembered, was to Israel. His baptism, as a prophet of Israel, was not Christian baptism (cf. Acts 19:1-6). It was to prepare Israel for the offered kingdom and the reception of the divine King. Mark briefly refers to John's ministry merely to introduce the Servant. In contrast to Mt 3:11 and Lk 3:16-17, Mark mentions only the baptism of the Holy Spirit, 8, effected at the first advent (cf. Acts 1:5 with 2:4 and 11:16), but omits the baptism 'with fire,' connected with judgment at the second advent. The reason is that Christ, as the humble Servant, did not execute judgment, as He will when coming as

King (Matthew) and Son of Man (Luke). (See notes on Mt 3:11; cf. Lk 3:16-17.)

9-11. The Servant's baptism. (See notes on Mt 3:13-17 and Lk 3:21-22.) The Sinless One as Servant-Saviour submitted to the baptism of sinners to identify Himself with them and with their need. The essence of His ministry was to seek and to save the lost (Mk 10:45). His baptism was His induction to this priestly redemptive work.

12-13. The Servant's testing. This was a divine necessity, because His humanity had to be tried as a servant, 12 (cf. Mt 4:1-11; Lk 4:1-13). Here, in combat with Satan (from Heb. *sâtân* 'adversary'), He proved victorious in conflict to be fit to 'give his life as a ransom for many.' 'The desert,' 12, and the 'wild animals,'13, witness of a creation marred by sin, showed the self-humbling of the Creator, who came to triumph over the fallen creature, Satan, and overcome amid conditions effected by the Fall.

1:14-4.5. Ministry in Galilee

14-15. The Servant's message. Matthew reports that both John (see note on Mt 3:2) and Jesus (see note on Mt 4:17) preached the same message, involving repentance and the kingdom of heaven at hand. Mark, slanted toward Gentiles, uses the larger, more embracive term

Galilee in the time of Jesus

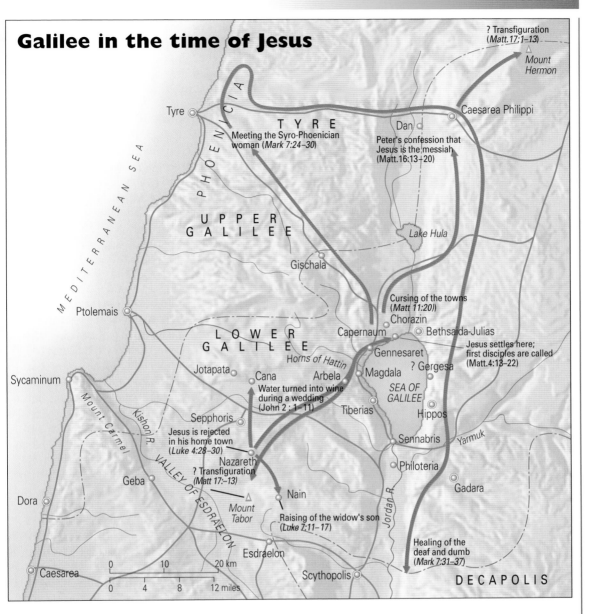

? Transfiguration
(*Matt.17:1–13*)

Mount
Hermon

Caesarea Philippi

Tyre

T Y R E

Dan

Meeting the Syro-Phoenician
woman (*Mark 7:24–30*)

Peter's confession that
Jesus is the messiah
(*Matt.16:13–20*)

P H O E N I C I A

M E D I T E R R A N E A N   S E A

U P P E R
G A L I L E E

Lake Hula

Gischala

Cursing of the towns
(*Matt 11:20)*)

Ptolemais

L O W E R
G A L I L E E

Chorazin

Capernaum

Bethsaida-Julias

Gennesaret

Jesus settles here;
first disciples are called
(*Matt.4:13–22*)

Horns of Hattin

? Gergesa

Sycaminum

Jotapata

Cana

Arbela

Magdala

SEA OF
GALILEE

Water turned into wine
during a wedding
(*John 2 : 1–11*)

Tiberias

Hippos

Mount Carmel

Kishon R.

Sepphoris

Jesus is rejected
in his home town
(*Luke 4:28–30*)

Sennabris

Yarmuk

Nazareth
? Transfiguration
(*Matt 17:–13*)

Philoteria

VALLEY OF ESDRAELON

Geba

Gadara

Dora

Nain

Jordan R.

Mount
Tabor

Raising of the widow's son
(*Luke 7:11–17*)

Esdraelon

Healing of the
deaf and dumb
(*Mark 7:31–37*)

Caesarea

0   10   20 km

Scythopolis

D E C A P O L I S

0   4   8   12 miles

'kingdom of God,' 15, as being more
appropriate. The simplest distinction may be
that the kingdom of God is universal, including
God's own of all ages (Lk 13:28-29; Heb 12:22-
23), in contrast to the kingdom of heaven which
is Davidic, mediatorial and messianic, having
its goal in the establishment of the kingdom of
God on the earth.

16-20. The Servant calls helpers. As a
humble servant Himself, He called lowly
fishermen, 16-20, to make them 'fishers of
men,' 17. Of the 12, four at least – Simon,
Andrew, James and John – were fishermen (cf.

Mt 4:18-22; Lk 5:1-11). These had believed
earlier an 1:35-42) and now were called to
commitment of life to service. (Cf. note on 'Sea
of Galilee' in Mk 6.)

**21-28. The Servant casts out demons
in Capernaum.** The Servant's ministry was
dynamic, not ritualistic, 21-22. Immeasurably
filled with the Holy Spirit (cf. Jn 3:34), He
challenged evil spirits, 23, i.e., demons (cf. Lk
4:33; Mk 5:1-20 and note on demonism).

**29-45. Other ministries of the
Servant.** These ministries included healing of
Peter's mother- in-law, 29-31 (cf. Mt 8:14-15; Lk

4:38-39); the healing of many, casting out demons, 32-34 (cf. note on Mk 5:1-20); the Servant's prayer life, 35; His tour of Galilee, 36-39; and the healing of a leper, 40-45.

2. Further ministry in Capernaum

1-12. Healing the paralytic. The Servant returned to His headquarters in Capernaum. His healing of the paralytic was proof of the deity of the Servant, for He alone could forgive sins, 5. The teachers of the law, copyists and interpreters of the Scriptures (scribes); realized this but refused to believe in His deity which had been manifested by His mighty miracles, 6-7. His miracles were selected to prove this, 8-11. The humble Servant was the world's Saviour, 10, who healed physical and mental sickness because He could deal with the great underlying problem of the forgiveness of sin, 12 (cf. Mt 9:1-8; Lk 5:18-26).

13-22. Calling Matthew. As a tax collector for Rome (publican), Levi was despised and counted as a common sinner, 14. Jesus' love for sinners, His holy desire to save them, 15, and His wonderful humility in associating with them advertised His character as a true Servant, 16-17, and aroused the ire of the scribes and Pharisees. The legalistic question of fasting revealed that Christ was 'the bridegroom,' 18-20 and 3:29), the bringer of God's grace. While the grace-bringing Bridegroom was with them, there was no occasion for mourning and fasting. Grace would supersede law. The occasion called for joy. The parable, 21-22, further elucidates the approaching change from the OT legal dispensation. The old cloth and old wineskins (legalistic Judaism) must not be mixed with the new cloth and new wine (the gospel of grace, Jn 1:17, to be brought in by Christ). (See note on Mt 9:16-17; cf. Lk 5:36-39.)

23-28. The Servant and the Sabbath. Closely connected with the coming change of dispensations is the episode showing the Servant as 'Lord even of the Sabbath,' 28. As Creator He rested on the seventh day. As a sign of His covenant with His people Israel, the Sabbath had become meaningless to them in its spiritual import. As the redeeming Servant, by His death and resurrection He was to supplant it by the Lord's Day. (See note on Mt 12:1-8.)

3. The Servant further displays His deity

1-12. Man with the withered hand healed. By this miracle in the synagogue the Servant proved what He had said about the Sabbath in 2:27-28. The empty legalism and utter hypocrisy of the Jews, 1-4, evoked His righteous anger, 5. They refused to believe, and the hardness of their hearts was what grieved the Lord. Pharisees (legalists) joined with Herodians (Hellenizing conformists) in common rejection and hatred of the Servant, 6, who went to minister to those who would receive His gracious ministry, 8-12.

13-19. The choosing of the twelve (cf. Mt 10:1-4; Lk 6:12-16; Acts 1:13).

Peter. His name Peter means 'stone' (Gr.). Cephas is Aramaic. He was married (Mt 8:14; Mk 1:30; Lk 4:38). Although he came from Bethsaida (Jn 1:44), he lived in Capernaum, and was a fisherman in partnership with James and John. He was a strange combination of cowardice and courage, impulsiveness and fearlessness. His association with the Servant, however, refined his character, making him an outstanding Christian.

James. Brother of John, both nicknamed Boanerges ('sons of thunder'). They and their father Zebedee conducted a fishing business partnership with the brothers Simon Peter and Andrew. James suffered martyrdom under Herod (Acts 12:2).

John. See introduction to John's gospel.

Andrew. One of the earliest of the Servant's converts, who led his brother Peter to Christ (Jn 1:40-42).

Philip, with Peter and Andrew, hailed from Bethsaida, a lake town NE of Capernaum. Philip brought Nathanael to Christ.

Bartholomew. Little is known of him. Some identify him with Nathanael.

Matthew. See introduction to Matthew's gospel.

Thomas ('twin') displayed zeal (Jn 11:16), but also a spirit of skepticism regarding Christ's resurrection (Jn 20:24-25). This, however, was completely dissipated by proof furnished by his contact with the living Christ.

James the son of Alphaeus. Some connect James (Heb. 'Jacob') with the James of the first church council (Acts 15) and writer of the book of James (cf. Acts21:18), though it is

Capernaum

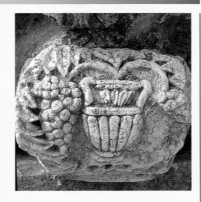

This busy fishing port on the NW shore of the Sea of Galilee, two and one half miles SW of the spot where the Jordan enters the lake, is identified with modern Tell Hum where extensive ruins exist (cf. Mt 11:23). It was also a toll-collecting station (Mt 9:9; 17:24-27), gathering tax revenue from caravans en route from Damascus to the Mediterranean coast and Egypt. Jesus' headquarters were located here. Excavations at Tell Hum have yielded one of the finest white limestone synagogues in Palestine, restored by the Franciscans. Ornamented with motifs of centaurs, lions, eagles, palm trees and vines, it is dated 2nd or 3rd cen. A.D. It was probably built on the site of the synagogue in which Jesus ministered.

Reliefs from Capernaum.

Remains of the third-century synagogue at Capernaum.

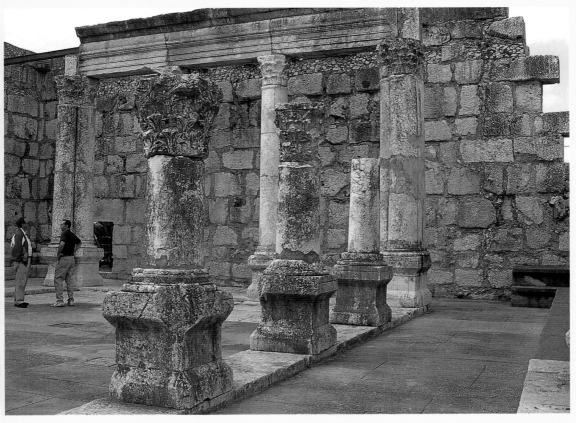

more commonly believed that Jesus' brother James was the Jerusalem church leader and writer referred to in Acts. He was called 'James the Less' (Mk 15:40), evidently because he was shorter in stature than James, the son of Zebedee.

Thaddeus. This is a Gr. form of Theudas, his surname being Lebbaeus (Aram. 'heart,' KJV). The name is likely a nickname for the Judas mentioned in Luke and Acts, selected to avoid confusion with Judas Iscariot.

Simon the Zealot had been a member of an extremely nationalistic sect of Judaism. Matthew the publican represented the opposite extreme. It is interesting that Jesus chose men of such diverse background.

Judas Iscariot. Judas is the Gr. form of Judah. He was the black sheep of the 12. Avaricious, greedy and ambitious, he chose to deny the Lord when hope of kingly position and reward failed (Mt 26:14, 47; 27:5; Acts 1:18).

20-30. The unpardonable sin. See note on Mt 12:24-37.

31-35. The Servant's new relationship. See note on Mt 12:46-50.

4. The Servant's seaside teaching

1-29. The parable of the sower. Mark develops only two of the seven parables elucidated in Mt 13, and connects them with the present kingdom of God, 11, 30, rather than as in Matthew, with the kingdom of the heavens. This is because Mark is presenting the gospel of the Servant, not the King, and the servanthood of Christ is related to the broader context of the inclusive kingdom of God rather than to the more national kingdom of the heavens, which involves the ultimate divine purpose for Israel.

This parable has to do with the reception given the Word of God (seed) in the world. Such truth was presented in a parable so that believers might be instructed without revealing the content of instruction to those who are spiritually blind and lack spiritual understanding, 11-12. The vivid contrast between mere profession and genuine possession of the Word may be clearly noted throughout the parable. Not only is the gospel to be appropriated, but it must shine forth in testimony, 21-25, and grow to fruitfulness, 26-29.

30-34. The parable of the mustard seed. Here the Servant describes the rapid growth of the present kingdom of God, for the common mustard seed is extremely small but when planted grows into a plant twelve feet high. The reference to the birds may suggest that, as the kingdom grows, things unsuitable for God's kingdom may attempt to lodge there (cf. Dan 4:20-22).

Probable site of Peter's House, Capernaum, later marked by an early Christian church and now covered by a Franciscan chapel.

35-41. The Servant and the storm.
The storm is a fitting close to this chapter which anticipates this present age. The Servant was with His servants in the boat. His fate was theirs, and His presence their security. His rebuke of the winds showed His power and deliverance, which are available for His own. (Cf. Mt 8:23-27; Lk 8:22-25.) See note on 'Sea of Galilee' in Mk 6.

5:1-20. The Servant's power over Satan

The Servant's sinless humanity challenged the demons. The place where the demoniac was healed, 1,is called 'the region of the Gadarenes' in Matthew (8:28). Luke (8:26) mentions 'the region of the Gerasenes,' and ancient textual authorities vary, calling the inhabitants of the region 'Gerasenes,' 'Gadarenes' or 'Gergesenes.' Some locate Gergesa (present-day Kursi, a tiny place) on the eastern shore of the Lake of Galilee just below the Wadi es-Semak, where steep hills jut into the lake. However, Gadara (Umm Qeis), five miles SE of the southern end of the lake, may be indicated. This important town of the Decapolis may well have extended in its settlements to the lake shore in that period. See note on Decapolis in Mk 7.

5:21-43. The Servant's power over disease and death

The Servant is the sinless Son of God, Lord of the spirit world, 1-20, having displayed His authority over Satan and demons, now displayed it over that which sin has introduced into the human race – disease and death.

6-7. The Servant's rejection

6:1-6. In his hometown. Unbelief in His person and work here expressed itself. The people saw Him as Joseph's actual son, as a carpenter, 3, as a mere sinful man with brothers and sisters (cf. Lk 4:16-30).

6:7-13. He sends forth the Twelve. (Cf. Mt 10:5-42; Lk 9:1-6.)

6:14-29. John the Baptist's martyrdom described. (See note on Mt 14:1-14; Lk 9:7-9.) Herod Antipas, son of Herod the Great, ruled Galilee and Perea as tetrarch 4 B.C.-A.D. 39. His incestuous marriage with his niece Herodias, former wife of his half-brother Philip, resulted in his murder of John the Baptist.

6:30-44. Miracle of the five thousand fed. See note on 'Miracles' in Mk 5.

6:45-52. Miracle of walking on the water (cf. Mt 14:22-32; Jn 6:15-21). The

Stormy weather arises over the Sea of Galilee. The lake was often subject to sudden and violent storms.

The Decapolis

The Decapolis (Ten Cities) was situated in the region SE of the Lake of Galilee. It was a confederation of Hellenistic towns (originally ten in number). All of them except Scythopolis (Beisan), just W of the Jordan at the entrance to Esdraelon, were located in Transjordan, S of tetrarch Philip's Gaulonitis, E of the N half of Herod Antipas' Perea and W and N of Aretas' sprawling kingdom of Nabatea. Pliny, a contemporary Roman historian, lists these Decapolis cities as Damascus, Philadelphia (Amman), Raphana, Scythopolis, Gadara, Hippos, Pella, Gerasa, Dion, and Canatha. (Cf. Mt 4:25; Mk 5:20; 7:31.)

The excavated remains of the Hellenistic city of Scythopolis (Bet Shean), one of the ten towns making up the Decapolis region, SE of the Lake of Galilee.

Servant is the mighty Son of God.

6:53-56. Healings at Gennesaret. Gennesaret is the fertile plain on the NW corner of the Sea of Galilee, where the rim of mountain wall flattens out. Though rejected by those of His own hometown and other, the Servant graciously continued His mission to seek and to save the lost (cf. Mt 14:34-36).

7:1-23. The empty religionism of the Pharisees. Concerned with mere outward forms of traditionalism, but devoid of faith or spiritual reality (2 Tim 3:5), the Pharisees were blinded in their rejection of and opposition to the Servant Son of God. They fulfilled Isa 29:13 (see 6-7; cf. notes on Mt 15:1-20).

7:24-30. The Servant and the Syrophoenician woman. See note on Mt 15:21-28. The Servant could not be hid, 24, because He was here manifesting His serving ministry (cf. Mk 10:45). This foreshadows the gospel going out to Gentiles after Israel's rejection of the King and the kingdom. Notice Mark does not allude to the woman's calling Jesus the son of David, properly recorded in the gospel of the King (Mt 15:22). See note on 'Demonism,' Mk 5:1-20, and on 'Miracles,' Mk 5. Tyre was on the coast, 25 miles N of Ptolemais, 20 miles S of Sidon.

7:31-37. The healing of the deaf and dumb man (cf. Mt 15:29-31). See note on 'Miracles' in Mk 5, and on 'Sea of Galilee' in Mk 6.

8. The Servant predicts His death

1-9. Miracle of feeding the four thousand (cf. Mt 15:32-39). See note on 'Miracles' in Mk 5.

10-21. The wicked unbelief of the Pharisees. Cf. comments on Mt 16:1-12,

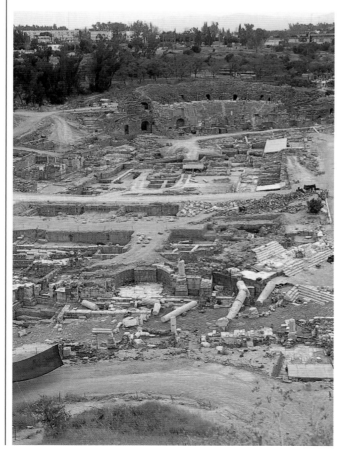

Caesarea Philippi

Caesarea Philippi, i.e., Caesarea of Philip, was rebuilt and enlarged by this son of Herod the Great. Its name had been Panias, in honor of the nature god Pan worshiped there, but was changed to Caesarea in honor of the then-reigning Caesar Tiberius. It was thus distinguished from the city of Caesarea built by Herod the Great on coastal Palestine. At this center sacred to paganism in proximity to the Paneion grotto in the foothills of Mt. Hermon it is significant that Jesus broached the subject of His deity (see notes on Mt 16:13-16; Lk 9:18-20). Nearby was an exquisite temple of marble built by Herod the Great in honor of Caesar Augustus.

Demonism

Method and purpose of the Servant's miracles

Demons are evil or unclean spirits (cf. Mk 1:23 with Mk 1:32-34; Rev 16:13-16), and are fallen angels, servants of Satan (Mt 12:26-27; 25:41). There is only one devil, but myriads of demons who serve the devil and make his power practically universal. A demoniac (Mk 5:1-20) is a person whose personality has been invaded by one or more demons, who at will can speak and act through their human victim, deranging both his mind and body. A number of such victims of Satan were delivered by the Servant (see 'Expulsion of demons' below). The unhindered power of God working through the sinless humanity of the Servant challenged the supernatural world of evil and explains the outburst of demonism during His earthly ministry.

The reality and personality of demons are attested in all eras of history since the Fall, as in the case of Saul and the spiritistic medium of Endor (1 Sam 28:7-20), in the case of ancient idolatry of which demonism was the dynamic (Ps 106:36-37; 1 Cor 10:20), in ancient divination and magic, and in ancient necromancy and modern spiritism.

Demons can derange mind and body (Mt 12:22; 17:15-18; Lk 13:16). They know the destiny and lordship of Christ in the spirit world (Mt 8:31-32; Mk 1:24; Acts 19:15; Jas 2:19), and realize their predestined fate (Mt 8:31-32; Lk 8:31). They have a conspicuous role in the government of the Satanic world

Expulsion of demons
Specific instances

Mk 1:21-28; Lk 4:31-37.

Demoniac in the synagogue at Capernaum.

Mt 9:32-34.

Dumb demoniac.

Mt 15:21-28; Mk 7:24-30.

Daughter of the Syrophoenician woman.

Mt 8:28-34; Mk 5:1-20; Lk 8:26-39.

Gadarene demoniacs.

Mt 12:22; Lk 11:14.

Blind and mute demoniac.

Mt 17:14-21; Mk 9:14-29; Lk 9:37-43.

Epileptic child.

system (Dan 10:13; Eph 6:12), in promoting cultism and false doctrine (1 Tim 4:1-3), and in opposing God's program and God's people (Eph 6:12; 1 Jn 4:1-6). Prayer is the believer's resource against Satan and demons (Eph 6:10-20). See also comments on 'Demonism' in Lk 11:14-28.

Miracles

Method and purpose of the Servant's miracles

Jesus did not work miracles solely by virtue of His deity, but in the person of His sinless humanity united to Deity. It was the Holy Spirit working in unhindered power through the medium of Jesus' undefiled human nature who wrought these mighty signs by spoken word, occasionally combined with physical agents such as clay or saliva.

The purpose of the Servant's miracles was to authenticate the King (Matthew), the Servant (Mark), the Man (Luke) and God (John) as the Creator-Redeemer, God become man, the eternal Word become flesh, Israel's King and the world's Saviour. Jesus' miracles were outward proofs of His deity and messiahship (cf. Jn 15:24). They also were the expression of His love for and identification with the human race, performed for its redemption from suffering, sin and death.

Most of Jesus' miracles are unrecorded (cf. Mt 4:24; Lk 4:40; Mk 6:53-56; Lk 6:17-19; Mt 15:30-31; Jn 21:25). Those that are recorded, as in John's gospel (cf. Jn 20:30-31) are highly selected for a specific purpose – to arouse faith in Jesus as 'the Christ, the Son of God, and that by believing you may have life in his name.'

Miracles of physical healing

A leper	Mt 8:2-4; Mk 1:40-45; Lk 5:12-15
A paralytic	Mt 9:2-8; Mk 2:3-12; Lk 5:18-26
Fever (Peter's mother-in-law)	Mt 8:14-17; Mk 1:29-31
Nobleman's son healed	Jn 4:46-53
Physical infirmity	Jn 5:1-9
A withered hand	Mt 12:9-13; Mk 3:1-6; Lk 6:6-11
Deafness and dumbness	Mk 7:31-37
Blindness at Bethsaida	Mk 8:22-25
in Jerusalem	Jn 9
Bartimaeus	Mk 10:46-52
Ten lepers	Lk 17:11-19
Malchus' severed ear	Lk 22:47-51
Hemorrhage	Mt 9:20-22; Mk 5:25-34; Lk 8:43-48
Drops	Lk 14:2-4

Miracles of resurrection

Jairus' daughter	Mt 9:18-26; Mk 5:35-43; Lk 8:41-56
Widow's son	Lk 7:11-15
Lazarus of Bethany	Jn 11:1-44

Miracles of nature

Water converted to wine at Cana	Jn 2:1-11
Stilling of a storm	Mt 8:23-27; Mk 4:35-41; Lk 8:22-25
Supernatural catch of fish	Lk 5:1-11; Jn 21:6
Multiplying food:	Mt 14:15-21; Mk 6:34-44
5,000 fed,	Lk 9:11-19; Jn 6:1-14
4,000 fed	Mt 15:32-39; Mk 8:1-9
Walking on water	Mt 14:22-33; Mk 6:45-52; Jn 6:19
Money from a fish	Mt 17:24-27
Fig tree dried up	Mt 21:18-22; Mk 11:12-14

noting 'leaven' there. 'Dalmanutha,' 10, is uncertain. After feeding the 4,000 somewhere in the NE region of the lake, Jesus took a boat to Magadan (Mt 15:39) in the 'region of Dalmanutha' (Mk8:10), probably to be identified with Khirbet Mejdel, three miles NE of Tiberias and located between it and Capernaum.

22-26. The blind man healed at Bethsaida. This was not the city just E of the place where the Jordan River enters the Sea of Galilee, enlarged by Philip the tetrarch who called it Bethsaida Julius, but the town in close proximity to Capernaum, just W of where the Jordan enters the lake. These two Bethsaidas can be illustrated by Kansas City, Kansas, and Kansas City, Missouri. (See Mk 1:16-17; Jn 1:44; 12:21.)

27-38. Peter's confession of faith. See notes on Mt 16:21-28.

9. The Servant's coming glory

1-13. The transfiguration. In one sense this was a confirmation of Peter's confession of Christ as the Son of the living God. It was a demonstration of the full deity of the Servant to three of the most discerning disciples, to prepare them against the shock of the Servant's approaching death. In another sense the transfiguration was a celestial testimony and climatic proof that this Jesus was the Christ – the Messiah, Servant, and Saviour to whom all OT prophecies pointed and in whom they were fulfilled. Again it was a visual illustration of the coming of the kingdom of God in power to the Gentiles (cf. notes on Mt 17:1-21).

14-29. The demon-possessed boy. See notes on 'Demonism' in Mk 5:1-20 and 'Miracles' in Mr 5:21-43. See also notes on Mt 17:14-19; Lk 9:37-43.

30-41. The Servant again predicts His death. Cf. notes on Mt 16:21-28. This subject was one of gradual unfolding to the disciples after the King and His kingdom were rejected, although it had been hinted at to Nicodemus at the beginning of Christ's ministry (Jn 3:14; cf. Mt 16:21; 17:9; 17:22-23; 20:17-19). The disciples quarreled among themselves as to who should be the greatest, 33-37, and their selfish bickering illustrated how little they understood the Lord's approaching death or its meaning, 38-41.

42-50. The Servant warns of hell. This is Gehenna, eternal hell, the 'lake of fire' (Rev 20:14-15), 'the second death' (Rev 21:8; cf. Jn 8:24), signifying eternal separation from God. Gehenna was the place in the valley of Hinnom, SW of Jerusalem, where human sacrifices were offered in OT times (2 Chr 33:6; Jer 7:31). Later it became a dumping ground where the worm

Mount Tabor, with its unmistakable profile, rises dramatically from the surrounding plain. The hill is regarded by many as the possible site of Jesus' transfiguration.

The Sea of Galilee

In Jesus' day this beautiful body of fresh water, 13 miles long and seven and one half miles wide, was dotted with populous towns, such as Capernaum (see note on Mk 1:21-28), Bethsaida, Chorazin, Magdala and Tiberias. The lake lies in a depressed cup 700 feet below sea level and enjoys a healthful semitropical climate. The lake was often subject to sudden and violent storms as the cold air from snowy Lebanon collided with the warmer air above the lake.

The lake abounds in fish, with fishing an imoprtant industry (cf. Mt 4:18-22; Mk 1:16-20). The sunny climate, with healthgiving sulphur springs near Tiberias, made it a mecca for the sick, and a fruitful scene for Jesus' healing ministry (Mk 1:32-34).

Remains of the synagogue at Chorazin.

Christ's Ministry in Galilee

Chorazin
Healing of the centurian's servant (Matt 8:5–13)
Healing of the paralyzed man (Matt 9:1–8)
Calling of Matthew `(Matt 9:1–13)
Raising the ruler's daughter from the dead (Matt 9:18–26)
Commissioning the twelve apostles (Matt 10)

Capernaum

Gennesaret
Sermon on the Mount (Matt 5–7)

Bethsaida
Feeding of the five thousand (Matt 14:

Magdala
Pharisees and sadducees test Jesus (Matt 15:39–41)
Home town of Mary magdalene

Sennabris
Healing of two demon possessed men and drowning of Gadarane swine (Matt 8:28–34)

Tiberias

Walking on water (Matt 14:22–36)

Calming of the storm (Matt 8:23–27)

?Gergesa
? Healing of two demon possessed men and drowning of Gadarene Swine (Matt 8: 28–31)

Hippos

Gadara

never died and the fire never was quenched, a graphic picture of the eternal destiny of those who reject Christ. Gehenna is in contrast to Hades (Lk 16:23), the intermediate state of the wicked dead before judgment.

10. The Servant's Perean ministry

1-16. Question of divorce. Perea, 1, was the territory across Jordan from Samaria, extending from the Decapolis E of the Sea of Galilee and S to the Dead Sea. It was ruled by Herod Antipas (see note on Mk 6:14-29). Jesus taught a monogamous standard on the subject of divorce, 6-8 (cf. Gen 1:27), teaching that God joins man and woman in marriage, 9, and that easy divorce is adultery, 10-12. Jesus' blessing of little children, 13-16, is closely connected in the context. They are also real victims of the hurt of divorce and adultery (Mt 19:13-15; Lk 18:15-17).

17-31. The rich young man. See note on Mt 19:16-26 (cf. Lk 18:18-30).

32-34. The Servant again foretells His death (cf. Mt 20:17-19; Mk 9:30-37).

35-45. James' and John's selfish ambition. Their desire to be served is contrasted with the Servant's aim to serve, 45. This verse is the key to Mark's presentation of the Son of God as Servant.

46-52. Bartimaeus receives his sight (cf. Mt 20:29-34; Lk 18:35-43). This miracle occurred near Jericho. See note on 'Miracles,' Mk 5:21-34.

11. The Servant's entry into Jerusalem

1-11. His presentation as King. This is in fulfilment of Zech 9:9 (cf. comments on Mt 21:1-11). It was a popular but superficial demonstration. The King and His kingdom had in reality already been rejected (cf. notes on Mt 3:2; 4:17; 13:12). The fickleness of the sinful human heart is here displayed. A few days later many of the same mob would jeer Him, proving they were not ready to receive the King nor the principles of His kingdom.

12-14. The barren fig tree. See notes on Mt 21:18-22. The fig tree of Palestine, if it has kept its leaves through the winter, usually contains figs also. The figure portrays the spiritual barrenness of the nation that would

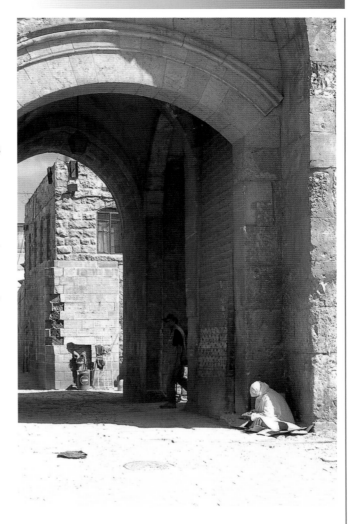

soon crucify the King it now so glibly hailed.

15-21. The cleansing of the temple is another proof of the apostasy of the nation (see note on Mr 21:12-16). The withered fig tree symbolizes this spiritual bankruptcy.

22-33. Faith contrasted with wicked unbelief. The prayer of faith, 22-26 (cf. Jas 5:15), starkly focused upon the unbelief of the scribes and elders who questioned Jesus' authority, 27-33, as further proof of their rejection of the King-Servant.

12. The Servant's teaching in Jerusalem

1-12. Parable giving a résumé of Israel's spiritual history. Israel, the vineyard (Isa 5:1-7), brought forth only wild grapes. The OT prophets and John the Baptist are alluded to, 2-5, as are Jesus Himself, 6-8, and the destruction

The Lion Gate leads into the Old City of Jerusalem from the Mount of Olives opposite. Jesus would have entered Jerusalem through a similar gate during his Triumphal Entry from Bethphage and Bethany.

Jericho

Jericho of Jesus' day was Herod's winter palace. He and his son Archelaus elegantly beautified it with magnificent Hellenistic buildings – palace, theater, fortress and hippodrome. Ancient ruins excavated from 1950 on the site of the present Tulul Abu el-'Alayiq lie one mile W of the modern city. The architecture and plan of the city resemble other cities of the Graeco-Roman world of the time. Herodian Jericho was a splendid city 17 miles from Jerusalem, 1,000 feet below sea level in the Jordan Valley, with a delightful winter climate.

Corner of the Hasmonean Palace, Jericho.

Overview of Herod the Great's winter palace at Tulul Abu el-'Alayiq.

of Jerusalem (A.D. 70), 9-10 (cf. Ps 118:22; 1 Pet 2:8). Verse 10 quotes Ps 118:22-23. (Cf. notes on Mt 21:33-46; Lk 20:9-18.)

13-17. Question of the tribute. The Pharisees and Herodians joined to trap the Servant Jesus with omniscient wisdom declared the principle of the separation of church and state, and so silenced both groups (see note on Mt 22:15-22; cf. Lk 20:19-26).

18-27. The Servant silences the Sadducees. The wealthy, rationalistic materialists did not believe in bodily resurrection. Their trap question seemed to favor polygamy in heaven. Jesus settled the question with one stroke – no marrying in heaven, but there is a resurrection, because Scripture so declares, and He quoted from the Pentateuch which the Sadducees claimed to believe (cf. Ex 3:6).

28-34. The great commandments (cf. Deut 6:4-5; Lev 19:18). God is to be first in our affection, our neighbor second (see Mt 22:34-40; Lk 10:25-37).

35-40. The Servant questions the Pharisees. From Psalm 110:1 He showed this psalm was penned by David, was inspired, was messianic and that He was David's son (man) as well as David's Lord (God). He silenced them and at the same time revealed their unbelief.

41-44. The widow's offering. The 'fraction of a penny' was about one-eighth of a cent. This widow first gave herself (Lk 21:1-4; 2 Cor 8:5).

13. The Servant's Olivet discourse

1-4. Prediction concerning the temple. On Olivet in full view of Herod's resplendent edifice, Jesus predicted its destruction. It is significant that from Olivet's strategic summit Titus poised his invincible legions for the siege of the city that was to eventuate in the complete ruin of the temple in fulfillment of Jesus' ominous words (cf. Mt 24-25; Lk 21).

5-23. Events of the tribulation (see note on Mt 24:4-26).

24-26. Second coming of the Son of Man (see note of Mt 24:27-30).

27. Regathering of Israel (see note on Mt 24:31).

28-33. The certainty of Christ's

The Jerusalem skyline viewed from the trees of the Mount of Olives. Here, in full view of Herod's resplendent Temple, Jesus predicted its destruction.

coming (see note on Mt 24:32-36 and note below on 'Time of the second coming').

34-37. Exhortations to watchfulness (see note on Mt 24:37-51).

14. Events leading to the Servant's death

1-2. The plot. On the Passover cf. Ex 12:1-28. This feast of redemption and that of unleavened bread which followed it speak typically of Him who was now being betrayed to die (Mt 26:2-5; Lk 22:1-2).

3-9. The Servant anointed for death. See comments on Mt 26:6-13; Jn 12:1-8. Mary of Bethany was the 'woman,' 3. She alone understood the full import of His approaching vicarious death, and only those who sit at His feet as she did (Lk 10:39) likewise understand.

10-11. Judas' plans to betray Jesus (Mt 26:14-16; Lk 22:3-6).

12-25. The last Passover and the Lord's Supper. The Paschal feast of redemption was prepared, 12-16 (cf. Ex 12:8), and celebrated, 17-21. Then the Servant instituted the Lord's Supper, a memorial speaking of His death and second coming (1 Cor 11:23-26), superseding and fulfilling the slain lamb typology of the Passover.

26-31. Peter's denial predicted (cf. Mt 26:31-35; Lk 22:31-34; Jn 13:36-38).

32-42. Gethsemane's agony. See notations on Mt 26:36-56.

43-52. Judas' betrayal and arrest of Jesus. Judas' base betrayal, 43-46 (cf. Mt

Jerusalem in the time of Jesus

Hinnom Valley

Palace of Caiaphas and Annas, the High Priest

City of David

Upper Room (possible site)

Herodian Aqueduct

Amphitheatre

Forum

Tyropoeon Valley (Lower City)

Hippodrome

Royal Portico

Weste

Garden of Gethsemane

Kidron Valley

Herod's Temple

Shops
and Market-Place

Herod's Palace

Upper City

Antonia Fortress

Mariamme Tower

Hippicus Tower

Phasael Tower

'Gordon's Calvary'

Tomb of Jesus?

Pool of Israel

Pool of Bethesda

Gethsemane

Above the present road from Jerusalem to Bethany four traditional sites vie for the site of Jesus' agony, all of them containing ancient olive trees. None of the sites is certain. Somewhere on the Mount of Olives Jesus agonized in prayer. Gethsemane (*gat semanim*) is assumed to mean 'press of oils,' but Jerome connected it with Heb. *gay' semanim* 'valley of oils' or 'fertile valley,' and may be correct in hinting that it was in a valley in which there were many olive trees.

Even today the Garden of Gethsemane remains a tranquil haven, with ancient olive trees and cultivated flowers.

26:47-56), was followed by Peter's flashing ire and show of courage, 47-52. Who the young man was who followed Jesus, 51-52, is not known.

53-65. Jesus before the Sanhedrin (cf. Mt 26:57-68; Jn 18:21-24).

66-72. Peter's denial (cf. Mt 26:69-75; Lk 22:56-62; Jn 18:16-27).

15. The Servant's death and burial

1-15. Jesus before Pilate. Pontius Pilate was Roman procurator of Judea (A.D. 26-36). Procurators were governors of the equestrian order (similar to medieval knighthood) subject to the emperor. They could summon help from the legate of Syria, if needed. They resided in Caesarea, but found it prudent to take up residence in Jerusalem on important feasts of the Jews. Procuratorial government proved unhappy. Roman businessmen were unable to understand the volatile Oriental people or their religious ceremonialism. As a result, they often resorted to cruelty, as Pilate did, when their patience was exhausted. Jesus' silence before Pilate, 5, fulfilled Isa 53:7. On Barabbas, 7-15, see

Mt 27:15-23. See note on 'Trials of Jesus,' Lk 23.

16-23. The king of the Jews mocked. Pilate's praetorium, 16, is probably to be identified with Herod's palace on the western side of the city wall, graced by the gorgeous towers Hippicus, Phasael and Mariamne. However, later tradition links the praetorium with the fortress of Antonia at the NW corner of the temple area. This structure was rebuilt by Herod the Great from an earlier Maccabean structure and named in honor of Mark Antony. On Golgotha, 22, see comments on Mt 27:33-44.

24-41. The crucifixion. See comments on Mt 27:33-56.

42-47. The burial. See Mt 27:57-61.

16. The Servant's resurrection

1-8. His resurrection. See notes on Mt 28:1-10. How gracious is the report of the angel of Jesus' resurrection, 6-7, with the appended note to Peter, the denier, who must have thought surely he was disowned — 'But go, tell his disciples *and* Peter,' 7. See note on 'The Resurrection Authenticated,' Jn 20.

9-20. His post-resurrection appearances. This portion is not found in the

Time of the second coming

Did the Son not know the time of His second coming? 'No one knows about that day or hour, not even the angels in heaven, nor the Son, but only the Father' (Mt 24:36; Mk 13:32). In Mark the Lord takes the

place of complete humiliation as a Servant and the servant is properly presented as he who 'does not know his master's business' (Jn 15:15). After His servantship was discharged in death and He was raised in

glory, the glorified Son omnisciently knew all, having this particular disclosure given to Him (Rev 1:1).

Order of the events of the crucifixion

Arrival at Golgotha (Calvary), Mt 27:33; Mk 15:22; Lk 23:33; Jn 19:17

Offer of a benumbing drink, Mt 27:34

Cry, 'Father, forgive . . . ,' Lk 23:34

The parting of Christ's garments, Mt 27:35

Jesus mocked, Mt 27:39-44; Mk 15:29

The thieves rail on Him, but one believes, Mt 27:44

Second cry, 'Today you will be with me . . . ,' Lk 23:43

Third cry, 'Dear woman, here is your son,' Jn 19:26-27

The darkness, Mt 27:45; Mk 15:33

The fourth cry, 'My Gof, my God . . . ,' Mt 26:46-47; Mk 15:34-36

Fifth cry, 'I am thirsty,' Jn 19:28

Sixth cry, 'It is finished,' Jn 19:30

Seventh cry, 'Father, into thy hands . . . ,' Lk 23:46

Jesus dismisses His spirit, Mt 27:50; Mk 15:37

Order of events of the resurrection

Mary Magdalene, Mary the mother of James, and Salome start for the tomb, Lk 23:55-24:1

Mary Magdalene goes to tell the disciples, Jn 20:1-2

Mary, the mother of James, draws near and sees the angel, Mt 28:1-2

She goes back to meet the other women following with spices

Meanwhile Peter and John arrive, look in and depart, Jn 20:3-10

Mary Magdalene returns weeping, sees two angels, then Jesus, Jn 20:11-18

The risen Christ bids her tell the disciples, Jn 20:17-18

Mary (mother of James) meanwhile returns with the women, Lk 24:1-4

They return and see the two angels, Lk 24:5; Mk 16:5

They also hear the angel's message, Mt 28:6-8

On their way to find the disciples, they are met by the risen Christ, Mt 28:9-10

Post-resurrection appearances

To Mary Magdalene Jn 20:14-18; Mk 16:9

To the women returning from the tomb Mt 28:8-10

To Peter later in the day Lk 24:34; 1 Cor 15:5

To the disciples going to Emmaus in the evening Lk 24:13-31

To the apostles (except Thomas) Lk 24:36-45; Jn 20:19-24

To the apostles a week later (Thomas present) Jn 20:24-29

In Galilee to the seven by the Lake of Tiberias Jn 211-23

In Galilee on a mountain to the apostles and 500 believers 1 Cor 15:6

At Jerusalem and Bethany again to James 1 Cor 15:7

At Olivet and the ascension Acts 1:3-12

To Paul near Damascus Acts 9:3-6; 1 Cor 15:8

To Stephen outside Jerusalem Acts 7:55

To Paul in the temple Acts 22:17-21; 23:11

To John on Patmos Rev 1:10-19

Sinaitic and Vatican manuscripts. Others have it only in part. Quite possibly Mark's original copy was transcribed and became a textual tradition before he finished it. Later he finished it, giving rise to another text (the fuller one, consisting of verses 9-20). This latter text is referred to by Irenaeus (c. A.D. 170) and is found in the Alexandrian and Cambridge manuscripts.

LUKE

The gospel of the Son of Man

The author. The writer is Luke, 'the beloved physician' (cf. Col 4:14; Phm 24; 2 Tim 4:11). He with Mark was a companion worker of Paul, shown by the 'we' sections of Acts 16:10-11; 20:5ff.; 21:1ff. That he wrote the gospel of Luke is shown by comparing Lk 1:1-4 with Acts 1:1-3 and by tradition. Luke very likely wrote his gospel while he was in Caesarea during Paul's imprisonment there (Acts 27:1), about A.D. 58, and before Acts was penned, about A.D. 63.

The synoptic gospels. Matthew, Mark and Luke constitute the synoptic gospels. Synoptic means 'seeing the whole together at a glance.' These three gospels, in contrast to John, present a common story and relate substantially the same incidents in the life of our Lord, with of course some omissions, additions and differences.

The explanation of the Synoptic Problem still occupies the energy of critical scholars. Many hypotheses have been devised, several of which deny the authentic historical nature of the narrative, the miracles, etc. The position which best fits the facts and honors the Christ of the synoptics is that the Holy Spirit presents, without contradiction, through three different human writers, the one Messiah-King, Servant-Saviour, God-Man. Each presents Him under a different aspect for a particular purpose, but the threefold presentation is of the one and same divine-human Person.

So multi-faceted is the glory of Christ's person and so far-reaching are the ramifications of His finished redemption that one gospel account could not portray His splendor. To view these accounts as mere human productions, mechanically pieced together from existing traditions, is to forfeit any real sense of their spiritual purpose and meaning. The so-called Synoptic Problem that results from such a view is both unresolved and unresolvable.

Outline

1:1–4:13 Birth, childhood, early ministry
4:14–9:50 Galilean ministry
9:51–21:38 Journey to and ministry in Jerusalem
22:1–23:56 Rejection and death
24:1–53 Resurrection and ascension

Characteristic features of Luke's Gospel

Luke compared with Matthew and Mark

Luke	Mathew	Mark
The human gospel	The kingly gospel	The servant gospel
Perfect manhood of Christ	Divine kingship of Christ	Divine servanthood of Christ
Basis of the saviourhood and present intercession Heb 5:1-2	Basis of His offer of Himself to Israel and His coming kingdom Acts 1:6	Basis of His giving His life a ransom for many Mk 10:45
Moral perfections and tender sympathies of the perfect Man	Kingly power and humble grace of Israel's Saviour-King	Miraculous power in sevice to man of the God-sent Servant
Our Lord in prayer cf Lk 3:21; 5:16; 6:12-13:9-18, stressing His depency as man	Our Lord in kingly manifestation	Our Lord in Spirit-empowered service
Appeal to Greek	Appeal to Jew	Appeal to Roman

1. Births of John and of Jesus foretold

1-4. Introduction. In polished Greek this prologue shows how spontaneous and adaptable to the human instrument divine inspiration is. 'Theophilus' ('God-lover') connects this gospel as well as the book of Acts (1:1) with Luke as the author. He was Luke's literary patron, doubtless a Roman or Greek of high rank, as his title, 'most excellent,' indicates.

5-25. Birth of John the Baptist foretold. The silence of the four centuries from Malachi to Matthew was broken. The ministering priest Zechariah ('whom the Lord remembers') heard from God through Gabriel, the archangel. This same angel had communicated to Daniel the vision of the seventy weeks (Dan 9:21). John was to be born of a barren couple and was to minister in the spirit and power of Elijah (1 Kgs 21:20; 2 Kgs 1:8; cf. Mal 4:5-6).

26-45. Birth of Jesus also foretold. Gabriel visited Mary at Nazareth, 26-27, announcing the most glorious event of human history, 28-33. Verses 32 and 33 are yet unfulfilled, and will be realized at the second advent (cf. Dan 7:27; Gen 12:2-3; Isa 9:67). Here was 'the virgin' of prophecy (Isa 7:14). Here was the divine-human Person whom Isaiah said was to be 'a child born' (human) and 'a son given'

Palestine in the time of Christ

SYRIA

Damascus

ITURAEA

PHOENICIA

Tyre

△ Mount Hermon

Caesarea Philippi

Lake Huleh

GAULANITIS

Ptolemais

GALILEE

Gamala

Raphana

TRACHONITIS

BATANEA

Kanatha

Sepphoris

Tiberias

SEA OF GALILEE

Hippos

AURANITIS

Mount Tabor

Dion

Geba

Gadara

DECAPOLIS

Caesarea

Scythopolis (Beth-shan)

Pella

Sebaste (Samaria)

Gerasa (Jerash)

SAMARIA

Sychar (Shechem)

Alexandrium

Antipatris

PEREA

Joppa

Phaselis

Archelais

Philadelphia (Rabbath Ammon)

JUDEA

Livias

Jamnia

Jerusalem

Cyprus

Esbus (Heshbon)

Azotus

Hyrcania

Ascalon

Herodium

DEAD SEA

Machaerus

NABATEANS

Gaza

Marisa

Hebron

IDUMEA

Masada

Capital

Boundary of Herod the Great's kingdom

Land given to

Philip

Herod Antipas

Archelaus

Province of Syria

Town of the Decapolis

Fortress of Herod the Great

Main route

0   25   50   75 km

0   15   30   45 miles

Incidents and events exclusive to Luke

1:5-25
Zechariah's vision and Elizabeth's conception

26-38
Mary's salutation

39-56
Mary's visit to Elizabeth

1:57-80
John the Baptist's birth and Zechariah's hymn of praise

2:1-3
The enrollment decree of Caesar Augustus

2:4-7
Christ's nativity in Bethlehem

2:8-20
Details of the Christmas story

2:21
The circumcision of the Child Jesus

2:22-24
The presentation of Christ in the temple

2:25-38
The story of Simeon and Anna

2:39-40
The silent years at Nazareth

2:41-52
Jesus at the Passover and among the rabbis

3:1-2
Dating of the beginning of John's public ministry

3:10-15
John's success

3:23-38
Human genealogy of Christ from Mary

4:15-30
Christ's rejection at Nazareth

5:1-10
Details of the call of Peter, James and John

6:17-49
Discourse of Christ on the plain

7:11-17
Raising to life of the widow's son at Nain

7:36-50
The woman who anointed Jesus in Simon's house

8:1-3
The women who ministered to Christ

9:51-56
Episode of James and John

10:1-12
The seventy sent out

10:17-24
Their return and report

10:25-37
Parable of the Good Samaritan

10:38-42
Christ at the house of Mary and Martha

11:5-8
Parable of the friend at midnight

11:37-54
Christ entertained by a Pharisee

12:1-53
Discourse to a great crowd

13:1-5
Pilate's murder of the Galileans

13:6-9
Parable of the barren fig tree

13:10-17
The woman afflicted 18 years

13:22-30
Problem of the number to be saved

13:31-33
Reply to the Pharisees concerning Herod Antipas

14:1-6
The man with dropsy

14:7-14
Parable of the ambitious guest

14:15-24
Parable of the great banquet

14:25-35
Difficulties of discipleship

15:3-7
Parable of the lost sheep

15:8-10
Parable of the lost coin

15:11-32
Parable of the prodigal son

16:1-18
Parable of the dishonest manager

16:19-31
The rich man and the beggar Lazarus

17:1-10
Instructions to the disciples

17:12-19
Healing of the ten lepers

17:20-37
Questions concerning God's kingdom

18:1-8
Parable of the persistent widow

18:9-14
Parable of the Pharisee and publican

19:2-10
Zacchaeus' conversion and call

19:11-27
Parable of the pounds

19:41-44
Christ's weeping over Jerusalem

22:31-32
Warning to Peter

22:35-38
Warning to buy a sword

22:43
Appearance of an angel in Gethsemane

22:44
The bloody sweat

23:6-12
Pilate's sending Christ to Herod

23:27-31
Christ's message to the women of Jerusalem

23:39-43
The penitent thief

24:13-35
The risen Christ's appearance to the Emmaus disciples

24:37-49
Details of His appearance to the eleven

24:50-53
Christ's ascension while blessing His disciples

Date of Christmas

Our traditional date of December 25 as the day of Christ's birth was set in the 4th cen. It was the day settled upon by the Western church. The Eastern church celebrates January 6. Actually the day is unknown. Apparently the nativity did not occur in the winter, since the shepherds in Palestine customarily do not remain in the open with their flocks, except from spring to autumn.

(divine) (Isa 9:6; Jn 3:16; 2 Cor 9:15). Mary quite naturally asked how this could happen, 34. 'The Holy Spirit will come upon you,' 35, means that the human nature of Christ (absolutely holy) was produced in the womb of a virgin by a creative act of God the Spirit (cf. Mt 1:18-20). 'The power of the Most High will overshadow you,' 35, means that the eternal Son of God united Himself with the miraculously generated human nature in the womb of the virgin. The result, 'the holy one,' was uniquely unclassifiable – deity and humanity were united for the redemption of the fallen race. Therefore His name was to be 'Jesus,' Lord-Saviour (cf. note on Mt 1:18-25).

46-56. Mary's ode of praise. Filled with OT Scripture and the Spirit of God, the virgin burst forth in praise, echoing Hannah's song (1 Sam 2:1-10; cf. Ps 34:2-3; 103:17; 111:9).

57-80. Birth of John and Zechariah's prophetic joy. Zechariah's tongue was loosed, 57-64, as Israel's will be when they see and believe. His prophecy, 67-79, like Mary's magnificat, was immersed in OT promises, which he saw would be fulfilled in the person and work of the coming King.

2:1-20 Birth of Jesus

1-3. Census of Quirinius. That Luke's census was part of an empire-wide enrollment is suggested by Egyptian papyri which tell of a periodic fourteen-year census. Moreover, evidence suggests also that Quirinius was twice governor of Syria, the first time about 8 B.C., when the first census was made. Household enrollment is also attested by the papyri, so there is every indication from increased archaeological knowledge that Luke is accurate in this passage frequently questioned by various NT critics.

4-20. Birth in Bethlehem. God's providence working through Caesar Augustus and the imperial enrollment decree made it possible for Mary and Joseph, living in Nazareth of Galilee, to fulfill the prophecy of Micah relating to Messiah's birth in Bethlehem (Mic 5:2).

This star on the floor of a cave beneath the Church of the Nativity in Bethlehem has for centuries been held to mark the place where Jesus was born to Mary.

Corrected calendar

In the 6th cen. A.D., when the Christian calendar, which reckoned time before and after the birth of Christ, replaced the old Roman calendar, which dated from the founding of Rome (753 B.C.), the monk Dionysius Exiguus made an error of at least four years. This mistake was not detected till long after the Christian calendar had been established in popular use. Dionysius reckoned 748 or 749 B.C. instead of 753 as the date of Rome's founding. Hence 5 or 4 B.C. must be reckoned as the birth of Christ.

Bethlehem

This ancient picturesque town, seven miles S of Jerusalem, called Bethlehem-Ephrathah in Mic 5:2, was the original home of the Davidic family, called Ephrathites (Ruth 1:2, 1 Sam 17:12), since they were residents of Ephrath, an early suburb of the city. Memories went back to Boaz and Ruth, ancestors of Christ. Ruth gleaned in the fertile fields of Bethlehem ('house of bread'). Under the ancient Church of the Nativity, originally built in the 4th cen. by Helena, mother of Constantine, tradition points out the manger room, which it also connects with the ancestral home of David, Boaz and Ruth. Just E of the town is the Shepherds' Field where the angels sang the joyous advent of 'a Savior . . . Christ the Lord,' 11.

The Church of the Nativity, Bethlehem.

Bethlehem is built on a hill a few miles south of the city of Jerusalem.

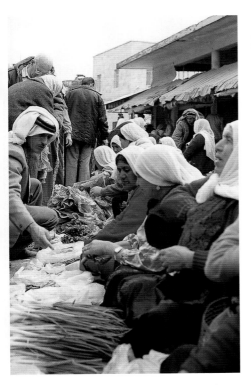

the Gentiles' (first advent) and 'glory to your people Israel' (second advent), 32 (Isa 42:6-7). Simeon's remarkable prophecy, 34-35, found fulfillment in Jn 19-25 (cf. 1 Cor 11:19; 1 Jn 2:9). Anna, 36-38, is a beautiful picture of devotion. She came in at the glorious moment, 38, to see the Babe, her faith in Him who could bring redemption being rewarded.

2:39-52. The boyhood of Jesus
39-40. Synopsis of his boyhood years. Little is told about Jesus' childhood, in contrast to the fantastic legends of the apocryphal gospels. Certainly the large family knew poverty and sacrifice, and Jesus knew the weariness of common toil, no doubt at the carpenter's bench.

41-52. His visit to Jerusalem at twelve. This is unique to Luke's account. Jesus must have regularly attended the three great feasts of Passover, Pentecost and Tabernacles, from 12 years of age and on. This incident is pivotal as our Lord's first self-witness to His deity.

Luke, presenting the perfect Man, omits the visit of the wise men and the flight into Egypt, which Matthew, describing the King, includes (Mt 2:1-21).

2:21-38. The infancy of Jesus
21-24. The circumcision and presentation. These rites were prescribed in the Mosaic law (Lev 12:3; Ex 13:12, 16; Num 8:17). They demonstrated that the perfect Man 'born of a woman' was 'born under law, to redeem those under law' (Gal 4:4-5). The circumcision made Him who was 'a servant of the Jews on behalf of God's truth, to confirm the promises made to the patriarchs' (Rom 15:8) 'obligated to obey the whole law' (Gal 5:3), which He alone could fulfill. Fulfilling it He redeemed us from its curse, 'becoming a curse for us' (Gal 3:13). For His name 'Jesus,' see Mt 1:21; Lk 1:31. The type of presentation offering indicates the poverty of Mary and Joseph (cf. Lev 12:8).

25-38. Simeon's and Anna's prophecies. These two aged saints belonged to the faithful remnant who believed the Word and waited for Christ at His first advent. Simeon recognized the Babe as the prophesied One, as God's 'salvation' and 'a light for revelation to

Chronology of this period

6-5 B.C.
John's birth announced to Zechariah Lk 1:5-25

6 months later
Jesus' birth announced to Mary Lk 1:26-38
Mary goes to see Elizabeth Lk 1:39-56

3 months later
Mary returns to Nazareth Lk 1:56
Joseph receives a message Mt 1:18-24
John born Lk 1:57-80

5 B.C.
Jesus born Mt 1:25; Lk 2:1-7

8 days later
Jesus is circumcised

33 days later
Jesus presented in the temple Lk 2:22-38

4 B.C.
Magi visit the King Mt 2:1-12
Flight to Egypt Mt 2:13-15
Murder of Bethlehem's children Mt 2:16-18

3-2 B.C.
Return to Nazareth Lk 2:39; Mt 2:19-23

Jesus' prayers in Luke

Lk 3:21	At His baptism
Lk 5:16	In the wilderness
Lk 6:12-13	Before calling the 12
Lk 9:18	At Caesarea Philippi
Lk 9:28-29	Before the transfiguration
Lk 11:1-4	When He instructed in prayer
Lk 22:31-32	For Peter
Lk 22:41	In Gethsemane
Lk 23:24	On the cross
Lk 24:30	At Emmaus

His mother had declared, 'Your father and I have been anxiously searching for you,' 48. He corrected His fallible mother by declaring that God was His Father: 'Didn't you know I had to be in My Father's house?' 49, and that His divine mission took all precedent. He accompanied them to Nazareth, and as the obedient One submitted to His parents.

3:1-20. John's ministry

1-14. John's ministry. In a passage remarkable for its accuracy and comprehensiveness, 1-2, Luke pinpoints the beginning of John's ministry. Tiberius (A.D.14-37) succeeded Caesar Augustus (27 B.C.-A.D.14). The fifteenth year of Tiberius was c. A.D. 29. Pontius Pilate was procurator of Judea (A.D. 26-36). Herod Antipas (4 B.C.-A.D.39), who killed the Baptist, was tetrarch of Galilee and Perea. Herod Philip (4 B.C.-A.D. 34) was tetrarch of Iturea and Trachonitis. Lysanias ruled Abilene, capital Abila, on the Barada River NW of Damascus. Joseph Caiaphas was appointed to the high priesthood by the procurator Valerius Gratus (A.D. 15-26) and was the acting official, while Annas was ex officio high priest, but very influential. Luke gives the fullest account of John's ministry, but cf. Mt 3:1-12;Mk 1:1-8; Jn 1:6-8, 15-36. John's rugged preaching of repentance (see note on Mt 3:2; 4:14) prepared the way for the ministry of Jesus. However, John's message was not the Christian gospel (cf. 14 with Acts 16:30-31) nor John's baptism Christian

baptism (cf. Acts 19:4-5). But John did prepare the way for these by announcing the Messiah-Saviour and His salvation.

15-20. John' s testimony to Christ. The baptism of the Holy Spirit (Acts 1:5; 2:4; 11:14-16; 1 Cor 12:13; Rom 6:3-4; Gal 3:26-27; Eph 4:5) is connected with Christ's death, resurrection and ascension at His first advent, 16-17. The baptism with 'fire,' 16, is connected with judgment at His second advent (see note Mt 3:11; Mk 1:8). On Herod Antipas and John's imprisonment see note on Mt 14:1-11.

3:21-38. Baptism and genealogy of Jesus

21-22. The baptism of Jesus. See comments on Mt 3:13-17 and Mk 1:9-11. Luke adds the detail that Jesus was praying when He was baptized and the heavens were opened, 21. Luke's gospel of the perfect Man often pictures Jesus praying, as the expression of human dependence upon God.

23-38. The human genealogy of Jesus. In Luke we have Mary's genealogy in contrast to Matthew, where Joseph's genealogy is presented (see note on Mt 1:1-17). Matthew's genealogy goes back to David and Abraham (presenting Christ's legal right to the throne of David and relating Him to the Abrahamic covenant). In giving Mary's line Luke presents the blood line of Jesus, 'who as to his human nature was a descendant of David' (Rom 1:3). In Mt 1:16 Joseph is called the son of Jacob, in Luke 'the son of Heli' (Lk 3:23), by which Luke means son-in-law of Heli, who like Joseph was a Davidic descendant. Cf. for this usage 1 Sam 24:16.

4:1-13. Jesus' temptation

1-12. The temptation. Luke presents the *order* of the temptation as it affected Christ's human nature, body, soul and spirit, in the perfect Man. The first temptation, 2-4, concerned the body; the second the soul, 5-8; the third the spirit, 9-12. The whole man was tested. Cf. notes on Mt 4:1-11; Mk 1:12-13. Matthew's order is different.

13. The devil routed. The accuser, however, left only temporarily. Satanic temptation in this life is not continuous but it is unrelenting.

Nazareth

Nazareth was a small little-known place (cf. Jn 1:46) until immortalized in the NT as the boyhood home of Jesus. Archaeology has shown that the town was not very old. There is no evidence of potsherds beyond Iron II (600 B.C.). It was just a small village of farmers and artisans, such as the carpenter Joseph. While not situated on the great trade routes from Damascus to Egypt, it did lie on a spur of road from Sepphoris on the N. While it was not a bustling emporium, it was far from being isolated from the busy Galilean towns and the stirring events of the day. Its scenic beauty and its opportunities for solitude made it an ideal spot for Jesus to grow up. Situated at an altitude of 1150 feet, the view above the village commanded a majestic panorama of snow-capped Hermon on the N, nearby Tabor on the E, the extensive Plain of Esdraelon on the S and Mt. Carmel and the blue Mediterranean on the W. At Nazareth Jesus received the regular training of a Jewish lad in home and synagogue (Lk 4:16).

Present-day Nazareth is a fair-sized town of about 22,000, the site of the synagogue traditionally marked by the Church of the United Greeks, but the Orthodox Greeks locate the site where the Church of the Forty Martyrs stood.

Inside the Synagogue Church, Nazareth.

View of Nazareth from the hillside above.

Satan

Gen 3:1-14
He was disguised under the Edenic serpent

Gen 3:15
He is the serpent's seed

Isa 14:12
He was Lucifer, son of the morning before his fall

Ezk 28:14
He was the anointed cherub that covers

I Chr 21:1
He energized David to evil

Job 1:7-2:10
He accused and afflicted Job

Zech 3:1-9
He opposes unbelieving Israel prefigured by Joshua the priest

Mt 4:3
He is the tempter

Mt 12:24; Acts 10:38
He is the prince of the demons

I Tim 4:1-6
He instigates false doctrine

Mt 4:4; Lk 4:10-11
He perverts the Word of God

Mt 12:22-29
He works in demon possession

Zech 3:1
He is Satan, the adversary

Lk 4:13
He is the devil, the slanderer

Jn 13:2, 27
He caused Judas to betray Christ

Acts 5:3
and Ananias to lie

2 Cor 4:4
He blinds people spiritually

I Pet 5:8
He seeks to harm believers

Eph 6:11-12
He heads a celestial hierarchy of evil

Eph 2:2
He indwells the unsaved

Jn 8:44
who are his "sons"

2 Thess 2:9
He works diabolic miracles

Jn 8:44
He was branded "a liar" and "the father of lies" by Jesus

Jn 8:44
He is a murderer

Jn 12:31; 14:30
He is the prince of this world

Lk 13:16
He blinds people physically and spiritually

Mt 25:41
He is a fallen angel

Mt 13:38-39
He sows tares

Mt 13:19
and snatches away the Word

Rev 20:1-3
He will be bound during the millennium

Mt 13:39
He is "the enemy"

Mt 13:38
"the evil one"

Eph 6:10-20
He is routed by spirit-directed prayer

I Pet 5:8-9
He is overcome by faith

I Thess 2:18
He hinders God's will in believers

Rev 12:9
He is the deceiver

Rev 12:9; 20:2
He is the dragon, that old serpent

Lk 10:18
He fell from a sinless high estate

Lk 22:31
He viewed Simon Peter as a target

Rev 2:9
He has a synagogue of legalists who deny God's grace in Christ

Jn 3:8, 10
His children are unsaved people

Mt 25:41; Rev 20:10
His ultimate fate is Gehenna

4:14-44. Jesus begins His Galilean ministry

14-15. He begins the Galilean ministry. This ministry, 4:14-9:50, curtailed by Luke, is given more attention in Matthew and Mark (cf. Jn 1:43-2:25; 4:1-54).

16-30. Rejection at Nazareth. Jesus' reading from Isa 61:1-2 is broken off at the point following the prediction of His first advent and the outgoing of the gospel of grace to Gentiles, 17-20. His preaching that divine grace is not confined to Israel, but will reach to Gentiles as in the case of Naaman and the widow of Zarephath, filled the people with wrath, 25-27 (cf. Kgs 17:9; 18:1; 2 Kgs 5:1, 14).

31-37. The demoniac healed (cf. Mk 1-28). See note on 'Demonism' in Mk 5:1-20, 'Miracles' in Mk 5:21-43, on 'Capernaum' Mk 1:21-28, on 'Satan' in Lk 4:1-13.

38-44. Peter's mother-in-law healed (cf. Mt 8:14-17; Mk 1:29-38). See note on 'Demonism' in Mk 5:1-20. On the kingdom of

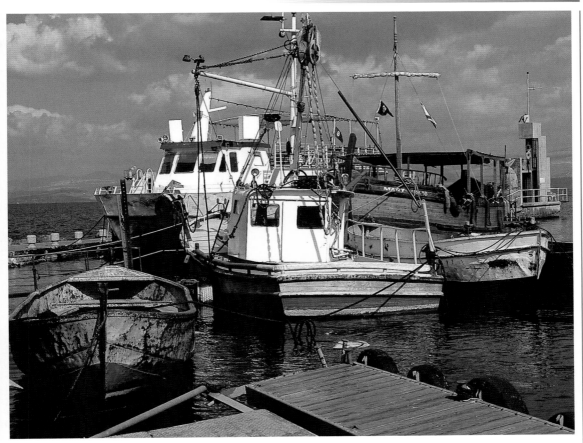

God, 43, see note on Mk 4:1-29. Jesus preached in 'the synagogues of Judea [Galilee],' 44.

5 Miracles and teaching in Galilee

1-11. The call of Peter, James and John (cf. Mk 1:16-20). On the Lake of Gennesaret, 1, see note on Lk 8:1-3. The miraculous catch of fish demonstrates His lordship as the last Adam over the animal creation lost by the first Adam. Peter's sinfulness was revealed. Cf. the other miracle of a large catch of fish in Jn 21, occurring after the resurrection.

12-26. The leper and the paralytic healed. See Mk 1:40-45; Mt 9:2-8; Mk 2:1-12. See note on 'Miracles' in Mk 5:21-43.

27-29. Call of Levi (Matthew). See comments on Mt 9:9; Mk 2:13-14.

30-39. Scribes and Pharisees answered. See notes on Mt 9:10-17; Mk 2: 16-22. For the parables of the garments and the wineskins, 36-39, see comments on Mt 9:16-17; Mk 2:21-22.

6. The twelve chosen; the Beatitudes

1-11. The Sabbath question. See comments on Mk 12:1-8; Mk 2:23-28. The healing of the atrophied hand (cf. Mt 12:9-14; Mk 3:1-6) showed our Lord transcended mere religious externalism. Religionism gloats in the letter of the law, but ignores the spirit, 6-11. On the synagogue, 6, see note on Lk 4:44.

12-19. Choosing the twelve. The perfect Man spent the whole night in prayer to God, 12, before this momentously important task. See notes on Mt 10:2-4, and especially Mk 3:13-19. On His miraculous healing ministry and expulsion of demons, 17-19, see notes on 'Demonism' in Mk 5:1-20 and 'Miracles' in Mk 5:21-43.

20-49. The Beatitudes. Many of the sayings echoed here are in the Sermon on the Mount (Mt 5-7), which are presented by Matthew as the proclamation of the King concerning the moral and spiritual principles which were to rule in His kingdom (see notes of Mt 5-7). See note on kingdom of God in Mk 4:1-29.

The synagogues of Galilee

Excavations in Capernaum (see note on Mk 1:21-28) have yielded the ruins of one of the finest white limestone synagogues in Palestine. The Franciscans have restored this structure. According to custom, the synagogue building was oriented toward Jerusalem. Rectangular in shape, the interior was 70 x 50 feet. It had a balcony for women, and colonnades on three sides. Other synagogues have been unearthed at Chorazin, Bethsaida Julias, Kefr, Birim, Meiron and Beth Alpha in the Plain of Esdraelon. All date from the 2nd cen. That at Beth Alpha is famous for its mosaics. See also note on 'The synagogue' in the section 'Between the Testaments.'

Artist's reconstruction of the synagogue at Capernaum, Galilee, probably dating to the third century A.D., but built on the foundations of the synagogue Jesus knew and taught in. Notice the women's gallery and the cupboard for the scrolls of the Torah, known as the Ark or tabernacle.

Women's gallery

Tabernacle for the Torah

Pulpit

Right: Remains of the old synagogue of Katzrin, northern Israel.

Cloister

7:1-35. Miracles of mercy

1-10. The centurion's servant healed.
See notes on Mt 8:5-13. On 'Capernaum' see note in Mk 1:21-28.

11-18. The widow of Nain's son raised. This episode is unique to Luke. Nain, still called by this name, is a Galilean town situated five miles SSE of Nazareth in the corner of Jebel ed Dahi (Little Hermon) two miles WSW of Endor. Its elevation (1690 feet) gives the hamlet a superb view of the Esdraelon plain on the S and SW and of Mt. Tabor on the NW. It is a cluster of ruins containing ancient sepulchers.

19-35. Jesus' testimony to John. John's languishing in prison tested his faith, 19-20, but the perfect Man strengthened it with a marvelous demonstration of miracles of healing and demon expulsion (see notes on Mk 5), followed by warm praise for John, 24-29, and an exposé of the irrationality of unbelief, 30-35.

7:36-50. Jesus anointed

36-50. The anointing by a sinful woman. This woman was neither Mary of Bethany (Jn 12:1-8) nor Mary Magdalene. She was an unchaste woman, 37, a prostitute likely converted under John's or Jesus' ministry, who gave public evidence of her conversion and gratitude for salvation. The Oriental banquet was in a Pharisee's house. Guests reclined, so it was easy for the woman to wash Jesus' feet with her tears and anoint them. The parable, 41-50, was a rebuke in response to criticism of the woman's demonstration of penitence.

8. Deliverances and instructions

1-3. Women who ministered to Christ. This is unique to Luke's gospel. The women were particularly demonstrative of their affection and devotion to the one who had delivered them. Mary Magdalene was from Magdala (Khirbet Mejdel), three miles NW of Tiberias and situated between it and Capernaum at the S end of the Plain of Gennesaret. The Lake of Galilee was sometimes called the Lake of Gennesaret (Lk 5:1).

4-15. Parable of the sower. See comments on Mt 13:1-23; Mk4:1-20.

16-18. Parable of the lamp (cf. Mt 5: 15-16; Mk 4:21-23; Lk 11:33).

19-21. The new relationship (cf. Mt

Roman centurion

The Roman centurion, corresponding roughly to a captain, commanded about 100 men ('century') which was one-sixtieth of a Roman legion of 6,000 men. Although a centurion often drilled and inspected men under him, his duties frequently corresponded to those of a noncommissioned officer. The centurion was the backbone of the Roman army and was required to be a good, brave, level-headed leader.

12:46-50; Mk 3:31-35).

22-25. Jesus stills the storm (cf. Mt 8:23-27; Mk 4:36-41).

26-39. Demoniac of Gadara. See comments on Mt 8:28-34, and note on 'Demonism' in Mk 5:1-20 and 'Miracles' in Mk 5:21-43.

40-56. A woman healed and Jairus' daughter raised. See comments on Mt 9:18-26; Mk 5:21-43.

9:1-17. The twelve sent out

1-9. The ministry of the twelve (cf. Mt 10:1-42; Mk 6:7-13). They were given power 'to drive out demons' and 'to cure diseases,' 1. There is one devil but many demons (see note on 'Demonism' in Mk 5:1-20 and 'Miracles' in Mk 5:21-43). On Herod the tetrarch, 7-9, murderer of John the Baptist, see note on Mt 14:1-11 and on Mk 6:14-29 (cf. also Lk 3:1-2).

10-17. Feeding of the five thousand. This miracle is told by all the gospel writers (see Mt 14:13-21; Mk 6:30-44; Jn 6:1-14). Bethsaida, 10 ('house or place of fishing') , was the hometown of Philip, Peter and Andrew (Mk 6:45 ; Jn 1:44; 12:21). The NT presents the Sea of Galilee dotted with thriving towns in Jesus' day, including Capernaum, Chorazin, Magdala, Bethsaida and Tiberias. On Bethsaida see Mt 11:20-24.

9:18-62. Prediction of death and coming glory

18-26. Peter's confession. See comments of Mt 16:13-20; Mk 8:27-30. Peter's confession of the perfect Man's deity, 20, did not settle his spiritual problem. So Jesus instructed in discipleship, 23, and its law of self-sacrifice and self-giving, 24-25, in the light of His approaching rejection and death 22, 31, 44.

27-36. The transfiguration. In the transfiguration, the three most spiritually perceptive disciples, Peter, John and James, 28, were given an audio-visual lesson in the law of losing and gaining oneself, 24. The glory of Christ's out-shining deity, 29, and the appearance of Moses and Elijah in glory, 30, talking about His 'departure' or death at Jerusalem, 31, were meant to show the disciples that the only way to glory for our Lord, as well as His disciples, was through self-giving to God's will and to others. Peter and the other disciples wanted the glory without the suffering and were living on the plane of self-saving, not self-losing. Hence the selfish suggestion of the three tabernacles, 33, and the cloud and fear, 34, relieved only by 'This is my Son whom I have chosen; listen to him,' 35.

37-50. Demonstration of the futility of the self-saving attitude. The self-centered, powerless disciples, 37-43, are contrasted with the selfless, powerful Christ, who again announced His death, 44-45. Results of the disciples' selfishness were the clash of believer with believer, 46-48; group with group, 49-50; race with race, 51-56. The only cure was giving up of self, 24, manifested in genuine

dedication to the kingdom of God, 57-62.

51-62. Journey toward Jerusalem. When Jesus finally left Galilee, 51, His ministry until the time of His death was performed in Perea, the territory ruled by Herod the tetrarch, E of the Jordan, and in Judea, under the Roman procurator Pontius Pilate, 9:51-19:27. Luke extensively details this Perean-Judean ministry, of which Matthew relates only a few incidents (Mt 19-20), Mark writes one chapter (Mk 10), and John includes five chapters (Jn 7-11).

10. The seventy-two sent; the good Samaritan

1-24. The seventy-two sent out. This sending of the 72 was in addition to Christ's sending out the 12 some nine months before. His purpose was to complete the proclamations of the King and the kingdom, so that those who disbelieved, 13-24, might have no plea they had not heard. (Cf. Mt 10:1-42; 11:20-24.) Our Lord's statement, 'I saw Satan fall like lightning from heaven,' 18, was a prediction (cf. Rev 12:8-9). Satan will not be cast out of the heavenlies till the second advent and the establishment of the kingdom (Rev 20:1-3), of which great event the 72 were announcers and precursors.

25-29. The lawyer's question. 'Who is my neighbor?' furnished the introduction to the

Remains of an ancient synagogue at Tiberias, on the Sea of Galilee. Although a thriving town and fishing center in New Testament times, it is not named in the gospels, probably because it was a Hellenistic city, regarded as unclean by the Jews.

parable following (cf. Mt 22:34-40; Mk 12:28-34).

30-37. The good Samaritan. This superb parable, exclusive to the gospel of Luke, reflects on our responsibility to care for others whether friend or stranger. In a spiritual sense it also pictures the saving ministry of our Lord, who is the consummate portrait of the Good Samaritan. The poor traveler, fallen among thieves, represents sin-despoiled humanity. The failure of the priest and the Levite to assist illustrates the inability of the law and the ordinances to save man from his sad plight. With superlative love and superb grace and kindness the perfect Man came to the place where the unfortunate man was and 'took pity on him,' bound up His wounds pouring on oil (typifying the Holy Spirit) and wine (speaking of the cleansing blood). The inn, 34, symbolizes the church, and the two pence speak of the rewards for those who minister in behalf of men's salvation. The promised coming again with a greater reward, 35, looks to the second advent.

38-42. Mary vs. Martha. This is another Lukan exclusive, which shows the primacy of spiritual worship over service. Service, if it is not to degenerate into mere fleshly busyness spoiled by frustrations and tensions, illustrated by Martha, must be grounded in true spiritual worship of Christ, illustrated by Mary, 39. Bethany is nestled on the eastern slope of Olivet, about one and five-eighths miles from Jerusalem.

11:1-13. Jesus' doctrine of prayer

1. Jesus praying. This gospel often presents the perfect Man in prayerful dependence upon God. See note on Lk 3:21-22, 'Jesus' prayers in Luke.'

2-4. Jesus instructing in prayer. This is more correctly the disciples' prayer rather than the Lord's prayer, since He was sinless and could never Himself pray, 'Forgive us our sins.' See comments in Mt 6:9-13. The prayer is based on the Father-child relationship and serves as a pattern for all those in His family.

5-13. The parable of the importunate friend, another Lukan exclusive, teaches persistence in petition. Prayer grounded in the fatherhood of God, 11-13, exhibits faith in this

relationship. Verse 13 was fulfilled at Pentecost. To ask for the Holy Spirit now that the gift has been given is like asking a friend for something he has already given you.

11:14-54. Demon expulsion and warnings

14-28. Jesus instructs in demonism. His expulsion of a demon, 14, brings the blasphemous accusation that 'by Beelzebub, the prince of demons, he is driving out demons,' 15. Beelzebub is another name of Satan. See note on 'Demonism' in Mk 5:1-20, 'Miracles' in Mk 5:21-43, 'Satan' in Lk 4:1-13. Satan is a king, 17-18, ruling over a kingdom of evil fallen spirits, 17-19. The kingdom of God, i.e., the rule of God upon mankind, comes upon a person when Satan and demons are cast out by the One stronger than he (Jesus the Christ), 20. This is in response to believing prayer, 11:1-13. The illustration of the demoniac, 24-26, is applied to the nation Israel by Matthew (see comments on Mt 12:43-45). Luke, however, applied the teaching to humanity in general, demonstrating the uselessness of self-reformation to save. External cleaning up without true regeneration invites Satan to return with seven viler spirits.

29-32. The sign of Jonah (cf. Mt 12:39-42; Mk 8:11). 'The queen of the south,' 31, was the Queen of Sheba (1 Kgs 10:1-13).

33-38. The lamp of the body (cf. Mt 5:15-16; Mk 4:21-22; Lk 8:16).

39-44. The Pharisees denounced (cf. Mt 23:13-35).

45-54. The lawyers denounced. 'Expert in the law' (*nomikos,* 'of the law') denotes one who was expert in the law of Moses and traditional Jewish law (Mt 22:35; Lk 7:30; 10:25; 11:45-46, 52; 14:3). 'From the blood of Abel' (cf. Gen 4:8) 'to the blood of Zechariah' (2 Chr 24:20-21), 51, follows the Hebrew order of books where Genesis opens the Scriptures and 2 Chronicles is the last book.

12. Parables and warnings

1-12. Warning against false doctrine. Yeast (Ex 12:8,15-20; Mt 13:33; 1 Cor 5:7-8) represents corrupt teaching. The teachings of the empty ritualists, the Pharisees, were nothing but sham and hypocrisy, 1-3 (see Mt 16:1-12). The Lord encourages His own, 4-14. He who has power to cast into hell (Gehenna) is Satan, who tempts to sin and Christ-rejection, 5. Five sparrows for two pennies, with no 'forgotten sparrow' before God, 6, shows His care of even the least of His creatures. For blasphemy against the Holy Spirit, 10, see note on Mt 12:31-32.

13-34. Warning against covetousness. A request from a man in the crowd, 13-15, occasioned the parable of the rich fool, 16-21, and a general warning against this cardinal sin of covetousness, 22-34 (cf. Mt 6:25-33; Col 3:5). On the phrase 'seek his kingdom,' 31-32, see note on Mt 3:2; 4:17; 13:1-2.

35-48. Watching for the second advent. See notes on the Olivet discourse, Mt 24:37-25:30.

49-59. Christ a divider of men. Christ's 'baptism,' 50, was His vicarious death for sinners (Mt 20:18, 22; Mk 10:38-39). He causes people to choose between good and evil, light and darkness. Therefore He is a divider.

13:1-21. Teachings and deliverances

1-5. Teaching on repentance and judging. This again is exclusive to Luke. Pontius Pilate (A.D. 26-36) frequently lost his Roman temper and severely dealt with the difficult Jews. Here is an example which Jesus used to enforce the necessity of repentance (Mt 3:2). He also referred to the collapse of the tower in Siloam in which 18 people perished.

6-9. The barren fig tree. Cf. Isa 5:1-7 and notes on Mt 21:18-20. The nation Israel was the fig tree. Because the nation displayed no repentance, the tree was to be chopped down (cf. Mt 24:32-34 and notes).

10-17. The woman delivered from infirmity. On the synagogues, 10, 14, see 'The synagogues of Galilee' in Lk 4:44. This episode is unique to Luke's gospel. Satan is represented as having bound this Jewish woman, called 'a daughter of Abraham' (see note on 'Satan' in Lk 4:1-13). The epithet indicates this woman had Abraham's faith.

18-21. Parables of the mustard seed and yeast. See notes on Mt 13:31-33; Mk 4:30-32.

13:22-35. Teachings on the way to Jerusalem

22-30. How many will be saved? This is also unique to Luke. The question was given a

practical turn by the Saviour, 24, to avoid presumption, 25-30. He would teach us to 'make our calling and election sure' (2 Pet 1:10 KJV).

31-33. Jesus warns of Herod Antipas. He was in Perea, which was Antipas' realm. Jesus called the wiley and wicked murderer of John the Baptist 'that fox.' The expression 'today and tomorrow' describes Christ's healing and delivering ministry. The 'third day' refers to His resurrection when He would be perfected (Jn 17:4-5; 19:30; Heb 2:10; 5:8-9). On Herod Antipas, see notes on Mt 14:1-14; Mk 6:14-29; Lk 9:7-9.

34-35. Jesus' lament over Jerusalem. The tender love of the perfect Man, the last Adam, shines through. (Cf. Mt 23:37-39; Lk 19:41-44.)

14. The cost of discipleship

1-6. Healing on the Sabbath. The Lord Jesus answered Pharisaic hypocritical ritualism and empty sabbath observance with a miracle of healing (see note on miracles in Mk 5:21-43).

7-15. Parable of the ambitious guest. This teaches the wisdom of humility, 11, and is peculiar to Luke's gospel. The phrase 'repaid at the resurrection of the righteous,' 12-14, hints at two resurrections, one to life (Rev 20:6) and the other to death (Rev 20:11-15).

16-24. Parable of the great banquet (cf. Mt 22:1-14). The self-righteous (unbelieving Jews), especially the Pharisees, made excuses to get out of attending the great supper of salvation provided by God, 18-20. All things were 'ready,' 17, looking forward to the finished work of the cross. Those in 'the streets and alleys of the town' and on 'the roads and country lanes,'

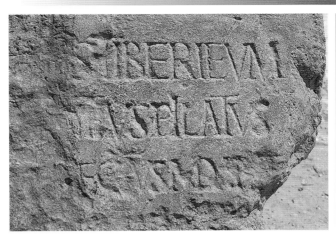

This inscription, found at Caesarea on the Mediterranean coast of Palestine, confirms that Pilate was prefect in the time of Jesus. It is translated: "Pontius Pilate, Prefect of Judaea, made and dedicated the Tiberieum to the Divine Augustus."

21-23, speak of the Gentiles to be brought in and the shutting out of self-righteous Israel, 24.

25-35. Conditions of discipleship. So primary was to be the disciple's love for Christ that his affection for his closest kin, and even himself, was to be as hatred in comparison, 26. This devoted love would weed out the superficial multitude, 25, and prepare for inevitable persecution, hardship and crossbearing, 27. Let the cost be counted! This is illustrated by the parable of the man building a tower, 28-29, a king waging war, 31-33, and the savorless salt, 34-35.

15. Parables: Lost sheep, lost coin, lost son

1-2. Occasion of the parables. The Lord answered the hypocritical complaint of the Pharisees, 2, illustrating the golden text of Luke's gospel: 'For the Son of Man came to seek and to save what was lost' (19:10). The willingness of tax collectors (or publicans) and sinners to hear Him, 1, proved His mission and elicited the complaint.

3-7. The lost sheep. The ninety-nine sheep represented the carping Pharisees; the one lost sheep, the publicans and sinners the Son of man came to save. The parable severely rebuked the Pharisees' empty religiosity and proud self-righteousness.

8-10. The lost coin. Again the one lost piece of silver represented the publicans and

Coin of the procurator Pontius Pilate, A.D. 30 (left); and of the procurator Antoninus Felix, A.D. 59.

sinners. The woman's rejoicing was like the rejoicing of the angels of God in heaven over one sinner who repents, 10, a severe rebuke again to the carping Pharisees.

11-32. The lost son. The prodigal represented the publicans, 11-22; the elder son, 25-32, the Pharisees. His self-righteousness and self-sufficiency were evident. He had never done anything wrong and considered himself above the poor sinful vagabond who had returned home. The rebuke of the Pharisees' criticism of Jesus as the Saviour and Friend of sinners was obvious.

16. The shrewd manager; the rich man and Lazarus

1-18. The parable of the shrewd manager. In this illustration Jesus commended the manager's provident foresight, not his dishonesty. The parable not only furnished an occasion to teach the right use of money, but afforded a means of rebuking the wrong, selfish use of it by the covetous Pharisees, who yet maintained they believed in the future life. If so, let them demonstrate their faith in the hereafter and use their money to befriend others, who would be at heaven's door to welcome them home, 9. Right use of money in this life demonstrates the genuineness of our salvation and will be rewarded in the life to come. The Pharisees' scoffing ridicule of Jesus' teaching about money, 14-17, proved their faith was empty and their belief in heaven an empty sham. Their covetousness proved it. Their boasted veneration for the law was also a farce, since they set aside the clear teaching of the law on divorce, 18, and granted it on trivialities.

19-31. The rich man and Lazarus. This parable (or as some suggest, a historical illustration) was also aimed at the sneering, unbelieving, self-righteous Pharisees. They boasted in their alleged law-keeping (cf. 15-17), and considered their wealth, which they covetously garnered, as evidence of this. Jesus proved the fallacy of this reasoning. The rich man's great wealth was on the contrary not evidence of divine favor, for he went to hell (Hades, Sheol, intermediate abode of departed human spirits between death and the resurrection). Lazarus, a penniless beggar, nevertheless went to 'Abraham's side,' 22, i.e., paradise, where the souls of all OT righteous went. He had no chance to make friends for himself by using 'worldly wealth' so as to welcome him to the 'eternal dwellings' (cf. 9). Yet he was there! And between him and the rich man was an impassable gulf, separating the lost from the saved. Let the covetous Pharisees take warning!

17. Forgiveness; second advent foretold

1-10. Instruction in forgiveness and service. Those who cause others to stumble, especially the young, are doomed to severe punishment, 1-2. Forgiveness and kindness are to be practiced if we are controlled by faith (cf. Eph 4:32). Service ought to be spontaneous and natural to one who confesses the lordship of Christ, 7-10.

11-19. The cleansing of the ten lepers. This episode is found only in Luke. All ten lepers were miraculously cured. While all ten exhibited faith and obedience, only one returned with an attitude of thankfulness. The Samaritan was the only one who worshipped the Healer rather than the healing. This proper spiritual focus resulted in spiritual as well as physical healing, 19.

20-37. When the kingdom of God should come. The question of the Pharisees, 20, was answered by our Lord's declaration that the kingdom of God came not with outward show but was among or in the midst of them, 21, i.e., in the person of the King, whom the Pharisees rejected. Christ then turned to the disciples and gave further instruction concerning the external manifestation of the kingdom's coming, at the time the King is accepted, 22-37. Then His coming will be evident to all, 24. However, His mission included suffering and rejection first, 25. Judgment would immediately precede the King's visible return, 26-37. Verses 34 and 35 refer to the instantaneous gathering out of offenders to end-time judgment. Verse 37 describes the terrible carnage of Armageddon (Rev 16:14; 19:17).

18. Parables and instructions

1-8. Parable of the persistent widow. This parable occurs in the context of Christ's second advent (17:20-37). Verse 8 asks, 'However, when the Son of Man comes, will he find faith on the earth?' In the dark apostate

Heaven and Hell

Jesus lifted the curtain to the life hereafter, revealing the place of departed souls, both saved and unsaved, between death and the resurrection.

Hades (Gr., Heb. 'Sheol') is the place all dead went in OT times of 'Moses and the Prophets,' 29. The righteous, however, went to 'Abraham's side,' 22, but were separated from the wicked OT dead by a 'great chasm,' 26.

The believing thief (Lk 23:43) was to be that day with Christ in paradise, which circumstance, in the light of Eph 4:8-10, seems to indicate that since the ascension of Christ, paradise, or 'Abraham's side,' has been transferred to the 'third heaven' (2 Cor 12:1-4), the immediate presence of God (1 Cor 15:53; 1 Thess 4:13-18; 2 Cor 5:2,8; Phil 1:23).

The unsaved both of the OT and NT period, however, still go to Hades, or intermediate hell, in conscious torment (Lk 16:24).

At the sinners' judgment (Rev 20:11-15) the wicked dead are raised and cast into eternal hell, together with death and Hades (Rev 20:14). This is the 'second death' or eternal separation from God (Rev 20:14), the final state of the wicked.

days of the Tribulation, faith will be found only in the faithful remnant of God's people. These, His elect, will suffer great persecution and cry continuously to Him for deliverance. He will avenge the remnant against their persecutors by His second advent.

9-14. The parable of the Pharisee and the tax collector. Like the preceding, this parable is exclusive to Luke's gospel. It was directed against the pride and empty ritualistic self-righteousness of the Pharisees, 9. The Pharisee was filled with egotism. Five 'I's' in this short prayer were directed to himself and not to God, 11-12, KJV. The publican was filled with humble contrition. 'God, have mercy on me, a sinner,' 13, had the mercy seat in mind (Ex 25:17-22; Heb 9:5), and means 'God be propitiated' or 'be toward me as You are when You look upon the blood-sprinkled mercy seat.' In Christ God is propitiated and merciful.

15-17. Jesus blesses little children (see Mt 19:13-15; Mk 10:13-16).

18-30. The rich ruler (cf. Mt 19:16-30; Mk 10:17-31).

31-34. Jesus again predicts his death (cf. Mt 20:17-19; Mk 10:32-34).

35-43. The blind man healed near Jericho (cf. Mt 20:29-34; see note on Jericho in Mk 10:46-52).

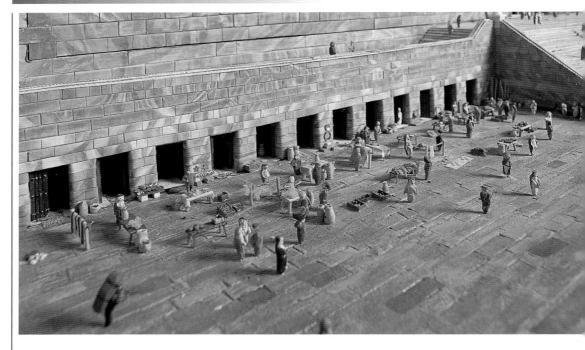

19:1-27 Zacchaeus; parable of the pounds

1-10. Conversion of Zacchaeus. As a rich tax collector, Zacchaeus was despised by his fellow Jews, 1-2. He sought to see Jesus, 3-4, but much more Jesus sought to see him, 5-6. Jericho streets in NT times were lined with sycamore trees, and wood has been preserved which archaeologists have analyzed as such. Zacchaeus' restitution, 8-9, proved the reality of his spiritual experience and admirably illustrates the fact that 'the Son of Man has come to seek and to save what was lost,' 10, the golden text of the gospel of Luke.

11-27. The parable of the minas. This parable was given to correct the false notion that the kingdom of God would immediately appear, 11. On the term 'kingdom of God' in Mark and Luke, see note on Mk 4:1-29. In this particular context Luke uses the term 'kingdom of God'; however, in the restricted sense in which Matthew employs the designation 'the kingdom of the heavens,' see notes on Mt 3:2; 4:17; 13:1-2. The kingdom, then rejected, is delayed (Lk 17:21; Acts 1:6-8), but will come in due time with visible manifestation (see notes on Lk 17:20-37). Therefore, in the parable the Lord Jesus is the 'man of noble birth,' 12, who goes into a far country (heaven) to receive for Himself a kingdom, to be established at His second advent. The ten servants represent the same groups as the ten virgins of Mt 25:1-13. Verse 27 describes the wrath of the Lamb and the slaughter of His foes in 'the great day of God Almighty' (Rev 6:9). The second advent will result in the reward of the righteous and the punishment of the wicked.

19:28-48. Triumphal entry; second cleansing of the temple

28-40. The triumphal entry. See comments on Mt 21:1-9; Mk 11:1-10. In 12:12-19, Luke gives the interesting detail, 'The whole crowd of disciples began joyfully to praise God in loud voices for all the miracles they had seen,' 37. Luke also reports their shout, 'Blessed is the king who comes in the name of the Lord! Peace in heaven and glory in the highest!' 38. Peace in heaven will come when Satan is cast out of the heavenlies (Rev 12:7-12) and bound in the bottomless pit (Rev 20:1-3). Peace on earth, the angelic announcement at Christ's birth (Lk 2:14), will be realized only at the second advent. **41-44. The perfect Man weeps over Jerusalem.** See notes on Mt 23:37-39. What tenderness and kindness our Lord manifested! His heart of compassion overflowed (Lk 13:34-35) as He prophesied the destruction of the city, 43-44 (cf. Lk 21:20-24). This was fulfilled in A.D. 70.

45-48. Second purification of the temple. See notes on Mt 21:12-16; Mk 11:15-18. Contrast the first cleansing at the beginning of Christ's ministry (Jn 2:13-17). The 'house of prayer,' 46 (cf. Isa 56:7), was made 'a den of robbers' (Jer 7:11).

20. Clash with the Jewish leaders

1-8. Jesus' authority questioned. See notes on Mt 21:23-27; Mk 11:27-33. Jesus exposed the empty hypocrisy and unbelief of the Jewish leaders by the test question concerning John's baptism, 14. Their inability to reply showed the quandary into which their sin forced them, between admission that they had refused to follow God's messenger and exposure to public disfavor.

9-18. Parable of the tenants. See exposition of it in Mt 21:33-46. Christ was the Stone that had been rejected, 17 (Ps 118:22-23). At His second advent He will be the 'capstone' (Zech 4:7). Whoever 'falls on that stone' in faith shall be broken in contrition and forgiveness, but 'he on whom it falls [in judgment] will be crushed,' 18, a clear reference to the Smiting Stone destroying Gentile world powers previous to the establishment of the kingdom (Dan 2:34-35).

19-26. Question of the tribute. See Mt 22:15- 22; Mk 12:13-17.

27-38. Sadducees silenced. See Mt 22:23-33; Mk 12:18-27.

39-47. The scribes interrogated. See Mt 22:41-46; Mk 12:35-37.

21. The Olivet discourse

1-4. The widow's mite (cf. Mk 12:41-44).

5-38. The Olivet discourse. Contrast Luke's record with Matthew's (ch. 24 and 25). The latter gives the fullest account (cf. also Mk 13). While Matthew gives full details of the end of the age immediately prior to Christ's second advent, Luke surveys this period, 5-19 and 25-36, but punctuates it with the prediction of the fall of Jerusalem (A.D. 70), 20-23, and the worldwide dispersion of the Jews during the intervening period, called 'the times of the Gentiles,' 24. During this period Jerusalem will be under Gentile dominion, and will not be fully delivered till the return of the Lord, 25-28, when this era, begun with the captivity of Judah under

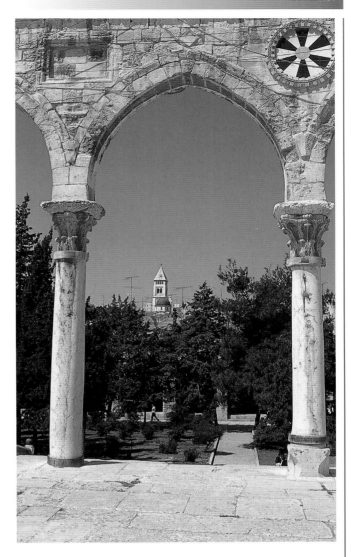

Nebuchadnezzar (606 B.C.), will end. 'The fig tree,' 29, is Israel. ' All the trees' are other nations that will also see a revival before the Lord comes – nations under the revived Roman Empire. 'Summer,' 30, is the mediatorial form (millennial) of the kingdom of God under Messiah, 30, at His advent. 'This generation,' 32, is the indestructible, unassimilable Jew, who will be preserved to fulfill God's prophetic word, 33. See notes on Mt 24 and 25; Lk 13.

22:1-23:26. Events prior to the crucifixion

22:1-2. Plot to kill Jesus (cf. Mk 14:1-21).

3-6. Judas' treachery (cf. Mt 26:2, 14-15; Mk 14:10-11).

The summit of the Mount of Olives, viewed from the Temple Mount, where Herod's Temple was situated.

Passion week April A.D. 30

Saturday

Supper at Bethany

Sunday

Disciples bring a colt
Triumphal entry into Jerusalem
Jesus in the city and temple
Retirement to Bethany

Monday

The fig tree cursed
Second cleansing of the temple

Tuesday

The last day in the temple
Christ's authority challenged
Parable of the two sons
Parable of the wicked husbandman
Parable of the rejected stone
Parable of the marriage feast
The question of tribute to Caesar
The question of the resurrection
The greatest commandment
David's son and lord
Denunciation of the scribes and
    Pharisees
Lament over Jerusalem
The poor widow's gift
Greeks desire to see Jesus
The Olivet discourse

Parables:

The fig tree
The porter
The master of the house
The faithful and evil servants
The ten virgins
The talents
The sheep and the goats
Judas bargains to betray Jesus

Wednesday

Day of quiet at Bethany

Thursday

Preparation for the Passover
The Paschal meal and the Lord's
    supper
Jesus washed the disciples' feet
Judas signaled as the traitor
Apostles warned against desertion
The great upper room discourse
    (Jn 13-17)
The great intercessory prayer
    (Jn 17)
The agony in Gethsemane
    (see note on Mt 26:36-56)
The betrayal and arrest
Peter and the healing of Malchus'
    ear

Friday

First Jewish trial: before Annas
Second Jewish trial: before
    Caiaphas
Third Jewish trial: before
    Sanhedrin
Jesus declared His messiahship
Jesus mocked; Peter's denial and
    remorse
First Roman trial: before Pilate
Second Roman trial: before Herod
Third Roman trial: before Pilate
    again
Pilate handed over Jesus to the
    Jews
Pilate again attempted to rescue
    Jesus
Judas' suicide
The road to the cross

On the cross

First three hours:
9:00-12:00 AM.

Three sayings:
'Father forgive them...'
'Today you will be with me in
    paradise'
'Dear woman, here is your son'

Second three hours:
12:00-100 PM.

Four sayings:
'My God, my God ...'
'I am thirsty ...'
'It is finished'
'Into your hands I commend my
    spirit

Supernatural phenomena accompanying Jesus' death:

darkness, earthquake
rending of the temple veil
Burial of the body in Joseph's
    tomb

Saturday

Body in the tomb, spirit in Sheol

Sunday

The resurrection (see 'Order of
    events' in Mk 16)

Trials of Jesus

	Trial	Scripture	Judge	Decision
Religious trials	JEWISH			
	First	Jn 18:12-14	Annas	Go signal given to liquidate Jesus
	Second	Mt 26:57-68	Caiaphas	Death sentence, charge of blasphemy
	Third	Mt 27:1-2	Sanhedrin	Death sentence made legal
Civil trials	ROMAN			
	Fourth	Jn 18:28-38	Pilate	Not guilty
	Fifth	Lk 23:6-12	Herod	Not guilty
	Sixth	Jn 18:39-19:6	Pilate	Not guilty, but turned Jesus over to the Jews

7-13. Preparation for the Passover (cf. Mt 26:17-19; Mk 14:12-16).

14-18. The last Passover (cf. Mt 26:20; Mk 14:17; Jn 13).

19-20. The Lord's Supper (cf. Mt 26:26-29; Mk 14:22-25).

21-23. Announcement of the betrayal (cf. Mt 26:21-25; Mk 14:18-21; Jn 13:18-30).

24-30. The apostles' place in the future kingdom (cf. Mt 19:28; Rev 3:21). Cf. notes on Mt 3:2; 4:17; 13:1-2.

31-34. Jesus' prediction of Peter's denial (cf. Mt 26:33-35; Mk 14:29-31).

35-38. Warning of coming conflicts.

39-46. Jesus on the Mount of Olives. See notes on Mt 26:36-46; Mk 14:32-42.

47-53. The betrayal (cf. Mt 26:47-56; Mk 14:43-50; Jn 18:3-11).

54-65. The arrest (cf. Mt 26:69-75; Mk 14:53-72).

66-71. Before the Sanhedrin (cf. Mt 26:59-68).

23:1-26. Before Pilate and Herod (cf. Mt 27:1-15; Mk 15:1-5; Jn 18:28-40).

23:27-56. The crucifixion and burial

27-38. The crucifixion. See notes on Mt 27:33-38; Mk 15:22-28; Jn 19:17-19. The cross of Christ not only judged the world (Jn 12:31) but uncovered what the world is. The people in general just stared in indifference, 35, the religious leaders scoffed, 35; the brutal mocked, 36; the convicted sinner prayed, 42; materialistic unbelievers gambled (Mk 15:24); the believing centurion glorified God, 47; the disciples stood afar off, 49.

39-45. The repentant robber. Here is the case of a deathbed repentance that was genuine. On 'paradise,' 43, see Lk 16:29-31 with notes. The story of the penitent thief is unique to Luke (cf. Mt 27:44; Mk 15:32).

46-49. Jesus dismisses His spirit, voluntarily performing an act of sovereign will, thereby differentiating the death of the God-Man from all other cases of physical death, 46 (Mk 15:37; Jn 19:30). 'No one takes it from me, but I lay it down of my own accord' (Jn 10:18).

50-56. Jesus' burial. See notes on Mt 27:57-61; Mk 15:42-47; Jn 19:38-42. Joseph was a member of the council, 50, i.e., the Sanhedrin, the official Jewish court, composed of 70 priests, scribes and elders, presided over by the high priest.' Waiting for the kingdom of God,' 51, indicates his messianic expectation, according to the great promises of the OT (see notes on Mt 3:2; 4:17; 13:1-2). The Sabbath, 54, began at sunset. Luke, addressing non-Jewish readers, explains the urgency of the burial according to Jewish custom.

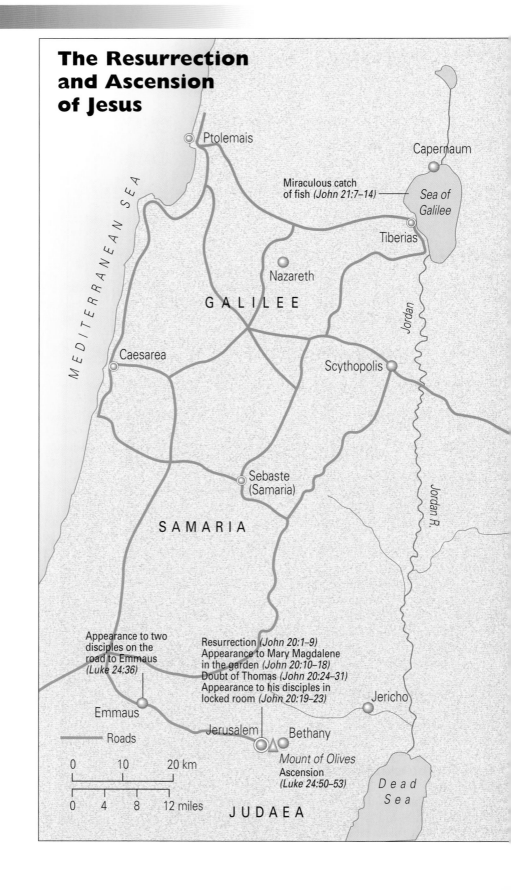

The Resurrection and Ascension of Jesus

MEDITERRANEAN SEA

Ptolemais

Capernaum

Miraculous catch of fish *(John 21:7–14)*

Sea of Galilee

Tiberias

Nazareth

GALILEE

Jordan

Caesarea

Scythopolis

Sebaste (Samaria)

SAMARIA

Jordan R.

Appearance to two disciples on the road to Emmaus *(Luke 24:36)*

Resurrection *(John 20:1–9)*
Appearance to Mary Magdalene in the garden *(John 20:10–18)*
Doubt of Thomas *(John 20:24–31)*
Appearance to his disciples in locked room *(John 20:19–23)*

Jericho

Emmaus

Jerusalem

Bethany

Roads

Mount of Olives
Ascension *(Luke 24:50–53)*

0   10   20 km

Dead Sea

0   4   8   12 miles

JUDAEA

This great circular stione was used to seal the 'Tomb of the Herods', found outside the city walls of Jerusalem. The tomb of Joseph of Arimathea, where Jesus was buried, featured a similar rolling stone door.

24. Resurrection and ascension

1-12. The resurrection (cf. Mt 28:1-6). For 'Order of the events of the resurrection' see note in Mk 16:1-8; cf. Jn 20:1-17. See note in Jn 20 for 'The resurrection authenticated.'

13-35. Post-resurrection ministry to the Emmaus disciples. Emmaus was 60 furlongs (one furlong equals 582 feet), hence about seven and one-half miles from Jerusalem. The village is probably to be identified with Amwas, which is about the distance specified by Luke W of Jerusalem. Its connection with NT Emmaus is very ancient and pre-Crusade. Luke alone reports in full this tender and sympathizing ministry of the risen Christ. 'Moses,' 27, refers to the Pentateuch, so full of messianic prophecy and typology; and 'all the Prophets,' 27, was the second part of the Hebrew Scriptures: Law, Prophets, Writings. The third division was also called 'Psalms,' 44, since this section was headed by Israel's devotional treasury.

36-43. Post-resurrection appearance to the eleven. The resurrected Christ proved He was not a mere spirit but possessed a glorified *body* of flesh and bones, 39. Proof resides in the fact they touched Him, talked to Him, and He ate before them, 43. All this befits the gospel of the manhood of Christ. The NT teaches clearly the physical resurrection of Christ. See note in Jn 20, 'The resurrection

authenticated.' for the 'Post-resurrection appearances' of Christ see note iin Mk 16:9-20.

44-49. The worldwide commission. The glorified Son of Man explained that Scriptural promises and predictions concerning Him had to be fulfilled, 44. He illuminated their minds to comprehend this, 45, and the meaning of His death and resurrection, 46. The end in view was that 'repentance and forgiveness of sins will be preached in his name *to all nations,*' 47. Thus Luke's narrative ends on its note of universal proclamation — salvation offered to *the whole world.*

50-53. The ascension. 'What my Father has promised,' 49 (the Holy Spirit), was to be given (Acts 2:1-4). Until they were thus clothed with power from on high they were to stay in the city (Jerusalem) and not attempt to fulfill their superhuman task by merely human means. The ascension was the final climax, 50-53 (see Mk 16:19-20; Acts 1:9-11). Bethany, 50, was a small village about one and five-eighths miles E of Jerusalem on the E slope of the Mount of Olives.

JOHN

The gospel of the Son of God

The author. From the time of the church Fathers the fourth gospel has been ascribed to John, the beloved disciple. Theophilus of Antioch (c. 180), Irenaeus (c. 200), Tertullian (c. 220) and Origen (c. 250) were in agreement on Johannine authorship. Even Porphyry and Julian the Apostate, two early sworn enemies of Christianity, apparently did not question the Johannine authorship. This they would certainly have done had there been grounds to deny the authenticity of the gospel which so signally emphasizes the absolute deity of Christ.

John the beloved. Both John and his brother James were Galilean fishermen, and members of a prosperous family, for their father Zebedee employed servants (Mk 1:20). John and his brother were fiery and impetuous. They earned the epithet 'sons of thunder' (Mk 3:17). John was in the inner circle close to Jesus (Mk 5:37; Lk 8:51; Mt 17.1),

The author in the gospel. (1) At the Last Supper John leaned on Jesus' bosom (Jn 13:23). (2) At the cross he stood faithful and was entrusted with the care of Jesus' mother (Jn 19:26-27). (3) At the tomb he was first to believe in Jesus' resurrection (Jn 20:1-10). (4) On Galilee's shore he was the first to recognize the Lord (Jn 21:1-7).

Date of the gospel. The date of John's gospel is after the synoptic gospels but not later than A.D. 85 or 90, shown by the following reasons. (1) It supplements the synoptics. It omits much that they record and records much that they omit; it is full where they are concise and vice versa. (2) It shows a maturity of Christian consciousness, unlikely in the earlier period of the church. (3) It shows no reference to the fall of Jerusalem in A.D. 70, either in prospect or retrospect, so was certainly written a number of years after that event. (4) Archaeology supports this sound dating, as shown by the special feature on the next page.

Outline

1:1–51 Introduction
2:1–12:50 Public ministry of the Son of God
13:1–17:26 Private ministry of the Son of God
18:1–20:31 Death and resurrection of the Son of God
21:1–25 Epilogue

Relief of the gospel-writer John from the Church of the Annunciation, Nazareth.

S. JOANNES

1:1-18. The prologue: The Word – who He was and what He became

1-13. The Word –who He was. These verses declare eight great truths concerning our Lord Jesus Christ. (1) He was and is the Eternal One, who always existed before time and matter: 'In the beginning *was* the Word.' (2) He was and is a Person distinct from God the Father: 'The Word [the preincarnate Christ] was *with* God' (the Father). (3) He was and is God: 'The Word *was* God,' 1. (4) He was co-existent with God (the Father) from eternity, 2. (5) He was the Creator of the universe, 3. (6) He is the Source of all life and light (both physical and spiritual), 4, 5, 9 (not to be confused with John the Baptist, 6-8, who was merely a witness to Him as the 'true Light,' 9). (7) He is the self-revealing God to a fallen universe and His self-disclosure is invincibly victorious, 5. (8) He entered the world of men and they ignored Him, 11. But those who receive Him are granted spiritual regeneration, 12-13.

14-18. The Word – who He became. 'The Word [the Eternal Creator God] became flesh [man],' 14. The mystery of the ages! God became Man, the God-Man. Deity united Himself to humanity in one glorious Person and dwelt in a tabernacle of flesh among us, 14. Those who saw the God-Man saw 'the glory of the only Son, who came from the Father,' 14, as John the Baptist bore witness, 15 (cf. 6-8). They actually saw God, who is invisible, in 'the only Son,' who made God known, 18, and introduced a new era of grace and truth, 17.

1:19-51 The testimony of Jesus' first disciples

19-28. Testimony of John the Baptist. The Jewish religious authorities of Jerusalem inquired, 'Who are you?' 19, 22. John denied he was the Christ, or Elijah (2 Kgs 2:11), who was expected to return before Christ, or 'the Prophet,' i.e., Messiah foretold in Deut 18:15 (cf. Jn 6:14; 7:40). John declared he was merely 'the voice' (Isa 40:3) prophetically announcing Messiah's advent, 23. The Jewish authorities then demanded why John was baptizing or performing an official rite without official status, 24. His answer was that the water ceremony he was performing was not an end in

John's baptism of repentance

John's baptism was a sign of repentance in preparation for the coming of the kingdom of God, which would be initiated by Jesus. It stood midway between the baptism of proselytes, an initiatory Jewish rite, and the baptism of the church, a rite of identification with the Christian community

The Dead Sea Scrolls

Discovered since 1947, these documents have shown the NT to be Jewish in background, with less Greek influence than Hebrew. They also furnish evidence to date the synoptic gospels, placing Mark between A.D. 60-65 and John not later than A.D. 90. The recovery of the Essenic literature from Qumran, the site on the NW shore of the Dead Sea where the first and most phenomenal manuscripts were discovered in 1947, demonstrates that John's gospel reflects the genuine Jewish background of John the Baptist and Jesus, and not the Gnostic background of the late 2nd cen. A.D. This is attested by the remarkable parallels to the conceptual imagery of the fourth gospel found in the Essenic literature from Qumran. These archaeological findings have discredited the rationalistic criticism which had removed John's gospel from the traditional date of the apostolic age (between A.D. 90-130), and thus treated it as essentially apocryphal.

Gnostic literature from Nag Hammadi

In 1945 thirteen codices containing 49 Gnostic documents were found in Upper Egypt at ancient Sheneset-Chenoboskion in the vicinity of Nag Hammadi, 32 miles N of Luxor. Dating from the 3rd cen. A.D. and written in Coptic, this material, rivaling the Dead Sea Scrolls in importance, proves that Gnosticism was much later than the gospel of John, and that the Gnostics based much of their material on this gospel, rather than the fourth gospel being a late Gnostic treatise.

Baptistery **Main entrance** **Scriptorium**

Plan of Qumran

It was in the caves in these cliffs above Qumran that the Dead Sea Scrolls were discovered.

Top: The cistern and in the background the watchtower of the Qumran community.

Bottom: The unique building, shaped like the top of one of the scroll-jars, which houses the Dead Sea Scrolls in Jerusalem's Israel Museum.

The Qumran region

Jordan R.

Jericho

Jerusalem   Caves   Nebo

Wadi Qumran   Qumran

Bethlehem   'Ain Feshka oasis

Herodium   *Wadi Kidron*

D E A D   S E A

W I L D E R N E S S   O F   J U D A H

Caves   **Machaerus**

En-gedi

Masada

0	10	20	30 km
0		10	20 miles

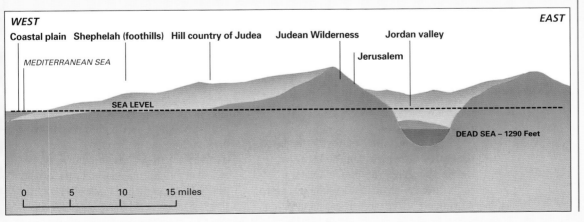

WEST   *EAST*

Coastal plain   Shephelah (foothills)   Hill country of Judea   Judean Wilderness   Jordan valley

MEDITERRANEAN SEA   Jerusalem

SEA LEVEL

DEAD SEA – 1290 Feet

0	5	10	15 miles

A baptism takes place near the spot in the Jordan river often linked with John's baptism of Jesus.

itself, but introductory and preparatory to a spiritual operation of far greater importance to be performed by Him whose way he was preparing, and whose sandal thong he was unfit to untie (a slave's job).

29-34. The baptism of Jesus. Jesus was the sacrificial Lamb of God, 29 (Ex 12; Isa 53:7; 1 Pet 1:19), outranking John because He existed before John, 30 (cf. 1-18). John's knowledge of Jesus' messiahship was divinely authenticated at Jesus' baptism by the dovelike Spirit coming and remaining upon Him, 31-33, confirming Him as the one 'who will baptize with the Holy Spirit,' 33, the Son of God, the Messiah, 34 (cf. 49; 11:27). John evidently recognized Jesus as the sacrificial Lamb who would die, 29, be resurrected and ascend to heaven, to give the gift of the Holy Spirit at Pentecost (Acts 2:1-5). This gift would contain the baptizing ministry of the Spirit (Acts 1:5; 2:4; 11:14-16). Since the baptizing ministry was made possible by Christ's redemptive death, He, the Redeemer, is styled 'He who will baptize with the Holy Spirit.' *After* the advent of the Spirit at Pentecost the Spirit Himself is the Agent of the spiritual baptism (1 Cor 12:13).

35-51. Testimony of Jesus' first disciples. John's testimony to Jesus' messiahship, 35-37, resulted in Andrew's conversion, 38-40. Andrew's testimony in turn won Simon, whose name Jesus changed to Cephas (Aramaic 'stone': Gr. *petros*, 'Peter'), 42. Philip was called, 43. He was of Bethsaida, on the Sea of Galilee near Capernaum, 44. He testified of the Messiah and won Nathanael, 45-51, of Cana near Nazareth (21:2).

2. Water turned to wine; the temple cleansed

1-12. The first miracle. 'This, the first of his miraculous signs,' 11, illustrates the basic *nature* of the *newness of life* which Christ came to give (cf. 20:30-31). This blessing of eternal life received by faith is seen in the water turned to wine at Cana, near Nazareth in Galilee. 'Signs' are mighty works or miracles *which symbolize spiritual truths.* The first sign shows that the Bestower of life is the omnipotent Creator of ch. 1, able to change water to wine. The wine is typical of the joy which He came to bring (1:17) and which issues in life. The Creator alone can be our spiritual Recreator. He alone can bestow the joyous exhilarations of eternal life prefigured by the wine (cf. Isa 55:1; Eph 5:18-20). It served as an exhibition of the glory of His person, 11.

13-25. The temple cleansed. This was the first cleansing of the temple at the commencement of Christ's ministry, not the second at the close mentioned by the synoptists (see notes on Mt 21:12-17; Mk 11:15-18; Lk 19:45-48). This act of Jesus manifested His authority as the Son of God and fulfilled Ps 69:9 ('my Father's house,' 16). The Jews surmised this and asked for a 'sign,' 18, and Jesus gave that of His death and resurrection, 19, which was completely misunderstood by His foes (cf. Mt 26:61), and not understood by His friends till after His resurrection (Mt 26:61; 27:40; cf. Jn 10:18).

3. Nicodemus and the new birth

1-21. Discourse on regeneration. From Jn 2:23 through 17:26 the Son of God imparts eternal life and describes what it is and what it does. 'Many people saw the miraculous signs He was doing and trusted in His name' (2:23). In His interview with Nicodemus, a rigid moralist and a Sanhedrin member, 1, Jesus showed the necessity of regeneration, 'You *must* be born again,' 7, and the necessity of His death to accomplish a basis for this spiritual transaction, 'so the Son of Man *must* be lifted up,' 14. In a most solemn fashion ('I tell you the truth,' 3, 5) Jesus declared that no one can 'see,' 3, or enter, the kingdom of God unless he is 'born of water' (figure of the cleansing Word, Eph 5:26; Jas 1:18; 1 Pet 1:23;) and of the Spirit (the Holy Spirit, the Agent in regeneration), 5. This is a supernatural imparting of eternal life on the basis of Christ's death, typified by the Mosaic serpent in the wilderness, 14 (see notes on Num 21:5-20; 2 Cor 5:21). The theme of John's gospel is clearly displayed in verse 16.

22-36. John the Baptist's testimony. 'Aenon near Salim,' 23, is probably Umm el-'Amdan, SE of Sychar. Here Jesus' disciples baptized under His direction (cf. 22; 4:2). John referred to himself as merely the 'friend who attends the bridegroom' (Christ), 29. Verses 31-36 constitute John's keen insight into the person and work of the Messiah, who had the Spirit in immeasurable fullness upon His sinless humanity, 34.

4. The Samaritan woman and eternal life

1-45. Jesus and the Samaritans. The hostile Pharisees, 1-3, evidently necessitated Jesus' leaving for Galilee and going through Samaria, which lay between. Samaria was populated by a mixed people, remnants of the northern tribes who had been taken captive

Miracles of the fourth gospel

	Application
2:1-11 Turning water to wine	Nature of eternal life
4:46-54 Healing the nobleman's son	Condition of eternal life – faith
5:1-9 Healing the infirm man at Bethesda	Power to live the life
6:1-14 The feeding of the 5,000 (also in Mt 14:13-21; Mk 6:32-44; Lk 9:10-17)	Food for the life
6:15-21 Walking on the sea (also in Mt 14:22-36; Mk 6:45-56)	Guidance for the life
9:1-41 Sight restored	Light for the life
11:1-44 Raising of Lazarus	Victory of the life over death
21:1-14 The catch of fish	Full fellowship of the life

when Israel fell in 722 B.C. They used the Pentateuch and worshiped the Lord. Racially and religiously mongrel, they were abhorred by the Jews, 9. Jesus' witness to the woman at the well of Sychar, in the heart of the Plain of Shechem under the shadow of Mt. Ebal, showed His compassionate concern for the lost which transcended all social and religious prejudices. The incident elicited His second great discourse, on the water of life, 4-26, following His first on regeneration (3:1-21). The woman's testimony had a remarkable effect upon the Samaritans, 27-39, and opened the way for Jesus' two-day ministry among them, 40-45.

46-54. The second sign. The healing of the nobleman's son sick at Capernaum illustrates faith as the *condition* for receiving eternal life. On Capernaum see note on Mk 1:21-28.

Discourses in John's gospel

Twelve discourses are unique to this gospel

1. **3:1-21** On spiritual regeneration
2. **4:4-26** On eternal life
3. **5:19-47** On the Source of eternal life and its witness
4. **6:26-59** On the true Bread of life
5. **7:14-29** On the Source of truth
6. **8:12-20** On the Light of the world
7. **8:21-30** On the true Object of faith
8. **8:31-59** On spiritual freedom
9. **10:1-21** On the Good Shepherd
10. **10:22-38** On the unity of the Godhead
11. **12:20-36** On the world's Redeemer
12. **Upper room teaching:**
    13:31-14:31 On the approaching separation
    15:1-27 On the union with Christ
    16:1-33 On the Holy Spirit and the future
    These discourses fall into two categories:
    1. Christ's public instruction, ch. 1-12, presenting Himself to the world as the *ultimate reality;* and
    2. Christ's private teaching, ch. 13-16, disclosing Himself to His own as *the eternal sufficiency.*

5. Infirm man healed

1-9. The third sign in John's gospel – the infirm man healed at Bethesda. This illustrates the divine power granted to live the new life (see introduction to John's gospel). This infirm cripple presents a vivid picture of man's complete helplessness as a sinner, and Christ's power to save and enable him to live the new life. Bethesda ('house of grace') was a rectangular spring-fed pool with five porticoes. It is likely the pool discovered in 1888 near St. Anne's Church in the Bezetha quarter of Jerusalem near the Tower of Antonia and the Sheep's Gate. It has a five-arched portico with faded frescoes of Christ's healing.

10-18. Opposition of the Jews. The Jews' empty ritualism carped at the healing and the healed man carrying his bed on the Sabbath, 10-11, and vented its rage on Jesus, 16. Christ claimed a unique relation to Deity, 'my Father,' 17, the Jews comprehending clearly that Jesus was claiming to be God, 18 (cf. Jn 10:30,33; Phil 2:6).

19-47. Discourse on the source of eternal life. In answer to Jewish opposition Christ set forth His unity in person and work with the Father, 19-23. This passage alone is sufficient to dispel foolish notions that Jesus never claimed to be God, or cult contentions that the Son is not very God of very God. He who is then one with the Father, God Incarnate, is the Source of eternal life. Verse 24 tells how eternal life is received; verses 25-26 show the effect of eternal life on physical death and resurrection. Verse 28 teaches literal physical resurrection. There will be a resurrection of the righteous (1 Cor 15 :22; 1 Thess 4: 13-18) and a separate resurrection of the unrighteous (Rev 20:4-6, 11-14).

Christ presented four witnesses to Himself as the Source of eternal life, 33-47: (1) John the Baptist, 33-35; (2) His mighty signs or works, 36; (3) the Father, 37-38 (cf. Mt 3:17); (4) the Holy Scriptures, 39-47 (cf. Lk 24:27, 44-46). For other discourses see introduction to John's gospel.

6. Five thousand fed; discourse on the bread of life

1-21. Feeding the five thousand. See note on 'Miracles' in introduction to John's gospel (cf. Mt 14:13-21; Mk 6:32-44; Lk 9:10-17). This furnishes the setting, after the episode of Jesus' walking on the sea, 15-21 (cf. Mt 14:23-36; Mk 6:45-56), for the next great discourse.

22-59. Discourse on the bread of life. See note on 'Discourses' in introduction to John's gospel. He who could walk on the sea was indeed the Bread of God who came down from heaven, and gave life to the world, 33. Clearly and unequivocally Christ announced Himself as the Divine One, the nourisher and sustainer of the eternal life which He gives. The unbelieving Jews could understand neither His deity, 42, nor how believers could feed upon Him spiritually, 52-58. On 'manna,' 31, 58, see Ex 16:14-22 comments. Christ fulfilled the type as giver and sustainer of life (cf. also Ex 16:35). On the Capernaum synagogue, 59, see note on Mk 1:21-28.

60-71. Discipleship tested: Peter's confession. In the face of large-scale desertion, Peter spoke for the twelve in declaring their trust in Jesus. John intimates that Judas, however, was never a true disciple.

7. The prophecy of the Spirit's advent

1-13. Jesus delays to go to Jerusalem. He remained in Galilee because the Jews in Judea sought to kill Him, 1. His brothers taunted Him in their unbelief, 2-5, urging Him in a selfish, worldly spirit to advertise and exploit his works for personal gain. He rebuked their spirit of selfish independence of action and showed the difference between them and Him in the matter of God's will, 6-9. But when the time was ready in the Father's will, He went up to the Feast of Tabernacles, 10-13. This section of the gospel, 7:1-11:53, introduces the period of conflict about His person – the unbelief of His brothers, 3-9, the bewilderment of the people, 10-13.

14-36. Jesus at the feast. The Feast of Tabernacles or Booths (Lev 23 :33-44, see comments) was the harvest festival memorial of redemption for Israel, prophetic of kingdom rest and blessings through Israel to the nations. The conflict over who Jesus was continued, as He taught in the temple. He propounded a paradox, asserting both His authority, 14, and subordination, 16, issuing in a controversy, 21-

Tiberias and the Sea of Tiberias

John refers to the Sea of Galilee (6:1; cf.21:1) as the Sea of Tiberias, and the city is mentioned in Jn 6:23. The city founded by Herod Antipas was named in honor of the then-reigning Emperor Tiberius (A.D. 14-37). It was built before A.D. 25, and was located on Galilee's western shore about six miles from the lower end of the lake where the Jordan River exits. Herod moved his court there from Sepphoris, N of Galilee. The lax Hellenistic Roman atmosphere of the hot bath resort was not conducive to the Jewish-slanted ministry of our Lord. Soon the city became so important that for a time it gave its name to the lake. After the fall of Jerusalem (A.D. 70) Tiberias became a Jewish metropolis and the center of rabbinical learning.

24. The confused reaction of the people appears in 20, 25-32, 35-36. Jesus' fifth discourse, on the Source of truth, 14-29, is given (see 'Discourses' in introduction to John's gospel).

37-39. The prophecy concerning the Holy Spirit. The last day of Tabernacles (Lev 23:36) was the most solemn and climactic of the entire festal cycle. It was the eighth day of rest and holy assembly. During the seven days symbolizing their wilderness wandering, water was drawn from the pool of Siloam and then poured out, commemorating the water supplied Israel in the desert. The eighth day signified the enjoyment of the springs of the land itself and

The town of Tiberias viewed from the southwest shore of the Sea of Galilee, or Sea of Tiberias.

An ancient well in the Holy Land. At the Festival of Booths, Jesus looked forward to the regathering of Israel, when the nation will joyously 'draw water from the wells of salvation.'

no water was poured out. That was the memorial aspect. The prophetic aspect looked forward to the regathering of Israel after her present worldwide dispersion and the fulfillment of the kingdom ode of Isa 12:1-6, when the nation will joyously 'draw water from the wells of salvation' (Isa 12:3; cf. Joel 2:28-32; Zech 14:8). Jesus stood and offered the spiritual reality of the kingdom to individual believers, 39, but national fulfillment to Israel of all that the festal ritual signified awaits His second advent. Verse 39 shows that the prophecy was realized in the advent of the Spirit at Pentecost (Acts 2:1-4). The idiom in 39 is, 'the Spirit was not yet' (Gr.). After Pentecost, when Jesus was glorified by resurrection and ascension, it could be said, 'The Spirit now is' (cf. Acts 19:2 where the same idiom occurs and is explained as referring to the advent of the Spirit at the introduction of a new era).

40-53. The people's confusion. The conflict over Christ was focused here in its intensity.

8. The adulterous woman; discourse on the light of the world

7:53-8:11. The woman taken in adultery. Many textual critics omit this incident on evidence from the oldest manuscripts. The RSV includes it, but sets it in small type to distinguish it from the main text. The NASB separates the story with brackets while the NIV separates it with dividing lines. Others place it after Lk 21:38. Still others think it was omitted in certain manuscripts on purpose because the grace in dealing with the woman was unpalatable to later legalists. Whether or not it appears in the earliest texts, the story is certainly authentic and is instructive as it highlights our Lord's tender compassion for the sinner.

12-20, 21-30. Discourses on the light of the world, and on faith. These were Christ's sixth and seventh discourses in the gospel. Unbelief which rejects Him involves eternal separation from God, 21-25. His identity is the acid test, 25-29. Many believed on Him, the true Object of faith, 30.

31-59. Discourse on spiritual freedom. This is the eighth discourse in John's gospel. Faith in Christ manifested by continuance in His Word, 31-32, is the gateway to spiritual freedom, not ritualism or human descent, 33. Whoever is enslaved by sin, 34, is not free. Only the Son can set the sinner free, 36. The Jews boasting in Abrahamic descent were children of the devil, 44. Jesus declared His eternity, 58. He was the 'I AM' (Ex 3:14; Isa 43:13) who existed before Abraham. The Jews proved their slavery to sin by their reaction to the Liberator from sin.

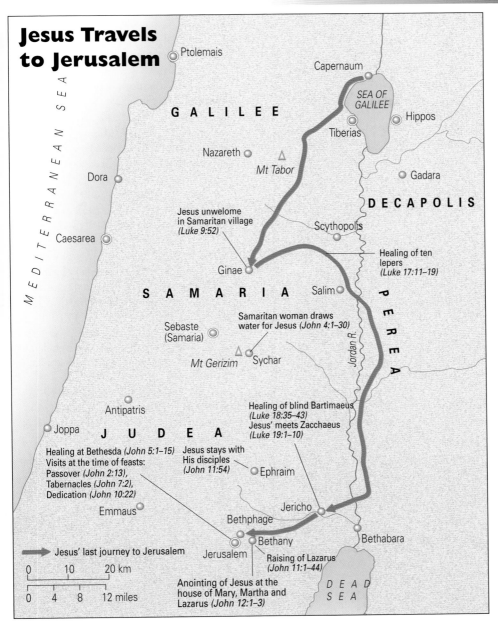

Jesus Travels to Jerusalem

MEDITERRANEAN SEA

Ptolemais

Capernaum

SEA OF GALILEE

GALILEE

Hippos

Tiberias

Nazareth

Mt Tabor

Gadara

Dora

DECAPOLIS

Jesus unwelome
in Samaritan village
(Luke 9:52)

Scythopolis

Caesarea

Healing of ten
lepers
(Luke 17:11–19)

Ginae

Salim

S A M A R I A

P E R E A

Samaritan woman draws
water for Jesus (John 4:1–30)

Sebaste
(Samaria)

Jordan R.

Mt Gerizim

Sychar

Antipatris

Healing of blind Bartimaeus
(Luke 18:35–43)
Jesus' meets Zacchaeus
(Luke 19:1–10)

Joppa

J U D E A

Healing at Bethesda (John 5:1–15)
Visits at the time of feasts:
Passover (John 2:13),
Tabernacles (John 7:2),
Dedication (John 10:22)

Jesus stays with
His disciples
(John 11:54)

Ephraim

Jericho

Bethphage

Emmaus

Bethany

Bethabara

Jesus' last journey to Jerusalem

Jerusalem

Raising of Lazarus
(John 11:1–44)

0   10   20 km

0   4   8   12 miles

Anointing of Jesus at the
house of Mary, Martha and
Lazarus (John 12:1–3)

DEAD
SEA

9. The blind man healed

1-34. The blind man restored to sight.
This is the sixth miraculous sign in the gospel, illustrating light and illumination for the new life to be found in Christ, 5. The clay and the spittle did not effect the healing, but symbolized what the creative power of Christ, the Creator-Redeemer, did, 6. The washing in the Pool of Siloam, 7, suggests the sign had the purpose of spiritual regeneration, 36-38 (cf. Eph 5:26). When Judaism cast the healed man out, 27-34, it cast him into the arms of a loving Lord.

35-41. Jesus reveals Himself to the man. This sign, like the other signs and discourses in John, anticipated the position of true Christianity outside the sphere of Judaism and that which has rejected Christ (Heb 13:13).

10. Discourse on the good shepherd

1-21. The discourse itself. This ninth discourse sprang out of the miracle of Christ's healing the blind man, who was cast out of Judaism. The true sheep of Christ, it is evident, would be cast out of the Jewish fold. The blind man restored to sight was so cast out, and became one of His sheep. Our Lord, therefore, gave parabolic instruction of the new order of God's sheep. Israel, as the Lord's true elect OT people in covenant with Him, were His sheep and He their Shepherd (Ps 23:1; 95:7; 100:3; Ezk 34:1-31; Zech 11:7-9; 13:7). In the parable, 1-6, Judaism was the sheepfold, 1. Christ the true Shepherd had come through the appointed door (the prophesied messianic line) into the sheepfold, 2. The doorkeeper (Holy Spirit) opened the fold to Him and His sheep responded (as the blind man of ch. 9) and He led them out, 3, of the apostasy and unbelief Judaism had degenerated into by rejecting Him, its true Shepherd, 4-5.

The lessons drawn from the parable, 7-21, are: (1) Christ now becomes the door of the sheep — a new order, 7. (2) All other presumed saviours (the leaders of apostate Judaism) are thieves, 8. (3) He alone is Saviour, Sustainer, Life-giver, 9-10. (4) He is the Good Shepherd who will die for the sheep (Israel), 11-15. The Good Shepherd has other sheep (Gentiles), who with the Jews will be brought into one fold (the church) with one Shepherd (Christ) , 16 (cf. 1 Cor 12:13; Eph 4:4-6). (6) This will be effected by the Good Shepherd's unique and voluntary death for the sheep, 17-18. Unbelief, 19-21, was incapable of anything except confusion and wicked blasphemy.

22-39. Discourse on the unity of the Godhead. The tenth discourse of John's gospel was delivered at the Feast of Dedication, 22, celebrated the 25th day of Chislev (Nov.-Dec.). It commemorated the reconsecration of the Jerusalem temple by Judas Maccabeus in 165 B.C. During the eight-day festival, the Jews demanded a statement of our Lord, if He were the Christ. His reply, 25-38, asserted: (1) Christ's sheep, who the unbelieving Jews were not, know His deity and messiahship, 25-27. (2) His sheep are saved, safe and secure, 28-29. (3) Jesus asserted His unity of essence with the Father, hence His unequivocal deity, 30 (cf. 14:9; 20:28-29), and the Jews so understood Him, 31. (4) He defended His deity by His works and by the Scriptures, 32-39. If Israel called its judges 'elohim' ('gods'), 34-35, because they represented God (Ps 82:6), why should they stumble at the true Son of God whom the Father sent, 36?

40-41. Jesus at the place where John had baptized. Many believed on Jesus because of the testimony John the Baptist had borne concerning Him.

This church at Bethany, on the outskirts of Jerusalem, commemorates the raising of Lazarus.

John and Isaiah

Subject	Isaiah	John
The shepherd and the sheep	40:11	10:1-21
Water for the thirsty	41:18; 44:3; 48:21; 49:10; 55:1	4:13-14; 6:35; 7:37
Food for the hungry	49:10	6:35
Guidance	42:16; 48:17	14:6
The divine Comforter	51:12	14:16
The gift of the Spirit	59:21	14:26; 15:26 16:13
Worldwide salvation	43:19; 45:22; 49:12; 56:7-8; 60:3	4:21-24; 10:16
Freedom from fear	4 1:10; 51:7	14:1
Sight for the blind	35:5; 42:7	9:39
Liberty for the bound	61:1	8:36
Divine teaching	50:4-5	14:10; 17:6-8

11. The raising of Lazarus

1-44. The Son's power over death.
This is the seventh sign-miracle of John's gospel, authenticating the Son of God as Life-giver (cf. 20:30-31). It was the last and greatest of Jesus' public miracles recorded by John proving His claim to be the resurrection and the life. The episode is supported by the most convincing evidence of details. Bethany was just beyond the brow of the Mount of Olives, less than two miles from Jerusalem. Jesus declared that Lazarus' illness would 'not end in death,' i.e., result in death alone; but was 'for God's glory so that God's Son may be glorified through it,' 4, through the resurrection from the dead. Jesus waited till Lazarus died and had lain in the grave for four days, so that He might perform a great and incontrovertible miracle. The great declarations of verses 25 and 26 will find their fulfillment in 1 Thess 4:13-18; 1 Cor 15:22-23.

45-57. The effect of this climactic sign. Many Jewish friends of Mary believed, 45. Others went to report the sign to the Pharisees, 46, who forthwith called the Sanhedrin, 47, and plotted to put Jesus to death, 48-57. Caiaphas' prophecy that one man should die for the nation rather than that the whole nation should perish, 49-52, was amazing, especially 52, 'for the scattered children of God, to bring them together and make them one,' i.e., the Gentiles (Ps 22:27; Jn 10:16; Rom 1:16; Eph 2:14-17). The city of Ephraim, 54, was a remote, isolated village N of Jerusalem.

12. Supper at Bethany; acclaim at Jerusalem

1-11. The anointing by Mary. See notes on Mt 26:6-13; Mk 14:3-9; cf. Lk 7:37-38. Martha as usual was serving. Mary as usual was worshiping. Others had come to His feet to have their needs met. Mary came to render Him His due. She anointed Him for His approaching death, 7, which she possibly glimpsed as a result of her worshipful communion. Judas' perfidy stood out in stark contrast, 4-6, as well as the wickedness of the chief priests, 10, in plotting to put Lazarus to death because of their venomous hatred of Jesus, 11.

12-19. The triumphal entry. See comments on Mt 21:4-9; Mk 11:7-10; Lk 19:35-38. Ps 1.18:25-26 was shouted, 13, by the populace who had been stunned by Lazarus'

Herod's Temple

Royal Portico

Court of the Gentiles

Place of Trumpe

Eastern gate

Huldah gate

Huldah

Possible bridge across
Kidron Valley to the Mount of Olives

Court of Priests

Herod's Temple

Court of the Gentiles

Solomon's Portico

Antonia Fortress

The Pool of Israel

being raised from the dead, 17-19. Zech 9:9 was fulfilled, 15. John adds the details of the reason for the public display of Palm Sunday – excitement over the climactic sign wrought at Bethany.

20-36. Discourse on the world's redeemer. This is the eleventh discourse in John's gospel. The occasion was the inquiry of 'certain Greeks,' 20, to see Jesus, 21-22, suggesting the outgoing of the gospel to the whole world as a result of Jesus' death, 23-24, authenticating by a voice from heaven, 28 (cf. Mt 3:17). In verse 31 the judgment of Jesus Christ as bearing the believer's sins is alluded to, resulting in the casting out of Satan, 'the ruler of this world' (Satanic world system). The sins of believers would be judged in the person of Christ lifted up on Calvary, 32. The result would be the justification of the believer, here embracing the extension of the gospel to the Gentile world.

37-50. Jesus' final words. Notice the prominence of Isaiah's prophecy in the quotations in 38 (Isa 53:1) and 40-41 (Isa 6:10).

13. Washing the disciples' feet

1-20. The meaning of the Lord's action. The Lord's washing of the disciples' feet illustrates the believer's continual need of cleansing after the once-for-all bath of regeneration. 'A person who has had a bath needs only to wash his feet; his whole body is clean. And you are clean, though not every one of you,' 10 (Judas being unregenerate). The figure is of a person returning from the public bath to his home. His feet would become defiled. So the believer is once-for-all cleansed in the bath of regeneration (Heb 10:1-12), but must confess the sins involved in his daily walk in a sinful world (Eph 5:25-27; 1 Jn 1:9). A defiled saint, 8, cannot have communion with Christ; that is why Peter had to have his feet washed. The command, 14, involves the exercise of a spirit of forgiveness of one saint toward another (Eph 4:32).

21-35. Prophecy of the betrayal by Judas (see Mt 26:20-25; Mk 14:17-21; Lk 22:21-22). Judas was never regenerated, 10 (cf. Jn 6:70-71; 13:27). He so surrendered himself to Satanic ambition and was so taken over by evil power that he is called a devil (Jn 6:70). Jesus' choice of him was an instance of divine overruling of evil for good. The name Judas (Gr. form of Judah) became popular after the time of Judas Maccabeus (166 B.C.).

36-38. Prophecy of Peter's denial (cf. Mt 26:33-35; Mk 14:29-31; Lk 22:33-34). Impetuous and well-meaning, Peter had to learn the hard way to gauge his weakness. His example is very human and therefore very helpful.

14. The second advent and the Spirit's coming

1-6. Christ's return for His own. This is part of the upper room discourse (ch. 14-16), involving the private instruction of Christ directed to His own whom He was soon to leave. His return here declared is His coming *for* His own (1 Thess 4:13-17; 1 Jn 3:1-3), not His return in glory *with* His own (Mt 24:29-30). It was Jesus' first instructions concerning the believer's heavenly hope (cf. Phil 3:20-21).

7-15. Christ expounds His deity. He declared His union with the Father, 7-11. Cf. the tenth discourse of John's gospel on the unity of the Godhead, 10:22-38. There our Lord had enunciated the same truth, 'I and the Father are one' (essence or substance, not one Person), 10:30. He who saw the visible Son saw the invisible Father (cf. 1:18). The 'greater things,' 12, are possible because our Lord in the flesh was confined to one place at a time. Now with outpoured Spirit (Acts 2) 'all that Jesus began to do and to teach' (Acts 1:1) can be continued world-wide by His faithful followers. Also the new promise and privilege in prayer, 13-15, makes the promise of verse 12 possible.

16-26. The promise of the Spirit. The Paraclete ('one called to assist') was the Holy Spirit, called 'another Counselor,' 16, because He would continue the ministry of Christ through His disciples after the Lord's death, resurrection and ascension. Called 'the Spirit of truth,' 17, because of His revelatory ministry in truth, the Holy Spirit was said to abide *'with'* the disciples, but at some future time (Pentecost, Acts 2) was promised to be *'in'* them (cf. Rom 8:9; 1 Cor 6:19). The advent of the Spirit would make up for Christ's departure, 18. 'On that day' (Pentecost), the disciples would be enabled to understand Christ's union with the Father because they would be baptized by the Spirit in vital union with Christ, 20. 'I in you' was the

Jesus' Burial

Jewish burial custom

There is no reference to a Jewish practice of embalming. Instead, the body was washed (Acts 9:37) and swathed in bandage-like wrappings of linen (*othonia,* 'strips of linen' 40; 20:5-7; Lk 24:12). Hippocrates and Aristophanes employ the word for 'bandages.' Thick layers of aromatic preservative were enclosed in the folds of the wrappings (Mt 27:59; Lk 23:53; cf. Jn 11:44).

Because evening was imminent with the high festal Sabbath commencing at 6.00 p.m., Joseph and Nicodemus chose a nearby garden tomb belonging to the former. Tomb burials were common. Ancient tradition from the early 4th cen. locates Jesus' tomb beneath the dome of the Church of the Holy Sepulchre. Archaeological excavations, except for showing that this spot was located outside the city walls in that era, however, have not

'Gordon's Calvary,' East Jerusalem.

confirmed this site otherwise. Ossuaries (stone boxes) holding the bones of the deceased when tombs were emptied for new burials have been found in large numbers in Jerusalem excavations dating from this era, and common names such

as Jesus, Judas, Ananias, Lazarus, even a Jeshua (Jesus) son of Joseph were found. These names are carved in the ossuaries in Hebrew, Aramaic or Greek.

Gordon's Calvary and the Garden Tomb

Another site known as the Garden Tomb near Gordon's Calvary rivals the Church of the Holy Sepulchre as the place of Jesus entombment Located outside the present north wall, this rock-cut chamber, originally sealed with a large rolling stone has been authenticated as a Jewish tomb of the Roman period However, epigraphic or archaeological evidence is lacking to prove it was Jesus' tomb. The exact location of these holy spots has been lost, probably by divine providence, God knowing the inveterate superstition of the human heart which tends to attach glory to places, while glory belongs to Him alone.

Church of the Holy Sepulchre, Jerusalem.

Spirit's predicted indwelling, 20. 'You in me' was the Spirit's predicted baptism. Verse 26 hints at the teaching ministry of the promised Spirit.

27-31. The bequest of peace. Cf. Phil 4:7.

15. Union with Christ and fruit-bearing

1-17. Abiding and fruit-bearing. The believer's relation to Christ is here prefigured as that of *union* (position) and *abiding* (experience). The *union* would be effected by the death, resurrection and ascension of Christ, and the advent of the Spirit (Acts 2) to baptize the believer into Christ (Rom 6:3-4), and into His Body, the church (1 Cor 12:13). The Spirit came at Pentecost to accomplish this (Acts 1:5 with Acts 11:14-16). The *experience* of *abiding*, 4, 5, 7 (Rom 6:11), is the result of knowing and reckoning that the position of union is reality (Rom 6:1-10). The result is 'fruit,' 2, 4; 'more fruit,' 2; 'much fruit,' 5, 8. As 'the true vine,' 1, Jesus was the true Israel, fulfilling the vocation in which the nation Israel had failed (Isa 5:1-7; Jer 2:21; Ezk 19:10-14). The branches are the new people of God, the church, issuing from union with Christ by the baptism of the Spirit. Fruit springs from abiding, or reckoning on that union, in faith, 5, and is manifested in prayer, 7, and loving obedience, 9-10; resulting in joy, 11, *love* toward fellow believers, 12-14, and a new intimacy as friends, not merely servants, 15-17.

18-27. The believer and the world. The world will hate and persecute the true abiding and fruit-bearing disciple. This refers to the evil Satanic world system organized under Satan's principles of greed, ambition, self-will and pleasure (Mt 4:8-9; Jn 12:31; 14:30; Eph 2:2; 6:12; 1 Jn 2:15-17). Satan is its organizational head; satanic principles underlie it. It is in deadly opposition to Christ and all joined to Him in *position* and in *practice*.

16. The work of the promised Spirit

1-6. Disciples warned of suffering. These verses connect with 15:18-25. Leaving His disciples shortly, the Lord was faithful to warn of dangers.

7-11. Threefold work of the coming Spirit. Jesus plainly announced that His death and ascension were necessary prerequisites for the Spirit's advent at Pentecost, 7. He outlined

the promised Spirit's work with the unsaved, 8-11: convicting sinners (1) 'about sin,' 8, 'because men do not believe in me,' 9, the one damning sin of rejecting Christ as Saviour; (2) 'about righteousness,' 10, because the Son's return to the Father was the evidence of the provision of a perfect righteousness for sinners through faith in Christ, without which there is no acceptance before a holy God; (3) 'about judgment,' 11, because rejection of Christ and His purchased righteousness results in the sinner sharing Satan's doom (Mt 25:41, 46).

12-15. Teaching ministry of the Spirit. This embraces Christ's authentication in advance of the NT Scriptures to be written, 12-13, including 'what is yet to come,' additional prophecies such as 2 Thess 2 and the Revelation. The Spirit to come at Pentecost was promised to guide into all truth, i.e., lead in the way to all the truth, the full NT revelation. He is the divine Teacher in this age.

16-33. Jesus predicts His death, resurrection and second advent. A new order in prayer, 'in Jesus' name,' was indicated, 26. This involves a new access to the Father on the basis of the finished work of Christ and the believer's position of dignity and power in union with Christ, the beloved Son.

17. Christ's great high priestly prayer

1-26. The seven petitions. (1) That the Son might be glorified, 1. *This involved our salvation.* He glorified the Father in His life and His finished work, anticipated in verse 4. In this our salvation resides. He had power to give eternal life to as many as the Father had given Him, 2. Our Lord defined salvation, 3. (2) Restoration to His preincarnate glory in union with the Father, 5. *This involved His glorious person.* He alone could be an efficacious Saviour. (3) Safety of His own from the world, 11, and the 'evil one,' 15. *This involved the security of the saved sinner.* (4) Sanctification of believers, 17. *This insured their fellowship with God and usefulness in this life.* (5) The spiritual oneness of believers, 11, 20-21. *This involved the advent of the Spirit* at Pentecost (Acts 1:5; 2:4; 11:14-16) to baptize all believers into vital union with Christ (Rom 6:3-4) and with one another in Him (1 Cor 12:13). (6) That the world might believe, 21. *This involved*

The Resurrection authenticated

The open tomb, Jn 20:1-2

The recovered grave clothing, Jn 20:3-8

The revelation of the risen Lord
1. To Mary of Magdala, Jn 20:11-18; Mk 16:9

2. To women returning from the tomb, Mt 28:8-10

3. To Peter later in the day, Lk 24:34; 1 Cor 15:5

4. To the Emmaus disciples, Lk 24:13-33:5.

5. To the apostles – Thomas absent, Lk 24:36-43; Jn 20:19-24

6. To the apostles – Thomas present, Jn 20:26-29

7. To the seven by the Lake of Tiberias, Jn 21:1-23

8. To a multitude of believers on a Galilean mountain, 1 Cor 15:6

9. To James, 1 Cor 15:7

10. To the eleven, Mt 28:16-20; Mk 16:14-20; Lk 24:33-53; Acts 1:3-12

11. At the ascension, Acts 1:3-12

12. To Paul, Acts 9:3-6; 1 Cor 15:8-13.

13. To Stephen, Acts 7:55

14. To Paul in the temple, Acts 22:17-21; 23:11-15.

15. To John on Patmos, Rev 1:10-19

Pilate's sealing and guarding the tomb, Mt 27:62-66

Removal of the stone by an angel, Mt 28:1-3

The terror of the Roman guards, Mt 28:4

The message of the angel to the women, Mt 28:5-6

The report of the guards to the chief priests, Mt 28:11

The chief priests' bribe to the Roman guards, Mt 28:12-13

The Roman guards spread the lie that Christ's body was stolen, Mt 28:15

The certainty of Christ's death, Jn 19:34-42

The certainty of His burial, Mk 15:42-47

The certainty His body was not stolen:

1. If His enemies had done so (Mt 28:4-15) they would have produced it.

2. If His friends had done so they would not have preached a lie nor been willing to die for it.

A hallucination? How could doubting Thomas have a hallucination, or 500 people imagine something at the same time?

A hoax? How does one then account for the wonderful change in all the disciples from deepest gloom to radiant joy, cowardice to valor, timid disciples to powerful witnesses?

The miracle of the Christian faith, personal regeneration

The conversion of Saul of Tarsus

---

recognition of the oneness of the church in its union with Christ and with all born-again believers, 20. (7) That believers might be with Him in heaven to behold and share His glory, 24. *This involved the security and assured eternal felicity of all who are His.*

18. The Son of God before His enemies

1-11. The arrest in Gethsemane. See comments on Mt 26:36-56; Mk 14:32-50; cf. Lk 22:39-53. In John's account there is nothing about the agony and the bloody sweat. These belong to a description of His humanity. The gospel of Christ's deity, however, describes what the synoptics omit – the momentary out-flashing of deity of Him who was the great 'I AM,' 5-6 (cf. Ex 3:13-14), prostrating the men who came to arrest Him. No power could touch Him till *His hour* had come!

12-27. Trial before Annas and Caiaphas (see Mt 26:57-68; Mk 14:53-65; Lk 22:66-71). Annas had been deposed as high priest by the Romans (A.D. 15) and had been succeeded by Caiaphas, his son-in-law, but Annas still wielded great influence, 12-13. During the trial Jesus was brought from the residence of Annas to the palace of Caiaphas, 24. The latter had predicted that Jesus should die for the nation(11:49-52). On Peter's denial, see 15-18, 25-27; cf. Mt 26:69-75; Mk 14:66-72; Lk 22:54-62.

28-40. Trial before Pilate (cf. Mt 27:1-14; Mk 15:1-5; Lk 23:17, 13, 16). See note on 'Passion week' and 'Trials of Jesus' in Lk 23. Jesus told Pilate that His kingdom (Ps 45:3, 6; Isa 9:6-7; Zech 9:9) was not from this world, i.e., of this Satanic world system, based on its principles of pride, lust and war, 36. If His kingdom were such, then His servants would fight. Jesus was emphasizing the true nature of His kingdom in stark contrast to Rome and other world governments.

19. The Son of God condemned, crucified, buried

1-15. Pilate brings Jesus before the populace. The scourging was a pitiless Roman atrocity, often itself fatal, 1. Pilate's words, 'Behold here is the man!' 5, recalls Zechariah's prophecy: 'Here is the man whose name is the Branch' (Zech 6:12), and John the Baptist's words: 'Look, the Lamb of God, who takes away the sin of the world!' (Jn 1:29). What shame and mockery were heaped upon Him who was the God-Man, especially the crown of thorns, the emblem of the curse being borne by Him who would someday come into His kingdom by bearing the curse of sin (Rev 19:12). Verse 7 reveals the full blind unbelief of the Jews: 'He claimed to be the Son of God' (cf. Lev 24:16). Verse 15, 'We have no king but Caesar,' uncovers the full terrible apostasy of the nation. The 'Pavement' (Aramaic *Gabbatha),* 13, was an exquisite inlaid floor, 2,500 meters square, designed as a parade ground for Roman

---

The blood and the water

Jesus' death was certainly unique and thought by many to be due to heart rupture, i.e., a 'broken' heart. The suffering and pressure of His sinless humanity in becoming a sin offering was too much for His physical body to stand, and so His heart ruptured, the blood collecting in the pericardium and separating in a sort of bloody clot and watery mass, 34.

---

military pomp and as the approach to the procurator's judgment hall. It was near the ancient Tower of Antonia, apparently part of the NW part of the temple area, now located under the present-day Church of the Dames de Sion.

16-30. The crucifixion. See notes on 'Passion week' in Lk 23 and 'Order of events of the crucifixion' in Mk 15. Above the cross, as was customary when executing criminals, the accusation was written in Hebrew (Aramaic), Latin and Greek, the three common languages of Palestine. Pilate apparently worded the charge differently in the three languages. Evidently Matthew and John report the Hebrew title, Mark gives the Latin and Luke the Greek, 19-20. The seamless robe (tunic), 23, a picture of Christ's perfect righteousness, was not torn, but gambled for, 24, fulfilling Ps 22:18. Jesus' loving committal of His mother to the beloved apostle John, 25-27, is unique to this gospel and exquisitely tender.

31-37. Fulfillment of Scripture. The 'special Sabbath' was especially holy since it fell on the Passover (Ex 12:16). 'The day of Preparation,' 31, 42, was the day before the Sabbath. Empty Jewish ritualism, 31 (cf. Deut 21:23), was over-ruled to fulfill prophecy: 'Not one of his bones will be broken,' 36 (Ps 34:20; cf. Ex 12:46; Num 9:12). 'They will look on the one they have pierced,' 37 (Zech 12:10), was *not* fulfilled then, but will be at the second advent (Rev 1:7). Breaking a criminal's legs was to hasten a horrible death that sometimes lingered for days.

38-42. Jesus' burial in a garden. Nicodemus, 39, must have become a real believer and here appears so (cf. Jn 3:1-2; 7:50-52). The burial of Jesus by these wealthy friends shows the reality of Christ's death.

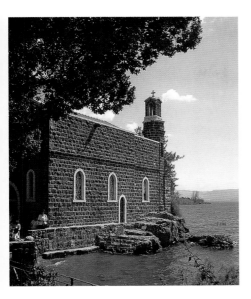

20. The resurrection

1-29. Evidence of the resurrection.

This stupendous event, the consummating fact of Christian faith, the capstone of the gospel of the deity of Christ, is here authenticated: (1) *By the open tomb,* 1-2. Its discovery was made by Mary, 1, who hastily returned to Jerusalem to report to Simon Peter and the other disciple, 2. Conclusion: 'They have taken the Lord out of the tomb,' 2. Reason: The huge stone which sealed the rock-hewn tomb was found moved. (2) *By the grave clothes.* 3-8. The two disciples Peter and John raced to the tomb and saw the linen clothes, 6-7. John *saw and believed,* 8. *The disciples, convinced, left the tomb,* 9-10. (3) *By the self-revelation of the Lord* to Mary Magdalene, 11-18. Her attitude of gloom and desperation was changed by the revelation of the risen Saviour to her. Jesus appeared also to the discouraged disciples, 19-20, Thomas being absent, 24-25; then a week later to the believing and rejoicing disciples when Thomas was present, 26-29. The latter's doubt answers the uncertainty of every honest skeptic ever since.

30-31. Purpose of John's gospel.
See 'Purpose of the fourth gospel' in the introduction to the book. The miracles reported are highly selected with practical intent: (1) to prove Christ as the Messiah, the God-Man; (2) to show Him as the Saviour and Life-giver; (3) to cause men to believe on Him; (4) that they might receive eternal life.

This purpose explains the fragmentary character and yet the essential unity of the book, its imagery, its symbolism and its characters, as well as its distinctive presentation of the Messiah, the Son of God.

21. Epilogue: instruction in spiritual service

1-2. Post-resurrection appearance.
The resurrected Christ directs our service for Him, 1-2. This can result only when the risen Lord reveals Himself to His own. For Sea of Tiberias, 1, see note on Jn 6:1.

3-25. Peter instructed in spiritual service.
Peter's 'I'm going out to fish' smacked of the old life of self-directed service before he yielded to Christ's call to leave his nets. The disciples, following human self-directed leadership, that night caught nothing, 3. Jesus' appearance, 4-5, showed their labors as fruitless (cf. Jn 15:1-17 comments). Service directed by Christ is fruitful, 6-11; revealing the inadequacy and shame of self, 7, and of the all-sufficiency of the risen Lord, 12-14 (cf. Lk 22:35; Phil 4:19). Love for the person of the risen Lord manifested in the primacy of His will in the life, 15-17, is the only acceptable motive for spiritual service (2 Cor 5:14; Rev 2:4-5). Peter was probed on the matter of the quality of His love for Christ. 'Feed my lambs' is pastoral work and demands love for the Good Shepherd of the sheep as the primary qualification. It is instructive that Christ probed Peter three times concerning his love, corresponding to the three times that Peter earlier denied Him. Commentators have also noted that John switches from *agape* (divine love) to *phileo* (brotherly love) as the dialog continues, suggesting that Peter now recognized that he was incapable of loving with *agape* love without divine help. It is quite possible, however, that John is using the terms synonymously.

After instructing Peter concerning his reponsibilities as a leader of the flock, Christ spoke of his eventual martyrdom. Peter would have the opportunity to fulfill his once proud boast that he would be willing to die for Christ (13:37). But before that day a great deal of spiritual maturity would be accomplished in Peter, 18-19. Jesus then spoke of John's own fate as a minister of the gospel.

Tradition has it that this chapel, on the shore of the Sea of Galilee, is built where Jesus told Peter, 'Feed my lambs.'

ACTS

The gospel to the ends of the earth

Author. The author of Acts is the same as the author of the gospel according to Luke. This is indicated by Lk 1:3-4 and Acts 1:1. The 'former book' addressed to Theophilus (Acts 1:1; Lk 1:3) is the third gospel. Internal evidence, particularly the 'we' passages of Acts (16:10-17; 20:5-21:18; 27:1-28:16), confirm Lukan authorship. Luke was a physician (Col 4:14), and presumably a Gentile, since he is not listed among those 'of the circumcision' in Colossians, being mentioned several verses later (cf. Col 4:11). As a Gentile, he wrote to Gentiles through a Gentile patron, Theophilus, narrating the extension of gospel privilege to Gentiles.

Date. This book was apparently written about A.D. 63, since it terminates with Paul's imprisonment in Rome (28-30). Since Luke devotes so much space to the account of Paul's trial and appeal to Caesar, it would have been very unlikely had the book been written later for the author not to have alluded to the outcome of the apostle's trial.

Scope and contents. The book of Acts, called the Acts of the Apostles since about the middle of the 2nd cen. A.D., bridges the period between the four gospels and the later epistles. In dealing with the history of Christian origins, it is the natural sequel to the gospels, and at the same time it is an indispensable introduction to the Pauline labors and epistles.

1. The book shows the progress of Christianity from Jerusalem, to all Judea, Samaria, and to the end of the earth (1:8).

This commission of the risen Lord had already been introduced by Luke in his gospel (Lk 24:46-49). Here it is again described and traced in its outworking as a result of the advent of the Spirit.

2. The book continues the acts of the risen Lord through the Holy Spirit. In the first account (the gospel of Luke) Luke says he dealt with 'all that Jesus began to do and to teach' (Acts 1:1). In the Acts he describes what Jesus *continued* to do and teach through His Body (the church), brought into existence at Pentecost (Acts 2), and indwelt by the Holy Spirit. This activity of the risen Christ in heaven working through the Holy Spirit on earth suggests the name 'The Acts of the Risen Christ' or 'The Acts of the Holy Spirit,' rather than merely 'The

Acts of the Apostles,' who were only human agents. This truth of Christ in glory working on the earth through the believer indwelt by the Holy Spirit, seen in historical outworking in Acts, is the subject of doctrinal revelation in the Pauline epistles. In addition to the human instruments in Acts, two supernatural Beings are found working: Christ in heaven, and the Holy Spirit on earth. Besides these, there is Satan, everywhere operating to hinder and thwart the work of God.

Outline

1-7 From Jerusalem to all Judea
8 To Samaria
9-12 To the Gentiles
13-28 To the end of the earth

The Parthenon, Athens, where the apostle Paul preached concerning the 'unknown god'. Acts shows the progress of Christianity from Jerusalem to the end of the earth.

I. The forty days

1-8. Post-resurrection teaching. On Luke's introduction, 1-2, see notes on author and date of the Acts, above. In verses 3-8 Luke presents a resumé of our Lord's 40-day post-resurrection ministry in which He instructed His own concerning the kingdom of God, 3. This teaching centered in 'the gift my Father promised,' i.e., the gift and advent of the Spirit, 4, to be realized at Pentecost (Acts 2). Thereupon our Lord mentioned the one unique ministry of the promised Spirit that would characterize the new age, 5, the Spirit's baptizing work, by which the church, Christ's Body on earth, shortly would be brought into existence (1 Cor 12:13; Rom 6:3-4; see notes on Acts 2). John the Baptist foretold this baptism of the Spirit (Mt 3:11). The reason Jesus omitted reference to the baptism with fire, which John also had foretold, was because this would be in connection with judgment at the second advent (Mt 3:12). The question of the restoration of the kingdom to Israel, 6 (cf. v. 3), was a natural query for a Jew, since instruction concerning the new age evidently had left this truth untreated (cf. notes on Mt 3:11; 4:17; 13:1-2). So far from denying such a restoration of the kingdom to Israel, our Lord reiterated His repeated teaching that the time was still future and was God's secret (Mt 24:36, 42-44; 1 Thess 5:1; cf. Mt 25:13; Mk 13:32).

9-11. The ascension and promised return. Christ's ascension, 9, was the capstone of His death and resurrection, as was His predicted second advent, 10-11. Each forms an unbreakable link in an inseparable chain of events. The 'cloud' which received Him, 9, was evidently the cloud of the Shekinah glory, so often seen in the OT, and to be seen when He returns again (Mt 26:64; Rev 1:7).

12-14. The ten-day wait for the Spirit. The disciples waited and prayed, and the Holy Spirit came on prophetic schedule to fulfill the divine type and timetable.

15-26. Choice of Matthias. This is not to be considered a mistake with Paul being regarded as the rightful twelfth apostle. The twelve had a ministry of witness to the entire Jewish nation. Not until Israel's final rejection of the testimony, as witnessed by Stephen's death (Acts 7), was Paul chosen as the apostle to the Gentiles and that by direct divine revelation (1 Cor 15:5-8).

Chronological Chart of Acts

All dates are approximate

Events	Acts	Dates
Ascension	1:9-11	A.D. 30
Pentecost	2:1-41	A.D. 30
Early church	2:42-67	A.D. 30
First persecution	4:1-31	A.D. 31
Second persecution	5:17-42	A.D. 32
Third persecution; Stephen's martyrdom	6:8-8:4	A.D. 35-36
Philip's ministry in Samaria and to the Ethiopian	8:5-40	A.D. 36
Paul's conversion	9:1-21	A.D. 37
Paul in Damascus, Jerusalem, Tarsus	9:22-30	A.D. 38
Peter at Caesarea	10:1-11:18	A.D. 41
Founding of Gentile church at Antioch	11:19-24	A.D. 41
Paul in Antioch	11:25-26	A.D. 43
Martyrdom of James; Peter imprisoned	12:1-19	A.D. 44
First missionary journey	11:1-14:28	A.D. 45-47
Jerusalem council	15:1-29	A.D. 50
Second missionary journey	15:36-18:22	A.D. 51-54
Third missionary journey	18:23-21:19	A.D. 54-58
Paul arrested in Jerusalem	21:20-23:22	A.D. 58
Paul a prisoner at Caesarea	23:23-26:32	A.D. 58-60
Paul's journey and arrival in Rome	27:1-28:31	A.D. 60-61

2. The Spirit's advent – birth of the church

1-13. The advent of the Spirit. This is a pivotal chapter opening a new era, witnessed by the wind, 2, fire, 3, and supernatural tongues, 4 (see notes on Acts 11). Pentecost marked: (1) The advent of the Spirit (Jn 16:7-8, 13). (2) The giving and reception of the gift of the Holy Spirit (Jn 14:16; Acts 2:38-39). (3) The abundant pouring out of the gift (Acts 10:45). The advent and giving of the gift involved the performing of all His ministries for this age, including (a) regenerating the believer; (b) baptizing him into the church as Christ's Body (cf. Acts 1:5; 11:16; 1 Cor 12:13) and into Christ the Head (Rom 6:3-4); (c) indwelling the believer (Jn 14:17); (d) sealing Him (Eph 4:30);

(e) giving him the privilege of infilling (Acts 2:4; Eph 5:18). (4) Thus Pentecost signaled the beginning of the church, since it marked the first historical occurrence of the baptism of the Spirit by which operation the church alone could be formed (Acts 5:13-14; 1 Cor 12:13). (5) It opened gospel opportunity to the Jew or Jewish proselyte (Acts 2:5). (6) It indicated Peter's first use of the keys of the kingdom of the heavens (Acts 2:14; cf. note on Mt 16:19). (7) It furnished an illustration of spiritual outpouring (Acts 2:16) prophesied upon Israel when restored to kingdom blessing in the coming age (Joel 2:28-32). (8) It signaled the worldwide proclamation of the gospel of grace to every race, prefigured by the supernatural languages (Acts 2:4-11), in fulfillment of the program of evangelization for the new age commanded by the risen Lord (1:8). See notes on Acts 8; 10; 11:1-18; 19:1-7.

14-47. The results of the advent of the Spirit. The reception of the gift of the Spirit as a deposit in the newly formed church was far-reaching. It furnished the dynamic for Peter's great sermon declaring the messiahship and lordship of Christ, 14-36. Three thousand were converted and became recipients of the blessings of the gift of the Spirit, 37-41. It brought power and unity to the newly formed community of believers, 42-46, and a sustained growth and increase, 47.

3-4. The first miracle and its results

3:1-11. The healing of the lame man. The miracle was a further testimony to the unbelieving Jewish nation of the lordship and messiahship of Him whom they had crucified, as Peter's sermon had been (2:14-36). It witnessed to the fact that the Crucified One was risen and ascended to glory, and that His omnipotence had been revealed through His name, 12-16, in the instant healing of the lame man.

3:12-26. Peter's second sermon. His words were addressed to the nation Israel. The nation was called to repent, 19, of its crime of killing the Author of life, 15. Repentance would have resulted in national deliverance, described as 'times of refreshing,' 20 (cf. Joel 2:28-32), and God's restoring 'everything, as he promised long ago by his holy prophets,' 21, i.e., the restoration of the kingdom to Israel alluded to in Acts 1:6 and the great theme of OT prophecy. The nation's official answer was complete impenitence (ch. 4), so that Israel's coming Saviour 'must remain in heaven' till this present age is past, 21. The outcome of not hearing the Prophet Jesus Christ (Deut 18:15-18) was to be utter destruction, 22-23, consummated in national decimation by the Romans in A.D. 70.

4:1-37. The result. The nation rejected the message of the miracle and of Peter's appeal, arrested the apostles, 1-4, and forbade preaching in Jesus' name, 13-22. Peter's address to the Sanhedrin, 5-12, was fearless, climaxed by a quotation, 11, from Ps 118:22, and a call to salvation, which was rejected. The high tide of spiritual life in the Jerusalem church appears in verses 23-37.

5. Discipline and persecution

1-11. Ananias and Sapphira's sin. Like Samson and Saul, Ananias and Sapphira sinned the 'sin that leads to [physical] death' (1 Cor 5:1-5; 1 Jn 5:16; cf. 1 Cor 5:1-5; 11:30). It was a direct yielding to Satan in the sense of lying to the Holy Spirit, 3, and tempting Him who was operating in such fullness of power in giving witness of the power of a crucified and risen Christ to the Jewish nation, 9. Peter was prominent in the discipline meted out (cf. Mt 16:19; 18:18).

12-42. Powerful witness to the Jewish nation. The place was prominent – Solomon's portico in the temple, 12. The results were public to the nation and miraculous, so much so that even Peter's shadow effected cures, 12-16. Jesus' works were continued by the Spirit through the apostles (1:1) as a further witness to the Jewish nation. These mighty miracles were directed toward Israel to give the nation a last chance to repent. They were only for the beginning of the age to authenticate the gospel of a crucified and risen Christ to Israel, and later to the first Gentile converts before the NT Scriptures were given. When these purposes were met, the miracles and sign gifts were superseded by a written revelation, which was to be the object of faith. Jewish rejection is seen in the second persecution, 17-42. Gamaliel was a well-known rabbi, 34-39. Theudas, 36, is mentioned by Josephus (*Ant.* XX.5.1). Judas, 37, revolted A.D. 6.

Where did the Pentecost pilgrims come from?

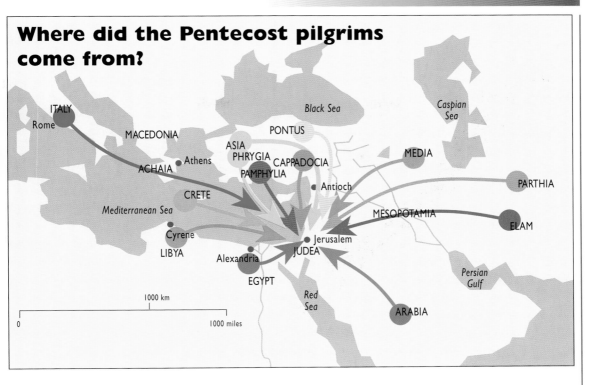

6. The first deacons

1-7. Choosing the seven. The 'Grecian Jews,' 1, were Hellenists who adopted the Greek language and customs. The Hebrews clung to Aramaic and Jewish practices. 'To wait on tables,' 2, included financial and temporal duties. 'Prayer and the ministry of the word,' 4, are always the principal responsibility for the pastor, presbyter, or bishop. The deacon's office was to guard this calling from encroachment by other necessary functions of a minister of Christ. The growth of the Jerusalem church, 7, is indicated. The laying on of hands, 6, speaks of simple identification of the apostles and the assembly with the chosen deacons in their work (cf. Lev 3:2).

8-15. Stephen's ministry and arrest. Stephen's Spirit-filled and miracle-attested witness to the nation's leaders was rebuffed, bringing final Jewish rejection of the testimony of the Triune God – God the Father in the OT, God the Son in the gospels, now God the Spirit in powerful appeal through Stephen. The Libertines (KJV), correctly 'Freedmen,' 9, were Jews who had been Roman slaves but were subsequently freed. The reference is apparently to a Jerusalem synagogue frequented by Jews from a number of the lands of the dispersion –

Cyrene in N . Africa W of Egypt, Alexandria in Egypt, Cilicia NW of Syria and proconsular Asia.

7. Stephen's martyrdom

1-53. Stephen's sermon. He was the chosen instrument to deliver the Lord's final testimony to the nation. He, the accused, became the accuser. He, the one judged by the nation, became the nation's judge. His defense cited Abraham's history through Isaac and Jacob, 2-8; Joseph's history, 9-16; Moses' rejection and deliverance, 17-38; Israel's apostasy, 39-50. His arraignment of his judges and sentence upon the nation follow, 51-53.

54-60. Stephen's martyrdom. The first martyr was remarkably like his Lord. He was filled with the Spirit and did 'great wonders and miraculous signs among the people,' 6:8. Like Christ he was accused of speaking against Moses, the law, and the temple, 6:13-14, and was put to death as a blasphemer, 7:56-58. Like Christ he was arraigned before the Sanhedrin and faced false accusers, 6:11-13. He gave witness to the truth of our Lord's confession that He was to sit at God's right hand, 7:55-56, seeing Him there. Like Jesus he prayed for his enemies' forgiveness and that the Lord might receive his spirit, 7:59-60. The first martyr was

Steps leading to the Temple of Augustus, Samaria, one of the non-Jewish places to which the gospel travelled owing to the persecution in Jerusalem.

transformed wonderfully by the Spirit into Christlikeness (2 Cor 3:18). Three manifestations of the glorified Christ are recorded: to Stephen (Acts7:55-56); to Paul (Acts 9:3-6; cf. 7:58 with 8:1); and to John (Rev 1:10, 12-16).

8. The Samaritans admitted to gospel privilege

1-17. Philip's ministry in Samaria.
The occasion was persecution, 1-3, resulting in the outgoing of the gospel to non-Jewish regions (Acts 1:8). Philip's ministry in Samaria, 4-13, prepared the Samaritans for admission into gospel privilege and the gift of the Holy Spirit, 14-25. It is particularly significant that Peter came to Samaria to pray for and lay hands upon believing disciples that they might receive the Holy Spirit, 15. The case involves the introduction of the gospel to another people (as to the Jew at Pentecost) and the initial bestowment of the Spirit upon them. Hence Peter's presence was necessary. To him alone was given the 'keys of the kingdom of heaven' (Mt 16:19). As he opened the gospel to the Jew (Acts 2:14) and to the Gentile (10:34), so in a similar sense he opened the gospel privilege to the racially and religiously mongrel Samaritans, who were a bridge to the Gentiles. The episode was *not* a second experience after salvation, but

marked the initial giving of the Holy Spirit to the Samaritans as an ethnic group. Until the Spirit was given to Jews at Pentecost, to Samaritans (Acts 8), and to Gentiles at Caesarea (Acts 10), no regenerated soul enjoyed the great salvation now experienced by every Christian, including baptism by the Spirit into Christ (Rom 6:34), sealing (Eph 4:30), and permanent indwelling (1 Cor 6:19-20) with the privilege of continuous infilling (Eph 5:18).

9. Conversion of the apostle to the Gentiles

1:1-19. Saul's conversion. Acts 1-8 presents the spread of the gospel from Jerusalem to 'all Judea and Samaria' (1:8). The rest of Acts is concerned with the preparation of the great evangelist to the Gentiles, ch. 9; the official introduction of the gospel to the Gentiles, ch. 10-11 ; and the extension of gospel witness 'to the end of the earth,' ch. 12-28. The conversion of Saul of Tarsus is significantly recounted immediately after the completed official opening of the gospel to Jews and Samaritans and just before the account of the introduction of gospel grace to Gentiles. Saul saw the risen, ascended Christ, 1-8, basic to his later apostleship; was filled with the Spirit, 17; and was baptized to show his identification with Christ and His people, 18-19.

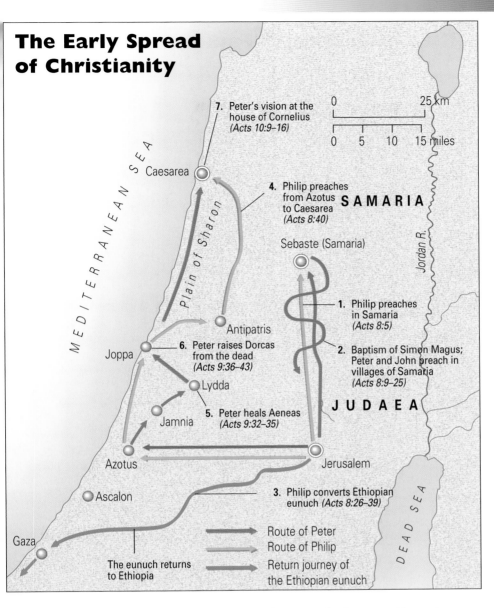

The Early Spread of Christianity

7. Peter's vision at the house of Cornelius (Acts 10:9–16)

Caesarea

4. Philip preaches from Azotus to Caesarea (Acts 8:40)

SAMARIA

MEDITERRANEAN SEA

Plain of Sharon

Sebaste (Samaria)

Jordan R.

1. Philip preaches in Samaria (Acts 8:5)

Antipatris

Joppa

6. Peter raises Dorcas from the dead (Acts 9:36–43)

Lydda

Jamnia

5. Peter heals Aeneas (Acts 9:32–35)

2. Baptism of Simon Magus; Peter and John preach in villages of Samaria (Acts 8:9–25)

JUDAEA

Azotus

Jerusalem

Ascalon

3. Philip converts Ethiopian eunuch (Acts 8:26–39)

DEAD SEA

Gaza

The eunuch returns to Ethiopia

Route of Peter
Route of Philip
Return journey of the Ethiopian eunuch

20-25. Damascus and the beginning of Saul's ministry. Saul's fearless preaching stirred Jewish persecution, 20-24. He was let down over the wall in a basket, 25. Damascus was a free city, a member of the Decapolis of free cities, but at this time may have been under Nabatean rule, for 'the governor under King Aretas had the City of the Damascenes guarded' (2 Cor 11:32) at the time. Aretas IV's (9 B.C.-A.D. 40) ethnarch probably waited outside the city, hoping to catch Saul as he emerged.

26-31. Saul's return to Tarsus. This was preceded by a visit to Jerusalem, 26-29. Intense hatred and persecution, 29, necessitated

Saul's return to his hometown Tarsus via Caesarea, Judea's capital and principal seaport. Tarsus was in Cilicia in SE Asia Minor across the Gulf of Issus from Antioch's seaport Seleucia. It was an important free city and a center of commerce.

32-43. Peter prepared for Gentile evangelism. Peter healed the paralytic Aeneas at Lydda (present-day Lod, 11 miles SE of Joppa), 32-35. At Joppa he restored Dorcas to life and resided with Simon the tanner, 36-43. Jewish law regarded a tanner as an outcast and his work defiling. Joppa was stoutly Jewish, a pharisaical center highly suitable for Peter's

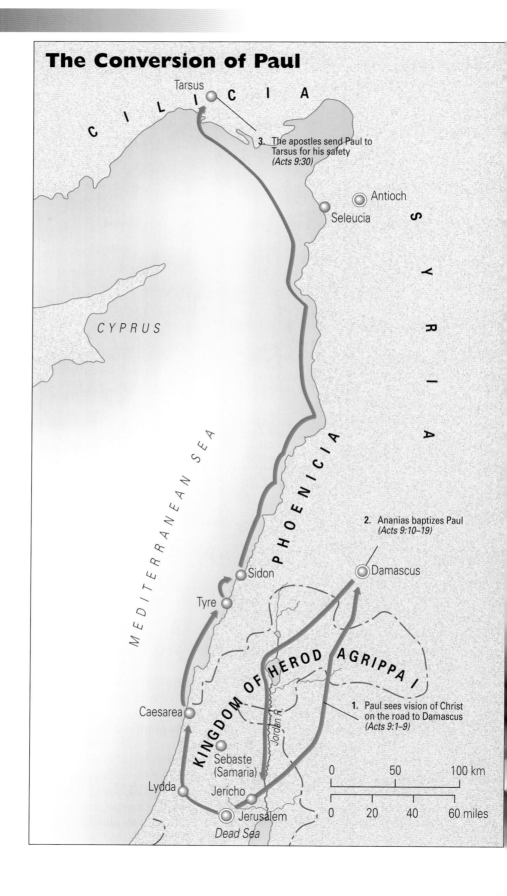

The Conversion of Paul

Tarsus

C I L I C I A

C Y P R U S

3. The apostles send Paul to Tarsus for his safety (Acts 9:30)

Antioch

Seleucia

S Y R I A

M E D I T E R R A N E A N   S E A

P H O E N I C I A

2. Ananias baptizes Paul (Acts 9:10–19)

Damascus

Sidon

Tyre

KINGDOM OF HEROD AGRIPPA I

1. Paul sees vision of Christ on the road to Damascus (Acts 9:1–9)

Caesarea

Jordan R.

Sebaste (Samaria)

Lydda

Jericho

Jerusalem

Dead Sea

| 0 | 50 | 100 km |
| 0 | 20 | 40 | 60 miles |

revelation of those clean and unclean, an indispensable prerequisite for his ministry to Gentiles, 9:43-10:33.

10. The Gentiles admitted to gospel privileges

1-33. Cornelius and Peter. The case of Cornelius, as a representative Gentile, 1-8, marked the giving of the Holy Spirit to the Gentiles. Cornelius, although devout and pious, did not enjoy the common salvation of the new age opened up at Pentecost (Acts 11:14). Peter's soul-transforming vision, 9-16, set forth the truth that Gentiles, unclean and long shut out from religious opportunity as 'dogs' (Mt 15:24-27), symbolized by the various ceremonially unclean animals, were to receive the 'same gift' God had given to the Jews at Pentecost (Acts 11:17; see notes on Acts 2 and 8).

34-48. Peter's last use of the keys. For the last recorded time Peter used the keys of the kingdom of heaven (Mt 16:19). It was he who preached the sermon, 34-44 (cf. Acts 2:14; 8:14), which opened the gospel and the gift of the Holy Spirit to Gentiles, establishing *the norm for the age.* With the events of verses 44-48, Jew, Samaritan and Gentile had been introduced to the gift of the Holy Spirit. Resident in the Body of Christ, the church, the Spirit becomes the blessing of *every one* who exercises faith in Christ as Saviour.

11:1-18. Peter defends his ministry to Gentiles

1-3. Peter called to explain his ministry to Gentiles. The fact that Gentiles received the Holy Spirit and were admitted to gospel privilege required explanation. The Judaizers (a group that required circumcision), 2, composed of conservative Jewish believers, came into existence as soon as Gentiles were saved (15:1-5; 21:20).

4-18. Peter's explanation. He recounted his experiences at Joppa and Caesarea, 4-14 (cf. 10:1-33). His interpretation to his Jerusalem colleagues, 15-18, included the following facts: (1) Salvation thereby was granted to Cornelius and his household as the first representative Gentiles, 14. (2) The Holy Spirit fell on the Gentiles as on the Jews at Pentecost, 15, referring to the mighty *infilling* (2:4) that characterized the initial giving of the Spirit at

The reconstructed Roman theater at Caesarea. Peter visited this important port city to explain the gospel to the Roman centurion Cornelius.

Pentecost and the introduction of the gift to Samaritans 18:16) and Gentiles (10:44). Cf. the term 'poured out' 2:17; 10:45. (3) The baptism of the Spirit, 16, was connected initially with Pentecost by Peter, as a comparison with Acts 1:5 shows, and also with the events of Acts 10. This demonstrated that the church began at Pentecost, since it was formed by this one spiritual baptism, as 1 Cor 12:13; Rom 6:3-4; Gal 3:26-27 show. (4) Peter declared the gift of the Spirit granted to the Gentiles was 'the same,' i.e., identical with the gift initially given to Israel in Acts 2. This included supernatural languages (2:4; 10:46; 19:6).

11:19-30. The church at Antioch

19-26. The disciples called Christians. The gospel began to be preached to non-Jews at Antioch, on the Orontes in Syria, 19-20. Great numbers of Gentiles were converted, 21, after the introduction of gospel privilege to them (see notes on Acts 10, 11). Barnabas (4:36) was from Cyprus and many Cypriots resided in Antioch, 20. He brought Saul from Tarsus, 25-26 (see note on 9:26-31). Believers were called Christians first in Antioch, 26. The term *Christiani* ('partisans of Christ') was probably an official name of Jesus' disciples given by Roman officials at Antioch. (Cf. *Pompeiani, Sullani, Herodiani,* Mt 22:16, and other party names.) See note on Antioch in ch. 13.

27-30. Relief sent to Jerusalem. The famine in the days of Claudius (A.D. 41-54)

Speaking in tongues

There are two aspects in the manifestation of tongues: first, the sign of tongues in Acts 2, 10, 19 (and probably in ch. 8); second, the gift of tongues in the early apostolic church. The gift under the second aspect evidently was not permanent (1 Cor 13:9-13), nor given to every believer. It required the concomitant gift of interpretation (1 Cor 12:10; 14:1-40). This sign gift with interpretation was meant to instruct the church before the completed NT Scriptures were given.

Under the first aspect tongues were a means by which the Holy Spirit witnessed to Israel on the day of Pentecost (2:4-13). They were a sign of the truth that Jesus was the Messiah and an indication of the new age of the Spirit.

The Jews were again challenged by the Samaritans' receiving the Holy Spirit (Acts 8:14-17), and, although this is not specifically mentioned, they may have been given the evidence that the despised Samaritans had actually received the same gift as the Jews, by the sign of their supernatural utterances (cf. 11:17).

This is the use of tongues in the introduction of the gift of the Holy Spirit to Gentiles (Acts 10:44-47). Nothing could have been more convincing to skeptical, unbelieving Peter and his Jewish colleagues than the fact that Cornelius and the other Gentiles spoke in supernatural languages just as the Jews at Pentecost.

The disciples of John the Baptist who received the Holy Spirit and spoke in languages they had never learned (Acts 19:6-10) were a similar witness to the strong Jewish community at Ephesus. For the disciples of John the Baptist, whom the Jews generally accepted as a God-sent prophet, to be blessed by the Holy Spirit after being baptized in the name of the rejected Messiah, was of the deepest significance. 'But some of them [the Jews] became obstinate; they refused to believe' as Isaiah (Isa 28:11-12) had predicted (1 Cor 14:22. Cf. notes on 1 Cor 14).

occurred probably in A.D. 46. Prophets like Agabus, possessing a supernatural gift of prediction, were common in the early church before a completed canon, as well as persons gifted with speaking in tongues and possessing other sign gifts.

12. Herod's persecution and death

1-19. Arrest of Peter and his deliverance. James the son of Zebedee was martyred. Peter was arrested. His persecutor was Herod Agrippa I, grandson of Herod the Great and the Maccabean Mariamne. Agrippa was made king over Judea and Samaria by Emperor Caligula, and from A.D. 41-44 ruled over practically the same territory as his grandfather, Herod the Great. For 'angel of the Lord,' 7, cf. Gen 48:16; Mt 18:10.

20-25. Death of Herod at Caesarea. On Caesarea see note on Acts 10:34-48. Herod evidently was in Caesarea to participate in the quadrennial festival in honor of the Roman emperor, which took place in the spring of A.D. 44. Josephus (*Ant.* XIX. 8.2) relates how that king was struck with a deadly malady after being hailed as divine.

13:1-12. First tour – Cyprus

1-3. Antioch the birthplace of foreign missions. Antioch-on-the-Orontes in Syria was the third largest city in the Roman Empire in Paul's day. The large Gentile church there was not only blessed with gifted teachers, 1, but with the free operation of the Holy Spirit, 2-3, who launched the pivotal gospel witness in the West. Seleucia, 4, was Antioch's seaport, situated five miles up the Orontes River from the Mediterranean. Two giant jetties jutting out into the sea are mute witnesses of the important harbor which connected the port city with its inland city.

4-12. The tour of Cyprus. Time: spring of A.D. 45. Destination: Salamis, 130 miles SW of Antioch on the E coast of Cyprus, third largest island in the Mediterranean. It was 148 miles long and 15 to 20 miles broad. It had a long pagan cultural history including the licentious worship of Aphrodite. Salamis was the largest city on the island, with a large Jewish population, 5. Paphos, 6, present-day Baffo near modern Ktima, was on the western part of the island. It was a cult center, capital of the senatorial province of Cyprus, residence of the proconsul (praetor) and mecca for the polluted worship of Aphrodite. Elymas (from the Arabic *alimun,* 'wise,' 'learned,' or

Caesarea

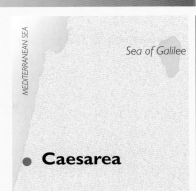

Sea of Galilee

● **Caesarea**

This brilliant capital of the Roman government in Judea was built (25-13 B.C.) by Herod the Great. He dedicated the city to Caesar Augustus in 12 B.C., changing the name Straton's Tower to Caesarea in honor of the emperor. Made a fine seaport, Caesarea had ready access to all parts of the Roman world. A huge sea mole 200 feet wide in 120 feet of water was constructed, remains of which are still visible. In 1960 the harbor was explored by the Link Expedition to Israel, opening up a chapter in underwater archaeology or aqueology. A coin depicting the harbor as two ships enter contains the letters KA, an apparent abbreviation for Caesarea.

Fine Graeco-Roman buildings included a forum, stadium and amphitheater. The latter was located by Israeli archaeologists by aerial photography. It was 300 feet by 200 feet, larger than the Colosseum at Rome. It was the scene of bloody gladiatorial contests when Herod inaugurated the town in 10 B.C. Here Graeco-Roman culture and customs prevailed in Palestine. Luke does well to highlight Caesarea in his account of the gospel outreach.

Top: Roman coin depicting a grain ship, similar to the vessel in which Paul sailed to Rome for his trial before Caesar.

Left: The reconstructed Roman aqueduct at Caesarea, which in New Testament times supplied the city's water.

Below: Columns and other remains of the Roman harbor, Caesarea.

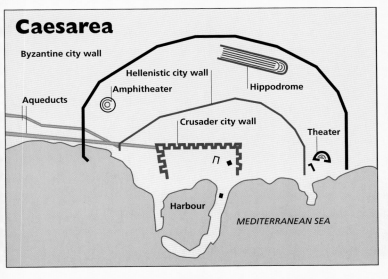

Caesarea

Byzantine city wall

Hellenistic city wall

Amphitheater

Hippodrome

Aqueducts

Crusader city wall

Theater

Harbour

MEDITERRANEAN SEA

Caesarea Harbor in the time of Paul

Aqueduct

City gate

Herodian harbour

Synagogue area

Lighthouse

Inner harbour

City Walls

Temple of Augustus

City gate

Theater

Herod's villa (probable)

Hippodrome

Antioch-on-the-Orontes and archaeology

Founded in 300 B.C. by Seleucus I Nicator, three centuries of cultural history prepared the great city for its famous role in Christian missions. Its suburb of Daphne was known for license and pleasure, the playground of the reprobate city. The seed of the gospel of grace found needy soil here, for Daphne morals were notorious even in blasé Rome.

The present-day site of Antakiyeh, in numerous excavations since 1932, has yielded gorgeous floor mosaics, as well as buildings, walls and other remains, enabling the history of the city to be outlined. The claim was formerly made that the famous Chalice of Antioch, found in 1910, contained the earliest figures of Christ and the twelve apostles and belonged to the latter part of the 1st cen. The inner chalice was supposedly the original communion cup of Christ. Scholars now generally place it anywhere from the 2nd to the 6th cen., as a product of early Christian art.

Famous churches excavated at Antioch include the octagonal edifice of Constantine and a cross-shaped edifice, both from the late 4th cen., showing that Christianity left its impress on Antioch's architecture. The city's patron deity was Tyche, whose memory is preserved in a marble replica in the Vatican.

Antioch

Seleucid palaces
Temple of Artemis
River Orontes
Theater
Aqueduct
Street of colonnades
Amphitheater
Daphne Gate

Aramaic 'powerful') was a demon-energized occultist, not pagan but Jewish, 8. At Soli, a city on the NW coast of Cyprus, a Greek inscription dated A.D. 52-53 was found reading 'Under Paulus the proconsul.' It doubtlessly refers to Sergius Paulus, Paul's famous convert.

13:13-52. First tour – Perga and Pisidian Antioch

13. From Paphos to Perga. Crossing the 180 miles of water from Paphos, Paul and Barnabas landed at Perga, chief city of Pamphylia in Asia Minor. This site, now called Murtana, is notable for the completeness and intactness of its ancient ruins. Artemis, the nature goddess, was worshiped here, as Pergan coins show. At Perga John Mark decided to quit the tour, 13 (cf. 15:38; 2 Tim 4:11).

14-52. From Perga to Pisidian Antioch and Iconium. The 100-mile trip to Pisidian Antioch was through rugged robber-infested terrain. Sir William Ramsay has adduced numbers of inscriptions from this area proving its banditry (cf. 2 Cor 11:26). But in bringing the gospel to Pisidian Antioch, Paul and Barnabas were planting the witness in a communication nerve center in the heart of Asia Minor through which an E-W traffic artery ran. Westward it connected with Apamaea, Colossae, Laodicea, Magnesia, Ephesus and the Greek world of the Aegean. Eastward it gave access to Lystra, Derbe and via the Cilician Gates led on to Tarsus, Issus and Antioch-on-the-Orontes. In verses 16-41 Paul's great message on justification by faith is reported in detail. Jewish rejection came into prominence.

14. First tour – Iconium, Derbe, Lystra

1-5. Iconium. Forced out of Antioch by malicious unbelieving Jews, Paul and Barnabas took the Royal Road toward Lystra, but turned aside to visit Iconium (present-day Konia) in Phrygia, 13:51. Archaeology has shown from inscriptions that the city was predominantly Phrygian racially and Galatian administratively. When Paul came to the town, it was one of the important cities in the southern part of the Roman province of Galatia. It attracted many Jews, being the center of a thriving weaving industry, for which the highland flax and Taurus sheep and goats furnished raw material. The city was also on a commercial artery, connecting it with Ephesus on the W and the Mesopotamian world on the E.

6-19. The work at Lystra. Driven out of Iconium by unbelieving Jews, the missionaries came to Lystra and Derbe, two other towns in the Roman province of Galatia. The site of

Iconium, Lystra and Derbe

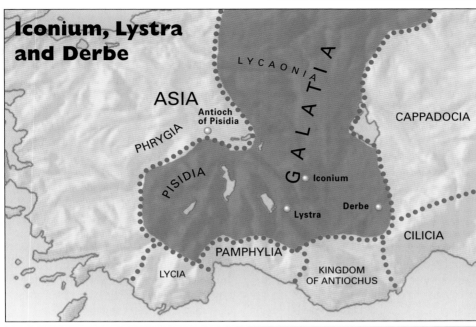

LYCAONIA

GALATIA

ASIA

Antioch
of Pisidia

CAPPADOCIA

PHRYGIA

PISIDIA

Iconium

Derbe

Lystra

CILICIA

PAMPHYLIA

LYCIA

KINGDOM
OF ANTIOCHUS

Paul's First Missionary Journey

G A L A T I A

A S I A

PHRYGIA

PISIDIA

Antioch of Pisidia

LYCAONIA

Iconium

L Y C I A

Ephesus

Derbe

Tarsus

Lystra

PAMPHYLIA

3. Paul and Barnabas are
mistaken for gods
(Acts 14:8–13)

Attalia

Perga

Seleucia

Antioch

C I L I C I A

Myra

S Y R I A

RHODES

CYPRUS

Salamis

Paphos

1. Paul and Barnabas
set sail for Cyprus
(Acts 13:4)

2. Elymas the sorcerer
is blinded (Acts 13:6–12)

M E D I T E R R A N E A N   S E A

Caesarea

Jerusalem

0   125   250 km

0   50   100   150 miles

E G Y P T

Area of Jewish settlement

Lystra was ascertained in 1885 by an inscribed Roman altar, still standing, which bore the name of the city in Latin – *Lustra,* with the notice that it had been a Roman colony under Augustus. Few if any Jews were there in Paul's time, as it was unimportant commercially. The uneducated and superstitious nature of the Lycaonians, not Greeks or Romans, is illustrated by their native cult, here appearing under a thin guise. Barnabas was viewed as Zeus and Paul as Hermes, 12. This identification is reminiscent of Moses and Aaron in Pharaoh's court where the Lord made Moses 'like God to Pharaoh' and Aaron was his prophet (Ex 7:1). Similarly, Paul as Hermes was considered to be the messenger for the older Barnabas (Zeus). One inscription from Lystra found in 1909 lists several priests of Zeus. Another refers to Hermes and Zeus. The brutal stoning of Paul by the natives distinguishes them from the educated Greek and Roman society of the colony. (Cf. 2 Cor 11:25; 2 Tim 3:11.)

20-28. Work at Derbe and the return to Antioch of Syria. Derbe was the last town in distinctively Roman territory on the road running through southern Galatia to the E. It was therefore a custom station, as Strabo declares. Paul visited it because of its strategic position on the great E-W military and commercial artery. Roman milestones dotted the road. Beyond Derbe on the E lay Commagene, under a Roman vassal but independent. The cult of Mithras prevailed there, and Paul avoided areas where kings were protectors of certain cults and could act drastically. The return trip to Antioch-on-the-Orontes, 23-28, covered the same ground the missionaries had crossed, and they visited and confirmed the established churches. At Perga, 25 (see notes on Acts 13:13), they preached and set sail for Syria at the port of Attalia, founded by Attalus in Philadelphus (159-138 B.C.).

15:1-35. The council at Jerusalem

1-12. The council and the issue. The question was whether Gentiles could be saved apart from circumcision and the legalism of the Mosaic system, 1, 5. That they could, and had been so saved, had been fully demonstrated on the first missionary tour, as Paul had reported to the Antioch church. The door of faith opened to the Gentiles (14:27) was an announcement that the gospel, apart from circumcision and Mosaic legalism, had been divinely authenticated as the medium of salvation to the nations. It was a summary declaration that Christianity was an international religion, completely separated from the legalism and narrow isolationism of the Hebrew faith, reaching out to the uttermost parts of the earth (1:8). The church at Antioch was to send a delegation to the mother church at Jerusalem, 2-4, and thus also witness the struggle of Christianity with Judaism (cf. Gal 2:1-10). Peter saw the futility of insisting that Gentiles had to become Jews to be saved, 7-11. He comprehended the irrationality of the Judaizers who desired to open the door to the Gentiles only halfway, admitting only those who in addition to faith in the Messiah submitted to Jewish rites, notably circumcision. Paul and Barnabas added their testimony, 12.

13-35. The council and the decision. The question of the first church council was happily settled in the form of the gospel of free grace Paul had seen so signally authenticated. James summarized the decision: 'It is my judgment, therefore, that we should not make it difficult for the Gentiles who are turning to God,' 19. They were merely enjoined to abstain from idolatry, from fornication, and from things strangled and from blood, 20-21. This decision was communicated by a delegation of the Jerusalem council to Antioch and to the Gentile world, 22-35.

15:36-16:11. Second tour – Asia Minor and the call to Europe

15:36-41. Paul and Barnabas separate. This epoch-making tour, which was to bring the gospel to Europe, began in sharp dissension. Paul and Barnabas separated over John Mark (Acts 12:12, 25; 13:13; 2 Tim 4:11). Barnabas, with Mark, sailed to his homeland of Cyprus. Paul and Silas set out for Asia Minor, this time by land via Mt. Amanus, the Syrian Gates, into Cilicia and on into Galatia, via the Cilician Gates (modern Gulek Bogaz), 3,575 feet above sea level across the Taurus Mountains.

16:1-5. Paul finds Timothy as he revisits Derbe and Lystra (see notes on ch. 14). This name is a shortened form of Timotheus ('God-honorer'). Timothy became Paul's 'true son'

Antioch of Pisidia

This city was one of 16 founded by Seleucus Nicator (312-280 B.C.), together with Antioch-on-the-Orontes in Syria. It is now commonly referred to as Pisidian Antioch because in the late 3rd cen. A.D. it was made the capital of a newly created province called Pisidia. In Paul's day it was a part of the Roman province of Galatia, district of Phrygia. Inscriptions point to Phrygian occupation. Rome took over the city when Galatia became a Roman province in 25 B.C. Augustus realized its strategic military location and made it one of his chief military colonies, officially calling it Colonia Caesarea Antiochia. The military highway, the Royal Road, linked it with a sister military colony of Lystra, 120 miles

SE. Antioch had a large number of Roman military personnel, numerous Greeks, and many Jews and Jewish proselytes (13:16, 26, 43). Members of the ruling military class (*coloni*) included the devout women of honorable position and the 'leading men' (13:50).

Pisidian Antioch and archaeology

The site was discovered in 1833 on the right bank of the Anthios River, on the slopes of a mountain called Sultan Dagh, near the Turkish town of Yalovach. Ruins of an ancient Roman aqueduct are still visible (see below). Coins display the river-god Anthios. Sir William Ramsay in 1910-13 excavated the

sanctuary of Men, the city's chief deity. The huge altar, 66 by 41 feet, was bounded by a sacred area 241 by 136 feet, enclosed by a 5-foot wall. Men was emblemized by a horned bull's head and was paired with Artemis (Diana), a Hellenized form of Cybele. Here the Phrygian mystery rites were celebrated (cf. Col 2:18). A significant inscription found at Antioch is engraved, 'To Lucius Sergius Paulus, the younger,' an important official at Antioch, who may have been a son of the Cyprus proconsul (13:7). Later excavations have uncovered an Augustan city and other buildings from the era of Tiberius. A magnificent frieze recovered depicts Augustus' victories by land and sea, adorned with Tritons, Poseidon, dolphins and other marine symbols. Representations of Men, symbolized by bulls' heads garlanded with leaves and fruit, graced the Square of Augustus and furnish very fine examples of Graeco-Roman art. Terracotta pipes of the water system of Antioch have been uncovered. These conducted the water from the aqueduct.

Ruins of the Roman aqueduct supplying water to Pisidian Antioch.

Importance of the first church council

The immense significance of the first church council consists, first, in saving the gospel from Judaistic mixture, thereby setting Christianity on its own course as a universal spiritual movement transcending all social, racial and religious barriers, offering spiritual regeneration to everyone who believes; and second, in the revelation of God's gracious purposes for the present age and the age to come, 14-18. The purpose of the present age is to take out of the Gentiles a people for God's name, 14, the called-out ones, the church, the Body of Christ. 'After this I will return,' 16; that is, Christ's second advent. When the called-out number is completed, Christ will return. Then Israel will be restored: 'I will . . . rebuild David' s fallen tent . . . I will restore it,' 16 (cf. 1:6; 3:21 with notes). The kingdom will be established – the world converted, 17, and God's plan for the ages will be fulfilled, 18.

On the second tour, Paul and Silas set out for Asia Minor by land via the Syrian Gates, into Cilicia and on into Galatia, via the Cilician Gates, 3,575 feet above sea level across the Taurus Mountains (below).

(1 Tim 1:2-18; 2 Tim 1:2) and 'our brother and God's fellow worker' (1 Thess 3:2). Apparently converted on Paul's first tour, Timothy was chosen as Paul's secretary and helper on the second tour. Paul's circumcision of Timothy, 3, was a matter of wisdom and loving concern for the salvation of his Jewish brothers, not compromise.

6-11. The call to Europe. Careful leading by the Holy Spirit, 6-7, indicates the tremendous spiritual import of the gospel going W into Europe. Asia, 6, was the province of proconsular Asia. Mysia and Bithynia were N of Asia. The Holy Spirit led to Troas, gateway by sea to Europe, 8, where the Macedonian (European) vision was given, 9. Following the Spirit's direction always leads to effective witnessing. Luke, the beloved physician and author of Acts, joined Paul's party, 10-17 (cf. 20:5-21:18; 27:1-28:16). Paul set sail from Troas, an old seaport town on the Aegean, a Roman *colonia* and a free city from the Augustan age, present-day Eskistanbul, where extensive ruins of the Roman period have been uncovered. Paul's ship touched at Samothrace, an Aegean island, roughly midway on the 175-mile trip between Troas and Neapolis, 11 (modern Kavalla), on the European mainland, the port of Philippi and terminus of the great Egnatian Road which ran through Philippi, and thence across Macedonia to Dyrrachium (Durazzo) opposite Brundisium in Italy. Across the Adriatic the Appian Way led to Rome.

16:12-40. Second tour – Philippi

12-15. First European convert. This convert was not a man, as in the vision, but a business woman of ability and means, 14. She was a dealer in purple dye, a native of Thyatira in the extreme S of Mysia, a colony of Macedonians and a thriving market for purple. Lydia's home became the first private home to

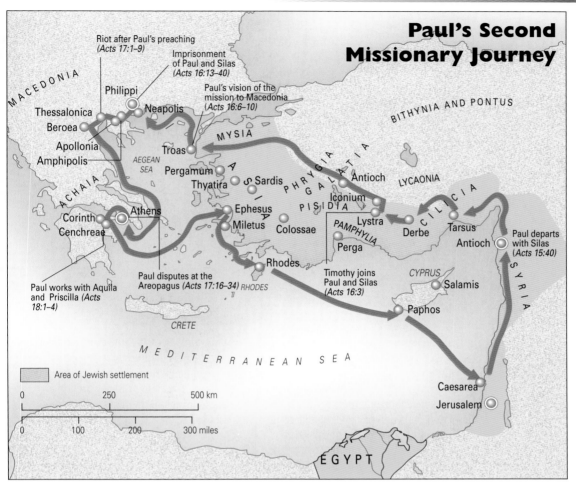

Paul's Second Missionary Journey

Riot after Paul's preaching (Acts 17:1–9)

Imprisonment of Paul and Silas (Acts 16:13–40)

Paul's vision of the mission to Macedonia (Acts 16:6–10)

MACEDONIA

Philippi
Neapolis
Thessalonica
Beroea
Apollonia
Amphipolis
Troas
AEGEAN SEA
Pergamum
Thyatira

MYSIA

BITHYNIA AND PONTUS

ACHAIA

Corinth
Cenchreae
Athens
Ephesus
Miletus
Colossae

Sardis

PHRYGIA
GALATIA

Antioch
LYCAONIA

PISIDIA

Iconium
Lystra
Derbe
PAMPHYLIA
Perga

Tarsus
CILICIA

Antioch

Paul departs with Silas (Acts 15:40)

SYRIA

Paul works with Aquila and Priscilla (Acts 18:1–4)

Paul disputes at the Areopagus (Acts 17:16–34) RHODES

Rhodes

Timothy joins Paul and Silas (Acts 16:3)

CYPRUS
Salamis

Paphos

CRETE

MEDITERRANEAN SEA

Area of Jewish settlement

0   250   500 km

0   100   200   300 miles

Caesarea
Jerusalem

EGYPT

be used as a meeting place for Christians in Europe. For two centuries the homes of wealthier Christians were to serve as places of Christian assembly. No synagogue apparently existed at Philippi because the Jewish element was small. Sabbath meetings were held by the Gangites River where Jews or proselytes gathered at a 'place of prayer,' 13. Most of those present were women. The first effect of the gospel in Europe was a happy harbinger of its emancipation of womanhood by Christianity in striking contrast to paganism and even Judaism.

16-24. Clash with demonism at Philippi. The progress of the gospel in strategic Europe was bound sooner or later to evoke Satanic opposition, 16-19. How could the gospel advance against the strongholds of paganism and not be challenged by demonism, the dynamic of heathenism (Deut 32:17; Ps 96:5; 1 Cor 10:20-21)? The young woman was a spiritistic medium with powers of oracular

utterance, 16, not a fake. The real enemy was not the girl but the evil spirit that controlled her and gave her powers of divination. Therefore Paul addressed 'the spirit' (demon), 18, not the girl, expelling the divining demon (Gr. 'spirit of Python') controlling her. In Greek mythology Python was the legendary dragon which was thought to guard Delphi, the most famous pagan oracular shrine of antiquity. 'The pythian spirit' became a generic term for the alleged source of inspiration of diviners in general. The Delphic oracle was originally a young woman from the surrounding countryside, and the god was claimed to enter the body and speak through the maid. Scripture recognizes the reality of this in its doctrine of demonism (1 Tim 4:1-6; 1 Jn 4:1-4).

25-40. Persecution at Philippi. Lethargic paganism was aroused when the promoters of the spiritistic medium saw their profit gone. The Roman element was prominent

The Stoa, Athens, where it is believed Paul delivered his Areopagus sermon.

in Philippi, as would be expected in a Roman colony, 12. The term *praetor* (Gr.), 20, is correctly employed by Luke as a courtesy title for the chief magistrate of a Roman colony. It was an office of great dignity (below a consul) and out of respect used instead of the more usual term *duumvir*. The *lictors* (translated 'officers'), 35, 38, were Roman, carrying the fasces or bundle of rods with an ax. With these rods the lictors soundly beat Paul and Silas. Two lictors attended each praetor, protecting him and executing his orders. The violation of the rights of Paul's Roman citizenship, 37, was a real cause for the praetor's fear, 38. The *lex Porcia* (248 B.C.) protected a Roman citizen from scourging for any reason whatsoever. Condemning a Roman citizen without regular trial and defense was also contrary to Roman law. But Paul used his citizenship not for selfish gain but to proclaim the gospel.

17:1-14. Second tour – Thessalonica, Berea

1-9. Paul at Thessalonica. Thessalonica lay 70 miles SW of Philippi on the Egnatian Way, running through Amphipolis and Apollonia. Under the Romans Thessalonica (modern Salonika with a population of more than 200,000) was a great emporium on the Thermaic Gulf, a center of trade both by land and sea. It attracted Jews, and Paul gained an

entrée for the gospel through the synagogue, 1-4. The rulers of the city were politarchs, a Macedonian term shown by inscriptions to be accurate. The Vardar Gate inscription particularly vindicates Luke's accuracy. Thessalonica was a free city with a *demos* or 'people's assembly' led by five or six politarchs, 5-9. Jason, 6, Paul's friend, was apparently a Jew whose Semitic name Jesus was complemented by a Greek name roughly comparable. Use of double names among Jews of the diaspora was common in this period (cf. Saul and Paul, Eliakim and Alkimos, Jesus and Justus, Col 4:11). Paul and Silas' labors resulted in a strong church in the city. The rabble-rousers, 5, employed by the Jews were common in the agora or forum of Graeco-Roman cities. They gravitated around a rostrum, applauding or heckling according to those who paid them.

Philippi and archaeology

The present-day site called Felibedjik was excavated by the Ecole Française d'Athènes between 1914 and 1938. Ruins mostly dating later than Paul have been recovered, including baths, a theater, the forum, and notably the colonial archway to the W of the city. This was probably the archway mentioned in Acts 16:13, 'outside the gate to the river,' under which the Via Egnatia ran as it left the city.

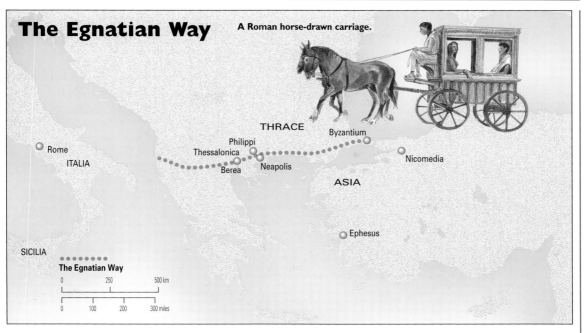

The Egnatian Way

A Roman horse-drawn carriage.

THRACE

Byzantium

Philippi

Thessalonica

Rome

ITALIA

Berea   Neapolis

Nicomedia

ASIA

Ephesus

SICILIA

The Egnatian Way

0   250   500 km

0   100   200   300 miles

Cicero aptly referred to them as *subrostrani* ('those-under-rostrum').

10-14. Paul at Berea. About three days of travel on the Egnatian Way brought Paul to Berea, an 'out-of-the-way city,' according to Cicero. It was W of the Thermaic Gulf, about 35 miles inland. Paul's experience here was a refreshing contrast to the treatment from the Jews elsewhere. Being 'of more noble character,' they searched the Scriptures with an open mind to see 'if what Paul said was true,' 11. Many believed, including some prominent Gentiles, 12.

17:15-34. Second tour – Athens

15-18. Paul and Athenian idolatry.
While Paul waited in Athens for Silas and Timothy, 'he was greatly distressed to see that the city was full of idols,' 16. To the apostle the artistic magnificence and cultural refinements of the city were seriously tarnished by superstition and spiritual ignorance. Since the Jewish community here was evidently small, Paul had discussions in the Agora (marketplace), 17. Luke accurately depicts the marketplace crowd in words which agree with pagan writers from Demosthenes and Thucydides to Pausanias: 'all the Athenians and the foreigners who lived there used to spend their time doing nothing but talking about and listening to the latest ideas,' 21. The Epicureans,

18, followed Epicurus (342-271 B.C.) in abandoning the search for pure truth by reason as hopeless and giving themselves to present pleasure. The Stoics, 18, followed Zeno and Chrysippus (3rd cen. B.C.) and embraced a philosophy of stern self-repression on the basis of human self-sufficiency. Paul had the answer for both in Christ's redemptive work. They called him a babbler (*spermologos*), meaning a talkative person with nothing important to say.

19-34. Paul's sermon to Areopagus. This court met on the 377-foot hill, the Areopagus, Hill of Area (Mars), god of war, a little NE of the Acropolis. In Paul's day this body functioned in matters pertaining to religion, culture and education. They evaluated the competence of visiting lecturers to speak, and so heard Paul as a promoter of a new religion. Paul's sermon to the court itself, whether assembled on Mars Hill or in the Stoa of Zeus Eleutherios or in the Temple of Apollo Patroos, was a masterpiece of perceptive adaptability to the Greek mentality. He quoted one of the Greek poets, Aratus, a Stoic of the 3rd cen. B.C., 28, arguing first from human reason, 22-29. When he went to revelation, preaching repentance and faith in a risen Christ, 30-32, these intellectual sophisticates viewed the matter as an amusing joke, 32 (cf. 1 Cor 1:18). Little spiritual result was visible, 33-34.

Archaeology and Athens

The marketplace or Agora, (Acts17) was the hub of Athens' culture. Its excavation since 1930 by the American School of Classical Studies constitutes an illustration of some of the finest example of archaeological study in the world. Among the famous buildings (some later than Paul's day) are the Odeion or Music Hall, the Stoa of Attalos, Stoa of Zeus, Temple of Apollos Patroos, the Bouleterion or Assembly of the Athenian Council of Five Hundred, the Tholos, the Temple of Ares (Mars), the Roman Forum and the Horologium or public clock.

On the 512-foot Acropolis are the ruins of the splendid Temple of Athena, Athens' patron goddess, called the Parthenon. There also are the Propylaea and the celebrated temples, the Erechtheum and the shrine of Athena Nike. The bronze statue of Athena, forged from the spoils of Marathon, towered above the Acropolis.

Below the Acropolis was the concert hall, the Odeion of Pericles, the Theater of Dionysus and SE toward the Ilissus River the huge Temple of Olympian Zeus 354 by 135 feet and 90 feet tall, one of the largest temples in antiquity.

Overall: The Acropolis, Athens, surmounted by the celebrated Parthenon, sacred to Athena, Athens' patron goddess.

The Odeion of Pericles, Athens.

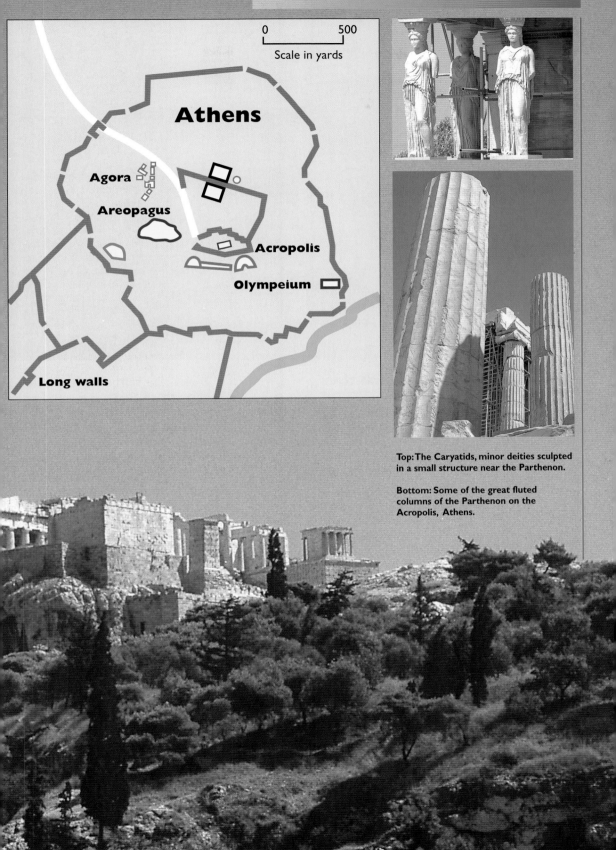

Athens

0   500

Scale in yards

Agora

Areopagus

Acropolis

Olympeium

Long walls

Top: The Caryatids, minor deities sculpted in a small structure near the Parthenon.

Bottom: Some of the great fluted columns of the Parthenon on the Acropolis, Athens.

18:1-22. Second tour – Corinth

1-11. Founding the church. See 1 Cor 1-4 for Paul's own account. His ministry in this dissolute thriving metropolis was begun in spiritual and financial testing. There was no word from Silas or Timothy concerning permanence of the work in Macedonia and little encouragement at Athens. What about Corinth? Paul's finding Aquila and Priscilla, with whom he lodged and found employment as a tent weaver, was providential, 2-3. Claudius' decree about A.D. 49 resulted in Aquila leaving Rome and settling in Corinth. Prosperous Corinth attracted numerous Jews. A stone inscribed 'Synagogue of the Hebrews' was uncovered at the foot of the Propylae. Paul's ministry to the Jews was rejected, so he turned to the Gentiles. The conversion of Justus and Crispus, 7-8, was a signal victory. Paul's encouraging vision from the Lord assured the success of the work in the city, 9-11.

12-17. Paul before Gallio. Gallio was proconsul, 12, in the summer of A.D. 51. This is now known from an important inscription found at Delphi in the form of a letter sent from Emperor Claudius containing a reference to Gallio 'as Lucius Gallio, my friend, and the proconsul of Achaia . . .' The date of the letter is A.D. 52, and Gallio must have arrived earlier to take up his office in A.D. 51, since he had been in office long enough to have given the emperor information important to the people of Delphi. Paul's arrival in Corinth was still earlier, in A.D. 50. The Jewish charge against Paul, 13, was treated lightly by Gallio, 12-17. He was unconcerned in a Roman court about altercations over minutiae of Jewish practice. His decision was a judicious one that saved Paul from the rage of Jewish bigotry.

18-22. End of second tour. Paul left Corinth by its seaport Cenchraea on the Aegean (c. autumn A.D. 51) for Syria. He landed at Ephesus and went on to Caesarea and to Jerusalem, and then back to Antioch.

18:23-19:7. Third tour begun – John's disciples

18:23. Beginning the third tour. Paul visited and reported to his home church at Antioch the results of the second tour as he had done on the first trip (14:26-28), giving a permanent lesson for missionary method, 23.

18:24-28. Apollos at Ephesus. Apollos was born in Alexandria, Egypt, 24, and although well-taught in the OT messianic Scriptures, 24, he knew only John's preparatory and introductory baptism, 25 (Mt 3:11; Mk 1:8;

Corinth of Paul's day

Corinth lay only one and a half miles from the narrow isthmus joining central Greece with the Peloponnesus. It was a great emporium with two seaports – Cenchraea on the E, and Lechaseum on the W. Sea cargoes were hauled overland across the strategic four-mile strip. This spared mariners the hazardous 200-mile jaunt around Cape Malea to the S.

The Corinth canal was not built till 1881-93, although Nero attempted such a venture in A.D. 66. Materialism and lust were two vices that plagued the city. Its brisk commercialism fostered the former; the entrenched cult of Aphrodite fostered the latter. The goddess of love (lust) had her temple above the Acrocorinth, served by more than a thousand religious prostitutes. Voluptuous and vicious forms of the goddess' worship made Corinth a notorious center of immorality (cf. the Corinthian letters, especially 1 Cor 5:1-5). Such terms as 'to corinthianize,' 'Corinthian sickness,' etc., were reminiscent of the moral debauchery of the city.

Beside the Forum of ancient Corinth stand great Doric columns from the Temple of Apollo.

Today, little remains at Ephesus of the great Temple of Diana, or Artemis.

which means they were introduced to NT salvation. The speaking in tongues, 6, was a sign to the large element at Ephesus that these Jewish men were admitted to gospel privilege. (Cf. notes on 11:1-18.)

19:8-41. Third tour – Ephesus
8-22. Paul's powerful Ephesian ministry. Paul first ministered in the synagogue, 8, then in the school of Tyrannus, 9, who apparently was a Greek rhetorician. Probably busy at his loom from dawn till about 11 A.M., Paul rented the lecture hall for the rest of the day. The Greek *schole* ('lecture hall'), 9, was a place for intellectual pursuits and instruction, and attained its finest use when Paul used it to teach Christ, the wisdom of God, 10. Paul's Spirit-empowered ministry of miraculous signs advertised the truth throughout the Roman province of pro-consular Asia, 10. It also clashed with the demonism energizing the city's idolatry and its paganistically contaminated Judaism. The result was the exposé of Jewish exorcism, 13-17, and the demon control in apostate Judaism (Mt 12:43-45) that had rejected the Messiah as well as the witness of Stephen. The clash also with demon-energized paganism resulted in the wholesale destruction of occult literature for which Ephesus was famous, 19. These scrolls were the *Ephesia grammata*, a term familiar in the Graeco-Roman world for magical writings in general. These magical formulas were associated with mutterings of temple soothsayers, and constituted an industry in the city. Fifty thousand drachmas of silver (about 9,200 gold dollars) was a large sum for those times, 19.

23-41. Clash with the cult of Diana.
The religious life of Ephesus centered around the worship of the fertility goddess Artemis or Diana, *Magna Mater* (the Great Mother), worshiped in a temple that was one of the seven wonders of the ancient world. Paul's success at Ephesus was so great that the cult of Artemis and its mighty temple were seriously affected, 25-27. Demetrius, apparently head of the silversmith guild or union, manufactured miniatures of the temple and the goddess. The rioters rushed to the theater, well-known from archaeology and inscriptional reference. The crowd's yell, 'Great is Artemis of the Ephesians,'

Lk 3:16), and nothing about the baptism of the Holy Spirit which occurred at Pentecost (Acts 1:5; 2:1ff.). Aquila and Priscilla, carefully taught in the gospel by close association with Paul (18:2-3), expounded to him the way of God more accurately, 26, i.e., gave him precise teaching concerning the gift of the Holy Spirit, particularly how the believer is now baptized into Christ and His Body, the church, the moment he believes in Christ.

19:1-7. Apollos' disciples become Christians. When Paul came to Ephesus, he found certain disciples of Apollos, 1. These disciples, because of Apollos' limited knowledge, knew nothing of the giving of the Holy Spirit (see note on Jn 7:39), nor of the ministries He undertakes for every believer. The trouble was not that the Ephesian disciples did not believe. It was *what* they believed, i.e., John's introductory and now superseded message of the coming Spirit. As a result of John's limited message, the disciples did not even know 'that the Holy Spirit has been given,' 2 (cf. the same idiom in Jn 7:39). Now that the Spirit *had* come, Paul proclaimed Jesus Christ and a finished redemption, 4-5. The result of faith in the gospel was that 'the Holy Spirit came on them,' 6,

Paul's Third Missionary Journey

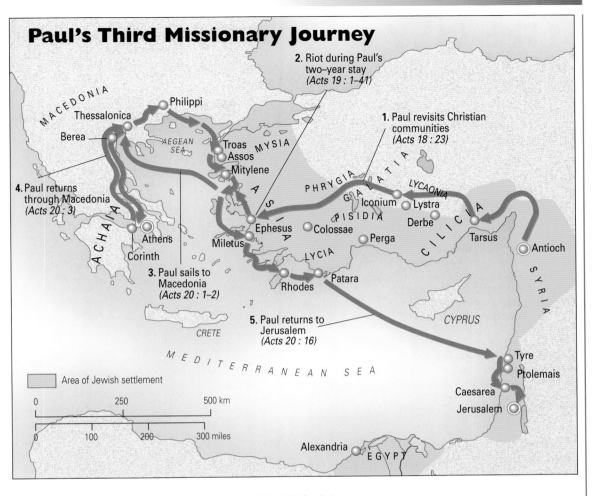

2. Riot during Paul's two–year stay (Acts 19 : 1–41)

1. Paul revisits Christian communities (Acts 18 : 23)

4. Paul returns through Macedonia (Acts 20 : 3)

3. Paul sails to Macedonia (Acts 20 : 1–2)

5. Paul returns to Jerusalem (Acts 20 : 16)

MACEDONIA
Philippi
Thessalonica
Berea
AEGEAN SEA
Troas
Assos
Mitylene
MYSIA
PHRYGIA
GALATIA
LYCAONIA
Iconium
Lystra
PISIDIA
Derbe
CILICIA
Tarsus
Antioch
ASIA
Ephesus
Colossae
Perga
Miletus
LYCIA
ACHAIA
Athens
Corinth
Rhodes
Patara
SYRIA
CYPRUS
MEDITERRANEAN SEA
CRETE
Tyre
Ptolemais
Caesarea
Jerusalem
Alexandria
EGYPT

Area of Jewish settlement

0   250   500 km

0   100   200   300 miles

28, is archaeologically corroborated. Many images and other objects of Artemis have been found and references to them occur in inscriptions.

The 'city clerk' *(grammateus)* is known from nonbiblical sources to have been an important administrative official in the city, 35-41. He drafted decrees submitted to the popular assembly and acted as chairman of popular meetings, often held in the theater. Such an authoritative voice was successful in quelling the riot.

When the town clerk called the city of Ephesus 'guardian of the temple' *(neokoros)* of Diana, 35, he was using a commonly attested term both for individuals and cities as temple keepers to a god. The crowd in the theater was called an 'assembly' *(ecclesia)*, 32, 39. This term also was used popularly, and frequently occurs on inscriptions from Ephesus.

20. Third tour
– Macedonia to Miletus

1-6. Last visit to Greece. After leaving Ephesus Paul returned first to Macedonia, revisiting the churches planted there, 1-2. He then went on to Greece, where he stayed three months. From Corinth he apparently wrote the epistle to the Romans. He planned to observe the Passover at Jerusalem. Discovery of a plot to kill him, probably as the ship was about to sail from Corinth's eastern port Cenchraea, 3, made him change his plan and return to Macedonia, celebrating the Passover and Unleavened Bread at Philippi. He then set sail from Neapolis to Troas (16:11-12), returning over the route by which he had entered Europe on the second tour.

7-16. From Troas to Miletus. At Troas Paul had received his great vision to evangelize Europe (16:8-10). Here the incident of the sleeping Eutychus falling out of a window

The city of Ephesus

Ephesus in Paul's day was the metropolis of proconsular Asia and vied with Alexandria of Egypt and Antioch of Syria among the top three cities of the East. Its ruins located at the mouth of the Cayster River three miles from the Aegean have been carefully explored and excavated. Its dredged harbor gave the city access by sea, and its easy connection with interior Asia by interlacing highways brought it commercial prosperity by land as well. The population has been estimated at 250,000.

Ephesus and the worship of Artemis

The worship of Artemis was the most distinctive source of Ephesus' prestige. The temple of Artemis was called the Artemision. This vast edifice was 340 feet long, 160 feet wide and was decorated with 100 columns more than 55 feet high. Richly adorned with treasures of art, the temple was also a bank, an asylum for fugitives and the center of an elaborate cult.

The discovery of the long-buried temple is an epic in archaeological research. Excavations and search began May 2, 1863, but not till December 31, 1869, at a depth of 20 feet, was the white marble pavement of the temple itself uncovered. During the next five years the fabulous finds that now adorn the Ephesian Gallery of the British Museum were dug up, including such exquisite works of art as Hercules struggling with the Queen of the Amazons, as well as hundreds of ritual inscriptions dealing with the cult. Later excavations (1904-5) uncovered a treasure trove of rich deposits of the goddess found under the pedestal which held the image of the deity.

Ancient Harbor

Marble street, Ephesus, flanked by marble pillars and buildings.

Ephesus and other archaeological discoveries

Continuous archaeological exploration has revealed the long checkered history of the city from its founding about 1044 B.C. The great theater of Paul's day, where the populace rioted, was situated in the hollow slope of Mt. Pion, and could accommodate about 24,500 spectators. Present-day ruins represent a reconstruction after Paul's time.

The chief street of Ephesus, called the 'Arkadiane,' marble-paved and monumented, was gorgeously colonnaded, shop-lined, and connected with the harbor by the beautiful Harbor Gate. The Greek agora (marketplace) lay S and SW of the theater. The larger Roman forum was situated N of the Arkadiane. The Magnesian Gate lay in the SE part of the city, NW of which was the odeum or lyric theater. Southeast of the Artemesion was the so-called Cave of the Seven Sleepers. Numbers of Christian

View from the tiered seating of the theater towards the stage.

churches of a later period attest the effectiveness with which Christianity took hold of the city. These include Justinian's Church of St. John and the double Church of the Virgin Mary.

Right: Cave of the Seven Sleepers, Ephesus.

Below right: Baptistery, double Church of the Virgin Mary, Ephesus.

Harbor gymnasium and baths

Stadium

City Wall

Theater

Arkadiane

Temple of Hadrian

Mount Pion

Library of Celsus

East gymnasium

Temple of Domitian

Mount Coressus

City Wall

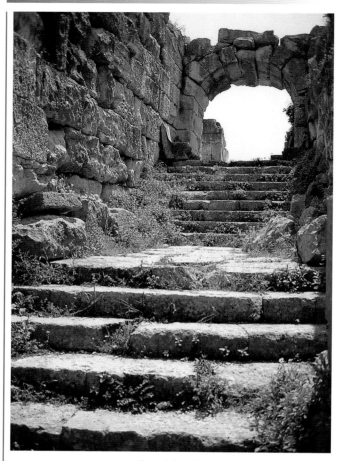

Steps leading to the ancient theater at Miletus, where Paul made a touching speech to the church elders before leaving for Caesarea.

also God-fearing,' which shows the secularization of the Jews of the city.

17-38. Farewell to the Ephesian elders at Miletus. Paul's touching speech to them and through them to the Ephesian church was his third discourse thus far reported by Luke. The first was addressed to *Jews* in the synagogue at Pisidian Antioch (13:16-41). The second was addressed to *Gentiles* in Athens (17:22-31). The third was addressed to the *church* (20:18-35). It was a masterful testimony of a true servant of Christ utterly yielded to his Master, and a touching warning against false doctrine and false teachers. Verse 35 is a quote from Jesus not found in the gospels.

21. End of third tour – on to Jerusalem

1-14. From Miletus to Caesarea. Cos and Rhodes, 21, are islands in the southernmost Aegean Sea NE of the island of Crete. Rhodes was both the name of the island and its capital city in the NE extremity of the island where Paul gazed upon one of the seven wonders of the world – the colossus of Helios, the sun-god, towering 105 feet above the fine harbor of the city. Strabo, the Greek geographer, lauded Rhodes' harbor, streets and walls. Patara was the seaport of Lycia, near the mouth of the Xanthos River, 1-2, a mecca for trading ships, a center of Apollo worship, and now a rich site for

occurred, and the Christians are seen celebrating the Lord's Supper on the first day of the week, 7 (cf. 2:42). For physical exercise, relaxation and spiritual communion Paul chose to go by foot from Troas to Assos, normally a six- to eight-hour walk, likely by the road through a valley from the N. Assos was a beautiful town on a high hill, with an admirable harbor sheltered by the island of Lesbos, occupying one of the most scenic sights in proconsular Asia. It has yielded rich archaeological treasures and numerous architectural remains, notably the Doric Temple of Athena. Mitylene, 14, the next stop, was the most important town of Lesbos, located on the eastern coast of the island. Chios and Samos, 15, picturesque islands in the Aegean Sea, were passed as the ship headed for Miletus, modern Palatia. Miletus, 17, was an important port at the mouth of the Maeander river, vying in importance with Ephesus at the mouth of the Cayster. In the great pagan theater there an inscription reads, 'Place of the Jews, who are

Archaeology and Paul's arrest

Had the charge been true that Paul had brought Gentiles into the temple, i.e., into the court of Israel in the inner precincts, to which only Jewish men who were not priests or Levites were admitted, it would have constituted a capital offense. On this point even Roman authorities were so conciliatory of Jewish scruples that they permitted the death penalty for this offense, even when infracted by a Roman citizen.

The warning notices in Greek at the gates to the inner courts read: 'No alien may enter within the barrier and wall around the temple. Whoever is caught [violating this] is alone responsible for the death [penalty] which follows.' One of these stones from Herod's temple was recovered in a cemetery in 1871. Another turned up near St. Stephen's Gate in 1935.

archaeological ruins. A triumphal arch reads: 'Patara the metropolis of the Lycian nation.' For Cyprus, 3, see notes on 13:4-12. At Tyre, 4-6, believers warned Paul of approaching trouble. This ancient city-state was a free city till 65 B.C. when it was annexed to Rome. Ptolemais is modern Acre, near Haifa, OT Accho (Jud 1:31). At Caesarea, capital of the province of Judea and contiguous regions, Paul was entertained at the home of Philip the evangelist, one of the seven deacons (6:1-7; 8:5-12). Agabus (11:28) imitated OT prophets in performing a symbolic act, 10-12 (cf. Isa 20:2-6). Caesarea was a magnificent Hellenistic town (see ch. 10). The fine harbor was called Port of Herod in honor of the city's builder, Herod the Great.

15-40. Paul in Jerusalem. The apostle's success among the Gentiles was narrated to James and the elders, 17-20. But a crisis came. Paul conformed to Judaism, 23-26, to allay suspicions of Jewish believers zealous for the law. The result was disastrous. He was arrested and taken prisoner. Agabus' prophecy was fulfilled. But in it all the apostle showed his tremendous love and concern for his Jewish kinsmen and proved that what he declared in Rom 9:1-5 were not idle words, spoken for mere rhetorical effect.

22. Paul's defense before the populace

1-21. Paul gives his testimony. He addressed the throng in Hebrew (Aramaic), 21:40, to show the Jews that their tongue was not alien to him, and to capture their attention. Gamaliel (5:34-37) was a famous rabbi, the grandson of Hillel, a Pharisee, 3. On Tarsus, 3, see note on 9:26-31. For Damascus, 5, see 9:20-25.

22-30. Paul appeals to his Roman citizenship. The examination by scourging, 24, was not for punishment but to get evidence. A Roman citizen uncondemned was protected from this cruel practice (cf. notes on 16:37-38). In the reign of Claudius (A.D. 41-54) Roman citizenship was frequently purchased for a large sum of money, 28.

23. Paul's defense before the Sanhedrin

1-10. Before the Sanhedrin. The tribune set Paul before the supreme Jewish court, not to try him but to get evidence, 22:30. Ananias, 2, was high priest in the reigns of Claudius (A.D. 41-54) and Nero (A.D. 54-68). He was assassinated in A.D. 66. 'Whitewashed wall,' 3, was an apt metaphor to apply to the hypocritical high priest, who broke Jewish law by commanding Paul to be struck even before he was proved guilty. It suggested a tottering partition whose rotten condition had been disguised by a generous coat of whitewash. Such undignified conduct obscured Paul's recognizing the high priest, 4-5 (cf. his quote of Ex 22:28).

Paul used wit and humor, 6-10, even though hard pressed. Sadducees were rational critics who denied resurrection.

11-22. Plot to kill Paul. Paul was sustained in his trials by a vision of the Lord, 11, even in the face of the plot to kill him, 12-22.

23-35. Paul sent to Caesarea. On Caesarea see notes on ch. 10; 21:8. The third hour was 9.00 to 10.00 P.M. The large bodyguard for Paul, 23, shows the seriousness of the tumult against him and the plot to kill him. Felix the governor, 24, was appointed procurator of Judea by Claudius (A.D. 52). He was cruel and had little moral principle. The letter of Claudius Lysias, 26-30, has the epistolary flavor of the period. Herod's palace, 35, was the sumptuous palace built by Herod the Great to grace his Hellenistic city of Caesarea. It was taken over by the Romans and used as the headquarters of the Roman procurators of Palestine.

24. Paul before Felix

1-23. Before Felix the first time. Ananias the high priest here appears again in a bad light in hiring the Roman lawyer Tertullus, who made the charge against Paul before Felix, 2-9. 'Nazarene sect,' 5, refers to Christians as followers of Jesus of Nazareth, but the term does not occur elsewhere in early Christian literature. Paul's defense before Felix is given in 10-21. 'The Way,' 14, 22, i.e., the true way of the Lord (Jn 14:6), was one of the first designations of Christianity (cf. 9:2).

24-27. Before Felix the second time. Felix's wife Drusilla was sister of Herod Agrippa II and Bernice (25:13). Felix's behavior was similar to that of Herod Antipas (Mk 6:20). Concerning him Tacitus declared, 'He exercised the power of a king with the mind of a slave' (*Annals* XII. 54). Felix's treatment of Paul's case well bears out this character analysis. He deliberately sacrificed duty and justice for his own selfish ambition. Paul had to languish in prison for two years on his account, 27.

25-26. Paul before Festus and Agrippa

25: 1-12. Before Festus. Porcius Festus was procurator A.D. 60-62. He showed the same compromising weakness, 9, as Felix. Paul, knowing the calamity of being turned over to a Jewish court, chose Caesar's tribunal, 9-10. He appealed to Roman justice in the person of the procurator. Festus decided the emperor himself should hear the matter. The apparent weakness of procuratorial government is seen in the conduct of Paul's case.

25:13-26:32. Paul before Agrippa Agrippa, 13, was Herod Agrippa II (A.D. 50-93). He and his sister Bernice were children of Herod Agrippa I (cf. ch. 12). In an attempt to clarify the case, Festus enlisted Agrippa's aid. The audience in the beautiful hall of the praetorium was a glittering affair, 23-27. After hearing Paul's testimony again, 26:4-23, Festus' conclusion was that Paul was unbalanced but harmless, 24. Both Festus and Agrippa agreed Paul was guilty of no crime worthy of death or even imprisonment, 30-31.

27. Paul's journey to Rome – Caesarea to Malta

1-6. From Caesarea to Myra. Paul's case was now out of the hands of the procurator of Judea. As a prisoner of Rome he had chosen to appeal to the emperor at Rome. Italy at this era had come to denote the entire Italian peninsula from the Alps on the N to the heel of the boot on the S, with the imperial city on the Tiber the governmental metropolis. The centurion commanded about 100 men, the basic unit of the Roman army. The Imperial Regiment was one of five stationed at or near the provincial capital. The term is attested in secular history. Caesarea was doubtless the port of departure. Sidon, 3, was on the Phoenician coast less than 70 miles N. This ancient Phoenician emporium had a Christian church and friends, whom Julius permitted Paul to visit. Cyprus, 4, brought a flood of memories of the first tour (13:4-13). The 'lee' of Cyprus, 4, was N and E of the island, since the westerly winds prevailed. Myra, 5, in Cilicia (modern Dembre) boasts imposing ruins today and was the maritime gateway to the eastern Mediterranean in early Christian times. There the centurion found an Alexandrian grain freighter bound for Italy and put Luke (indicated by the 'we' passage) and Paul's party aboard.

7-12. From Myra to Crete. Adverse winds made the 130-mile trip to Cnidus (a fine harbor) difficult and lengthy. The time of the Fast (Oct. 5), 9, signalized that dangerous weather had set in, which could be expected

Paul's voyage to Rome

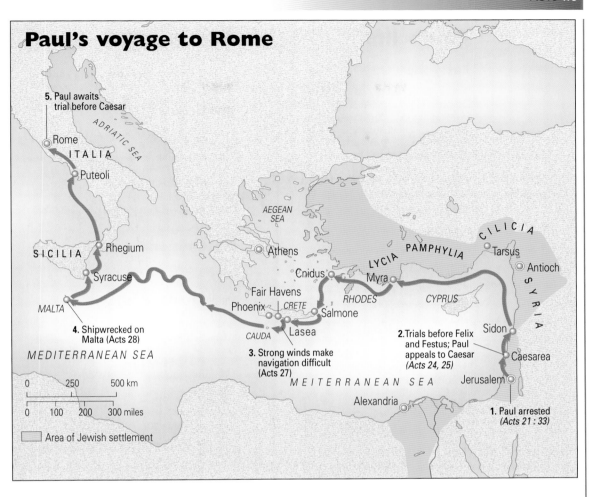

5. Paul awaits trial before Caesar

Rome

ITALIA

ADRIATIC SEA

Puteoli

AEGEAN SEA

CILICIA

SICILIA Rhegium

Athens

PAMPHYLIA Tarsus

LYCIA

Antioch

Syracuse

Cnidus

Myra

S Y R I A

Fair Havens

RHODES

CYPRUS

MALTA Phoenix *CRETE* Salmone

Sidon

4. Shipwrecked on Malta (Acts 28)

CAUDA Lasea

2. Trials before Felix and Festus; Paul appeals to Caesar (*Acts 24, 25*)

Caesarea

MEDITERRANEAN SEA

3. Strong winds make navigation difficult (Acts 27)

MEITERRANEAN SEA

Jerusalem

0   250   500 km

0   100   200   300 miles

Alexandria

1. Paul arrested (*Acts 21 : 33*)

Area of Jewish settlement

after September 14. Phoenix, 12, is probably Lutro, a harbor 34 miles W of Cape Matala in Crete; but Phineka, just W of Lutro on the other side of the peninsula of Muros, is likely the specific place.

13-44. The storm. This account is a classic of graphic precision and accuracy. The tempestuous NE gale which struck the ship, 14, was called by a hybrid Greek-Latin term *Euraquilo,* from *euros* ('east wind') and Latin *aquilo* ('north wind'), i.e., an east by northeast wind. Cauda, 16 (modem Ghaudo, Gozzo), is an island some 23 miles SE to the leeward. The 'sandbars of Syrtis,' 17, were the quicksands off the African coast W of Cyrene. Paul displayed faith and moral strength in the terrible ordeal, 21-26, and was strengthened by God through an angel. The distance from Cauda to Malta is 476 miles, and the ship's forward progress averaged about one and a half miles per hour. By midnight of the fourteenth day the ship would be

less than three miles from St. Paul's Bay on Malta. The Adriatic Sea, 27, was the central portion of the Mediterranean bounded by Italy on the N, Sicily on the W, the Cyrene coast of Africa on the S and Crete on the E. The Gulf of Adria was the smaller sea between Italy and Greece.

28:1-16. Malta to Rome

1-10. Paul in Malta. Malta is S of Sicily in the mid-Mediterranean. It was sometimes called 'Melita', a Phoenician word meaning 'escape': this island had often proved a haven of escape for early Phoenician sailors. The natives welcomed the bedraggled victims of shipwreck. Publius, 7-8, was the propraetor's immediate subordinate in Malta, since Malta was under the province of its propraetor Sicily, only 60 miles away. Paul's experience with the viper was providential. His healing of Publius' father and others gave the apostle opportunity to show his gratitude for Publius' kindness, 7-9. Maltese

Paul's life

Early life

Born in Tarsus (Acts 22:3), c. A.D.10
Educated in Judaism (Acts 22:3), A.D.20-30
Saw Stephen's death (Acts 7:58), c. A.D.35
Persecuted Christians (Acts 9.1-2), A.D.35-36
Conversion near Damascus
(Acts 9:3-18), A.D.37
Sojourn in Arabia (Gal 1:17), A.D.37-39
Visit to Jerusalem (Acts 9:26-29), A.D.39
Return to Tarsus (Acts 9:30), A.D.39
Brought to Antioch (Acts 11:25-26), A.D.43

First tour

Cyprus crusade (Acts 13:4-12), A.D.45
Perga (Acts 13:13)
Pisidian Antioch (Acts 13:14-50), A.D.46
Iconium (Acts 13:51-14:5)
Lystra (Acts 14:6-19)
Derbe (Acts 14:20)
Return to Lystra, Iconium, Pisidian Antioch
(Acts 14:21-24), A.D.47
Perga, Attalia (Acts 14:25), A.D.47
Syrian Antioch (Acts 14:26-28), A.D.47-50
Jerusalem council (Acts 15) A.D.50

Second tour

Antioch by land through Syria and Cilicia
(Acts 15:41), A.D. 50
Derbe and Lystra (Acts 16:1-5)
Phrygia and Galatia (Acts 16:6)
Troas, Samothrace, Neapolis, Philippi
(Acts 16:8-40)
Thessalonica (Acts 17:1-9)
Berea (Acts 17:10-14)

Athens (Acts 17:15-34)
Corinth (Acts 18:1-17)
1 and 2 Thessalonians
Ephesus, Caesarea, Jerusalem (Acts 18:18-22)
Return to Antioch (Acts 18.22), A.D.53 or 54

Third tour

Galatia and Phrygia (Acts 18:23), A.D.54
Ephesus (Acts 19:1-41), A.D.54-57
1 and 2 Corinthians, Romans, Galatians
Macedonia and Achaia (Acts 20:1-5), A.D.57
Troas (Acts 20:6-12) , A.D.58
Miletus (Acts 20:13-38)
Journey to Jerusalem (Acts 21:1-17), A.D.58
Arrested in Jerusalem (Acts 21 :27-36), A.D.58

Prisoner and death

Prisoner at Caesarea (Acts 23.23-26:32),
A.D.58-60
Journey to Rome (Acts 27), A.D.60
Arrival in Rome (Acts 28:16), A.D.61
First imprisonment, A.D.61-63
Prison epistles:
Philemon, Colossians, Ephesians, Philippians
Release, A.D. 64-67 (?)
1 Timothy, Titus
Spain (?) Crete (Tit 1:5)
Asia (2 Tim 4:13)
Macedonia (1 Tim 13)
Greece (2 Tim 4:20)
Second arrest (?), A.D.67
2 Timothy
Martyrdom, A.D.68

Dates are approximate

---

fever, due to an organism in goat's milk, is a notorious sickness on the island.

11-13. Malta to Puteoli. Another ship of Alexandria, doubtless also a grain freighter, had been forced to winter in Malta, probably in the harbor of Valetta. Around March 5, with the opening of the navigation season, Paul sailed for Sicily, 11. Castor and Pollux were worshiped by sailors. As legendary sons of Zeus, they were patrons of distressed mariners. Connected with the constellation Gemini, the Twins, the two chief stars being Castor and Pollux, if glimpsed in a storm, were considered harbingers of good fortune. Syracuse, 12, was described by Cicero as 'the greatest of the Greek cities and the most beautiful of all cities' (*In Verrein* IV, 52). Rhegium, 13, was on the toe of Italy (modern

Reggio di Calabria), across the strait of Messina, some six miles from Messina on the Sicilian side. Puteoli, 13, is modem Pozzuolinear Neapolis (Naples). In Paul's time, Puteoli was the gateway to Rome for large grain ships before Ostia was dredged sufficiently a little later to become Rome's port, supplanting Puteoli.

14-16. Puteoli to Rome. The first Augusteum (temple of the imperial cult) was located at Puteoli. Little remains of the old port city, except ruins of the mole where Paul first stepped on Italian soil and the amphitheater where Nero performed as an actor. The Forum of Appius, 15, was 43 miles from Rome. Here an official welcoming party of Roman Christians greeted Paul. Three Taverns, 15, was 33 miles from Rome. Both were on the famous Appian

Way which Paul had taken to Capua, from which point it was 132 miles to Rome. Some of the delegation were so eager to meet the apostle they came the extra ten miles to the Forum of Appius.

28:17-31. Paul in Rome

17-22. Paul contacts the Jews. He doubtless entered by the Porta Capena. At last he was in the world's capital. Although a prisoner, he trusted for an open door to all parts of the Empire (cf. Rom 15:23-28). His great love for his kinsmen the Jews was demonstrated. Despite their terrible treatment of him in many parts of the East and especially in Jerusalem, his concern went out to them in Rome (Rom 9:1-5). These Jews desired to hear his views.

23-31. Final Jewish rejection of the gospel. This is the last demonstration in Acts of the principle 'to the Jew first.' Paul's 'chain,' 20, was a proof of his love for Israel; but here in Rome the final crisis was reached. Rejection of the message of him who was such a trophy of grace and who manifested such love toward Israel could result only in judgment. What insight and wisdom were revealed as Paul opened up 'the kingdom of God,' 23, the new order for the age as it affected the Gentiles particularly. He expounded from Moses and the prophets, 23. Unbelief caused Paul to quote Isa 6:9-10 and to announce the outgoing of the

gospel to Gentiles (cf.13:46; 18:6). This final appeal to Jews in the world's capital constituted a scene of immense significance. It was a signal that the new age was fully established and God's purpose for it, to visit the Gentiles, fully launched (cf.15:14-15).

Rome of Paul's day

Size of the city

In Paul's day Rome was the greatest city in the world. An inscription discovered at Rome's seaport Ostia in 1941 gives the population of the capital as 4,100,000 in A.D. 14. Although this figure is more than three times the usual estimate, it at least gives an idea of the vast size of the metropolis on the Tiber. Most of these teeming millions lived in large tenement houses, multi-storied, called *insulae*. The wealthy lived in *domi,* with rooms opening on an inner court.

Palaces and temples

The Forum was a maze of exquisite temples and altars. The Palatine Hill was graced with the palaces of the emperors, notably the house of Augustus' wife Livia,

The Forum, ancient Rome.

with its superb murals, and the fabulous palace of Nero, which sprawled to the foot of the Esquiline and was one of the wonders of the Empire. The Temple of Apollo and the Temple of Cybele also adorned the Palatine. Innumerable temples graced the city, such as those of Jupiter, Augustus, Saturn, and the Divine Julius.

Avenues and hills

Built on seven hills, the city was famous for its roads and scenic avenues which interwove among the hills and along the Tiber. The more famous hills were the Palatine, Esquiline, the Coelian, Aventine, and Capitoline. Famous roads and avenues, often 15 to 20 feet or more in width, opened up into the heart of the city. These

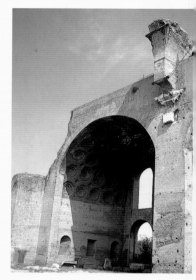
Part of the remains of ancient baths in the Roman Forum.

included the Via Appia, Via Flaminia, Via Nomentana, Via Salaria and Via Pinciana, Via Ostensis, Via Latina, Via Labicana and Via Tiburtina.

Theaters and places of pleasure

The Rome of Paul's day was given to pleasure. 'Bread and circuses' were the concern of the populace, according to Juvenal. Holidays amounted to 159 a year, with 93 supplied with public spectacles at government expense. Famous circuses included the mammoth Circus Maximus, enlarged to seat some 200,000 in Nero's time. Others were the famous Circus of Caligula, Circus Flaminius and the so-called Circus of Nero. Theaters of Paul's day included Pompey's Theater (55 B.C.) seating 10,000, the Theater of Balbus (13 B.C.) seating 8,000, and the Theater of

Ancient Rome

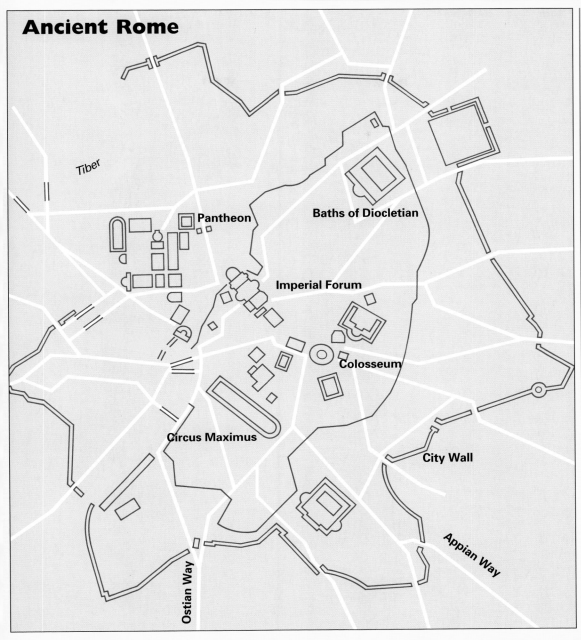

Tiber

Pantheon

Baths of Diocletian

Imperial Forum

Colosseum

Circus Maximus

City Wall

Ostian Way

Appian Way

Marcellus (11 B.C.) seating 14,000. Amphitheaters such as the Colosseum, except that on the Campus Martius (29 B.C.), date after Paul's time. Rome rapidly degenerated and bloody orgies became common from Nero's day on.

Gardens and public parks
Numerous recreation areas dotted the city. In the Vatican district the estates of Domitia, Nero's aunt, were fabulous and became known as Nero's Gardens. Sumptuous public baths (*thermae*) were also common. Many of these with impressive ruins date after Paul's time, such as the Thermae of Titus, the Thermae of Trajan and the Thermae of Diocletian.

Marble sculpture of a Roman officer.

The Epistles of Paul

Distinctive character of Paul's epistles

The Pauline epistles present the calling, hope and destiny of the church of Jesus Christ. In the four gospels the person and work of Christ are presented historically, eventuating in our Lord's death, resurrection and ascension. In the Acts the result of these historical events is traced in the founding and growth of the church. In the Pauline epistles the *doctrinal* revelation and *theological* significance of all these events are expounded.

To Paul was given the disclosure of God's heretofore hidden purpose (Eph 3:9) for this present era between the ascension of Christ and His return. This involves the calling out principally from the Gentiles a people for God's name to be the Body and the Bride of Christ (cf. Acts 15:14-15). In Mt 16:18 our Lord has preannounced this divine purpose concerning the church. However, the how, why and when of this new spiritual entity, as well as its position, relationships, duties and destiny were wholly unexplained. To Paul was given the distinctive revelation of these matters. To Paul also was given the revelation of the doctrinal meaning of the cross and salvation by faith *alone* through grace (Eph 2:8-10). By him the gospel of God's grace was expounded in the great doctrines of justification, sanctification and glorification (Rom 1-8) as these affect every believer, including the Jew (Rom 9-11), and also as they relate to the law of Moses (Gal 1-6).

Artist's impression of the apostle Paul writing one of his epistles from prison.

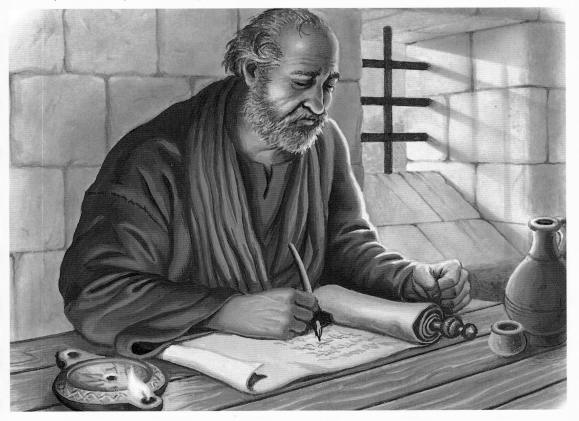

ROMANS

The revelation of the gospel of God

Importance. Romans is the greatest and most influential of all Paul's epistles, the first great work of Christian theology. This doctrinal exposition of the meaning of the cross of Christ has had an immense effect on the thought of the West from Augustine's time on. It was the bulwark of the Reformation, the great corrective against the errors of medieval Catholicism, the protective against modern cultism. The divinely revealed gospel of God in Romans is the antidote for the babel of false gospels of our day or any day. Called the profoundest and yet the simplest document, the epistle is for sinful mankind *as it is*. It points out how lost, helpless humanity can find deliverance in Christ and what this deliverance includes. All focuses in Christ's cross. Christ's redemption is shown to be humanity's *only* hope. But what a glorious, exhilarating hope!

Place and occasion of writing. The epistle was apparently written from Corinth after Paul had completed collecting contributions for the Jerusalem church from the Gentile churches of Greece and Asia Minor (Rom 15:25-27; cf. 1 Cor 16:3-5). He was waiting to go to Jerusalem with it, intending afterward to visit Spain (Rom 15:28), and on the way to visit the church at Rome. He wrote his doctrinal masterpiece to the members of the church in the Imperial City to announce his intention to visit them

and to enlist their prayer and interest in evangelizing the West. The epistle is dated about A.D. 57, toward the end of the third missionary tour.

Outline

1-8 Doctrinal
1:1-17 Introduction
1:18-3:20 The sin of man
3:21-5:21 Justification of the sinner
6:1-8:39 Sanctification of the believer
9-11 Dispensational (the case of Israel)
9:1-33 God's past purpose for Israel

10:1-21 God's present purpose for Israel
11:1-36 God's future purpose for Israel
12-16 Practical (duties and privileges of the believer)
12:1-13:14 The Christian's service
14:1-15:3 Christian service and questionable things
15:4-13 Christian service and God's worldwide glory
15:14-16:27 Christian service and fellowship

Marble sculpture of a Roman soldier's costume.

1:1-17. The theme – the gospel of salvation

1-6. Paul and his gospel. The author of the epistle presents himself as 'servant' in his personal relation to Jesus Christ, 'apostle' in his official relation to Him and 'set apart for the gospel of God' in relation to the message committed to him, 1. The 'gospel' or good news he expounds, 1-6, is *divine* in origin, 'the gospel of God,' 1; *promised* in the OT prophetic Scriptures, 2; *centered* in the incarnation of Jesus Christ, the Son, 3; authenticated in His resurrection, 4; and accredited by the Son for worldwide proclamation, 5-6.

7-17. Paul and his readers. The salutation of grace and peace is made to his readers at Rome, 7. It includes: thanksgiving for them, 8; petition concerning his proposed trip to them, 10; desire to minister to them, 11-15; and conviction that the gospel of Christ presented to them is worthy of pride even at imperial Rome, 16, because it is effective to save and is a revelation of the divine righteousness on the basis of faith (cf. Hab 2:4). On Rome of Paul's day see note on Acts 28:17-31. In Paul's statement of his theme, 16-17, the great words of the epistle emerge – 'the gospel,' 'power of God,' 'salvation,' 'faith' (believe), 'revealed,' 'righteousness,' 'live.' Paul's comprehension of the glory of the gospel was the basis for his

enthusiasm for it. 'By faith from first to last,' 17, means faith is the sole condition of salvation.

1:18-2:16. The revelation of man's sin – the Gentile

1:18-32. God's wrath against man's sin revealed. This divine wrath is a revelation God has made. It is not based on fallen man's faulty reasonings as to his own supposed goodness. The divine arraignment of the fallen race is on two counts: man's guilty abandonment of God's glory, 18-23; and his progressive moral decline, 24-32. Hence man is under God's wrath, 18, i.e., under the necessary expression of divine displeasure against human sin because of God's infinite holiness. The reason: (1) man changed the divine glory into idolatry, 19-23; as a result, God gave him up to uncleanness, 24; (2) man 'exchanged the truth of God for a lie', 25; as a result God abandoned him to gross immoralities, 26-27; (3) man forsook the knowledge of God, 28; as a result, God abandoned him to a base mind and perverted conduct, 29-32. What a horrible picture of human depravity!

2:1-16. The sin of the Gentile revealed. Immediately the Gentile begins to plead 'not guilty' to God's indictment of his sin, seeking to gloss over it with the claim of morality. This claim is refuted because unsaved man really

Brothel sign from ancient Ephesus. In Romans Paul demonstrates sin is universal and total, involving man's speech, actions, deeds, and vision

Relief from Titus' Arch, Rome showing the Roman army carrying the Jewish Menorah in triumph after the destruction of Herod's Temple. Paul deals specifically with God's purpose for Israel in Romans chapters 9—11.

has no consistent morality. He does the things he condemns, 1. The divine sentence, 16, in contrast to man's judgment, is on the basis of truth, 2-5; according to deeds, 6-10; without personal bias, 11-15; and in accord with the gospel, 16.

2:17-3:20. The revelation of man's sin – the Jew

2:17-3:8. The sin of the Jew revealed. Immediately the Jew under the Mosaic law also begins to plead 'not guilty,' attempting to gloss over his sin with the claim of religion, boasting in his spiritual privileges, 17-20. Yet his unchanged life nullifies any such claim, 21-29, netting him only increased condemnation, 21-22, as he causes evil to be spoken of God's name by the Gentiles, 23-24. Being victimized by mere ritualism, 25-26, he thereby nullifies any claim of superior religious standing, 27-29.

Several Jewish objections are offered, 3:1-8. Has the Jew then no profit or advantage, 1? The answer is 'Much in every way,' chiefly in the fact that 'they have been entrusted with the very words of God,' 2. They were not made a mere Bible depository, but as Jews God gave them promises *peculiarly their own, and yet to be fulfilled* (cf. ch. 9-11). But does not Jewish unbelief nullify God's faithfulness, 3? By no means; these promises will yet be fulfilled (cf. 11:29). There *is* a future for Israel based upon OT covenants and promises made to the nation (ch. 11). The unbelief of some will not make God untrue to His promises to the nation, 4 (cf. Ps 51:4). Then another Jewish objection is raised, 5, 'But if our unrighteousness brings out God's righteousness more clearly, what shall we say? That God is unjust in bringing his wrath on

us?' Paul answers, 'Certainly not! If that were so, how could God judge the world?', 6. For the world is unrighteous, too, and sin reveals God's love toward it. Such false reasoning would rule out God's righteous judgment toward Jew or Gentile.

3:9-20. The universality of sin. Man's condemnation under sin is summarized. God's case is proved, 9. All, both Jew and Gentile, are 'under sin.' Sin is demonstrated to be universal, 10-12, and total, 13-18, involving man's speech, 13-14; his actions and deeds, 15-17; and his vision, 18. The final verdict, 19-20, is that all opposition is removed, 19, no flesh is justified, and the whole world is found guilty before God, 20.

3:21-31. Justification defined

21-23. Justification involves the revelation of God's righteousness. The righteousness which God's infinite holiness requires is apart from the law, 21; it is by grace, yet is witnessed to by the law and the prophets, i.e., the OT Scriptures. From Genesis to Malachi the grace of Christ is prefigured by symbol, sacrifice, promise and prophecy. This righteousness is not only apart from the law of Moses, 21; it is made available to all, 22, and needed by all, 23.

24-28. Justification involves the imputation of God's righteousness. Justification is God's act of declaring the sinner righteous, so that the divine righteousness is judicially reckoned to his account. This divine transaction is on the basis of *grace,* or the unmerited favor of God the Father revealed in Christ, which provides it, 24; *blood,* or the death of Christ, which procures it, 25-27; and *faith,* produced in man by the Spirit, which appropriates it; 28. This all-sufficient basis for the sinner's being justified, 26, strips away all ground for human boasting, 27.

29-31. Objections to justification answered. Justification is a universal remedy for sin. By this means God justifies all, both Jew and Gentile, 29-30. Justification honors the law, 31. How it establishes the OT Scriptures is seen in ch. 4.

4. Justification illustrated

1-5. By God's dealings with Abraham. In defending justification from the OT Scriptures, the apostle shows it was a well-

established principle in God's dealings with men as far back as Abraham, so that it was not some novel idea the apostle had invented. Moreover, it was in operation prior to the Mosaic law, so it is not dependent upon legal observance. Abraham was so justified, 3 (cf. Gen 15:6), and righteousness was 'credited' to him (cf. Phm 18) on the basis of grace, 4-5.

6-8. By the case of David (parenthetical).
David was not only devoid of the works of righteousness but loaded down with sins of adultery and murder. Out of this awful plight he could claim forgiveness because he was justified by faith (Ps 32:1-2).

9-25. Resumption of the case of Abraham.
He was justified by faith, not by religious rites, 9-12, before he was circumcised, 9-10. His subsequent circumcision was indicative of the acceptance with God he already enjoyed, 11-12, so that he might be 'the father of all who believe,' 11. Abraham was justified by faith, not by legal observances, 13-25. The promise given to him was long before the giving of the law, 13. This was a necessity because of the intent and effect of the law, 14-15. Moreover, the law was delivered to only one nation, but the promise of faith through Abraham extends to all, 16-21 (cf. Gen 17:5). Through Isaac, the child of faith, came Christ, the Justifier. He was delivered up because of our transgressions and 'raised to life for our justification,' 25. His resurrection, ascension and present intercession at God's right hand (cf. Heb 9:24) are the proof that our sins are remitted. Because His work is completely accepted by the Father, we stand fully acquitted in Him.

5:1-11. The results of justification

1-5. Our present possessions.
'Therefore, since we have been justified by faith, we have *peace*,' i.e. reconciliation or a state of harmony with God, 1. We have '*access* by faith into this grace,' 2. We also have joyful '*hope* of the glory of God,' 2, since that hope is based on what God has done for us, not what we may or may not do for Him. This certainty of our destiny in Christ gives spiritual backbone in suffering, 3; for we realize that tribulation for Christ cannot be futile in the life to come, or unrewarding in its beneficial effects in this life, 3-5.

6-11. Our future security.
Justification gives conviction of security. It gives assurance of salvation by contrasting what we were *before* being justified, 6, 8, 10, with what we are *after* being justified, 9-11. The climax is a twice-repeated 'much more . . . shall we be saved,' 9-10. 'Saved from God's wrath,' 9, expresses what we have been saved *from*. 'Saved through his life,' 10, expresses what we have been saved *to* – a life of holiness and power through the manifestation of His' resurrection life in us (8:11). 'Reconciliation,' 11, is manward, and removes our enmity toward God. It is that which we need and receive in justification.

5:12-21. Justification summarized
The gracious results of justification are brought to a climax in this incisive contrast between what the sinner was in condemnation and what he becomes in justification. This prepares the way for the higher subject of sanctification.

The new headship. Being in Adam relates one to the fallen race in sin. Being in Christ is the new position in the Second Adam, the Head of the new creation. This new position is the ground for a holy life as unfolded in ch. 6. It is an effective answer to the objection that justifying grace leads to looseness of life.

6:1-11. Sanctification – The method

1-10. Positional sanctification by union with Christ.
The problem raised against God's method of saving men by justifying grace, 1, is answered, 2-11. Similar objections are dealt with in 6:15; 7:7; 7:13. The first objection is: Salvation by grace alone will encourage men to go on living in sin, taking advantage of free, exhaustless grace as a self-indulgent son presumes upon a father's generosity. The answer given in verse 2 involves the principle of being cut off from sin by 'death.' In His birth Christ became identified with us, that we might become identified with Him in His death. This is effected by our union with Christ by the baptism of the Spirit, 3-4 (cf. 1 Cor 12:13), which places us in the Body (1 Cor 12:27) with Christ Himself the Head. This is the position of the justified believer, i.e., his status as God sees him and as he is in God's purpose.

This divinely administered baptism of the Spirit, of which water baptism is an outward symbol, makes us one with Christ in a Body that has passed through death, burial and resurrection into new life, 4. Thus we are no longer in Adam but in Christ. 'United with him' ('planted together,' KJV), 5, means caused to grow together as a graft, so that life and nature merge into one. The 'old self,' 6, is what we were in Adam. The 'body of sin' which was made powerless, can be viewed either as the human body enslaved by sin in its unjustified state in Adam, or as the sin nature working through the body. In either case, verse 7 declares that 'Anyone who has died has been freed from sin.' Since this is the justified believer's position, 2-10, he is delivered from sin's domination and enabled to live a holy life in resurrection power, 8. He is united to the risen Christ, who won a judicial victory for him over sin in the flesh, 10 (cf. 8:3).

11. Experiential sanctification by knowledge and faith. Converting our position, i.e., what we are in God's sight, into possession, i.e., what we enjoy in our experience, is on a twofold basis: we must know what we are in our position in Christ, 2-10; and we must act in faith on what we know. We are to constantly 'count' as true (present tense), a word of *faith* based on knowledge, 11. As we count on the twin truth that we are 'dead to sin' and 'alive to God in Christ Jesus,' our position becomes an experiential reality. Justified believers *are* 'dead to sin' and 'alive to God' unchangeably in their position. They become so in their experience only as they momentarily count upon their position in faith. This requires yielding, 13, to God's will.

6:12-7:6. Sanctification by grace and legalism

6:12-23. Sanctification by grace dispenses with the problem of legalism. The gospel of grace which Paul expounds does not give license to sin, 12-14. 'For sin shall not be your master, because you are not under law [the legal principle] but under grace [grace principle],' 14. Law says, 'Do and live.' Grace says, 'Live and do,' conferring blessed enablement so that deeds and fruit may follow.

The abuse of God's declaration that the believer is not under a principle of legalism, 15, is answered by the truth that not only does sanctification by grace not give license to sin, 14-15, but *actually provides freedom from sin,* 16-23. The servitude it delivers from and the freedom it gives are contrasted: *with regard to masters,* 16-20, and *with regard to results,* 21-23. The two masters, 'sin' personified, 16, and God in Christ, are contrasted. The servitude is unto death, but the freedom is unto life. Men are either slaves of sin or servants of righteousness. The *results* are either death, 21, with NO fruit, 'holiness' and 'eternal life,' 22. The 'wages of sin,' death, is contrasted with the 'gift of God,' eternal life, 23.

7:1-6. Sanctification by grace delivers from the principle of legalism. In ch. 6

Condemnation and Justification contrasted

	Condemnation	**Justification**
Source	From one: first Adam	From one: second Adam
Extent	To all: the many	To all (by faith): the many
Cause	Disobedience Trespass	Obedience Grace
Nature	Judgment deserved	Free gift undeserved
Measure	Abounded	Abounds much more
Result	Sin Death	Righteousness Life

sin is viewed as a master to whom the sinner belongs as a slave. This bond is dissolved by death of the slave. In 7:1-6 the figure of the marriage bond is introduced to show the believer's relation to the legal principle. Sanctification by grace delivers from the legal principle *by the death of the believer*, 4*a*, and *by the marriage of the believer*, 4*b*. The illustration of the law of marriage simply points out that death alone dissolves legal obligation. The marriage bond is for life. Only the death of husband or wife annuls it. But in this case who dies? The law? Christ? The believer? Although Christ died, His death is not in view except as it effected the believer's death in union with Him. Therefore, the believer 'died' and so becomes released from the legal principle by incorporation into the Body of Christ, 4.

But the release of the believer from legalism by death is only half of Paul's illustration. The believer is now free to be 'married to another,' (4, KJV), that is, to Christ, the New Man, risen from the dead. But if we died, how can we be married? The point is that our union (in resurrection) is with the risen Lord, who has obtained through death and resurrection a bride akin to Himself (Eph 5:25-32). What a climax of Christian revelation! Married to the risen Christ! Sharing His past triumphs, His present life, His future glory! The Father has taken the hand of His Son and that of His child and joined them for time and eternity.

7:7-25. False sanctification – its defeat

7-14*a*. Sanctification by grace and the law. Another objection (cf. 6:1, 15; 7:13) arises. If the law arouses sin, 5, is it not sinful, 7? Paul dismisses this error with abhorrence and shows the good purpose of the law in revealing man's sin, 8-9. The law is blameless, 12. It is sin that is to blame. Just because the law cannot sanctify does not make it sinful, 9-11. So the law reveals sin to be sinful, 7-13, and condemns the carnal nature, 14.

14*b*-24. False sanctification by the self-effort of legalism. Whether legalism is the law of Moses for the Jew or the general moral law of the non-Jew, sanctification cannot be realized by legalistic self-effort. A new standard of conduct is obtained. Not an external standard (law) to live up to, but an indwelling

Person to please. Not self-occupation, but occupation with Christ. Not what I am in myself, but what I am in Him. Not I, but Christ. This is the struggle of self to live the Christian life. In these 11 verses the pronouns 'I,' 'me' and 'my' occur 35 times. 'I' trying to sanctify itself is the reason for the dismal defeat here outlined. The story is 'I' the new man attempting to live the Christian life, but defeated by 'I' the old man. Portrayed is the struggle of the new nature over the old. The defeat is that of legalistic self-effort or false sanctification.

25. True sanctification. Victory alone is 'through Jesus Christ our Lord.' Not through suppression of the old nature (futile legalism); nor eradication (pure imagination), since if this were true one could not sin if he wanted to, for the new nature never sins (1 Jn 3:9). The answer is the deliverance which Christ has wrought, expounded in Rom 6 (see comments). Defeat is due to failure to realize and act upon our gracious position in Christ, converting it by faith into experiential reality.

8:1-25. True sanctification – its victory

1-4. The new law. The victory is by knowing and acting on our position of grace in Christ and thus experiencing its power. This involves triumphant life in the Spirit. No objections are offered, no defeat appears in Rom 8. Basic to all victory is the assurance of 'no condemnation' in our new position in Christ, 1. 'Therefore' is cumulative of the truth presented in ch. 1-7. The phrase in the KJV, 'who walk not after the flesh, but after the Spirit' obscures the radiant truth of verse 1, and is interpolated from verse 4, where it belongs. The new 'law of the Spirit of life,' 2, is the Holy Spirit operating in the sphere of the believer's new position in Christ as a higher principle, counteracting and overcoming the lower 'law of sin and death,' producing righteousness and life. What the law of Moses, or any legal principle, was unable to do because of human sin, God accomplished through the incarnation of His Son, 3. He, through His sinless humanity, condemned sin as a master criminal and secured a judicial sentence against it. Accordingly, God can righteously undertake to fulfill the just requirements of the law in us through the gracious operation of the Holy Spirit, 4.

Sanctification
The Bible teaching on sanctification

Largely misunderstood and abused, sanctification (a setting apart for God's worship and service), as taught by the Scripture, is in three aspects: past, present, future. The following chart will illustrate.

Past aspect of sanctification	Present aspect of sanctification	Future aspect of sanctification
Positional (I Cor 1:2, 30). All believers were so sanctified as saints, the youngest as well as the oldest, the most carnal as well as the most spiritual.	Experiential. Depends upon our knowledge of and faith in our position in Christ (Rom 6:1-11), converting our position into experience.	Final. When we see the Lord and are made like Him - sinless sickless, deathless (I Cor 4; 15:54; I Jn 3:2).
Static, unalterable, inseparable from justification, and the result solely of our union with Christ	**Progressive, changeable,** depends upon yieldedness to God's will (Rom 6:13) and conformity to God's Word (Rom 12:2).	**Eternal.** Will result in our final state in eternity (Phil 3:21).
As God sees us in Christ (I Cor 1:2, 30, with Phil 1:1, etc).	**As we are in our conduct** (2 Thess 2:13).	**As we shall be in glory** (Rom 8:29; I Cor 15:49).

5-25. The new victory. The Holy Spirit takes over the conflict with sin, 5-13. The combatants are the 'sinful nature' and the 'Spirit.' The Spirit supplants the 'I' of ch. 7, and victory instead of defeat is the result. Proof is abundant that true sanctification is by grace through faith (6:1-11) which brings the power of the Spirit in victorious operation against the 'sinful nature,' i.e., sin working through the human body. The new victory brings also a new realization of sonship, 14-17. Not only does the believer become a child by birth, but a son by adoption (cf. Gal 4:5), with mature status and full legal rights; with guidance, 14; full family fellowship, 15; assurance, 16; heirship and stamina to suffer, 17, in view of coming glory, 18-25. Creation itself will be delivered, 20-22. 'The sons of God,' 19, will be revealed with God's Son Jesus Christ. Our 'adoption,' 23, is our future physical resurrection of which our present spiritual adoption is a pledge and prospect, 15. 'Saved' by 'hope,' 24-25, is the future aspect of our salvation as we who are in Christ look toward the glory ahead, 14-23. Faith produces this hope. Without faith there is no such hope.

8:26-39. True sanctification – its power and assurance

26-27. True sanctification – its power in prayer. Acting on our position in Christ brings the power of the Spirit in the realm of our prayer life, enabling us to overcome our notable weaknesses in this area, making possible the Spirit's intercession *in* us on behalf of the saints according to God's will, 26-27.

28-34. True sanctification – its assurance. In these verses the Father provides *for* us. His providence includes 'all things,' 28, cf. 32. True sanctification gives assurance amid life's providences of God's unfailing purposes for good toward us. But the magic lens which enables us to see all things working together for our good is love. His love for us in Christ, which gives us 'all things,' evokes our love for Him, enabling us to trust Him through trials. The basis for this assurance is His sublime purpose toward us spanning eternity. He foreknew us, 29*a*; predestined us to Christ-likeness, 29*b*; called us, 30*a*; justified us, 30*b*; glorified us, 30*c*, the latter even put in the past tense to show the certainty and immutability of His age-spanning plans for us. The conclusion is, 'God is for us!' Who then can be against us, 31? The grand proof of this is the sacrificial gift of His Son 'for us all,' 32. This supreme demonstration of His love in the greater realm is a guarantee that such love may be trusted to 'graciously give us all things,' 32, for our good in this earthly sphere – to defend us, keep us safely, and bring us to Himself in glory, 33-34.

35-39. True sanctification – its climactic triumph. So wonderful are the notes of triumph just sounded, 33-34, that the apostle breaks forth into ecstatic exultation. Man's awful condemnation (1:18-3:20), triumphed over by God's glorious justifying grace (3:21-5:21), logically leads up to the exultant triumph of sanctification (6:1-8:39). The safety and security of the believer is strongly emphasized. The new life in Christ is inseparable from Christ, 35-39. Every possible type of experience that might be conceived of as separating from Christ is called up. The conclusion is '. . . *more than* conquerors through him who loved us,' 37. Nothing in time or eternity can separate one from God's love manifested in Christ, 38-39. This is the dramatic and soul-thrilling climax to the grand exposition of 'the gospel of God,' 1:1. This is the summit where *true* sanctification leads.

9:1-13. God's past purpose in Israel – her position

Romans 9-11 is parenthetical. In the unfolding of the gospel of grace, what about the Jew? The gospel as 'the power of God for the salvation of everyone who believes' had been announced in the apostle's theme (1:16) to be *'first* for the Jew.' What about the Jews' rejection of Messiah at the cross as well as their rejection of the program 'first for the Jew' (Acts 13:46)? Are the covenants and promises God made with His ancient people empty words? Has God failed them because they failed Him? How do they fit in to God's glorious plan of salvation (ch. 1-8)?

1-5. Israel's national position. Paul's deep love and intense anguish of heart for Israel are expressed, 1-3. His words are strikingly reminiscent of Moses' intercession (Ex 32:1-34) and recall our Lord's weeping over rebellious Jerusalem (Mt 23:37-39), The same Spirit that gripped the heart of Moses and that of our Lord for Israel gripped Paul's heart.

Paul follows with a statement that distinguished Israel from any other nation, 4-5. Eight distinguishing privileges are mentioned:

(1) the adoption or sonship (Ex 4:22; Deut 14:1); (2) the glory – on Mt. Sinai and among the people in the holiest place (Ex 40:34-35; Ps 147:20); (3) the covenants – the *Abrahamic* (Gen 12:1-3; 13:14-17, etc.), the *Mosaic* (Ex 20-31), the *Palestinian* (Deut 29-30), the *Davidic* (2 Sam 7), and the *new* (Jer. 31:31-33); (4) the law at Sinai; (5) service of the tabernacle; (6) the promises, the messianic kingdom, etc.; (7) fathers – the patriarchs to whom God revealed Himself; (8) Christ – born of Israel as her anointed Saviour-King and given as the world's Redeemer.

6-13. Israel's spiritual election. God has not failed in Israel's unbelief, 6. This people is distinctively *His*. This truth is expounded as the basis of the absolute sovereignty of God over those who are so peculiarly His chosen ones. The spiritual remnant of the nation, 6-7, are the recipients of the promise, 8, descended from a supernaturally generated posterity through Isaac, 9. In addition, from among this line God makes a sovereign choice, selecting Jacob the younger, and setting aside Esau the elder, 10-13. The conclusion? Israel is His. He is sovereign over His people.

9:14-33. God's past purpose in Israel – His sovereignty

14. An objection offered. God's righteousness (justice) is challenged. Has Jewish unbelief placed God in the position of not being able to keep His word and agreement?

15-29. The objection answered – God's righteous sovereignty. Since Israel is distinctively His, 6-13, cannot God do as He wishes with His *own*? Is He not free to show His mercy, 15-16, or power and wrath, 17-18, as the case may warrant in His divine wisdom? *His* is the clay. The divine Potter can make of it that which He sees fit, 21-24, Moreover, the Potter had proclaimed His purpose through the prophets, 25-29, to show that the Gentiles were to become God's people, 25-26 (Hos 2:23; 1:10; cf. 1 Pet 2:10). At the same time the Jews were forewarned against becoming like Sodom and Gomorrah, 27-29 (cf. Isa 10:22-23 with Isa 1:9).

30-33. Israel's rejection of God's righteousness. In His infinite wisdom and love the Potter selected the cross as the mold for His redemptive purposes. The Gentiles in faith accepted that mold and obtained 'a righteousness that is by faith,' 30. In contrast, Israel stumbled through unbelief, seeking legalistic righteousness by works, 31-33. Rejecting the principle of faith declared even in their own Scriptures (Hab 2:4), they stumbled at the stumbling stone (cf. 1 Pet 2:8), plunging headlong out of their land to be weary wanderers over the earth ever since.

10. God's present purpose for Israel

1-5. Israel's present condition. As individuals they need salvation, 1, which is the burden of Paul's heart (cf. 9:1-3). They are zealous, but ignorant of God's righteousness, 2-3 (cf. 3:21-5:11). They are busy seeking their own righteousness by law, and have bypassed God's righteousness, 3. For 'Christ is the end of the law so that there may be righteousness for everyone who believes,' 4.

6-21. Present salvation for both Jew and Gentile. This requires no effort, 6-7, such as bringing Christ from above or from beneath. The righteousness of faith, which is judicially reckoned to all who trust Christ, has as its key words, 'believe,' 'confess,' 'call on the name of the Lord,' 9-13. It results in salvation and is available to both Jew and Gentile without any distinction, 12. This divine plan for bringing God's righteousness to everyone, 14-15, involves the sending of men to preach, 15. People are to hear and believe, 14. Believing they are to call, and calling they are to be saved, 13. This method of gospel propagation renders man's unbelief inexcusable, 16-21. Faith is produced by hearing God's Word, 17, in the case of 'all the earth' (the Gentiles), 18 (cf. Ps 19:4). Israel, from her Scriptures, should have recognized the extension of this message to the Gentiles (Deut 32:21; Isa 65:1; cf. 42:6-7). While Gentiles have found God, 20, the Jews have rejected God's righteousness through disobedience, 21 (cf. Isa 65:2).

11. God's future purpose for Israel

1-10. Israel's national setting aside not final. God's faithfulness is guaranteed in a future restoration of the nation. The present setting aside of Israel in her national election is only temporary, 1, because: (1) Paul himself as a Jew was saved in this age, 1; (2) the Lord foreknew Israel's unbelief, 2; (3) God has always had a remnant of faithful believers as in Elijah's day, 2-4; (4) in this present age God has a saved remnant, 'chosen by grace,' 5. This remnant is composed of believing Jews who become one with Gentiles in the Body, the church, and obtain the blessing, 6-10, while the rest of Israel is blinded and hardened in unbelief (cf. Isa 29:10; Ps 69:22). Hence Israel's present blindness is only partial.

11-24. Israel's present national rejection has a divine purpose. (1) It has brought salvation to the Gentiles, 11, hence has been beneficial to the world. (2) The future restoration of the Jews will also bring untold world blessing even as their present rejection has, 11-15. (3) Gentile salvation will provoke Israel to jealousy, 11. (4) Their rejection serves as a warning to the Gentiles, 16-26. The 'dough' and the 'root' (Num 15:19-20; Jer 11:16-17) symbolize the patriarchs through whom Israel has been consecrated. The good olive tree prefigures Israel in covenant relation with God through Abraham (Gen 12:1-3), the root. The tree is ever green as the covenant is unchangeable. The broken-off branches represent the nation's unbelief. The wild olive graft represents Gentiles brought into spiritual privilege. Unless Gentiles cherish their privilege, like unbelieving Israel they will be broken off. God will graft back the real olive tree, Israel, when unbelief gives way to faith.

25-36. Restoration of the nation certain. It is assured *by special revelation,* 25. A 'mystery' is a truth once hidden but now revealed. This truth is that of Israel's partial blindness during this age, which is to last till 'the full number of the Gentiles' has been brought in, 25. This means the completion of God's purpose in calling out a people from the Gentiles in this age (Acts 15:14). The restoration of the nation is the *subject of prophecy.* The kingdom is to be restored to Israel, 26 (Acts 1:6; 15:15-17). All Jews living at the second advent will be saved when Christ the Deliverer shall come out of Zion, 26, as Isaiah predicted (Isa 59:20-21). The new covenant with converted Israel, 27, was foretold by Isaiah (27:9) and Jeremiah (31:31-37; cf. Heb 8:8; 10:16). The restoration of the nation is *according to the divine plan,* 28, and *the divine principle,* 29. Although she is temporarily hostile to the gospel, the election of Israel as a nation is irrevocable. God has not changed His mind about the covenants and promises made to the nation. The restoration of the people will constitute a *fulfillment of God's purpose,* 30-32, and will *contribute to God's glory,* 33-36.

12. Practical Christian service

The last five chapters constitute the practical part of the epistle. Now the doctrine of salvation is to be worked out in experience. Service is to be expressed in the outliving of the inliving Christ.

1-2. Christian service and self. Self is to be sacrificed. The body is to be presented to God the Father. This is a privilege. 'I urge' expresses exhortation and responsibility. 'Therefore' is logical because of God's salvation, ch. 1-11, and 'God's mercy' in redemption. The sacrifice is 'living,' involving our life. It is 'holy' and 'pleasing' because it is cleansed by Christ's blood. The results will not be a conforming to or fitting into the mold of the world, 2, but a change of mind so that we may know and prove the will of God, the only valid sphere of spiritual, God-glorifying service.

3-8. Christian service and gifts. Exercise of spiritual endowments in service calls for humility and proper evaluation of oneself, 3. In relation to the church, the Body of Christ, we are to remember we are many members, with different duties and functions, 4-5. Our varied service is to be discharged as a gift from our Lord, 6-8.

9-16. Christian service and fellow believers. Love is to be genuine. Evil is to be hated. That which is good is to be held fast, 9. Love is again commanded, 10. Christians should not be 'lacking in zeal,' but should have 'spiritual fervor, serving the Lord,' 11.

17-21. Christian service and unbelievers. General exhortations to kind conduct toward Christians are followed by special pleas to loving forbearance under provocation from unbelievers. It is God's part to administer wrath, 19. Man's responsibility is to serve in love, 20.

13. Christian service and government

1-7. The Christian and the state. This important relationship requires submission to governing authorities, 1. The reason? Human government represents God's authority, 1-7. To resist it is to resist God, 1-2, and to incur judgment. Governmental authorities are agents of God for good, 3-4. Good citizenship is required of a Christian, 5-7, to avoid God's displeasure and to have a good conscience.

8-14. The Christian and good citizenship. God's law of love is a potent force for a law-abiding life, 8-10. It crystallizes our duty to fellow citizens, 9-10, and fulfills the law of God, 10 (Lev 19:18; cf. Ex 20:13-17). The urgency of the times is a call to good citizenship, 11-13. It is time to be awakened, 11-12, time to live soberly, 13. 'Salvation is *nearer* now than when we first believed,' 11, means we are closer to the full result of salvation in glorification. The essence of good citizenship is outlined, 14, involving putting on Christ as a garment, putting off lusts as a soiled garment.

14:1-15:3. Christian service and questionable things

14:1-13. The principle of personal liberty. This problem involves the Christian and doubtful practices, 1-2. The strong believer has a duty to welcome a weak believer, but 'without passing judgement on disputable matters,' 1, such as eating or not eating certain foods, 2. In matters of conduct over which Christians differ, 2-6, the principle of personal liberty is to operate, 3-13*a*. This prohibits our despising or judging a weaker brother, because (1) God has received him as a believer, 3; (2) he is the servant of Another (Christ, the Master) not us, 4; (3) there are allowable conscientious differences, 5-6; (4) we answer to the lordship of Christ under whom we live, 7-9; (5) we shall be judged at the judgment seat of Christ, 10-12; (6) human judgment, therefore, is not to limit our brother's liberty in Christ, 13*a*.

14:13b-21. The principle of our neighbor's welfare. This consideration rules out putting a stumbling block in his path, 13*b*-15, even though something may seem good in itself, 16-20. The weaker believer's welfare must be valued above one's own desires, 21.

14:22-23. The principle of God's glory. God the Father is to be glorified in a life of faith, 22. We are to live in God's sight by faith, 22*a,* free from a spirit of condemnation, 22*b*-23 (cf. 1 Cor 10:31).

15:1-3. Plea to observe these

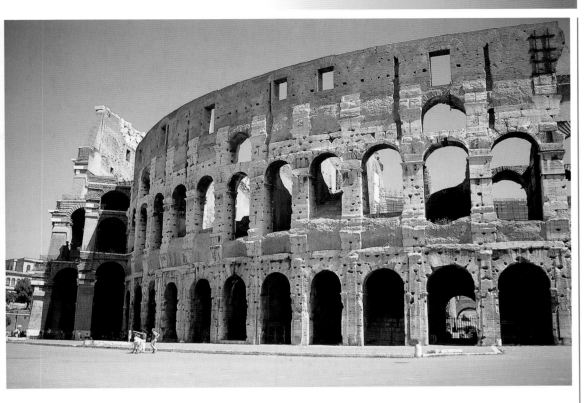

principles. The strong believer ought to put up with the failings of the weaker brother, sacrificing personal pleasure, 1*b* (the principle of personal liberty). Furthermore, the strong believer is to please his neighbor for his good and upbuilding, 2 (principle of our neighbor's welfare). He also is to imitate Christ's example for God's glory, 3*b* (principle of God's glory).

15:4-13. Christian service and God's worldwide glory

4-7. The hope of God's worldwide glory. All Scripture inspires hope, 4, by instructing us in the divine redemptive purposes for man and the earth. Human relationships of God's redeemed ones are to glorify the Father, 5-7, promoting His praise and honor. Harmony among God's people is for the purpose of a united voice of praise to God.

8-13. The world is the ultimate outreach of the gospel. God's plan embraces the extension of the gospel to the entire globe in which both Jew and Gentile are glorifying God. For this purpose Jesus ministered to one nation, 8, so that eventually in the future kingdom all nations might join in glorifying God the Father, 9-12. As 'a servant of the Jews on

Quotations from the Old Testament

Paul quotes extensively from the Old Testament to support his argument in Romans. Like several of the NT writers, he draws his quotations from the LXX (Greek) rather than the Hebrew text of the OT that serves as the basis for our English translations. Furthermore, the NT writers, under the inspiration of the Holy Spirit, did not feel compelled to always quote the text verbatim, often choosing rather to paraphrase and comment on the text as necessary for their own context.

behalf of God's truth,' 8, Christ had as His ultimate purpose not only the calling out of a people for His name in this age but the confirming (not abrogating) of His promises to the patriarchs. These promises guarantee worldwide Gentile conversion when the kingdom is restored to Israel. Their fulfillment awaits the second advent. The promises are taken from the Psalms (18:49; 117:1), from Moses (Deut 32:43), and the prophets (Isa

God's glory lost and regained

	In the Bible as a whole	In the book of Romans
Paradise lost	Ruin Gen 1–3	God's glory forfeited 1:18–38; whole world under sin 3:9-20
God's plan of salvation	Redemption Gen 4–Rev 20	Gospel of God 1:1 – justification, 3:21-5:21; sanctification, 6:1–8:28; glorification, 8:29-39
Paradise regained	Restoration Rev 21–22	Glory of God regained 15:9-12; 16:27

Women in Paul's greetings

Modern critics have often faulted Paul for his 'male chauvinist' attitude towards women in the church. It is notable that at least nine women are mentioned by Paul among those who had done much for him and in service to the Lord.

11:10). They show that God's goal all the while is the nations of earth glorifying Him in worldwide adoration. The apostle appends his quotation of these promises with a benediction of hope, 13.

15:14-16:27. Christian service and Christian fellowship

15:14-33. Paul greets the saints in Rome. (On city of Rome, see note on Acts 28:17-31.) The apostle expresses assurance of their spiritual growth, 14. In order not to be misunderstood, he outlines his devotion to his ministry for Christ, 15-21. Its source is in God, 15-17. Its accreditation is by miraculous signs, 18-19*a*. Its extent is broad, 19*b*. Its aim is to be a pioneer for Christ, 20-21. What a confession of a faithful ministry! Paul also expresses his longing to visit the church in Rome, 22-29, and the circumstances delaying his visit. He makes request for their prayer support, 30-32, ending with a benediction of peace, 33.

16:1-27. Closing greetings and warnings. He mentions many saints by name –trophies of the gospel of God, 1-16 (cf.1:1). His salutations are full of the grace and the love of

Christian fellowship. He warns against schismatics and false teachers, 17-20. He asserts they will be defeated, 20*a*, and breathes a triumphant benediction, 20*b*. The apostle includes his colleagues in his salutation, 21-23. His closing benediction ends in an outburst of praise to God, 25-27.

1 CORINTHIANS

Worldly vs. spiritual Christian living

Date and purpose. This epistle was written from Ephesus, probably in A.D. 55. It was penned to instruct recent converts from the lowest and grossest paganism with its vice and sin, so notably practiced at Corinth. See note on the city in Acts 18:1-17. It was not easy for these converts to break with their degraded past. Their carnality and spiritual immaturity needed patient instruction on the part of the apostle. As a center of commerce and wealth, as well as covetousness and unbridled lust, Corinth, with its vain worldly wisdom, offered a challenge to Christianity. If a church could be planted here where East and West met on the crossroads of the Graeco-Roman world, its influence could be expected to be far-reaching. Moreover, a large Jewish element in the city provided an initial audience for Paul, who followed his policy 'first for the Jew' (Rom 1:16).

The 'Street of the Curetes', Ephesus. 1 Corinthians was written from Ephesus, probably in A.D. 55 to instruct recent converts from the vice and sin notably practiced at Corinth.

Outline

1-3 The unity of the church vs. divisions
4-11 The order of the church vs. disorders
12-16 The gifts and doctrines of the church vs. their abuse

I. Christ the basis of unity

1-9. The preeminence of Christ. The spotlight is focused upon Christ in these opening verses. He is the basis of the church's unity and of the individual believer's position, i.e. the sphere in which God sees the believer and deals with him. Christ must be central and preeminent in any church to correct its abuses. This is the lesson of the epistle. Correction of faults in the assembly must begin, as Paul begins, with the fact of Christ: (1) His authority – 'an apostle of Christ Jesus,' 1; (2) His power to give us a new position – 'sanctified in Christ,' 'called to be holy,' 2*a*; (3) His ministry to create spiritual unity among believers everywhere, 2*b*; (4) His granting of grace and peace, 3; (5) His giving the believer full sufficiency, 4-5; (6) His being the object of the believer's witness, 6, and expectation, 7; His being the confirmer of the believer's destiny, 8; and (8) His being the focus of the believer's fellowship, 9. Therefore, the believer's position in Christ, 1-9, is the basis of

Marble sculpture of a Greek discus-thrower. The Isthmian Games, celebrated throughout Greece, were held in Corinth.

appeal to correct the faulty practices of the Corinthians.

10-17. The presence of factions. The faults and abuses in the Corinthian church were due to Christians behaving as unregenerate men, as carnal believers instead of spiritual. The result was disunity, occasioning a plea for unity, 10, against the evil of factionalism, 11, brought about by a perversion of Christian liberty, 12-13. The legitimate likes and dislikes of teachers and leaders were perverted into parties and cliques. The corrective is Christ. Is He 'divided,' 13? See comments on 1:1-9. Let Christ be central! Party spirit will flee! To this end Paul stresses the priority of preaching Christ, 14-17. Paul's primary duty was to 'gospelize,' to evangelize, not ceremonialize. He was not belittling baptism, but He was exalting Christ. Only in Christ does the church's true unity appear. Occupation with Him and not with ceremonies is the only sure cure for divisions in the Body of Christ, the church.

18-31. The corrective of the cross. Only at the cross can the sin of dividing over men instead of uniting around a message be avoided. Only the cross can save us from man's philosophies and bring us the true wisdom of God. The preaching of the cross is 'foolishness' to the lost, 18, but 'the power of God' to the saved. The futility of worldly philosophy, 19-20 (cf. Isa 29:14), is contrasted to the triumph of preaching the cross, 21-25. Faith in the message of the cross releases both the wisdom and the power of God that humanity might not boast before God, 26-29. God is the source of our life in Christ Jesus. God has made Him our wisdom, our sanctification and redemption, 30. He who boasts must therefore boast in the Lord Jesus, 31 (cf. Jer 9:23-24), i.e., in his position in Christ, not in what he is in himself.

2. The Holy Spirit the agent of unity

1-13. The Spirit reveals true wisdom. This wisdom, the touchstone of Christian unity, is not to be obscured by flowery rhetoric and molded by human philosophy to make it palatable to the unregenerate, 1. It centers in the person and death of Jesus Christ, 2; is nurtured in human weakness, 3; is marked by the effective witness of the Holy Spirit, 4; and concentrates faith in God's power, 5. This

Ruins of the Temple of Apollo and surrounding buildings, ancient Corinth.

wisdom is distinctly God's wisdom, 6-7, 'a secret wisdom that has been hidden' and revealed only by the Holy Spirit, 7. It is in striking contrast to the wisdom of this world and that of the intellectual leaders of this age, 6. It is comprehended only by the mature believer, 6. The proof that the leaders of this world were ignorant of this true wisdom is the fact they crucified the Lord of glory, who is the true wisdom of God, 8. This wisdom is absolutely dependent upon the Spirit's revelation and illumination. 'However, as it is written, "No eye has seen, no ear has heard, no mind has conceived what God has prepared for those who love him,"' 9 (cf. Isa 64.4); 'God has revealed it to us by his Spirit,' 10. Therefore, apart from the teaching ministry of the Spirit (cf. Jn 16:13-15) true wisdom is unknown and unknowable, 11-13. These truths are imparted 'not in words taught us by human wisdom but in words taught by the Spirit,' 13.

14-16. The unregenerate man is totally ignorant of true wisdom. The 'man without the Spirit,' i.e., the unbeliever, who does not possess the Spirit (Jude 19), does not receive true wisdom, because it is mere folly to him, nor does he comprehend it, because it is discerned or understood only on the basis of the teaching ministry of the Holy Spirit, 14. By contrast, the *pneumatikos* (the mature believer controlled by the Holy Spirit) discerns or comprehends 'all things,' i.e., true wisdom, yet he himself is judged by no one except God. No one can instruct God, but the believer can be taught by God because he possesses 'the mind of the Lord.' Unity resides in Him, 16.

3:1-8a. The spiritual Christian
1-3a. The spiritual vs. the worldly.
The worldly and spiritual believers are contrasted, 1-2. (1) The 'worldly' or fleshly believer lives under the power of the Adamic or old nature working through the human body. The 'spiritual' believer lives under the power of the new or Christlike nature with his body controlled by the Holy Spirit. (2) The worldly believer is a 'mere infant in Christ,' 1, i.e., born again but immature and undeveloped in the Christian life when he should be mature. The spiritual Christian is mature. (3) One can feed only on milk, simple teaching. The other can take the solid food of full doctrinal instruction with personal application.

3b-8a. The results of worldliness.
Jealousy, bickering and divisive cliques were formed, the result of 'acting like mere men,' 3,

Roman copy of a Greek sculpted head of Apollo. The major temple at Corinth was dedicated to Apollo, the sun-god.

i.e., as unregenerate men instead of mature Christians. Following human leaders, 4, was a direct violation of the principle of the unity of the Lord's people, 5-8. Christian servants, although possessing different tasks to perform, are one — have one Lord, one aim, one goal, 8. Spiritual maturity alone realizes Christian unity.

3:8b-23. The judgment of the believer's works

8b-9. Christian service to be judged. This judgment will determine the believer's reward, 8b, or loss of reward, 15. In *no sense* does this judgment involve the issue of sin, condemnation or eternal life (Rom 8:1; Jn 5:24). It concerns works solely, *not* salvation. It involves the issues of the worldly and the spiritual believer, but *only the believer* and the quality of his life and service after salvation (*cf.* 2 Cor 5:10; Rom 14:8-10). It judges the faithfulness or unfaithfulness of the believer as a *servant.* hence 'God's fellow *workers* . . . God's field, God's building,' 9. We work *for* God, but also *with* Him in dignity. More than that, He works in us, through us and upon us for His glory, 9.

10-15. The believer's judgment for service. The basis is the gospel of salvation from sin through Christ. Christ is the foundation, 10. Building upon Him as a

foundation is a metaphor for Christian service which is only for born-again believers, 11. There exist two kinds of service. One is illustrated by gold, silver and precious stones, built by the spiritual believer, and indestructible by the fire of judgment, 12. The other is set forth by wood, hay, stubble, built by the worldly Christian. This is destructible and will not stand up before Him whose eyes are like a flame of fire (Rev 1:14). The issue for the truly born-again servant will be either reward for the spiritual believer, 14, or loss of reward for the worldly believer, 15. However, the fleshly worker will still be saved, since the issue is not condemnation or eternal life. Yet he will be saved so as through fire with all his works burned up, as a man escapes with his bare life.

16-23. Solemn warning to worldly believers. The body of *every* believer is a sacred temple in which the Holy Spirit dwells, 16. If a worldly believer scandalously (*cf.* 5:1-5) desecrates this holy precinct, God will destroy him by *physical* death, 17 (*cf.* 1 Cor 5:5; 11:29-30; 1 Jn 5:16). Not only are fleshly sins of the body warned against, but intellectual sins, 19-23. (Cf. v. 19 with Job 5:13; v. 20 with Ps 94:11.) Christians are not to be ensnared by worldly wisdom, nor are they to glory in men, but in the Man Christ Jesus in whom the believer possesses everything, 21-23 (cf. Rom 8:16-17).

4. The church and its leaders

1-8. The sin of judging God's servants. The church's leaders are to be highly esteemed as ministers of Christ and stewards of the truths revealed by God, 1. Their supreme duty is to be faithful to God in this trust, 2. They are to be judged in this matter by Him alone, and not by any human being, 3-4. Therefore judgment must be suspended till the corning of the Lord and the divine assessment of the believer's works, 5 (cf. 3:11-15). The Corinthians must cease their worldly judging of their church leaders, 6-7, prompted by worldly pride, which the apostle rebukes with keen sarcasm, 8.

9-21. The holy dedication of the apostles. Apostolic sacrifice and suffering are used to shame the carnal self-secure critics in the Corinthian church, 9-13. Paul writes incisively but lovingly, 14, appealing to his begetting them in the gospel, 15, his sacrificial example of life, 16, and his concern for them in sending Timothy, 17. Nevertheless he sternly warns the unrepentant, 18-21.

5. The problem of the immoral believer

1-5. Carnality blinds to the presence of gross immorality. A case of vile incest, alien even to sinful Corinth, was reported in this church, 1. The apostle directed the disordered saints, completely unconcerned about disciplinary action, 2, on their responsibility, 3-5. The incestuous brother was to be abandoned to Satan 'so that his sinful nature [body] may be destroyed' (physical death, cf. 1 Cor 11:30; 1 Jn 5:16) that his 'spirit' may be 'saved,' i.e., he might be disciplined as a believer possessing eternal life, 5.

6-13. The principle of the yeast of sin. Yeast, as a type of sin in Scripture, spreads through the whole batch of dough, 6. Sin condoned or unjudged likewise spreads. It must, therefore, be purged out, 7. The reason? Christ, the Passover Lamb, who takes away the sin of the world (Ex 12:1-13; Jn 1:29), has been offered, by which the believer is saved. The result is the Feast of Unleavened Bread, which the Paschal sacrifice inaugurated (Ex 12:12-22). This is typical of the Christian life to be lived in separation from sin, 8. Therefore, the incestuous brother must be excommunicated, 9, 11. Yet personal separation must be on the principle of 'in the world but not of it,' 10-11. Discipline is to be exercised within the church, but judgment of those outside the church rests with God, 12-13.

6:1-8. The disorder of legal suits

1-8. Christian suing Christian. Christian going to law against fellow Christian in pagan courts before pagan judges, 1, is a violation of Christian truth. 'God's people' are to judge the world (unsaved humanity), 2, and even the fallen angels, 3 (cf. 2 Pet 2:4; Jude 6). Since this judicial dignity is a result of the believer's union with Christ, the Judge, are there not wise saints to act as judges in cases involving Christian with Christian, 4-5? The worldly Corinthians clearly manifested their worldliness in going to law against each other and wronging each other, 7-8.

6:9-20. The snare of fornication

9-20. The Christian tempted by fornication. This problem was acute in this church because it had been recently saved out of the polluted moral atmosphere of Corinth. As a commercial emporium this city united East and West in a veritable cesspool of uncleanness. The apostle warns that believers failing to separate from this polluted paganism, 9-10, 'will not inherit the kingdom of God,' i.e., will suffer loss of reward (cf. 3:11-15), even inviting premature physical death as the penalty of scandalous sin. Fornication is utterly at variance with the Christian because (1) He has been sanctified and justified from this and other sins in *his position* (as God sees him in Christ), and is to realize his position in *his experience* (as he acts toward men), 11, under grace, 12. (2) The believer's body is for the Lord's use, 13, and when so used the believer can claim the Lord's care of his body. (3) The body is holy and is to be resurrected, 14. (4) The body is joined to Christ, 15-17, not to a harlot. (5) Fornication is a sin against the sanctity of the believer's body, 18. (6) The believer's body is 'a temple' (*naos,* 'a dwelling place of God'), specifically the most holy place or inner sanctum where the Shekinah glory was manifested in the tabernacle and temple, 19. (7) The believer's body is God's property, 19. (8) It is for God's glory, 20. (9) God-ordained marriage is the antidote against fornication, 7:1-3.

7:1-24. Regulations of Christian marriage

1-9. The purpose of Christian marriage. The unmarried state is good; but Christian marriage is for the purpose of avoiding fornication and establishing a mutually satisfactory monogamous relationship, 2-3, in which both partners express full bodily powers in normal satisfactory physical union. Depriving either partner of sexual intercourse is to be only by mutual consent for the purpose of special time of prayer, 5*a*, after which normal sexual union is to be enjoyed in order to avoid satanic temptation to some illegitimate sexual outlet, through reduced self-control, 5*b*. This is a concession to human weakness, rather than a divine commandment, 6. Celibacy is best for some, 7-8, but marriage is

God-ordained, and designed to meet physical and psychological needs as constituted by the Creator, 7, 9.

10-24. Regulations governing Christian marriage. Marriage of believers is for life, 10-11. The Christian wife is not to leave her husband. If she does, she is to forfeit marrying again. Likewise the Christian husband is not to leave his wife. Loose pagan views of marriage must be abandoned. These regulations that are given by the apostle, so far from not being inspired, are associated with our Lord's instruction, 12 (cf. Mt 5:31-32; 19:59), and designed to meet new situations arising with the outflow of the gospel to the Gentiles. The general principle is that insofar as possible every effort is to be made to maintain the status quo at the time of becoming a believer, 12-24. Applied to the marriage union, it means the saved partner is to do everything possible to maintain the union, and win the unsaved partner to the Lord. The children are privileged to be in a circle of Christian instruction when even one parent is saved, 14.

7:25-40. Married vs. the unmarried state

25-31. The general principle. The general rule is that the unmarried are well-off as they are, particularly at times when believers are subject to economic and social stress, 25-26. At such times they are to remain in the general state in which they were when saved, 27-28. There are, however, certain advantages of the unmarried state for a believer. He is free from economic cares, 26. He is spared 'many troubles in this life,' i.e., the inevitable responsibility of the health and welfare of his family, 28. He is in a better position to realize the brevity of life in the light of eternity, 29-31.

32-40. Contrast between the married and unmarried state. The unmarried believer of either sex is more at liberty to please the Lord, 32-34, and to serve Him without distraction, 35. Physical and psychological makeup may require one to marry, 36. On the other hand, those who can are to remain single, 37-38. Marriage is till death parts, 39-40. Remarriage is limited to those whose former mates have died, and then only between believers. Even in such cases, remaining single is the better course.

8. Christian liberty

1-3. The law of love the solution. Paul faces the problem of a Christian's eating food offered to idols, which involves the principle of a believer's liberty in non-moral questions. In such matters knowledge about an issue is common, but love is often lacking, 1. Knowledge may be incomplete and superficial, leading to pride. It cannot solve such problems as those involved in the limitations of Christian liberty. Love, however, does solve these problems, 3, and God is fully cognizant of the principle operative in His own.

4-13. The law of knowledge inadequate. To most believers, the knowledge of the nothingness of an idol and the sole existence of the one true God was such an obvious fact of revelation, 4-6, that they were not offended by eating meat first dedicated to a heathen deity, as was often the case in a pagan city like Corinth. Other weaker believers did not have this conviction of the nothingness of an idol, and were offended, 7. Love must control over knowledge if a weaker brother is not to be offended, 8-13. Christ in love died for him, 11, and Christ's love is to rule our hearts, 12, as it did the apostle's heart, 13.

9. The church and its workers

1-15. Church leaders are to be honored and supported. Paul had to defend his office as an apostle before a carnal, critical element at Corinth. This ought not to have been the case. Rather, God-ordained church leaders ought not only to be honored as such, but financially supported as well, 7-18. As illustrations of the latter the apostle uses the cases of the soldier, the farmer, and the dairyman, 7, and the law of 8-9 (cf. Deut 25:4). Even the ox is not muzzled when he stamps out the grain, so that he can eat his fill as a reward for his labor. Plowing and threshing are in hope of a return for labor, 10; and so it ought to be in the spiritual realm, 11. Paul forbears this privilege for a definite purpose, 12, 15, but uses another illustration, the temple and its Levitical priesthood, 13, to prove the thesis that 'those who preach the gospel receive their living from the gospel,' 14.

16-27. True church leaders are to be rewarded. They are under a divine commission and constraint, 16; and if they serve willingly, they will be rewarded in this life, 18, and in the life to come, 19-27. This calls for work performed as a genuine 'slave to everyone,' to win more for Christ, 19. This is dedicated adaptability, 20-23, for the high purpose to 'save some,' i.e., be the human medium through which the divine Spirit moves in regeneration, 22-23. Reward at the judgment seat (*bema*) of Christ will crown such dedicated service, 24-27 (cf. 1 Cor 3:11-15; 2 Cor 5:10). Paul uses the athletic figure of the famed Isthmian games, 25, held near Corinth. The footrace, 24, 26, and the boxing match, 26, are selected. Self-control and rigid discipline, 25, are necessary to win a perishable victor's crown. Verse 27, 'I beat my body and make it my slave so that after I have preached to others, I myself will not be disqualified,' concerns rewards, *not* salvation.

10:1-15. The church's heritage

1-5. OT typology and its lessons. The Egyptian redemption, the wilderness wandering and entrance into the land were types or shadows of spiritual truths applicable to NT saints, 6, 11. Moses prefigures Christ, 2, while Israel's passing through the cloud and sea were typical of the baptism of the Spirit into Christ (Rom 6:3-4). The 'fathers' prefigure NT saints, and the bread they ate and the water they drank in the desert point to Christ, 3-4 (Ex 13:21; 14:22; Ps 105:39; Ex 17:6).

6-15. The warning. Despite God's grace, Israel fell into idolatry, 5, 7, 8 (cf. Ex 32:6; Num 25:1, 9); tempted the Lord, 9 (cf. Ex 17:2, 7; Num 21:6); murmured, 10 (Num 14:2); and were destroyed, 9-10 (cf. Num 25:1-9). Verse 8 says 23,000 fell 'in one day' (cf. Num 25:9 which gives 24,000 having included the 1,000 Israelite leaders whose execution is recorded in Num 25:4). The warning against proud self-sufficiency follows, 12, together with encouragement to trust God, and an injunction to flee from idolatry, 13-14. Appeal is made in verse 15 to a wise course.

10:16-33. The Lord's Supper

16-22. Fellowship at the Lord's Table requires separation. The communion, symbolizing the death of Christ and the fellowship of the Body of Christ, 16, portrays our oneness as believers in union with Christ, 17.

The apostle uses the example of the Israelite priesthood fellowshiping at the altar by eating of the sacrifice as a case in point of separation and communion, 18. Hence, believers must be separate from idolatry, not because the idol is anything, 19, but because idolatry is demon-energized, 20, and represents fellowship with demonic powers, 21. Behind the lifeless idol is the demon, 21, from which the Lord's Supper in all that it portrays demands rigid separation. Involvement with idols is folly, since the Lord is righteously jealous of sole worship and is omnipotent to deal with offenders, 22.

23-33. The law of love and Christian liberty. The believer is not under a legalistic principle, but the law of unselfish love, 23-24. A Christian is not to quibble over eating what might have been offered to idols, since he recognizes the earth is the Lord's by creation and redemption, 25-26 (cf. Ps 24:1). If, however, the circumstance involves offense to a weaker believer, he is to abstain (cf. Rom 14:1-23). A believer must always act to God's glory, 31, giving no cause for stumbling, 32, in a spirit of selfless love, 33.

11:1-16. The church and its women

1-10. The headship of the man. Verse 1, urging the Corinthian believers to be imitators of the apostle, belongs to the preceding chapter. In urging the headship of the man, 3 (cf. Gen 3:16), Paul presents the woman's headdress as a symbol of her subordination to the man, as the man in turn is subordinated to Christ, 4-6. The apostle uses the OT to show that

A Greek panel dedicated by women officials of a religious cult. In Greek worship men prayed with covered heads but women did not cover their heads; Paul taught the reverse for Christian worship.

man is made in the image and for the glory of God (Gen 1:27), and when praying or preaching he should not have his head covered, in token of God's order among the sexes, 7. Man was created first. The woman was made from man, 8. Hence, man's headship. Therefore, the Christian woman ought to have the badge of her husband's authority on her head 'because of the angels,' 10, i.e., because of the divine order that prevails among the elect unfallen angels (cf. Ps 103:20), who are looking on the human scene.

11-16. Order under grace. 'In the Lord,' man and woman are one, and mutually dependent, 11-12. Order and propriety are to be observed, 13-15, but not in any legalistic sense, 16. The freedom of grace is never to be compromised, but believers ought to be willing to submit to that which is proper, even if it is not mandatory.

11:17-34. Disorders at the Lord's Supper rebuked

17-22. The disorder exposed. The holy ordinance of the Lord's Supper was marred by irregularity, 17; schisms, 18; divisive sects, 19; and gluttony, 20-22.

23-34. The disorder corrected. The sacred institution of the Supper is indicated, 23-25 (see notes on Mt 26:26-29; Lk 22:17-20). Its doctrinal import is specified. It declares the Lord's death (retrospect) until He comes (prospect). It looks backward to salvation provided in redemption and forward to salvation realized in glorification, 26. Its violation is described, 27, as partaking of it 'in an unworthy manner.' This means in an attitude of unconfessed sin, and thus being 'guilty of sinning against the body and the blood of the Lord,' transgressing against the very essence of the meaning of Christ's death, which liberates the believer from sin, 27. Self-examination is necessary, 28, to avoid condemnation and consequent chastening, entailing physical weakness, sickness and even death, 30. This judging of self, with its consequent confession, not only avoids the Lord's disciplinary action against the sinning saint, but is for the distinct purpose of sparing him as a son from condemnation (eternal hell), the portion of every unbeliever, 32. Hence let the believer avoid abuse of the Lord's Table, 33-34.

12:1-11. The believer and the sign gifts

1-3. The Giver of the gifts. The apostle now sets forth much needed instruction of the operations and manifestations of the Spirit through the individual believer. The Corinthian Christians were appallingly ignorant of this subject. Abuses abounded among them, since they were saved so lately out of paganism and demon-inspired idolatry, 2 (cf. 10:20-21). They who had been controlled by demon spirits must now be taught the operations of the Holy Spirit, called also the Spirit of God, to emphasize the importance of His working in the believer in the manifestation of gifts, 3. Let them also beware of demonic counterfeit.

4-11. The enumeration of the gifts. There are *numerous* and various gifts, but only *one* and the same Spirit who gives the gifts and operates them through *each* believer, 4. There are numerous and different administrations or operations of these gifts through gifted believers, but the same Lord, 5 (cf. Eph 4:4-6). *The Spirit* gives the gifts to believers for service. *Christ* gives the gifted believers to the church (cf. Eph 4:8-12). *God the Father* controls the numerous and various operations or workings, 6. Thus the Triune God works in each believer, to whom the Spirit's manifestation is given for profit and edification, 7.

Some of the various gifts are enumerated, 8-11. Although under the sovereign control of the Spirit, 11, these are mainly and more particularly the *sign* or *miraculous* gifts with which the early church was endowed before the full NT written revelation was given to guide believers. They included: (1) *intellectual gifts* – wisdom, knowledge, 8, and faith, 9, chiefly to instruct the church before it had the authoritative, complete, once-for-all written revelation; (2) *volitional gifts* – healing, 9; miracles, as a sign to the Jews and authentication to Gentiles, and prophecy, chiefly a supernatural receiving and declaring of truths not yet given in full and final written form, 10; (3) *emotional gifts* – 'ability to distinguish between spirits,' 10 (cf. 1 Jn 4:1-4), given to ascertain whether supposed truth was from God the Holy Spirit or from Satan (1 Tim 4:1-4); speaking in supernatural tongues (either known languages or mystic utterances), as a sign to the Jews (cf. Acts 2:4; 10:46; 19:6 and notes); and

Judgments mentioned in Scripture

Judgment	Nature	Occasion	Result
Of Jesus Christ Jn 12:31	Bearing the believer's sins, 2 Cor 5:21; Heb 9:26-28; 1 Pet 2: 24; 3:18	Christ lifted up on the cross, world judged, Satan defeated, Jn 12:31	Death of Christ; justification and security of the believer, Jn 5:24; Rom 5:9; 8:1; 2 Cor 5:21; Gal 3:13
Of the believer's works 2 Cor 5:10	Quality of the believer's life as a servant, 1 Cor 3:11-15; Mt 12:36 (in *no* sense for sins, Heb 10:17)	At the coming of the Lord, 1 Cor 4:11-5; 9:24-27; Rom 14:10; Gal 6:7; Col 3:24-25; 2 Tim 4:8	Reward for faithful service; loss of reward for unfaithfulness, 1 Cor 18:14-15; Rev 22:12
Of the believer by himself 1 Cor 11:31-32; 2 Sam 7:14-15	The believer's condemnation of himself for permitting his own sinful ways and habits, 2 Sam 12:13-14	Self-judgment of the believer as a son to avoid chastisement by his heavenly Father, Heb 12:7	If neglected, the Father's chastening follows, but never condemnation, 1 Cor 11:32; 5:5
Of the nations Mt 25:31-46; Joel 3:11-16	Point of testing is the treatment of Christ's 'brothers,' i.e., the Jewish remnant of the end time	At Christ's return in glory to set up the kingdom over Israel, Acts 1:6	Entrance into or exclusion from the kingdom as individuals in the nations
Of Israel Ezk 20:33-44	Subjects will be living Israelites at the end time regathered from worldwide diaspora	Similar on the Israelite plane to the judgment of the nation with regard to the Gentiles	Entrance or non-entrance into the land for kingdom blessing, Ps 50:11-7; Mal 3:23; 4:1-2
Of the fallen angels Jude 6; 2 Pet 2:4; 1 Cor 6:3	Subjects will be the angels who rebelled with Satan, Rev 12:3-4	Evidently after the millennium, at the end of history	Satan and evil angels relegated to the lake of fire, Gehenna, eternal hell, Rev 20:10
Of the unsaved Rev 20:11-15	Only the wicked dead. Perhaps Satan and fallen angels are finally judged also at this time	Basis of judgment is according to works to determine degree of punishment of the lost	Second death or lake of fire – *not* annihilation, Rev 19:20; 20:10, 14-15

'interpretation of tongues,' giving the content of the supernatural message in the common parlance of the people.

12:12-31. The church and the sign gifts

12-27. The church as the Body of Christ.
The *unity* of the church is presented under the illustration of a human body, 12*a*. *One* body but *many* members of that one body is the figure used to portray Christ, 12*b*. This is not Christ merely as a person, but also in His people united to Him (Rom 6:3-4) by the baptism of the Holy Spirit, 13. Just as the human body is a unit with many members, 14, such as the foot, the hand, the ear, 15-16, so also is the church, the Body of Christ, 27. *One* church, *one* body, *many* members, *many* functions, but all a vital part of the *one* Body.

28-31. The church and the sign gifts.
As the apostle had related the individual Christian to the sign gifts, 1-11, he now relates the church, the Body, the aggregate of individual believers, to these gifts. Although some of the permanent gifts are again included, the list stresses once more the temporary sign gifts, such as apostles, prophets, miracles, gifts of healings, diversities of tongues, 28. Note particularly that all do not have the same gift, 29-30, nor are they expected to have.

13. The church and the permanent gifts

1-8*a*. Love must control the exercise of all spiritual gifts.
This is true of the sign gifts as well as the non-sign or permanent gifts of the church. The 'greater gifts,' 12:31, are the permanent, necessary, edifying gifts. These are to be earnestly sought. The 'most excellent way' is the 'love' way, which the worldly, emotional Corinthians had completely missed in their childish desire for the showy gifts to be used for selfish ends. In this classic passage, 1-8*a,* love is shown to be the essential condition of the exercise of all gifts such as tongues, 1, prophecy, knowledge and faith, 2 (cf. 12:8-11). Even charitable almsgiving and martyrdom are useless without love, 3. Love is personified and its exellencies detailed in 4-8*a*.

8*b*-13. Permanence of love.
Love is contrasted with the gifts which would be superseded and would cease, 8. They would cease because a time of complete or perfect knowledge and prophecy would come, 9. The partial revelation through *direct inspirational* knowledge, prophecy, and tongues would then give way to that which is perfect (Gr. 'the complete and final thing'), 10, an event many have linked with the completion of the NT Scriptures. Paul illustrates the period of the church's infancy, when it had to depend on piecemeal revelation through special gifts, by the figure of a child growing into adulthood, 11, and a person seeing himself indistinctly in a metal mirror which reflected only a blurred image, 12. However, faith, hope, and especially love would remain and always be necessary, 13, in contrast to the impermanent gifts.

14. Abuse of the sign gifts

1-11. The superiority of prophecy over tongues.
'Keep on pursuing love' (Gr.), 1, and 'eagerly desire spiritual gifts' – particularly prophecy, i.e., inspired verbal utterances of truth not yet written down. This is superior to speaking in tongues by contrast, because it is more *comprehensible* to men, 2, 6, than are difficult sounds or voices, 10-11; and it is *edifying* to the church, 3 (cf. 12; Rom 14:19; Eph 4:29).

12-40. Correction of the abuse of tongues.
The corrective for the situation in the primitive church where there were liberty and a need for the ministry of all the gifts outlined in 1 Cor 12:8-11 includes the following important regulations. (1) The believer was to desire the superior edifying gifts, such as prophecy, and was to seek to be richly furnished or abundantly gifted in these gifts to the upbuilding of the church, 12, 23-26. (2) The believer was to pray for the gift of interpretation if he had the gift of tongues, 13-18. (3) The church was to use tongues only with great restraint, 19, and in any case, only if an interpreter was present, 27-28. (4) Childish immaturity manifested in the abuse of this gift was to be outgrown, 20. (5) The principal purpose of the gift, 21-22 (cf. Isa 28:11-12) as a *sign* to unbelieving Jews was to be held in mind (Acts 2:6-13; 10:45-46; 11:15-18). (6) Prophecy, especially in its character as a vehicle of revelation before the objective written Word was completed, was to be given the prominent place, but also regulated orderly, 29-33. (7) In public meetings women

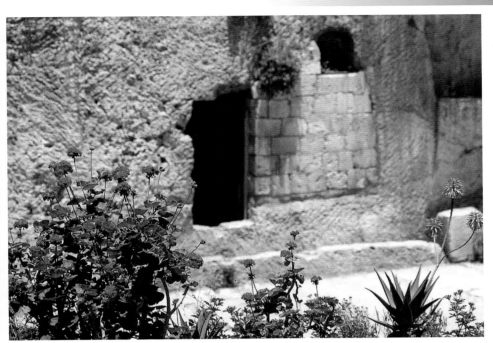

The empty 'Garden Tomb' Jerusalem. Paul presents Christ's resurrection as central to the gospel of salvation which he proclaimed to the Corinthians.

were to keep silent, 34-35, not only in the matter of tongues, but in declaring divine revelation (i.e., prophesying). (8) Tongues and the sign gifts were seemingly to cease after the initial need for them in the apostolic church was met, 19, 21-22. (9) These injunctions were to be recognized as divinely corrective, 36-37. (10) Decency and order were to prevail, 40.

15. The doctrine of resurrection

15:1-19. The fact and import of Christ's resurrection

1-11. The fact of Christ's resurrection. The doctrine of the resurrection of the body was specially denied by the pagan intellectualism of Corinth. By contrast Paul presents Christ's resurrection as central in the gospel of salvation which he proclaimed and which the Corinthians received, 1-4a. It was a fulfillment of Scripture, 4b (cf. e.g., Ps 16:10), and authenticated by Cephas (the Aramaic name of Peter); the twelve, 5; more than 500 brethren, 6; James; all the apostles, 7; and by Paul himself. Paul considered his own spiritual birth 'as to one abnormally born,' either because he prematurely foreshadowed the national spiritual rebirth of Israel or because he considered himself unfit to be listed alongside the other apostles, who spent time under Christ's personal teaching.

12-19. Christ's resurrection the basis of ours. Some Corinthian believers were contaminated with the prevailing pagan denial of bodily resurrection, 12. The apostle argues for the importance of the doctrine by facing the alternatives to denying it. These are: (1) Christ would not be risen, 13; (2) Paul's preaching would be useless, 12, 14; (3) the Corinthians' faith would be empty, 14, 17; (4) the apostle would be a false witness, 15-16; (5) the Corinthians would still be unsaved, 17; (6) the dead in Christ would have perished, 18; (7) hope would be limited to this life, 19; (8) the Christian's lot would be most pitiable, 19. So ridiculous are the alternatives, Paul uses these arguments as the basis for his declaration of the doctrine in the verses following.

15:20-23. Christ's resurrection and ours

20-23. Christ's resurrection a guarantee of ours. It is declared a fact, 20a, which guarantees our resurrection, 20b. Christ is the 'firstfruits of those who have fallen asleep.' On the Feast of Firstfruits (Lev 23:10-14), the first sheaf of ripened grain was presented to the Lord on the day after the Sabbath (the day of Christ's resurrection), a pledge of the ingathering of the whole harvest ('those who belong to him'), 23 (1 Thess 4:13-18).

21-23. Christ's resurrection the divine remedy for the Fall.

'For since death came through a man, [Adam] the resurrection of the dead comes also through a man [God incarnate],' 21. All in Adam, i.e., all members of the human race, die (physically). All in Christ, *all* redeemed humanity, will enjoy victorious resurrection. OT saints, NT saints and Tribulation martyrs will enjoy the benefits of Christ's resurrection (cf. Dan 12:2; Rev 7:9, 13), but will be raised in the various steps of the first resurrection, 'each in his own turn.' But Paul here is thinking in particular of Christian believers, and so limits the complex picture of resurrection to that which affects them, namely, the coming of Christ for the church (1 Cor 15:53-54; 1 Thess 4:13-18).

15:24-28. Resurrection and the final consummation

24-26. The final abrogation of death.

'The end,' 24, is not the commencement of Christ's earthly reign at His second advent, but the end of that reign. It is the termination of time and its ordered ages, and the dawn of the eternal state, and has as its goal the restoration of the divine authority in all creation, 24-25, with the abolition of death, 26. The destruction of death is the last result of Christ's mediatorial reign, and the climax to His initial victory over death in His own resurrection.

27-28. The eternal state.

This will entail paradise regained (Rev 22) as it was lost in Gen 1-3. Satan, demon powers, and unregenerate men, as well as sin and death, will be done away. God 'all in all' (absolutely supreme) will be realized in a sinless, deathless universe *glorifying the one Triune God,* with all evil confined and quarantined in *one* place (Rev 20:14-15), never to disturb a sinless universe again.

15:29-34. Christ's resurrection and new incentives

29. The incentive to be baptized for the dead.

If Christ's resurrection is not a fact, and ours consequently not a living hope, 12-19, then what purpose is there for the rite of Christian baptism? What course of action shall believers take who through this introductory ceremony have publicly taken their places in the ranks left vacant by believers who have died, 29? If there is no resurrection, and really no divinely authenticated Saviour and gospel of salvation, might they not better give up a rite that portrays their identification with such a Saviour and such a salvation?

30-34. The incentive to live dangerously.

'Why do we endanger ourselves every hour?' If Christianity is a mere resurrectionless, hopeless religion, why risk one's life, as the apostle did, in fighting against violent beastlike opposition such as that at Ephesus (Acts 19:23-41)? Why not renounce Christian sacrifice and get all the selfish enjoyment possible out of a life in which death ends all? But the apostle knows the reality of the gospel of the resurrection and 'dies every day,' 31, i.e., exposes himself constantly to physical death for Christ (Rom 8:36-37). Moreover, he separates himself from evil, 33 (cf. Prov 13:20; Eph 4:29) and bestirs himself to righteousness, 34.

15:35-58. Resurrection and conquest over death

35-49. The character of the resurrection body.

The question of the 'how' of the resurrection is broached, 35. The process is described as death, 36. Death is the prelude to life. In nature nothing lives except it dies (cf. Jesus' illustration in Jn 12:24). The product of this resurrection process is a new kind of body fitted for a new type of life. Three illustrations from nature are used to demonstrate the reasonableness of the new resurrection body: plants, 37-38; flesh, 39; heavenly bodies, 40-41. The resurrection body will likewise be similar to and different from the natural body, 42, but will be a spiritual body, 42-44, freed from the characteristics of corruption, dishonor and weakness of the natural body. It will spring from Christ, the Head of the new creation, the Lord from heaven, 45-49, and will bear His heavenly image.

50-58. The change that produces the resurrection body.

The need for the change is indicated by the creation of our bodies for the natural realm and their fallen corrupt nature, 50. The mystery of the resurrection is set forth, 51, a divine secret that becomes known to the one who enjoys eternal life. All believers will be changed, but all will not 'sleep' (die, since death is really no more than a nap for one redeemed), 51. The change will take place in a split second, at the 'last trumpet' (cf.1 Thess 4:13-18), which has no connection with the last of the seven judgment trumpets sounded by angels (Rev 11:15-19). This trumpet blast is a trumpet of blessing sounded by God. The imperative necessity of the resurrection, 53, preludes the triumph of the event, 54-57, producing the great incentive to holy steadfastness and achievement in the Christian life.

16:1-4. The doctrine of stewardship

1-2a. The principles involved. The occasion of the instruction here given is an offering for the poor believers in persecution-ridden Judea, 1. Giving to God involves: (1) The principle of *regularity.* It is to be done periodically. 'On *the first day* of every week,' 2. (2) The principle of *individual responsibility.* 'Each one of you should set aside a sum of money.' Specifically, every believer is to be a steward. The *giver* is as important as the gift. (3) The principle of *proportion.* 'In keeping with his income.' The basis is to be according to personal prosperity. Periodic, personal, proportionate giving is not to be mere legalistic tithing, though certainly presupposes giving a

tenth as a minimal standard. It is rather a gracious giving of all, on the basis of love for the Saviour.

2b-4. The reason and application. 'That when I come no collections will have to be made,' 2b. Christian giving is not to be on the basis of emotional appeals or under pressure of financial crises. It is to be a spiritual ministry based on scriptural principles. The application, 3-4, involves the very highest motive for giving and wise handling of the gift.

16:5-24. The illustration of brotherly service

5-14. Brotherly concern. This is illustrated by the mention of three contemplated visits: Paul's own visit, 5-9; that of Timothy, 10-11; that of Apollos, 12. It is emphasized by an appeal to manliness and maturity on the part of the Corinthians as they serve, 13-14. True growth will manifest itself in such service (cf. 13-18).

15-24. Service and final salutation. Verses 15-18 offer a beautiful illustration of brotherly service, as do the closing salutations, 19-24 – one from the churches, 19-20, and the other from the apostle, 21-24.

Relief of a gladiator from Ephesus. Paul speaks of fighting 'wild beasts' at Ephesus.

2 CORINTHIANS

The glory of the Christian ministry

Author and genuineness.
Evidence that Paul is the writer and
that the letter is genuine is strong.
Polycarp, Irenaeus, Theophilus of
Antioch, Clement of Alexandria,
Tertullian, Cyprian, Marcion and the
Muratorian Canon all testify to
Pauline authorship. The intimate
details of Paul's life and ministry
contained in the epistle are beyond
the reach of the forger. Links with
1 Corinthians, Galatians, Romans
and Acts abound in the
biographical touches. It is saturated
with characteristic Pauline
concepts. The epistle was likely
written shortly after 1 Corinthians,
in A.D. 56, from Macedonia (cf. 2:13;
7:5-7; 8:1; 9:2-4).

Character of the epistle. It
is the most personal and the least
doctrinal of all the Pauline epistles,
Philemon excepted. It lays bare the
life and ministry of the great
apostle. In intensity of emotion,
expression of the writer's
idiosyncrasies, and individuality
of style it stands in the forefront of
Paul's letters.

Contents. Attacked by critics,
Paul presents a grand defense of his
life and ministry in ch. 1-7. Chapters
8 and 9 concern the collection for
the impoverished believers in
Jerusalem, with instructions in
proper giving. Chapters 10-13
further defend Paul's apostleship
and authority against false legalistic
teachers. While the apostle is forced
by enemy attack to lay bare his life
and ministry, the occasion furnishes
the highest instruction and
inspiration to every minister of
Christ.

The remaining columns of the temple of the sun-god Apollo, ancient Corinth.

Outline

1:1-2:13 Introductory, personal
testimony
2:14-7:16 The glory of the
Christian ministry
8:1-9:15 The glory of the
ministry of giving
10:1-13:14 The glory of the
Christian ministry defended

1:1-11. Divine comfort and its purpose

1-7. God's comfort abounding in times of trouble. After a usual salutation, 1-2 (cf. Rom 1:1-7; 1 Cor 1:1-3), the apostle presents a benediction to God as (1) 'Father of our Lord Jesus Christ,' (2) hence 'Father of compassion,' since all divine grace flows through the Son, and (3) the 'God of all comfort,' since comfort follows grace. Comfort (Gr. *paraklesis*, 'a calling alongside') is divine aid which comes to our side to help us in extremity or sorrow (cf. Jn 14:16, 26; 15:26; 16:7; 1 Jn 2:1). The purpose of God's comfort is that we in turn may go to the side of a needy one and help him in the strength of the divine consolation and solace which we have received, 4. When extremities and sufferings abound, experience of God's comfort multiplies, and so does our usefulness in comforting others, 5-7.

8-11. Thanksgiving for recent deliverance. Paul's harrowing experience in proconsular Asia at Ephesus (cf. Acts 19:23-20:1) is selected as an example of the tribulation through which God's servant passed, 8. Its severity was almost to the point of death, 9, but comfort abounded through concerted prayer, 11.

1:12-2:13. Testimony of sincerity

1:12-24. Paul's reason for joy. His 'conscience' was clear concerning the simple, sincere manner of his life and specially of his conduct toward the Corinthian believers, 12-14. 'The day of the Lord Jesus,' 14, is the time of blessing and reward for the saints at Christ's coming for His own (cf. 1 Cor 1:8; 5:5; Phil 1:6, 10; 2:16).

The second 'benefit' (Gr. *charin*), 15, the only use of this expression in Scripture, has reference to an additional spiritual benefit that would accrue to the Corinthians as the result of another visit from Paul, 16-24. The sealing of the Spirit, 22, is the guarantee of the believer's security (Eph 1:13; 4:30); the Holy Spirit is the 'seal.' A seal signifies ownership (Jer 32: 11-12; 2 Tim 2:19), security (Est 8:8; Dan 6:17; Eph 4:30), and a completed transaction (Jer 32:9-10; Jn 17:4; 19:30).

2:1-13. Paul's desire to visit them in joy. To avoid a sad visit, 1-2, he wrote to them correctively, 3-13. The case of the incestuous

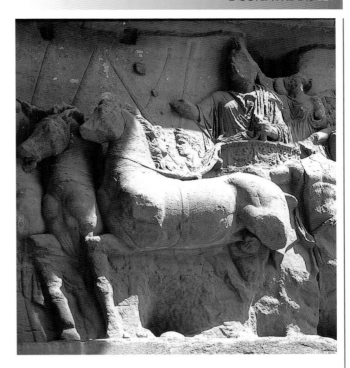

brother, 6-8 (cf. 1 Cor 5:1-5), needed further direction from the apostle, and he gives such instruction. The apostle's mention of Satan's devices or stratagems, 11 (cf. 2 Cor 11:3; Eph 6:10-12), shows the crucial importance of the believer's knowledge of biblical demonology.

Relief of a Roman triumph from Titus' Arch, the Forum, Rome. Paul uses the metaphor of a Roman general's triumphal procession in 2 Corinthians 2:14.

2:14-17. The glory of the ministry – its triumph

14. The Christian's march of triumph. The figure is that of a triumphal march through the city of Rome to honor a Roman conqueror. The public honor was voted by the senate. The procession included victors and victims. The conquerors, with the commander at the lead, were followed by the conquered, led in chains to death or captivity. Perfume of incense ascended from multitudinous censers borne by captives and from aromatic herbs strewn along the way. The scent of victory's perfume filled the air. Such is an illustration of the Christian minister-warrior's constant victory march.

15-17. The Christian's powerful influence. Every true minister of Christ is a censer of sweet incense wafting Christ's fragrance abroad upon a corrupt and ill-smelling world – not only as a future anticipation but as a present experience. This influence of gospel presentation has a two-fold effect. To them 'who are being saved,' i.e., who *have* accepted Christ and *are* walking in Him, it is 'the fragrance of life,' giving life and fullness of life (Jn 10:10). To them 'who are perishing,' who have rejected Christ and continue to reject Him, it becomes 'the stench of death' bringing eternal death and confirming the rejecter in death. So vital is a true minister's vocation, involving such tremendous issues for eternity, that the question is, Who is adequate for such a task, 16? The answer, only those whom God calls and equips. Only those who do not 'peddle the Word of God for profit,' 17, but declare it with utmost sincerity as in God's omniscient presence.

3:1-6a. The glory of the ministry – its accreditation

1. It is not accredited by self-commendation. The apostle found it both unwise and unnecessary to justify himself or commend himself by letters of commendation to them or from them. Personal performance for Christ is to be a self-evident credential and our best recommendation.

2-3. It is accredited by Paul's witness and work. Paul's Corinthian converts were his credentials, 2, as well as Christ's credentials, 3. They were his 'letter,' written in his heart, which everyone could see, 2. They were also Christ's 'letter,' written not with pen and ink but by the supernatural working of the Spirit upon human hearts, 3.

4-6. It is accredited by God. Paul's qualification was divine. His ministry was attested by Christ, 4, dating back to the Damascus road experience. It was made possible by divine enablement, 5. His competence (cf. 2:16) was 'from' (*ek*) God. It had its source in God. God 'enabled' him to be sufficient as a minister, 6*a*.

3:6b-11. The glory of the ministry – its message of grace

6*b*-11. Its message was spiritual and life-giving. As the gospel of grace is energized by the Holy Spirit, it is contrasted with the law of Moses, a code written on stone. The power of the minister of the new covenant does not lie in the letter of the law, the old covenant, which convicts of sin and serves only to manifest our death, but in the Spirit of God who grants us

eternal life. The old legal covenant that kills is thus 'the ministry that brought death,' 7, 'that condemns men,' 9, since it merely points out our sin. The new covenant of grace 'gives life,' 6, as a 'ministry of the Spirit,' 8, and as a 'ministry that brings righteousness,' since it also provides for the removal of our sin, 9. One is graven on stones, 7; the other on the human heart. One is glorious, 7; the other is much more glorious, 8-11.

3:12-18. The glory of the ministry – its transforming power

12-17. It is to exercise great boldness, illumination and liberty. The glory of the Christian ministry produces such hope that plainness without fear is demanded when proclaiming its message, 12. Ministers of the new covenant are not to be like Moses, who put a covering over his face after he received the law on Sinai (Ex 34:28-35). The glory that shone from his face was a fading, temporary glory that represented the law, which was to pass away, 13. In its place the gospel of grace would come to reflect the face of Christ with a permanent glory. Judaism has a veil over it (Ps 69:22; Isa 6:9-10; Rom 11:7-12), which has been removed away in Christ, 14-15. When Israel turns to the Lord, however, the veil will be taken away, 16 (Zech 12:10-13:1; Rom 11:26-27). Meanwhile, the believer who gives Jesus Christ His rightful place finds himself moving in the realm of liberty. Instead of the regulation of outer law, he finds the dynamic of inner law, 17, 'the law of the Spirit of life' (Rom 8:2).

18. It is to enjoy wonderful transformation. Three steps are involved: (1) *the seeing* – we will 'reflect the Lord's glory,' having a clear image presented of the glory of the Lord with an unveiled or uncovered face (unlike Moses); (2) *the changing* – 'we are being transformed into his likeness with ever-increasing glory'; (3) *the transforming* – this 'comes from the Lord, who is the Spirit,' the change being God's work in us, not our own work or effort.

4:1-7. The glory of the ministry – its sincerity

1-2. It renounces all sin and sham. Such a ministry is grounded in a personal experience of God's mercy in Christ. This becomes the powerful incentive for unselfish service in carrying the message to others, 1. Negatively, it rejects every semblance of a false life; and positively, commends itself by a true testimony lived before God as well as men, 2.

1-7. It advertises Jesus Christ. He must be proclaimed and set forth, for unless He becomes visible, our gospel is veiled to those that are lost, 3, Satan, the god of this present age (cf. Jn 12:31), has blinded the minds of unbelievers to the light of the gospel. It is, therefore, essential that if this blindness is to be penetrated, Christ, not we ourselves, must be proclaimed. He is the divine source of light, 5 (cf Jn 8:12). We are the human source, 6 (cf. Mt 5:14). The light must shine from God through us. The 'treasure' of the indwelling Spirit is 'in jars of clay' (the believer's body), that the excellency of the power might be from God, and not from us, 7.

4:8-18. The glory of the ministry - its sufferings

8-11. It suffers but is spiritually benefited. 'We are hard pressed on every side, but not crushed; perplexed, but not in despair; persecuted, but not abandoned; struck down, but not destroyed,' 8-9. The believer experiences suffering and death, as did his Lord, so that Christ's life may be revealed and seen in him, 10-11.

12-18. It has an inner secret of spiritual stature. This secret comprehends self-crucifixion, 12; intense faith, 13; radiant hope, 14; self-forgetfulness, 15; spiritual strength, 16; proper perspective, 17; and a wise life goal, 18.

5:1-13. The glory of the ministry - its fearlessness in the face of death

1-8. Its conviction of the resurrection of the body. The Christian has the strong assurance, 1, 6, of a future life. His redeemed body is called an 'earthly tent.' Death is the taking down of the tent, 1. The resurrection body is not built by human hands. Immortal, it is described as, 'an eternal house in heaven', 1. The believer's earnest desire for the resurrection body, 2-4, is answered in God's redemptive work for him in Christ, particularly

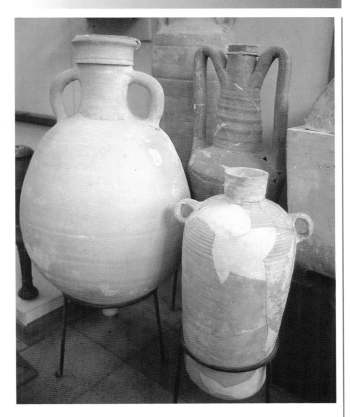

A selection of ancient clay pots and wine jars. Paul writes that the 'treasure' of the indwelling spirit is 'in jars of clay' – the believer's body.

the Spirit of God indwelling the believer's body as a forepayment and guarantee of the glorification of the body, 5. This fact of the gospel of redemption gives great confidence, 6-8. Whether still in this body (life) or absent from the body (death), we are of good courage, boldly cheerful in the face of our glorious hope. Faith, not sight, becomes the manner of our living, 7. We know that what we do not see is often more important and lasting than what we do see (cf. 4:17-18). Absence from the body (death) for the believer means to be present with the Lord (in heaven). Could there be a greater incentive to valor?

9-13. Results of the conviction of bodily resurrection. (1) It makes us labor, i.e., constantly bend every effort to be well-pleasing to the Lord, 9. (2) It makes us reckon on the fact that all believers must face a judgment of their life and works since they have been saved. This is to be the *bema* (judgment seat) of Christ. Reward or loss of reward (cf. 1 Cor 3:12-15; 4:5; 9:27) will be the issue, 10. (3) In the light of the judgment of our works before Christ, we plead with believers to be faithful to the Lord in their life and testimony,

11. The 'fear' of the Lord is reverential awe and deference due Him. (4) It leads to selfless, dedicated service to God and men, 12-13.

5:14-21. The glory of the ministry – its motives and dignity

14-17. Its glorious motive. This is 'love' (cf. 1 Cor. 13:1-8), both Christ's love for us and our love for Christ. This mighty dynamic constrains or impels us. Love is the constant drive of the true minister of Christ. He concludes that because one (i.e., Christ) died, all (believers) died *in Him.* by virtue of spiritual union with Him (1 Cor 12:12-13; Rom 6:3-4), and are thus 'dead' in their position, i.e., as God sees them. Therefore, love should be the impelling motive, since we know one another as fellow members of Christ in spiritual union and not after the flesh, 16. Being in Christ involves a new creation with a *completely* new order, 17.

18-21. Its wonderful dignity. We have been reconciled to God, 18. We have been given the ministry of reconciliation, 18-19. Reconciliation describes the effect of Christ's death upon man as a sinner alienated and estranged from God by the Fall. In response to the believing sinner's faith in Christ, divine power works in him a complete transformation toward God, from enmity and aversion to loving trust. We are Christ's ambassadors, 20-21. To be an ambassador means to represent one's country (heaven) and government (the Lord) with prestige, wisdom, maturity and dignity.

6:1-10. The glory of the ministry – its character

1-3. It is to be blameless. (1) Because it involves cooperation, both with God and with fellow Christian workers, 1*a*. (2) Because it entails the proclamation of the free grace of God, 1*b*-2 (cf. Isa 49:8), which can be so easily abused by license – the grace of God received 'in vain' – to *no purpose* in practical holiness. (3) Because there is an urgency in Christian evangelism that must not be nullified by inconsistency in the evangelist, 2. (4) Because the ministry is peculiarly liable to criticism and blame from sinful men, as well as from worldly believers, 3. Stumbling blocks are easily erected by wrong conduct.

4-10. It is to be approved. Negatively the ministry is to be blameless, 1-3. Positively, it is to be highly approved, 4-10, by the loftiest type of devoted and selfless service to God and man. The apostle names *nine testings of a minister* in which he is to honor God: in afflictions, hardships, distresses, beatings, imprisonments, riots, hard work, sleeplessness, and hunger, 4-5. Then he proceeds to indicate *nine ways by which the minister of Christ is to be characterized:* by purity, by understanding, by patience, by kindness, by the Holy Spirit, by genuine love, by the word of truth, by the power of God, by the weapons of righteousness, 6-7. He lastly names *nine paradoxes,* 8-10, which occur in the life of the true minister who honors God in the nine testings and nine characteristics just outlined. These paradoxes are: 'through glory and dishonor, bad report and good report; genuine, yet regarded as imposters; known, yet regarded as unknown; dying, and yet we live on; beaten, and yet not killed; sorrowful, yet always rejoicing; poor, yet making many rich; having nothing, and yet possessing everything.' The blameless and approved ministry is one of miracle and paradox. It gives the God of miracle and paradox a chance to work.

6:11-7:1. The glory of the ministry – its purity

6:11-13. Purity is the basis of affection among believers. Paul pleads for the complete affection of the Corinthians. He poured his sincere love upon them. He pleads for a return in kind. But this manifestation of love among believers is dependent upon their separation from sin and from alliances with unbelievers. To achieve Christian unity and to love one another, God's people must be separate from that which is contaminating.

6:14-7:1. A plea for purity. The unequal yoke is anything that unites a believer with an unbeliever in a common purpose, 14 (cf. Deut 7:2-3; 22:10). It undermines fellowship and communion, 14, concord and agreement among Christians, 15-16. Separation is not from *contact* with evil in the world, but from complicity with it and conformity to it (Jn 17:15; Gal 6:1). The result of separation from evil is the full manifestation of God's fatherhood, with unhindered worship and communion, 17-18; therefore the exhortation to cleansing from all uncleanness, 7:1, in the light of the promise of blessing in the preceding verses.

7:2-16. The glory of the ministry – its reflection in Paul's life

2-11. Paul's loving concern for the Corinthian believers. He urges them to open their hearts toward him, 2, protesting his interest in their welfare, 3-7. He mentions his severe dealing with them in a former letter, 8, but rejoices that it produced godly sorrow, 9, which works repentance to salvation in contrast to the sorrow of the world which produces only death, 10. The apostle is glad because the Corinthian believers really were sorrowful to repentance, 11.

12-16. He desires them to be assured of his love. He solicits their recognition of the fact that he cared for them, 12. Their welcome of Titus assured the apostle that his confidence in them was not misplaced, 13-16.

8:1-15. Example and exhortation in giving

1-8. Christian giving and the example of the Macedonian Christians. Paul uses the example of the generous Macedonian churches in demonstrating the grace of giving, 1. Their giving was miraculous for its rich liberality out of deep poverty, 2-4. The reason was basic, they *first* gave *themselves* to the Lord, 5. All charity and Christian giving should begin where the Macedonian believers began. It was there that the Corinthian believers were exhorted to begin, 6-8. Giving ourselves to the Lord should always be done *first*. If God *has* us. He has our *all*, including our pocketbooks.

9-15. Christian giving and the example of Christ. The apostle sets forth: (1) The *grace of giving,* i.e., a disposition wrought in the heart by the Holy Spirit, 9 (cf. v.

7). (2) *The example of Christ in giving:* 'Though he was rich, yet for your sakes he became poor, so that you through His poverty might become rich,' 9*b.* (3) *Pledging in giving,* 10-11. A pledge to aid in the offering for the impoverished saints in Jerusalem had been made by the Corinthians a year previously. Something had hindered. Let them now keep their pledge. (4) *Willingness in giving,* 12. This is a prime requisite. Spiritual giving is willing giving based on what we have, not on what we do not have. (5) *Equality in giving,* 13-15 (cf. Ex 16:18). One is not to be burdened while another is eased. There is to be willingness to share abundance with the needy.

8:16-9:5. Instruction in wise handling of funds

8:16-24. The Lord's money is to be handled in a manner above reproach. Funds are to be administered by approved men of integrity, 16-18. These men are to keep such records as can be mutually checked, 19. The management of funds is to be in such a business like manner as to avoid any blame or suspicion, 20, in accordance with principles of strict honesty before the Lord as well as before men, 21. The character of the men chosen to administer the offering, 22-24, should be sufficient evidence of integrity of management.

9:1-5. The Corinthians are urged to meet their share. Paul tactfully commends them, 1-2, yet sends delegates to them to make sure they will be ready, 3-4, and their gift in hand, 5.

9:6-15. Principles of spiritual giving

6. The principle of harvest. The apostle has already hinted at the principle of readiness,

This inscription from Corinth, which would originally have been inlaid in bronze characters, names the city magistrate Erastus. Paul also mentions a city official bearing the identical name.

1-5. Now he adds the principle of sowing and reaping. A bountiful sowing will mean a bountiful reaping. More is reaped than is sown.

7. The principle of free-will donation. There is to be no constraint, no pressure, no high-powered clever methods. Giving is to be a matter of personal decision. Joyful, spontaneous gratitude to God for what He has done for us in Christ alone can make a 'cheerful' (hilarious) giver. This is the kind of giving that delights God, because its motive is love.

8-10. The principle of grace. Spiritual giving taps God's boundless resources. The grace He is able to make abound toward us is His blessing in our lives, that will enable us in His sufficiency to minister to needy people in their deficiency, 8-9 (cf. Ps 112:9). He gives to us that we may give to others. This is a tremendous promise, opening up new vistas of challenge to *every* believer, 10.

11-15. The principle of thanksgiving. Observing the *law* of spiritual giving and spiritual receiving engenders an attitude of gratitude to God, 11. Not only is the receiver blessed, but the giver also, 12 (cf. Acts 20:35). The receiver is particularly positioned to glorify God, 13, and to be stirred up to prayer, 14. Thanksgiving ultimately goes back to God's supreme gift of salvation through Christ, 15, the ground of all spiritual grace. This gift is so wonderful it is said to be 'surpassing' and 'indescribable,' 14-15.

10. The glory of the ministry defended – commended by the Lord

1-6. The minister commended by his attitude. He is to be characterized by 'the meekness and gentleness of Christ,' 1, yet by godly boldness, 1-2, and a disciplined prayer life, 3-4 (cf. Eph 6:10-20), that is highly effective in spiritual results, 5. This prayer power overthrows human reasonings and leads every thought into submission to Christ. It also imparts spiritual stamina to punish disobedience, 6.

7-11. The minister commended by his authority. The authority is not idly presumptuous or dependent upon outward appearance, 7-10, but is from the Lord and genuinely real, 11. It is for the purpose of

'building up' and not for 'pulling down', 8.

12-18. The minister commended by the Lord. Self-commendation as well as comparison with others is unwise and not to be engaged in, 12. Like Paul, our ministry is to be reviewed not in the light of our own self-elected standards but according to Christ's norm, 13-14, not claiming credit for others' labors, 15-16, but glorying in the Lord, 17. The fact must be recognized that he is approved whom the Lord approves, not the one who commends himself, 18.

11:1-15. The glory of the ministry defended by sincerity attested in service

1-6. The sincere motives of service. Like Paul, the true servant of Christ is often criticized falsely and wrongly accused. Sincerity, which is one of the greatest assests in life, is here referred to by the apostle as a quality to answer his critics and to show that his life was right. He was sincere in his jealous love for the spiritual welfare of the Corinthians, and it was his desire that they might be chaste and pure in Christ, 2, with an unspoiled, 'sincere and pure devotion to Christ,' 3, by false teachers, 4. Against these Paul pits his eminence and knowledge as an apostle, 5, and also the proof of his faith in Christ exhibited by his works for Christ and for the Corinthians, 6.

7-11. The rewards of sincere service. Sincere service abases self and serves unselfishly, 7-9. It enables the servant of the Lord to boast in the Lord and to be offenseless in his service for others, 10. It proves the reality of the servant's love for those to whom he ministers, 11.

12-15. The counterfeits of sincere service. The apostle determines to persist in a blameless ministry, thereby cutting off occasion for criticism from counterfeit servants who eagerly look for some cause to attack him, 12. He describes these insincere ministers, branding them in their true colors as 'false apostles, deceitful workmen,' 13, under Satan's delusive, transforming power, 14, whose end will be according to their evil works, 15.

11:16-33. The glory of the ministry defended by sincerity attested by suffering

16-23a. Paul answers his critics. The

Central Corinth

Theater

Temple of Apollo

Odeum

Forum

Temple

Shops

apostle resorts to a legitimate type of ridicule and satire to answer his critics forcefully and to prove to them his utter sincerity. They boasted. He also would boast for argument's sake, 16, even though foolishly, 17. They gloried in the flesh. He also would glory for argument's sake, 18, and adds a note of penetrating sarcasm to shame the Corinthians out of being imposed upon by false, insincere ministers, 19-21. They boasted what they once were, 22. They prided themselves in being Hebrews racially, nationally and religiously. He could claim the same and more! They prided themselves in what they were now, 23. They boasted of being 'servants of Christ.' He could claim the same and more! How? By citing his sufferings and testings for Christ.

23*b*-33. Paul cites his sufferings to prove his sincerity. In these verses he summarizes his entire ministry and glories in his sufferings for Christ in contrast to the false apostles who gloried in themselves and their personal accomplishments. Adversity is the real test of sincerity in spiritual matters. The multitudes follow the easy road; only the sincere glory in their sufferings for Christ. Acts 13-28 is a commentary on Paul's sufferings, here cited to answer his worldly critics.

12:1-10. The glory of the ministry defended by experience of God's dealing
1-6. The experience of God's glory. Experience is important in any work or job. So it is in commending the Lord's servant. Paul uses his sublime experience of God's revealed glory to him, 1, to defend his ministry against false workers. Paul recounts one of his many visions and revelations. 'A man in Christ' was the apostle himself, 2-3. He was caught up to 'the third heaven,' the place of God's abode, 2, or paradise, 4 (see notes on Lk 16:19-31). Paul could not tell whether he was 'in the body,' i.e., still alive in the flesh, or momentarily dead, with his soul and spirit released temporarily from the physical body. This may have occurred when he was mercilessly stoned at Lystra and dragged out of the city for dead (Acts 14:19-20).

Besides the experiences of God's glory are experiences of his testing and chastening.

7-10. The experience of God's testing. Paul's 'thorn' (Gr. *skolops,* 'anything pointed,' like a stake for impalement or a sharp brier to prick) was a real pain or experience of suffering with a definite purpose to keep him humble, 7. In the case of God's servants, suffering is never pointless. It tests to strengthen or chastens to correct, after acting as a deterrent to sin. In this case it was an angel or messenger (*aggelos*) of Satan – perhaps some physical weakness or disability caused by Satanic or demonic power, but permitted by God. What it actually was is pure conjecture, for it is not specified. It was in God's will and not removable by prayer or faith, 8. Its purpose was to teach that: (1) God's grace is fully sufficient for His tested servant; (2) divine strength is fully realized only in human weakness; (3) God's servants are to glory in human weakness so that God's power may rest upon them; (4) when they are weak in themselves, they are strong in Christ, 9-10.

12:11-21. The glory of the ministry defended by experience of effective service

11-12. Ministry for Christ is to be effective for Christ. We either help or hinder the cause of Christ. Simply because we make extravagant claims to be ministers, 11, is no proof that we produce the true works of a minister. Paul authenticated his apostleship by the genuine works of a true apostle, including miracles and the sign gifts, 12 (cf. 1 Cor 12:8-11).

13-19. Effective service excels in helping others. It does not seek its own advantage and good, 13, but the good of others, as a father seeks the welfare and security of his children, 14. It willingly spends and is spent for others, irrespective of the requital of love, 15-16. It acts in sincerity before God in Christ for the edifying of God's people, 17-19.

20-21. Effective service warns against sin. It does not gloss over sin in the saints, but demands a clean break with iniquity.

13:1-10. The glory of the ministry defended – commended by honesty

1-6. Honesty to correct faults. The true minister is no coward. He is willing to face a battle. He will not back down to sin, 12. Witnesses must support a testimony against a sinning saint (cf. Deut 19:15). The apostle gave proof of Christ's speaking through him and the power of God operating in him, 3-4. He pleaded for self-examination (1 Cor 11:28; 1 Jn 3:20). This was not a morbid introspection, but a healthy scrutiny and taking stock of one's spiritual condition. There is such a thing as a believer *failing* the test in the race before him, 5-6 (1 Cor 9:27), facing loss of reward or possible physical death (1 Cor 3:14-15; 5:5; 1 Jn 5:16).

7-10. Honesty to demand honesty. He was honest himself and demanded honesty in those to whom he ministered, 7. He warned that truth cannot be fought against successfully, 8. His delight was the strength and maturity of God's people, 9, and he would not compromise to achieve this goal, 10.

13:11-14. Benediction and farewell

11-13. The exhortation. The apostolic call is to be made complete, of good comfort, of one mind, to live in harmony and to enjoy God's love and peace.

14. The benediction. The blessing of the Triune God is invoked upon the Corinthians.

GALATIANS

Maintaining our freedom in Christ

Date and occasion. Written by the apostle Paul about A.D. 58 (some argue that Galatians was written much earlier as the first of the Pauline epistles), the epistle was necessitated by serious defection among Paul's converts in the Roman province of Galatia made on his first (Acts 13:4-14:28), second (Acts 16:6) and third (Acts 18:23) missionary journeys. Opinions are divided concerning the recipients of the letter. Early study suggested it was directed to N. Galatia, but following Sir William Ramsay, most believe the letter was sent to the S. Galatian churches of Lystra, Derbe, Iconium, and Pisidian Antioch. The apostle is called upon to defend the gospel of free grace that he had proclaimed to the Gentiles (Acts 14:27). Judaistic teachers had come in to adulterate Paul's gospel with a mixture of human works and some form of legalism.

The purpose. The situation made it incumbent upon Paul to defend his apostleship as genuine, the gospel he preached as divinely authoritative, the doctrine of justification by faith alone apart from any admixture of works or law-keeping as valid, and the principle of Christian living on the basis of freedom in Christ, and by faith appropriating their resources in Him as effective in practice.

Contrasts presented in the epistle. The apostle presents the gospel in a series of contrasts, things that ought not to be mixed because they are incongruous. The cross of Christ produces the contrasts.

Outline

1:1-2:14 Personal – Gospel revelation
2:15-4:31 Doctrinal – Justification
5:1-6:18 Practical – Sanctification

Contrasts in Galatians

Chapters 1-2 Personal

Lost in Adam	Saved in Christ
All die physically in Adam	All live spiritually in Christ
Another (false) gospel	The genuine gospel
Man's reasoning	God's revelation

Chapters 3-4 Doctrinal

Law	Grace
Works	Faith
The curse of death	The blessing of life
Condemnation by works	Justification by faith
Servants in bondage (defeat)	Sons in freedom (victory)
The old covenant (symbolized by Hagar)	The new covenant (symbolized by Sarah)

Chapters 5-6 Practical

Living in the flesh	Walking in the Spirit
Works of the flesh	Fruit of the Spirit
Falling from grace	Standing firm in grace
World or self the object of glorying	The cross the sole object of glorying

1:1-9. Salutation and theme

1-5. The greeting. The apostle combines his personal greeting with that of his colleagues in gospel ministry, 1-2. He stresses the divine origin of his apostleship, because his enemies in Galatia attacked both him and the gospel he preached. His salutation, 3-5, stresses the redemptive self-giving of Jesus Christ (Gal 2:20; 1 Cor 15:3; 1 Pet 2:24) issuing in deliverance from this 'present evil age.' In this phrase Paul refers to this age or era in which evil is allowed to work and in which Satan, demons and evil men are permitted a large sphere of activity. From all this Christ has rescued and set us free.

6-9. The gospel – true and false. The apostle is astounded or amazed that his converts in Galatia have been so quickly changed over to or transferred from the gospel of free grace to 'a different [(*heteros*)] gospel – which is really no gospel at all' (*alios,* of the same kind; but heterodox, not of the same class or category). It is a false gospel and hence not the gospel at all, only a perversion of it, 7. Here for all time Paul finalizes and fixes the true gospel of redeeming grace from any admixture of legalism or human works, 8-9. His solemn 'anathema' does not express narrowness or personal pique, but emphasizes the tremendous importance of safeguarding the gospel, which involves issues of eternal destiny.

1:10-2:14. Paul's true gospel – a divine revelation

1:10-24. Proved by Paul's early experiences and ministry. The Galatians had the fact fully demonstrated to them that the apostle was not a pleaser of men, 10. He backs up his declaration of the divine origin of his gospel of grace with his character, which had been fully manifested to the Galatians, 11-12. Paul declares that he himself had once been a foremost protagonist of Judaism, which his legalistic foes were trying to mix with the gospel of grace, 13-14, but he had left it for something better. He had divinely received the revelation of grace and proclaimed it long before he saw any of the other apostles, 15-24.

2:1-14. Proved by Paul's later experiences and ministry. Nothing was added to the divine revelation of Paul's gospel of grace by subsequent contacts with the apostles, 1-6. His apostolic authority and message were fully owned by them, 7-10. If appeal was made to Peter's authority, his course of action among Gentile believers, and his failure to claim any such authority when rebuked, were sufficient answers that Paul's message was completely independent of men, 11-14.

2:15-21. Justification and the Jewish law

15-18. Jews (not just Gentiles) must be justified by faith. Paul here proves to the Galatians that whatever false claims were made by the legalistic perverters, he and Peter were in complete concord doctrinally. Paul cites his words to Peter, 15-16, when he rebuked that apostle's inconsistent practice at Antioch, 11-14, to emphasize the fact of their mutual agreement that justification by grace through faith is entirely apart from observance of the Mosaic law, 16. In verses 17-20 Paul's declaration may be thus paraphrased, 'But if we *Jews* (cf. Rom 3:19-23), in trusting in Christ fully to be justified, are thus placed in the position of being lost sinners like the Gentiles, is it therefore Christ who makes us sinners? Of course not! It is rather by placing ourselves again under law after being justified freely by Christ, that we build again that which we destroyed and make ourselves transgressors against the gospel of grace.'

19-21. Justification by faith cuts us off from legalism. Dead to the law, 19, means to be completely out of the sphere of the law of Moses or any principle of legalism. This is accomplished through the law which has already executed its sentence of condemnation upon the one who trusts in Christ, 19. Thus, the law has no more claim on the Christian. The result of having 'died to the law' is enablement to 'live for God' (cf. Rom 7:4), because of a new position in Christ of co-crucifixion and co-resurrection, whereby the indwelling Christ lives out His life in the believer, 20. The principle is faith (Rom 6:11) in the believer's new position in the Son of God. As I believe *I am what I am* in union with Him, I enjoy the experiential reality of that new position, 20. This is the Christ life. To mix law works with this grace frustrates it, i.e., sets aside or abrogates it. In a fallen sinner, God's imputed righteousness can come only by Christ's death. Otherwise His death was useless, 21.

3:1-5. Justification and the Holy Spirit
1-3. The gift of the Spirit is by faith. The Galatians in lapsing from grace into legalism were senseless or irrational and bewitched or deluded by its spell. Especially so since Christ's all-sufficient death had been so fully and distinctly expounded before them, 1. Paul, in contrasting several completely antithetical principles – law vs. grace, works vs. faith, flesh vs. Spirit – asks several pivotal questions. Upon

what principle did they 'receive the Spirit'? (Cf. Acts 2:38-39; 8:14-15; 10:45, and see notes on these passages.) The answer was the fact that the Spirit from the time of Pentecost has been given purely on the basis of faith in a crucified and risen Redeemer.

4-5. Christian living is by faith. They began the Christian life in faith, relying on the Spirit. Were they to be made mature or complete in it by the flesh, 3? Was all their suffering for Christ to no purpose, 4? Was the apostle's dynamic ministry among them by faith to be ignored and counted as mere human activity and legalism? Or did the Spirit of God minister to him and through him to them?

3:6-9. Justification and the Abrahamic covenant
6-9. The Abrahamic covenant is on the basis of faith. Abraham believed God, 6 (cf. Gen 15:6), and so was justified, as are all those who like him believe God, 7. The Scripture foresaw the justification of the Gentiles by faith and proclaimed the gospel in the Abrahamic covenant promises, 8 (cf. Gen 12:3). This has been realized in the justification of Gentile believers, 9.

3:10-18. Justification and blessing

10-13. Redemption from the curse.

What is the 'curse,' 10 (cf. Deut 27:26)? It is the result of the law's requirement of obedience from men who are sinners by nature, 10 (cf. Jas 2:10). Breaking one of its commands is being guilty of breaking the whole law. The purpose of the law was not to justify, 11 (cf. Hab 2:4), or to be a way of salvation. The law was intended to demonstrate man's helpless sinfulness, 12 (cf. Rom 3:20; 7:13), that he might be saved by Christ, 13. The curse of the law fell upon our Lord, 13. By His death on the tree (the cross) the Sinless One became the Sin Bearer, the Sin Offering (2 Cor 5:21; 1 Pet 2:24; cf. Isa 53:4, 11; Ps 22:1). He took the curse that was ours because of a broken law and bore it in His sinless person, thereby buying and setting us free from the curse and condemnation of the law.

14-18. Reception of the blessing.

The blessing of justification includes:

(1) *The blessing given to Abraham,'* 14-16, the benefit accruing from faith, 8 (cf. Rom 4:2-5). Abraham is the great example of faith, 'the father' of all those who believe (Rom 4:13-25). He honored God by faith that credits God and God's word. He believed in the promise concerning Isaac and a physically impossible posterity which was the link to faith in the promised Seed, Christ. The blessing of salvation Abraham enjoyed has come to the Gentiles through Christ. This salvation described with regard to the Holy Spirit (cf. Lk 24:49; Acts 2:38-39, see comments) is called 'the promise of the Spirit,' 14. The reason is that the salvation brought by Christ entails a wider and fuller bestowment of the Spirit (cf. Jn 7:37-39 Lk 24:49; Acts 1:5-8; 2:1-4) than was ever possible in pre-Pentecost experience.

(2) *The promise through faith,* 14. The 'promise' is important (cf. its recurrence, 14, 16, 17, 18, 21, 22, 29). Neither law nor law-keeping offered any real promise, since fallen man could not keep its injunctions. But grace and faith bring promise upon promise. Abraham and his Seed (Christ) is the one channel through which the promises pass, 16.

(3) *The covenanted blessing of an inheritance,* 17-18. An inheritance is not worked for or earned. It is obtained entirely by birthright or adoption. The promise to Abraham, confirmed to Jacob when he went down to Egypt, was given

430 years before the law at Sinai (cf. Ex 12:40-41). The law therefore does not disannul the promise. Grace and faith precede law and works and supersede them in Christ to fulfill Abrahamic promises. The covenant blessing, therefore, is *wholly by faith.* Salvation is by faith *plus nothing.*

3:19-29. Justification and the purpose of the law

19*a*. The question.

If justification is by faith plus nothing, 14-18, and not at all by works of the law, what then is the purpose of the law?

19*b*-29. The answer.

(1) It was 'added' (i.e., put or placed by the side of grace) 'because of transgressions,' i.e., for the divine purpose that it might *clearly reveal sin* as transgression or personal guilt (Rom 5:13). It was also to show the utter sinfulness of man's old nature, since the law could not keep man from sinning, but actually provoked him to sin more. Its introduction after covenant grace was to be *strictly* temporary, 'until the Seed to whom the promise referred [Christ] had come.' The promise channeled through Him would then be realized.

(2) It was added to show that all, both Jew and Gentile, are chained to sin, 22 (cf. Rom 3:19-23).

(3) It imprisoned sinful men until faith appeared as the only medium of salvation, 23.

(4) Dispensationally it marked a period of child-training for the Jew. It was a supervisor to train him as a minor with childish 'do's' and 'don'ts,' till he came to spiritual adulthood in Christ, 24-25, where the responsibility of love responds spontaneously to the benefits conferred by grace.

(5) It was thus introductory to the present age of spiritual adulthood, 25-29, in which (a) 'faith [the faith principle of salvation, faith plus nothing] has come,' i.e., has been proved by the law of Moses to be the *only* way of salvation for guilty sinners, 23, 25; (b) all believers have the adult status of 'sons of God' under faith and not prisoners as under law, 26; (c) all believers have been baptized by the Holy Spirit into spiritual union with Christ, 27 (cf. Rom 6:3-4); (d) and thus 'have been clothed with Christ,' 27. Spiritual union with Christ means all human distinctions are laid aside, 28, and the believer inherits through Christ the promises of faith given to Abraham, 29.

4:1-7. Justification and sonship

1-3. Sons under faith vs. servants under the law. The apostle illustrates the difference between the Mosaic (legal) age and the gospel (grace) age inaugurated by the death and resurrection of Christ with the figure of a child heir in a family. Although the child is heir, as long as he is a minor he does not differ from a slave, despite the fact that he is destined to inherit all. He is under child-training discipline ('the pedagogue,' 3:24) until the father constitutes him heir. The comparison is with the Jews ('we') who when under the law were children and servants – not sons – and in servitude to he legalistic elements of the world, not free in the grace of Christ.

4-7. Sonship by redemption from the law. Christ's incarnation was in 'the fullness of time,' i.e., when the law had fully discharged its task as a pedagogue to bring us to Christ, 4. Then God sent His son to redeem us from the law, that we might have the placement of full grown sons in the new age of grace. Placement as full adult sons (*huiothesia,* Rom 8:15; Eph 1:5) means full deliverance from the child-servant status of the legal age with the Spirit sealing the filial relationship, 6-7.

4:8-18. Justification and freedom

8-14. Losing our liberty in Christ. Before they became acquainted with God, the Galatians were in bondage to the enslaving deities of paganism, 8. Being set free by a knowledge of the one true God revealed in Christ (cf. Jn 8:32, 36), were they not to be again victimized by a religion of *doing something* to gain favor with the Deity, 9? These elementary religious regulations are stated, 10, badges of religious bondage, insignia of pagan religions and false cults (cf. Col 2:14-17). Their lapse back into their elemental legalism has caused the apostle concern, 11. The result in conduct contrasts sharply with the Galatians' original joyous reception given Paul and his message of grace, 12-14.

15-18. Losing the blessing of liberty. What a boon is liberty, especially spiritual emancipation! How easily lost! How jealously to be guarded! The Galatians once enjoyed this blessing and were willing to prove it by any sacrifice, 15. Would their loss of that liberty result in rejection of the apostle and the liberating truth he proclaimed, 16? The legalists made a show of affection; however, not for the good purpose of liberating but for enslaving. Indeed, they were determined to shut out or separate their victims from the liberating troth of the grace of Christ that their dupes might show them obedient affection, 17. But obedient affection must be shown in a good thing (the liberating grace of Christ), not in a bad thing (the enslaving legalism of the false teachers), 18.

4:19-31. The new covenant vs. the old

19-26. The illustrating allegory. The allegory, 22-27, is directed as an illustration to confused but justified *believers,* 19-21, who were attempting to mix two mutually exclusive systems, law and grace. For the fifth time in this letter the question of whether the believer is under the law is discussed (cf. 2:19-21; 3:1-3; 3:25- 26; 4:4-6; 4:9-31). The allegory presents Sarah and her son versus Hagar and her son, 22-24 (cf. Gen 21:9-21). The two mothers represent two covenants, Sarah the new covenant, Hagar the old covenant; one gracious, the other Mosaic and legal (Jn 1:17). Their sons, Isaac and Ishmael, are the children of those covenants, with their spiritual status fixed before God.

27-31. The meaning of the allegory. (1) The believer loosed from the law is free in Christ under grace. (2) Sarah (the new covenant of grace) is productive of a great spiritual progeny, occasioning intense joy, 27, in contrast to Hagar (the old covenant), now unproductive and spiritually barren (cf. Isa 54:1). (3) As Sarah's posterity, believers are 'children of promise,' 28. The new covenant is a covenant of promise – promise of divine favor, of life eternal, of the Holy Spirit, of sonship, of freedom, etc. (4) Sarah's descendants are persecuted by Hagar's descendants. There is bitter antipathy between the children of the Spirit and the children of the flesh, between the spiritual believers free in Christ and the worldly believers enslaved by legalism, 29. One suffers persecution, the other avoids it (cf. 2 Tim 3:12). (5) The believer is to realize his freedom from the law, 30-31. Therefore as the epistle proceeds from *doctrine* to *duty,* his privilege and obligation is not to the Mosaic law, nor indeed to any

Allegory: law vs. grace

Hagar	Sarah
Old covenant (law)	New covenant (grace)
Mt. Sinai	Mt. Calvary
Bondage, her children were slaves performing the rites of the Sinaitic law	Freedom
Jerusalem that now is	Heavenly Jerusalem (cf. Heb 12:18-24)
Bondwoman	Freewoman
After the flesh	Divine promise
Her children born into slavery	Her children born into freedom
Powerless to change their status	Dignity of sons with a preferred status
Works	Faith

principle of legalism, but to live out his freedom in Christ by the power of the Spirit.

5:1-9. The peril of falling from grace

1-3. Falling from grace. The apostle now leaves the *doctrinal* discussion, 2:15-4:31, to deal with the *practical* issues of experiential sanctification, ch. 5-6. Having proved the truth that the believer is not under law but under grace (cf. notes on 4:19-26), the apostle warns of the peril of being entangled once more or held fast in 'the yoke of slavery.' By this latter expression Paul means legal rites or ceremonies of Judaism, particularly circumcision, 2-6. Given as a sign of the Abrahamic covenant (Gen 17:9-14; Rom 4:11) and a part of the Mosaic covenant (Lev 12:3), the reality of all that this sign of separation in the flesh stood for was fulfilled in Christ (Col 2:8-10). The legalists were declaring that circumcision was necessary to salvation in addition to faith in Christ (Acts 15:1).

4-9. The sad results of falling from grace. (1) This meant leaving the principle that faith *alone* leads to salvation. They had 'fallen away from grace,' 4 (cf. 4:9). (2) It meant being entangled again in the yoke of slavery, and (3) nullifying the full efficacy of Christ's atonement, 4. (4) It meant losing sight of the position of spiritual oneness in union with Christ, 6, and (5) the importance of one thing – 'faith expressing itself through love,' 6. (6) It meant losing the race, 7; (7) disobeying the truth, 7; (8) listening to false teachers rather than the Spirit; and (8) accepting the dangerous 'yeast' of false doctrine (legalism) that could corrupt the whole gospel of truth, 9 (cf. Mt 16:6, 12; 1 Cor 5:6-8).

5:10-15. The call to freedom under grace

10-13a. The call. The apostle expresses assurance that the Galatians will heed his warning and the false teachers will be dealt with as they should, 10-12. He shows how the legalists avoid persecution at 'the offense of the cross,' 11 (1 Cor 1:23; 2 Tim 3:11-12), by insisting on circumcision and law-keeping.

13b-15. The warning against license. The call is to 'freedom.' But Christ-bought liberty is not to be used as an opportunity for fleshly indulgence or as a cloak for sin, but for love manifested in service, 13. The law is thus fulfilled in love (Lev 19:18). But a lack of love will result in biting and devouring one another (Jas

Cows graze in the ancient stadium of Perga, Galatia. In ancient times the arches housed shops.

3:13-16) and mutual destruction, 15 (Isa 9:18-21).

5:16-18. Sanctification and the Holy Spirit

16a. The human condition. 'Live by the Spirit.' This involves not fleshly striving, legalistic ordinances, or works of the law, but simple adjustment to the Spirit. The imperative (command) is in the present tense and involves a *continuous* reliance upon the Spirit, i.e., faith in the Spirit's operation. 'Live by the Spirit,' i.e., by means of (agency) the Spirit, indicates the divine agent and dynamic of victory under grace. Sanctification is thus by faith not by works; by the Spirit of God, not by morality or self-effort.

16b-18. The divine undertaking. 'You [by the aid of the Holy Spirit] will not gratify the desires of your sinful nature,' i.e., the body as controlled by the old, unrenewed nature, which always exists side by side with the new nature in the believer, 16b-17. When we believe, God undertakes. It is God, not we ourselves, who does the sanctifying work. The unceasing struggle between the old nature and the new, 17, and the futile self-effort of the flesh versus the effective inworking of the Spirit, demonstrate that those who are 'led by the Spirit,' alone have complete

victory, 18. They alone are delivered from the bondage of self-effort which seeks to please God by law-works.

5:19-26. Acts of the sinful nature vs. fruit of the Spirit

19-21. The acts of the sinful nature listed. These are the outcome of unbelief – failing to walk by means of the Spirit, which involves faith. They are the results of the activity of the old, unrenewed nature being made manifest (i.e., being openly revealed), laying its defiled nature bare through the vehicle of the human body. *All* these sins may be manifest in a believer unless he lives continually by the Spirit. The old nature in him is just as vile as the old nature in the unregenerate. If he commits or practices such fleshly sins in not living by the Spirit, he may expect the heavy chastening of God in this life (1 Cor 5:5; 11:30-32; Heb 12:5-11), and the forfeiture of rewards and honors in the life to come (1 Cor 3:11-15; see notes on 1 Cor 6:9-12).

22-26. The fruit of the Spirit specified. 'Fruit' is in contrast to 'acts.' One is by faith, the other by human effort; one by the Spirit, the other by the flesh. One is holy, the other polluted. One springs out of the renewed everyone has a burden to bear, 5. 'The law of Christ,' 2, is the law of love for one's neighbor (Lk 6:27-38). A *teaching* brother is to be supported financially by one who is benefited by his ministry, 6.

7-9. Sowing to the Spirit. The new life in Christ is presented under the figure of farming or husbandry. Deception is easy for a believer. He is not to forget that the inexorable law of sowing and reaping applies to him as spiritual or worldly, as well as to the unsaved, 7-8 (cf. Jas 1:16; 1 Cor 3:10-13). The spiritual believer is, therefore, not to become weary in the work of faith, 9 (1 Cor 15:58; 2 Thess 3:13). He will reap at the time of harvest (Jas 5:7-8) if he does not faint or despair, i.e., be unloosed or exhausted spiritually, 9 (Heb 12:3, 5).

10-13. Manifesting spirituality. Spirituality is shown by doing good to all, particularly to fellow believers, 10 (cf. 6:1-6; cf.Rom 12:13; 1 Jn 3:17), and by exemplifying a spirit of sacrificial love, 11-13. This the apostle did in the matter of fidelity to the gospel of grace against legalistic contamination (insistence on circumcision as necessary to salvation). Verse 11 refers to the apostle's writing this epistle (or at least the final section) in very 'large letters,' possibly because of poor eyesight (cf. Gal 4:13-15). He wrote it himself, rather than dictating it, as a token of his sacrificial love for the Galatians.

14-18. The basis of true spirituality. This is the cross, 14 (cf. 1 Cor 1:18). The reason is that it separates the world from the believer by his death-to-sin position in Christ (Gal 1:4; 2:20), and the believer from the world, i.e., the Satanic world system which is the chief foe of true spirituality, 14-15. In this 'new creation,' Christ is all. Human merit and legalistic self-effort are of no use or relevance. The 'Israel of God,' 16, are saved Jews who believe that salvation is by grace through faith, totally apart from the works of the law (Rom 4:12; 9:6-8; Eph 2:8-10). For this truth the apostle has suffered, proving his utter sincerity in proclaiming the message of grace. The brands or scars in his body, the tokens of his suffering for the gospel of grace, are the evidence. He closes with a benediction, 18.

nature, the other is produced by the old nature. One is singular 'fruit,' a blended whole; the other is plural 'acts,' discordant confusion. One is contrary to law because it is criminal; against the other there is no law because it is virtuous, 23. The basis for the production of the fruit is the believer's once-for-all recognition of the fact of his death-to-the-sinful-nature *position* in Christ and his *reckoning* on that position, 24 (cf. Rom 6:11), permitting the Spirit to produce the fruit. 'If we live by means of the Spirit (instrumental), let us frame our conduct in accordance with this truth by the Spirit' (Gr.), 25. This will liberate us for the Spirit's production of 'the fruit,' not the flesh's production of its 'acts,' 26.

6:1-18. Sanctification in action
1-6. Dealing with fellow Christians.
The spiritual believer, i.e., one in whom the fruit of the Spirit is produced (5:22-23), and who is being sanctified experientially by the Spirit, is instructed in his conduct toward the *erring* fellow believer, whom he is to restore with humility, considering his own exposure to temptation and sin apart from the Spirit's ministry. The *burdened* fellow believer, 2-5, is to be helped, 2, in all humility, 3, and faithfulness, 4, realizing

EPHESIANS

Blessed in the heavenly realm in Christ

Date and author. This magnificent epistle was evidently addressed to the church in Ephesus (cf. Acts 19), but intended also as a circular letter to neighboring churches. The omission of the phrase 'in Ephesus' (1:1) in two of the oldest manuscripts suggests that early copyists shied away from localizing the letter when it was intended for reading in other churches in the vicinity. Paul had spent three years in the Ephesian metropolis (see notes on Acts 19:8-41). He wrote this letter, the first of his so-called prison epistles, about A.D. 61 or 62 from prison in Rome, and sent it to Asia, together with Colossians and Philemon.

Significant words in Ephesians

In occurs about 90 times. It stresses the truth of the believer's union with Christ in death, resurrection, ascension and present position. The fact of the believer's 'position *in* Christ' permeates the entire thought of the epistle.

Grace shows that this epistle is an exposition of 'the gospel of God's grace' (cf. Acts 20:24).

Spiritual (or *Spirit*) defines both the sphere of truth dealt with in the epistle and the realm of life in which believers are living.

Body is a metaphor describing our positional union with Christ.

Live refers to our behavior within the Body of Christ, how we act in union with Him, the Head. This term is the heart of the practical appeal of the epistle.

The great theater of Ephesus viewed from an audience entrance high in the tiered seats.

Heavenly realms sets forth the exalted *sphere* of the believer's *position* in Christ and the *realm* of his walk and warfare.

Mystery does not denote something inscrutable, but a hidden truth held in secret till the proper time for its revelation in the divine program.

Outline

1-3 Our position in Christ (What we are before God)
1:1-23 The believer as God's child
2:1-18 The believer as a member of Christ's Body
2:19-3:21 The believer as God's building
4-6 Our practice of Christ (How we are to act before men)
4:1-6:9 A worthy walk
6:10-24 A continual conflict

Divine election

This is the sovereign act of God in grace by which from eternity certain are chosen from the human race for Himself (Jn 15:19; Eph 1:4). Election pertains only to God's people, not to the lost. Men are not elected to perdition. Christ is the Chosen of God par excellence (Isa 42:1-7). God the Father chose us in eternity past in Him. All elect are selected to a holy life of separation to the Chooser (Jn 17:16; Eph 1:5). Election may be corporate, as in the case of the nation Israel (Isa 45:4) or the church (Eph 1:4), or individual (1 Pet 1:2), being based on divine decree and foreknowledge.

Foreordination

Foreordination is that exercise of the divine will by which that which has been determined by God from eternity past is brought to pass by Him in time. It is our guarantee that what He has predetermined for us shall not be nullified.

Foreordination and free will

Foreordination concerns only God's people. So far as the human race is concerned, every man not only may accept Christ as Saviour but is urged and invited to do so. The ground of this invitation is the work of the incarnate Son, which made the human race savable (Heb 2:9; Jn 3:16). Free will concerns the man outside of Christ. Once he accepts the gospel and is 'in Christ' his viewpoint changes, as God from His side shows him why the believer is accepted. Divine foreordination and human free will are humanly irreconcilable, but like two parallel lines that meet in infinity, they have their solution in God. Only when the sinner exercises personal faith in Christ and enters the portals of salvation does he discover emblazoned on the inside of the doorway 'Chosen in him before the foundation of the world' (Eph 1:4, KJV).

1:1-6. Chosen in Christ by the Father

1-6. Blessed, chosen and adopted in Christ by the Father. After the salutation, 1-2, the apostle presents God the Father's role in our salvation, 3-6. This includes: (1) Blessing us with all spiritual blessings in 'heavenly realms,' 3, i.e., in the realm of the believer's position and experience as a result of his being united to

Salvation in panorama
Work of the Triune God

Father	Son	Holy Spirit
Past		
Chose us in the Son	Purchased us with His blood	Persuaded us to believe the gospel
Present		
Places us as sons	Reveals the Father's purpose and will	Seals us as God's own
Future		
Will fully accept us in Christ	Will inherit us as His own	Will claim us in final Possession

Christ by the baptism of the Spirit (Rom 6:3-4; 1 Cor 12:13). (2) Choosing us for Himself (election) *before* the foundation of the world (earth) 'in him' (the Son). (3) Choosing us for glory hereafter 'to be holy and blameless in his sight,' 4b. (4) Foreordaining us in love to sonship by adoption, 5a, or 'placement as adult sons' (cf. 1 Jn 3:2), according to His sovereign will and pleasure, 5b. (5) Assuring us of His present and future delight, the goal of His electing love being centered in Himself, the Chooser, 6.

1:7-12. Redeemed by the son

7. Purchased by Christ's blood. Our redemption was *planned* by the Father, 3-6, and *provided* by the Son. Christ's role in our salvation is now outlined, 7-12. 'Redemption' is deliverance by means of a price paid, in this case Christ's blood (Lev 17:11; Mt 20:28). The result is 'forgiveness of sins,' 7 (cf. Heb 9:22), because His blood, being that of the God-Man, was infinitely efficacious (Jn 1:29) and accomplished a completed redemption (Jn 19:30).

8-10. Enlightened by his grace. The wisdom and knowledge of God center in Christ, 7b-8 (Mt 11:27; Jn 1:18; 14:8-9; 1 Cor 1:30). His redemption purchased us out of the ignorance of the slave-to-sin category into the intimacy of a relationship as a son (Jn 15:15). The purpose is that during the last of the ordered ages of time, He might 'gather into one all things in Christ,' 10 (KJV), thus making way for the eternal state (1 Cor 15:24-28, see notes).

11-12. Given an inheritance in his purpose. The King James version renders verse 11, 'We have obtained an inheritance.' How wonderfully true! (Cf. Rom 8:17; 1 Cor 3:21, 23.) The expression, however, may mean that we were made a heritage, His inheritance in us being meant rather than our inheritance in Him. The purpose is that we 'might be for the praise of his glory,' 12. He shall be glorified in us, as well as we in Him.

1:13-14. Sealed by the Spirit

13a. The Spirit energizes faith to salvation. The Father planned, 3-6; the Son provided, 7-12; and the Holy Spirit *applies* our salvation in persuading us to appropriate it (cf. Jn 16:13-15). 'The word of truth' is called 'the gospel of your salvation' since it results in deliverance on the basis of faith.

13b-14. The Spirit seals the believer. The Spirit Himself indwelling the believer is the seal. This marks: (1) *Ownership*– that we belong to God (1 Cor 6:19-20). In this connection the Sealer is called 'the promised Holy Spirit,' since He is the pledge or deposit (part payment guaranteeing a complete transaction) of full possession of that which has been purchased (cf. 2 Tim 2:19). (2) *Security,* guaranteeing safe delivery to heaven (Eph 4:30) and assurance of full redemption in glorification. (3) *A completed transaction* (Jer 32:9-10; Jn 17:4; 19:30).

1:15-23. Prayer for realization of the believer's position in Christ

15-16. The apostle's prayer interest. The faith and love of God's people aroused prayer and thanksgiving on the part of the apostle.

17-23. The apostle's prayer. He petitions (1) for *knowledge* on the part of God's people concerning their position and possessions in Christ, and concerning Christ's position toward them and inheritance in them, 17-18; and (2) for *power* of that position to be

manifested in their lives by faith, 19-23 (cf. Rom 6:11). The basis of that power is the resurrection, ascension and exaltation of Christ 'far above' every power, angelic or demonic, 20-22, and Christ's leadership of the church, 23, His Body, composed of all those baptized into vital union with Him (1 Cor 12:13) the Head (Rom 6:3-4).

2:1-7. The believer as a member of Christ's Body

1:22-23. The Body defined. See above.

2:1-7. The Body brought into being. All in the Body are regenerated, 1-5. They were dead in sins, 1; disobedient to God, 2-3a; and deserving of wrath, 3b. This is *what they were,* 1-3, utterly lost, cut off, helpless, fallen under demon control and divine displeasure. *What God has done* in Christ, 4-7 (cf. Rom 3:21-5:21), is summed up in His marvelous *remedy* in Christ. This comprehends God's mercy, 4 (cf. Ps 103:8-18), His love, 4, and grace, 5. Mercy is God's love in action, resulting in grace, which is His undeserved favor toward lost, helpless sinners, the objects of His love. The results of the operation of grace are threefold – past, present and future, 5-7. (1) *Past* – we *were* raised from the dead *with* Christ, 5-6a. In the plan of God this occurred when Christ was raised. By virtue of our union with Him by the baptism of the Spirit (Rom 6:3-4), we were raised with Him. So all in the Body are not only *regenerated,* 1-5, but also *baptized by the Spirit* into union with Christ, 6. This is what is meant to be saved, 5 (cf. 8). (2) *Present* – we *are now* seated in the heavenly realms *in union with* Christ, 6b. This is true because we have been baptized by the Spirit into Christ's Body (into union with Him, the Head of the Body, Rom 6:3-4). Hence we share the death, burial and resurrection position of the Body. (3) *Future* – God will display to the universe the unfathomable wealth of His gracious kindness to us *through* Christ, 7. The divine triumph over sin through grace will be put on exhibition to every created being – fallen and unfallen alike. The divine glory will thus be demonstrated.

2:8-10. The way of salvation in the Body

8-9. Saved by grace. This is the indubitable conclusion resulting from verses

1-7. The emphasis is (1) on the *divine method* of salvation – 'by grace' ; (2) on its *assured certainty* – you have been saved (a past fact and present certainty) and are being saved (a continuous unfailing present operation), no uncertainty or lack of assurance here; (3) on its *human medium* – 'through faith'; (4) on its *non-meritorious basis* – 'not from yourselves,' not 'by works'; (5) on its *free, undeserved character* – 'the *gift* of God'; (6) on its *God-glorifying end* – 'so that no one can boast.'

10. Saved to serve. Saved *apart* from works, but unto good works. These truths emerge: (1) To be saved, 'created in Christ,' is for the purpose of entering God's plan for the redeemed life, 'to do good works.' (2) This plan has been divinely foredetermined for us, and is not a hit-or-miss proposition: 'which *God prepared in advance* for us to do.'

2:11–18. The Body made one by Christ's blood

11-12. What we were in ourselves. Salvation, as it pertains to the individual, 1-10, now is seen as it affects the collective. The race in its twofold division, Jew and Gentile, comes into view. The sacrifice of Christ goes beyond meeting the individual's need and meets that of society, removing all obstacles to the unity of the new Body in doing away with all distinctions of race, class, or even sex (cf. Gal 3:28). The moral and spiritual plight of the individual seen in 2:1-3 is now applied to the corporate, and we are seen to have been dispensationally and collectively undone as well, being (1) 'Gentiles by birth,' 11*a,* and belonging to the vast unsaved mass of humanity (cf. Rom 1:18-32); (2) outside of Jewish spiritual privilege through the Abrahamic covenant sealed by circumcision, 11*b*; (3) without Christ, without hope, without God; (4) aliens to the covenants and promises made to Israel, 12.

13-18. What we are in Christ. In strong contrast to what we were: (1) We are now united to Him instead of being separated from Him. (2) We have been brought near by Christ's finished work instead of remaining far off as unsaved Gentiles. He has broken down 'the dividing wall of hostility,' referring to the outer court of the temple for the Gentiles who were excluded from the inner court into which Jews alone might enter. (3) We are given full

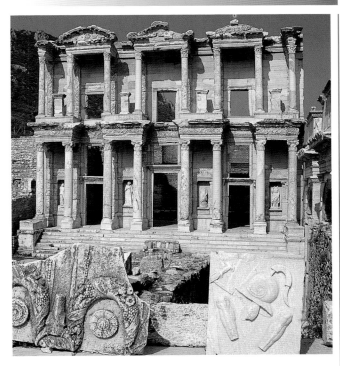

The magnificently restored Library of Celsus, Ephesus.

acceptance with God through Christ apart from legal ordinances, 15*a*. (4) We have been made a new community of His people, the church, Christ's Body, here called 'one new man,' 15*b* (cf. Eph 1:22-23; 1 Cor 12:12-13; Col 3:10:11; Heb 12:23). (5) He has abolished the old enmity between Jew and Gentile by being 'our peace,' 14- 15a, and preaching 'peace,' 17, reconciling both to God. (6) Both have been given access to God by one Spirit, 18 (cf. 4:4-6).

2:19-22. The believer as God's building

2:19-22. The building described. Believers are also parts of a single 'building.' This involves the Triune God. It is God the Father's 'household' into which the believer is born, 19. The holy 'temple' into which the believer is corporately built is the Lord's, the Son's 21. The dwelling or abode which He has chosen to indwell is the Spirit's, 22. The Lord's 'temple,' 20-21, has its foundation in both the Old Testament and the New Testament 'apostles and prophets,' in the truth entrusted to these men concerning the one foundation (cf. 1 Cor 3:10-11). Jesus Christ Himself is the cornerstone (Ps 118:22). All prophecy and the apostolic message center in Him, who binds the building together. The building is composed of living stones – born-again Jews and Gentiles made *one* in Christ. Completion of the building will be at the Lord's coming. It (not any earthly cathedral or shrine) is the real building of God in this age.

3:1-12. The foundation of the building revealed

1-6. The mystery and its meaning. It was revealed to the apostle Paul, now a prisoner, 1, 3. It involves the 'administration' (economy) of the grace of God, 2, and is called 'the mystery of Christ,' 4, 'hidden in God,' 9. It is the divine purpose to make from both Jew and Gentile a new entity called the church, the Body of Christ, formed by the baptism of the Holy Spirit (cf. 1 Cor 12:12-13). This mystery was latent in OT typology and prophecy but not revealed, and was foretold by Christ (Mt 16:18). The revelation of its meaning was divinely made known to Paul, who expounds the mystery of the church in his epistles.

7-12. The mystery and Paul's ministry. Paul was especially equipped to be a minister of the mystery, 7-8. The mystery involves the unfathomable riches of Christ, 8, including His person, His work, His intercession, His coming again, His eternal kingdom, His inheritance in us. The purpose of this ministry, 9-12, is to make known the 'administration of this mystery' (that Gentile with Jew had become one by faith in Christ) to all the earth and to all the heavenly realms.

3:13-21. Prayer for knowledge and power

13-19. The petition. The prayer is addressed to the Father, 14-15, seeking the threefold fullness of the Triune God, 16-19. Paul asks that God's *Spirit* would make the Ephesians strong in the inner man, 16; that by *Christ's* indwelling their hearts by faith, 17*a,* and rooting and grounding them in love, 17*b,* they would know His full love consonant with their position in grace, 18-19*a*; and that they would be 'filled to the measure of all the fullness' by *God the Father,* 19*b.* This threefold fullness of God is the believer's *state* in Christ. The apostle prays for an experiential comprehension of this position with its resultant *power* realized in everyday living.

20-21. The benediction. The practical realization of the believer's position in Christ is made possible by our omnipotent God. He is willing and able to bring this about in response to our knowledge of and faith in this truth, 20. Such a God and Saviour is worthy of all glory, 21.

4:1-6. A life worthy of Christ

1-3. The life described. Living in accordance with one's *position* in Christ is the believer's gracious privilege, the response of his love to God's love displayed in saving him with the wonderful salvation outlined in ch. 1-3. Hence the language of the book is that of beseeching or imploring, not legalistic commanding. The virtues of humility, gentleness, patience, and forbearing love, 2, are basic in maintaining the practical unity of the Body of Christ. The Spirit alone can effect this experiential oneness – hence it is 'the unity *of the Spirit,'* 3.

4-6. The basis of the worthy life. Sound doctrine, 4-6, always underlies right conduct, 1-3. Doctrinal defection forfeits a worthy life. The doctrinal *sine qua non* of such a walk is the recognition of: (1) 'one body' composed of *all* who are born again; (2) 'one Spirit' – the Holy Spirit of God; (3) 'one hope when you were called,' the divine call to sainthood; (4) 'one Lord,' Jesus Christ, the Head of the Body and the center of our unity; (5) 'one faith,' that body of truth 'once for all entrusted to the saints' (Jude 3), and focusing on the death and resurrection of Christ (1 Cor 15:3-4); (6) 'one baptism,' that of the Spirit (1 Cor 12:13), which forms the 'one body' in union with Christ the Head (Rom 6:3-4), the entity of the unity; (7) 'one God and Father of all [believers], who is over all [created intelligences], and through all [His plans], and in all.' This is scriptural ecumenicity.

4:7-16. The ministry and a worthy life

7-11. Christ's gifts for a worthy life. Every individual in the Body is given grace or spiritual enablement and blessing to live worthily of his high calling and position in Christ. This is made possible because 'grace has been given as Christ apportioned it,' 7, i.e., His great ascension gift of the Holy Spirit (Jn 14:16-17; Acts 2:38-39). This gift of the Spirit was the direct result of Christ's glorious victory, 8-10, over all His foes and ours, none excepted, 9-10. His ascension, a proof of His resurrection, marked His *complete triumph:* by His redemptive conquest He captured the powers of evil that once held us captive (cf. Ps 68:18). It also resulted in His *dispensing 'gifts to men,'* 8. *The* gift par excellence, 7, is the Spirit (Lk 24:49), but other gifts which make possible a worthy life are also included, notably gifted men, 11. They all remain except the apostles, which were meant to be temporary. Cf. 1 Cor 12:8-28 where the gifts or spiritual enablements (not the men) are in view.

12-16. Purpose of the gifts. In general the gifts (including gifted men) are given 'to prepare' the saints for the work of ministering on the Lord's behalf and building up the Body of Christ, 12, and producing maturity, 13, especially in doctrinal matters, 14, manifested by love, 15-16. As a result Christ becomes the center of unity and the purpose of occupation.

4:17-29. The new self and a worthy life

17-22. The old self put off. The 'old self,' 22, is the unregenerate man ruled by his corrupt, fallen nature (Rom 6:6). Verses 17-22 describe his conduct, characterized by (1) a heathen or pagan way of life; (2) futility of thinking, 17; (3) a darkened mind alienated from God, 18*a;* (4) spiritual ignorance and blindness, 18*b;* (5) moral insensitivity and ethical debasement, 19. In God's reckoning, the old self *in the believer* has been crucified and is dead. As an old, worn-out soiled garment, the old man has been put off through learning Christ, having been taught by Him, 20-21. 'Truth' in Jesus, i.e., positional truth concerning our union with Him as Saviour from sin, forms the basis of deliverance from the corruption of the old nature, 21-22.

23-29. The new self put on. 'The new self,' 24, is the regenerate man with a new nature in whom Christ is formed (Col 1:27). In the reckoning of God, the believer has put on the new self as a clean garment. This new self is characterized by a renewed mind, 23, in contrast to the blind ignorance of the old self, 18; and he is divinely created in the likeness of God, in true righteousness and holiness. This new position is the basis for deliverance from falsehood, 25;

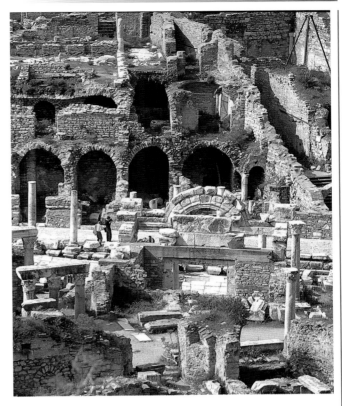

Ruins of shops and houses adjoining the important Curetes Way, Ephesus.

sinful anger and grudges, 26-27; theft and laziness, 28; and impure speech, 29. Deliverance comes by claiming our in-Christ position by faith, making it an experiential reality.

4:30-32. The Holy Spirit and worthy life

30. The Holy Spirit is grieved by an unholy life. He is the dynamic of a worthy life. Stop grieving Him or causing Him pain or distress! Why? (1) Because He is the *holy* Spirit. Unholiness distresses Him. (2) He is the 'Holy Spirit *of God,'* a divine person. (3) He has sealed or stamped us as God's own, and God's honor is brought into disrepute by our sinning. (4) He has sealed us 'for the day of redemption' (full glorification). Our safety and security are not to be abused by license.

31-32. The Holy Spirit effects a holy life. He enables us to put away sin — bitterness, wrath, anger, clamor, slander and all malice, 31. He enables us to be kind, compassionately tender-hearted, forgiving, because He makes us acutely conscious we have been forgiven by grace, 32 (Col 2:13).

5:1-17. Imitators of God and a holy life

1- 7. Imitating God as children of love. Since 'God is love' (1 Jn 4:8), family likeness requires that we imitate our Father in worthy behavior as children of love, 1-2. God's love is most clearly revealed in the sweet savor offering of Christ, 2 (Lev 1:9, 13). Sexual impurity, greed, 3; filthiness, silly talk and coarse jesting, 4, are unsuitable to children of love because they are harmful to others. Thus they deny the very essence of love to God and to one's neighbor (Lev 19:18). These sins characterize the unsaved, 5-7, upon whom the wrath of God rests, 6 (cf. Rom 1:18). Should they characterize the professing believer, if truly regenerate, he forfeits any reward or inheritance in the kingdom of God, 5 (see notes on 1 Cor 3:12-16; 6:9-12); if one is still unsaved, he merely deceives himself with an empty profession.

8-17. Imitating God as children of light. Since God is light (1 Jn 1:5), family resemblance necessitates that we imitate our Father in a worthy life as 'children of light,' 8 (cf. 1 Thess 5:5). This means (1) walking 'in the light' (1 Jn 1:7); (2) exhibiting the fruit of the Spirit, 9 (cf. Gal 5:22-23); (3) ascertaining what is well-pleasing to the Lord, 10; (4) separating from fruitless works of darkness; (5) reproving such works, 11-13; (6) being spiritually alert, 14 (cf. Isa 60:1-2); (7) living wisely and exemplarily, 15; (8) taking every opportunity to do good, 16 (Col 4:5); and (9) clearly perceiving the will of God, 17 (Rom 12:2).

5:18-20. The filling of the Spirit and a worthy life

18. The true elixir of life and the false. Paul warns against intoxicants that give momentary natural exhilaration and often lead to excess, 18*a*, which he contrasts with the true stimulant of God, the Holy Spirit. The injunction is to be continually filled with Him (completely submitted to His presence and control), instead of wine.

19-20. The results of being Spirit-filled. These are productive of the greatest good, and involve a life overflowing with joyful song and praise to the Lord, and a thankful spirit, the result of clear appreciation for all

God's blessings given to us in Christ's redemption, 20 (cf. Ps 34:1; Phil 4:6).

5:21-33. Husbands, wives and a worthy life

21. The general principle. We are to submit to one another 'out of reverence for Christ.' This is a broad guiding directive involving all earthly relationships of believers as husbands-wives, 22-23; children-parents, 6:1-4; and servants-masters, 6:59.

22-24. The duty of wives. Christian wives are to be in subjection to their husbands as 'to the Lord,' 22*b*, because the husband is the head of the wife, 23*a* (cf. Col 1:18). The illustration used is the relation between Christ and the church. Christ is the Head of the church, 23*a*. He is its Saviour, 23*b*, since He purchased it with His own blood, 25. A Christian wife is to be in subjection to her Christian husband 'in everything.' The dominating note is love – a loving subjection, not a mechanical 'obey,' a word reserved for children, 6:1, and servants, 6:5.

25-33. The duty of husbands. They are to love their wives, 25, as Christ loved the church and died to sanctify and glorify it, 25-27, because a husband is joined to a wife as one and is one flesh with her, even as the church is united to Christ in one Body joined to the Head, 28-31 (cf. Gen 2:24). Taken from Adam's side, Eve was actually his flesh and bones. But also being his wife, in a relationship that made the 'two . . . one flesh' (Mt 19:5-6), she typifies the church as Christ's Bride. This is a mystery, 32, a glorious, God-revealed secret unfolded in the NT. The union of Christian husband and wife is to be permanent, intimate, and indissoluble, 31.

6:1-4. Children, parents and a worthy life

1-3. The injunction to children. Family relations are to be such as to reflect our position in Christ. Children are to obey parents, the only qualification being 'in the Lord.' This injunction contextually applies to saved parents and children. Children are to obey, providing such obedience does not violate prior duty to God. The Decalogue is cited to enforce the command, 2-3 (cf. Ex 20:12; Deut 5:16).

4. The injunction to fathers. This is twofold: negatively, do not provoke your children to anger by unreasonable demands (Col 3:21); positively, rear them in the discipline and instruction which the Lord gives in His Word against sin and wrongdoing.

6:5-9. Servants, masters and a worthy life

5-8. Servants are to obey. Slavery was common in the ancient biblical world. Many slaves were converted to Christ. They are enjoined to obey their masters, living for Christ in the social status in which they were saved, 5*a*. This obedience is to be genuine, 'with sincerity of heart,' not just working when watched to impress people, but as obedient to Christ Himself, as 'slaves of Christ, doing the will of God from your heart,' 5-7. The servant is to be fully conscious of the reward for good service which belongs to *every* believer, whether slave or freedman, 8 (Col 3:24-25; cf. 1 Cor 3:11-16).

9. Masters and employers. The same sincere, Christ-honoring conduct is enjoined upon masters as upon slaves. They are to stop threatening, perhaps suitable for pagan but not Christian conduct. They are to act in the light of Christ's mastery over their lives, bearing in mind there is no respect of persons or earthly positions with Him (cf. Acts 10:34).

6:10-20. Spiritual conflict and a worthy life

10-12. The warrior's resources. The Christian inevitably engages the opposition and spiritual resistance of Satan and his hosts. Thus, as a Spirit-filled warrior he must continually 'be strong' or strengthen himself with the armor provided for him. The ground of the warrior's strength is his position 'in the Lord.' His strength is 'in his [Christ's] mighty power.' When the Christian takes into account his position in Christ and appropriates the provided armor, the Holy Spirit empowers him to make good the new life in resisting Satanic attack.

13-20. The warrior's use of his resources. The believer's resources are described under the figure of a Roman soldier's equipment in full battle dress. His secret of victory in spiritual battle is reckoning or counting by faith on those resources which are actually his in Christ, the Victor (Col 1:13; 2:15). 'Put on the full armor' emphasizes the responsibility of so reckoning, 13. This the Christian must do if he is to wage effective warfare.

Christ is the believer's defense, and therefore all pieces of the armor may speak of Him; but they also speak of the resources which are given to the believer by Him. The belt of truth gives confidence against the onslaught of error, while the breastplate of righteousness (the practical outgrowth of imputed righteousness) gives protection against the subtle temptations of unrighteousness, 14. The good news of peace with God produces firm-footed stability when facing the enemy, 15, and the shield which consists of faith offers a defense against the devious attacks of Satan, 16. Salvation constitutes the helmet or headgear, protecting the vital organs which have to do with the believer's thought life and spiritual senses, 17*a*. The only offensive weapon is the sword which the Spirit provides, the Word of God, 17*b*. Personal knowledge thereof is used by the Holy Spirit both offensively and defensively (e.g., Mt 4:1-11; Heb 4:12).

Prayer is the capstone of the believer's armor in that it is to be his uninterrupted activity. It is in this realm that the armor Christ has provided is appropriated to the immediate conflict being waged, 18. Paul makes personal application in verses 19 and 20.

6:21-24. Personal note; closing salutation

21-22. Personal note. Tychicus, a beloved brother and faithful helper of Paul, is mentioned and his ministry made known.

23-24. Closing salutation. Peace, love, faith and grace are mentioned in benediction and blessing.

PHILIPPIANS

The joy of knowing Christ

Author and theme. This epistle is one written while Paul was a prisoner at Rome, perhaps A.D. 62. Its theme is the adequacy of Christ for all the experiences of life – privation, persecution, hardship, suffering, as well as prosperity and popularity. Christ gives joy and triumph whatever may come, if He is allowed to be the center of life. This is mottoed in Paul's testimony: 'For to me, to live is Christ' (1:21).

Historical background. The account of the Philippian mission (Acts 16:6-40) shows the church there was founded under divine leading (Acts 16:6-7) as a result of a directing vision (8-11). It was born in a prison (Acts 16:25-34), and this letter written to it a decade or so later was penned from a prison. A note of triumphant joy in Christ permeates it, despite the apostle's severe testings in the interim (cf. 2 Cor 11:23-33). The note of joy is sounded more than 18 times in the course of the short letter. 'Rejoice in the Lord always. I will say it again, rejoice!' (4:4) may be taken as the golden text.

Outline

1 The joy of Christ our life
2 The joy of Christ our example
3 The joy of Christ our goal
4 The joy of Christ our sufficiency

Philippi

Acropolis

Scale
0   200 yards

Reservoir
Egnatian Way

Theater

Forum

Baths

The remains of ancient Philippi.

1:1-11. Paul the pastor's joy in Christ

1-2. His pastoral salutation. Paul addresses the local church in Philippi, Macedonia (cf. Acts 16:6-40). It was organized with 'overseers' (bishops) and 'deacons' (cf. Acts 6:1-7). He greets it as composed of 'saints in Christ,' but it doubtless, as other local churches, contained some professing members who were not born again.

3-11. His pastoral joy. Paul's remembrance and prayer ministry for the Philippians were characterized by joy, 3-4 (1) because of their continued fellowship in the gospel, 5; (2) because of the apostle's assurance of God's effectual working in them until 'the day of Christ Jesus,' i.e., the time of judgment of the believers' works at the Lord's coming when the rewards for faithful service are dispensed, 6; (3) because they shared with Paul his experience of the joy of Christ, 7; (4) because of his great interest in their spiritual welfare, 8-11.

1:12-30. Paul the prisoner's joy in Christ

12-20. His confident joy in tribulations. He is assured his sufferings will result in promoting the gospel, 12, even in the emperor's court itself, 13 (cf. 4:22). His imprisonment in Rome has inspired a fearless confidence in many to speak the Word, 14. He even rejoices that the Word is proclaimed by those who preach Christ contentiously, opposing him, 15-19. Paul's confidence is confirmed by his realization that Christ will be magnified in his body, whether he lives or dies, 20.

21-30. The secret of Paul's confident joy is his Christ-centered life. For him 'to live is Christ,' 21. Outwardly his one goal was Christ; inwardly Christ was living out His life through him. Living, he was blessed with radiant joy. Dying was 'gain' because it meant to 'be with Christ,' which was 'better by far,' 22-23. To remain in this life was, however, more helpful for the spiritual progress of the Philippians, 25-26. In the light of his own conflicts, the apostle admonishes them to endure sufferings joyfully, 27-30.

2:1-11. Exhortation to unity and humility

1-4. The exhortation. The basis for the exhortation is the Philippian believers' position in Christ, 1. If they act upon this position they will fulfill the apostle's joy, 2, by realizing their unity which will be effected by genuine selflessness and meekness, 3-4.

5-11. The example of Christ. His self-humbling, 5-8, led to His exaltation by the Father, 9-11. This great 'kenotic' or self-emptying, passage is the basis for the apostle's exhortation, 5, to share Christ's state of mind.

The passage teaches (1) the deity of Christ. He was 'in very nature God,' the second Person of the God-head, absolute Deity, on an equality with God, 6*b*. (2) This equality was His by right of His glorious person, not something He needed to grasp after. (3) As God He 'made himself nothing' ('emptied Himself,' NASB), giving up not His deity but His heavenly glory and privilege, 7*a*, (4) becoming incarnate in order to be a 'servant,' 7*b*, (5) as a man among men, 7*d*. (6) He then humbled Himself further, 8*a* (Ps 40:6-8), by dying, (7) even to the point of dying for sinners on the cross, 8*b*. (8) As a result, He was gloriously exalted in resurrection, ascension and His heavenly session. This exaltation will be furthered still more in His return and subsequent mediatorial reign, defeating His enemies and bringing great glory to the Father, 9-11 (cf. Heb 2:9; Rev 3:21; Ps 2:8-12).

2:12-16. Working out salvation

12-13. The exhortation. Working *out* salvation is vastly different from working *for* salvation. Salvation can be worked out only by those to whom God has first given it (Eph 2:8-10). Personal salvation is completed by God Himself – by faith apart from works. Working it out in daily experience is on the basis of obedience to God's Word, 12*a,* and by 'fear and trembling.' Fear is necessary because it is possible to fail to work out that which is inwrought by God. God works in us by the Spirit to enable us to work it out.

14-16. The result. This will be: (1) spiritual accomplishment without complaining and friction, 14 (cf. 1 Cor 10:10); (2) blamelessness of life, character in keeping with the position of God'5 children, 15; (3) proper testimony by bearing light in a sin-darkened world made perverse by sin; (4) effective soul-winning in holding forth, as exhibited wares, 'the word of life' to those dead in sin; (5) furnishing the apostle joy 'on the day of Christ' (cf. notes on 1:3-11).

2:17-30. Paul's example of humble service

17-18. The joy of such service. To realise fully such joy, the apostle is willing to be poured out as a drink offering sacrificially in service, 17, and desires the joy of the Philippian believers to be realized in such a manner also, 18.

19-30. The service exemplified. In Timothy, 19-23, in himself, 24, and in Epaphroditus, 25-30 (cf. Phil 4: 18), joyful self-humbling service is seen.

3:1-6. Christ the true goal vs. false goals

1. The true goal in life presented. Christ is the true end in life. He alone brings genuine joy. All real rejoicing concentrates in Him and what He has done, 1*a* (cf. 1 Thess 5:16). To point this out and warn against spiritual counterfeits which steal away this joy is not tedious for the apostle, and is safe for the Philippian believers.

2-6. False goals warned against. Those who proclaim these false goals, particularly legalistic teachers, violate grace and detract from the all-sufficiency of Christ. They are termed 'dogs,' 'men who do evil,' 2, since they cause much harm to believers in God's grace. The term 'mutilators of the flesh' involves a play on the word' circumcision.' Paul uses *katatome* ('a cutting up' or 'mutilation') instead of *peritome* ('a cutting around' or 'circumcision') in order to emphasize the error of the Judaizers who required circumcision of the Gentile believers. The legalists said one had to be circumcised and keep the law to be saved, in addition to faith in Christ (Acts 15:1; Gal 5:1, 3). Paul shows that true circumcision involves faith in Christ without any recourse of legalism, 3. He uses his own example as a warning against the false goal of trusting in legal righteousness instead of the righteousness of Christ alone, 4-6.

3:7-9. Christ the one goal in life

7-8. Counting all lost. All the things Paul formerly valued 'in the flesh' as a natural religionist, 4-6, which were gains in the old unregenerate life, he now reckons total loss, pure liability, 'for the sake of Christ.' 7. He counts all as rubbish (Gr. 'excrement'), 8*b*.

8*b*-9. Reckoning the gain. On the credit ledger appears (1) 'the surpassing greatness' of knowing Jesus Christ as his Lord; (2) winning Christ as the ultimate prize or treasure; (3) to be 'found in him,' a position of perfect acceptance in the righteousness of God gained by faith, 9.

3:10-14. Concentration of spiritual purpose

10-11. The object of concentration.

The apostle's object is Christ. His purpose is to know Him experientially in a threefold way: the power of His resurrection (victory over sin and death); and what is inseparable, the fellowship of His sufferings (the cross); and what follows, 'being like him,' i.e., being continually molded into the form of Christ's death. Thus he will possess the experience *of* Christ.

The 'resurrection from the dead,' 11, has reference to the resurrection of believers when separation from sin will be final and conformity to Christ complete. This was Paul's prospect while his life hung in the balance, a prospect deepened by his life purpose, 10. 'Somehow' voiced no uncertainty as to his participation in the resurrection, but simply echoed his desire to submit to any means (imprisonment, suffering, death) which would hasten the day of complete conformity to Christ.

12-14. The reason for concentration.

Paul did not presume to have gained absolute or final knowledge of Christ as outlined above. Such knowledge requires diligent and constant pursuit, having as the ultimate goal the possession of Christ as He had taken possession of Paul, 12. Although the apostle's wonderful career for the Lord was drawing to a close and he had not yet grasped in experience the fullness of what he was in Christ, still he exerted the utmost concentration in pursuing the goal of God's upward call in Christ Jesus, 13-14. This probably has reference to the *bema,* or judgment seat of Christ, when the believer's works shall be judged. Paul's aim was evidently to possess such intimate knowledge of his Lord, and his position in Him, that the day of judgment would be one of approval and victory instead of shame and defeat. Every effort was bent with this focus in view.

3:15-19. Another appeal for unity

15-16. The appeal.

Those who are 'mature' *(teleiot),* i.e., grown-up both doctrinally and experientially, are to have the attitudes that Paul had just expressed in his testimony concerning his own struggle of faith, 15 (see comments on 10-14; cf. Gal 5:10). Unity is essential and patience necessary.

Depiction of a Roman chariot race, from the top of an ancient clay lamp. Paul described his life in Christ as pressing towards the goal to win the prize.

17-19. The example.

The apostle is able to offer his own manner of life as an example. join with others in following my example,' 17*a* (cf. Eph 5:1). He urges continual observation of those who live by God's grace, 17*b,* because many do not walk thus. Those who do not walk in grace are 'enemies of the cross of Christ,' i.e., they are hostile in some degree to the complete sufficiency of the death of Christ as the basis of justification before God, adding some other requirement to grace through faith as the way of salvation (Eph 2:8-9). Paul strongly denounces them, 18-19.

3:20-21. Christ the believer's expectation

20*a*. Our heavenly citizenship.

Our commonwealth or native land is in heaven. We are a heavenly people (Col 3:1-4), citizens of a country in keeping with our high calling.

20*b*-21. The privileges of our citizenship.

We are expecting or awaiting our Saviour from heaven (Acts 1:9-11; 1 Thess 1:9-10;

4:13-18). He will then complete our salvation in its future sense of glorification, 21. This involves changing 'our lowly bodies' i.e., our present physical bodies, still subject to sin, disease and death, 21. This remodeling or transforming will result in a body that is like the resurrection body of our Lord (cf. 1 Thess 4:13-18; 1 Cor 15:52; Lk 24:39). It will be deathless, diseaseless, sinless, indestructible, designed for heaven and the spiritual world. Such a change will be effected by Christ's omnipotence.

4:1-5. Standing fast in Christ's sufficiency

1. The reason for the injunction. 'Keep on standing firmly (present imperative), constantly persevere in Christ' (Gr). Why? Because we are a heavenly people enjoying a sure salvation (3:20-21) and are to be rewarded for such firm adherence to our position in Christ. 'My joy and crown' refers to Paul's fruit borne in lives, which will be recompensed at the Lord's coming, 1b.

2-5. The result of the injunction. Their constant perseverance will heal personal rifts and cause them to 'agree with each other in the Lord,' 2 (cf. 2:5). It will produce a spirit of helpfulness among believers, i.e., those whose names are 'in the book of life,' 3 (Col 1:27), and will produce double joy, 4. Rejoicing in anything or anyone other than in Christ and in the matter of His atoning work of salvation, always decreases joy. A firm stand also generates the 'gentleness' of Christ and the expectation of the imminent return of the Lord, 5 (cf. 3:20-21).

4:6-9. The secret of God's peace

6-7. The prescription for receiving God's peace. The direction is twofold: don't worry about anything; and pray about everything in a spirit of thanksgiving and gratitude, 6. The result will be 'the peace of God.' This is the peace with which God fills the believer as he stands firmly in his position in Christ, 1. It is to be distinguished from 'peace with God' which is the result of justification (Rom 5:1) and the portion of *every* believer. This deeper peace of walking with God is said to be incomprehensible to the merely natural mind. It surpasses anything the unspiritual mind can grasp; it 'keeps on guarding' (Gk),

protecting the mental, emotional, and spiritual life from enemy intrusion of that which would spoil God's peace.

8-9. The prescription for maintaining God's peace. The secret is (1) to guard our mental life, i.e., what we allow ourselves to think upon or ponder, 8. We are to meditate continually on the things that are true, noble (honorable, reputable), right (just, righteous), pure, lovely (acceptable), of good report (commendable, laudable). (2) To practice the things which were taught by the apostle and were exemplified in his personal contact with them. The result will mean not only possessing 'the peace of God,' 7, but 'the God of peace' Himself, 9.

4:10-23. Paul's testimony of God's peace

10-14. His contentment in the Lord. He rejoices greatly that the Philippians' care for him has flourished once again, like vegetation revived by a shower, 10. He stresses the fact that he has learned to be satisfied in whatever state he found himself while in the pathway of service for the Lord, 11-12. In Christ he has unlimited potential, 13 (cf. Jn 15:5; 2 Cor 12:9). He is grateful for help in time of necessity, 14.

15-23. His gratitude for benefit received. He commends the early liberality of the Philippian church, 15-17, and is grateful for their recent gift via Epaphroditus, 18. They are assured that God will honor them as they honor Him in their giving, 19 (cf. Ps 23:1). Paul closes with a benediction, 20, 23, and personal salutation, 21-22. The saints of Caesar's household were converts from the imperial Roman court itself.

COLOSSIANS

The supreme glory of Christ's person

Colossae

Mediterranean Sea

Date and author. One of the Roman prison epistles written by the apostle Paul (1:1), this letter was dispatched to proconsular Asia by Epaphras, who also delivered Ephesians and Philemon. This letter therefore dates about the same time, probably A.D. 61 or 62.

Purpose and theme. This epistle was penned to the church at Colossae, a town near Laodicea and Hierapolis. The apostle had learned of two serious doctrinal errors that were threatening the church. One was a form of ascetic legalism (2:14-17). The other was a type of unsound mysticism (2:18-23). To combat both, the epistle exalts Christ in His person and work and the believer's union with Him as the answer for all time to errors of this sort.

Outline

1:1-14 Paul's interest in the Colossians
1:15-29 The glory of Christ's person and work
2:1-23 Christ the answer to doctrinal errors
3:1-4:18 Union with Christ the basis of Christian living

1:1-8. The apostolic greeting

1-3. Paul's pastoral solicitude. Paul associates Timothy with himself, 1, in this introductory greeting to the believers at Colossae, a small town in Asia Minor. He did not establish the church there but greets it as his own, 2, and declares his earnest prayer interest in it, 3.

4-8. Reasons for Paul's interest. He was impressed with their faith in Christ, their love for Christ's own, 4, and the fruitfulness of the gospel in their lives, 6. He also had a personal connection with them through Epaphras, 7, who had made known their 'love in the Spirit', 8.

1:9-14. The apostolic prayer

9-11. The petitions made. Paul's prayer for the Colossians was continuous, 9 (cf. 3). The apostle intercedes (1) for full knowledge of God's will and spiritual perception, 9; (2) that this knowledge might be translated into a 'worthy' form of life (cf. Eph 4:1), productive of good works (cf. Eph 2:10); (3) that further knowledge might be granted, 10; (4) that spiritual power might be given, 11a; (5) that Christian virtues such as patience and endurance might be exercised with joyfulness, 11b.

12-14. The name in which the petition is made. The prayer is directed to God the Father, who is said to have qualified us to share the portion which is the inheritance of the saints who dwell in the realm of light, 12 (cf. 1 Jn 1:5). He has rescued us from the dominion of Satanic and demonic power, 13a (cf. Eph 6:10-20) and 'brought us into the kingdom of the Son he loves,' 13b. In this One we possess redemption through His death, namely, 'the forgiveness of sins,' 14.

1:15-17. Christ's deity and creatorship

15a. Christ's deity. He is the image (*eikon*), the exact likeness or representation, of the invisible God. He is very God of very God, one with the Father, so that he who sees the Image sees the identical likeness of God reflected (Jn 14:9). Apart from the Image, God the Infinite Spirit cannot be seen by a human being (Jn 4:24; Rom 1:20). In Christ preincarnate and then incarnate, God became visible to man (Jn 1:1, 14, 18).

15b-17. Christ's creatorship. As Creator, (1) Christ is prior to all creation, being the Creator Himself – 'the firstborn over,' antecedent to, every creature or all creation, 15b. He is 'before all things,' 17a (cf. Jn 17:5), having existed eternally before all creatures and creation. (2) He is the *Agent of creation* – 'for by him all things were created,' 16a. This statement is repeated, 16b. (3) He is the *Goal of creation*. 'All things were created for him,' 16c. All creation centers in Him and has its consummation in Him. (4) He is the Sustainer of creation. 'In him all things hold together.'

1:18-19. Christ's headship over the church

18a.He is Head of the church. The church is *His Body*. As the head of the human body is one with the body, so Christ is corporately one in life and destiny with His redeemed of this age. The Holy Spirit baptizes the believer into the Body (1 Cor 12:13) and at the same time int0 Christ the Head (Rom 6:3-4). As the head directs and controls all the activities of the human body, so Christ directs and controls all the activities of the church, His spiritual Body (1 Cor 12:12; Eph 1:22).

18b-19. He is the beginning of the new creation. As the crucified and risen Redeemer He is 'the firstborn from among the dead' and as such 'the beginning' of the new creation (2 Cor 5:17; Rev 1:5). As 'the firstborn of all creation,' 15, He is the Creator and imparts natural life. As the 'firstborn from among the dead' He is the Redeemer and imparts new resurrection life. Through His redemptive work the new creation is brought into being, by virtue of which He is its Head. He is to have the first place in everything, for 'God was pleased to have all his fullness dwell in Him,' 19. He was very God become man, to create a new people through redemption.

1:20-23. Christ's work of reconciliation

20-21. The meaning of reconciliation. Reconciliation is Christ's making peace between God and man, who was alienated from and at enmity with God as a result of the Fall. This was accomplished by the blood (Christ's death) on the cross, 20a. Alienation and enmity were centered in man's mind (his thoughts) and were expressed in wicked works, 21. The sinner is reconciled (thoroughly changed) by divine power from a state of hostility and aversion toward God to loving trust (cf. Rom 5:10; 11:15; 2 Cor 5:18-20).

22-23. The purpose of reconciliation. The end in view in Christ's reconciling work, realized in His finished sacrifice, is to present the believer holy, faultless and beyond reproof before God, 22 (cf. Eph 5:27).

1:24-29. Christ's glory proclaimed in Paul's ministry

24-25. By Paul's sufferings. The apostle rejoices in these sufferings, which are for God's people, 24*a*. By so doing he 'fills up' or completes that which is lacking in his afflictions for Christ endured in his physical body for the sake of Christ's mystical Body, the church, 24*b*. Of this church Paul has become a 'minister' (*diakonos*) in accordance with the stewardship or apostolic commission divinely committed to him for the Colossians' benefit, that he might thereby fully execute the preaching of God's Word, 25*c*.

25*d*-29. By his fulfilling the word of God. The complete preaching of the Word of God, 25*d,* involves the revelation and exposition of the 'mystery,' 26. This mystery, or divine truth now made known, was unrevealed in ages previous to the church period, 26*a* (cf. Eph 3:2-6). It is now revealed through the apostle, 26*b,* and contains 'the glorious riches' of God's glory among the Gentiles, involving their salvation, 27*a* (cf. Acts 15:14). The epitome of this mystery is 'Christ in you,' which is the truth that the crucified, resurrected and ascended Christ dwells in the believer, 27*b.* It comprehends the fact that Christ is formed in the regenerate or 'new man' (cf. Gal 2:20; 4:19; 1 Jn 4:12; cf. Eph 4:24). The indwelling Christ is the believer's 'hope of glory ,' 27*c* (Col 3:3-4), since the believer is identified with Him and made one with Him in life and glorious destiny. Christ's glorified humanity in heaven is the guarantee that the believer will be glorified for eternity (1 Jn 3:2). The goal involved in proclaiming this mystery is adulthood or maturity in Christ, 28. It requires labor and conflict, but is wrought by the power of God, 29.

2:1-7. Christ the answer to doctrinal error

1-2. The conflict with error. This involves intense conflict (Gr. *agonia,* 'agony'), 1*a,* because of demonic opposition directed against God's truth (cf. 1 Tim 4:1-5; 1 Jn 4:1-4), especially against that so sublimely glorious as 'the mystery of God,' 2. This spiritual struggle was to the end that God's people at Colossae and Laodicea (see introduction) might be comforted or consoled by the truth, 2*a;* that they might be united in love, 2*b;* that they might have full assurance of salvation brought by understanding the mystery of God, which centers in the grace of God in Christ, 2*c.*

2*c*-7. The answer to error. This is 'the mystery of God,' 2, which is Christ, in whom the fullness of the Godhead became incarnate for the redemption and reconciliation of man. In the incarnate One are 'hidden *all* the treasures of wisdom and knowledge,' 3 (cf. Eph 1:9; 3:9). God incarnate is thus the answer to all error (cf. 1 Jn 4:2-3) including any persuasive speech that shoves Christ from the center of spiritual thought and activity, 4. Paul's desire is that the Colossians will not make this mistake, 5, but will continue to live with Christ focal in their doctrine and conduct, as they had received Him, 6-7.

2:8-13. The peril of false philosophy

8. The warning. 'Philosophy,' literally 'love of knowledge,' is here any system of religious thought that does not make the person and work of Christ central. Unless the believer is extremely wary, he will be 'taken captive,' i.e., victimized by deception, carried off as the prey of empty delusion. Such vain systems of thought are built on that which has been handed down by learned but unbelieving men and are framed according to the elementary principles of the Satanic world system 'rather than on Christ.' In Him alone are hid all the treasures of wisdom and knowledge, 3.

9-13. The remedy. The remedy to false religion centers in Christ and involves: adherence to the truth of His *full* deity in humanity, 9 (Jn 1:14; Col 1:19); recognition of the believer's complete spiritual life in union with Him, 10*a*; recognition of Christ's authority as Head of the Body, the church, as well as all earthly rule and authority, 10*b*; recognition that union with Christ gives the believer a new position. This new position is that of true spiritual circumcision, i.e., the putting off of the 'sinful nature,' 11. The believer is now able to live a life of victory over sin because he has been made alive by the resurrection life Christ has imparted to him, 11-13.

2:14-17. The peril of legalism

14-15. Legal observances were done away in Christ. When the veil of the temple was ripped from top to bottom at Christ's death (Mt 27:51; Jn 1:17; Heb 9:3-8; 10:19-20), the termination of the legal age was indicated. Christ fulfilled the law (Mt 5:17), and by His death liberated us from its condemnation, 14. He erased or blotted out the legal ordinances that condemned us, nailing as it were the certificate of debt that was against us as sinners to the cross (cf. Eph 2:15-16). Moreover, He defeated Satanic and demonic powers which bound us (Eph 6:12; Heb 2:14), making a public spectacle of them in His triumph, 15. In Him we have full emancipation.

16-17. The conclusion. Therefore, no believer is to pass judgment upon another believer in matters of food, observance of a festal day, monthly new moon, or sabbath, 16 (cf. Rom 14:3). The believer is complete in Christ and has been accepted by Him, 10. No brother is, therefore, to reject such a believer because of non-observance of legal minutiae. These legal ceremonies were only types or shadows of the real things that were to come in Christ. Therefore they can neither add to nor subtract from the completeness which the believer enjoys in Him, 17.

2:18-19. The peril of false mysticism

18. The form of the error. This pseudo mysticism took the form of Gnosticism, a spurious knowledge (Gr. *gnosis*) which inculcated a false humility and a worship or veneration of angels, 18*a*. In doing so it looked upon Christ as merely the highest in rank in the order of spirits, impinging upon the full dignity of His person and work by venerating angels. Paul's warning against Gnosticism had called forth magnificent statements of Christ's sublime person (1:15-19) and complete work (1:20-23; 2:9-10). Now he brands its false teachers as audacious intruders, prying into a realm of which they were ignorant and impelled by inflated pride, 18*b*.

19. The reason for the error. This false mysticism resulted from having 'lost connection' to the supreme headship of Christ, 19*a*. Only when the absolute supremacy of Christ is adhered to can the Body, the church, function normally and grow. As is the case of the human body, the Head must direct all the other functions of the Body, 19*b*.

2:20-23. The peril of asceticism

20*a***. The believer's emancipation from legalistic ordinances.** The medium of emancipation is death, the final separation. This is the *position* the believer enjoys in Christ by virtue of identification with Him (Rom 6:3-4). This position of death to legalism of any sort is to be reckoned on (Rom 6:11) and converted into the *experience* of deliverance from legalistic 'do's' and 'don'ts.' These the apostle calls 'the basic principles of this world' (Gr. *kosmos,* 'world system'). It instills a works-merit basis of acceptance with God in opposition to a faith-grace basis founded on the all-sufficiency of Christ's person and work. The tendency is for these elementary principles to produce a legalistic asceticism, dishonoring to the freedom Christ has purchased for those in Him.

20*b***-23. Result of this emancipation.** If freed, why then 'still belong,' i.e., suffer laws to be imposed on oneself or permit oneself to be bound by ordinances, 20*b*? On the contrary, let there be a thorough separation from such regulations as 'Do not handle! Do not taste! Do not touch!' 21. Such legalistic ordinances (as those under the Mosaic law) were divinely intended 'to perish,' in the sense of cessation after Christ came, being used up or consumed when they had discharged their intended function, 22*a*. The imposition of such ordinances now, under grace, is the result of men's commandments and teachings, not God's, 22*b*. Legalism has a wordy show (*logon*), a mere talkative demonstration, but no real manifestation of wisdom, i.e., true wisdom, which makes Christ all in all, 23*a* (cf. 1 Cor 1:30). It is mere 'will worship' (KJV), not Spirit-directed communion with God; 'false humility,' not true submission to the grace of God in Christ, 23*b*. Grace humbles man and exalts God. Such asceticism neither honors God, nor does it gratify the flesh, 23*c*. It is futile in every direction.

3:1-4. Union with Christ and a holy life

1. Basis of a holy life. The basis is the *fact* of union with Christ in resurrection, 1*a,* and in His present heavenly position, 1*b* (Rom 6:5; Eph

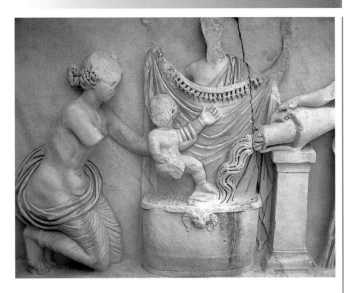

Relief of a child being bathed, from Perga. In Colossians 3, Paul teaches about good relationships within the family.

2:6; Col 2:12; Ps 110:1). Our union is heavenly (*position*). Therefore, our manner of life (*experience*) is also to be heavenly.

2. Exhortations to a holy life. (1) a continuous seeking or striving for spiritual attainments; 'keep seeking (emphatic) the things above,' 2*a;* (2) a continuous 'setting one's thought life upon *the things above, the things above* [doubly emphatic by word position and by repetition] set your mind upon' (Gr.), 2*a*; (3) a clear-cut break with earthly or material things, 'not on earthly things.'

3-4. Reasons for these exhortations. These are: (1) because of the believer's death-to-sin position in Christ, sin thus having no claim on him, 3*a*; (2) because his life is now Christ's and thus 'hidden (laid up in store) with Christ in God,' 3*b*; (3) because Christ is the believer's life, 4*a*; (4) because Christ's manifestation in glory will mean our manifestation with Him, 4*b*. A holy life is possible *now* if we *know* and act on our position in Christ. It is assured *in the future* by our glorification.

3:5-7. Pronouncing death on a sinful life

5*a***. Death sentence declared.** 'Put to death, therefore, whatever belongs to your earthly nature,' or once for all pronounce the death sentence upon any organ or part of the body which may be yielded to sin before the redeemed body has been glorified (cf. Rom 8:13; Gal 5:24).

5*b***-7. Results of failure to pronounce**

Christianity and slavery

Although Paul never condones slavery, arguing to the contrary in Gal 3:28 that the slave and the free man are one in Christ, he does recognise it as part of the law of the land and an inherent part of Roman culture. As a result, he offers instructions to both slaves and slave owners concerning their behavior under Christ. This should not be interpreted, however, as an acceptance of the practice (cf. Philemon and Onesimus).

the death sentence. The organs or members of the redeemed body will fall into the sins enumerated in 5*b*. 'Immorality' is any illicit sexual intercourse, 'impurity' any sexual or bodily perversion. 'Lust' (inordinate affection) is any perverted or unnatural passion (Rom 1:26). 'Evil desire' is the insatiable craving or burning desire generated by such indulgence. 'Greed,' the desire to have more and more, is idolatry because it relegates God to a secondary place or ostracizes Him altogether (Eph 5:5). These sins bring 'the wrath of God' upon the unsaved, 6. Pollution by them will result in severe chastening of believers,7 (cf. 1 Cor 3:12-17; 5:1-5).

3:8-17. Putting on the new self

8-9. Putting off the old. 'The old self' is the unregenerate man with his corrupt human nature (Rom 6:6; Eph 4:22). In position, as *God sees* the believer in Christ, the old man was crucified and *is* dead. The believer is here exhorted to make this good in his *experience* by reckoning or counting it so as a once-for-all act of faith, 8*a*. The figure of an old soiled garment laid aside is used to describe the old life of anger, wrath, malice, evil speaking, filthy talk, and falsehood which has been abandoned, 8-9.

10-17. Putting on the new. For the new self see note on Eph 4:23-30. He is put on as a fresh clean garment, 10. The new man involves (1) a new divine nature (regeneration), 10*b*; (2) a new unity transcending race, social position, etc., 11*a*; (3) a new sphere where Christ is absolutely central, 11*b* (Eph 1:23). His behavior is to be based on the fact that God has chosen, loved and sanctified him, 12*a*; therefore every Christian virtue and grace should be manifested, 12*b*-17.

3:18-4:6. A heavenly walk and domestic relationships

3:18-21. Wives, husbands, children. Wives are to act under two principles: (1) submission to their husbands (cf. Gen 3:16) and (2) what is suitable or proper 'in the Lord,' 18 (cf. Eph5:22; 1 Pet 3:1). No Christian wife is to give blind submission to an unsaved husband if such obedience violates her conscience before God. The supreme duty of a husband is to love his wife, 19 (Eph 5:25), and everything else will follow in due order. Children are to be obedient in all things, because this particularly pleases God, 20 (cf. Eph 6:1). Fathers are to be reasonable with their children to avoid exasperating them and thus discouraging them, 21.

3:22-4:1. Servants, masters. This lengthy instruction must have been partially dictated by the experience of Philemon, a Christian at Colossae, with his runaway slave Onesimus (cf. 4:9; also book of Philemon). Slaves (servants) are to act under a Christian spirit of service, obedience, fidelity and sincerity, 3:22-25. Masters are to act in light of the example set by their supreme Master in heaven, 4:1 (cf. Eph 6:5-9).

4:2-6. General principles. Prayer is to be practiced, 2-4. Wise conduct toward the unsaved, 5*a*; discreet use of time, 5*b*, coupled with sound gracious speech, are to be cultivated, 6.

4:7-18. A holy life and Christian fellowship

7-15. The commendation of fellow workers. A heavenly walk generates warm Christian fraternity.

16-18. Instructions and salutation. Directions are given concerning the public reading of the letter to the Colossians at Laodicea, a nearby town. Paul also requests that the epistle from Laodicea (contents unknown to us) be read at Colossae. Archippus is admonished, 17 (cf. Phm 2). A closing word of greeting is given by Paul, 18.

I THESSALONIANS

Picture of an exemplary church

Writer and date. The first letter to the Thessalonians is likely the earliest of the Pauline epistles. It was penned from Corinth not long after Paul left Thessalonica on his second missionary tour (Acts 16-17, perhaps A.D. 52).

Purpose of the epistle. This letter was written to encourage and establish a young church in the basic truths of the gospel, to inspire it to progress in the power of holy living, and to instruct it in the matter of the coming of the Lord for His own and the relation of this event to the events of the Day of the Lord.

Outline
1:1-10 An exemplary church
2:1-20 A model minister
3:1-4:12 A holy life
4:13-5:28 The coming of Christ and the Day of the Lord

Roman theater and street at Thessaloniki, biblical Thessalonica, capital of the Roman province of Macedonia.

1:1-4. An elect church

1-3. A model assembly. Thessalonica was a very important city on the Thermaic Gulf, SW of Philippi. The apostle, however, takes pride in the Christians there rather than in the great city. The model church recently established, 2, was cause for thanksgiving because of its 'work produced by faith,' its 'labor prompted by love' (love proved by toil) and 'endurance inspired by hope' (in waiting for God's Son from heaven, 1:10), 3.

4. An elect assembly. Election is both individual and corporate. The latter is in view here. The divine order is foreknowledge (1 Pet 1:2), election (choice) and predestination. The foreknown are elected, and the elect are predestinated. This election is certain to every believer. It is wholly by grace (Rom 9:11; 11:56) apart from human merit, and proceeds from the divine will (Jn 15:16; cf. Eph 1:5).

1:5-8. A missionary church

5. Objects of effective evangelism. The gospel which Paul and his fellow workers preached, called 'our gospel', did not come to the Thessalonians in word only, i.e., merely theoretically, but effectively – 'with power,' 'with the Holy Spirit,' and 'with deep conviction,' 5a. Paul himself was an example of this manifestation of God's power, 5b.

6-8. Subjects of effective missionary work. Their effective conversion led to: (1) their following Paul and his fellow workers, and the Lord, 6a; (2) their receiving the Word of God in the midst of tribulation with the joy the Holy Spirit gives, 6b (cf. Acts 13:52); (3) their becoming an example of what Christians should be like to the believers in Macedonia and Achaia (Greece), 7; (4) their missionary zeal in spreading the gospel to the regions beyond, 8 (cf. Rom 10:18).

1:9-10. A serving and waiting church

9. They served God. To do this they manifested their 'work produced by faith,' 3, in that they 'turned to God from idols,' and their labor of love in that they served 'the *living* and *true God*' in contrast to the false, dead idols.

10. They waited for Christ. They manifested their patience of hope in that they waited 'for God's Son from heaven.' He will deliver us from the wrath which is to come upon the unsaved.

2:1-4. Model ministerial conduct under persecution

1-2. Boldness engendered by suffering. It was well known among the Thessalonians that the presentation of the gospel to them was not fruitless or ineffectual, 1. It was characterized by boldness. The suffering which Paul and his associates endured at Philippi (Acts 16:12-40), which involved cruel beating and imprisonment, had emboldened them to declare the gospel of God with great confidence. The result was twofold: abundant spiritual fruit, 1b; and 'strong opposition' (Gr. *agonia),* spiritual struggle and warfare, 2. Far from being cowed and silenced, persecution spurred Paul on to greater liberty and power in preaching.

3-4. Faithfulness called forth by responsibility. Paul's hortatory instruction, i.e., his earnest entreaty, did not have its origin in the desire to deceive or defraud, nor in impurity of motive; nor was it an attempt to bait or entrap its hearers by insidious artifice, 3. Far from such a show of infidelity, it was a model of fidelity. It viewed the gospel as a sacred trust and its heralds solemnly entrusted with it as something exceedingly valuable and easily despoiled, 4. Its heralds viewed themselves as 'approved by God' to be entrusted with the gospel only after rigid testing and approval. Therefore they spoke boldly, not pleasing men but God, who tests men's hearts (Jer 11:20) and who had approved them for this gospel trust.

2:5-8. Unselfish ministry in love

5-7. The proof of selfless love. Negatively, Paul and his colaborers never employed flattery, i.e., insincere praise for unworthy ends as a 'mask' or pretext (that which appears in front or is put forward to hide the true state of things) for covetousness. They never flattered people for material gain, as so many ministers are tempted to do. They could call God to witness this fact, 5. They never sought men's glory, 6a; never were financially or otherwise burdensome, which they might have been under the circumstances, 6b. Positively, they were gentle, i.e., mild or kind as a nursing mother who nourishes her own little children and hence showers real love upon them, 7.

8. The expression of selfless love. Having a strong love for the Thessalonians, Silvanus (Silas, cf. Acts 15:22, 40) and Timothy (1:1) were 'delighted' (heartily willing) to communicate not only the gospel but their very own lives. Why? Because the Thessalonians became 'dear' to them. Love gives the magic touch to ministry for God and others.

2:9-20. Devoted ministry for others

9-12. Devoted ministry described. It is marked (1) by sacrifice, labor and self-denial for others' good and the success of gospel witness, 9; (2) by blamelessness in one's personal life, 10; (3) by fatherly love and patience in instructing and comforting, 11; (4) by the high goal of establishing believers in a life 'worthy of God' and His high calling to His 'kingdom and glory,' 12.

13-20. Results of a devoted ministry indicated. Such service is always God-blessed and fruitful, as it was with the Thessalonians. (1) They received the Word preached as the Word of God, not the word of men, 13*a,* and it operated effectually in them in response to faith, 13*b* (1 Pet 1:23). (2) They became followers (imitators) of the churches of God in Judea, which likewise suffered persecution from apostate Jews, whose unbelief and sins are mentioned, 14-16 (cf. Acts 7:52; 17:5, 13; 18:12). (3) They endeared themselves to the apostle who so earnestly desired to see them again, 17, but was hindered by Satan in his proposed visit, 18. (4) They were Paul's 'hope,' 'joy,' and 'crown,' his reward at the judgement seat of Christ, when the Lord rewards His saints at His coming, 19- 20 (1 Cor 3:12-15; 4:5; 2 Cor 5:10).

3:1-8. Standing fast in the Lord

1-5. The apostle's concern. When Paul had arrived in Athens (cf. Acts 17:15; 18:5), he so desired the Thessalonians' spiritual welfare that he preferred to remain alone, 1, in order that Timothy might be sent to look after their spiritual interests, 2, and to steel them against the afflictions they were called to endure, 3 (2 Tim 3:12). On Paul's visit to Thessalonica he had warned them concerning suffering

Reliefs on the triumphal Arch of Galerius, Roman Thessalonica.

tribulation, 4. Now he is anxious to find out how they had fared. He knew the subtlety of Satanic temptation (2 Cor 11:2-3) and how the results of spiritual labor could be brought to nought, 5*b* (cf. Gal 4:11).

6-8. The apostle's reward. His godly concern for them was rewarded by a good report from Timothy. He 'brought good news' of their faith and love, indicating that the Thessalonians held the apostle in happy memory and that they were as earnestly desirous of seeing him as he was of seeing them, 6. This greatly consoled the apostle, 7. He declared, 'For now we really live, since you are standing firm in the Lord,' 8 (Eph 6:13-14; Phil 4:1). Such standing is the key to spiritual health. It is the antidote against all error.

3:9-13. Apostolic prayer for holiness

9-10. The question. The petition, 11-13, is prefaced by a question, 9-10. How can God be thanked enough for all the joy the

Thessalonians have given Paul by their spiritual perseverance, 9? This thanksgiving accompanies his request to see them again that he might complete anything that might be deficient in their faith, 10.

11-13. The petition. He prays that God might direct or clear the way for them, 11. Further, he asks that the Lord might make them 'increase' (have abundance) and 'overflow' in love, 12, to the end that God might establish their hearts blameless in holiness (separation to God). The time of reckoning before God will come at the second advent when those who have died in Christ (as in 4:14) are brought with the descending Lord when He catches His living saints up to meet Him in the air (4:13-17).

4:1-8. Divine call to holiness
1-3. The authority behind the call. The authority is God's. 'We ask you and urge you in the Lord Jesus,' 1. Cf. God has called us 'to live a holy life,' 7. He therefore that rejects this call rejects God, 8.

4-8. The call itself. We are called to a life pleasing to God, 1. This involves a life set apart unto God (experiential sanctification), 3a, which is characterized by abstention from sexual immorality, 3b; by sexual temperance, 5; and by rigidly avoiding adultery, 4-5. This call to holiness emphasizes sexual purity because: (1) the Lord is the avenger (punisher) of all who practice sexual promiscuity, 6; (2) He has called us to holiness, 7, emphatically not to uncleanness; (3) His authority is behind the prohibition, 8a; (4) God has provided the Holy Spirit to give each believer victory and sanctity in this area of life, 8b.

4:9-12. The elements of a holy life
9-10. The basic element of love. 'Brotherly love' is so indispensable and obvious to a holy life that the apostle declares the Thessalonians have no need for written instruction. They have been taught by God to love one another, 9 (cf. Jn 15:12, 17; Jas 2:8; 1 Jn 3:11-18), and are commended for the exhibition of their love, but urged to increase more and more, 10.

11-12. Other elements enjoined. (1) *Quietness.* 'Make it your ambition to lead a quiet life,' i.e., to live peaceably or have a tranquil spirit. (2) *Industry.* 'Mind your own business' (1 Pet 4:15), rather than being a meddler or a busybody in others' affairs. (3) *Responsibility.* 'Work with your hands,' i.e., not be lazy, shiftless, nor a parasite on others, 11-12b (cf. 2 Thess 3:10- 12). (4) *Honesty* in one's life and testimony toward the unsaved, 12.

4:13-18. The believer's hope
13-15. The blessed hope. Hope is faith-produced confidence and expectation of the future. The great obstacle to hope for the unbeliever is death. This obstacle is removed in Christ. Believers do not really die, they merely 'sleep,' 13. This is true because Jesus died and rose again (1 Cor 15:20, 52). Therefore, since believers are united to the risen Lord (Rom 6:4; Col 3:1-4), when they die physically they fall asleep 'with Jesus.' When Christ returns He will bring their souls and spirits with Him to be united with their risen bodies, 14. But the saints still alive physically when the Lord returns for His own shall not go before those who have fallen asleep in Jesus, 15.

16-18. The Lord's coming. The answer to the Christian's hope is the return of the resurrected, ascended Christ to raise the bodies of those who died in the Lord and to glorify the living saints. 'The Lord himself,' personally, bodily, 'will come down from heaven, with a loud command, with the voice of the archangel and with the trumpet call of God.' The 'loud command' is the shout of triumph over death (1 Cor 15:54-57), manifested in the raising of the dead saints and in the instantaneous glorification of the living saints, who will never taste physical death. 'The voice of the archangel' is evidently that of Michael (cf. Dan 12:1-2). The dead in Christ rise first, then immediately the saints who are living when the Lord comes and remain to that hour 'will be caught up,' suddenly conveyed away in the 'clouds' to meet the Lord in the air. In this manner the saints will forever be with the Lord. This is the comfort and hope of the Christian, 18.

5:1-11. The Day of the Lord
1-3. The Day of the Lord – what it is. The apostle has just described the coming of the Lord for His own. This inaugurates 'the day of Christ' with glorification and reward for the

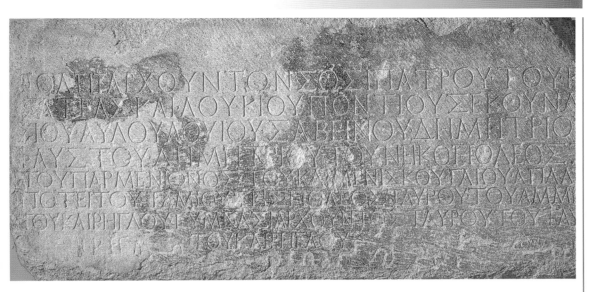

This important inscription, found at the Gate of Vardar at Thessalonica, names six of the 'politarchs' who ruled the city.

translated church saints (1 Cor 1:8; 5:5; 2 Cor 1:14; Phil 1:6, 10; 2:16). Now Paul turns to the subject of the 'Day of the Lord.' By contrast, it concerns the restoration of the kingdom to Israel (Acts 1:6-7; 3:19-21), and the earth judgments which take place prior to the setting up of that kingdom (cf. Isa 2:6-22; Jer 30:5-9). It was no new revelation, hence Paul had no need to write about it, 1. It will come unexpectedly, like a thief, upon the ungodly, i.e. those in darkness (cf. Mt 24:36-51; 25:5), when mankind will have hoped to attain world peace, 3.

4-11. The Day of the Lord and the believer. These earth judgments and the outpoured divine wrath do not fall upon believers, 4, because they are sons of light, 5-8 (cf. Eph 5:8), and because God has not appointed them to wrath but to 'salvation through our Lord Jesus Christ,' 9. The wrath of God will not fall upon those 'in Christ,' 10, because they will be glorified and removed (1 Thess 4:13-17) before these end-time manifestations of God's wrath (Rev 3:10). This is their comfort and edification, 11.

5:12-15. Exhortations toward mutual harmony
12-13. Showing honor to those in places of responsibility in the Lord. Believers are to regard or recognize these brethren with the favor and respect due them: (1) because of their consecrated labors in the cause of Christ, 12a: (2) because of their God-ordained position as those set or appointed with authority over believers, 12b; (3) because of their wisdom and counsel (they 'admonish,' i.e., put in mind or warn, God's people), 12c; (4) because of their good 'work,' 13a.

13b-15. General admonitions for harmony. (1) The basic principle of living in peace is to rule in all relationships, 13b. (2) Believers are to admonish or warn the idle, that is, those neglectful of duties, derelict in responsibility, 14. The word 'idle' (*ataktos*) is used of soldiers who desert their ranks. Other responsibilities include: (3) comforting the faint-hearted or discouraged (*oligopsuchoi*, literally 'little souled'); (4) supporting or exercising a zealous care for the weak, the infirm, those deficient in mental, moral or spiritual strength; (5) being patient (long tempered) toward all (cf. Eph 4:2); (6) seeing (take care, see to it) that none render evil for evil, 15a (cf. Prov 20:22; 24:29; Mt 5:39, 44), 'but always try to be kind to each other and to everyone else, 15b.

5:16-22. Various exhortations
16-18. Rejoice, pray, be thankful. Literal translations: '*Always* (the emphasis) keep on rejoicing,'16 (cf. Phil 3:1; 4:4); '*unceasingly* (emphatic) go on praying,' 17; '*in everything* be grateful.' The reason is that thankfulness is God's will for His people, 18.

19. Do not quench the Spirit. We grieve the Spirit by unconfessed sin (Eph 4:30). We *quench* (stifle, dampen) the Spirit by disobedience to God's will.

20-22. Other injunctions. 'Do not treat prophesies [the truth of God as declared by a prophet] with contempt,' 20. Examine everything carefully. Adhere to the good, 21. 'Abstain from every kind (emphatic) of evil,' 22.

5:23-24. Sanctification for the whole man

23. The whole man set apart for God. To be set apart for God is the idea of the Gr. adjective *hagios* ('holy') which in its verbal form means sanctify or make holy. This work of sanctification is the operation of God Himself. It is not a human accomplishment.

Sanctification results in 'the peace of God' (Phil 4:7); therefore the divine Sanctifier is called 'the God of peace.' It involves the whole nature of man: *body,* the material tent (2 Cor 5:1-8) in which man pilgrims in this world and with its five senses has communication with the natural world; *soul,* the seat of affections, desires, will and emotions (Mt 11:29; 26:38; Jn 12:27); *spirit,* the higher part of man which knows (1 Cor 2:11) and has communion with God (Job 32:8; Ps 18:28; Prov 20:27).

Sanctification itself is in three tenses: *past,* the believer *was* sanctified positionally in Christ at regeneration (1 Cor 1:2), so that every believer is called a saint; *present,* the believer experientially should be continually being set apart unto God (2 Thess 2:13); *future* – full conformity to Christ in glorification (1 Jn 3:1-3).

24. The certainty of complete sanctification. God effects sanctification. He guarantees our past unchangeable position as complete in Christ and thereby makes certain our future glorification. The Holy Spirit makes it possible for the believer to realize the present experiential or practical sense of sanctification in his daily life (1 Cor 10:13; 2 Thess 3:3; Gal 5:16).

5:25-28. Closing charge

25-26. Request for prayer. 'Brothers, keep on praying for us,' 25 (Gk.). The Lord's servants need the constant prayers of God's people. 'Greet all the brothers with a holy kiss,' 26. This was customary among early Christians, especially in the high tide of spiritual love/which often prevailed.

27-28. Charge concerning reading. 'I charge you before the Lord to have this letter read to all the brothers,' 27. The closing salutation, 28, is characteristic of the Pauline epistles.

2 THESSALONIANS

Comfort in persecution

Writer and occasion. Paul was the writer (1:1). The occasion was a misunderstanding among the Thessalonians regarding the coming of Christ for His own. (1 Thess 4:13-17) and the Day of the Lord (1 Thess 5:1-10). Because these believers were being persecuted severely, they erroneously concluded that the Day of the Lord had arrived (2:2). Paul writes to correct this misconception.

Date. This epistle was written after 1 Thessalonians in the early 50's.

Outline

Chapter 1. The coming of the Lord and comfort in present persecution
Chapter 2. The coming of the Lord and the Day of the Lord
Chapter 3. The coming of the Lord and practical Christian living

Bust of the Emperor Nero, A.D. 54-68. Nero was a notorious persecutor of the Christians. The church at Thessalonica was being severely persecuted when Paul wrote this epistle.

1:1-4. The church recommended

1-2. The greeting. As in the first epistle, the apostle associates Silvanus (Silas, cf. Acts 15:22, 40) and Timothy with himself in saluting 'the church of the Thessalonians' (see 1 Thess 1:1).

3-4. The commendation. Paul was bound to express thanks to God for the Thessalonians because their faith was growing and their love was abounding toward one another, 3. The result was that the apostle was able to 'boast' of them (cf. 2 Cor 9:2) and thus give a laudatory testimony concerning them in the church of God (local assemblies) for their patient and faithful conduct under persecution, 4 (cf. Jas 5:11).

1:5-10 The church comforted

5-6. The reason for their sufferings. Their tribulations were not an accident or piece of ill luck but clearly the will of God, 'evidence' of the righteous decision of God, 5*a*, to test or prove them worthy of the kingdom of God, 5*b*. It was really for the kingdom of God that they suffered, 5*c* (1 Thess 2:14; Heb 10:32-33).

7-10. The basis of comfort. The second advent of Christ in glory, 7-8, will witness the vengeance of God on those who do not know Him and have not obeyed the gospel of salvation by believing, 8. Those who persecuted the Thessalonians belonged to this category. This will involve eternal dismissal (not annihilation) from God's presence in a separate eternal isolation ward reserved for sinners (cf. Rev 20:10-15) called Gehenna or eternal hell, which is eternal separation from God, 9-10.

1:11-12. Intercession for the church

11. The prayer. Paul constantly interceded for the Thessalonians, asking that God would count their conduct and Christian achievement worthy of their high calling (cf. Eph 4:1-3; Col 3:14), each believer fulfilling God's will in His power through faith manifested by good works.

12. The purpose. That the Lord might be magnified in them and they in the Lord according to the grace given them.

2:1-5. The church's outtaking and the Day of the Lord

1-2. A misunderstanding exposed.

The Thessalonians thought their sufferings (1:5-12) meant that the Day of the Lord had arrived, 2, that the end-time period of worldwide judgment (Rev 6-19) had dawned, making way for the setting up of Christ's kingdom (Rev 19:16-20:10). The apostle pleads against this mistake by citing again the truth that Christ's coming would be *before* the day of the Lord, 1, a teaching he had outlined in the first epistle (4:13-18). He warns clearly against the speciousness of the error, 2-3*a,* and describes the first phase of Christ's coming *for* His saints as the personal presence (*parousia*) of our Lord Jesus Christ, coupled with our gathering to Him (*episunagoge*), as outlined in 1 Thess 4:13-17.

3-5. The error refuted. *Before* the Day of the Lord bursts upon a Christ-rejecting world, there must *first* come the apostasy or falling away. This is not simply the departure from the faith often characterizing the church age (1 Tim 4:1-5; 2 Tim 3:1-8; Rev 3:14-22), but the wholesale rebellion and thoroughgoing lapse into error and demonism of the period just preceding Christ's advent in glory (Lk 18:8; Rev 9:20-21). There must also come the revelation of the Antichrist, here called the 'man of lawlessness,' the last great demon-inspired ruler (Dan 11:36; Rev 13:1-10; 19:20; 20:10). He will arrogate to himself divine honors and deceive end-time Jewry regathered to Israel, 4. The apostle had plainly taught these truths when he founded the Thessalonian church, 5.

2:6-9. The church's outtaking and the man of sin

6-7. The church's outtaking and the Holy Spirit. The One who holds back the full development and manifestation of the demonic forces of evil in this era (cf. 8-10), is the Holy Spirit. He has been forming and indwelling the church ever since Pentecost (Jn 14:16; Acts 2:1-4; 1 Cor 6:19), and will do so until He 'is taken out of the way,' literally comes out of the midst, when He leaves in the distinctive sense in which He came at Pentecost. This takes place at the time the church, indwelt by the Spirit, is taken to meet Christ in the air (1 Thess 4:13-17). Only when the divine Restrainer is taken away with the glorified church can and will the Antichrist be made manifest, 6, and 'the secret power of lawlessness' come to the full.

**8-9. The church's outtaking and the

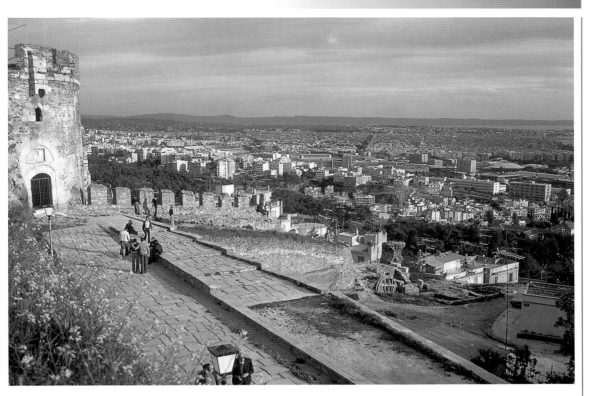

man of sin. 'Then,' *after* the Holy Spirit is taken out of the way, the lawless one will be revealed. This sinister personage sums up 'the secret power of lawlessness,' or the full development of last-day miracle-working demonism (Rev 9:1-21; 12:7-17; 16:13-16). He will be destroyed by Christ's advent in glory (Rev 19:20; 20:10) and Satan will be bound in the abyss (Rev 20: 1-3).

2:10-12. The church's outtaking and latter-day truth rejecters

10. The doom of truth rejecters. Demonic deception, operative during the church age in a restricted sense because of the Holy Spirit's restraining operation, 6-9 (cf. 1 Tim 4:1-4; 1 Jn 4:15), will burst forth with irresistible power. Those 'who are perishing,' 10*a,* are the unsaved multitudes still living on the earth after the church is translated. Rejecting truth when it was available results now in demonic delusion 'because they refused to love the truth and so be saved,' 10, i.e., before the church was glorified.

11-12. The reason for their doom. Because they did not love and accept the truth when it was available, 10*b,* God sends them a 'powerful delusion,' an inworking or energy of deception, to believe 'the lie,' i.e., the supreme deception of accepting the Antichrist, 11 (Jn 5:43; Rev 13:8, 16-18). The delusion is sent so that they all might be judged and found guilty for not having believed the truth, but having had pleasure in unrighteousness instead, 12.

2:13-17. The church's outtaking and the Thessalonians

13-14. The Thessalonians were a cause for thanks because they were God's beloved and elect (see notes on 'Divine election' and 'Foreordination' in Eph 1:1-6). They were chosen to salvation and sanctification. In contrast to the deceived of the last days, they loved and hence believed 'the truth.' They were saved under the preaching of Paul's 'gospel,' 14*a,* to be sharers of Christ's glory 14*b* (Rom 8:17; 2 Tim 2:12).

15-17. They were objects of exhortation and prayer. The exhortation is to steadfastness and fidelity to the 'teachings or traditions' taught them, 15. The prayer is for comfort and establishment or grounding 'in every good deed' (practice) 'and word' (doctrine).

3:1-5. Apostolic request for prayer

1-2. The request. The petition is twofold: (1) That the Word of God may run without obstruction and victoriously, as an athlete in a race (1 Cor 9:24, 26), that it may progress freely and advance rapidly and be glorified. The Word is always glorified when it has free course because the God of the Word is thereby exalted. (2) That the apostle might be delivered (rescued) from 'wicked and evil' men, men out of place or order, i.e., not being where God would have them. Being unoriented toward God they are troublesome and wicked. Being without faith (cf. Heb 11:6), they lacked the starting point for deliverance from sin and orientation toward God.

3-5. The basis for the request. The Lord's faithfulness and Paul's confidence in the Thessalonians constituted the ground for the apostle's prayer, 3-4. He asks that the Lord would direct them along the straight path 'into God's love and Christ's perseverance,' 5 (cf. 1 Thess 4:13-17; 2 Thess 2:1-3).

3:6-15. Instruction concerning disciplinary separation

6. The general principle of separation. The injunction is to withdraw oneself from every believer who goes on living disorderly, in neglect of the common duties of life, like a soldier who deserts his regiment and disregards 'the teaching,' i.e., the transmitted tradition (cf. 2 Thess 2:15) he has received from the apostle, 6.

7-9. The apostolic example. Paul gave not only doctrine to guide, but his life as an example, 7-8. He toiled with his own hands as a tentmaker, that he might not be an expense or burden upon any of those to whom he ministered, 8. He did this not because he had no right to expect support, but in order to furnish an example that the Thessalonians might follow, 9.

10-11. The disorder specified. A disturbing attitude was evidently present among the Thessalonian believers. It was apparently a presumptuous piety that attempted to be heavenly minded but shirked the common duties of earthly existence, such as working and supporting oneself and one's dependents. Paul gives a straightforward cure. No work – no food, 10. He puns on the word 'work,' 11 – not just workers (*ergazomenoi*) but workers-around

(*periergazamoi*), i.e., intensive workers in the wrong way or 'busybodies,' 11*b* (cf. 1 Tim 5:13; 1 Pet 4:15).

12-15. The cure indicated. The cure was plain. (1) First, they were to 'settle down and earn the bread they eat,' not complaining, gossiping, or prying into others' business. (2) Secondly, they were to eat *their own* food and not be a parasite on others, 12. (3) The orderly believers were to be unwearied in continuance of their well-doing, furnishing an example to the disorderly, 13. (4) The obstinately disobedient were to be marked or noted, 14*a*. (5) The faithful were not to mix or associate intimately with the disorderly, in order to shame them, 14*b*. (6) Yet such a disorderly brother was not to be reckoned as an enemy, but warned as a brother, 15 (cf. 2 Cor 6:14-17; Lev 19:17).

3:16-18. Concluding benediction

16, 18. The benediction. 'The Lord of peace' (Jn 14:27; Heb 13:20) was to grant them peace by His personal presence, 16. 'The grace of our Lord Jesus Christ' is pronounced upon 'all' (God's people), 18, 17. The salutation was Paul's own signature, which was the token or pledge and assurance of the genuineness of his letters.

I TIMOTHY

Directions for church order

The writer and date. Paul is the writer (1:1). The epistle is one of the pastoral letters and dated later in Paul's life; how late depends upon the question of whether the apostle had one or two imprisonments. If there were two, it was apparently written during the interval between the two, not later than A.D. 66. If there was but one, the letter was penned not long before the apostle's last trip to Jerusalem, probably A.D. 64.

The theme. The central thought of I Timothy is on church order, soundness of faith, and ecclesiastical discipline (ch. 1-3). This was natural after numerous churches were established and the government of local assemblies came to the fore. It was also inevitable that instruction to settled pastors should be given after the churches were founded (ch. 4-6).

Outline

Chapter 1 The discipline of sound doctrine
Chapter 2 The discipline of prayer and public worship
Chapter 3 The discipline of church government
Chapter 4-6 The discipline of the local pastor

View of the stage of the theater, Ephesus. Timothy was a leader of the church in this major city of Asia Minor.

teachers, they are characterized by ignorance of true knowledge or genuine experience, 7.

1:8-11. The law and the gospel of Christ

8-10. The purpose of the law. The law itself is good, 8a (cf. Rom 7:12), but it must be employed (made use of) lawfully, i.e., properly or legitimately, in line with the glorious gospel committed to Paul's trust, 11. Its purpose is to convict the sinner (the unrighteous) and to lead him to the Saviour that he might be declared righteous by faith (Rom 3:21-28; Eph 2:8-10). In no sense is the law to be used for the righteous (justified) man, either to justify him or to sanctify him. It is intended to reveal to the sinner his sin and its penalty apart from Christ, 9-10.

11. The purpose of the gospel. It is 'the glorious gospel of the blessed God,' 11a. It is the good news which heralds God's excellence in manifesting His gracious love for sinners by providing for their salvation (Jn 3:16). What the law could never do, grace does (Jn 1:17; Tit 3:4-5).

1:12-17. The gospel of Christ and the sinner

12-15. Salvation and commission of Paul the sinner. The apostle's ministry of salvation was the result of God's saving grace, 12, manifested toward a great sinner, a blasphemer, a persecutor of God's people and 'violent man' 13a (Acts 8:3; 1 Cor 15:9). He received God's mercy because he committed his sin in ignorance and unbelief, 13b, the abundance of God's grace being shown toward him, 14. Paul was an illustration of the great truth that the incarnation of God in Christ was for the purpose of saving sinners, in which category he placed himself first, 15. This grand fact is a 'trustworthy saying' i.e. true and indubitably sure, worthy of hearty reception and universal cordial assent.

16-17. Paul's salvation an example for all believing sinners. The apostle was to be a pattern of God's gracious patience and love toward sinners in Christ, 16. God is 'the King eternal, immortal, invisible [Jn 1:18], the only God' to whom all honor and glory are to be given forever, 17, because of the salvation He has provided in Christ.

1:1-7. The pastor and sound doctrine

1-4. The pastor and unsound teachers. Paul greets Timothy as a pastor and as 'my true son in the faith,' 1-2. In such a capacity he urges the younger man to assume responsibility against unsound teachers, 3-4. A pastor must first be sound himself before he can assume such responsibility. Timothy was urged to remain at Ephesus (cf. Acts 20:1-3) that he might instruct the leaders that they not 'teach false doctrines,' i.e., 'false' in the sense of different from and at variance with sound Christian truth, 3; and that they not 'devote themselves to myths,' i.e., religious fictions, such as the myths that honeycomb paganism, nor 'endless [interminable] genealogies,' in which Judaism prided itself. Why? These unprofitable exercises offer only fruitless questionings rather than the acceptance of God's stewardship, i.e., the discharge of His plan and purpose as seen in the gospel. Their stewardship is known by faith, 4.

5-7. The pastor and legalists. In contrast to the unsound teachers' empty legalism, the goal of Christ's commandment (cf. Jn 13:34; 15:12; Gal 6:2) is love, born out of a pure (clean) heart, out of a good conscience, and out of sincere faith, 5. Those who have missed the mark through legalism have turned aside to 'meaningless talk' – discussion of meaningless words, 6. Desiring to be law-

Ephesus

Harbor gymnasium and baths

Stadium

City Wall

Theater

Arkadiane

Mount Pion

Temple of Hadrian

Library of Celsus

East gymnasium

Temple of Domitian

Mount Coressus

1:18-20. The charge to Timothy the pastor

18-19a. The charge. The solemn exhortation and injunction to Paul's 'son' Timothy, since he was evidently Paul's convert, is that he might wage a successful spiritual conflict, 18b (cf. 2 Tim 4:2; Heb 9:14). Predictions of such a ministry were made earlier in the younger man's life and would not fail to be realized in him.

19b-20. The warning. The case of Hymenaeus and Alexander (2 Tim 2:17-18) offers an example to the contrary. Teaching error concerning the resurrection, Hymenaeus had destroyed the faith of some. By apostolic authority Paul had delivered these false teachers to Satan, 20 (cf. 1 Cor 5:5; 11:30-32; 1 Jn 5:16). This involved serious chastening (Heb 12:6), even to the point in some cases of physical death.

2:1-8. The church and public prayer

1-2a. The general injunction. Prayer both public and private has a primacy. Paul exhorted, therefore, that 'requests, prayers, intercession and thanksgiving be made for everyone,' 1, especially for civil rulers and authorities, 2a (Rom 13:1).

2b-8. Reasons for prayer. (1) That Christians may lead a tranquil and quiet life in godliness and dignity, 2b, in accord with God's will, 3. (2) Because God's desire is the salvation of men in which prayer has an important place, 4. (3) Because the incarnation and redemptive work of Christ gave new power and outreach in prayer, 5-6 (cf. Jn 16:23-28). Paul was divinely commissioned as a preacher (herald or proclaimer) and an apostle (delegated one) of these truths concerning prayer, 7. He was to instruct believers in the proper prayer attitude and exercise, 7-8.

2:9-15. The order of women in Christian society

9-10. A Christian woman's demeanor and dress. As the Christian man's life is to be adorned by prayer, so the Christian woman is to beautify herself with the proper 'cosmetic.' Positively, this is well-ordered (i.e., proper) dress. Without, there is to be befitting dress; within, proper adornment of heart manifested

Artist's impression of Luke the physician and gospel writer. It is through Luke's account of Paul's missionary tours in Acts that we know a little about Timothy, companion to Paul on the second tour.

the sense of acting in independent power or domineering over them, 12.

The reason for subjection is outlined, 13-15. (1) Adam was created as federal head of the race before Eve was formed, 13. (2) Eve was formed from Adam, not Adam from Eve. (3) The woman, not the man, was deceived, 14, and is still peculiarly subject to doctrinal deception. (4) She will be 'kept safe,' i.e., be rescued and preserved from the dangers of insubordination, deception, and teaching doctrinal error which the apostle hints at, by cultivating her highest call of childbearing. Her real honor is in producing and training godly offspring, 15.

3:1-7. The qualifications of overseers

1. The honor of the office. It is a fact that if anyone earnestly desires, in the sense of setting his heart upon, the office of an overseer (*episkopes*), he desires 'a noble task' (office, position of watching over the flock of God).

2-7. The qualifications of the office. The ideal overseer must be: (1) above reproach, not to be laid hold of by some blot on his character; irreprehensible; (2) a one-wife man, not an adulterer, divorced or polygamous, although he may be an unmarried man; (3) vigilant, watchful, circumspect; (4) sober, serious-minded; (5) of good behavior, well-ordered with a life focused on Christ; (6) given to hospitality, literally a stranger-lover; (7) gifted and qualified to teach, 2; (8) not addicted to wine and hence not intemperate and violent; (9) not quarrelsome, that is, not a violent, quick-tempered person apt to give a blow in a fit of anger; (10) not covetous or greedy; (11) patient, mild or gentle; (12) not a brawler, literally a nonfighter; (13) one who controls his own family well, having his children well-disciplined, 4. If a man is defective in the control of his own family how can he be qualified to take care of the house of God (the local church), 5? (14) An elder must not be a novice, one newly planted in the Christian church, a new convert. Such an inexperienced, untested believer is peculiarly exposed to the sin of pride that caused Satan's original fall and still characterizes him, 6 (Isa 14:12-14; Ezek 28:12-19; 1 Tim 6:9; 2 Tim 2:26). (15) He must also be one having a good reputation (testimony) among the unsaved, 7.

by modesty and a serious attitude toward her place in Christian society, 9a. Negatively, to spell out the positive injunction, Christian women are not to adorn themselves with 'braided' hair (from root *pleko,* to interweave or plait), or with costly jewelry, 9b. This does not suggest drab dress, but modest adornment, becoming a woman's position as a Christian. That which is worldly or unbefitting these criteria is to be avoided, whether a woman is queen or commoner. Positively again, the real adornment or cosmetic of the godly woman is to be her good works.

11-15. A Christian woman's reaction to men. A Christian woman is to be characterized by a spirit of teachableness and of quiet submission to her husband, 11 (1 Cor 14:34-35; cf. Gen 3:16). The opposite attitude is most unbecoming to a woman professing godliness. Paul himself did not permit women to teach men or usurp authority over them, in

3:8-13. The qualifications of deacons

8-12. Their qualifications. The deacons were charged with the financial and temporal administrations of the local church, as the overseers were charged with the more directly spiritual aspects. The deacons' qualifications are largely the same as the overseers, 8-10, 12 (cf.2-7). The qualifications of their wives, 11, doubtless also apply to overseers' wives.

13. Their reward. They who discharge the office well acquire (gain or earn) for themselves an 'excellent standing,' literally a step, or stair, in the sense of dignity of rank. They also attain boldness and freedom of speech which the Spirit gives to those who gain confidence and assurance by virtue of fidelity to a Christ-centered faith.

3:14-16. The church and revealed truth

14-15. The church and its relation to revealed truth. Paul intends Timothy to be instructed in church management and discipline. If the apostle cannot do this orally, he will write, 14-15a. It is important to know how one, particularly a pastor, ought to conduct himself in the house of God (the local church). 'The church of the living God' (the Body of Christ) is the pillar or column in the sense of the support holding up the root of truth. It is also the ground or foundation of truth in that the Holy Spirit teaches the revealed truth of God (the Bible) only to believers, members of the true church.

16. The gist of revealed truth. This verse refers to the basic body of divine revelation made known in Scripture and may well have constituted an early Christian hymn. It is avowedly 'great' because it embraces God's eternal plans and purposes in Christ centering in redeemed man. It involves a 'mystery,' i.e., revealed truth previously hidden but now made known, which still transcends man's full comprehension. This mystery has its goal in godliness, that is, restoring lost mankind to a state of godlikeness where man is united to Christ and enabled to fellowship with and worship his Creator. It centers in Christ: (1) His *incarnation* – God 'appeared in a body' (Jn 1:1, 18); (2) His *resurrection* by the power of the Holy Spirit vindicating and proving true all His claims (Rom 1:4); (3) His *post-resurrection appearances* witnessing to the spirit world of

Remains of the Temple to the Emperor Hadrian, Ephesus. Emperor worship remained a challenge to the early Christians.

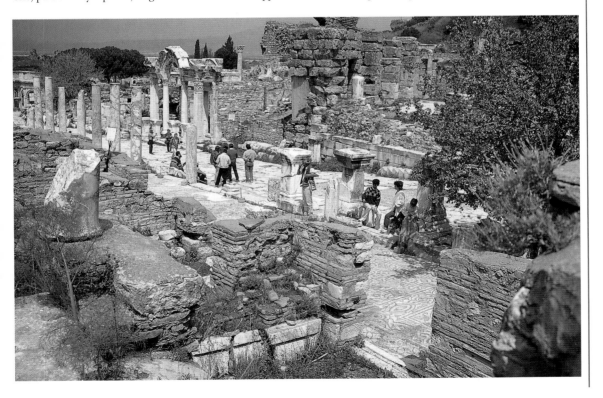

His person (Mt 28:2- 7); (4) His *gospel* – 'preached among the nations' (Gal 1:16); (5) His *church and Body* – constituted by those who 'believed on [Him] in the world'; (6) His *ascension* – 'taken up in glory' (Acts 1:9-11).

4:1-6. The pastor and doctrinal error

1-2. Demonism the source of doctrinal error. The well-instructed pastor must know the real origin of false teaching to deal with it adequately. Therefore the Holy Spirit speaks plainly on this point. He declares unequivocally that error is instigated *not* primarily by the false teacher but by the evil spirits or demons energizing the false teacher. This truth is enunciated by the fact that when some depart from the faith (Jude 3), they are said to give heed to (take up with) seducing spirits rather than the false teachers. The result is doctrines of demons – not teachings about demons (demonology) but errors originated by demons. These teachers, teaching falsehoods in hypocrisy, are mere insincere actors or pretenders, whose conscience is cauterized into insensitivity to differentiate good from evil, error from truth.

3-6. An illustration. The apostle selects a current error, a kind of legalistic asceticism, to illustrate the fact that false doctrine is demon-originated. It forbids marriage (as if this God-ordained institution were evil, and thus incriminates God), and the eating of certain foods, which the apostle shows were created by God to be received with thanksgiving and prayer, 3-5. The demonic impress in this doctrine is apparent, displaying Satanic pride (Isa 14:12-14), slander of God's goodness (Gen 3:5), and clear falsehood (Gen 3:4). As a good pastor Timothy is to show the source of error and teach truth, 6.

4:7-16. The pastor and self-discipline

7-11. Self-discipline in public ministry. This involves faithfully teaching truth (cf. 6); refusing or rejecting 'godless myths and old wives' tales,' which are profane, not being connected with holiness or godliness; and exercising toward a goal of godliness rather than toward mere physical conditioning, the benefits of which are temporary in contrast to both the temporal and eternal benefits of godliness, 8. This is a completely reliable directive, 9, for the reason given in 10. Our hope is in the 'living God,' who through Christ's sacrifice has made humanity 'savable,' and who actually saves those who believe. Self-discipline also involves the diligent teaching of these things, 11.

12-16. Self-discipline in private ministry. Timothy, the young man, is to give no occasion for anyone to look down upon his youth. He is rather to be an example or model to God's people, 12. In his ministry he is to emphasize reading (scholarly study of the Scripture), exhortation (preaching) and doctrine (teaching). He is not to neglect the spiritual gift he possesses. There is evidently reference here to the charge given him at his ordination, 14. He is to meditate or continually bestow careful thought upon these matters, so that his progress or advancement in spiritual maturity may be apparent to everyone. This means he must pay particular attention to this living as well as to his teaching. In persevering in these matters he will save himself in the sense of deliverance from pastoral pitfalls, and rescue the people to whom he ministers from common snares in the Christian life.

5:1-16. The care of widows

1-2. Conduct toward various Christians. *Elders* are not to be the objects of verbal violence. The *young men* are to be treated as 'brothers,' the *older women* with parental respect and love. Sisterly purity is to mark Timothy's relations with the *younger women.*

3-16. Treatment of Christian widows. Widows who are really destitute are to be honored and provided for, 3. Those who have children or other relatives ought to be supported by them, 4. Real widows trust God, 5, something which is not true of those who live in voluptuous pleasure and luxury, 6-7. Such are not to be supported by the church. Relatives are under obligation to support widows within their families, 8. No widow under 60 was to be church-supported. Those who are, must fulfill certain conditions, 10. Younger widows are not to be supported for various reasons, 11-13, but are encouraged to marry and bear children, 14-15. Insofar as possible the church is to be responsible only for real widows, 16.

they precede the sinner to judgment. In the case of others, their sins follow after or catch up with them and appear as the sequel to their evildoing, 24. In like manner the good works of some believers are obvious and manifest. However, those good works and deeds of love which are not open to everyone's sight cannot be hid, certainly not from God, and not even altogether from men, 25.

6:1-5. Directions for servants and masters

1-2. The general directive (cf. Eph 6:5-9 with comments). The apostle takes the social custom that prevailed and inculcates the Christian ethic as applicable to the prevailing institution, as wrong as the institution itself may have been, 1-2. (Cf. also Col 3:22-4:1 with comments).

3-5. Denunciation of false teachers. Those who reject wholesome (sound) words and doctrines which result in godliness, 3, are described in their true light. They suppose that gain is godliness, 4-5.

6:6-10. Warning directed to the rich

6-8. The blessing of godly contentment. Gain is not godliness, 5, but godliness with contentedness is *great gain* (emphatic), 6. Contentment is satisfaction with one's lot in the will of God (Heb 13:5). Since we brought nothing material into this world nor do we take anything material out, 7, having food and clothing we should be satisfied, 8 (cf. Gen 28:20-21).

9-10. The curse of ungodly wealth. The curse is not in wealth itself, but in the wrong attitude toward it. They that make a deliberate choice to be rich, select a course of life motivated by the desire for worldly wealth. As a result they pay the penalty of falling into temptations others never have to face. Such ungodly wealth also proves to be a snare. Like a trap that deprives an animal of freedom and life, it traps men in 'many foolish and harmful desires' so strong they become irresistible and result in personal and moral ruin. Instead of bringing contentment it is '*a root*' (emphatic) of all sorts of evils, such as covetousness, apostasy from the faith, and piercing sorrows.

5:17-22. Concerning elders

17-20. Honor due them (cf.5:1). Teaching elders (pastors) are to be considered worthy of 'double honor' – honor of position and honor of financial support, 17-18 (cf. Deut 25:4; 1 Cor 9:7, 11; Lk 10:7). They are not to be irresponsibly accused, 19 (cf. Deut 19:15). However, those who sin are to be publicly rebuked for the sake of others who may be tempted, 20.

21-22. Timothy's responsibility. Like all pastors, Timothy is solemnly warned against partiality and prejudice in dealing with God's people, 21 (cf. Jas 2:1-12). He is also warned against ill-advisedly ordaining young men to the ministry, 22 (cf. Acts 13:3).

5:23-25. Paul's personal advice to Timothy

23. Regarding Timothy's health. Paul suggests that Timothy no longer be a water drinker, i.e., no longer confine himself to drinking water only, but use a little wine for its medicinal value, 23.

24-25. Regarding the question of men's sins and good works. Some men's sins are so plainly manifest and evident that

6:11-16. Warning directed to the man of God

11-12. His ambition. The man of God is to run away from the snares of worldly wealth, to shun them in rigid separation (2 Cor 6:14-17; 2 Tim 2:19-21). He is to diligently pursue Christian virtue, 11. He is also to fight, 12*a,* and this means spiritual conflict (Eph 6:10-20; 2 Tim 2:3-4). The battle rages around the good fight of faith. Lastly, he is to lay hold of eternal life, 12*b.* This suggests the athletic figure of running for a prize (Phil 3:12-14), the reward being the full realization of the meaning of eternal life in the believer's early race, 12*c.*

13-16. The apostle's charge to him. Paul charges the man of God, i.e., the person who permits God to control his life, to keep this commandment, 14, concerning worldliness and worldly wealth (6-13) without stain or cause for rebuke till Christ's appearing (1 Thess 4:13-17). His life ambition is to be above reproach.

6:17-19. Instructions for wealthy believers

17-18. The charge. They are solemnly commanded not to be conceited, nor fix their hope on material wealth, which is always characterized by a degree of uncertainty and insecurity. Faith is to be reposed rather in the bounty of the *living* God, 17. They should rather be rich in good works, ready to use their wealth to advance God's work and to share with poor believers, 18.

19. The purpose. The goal in view is: (1) *Future reward* for faithfulness (cf. 1 Cor 3:9-15; 9:23-27; 2 Cor 5:10-11). They are to lay up in store the treasure of a good foundation (imperishable eternal wealth) for 'the coming age.' (2) *Present enjoyment of the spiritual life.* 'That they may take hold of the life that is truly life' (cf. Phil 3:14), that is, life more abundant here and now (Jn 10:10).

6:20-21. Appeal to Timothy

20*a.* The positive injunction. 'Guard what has been entrusted to your care.' The young pastor was entrusted with a life and ministry which he was commanded to watch over jealously.

20*b*-21. The negative warning. He was to avoid or shun worldly and empty discussion and pointless argumentation. He was likewise to avoid points of controversy with pseudo-science, the realm of false knowledge. Man's unproved theorizing has many so-called conflicts with revealed truths. The wise minister will shun these and give himself wholly to proclaiming God's revealed truth, 20. Some, however, in Paul's day as in ours, became involved with man's theorizing and subsequently have 'gone astray' from the faith, 21*a* (Jude 3). The closing benediction follows, 21*b.*

2 TIMOTHY

A good soldier of Jesus Christ

The writer and date. Second Timothy was written, as was 1 Timothy, by Paul the apostle to his 'dear son' Timothy (1:1-2). If there was only one imprisonment of Paul, this touching epistle containing the last recorded words of the apostle was penned about A.D. 64. If there was another and later imprisonment it was penned about A.D. 67.

The purpose. The letter was written to outline the course of a true servant of Jesus Christ in a time of doctrinal declension. The churches in Asia (1:15) had defected from the gospel of grace which the apostle had proclaimed and had lapsed into legalism. Paul encourages Timothy to use the divine resources available to the faithful pastor in such a time of apostasy.

Outline

Chapter 1 Apostasy and pastoral fidelity
Chapter 2 Apostasy and spiritual conflict
Chapter 3 Apostasy and the Word of God
Chapter 4 Apostasy and a faithful Lord

A Roman centurion and infantryman. In 2 Timothy Paul encourages Timothy to suffer opposition as a good soldier of Christ Jesus. No one serving as a soldier, says Paul, entangles himself with the affairs of this life.

1:1-5 The integrity of a faithful pastor

Paul's love and prayers for Timothy.
In his greeting, 1-2, Paul calls Timothy his 'dear son,' showing his deep affection for this true child in the faith. His interest in Timothy is revealed by his constant prayer on his behalf, 3, and his love is displayed by his earnest desire to see him, 4 (cf. 4:9, 21), which in turn would fill him with joy. This is one of the great friendships of Scripture.

5. Paul's confidence in Timothy. He calls to mind Timothy's 'sincere faith,' and how genuinely real it was, with no hypocrisy or make-believe sham. He was persuaded with full confidence that the same genuine faith which resided in his mother and grandmother was present in Timothy also.

1:6-8. The afflictions of a faithful pastor

6-7. Afflictions demand a spirit of courage. In the light of Timothy's background and faith, he was to 'fan into flame the gift of God' in him. This divinely conferred endowment (*charisma,* 1 Cor 12:4, 9, 28) was bestowed upon him through the laying on of the apostle's hands (1 Tim 4:14) at his ordination as a pastor. A spirit of ardent courage is needed to combat declension in a day of apostasy. Timothy's God-given endowment was not a spirit (attitude) of fear (Rom 8:15; 1 Jn 4:18), but of power (the dynamic inworking of an omnipotent God), love and a sound mind. This last phrase refers to a tranquil mental health that displays fearless courage to stand for truth and righteousness, 7.

8. Afflictions are part of faithful gospel testimony. Timothy was accordingly to expect afflictions and not try to avoid them by being ashamed 'to testify about our Lord,' which involves the full declaration of Christ's person and saving work. Nor was he to be ashamed of Paul, 'his [Christ's] prisoner' (because Paul was imprisoned for his faithfulness to Christ). 'Suffering for the gospel' is inseparable from the declaration of the good news itself. When they are endured for the sake of the truth, the power of God can be expected to be manifested in the ministry of the one afflicted.

1:9-11. The appointment of a faithful pastor

9-10. The gospel described. Several phrases describe the gospel or good news which the faithful pastor must proclaim, and to which he is appointed. Essentially it is a message which declares the parallel work of God in saving and calling the sinner. The call is emphasized here as being: (1) *divine,* God 'called us'; (2) *sanctifying,* 'a holy life,' setting the called ones apart from God's own possession and use; (3) *gracious,* 'not because of anything we have done but because of . . . grace'; (4) *purposeful,* 'because of his own purpose'; (5) *preplanned,* 'given us . . . before the beginning of time'; (6) *revealed,* or made known, by Christ's incarnation. God's call was effected through the work of the divine-human Son, who rendered death powerless and provided life eternal and incorruptibility. These great gifts are brought into clear light through the gospel.

11. The appointment illustrated. Paul himself furnishes an illustration of one who has been divinely appointed as a herald, an apostle – delegated one –and an instructor of the gospel.

1:12-14. The holy confidence of a faithful pastor

12. The testimony of assurance. 'I am suffering as I am. Yet I am not ashamed,' 12*a.* Why? The apostolic confidence is the answer. 'I know . . . I have believed and am convinced.' Assurance is basic to an effective witness. It is the believer's unswerving conviction not only that he possesses salvation, in which he will be eternally kept through the merits of the work of Christ alone, but that the commitment of his life to the Saviour will be safely guarded and his investment blessed and increased.

13-14. The results of assurance. One sound in the faith is able (1) to enjoin soundness of doctrinal teaching and terminology on others. 'Keep as the pattern [type, impress] of sound 'teaching,' 13*a;* (2) to put sound (healthful) doctrine into practice, 13*b;* (3) to guard or keep his ministry for Christ intact, 14*a.* This is accomplished by means of the Holy Spirit (not self-effort) 'who lives in the believer, 14*b* (cf. 1 Cor 6:19).

1:15-18. The trials and joys of a faithful pastor

15. The trials. The churches of proconsular Asia had declined doctrinally. They had 'deserted' from the apostle, i.e., turned away from his message of grace, going back to some degree of legalism. To that degree the apostasy had already set in, 15*a*. Two who had defected are especially named, 15*b*.

16-18. The joys. The household of Onesiphorus is mentioned on the other side of the pastoral ledger. This brother had refreshed the apostle by not being ashamed of Paul's imprisonment in Rome, and by previous help at Ephesus, 17-8.

2:1-3. The message of grace and spiritual warfare

1-2. Strength is required to proclaim the gospel of grace. *'You* (emphatic) then, my son, be strong [or strengthen yourself] in the grace that is in Christ Jesus,' because the Asian churches have defected from it, 1 (see 1:15). This injunction was especially necessary because the truth that salvation is wholly the result of the finished work of Christ without any admixture of works, human merit, or legalistic observance is subject to Satanic attack (cf. 1 Tim 4:1-5).

The truth of grace was divinely revealed to the apostle (Eph 3:1-10) and committed to Timothy in the presence of many witnesses. Timothy, in turn, was to transmit this truth to other faithful men who would, in like manner, instruct others, 2. This is the biblical pattern for Christian education, the method of promulgating the gospel to the ends of the earth.

3. Preaching grace arouses conflict. An adherent to this message may expect opposition. Paul enjoins Timothy to suffer opposition along with him, as a good soldier of Christ Jesus.

2:4-7. Separation and success in God's work

4. The necessity of separation. The military figure of a soldier, 3, continues. No one who serves as a soldier in performing military duty entangles or implicates himself with the business and affairs of this life. The purpose is that he might be pleasing to the one who enlists troops. In the conflict which the message of grace arouses there must be disentanglement from worldly pleasures and pursuits on the part of the Christian soldier, for his singular aim must be that of pleasing his Lord (2 Cor 5:9).

5-7. The necessity of obedience and effort. Reward for achievement in the

Timothy was a leader of the church at Ephesus. This view of the ancient city shows the reconstructed Library of Celsus (left) and, in the distance, the site of the ancient harbor, long since silted up.

Christian race demands (1) separation from sin (Heb 12:1); (2) discipline and obedience to God's Word (the figure of an athlete running according to the rules of the contest), 5 (cf. 1 Cor 9:25-27); and (3) labor and effort (the figure of a hard-working farmer who must labor first before sharing the fruits of his toil), 6. (See the distinction between salvation and rewards in 1 Cor 3:10-15.) The apostle implores comprehension of these examples as a result of the Lord's instruction, 7.

2:8-10. Suffering and soul-winning

8-9a. The cause for the suffering. Paul's gospel of grace, at the very center of which were the doctrines of the resurrection of the incarnate Christ and His messiahship (of the posterity of David, 8; Rom 1:3-4), led him to suffer hardship even to the extent of imprisonment (Eph 6:20).

9b-10. The results of the suffering. He was in chains, but the Word of God was not, 9b. As a result, the unbound Word which he had preached would effect salvation in the lives of many. 'The elect' are believers or believers to be (Eph 1:4-6). He endured suffering that these elect might be saved and be eventually glorified.

2:11-14. Union with Christ and coming glory

11. The believer's position of union. This is a trustworthy statement, a reliable fact, that the believer has been baptized (placed) by the Holy Spirit into a *position* of union and identification with Christ in death, burial and resurrection (Rom 6:3-4; 1 Cor 12:13; Col 2:8-10; Gal 3:27). Here the apostle dwells on the death and life aspects of that position. 'If [since] we *died* with him . . . we will also *live* with him.' The death aspect is inseparable from the life aspect. As the believer died in Christ to sin, so he also possesses life in and with Him.

12a. The believer's experience of union. If we suffer in our experience of living in Christ, we shall also reign with Him, both presently as an experience of power and authority (Phil 3:10-15), and hereafter as a reward (Rev 2:26-27; 20:6).

12b-14. The problem of the believer's unfaithfulness. 'If we disown him, He will also disown us' – reject us, count us as dis-

qualified for a prize, disapproving us for reward in the Christian race (1 Cor 9:27, see notes). If we continue to be unfaithful, so that our experience is inconsistent with our position, yet 'He will remain faithful, for He cannot disown himself,' 13 (cf. Num 23:19). He cannot go back on His word, His promise of our safety and security in Christ (Jn 10:28-29; Rom 8:1). Timothy was to remind his flock of these truths of grace, meanwhile warning them against petty debates which result in the subversion and ruin of the hearers from 'the grace that is in Christ Jesus,' 14 (2:1).

2:15-19. Bible study and godly living

15 -18. A discerning use of Scripture – the antidote to error. Study, be diligent or zealous, to present yourselves 'approved' (qualified) before God. The workman is not to be ashamed or embarrassed by faulty workmanship, for he is to 'correctly handle,' literally 'cut straight,' the revealed Word of God, here called 'the word of truth.' This setting forth of divine revelation without distortion, perversion or contradiction is possible only as God's workman diligently labors to discern the various subjects in Scripture and to make application accordingly. Only in this way can error and cultism, 16-18, be answered, illustrated here by the false teaching mentioned concerning the resurrection.

19. Bible study – the key to godly living. Revealed truth disclosed that 'God's solid foundation,' the essence of His character, 'stands firm,' steadfastly immoveable. This divine foundation has a twin seal (mark or token) guaranteeing it: (1) the Lord knows His own (Num 16:5; Jn 10:14); and (2) the Lord's own are to abstain from wickedness. Holy living is to be the external evidence of one's personal relationship to God. These two principles run through the fabric of all Scripture.

2:20-23. Separation and spiritual usefulness

20-21. The principle illustrated. The illustration is that of a large household with many utensils, some valuable, others less so. Some are for honorable uses, others for dishonorable purposes. The 'Lord's servant' is a vessel. If he is to be used by God, he must separate from evil – purge himself from dishonorable utensils. He will then become a vessel for honor, experientially as well as positionally sanctified (made holy), 'prepared to do any good work.'

22-23. The principle enunciated. 'Flee the evil desires of youth' (the intense burning desires or passions of youth), but pursue Christian virtues practiced by those 'who call on the Lord.' Only by such means can a pure (clean) heart be maintained. Foolish and unprofitable questions are to be avoided, for they produce only quarrels and dissensions, 23.

2:24-26. Spiritual victory

24-25a. The servant of Jesus Christ. Here the pastor is called 'the Lord's servant.' Although called to spiritual battle, he must not strive – quarrel or dispute in a natural sense. Rather he must display traits of victory over himself, being gentle, gifted and trained to teach, enduring, and patient under evils and injuries, 24. With gentleness he is to instruct and correct those that are of an opposite opinion to his, 25a.

25b-26. The servant's conquests over Satan. The servant's personal victory, 24-25a, has a twofold strategy: (1) that the Lord might grant his opponents repentance, leading them to a full comprehension of the truth, 25b; (2) that they might recover their senses. Those caught in the devil's snare of false doctrine become infatuated and intoxicated. When in such a state they are captured by the devil at his pleasure, 26.

3:1-5. The apostasy

1. The time of the apostasy. The importance of this revelation is seen in the phrase 'But mark this.' It was something to which Timothy was to give special attention. The time described as 'the last days' often refers in Scripture to the messianic period. NT writers viewed Christians as living in the last days, which were to be days of departure from the truth. Within the period of these 'days' were to be 'terrible times' which would be particularly spiritually and morally trying. Conditions will become progressively worse as the church age draws to a close (v. 5).

2-5. The nature of the apostates. The difficult times, 1, are made so by the character of the people involved. They will be: (1) self-lovers; (2) money-lovers; (3) boasters who are ostentatiously arrogant; (4) proud, haughty; (5) blasphemers, impiously irreverent toward God and holy things; (6) disobedient to parents, self-willed and undisciplined; (7) unthankful for blessings received from God and man; (8) unholy, repudiating the distinction between good and evil; (9) without natural affection, devoid of love for their own kindred; (10) irreconcilable, unwilling to be placated; (11) false accusers, slanderers who are literally devils; (12) incontinent, intemperate and uncontrolled, lacking mastery of self; (13) fierce, savage or ferocious in attitude and action; (14) despisers of those who are good, literally of the good; (15) traitors, betrayers; (16) heady, headstrong ones who rush forward pursuing their own will; (17) high-minded, imbued with the fumes of conceit, puffed up; (18) pleasure-lovers rather than God-lovers; (19) 'having a form of godliness, but denying its power,' possessors of mere formal religion which resembles the real, but continuing to reject the genuine dynamic which energizes the Christian life.

5b. The attitude toward apostates. Rigid separation (cf. 2:4-5, 20-23) is enjoined: 'Have nothing to do with them.' This injunction needs to be pondered in our day.

3:6-9. Results of apostasy
6-7. Immorality and false intellectualism. Apostates gravitate into immorality (2 Pet 2:10-14; Jude 4, 8, 10). Here they are represented as entering homes and seducing weak-willed women. Literally, these are 'little women,' lacking in true womanhood, laden with sins and led away from virtue by various lusts, 6 (cf. Tit 1:11). Apostates also are victimized by false intellectualism. They are ever learning (philosophical and kindred disciplines) but are never able to come to any accurate or real knowledge of the truth.

8-9. Opposition to the truth. Not only are apostates unable to arrive at the precise knowledge of the truth, they stoutly 'oppose' or stand against the truth, as Jannes and Jambres (cf. Ex 7:11-12). These names are preserved in Hebrew extrabiblical tradition as opposers of Moses. (Cf. those who suppress the truth, Rom 1:18.) They are men in a state of corruption, perverted in their thinking, reprobate concerning the faith, 8 (Jude 3). Their judgment and doom are indicated, 9. Apostasy is irremediable and awaits divine judgment.

3:10-13. Persecution and apostasy
10-11. Apostasy leads to persecution. The apostle's life and ministry are an example, 10. Persecutions and troubles befell him at Antioch in Pisidia, 11 (Acts 13:45-50), Iconium (Acts 14:5-6), and Lystra (Acts 14:19). In his patient endurance he saw the Lord's delivering hand.

12-13. Godliness and persecution. All those who determine to live in a godly manner in union with Christ Jesus, i.e. determine to realize their *position* in Christ by an

experience of Christ, shall suffer persecution, 12. This will be particularly true in the difficult times preceding Christ's return, because evil men and imposters (literally diviners) shall grow worse and worse, deceiving, and being deceived, 13.

3:14-17. Scripture and apostasy
14-15. The role of Scripture in Timothy's life. He had learned Scripture and been assured of its truths by his grandmother, mother (1:5-6) and the apostle himself (1 Tim 1:1-2; 2 Tim 1:12). From childhood he had been taught the holy writings (the OT). These have the power of making one wise to salvation through faith centered in Jesus Christ (Rom 10:17).

16-17. The inspiration and use of Scripture. This declares: (1) The full inspiration of the entire OT and by implication all canonical Scripture. (2) All Scripture is a product of God – God-breathed. God actually produced it, 'breathed it *out*.' It remains so whether man believes it or not. It has this unchanging quality *objectively* inherent in it. (3) As God-breathed it is inerrant and fully authoritative, since God produced it and actual error is inconsistent with God. (4) The whole of Scripture is useful (a) for doctrine (teaching); (b) for reproof or censure of wrong and sin; (c) for correction, setting aright or reformation; (d) for instruction (disciplinary education) in righteousness, both God's inherent righteousness and the righteous conduct He requires of His own; (e) that 'the man of God may be thoroughly equipped' in the sense of complete with nothing lacking, completely equipped and furnished 'for every good work.' This view of the full inspiration of the Bible is the citadel against error and apostasy.

4:1-4. The preached word and apostasy
1-2. The solemn charge. Paul enforces the command, 'Preach the Word,' 1a, with a most serious and weighty appeal to the divine witnesses, God the Father and Christ Jesus the Judge of all, 1 (cf. Jn 5:22). So pivotal is the matter of heralding the Scripture, 2, that the apostle stresses the accounting which Christ's ministers will render as to how they have han-

A writing scroll. In this letter, Paul asks Timothy for 'my scrolls,' but especially the 'parchments,' vellums, made of polished fine leather.

dled the Word of God. The preacher is to have *one* ambition — to herald and proclaim *the Word.* This means the systematic and orderly exposition of the plans and purposes of God for lost humanity centering in Christ. Such a task is to be executed 'in season' (conveniently) as well as 'out of season' (inconveniently); in other words, *always.*

3-4. The reason for the charge. The Word of God alone is the antidote against apostasy. In these verses apostasy is described as it relates to Scripture. (1) Apostates will not endure healthy teaching ('sound doctrine'). (2) They will 'gather round them' teachers who will pander to their lusts. (3) They will have 'itching ears,' burning to be titillated by some novel error, 3. (4) They will turn their ears from the truth (the Word) to fables or myths.

4:5-8. The reward of the faithful preacher

5. Advice for a faithful preacher. The advice is (1) 'keep your head,' be alert; (2) 'endure hardship' (2:3); (3) 'do the work of an evangelist' (an announcer of the good news that Jesus died to save sinners); (4) 'discharge,' or fulfill, your ministry. Serve God in full measure, completely discharging your service through maximum effectiveness.

6-7. Testimony of a faithful preacher. This is the triumph of one who preached the Word. Paul states that he is 'now ready to be offered' (KJV), i.e., to pour out his life as a libation or drink offering, having spent it in sacrifice to make known the gospel (cf. Phil 2:17). The time of his departure by death was at hand. He had fought a good fight (*agonia,* a spiritual struggle, cf. Eph 6:10-20), and now had finished his course. The 'race' (*dromos*) refers to a race in the public games and is used figuratively of one's career or ministry. The apostle had 'kept the faith' (Jude 3), guarded it against error and apostasy.

8. The reward of the faithful preacher. Here faith becomes vocal in radiant hope. 'The crown of righteousness' is a reward for faithfulness and is reserved for those who particularly love Christ's appearing. The 'crown' is the *stephanos* or victor's crown, the garland of wild olive or pine, given to the winner in the Greek games.

4:9-15. Personal warnings of a faithful preacher

9-13. Advice concerning fellow workers. Timothy is urged to bend every effort to come to the apostle immediately, 9. The reason was that Paul was almost alone. Demas had abandoned him because of love for the present age (or world system). Crescens had gone to Galatia in Asia Minor, Titus to Dalmatia across the Adriatic Sea from Italy, 10. Only Luke remained. Paul requests Mark to be brought, 11 (cf. Acts 15:37-39). The request for Mark is particularly significant since Paul had earlier refused to take him on the second missionary journey because of his unreliability. Apparently Mark had matured and Paul had forgiven. Paul had sent Tychicus (Tit 3:12) to Ephesus, 12. He asks for 'the cloak,' a warm coat with hood used in travel, and 'my scrolls,' but especially the 'parchments,' vellums, made of polished fine leather, 13.

14-15. Warnings concerning evil workers. Timothy is warned to beware of Alexander the coppersmith because he had stoutly resisted Paul's message, 15.

4:16-18. Testimony of the Lord's faithfulness

16. Man's unfaithfulness. At his first defense (preliminary hearing) before Caesar, all had abandoned Paul and no one vouched for him and his statements. Although disappointed, he was not vengeful, and prayed that their neglect would not be held against them.

17-18. God's faithfulness. By contrast, the Lord stood with Paul and stengthened him, apparently securing his acquittal and further ministry. 'Delivered from the lion's mouth' refers evidently to the Roman power. Those who date 2 Timothy after Paul's release from his first imprisonment use this passage as evidence of that release. Paul's confidence in the Lord's continued faithfulness is asserted, 18.

4:19-22. Greetings and closing salutation

19-21. Greetings. Among others Priscilla and Aquila, Paul's colaborers in the gospel and in the trade of tentmaking in Corinth and Ephesus (Acts 18:2-3), are named, together with 'the household of Onesiphorus' (1:16-18), Erastus (Acts 19:22) and Trophimus (Acts 21:29).

22. Closing salutation.

TITUS

The order of God's house

Writer and date. The author is Paul (1:1). His letter to Titus was written about the same time as 1 Timothy (see discussion there), approximately either in A.D. 64 or in 66, depending on whether Paul had one or more imprisonments.

Theme. Titus had been left on the island of Crete to organize the churches there (1:5). The letter therefore has much in common with 1 Timothy, but with greater emphasis on church organization and administration.

Outline

1 Scriptural church organization
2 Pastoral ministry toward various groups
3 Pastoral ministry and general teaching

CRETE

Mediterranean Sea

1:1-4. Greeting to Titus

1-3. Paul's ministry defined. The apostle defines his offices as being those of God's bond-servant and Christ's apostle. His performance of these offices was to be evaluated in accord with 'the faith of God's elect' (the personal faith which the believers possessed) and 'knowledge of the truth' which had produced godliness and assurance of eternal life in the lives of the Cretan believers. Paul views his commission as being the proclamation of God's promise of eternal life as embodied in the redemption and life which Christ the divine Word provides, 2-3.

4. Paul's greeting to Titus. He is called 'my true son in our common faith,' called common because it was meant for all sinners to embrace and enjoy (cf. 1 Tim 1:1-2).

1:5-9. Qualifications of elders and bishops

5. Titus' task outlined. Paul left Titus in Crete to organize the assemblies there according to divine order and appoint church officers (elders and bishops). These officers are called bishops (*episcopoi,* 'overseers') and deacons (*diakonoi,* 'servers') in 1 Tim 3:1-13. Bishops and elders (*presbuteroi*) are terms apparently used to designate the same office of one who both preached and taught, in addition to being an administrator. Deacons, on the other hand, were concerned with finances and benevolences (Acts 6:1-7). However, evidently not all elders were teaching elders or more specifically pastoring elders, with the chief oversight of a church.

6-9. Qualification of elders (see 1 Tim 3:1-13). The 'overseer,' literally 'God's steward,' is one who holds a commission from God to serve in the gospel, a trustee of spiritual truth, 7. Among other essential qualifications, he must adhere firmly to the faithful Word of God, 9. This is possible only as the teaching elder is a careful Bible student. He will then be able by healthful teaching to exhort and convince opposers, 9.

1:10-16. Warning against false teachers

10-13a. The legalists especially cited. The churches in Crete were endangered by many who were 'rebellious people, mere talkers,' given to arguing and trivial disputation; 'deceivers,' leading people astray in their thinking. Especially guilty were those of the circumcision, i.e., Jewish legalists. Paul asserts that a curb or muzzle *must* be applied to their mouths to silence them. They corrupt or overturn whole families, teaching 'things they ought not to teach' for vile or dishonorable financial gain, 11. Paul quotes one of their own prophets (Epimenides, '*de oraculis,*') as saying: 'Cretans are always liars [delinquents], evil brutes [wicked beasts], lazy gluttons.' Paul agrees, 13.

13b-16. The remedy. A severe reprimand is called for. 'Rebuke them sharply, so that they will be sound in the faith' and unlegalistic, 13b-14 (cf. 1 Tim 1:4). Then a positive note is sounded: Inculcate purity. 'To the pure all things are pure; but to those who are corrupted and do not believe, nothing is pure.' The reason for impurity is that they are not regenerated, 15-16a. 'Easy believism,' 16a, not supported by works, is no credential of being saved (2 Tim 3:5, 7; cf. Jas 2:14-20).

2:1-4a. The aged adorning the gospel

1-2. Aged men. The general responsibility of a true pastor is to teach that which is proper for sound doctrine, 1. Older men are to be 'temperate, worthy of respect, self-controlled, and sound in faith, in love, and in endurance' (the quality of remaining under a trial gracefully).

3-4a. Aged women. Older women are to be reverent in their behavior; not 'slanderers' (literally, not devils, controlled by the devil the accuser [from *diaballo,* 'to accuse']); not enslaved to excessive wine; teachers of what is good to the young.

2:4-6. The young adorning the gospel

4-5. Young women. The older Christian women are to train the young women to be 'self-controlled' (serious-minded); lovingly devoted to their husbands and to their children; holy or chaste; workers at home; 'kind'; subjecting themselves to their own husbands. The purpose or motive for such action is that God's Word may not be blasphemed because of unruly, insubordinate wives.

6. Young men are also exhorted and urged

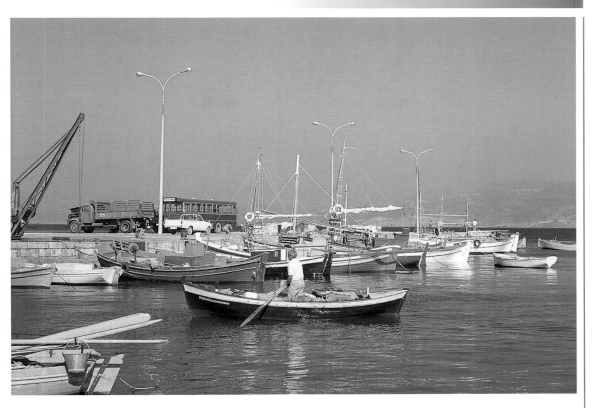

to be serious-minded and sensible. This quality is expected of all ages (cf. 1:8; 2:2, 5) and is a mark of spiritual maturity.

2:7-8. Titus, the pastor, adorning the gospel

7-8*a*. The pastoral example. Titus was to be an example for the young men, 6, to imitate (1 Cor 11:1). 'In everything' he was to be a model of good works, 7; displaying the quality of not being corrupted or vitiated by error in doctrine. His attitude or manner was to exhibit 'integrity' and 'seriousness' (genuineness). 'Soundness of speech' included all his conversation and meant that nothing capable of being condemned should be found in it, being irreproachable.

8*b*. The purpose of the pastoral example. Titus was to be so exemplary that the opponent would be put to shame, having nothing bad to say concerning the young pastor.

2:9-10. Servants adorning the gospel

9-10*a*. Their conduct enjoined. Servants were to be voluntarily submissive to their own masters, pleasing them in everything without being impudent or insubordinate, 9. Pilfering or stealing was forbidden, but displaying all good faith was enjoined, 10*a*.

10*b*. The purpose stated. 'That in every way they [bondslaves] will make the teaching about God our Savior attractive.' How significant it is that common slaves should be selected for this high purpose of adorning the gospel, i.e., honoring or dignifying it, decorating or embellishing it, so that men can see its glory displayed in humble human lives. The word for 'make attractive' (*kosmeo*) gives us our English word 'cosmetic.'

2:11-15. The gospel and adorned living

11-14. The basis of adorned living. 'The grace of God' — the unmerited divine favor and mercy bestowed upon helplessly lost sinners who trust in Christ's vicarious atonement (Rom 3:24) constitutes the foundation of godly conduct. This grace, which brought salvation and was displayed in Christ's person and work, teaches by disciplining and instructing us as a child is instructed, 11-12*a*. Its lesson is that we

The harbor, Sitia, Crete. Titus was left on the island of Crete to organize the churches there.

are saved by His grace from sin to righteous holy living, and are thus to deny or reject ungodliness and worldly lusts. This life is to be a positive one, characterized by a mind set in proper balance ('self-controlled'), by conduct which meets with God's approval ('upright'), and by reverence toward God ('godly'). The sphere of this activity is 'this present world' or age, the testing ground of our faith, 12.

Motivation for godly conduct is to be found in the believer's anticipating Christ's return for the saints ('blessed hope – the glorious appearing'), 13. This hope is even more blessed when the work of the Coming One is realized. His was a vicarious sacrifice. By His atoning death He paid the ransom to rescue sinners from the slavery of sin ('redeem') so that they might be uniquely His own possession, zealous of good works, 14. Such grace demands a life of adorned living in response.

15. The injunction to enforce these truths. Paul emphasizes the need to continually urge the foregoing directives upon Christians, using whatever authority necessary. They are incumbent on every believer ('don't let anyone despise you').

3:1-7. Adorning the gospel before the world

1-2. The nature of exemplary behavior. (1) Believers are to remember that they are subject to established government (Rom 13:1) and are to obey civil authorities, being ready to assist in worthy civil or educational projects, 1. (2) They are to speak evil of no one. (3) Instead of being contentious, a Christian must be 'peaceable,' displaying all meekness to all men (both believers and unbelievers), 2.

3-7. The reason for exemplary behavior. First of all, the gospel of grace is to be adorned before the world because we *ourselves* (emphatic) were once in the same unsaved state, 3. Thus we are to be examples of God's grace, not judges of the world. We ourselves were once 'foolish' (unwise, without spiritual understanding); 'disobedient' (refusing to believe and submit to God's will); 'deceived' (led astray, caused to wander in spiritual darkness); 'enslaved' by various lusts and pleasures; living 'in malice and envy' (in ill will and jealousy) ; 'being hated and hating one

another' in distrust. People in this state need the gospel advertised to them *by life,* if they are to see the glory of God's grace.

The second reason for proper behavior is seen in the realization that our present condition is entirely due to the grace of God, 4-7. This involves: (1) our understanding God's love for men ('kindness and love of God,' *philanthropia,* i.e., God's special love for mankind), 4; (2) our understanding that salvation is a free gift given, entirely apart from human merit, on the basis of God's mercy and grace, 5*a*; (3) our realizing that Christ is the exclusive channel of salvation and secures for us 'the washing of rebirth' (the cleansing of the believer from the guilt of sin) and 'renewal by the Holy Spirit' (the impartation of new life in the person of the indwelling Holy Spirit), 5*b*-6; (4) our realizing the possessions which are ours in Christ, 7. These include 'having been justified' (pronounced guiltless from sin), made 'heirs' (in line for the full inheritance of salvation), 'having the hope of eternal life' (the hope which eternal life gives).

3:8-11. Adorning the gospel with good works

8. The continual affirmation of profitable things. Paul sets forth a basic principle based on the summary of truth given in 4-7: good works are to follow personal faith. 'Those who have trusted in God' must be careful to take the lead in the diligent practice of good works. Such a fact is to be affirmed constantly.

9-11. The avoidance of unprofitable things. Legalistic snares such as 'foolish controversies,' with which Judaism was honeycombed, and 'genealogies,' to which the Jews attached great importance (1 Tim 1:4; 2 Tim 2:23) are to be shunned because they have no value and are useless. 'Arguments and quarrels' (contentions and disputes) about the law are also to be avoided, for they too are without value and gain no end, 9.

A heretic, one who creates factions and fosters divisions as a result of false doctrine, is to be shunned after he fails to respond to a first and second admonition or warning (cf. Mt 18:17). Such a one is a serious sinner because he destroys the unity of God's people (cf. Eph 4:3-6). He is a divisive person who is 'warped' (turned aside or away from the truth) and goes on sinning, being self-condemned, 11.

3:12-15. Closing greetings

12-13. Instructions concerning fellow workers. Paul desires Titus to come to Nicopolis, where the apostle plans to spend the winter. This may have taken place between the first imprisonment and die possible second (see introduction to 1 Timothy). Zenas and Apollos are to accompany Titus, 13.

14-15. Instruction concerning Christian industry. 'Our people must learn to devote themselves to doing what is good, in order that they may provide for daily necessities and not live unproductive lives.' There is to be no abuse of grace; no thinking that because one is saved by grace apart from works and human merit therefore there are to be no good works produced. One is saved without works (Eph 2:8-9) but 'to do good works' (Eph 2:10). A practical result also appears. Believers must have funds for essential needs. Their lives are not to be unfruitful and barren of the rewards of common labor. A closing benediction is given, 15.

PHILEMON

Christian fellowship in action

Artist's impression of Philemon with his slave Onesimus.

Writer and date. The apostle Paul is the author of this personal epistle, written probably in A.D. 61 or 62. The letter is one of the so-called prison epistles (see introduction to Ephesians and Colossians). It was dispatched by Paul from his prison in Rome by Tychicus, as were Ephesians and Colossians.

Theme. Philemon was a Christian of Colossae, a small city in Asia Minor SE of Laodicea and S of Hierapolis. His slave, Onesimus, had apparently robbed him and consequently fled to Rome. There the renegade slave came in contact with Paul and was saved. The apostle sent him back to his master with this priceless letter preserved for us.

Outline

1-7 Paul's greeting and commendation of Philemon
8-21 Paul's intercession for Onesimus
22-25 Concluding word and greeting

1-3. Paul's greeting to Philemon

The greeting. Paul describes himself as a 'prisoner of Christ Jesus,' 1a, not of the Roman emperor (cf. Eph 3:1, 4:1), for he viewed his imprisonment as being the direct will of God. He calls Philemon 'our dear friend and fellow worker,' identifying him as one with himself in the fellowship of the gospel. Mentioned is the church which met in his house. The homes of believers were the customary meeting places of all the early assemblies.

3. The benediction is characteristic of the Pauline letters (cf. Eph 1:2).

4-7. Paul's commendation of Philemon

4-5.Philemon's love and faith. Paul thanks God and commends Philemon for his love and faith directed toward the Lord and toward all believers.

6-7. Paul's prayer for Philemon. The apostle prays that the 'sharing' of Philemon's faith may be 'active' in the sense of being efficiently adapted to work toward others in blessing (cf. Jas 2:14, 17). As a result others may acknowledge every good thing in him in Christ Jesus (cf. Phil 4:8; 2 Pet 1:5, 8). Paul further commends Philemon for his love because the hearts (Gr. 'bowels') of the saints had been refreshed by his testimony.

8-13. Paul's plea for Onesimus

8-10. The plea. Philemon's runaway slave is the object of Paul's intercession. Although by virtue of his apostolic authority, Paul was free to 'order' Philemon concerning the proper action to take with regard to Onesimus, 8, yet out of Christian love he rather pleads with him, as the aged friend and the 'prisoner of Christ Jesus.' Paul calls Onesimus 'my son,' literally, 'my very own child whom I have brought to spiritual birth while imprisoned,' 10 (1 Cor 4:15).

11-13. Paul's defense of Onesimus. The apostle freely acknowledges that Onesimus had been unprofitable in the sense that he caused his master loss. But he also stresses the change conversion makes in a life and asserts, 'But now he has become useful both to you and to me.' Paul would have desired to keep Onesimus because of his usefulness in assisting and encouraging him while in prison, and also

because of the deep affection Paul had for him, but gives him back to his master, 13. It is a powerful plea for Philemon to forgive and reinstate his runaway slave.

14-16. Not as a servant but as a brother

14. Paul's courteous tact. 'But I did not want to do anything without your consent so that any favor you do will be spontaneous and not forced.' Forced service for Christ is not genuine. Paul's aim was to motivate the best in a man.

15-16. Paul's skillful analysis. The apostle suggests a deeper purpose in the matter (cf. Rom 8:28). Maybe Onesimus was separated from Philemon for a while that his master might have his complete loyalty and permanent service, 15. This was now possible because Onesimus was no longer just a servant (a common slave or bondman), but above a slave a 'dear brother' in Christ and united with Philemon in a bond stronger than any other, the Body of Christ – the church. Onesimus was especially beloved to Paul because Paul was his spiritual father. How much more beloved was he to Philemon, his master, because 'as a man' (on the natural plane) he was now a dependable Christian servant, and 'in the Lord' (on the spiritual plane) he was a fellow believer, 16.

17-19. Reckon to my account

17. Welcome him as me. Paul gives a further appeal, 'So if you consider me a partner (sharer of salvation, a partaker of eternal life with you), welcome him as you would welcome me,' 17. The 'if' does not express a doubtful contingency. 'Therefore, since you do esteem me as a fellow partner in salvation, esteem your repentant slave as a fellow believer also, for such he is now.'

18-19. Put any demerit to my account. This is a beautiful illustration of the principle of imputation by which the sinner's sins are reckoned or imputed to Christ's account, and His righteousness is credited or imputed to the sinner's account, all by faith. The apostle states, 'Welcome him as you would welcome me' – *reckon to him my merit*. 'If he has done you any wrong or owes you anything' – put that on my account – reckon or *impute to me his demerit* (cf. Jas 2:23). Paul will pay any debt owing, 19*a*; but he tactfully suggests that Philemon owes himself to him for the benefit not only of returning a runaway slave, but even more, now a brother in the Lord. It may be that Philemon also was a convert of Paul's, in which case an even greater debt was owed the apostle.

20-21. Paul's confidence in Philemon

20. The request. Philemon's reception of Onesimus would bring joy to Paul in that his action would gladden him and refresh his inmost self.

21. The confidence. Paul has confidence that Philemon will do even more than has been suggested to him.

2-25. A request and closing greetings

22. The request. The imprisoned apostle asks Philemon to find him lodging, for he, in faith, looks forward to release.

23-25. The greetings.

The Jewish-Christian epistles

Hebrews, James, 1 Peter, 2 Peter, Jude

These inspired epistles are addressed principally to Jewish believers. In the case of Hebrews the purpose is to set forth the finality of Christ's salvation and warn against the peril of Jewish believers going back to the fulfilled types and superseded ritualism of Judaism. James instructs them in the practical virtues familiar to OT saints. First Peter is also addressed to Jewish Christians of the dispersion (1:1-2). Second Peter and Jude are more general, like the catholic (universal) epistles of 1, 2 and 3 John.

All these Jewish-Christian writings differ from the Pauline epistles in their omission of those distinctive elements which were revealed particularly to the apostle to the Gentiles, such as the nature, position and destiny of the church, the Body of Christ. For instance, the epistle to the Hebrews presupposes these truths but it does not expound them. Instead, it approaches our 'so great salvation' from the point of its superiority to Judaism, since the letter is directed primarily to Jews, not Gentile believers as were the Pauline letters.

It may be said that these Jewish-Christian epistles deal more with the inculcation of the practical expression of salvation in consistent living grounded in the basic doctrines of biblical Christianity. By contrast, the Pauline letters base the same conduct on the more complex disclosures of the Christian's *position* and *possessions* in union with Christ (Eph 4:1-3), in His death, resurrection, ascension, and return in glory (Rom 6:1-11; Eph 1:1-14; Col 3:1-4). The difference then is not that of disagreement or conflict in any sense. Both present the same Christ, the same salvation and the same hope. But the distinction is that of development and extension.

Relief of a Jewish Menorah, or seven-branched candlestand, often used to symbolize the Jewish faith.

HEBREWS

Christ superior to all

Authorship. This great epistle is anonymous. Paul has been claimed as its author (cf. 2 Pet 3:15; Heb 13:23), and there is internal evidence pointing to this possibility. But in the absence of direct statement or indubitable proof, the question must remain unsettled. This, however, does not affect the genuineness of the epistle. No book contains grander truth, nor attests itself as being more divinely inspired.

Theme and date. Hebrews meets a pivotal need in showing the relationship of Christianity to Judaism, a burning issue in the Christian church since the apostolic period. The book was written before the destruction of Jerusalem and the temple by the Romans in A.D. 70 (cf. 10:11).

Outline

1:1–2:18 Superiority of the Son to prophets and angels
3:1–4:16 Superiority of the Son to Moses and Joshua
5:1–8:5 Superiority of Christ's priesthood
8:6–10:39 Superiority of the new covenant to the old covenant
11:1–13:25 Superiority of faith

Authentic scale model of Herod's Temple, showing the central sanctuary and the surrounding courts. This building was destroyed by the Romans during the first Jewish war.

1:1-3. The Son superior to the prophets

1. The ministry of the prophets. The word through the OT prophets came in many ways and in various modes (dreams, visions, audible voice, theophany, angels, men, etc.). Although it was the inspired, infallible Word ('God spoke'), it was ministered by weak, fallible men ('the prophets') to those who proved disobedient ('our forefathers').

2-3. The superior ministry of the Son. The Son's ministry is superior to that of the OT prophets because of His glorious person and His creative and redemptive work. That superiority is seen in the following declarations. *Christ's eternal deity* is seen in the reference to 'Son,' 2a, the Word who was God and who became flesh (man), the only begotten of the Father (Jn 1:1, 14). He was *God's full and final revelation* of Himself to man, for '[God] has spoken to us by His Son,' 2a; not through mere man but through Himself become man. 'Whom he appointed heir of all things,' 2b, has reference to *the Son's eternal heirship.* God's heir is Christ (Rom 8:17). His inheritance is over all things and is eternal as well as universal. The Son is also superior because of *His creatorship,* 2c, for He not only created the material universe but fashioned the ages of time. His *full divine glory* is that which is referred to when it is said that He was 'the radiance of God's glory,' 3a. Christ is the absolute expression of the collective attributes of Deity (Jn 1:18; Rom 9:5). All that God is and does is revealed in full splendor in the divine Son. 'The exact representation of his being,' 3b, has reference to the Son's being the incarnation of God Himself. God is seen, or is made visible, in the person of Jesus Christ. The Son is also *the sustainer* (Col 1:17b) *and the maintainer of the universe,* 'sustaining all things by his powerful word,' 3c. In His redemptive act He did what no other priest had ever done. He completely removed sin from the sinner, not merely covering it temporarily (Jn 1:29; 19:30; Heb 5-7). 'He provided purification for sins,' 3d. His was *a finished redemption.* Finally, it is said that He 'sat down at the right hand of the Majesty in heaven,' 3e, becoming, in *His present position,* an interceding priest on the basis of an accomplished redemption (Heb 8:1-2; 10:12; 12:2).

1:4-14. The Son superior to the angels in His person and work

4-9. Superior in His person. He is *uncreated* Deity; the angels are mere creatures, though lofty celestial spirits. He has inherited a name which is 'superior' to the angels, 4 (cf. 1-3). He received this name as the result of His redemptive work (Rom 1:4; Phil 2:5-8). It is an inheritance of the Father who has highly exalted Him and given Him this *'name' that is above every name'* (Phil 2:9).

God addresses Him 'my Son' (Deity), 5, in Father-Son relationship (Sam 7:14), which is in contrast to the angels (mere creatures) who are never so addressed. Furthermore, Christ is styled 'firstborn,' 6, a title of uncreated Deity (Col 1:15), and 'all God's angels' are commanded as creatures to *worship Him,* their Creator. They are designated His (created) 'servants,' 7 (Ps 104:4). The Son is addressed as 'God' in verses 8-9; attributes of Deity are ascribed to Him; His righteous kingdom rule is intimated; and His immeasurable anointing with the Holy Spirit is noted (Ps 45:6-7).

10-14. Superior in His work. Christ is superior to angels in His work as *Creator,* 10-12, and *Redeemer,* 13-14. As the crucified and risen Lord He sits at the Father's right hand, until His enemies are made the footstool of His feet (Ps 110:1). No angel was ever addressed in this fashion, 13. Angels have a blessed but much lower status, 14. As creatures they are all engaged in sublime but subordinate service, 'ministering [serving] spirits,' delegated and sent forth to assist 'those who will [in the sense of a sure and settled future] inherit salvation.'

2:1-4. Warning against drifting

1. The warning. Since the infinitely superior Son of God has spoken, we ought of necessity to give the more earnest attention to the things which we have heard from Him and concerning Him (the gospels and the Acts). If Hebrew believers thought the OT prophets should be heard, how much more the Lord of glory Himself! The danger was that they might imperceptibly *drift away* from these truths in the strong currents of legalistic ritualism.

2-4. The reason for warning. The writer now argues from the lesser to the greater. If judgment fell on those who transgressed the

Artist's cutaway impression of worship in a first century Jewish synagogue.

law given through the mediation of angels, how much more serious will be the state of the one who rejects the word of God's Son! Then an unanswerable question: 'How shall we escape if we ignore such a great salvation?' 3. Those who perished under the judgment of the Mosaic economy serve as a warning to us. This word of 'great salvation' was first proclaimed by Christ Himself; then by His commissioned disciples, attested by miraculous signs and gifts of the Holy Spirit (1 Cor 12).

2:5-9. The Son superior to the angels in His authority

5. The Son's kingdom authority. 'The world to come' refers to the inhabited earth in the coming age when Christ the Son returns in His glorified humanity to rule as King of kings and Lord of lords (Rev 19:16). This future world will not be subject to angels, but to Christ in its totality . Such authority is His alone.

6-9. The basis of the Son's authority. This quotation from Psalm 8:4-6, referring to the original estate of the first Adam (man), is applied to Christ the 'second man' (1 Cor 15:47). Adam, the representative man, forfeited his dominion over the earth through sin, but the last Adam (Christ, the perfect man) regained it by virtue of His humiliation and death for every man. He was made 'a little lower than the angels,' 9, God becoming man, submitting to human limitations to which angels are not subject, and foregoing the glories which were His as the Prince of heaven. Undergoing the suffering of death, He, the Sinless One, tasted death for every man. His was a vicarious and a substitutionary death for sinners. From such humiliation He arose to the heights of exaltation and is crowned with glory and honor, far above that of angels.

2:10-13. The Son superior to the angels in His perfect humanity

10. Bringing sons to glory. It was the purpose of God the Father 'in bringing many sons to glory,' i.e., consummating their salvation in resurrection and glorification, to make complete the work of the Pioneer (Leader) of their salvation through suffering. He was thus advanced to completeness in His role of suffering Redeemer. Because He suffered He is qualified to serve as the Leader of those who are heirs of salvation, those being brought to glorification.

11-13. Union of the redeemer and the redeemed. Both 'the one who makes men holy' (the Son through whom the Father is bringing many sons to glory) and 'those who are made holy' (the sons who are being brought to glory) are 'of the same family,' 11. They have a common origin in God; therefore, because of this unity, the Son is not ashamed to call them His brothers. As sons of glory, 10, they are destined for glorification even as Christ their Pioneer is already glorified.

The reference to Psalm 22:22 in verse 12 prophetically sets forth the eternal priestly work of Christ in which He continually reveals God's name to us and sings the praises of God among us His 'brothers' (cf. Jn 20:19). 'I will put my trust in him,' 13*a* (cf. Isa 8:17), expresses the personal faith of the Son in the Father. 'Here am I, and the children God has given me' (Isa 8:18) actually refers to Isaiah's two sons, but is here, 13*b,* applied by the Holy Spirit to represent the unity of the Son with His brethren. The angels do not sustain such unity with the redeemed; it uniquely belongs to the perfect Man, the Redeemer.

2:14-18. The Son superior to the angels in His conquest of sin and death

14-16. The purpose of the incarnation. This purpose is threefold: (1) that the Incarnate One might render null, void and completely powerless the devil's power over death (Gen 3); (2) that such might be accomplished through the death of the Incarnate One, 14; (3) that those who were held in bondage to the fear of death all their lives might be delivered, 15. Help was not given to angels, but to the descendant of Abraham, and for such a task the incarnate God-Man was necessary, 16. Only He could fulfill the great divine purposes of the Abrahamic covenant (Gen 12:1-3).

17-18. The purpose of His priesthood. The Son's incarnation was a necessary prelude to His priesthood. He must, in order to be a qualified high priest in behalf of men before God, 'be made like his brothers,' whom He was bringing to glory. This involved His becoming a human being, laying aside His heavenly splendor and glory, and sharing man's sufferings and temptations, 17*a*, 18. Only thus could He be a 'merciful and faithful high priest.' As such, Christ made 'atonement (satisfaction) for the sins of the people' at the cross (Jn 19:30), giving man access to God, 17.

3:1-6. The Son superior to Moses

1. Holy brothers. For the first time the readers are addressed as 'holy brothers, who share in the heavenly calling,' 1. They were no longer simply Jews with an earthly inheritance but members of the church, the Body of Christ, with a 'heavenly calling.' This is emphasized throughout the book.

1-2. Consider the Son. The exhortation here is to consider Christ, to contemplate our faithful High Priest so as to perceive and fully understand Him as the delegated One sent by the Father. He is the High Priest of our confession, to whom confession is made by believers, 1.

In comparing Christ with Moses, emphasis is given in verse 2 to the faithfulness each exercised in his calling. Christ 'was faithful to the one who appointed him, just as Moses was faithful in all God's house' (Num 12:7; Mt 26:42).

3-6. The Son contrasted with Moses. Christ is esteemed, deserving of more honor than Moses, for although both were faithful in administrating the divine economy (the spiritual household) committed to them, Christ built the house (the divine economy) while Moses only served therein, 3-5*a*. Moses was faithful as a free and dignified servant; Christ was faithful as Son. Moses' ministry was typical and prophetic of Christ, and of the truths and blessings to be realized in Him, 5 (Deut 18:15, 18-19). He was the fulfillment of all that Moses and the law looked forward to in redemption. The saved now constitute God's 'house' (1 Cor 3:9; Eph 2:19-22). Their faith is expressed by their confidence in Christ, which constitutes their hope until the day of complete redemption, 6.

3:7-19. Warning against departing from the living God

7-10. The sin of heart-hardening. This warning is addressed to the brethren of verse 1. It is *urgent* ('today') and *authoritative* ('as the Holy Spirit says'). Faith and obedience to God's Word ('if you hear his voice,' Ps 95:7-11) are involved, 7. The danger is that of an omnitemporal peril – hardening the heart – becoming stubbornly insensitive and rebellious against God, 8*a*. Illustrated by God's people in the wilderness, 8*b,* the warning concerns tempting God, refusing to believe Him in the face of gracious signs and miraculous provisions, and at the same time evidencing unbelief by demanding new signs and miracles, 9. Such sin leads to error, wandering, and ignorance of God's ways, 10.

11. The penalty – forfeiture of God's rest. Unbelief, 7-10, stirs up God's anger, 11, and provokes His wrath, i.e., the suitable response of His gracious and infinitely holy nature. God's 'rest' is the quiet inner assurance and triumphant sense of peace He gives those who trust Him. It is the reward of believing God and is typified by Israel's entrance into Canaan.

12-16. The deceitfulness of sin. So treacherous is sin in rendering the heart insensitive and unresponsive to God and His Word, that constant exhorting and urging are necessary while opportunity affords, 13. That those addressed were genuine believers is indicated by the fact that they had been made 'partakers of Christ,' 14. They must continue to hold to the full efficacy and finality of Christ's priesthood, not lapsing back into Jewish ritualism. To do so would have been to harden their hearts as in 'the rebellion' – Israel's rebellion in the desert for 40 years, 15-16 (Ps 95:8; Ex 17:1-7; Num 14:1-45).

17-19. The tragedy of unbelief. The Israelites 'rebelled,' 16, and angered God, 17. Their bodies fell in the desert. They forfeited God's rest, 18, because of unbelief, 19. Redemption, typified by sprinkling the Passover blood (Ex 12:12-13) and crossing the Red Sea

(Ex 14:13-31), was meant to have its consummation in 'rest,' illustrated by the conquest and settlement of Canaan. This aspect of salvation was forfeited because of unbelief. The chastening which resulted was physical death – their corpses fell in the desert (cf. 1 Cor 11:30-31; 1 Jn 5:16).

4:1-8. The Son superior to Joshua in the rest He gives

1-3*b*. The gospel, the source of rest. A believer should 'be careful' (have godly concern) lest he die in unbelief in the 'wilderness' like Israel, and never enter Canaan, the place of rest (cf. Num 14). Canaan rest (Mt 11:28-30) is that *full trust* in the finished work of Christ, both for salvation of the soul and sanctification of life, which brings not only 'peace with God' (Rom 5:1) but the 'peace of God' (Phil 4:7). The gospel is the source of this peace, because it centers in the atoning work of the Son. It (the good news) was preached to 'us,' as well as 'to them,' referring to Israel in the OT. The difficulty was that 'those who heard did not combine it with faith.' The gospel then pointed forward to the atonement of Christ as it now points back to it (1 Cor 15:1-4). Faith in the gospel is the key to this rest, 3*a* (Ps 95:11).

3*c*-8. God's creation rest is a type. On the seventh day of creation God rested and was refreshed (Ex 31:17; cf. Gen 1:31-2:3). This serves as a type of the rest that the believer may enter spiritually now, in the midst of persecution and conflict, as he fully relies on the finished work of Christ. This rest was not entered into by the generation that came out of Egypt (except Caleb and Joshua) because of unbelief, 6. Neither did Joshua (here called Jesus, the Gr. form of Joshua) give Israel this rest from the harassment of their enemies. Only Christ, the greater Joshua, can provide true rest, 8.

4:9-13. The Son superior to Joshua in the redemption He provides

9-10. Redemptive rest is available for God's people. These verses refer to the rest called sabbath-keeping (*sabbatismos,* 'a state of rest from labor'), 9. It involves the believer's resting completely in a perfect work of redemption (3-4) as God rested from a perfect work of creation, 10. This rest of redemption reposes *wholly* in the work of the cross, and ceases from all self-effort, human merit or legalistic claim as a means either to salvation or sanctification, 10 (cf. Eph 2:8-10). It projects the victory of faith in conquest over spiritual enemies (the world, the flesh and the devil).

11-13. The rest to be diligently realized. The believer is exhorted to be eager to enter into this rest through quiet believing with the reminder that some in Israel failed to enter the rest of the Promised Land because of their unbelief, 11. Faith is necessary in order to possess the rest which Christ provides, while unbelief will rob us of such blessing.

The instrument which God uses to bring men into the rest of faith is the living and dynamic Word of God, 12-13. This Word, keener than a sharp two-edged sword, severs to the point where attitudes and motives are laid bare, where one's innermost thoughts are judged, 12. It strips away all pretense and sham, revealing us as we truly are, 13. Faith that leads to rest in Christ is distinguished thereby from mere assent and formalism.

4:14–5:10. Christ's priesthood superior to Aaron's

4:14-16. Our great high priest. Christ, our 'great high priest,' is great because of *His finished work of redemption,* attested by His having 'passed through the heavens' (ASV), 14. This means that worship and intercession are now carried on in the heavenly sanctuary alone, the believer being brought directly into God's presence (Phil 3:3; Heb 10:19).

Christ is also great because *He is Jesus, the Son of God,* qualified to represent man before the throne of God the Father. He is able to 'sympathize with our weaknesses,' because He was tested in all particulars as we are, sin excepted; that is, He had no connection with sin (cf. 7:26). He was perfect man, tempted in every way as the absolutely Sinless One.

Further, Christ is great because *He transforms God's throne* of holy judgment against sinners *to a throne of grace* for believers, His blood being sprinkled thereupon. There the believer finds a continual supply of mercy and grace for help in all times of need, 16. The greatness of our High Priest calls for adhering to (holding fast) our confession to

Him, 14. He is the One to whom confession is made, and to whom we may draw near with confident assurance that grace may be expected from His throne, 16.

5:1-4. Qualifications of Aaronic priests. Israel's high priest (1) was *chosen from among men,* 1*a*; (2) was ordained or *appointed to minister on behalf of his fellow men* before God, 1*b*; (3) *offered gifts and sacrifices* for sins, representing the sinner, 1*c*; (4) was *compassionate with sinners* because he himself 'is subject to weakness,' 2; (5) also *offered sacrifice for his own sins* as well as those of the people (Lev 16:11) because he, too, needed atonement, 3; (6) was *God-called,* not self-chosen (Ex 28:1; Num 16:40).

5:5-10. Superiority of Christ's qualifications. Christ was fully qualified to be a high priest because He was: (1) *divinely chosen* by God the Father, 5; (2) *divinely appointed* to be *an eternal High Priest* of the order of Melchizedek, 6; (3) a *true man* with a genuinely human nature while He was on earth, therefore able to represent men, 7*a*; (4) the *actual sacrifice* or offering for sin, facing death for sinners, 7*b*; (5) the *final victor over sin* and death in His resurrection, 7*c*; (6) the *perfect substitute* for man and his sin in that Christ's sufferings taught Him the full obedience necessary for His redemptive work, 8. As a result of His perfect qualifications, He became the source of eternal salvation, not a mere covering for sin (as did the Aaronic high priest's sacrifice). His salvation is eternal because His status as a priest is eternal – after the order of Melchizedek (see Heb 7), 9-10.

5:11-14. Appeal to maturity

11-13. Characteristics of the immature. Before developing the truth of the Melchizedek priesthood of Christ the writer introduces another warning or rebuke in the epistle, this time concerning spiritual immaturity. Many of the Hebrew believers addressed were characterized as being dull of hearing in their acceptance and understanding of the truths of the faith, 11. They were still untaught at a time when they should have been qualified to be teachers of the deeper truths, such as the Melchizedek aspect of Christ's priesthood, 12*a*. As babes, they could receive only milk, or elementary truths, and

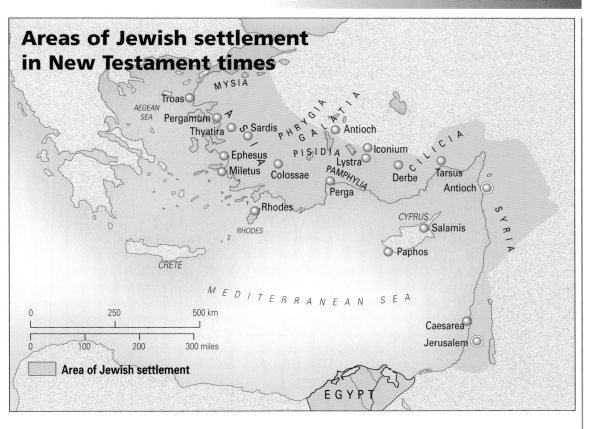

Areas of Jewish settlement in New Testament times

(Map showing cities including Troas, Pergamum, Thyatira, Sardis, Ephesus, Miletus, Colossae, Rhodes, Antioch, Iconium, Lystra, Derbe, Perga, Tarsus, Antioch, Salamis, Paphos, Caesarea, Jerusalem. Regions labeled: MYSIA, PHRYGIA, GALATIA, PISIDIA, PAMPHYLIA, CILICIA, SYRIA, CYPRUS, RHODES, CRETE. Seas: AEGEAN SEA, MEDITERRANEAN SEA. EGYPT. Scale: 0, 250, 500 km; 0, 100, 200, 300 miles. Legend: Area of Jewish settlement)

were unqualified because of a lack of knowledge of the truth of the Word, 12*b*-13.

14. Contrast of the mature. Those who are mature have an adult diet, able to take the solid nourishment of the Word as applied to life and doctrine. They are trained athletes in the spiritual life because of the discipline under which they have gone. In addition, they are doctrinally discerning, able to distinguish between truth and error because their mature experience has made them spiritually discriminating.

6:1-3. Pressing on to full growth

1*a*. Exhortation to spiritual progress. 'Therefore [because of the danger of immaturity, 5:11-14], let us leave the elementary teachings about Christ, and go on to maturity.' 'Leaving,' in this passage, means advancement – advance beyond the elementary truths concerning Christ toward completeness or full growth (*teleiotes*). Perhaps the writer had in mind advancing to the experiential knowledge of Christ's life, death and resurrection, etc.,

beyond the simple historical facts, to the realization of one's position and possessions in Christ as revealed in the NT epistles.

1*b*-2. Danger of spiritual retrenchment. The peril endangering maturity is that of relaying the foundation instead of proceeding to build the superstructure thereupon. Those basic truths constituting the foundation, while absolutely necessary but not ends in themselves, are: (1) 'repentance from acts that lead to death,' 1*c*, i.e., those works which were involved in obedience to the Mosaic law, 'dead' because they were valueless in obtaining eternal salvation (Acts 15:10; cf. Deut 6:24-25 with Gal 3:11-12); (2) 'faith in God,' 1*d*, *not* faith in their privileges as Jews (1 Pet 1:18-21); (3) 'instruction about baptisms,' 2*a*, which for the addressees included OT washings and purification rites as well as Christian water baptism; (4) 'laying on of hands,' 2*b*, a ceremony symbolizing identification and transfer in the OT (Lev 16:21) with similar meanings in the NT (Acts 5:12; 8:17-19; 9:41; 13:3; 19:6; 1 Tim 4:14; 2 Tim 1:6); (5) 'resurrection of the dead,' 2*c*, a doctrine believed in the OT (Job 19:25; Ps 16: 10; Dan 12:2) and a cardinal element of NT preaching which proclaimed the believer's hope (Lk 24:39,43; 1 Cor 15:20-22); (6) 'eternal judgment,' *2d,* the teaching that lost mankind and rebellious angels will experience eternal punishment (Mt 25:41; Rev 20:10).

3. The dynamic of spiritual progress. With God's permission, these Jewish believers must press on toward maturity, advancing from the elementary doctrines just mentioned. God can only allow such blessing as believers trust Him in faith and allow Him to work in them. 'Pressing on' is the Christian's working out God's inwrought salvation (Phil 3:14).

6:4-8. The sin of lapsing back into Judaism

4-5. The subjects – Hebrew believers. These verses give evidence that those being discussed were believers, but they had drifted away from the experiential knowledge relating to Christ's person and work, thereby neglecting to claim God's rest and remaining immature.

6. The nature of the sin – defection from the all-sufficient nature of Christ's death. This sin involved their falling away from grace (salvation in Christ by faith alone) to Judaistic ordinances in the maintaining of their relationship to God. It was a denial of the Hebrew believer's initial repentance from the dead works of the law, which in reality was a denial of the complete efficacy of Christ's death for all sin (Jn 19:30). Evidently the Christians in view were those who fell back of Judaistic ritual and sacrifices to atone for their sins. This was tantamount to crucifying the Son of God again, considering Him an impostor and subjecting Him to great indignity and public shame, because it slighted both His person and His work. For such there was no repentance, no about-face, only divine judgment.

7 -8. The result of the sin – divine rejection. Defection calls forth God's disciplinary action because there is lack of fruitfulness in the life, 7, and instead, the presence of unbelief and sin ('thorns and thistles' being tokens of unbelief and the curse of sin), 8. The result is rejection (*adokimos*) disapproval or disqualification (1 Cor 9:27) for

a prize, with the believer's work being burned, as wood, hay or stubble, at the judgment seat of Christ (1 Cor 3:13-15).

6:9-12. The contrast of maturity in Christ

9-10. The better things of salvation. Although very much aware of the dangers which were present to thwart these Hebrew Christians in their growth toward maturity, the writer expresses his confidence in them. Their past lives gave him a basis for this confidence, 10. Not only he but God Himself would not forget their many acts of kindness which they had shown toward their Christian brethren even in the face of tribulation and temptation. 'Things that accompany salvation' evidently has reference to the fruitful works which resulted from their inwrought faith.

11-12. The author's desire. It was the writer's longing that their good start (9-10) might continue toward full maturity, 11. This would be accomplished by each manifesting through outward conduct the same earnestness which had been displayed to this point. Such diligence would result in the full assurance that they would possess or inherit the promises in the end, at the consummation of the age. There would be the temptation to slothfulness or sluggishness, but they were to be imitators of those saints who inherit the promises, 12.

6:13-20. Encouragement to maturity in Christ

13-18a. God's faithfulness to Abraham. Those who anticipated inheriting the promise, 12, had God's covenant with Abraham as their assurance. This patriarch is introduced here to serve as an example of perseverance in waiting for the promise of God. Abraham persevered because God guaranteed by His own name the covenant He made with Abraham, 13. The divine oath, 14, involved a Hebraism, 'I will surely bless [superabundantly bless] you and give you many descendants [superabundantly multiply].' Given to encourage Abraham in patience, it accomplished its purpose and he obtained the promise, 15, that is, he received the full guarantee of its complete fulfillment.

Using the human custom of an oath as settlement of a controversy, 16, God, being more abundantly willing to demonstrate the unchangeableness of His purpose, confirmed His promise by an oath. Having sworn by His own name, it was impossible for God to lie. His authority and integrity were at stake. His oath, thereby, gave Abraham absolute guarantee of fulfillment, 17-18. Since God is unchangeable, we have as strong an encouragement as did Abraham.

18b-20. God's faithfulness in Christ. Christ, who is the fulfillment of the Abrahamic covenant, is our assurance, the object of our hope, 18b. This hope we continually have as an anchor (emphatic) for the soul which keeps us from drifting. It (Christ) is within the veil in the heavenly sanctuary, 19, and He, as our Forerunner and High Priest, enables us to follow after Him and through Him to enter within the veil – heaven itself, 20.

7:1-3. Melchizedek, the type of Christ as king-priest

1-3a. The identity of Melchizedek (cf. Gen 14:17-24). This man was 'king of Salem,' an ancient name for Jerusalem, in the patriarchal era. But more important, he was 'priest of God Most High' (*El Elyon,* 'creator [or 'possessor'] of heaven and earth,' Gen 14:19, 22), 1a. His eminence or superiority to

Abraham is revealed in his blessing, 1b, and in his receiving tithes from Abraham, 1a. Perhaps a clue to his character is given in the translation of his name, which means 'king of righteousness,' and in the meaning of his title as 'king of Salem,' that is, 'king of peace,' 2b. Neither Melchizedek's parentage nor his genealogy is recorded; nor are his birth and death specified, not because he was eternal, but because these details are extraneous to his position as a type, 'like the Son of God,' 3.

3b. Melchizedek, a type of Christ. Melchizedek was made like, or made to resemble, Christ in description and typical significance. The focus is thus placed on Christ's royal authority and the unending duration of His priesthood, which, in turn, are based on His person (the Son of God) and His work in redemption (as King of righteousness, Rom 3:25-26; then as King of peace, Rom 5:1). Our King-Priest now sits 'at the right hand of the throne of the Majesty in heaven' (8:1); He 'always lives to intercede' (7:25b).

7:4-22. The superiority of Melchizedek's priesthood to Aaron's

4-7, 9-10. Aaron paid tithes to Mechizedek. The reader is urged to observe

The third century synagogue at Capernaum stands over the site of a first century synagogue.

the greatness of Melchizedek, who was so great that even Abraham gave him tithes of the best produce of the land, 4. The theme emhasized is that Melchizedek's priesthood was greater than Aaron's because the Aaronic priests (who received the tithes of the people) as descendants of Abraham offered tithes through Abraham to Melchizedek, the greater. In this manner Melchizedek, 'the greater,' blessed the Levites, 'the lesser,' 7.

8. Aaron's priesthood was temporary, Melchizedek's permanent. The Levitical, or Aaronic, ministry was temporary because it was served by mortal men who died. By contrast, the Melchizedek priesdy ministry was enduring and contained no hint of death. Christ, the antitype, is emphasized in the last phrase. His ministry is eternal because it is served by the immortal, death-conquering King-Priest.

11-14. The Aaronic priesthood was limited. The Levitical priesthood lacked 'perfection' in the sense of finality of function and completeness of operation and effect. It could neither remove sin, nor grant righteousness or favor and position with God, 11*a*. This lack of perfection is recognized: (1) in the need which existed for 'another priest,' i.e., one of a *different* order, the order of Melchizedek, 11*b*; (2) in the necessity of a change in the law with which the Aaronic priesthood was unseparably bound, 12; and (3) in the need for a change in the exclusive regulations of the law which limited the priesthood to the tribe of Levi, and thereby excluded Christ on the human plane from serving, since He was from the tribe of Judah, 13-14*a*. Moses gave no priestly authority to Judah, 14*b*.

15-22. The Melchizedek priesthood is final. Christ's priesthood, after the order of Melchizedek, is final and complete because of: (1) its superior nature, 15 (cf. 4-11); (2) its qualification by the power of an indissoluble life and not by physical regulations, 16; (3) its institution by the authority of the Word of God, 17; (4) its bringing in a better hope with immediate access to God, 19; (5) its finalization by a divine oath establishing and ordaining Christ's eternal priesthood, 20-21 ; (6) Christ, the guarantee of a new and better covenant by virtue of the oath's better validity, 22 (Jer 31:31-33; Mt 26:28; 1 Cor 11:25).

7:23-28. The superior efficacy and perpetuity of Christ's priesthood

23-24. Its perpetuity. The Aaronic priests were many in number, death necessitating that they frequently be replaced by their descendants. They contrasted to Christ's one permanent priesthood (*aparabaton,* 'not to be superseded' in the sense of not passing from one to another), because He continues forever, 24.

25-28. Its superior efficacy. The superior nature of the efficacy of Christ's priesthood, based on its perpetuity, consists, first in its *complete ability to save* 'completely,' or forever (*eis to panteles,* 'through all time'), 25*b*. This is possible because those coming to God through Him enjoy His uninterrupted intercession which guarantees their salvation forever. 'He always lives to intercede,' never interrupted by death.

Second, it is superior because *its Priest is perfectly suited to our need,* 26. He is: (1) 'holy,' perfectly aligned with God's will in reverent piety (Ps 16:10); (2) 'blameless'; (3) 'pure,' in the sense of being unstained by blemish from sinful men; (4) 'set apart from sinners,' being in a different class from sinners when He was on earth and now separate from them as their High Priest in heaven above (cf. Lev 21:12); (5) 'exalted above the heavens,' for He literally 'passed through' the heavens (4:14).

Third, the *sacrifice* of this priesthood is *final.* 27. In contrast to the day-by-day sacrifices of the Aaronic priests (9:6; 10:11; cf. Ex 29:38-42), Christ's sacrifice was a *once-for-all offering* of Himself. He did not need to offer daily, nor to offer for His own sins. He offered Himself as a final and complete efficacious sacrifice, the Sinless One alone offering for the sinful (cf. Lev 16:11).

Fourth, the efficacy of Christ's priesthood is superior because *it is sealed by divine oath.* 28. In contrast to the Mosaic law, which constituted men priests who themselves were sinners, God's oath in Ps 110:4 (which was made after the law was given) makes the sinless Son Priest perfected forevermore.

8:1-5. Christ, high priest in the heavenly sanctuary

1-2. The reality of his ministry. The main 'point' in what has been said is that Christ 'sat down at the right hand of the throne of the Majesty in heaven,' completely superseding the Levitical priesthood, 1. He is infinitely above all other priests, exercising His priesthood in heaven, not on earth (10:12). The high priest, even when he entered the holiest annually, only *stood* for a moment before the *symbol* of God's throne. By contrast, our Lord *ever sits* on the throne of the Majesty on high till His enemies are made His footstool (Ps 110:1). Further, Christ sits as a minister in the sanctuary – the administrator of the holy things in the real tabernacle in heaven. The early tabernacle was a mere foreshadow of the heavenly, being pitched not by man but by the Lord, 2.

3-5. The typical foreshadowing of His ministry. 'Every high priest . . . appointed to offer both gifts and sacrifices' was a type of 'this one,' who must also have something to offer, 3, viz., He offered Himself once for all as a completed, final sacrifice to remove sin. As the high priest did not enter the most holy place apart from blood, so Christ did not enter the holiest (heaven) apart from His own blood (1 Pet 1:2). He ministers thus in heaven. If He were here on earth He would not even be a priest, not being from the tribe of Levi, 4. But He ministers the real, while the Levitical priests ministered only 'a copy and shadow of what is in heaven,' 5 (Ex 25:40).

8:6-13. The satisfactory nature of the new covenant

6-9. The limitations of the old covenant. The 'old covenant' refers to the legal or Mosaic covenant. It was *enacted on promises inferior* to those upon which the new covenant was established, 6. These promises entailed conditions ('if . . . ,' Ex 19:5-7), with promises of blessing following obedience, but furnishing no dynamic for such obedience. By contrast, the new covenant is unconditional, final, and irreversible, since God does everything, 8-10. It rests upon the finished work of Christ and secures eternal blessedness, under the Abrahamic covenant, to all who believe (Gal 3:13-29).

The old covenant *lacked finality,* 7. It was not without defect. The law as a method of divine dealing made nothing perfect or final (Rom 8:3; Heb 7:18-19) because of man's sinfulness. Had the old covenant been

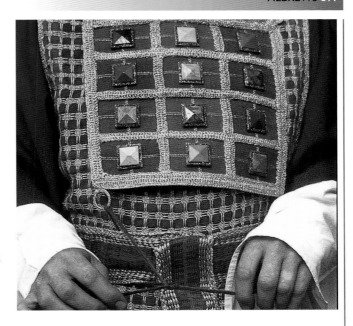

satisfactory, a second covenant would not have been needed.

The old covenant also *lacked efficacy,* 8-9. It provided no power to the sinner to keep its conditions. Although a standard for conduct was provided, enablement to maintain it was lacking, and Israel disobeyed and fell under the judgment of God, 8*a*, 9*b*.

10-13. The satisfactory nature of the new covenant. In contrast to the old, the new covenant is *gracious and unconditional,* 10*a*. This is the result of what God does sovereignly and unconditionally for Israel at the second advent, not what they helplessly attempt to do for God (cf. the 'I wills,' 10-12). The new covenant is also *spiritually efficacious,* 10*b*-11, resulting in spiritual regeneration, 10*b*, and universal knowledge of the Lord, 11. Then, too, this covenant is *faultless and final,* 12, based as it is upon the complete redemption of Christ, settling forever Israel's sin question and superseding the old covenant, 13 (see notes on 10:15-17).

9:1-10. The typical nature of the old covenant

1-5. The ordinances of the sanctuary under the old covenant. The ministry of the priests under the Mosaic covenant is described in relation to the pieces of furniture in the tabernacle. It is selected for special description here because the priestly ordinances

Replica of the high priest's breastplate.

were observed therein. The outer room (the Holy Place) is described in 2, the inner room (the Most Holy Place) in 3-5. Each piece of furniture spoke typically of Christ, His person and work (see notes on Ex 25-30).

6-10. The sacrifices of the old covenant. The daily repeated activities relating to sacrifice and worship which were performed by the priests in the holy place, 6, and the sacrifices on the Day of Atonement which were offered by the high priest once a year in the holy of holies, 7, intimated that the way of access directly to God for every believer was not yet open, 8. These were regulations for the body, 10, early and external observances related to an imperfect tabernacle. Such ordinances served as symbols, or typical illustrations, for that pre-cross era of the future glorious ministry of Christ and the spiritual realities which He would effect, 9. They were external and temporal symbols imposed by the old covenant (Mosaic law) until the time of reformation (of setting things right) by the new covenant in the death of Christ, 10.

9:11-14. Reality under the new covenant

11-12. The essence of the reality. Christ's appearance as High Priest fulfilled the types of both the Melchizedek and the Aaronic priesthoods in bringing 'the good things that are already here,' 11a. He fulfilled the type of the high priest's entering the holiest once a year (Lev 16) by having entered *once for all* into the real holy place in the tabernacle in heaven, 11b. There He presented His own infinitely efficacious blood on the heavenly mercy seat, showing His one sacrifice to be incomparably superior to the *many continued* sacrifices of the blood of goats and calves 12a (cf. 9:13-14). This once-for-all sacrifice secured eternal redemption, not merely a temporary covering and passing over of sin for the time being, as under the old covenant, 12b. 'Eternal redemption' has reference to the safety and security which the believer possesses in Christ, and his future eternal glorification.

13-14. The meaning of the reality. This eternal redemption, purchased by Christ's own blood, purifies not only externally and ceremonially (as did the Levitical sacrifices on the Day of Atonement), but inwardly and vitally for service rendered to a 'living God.' If the sprinkling of ceremonially defiled persons with animal blood and the ashes of a red heifer (Num 19:16-18) could purify outwardly to any degree, to how much greater degree shall the blood of Christ effect inward cleansing and obtain an eternally complete salvation, 14?

9:15-22. The new covenant sealed by Christ's blood

15-17. Christ's death a necessity. The sacrificial offering of Christ in death constituted the beginning of a new covenant based thereon. Without His death there could have been no 'will' or covenant, 16, nor could He have become the Mediator, acting between a holy God and guilty sinners to the end that they might be reconciled, 15a (cf.8:6; 1 Tim 2:5). As a result of His redemptive death, those whose sins were simply covered under the old covenant (Rom 3:24-25) have now received 'the promised eternal inheritance,' 15b.

In the OT the only way a covenant could be sealed was by the blood of sacrifice, 16. Similarly, Christ's death sealed the new covenant and set it in force (made it valid), 17. Even among men, a covenant (*diatheke,* testament or will) is invalid until the testator dies, and then it becomes operative.

18-22. The necessity of Christ's death foreshadowed by the law. The first or legal covenant was inaugurated by blood, 18, beginning only when Moses had sprinkled with blood both the book of the law and the people, 19, and had pronounced the words, 'This is the blood of the covenant, which God has commanded you to keep,' 20 (Ex 24:1-8). The tabernacle and all the vessels of worship were similarly blood-sprinkled, 21 (Ex 29:12, 36), as were practically all things under the old dispensation, 22a, thus typically showing the necessity of Christ's death. (For exceptions see Ex 19:10; Lev 15:5, etc). This emphasized the great truth, 'Without shedding of blood [death] there is no forgiveness' (Gr. *aphesis,* 'no sending off or away,' i.e., no separation of sin from the sinner, cf. Mt 26:28, 22b).

9:23-24. The better sanctuary of the new covenant

23a. The Mosaic tabernacle purged with animal sacrifices. This tent and its personnel and ritual were only 'copies' (in the

The covenants of Scripture

Covenant and significance

Eternal covenant Heb 13:20
The redemptive covenant before time began, between the Father and the Son. By this covenant we have eternal redemption, an eternal peace from the 'God of peace,' through the death and resurrection of the Son.

Edenic covenant Gen 1:26-28
The creative covenant between the Triune God, as the first party (Gen 1:26), and newly created man, as the second party, governing man's creation and life in Edenic innocence. It regulated man's dominion and subjugation of the earth, and presented a simple test of obedience. The penalty was death.

Adamic covenant Gen 3:14-19
The covenant conditioning fallen man's life on the earth. Satan's tool (the serpent) was cursed (Gen 3:14); the first promise of the Redeemer was given (3:15); women's status was altered (3:16); the earth was cursed (3:17-19); physical and spiritual death resulted (3:19).

Noahic covenant Gen 8:20-9:6
The covenant of human government. Man is to govern his fellowmen for God, indicated by the institution of capital punishment as the supreme judicial power of the state (Gen 9:5-6). Other features included the promise of redemption through the line of Shem (9:26).

Abrahamic covenant Gen 12:1-3; confirmed, 13:14-17; 15:1-7; 17:1-8
The covenant of promise. Abraham's posterity was to be made a great nation. In him (through Christ) all the families of the earth were to be blessed (Gal 3:16; Jn 8:56-68).

Mosaic covenant Ex 20:1-31:18
The legal covenant, given solely to Israel. It consisted of the commandments (Ex 20:1-26); the judgments (social) (Ex 21:1; 24:11) and the ordinances (religious); (Ex 24:12-31:18); also called the law. It was a conditional covenant of works, a ministry of 'condemnation' and 'death' (2 Cor 3:7-9), designed to lead the transgressor (convicted thereby as a sinner) to Christ.

Palestinian covenant Deut 30:1-10
The covenant regulating Israel's tenure of the land of Canaan. Its prophetic features include dispersion for disobedience (Deut 30:1), future repentance while in dispersion (30:2), the Lord's return (30:3), the restoration (30:4-5), national conversion (3:6), judgment of Israel's foes (30:7), national prosperity (30:9). Its blessings are conditioned upon obedience (30:8, 10), but fulfillment is guaranteed by the new covenant.

Davidic covenant 2 Sam 7:4-17; 1 Chr 17:4-15
The kingdom covenant regulating the temporal and eternal rule of David's posterity. It secures in perpetuity a Davidic 'house' or line, a throne, and a kingdom. It was confirmed by divine oath in Ps 89:30-37 and renewed to Mary in Lk 1:31-33. It is fulfilled in Christ as the world's Saviour and Israel's coming King (Acts 1:6; Rev 19:16; 20:4-6).

New covenant Jer 31:31-33; Mt 26:28; Mk 14:24; Lk 22:20; Heb 8:8-12
The covenant of unconditional blessing based upon the finished redemption of Christ. It secures blessing for the church, flowing from the Abrahamic covenant (Gal 3:13-20), and secures all covenant blessings to converted Israel, including those of the Abrahamic, Palestinian, and Davidic covenants. This covenant is unconditional, final and irreversible.

sense of suggestive tokens) of the heavenly things in the heavenly tabernacle. Animal sacrifices might typically purify this inferior earthly sanctuary, but not its antitypical and superior sanctuary in heaven, 23.

23b-24. The heavenly tabernacle purged with better sacrifices. 'The better sacrifices' (plural) comprehend and sum up the *one* final sacrifice of Christ. This *one* sacrifice is more than equivalent to all the numerous Levitical sacrifices. Our Lord, as both Priest and Sacrifice, has entered into 'heaven itself,' to present Himself in the immediate presence of God on our behalf, 24, thus securing eternal redemption.

9:25-10:4. The better sacrifice of the new covenant
9:25-28. Christ's sacrifice is final. This finality is indicated by Christ's complete and unrepeatable offer of Himself in contrast to the early high priest who entered the holiest every year 'with blood not his own,' 25 (Lev 16). If Christ's sacrifice had not been final He would then often have had to suffer, since the continued sins of men would entail repeated suffering on earth 'since the creation of the world,' 26a. But His sacrifice once for all at the consummation of the ages has put away and abolished sin — thus there is no need for further sacrifice, 26b.

The sacrifice of Christ is final because: (1) it involved the blood of His own glorious person, 26c, satisfying all the claims of an infinitely holy God against sinful men; (2) it perfectly meets the needs of the sinner who faces death and judgment, 27; (3) it perfectly meets the needs of the believer. Christ was once offered to bear the believer's sins, 28a (1 Cor 15:3; 1 Pet 2:24), and the believer will never have to face the sin question again (Jn 5:24). Christ's coming for His own will not involve the sin question, but rather 'salvation,' consummating in glorification (1 Cor 15:51-57; 1 Jn 3:1-2), 28b.

10:1-4 Levitical sacrifices imperfect and repeatable. These sacrifices were directly related to the law of Moses and were only 'a shadow' (*skia,* 'a dim shadowing forth') of 'the good things that are coming' (cf. 9:11), i.e., the blessings of Christ's salvation, 1a. They lacked the perfection and finality of Christ's once-for-all

sacrifice, 10b, in that these typical sacrifices continued to be offered and never really cleansed away the consciousness of guilt and sin in the worshipers, 2. On the contrary, they only brought a fresh remembrance of sins to be atoned for, 3, because of the utter inability of animal blood to remove sin and guilt, 4.

10:5-10. The new covenant based on Christ's perfect sacrifice
5-7. Christ's perfect sacrifice foretold. His sacrifice was prophesied in Ps 40:6-8 by David, who expressed the truth that animal sacrifices were powerless to remove sins (see v. 4). This prophecy envisioned the coming of One who would enter the world (by incarnation) to effect the removal of man's sins, 5a, and enunciated God's dissatisfaction with the sacrifices and offerings of the Levitical system, 5b-6. It predicted the incarnation, 'a *body* you prepared for me,' 5c. The Heb. of the OT has, 'my ears you have pierced' (Ps 40:6), alluding also to the incarnation and willing servitude of Christ (Ex 21:5-6).

Verse 7 predictively sums up our Lord's redemption work: God the Son entering the world to become incarnate, 'I have come' (cf. Lk 1:35); and His utter obedience to the Father's will, even to death, 'to do your will, O God' (cf. Lk 22:42; Phil 2:8).

8-10. Christ's perfect sacrifice annuls the old order. The Father's dissatisfaction with the Levitical ritual, 8, is contrasted with His will for the Son, 9. This will involved the Son's sacrifice of Himself in order to establish the new covenant of perfect redemption. It also has resulted in the formation of a new company of redeemed, those who are positionally sanctified (set apart unto God as holy) through the once-for-all offering of Christ's own body, 10.

10:11-14. The new covenant superior because of Christ's present position
11. The inferior position and ministry of the Levitical priests. The incompleteness and inefficacy of the Levitical priest's ministry were seen in the repetition of his ritual and in his position as standing before the altar. The repeated offering of the same sacrifices could never *take away* sins (could

never remove sins in the sense of stripping them away, as one would strip off an old soiled garment closely wrapped around a body).

12-14. The superior position and work of Christ. In striking contrast to the inadequacy of the Levitical priesthood, Christ offered 'one sacrifice,' a single efficacious sacrifice for sins which availed for all time, 12*a*. The completeness of His work was signified by His having 'sat down,' thus assuming an exalted position of authority and priestly service 'at the right hand of God,' 12*b*. He now awaits the wider results of His redemptive work, when His enemies will be vanquished and His rule established throughout the whole earth, 13. The superior efficacy of Christ's sacrifice is noted in that 'by one offering He has made perfect *forever* those who are being made holy,' 14. See note on verse 10.

10:15-18. The new covenant is superior because of the finality of Christ's sacrifice

15-17. The witness of the Spirit. The Holy Spirit's testimony to the finality of Christ's sacrifice is quoted from Jer 31:33-34. This prophecy of the new covenant envisions Israel's conversion at the second advent, but inasmuch as the new covenant is based on the finality of Christ's sacrifice its blessings are enjoyed by both the church (Mt 26:28; 1 Cor 11:25) and Israel.

Christ in His sacrificial atoning death accomplished remission of sins and transformation of life for all who place their faith in Him, 16-17. It was to this that the Spirit gave witness.

18. A summary statement. Christ's sacrifice is final and complete because it secured *aphesis,* complete 'dismission' of sin from the sinner in the sense of unqualified forgiveness. The guilt and penalty of these ('sins and lawless acts,' 17) were cancelled. Where these sins are completely forgiven a need no longer exists for further 'offering for sin.'

10:19-25. Appeal to a life of faith

19-22. The basis for the appeal. Underlying this exhortation, 22, is the description of all that Christ is and has done as found in the preceding argument of this epistle. Confidence (assurance, boldness) is enjoined for these fellow Hebrew believers as they enter the very presence of God because: (1) the blood of Christ – eternally acceptable to God and totally sufficient – has made such access possible, 19; (2) Jesus has inaugurated a new and living way through the veil into the immediate presence of God, 20; and (3) we have a High Priest, superior to all other priests, who serves 'over the house of God,' the real sanctuary in heaven, 21 (see notes on 9:11-12, 23-24). Such privileges enable the believer to 'draw near [come to God intimately and frequently] with a sincere heart in full assurance of faith,' freed from the doubts of an evil conscience and cleansed from defilement, 22.

23-25. The further appeal. In appealing to a life of faith, the writer not only emphasizes the necessity of possessing assurance to enter God's immediate presence (19-22), but urges: (1) steadfastness in the hope Christ has given us, 23, i.e., complete reliance on God's faithfulness in giving the future inheritance He has promised (1 Pet 1:3-5); (2) consideration for one another, 24, which will result in stimulating each other to love and good works; and (3) constancy in public worship, 25, which will encourage one another in view of the Lord's coming ('the Day') and His judgment of the believers' works.

10:26-31. Warning against lapse into Judaism

26-29. The problem of presumptuous sinning. This sin, which faced the Hebrew believers to whom the epistle is addressed, consisted of a willful and deliberate course of action against the full knowledge (*epignosis*) that they had received of the truth – Jesus Christ and His salvation as the way to God (cf. 2:1-4; 3:7-19; 5:11-6:20; 12:3-17, 25-29), 26*a*. It evidently involved a return to worn-out forms and ceremonies to atone for sins, things that had been fulfilled in Christ's sacrifice. Rejecting His *one* and *only* sacrifice, 'there no longer remains a sacrifice for sins' – no other sacrifice is left on which to depend, 26*b*. Such sin incurs the judgment of God, a fearful and terrifying thing which all adversaries (those opposed to God's method of salvation by grace through faith in the atoning death of Christ) may expect, 27. The charge placed against these rejectors included: (1) trampling under foot (spurning and treating shamefully) the Son of God, who purchased so great salvation; (2) rejecting as common and unholy the covenant blood of Christ by which the believer is consecrated; and (3) insulting the Holy Spirit who imparts the gracious blessing of God, 29.

30-31. The punishment. If one who despised the old covenant faced severe judgment, 28 (Deut 17:2-6), how much worse will be the punishment of those who despise the new covenant, 29? Deut 32:35-36 is quoted to give additional evidence of the judgment which rejectors may expect, 30. This punishment is in reference to 'his people,' and may be executed by present disciplinary action or at the future judgment seat of Christ (see notes on 1 Cor 3:11-17). In either case it involves falling into the hands 'of the living God,' the Judge of all the earth, 31, a terrifying and fearful thing.

10:32-39. A call to patient faith

32-34. The call to remember their early faith. These vacillating Hebrew believers, endangered by a return to Mosaic ordinances and ritual, are called upon to remember the days past, in which, after they had been spiritually enlightened concerning Christ's eternal redemption, they *proved* their faith by enduring a 'great contest in the face of suffering,' 32. This involved being publicly exposed to abusive insult from unbelieving Jews, or sincerely sharing in sympathy with those fellow believers who were so treated, 33. They had further *demonstrated* the genuineness of their faith in Christ by expressing sympathetic compassion for those imprisoned (including the writer of the epistle) and by accepting with joy the seizure of their property—looking with the eye of faith at a better and abiding possession, 34.

35-39. The call to continue in patient faith. These believers, in the light of their expression of past faith, are urged not to 'throwaway' their intrepid confidence in Christ, which carries with it a great reward, 35. Their present need is perseverance (*hupomone,* that quality of remaining under trial and difficulty with persevering endurance), so that having accomplished the will of God they may 'receive what he has promised,' the promised reward related to the imminent return of the Lord, 36-37.

Faith is to be the theme of the believer's life, not legalistic forms and works (Hab 2:3-4; Rom 1:17; Gal 3:11). But if any, to escape persecution or ostracism, draw back from professed faith to legalism, God shall voice His displeasure, and judgment may be expected (cf. 26-31), 38. The writer realizes his readers have genuine faith that will not permit them to draw back to eternal ruin; rather, they are 'of those who believed and are saved,' 39.

11:1-3. The superiority of persevering faith

1. The definition of persevering faith. The faith here defined is not faith in its widest sense or entire nature but specifically persevering faith. It is urged upon tried and tested believers so that they might go on to perfection (6:1-20), avoiding defection (10:19-39). Such faith is said to be: (1) the assurance (*hupostasis*, that which stands under as a foundation or basis, giving assurance of realization) of things hoped for – hope being faith in action with regard to the future reality of present promises; and (2) a settled conviction or persuasion of things not yet actual but certain to become so (cf. 2 Cor 5:7).

2-3. The accomplishments of persevering faith. Faith enables men *to receive divine approval.* 2, and *to understand spiritual truth,* 3. We believe, therefore we know (Anselm's *credo ut intelligam*), through a Spirit-enlightened intellect. Such knowledge brings understanding concerning God's creative acts and His ordering of the ages for His own purpose and glory.

11:4-40. Faith that envisioned the promise – Christ

Abel and Enoch

4. Abel's sacrifice of faith. His sacrifice was 'better' in the sense of being greater and of higher value. It involved the shedding of atoning blood, speaking of Abel's faith and obedience to God's revelation that fallen man was a sinner and needed the interposition of a substitute (Gen 13:15, 21; Heb 9:22). Cain's offering was a presentation of his own works and secured no acceptance with God (see notes on Gen 4). In contrast, Abel's sacrifice secured God's declaration that he was righteous, and testified to all men for all time that salvation is by faith in the atoning death of an acceptable substitute (Jn 1:29).

5-6. Enoch's walk of faith. (Cf. Gen 5:23-24.) His walk in unbroken fellowship with God resulted in his being translated to heaven without so much as a glimpse of death. The character of his life had been such that God could testify that Enoch had pleased Him, 5. Thus, his life was an illustration of the truth that the way of faith is the *only way* of pleasing and approaching God, 6.

Artist's impression of the Jewish high priest sprinkling blood on the horns of the altar.

Noah

7. Noah's action of faith. Noah built the ark because of his faith in God's predictive word concerning events of which there was as yet no visible sign. As a result of this act: (1) his household was saved from judgment; (2) his 120-year witness condemned the world because of its unbelief; and (3) he became an heir (possessor) of righteousness because of his faith (later exhibited in his offering, Gen 6: 13-22).

Abraham and Sarah

8-10. Abraham's obedience of faith. In leaving his home in Ur, and later Haran (Gen 11:31-12:4), for Canaan, Abraham displayed an obedient faith which was *unwavering* in that the land he set out for was still not promised to him, and when it was, the Canaanites still possessed it. His was also an *unquestioning* faith, for he did not know where he was going, 8b, and a *pilgrim* faith in that he lived in a foreign land without a permanent dwelling, 9. *Expectantly* in faith 'he was looking forward to the city with foundations, whose architect and builder is God,' 10 (Rev 21:19-20; cf. Jn 8:56; Heb 11:16; 12:22; 13:14).

11-12. Sarah's strength of faith. By faith Sarah received physical strength to conceive Isaac, the child of promise in the line of Christ, even when she was long past the age of childbearing, because she considered God, who had given her the promise, faithful and trustworthy in keeping His word, 11 (cf. Gen 17:19; 18:11-14; 21:1-2). Because of their trust in God, Abraham and Sarah, even though physically they were 'as good as dead,' became the parents of multitudes as numerous as the stars of the sky and the sand of the seashore, 12. All Jews trace their physical lineage to them, and all believers trace their spiritual lineage to this blessed couple.

The reality and hope of faith

13-15. Its reality. The genuineness of the faith of OT saints is shown: (1) by *their death,* all died in faith, for they were controlled and energized to the end by their confidence in God, 13a; (2) by *their unwavering trust,* despite the fact that they did not receive the visible fulfillment of the promises, 13b (Gen 3:15; 12:1-4, 7); (3) by *their separated and pilgrim walk,* as a result of their having been given the promises, 13c (cf. Gen 23:4; Ps 39:12); and (4) by *their words and actions,* proving they sought a heavenly country (14-15), for they had ample opportunity to return to Mesopotamia and Ur had they desired.

16. Its hope. The genuine faith of the OT saints expressed itself in their hope for a better country (heaven). God responded by being identified as the God of Abraham, Isaac, and Jacob (Ex 3:6, 15; 4:5). In fulfilling their hope 'he has prepared a city for them,' the New Jerusalem (Isa 2:2; Ezk 40-48; Heb 12:22; 13:14; Rev 21-22).

Abraham and Isaac

17-18. Abraham's severely tested faith. The supreme test of Abraham's faith was his presenting of Isaac as a sacrificial offering (Gen 22:1-10). In intention he actually did sacrifice his 'one and only' son, typifying the Father 'who did not spare his own Son, but gave him up for us all' (Rom 8:32). The test was intensified because God had said to Abraham face to face, 'through Isaac your offspring will be reckoned' (Gen 21:12).

19. Abraham's uniquely triumphant faith. His faith met the supreme test because: (1) it conquered the fear of death, 'he considered that God is able to raise men even from the dead' (Gr.); and (2) it retrieved Isaac from death by what was a parable of the resurrection, in the sense that Isaac was figuratively dead by being potentially sacrificed.

Isaac, Jacob, and Joseph

20-21. Isaac and Jacob's blessing of faith. Isaac by faith, when blessing Jacob and Esau, assigned things still in the future as if they were present (Gen 27:27-29, 39-40). Jacob had the precedence because his blessings were spiritual. 'By faith Jacob, when was dying, blessed each of Joseph's sons' (Gen 47:29; 48:8-20). Unable to distinguish them by sight, he did distinguish them by faith and intentionally placed his right hand on Ephraim, the younger, faith showing him that Ephraim would be greater than Manasseh. The aged dying Jacob did this, 'and worshiped, as he leaned on the top of his staff,' the emblem of his God-sustained pilgrimage to the heavenly city.

22. Joseph's instructions of faith. 'By faith Joseph, when he was dying, made mention of [by reminiscing upon the promise of God] the exodus of the sons of Israel, and gave orders concerning his bones' (Gr., Gen 50:24-25). His exalted position did not blind him to the fact that Egypt was not his home (cf. Josh 24:32). He believed God would keep his word in bringing about the exodus and Israel's restoration to Canaan (Gen 15:13-21), and ultimately would resurrect his physical body for the heavenly Canaan.

Moses in Egypt

23. His parents' act of faith (cf. Ex 1:22-2:2). Moses' unusual appearance (perhaps great beauty) as a baby was likely the divinely appointed sign by which God aroused the faith of Moses' parents to the conviction that this boy was destined to be the deliverer – because 'they saw [by faith] he was no ordinary child' (cf. Acts 7:20).

24-26. Moses' choice of faith. After he was grown, Moses willingly refused to be identified as 'the son of Pharaoh's daughter' together with the eminence and royal position which would have been his (Ex 2:10), 24. He preferred to share the hardships and endure ill treatment with God's people rather than enjoy the passing pleasures of a sinful life, 25. This choice was made because faith gave him a glimpse of the Messiah to come, and Moses considered suffering for Him to be of 'greater value than the treasures of Egypt,' 26.

Moses quitting Egypt

27. Moses' flight of faith (cf. Ex 2:14-15). Moses' flight represented the irrevocable choice of faith that forever severed him from Egypt and joined him to God's people as their deliverer. He fled without fear of Pharaoh, enduring because he saw 'him who is invisible.' He acted as though he were dealing not with men but with God alone, who was ever in faith's eye.

28-29. Moses' Passover of faith. Simple faith in God prompted Moses to institute the Passover and the sprinkling of the blood on the doorposts, so that the destroyer of the firstborn might not touch the Israelites (Ex 12:21-30). By the same trust in God Israel crossed the Red Sea with walls of water on each side. What was faith to God's people was presumption to their enemies, who were engulfed in the sands as well as the waves of the sea (Ex 14:21-31; 15:12).

Joshua and Rahab

30. Joshua's march of faith. By faith the walls of Jericho fell down after the Israelites had marched around them seven days, in contrast to sieges which often lasted for years. Faith, not the

Artist's impression of Moses before Pharaoh. After he grew up, Moses refused to be identified as 'the son of Pharaoh's daughter;' he preferred to share the hardships with God's people rather than enjoy the passing pleasures of a sinful life.

marching or the trumpet blaring, released the power of God to level the walls (Josh 6:12-21).

31. Rahab's hospitality of faith. Rahab, the Jericho prostitute, did not perish with her unbelieving fellow inhabitants of the city, because she received the Israelite spies into her home and thus exhibited personal faith in her confession (Josh 2:9-11).

From Gideon to Samuel and the prophets

32. Other heroes of faith. In summary, the writer mentions Gideon (Jud 6-8), Barak (Jud 4-5), Samson (Jud 13-16), Jephthah (Jud 11-12), David (1 Sam 16-30; 2 Sam 1-24,1 Kgs 1-2), and Samuel (1 Sam 1-16).

33-34. Their exploits. These who were robust in faith: (1) conquered kingdoms – e.g., David (1 Sam 8); (2) performed acts of righteousness – e.g., Samuel (1 Sam 12:3-23; 15:33) and David (2 Sam 8:15); (3) obtained promises – e.g., the prophets (Josh 21:45; 1 Kgs 8:56); (4) shut the mouths of lions – e.g., Samson (Jud 14:5-6), David (1 Sam 17:34-37), Benaiah (2 Sam 23:20), Daniel (Dan 6:22); (5) quenched the power of fire – e.g., the three Israelites (Dan 3:25); (6) escaped the edge of the sword – e.g., Jephthah (Jud 12:3), David (1 Sam 18:11; 19:10), Elijah (1 Kgs 19:1-2), Elisha (2 Kgs 6:14-17); (7) from weakness were made strong – e.g., Samson (Jud 16:28-30); (8) mighty in war . . . routing armies – e.g., Barak (Jud 4:14-15), Maccabees (1 Macc 15); (9) women received back their dead by resurrection – e.g., the widow of Zarephath (1 Kgs 17:17-24), the Shunammite (2 Kgs 4:17-35).

35-37. Their sufferings. Many of the faithful suffered by: (1) being tortured – e.g., Eleazar (2 Macc 6:18; 19:20, 30), who was stretched out on the wheel and beaten to death – and not accepting release, in order that they might attain a better resurrection, i.e., the first resurrection to life, their martyrdom being the supreme proof of their saving faith; (2) being scourged and imprisoned – e.g., Hanani (2 Chr 16:10); (3) being stoned – e.g., Zechariah, son of Jehoiada (2 Chr 24:20-22; Mt 23:35); (4) being sawed in two – e.g., Isaiah by Manasseh, according to tradition; (5) various other inflictions such as being tempted to sin, put to death by the edge of the sword, ill-treated, destitute.

38. Their evaluation. The world was not worthy of them. In treating them as it did the world condemned itself.

39-40. The faith of Old Testament saints and ours. Old Testament saints gained approval as a result of their faith; but they did not receive the realization of Christ's complete salvation nor the fulfillment of the new covenant with its personal and national blessings. This perfection will come for both OT and NT saints when Christ returns to complete salvation and reign as King of kings and Lord of lords.

12:1-4. The race and goal of faith

1. The race of faith. The figure of an amphitheater filled with OT saints (11:4-38) witnessing NT believers run the race of faith constitutes an incentive for the Christian as he runs. 'Therefore,' since we have surrounding us such a great company of OT witnesses who themselves performed so well in their lives, 'let us run [keep on running] with perseverance the race [*agona,* a contest demanding full expenditure of energy] marked out for us.' To run with full energy demands that we first lay aside every encumbrance, as a runner would strip off clothing, 'and the sin that so easily entangles.'

2-4. The goal of faith. The goal is 'Jesus,' the all-sufficient Saviour; therefore sight is to be *fastened on Him* during the entire course of the race. The believer is to run 'fixing our eyes on Jesus,' and away from every other would-be saviour, because: (1) He is the only Saviour, 2*a*; (2) He is the originator and the perfecter of our faith, 2*b*; (3) He is the supreme example of steadfast faith – 'who for the joy set before Him endured the cross,' 2*c*; (4) He won the race and as a result He 'sat down at the right hand of the throne of God,' 2*d*; (5) His example is the antidote against discouragement, 3; (6) His struggles were infinitely greater than ours, yet He was victorious, 4.

12:5-11. Chastening as an incentive to faith

5-9. The discipline of faith. Divine chastening is an encouragement to press on toward the goal because it is a token of the Lord's love for His own, 5-6 (cf. Prov 3:11-12). Therefore, it is not to be regarded lightly, or wrongly interpreted as being ground for discouragement. The Lord's chastening is a necessary discipline in the Father's treatment of His sons, 7, the absence of which would prove that we were illegitimate children and not genuine sons, 8. If a human father's discipline of his son is beneficial, of how much greater value is it for us to be submissive to our heavenly Father's discipline and thus receive fullness of life, 9?

10-11. The results of disciplined faith. The first result is our permanent eternal good, not merely temporal welfare, which may have seemed fit to our human father, 10a. The second result is the sharing of God's holiness, 10b. Chastisement is inflicted so that we may share God's holiness experientially (2 Pet 1:4), here and now, in preparation for future glorification in His presence, 10b, 14 (cf. 1 Jn 3:2-3). To those so trained, discipline seems painful rather than pleasant; later it yields the peaceful fruit of righteousness, 11.

12:12-17. A warning from Esau

12-14. The exhortation. In the light of the great incentives to run the Christian race with patience, 1-11, the Hebrew believers are urged to lift up their drooping hands and strengthen their weak knees, 12 (cf. Isa 35:3).

They are to make straight paths for their feet so that 'the lame' [the weak believer tempted to forget grace] may not be disabled [by yielding to such temptation] but rather healed' by being encouraged to persist in the gracious race of faith, 13 (Rom 14:19; Gal 6:1). The call is to pursue peace in the sense of constantly and diligently following it, 14a (cf. Ps 34:14), so as to live harmoniously with everybody. Urged also is the diligent pursuit of holiness, 14b. Believers are to be daily set apart as holy unto God (present sanctification) by earnestly pursuing a course of separation from sin, claiming by faith their position in Christ and converting it into the experience of Christ (Rom 6:11-12) through yieldedness to the Holy Spirit. Only as the Holy Spirit sanctifies us are we fit to see the Lord, in the final sense, and to be ever with Him. A right relation with God must be coupled with a proper relation with fellow believers.

15-17. The warning. Verse 15 is a warning against defaulting from the grace of God, resulting in a bitter spirit which poisons many in the Christian community. An illustration is given in the example of Esau, 16-17, whose godless or secular interest through the forfeiture of his birthright led to a hopeless condition (Gen 27:30-40). He exchanged spiritual well-being for momentary fleshly

Relief of Jews sorrowing in exile in Babylon, from the menorah outside Israel's Knesset building in Jerusalem.

gratification. Default from God's grace back to Mosaic ceremonialism leads to similar despair. Believers may, through carnal sin and unbelief, miss the privileges of their access into the holiest through their great High Priest and the promises of blessing in Him.

12:18-24. The result of faith that has obtained the promise

18-21. It delivers from a law of terror. The realities of the old covenant are contrasted with the glories of the new, pointing out once more the advantages of 'going on in Christ' over a return to Judaism because of persecution. God's presence, under the law, brought fear and trembling, even to Moses, 21.

22-24. It brings the blessings and relationships of grace. Grace, under the new covenant, brings Hebrew believers to *Mount Zion,* the city of the living God, the New Jerusalem, in contrast to the earthly Jerusalem and the fearful Mount Sinai, 22*a* (cf.11:10; Rev 21:2ff.). They are also brought into the company of 'thousands of angels in joyful assembly, to the church of the firstborn, whose names are written in heaven,' 22*b*-23*a*. The firstborn is a reference to Christ (Rom 8:29; Col 1:15-16; Heb 1:6), and the church is His Body, His possession, the members of which are heavenly citizens (Eph 2:19; Phil 3:20). These relationships also include one of access to *God, the Judge* of all men, 23*b*; association with *just men made perfect,* 23*c,* a reference to OT saints now made perfect by the cross of Christ (11:39-40); and identity with *Jesus, the Mediator* of the new covenant, 24*a,* and His *sprinkled blood* which has obtained eternal forgiveness from sin, 24*b.*

12:25-29. Warning against refusing to heed God's voice

25-27. The danger of the sin. Warning is given lest some refuse to hear the voice of Christ through the gospel of grace and therefore shun Him, 25*a.* For such there is no escape, 25*b*-27, judgment will come. If the Israelites who refused to listen and obey Moses' warning on earth suffered the judgment of God, how much greater peril do those face who refuse to heed the voice of God's own Son from heaven, 25*b*? Then reference is made to the day of judgment when the impermanent will be

shaken and only the permanent and eternal will remain, 26-27, including the kingdom which will be the inheritance of believers, 28*a.*

28-29. The preventive against the sin. Realising that they are heirs of the unshakable kingdom, believers are to show their gratitude for the grace they have received through the gospel by serving God with reverence and awe. 'God is a consuming fire,' 29, but Christ is our haven from judgment. Recognition of the blessings one has in Christ will prevent the sin of refusal (25).

13:1-6. The expression of faith in daily living

1-4. In social relationships. Faith must have its outward manifestations in the believer's relations with others. *Love for the brethren* is to be a normal course of action, 1, which may express itself in such ways as the offer of hospitality to strangers – who might indeed be angels (Gen 18:1-8; 19:1-3), 2, and in caring for those in prison and others who have been persecuted or ill-treated, 3. The thought is that of genuine sympathy, true identity, with these brethren, suffering as if you were in their place. The *marriage bond,* and the *sexual life* within that bond, are to be held in high honor, 4. Those who break such, face the judgment of God.

5-6. In financial matters. The life of faith makes no provision for covetousness. Freedom from the love of money and contentment with present possessions are to characterize the believer's way of life. He is to take comfort in the Lord's presence and provision, both of which are constant.

13:7-9. Faith's expression in a stable testimony

7-8. The example. Both the spiritual leaders who had spoken the Word of God to these Hebrew believers and the Lord Jesus Himself constitute examples of stability. The outcome of the lives of such leaders as Stephen, James the brother of the Lord, James the brother of John (Acts 12:2), and others who faced suffering and martyrdom, testifies to their faithfulness to the end. Their faith is to be imitated, 7. The immutable Christ, always the Changeless One, serves as the perfect example for all believers.

9. The exhortation. 'Do not be carried

away by all kinds of strange teachings' is an obvious reference to Judaism. Such legal observances as the dietary laws brought no lasting spiritual benefit, while, in contrast, the heart *is* strengthened by God's grace. Legalism was barren of spiritual reality, grace is full of it. Feeding on grace will lead to stability of life and testimony.

13:10-14. Faith expressed in separation from Judaism

10-12. The basis of separation. The life of faith was no longer related to the practices of Judaism. Instead, the distinctiveness of Christianity from Judaism, shown by a new and different altar, 10, and a greater and antitypical sacrifice (Christ's), 12, makes faith and legalism mutually exclusive under the new covenant.

13-14. The exhortation to separation. 'Let us, then, go out to Him outside the camp' meant separation, for these Hebrew believers, from Judaism to Christ. It would entail persecution and rejection by the Jews, and this was the reproach they would have to bear, 13 (Acts 5:41; Heb 11:25-26). Separation would also require pilgrim faith, fixing their hope not on the temporal but on the eternal, 'the city that is to come,' 14.

13:15-17. Faith expressed in spiritual worship and obedience

15-16. Sacrificial worship. The believer-priest (10:19) is to offer continually spiritual sacrifices to God. These include: the *sacrifice of praise* in joyful ascription of glory to God, called 'the fruit of lips' because the lips are a sensitive spiritual barometer of the condition of the heart, 15; and the *sacrifices of substance and of good works,* 16, sharing oneself with others in need. With such sacrifices God is pleased because they are proof of spiritual reality in worship (Phil 4:18).

17. Humble obedience. Believers are urged to be submissive to their leaders because 'they keep watch over you as men who must give an account.' Obedience to them will result in spiritual maturity, bringing joy in the day of reckoning to those in authority.

13:18-25. Concluding benediction

18-19. Personal request. The writer requests specific prayer from the addressees of this epistle, particularly for honorable conduct and for restoration to their immediate company.

20-21. Benediction. This prayer of the writer contains essential elements for the spiritual well-being of the Hebrew believers to whom he has been writing: (1) 'the God of peace,' who has established or made peace between man and Himself through the sacrifice of Christ, and who gives peace of mind and soul to those who trust in Him; (2) the hope of resurrection founded on God's raising Christ from the dead; (3) the shepherd care of Christ for His own; (4) the assurance of covenant relationship based on Christ's shed blood; (5) a request for each believer's fitness for his task in the will of God – 'equip you'; (6) a request to allow the indwelling Christ to work in the believer that which is pleasing to God. Such matters would have particular relevance for Hebrew believers, who would contrast them with the inferior blessings of Judaism.

22-25. Concluding salutation.

JAMES

The necessity of a living faith

The author. There is strong evidence for the traditional view that James the half brother of our Lord (Mk 6:3) was the author of this epistle. He was an unbeliever during our Lord's earthly ministry (Jn 7:3-10), and after the crucifixion he apparently remained in Jerusalem with his mother. Following the resurrection, Christ appeared to him also (1 Cor 15:7), doubtless in connection with his conversion, for he was among those in the upper room (Acts 1:14). Paul, after his stay in Arabia, visited him in Jerusalem, about A.D. 35 or 36 (Gal 1:18-19).

By A.D. 44 James was a leader in Jerusalem (Acts 12:17), heading up the first church council (Acts 15:13, 19; Gal 2:1, 9-10) and overseeing the Jewish church there (cf. Gal 2:12). Paul talked with him on his last fateful visit to Jerusalem (Acts 21:18-25). According to Josephus

and Eusebius, James was martyred at Jerusalem in A.D. 62 or 63.

The date and character of the epistle. Several considerations place this book as one of the earliest, if not the earliest, epistle addressed to (Jewish) Christians, dated possibly as early as A.D. 45.

The internal evidence. The church order and discipline it displays are very simple. The leaders are called 'teachers' and 'elders,' with no mention of 'bishops' or 'deacons.' Believers still met in the synagogue, with little organization since various members set themselves up as teachers.

The doctrinal character of the letter. The epistle is silent with regard to the relation of the church to the non-Jewish world and doctrinally is elementary in character. It shows

no evidence of the church as the Body of Christ. Indeed, in the Judaic tone displayed throughout the epistle the question of the admission of Gentile believers does not even seem to have come up, indicating a date of authorship before the Jerusalem council, A.D. 48 or 49.

There is no more Jewish book in the NT. If the several passages referring to Christ were eliminated, the whole epistle would be as proper in the canon of the OT as it is in the NT. In fact, the epistle could be described as an interpretation of the OT law and the Sermon on the Mount in the light of the gospel of Christ.

The external evidence for the acceptance of the book. It tallies with what appears concerning James in Josephus (*Ant.* XX, ix), in the Acts (15:13-21; 21:17-25), in Galatians (1:19; 2:9-10), and from the known circumstances of Jewish Christians in the dispersion. In the East the epistle early appeared in lists of accepted books from Asia Minor and Egypt. Not being written by an apostle, or addressed to Gentile churches, and seeming to contradict Paul, the question of the epistle's reception at Rome and Carthage until the 4th cen. can be better understood.

Outline

1 Living faith tested by trial
2 Living faith proved by work
3-4 Living faith evidenced by conduct
5 Living faith exercised by persecution

The Damascus Gate, Jerusalem. The author of this epistle was probably Jesus' brother James, who after the crucifixion apparently remained in Jerusalem with his mother.

1:1-4. The purpose of trials

1. The author. Although he was the brother of our Lord (see introduction) and one of the most prominent and influential leaders in the early church of Jerusalem and Judea, James humbly styles himself simply 'a servant (*doulos,* 'slave') of God and of the Lord Jesus Christ.' He addresses Jewish believers as Peter (1 Pet 1:1) and the author of Hebrews do. As leader of the Jerusalem church James was overseer of Jewish believers everywhere, since these came annually to the great feasts held in the capital city (cf. Acts 2:5-11) from every part of the Roman Empire.

2-4. His message. James' chief ministry was to comfort Jews who had turned to Christ. These were targets of intense persecution and ostracism from their unbelieving countrymen. Addressing these sufferers for Christ as 'brothers,' James urges them to 'consider it *pure joy*' (emphatic), unmingled by any regret, the occasion of becoming involved for Christ's sake in diversely manifold temptations. These are experiences that test or prove by trial, calamity or affliction the reality of their faith in Christ and are designed to strengthen it, 2. Therefore they are to rejoice because: (1) testing gives knowledge and experience; (2) testing brings conviction that the testing of faith continually produces and results in a patient endurance that remains under trial until such testing has worked out its divinely designed blessing; and (3) testing leads to full maturity of Christian character, 4. 'Perseverance must finish its work so that you may be mature and complete (all parts fully developed), not lacking anything,' 4.

1:5-12. Wisdom for trials

5-8. The need and supply of wisdom for trials. In no sphere is wisdom so essential and folly so disastrous as in the matter of life's reverses. If anyone is deficient in the matter of this God-given faculty let him: (1) ask or petition it *from God,* its source and bounteous Bestower, 5a (Prov 2:3-5), who does not 'upbraid' (Gr.) the ignorance of the petitioner as a teacher might scoldingly censure a dull student, 5b; (2) ask liberally, for God bestows bounteously, 5c; (3) ask without doubting, for God gives in response to faith, 5d-6. He who doubts and hesitates because of mental reservations is as unstable as a wave of the sea,

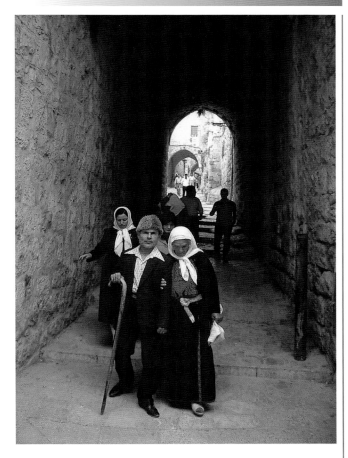

at the mercy of the wind and utterly changeable. Such a person is not to imagine 'he will receive anything from the Lord,' 7, being 'double-minded,' hence inconstant and fickle because one mind continually counteracts the other. Thus he is characterized by an unsettled state of disorder in all his ways, i.e., all the roads of life he journeys.

9-12. The rewards of exercising wisdom in trials. (1) Wisdom enables the brother of 'humble circumstances' (he who is in a poor or depressed condition in this life) to see and rejoice in his high and exalted position as Christ's own, having a place of eminence and dignity with his Saviour, 9. (2) Wisdom enables the rich brother, on the other hand, to see and rejoice in his lowliness apart from his salvation, the low estate of all his wealth apart from God (Isa 57:15), in the light of the transiency of mortal life and material possessions, 10-11. (3) Wisdom reveals the blessedness of the believer who endures testing, because it shows him that when he is approved as the result of

A blind man is helped through the narrow streets of the Old City of Jerusalem. James teaches that the practice of genuine religious service is exhibited in compassionate love and separation from sin.

his wise reaction to testing, he shall be rewarded, 12*a*. The 'crown of life' is the reward of those who love the Lord and prove it by trial even to death, 12*b*. See notes on 1 Cor 3:12-17; 9:25-27; 2 Cor 5:10 for rewards.

1:13-18. God and trials
13-15. God tempts no one to sin.
Wisdom (cf. 5-12) alone can show us God's relation to temptation, which is employed in this context in two senses: (1) testing under trial, 2-12 (cf. Gen 22:1; Lk 22:28; 1 Pet 1:6); (2) solicitation to evil, 13-15 (cf. Gen 3:1-6; Mt 4:1; 1 Cor 10:13; 2 Cor 11:3-4). Wisdom shows us that *solicitation to evil is not of (from) God as* the source and initiating agent. He 'cannot be tempted by evil,' being infinitely holy, nor does He tempt (solicit anyone to evil), 13. The *cause of sin is in ourselves,* 14. Each one is tempted by his own peculiar lust, that intense impure desire proceeding from sin working through the old fallen nature and expressing itself in the flesh. This occurs 'when [one] is dragged away [allured] and enticed' (entrapped as with a snare, or caught as a fish with bait). *The progress of sin is inexorable,* 15. 'Then, after desire [personified as a harlot] has conceived, it gives birth to sin [expressed in word and deed] ; and sin, when it is full-grown, gives birth to death.'

16-18. God is good to men.
Under trial and temptation it is easy to be misled or deceived on this point, 1*b*. But do not be led astray about the source of temptation; it is in ourselves, not in God. His goodness is shown by *His gifts,* 17. So far from bringing temptation and sin into our lives, He is the Bestower of every benefit we enjoy. 'Every good and perfect gift is from above, coming down from the Father of the heavenly lights' (Creator of the lights of heaven as well as the spiritual lights in the kingdom of grace). Because He 'is light,' in him there is no darkness at all' (1 Jn 1:5), He cannot be the author of sin, 13, nor be characterized by variation, not even the shadow of a turning as when the sun is eclipsed by the body of the moon and the moon by the shadow of the earth.

God's goodness is further shown by *His greatest* gift of eternal life in Christ an 1:12-13; 3:16), which becomes ours as He gives us birth by the word of truth (the gospel), 18*a* (1 Pet 1:23). Thus born again, we become 'a kind of

first fruits of all he created,' 18*b,* the pledge and earnest of a redeemed race (Rom 8:19, 23). The figure goes back to the OT consecration of the first fruits of man, cattle and fruits to God (Ex 23:16-19; Deut 26:1-19).

1:19-25. God's word and trials
19-21. God's goodness and the believer's responsibility.
Because God graciously grants wisdom to face the testings of life, 5-12; does not tempt us to sin, but rather tests us to strengthen us against sin, 13-16; and has made us His children through the new birth, 17-18, let us heed the injunctions of verses 19-21. These are: (1) be quick to listen; (2) be slow to talk; (3) be slow to get angry, for man's anger does not promote the righteousness God requires; (4) get rid of everything vile and the remains of evil, as a dirty garment is discarded; (5) receive the Word of God which cleanses (Jn 15:3) and which, engrafted and living in the heart, is able to save the soul by separating from sin so that the believer may enjoy fullness of life in Christ (Jn 10:10).

22-25. God's Word and the believer's obedience.
So important is God's Word in living and facing life's trials that we must be 'doers,' practiced exponents, of it rather than mere 'hearers' who know the Word only theoretically (cf. Heb 4:2) and are deluded by the logical fallacy that mere hearing is enough. Such a deceived reader is like a man looking at his face in a mirror (the Word, which shows us ourselves), but goes away and immediately forgets what he looks like, 23-24. In contrast, whoever looks carefully into the flawless law of liberty, i.e. the law of Christ which is applied to those freed from the law of sin (cf. Gal 6:2; 1 Jn 2:7, 8, 15; 2 Jn 5), and habitually does so, will become an active doer who obeys and will find happiness (blessedness) in his obedience, 25.

1:26-27. True religion and trials
26. False religion.
Outward religious service (religion) may be genuine and thus the expression of true faith, or it may be false and the expression of dead works. Since man is created religious, he is so even in his fallen state. Therefore the world is full of vain religion. James gives a sample. If anyone seems or appears to be religious, meticulously observant

of the externalities of his faith, and does not curb or bridle his own tongue, as a bit controls a horse, this person's religion is vain (deceptively useless, fruitlessly barren and ineffective). Religion (external) must be accompanied by godliness (internal) to be genuine.

27. True religion. The practice of genuine religious service, in contrast to mere external ritual, 26, is exhibited in compassionate love (looking after orphans and widows in their trouble) and in separation from sin (keeping personally free from the world's smut).

2:1-9. Dead faith manifested in partiality

1-5. How the sin nullifies genuine faith. Partiality is the sin of displaying undue respect or disrespect for certain persons. It nullifies genuine faith by violating equality within the Christian brotherhood ('my brothers,' 1*a*), and by detracting from God's glory revealed in Christ, 1*b*. 'Do not hold your faith in our glorious Lord Jesus Christ with an attitude of personal favoritism.' Christ is 'the radiance of God's glory' (Heb 1:3), taking the place of the Shekinah of the OT, and in His presence earthly distinctions disappear. Regarding mere external appearances, such as social status and wealth, ignores internal and more basic considerations, 2-4 (cf. Acts 10:34; Rom 2:11).

6-7. Why the sin is serious. Partiality misrepresents God's choice, 5*a*. 'Has not God chosen those who are poor in the eyes of this world to be rich in faith and to inherit the kingdom?' This choice is spurned by those showing partiality. It also ignores inner spiritual worth, 5*b*, that these who are poor outwardly are rich in faith inwardly; though refused on earth they are heirs of heaven; though unloved by believers, they belong to those who love Christ. Furthermore, it dishonors the poor, 6, and honors the rich, who so frequently are oppressive and godless, 7.

8. Partiality breaks the royal law. This is the law of love, 'royal' or 'kingly' because it is the monarch of all laws, the quintessence of the Ten Commandments. It is the law of God, the great King, who is love and whose royal law of love reigns supreme as He Himself. The sign of partiality infringes upon this royal law, 'love your neighbor as [you love] yourself' (Lev 19:18).

9. The royal law convicts of guilt. 'But if you display respect of persons by paying regard to mere external appearances, you are committing sin, all the while being convicted by the law as transgressor' (Gr.), 9.

2:10-13. Dead faith results in judgment

10-11. The reason for judgment. Under the Mosaic system infraction of any part of the law makes one a lawbreaker and a guilty sinner before God. The law is like a chain. The chain is broken when one link of the chain is broken, 11. A man is a guilty sinner before an infinitely holy God under the legal principle whether he breaks the royal law of love, 8-9, or some minor offense. Unless man has saving faith in Christ, he stands condemned by the law, 12. Dead faith cannot save him.

12-13. The reason for mercy. The man who has faith that saves is not under the Mosaic law of condemnation, but under 'the law that gives freedom,' 12, i.e., the principle of free grace and mercy in Christ. Therefore he is to so speak and so act as those who are to be judged under the grace principle, 12. This means, although he will never be judged (condemned) as a sinner (Jn 5:24; Rom 8:1), he will be judged for his works as a believer (cf. note on 1 Cor 3:11-15; 9:27; 2 Cor 5:10). Because God has shown him mercy, he is to be merciful in his dealings with others, 13.

2:14-20. Dead faith is useless

14-16. The principle stated and illustrated. What is the advantage, James asks, if someone claims to possess faith but does not possess works? Can *such a faith* save him, 14? Combatted is the Jewish tendency (transferred to Christianity) to substitute a lifeless knowledge of the law for a practical holiness of life, as if justification before God could be secured in this manner (Rom 2:3, 13-23). The uselessness of dead faith is illustrated by the case of a fellow believer who is destitute, 15-16. The believer is particularly obligated to lend assistance to this brother, yet he not only does not help him but uselessly tells him to be fed and clothed.

17-20. The inseparability of faith and works. Faith is declared to be dead in itself when separated from works, 17. James concerns himself here with proving that faith and works are inseparable. He does not question that faith is *the* way of salvation, and *the only way.* But he does question that such saving faith can ever be divorced from works, which prove its existence. To offer God a faith separated from works is little better than the faith of demons who believe and shudder, but such faith produces no good works of repentance or virtue, 19-20.

2:21-26. Living faith proves a man righteous

21-24. The case of Abraham. James presents two examples of living (saving) faith – faith with works: Abraham, one of the greatest men of faith in the Word of God, 21-24; and Rahab, the harlot, 25. He asserts that Abraham was justified by works when he offered up Isaac, 21 (Gen 22:9-12). That James is not contradicting Paul, who declares that Abraham was justified by faith apart from works (Rom 4:2-4), appears from the following considerations.

(1) James uses the term 'justified' (NASB) in the sense of actually proved or demonstrated to be righteous *before men;* Paul uses the term in the sense of being judicially declared righteous *before God.* James is speaking manward, Paul Godward. (2) James offers the corrective of an abused truth, Paul sets forth the truth itself. (3) James' epistle is aimed toward Jewish believers tempted with a tendency to substitute a head knowledge of the law for a heart experience manifested in holiness of life. Paul's epistles are aimed toward Gentiles lost in sin with no legal righteousness to offer God. (4) James' justification by works does not contradict Paul's justification by faith, because Abraham enjoyed the latter blessing (Gen 15:6) long before he enjoyed justification by works as a result of his offering of Isaac (cf. Gen 22:1-12).

25-26. The case of Rahab. Her saving faith was proved before men when she hid the spies, sent them back another way, and hung out the red cord (Josh 2:1-21; Heb 11:31). The analogy is given in verse 26. As the body is lifeless when the spirit departs in death, so faith separated from works is dead (cf. 17-20), being a lifeless, useless thing which cannot secure our righteous standing before God or demonstrate that position before men.

3:1-5. Living faith and the influence of the tongue

1-2. Our weighty responsibility for what we say. The tongue has great influence for good or bad. For this reason James warns against haste in becoming a teacher, 1a, since a teacher instructs and influences lives to a large extent by what he says. He therefore should be conscious of his tremendous responsibility, knowing that 'we who teach will be judged more strictly' if we discharge our heavy obligation wrongly or influence people against God and His Word.

The sins of the tongue are commonest and hardest to control, 2. 'We all stumble' (*ptaiomen*), in the sense of making a slip of the tongue, and so transgress, 1a. 'If anyone [believer] is never at fault in what he says, he is a perfect man' (*teleios*) spiritually developed, 2b, and able to control his body as a horse is controlled by a bit.

3-5. The power of the tongue illustrated. Three analogies are employed to illustrate that in the natural world a great effect can be produced by a relatively insignificant cause: the horse's bit, 3; the ship's rudder, 4; and the spark of igniting fire, 5.

3:6-12. Living faith and the treachery of the tongue

6-8. Its unruly nature. Not only is the tongue powerful and influential but treacherous as well. Its treachery is shown by: *its distinctive character* as a fire, a blaze uncontrolled and devastating; *its defiling character,* defiling or staining the whole body as smoke tarnishes and soils; *its corrupting quality,* being 'a world of evil' in the sense that it sets on fire the whole machinery of existence, reacting harmfully on both the speaker and on the hearer; and *its evil source,* it is kindled by Gehenna, eternal hell (Mt 5:22). Unlike any beast, 7, the human tongue is untamable, 8a, being 'a restless evil, full of deadly [death-causing] poison,' 8b.

9-12. Its unpredictable inconsistencies. The tongue is used both to bless God, our Lord and Father, and to curse men, who are made in God's likeness, 9 (cf. Gen 1:26; 1 Jn 4:20). From the same mouth proceed blessing and cursing. This is a glaring inconsistency which ought not to be, 10. James shows how inconsistent this is by illustrations from nature. The sweet-water spring does not send forth the brackish water of the mineral spring, nor does the fig tree bear olives or the grapevine produce figs. Neither can salt water yield fresh. Yet the tongue is guilty of that which is absolutely contrary to nature, 12.

3:13-18. Living faith and wisdom

13-16. Earthly Wisdom. The wise man (*sophia*), the technical term for teacher (cf. v. 1), as well as every believer, must choose which wisdom will control his life, earthly, 13-16, or heavenly, 17-18. Earthly wisdom cannot produce a truly wise teacher, endued with discreet knowledge (*epistemon*), who demonstrates by good behavior his works with genuine humility, 13. It rather produces bitter jealousy and selfish ambition, boasting, and disloyalty to the truth, i.e., to the Word of God as centered in Jesus Christ, 14 (Jn 14:6; Eph 4:21). Moreover, such wisdom is not from above, not taught by the Holy Spirit (Jn 16:13). Rather, it is earthly, belonging purely to this natural terrestrial sphere. It is sensual or animal-like (*psuchiche*), the learning of the natural, unregenerate, purely *soulish* man (Jude 19), and is demonic, having its origin in Satanic activity, 15 (cf. 1 Tim 4:1-5; 1 Jn 4:1-4). As a result such wisdom produces confusion and every evil work, 16 (cf. Gal 5:17-21).

17-18. Heavenly wisdom. The teacher, and every believer, is to be controlled by heavenly wisdom (1 Cor 2:6-7), which is divine in its origin, literally, 'the *from above* [emphatic] wisdom.' It is *pure* in the sense of being chastely modest, blameless from the sin of intellectual pride, so characteristic of teachers; *peaceable,* tending to tranquility and concord, not divisive and heretic; considerate, patiently mild so as always to be modestly fair and reasonable; submissive, being pliant so as always to be bendable to further truth and increased light; *full of mercy and good fruits* of the Spirit (Gal 5:22-23); impartial, manifesting conviction on matters of truth; sincere, stripped of the actor's role and utterly *without hypocrisy,* 7. True or heavenly wisdom, which has righteousness as its fruit, sows in peace because possessors of this wisdom are those who make peace, 18.

Near Mount Sinai. We may approach God, not as Moses once did on Sinai, but through Christ.

4:1-5. Living faith and worldliness

1-4. The manifestation of worldliness. This sin rooted in unbelief is evidenced by: (1) *tensions,* which are generated by the lustful pleasures that are at war, as an army of soldiers, in the members or organs of the physical body, 1; (2) *dissatisfaction,* 2*a,* the result of yielding to the lusts of the flesh with their insatiable cravings even to the point of committing murder by hating (cf. 1 Jn 3:15); (3) *prayerlessness,* 2*b*; (4) *prayer with the wrong motive,* 3, asking only for selfish and lustful gratification; (5) *spiritual adultery,* 4*a,* disloyalty to the Lord; (6) *hostility against God* – love (*philia*) for the Satanic world system is hostility against God. He who chooses to be the world's friend constitutes himself the Lord's enemy.

5. The cure for worldliness. This is submission to the Holy Spirit who resides in the redeemed body of every believer (1 Cor 6:19), allowing Him to control the whole life. 'The Spirit who dwells at home in us has keen desire [for our spiritual welfare] to the point of jealousy.' The Spirit's dynamic in the life is the sure cure of worldliness in the believer.

4:6-10. Living faith and humility

6. The source of humility. God is the source of this grace which is greater than anything the world can bestow.

7-10. The way to humility is to submit to God, 7*a*; resist the devil, 7*b*; draw near to

God, 8*a*; separate from evil, 8*b*; repent in abject contrition, 9; humble yourself, 10, and God will grant His grace of humility, and will then exalt you.

4:11-12. Living faith and evil speaking

11*a*. The injunction is to stop speaking loosely against fellow believers in a spirit of criticism (cf. ch. 3). Such a practice is not the result of living faith.

11*b*-12. The reason for the injunction. Such evil speaking is sinful because it not only is against Christian brothers, 11*a*, but against the law. It makes the speaker a self-appointed judge of the law. God alone is the one Lawgiver and Judge whose prerogative it is to judge another. He has the authority to save and to destroy, 12. The man who judges his neighbor does not have such authority, thus he has broken the law when he usurps this authority.

4:13-17. Living faith and secularism

13. The spirit of secularism. Supreme and well-nigh exclusive attention to the affairs of this life with little or no thought of God is denounced. Such secularism is the result of a lack of living faith.

14-17. The folly of secularism. Secularism is foolish because: (1) it is presumptuous and based on ignorance of the future – 'you do not even know what will happen tomorrow,' 14*a*, (2) it is a violation of the meaning of life, which is to serve God, not self, 14*b*; (3) it forgets the brevity and uncertainty of life, 14*c*; (4) it forgets God and His will, 15; (5) it is guilty of arrogance and pride, 16; (6) it is sinful. 'Anyone, then, who knows the good he ought to do [to put God first in the life] and doesn't do it, sins,' 17.

5:1-6. Living faith exercised by persecution

1-3. Oppressors' doom predicted. These oppressive rich people represent the unsaved. They persecute genuine believers ('brothers,' 7), victimizing them by the sin of secularism, which was denounced in 4:13-17. Both they and believers are confronted by the coming of the Lord, 7-9, which will right all

wrongs and judge all unrighteousness (cf. Rev 19:11-16). Oppressors will face judgment in the last days, 3, i.e. the end of this present age (1 Jn 2:18).

4-6. Oppressors' crimes exposed. Their oppression of the godly poor has reached the ears of 'the Lord Almighty' ('Lord of Sabaoth,' or' of hosts'). This expression, common in the prophets, is a prophetic title of Christ in His role of coming Conqueror and Restorer of righteousness upon the earth. The same spirit that led these wicked men to crucify the Righteous One leads them to persecute the righteous ones who belong to Him, 6. Therefore, their judgment is sure (cf. v. 3).

5:7-1.1. Living faith exercised by patience under persecution

7-9. Ground for patience. Note the double, and therefore emphatic, exhortation: 'Be patient . . . be patient,' 7-8. Why? Because such patient endurance and long suffering will surely receive its reward at the *parousia,* the personal presence or coming of the Lord. The certainty of this reward is illustrated by the farmer who waits for the precious fruit of the earth, being patient until the ground receives the early (Oct.-Jan.) and latter (Feb.-Mar.) rains. James refers to the coming of the Lord as being 'near,' the Gr. expressing present time and a settled state, so that the event is always imminent, 8, with the Judge (the returning Christ) standing at the door (cf. Mt 24:33). He will judge all wrongs, right all inequalities; thus believers are not to try to do what is the Lord's prerogative alone to do, 9.

10-11. Encouraging examples of patience. James cites the case of the OT prophets, who were especially persecuted and therefore exceptionally blessed, 10-11*a*. The case of Job is the classic illustration of God's purpose in the trials and afflications of His people and man's steadfast endurance, 11*b*.

5:12. Living faith exercised by avoiding oath-making

12*a*. The warning. 'Above all' do not swear (Mt 5:34, 37), because swearing or cursing manifests impatience and pride which are foreign to the meek endurance just commanded. Let your 'yes' be 'yes' and your

Divine healing

1. Does the Lord heal today? Of course He can and does heal today, but not always.

2. God is completely free to heal or not to heal according to His will (cf. 1 Jn 5:13-15).

3. His will may include physical infirmity and sickness in His plan for the testing, strengthening or chastening of His own (1 Cor 11:30-32; 2 Cor 12:7-10). A Spirit-filled believer may be thus tested.

4. The principle of optimum benefit for the believer is the divine method.

'no' be 'no,' avoiding oaths. In everyday speech simple affirmation or denial is to be considered sufficient to establish one's word, and it will result in a reputation for honesty.

12*b*. The reason for the warning.

5:13-18. Living faith exercised in prayer

13. Exhortation to the suffering. Affliction or calamity of any sort is to lead the suffering saint to prayer, while those cheerful or joyous in mind are to sing psalms of praise, as Paul and Silas did in the Philippian jail (Acts 16:25).

14-15. Instructions for the physically ill. This passage concerns what is commonly called divine healing. The sick believer was to call the elders of the assembly, never one elder. The use of oil for anointing the sick was a general Jewish practice, as shown by the Talmud, and a Jewish custom the Lord's disciples adopted (Mk 6:13). However, the emphasis is not on the oil, but on 'the prayer offered in faith' which saves the sick. Such a prayer is divinely given and operates *when it is God's will to heal.* Chastening, testing and other factors condition the Lord's healing of a Christian's sicknesses (cf. 1 Cor 11:30-32; 2 Cor 12:7-9; 1 Tim 5:23; 2 Tim 4:20).

16. Exhortation to persevering prayer. 'Confess your sins to each other [if you have offended someone], and pray for each other so that you may be healed' (of bodily sicknesses). Power in prayer is evidently conditioned upon one's being in fellowship with both the Lord and fellow believers. This being

met, the persevering prayer offered by a 'righteous man,' one accepted by God on the basis of his faith in Christ, is powerful and effective.

17-18. The example. Elijah so prayed, being a man with a nature like ours, 17*a.* He prayed 'earnestly' ('prayed with prayer,' a Hebraism for 'prayed intensely,'cf. 1 Kgs 17:1); he prayed effectively, with God's glory in mind for a national drought in recompense for a national sin (1 Kgs 19:10). His prayer was also answered for the removal of the drought, 18 (1 Kgs 18:42-45).

5:19-20. Living faith exercised by a diligent witness

19. The need for witnessing. The blessing of reclaiming a brother who errs in being led astray from the truth of the gospel and its precepts is set forth. One who brings such a one back to the truth has performed a useful service, to God and to the church.

20. The results of witnessing are twofold: (1) the salvation of the sinning brother from physical death (1 Cor 11:30), and (2) the hiding of his multitudinous sins, such sins being covered before God (or forgiven) by Christ's finished work on the cross.

I PETER

Living in the light of future glory

Authorship. That the epistle was written by the apostle Peter is indicated by the intimate acquaintance the author shows with the life of Christ and His teachings (cf. 5:5 with Jn 13:3-5; 5:2 with Jn 21:15-17). He enlarges on the sufferings of Christ as an eyewitness (5:1; cf. 3:18; 4:1), and features the person of Christ in relation to these sufferings (2:19-24; cf. 4:13). There is also a noteworthy similarity between Peter's speeches in Acts and his words in the epistle (Acts 2:32-36; 10:34, 41 with 1 Pet 1:21; Acts 4:10-11 with 1 Pet 2:7-8; Acts 10:34 with 1 Pet 1:17). Petrine authorship of the epistle was universally recognized by the early church. Polycarp quotes 1:8; 2:11; 3:9 in his Epistle to the Philippians. Irenaeus quotes it by name in *Against Heresies* (IV:9; IV:16, 5; V:7, 2).

Occasion and date. The epistle is predominantly, if not entirely, addressed to Jewish believers (but cf. 4:3-5). It was written perhaps as late as A.D. 65, for the letter shows knowledge not only of very early epistles such as James, 1 Thessalonians and Romans, but seems also to be acquainted with Paul's later prison epistles (Colossians, Ephesians and Philippians). The date, of course, depends on the time of Peter's martyrdom, which Eusebius places in Nero's thirteenth year, A.D. 67-68.

Theme. The subject of the epistle is 'suffering,' with seven different words used for it in the one letter. Hope in the midst of suffering is engendered by the prospect of a future inheritance (1:4-5) and the

coming of the Chief Shepherd (5:4). Suffering is purposeful (1:6-7; 2:19-20; 3:14; 4:14). It is to be expected (4:12), not to be dreaded (3:14); borne patiently (2:23; 3:9) and rejoiced in (4:13). The sufferings of Christ are featured (1:11; 2:21; 5:1) as the believer's example (2:21; 4:12). Suffering is often in God's will (4:19).

Peter's later life and ministry. At Pentecost Peter's preaching opened gospel opportunity to the Jews (Acts 2:14-41). Later, at the temple he and John healed the lame man (Acts 3:1-10), following which he preached a sermon on the theme of the future fulfillment of Israel's covenants (3:11-26). News of his distinctive ministry and message spread and he, along with John, was arrested and tried before the Sanhedrin (Acts 4:1-22). As the leader of the church at Jerusalem the responsibility of dealing with Ananias and Sapphira fell on his shoulders (Acts 5:1-11). Peter, along with other apostles, was subject to further persecution and imprisonment by the Jewish leaders following a period of spectacular power in the early church (5:12-41).

Peter was the chosen instrument (Mt 16:16-18) to open gospel oportunity to the Samaritans (Acts 8:14-25), and later to the Gentiles (Acts 10-11). The desire to placate the Jews led Herod Agrippa I to kill James, the brother of John, and to imprison Peter, between A.D. 41 and 44 during his reign over Judea (Acts 12:1-17). After his miraculous release, and following Paul's first missionary journey, Peter took a leading role in the first church

council in Jerusalem (Acts 15:7-11; Gal 2:6-10). At Antioch he was rebuked by Paul for hypocritically withdrawing from fellowship with Gentile believers (Gal 2:11-14). He traveled extensively, often with his wife (1 Cor 9:5), apparently visiting Asia Minor, especially Pontus, Cappadocia and Bithynia, areas Paul did not visit. Peter's martyrdom is hinted in John 21:18-19.

The tradition that Peter was the founder of the church at Rome and its first bishop lacks historical evidence. The Bible gives no indication of such. In fact, there is no historical proof that Peter was ever in Rome, although historians grant the possibility of his going there toward the very end of his life. If so, he probably suffered martyrdom there.

The Quo Vadis tradition represents Peter as fleeing from Rome to avoid martyrdom. On the Appian Way he met Jesus, and asked '*Quo Vadis?*' ('Where are you going?'). Jesus replied that He was returning to the city to be crucified. Thoroughly rebuked at his own cowardice, Peter returned to be crucified head downward, considering himself unworthy to be crucified as his Lord was.

Outline

1:1-25 Present suffering and future inheritance
2:1-4:6 The Christian's suffering in view of Christ's passion
4:7-5:14 The Christian's suffering in view of Christ's advent

Entrance to the ancient synagogue at Sardis, Asia Minor, decorated with a mosaic floor. Peter's letter was addressed to Jewish believers who were dispersed throughout the Roman Empire.

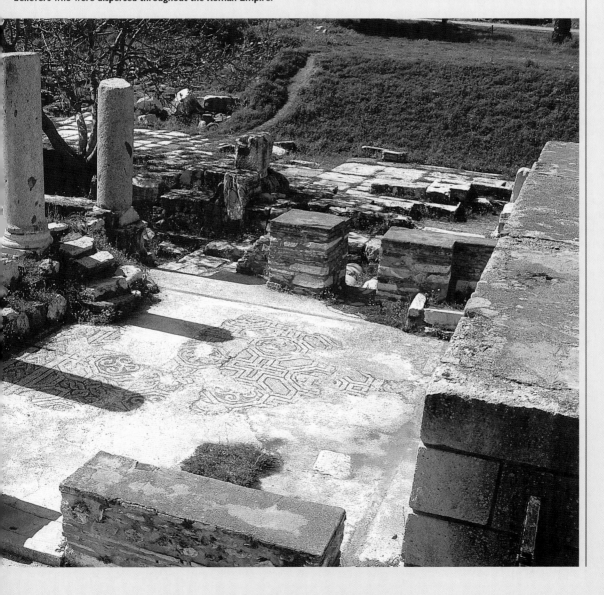

1:1-5. Encouraged for suffering

1-4. A basis for courage. The strangers (sojourners) of the dispersion were believing Jews (spiritual pilgrims) scattered throughout Roman provinces in Asia Minor. These believers were often subject to severe persecution from fellow Jews. Their spiritual wealth provided a basis for courage in the midst of their trials. It included: (1) their *election*, 2, for God had sovereignly chosen them for His very own possession; (2) their *sanctification* by the Holy Spirit, 2, giving the believer the holy position of being set apart unto God, the result of the sprinkling of the blood of Jesus Christ, which is to issue in 'obedience'; (3) their *new birth*, 3, a result of God's abundant mercy; and (4) their future *glorification* and *inheritance*, 3-4. This living hope is imperishable; not subject to decay; inviolately intact; kept in heaven, or, better translated, 'which has been and is reserved [laid up in trust] for you.'

5. Present status of the sufferers. Further encouragement was given by the reminder that these believers were 'shielded by God's power' in the sense that they were continually guarded and thus maintained in a state of security. Their response was to be 'through faith' in the provision God had made. The full revelation of this salvation awaits 'the last time,' i.e., the coming of the Lord.

1:6-9. Tested for suffering

6. The proper attitude toward suffering. Suffering should be *endured with joy*, 6a. The word 'rejoice' is strong, i.e., 'in this be exuberantly glad.' Salvation is a thing so vitally present as to cause exhilarating joy, despite present trials. Furthermore, suffering should be *seen as transient, 6b,* 'for a little while,' viewed in the larger perspective of coming glory. Self-inflicted pain outside God's will is never virtuous (cf. 2 Tim 3:12). One may expect suffering in God's will to be occasionally severe and varied, 6c.

7-9. The purpose of suffering. God's aim in suffering is that the believer's faith may be *proved genuine, 7b;* that this genuine faith may *result in 'praise, glory and honor'* to Christ at His unveiling (second coming), 7c; that the believer may see the great *external value of his faith,'* of greater worth than gold,'

7a; that the believer may *grow in his love for the Lord,* thus knowing Him as the *source of full joy,* 8. As the outcome of his genuine faith in Christ, the believer receives the salvation of his soul, a present reality, 9.

1:10-12. Salvation and suffering

10-11. The search of the prophets. The OT prophets were intrigued by the plan of salvation which was hinted in their prophetic utterances concerning God's grace, 10. This grace was to be displayed in the vicarious sufferings of Messiah-King, 11, something which was a mystery to the Jews. The readers of this epistle, with their Jewish background, were brought back to the subject of suffering by this reference to the sufferings of Christ. The grace of God involved Christ's sufferings to secure salvation. So also may His grace involve suffering for those who possess His salvation.

12. The benefactors of the prophetic message. It was revealed to the prophets that their message and ministry were intended for a future age (ours). The marvelous gospel of God's grace to sinful men was prophesied by OT prophets who failed to comprehend its truths; it was preached by NT Spirit-filled apostles, and is of great wonder to angels.

1:13-21. Holy living and suffering

13-17. The exhortation to holy living. This so great salvation 10-12, demands a once-for-all attitude of separation from sin. Such holiness of life involves mental alertness ('prepare your minds for action'), 13a; sobriety or seriousness, 13b; mature patience in light of future blessing, 13c; obedience, 14a; nonconformity to former passions, 14b; a likeness in behavior to the holiness of God Himself, 15-16 (cf.Lev 11:44-45); recognition of God's justice amid persecution, 17a; and conduct prompted by godly fear, 17b.

18-21. The reason for holy living. Our great redemption is the essential basis for a holy life. The apostle again reminds his readers of its greatness by reference to: (1) *its infinite cost and worth,* 18-19; (2) *its effectiveness* in redeeming the believer from empty legalistic religion and mere human piety, 18b; (3) *its Redeemer, Christ,* whose blood is 'precious' (infinitely valuable and inestimably costly) in that He was 'without blemish' in His own character and 'without defect' from contact with men, thus He was able to redeem, 19, and His redemptive work was in the eternal plan and purpose of God, 20, its efficacy being sealed by His resurrection and subsequent glory, 21*b*; (4) *its impartation to man* through faith in Christ, 21*a*, totally apart from human merit.

1:22-25. Regeneration and behavior

22. The responsibility of regeneration. The new birth, 23*a*, is to be manifested in transformation of character. The addressees of this epistle had realized the cleansing of their souls, effected by obedient response to the truth of the gospel. This had issued in a genuinely sincere or unhypocritical love for fellow believers. Now they were enjoined to continue the practice of this same principle as evidence of their new birth. Such love is to be 'from the heart' a genuine and permanent attitude and 'deep' (*ektenos*, 'with internal earnestness').

23-25. The means of regeneration. Being 'born again' (Jn 3:1-5), that is, being given spiritual life and birth by God, rests on the authority and the testimony of the Word of God. This Word is characterized as imperishable, living and eternal, outlasting all natural phenomena (Isa 40:6-8). Realizing its character gives assurance to the believer, 25*b*.

2:1-3. The believer's growth and suffering

1. Separation from evil. Successfully meeting the trials of the believer's life, so prominently featured in this epistle, is possible only in the case of the spiritually mature. Accordingly, Christian growth calls for a negative and a positive response from the believer. Negatively, he is to exhibit a distinct separation from evil, 1, being permanently done with 'all malice' (ill will), 'all deceit' 'hypocrisy' (insincere acts for outward effect), 'envy' and 'slander of every kind.' These violate the principle of love which is to characterize the behavior of the regenerate (1:22).

2-3. Desire for the Word of God. Positively, the believer is to exhibit an intense appetite for the Word of God, 2. It is the nourishment which makes growth and development possible. Growth is the anticipated response of those who have tasted God's grace, 3.

2:4-10. Spiritual identity, an encouragement in suffering

4-8. Identity with Christ. The apostle now brings to his Jewish readers assurance that, though they may be ostracized by the world and by unbelieving Jews, they are gloriously identified with their Lord and His church in a personal and intimate way. The figure of a building is used to describe this relationship. Christ is the chosen, precious living Stone, 4. Believers, possessing His life, are living stones which constitute a spiritual house (in contrast to the earthly temple) of priests who offer spiritual sacrifices to God, 5. Their superiority to the order of the old covenant is obvious. Jesus Christ is the cornerstone, the keystone, of this building made up of living stones (the church), 6-7. He is the superlatively precious One to believers, 7*a*, but 'a stone that causes men to stumble and a rock that makes them fall' to those Jews who rejected Him, 7*b*-8. (Cf. Isa 28:16; Acts 4:11.) This doubtless explains why many Jewish believers were subject to suffering for His sake.

9-10. Identity with God's own. Identification with Christ also brings one into living relationship with the whole company of believers. Peter refers to this body as '*a chosen* [elect] *people,*' '*a royal priesthood*' (priests of royalty directly related to the King with immediate access through Him to God), '*a holy nation*' (a sanctified nation, set apart in Christ unto God, as Israel was meant to be but never was), '*a people belonging to God.*' 'Not a people . . . had not received mercy' refers to their former condition as alienated from God in the dead religiosity of Judaism.

The responsibility of those who possess such a relationship is to declare the gracious goodness of God in calling lost men out of spiritual darkness into His 'wonderful' light, 9*b*. The light of redemption is to shine from those who are so lighted.

2:11-20. The believer's pilgrimage and suffering

11*a*. Pilgrim character described. In a threefold designation Peter describes his Jewish fellow believers as: (1) 'dear friends,' showing his love for them; (2) 'strangers' (*paroikous,* 'temporary residents') on earth with heaven as their real home; and (3) 'foreigners' (KJV 'pilgrims,' *parapidemous,* 'residents in a country not one's own').

11*b*-18. Pilgrim conduct enjoined. This includes abstaining from 'sinful desires,' 11*b* (cf. Gal 5:19-21), because these fight against the regenerated soul by opposing its high endeavours (Rom 8:13). Pilgrims are to maintain good 'lives among the pagans,' among whom these Jewish believers were scattered, that the unsaved might glorify God by the good works of His own in the 'day he visits us,' the day of Christ's coming in judgment, 12. Also expected from these sojourners are: submission to constituted civil government, 13-14 (cf. Rom 13:1, 7); a good defense against those who wrongly accuse them, 15; the exercising of the freedom God's own have in submitting to His mastery, not using such freedom as pretext for evil, 16; giving honor to all men, 17; love for fellow believers; reverence for God; giving honor to the king; obedience to masters, 18 (Eph 6:5).

19-20. Pilgrim conduct and suffering. Maintaining a good conscience toward God as a pilgrim, often calls for enduring pain as a result of suffering unjustly, 19. This sort of suffering 'is commendable before God,' 20.

2:21-25. The believer's suffering and Christ's example

21a. The believer's call to suffering. Suffering righteously is an intrinsic part of the Christian vocation.

21*b*-25. The example of Christ's suffering. Believers are called to suffer in the same spirit of placid faith and patient endurance Christ displayed. He left us an example for imitation, a pattern for guidance, desiring His redeemed ones to 'follow [closely] in His steps,' 21*b*. Christ was absolutely sinless and without deceit, 22 (Isa 53:9), yet suffered, and that with calm trust and patient endurance, 23 (Isa 53:7; Mt 26:59-68; Jn 18:19-23). So far from suffering for wrongdoing Himself, His suffering unto death vicariously redeemed us sinners, making Him much more than a mere example. He, alone being able and willing, sacrificially carried and offered up *our very*

own sins in His own body on the cross, 24*a,* providing us not only redemption from the penalty of sin but also deliverance from the power of sin, so that we might live righteously, 24*b* (Rom 6:1-11; 8:3-5). Thus His sufferings unto death provided us spiritual healing, 24*c,* and spiritual restoration, 25.

3:1-7. God's pattern for wives and husbands

1-6. Pattern for wives. Wives are to be in subjection to their own husbands so that an unbelieving husband might be won to Christ by the godly behavior of his wife, 1-2. She is to be outwardly *pure* in life, *reverential* in her attitude toward her husband, *modest* in dress, 2-3, and inwardly spiritually adorned 'with the incorruptible, fadeless charm of a gentle and tranquil spirit which is priceless in God's estimation' (Gr.), 4. Following OT examples, particularly Sarah (Gen 18:12), she is to be a woman of faith, inner adornment, submission, obedience, and courage, 5-6.

7. Pattern for husbands. The husbands are to live with their wives with the understanding of what marriage means. They are to purposefully bestow honor on the woman as the physically weaker sex, recognizing that both are equal heirs of God's gracious bestowment of life, physical and spiritual. Domestic tranquility is to prevail, so that their prayers may be unhindered; thus they may enjoy the blessing of united faith.

3:8-12. The believer's suffering and harmonious living

8-11. Requirements for harmonious living. In order for believers to live harmoniously, especially under trial, they must be likeminded in the faith, sympathetic in their attitude toward one another, brotherly, compassionately tenderhearted (Eph 4:32), humble in spirit, 8; not vengeful toward others, but beneficent, and thus in line for personal blessing, 9 (Ps 34: 12-15).

12. Reason for harmonious living. Using the words of the psalmist in Ps 34:15-16 the apostle assures believers that *they* are the objects of the gracious care of the Lord, not enemy pawns. Living harmoniously under suffering may invite the cruelty of their enemies,

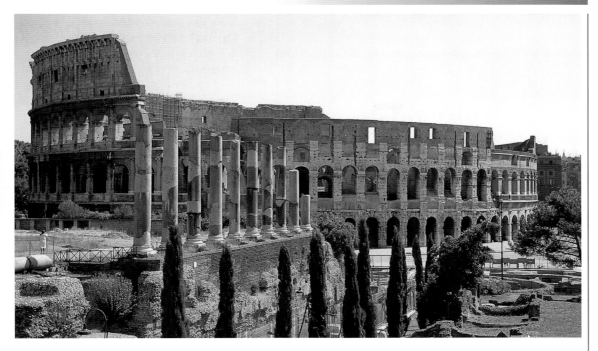

but it also invites the Lord's personal attention.

3:13-17. Maintaining a good conscience under suffering

13-15. The way to a good conscience. One's conscience may be considered good when void of offense toward God and man (Acts 24:16; 1 Tim 1:5), or it may be considered evil when it is defiled (1 Tim 4:2; Tit 1:15; Heb 10:22). Keeping a good conscience entails: (1) personal integrity, 13; (2) a proper attitude toward suffering righteously, 14*a*; (3) facing persecution fearlessly, 14*b*; (4) giving God the proper place in your life, 15*a,* for Christ must be reverenced as *Lord* before the conscience can be void of offense toward God; (5) maintaining a proper witness before men, 15*b*.

16-17. The result of a good conscience. A good conscience will put persecutors to shame, 16*a*; it will prompt good behavior, 16*b*; and it will give the persecuted believer conviction of the value of suffering righteously, 17.

3:18-22. Christ's example of triumph and encouragement

18. Christ's triumph over suffering. Christ's example argues for patience under suffering because He Himself chose not to be exempt from suffering. If He was not exempt

from suffering, even to death, why should believers expect to be? He was sinless; we are sinners. He was to expiate sin and reconcile us to God; we are merely to be tested and corrected. He was to enter into glory; we are soon to follow Him.

19-20. Christ's encouragement in suffering. The Jewish believers to whom Peter wrote were almost engulfed in the pagan world around them. He encourages them by a reference to Christ's ministry to the antediluvian generation through Noah. This ministry was by the same Spirit, 18 (Rom 8:11), that effected Jesus' resurrection, 19*a.* It was a preaching ministry in which Christ went by special operation (Gen 11:5; Mic 1:3) and preached 'to the spirits now in prison,' (Gr.), those who were sinners in the flesh in Noah's day. Christ, through His Spirit (Gen 6:3), preached to them through Noah. Their sin was that they were disobedient (rebellious and unpersuadably unbelieving), their crime being aggravated by God's patient longsuffering during the 120 years that the ark was being built, 20. This rebellion resulted in their bodies being drowned and their spirits cast into 'prison' (called *Tartarus,* 2 Pet 2:4-5; Job 1:6; see notes on Gen 6:1-6), 19.

21-22. Christ's triumph in providing salvation. Christ's sufferings resulted in our salvation. This makes our suffering not only

The Colosseum, Rome, viewed from the Forum. When Peter refers to 'Babylon' this is probably a coded reference to Rome.

bearable but glorious. The outward figure of this salvation is water baptism. The ark on the flood waters is the type; our salvation in Christ (the true Ark) the antitype. The water simply cut off the righteous from the sin and sinners of that day. The ark alone saved. So baptism is for the saved, but cannot itself save, except as a picture of the *saved* candidates having been cut off from sinners and their doom. Christ alone can save, and that by virtue of His resurrection (Rom 4:25), 21*c.* No mere external rite can save – 'not the removal of dirt from the body,' 21*b*: 'but the pledge of a good conscience toward God' – by the consciousness of sin *removed* by Christ's blood (cf. Heb 9:14).

4:1-6. Suffering and Christ's example for victorious living

1-2. The basis for victorious living. As Peter has previously used Christ's example to enforce patience in suffering, he now employs it to urge the putting to death of sin. The believer is to arm himself, as a soldier putting on his armor, 'with the same attitude' (and purpose) Christ had – purposing to suffer rather than to sin (cf. Phil 2:5-8), 1. As physical death frees a man from sin, so he who identifies himself with Christ's redemptive suffering should reckon on that fact, no longer responding to the strong sinful passions of men while he lives on earth, but responding to the will of God for his life, 2.

3-6. The case against sinful living. The apostle goes on to contrast the lustful living of the Gentiles with the life lived in the will of God (cf. v. 2). Such sinful living took its toll before conversion and should be given no further opportunity, 3*a.* Six sins are cataloged, 3*b,* characteristic of the unregenerate. Believers, because of their changed lives, bring condemnation to the ungodly, resulting in Christians being maligned for their purity of life, 4. However, unbelievers are sure to face the judgment of God, both in this life (the 'living') and in the final Great White Throne judgment to come (the 'dead,' Rev 20:11-15), 5. Because unregenerate man must face God's judgment, the good news (the gospel) has been preached, even to those who are now dead. If a man believes the gospel, even though he is judged in this life according to the judgment of men, he lives spiritually according to the will of God, 6.

4:7-11. Judgment and service amidst suffering

7. Living in the light of coming judgment. Peter's statement, 'The end [consummation] of all things is near' (cf. Jas 5:8-9), still has the subject of judgment in mind (cf. 5-6). In light of its nearness the believer is enjoined to 'be clear- minded and self-controlled so that you can pray.'

8-11. Serving in the spirit of love. Foremost is the injunction to 'love each other deeply, because love covers over a multitude of sins,' 8. Lack of love broadcasts and uncovers these sins to the detriment of God's work. Peter is speaking merely of a loving spirit of forgiveness versus an unloving spirit of criticism, not of the expiation of sins. He also enjoins the practice of ungrudging hospitality, 9, and the use of one's spiritual gifts (cf. 1 Cor 12:8-12) for the welfare of one another, 10 (cf. Rom 12:6, 8; 1 Tim 6:17-18). Such service is to bear the marks of God's authority and of humility, 11. The goal of all service is to be God's glory, 11*c.*

4:12-19. The Lord's return and trials

12-14. The source of courage for trials. A proper attitude toward trials, and understanding of their purpose and benefits for the Christian, will engender courage. They are to be expected, not viewed as unusual in the believer's life, and are allowed in order to test the genuineness of his faith, 12. Continual rejoicing under trial is enjoined, because one thereby now has fellowship with Christ in His suffering, 13*a,* and at His revelation (coming) will have cause for even greater joy, 13*b.* *Present* trials bring special happiness or blessedness because the Spirit of God therein effects spiritual unction and testimony to God's glory, 14.

15-19. Courage for trials and Christian duty. The believer's responsibility is to avoid suffering that is the outcome of sin, 15. Also, he is not to be ashamed of suffering as a 'Christian,' a contemptuous nickname invented by the Gentiles at Antioch (Acts 11:26; 26:28). By suffering righteously he honors the name 'Christian' (a believer in and a follow of Jesus Christ the Messiah), and glorifies God thereby, 16.

The Christian is to realize that the judgment of his works at the Lord's return is imminent, 17 (cf. 1 Cor 3:11-15; 4:1-6; 2 Cor 5:10), and if he, a member of God's household, is subject to judgment, the ungodly have an even more severe judgment to anticipate. Perdition alone can be their portion since they do not know Christ and are lost sinners, 18. The apostle summarizes this section by stating that suffering is to be welcomed when it is 'according to God's will,' and the sufferers are to commit their souls to a faithful Creator, who made them and can certainly take care of them in suffering, bringing them through it to His glory, 19.

5:1-5. The Lord's return and daily duty

1-4. Duty of elders. The elders (or bishops, evidently the same office) are exhorted to tend the flock of God, assuming the responsibility of overseeing 'God's flock' (the body of believers) voluntarily, not under compulsion, and eagerly without being motivated by thoughts of personal (base) gain, 1-2. They are to prove themselves examples for the flock to follow, not exerting autocratic domination over those placed under their supervision, 3. The reward for faithful shepherding will be 'the crown of glory that will never fade away' when Christ the Chief Shepherd appears for His own (cf. 1 Cor 3:11-15; 2 Cor 5:10), 4.

5. Duty of the young. The young are to be subject to their elders (1-4), and all members of the flock are to clothe themselves with humility toward one another (Prov 3:34; 18:12; Jas 4:6).

5:6-11. The Lord's return and Christian maturity

6-9. Developing maturity. This entails a spirit of continued submission to God, 6-7, and an attitude of continued resistance to Satan, 8-9. With respect toward God, believers are to *humble themselves* in full submission 'under God's mighty hand,' 6a, no matter what of good or evil it may at the moment seem to mean in suffering (cf. Isa 57:15); *trust God* to exalt them at the proper time, 6b; *cast all their anxieties on Him,* 7a, assured that He cares about them, 7b (Ps 55:22).

With respect to Satan, believers are to be sober (serious-minded) and alert, because their opponent the devil prowls around 'like a roaring lion' in search of some one to devour, 8. The believer must be firm in his faith to 'resist him' who resists them (cf. Zech 3:1; Rev 12:10). For the believer's encouragement he is to realize that it is a sign of God's favor, rather than disfavor, that Satan is permitted to hound him as he did Job. All fellow believers have the same conflict in the world (where Satan operates), 9.

10-11. Enjoying maturity. This is possible because: 'the God of all grace' deals graciously with us, 10a; He has called the believer to His eternal glory in Christ, 10b, assuring him of ultimate perfection; His purpose in allowing suffering is to 'restore' the Christian, to make him 'strong, firm and steadfast, 10c. The response of the believer in all of this is to be perpetual recognition of God's glory and dominion, 11.

5:12-14. Concluding salutation

12. Personal testimony. Exhortation and sincere explanation have been given throughout the epistle; now Peter adds personal testimony: 'I have written . . . encouraging you and *testifying that this is the true grace of God,'* 12. Peter wrote with ringing authority because he himself was a brilliant trophy of God's grace. Silas (Gr. Silvanus) was one of Paul's companions (Acts 15 :22, 40).

13-14. Final greetings. 'She who is in Babylon' probably refers not cryptically to the city of Rome but to the church (2 Jn 1) of Jewish converts at Babylon on the Euphrates (Acts 2:9), the center from which the Asiatic Jewish dispersion was derived. It was the location of a large Jewish community in the apostolic era, according to both Philo and Josephus. Mark is John Mark (cf. Col 4:10; 2 Tim 4:11). 'A kiss of love,' 14, has singularly been discontinued by most Christians (Rom 16:16; cf. Acts 20:37).

2 PETER

Growing in grace

Authorship. Because of a difference in style between 1 and 2 Peter, some of the early Fathers, Reformers, and modern critics have questioned the Petrine authorship of 2 Peter. It was not generally recognized as an authentic writing of the apostle Peter until Origen's time (c. A.D. 250) or later. However, the evidence seems to favor its having been written by the apostle (1:1).

The lack of recognition by the early church and the consequent neglect by the Christian public are explained by the brevity of the epistle, its general nature (not being addressed to any specific person or church), and the fact that it contains little new material. Some have charged that Simon Peter's name (1:1) is a forgery or interpolation, but this charge lacks support and is rather improbable. It is quite unlikely that a forger writing in the interest of truth to warn against false teachers should himself be a deceiver. On the other hand, there is no real motive for pseudonymous authorship. The epistle is orthodox, advancing no new teaching. It tells nothing new of Peter, in contrast to the spurious Gospel of Peter and the Apocalypse of Peter. The autobiographic allusions are true to fact (cf. the reference to the transfiguration, 1:16-18, and Peter's martyrdom, 1:12-14, the latter written before Jn 21:18-19 which predicts it). The Christian earnestness, the apostolic zeal and the general worth of the epistle, in contrast to the valueless products of those who forged the name of an apostle, argue for the genuineness of 2 Peter. Jude apparently alludes to 2 Peter (cf. 2:6-3:3; Jude 4-16).

---

1 Peter and 2 Peter in contrast

1 Peter	2 Peter
Emphasis on suffering	**False teaching and false teachers**
The sufferings of Christ	**The glory to follow**
Redemptive title - Christ	**Title of dominion - Lord**
Consolation	**Warning**
Hope to face trial	Full knowledge to face error
Seven different words for 'suffering' occur, and theme occurs over and over again	The word 'know' and its cognates occur 13 times 1:2, 3, 5, 6, 8,12, 14, 20 2:9, 20, 21 (twice); 17, 18

Occasion and date. Second Peter was evidently penned to the same people as 1 Peter, namely, Jewish Christians (see note on 1 Pet 1:1). It was apparently written after 1 Peter and before Jude, as the doctrinal defection it describes is not as fully developed as in Jude. The date is probably A.D. 66 or 67.

Outline

1 Secret to Christian growth
2 Antidote to error
3 Key to certainty of the future

1:1-4. The basis of Christian growth

1-2. The common faith of believers.
Simon is the Gr. form of the Heb. *Sim'on* ('hearing') (Acts 15:14; cf. Mt 16:16-18), and identifies Peter as a Jewish Christian, 1. The use of his earlier name is in keeping with the purpose of this second letter, which is to warn against the rise of false teachers through the testimony of original apostolic eyewitnesses, counteracting the error of the false teachers with the full knowledge of Christ, 2.

The apostle addresses those who have received 'a faith as precious as ours,' that is, a faith equally precious to all believers. This faith, the basis of Christian development and growth, is obtained or received from God, and is not a human attainment. It rests on the basis of the righteousness of God through the redemptive work of Christ (cf. 1 Cor 3:11). 'Grace' and 'peace' are multiplied (increased) to believers through 'the knowledge of God and of Jesus our Lord,' 2.

3-4. The spiritual endowment of believers.
Facilitating Christian growth, this endowment consists of: (1) 'His divine power' (the dynamic of the Holy Spirit), bestowing on us everything necessary for the realization of life and godliness, 3*a*; (2) 'knowledge of him,' 3*b*, full, personal, accurate knowledge (*epignosis*) of Christ, made possible by the Spirit's teaching ministry (Jn 16:13-15); (3) His Word, 4*a*, infinitely valuable and exceedingly great promises having been given to us; (4) a new nature, 4*b*, the privilege to 'participate [*koinonoi,* 'fellow partners'] in the divine nature' (Jn 3:1-5); (5) ability and means to live in a holy manner, 4*b*, to 'escape [by the preceding resources] the corruption in the world caused by evil desires.'

1:5-9. The way to Christian growth

5-7. Employment of one's spiritual endowment.
'For this very reason,' because of the spiritual endowment God has committed to us, 3-4, let us 'make every effort' to cooperate with Him. This involves supplying in your faith (the starting point of all spiritual knowledge and growth) 'goodness, and to goodness, knowledge [of God's truth and will]; and to knowledge, self-control; and to self-control, perseverance; and to perseverance, godliness [devotion to God in fellowship and service, so your perseverance is not mere stoicism, but the outflow of the indwelling life of God]; and to godliness, brotherly kindness, and to brotherly kindness, love.' Love fittingly completes the choir of graces as in Col 3:14, and encompasses them all, being the badge of spiritual adulthood (cf. 1 Cor 13).

8-9. The resultant manifestation of spiritual maturity.
This adulthood will reveal itself in fruitfulness, 8, and will shield the believer from spiritual shortsightedness (*myopadzon,* a state of being dim-visioned, seeing only what is near at hand), 9. A shortsighted person has forgotten that he was purged from his sins (cleansed once for all, at the time of regeneration, Jn 13:10; Heb 10:2).

1:10-15. The consummation of Christian growth

10. Assuring our calling and election.
'Therefore [because of the danger of lapsing into spiritual shortsightedness, 9], my brothers, be all the more eager to make your calling and election sure.' Although their election was certain from the divine point of view, being the result of God's sovereign choice and based on the efficacy of Christ's finished redemption, believers are to employ their spiritual resources, 5-7, in manifesting maturity, 8-9, in order to make their calling and election certain to men. The result will be that 'you will never fall,' causing failure in the Christian life, 10*b*. (See notes on Eph 1:1-6.)

11-15. Entering the eternal kingdom.
Believers spiritually enter the kingdom of God when they are born again (Jn 3:5). The entrance spoken of here is the actual entrance into the eternal kingdom of our Lord and Saviour Jesus Christ at the resurrection of the body and its consequent glorification (1 Thess 4:13-17; 1 Jn 3:1-3; Phil 3:20-21). The work of grace in this life shall be crowned with the reward of grace in the life to come.

This glorious future demands constant reminding in order to arouse God's people, 12-13. Peter's reference to 'the truth' means the gospel truth now present, formerly promised to the OT saints and now in NT times actually present with and in believers as an arrived reality. Furthermore, the apostle considers his reminding ministry urgent in view of his impending death, 14. As a result of such responsibility he assures his readers that after his death his writings will serve to call to mind the truths of the gospel which he had taught them, 15.

1:16-21. Christian growth and biblical authority

16-18. The authority of apostolic testimony. Peter himself points believers to the real authority of the Word of God, declaring that the inspired testimony for the apostles rules out deception or imposture ('we did not follow cleverly invented stories,' i.e., myths devised by human wisdom in contrast to Holy Spirit inspiration, cf. 1 Cor 3:13), 16a. Furthermore, apostolic testimony comprehends the revelation of the power and coming of Christ, embracing the evidence of eyewitnesses, 16b (Mt 17:1, 5). T o have seen the risen Christ was a requirement for being an apostle (Acts 1:21-22). On the mount of transfiguration Peter was such as eyewitness' of that great One's majesty' (this is the emphasis in Gr.). The transfiguration was the second advent in miniature (see notes on Mt 17:1-8; Mk 9:2-10; Lk 9:27-36). Peter also heard the voice of 'the Majestic Glory' (God) when he, with James and John, was on the 'sacred mountain,' 17-18.

19-21. The authority of the written word. This is now the sole and all-sufficient authority for faith and practice. The written Word not only contains and preserves the authority of apostolic testimony (16-18), but it has been proved inspired by fulfillment, 19a ('And we have the word of the prophets [the OT Scriptures] made more certain,' attested or confirmed by fulfilled NT events. The prophetic Scriptures are to be diligently heeded in our hearts, 19b. The morning star is Christ in His coming for His own (Jn 14:1-3; 1 Cor 15:51; 1 Thess 4:13-18). The Scriptures also are of divine origin, for they are divinely inspired, 20-21. An expanded translation of the Gr. text would read: 'For *not by the will of man* [emphatic] was any prophecy ever borne to us, but, on the contrary, men being borne along by the agency of the Holy Spirit spoke *from God* [emphatic],' 21.

2:1-3a. False teachers – their rise

1. Their activity. In contrast to the true prophets who spoke for God, Peter refers to the opposition of false prophets (Mt 24:5; 1 Tim 4:1; Jude 4). They would stealthily introduce destructive heresies, even denying the very Lord who bought them, i.e., made them savable.

2-3. Their influence. The influence of these false prophets is shown by their popularity ('many will follow their shameful ways'), 2a; their apparently *successful opposition* to the truth, 2b; and their *financial exploitation* of their victims ('in their greed these teachers will exploit you with stories they have made up' – *plastois,* 'formed' or 'fashioned' to deceive, 'fabricated' to be counterfeit), 3a.

2:3b-9. False teachers – their doom

3b. Their certain judgment declared. The sure ruin of these false teachers is emphasized by the following graphic personification: 'Their condemnation has long [in God's purpose and plan, Jude 4] been hanging over them, and their destruction has not been sleeping.'

4-8. Their certain ruin illustrated. The first illustration is that of the *fallen angels,* 4. These were evidently those who at the time of the Flood intermarried with mortal women, corrupting the race, and breaking down God's orders of being (Gen 6:1-6; Jude 6). Their doom was imprisonment in 'gloomy dungeons.' The second example is that of the *ancient world,* 5. Only Noah and his family were saved (Gen 6:1-8:22). The third illustration is that of *Sodom and Gomorrah,* 6-8, in which righteous Lot was spared (Gen 19:1-29; Jude 7).

9. The divine principle enunciated. The Lord is at no loss for means to rescue the godly from temptation (trial) nor to keep the unrighteous under punishment.

2:10-16. False teachers – their presumption and greed

10-12. Their sin of presumption specified. These ungodly teachers, kept under judgment, 9, are given particularly to *sensuality,* indulging the flesh (the corrupt sinful nature) in the lust of moral defilement, 10a. They are given to *lawlessness,* despising authority – especially that of God and His Word, 10*b*. Both of these sins, however, seemingly stem from the more basic sin of *presumption,* 10*c*-12. Because they are presumptuous (Gr. 'darers') and self-willed, seeking to please themselves in willful obstinacy, they are not afraid to speak evil of angelic majesties (the order of angels). On the other hand 'angels, although they are stronger and more powerful [than these lawless human beings], do not bring slanderous accusations against such beings [the false teachers] in the presence of the Lord,' 11. Such presumption leads these false teachers to malign those things of which they have no knowledge, 12*a*.

12*b*-13*a*. The punishment of their sin. They shall 'perish,' the Gr. word expressing 'corruption' and 'destruction,' 12*b*. Their recompense will be the reward of unrighteousness, 13*a*.

13*b*-14. Their moral obliquity. The false teachers' love of luxurious pleasure leads to lives addicted to revelry, 13*b*-14*a*. They are moral blots and blemishes, disgraces to society, living in riot and revelry, and deceptively feasting together with believers at their love feasts. Their mercenary character is revealed by their being 'experts in greed.'

15-16. Their mercenary character illustrated. Having abandoned the right path of obedience to the Lord, they have gone astray, following the way of Balaam – the course of easy world conformity taken by this hireling prophet who was eager only to commercialize his spiritual gift. They are like him 'who loved the wages of wickedness' and was willing for gain from Balak to curse Israel whom God had blessed. Failing this, he was willing to lure Israel into idolatry and fleshly lust in order to realize material gain. The dumb ass spoke with a man's voice to rebuke the prophet's madness (Num 22:21-31). What a contrast – a dumb animal reproving an inspired prophet!

2:17-18. False teachers – their empty intellectualism

17. They are devoid of God's Spirit. Several metaphors show this emptiness: (1) wells (springs or fountains) without water, water being a symbol of eternal life by the Spirit (Jn 4:14; 7:37-39); (2) tempest-driven mists, unalterably unstable in spiritual issues; (3) 'blackest darkness is reserved for them,' thus they are doomed to spiritual ignorance.

18. They are snared by empty intellectualism. These teachers of error employ arrogant language with a view to deceive. Their appeal is to the base desires of the flesh whereby they entrap young converts, those who have scarcely escaped from those who live in the ungodly world.

Mount Hermon, northern Israel – possible location of Jesus' Transfiguration. Peter refers in this epistle to his presence at that awesome event.

2:19-22. False teachers – their bondage to sin

19-20*a***. Their empty promise of liberty.** This promise is worthless because they themselves are enslaved by sin, 19*a*. They are common slaves (*douloz*) of moral depravity, and thus helpless to free others. Having rejected the truth of the gospel, they have spurned the only source of true liberty (Jn 8:32; Gal 5:1, 13; Rom 6:12-22). The liberty they offer is spurious. It is not a deliverance from sin, but a promise of liberty from every yoke, as if the service of God were not perfect freedom. Such a promise appeals to mere professors of the faith, 20, those who have in their outward conduct escaped the pollutions of the world because of fear, but as unregenerate still hanker after the old lusts.

20*b***-22. The plight of their victims.** As enlightened but unsaved moralists, the followers of these false teachers at least avoid the more obvious sins, but by rejecting the light of Christ they are exposed to greater darkness and deeper sins (Phil 3:18-19). Having turned from 'the sacred commandment that was passed on to them' (failing to repent toward God and exercise faith toward Christ), they are like the dog turned again to his own vomit (Prov 26:11) and like the sow, after a washing, turning again to her wallowing in the mire, 22. The washing of the swine speaks of mere outward reformation.

3:1-7. Last-day scoffers and the second advent

1-3. The warning concerning scoffers. Peter refers to 'my second letter,' which we call 2 Peter, in which he again seeks to arouse his readers spiritually by reminding them of 'the words spoken in the past by the holy prophets [of the OT] and the command given by our Lord and Saviour through your apostles.' (Cf. Mt 24:11; 2 Tim 3:1-9; 1 Jn 4:1-6.) His specific purpose in writing was to alert them to the peril of last-day scoffers, scorners and mockers who laugh at or make jest of anything (Jude 18).

4-7. The nature of their scoffing. These mockers will scorn the truth of the second advent, 4*a*. After all these centuries Christ's coming has not occurred and their sneer is, 'It never will!' They boldly question the reliability of God's Word, which has this truth emblazoned in the pages of the OT prophecy as well as NT.

Furthermore, they espouse a natural order of events versus supernatural catastrophism, 4*b*, assuming that natural world' goes on as it has since the beginning of creation.' The inference is, 'All things will always continue thus.' Such an assumption is *refuted by Bible history,* 5-6, and Bible prophecy, 7. The restoration of the earth (Gen 1:1-31), the Noahic flood, 6, and the coming earth-renovating catastrophe by fire, 7, exhibit the truthfulness of God's Word versus the scoffer's claim, 4.

3:8-10. God's patience and the Day of the Lord

8-9. God's time schedule. The apostle proceeds to answer the scoffers, pointing out that our time concepts are not the limited context in which God operates to bring His purposes to pass. He quotes from Ps 90:4 to show that God works in eternity and is not bound by time limitations as is man, 8. Yet God is always on time, 9. He is not 'slow,' i.e., He does not delay in the sense of being indecisive or slow in keeping His promises, as some men by natural reasoning reckon the matter. By contrast 'He is patient with you, not wanting anyone to perish, but everyone to come to repentance' (Mt 20:28; 1 Tim 2:4; cf. Gen 6:3; 1 Pet 3:20).

10. The certainty of the Day of the Lord. Peter gives a new revelation concerning the Day of the Lord as it relates to the cataclysm of fire (cf. v. 7). OT prophecy clearly related that day to judgment, the second advent, and the subsequent reign of Messiah (Isa 2:6-22; 4:1-6; cf. Rev 4-19, etc.). This new revelation focuses on the *consummation* of the day, its climactic final catastrophe in the destruction of the earth in a fire bath, as it had a flood bath in Noah's day. The tremendous heat generated will effect the change indicated by Peter, an event which can be rather clearly visualized in this atomic age.

3:11-13. Present conduct and the eternal state

11-12*a***. The impetus to holy living.** The coming judgments of the Day of the Lord furnish ample reasons for godly living. Such piety will be exhibited by a constant anticipation of and desire for the arrival of 'the day of God,' 12*a*. This 'day' is the final event of time when death, sin and hell are fully conquered and

Christ surrenders the mediatorial kingdom to the Father (1 Cor 15:24-28; Rev 20:7-22:21).

12*b*-13. The glorious expectation. This anticipated event will put an end to the mockery of all scoffers (v. 4). Promised by God's own Word, 13*a,* and expected by faith, 13*b,* it entails a sin-cleansed universe, 13*c* (Isa 65:17; 66:22; Rom 8:21; Rev 21:1, 27). As the Noahic flood resulted in a renovated earth purged of sinners, so the baptism of fire will cleanse the earth for the habitation of man wholly delivered from the curse; thus righteousness will dwell therein, 13*d.* The heavens will be cleansed of Satan and demonic forces (Eph 6:10-12; Rev 20:1-3, 10) and the earth of wicked men (Rev 20:11-15). The lake of fire will be the place of eternal confinement of all evil, so that righteousness alone may fill the universe in eternity (Rev 20:10; 21:1-4, 8).

3:14-18. The believer's hope and growth in grace

14-17. The incentive to growth. The realization of this hope (of new heavens and a new earth in which righteousness dwells) is a further stimulus for a holy life, 14. In the meantime, the believer is to understand that our Lord's long-suffering is designed for sinners' salvation, 15*a.* Peter refers to the enunciation of these foregoing truths in Paul's epistles, 15*b*-16, a statement which authenticates the Pauline letters as inspired of God. Peter concludes by warning that error must be avoided, 17.

18. The plea for growth. Believers are urged 'to keep on growing in grace' (Gr.) – God's method not only of saving men but maturing them – and 'in the grace and knowledge of our Lord and Saviour Jesus Christ,' the twofold sphere of true spiritual growth.

I JOHN

Fellowship of the father and children

Outline
1-3 Family fellowship and the Father
4-5 Family fellowship and the world

Emphasis of John and Paul compared	
John	**Paul**
Regeneration	Justification
Sonship in the family	Membership of the body
Sin as a child's offence against the Father	Sin as unworthy of position in Christ
Our private relation as children of the Father	Our public position as sons

Author. The writer was the apostle John, also the author of the fourth gospel. This fact is demonstrated by such internal evidence as a similar vocabulary in both the gospel and the epistle. They contain such expressions as light, new commandment, works of the devil, take away sins, eternal life, love, abide, lay down one's life, Paraclete, Saviour of the world, born of God. Both also have the same simple, direct Hebraic parallelism and sentence construction.

Johannine authorship is also attested by external evidence which is both early and substantial. Polycarp, Papias, Irenaeus, Clement of Alexandria, Tertullian, Cyprian, the Muratorian fragment, the Syriac Peshitta, Origen, Dionysius of Alexandria and Eusebius all lend their testimony to the authenticity of the epistle and Johannine authorship.

Occasion and date. The epistle was written about A.D. 85-90, apparently from Ephesus, where Irenaeus says John lived during the latter part of his life, and where he seems to have overseen surrounding churches (cf. Rev 2-3). We gather from Irenaeus that it was occasioned by the invasion of several errors. One was associated with moral laxity and the Nicolaitans, whom Irenaeus tenuously connects with Nicolas (Acts 6:5; cf. Rev 2:14-15). The other was an error concerning the person and work of Christ, attributed to Cerinthus, who taught a form of Gnosticism.

Archaeological light

John and the Qumran Community.

It was long a popular notion that John's writings betrayed the influence of Greek philosophy (the 'logos,' etc.) and that this pointed to a late date for these writings. Discoveries at Qumran have radically changed that assessment, however. Similarities between John's writings and those found at Qumran demonstrate that John's thinking is thoroughly Jewish. Dualisms like 'light' and 'darkness' are prominent in both, though John is quite different in his application, as he repudiates dualism.

1:1-4. The basis of fellowship

1-2. The incarnation and eternal life.
The apostle John presents his authority as an eyewitness to the central fact of the gospel, viz., the incarnation of the Eternal Living Word (Jn 1:1, 14; Prov 8:23). He particularly refers to the evidences which the senses provide in proving the *real* humanity of Christ, the Living Word, thus refuting the Gnostic claim that Christ was not truly human. 'The Word of life,' 1, is a reference to Christ as the One who came to bring eternal life to sinners dead in sin (Jn 3:16). He was eternally coexistent with the Father, 2, and manifested to men in the incarnation (Jn 1:1-2).

3-4. The incarnation and fellowship.
The purpose of the incarnation was to give 'life,' which constitutes the basis, or necessary prerequisite, of fellowship between regenerated sinners and God the Father and God the Son. The aim of John, as well as the other apostles, in writing was that their Christian readers might have fellowship (*koinonia,* partnership in common participation of an experience) with them in sharing intimate contact and communion with God, 3, which is turn would bring 'complete' joy, 4. Fellowship with the Father and the Son brings such joy!

1:5-10. The conditions of fellowship

5-8. Walking in the light.
This walk of fellowship 'in the light' (a metaphor for life) depends upon the believer's having a *right*

concept of God, i.e., that 'God is light' (Jn 3:20-21; 1 Tim 6:16), 5. He is absolute holiness without taint of evil, 'no not even one iota of darkness' (Gr). What light is to the world of nature, so God is to the world of the spirit. Other requirements for a walk in fellowship are: having *a life separated from sin,* 6; *claiming the cleansing power of Christ's sacrifice* from daily sins of defilement, 7 ; and *recognizing the presence of the old nature,* 8, lest believers lead themselves astray, shutting out the light because of self-deception. The apostle states, 'If we claim to be without sin [nature, principle or root], we deceive ourselves, and the truth is not in us.' Each requirement cited above is revealed by the apostolic message, 5*a*. This Word must be believed if one is to act thereon and thus 'walk in the light.'

9-10. Confessing our sins.
Confession of our sins to God brings forgiveness and cleansing. Such involves our frankly admitting and openly avowing our known sins, 10, realizing they spring from the old sin nature which is still with us (v. 8), and also realizing that they have broken our fellowship with an infinitely holy God. In true confession admission must be accompanied by repentance, a turning from our sins to the sacrifice of Christ as the means of cleansing from their defilement. God promises, in response to such confession, to remove these sins as a barrier to our fellowship through the blood of Christ (v.7, for He bore our sins in His redemptive work – sins past, present and future (Rom 3:4, 25-26; 2 Cor 5:21; 1 Jn 5:10), 9. Personal confession involves an acknowledgment that we have sinned in thought, word, and act. Failure to admit this makes God a liar, for His Word clearly states that man has sinned. The life of victory and fellowship is possible only when sin is admitted, confessed and forsaken.

2:1-2. The advocacy of Christ and fellowship

1. Fellowship maintained Godward by Christ's advocacy.
The apostle explains to his readers that what has been said in the foregoing chapter about sin and its forgiveness was stated 'so that you will not sin' at all! He now proceeds to explain the nature of the remedy for sin through infirmity, because the old nature can still be active unless continually

reckoned dead (Rom 6:6). This remedy is based upon the work of *a continually present advocate* who is none other than Jesus Christ the righteous. An advocate is one who is summoned alongside to serve as a helper. Advocacy, then, is that work of our Lord in heaven carried on before the Father's throne by which He represents sinning saints on earth and restores them to fellowship with the Father on the basis of His eternally efficacious sacrifice (Ps 23:3; Jn 13:10). He pleads the cause of the believer against Satan, the 'accuser of our brothers' (Rev 12:10). It is because our Lord is *righteous* that He can plead with the righteous Father.

2. The efficacy of Christ's advocacy. Christ Himself is the all-sufficient Advocate because *He Himself* (Gr. intensive) is the personal 'atoning sacrifice.' Atonement means satisfaction, and Christ is the satisfaction for our sins. His redemptive sacrifice constituted the satisfaction which God demanded for sin, and it was sufficient for the sins of the whole world, the entire human race (making them savable). God the Father does not break fellowship with the sinning believer, because Christ the Advocate pleads the satisfaction of His sacrifice as sufficient for all the believer's sin.

2:3-6. Obedience and fellowship

3-5. Assurance of being in fellowship. The believer may be assured, or may know that he is in fellowship by the proof of obedience, 3-5. Knowledge of Christ is inseparably linked to obeying Him and loving Him, 5b.

6. The duty of the believer claiming to be in fellowship. The Christian is *bound* to ('must') imitate Christ in His walk (humility and self-sacrifice) if he claims to 'live in Him.' *Abiding* may be defined by using John's definition in 3:24: habitual fellowship maintained by continual obedience to His commandments. 'Even as' or 'in the same manner' (Gr.) indicates that the imitation of Christ is to be exact and true to pattern.

2:7-11. Brotherly love and fellowship

7-8. Love, the expression of fellowship. This indispensable ingredient of fellowship in one sense does not involve a new commandment, 7. It is the one we had from the beginning (Lev 19:18; Deut 6:5; Mt 22:37-40: Mk 12:28-31; 2 Jn 5). Yet in another sense it does involve a new commandment, 8. Jesus also called it 'new' and gave it a new motive, '*as I have loved you,* so you must love one another' (Jn 13:34-35; 15:12). It was new with a fresh dynamic, because it was realized in Christ, and is realized in the believer when he walks as Christ walked, 8b.

9-11. Hatred, the denial of fellowship. Hatred destroys fellowship because it belongs to the spiritual realm of darkness where fellowship with the God of light is impossible, 9. Love, on the other hand, belongs to the realm of light where fellowship with God and with the brethren flourishes, 10. The loving Christian gives no occasion for a fellow believer to stumble because of him. Hatred not only kills fellowship but breeds spiritual ignorance and blindness, 11.

2:12-14. Spiritual maturity and fellowship

12. The Father's family. The addressees of this letter of John's were all God's children. He describes them as 'dear children' (*teknia,* 'born-again ones') whose sins have been remitted. Thus, they all have the privilege of fellowship in the family, irrespective of growth or maturity.

13-14. Fellowship and Christian growth. Those who develop spiritually and enjoy the full privilege of fellowship are described in these verses from the most mature to the babies. The mature, 'fathers,' are characterized by a seasoned knowledge of Christ – 'him who is from the beginning' (Jn 1:1, 14). This knowledge is experiential and the result of intimate fellowship with the Father and the Son. The 'young men,' those growing in maturity, are commended because they emphatically overcome the wicked one (Satan), the outcome of being strong spiritually and of having the word of God abiding in them. The immature, 'dear children' (*paidia,* 'infants'), are spiritually undeveloped. Although some are immature, all believers are in the family of God and know Him as Father and Christ as the Forgiver of their sins, 12. The need is for all to grow up and enter the full privileges of fellowship.

2:15-17. The peril of worldliness and fellowship

15*a*. **The peril warned against.** This warning is couched in a twofold command; (1) 'Do not love the world' (*kosmos*), the world system under which Satan has organized fallen mankind upon his God-opposing principles of pride, selfishness and ambition (Mt 4:8-9; Eph 2:2; 6:12); (2) 'or anything in the world,' such as its wealth, pleasure or honors. It is useless to claim we do not love the world yet love what it offers.

15*b*-**17. The reason for the warning.** (1) Love for the world excludes love for God, 15*b*-16. 'If anyone goes on loving the world, the love of the Father is not in him!' (Gr.) So contrary is the evil world to all that God is, both cannot be loved at the same time. 'The world' embraces 'the cravings of sinful man,' the keen desire of the unregenerate man centered upon self and opposed to God (cf. Rom 7:18); 'the lust of his eyes,' those keen appetites which master our body, soul and spirit through the senses (2 Sam 11:2; Josh 7:21; Ps 119:37); 'the boasting of what he has and does' i.e., the vainglorious display of godless living. Thus the evil world is completely at variance with our infinitely holy God, 16*b*. (2) The world is fleeting and impermanent, 17*a*. It is even now passing by, in a state of transition like a parade and it will soon be gone, as well as 'its desires.' By contrast, the doer of God's will is destined for permanence, 17*b*. 'But he who continually does the will of God remains forever,' as God abides forever (Ps 90:2), for he is linked eternally with God in Christ and in present unbroken fellowship.

2:18-23. Loyalty to the faith and fellowship

18-21. Doctrinal defection, the foe of fellowship. John again addresses 'dear children,' perhaps emphasizing their immaturity in contrast to the writer's authority and spiritual experience. He reminds them that it is the last hour, furthering the idea of the passing away of the present world (v. 17). This entire present age may be characterized as 'the last hour' with an acceleration of defection as the second advent draws nearer (1 Tim 4:1-5; 2 Tim 3:1-5; Jude 17-18). The apostle then identifies the source of much opposition to the

truth by affirming both the presence of many *antichrists* in his day and the coming of *the Antichrist* at a future time (2 Thess 2:3-10; Rev 13:1-10). 'Antichrist' means one who is opposed to Christ but who deceitfully comes under the guise of Christ, 18.

These Christ-opposers belonged to the church outwardly, but 'did not really belong to us' – not organically identified with the body of believers, 19. For them defection or apostasy was natural and 'they went out.' Their *defection proved their false profession*. Fellowship with Christ and His church is never possible for those who deny Him.

On the other hand, God's children are protected from the peril of defection and the influence of false teachers by the anointing of the Holy Spirit given by 'the Holy One' – Christ Himself. This anointing enables believers to discern between truth and error, and to discover those who are antichrists, 20, by the Spirit's help. This epistle was written because of the existence of the antichrists who stood opposed to the truth and because John's readers knew the truth, 21.

22-23. The essence of doctrinal defection. Writing against the background of the Gnostic heresy, John identifies the defectors as those who deny the deity of Jesus, 22. The Gnostics ('liars') denied that Jesus was the God-Man, stating that the Christ-spirit came upon Jesus at His baptism and departed before His death. By denying the Son they also denied the Father, since the Son is the revelation of the Father and the only way to the Father (Jn 14:6, 9), 22*b*. This last thought is given emphasis in 23. Fellowship with God the Father and the Son is never possible to those who deny the Son. To deny Him by refusing to accept His deity is to forfeit the privilege of a living relationship with Him. Doctrinal defection gives evidence of personal rejection.

2:24-29. Abiding in Christ and fellowship

24-26. Adherence to the truth. In contrast to those who promote error (vv. 18-23), believers are to allow the foundational truths of the gospel ('what you have heard from the beginning') to abide in them. Such adherence results in fellowship (abiding) with the Son and the Father, 24. The promise and present possession of those who abide, is eternal life, 25. In addition, adherence to the truth will deliver believers from 'those who are trying to lead you astray' – those actively attempting to deceive, 26.

27-29. Reliance upon the Holy Spirit. The Holy Spirit is the anointing (v. 20) which believers receive at the time of conversion. He abides in the believer and teaches him 'all things,' guiding him into 'all truth' (Jn 16:13), 27. Abiding results in one's having confidence and in not being ashamed at the coming of Christ, 28. The fruit of abiding is the practice of righteousness, which gives evidence of one's relationship to and fellowship with the Righteous One, Christ, 29.

3:1-10. Righteous living and fellowship

1. God's bestowed love, an incentive to a holy life. The germane thought of 2:29 concerning righteous living is expanded in 3:1-10. John states that there are two reasons why the Christian's life should be a holy one. The first is related to God's past work for us (v. 1), the second is related to His future work (vv. 2-3).

The apostle calls attention to the marvel of God's bestowed love – 'How great!' It should call forth continual admiration and praise. God's bestowal of His superlatively excellent love in making us His children (*teknia*) should lead to behavior which befits the family likeness. Such a relationship is unknown by the world because it does not know the Saviour, and such knowledge comes only through personal experience.

2-3. Christ's coming, an incentive to a holy life. God's future work of transforming the believer by glorification at the coming of Christ should also motivate him to a righteous life. Because we are 'children of God' (v. 1) we shall be glorified when Christ is visibly manifested. This glorification includes a new resurrection body, sinlessness, complete righteousness, and full purity, 2. Whoever has this hope continually purifies himself in his daily walk, 3.

4-5. A holy life, the intent of salvation. Sin is lawlessness, and it follows that everyone who continually practices sin transgresses the law (law in its broadest scope), 4. Christ appeared as the answer to the sin problem – to remove sins, making a holy life possible for those who possess His salvation, 5. He, the sinless Saviour, is our example, 5*b*.

6-10. A holy life and fellowship. The person who is abiding in Christ does not sin habitually (present tense, 'does not go on sinning continually'), 6*a*. On the other hand, the one who sins continually (also present tense) has never seen Christ with the eye of faith nor known Him experientially as his own Saviour, 6*b*. Righteous deeds are the fruit of a righteous character and proof of regeneration, 7. Such *holiness is the family likeness,* 7*b*.

As righteousness is the family image for God's family, so the continual practice of *sin is the image of the devil's family,* 8*a*. Sin has been the constant mark of Satan's character, 8*b*, 'from the beginning' (Isa 14:12-14; Ezek 28:11-15). Since Christ's redeeming work was purposed to destroy Satan's works, Christians cannot practice what their Lord and Saviour came to destroy, 8*c*. Furthermore, no member of God's family habitually practices sin, because the new nature (God's 'seed') abides in him and he cannot sin as a pattern of life, 9. The new nature (bestowed at the time of regeneration or new birth), by its very presence in the believer, will never permit continual sinning. The apostle then climaxes this section by furnishing the criterion for distinguishing the redeemed from the unconverted—the family of God from the family of the devil, 10. That standard is *the practice of righteousness* which is expressed through brotherly love.

3:11-18. Brotherly love and fellowship

11-15. The fellowship of love. A constant exhortation of God's Word is, 'Love one another,' 11. The fellowship of God's family is to be permeated by the atmosphere of love. The example of Cain is given as an illustration and warning of one who was unregenerate, of the Evil One (the devil, cf. 8, 10), and thus without God's love, 12. His hatred found its logical outcome in murder, proving his deeds evil and his brother's righteous (cf. Gen 4:1-16; Heb 11:4). The attitude of the world toward God's own is one of hate because love is alien to it – the prince of this world (Satan) being the father of hate (v. 10), 13. Love gives evidence of regeneration and new life, 14, while hate furnishes evidence of spiritual death, 15.

16-18. The manifestation of love. The supreme manifestation of love was Christ's incarnation and death (Jn 3:16; Rom 5:8), which furnishes an example of love in action, 16. Such evidence of love should be practical, not merely theoretical, 17-18. 'To lay down our lives' may take the practical turn of sacrifice for others in need, 17. Loving 'with words or tongue,' with intention but without deed is hypocrisy, not genuine love, 18 (Jas 1:22).

3:19-24. Christian assurance and fellowship

19-21. The nature of assurance. Assurance, or certainty of salvation and acceptance with God, depends on the practice of genuine love, 19. By our loving 'with actions and in truth' (v. 18) we know that we are really Jesus' disciples and belong to the truth as it is in Jesus, and shall reassure our hearts that all doubts as to our acceptance before God have been removed. *But* if our 'hearts' (the seat of our emotions and will, our inner judge) accuse us because our brotherly love is inadequate, 'God is greater than our hearts,' since He is omniscient, 20. We then appeal to Him for correct judgment about ourselves. If, on the other hand, our hearts do not condemn us, then we have double assurance of approach and freedom of speech ('confidence') before God, 21.

22-24. The realization of fellowship. Experiential communion with the Father is enjoyed through a *dynamic prayer life* and *constant obedience,* 22-23. This latter involves believing in Christ's finished redemptive work and the subsequent practicing of brotherly love. Obedience results in abiding in Him, 24. The Christian knows he is abiding when he is obeying. The Holy Spirit witnesses to Christ's abiding in the believer (cf. Jn 14:16-21; 15:1-10).

4:1-6. Discernment of error and fellowship

1. The presence of error. Error threatens the fellowship of God's own. Believers are here enjoined to 'test the spirits' – those spiritual powers which energize all teachers – 'because many false prophets have gone out into the world' and the consequent threat to the fellowship is a grave one. The origin of all teachers must be tested, 'whether they are from

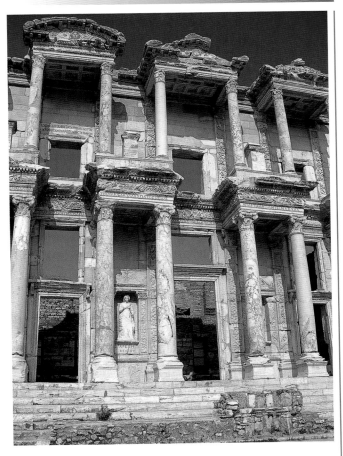

God.' Teachers who are not from God are false prophets, energized by demon spirits.

2-6. The acid test of error. The essence of this test is the confession of *Christ's deity and incarnation,* and it is this confession which distinguishes between those energized by the Spirit of God and those false teachers empowered by the spirit of error (Antichrist), 2-3a. Every Christian heresy can be traced to a faulty view of Christ's person and consequent work. The immediate danger of error is again stressed by the reminder that the spirit of Antichrist is already in the world, 3b. However, God's own have living in them a greater power (the Holy Spirit) than that at work in the world (Satan's power), and the Spirit enables them to overcome false teachers, 4, whose source of speech is 'from the world' and whose audience is 'the world,' 5. A teacher's hearers are a further test of his source of power – only those who are increasing in the knowledge of God continue to listen to the apostles ('us'), 6.

The impressive reconstruction of the Library of Celsus, Ephesus. I John was probably written from this city.

4:7-18. Love and the manifestation of fellowship

7-8. Love, a family characteristic. This is the third time the apostle has dealt with the subject of love (2:7-11; 3:10-18). It is introduced at this point perhaps because love is the great bond of fellowship which binds believers to one another, and to their Lord, in the face of Satan's threats. True love (*agape*) has its source in God and is a characteristic of every one who has been begotten of God, those who personally know Him, 7. Their behavior is to reveal their character in their loving one another, 7*a*. On the other hand, those who do not habitually love as a pattern of life reveal the fact that they are unrelated to God, not having experiential knowledge of Him, 8*a*. God, by His very nature, is love, 8*b*. His children bear this likeness.

9-10. The supreme manifestation of love. The greatest manifestation of God's love for men was His giving of His only begotten Son (Jn 3:16), 9*a*. Christ was His only born Son in a totally unique sense, sent so that we who were dead in sin might live through Him, 9*b*. The nature of God's love is seen in His loving us apart from any reciprocal love on our part – it is impossible for fallen men to love God, 10*a*. Because He is such love, God sent Christ to be the 'atoning sacrifice' (satisfaction) for our sins, 10*b*.

11-12. The obligation to love. Believers have a moral obligation ('ought') to love one another since God loved us to the extent of giving His only born Son, 11. Since no one has ever seen God, the only way He who is love can be seen is by His children's loving one another and thus revealing the family likeness, 12*a*. By our so doing, His love (the love which is His nature) accomplishes its full purpose ('is made complete'), 12*b*.

13-16. Love and the indwelling presence of God. The Holy Spirit, who indwells each believer, imparts knowledge of God's presence and of our union with Him (cf. Jn 15:1-10), 13. As a result the Spirit enables us to testify of Christ's saviourhood, 14. Confession of Christ's deity (implying also surrender to Him) establishes union with God, 15. Those who respond to God's love find that love becomes a working force in their lives, bringing the attendant blessings of fellowship with Him and His abiding presence in them, 16.

17-18. The perfection of love in us. The Holy Spirit brings the love which God produces in us to maturity and full development so that we may have confidence, or boldness, in the day of the judgment seat of Christ, 17. *Mature love results in the* assurance that we will be unashamed in that day because of our likeness to Christ – particularly with reference to love ('we are like him'), 17*b*. Also, mature love *gives fearlessness,* for fear and love cannot be mixed, 18. Love involves the self giving of one for the highest good of another; fear involves shrinking from another because of guilt. God's love has removed our guilt, thus fear of punishment is also gone.

4:19-21. The incentive to love and fellowship

19. The incentive to love. God's love for us, demonstrated by His giving His Son, is the great incentive for our loving continually (present tense). If His love was so great 'first,' then it is expected that His children will love as a result.

20-21. The fellowship of love. Our love for our brother proves our love for God. It is humanly easier to love one whom we can see than God whom we cannot see. Then how inconsistent to say that we love God but hate our brother. We cannot love God if we hate our brother. The circle of fellowship is complete when we show our love for God by loving our brother. This is the express command of God, 21. (Cf. Lev 19:18; Mt 22:39; Jn 13:34; 15:12.)

5:1-5. Faith and fellowship

1-3. Faith introduces us to fellowship. Faith in Christ, bringing the experience of the new birth, is the basis of fellowship, 1. This is a *fellowship of love,* 1*b*-2*a*. 'Everyone who loves the father [God] loves his child [the believer].' It is also a *fellowship of obedience,* 2*b*-3. The proof that we love God and His children is that we also keep His commandments (2:3; 3:22-24; 2 Jn 6). Observing God's commandments is not 'burdensome' (Gr. *bareiai,* 'severely oppressive'), because we love God and show our love for Him by obedience.

4-5. Faith gives victory. Faith operates through believers to overcome the world, the foe of God's family, 4*a*. 'Overcome' is in the present tense and conveys the thought of habitually conquering in victory, wrought by faith. This victorious faith is centered in the person of Christ, 5. He conquered the world Himself (Jn 16:33); therefore we overcome the world through Him.

5:6-12. Testimony and fellowship

6-10. The testimony concerning the son. The *first witness* is external and is to Christ's righteousness and to His redemption, 6. 'This is He who came through water and blood' (Gr.). 'Through water' refers to the inauguration of our Lord's public ministry by His baptism in the Jordan (Mt 3:13-17), by which He identified Himself with a ministry of *righteousness.* 'Through blood' refers to His vicarious death on the cross (Heb 9:12) by which *redemption* from sin was accomplished.

The *second witness* is internal and is that of the Holy Spirit, 6b. He continues to bear witness to Jesus' righteousness and redemption, and because He is truth His testimony is absolutely true. The witness to Christ's person and work is threefold and consistent, 8. Accordingly, there are three witnesses, 'the Spirit, the water, and the blood; and the three are in agreement' (Gr. 'attest the same truth'). This witness is wholly reliable, 9, for if we receive the testimony of men on the strength of two or three witnesses (Deut 19:15; Mt 18:16; Jn 8:16-18), how much more should we receive the greater and better attested witness of God concerning His Son? Furthermore, when received by faith this testimony becomes one's own personal witness, 10a. But refused, it means the unbeliever, in rejecting God's plan of redemption, makes God a liar, 10b. In effect the rejecter is saying, 'I don't believe it!'

11-12. God's testimony believed. The testimony is: 'God has given us eternal life, and this life is in his Son,' 11. The result deduced is that he who has the Son possesses eternal life. The converse is also true, he who rejects the testimony does not have the Son of God and hence does not possess eternal life, 12. God's entire program of salvation is centered in His Son. Man must make a choice regarding Him!

5:13-15. Prayer and fellowship

13. The importance of assurance. The apostle's purpose in writing to believers was that they might have assurance of eternal life. Such confidence provides the basis for joyful prayer and fellowship.

14-15. Power in prayer. Assurance of salvation gives: (1) confidence of access to God's presence (*pros,* 'face to face with Him'), 14a; (2) breadth of petition, 14b, 'if we ask *anything*'; (3) consciousness of God's will, 14c, 'according to according to his will'; (4) faith to believe, 14*d*, 'assurance . . . he hears us'; (5) confidence we will receive an answer to the requests made, 15.

5:16-21. Prayer fellowship and the sinning Christian

16-17. Prayer and the problem of serious sin. It is possible for a true believer to fall into sin, 16*a*. If and when this happens, a fellow believer is to pray for him, 16*b*. As a result God will give the sinning Christian preservation of physical life (not eternal life, for this life is eternal and unforfeitable). However, this intercession is effective only in the case of sin not unto physical death, 16*c*.

'There is a sin that leads to death,' 16*d*. This is persistent, willful sinning in a believer in which the body is destroyed so that the spirit might be saved (1 Cor 5:1-5; Acts 5:1-11; 1 Cor 11:30). Both Saul and Samson are types of this very severe chastening in the OT. 'All wrongdoing is sin, and there is sin that does not lead to [physical] death' (involving lesser chastisements, cf.1 Cor 11:30).

18-20. Sin and its remedy. The primary remedy for habitual sin is *the new birth,* 18. 'We know that everyone who has been born of God does not go on practicing sin as a habit. He having been begotten of God, this divine life keeps him from continually practicing sin, and Satan does not touch him' (Gr.). The believer's *new position* is also a remedy for sin, 19. He is born of God and into His family. In contrast, the world (all unsaved) is in the power of Satan, 19b. Finally, *our understanding of the truth* is a deterrent to habitual sin, 20. Truth and life mark the realm of the child of God.

21. Concluding charge. The aged apostle adds a final note for his 'dear children': 'keep yourselves from idols.' An idol is anything that usurps God's place in one's life. Ephesus was full of idolatry and its practices, making these words very appropriate.

2 JOHN

Living in truth and love

Writer and destination.
Second John is a personal note, sent by the apostle John to 'the chosen lady and her children.' The identity of this woman (or church?) is not known, though some scholars maintain the name is 'Lady Electa' (the Gr. for 'chosen,' or kyria, the Gr. word for 'lady'). This Christian matron lived somewhere in the circuit of churches over which the aged apostle John had the oversight. That John was the writer is apparent from the style and content of the note, which strikingly resembles 1 and 3 John and the gospel of John.

Date and purpose. There is no suggestion of any great interval between the writing of 1 John and 2 John. John's purpose in penning the letter was to warn this influential and esteemed lady (1-2) against false teachers. She apparently sponsored meetings with visiting preachers in her home (10), like Nympha in Laodicea (Col 4:15). The apostle encourages her and warns against unsound doctrine by suggesting she sponsor no one who teaches less than the full deity and humanity of Christ.

Part of the ancient Roman theater, Laodicea. John's purpose in this letter was to warn 'the lady' against false teachers. She apparently sponsored meetings with visiting preachers, like Nympha in Laodicea.

1-6. Living in truth and love

1-3. The salutation. John, in this more intimate epistle, styles himself simply 'elder' (Acts 11:30; Tit 1:5-9), using a less authoritative designation than 'apostle.' He professes to love the chosen lady and her children 'in the truth,' 1*a*. True Christian love rests on 'the truth,' i.e., the revealed Word of God focused in the person and work of Christ (Jn 14:6), and contrasts with false teaching, which errs at this point (see 7-11). Fellowship in the truth produces a breadth of love as wide as the communion of faith, 1*b*. Such truth is the only sure basis of genuine love, both in the present and in the future, 2. Grace, mercy and peace have their source in God the Father and Jesus Christ the Son, 3. Thus, they are founded in truth and love.

4-6. The exhortation. The apostle greatly rejoiced that he found some of her children living their entire daily lives in truth – the truth of the gospel. Their conduct conformed to the truth as it was manifested in Christ. John urges the practice of Christian love as the natural outcome of the truth, as he did in the first epistle (see notes on 1 Jn 2:7-8).

7-13. Refusing the false fellowship of error

7-9. The presence of error indicated. There is a great contrast between the preceding verses and those which follow, showing that error violates the revealed truth of God and the commandment of love. Such false teaching is promulgated by 'many deceivers' who 'have gone out into the world,' 7. Essentially, their error is a refusal to acknowledge that Jesus Christ has come in the flesh, thereby denying the *possibility* of the incarnation and by implication also denying both advents of Christ.

The presence of error also calls for self-examination on the part of the believers, lest the false teachers undo in the fellowship what the apostles had accomplished, thus resulting in loss of reward for the Christian, 8. Those who go too far ('run ahead') in professing identity with the Christian fellowship must also be examined, especially when they do not 'continue in the teaching of Christ.' To so fail indicates lack of relationship to God and spiritual bankruptcy, 9.

10-11. Refusal to admit false teachers. Evidently the above teachers of error were being entertained in Christian homes under the cloak of hospitality. The apostle sternly forbids the continuance of this practice and commands believers not to grant such fellowship and Christian hospitality, 10. Even the giving of a customary greeting is forbidden, for this would show identification and participation with the person's evil deeds, 11. Separation from error is necessary (2 Cor 6:14-17).

12-13. Conclusion. The apostle anticipates a personal visit, 12, and sends greetings from 'the children of your chosen sister,' 13.

3 JOHN

Help and hospitality toward itinerant ministers

Author. Similarity of tone, ideas and style, as well as evidence from Irenaeus, Clement of Alexandria, Dionysius or Alexandria, Cyprian and others, indicates that this epistle was written by the same author as 1 John, namely, John the beloved disciple.

Date and place of writing. According to Eusebius (*Ecclesiastical History* 3:25) John returned from the Patmos exile to Ephesus after the death of Domitian (A.D. 96), spending his closing years visiting the Asiatic churches (cf. 2 Jn 12; 3 Jn 10, 14), ordaining elders and ministering. Therefore, 2 John and 3 John were written after the Apocalypse, if Eusebius is correct.

The marshy site of the now ruined Temple of Artemis, Ephesus. 3 John, a true letter, was probably written from this city.

1-8. Gaius' example of living in truth and love

1-4. The apostle's salutation to Gaius.
The epistle is addressed from 'the elder' (see 2 Jn 1) to 'my dear friend Gaius,' who was possibly Gaius of Derbe (Acts 20:4), Gaius of Corinth (Rom 16:23; 1 Cor 1:14), Gaius of Macedonia (Acts 19:29), or Gaius the bishop of Pergamos (mentioned in the *Apostolic Constitutions* 7:40). Whoever is meant, the apostle professes his genuine love for him, 1; wishes him physical health, 2*a*; and expresses confidence in his spiritual vitality, 2b. John's greeting includes a prayer for Gaius' spiritual and physical well-being, and expresses joy for his life in the truth, 3-4 (cf. 1 Thess 2:19-20).

5-8. Gaius' life in the truth.
This manner of daily living is demonstrated by *the good works such a faith produces,* 5, for the brethren, especially traveling Christian workers ('strangers') who were dependent on the church for support rather than on pagans; *the hospitality and love such a life shows,* 6; *the consideration such a life displays,* 7.

9-11. Example of a contrary life

9-10. The example.
Diotrephes, in contrast to Gaius and Demetrius, 1-8, 12, did not walk in love and the truth because he was carnally ambitious, 9. John had written to the church of which Diotrephes was a member. The latter had rejected some suggestions the apostle had made because he 'loves to be first.' He also manifested the works of the sinful nature, 10*a,* and was uncharitable and domineering, 10*b*.

11. The warning.
Diotrephes' life was evil and not to be imitated. He was not 'from God' nor had he 'seen God,' his evil life proving this.

12-14. Demetrius' good example

12. Demetrius' good report.
The good testimony to the life of Demetrius (unknown) was universal, including the witness of the truth itself and that of John. This was in stark contrast to the report given of Diotrephes.

13-14. Closing observations (cf. 2 Jn 12).

JUDE

Contending for the faith

The author and attestation. The author was evidently the brother of James, who was the bishop of Jerusalem and the writer of the epistle of James (Jas 1:1; cf. Mt 13:55; Mk 6:3), and the (half) brother of our Lord, 1. At first an unbeliever (Jn 7:3-5), he became convinced of Jesus' deity (Acts 1:14). Some scholars, however, identify him as the apostle Judas (Jude; Mt 10:2-3), called Lebbaeus or Thaddaeus (Lk 6:16; Acts 1:13). Echoes and allusions to the epistle occur in the writings of Hermas, Polycarp, Athenagoras, Theophilus of Antioch and Tertullian, so that Jude has stronger external attestation than 2 Peter.

Occasion and date. Little is known of the circumstances or date of writing, except that the decline it protests is more developed than in 2 Peter and hence appears to be written later, after A.D. 66 or 67. The deep apostasy it describes furnishes background for the Apocalypse, before which it is placed in English Bibles. The Spirit of God gave both Jude and Peter a similar note of warning, so sorely needed by the church.

The shore of the Dead Sea near the probable site of ancient Sodom. Jude reminded his readers of the solemn fate of the cities of the Plain.

1-4. Contending for the faith

1-2. Salutation. Jude addresses believers in general, citing their election, their preservation, and their status as 'loved by God the Father.'

3-4. The occasion of the epistle. The author's original purpose was to write a doctrinal epistle, 3*a*, 'about the salvation we share.' This 'common' *(koines,* 'belonging equally to more than one') salvation was for *all* believers. False teachers threatened the teaching of this general truth involving Christ's person and finished work. Jude, therefore, found it necessary to switch to *an exhortation to militantly defend the faith. 3b.* 'The faith' is that which was once for all delivered to the saints. No other revelation or faith is needed, for it is complete and final. It is the answer to those who claim revelation and truths in addition to the canonical Scriptures. The intrusion of false teachers brought error concerning the doctrine of the person and work of Christ, especially with respect to His sovereignty and lordship, 4. This is the primary error of all false teaching (cf. 2 Pet 2:1).

5-7. Historical warnings of God's judgment

5. The Israelites in the wilderness. Since those addressed in this epistle already knew all the facts once for all, Jude needed only to remind them of these things, 5*a.* These facts are: that 'the Lord delivered his people out of Egypt, but later destroyed those who did not believe,' i.e., at Kadesh-barnea (Num 14:1-45; 1 Cor 10:1-5; Heb 3:17-19). This divine judgment for disobedience was upon God's own people and involved the sin unto physical death (cf. 1 Cor 5:1-5; 11:30-32; 1 Jn 5:16).

6. The fallen angels. Evidently, the sin of these specially designated angels was that they 'did not keep their positions of authority;' their own initial distinctive order as purely spirit beings, but 'abandoned their own home' by cohabiting with mortal women and thus producing the condition which necessitated the Flood (Gen 6:1-6; 2 Pet 2:4-5). Their punishment for disobedience is imprisonment 'in darkness, bound with everlasting chains' (see 2 Pet 2:4). Their judgment will be at 'the great Day,' probably in association with Satan's judgment (Rev 20:10).

7. The sinners of Sodom and Gomorrah (cf. Gen 19; 2 Pet 2:6-8). Their sin, 'in a similar way' as the angels of verse 6, was that they 'gave themselves up to sexual immorality and perversion, i.e. unnatural vice.' Their judgment served as an example to warn others of the judicial punishment of eternal fire. The literal fire by which they were consumed is a symbol of the eternal fire to which the wicked have been consigned (Rev. 19:20; 20:10, 14; cf. Mt 25:41).

8-16. False teachers

8. Their presumption indicated. This sin of false teachers (v. 4) is revealed by their *failure to heed the historical warnings* of divine judgment illustrated in 5-7 (Gr. 'in the same manner notwithstanding' the warnings given), 8*a*; *their dreaming state* – dreaming, as natural men who are spiritually asleep; their *sexual immorality* – 'pollute their own bodies' (cf. v. 7); their *insubordination* – they 'reject authority,' particularly that of God's Word; their *slander* – they 'slander celestial beings.'

9-10. Their presumption illustrated. When Michael the archangel contended with the devil about the literal body of Moses, because it was raised for the transfiguration (Mt 17:3-4) previous to its allotted time, he did not presume to bring an abusive judgment upon Satan, out of reverence for his former dignity (v. 8*c*), but simply said, 'The Lord rebuke you' (Zech 3:2). In contrast, these men 'speak abusively against' anything which they do not understand, showing no reverence for any authority. By those things that they do know, by animal instinct, they corrupt themselves and are destroyed.

11. Reasons for their woe. These teachers of error are *self-willed religious naturalists,* gone 'the way of Cain' (Gen 4:3-8). Cain was a type of the religious natural man who rejects God's plan of redemption and molds his own religion of human merit and works to suit himself, 11*a.* They are *mercenary religious moralists,* having 'rushed for profit into Balaam's error,' 11*b* (Num 22-24). This error was the mistake of supposing that a righteous God must curse sinning Israel and displayed ignorance of the higher morality of the cross, whereby God can be righteous and at the same time eternally justify the believing sinner (cf. 2 Pet 2:15; Rev 2:14). They are also *lawless religionists,* having 'been destroyed in

Korah's rebellion' (Num 16:1-50; 26:9-11). Korah's sins were a denial of God's authority through Moses as His chosen mouthpiece, and Korah's consequent intrusion into the priests' office. Rejection of the authority of God's Word is characteristic of all false teachers.

12-13. Their spiritual sterility. The spiritual emptiness of these teachers is indicated by their *peril, 12a.* 'They are wild-waves of the sea' on which the Christians' love feasts were in danger of being wrecked by their selfish and carnal carousing (cf. 1 Cor 11:30-32). Their sterility is also seen in their *barrenness, 12b.* They are 'clouds without rain, blown along by the wind; autumn trees, without fruit, and uprooted,' being spiritually lifeless to begin with, and when plucked up by the roots, visibly proved dead. Their *shame, 13a* (Isa 57:20), and their *deception, 13b,* further reveal the lack of spiritual reality.

14-15. Their judgment predicted. This prophecy, preserved as tradition in the noncanonical book of Enoch (1:9), is here given by the Holy Spirit as divine truth. Jude declares that Enoch prophesied of these false teachers in dim antiquity, and that judgment will take place at Christ's second advent when latter-day apostates will be judged, 15.

16. Their character reviewed. False teachers are declared to be 'grumblers'; 'fault-finders' (malcontents); loose-livers; arrogant in speech; following those who flatter people 'for their own advantage.'

17-25. Exhortations and closing benediction

17-23. Exhortations to God's own. The children of God are to remember the apostolic prophetic warnings, 17-18 (such as 1 Tim 4:1-6; 2 Tim 3:1-10; 2 Thess 2:1-12; 2 Pet 2:1-22). They are to evaluate false teachers correctly, as those who 'divide,' who 'follow mere natural instincts,' without the new nature, and devoid of the Spirit (Rom 8:8-9), hence unsaved.

Believers are to cultivate spiritual growth, 20a, and a Spirit-energized prayer life, 20b; to keep themselves in the sphere of God's love, 21a; to be keenly expectant of God's mercy in the consummation of eternal life, 21b; to show compassion toward those who have honest doubts regarding the faith, those probably influenced by false teachers, 22; to be evangelistic, 23a; and to separate from carnal sins, 23b.

24-25. Closing benediction. Praise is ascribed to God for His ability to keep us from stumbling into sin and to present us in a glorified state in His glorious presence. Our safety and security in Him are indeed causes for praise!

REVELATION

Christ's unveiling and kingdom

The title. This great prophetic unfolding is called 'the Revelation [Gr. *Apocalypse*] of Jesus Christ.' It is *His* revelation given to Him by the Father to be made known to His servants, 1:1. The title 'Apocalypse of John' is a traditional designation early used to differentiate it from other apocalypses, the epithet St. John 'the Divine' being added in the 4th cen.

Attestation and authorship. Clear attestation comes from Justin Martyr, Irenaeus, Tertullian and Hippolytus, both as to genuineness and authorship by 'John, the apostle and disciple of the Lord.' The same is true of Clement of Alexandria, Origen, Victorinus (who wrote a commentary on Revelation), the Muratorian Fragment, Ephraim Syrus, etc. Rejection of the book as nonapostolic by the reformers Luther, Zwingli and Erasmus, in the face of early evidence, seems arbitrary and weightless. Johannine authorship is established by the writer, who calls himself John (1:1, 4, 9; 22:8). The early church Fathers Clement of Alexandria, Irenaeus and Eusebius declared it was John the apostle who was banished to Patmos (1:9).

Background and date. Evidence both internal and external (e.g., Irenaeus) places the book toward the end of Emperor Domitian's reign (A.D. 81-96). It was Domitian who had the apostle banished to the rocky island of Patmos in the Aegean Sea (1:9).

Great prophetic themes consummated here

Gen 3:15; Rev 1:1
The Lord Jesus Christ, the central subject of all Scripture

Mt 16:18; Rev 2-3
The Church

Rev 20:4-6
The resurrection and glorification of the saints

Deut 4:29-30; Jer 30:5-7; Rev 4-19
The Great Tribulation

Isa 14:12-14; Ezk 28:11-18; Rev 12:3-17; 20:1-3, 10
Satan and the world system

Joel 3:1-10; Mt 25:31-46; Rev 16:13-16
The judgment of the nations

Ezk 28:1-10; 2 Thess 2:7-10; Rev 13:1-10; 19:20
The Antichrist

Isa 11:1-16; Acts 1:6; Rev 20:4-7
The kingdom of Messiah over Israel

Dan 2:37-44; Lk 21:24; Rev 6:1-19:16
The times of the Gentiles

Gen 3
Paradise lost

Rev 21-22
and paradise regained

Israel's covenants

Abrahamic Gen 12:1-3;

Palestinian Deut 30:1-10;

Davidic 2 Sam 7:4-17;

new Jer 31:31-33 Zech 14:1-14;

Rev 19:11-16
The second advent of Christ

Ps 9:17; Rev 20:11-15
The judgment of the wicked

Isa 65:17; 66:22; Rev 21-22
The eternal state with the new heaven and earth

Nature of the Book. Revelation is the central terminal where all the great trunk lines of the prophetic Word converge, and is thus the consummation of all revealed truth. It was meant to be understood for the following reasons: (1) It is revelation (an apocalypse), 'a making known' or 'unveiling.' (2) It promises blessing to those who read, hear, and keep its words of prophecy (1:3). (3) The book is not sealed (1:3*b*; 22:10; cf. Dan 12:9). (4) A simple key is furnished to understand the book (1:19). (5) The apocalyptic symbols of prophecy, which are the vehicles of its interpretation, are found explained elsewhere in Scripture, which in turn furnishes the commentary on this crowning book of consummation.

Methods of interpretation

The spiritualizing method.
This interpretation takes a mystical or allegorical approach to most of the book. Clement of Alexandria, Origen, and later Augustine and Jerome followed this method. Recent interpreters who accept this method find the book dealing primarily with the general struggle between the church and evil throughout the entire age, thereby giving encouragement to tested saints. Such an interpretation, however, fails to expound the book meaningfully, and practically ignores the claims to its prophetic nature (1:3; 10:11; 22:7, 10, 18-19). It fails to recognize the interpretive key to the book (1:19) and the focus of Revelation on the second advent, including the climactic events which follow (1:7; 3:11; 16:15; 22:7, 12).

The praeterist method.
This interpretive school holds that the book has already been practically fulfilled. The older praeterist view maintained it was fulfilled in the defeat of the Jewish enemies of the early church and in the reign of Nero (ch. 6-11), the remaining chapters being vaguely future. From the 17th cen. on, praeterists have held that the church's conflict with Judaism (ch. 4-11) and with paganism (ch. 12-19) is depicted, ch. 20-22 describing her present triumph. This position ignores the interpretive key of 1:19, gives arbitrary meanings to the symbols found in the book, and fails to account for the indications of a *short* span of time covering the events of ch. 4-19 preceding the second advent.

Patmos from the Monastery of St John. John the apostle was banished to the rocky island of Patmos in the Aegean Sea by Domitian.

The continuous-historical method.
Those who hold to this method maintain that Revelation covers the entire span of church history from John's time to the end of the world. The view has been popular since the time of Berengaud (9th cen.) and Joachim (12th cen.). Wycliffe, Luther, Joseph Mede, Isaac Newton, Bengel, Barnes and others held it. The inadequacies of the preceding two methods apply to this interpretation as well. It fails to correlate the book with Bible prophecy as a whole, and leaves the details of Revelation without adequate explanation.

The futurist method of interpretation.
This school uses the key of 1:19 as a guide in placing most of the book (ch. 4-22) still in the future, grounding interpretation in OT prophecies, such as those relating to the Day of the Lord (Isa 2:10-22; 4:1-6; 34:1-17), the kingdom (Isa 35:1-10), and Christ's second advent (Zech 14). NT prophecies which refer to Christ's return are correlated with the events recorded in Revelation (e.g., Mt 24-25; Mk 13; Lk 21).

View of the early church.
The early church Fathers evidently favored the futurist view because of their belief in the imminent return of the Lord, His subsequent earthly kingdom (cf. Acts 1:6), and a period of great trouble preceding and inaugurating that kingdom. Justin Martyr, Irenaeus, Hippolytus, Tertullian, and Victorinus held literal views of the future kingdom.

Outline

1 The Patmos vision (*the things seen,* 1:19*a*)
2-3 Letters to the seven churches (*the things which are,* 1:19*b*)
4-22 Climactic events of history (*the things which shall be hereafter,* 1:19*c*)
4-5 The divine throne in heaven
6-18 The Great Tribulation on earth
6:1-8:1 Seal judgments
8:2-11:19 Trumpet judgments
12:1-13:18 Seven personages
14:1-20 Preview of the end of the Great Tribulation
15:1-16:21 Bowl judgments
17:1-18:24 Judgment of Babylon
19 The second advent and Armageddon
20-22 The millennium, the last judgment, the eternal state.

Seven-branched candlestand. In the early chapters of Revelation, Christ appears in the midst of the church, denoted by the seven lampstands, He Himself being the Light.

1:1-3. Introduction

1-2. The nature of the book. It is the Revelation, the great unveiling *par excellence* of the future, which is '*from* Christ' (subjective genitive), 'which God gave him.' In no sense is Revelation a sealed book, nor a book which is not to be studied and understood. It deals with things which 'must' come to pass 'shortly' or 'soon' and so are of vital import to God's people *now*. It is an unveiling from Christ, given through an angel to John in signs or symbols.

3. The purpose of the book. Its purpose is to bless or make happy the one who reads its words and also 'those who hear it and take to heart what is written in it.' The reason given for so doing is that the time of the fulfillment of its predictions is near. Hearing and keeping will result in faith and stabilizing hope while facing the trials and persecutions of this sinful age, in view of the triumph of Christ and the ultimate triumph of His own.

1:4-8. Salutation from the author

4a. The author and recipients of the book. John the apostle is evidently the human author. The recipients are *seven* representative churches in the Roman province of Asia in western Asia Minor. These are representative of conditions in the universal church in every locality during the *entire* church age. Some commentators have attempted to identify the seven churches with seven successive periods of church history, typically suggesting that we are in the Laodicea age now. This interpretive program has little textual warrant, however.

4b-8. Benediction from the Triune God. 'Grace and peace' are the two great possessions of the church in Christ (2 Thess 1:2). They come from (1) *God the Father, 4b,* 'Him who is, and who was, and who is to come,' a periphrasis for the unspeakable name Jehovah (Yahweh), the unchangeable, eternally self-

The seven sevens of the Apocalypse

1. THE SEVEN CHURCHES
2:1-3:22

2. THE SEVEN SEALS 6:1-8:1

3. THE SEVEN TRUMPETS
8:2-11:19

4. THE SEVEN PERSONAGES
12:1-13:18

The woman, 12:1-2

The dragon, 12:3-4

The Man Child, 12:5

The archangel Michael, 12:7

The remnant, 12:17

The beast out of the sea 13:1-8

The beast out of the earth 13:11-18

5. THE SEVEN BOWLS
15:1-16:21

6. THE SEVEN DOOMS
17:1-20:15

Ecclesiastical Babylon, 17:1-18

Political Babylon, 18:1-24

Antichrist and the false prophet, 19:20

Antichristian nations, 19:21

Gog and Magog, 20:8-9

Satan, 20:10

The wicked dead, 20:11-15

7. THE SEVEN NEW THINGS
21:1-22:21

New heavens, 21:1

New earth, 21:1

New city, 21:9-23

New nations, 21:24-27

New river, 22:1

New tree, 22:2

New throne, 22:3-5

existing One (Ex 3:13-14); (2) *God the Spirit,* 4c, symbolized in the completeness and totality of His activities as 'the seven Spirits before His throne' (cf. Isa 11:2; 1 Cor 12:4, 13); (3) *God the Son – Jesus Christ,* 5-8. Jesus, as the center of the book, is described in full detail, including (a) *His obedient earthly life,* 5a, 'the faithful witness' (Isa 55:4); (b) *His glorious resurrection,* 5b, 'the firstborn from the dead' (Col 1:18); (c) *His future title and kingdom glory,* 5c, 'ruler of the kings of the earth' (Ps 2:2, 9); (d) *His redemptive work,* 5d, 'to him who loves us, and has freed [KJV 'washed,' based on later MSS] us from our sins by his blood' (Rom 3:25-26; 1 Pet 1:18-20); (e) *His redemptive accomplishment,* 6a, 'and [He] has made us to be a kingdom and priests to serve his God and Father'; (f) *His worthiness of all praise,* 6b; (g) *His second advent,* 7; (h) *His personal testimony,* 8, 'I am the Alpha and the Omega' (the first and last letters of the Gr. alphabet, like our ' A to Z'). Hence He is the beginning and end of all things which are consummated in this book (Isa 44:6). He is the real Author of the Revelation (1:1).

Part 1.
The things seen –
The Patmos vision, 1:9-20

1:9-20. The circumstances and the vision

9-11. The circumstances. The apostle was in banishment on Patmos, an Aegean island ten by six miles, about 37 miles SW of Miletus, off the coast of Asia Minor. He was exiled there by Emperor Domitian in A.D. 95, according to Eusebius, because of his loyalty to the Word of God, 9. The trumpetlike voice is that of Christ, 10, the Alpha and Omega. The seven churches are listed by name, 11 (see notes on ch. 2-3).

12-16. The vision itself. Christ, the glorified One, appears intimately associated with His church on earth, 13. He is in the midst of the church, denoted by the seven lampstands or lightholders, Christ Himself being the Light (Jn 8:12). He appears as 'son of man,' here primarily as Judge, evaluating the service of His church on earth.

His snow-white hair, 14a, portrays His eternity, His infinite wisdom, experience and venerableness of character. *His flaming eyes,* 14*b* (cf. 19:12), bespeak His omniscient insight as Judge, while *His feet like glowing brass,* 15*a,* speak of Him who not only walks in the midst of His church to evaluate her service, but who will 'tread the winepress of the fury of the wrath of God' (19:15) at His advent to judge sinners and to make war against Satan and the Antichrist (19:11). *His voice like the sound of rushing waters,* 15*b,* symbolizes the awe-inspiring pronouncement of the Judge's verdict, whether of commendation of His own (Mt 25:34) or condemnation of the wicked (Mt 25:41). *His right hand,* 16*a,* once nail-pierced and still bearing the scars as credentials of His divine-human person and finished work (Jn 20:27), qualifies Him for judgment. *His mouth,* 16*b,* out of which proceeds His sharp two-edged sword of judgment and justice (19:11-15), sets forth the truth that He will pronounce judgment and execute justice on the basis of the Word of God (Eph 6:17; Heb 4:12). *His face like the sun,* 16*c* (cf. Mt 17:2), sets Him forth in the glory of His second advent as Judge (Mal 4:2) and as He will appear in His eternal glory (Rev 21:23).

17-18. John's response to the vision. Prostrated at the sight of the glorified Son of Man appearing as Judge, 17 (cf. Isa 6:1-10), John is given assurance by the resurrected and glorified Christ, who accordingly has 'the keys of death and Hades' (the unseen realm where the dead go at death), 18. 'The keys' (Mt 16:19) are emblems of authority and access, showing that He alone can open and shut the unseen world, having conquered death Himself.

19. The key to all the visions of the book. This verse, indispensable to the correct interpretation of Revelation, suggests a threefold division of the book: (1) 'what you have seen,' i.e., the vision of the Son of Man as Judge (1:10-20); (2) 'what is now,' i.e., the seven churches then existing in the Roman province of Asia, representative of the church during the entire church age (ch. 2-3); (3) 'what will take place later,' i.e., after the church period ends (ch. 4-22).

20. The meaning of the first vision. The 'mystery,' a truth previously hidden but now revealed, which nevertheless still has an inscrutable element in it (cf. Mt 13:11), is twofold. (1) *The seven stars* are the messengers, probably not actual angels but more likely men,

sent by the seven churches to Patmos to ascertain the aged apostle's condition, and who subsequently became bearers of his message. (2) *The seven lampstands* are the churches (see 1:4, 11). 'Stars' and 'lampstands' are the luminaries of this dark age, symbols of God's people who are to reflect the One who is the Light of the world (Mt 5:14; Jn 8:12; Eph 5:8; Phil 2:15).

Part 2.
The things which are
– The church age, Ch. 2-3

2:1-7. Ephesus
– the loveless church
1-3. Salutation and commendation. The letter is addressed to the 'angel' (messenger, see note on 1:20) of the church in Ephesus, the great metropolis of proconsular Asia and the Vanity Fair of the ancient world (see note on Acts 19:8-41 and 'Ephesus and Archeological Discoveries'). The message is from the glorified Judge (Christ), 'who holds the seven stars in his right hand' and 'walks among the seven golden lampstands' (His church on earth). The church is commended for its good works, patient endurance and intolerance of evil, especially evildoers and impostors, 2-3 (cf. Acts 20:29-30).

4-5. Complaint and warning. The Ephesian church's sin was departure from its initial heartfelt affection for the Lord. 'Nevertheless, despite your other excellencies [v. 2], I have this against you that you have abandoned, by imperceptibly quitting, your first love' (the spontaneous affection you had for Me at the first), 4. The warning is sounded in verse 5. They were to *remember* from where they were fallen, 5*a.* Spontaneous love for the Lord is the height of true spirituality. To leave it is the first step toward a very serious fall. The Lord further enjoins them to *repent,* 5*b* (change their attitude), and '*do the things you did at first,*' 5*c,* as a proof of the genuineness of their love. The alternative is forfeiture of testimony, 5*d.*

6-7. Praise and promise. The church is again commended for detesting 'the practices of the Nicolaitans,' a symbolic name apparently of a party attempting to introduce a false freedom into the church. They abused grace, which led

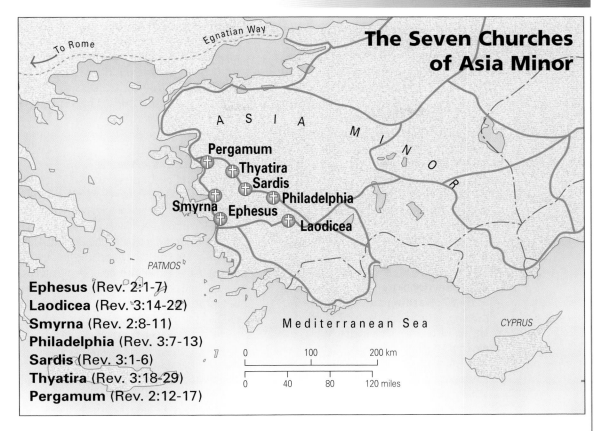

The Seven Churches of Asia Minor

To Rome

Egnatian Way

A S I A

M I N O R

Pergamum
Thyatira
Sardis
Philadelphia
Smyrna
Ephesus
Laodicea

PATMOS

Mediterranean Sea

CYPRUS

Ephesus (Rev. 2:1-7)
Laodicea (Rev. 3:14-22)
Smyrna (Rev. 2:8-11)
Philadelphia (Rev. 3:7-13)
Sardis (Rev. 3:1-6)
Thyatira (Rev. 3:18-29)
Pergamum (Rev. 2:12-17)

0	100	200 km

0	40	80	120 miles

to licentiousness, 6 (cf. v. 2; 2 Pet 2:15-16, 19; Jude 4, 11). Some take this symbolism, however, as indicating the origin of clericalism *(nikao,* 'conquer,' and *laos,* 'people'), making them a group that early favored a clerical system which later developed into the papal hierarchy. To the individual overcomer is promised reward in the eternal state (cf. Gen 2:9; Rev 22:2, 24).

2:8-11. Smyrna – the persecuted church

8-9. The persecution. The risen Christ as the Conqueror of death, 1, is the speaker. Smyrna (modern Izmir) is 40 miles N of Ephesus. The city was called the 'glory of Asia' because of its planned development, its beautiful temples and ideal harbor. It was a center of Caesar worship and included a large Jewish community among its populace. The Jews of the 'synagogue of Satan,' 9 (3:9), were Jews nationally but not spiritually. They bitterly blasphemed Christ as 'the hanged one' and opposed Christianity, so that in rejecting the truth their synagogue became that of Satan (cf. 1 Tim 4:1-4; 1 Jn 4:1-4). Contrast 'the

congregation of the Lord' (Num 16:3; 20:4).

10-11. The encouragement. The exhortation given is not to fear, 10a (Gr. 'Do not fear these things which you are about to suffer'). Why? (1) *God will overrule the devil's temptations.* 'The devil will put some of you in prison to test you,' 10b. On God's side, however, you will be 'tested' to be approved and rewarded. (2) *The time of the persecution will be short,* 10c. The 'ten days' (cf. Dan 1:12) symbolize a short period (cf. Gen 24:55). (3) *Faithfulness even to physical death will be rewarded by 'the crown of life,'* the martyr's reward, 10d (cf. Jas 1:12). (4) *The overcomer will not be hurt by the second death,* 11. This is the lake of fire, Gehenna, the place of eternal separation from God (Rev 20:6-15; 21:8).

2:12-17. Pergamum – the worldly church

12-13. Where Satan's throne was. Pergamum was a notable center of idolatry and demon-controlled religion, with splendid temples to Zeus, Athena, Apollo and Asclepias (the god of healing). It was located on the

Aegean Sea about 60 miles N of Smyrna. As a brilliant center of pagan religion, including Caesar worship, it was called 'where Satan has his throne' and 'where Satan lives' (cf. 1 Cor 10:19-20; Rev 9:20-21; 16:13-16 for the connection of idolatry with demonism). Antipas was one of the faithful martyrs.

14. The doctrine of Balaam. This was Balaam's teaching Balak to corrupt God's people who could not be cursed (Num 31:15-16; 22:5; 23:8). The strategy was to entice them to intermarry among the Moabites, violate their separation from the world and give up their pilgrim walk.

15. The doctrine of Nicolaitans. What were hated 'practices' of the Nicolaitans in Ephesus (2:6) was a strongly held doctrine in Pergamum (see note on 2:6).

16-17. Warning and promise. The *warning* is to 'repent,' 16 (cf. 2:5). The alternative of repentance for the Nicolaitans was the Lord's fighting against them with the sword of His mouth (cf. 1:16). The sword alludes to the drawn sword with which the angel confronted Balaam (Num 22:23) on his way to curse Israel, and was an earnest of the sword by which he and the deceived Israelites eventually fell. The *promise* entails Christ as 'the hidden manna,' 17 (Jn 6:31-35), His glorified humanity preserved in the heavenly tabernacle until manifested at His second advent. The promise also embraces the 'white stone.' It may refer to the precious diamond on the high priest's breastplate, the 'new name' engraved upon it being Christ's (3:12), containing some new revelation then to be made known.

2:18-29. Thyatira – the paganized church

18-23. Commendation and complaint. Thyatira was a commercial center honeycombed with pagan religion. Its many trade guilds periodically sponsored idolatrous feasts. Christ, depicted again as Judge (1:14-15; Dan 10:6), 18, charges the church with tolerating the false prophetess Jezebel, 20, even though it was a church of good works, 19. This woman is so designated because she resembled Ahab's wicked consort who introduced depraved Phoenician cults into Israel (1 Kgs 16:31-32; 2 Kgs 9:22, 30-33).

24-29. Promise to the overcomer.

'Satan's so-called deep secrets,' 24, is an arresting reference to the shocking depth of demonism (1 Tim 4:1-6; 1 Jn 4:1-6; Rev 9:20-21; 16:13-16) and false doctrine (2 Tim 3:1-8; Jas 3:15; 2 Pet 2:1-3) to which this system sank. Overcomers will participate in Christ's messianic rule, 27 (Ps 2:8-9).

3:1-6. Sardis – the lifeless church

1-3. Dead orthodoxy. Located 50 miles NE of Smyrna, Sardis was noted for its wealth because of its textile and jewelry industries. The church there had a 'reputation' for spiritual life, just as the city had a reputation historically and politically; but Christ the Judge who has 'the seven spirits' (i.e., the Holy Spirit in sevenfold fullness) and holds 'the seven stars' (the messengers of the seven churches) judged it spiritually dead, 1. It is called upon to 'wake up,' to 'strengthen what remains,' 2, to 'remember' what it has 'received and heard' (recovery of God's Word), keep it, and repent (change its present course toward total spiritual death), 3. Failure to do so will mean judgment instead of blessing, at the Lord's coming, 3*b*.

4-6. Blotting names out of the book of life. The church is characterized by nominal Christianity (v. 1), with perhaps many admitted to the fellowship mechanically without regeneration, hence the bold figure of 'erasing' names from 'the book of life,' 5. This symbolism refers to the ancient practice of a city enrolling its citizens with the names of the dead erased. So, by analogy, those who have a 'name' (as belonging to the visible church) but are 'dead' (unregenerate) are 'erased' from God's roll of heavenly citizens. They are in the book in the sense of being *called* to salvation, their erasure being in the sense of *not* being *chosen* for salvation. 'The book of life' in 20:15 and 21:27 appears, however, strictly as the book of the elect alone, those whose names remain after the erasure of mere professors (Mt 22:14). The few true believers in Sardis, the 'overcomers,' are those 'who have not soiled their clothes' by dead works, but 'are worthy' because they trust in Christ and are in Him, 4, clothed in the white garments of His righteousness, 5. The importance of the garment industry in Sardis doubtless led to this double reference to clothing.

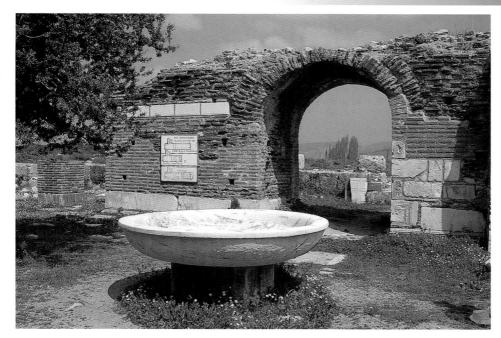

The Double
Church of Mary
the Virgin,
Ephesus. The
Ephesian church's
sin was its
departure from
its initial affection
for the Lord.

3:7-13. Philadelphia
– the missionary church

7-9. An open door of witness. This letter, together with the one addressed to the church at Smyrna, contains no word of rebuke. The name of this city, located 25 miles SE of Sardis, means 'brotherly love.' Although threatened by severe earthquakes, almost to the point of complete destruction, the city still remains and a Christian group meets regularly there. Christ, the 'holy' (Lk 1:35; Jn 10:36), the 'true' (Jn 14:6; Rev 19:11), the One who has 'the key of David' (Isa 22:22), set before this church an open door, 7, and it was impossible for anyone to shut it, 8*a*. Although it had 'little strength' (*dunamin,* 'spiritual power') to take advantage of the opportunity for witness, it had kept Christ's Word and had not denied His name, 8*b*. The Philadelphian church's vigorous missionary activity won many Jews of the city, resulting in the violent opposition of the local Jewish populace, whose members, though claiming to be the people of God, were proved by their actions to be of Satan's synagogue (see note on 2:9).

10-13. Kept from the hour of testing. This promise, 10*b,* seems to indicate that the church, of which the Philadelphian church was representative, will be glorified and taken to heaven before the Great Tribulation begins, 10.

The promise applies to all who are Christ's, 'since you have kept my command to endure patiently.' The expression, 'I will also *keep you from'* means to 'protect someone from something' (Prov 7:5; Jn 17:15). Since that 'hour' from which they are to be kept is worldwide and inescapable for all earth dwellers, 10*c,* 'kept from' suggests removal from the scene upon which the 'hour' transpires. The 'test,' 10*d,* has reference to the Day of the Lord, Daniel's 70th week, the final seven years of terrible trouble which will engulf the earth, the time described in Rev 6-19. The promise relates to Christ's advent for His own, 11*a* (Jn 14:1-3; 1 Thess 4:13-17; 1 Cor 15:51-52) and the rewards of Christians, here called overcomers, 11*b*-13. Believers will be clearly identified as God's own possession and the inhabitants of the New Jerusalem, 12 (cf. 21:2-3, 10). Christ's 'new name' will then be revealed.

3:14–22. Laodicea
– the lukewarm church

14-19. Insufferable lukewarmness. Christ as Judge is here styled 'the Amen,' 14 (cf. 2 Cor 1:20), 'the faithful and true witness' (in contrast to this church's compromising infidelity). The 'ruler of God's creation' denotes Christ's complete sovereignty over all creation (cf. Col 1:15-18). He gives no commendation to this inclusivist church in the proud and wealthy city of Laodicea, located near Colossae (Col 4:13-16) and about 40 miles from Ephesus. This city's wealth was so great that in A.D. 60, when it was almost completely destroyed by an earthquake, its citizens refused Rome's aid and rebuilt the city at its own expense. As an industrial center, it was known for the production of fine black wool and its Phrygian powder, used to treat eye diseases; and hot mineral springs made it a medical center as well. These features are used in the letter to illustrate the Laodicean church's true spiritual condition; for Christ calls its lukewarm profession nauseating, 15-16, and utterly deceptive of its true spiritual condition, 17. He advises the church 'to buy from me gold refined in the fire,' 18, the real wealth of a divine-human Saviour cleansing the heart and thus giving the 'white clothes' of a truly regenerated and sanctified life, and the eye salve of faith granting true spiritual insight and knowledge. Chastening is promised for those in Laodicea who are Christ's, 19. They are to repent of the compromising disloyalty of their unbelief.

20-22. Christ shut out. The church had ousted their Saviour and Lord. He was not even missed by this worldly-wise group. He therefore appears on the outside knocking on the doors of individual hearts, waiting for them to receive Him and to enter into fellowship with Him, 20. To the overcomer is promised the right to sit with Christ on His own throne in the coming kingdom, 21.

Part 3.
The things which shall be hereafter, Ch. 4-22

4-5. The divine throne in heaven

Chapters 4 and 5 introduce the source of the visions and judgments which are to follow. The setting is in heaven and the chief personage is Christ. The actual chronology of the book commences with ch. 6.

4:1-5. The throne introduced

1. The heavenly door. 'After this,' *1a,* refers to the church age represented by the seven churches in ch. 2 and 3. The scene is changed from earth to heaven, *1b,* as the trumpet call of Christ summons John to heaven (cf. 1:10-13).

2:2-5. The heavenly throne. Christ now occupies the throne of God the Father, 2, until His second advent (3:21). God's glory is symbolized in terms of precious gems, 3 (Ezk 1:26-28; cf. 1 Jn 1:5). The rainbow, *3b* (Ezk 1:28), is a token of God's mercy based on the accepted sacrifice of His Son, as the Noahic rainbow was the sign of a covenant based on the sacrifice offered by Noah (Gen 8:20-22) which looked forward to Christ. John's bow was emerald colored (green) guaranteeing God's fidelity to His covenant with Noah not to destroy the earth again, as in the Flood, despite the terrible judgment to come (ch. 5-19) and despite the fact that the throne is a throne not of grace but of judgment, 5.

4:4. 10-11. The twenty-four elders

These 'elders' evidently represent redeemed OT and NT saints, for the term 'elder' is never applied to angels or other heavenly and unfallen order of beings, nor do angels have crowns or occupy thrones; only redeemed men are promised such (Mt 19:28; 2 Tim 4:8; 1 Pet 5:2-4; Rev 2:10; 20:4). The crowns they wear are *stephanoi* (victors' crowns), 4, and the thrones they occupy show that these saints are viewed as having already been judged for their works (see notes on the believer's judgment, 1 Cor 3:11-15; 2 Cor 5:10) and have received their rewards (cf. Dan 7:9-10). Their being 'dressed in white,' 4, displays them as a *redeemed* royal priesthood (1 Pet 2:9), engaged in priestly services (Rev 5:8). They await *judicial* and *royal* functions to be given them at Christ's second advent (20:4-6).

The term 'elder' is commonly employed in Scripture of the representative head of a nation, tribe, city or family. The number 24 represents the OT saints under the 12 tribes of Israel and the NT saints by the 12 apostles of the Lamb (cf. the 12 foundation stones of the 12 apostles of the Lamb and the 12 gates of the 12 tribes of Israel, Rev 21:10-14). The number 24, moreover, is thus representative in a redeemed priestly capacity. When David formed the priests into courses, he founded 24 heads of priestly families, and made these representative of the entire priesthood (1 Chr 24:1-19).

The agora, ancient Smyrna, modern Izmir, Turkey. John's vision spoke of the church here as persecuted by the Jewish synagogue in the city.

4:6-11. The four living creatures

6-8. Their identity. They are a *special order* of created beings associated with the throne of God, apparently combining characteristics both of the cherubim, concerned with the public *governmental glory of God* (Gen 3:24; Ex 25:17-20; Ezk 10:1-22), and the seraphim, concerned with the *holiness of God* (Isa 6:1-7). Their intelligence and insight into God's plan for the earth are seen in their being 'covered with eyes,' 6, 8. Their likeness to animals and man indicates the character of God's judicial government toward the earth, since the whole earthly scene is about to be visited with judgment (ch. 5-19).

8-11. Their worship. They adore the Lord God Almighty, 8-9, and are joined in worship by the 24 elders, 10-11.

5:1-4. The seven-sealed book

1. What the book is. The seven-sealed book is the *title deed* to the forfeited inheritance of the earth lost by Adam when he fell. This legal document, guaranteeing the dispossession of Satan and wicked men from the earth (cf. Eph 1:13-14; Rom 8:22-23), and provided by Christ's atoning death, is seen lying 'upon' (Gr.) the opened right hand of the One sitting on the throne (God the Father), 1*a*. 'A scroll with writing on both sides' implies the completeness

of legal provision for dispossession, 1*b*. 'Sealed with seven seals' symbolizes the completeness of the sealing till one legally qualified to open the tightly closed legal document should appear.

2-4. Who is worthy to open it? This question looms large, 2. 'No one' was able to open it. Not angelic beings, because the inheritance was lost by a human being and a man must therefore open it. Not any of Adam's descendants, because they are all sinners. John's keen desire to know the revelation promised herein seems frustrated, 4.

5:5-10. The one worthy to open the book

5-6. The Lion of the tribe of Judah. He alone is worthy because (1) He is the 'Lion of the tribe of Judah' (the royal tribe), a second advent title of Messiah as 'King of kings' (19:16; Gen 49:8-10), who in majestic might would secure the blessing of Israel and the whole earth and in His lionlike character crush His foes; (2) He is 'the Root of David' (*divine,* David's Lord and Creator, Ps 110:1; Mt 22:42-45; and 'the Offspring of David,' 22:16, i.e., *human*); (3) as the God-man He 'has triumphed,' so that 'He is able to open the scroll,' 5; (4) He is the Lamb 'slain,' 6. The death of Christ is the basis of the redemption not only of sinners but of the earth (Rom 8:18-22). The 'seven horns' denote the fullness of efficacy and the 'seven eyes' completeness of intelligence in the Spirit's judicial administration over the earth, based on Christ's redemption, 6.

7-10. His sublime action. 'He [Christ] came and took the scroll from the right hand of him who sat upon the throne' (cf. Dan 7:13-14, where the same grand scene is envisioned). It was the case of a kinsman (the God-man) being able to do what no one else could do (3-4; cf. Lev 25:23-34), the redemptive price being Christ's own blood (1 Pet 1:18-20;cf. Ruth 4:1-12). This act calls forth the worship of the living creatures, 8-10.

5:11-14. Universal worship of the Lamb

11-12. Worship of the heavenly beings. This great scene depicting the kingdom rights and glories of Christ (ch. 4-5), climaxed by His taking the seven-sealed book to claim possession of the earth, evokes the praise and worship of myriads of angels, the living creatures and redeemed humanity in heaven, 11. Their great theme is 'Worthy is the Lamb' (cf. 5:2-3, 9; cf. Phil 2:9-11).

13-14. Participation of all creation. All creation worships and praises the Lamb. This adoration is repeated by the four living creatures, 14*a,* and the elders, 14*b* (see 4:4).

6:1-8:5. The seven-sealed book opened

6:1-17. Seals one to six

1-4. Seals one and two. The opening of the seals precipitates the Day of the Lord and the period of tribulation on the earth to dispossess Satan and wicked men. With each of the first four seals, one of the living creatures associated with God's judicial government toward the earth cries, 'Come!' Thus they call forth the first judgments, symbolized by four horsemen. The rider on the white horse, 2, is the Antichrist who imitates Christ (19:11), the 'bow' and 'crown' symbolizing his great *conquests.* The rider on the red horse, 3-4, symbolizes war and carnage (cf. Zech 1:7-11; 6:1-8).

5-8. Seals three and four. The rider on the black horse symbolizes *famine.* which follows war. Bread is rationed: ' A quart of wheat for a day's wages (a denarius), and three quarts of barley for a day's wages,' 5-6. A denarius

ordinarily had the purchasing power to buy 8 quarts of wheat or 24 quarts of barley. The rider on the pale horse represents *pestilence* and is called 'Death,' 7-8 (cf. 20:14).

9-11. Seal five. The souls under the altar (the altar of sacrifice where the sacrificial blood was poured out) represent *martyrs* of the first half of the Tribulation period. 'The word of God' is that for which they suffered death, and their 'blood' cries for vengeance, 10 (cf. Gen 4:10). They are the Jewish remnant whose cry is that of the prophetic imprecatory Psalms 35, 55, 59, 94, etc. The 'white robes' indicate the redemption of their souls. They are to rest for a little season (the short period of the Great Tribulation on earth, Dan 9:27) until 'their fellow servants and brothers' (fellow believing Jews) should share their martyrdom (cf. Rev 20:4-6).

12-17. Seal Six. This seal apparently symbolizes *governmental anarchy* under the figures of earthquake, darkening of sun and moon, and the falling of stars. The collapse of all human government occasions awful terror as the great day of God's wrath arrives (cf. 14:10; 15:1; 16:1; 19:14).

(Ch.7. First parenthesis)

7:1-8. The sealing of Israelites

1-3. A remnant of Israel preserved. These elect on the earth are preserved from the end-time Tribulation judgments which befall the earth, 1. The preservation is symbolized by a 'seal,' 2*a* (cf. Eph 1:13-14). It is a public preservation, for 'the servants of our God' are to be sealed on their foreheads, 3, involving no secret discipleship.

4-8. The number of sealed Israelites specified. These are earthly Israelites living in the time of 'Jacob's trouble' (Jer 30:5-7). Though the tribal genealogies have ceased, God knows who the tribes are and where they are (Isa 11:11-16), and will preserve an elect remnant, returning them to the restored kingdom (Acts 1:6). The event will occur when 'the times of the Gentiles' have run their course (Lk 21:24) with the full number of Gentiles gathered in (Acts 15:14; Rom 11:25). In the enumeration the tribes of Dan and Ephraim are omitted, probably because of their complicity in idolatry (Deut 29:18-21; 1 Kgs 12:25-30, but cf. Ezk 48:1-7, 23-29).

The Roman theater, Pergamum. Christ spoke of the church here as worldly and compromised.

7:9-17. The salvation of Gentiles

9-14. Elect Gentiles preserved. This company of saved people is an elect body of Jews, 1-8, which will be preserved through the end-time tribulation, 14, to enter the kingdom. Like the sealed remnant of Israel, they show that in the midst of His wrath God remembers mercy (Hab 3:2). They are apparently *unglorified people on the earth,* envisioned as 'saved' and therefore seen 'before the throne and in front of the Lamb. They were wearing white robes and were holding palm branches in their hands,' a symbol of millennial joy and triumph, 9 (Lev 23:40; Jn 12:13). They have experienced unparalleled suffering in the Great Tribulation, 14 (Dan 9:27; Mt 24:15-51; 2 Thess 2:1-12) having been brought to salvation by the preaching of the gospel of the kingdom (Mt 24:13-14; also called the 'eternal gospel,' Rev 14:6).

15-17. Their kingdom bliss assured. They are 'before the throne of God,' denoting not their local place but their moral position, and they serve God ceaselessly 'in his temple' (the millennial temple, Ezk 40-44), 15*a.* God will dwell among them (Gr. *scenosei ep autous,* 'shall be a tabernacle over them'), 15*b* (cf. 21:3; Lev 26:11; Isa 4:5-6). The sufferings of their tribulation experiences will be past, 16, and Christ the kingdom Shepherd (Ezk 34:23) will provide for them, 17 (Ps 23:1-6; Isa 12:1-6).

8:1-5. Seal seven

1. Seal seven opened. This concludes the complete opening of the seven-sealed book (5:1) so that its full contents (the trumpets and bowls) might be released upon the earth and its wicked inhabitants. The half hour of silence is the lull after a preceding tempest and the prelude to a more terrible one.

2-5. The prayer of the saints answered. 'Another angel,' 3, is taken by some to be Christ, but probably the incense offerer is an angelic being acting in priestly capacity. The saints' prayers are answered by earth judgments upon the wicked.

8:6-11:19. The seven trumpets blown

8:6-13. Trumpets one to four

7. Trumpet one. The first six trumpets introduce more severe judgments, perhaps beginning the second half of the Tribulation period. Trumpet one is blown resulting in hail and fire mixed with blood being thrown to the *earth* which affects vegetation and suggests *severe drought.*

8-9. Trumpet two. The second trumpet results in judgment upon the *sea,* affecting the sea *food supply* and the ocean *transportation* lines.

10-11. Trumpet three. The blowing of the third trumpet affects the *fresh water* supply, a third of which is *made* deadly *bitter* by the drug 'wormwood.'

12-13. Trumpet four. The *heavens* themselves are affected by the judgment resulting from the blowing of the fourth trumpet. Creation is reversed as a third of the *lights of heaven* are touched and *darkened,* 12. Three calamities ('woes') are announced, 13, which are terrible judgments falling directly on men. These three woes constitute the final three trumpet judgments.

9:1-12. The fifth trumpet – the first woe

1. The abyss opened. The seer sees 'a star that had fallen from the sky to the earth.' This 'star' is the angel custodian of the pit of the Abyss, the prison house of the demons (Lk 8:30-31). That he cannot be Satan, or even an evil angel, is shown by the fact that he is the same angelic personage who once again opens the pit of 'the Abyss' to bind and imprison Satan prior to the millennium (20:1-3). He is an angel *fallen* from heaven, not a fallen angel, the past participle 'fallen' describing the swiftness of the angel's descent and the suddenness with which this first woe bursts upon wicked earth dwellers.

2-12. The loosing of myriads of demons. The symbolism, 2-11, is descriptive of the invisible spirit world in terms visible and comprehensible to men. The locusts represent demons and the way they will possess, drive and torment men in the end time. (See note on 'Demonism,' Mk 5:1-20.) While multitudes of demons have been free to torment the human race during previous ages (Mk 1:23-27; 5:1-17; 1 Tim 4:1-6; 1 Jn 4:1-4), many of them are so viciously depraved and harmful that God has imprisoned them in the abyss. These are the terrible demons let loose under the first woe. The name of the king of the demons is *Abaddon,* meaning 'destruction,' 11 (Job 26:6; Prov 15:11), or in Gr. *Apollyon,* meaning 'destroyer' (cf. 2 Thess 2:7-12).

9:13-21. The sixth trumpet – the second woe

13-19. Gathered armies loosed. From the altar of intercession, the golden altar of incense, God answers the prayers of His suffering and martyred saints. Toward the altar their prayers ascend (8:3). From it the answer goes forth, 13, specifically from the 'four [expressing universality] horns' (denoting power and efficacy of the saints' prayers and the answer). This loosing of the armies is effected by the release of the four angels (ministers of judgment under divine control). The place of their loosing, the Euphrates, was the location of ancient Babylon. The very hour of their release is determined as well as the extent of their destruction, 15. The number of the cavalrymen is 200,000,000, as John heard it, 16. Some think the description of the army, 17-19, like the locusts, indicates denizens of the spirit world. Such armies of the spirit realm appear in Scripture (cf. 2 Kgs 2:11; 6:13-17; Rev 12:7; 19:11-16). Belonging to the sphere of the spirit world, which is ordinarily invisible to men, the torment and destruction of this infernal host will be so much more terrible. Others feel that the event of Daniel 11:44 is referred to here.

20-21. The purpose of the woe. The divine design is twofold, punishment and reformation. But those who survive this dreadful calamity do not repent of their evil works and idolatry. The rampant demonism of that day (1-12) turns them away from worship of God to worship of demons. The awful results of demon-energized idolatry are enumerated: murders (violence), magic (traffic in demonism), sexual immorality, and thefts (robbery), 21.

(10:1-11:13. Second parenthesis)

10:1-7. The angel and the little scroll

1-6. The identity of the mighty angel. This angel is an *actual* angel who symbolizes Christ (cf. 5:2; 8:3). As representative of Christ, the angel reflects His glory and bears the insignia attributed in 1:15-16 and 4:3 to Christ Himself, 1. His stupendous act of setting his foot on land and sea shows Christ's right to claim the earth as His own, 2 (Ps 95:5; Eph 1:13-14). The angel's loud cry and the seven thunders give full testimony to Christ's authority over the earth, 3-4*a*. His oath that 'there will be no more delay' shows Christ's divine sovereignty and control in these matters of judgment, 6.

7. The mystery of God fulfilled. 'The mystery of God' is the theme of the 'little scroll,' and concerns Christ as incarnate Redeemer of the earth. It is a previously hidden truth, now fully revealed, which focuses upon Christ, in whom God's plan for this earth is centered and unfolded. This truth is the grand theme of the rest of Revelation where 'the mystery of God' is 'accomplished,' i.e., completed. It will be 'as He [God] announced [Gr. 'evangelized; announced the good news'] to his servants the prophets,' who declared the grand themes of Christ's redemption, kingdom and eternal glory.

10:8-11. John and the little scroll

8-10. What the little scroll is. The little scroll (book) is not only the record of the fulfillment of the mystery of God, 7, and distinguished from the seven-sealed book of 5:1, but it seems to be, in part at least, the book Daniel was told to seal up till the time of the end (Dan 12:4, 9). This passage in Daniel appears to be the foundation for these verses. This is the reason the scroll was 'sweet as honey' when first eaten (Ezk 2:8-9; 3:1-3; Ps 19:10;

119:103), but when digested, 'sour' (Jer 15:10; 20:14-18). The bright promises of deliverance for Daniel's people were preluded by terrible suffering and judgment.

11. Its effect on John's ministry. As a result the seer must prophesy again, as he had done in the previous section, 'about many peoples.'

11:1-2. The end of the times of the Gentiles

1-2*a*. Restoration of temple worship. This point marks the Lord's dealing again with Israel and its worship in a restored temple in 'the holy city,' Jerusalem (cf. 2 Thess 2:3-4). This is by the seer's measuring 'the temple of God' and 'the altar,' and the worshipers,' 1. Whereas the Lord accepts the godly remnant, the true worshipers, the apostate Jews who have linked themselves with the Gentiles (symbolized by the outer court) God rejects.

2*b*. End of the times of the Gentiles. This period, which began with Judah's captivity under Nebuchadnezzar (605 B.C.), will not end until the second advent (Dan 2:34-35, 44; Rev 19:11, 21). During this time Jerusalem has been subject to Gentile rule (Lk 21:24). Divine recognition of temple worship signalizes the swift close of 'the times of the Gentiles,' specified as 42 months. This is the middle of Daniel's seventieth week (a week of seven years, Dan 9:27) with the last three and a half years yet to run (cf. Dan 7:25; Rev 12:14; 13:5).

11:3-13. The two witnesses

3-7. Their identity. Although the two witnesses are commonly identified as Moses and Enoch or Moses and Elijah, such identifications are unlikely since both of the witnesses are killed and resurrected, something which could not be true of these OT prophets as glorified men (Mt 17:3). These witnesses are evidently two members of the latter-day remnant. They are Christ's witnesses, 3, 'my witnesses' referring to the mighty Angel (Christ) of ch. 10. They preach 'clothed in sackcloth,' a symbol of mourning, because they identify themselves with Israel's grievous sin and Jerusalem's wickedness, 3b, 8 (cf. Joel 1:13; Jer 4:8). Their *message* is Christ's lordship over the earth, 4, proclaiming the soon coming of the King of kings to take possession of the earth. 'The two olive trees and the two lampstands' (Zech 4:2-3) connect them with testimony that Messiah as King-Priest (the two olive trees in Zech 4 denote these two offices) will shortly reign over restored Israel as the light of the world. They have *miraculous powers* like Elijah and Moses, 5-6. Fire comes out of their mouths (cf. 2 Kgs 1:10, 12; Jer 5:14; cf. Lk 9:54-55). They command drought like Elijah, 6a (1 Kgs 15:17); turn water to blood (Ex 7:19) and work other signs like Moses, 6b (Ex 7-10). They are *killed by the beast* (head of the revived Roman Empire, Rev 13:1-10; 17:8), who ascends out of the abyss (cf. 9:1-12), but not until they have completed their testimony, 7.

8-13. Their destiny. Their corpses are dishonored in Jerusalem, 8, but God resurrects, 11, and translates the two witnesses in *'the cloud'* (Gr.), 12, i.e., the Shekinah glory (cf. Ezk 10:19; Mt 17:5). Meanwhile their enemies are punished with an earthquake that kills 7,000 and destroys one-tenth of Jerusalem, 13, which causes those who remain to give glory to the 'God of heaven' because of His power, not because of their repentance.

11:14-19. The seventh trumpet – the third woe

14-18. Anticipation of Christ's worldwide kingdom. The second woe (9:13-21) is here repeated after the parenthesis,

10:1-11:13, to bridge the gap of the parenthesis and to connect the first two woes with the third and final woe, 14. This woe is said to come 'soon,' and includes all the remaining judgments prior to the establishment of the kingdom (11:14-20:3). Verses 15-19 give a panorama of the rest of the book, future events being seen as already present. They envision the establishment of Christ's worldwide kingdom and reign, 15-17; the judgment of the raging nations at Armageddon, 18a; the judgment of the dead (20:11-15) when the destroyers of the earth will be destroyed, 18c; and the rewarding of prophets and saints in millennial positions of rule and dominion, 18b (20:4-6).

19. God's temple in heaven opened. 'The ark of His covenant' seen within the temple speaks of God's faithfulness to His covenants and promises to Israel (Rom 9:4-5): The last apocalyptic judgments and the second advent will realize the consummation of all these commitments made to God's covenant people Israel. (See 'The Covenants of Scripture,' Heb 9.)

12-13. Seven personages performing during the last days of the tribulation

12:1-2 Person one – the woman, Israel

1. The woman. The characters who will be on the stage during the final days before Christ's return are introduced. Not only are the outward events of the final conflict recorded, but the hidden spiritual aspects as well. The great 'wondrous sign' is the 'woman,' 1. She evidently symbolizes Israel, for she is dressed in regal and governmental splendor, the 12 stars illustrating her 12 tribes, as Joseph's dream shows (Gen 37:9). Israel was often portrayed as a married woman in the OT (Isa 54:1), and as an adulterous divorced wife in her sin and rejection (Isa 47:7-9, 50:1; Jer 3:1-25, Hos 2:1-23).

2. The woman's travail. This travail refers to Israel's agony during the Great Tribulation, as the context clearly illustrates. The symbol of birth was a common OT figure used to portray acute suffering, especially 'the time of Jacob's trouble' (Jer 30:5-7, Isa 26:15-18, 66:7). During this supreme travail the nation will give birth to the godly Jewish remnant, 17 (cf. Mic 5:2-3), which will be closely associated with the male child, Christ, 5.

12:3-4. Person two
– the dragon, Satan

3. Dragon in prophetic view. The dragon is identified as 'that ancient serpent [cf. Gen 3:1-10], called the devil [accuser] or Satan' (opposer) in verse 9. He is 'an enormous red dragon,' which symbolizes him as the proud, cruel energizer of the 'beast.' 'Red' portrays his murderous character an 8:44), which is now featured. His seven diademed heads and ten horns identify him with the final form of Gentile world power centered in the beast (13:1-10; cf. Dan 7:8).

4. The dragon in historical perspective. This includes a panoramic sketch of his original fall, 4a (Isa 14:12-14; Ezk 28:12-15), suggested by verses 7-9, and of Satan's hostility to the woman's posterity, 4b (Gen 3:15; Mt 2:16).

12:5-6. Person three
– the male child, Christ

5. The male child. Four things are declared: (1) His *birth,* 5a; (2) *His destiny,* 5b, which is to break His foes to pieces (Ps 2:9) and then to rule in righteousness; (3) His *ascension,* 5c; (4) *His position* on God's throne, 5d (3:21). He is destined to rule yet. Satan knows this, and pursues the woman (godly Israel).

6. The woman's flight. The long gap of the Christian era is between verses 5 and 6. Verse 6 describes Israel's flight into the wilderness (possibly Petra in Edom; cf. Mt. 24:16; Dan 11:41), to be sustained for three and a half years during Satan's terrible persecution, which he effects through the beast (2 Thess 2:3-7).

12:7-12. Person four
– Michael, the archangel

7-9. Michael. Michael is the especial protector of Daniel's people the Jews, 7a (Dan 12:1; cf. Dan 10:13-21). He is involved in the war when Satan's expulsion from the heavenlies is at hand, 7b. Since his original rebellion, Satan and his hosts have been loose in the heavenlies (Job 1:6; 2:1; Gen 3:1-10; Eph 2:2; 6:10-12). In the middle of the Great Tribulation he and his angels will be expelled and cast on the earth, 7-9 (cf. Dan 10:10-14).

10-12. Rejoicing over Satan's expulsion. This joyous shout is a prelude to the establishment of Christ's kingdom, 10a, which begins with the return of Christ. Victory over last-day malignity will be on the basis of the accomplished sacrifice of Christ, 11a, by a faithful testimony, 11b, and by martyrdom, 11c. Satan's expulsion means terrible woe to the earth, 12. His wrath is spurred on by the shortness of the time (cf. 10:6; 11:14).

12:13-16. Satan persecutes
the woman

13-14. Reason for Satan's persecution. Knowing that his defeat has been occasioned by the exaltation of the Man Child, Christ, the dragon vents his fury upon the sun-clothed woman (Israel) who gave the Man Child birth, 13. The eagle wings given to the woman to escape to the wilderness recall how the Lord delivered Israel from Egypt and bore her on eagles' wings (Ex 19:4; Deut 32:11-12; Isa 16:20; 27:1). This is the period of the 'abomination of desolation' (Dan 9:27) and the Great Tribulation spoken of by our Lord (Mt 24:15-22; Lk 21:20-24).

15-16. Israel's preservation. The serpent (Satan) cast out of his mouth 'water like a river,' 15, symbolizing Gentile nations (17:15) energized by Satan with anti-Semitic hatred to destroy the Jew. 'But the earth helped the woman by opening its mouth and swallowing the river,' 16. This points to friendly nations, who having heeded the preaching of the gospel of the kingdom, protect these persecuted Jews.

12:17. Person five
– the Israelite remnant

17. The godly remnant. Satan now turns against the godly remnant of Jews still in the land (cf. Isa 1:9; 6:13; Rom 11:5). These are individual godly Jews who had not escaped to safety when the Tribulation broke out (Mt 24:15-20). These 'keep God's commandments,' the mark of godliness common to true believers of all ages, and 'hold to the testimony of Jesus,' i.e., bear faithful witness to Him.

13:1-10. Person six
– the beast out of the sea

1-5. The beast – the Roman prince. This last great ruler of Gentile world power arises out of an unsettled political condition ('the sea,' Isa 57:20), 1a. He heads a confederated ten-kingdom empire covering the sphere of the ancient Roman Empire, Daniel's fourth beast (Dan 7:24-28). The 'ten horns' are ten kingdoms (kings, 17:12) and the 'crowns' on the horns speak of despotic power. The dragon, having 'seven heads and ten horns and seven crowns on his heads' (12:3) is the dynamic behind the beast, 1b, 2b. The beast is in complete defiance of God indicated by the 'blasphemous name' upon each of his seven heads, 1c. His empire partakes of all the beastly qualities of the preceding world empires of 'the times of the Gentiles,' 2 (cf. Dan 7:4-6) – leopardlike agility of conquest (Macedonian), bearlike voracity (Persian), lionlike strength (Babylonian). His kingdom represents the restoration of the imperial power of the Roman Empire, 3b. The head wounded to death symbolizes the seventh (and last) form of government of the Roman Empire, the imperial, destroyed in war; but 'the fatal wound' yet to be healed indicates the imperial form of government will be restored under the beast (Dan 7:8). The beast is worshiped together with the dragon who energizes him, 4. He becomes utterly God-defiant and destructive during the final three and a half years of the Great Tribulation, 5.

6-10. The beast's wicked career. He blasphemes God and those who are His, 6. To this end he wars against the saints, 7a (Dan 7:21-22; Rev 11:7, 12). He is permitted unrestrained power over all earth dwellers except over the elect, 8-10 (cf. Mt 24:13, 22). He is the Antichrist, the man of sin (2 Thess 2:3-12; 1 Jn 2:22; 4:3).

13:11-18. Person seven – the beast out of the earth, the false prophet

This third member of the unholy trinity arises out of the earth, 11a. He is the first beast's (Antichrist's) prophet, 11b, though disguised as a lamb. As such he directs worship to 'the first beast' by miraculous powers, 12-14, giving life to the image of the beast and killing those who do not worship the image, 15 (cf. Dan 3:1-30). Despite numerous attempts to identify the 'mark of the beast' with names, computers, monetary systems and the like, its precise nature is

unknown, remaining to be disclosed as the end draws near.

14. Foreview of the end of the Tribulation

14:1-5. The Lamb and the 144,000

1-3. Identity of the 144,000. These are evidently the living Jewish remnant spared from death and moral contamination during the Great Tribulation. They are associated with 'the Lamb' (Christ) upon Mount Zion, 1a, the early Zion in Jerusalem, the seat of royal power in the kingdom. It seems evident that the 144,000 here are identical to the Israelites of 7:1-8, who have been sealed for preservation from death during the Tribulation (7:3). They belong to the Lamb and have His mark on their foreheads, 1c. Having gone through great tribulation, their song of God's grace is a 'new song,' a song of redemption at the cost of the Lamb's blood, 3 (cf. Rom 3:24).

4-5. Their character and destiny. Their practical godliness is shown in: (1) *their separation* in virgin purity from the wickedness and idolatry around them, 4a (cf. 9:20-21); (2) *their obedience and discipleship,* 4b; (3) *their redemption,* 4c; (4) *their destiny,* 4d, to be the 'first fruits to God and the Lamb,' an earnest of earth's coming kingdom when all will bow to God and the Lamb; (5) *their truthfulness,* 5a, clinging to the truth of God's Word by profession and life when the whole world believes '*the* [devil's] lie' (2 Thess 2:11).

14:6-8. The fall of Babylon foreseen

6-7. Proclamation of the everlasting gospel. This gospel proclaims *mercy in the midst of judgment,* calling men in this terrible period to abandon the worship of the beast and reverence God (Prov 1:7), giving glory to Him, not the beast, 'because the hour of his judgment has come.'

8. Fall of Babylon anticipated. Babylon is a symbol of the Satanic world system, the center of all that is false and evil, of idolatry and oppression. It consists of the order of unregenerate humanity organized under evil principles with Satan as its head (cf. 1 Jn 2:15-

A few arches are all that remain from the stadium of Laodicea. The church here had ousted their Saviour. He therefore appears outside knocking on the doors of individual hearts.

17), with emphasis given to the ecclesiastical (ch. 17), political and commercial (ch. 18) aspects of this system. 'Fallen, fallen' is a Hebraism for 'completely fallen.'

14:9-13. The punishment of the wicked

9-11. Worshipers of the beast and their fate. The doom of these rebels is announced by an angel with 'a loud voice' so all may hear and be without excuse, 9. It entails the full fury of God, 10*a* ('He too will drink of the wine of God's fury, which has been poured full strength into the cup of his wrath' (Isa 51:17; Jer 25:15; Ps 75:8; Job 21:20). Unutterable anguish is symbolized by the 'burning sulphur,' 10*b* (cf. Isa 30:33; Rev 20:10). Eternal punishment is portrayed by 'the smoke of their torment' rising up 'for ever and ever,' 11. Ceaseless torment is prefigured by the expression 'day and night.'

12-13. The bliss of the martyrs. In this dread day the 'endurance on the part of the saints' will be supremely tested. Perseverance is by the remnant's keeping the commandments of God and maintaining faith in Jesus, 12. The blessedness of those who die rather than worship the beast is indicated, 13.

14:14-20. Preview of Armageddon

14-16. The harvest. This is heaven's view of the climax of God's judgment. The figure of the harvest portrays judgment which separates the righteous from the wicked. The judge is the one who sits upon 'a white cloud,' white signifying the purity and absolute righteousness of the judgment to take place, the cloud indicating the divine presence (10:1; Ezk 10:4; Mt 17:5; 24:30). The judge is the Son of Man, the title under which Christ deals with the earth and earth dwellers (Mt 25:31; Jn 5:27) and claims universal dominion (Dan 7:13-14; Rev 1:13-14). His divine Kingship is shown by the golden crown on His head (Rev 19:12), the 'sharp sickle' being a symbol of a thorough harvest (Joel 3:13). The judgment proceeds from the temple, 15*a,* the immediate presence of God, and the call is for immediate reaping because the harvest is 'ripe' and the appointed time has arrived, 15*b*-16. The angels are the actual reapers (cf. 19; Mt 13:39); the Son of Man reaps through the instrumentality of the angels, 16 (Joel 3:9-14).

17-20. The vintage. This is God's wrath outpoured on sinners. It issues from God's presence, the temple, 17, and from the altar, 18, i.e. the brazen altar of sacrifice. The angel who comes out has power over fire, for this altar of sacrifice has now become the altar of judgment, 18 (cf. 16:5, 8). The judgment of the wicked is fully ripe, 18*b* (cf. 2 Thess 2:7-12). It is unsparing, signified by the figure 'trampled in the winepress' in which unmitigated divine wrath falls upon sinners (19:15; cf. Isa 63:36), and is executed 'outside the city' (Jerusalem), 20, in the valley of Jehoshaphat (Joel 3:12-13). The terrifying carnage of Armageddon is symbolized by the picture of blood flowing as high as a horse's bridle for 1600 stadia (about 200 miles), 20*b*. Vast destruction over a circumscribed area centering in Palestine-Syria is indicated.

15-16. The seven bowls

15:1-8. Preparation for the final plagues

1. The sign of the seven angels. This sign (symbol) is called 'great and marvelous' because these angels have the seven last plagues and in them the fury of God is completed. Attention is directed in this sign to the Antichrist, who attempts to take over the earth for himself and destroy the woman (Israel).

2:2-4. The victorious martyrs. The fire mingled with the glass recalls the tribulation martyrs' fiery persecution under the beast, 2. The harps of God symbolize their victorious joy as a result of their triumph over the beast (5:8). The song of Moses (concerning redemption out of the Red Sea, Ex 15) combines with the song of the Lamb (redemption from sin and the exaltation of the Lamb of God). The subject of the song, 3-4, is the equity of God's works and ways as 'King of the ages.' The reverence and glory due the name of Him whom all nations will soon worship, are celebrated as His final judgments are revealed, 4.

5-8. Ministers of God's wrath. These final judgments (11:19-18:24) originate from God's temple because they are more severe than those earlier judgments which originated from His throne, 5-6. The angels' clothing of shining linen (cf. 19:8, 14) shows the righteous character of their mission, 6*a*. They come to sacrifice to the offended holiness and justice of God. The golden bowls were temple vessels for pouring drink offerings, and here describe the fullness (seven) of God's wrath poured out. The

four living creatures (see notes on 4:6-11), as executors of the judicial government of God, perform accordingly, 7. The smoke is the result of the fire of God's wrath, now hiding His grace because sin is fully ripe and must be judged without mercy, 8.

16:1-12. Bowls one to six

1-3. Bowls one and two. The bowl judgments are the consummation of the wrath of God poured out on the wickedness of men and are characterized by severity, finality and brevity. Evidently they continue to the very end of the Tribulation period, for the angels do not return to the temple in heaven. Chronologically, the next event following the outpouring of the bowls is the coming of Christ in victory, ch. 19.

The command from heaven, 1, indicates that God's long-suffering is ended and His judgment can no longer be delayed. His glory demands that His name be vindicated. The *first bowl*, 2, is poured out upon the earth-organized government under the leadership of the beast. A malignant sore is inflicted on those bearing the mark of the beast. This constitutes God's judgment on those who have rejected His grace and rebelled against His worship. The affliction may well be moral and spiritual as well as physical. The *second bowl*, 3, is poured out upon the sea, which becomes blood and is symbolic of the complete moral and spiritual death of godless society.

4-9. Bowls three and four. Fresh waters become blood in the pouring out of the *third bowl*, 4. But in the midst of such judgment there is a proclamation of the righteousness of the Eternal God who has judged, 5. The sympathy of the heavens is with the Judge! Justice has been done, for earth dwellers on whom such retribution falls have shed the innocent blood of prophets and saints, 6; thus they deserve to drink blood. The altar adds its testimony, 7, perhaps because the prayers of the saints (6:9-10) under the altar are now answered. God's absolute authority over creation is exhibited in the *fourth bowl*, 8, increasing solar heat so that men in their frightful anguish cry out in blasphemy, 9. Their hearts are hardened thereby, and their true character revealed.

10-11. Bowl five. Darkness falls over the empire of the beast, 10, as his center of power (throne) is affected and God's answer to the taunt of the beast's followers is given (13:4). Morally, politically and spiritually his kingdom is plunged into solitary darkness, and men gnaw their tongues in fearful agony. Their blasphemy, 11, reveals the completeness of their spiritual blackout.

12. Bowl six. The drying up of the Euphrates River, 1,780 miles in length, the largest stream in western Asia, symbolizes the removal of every barrier for the advance of 'the kings from the East' to Armageddon. This great river formed the eastern boundary of the Roman Empire and is stipulated as the eastern limit of enlarged Palestine (Gen 15:18). It was a natural barrier in antiquity to invading armies from the east. No longer shall it be a barrier when the Lord gathers the hosts to Armageddon or when He gathers Israel back into the kingdom (Isa 11:15-16). The kings from the east are the rulers of powers east of the Euphrates.

(16:13-16. Third Parenthesis)

16:13-16. The three frogs
13-14, 16. Satanic trinity and Armageddon. 'Frogs' symbolize the demons who will be the *spiritual dynamic* behind Armageddon (cf. 1 Kgs 22:20-28). The dragon (Satan), the beast (the Antichrist) and the false prophet symbolize the Satanic trinity of evil, the source of the 'spirits of demons,' 14, i.e., demon spirits. (See note on 'Demonism,' Mk 5:20.) These demons form the delusive means of persuading the nations to gather for the supreme folly of Armageddon – man's insane fight against God and Christ's sovereignty over the earth. Armageddon, 'Hill of Megiddo,' is the ancient battlefield and site of several decisive battles in Israel's history (cf. Jud 5:19; 2 Kgs 9:27; 2 Chr 35:22). It symbolizes the place of the *gathering* of the nations, as the valley of Jehoshaphat (Joel 3:2, 12) symbolizes the place of *slaughter* in the final age-end battle. This battle decides the governmental question of the sovereignty of the earth.

15. Warning to the remnants. This is a parenthesis between verses 14 and 16. So dense will be the darkness and deception of that hour, that earth's hordes gathered at Armageddon will be suddenly surprised by Christ's glorious advent (1 Thess 5:2-3). The saints of Israel (7:1-8; 14:1-

5) and the saints from among the Gentiles (7:9-17) will need warning and encouragement in these days of gross darkness (Isa 60:2) to watch their conduct and be prepared for Christ's advent.

16:17-21. The seventh bowl
17-18. The consummation of judicial wrath. The seventh angel pours out his bowl 'into the air,' the realm of Satan (Eph 2:2), who now has been driven out of the heavenlies onto the earth (12:9) and operates through the beast, the false prophet and their followers. The judgment (hailstones, 21) falls on the organized systems of evil on the earth. 'It is done!' announces the completion of the wrath of God upon those who have refused the cry from the cross, 'It is finished!' (Jn 19:30). God's voice from both temple (*naos,* 'place of His presence') and throne (seat of His administration) is heard. His judicial action symbolized by voices, thunders and lightnings, precedes the great earthquake, 18. This earthquake is a physical reality, for in no other way could there result the complete overthrow of which all previous judgments have been precursors. Other prophecies foretell such an earthquake (cf. Zech 14:4-5), and indicate results which only a literal cataclysm could effect.

19-21. The results of God's wrath. Jerusalem, 'the great city,' is divided into three parts. 'The cities of the nations' also fall. 'Babylon the Great,' the counterfeit political and religious center of ch. 17 and 18, experiences God's full wrath, 19*b*. The earthquake is worldwide, 20, and only one kingdom escapes, for it cannot be shaken (Dan 2:44). The great hail (about 100 pounds in weight), 21, recalls the defeat of Israel's enemies at Beth-horon (Josh 10:1-11).

17-18. Judgment of Babylon

17:1-6. The vision of the harlot, ecclesiastical Babylon
1-5. The harlot and her identity. Chapters 17 and 18 fully supplement the previous passing prophetic notices (14:8; 16:19). The harlot represents ecclesiastical Babylon (personified religious revolt against God) in its final form, ripened for judgment. (1) *She stands for corrupt religionism,* 1, a 'great

prostitute' (Nah 3 :4), denoting a religious system that compromises truth for worldly power. (2) *She exploits the peoples* ('waters') *of the earth,* 1. (3) *She is guilty of prostituting truth and purity,* 2c, intoxicating men by her doctrines and practices which violate the Word of God. (4) *She is spiritually destitute,* 3a. The wilderness (desert) symbolizes the place of drought, where those who are thirsty (cf. Jn 7:37-39) can never be satisfied. (5) *She dominates and uses the state whenever possible,* 3b. She rides into power on political Babylon, the beast's kingdom, the final form of Gentile world government (13:1-10, see notes). (6) *She heads up the corrupt religious system of the end time,* 4. Scarlet denotes her sin and adultery (Isa 1:18). She is rich and influential. The 'golden cup' being filled with 'abominable things' (idolatries) and 'the filth of her adulteries' tells of her gross infidelity to God and His Word. (7) *She represents in fullest scope all apostate religious movements,* from their inception in the ancient Babylon of Nimrod (Gen 10:8-10) to their terrible consummation in apostate Christianity, and other evil religious forces of the last days, 5.

6. The woman and her crimes. Her most horrible sin is her murder of the true saints of God. Both OT 'saints' and NT martyrs of Jesus suffered under this harlot. In the end-time persecution, this evil system will participate with the beast in the wholesale murder of the true followers of Jesus.

17:7-18. The harlot and her doom

7-14. The instrument of her doom. The *revived* Roman Empire with its end-time emperor (the beast) appears as the agent of the harlot's destruction (16-18). Its last-day revival is predicted, 8a. It 'was' (it existed) in John's day, and 'now is not' (was prophesied to cease, and did as a united empire in A.D. 476). It returns in the end-time worse than ever with Satanic powers from the abyss (cf. 2 Thess 2:8-9; Rev 9:1-12; 11:7; 13:2), but its continuance is brief, 8b. It shall go into perdition at Christ's advent (19:20). This revival of the Roman power under the beast will occasion great wonder and deception, 8b-9 (13:3-4; 2 Thess 2:8-12). The woman (ecclesiastical Babylon) has her headquarters in the beast's capital, 9b, which is

the seven-hilled city of Rome (cf. 18).

The type of government of the revived Roman Empire is indicated, 10. The seven heads are not only seven hills (on which Rome is built and the harlot sits, 9), but they are also seven kings. These 'seven kings' evidently refer to seven distinct forms of government which characterized the empire (32 B.C.-A.D. 476). The five which have fallen are kings, consuls, dictators, decemvirs, tribunes. 'One is,' the imperial . . . 'The other,' the seventh as following the sixth *imperial* form of government, has yet to come, and when it comes it must remain only 'a little while' (its full power is only three and a half years, 13:5).

The last ruler of the revived empire is specified, 11: ' And as for the beast which was and is not [the revived empire, 8a], even he [*autos,* 'he himself,' the personal beast-emperor now coming into view] is the eighth, and is of the seventh [the imperial government, 10]; and he goes into perdition' (Gr.; cf. 8). This diabolical head is unique, 12-14. He rules over a ten-kingdom federation, 12-13, unknown to imperial Roman government, and makes war against the Lamb (16:14; 19:19) in the gigantic conflict for sovereignty over the earth (19:16; cf. 1 Tim 6:15).

15-18. The account of her doom. The prostitute who has dominated and exploited the peoples of the earth, 15, and who has ridden into last-day power on the beast, shall find the beast turning against her at the end to utterly destroy her, 16. This will occur by God's providential overruling to fulfill His Word, 17. Destruction is her judgment (18:6) because of her evil desire to dominate earthly rulers for her own selfish and deceptive interests, 18.

18:1-24. Judgment of commercial Babylon

1-8. Her destruction announced. A great angel announces her utter ruin 1. She is 'fallen, fallen' (completely fallen) because of her corrupting sin of commercialism, 2-3. God's people are commanded to separate from her (2 Cor 6:14-17), 4, for her iniquity is full, 5, and her pride calls for full and immediate punishment, 6-8.

9-19. Her destruction is lamented. Those who grew wealthy on her traffic bewail her, 9-11. Her rich commerce is outlined, 12-19 (cf. Isa 13:21-22), and echoes the taunt songs in Isa 23-24, 47;Jer 50-51; Ezk 26-27.

20-24. Her destruction is effected. All heaven is summoned to rejoice over her destruction together with 'saints and apostles and prophets.' The reason for such joy is that 'God has judged her for the way she treated you.' This shows that God alone is the real destroyer of the Satanic world system, both ecclesiastical and commercial. The boulder thrown into the sea symbolizes Babylon's utter destruction, 21-23, for she is guilty of the blood of God's people, 24.

19. The Return of Christ

19:1-5. Rejoicing at Babylon's fall

1-4. Heaven rejoices. Ecclesiastical Babylon (ch. 17) , together with commercial Babylon (ch. 18), must be judged before the true Bride (19:6-10; 21:9-21) is revealed, *1a.* Wicked earth dwellers lament (18:9-19) but heaven rejoices (18:20-19:6) over Babylon's fall. Heaven's rejoicing is celebrated by the great multitude (representing all the glorified saints in heaven), angels, and the 24 elders. They ascribe deliverance, glory and power to God, *1c,* employing the Heb. word 'hallelujah' (Gr. 'alleluia'), 'praise Yah' (i.e. Yahweh, the Lord), 1, 3, 4, 6, in celebration of Babylon's eternal ruin, 2-4.

5. The throne speaks. This symbolizes God Himself speaking from the center and source of His government. A new cause for rejoicing, too, comes into view. The marriage of the lamb is about to be announced.

19:6-10. The marriage of the Lamb

6-8. The wedding. This grand event is preluded by the announcement that God Almighty assumes kingly power in Christ, *6a,* and occasions the fourth and last 'hallelujah,' *6b,* and supreme exultation, *6c-7a.* It calls for honoring the lamb, for this event is not said to be the marriage of the Bride, but 'of the lamb.' The Bride, spoken of as wife to be, represents the NT Church (Jn 14:3; 1 Thess 4:13-17; Eph 5:32). The figure of 'wife' symbolizes the glorified church joined to Christ her Head in royal administration and dignity in the

Babylon

The Babylon of ch. 18 is the Satanic world system in its godless commercial and economic aspects. This system honeycombs all phases of the life of unregenerate mankind organized as a system under Satan. Chapter 17 highlights the religious aspects of Babylon, but its ramifications are cultural, scientific, educational and governmental as well. The Satanic world system of Babylon is mentioned in more than 30 NT passages. Satan is its directing head (Jn 12:31; 14:30: 16:11; 1 Jn 5:19; Rev 2:13). The system is pronounced by God as wholly evil (Gal 1:4; Col 1:13; 2 Pet 2:20; Jas 4:4; 1 Jn 4:3). It is shown to be limited and temporary (1 Jn 4:4), as Rev 17-18 proves. It is doomed to destruction at Christ's second advent (1 Jn 2:17; Rev 17-18; 19:11-16; 20:1-3). It is characterized by greed, pride and war (Jas 4:1-4), and is a perpetual snare to God's people (1 Jn 2:16; Rev 18:4-5).

kingdom. The figure of marriage symbolizes the outward, public consummation of the inner spiritual union between Christ and His church (1 Cor 12:13; Rom 6:3-4; Gal 3:27; Eph 5:25-27, 30; Rev 21:9). The Bride making herself ready presupposes her being made fit by God through Christ (Col 1:12) and having her works reviewed at the *bema* (judgment seat) of Christ (see notes on 1 Cor 3:11-14; 2 Cor 5:10). The Bride's robes prefigure the righteousness of Christ (Rom 3:21-22), graciously given to her both by imputation and sovereignty on the basis of Christ's works ('righteous acts') performed in and through her (Phil 2:13), 8.

9-10. The guests. This feature of the wedding is important, hence the command to 'write,' *9a.* The bliss of the invited guests is stressed in *9b,* 'Blessed [happy] are those who are invited.' They are clearly distinguished from the Bride, evidently OT saints (Jn3:29). It is called a 'wedding supper,' *9b,* as it is a blessed reward for God's own in contrast to the supper of judgment (19:17). John the seer is overwhelmed by both the message and the messenger, and is reminded that the focus of prophesy is in Jesus, 10.

19:11-16. Christ's second advent

11-14. The conqueror and his victorious army. Christ's coming is described in a symbolic vision. John sees 'heaven standing open,' 11a (cf. 4:1 where there is only 'a door opened in heaven'). The vision is the departure of Christ from heaven with His saints and angels to claim His kingship over the earth. His victory is denoted by His sitting on 'a white horse,' 11b, symbolic of victorious conquest (cf. 6:2; Ps 45:4). His triumph is on the basis of His being faithful and true to the will of God in an unqualified sense, 11c (Phil 2:5-11). He comes to judge and wage war, 11d; but contrary to many other warriors, when Jesus comes He comes absolutely 'with justice.' He exercises omniscient judgment, 12a, symbolized by 'His eyes are like blazing fire' (cf. 1:14; 2:18), and has absolute authority, 12b, shown by His many crowns (diadems). These saints wear a victor's crown (*stephanos*), not a monarch's crown (diadem) (4:4-10). Christ has a humanly inscrutable name, 12c (cf. Mt 11:27). He comes in vengeance upon His enemies, denoted by His garment 'dipped in [His enemies'] blood,' 13a (cf. Isa 63:1-4). His name is 'the Word of God,' 13b, proclaiming Him as God and Creator (Jn 1:1, 3) as well as Redeemer (Jn 1:14), and hence with double right to rule the earth as Creator-Redeemer (Eph 1:13-14; Rev 5:1-7). The armies of heaven (saints and angels) are associated with Him in His victory, 14. He comes on a white horse in victorious conquest. His redeemed share His triumph, and are also seen coming on white horses.

15-16. The conqueror and His conquest. *He conquers supernaturally, 15a.* The 'sharp sword' is the omnipotent, irresistible Word of God that spoke the universe into being. It slays His enemies (Isa 11:4; cf. Jn 18:5-6; Heb 11:3). *He rules with stern judgment, 15b.* He shall rule peacefully, as a shepherd, but those who are rebellious will find His shepherd's staff a rod of iron (12:5; Ps 2:9), a symbol of unflinching severity against sin. *He will deal with unsparing vengeance on evil, 15c* (cf. 14:17-20). The figure of the vintage signifies the unrelieved judgment of evil (cf Isa 63:3, 6; cf. Mt 21:44). *He comes with absolute royal sovereignty, 16.* Universal dominion is His (Ps 45:3; Rev 1:5; 17:14; cf. 1 Tim 6:15). His name, denoting His full kingship and lordship over all the earth and men, is His right as Creator and Redeemer. The descriptive title 'King *par excellence* and lord *par excellence*' is on His 'robe' and on His 'thigh,' where one would

expect His sword (instead of issuing from His mouth, 15). This fact intimates that His sovereign dominion is that which is His by the word and will of God, not that which He must win through a literal sword.

19:17-21. Armageddon

17-18. The great supper of God. This 'great supper' contrasts with 'the wedding supper of the Lamb' (19:9). One denotes the blissful fellowship and glorious destiny of the righteous in heaven. The other symbolizes the destruction of Christ's enemies on earth (cf. Dan 7:5; Ezk 32:21-32). The catastrophe of Armageddon (see 16:13-16) is effected by the word from the mouth of the returning Christ.

19-21. The total destruction of Christ's foes. The beast (see 13:1-10) and his confederate kings and armies are seen gathered to make war against the Lamb. The beast and the false prophet (13:11-18, see notes) are both cast alive into Gehenna (eternal hell, the eternal abode of *all* evildoers, 20:15), 20. 'Burning sulphur' signifies terrible torment (14:10). The portrait of the fearful slaughter is repeated, 21.

20. The millennium and final judgment

20:1-3. Satan bound

1. The vision of the angel. This vision symbolizes an event which is the natural outcome of the events of ch. 19. Satan, the prime instigator of earth's evils and opposition to God, must be dealt with before Christ's kingdom can be established on earth (4-6). The angel represents the agent of God's authority over the underworld. The 'key' and the 'chain' portray in figurative language the divine authority itself.

2-3. The binding of Satan. This is signified by an angel's laying hold of the dragon in the sense of subduing and vanquishing him. The angel is seen 'coming down' from heaven to take Satan, because Satan has been expelled from the heavenlies to the earth (cf. Eph 6:10-12; Rev 12:9). Satan's character is represented by: (1) 'the dragon,' to denote his cruelty; (2) the 'serpent,' to represent his cunning deception; (3) 'ancient,' because he operated thus in Eden (Gen 3:1); (4) 'the devil,' to indicate his malicious slander (12:10); (5)

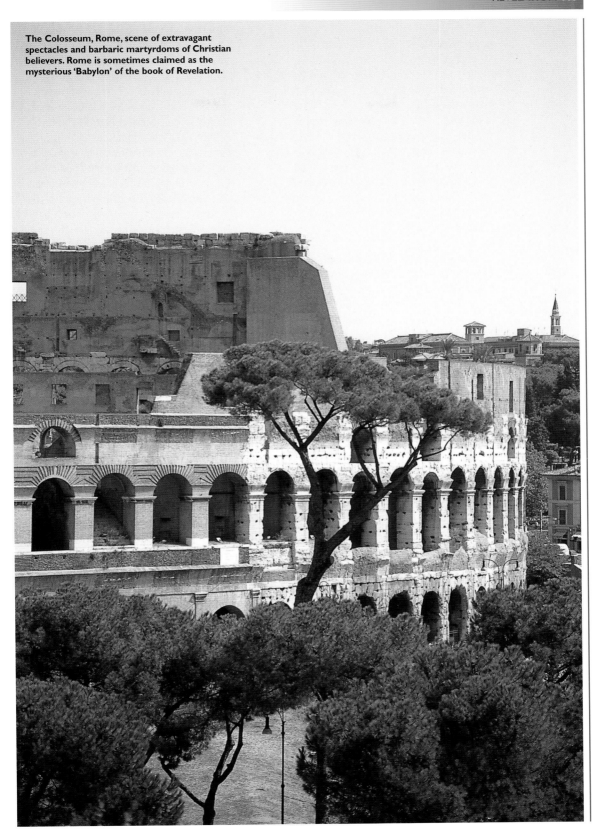

The Colosseum, Rome, scene of extravagant spectacles and barbaric martyrdoms of Christian believers. Rome is sometimes claimed as the mysterious 'Babylon' of the book of Revelation.

Satan ('opposer'), because of his rebellion against God's will, 2. The duration of Satan's binding is the length of the millennium. This binding is necessary because the kingdom has for its object the restoration of the divine authority over the earth (Acts 15:14-17), against which Satan is the chief opponent and the principal rebel. The place of imprisonment is the abyss, the prison of the demons (Lk 8:31; Rev 9:2; 17:8). Satan is loosed for a final revolt after the millennium (7-9); then cast into eternal hell, Gehenna (10) to share the fate of the beast, the false prophet (19:20) and unsaved men (20:15; Mt 25:41).

20:4-6. The saints reign

4. Classes of saints reigning with Christ. *The first company, 4a,* consists of all the redeemed from Abel to the translation of the church (1 Cor 6:2-3; cf. Dan 7:9-10). The *second company, 4b,* consists of the souls of the martyrs of the early part of the Tribulation period in their disembodied state (cf. 6:9-11). The reason for their death is their 'testimony for Jesus' and their faithful adherence, as a remnant, to the Word of God. The *third company, 4c,* consists of the individuals (souls) who had not worshiped the beast (13:15-17) and belong to the martyrs of the last part of the Tribulation period.

4d-6. **The first resurrection.** 'They,' the martyred of the Tribulation period, *4b, c,* 'came to life,' i.e., were resurrected. Their resurrection thus occurs *after* the marriage of the Lamb (19:7-9) and at the beginning of the kingdom. Hence they are distinct both from the Bride (the church) and the guests (OT saints) but all three companies (*4a-c*) comprise those in the *first resurrection, 6a,* who are 'blessed and holy.' They are to be distinguished from the unsaved ('the rest of the dead') who are not resurrected till the second resurrection to eternal punishment (11-15) after the millennium, 5 (cf. Jn 5:29). 'The second death,' Gehenna (the lake of fire), has no power over these, *6b,* but they shall be king-priests of God associated with Christ the King-Priest (Zech 6:9-15), and shall reign during the thousand-year Kingdom Age, *6c* (cf. 11:15).

20:7-10. Satan loosed

7-9. Satan's last rebellion. Verse 7 resumes the history of Satan begun in verse 3, interrupted by the account of the saints' reign during the millennium. After His thousand-year imprisonment, Satan is liberated from the abyss to test man's loyalty to God under the ideal conditions of the last of God's ordered ages, before the eternal state, 7. The result is his successful deception of 'the nations' in the final human confederacy. This postmillennial rebellion will be similar to the premillennial one (Ezk 38-39) and therefore metaphorically called 'Gog and Magog' (see notes on Ezk 38-39). However, this rebellion will be worldwide and compose the final coalition against God, His people and the Holy City, Jerusalem, 8-9. The rebels will evidently be individuals among the nations who, to a large extent, yielded only feigned allegiance to Messiah's iron rule (Ps 2:9; 18:44; 66:3; 81:15). Israel will be loyal to her Messiah (Jer 31:31-34; Rom 11:26). The result of the revolt will be the complete supernatural destruction of the rebels and the end of divine toleration of evil upon the earth, 9.

10. Satan's final doom. Satan's predestined judgment (Gen 3:15) is now executed. First cast out of the heavenly realm (12:9), then imprisoned in the abyss (20:1-3), he is now consigned to his eternal fate, the lake of fire. 'Burning sulphur' speaks of inexpressible conscious torment (14:10; Isa 30:33). The lake of fire will contain (1) the beast and the false prophet, who are already there, 10, preserved 'with fire' (Mk 9:49) and punished in proportion to their sin; (2) the devil and his angels, and (3) the unsaved (Mt 25:41).

20:11-15. The final judgment

11. The throne and the judge. This scene of judgment closes the millennium and marks the beginning of eternity. The judgment concerns the wicked dead. 'A great white throne' describes the *greatest* judgment ever held, 'white' depicting divine purity and righteousness, which characterize God's decisions, 11*a*. 'Him who was seated on it' is Christ (Jn 5:22), to whom all judgment is committed, 11*b*. The living He has already judged (Mt 25:31); now He is about to judge the dead (cf. 2 Tim 4:1).

12-15. The dead and their judgment. The subjects of this judgment are those who are both physically and spiritually dead, 12*a*. All the *unsaved are included* – 'the great and the small,' no matter what their position on the earth may have been, 12*b*. They stand, in the agony and shame of their sins, before a throne which is 'great' and 'white.' They have neither altar nor blood for forgiveness. Each sinner is face to face with God alone, 12*c*. They are faced with their works, 12*d*, but are lost because they did not accept God's salvation. As lost souls, they are judged on the basis of what they did (Eph 5:6). The book of life is opened, 12*e*, which is the register of the saved (13:8; 17:8). It contains the name of not one unsaved person, demonstrating that this is purely the sinner's judgment, 15. The wicked dead are raised, 13, as death holding the body and Hades the soul surrender their prisoners (cf. Jn 5:28-29). Death and hell (Hades) are finally done away with, 14, at the completion of the first resurrection (1 Cor 15:26). The doom of the unsaved is 'the second death . . . the lake of fire,' the place of the isolation of evil and all sinners from God in eternity.

21:1-22:5. The City of God and the eternal state

21:1-8. The eternal state
1-7. Eternity and the righteous.
Revelation 21:1-8 belongs with 19:1-20:15, to which it forms the natural conclusion in a sequence of events issuing in the eternal state (cf. Isa 65:17; 66:22; 1 Cor 15:24-28; Eph 3:21; 2 Pet 3:13). Eternity is characterized by a new heaven and a new earth, 1. The new Jerusalem, 2, represents the glorified church (3:12) *after* the millennial reign. She is called 'holy' because she is glorified and sinlessly joined to Christ in administrative and ruling dignity (1 Jn 3:2; Rom 8:29; Phil 3:21). She comes 'down out of heaven, her home (Col 3:1-4). God's dwelling with men, 3, is now possible (1 Cor 15:24-28) because Adam's curse has been removed, Satan judged, the wicked punished, and the universe sinless, except for 'the lake of fire' (20:15). In the millennium God spread His tabernacle *over* His people (7:15); now He tabernacles *with* them. All traces of sin are removed, 4. The authentication of this grand finale of divine redemption is by God Himself, 5. Meanwhile, an offer of salvation is made to the sinner, 6 (cf. Jn 7:37-39), and of rewards to the saint who overcomes, 7, all in the light of eternity.

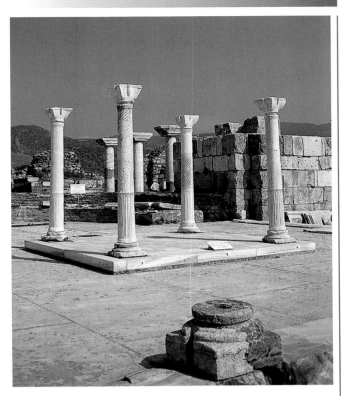

8. Eternity and the unrighteous. God's sinless, blissful eternity will have only one isolation ward for sin and sinners. It is 'the second death' or 'lake of fire' (20:14). This is the eternal abode of the wicked. It is called 'second' in reference to the sinner's preceding physical death while in a state of spiritual death and because it represents eternal death in separation from God. It is as eternal as the throne of God (Heb 1:8) is eternal (cf. 19:20; 20:10). The unsaved, who are described at length, 8, are its tenants.

John is reputed to be buried here, in the basilica church dedicated to him, at Ephesus. It is said that, following exile on Patmos, he finished his life in the city of Ephesus.

21:9-10. The vision of the city introduced
9. The angelic invitation. 'One of the seven angels,' the same angel who had invited John to view the judgment of ecclesiastical and political Babylon (17:1), here invites the seer to view the Lamb's wife, the Bride. This is a reference to the city of the Lamb, an orientalism which saw the city of a ruler as wed to him.

10. The view of the great city. John is carried away in 'the Spirit,' i.e., in the vision, to a suitable vantage point from which he views the descent of the holy Jerusalem. The greatness of the city is seen in the following dimensions and splendor, 11-23. This city takes the place of and supersedes the historical Jerusalem which passed away with the first earth, 1*b,* and becomes part of the new earth, 2*a.*

21:11-21. A description of the city

11-14. Her identity. The city is the magnificent symbol of the eternal abode and destiny of the redeemed of all ages. God's saints have always envisioned such a city (Heb 11:10, 16; 13:14; Jn 14: 1-3). Its inhabitants will be God the Father in full revelation of divine light and glory, 11, glorified OT saints (Heb 11:40), NT church saints (the Bride, the Lamb's wife), myriads of unfallen angels, and our blessed Lord Himself (Heb 12:22-23). Both Israel and the church appear prominently in the city, 12*c,* 14, the great high wall, 12*a,* denoting the safety and security of all its inhabitants, who are bathed in God's radiant and unveiled majesty.

15-17. Her size. The dazzling city's measurements reveal a solid cube of golden construction 1500 miles broad, wide and high. This could mean 2,250,000 square miles on each tier of the cube extending 1500 miles upward, like a huge skyscraper with innumerable floors.

18-21. Her splendor. The glorious destiny of the redeemed in eternity is symbolized by the city's adornment with every divine beauty, her wall being of jasper, and the city itself of pure gold, both crystal-clear, 18. Each of the 12 foundations is a spectacular gem of unusual brilliance and color, 19-20. These foundations are not sections divided into three on each side of the city, but 12 layers, each of which encircles the city. Looking at them would give a rainbow or prism effect of symmetrical beauty. Each gate is a pearl, 21, and the street is transparent gold.

21:22-22:5. Life within the city

22. Her temple. No visible temple will adorn the city of God, for there is no need for a place of worship. God the Almighty and Christ the Lamb dwell in the midst of the redeemed and there is direct access. Indirect approach through a temple with its altar is entirely unnecessary.

23-24. Her light. There is no need for the heavenly luminaries to give light, for the radiant glory of God will illuminate the city. All will be bright with His light.

24*b,* 26. Her honor. The nations and kings of the earth will bring their glory to her, and her authority will be universally acknowledged.

25. Her gates. Her gates need never be closed, for her enemies have all been destroyed, and there is no darkness to hide them, if there were enemies.

27. Her citizenry. Nothing unclean will find lodging in the city, for moral and spiritual uncleanness will be unknown within her walls. The redeemed righteous, totally free from sin's defilement and presence, will constitute her inhabitants. Their names are on God's roll, 'the Lamb's book of life.'

1-5. Paradise restored. The complete removal of the curse brings even more than paradise ever enjoyed before the Fall. The environment will be perfect. Fullness of life ('river of the water of life') flows from the source of eternal life, God the Father through the Son (the Lamb), 1. It is readily available to all ('down the middle of its street'), 2*a.* Every desire is met in the kinds of fruit available, 2*b,* and spiritual blessing becomes a reality for all, 2*c.* The curse is removed and with it all the laborious toil, futility, and rebellion which marked and marred man's history, 3. The redeemed will readily submit to the Lord's sovereignty, and as His bond servants they will serve Him, seeing His face in intimate fellowship and being identified by His name on their foreheads, 4. What perfect occupation! Light will mark life in the eternal state, resulting in complete happiness and fellowship, with the redeemed reigning for endless ages, 5. In all this the Lamb is focal!

22:6-21. Closing Testimonies

22:6-11. The testimony of the angel and of Christ

6. The angel authenticates the prophecy. The truth of these great predictions is attested, 6*a,* and the OT foundation and NT fulfillment are declared, 6*b.* The same God who inspired the ancient seers has sent His angel to reveal these prophecies to His NT servants, because the prophecies are soon to be fulfilled, 6*c.*

7. Christ Himself announces His soon coming (cf. vv. 12, 20). The blessing of him who treasures the words of the Apocalypse is promised and repeated (cf. 1:3; 22:7).

8-11. The angel pronounces the book unsealed. John made a similar mistake previously of worshiping an angel, 8-9 (19:10). Worshiping any creature is an affront to the Creator. The angel declares the book of the Revelation is to be unsealed, 10, in contrast to the command to seal Daniel's prophecy (Dan 12:4, 9). The reason for not sealing this prophecy is that 'the time is near.' Verse 11 describes the permanency of human destiny. There is no second chance after death or the Lord's return.

22:12-21. The concluding testimony of Christ

12-15. His coming and rewards. Christ announces once again the certainty and nearness of His coming, 12a. He declares the rewards He will render for works, 12b. These rewards are dispensed at the judgment seat of Christ (see notes on 2 Cor 5:10; 1 Cor 3:11-15; 9:24-27). He, the Rewarder, is the eternal Christ, 13. Living faith in Christ alone gives access to the tree of life (Jn 3:16; Eph 2:8-9) and entrance into the eternal city, 14. Unsaved people are debarred, 15.

16-19. His person and relationships to mankind. He who has sent His angel to give 'this testimony' (the whole content of the book) to the churches, 16a, describes Himself *in His relation to Israel,* 16b: 'I [emphatic] am the Root and the Offspring of David.' As the 'Root' He is divine, David's Lord. As the 'Offspring' He is human, David's son (Ps 110:1). By virtue of who He is, the crown of Israel is His, both by promise and prophecy. Born as King of the Jews (Mt 2:2), He died as King of the Jews (Mt 27:37). He will yet reign as King of the Jews (Zech 9:9). *In His relation to the church,* 16c, He is 'the bright Morning Star' (cf. 2:28). This presents Him in His second advent when He returns for His Bride before the dawn of the millennial day. *In His relation to every soul that thirsts,* 17, He invites them to come and take of 'the free gift of the water of life' (cf. Jn 7:37-39). He warns against taking away or adding to the book of the Revelation, 18-19.

20a. Christ declares His soon coming. 'Yes, I am coming soon.' These words are His final message to the church. They assert His soon coming, repeated (for emphasis) for the last time.

20b. The church replies to her Lord. John, representing the church, as well as his own keen desire, cries, 'Amen. Come, Lord Jesus,' or, 'Yes, indeed, come, Lord Jesus.'

21. The closing benediction. John, the beloved apostle and seer, also adds a benediction. 'The grace of the Lord Jesus be with God's people' (the saints). So ends this magnificent prophetic panorama of God's ways with man, as well as the completed sacred revelation itself.

How the Bible came to us

The earliest Hebrew Scriptures

The OT Scriptures were penned over a period extending more than a millennium, from c. 1450 to c. 400 B.C. According to conservative scholars, Moses was the first inspired writer, producing the Pentateuch around 1450-1400 B.C. (see p. 15, 'Authorship of the Pentateuch'). Malachi, the last of the writers, wrote not later than 400 B.C. For a discussion of more technical matters relating to authorship, date, etc., of the various OT books, see Gleason L. Archer, *A Survey of Old Testament Introduction* (1964), and R. K. Harrison, *Introduction to the Old Testament* (1969).

The text of the Old Testament

The earliest parts of the OT were originally inscribed on leather or papyrus in old Hebrew with the archaic prong-shaped letters similar to the script of the earliest recovered Phoenician inscriptions, e.g., b = 𝈵; h = 𝈵; m = 𝈵. This archaic writing gradually developed, after 400 B.C., into the square script found in the Dead Sea Scrolls, later Hebrew MSS., and in printed Hebrew Bible since 1477, e.g., b = ב; h = ח; m = ל.

Canonization of the Old Testament

The canon of Scripture is a phrase by which the catalog of the authoritative sacred writings is designated. The word *kanon* in the Greek originally signified a reed or measuring rod. Actually it indicated 'that which measures,' that is, a standard or norm or rule; specifically, 'that which is measured' by that standard or norm. Those books which were measured by the standard or test of divine inspiration and authority, and were adjudged to be 'God-breathed,' were included in 'the canon.'

Conservatives hold that inspired Scripture had the impress of canonical authority from the moment of inspiration by the Spirit of God, independent of formal collection or mere human recognition. The higher critical view, however, is that canonization took extensive time. According to this theory, the Law was first canonized by 444 B.C., the Prophets not until 300-200 B.C., and the Writings about 165-100 B.C. (see 'Order of Books in the Hebrew Old Testament' pp. 9-10). Higher criticism thus assumes that the threefold division of the Hebrew canon is due principally to chronology. It is held that the Prophets did not become popular until after 300 B.C., and as a result their writings were collected and canonized within the next century. Alleged 'Second' and 'Third' Isaiah (ch. 40-66 mainly) were attached to Isaiah because their authors were completely forgotten. Daniel was supposedly not written until 167 B.C. and assumed to be too late to be included in the second or prophetic section. Other books, such as Esther, 1 and 2 Chronicles, and Ezra-Nehemiah, are said to have been composed too late to be included in the historical section.

Conservative criticism, however, maintains that the threefold division of the Hebrew canon can be explained by either the status of the writer, or the arrangement of the books for liturgical convenience. Early dates for the OT books which maintain their integrity are accordingly held. Strict adherence to the Jewish canon has always been the Protestant position.

The work of the Masoretes

Before A.D. 500 Hebrew manuscripts had

no system of vowel indication, except certain consonants to indicate long vowels. Between A.D. 600 and 950 Jewish scholars, called Masoretes (Traditionalists), invented a full system of vowels and accents to punctuate the text. They also standardized the text, including marginal readings (called *qerê*) and textual variations (called *ketîb*). The work of the Masoretes on the Hebrew Bible providentially prepared it for the advent of the printing press five centuries later.

Printed Hebrew Bibles

The Psalter was the first part of the Hebrew Bible put into print. It appeared in 1477. In 1488 the first edition of the entire Hebrew OT appeared printed with vowels and accents.

The earliest Christian scriptures

For almost two decades after our Lord's ascension, the OT Scriptures, mainly in Greek, constituted the only Bible in existence (see pp. 9-10). The first NT book was apparently James, written perhaps as early as A.D. 45. The Apocalypse is commonly viewed as the latest, dating about A.D. 95. During this early period the church employed the OT as its Bible. Peter preached from the OT (Acts 2:14-36), as did Stephen (Acts 7:2-53), Philip (Acts 8:32-35) and Paul. *All* the NT writers were imbued with the OT and their inspired writings were grounded in its inspired revelation.

Origin of the New Testament books

The gospel (1 Cor 15:3-4) was first preached by word of mouth and interpreted in the light of OT history and prophecy. Oral accounts of the life and work of Christ were written down and finally gave way to the inspired synoptic gospels sometime before A.D. 70. The need for doctrinal interpretation of Christ's person and work soon became a necessity, accentuated by the need to define Christianity against such errors as legalism and antinomianism. The Pauline and other epistles were written to meet this need. The demand for a historical sketch of the development of the church was met by the book of Acts. The Apocalypse was penned to consummate the revelation of God's plan and purposes for time and eternity.

Artist's impression of Jewish scribes working with manuscripts.

CANONIZATION OF THE NEW TESTAMENT

Some early noncanonical New Testament books

1 Clement, an epistle penned by Clement of Rome (*c*. A.D. 96) to the Corinthian church, was highly esteemed. It was considered of canonical authority by some and was publicly read in the church at Corinth around 170. Various writers in Egypt used it, such as Clement of Alexandria and Origen. It was attached to Codex Alexandrinus.

2 Clement was an epistle also attached to Codex Alexandrinus. It was falsely ascribed to Clement of Rome and never was widely read. Neither it nor 1 Clement ever enjoyed canonical recognition in the West.

The Didache (The teaching of the twelve Apostles) (*c*. 120) was regarded as Holy Scripture by some in Egypt, notably Clement of Alexandria and Origen. It had a wide circulation.

The Epistle of Barnabas (*c*. 130) was included in the Codex of Sinaiticus and was accounted authoritative in Egypt. Jerome (*c*. 400) regarded it as apocryphal, and it gradually lost any claim to the status of Holy Scripture.

The Shepherd of Hermas (*c*. 140) was written by Hermas, the brother of Pius, bishop of Rome. It was also included in Codex Sinaiticus and was looked upon highly by the Muratorian Canon, but never established itself as Holy Scripture.

Apocalypse of Peter (*c*. 145), of less importance than the preceding books, was nevertheless highly regarded in the East and known in the West. It was not approved by the Muratorian Canon and regarded as spurious by Eusebius.

Acts of Paul (*c*. 170) was circulated widely and viewed by some as canonical, but enlightened scholarship saw its apocryphal nature and gradually it was rejected. Numerous other later gospels, acts, epistles and apocalypses appeared under apostolic names. These were obviously forgeries and never received serious consideration of the church.

Factors fostering New Testament canonicity

The recognition of 1 Clement, the Didache, the Epistle of Barnabas and the Shepherd of Hermas as canonical or semi-canonical, especially in the East, by the end of the 3rd cen. focused attention on the need of a clearly defined canon. Also, the incomplete canon of the heretic Marcion (*c*. 140) was widely subscribed to. Marcion was a Gnostic and on doctrinal grounds accepted only Luke's gospel and ten of the Pauline epistles, after seriously mutilating them. The appearance in time of other apocryphal and pseudepigraphal books clamoring for recognition demanded a clearly delimited canon. Somewhat later the edict of Emperor Diocletian (303), ordering the burning of all sacred books, necessitated carefully defining the canon.

Criteria for New Testament canonicity

The first criterion was *apostolicity*. Was the writer a bona fide apostle? If not, did he have close associations with an apostle, as was true of the writers of the gospel of Mark, the gospel of Luke, the book of Acts and the epistle to the Hebrews?

The second criterion was *content*. Were the subject matter and the treatment of it of the high order and spiritual stamp demanded by the test of Holy Scripture? By this criterion the spurious books were eliminated.

The third criterion was *universality*. Did the church as a whole receive the book? Did it have a universal appeal?

The fourth criterion was *divine inspiration*. Did the book give unmistakable evidence of being 'God-breathed' (2 Tim 3:16)? And did the Holy Spirit give this conviction to men of God that this was true? This was the final test. Without providential guidance the NT canon would never have been correctly delimited.

Books early received as canonical

These recognized books were called by Origen (*c*. 245) *homologoumena* ('confessed' or 'acknowledged' books). They were the NT writings universally owned as inspired Holy Scripture. Origen included the four

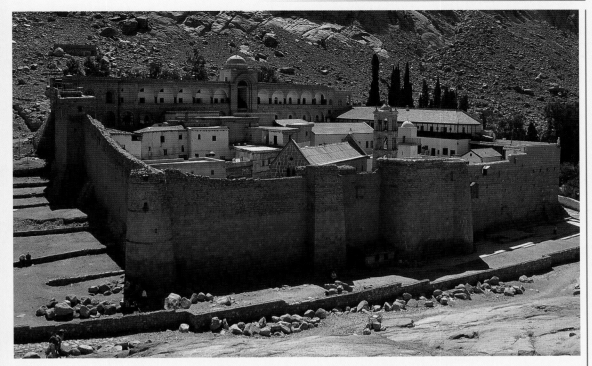

gospels, Paul's epistles, 1 Peter, 1 John, Acts and the Apocalypse. Although he did not include Hebrews among the *homologoumena,* he cited the epistle as Pauline, and canonical. In fact, the only books he did not cite as Scripture were Jude and 2 and 3 John.

Eusebius of Caesarea (*c.* 300-325), the church historian, included among the *homologoumena* the four gospels, Acts, the Pauline epistles, 1 John, 1 Peter and the Revelation. He seems to have inadvertently omitted Hebrews.

New Testament books at first questioned

Origen called these questioned books the *antilegomena* ('spoken against' or 'disputed'). Among these he placed Hebrews (see above), 2 Peter, 2 and 3 John, James, Jude, and the apocryphal epistle of Barnabas, the Shepherd of Hermas, the Didache, and the gospel of the Hebrews.

Eusebius of Caesarea divided the *antilegomena* into (1) those merely disputed or questioned – James, Jude, 2 Peter, 2 and 3 John; (2) those actually spurious or uninspired – Acts of Paul, the Shepherd of Hermas, the Apocalypse of Peter, the epistle of Barnabas, and the Didache.

Reasons for doubting certain New Testament books

The seven books that at first were challenged are James, 2 Peter, Hebrews, 2 John, 3 John, Jude and the Revelation. The hesitancy of some early church leaders to accept these books is explainable on the basis of their peculiar internal evidence. (1) James and Jude style themselves mere 'servants' of Christ, not apostles, while the author of 2 and 3 John refers to himself as a 'presbyter' or 'elder,' not an apostle. John in the Apocalypse calls himself 'servant' and 'brother.' (2) Hebrews is anonymous and differs in vocabulary and style from the recognized Pauline epistles. Peter's second epistle, while not anonymous, differs from 1 Peter in the same way. (3) James, too, was written to early Jewish converts and not addressed to the great universal Gentile church. (4) Jude was questioned also because it used the apocryphal book of Enoch (1:9; 5:4; cf. Jude 14-15). Gradually, however, all these controversial though genuine books came to be universally accepted by the church. In the West this was accomplished by A.D. 400 and in the East by 500.

St Catherine's Monastery, in the Sinai, where Count Tischendorf discovered one of the oldest extant New Testament manuscripts, the *Codex Sinaiticus,* in 1844.

Early growth of the canon in the West

The witness of Clement of Rome (c. A.D. 96). In his highly revered letter (known as 1 Clement) to the church at Corinth while bishop of Rome, he shows knowledge of Matthew, Romans, 1 Corinthians, and refers over and over again to Hebrews.

The witness of Marcion (c. 140). As a Gnostic heretic he accepted only Luke's gospel and ten of Paul's epistles. But his testimony, though erroneous, is illuminating and constitutes an important milestone in the church's collection and approval of the present NT canon.

The witness of Hermas (c. 150). As the reputed author of the highly revered Shepherd of Hermas he authenticates Matthew's gospel, Ephesians, apparently Hebrews and James, and notably the Apocalypse.

The witness of Irenaeus (c. 140-203). As one who in his youth came in contact with Polycarp at Smyrna and as later bishop of Lyons in Gaul, he bears witness to the four gospels, Acts, 1 Peter, 1 John, all Paul's letters except Philemon, and the Revelation.

The witness of the Muratorian Canon (c. 172). The fragment was discovered by Muratori, an Italian, in the Ambrosian Library at Milan in 1740. The mutilated beginning contained apparently Matthew and Mark. It attests all the NT books except 1 Peter, 2 Peter, James and Hebrews.

The witness of the Old Latin version before 170.

It attests all the books except James and 2 Peter, Hebrews being added before Tertullian's time.

The witness of Tertullian (c. 150-222). This voluminous Latin writer of Carthage attests the four gospels, 13 Pauline epistles, Acts, 1 Peter, 1 John, Jude and the Apocalypse. Following the principle of apostolic authorship, he rejected Hebrews since he believed that Barnabas was the author.

The witness of Cyprian (c. 200-258). As bishop of Carthage he closely followed Tertullian regarding Hebrews, and did not quote from Philemon, James, 2 or 3 John, or Jude.

Later growth of the canon in the West

The witness of Jerome (c. 340-420). The great translator of the Latin Vulgate and renowned scholar attested *all* our canonical NT books. He accepted Hebrews as written by Paul, and explained how James and 2 Peter came to be recognized. His opinion is of superlative value.

The witness of Augustine (354-430). His opinion, unlike Jerome's, was uncertain. Although he accepted all the seven books which had been questioned, he posited different degrees of scriptural authority and was largely responsible for the wider OT canon of the Roman Catholic church, including the Apocrypha.

Action of church councils. The delimitation of the NT canon was not the work of any council or councils. The inspired worth and intrinsic authority of each individual book were the deciding factors. This fact is strong proof of the genuineness and authenticity of the books that have come down to us in the canon. Not until the close of the 4th cen. did any council make any pronouncement on the subject.

The third Council of Carthage (397) rendered the first decision on the canon. One of the canons of this body stipulated that only 'canonical' books be read in the churches. Then it listed exactly our present-day 27 books. Hebrews was recognized on the ground of being Pauline. The Council of Hippo (419) repeated the list of the Third Council of Carthage. The selection of the canon was thus a spontaneous process that went on in the church till each book proved its own worth.

Growth of the canon in the East

Ignatius, bishop of Antioch (c. 116); Polycarp, bishop of Smyrna (c. 69-155), and Papias, bishop of Hierapolis (c. 80-c. 155), testified to Matthew, John, Paul's epistles, 1 Peter, 1 John and likely Acts.

The Didache (c. 120) features Matthew and knows of Luke, as well as the majority of our NT books.

Melito, bishop of Sardis (c. 170), quoted from all the NT books except James, Jude, 2 and 3 John.

Theophilus of Antioch (c. 115-c. 188) adhered to most of the NT books and held them in the same esteem as the OT canon. However, his successor Lucian (martyred 312) in his 'Antioch Canon' excluded Revelation, 2 Peter, 2 and 3 John and Jude in his revised OT and NT text.

Basil the Great of Cappadocia (c. 329-379) and Gregory of Nazianzus (c. 330-390) recognized all the books of our present canon, except the Revelation, although he quoted it as written by John.

John Chrysostom (347-407) accepted all but 2 Peter, 2 and 3 John and Revelation.

Theodore of Mopsuestia (c. 350-428) rejected the Catholic epistles and the Revelation. The opinion of this part of the church was thus strongly influenced by the canon of Constantinople, which rejected 2 and 3 John, 2 Peter, Jude and Revelation, and which developed from the 'Antioch Canon' of Lucian.

The Peshitta (411-435) likewise followed the canon of Constantinople. Not until Philoxenus (c. 508) had the Syriac Peshitta been revised to add the rejected books was the unsound influence of the canon of Constantinople broken.

Early growth of the canon in Egypt and Palestine

Justin Martyr (c. 100-165) gave important testimony concerning the Revelation, which he considered the work of the apostle John. He also knew Hebrews and probably referred to Mark's gospel under the title 'Memoirs of Peter.'

Clement of Alexandria (c. 155-c. 215) was very well read and accepted all the books in our NT, including Jude, Hebrews, the Catholic epistles and the Revelation.

Origen of Alexandria (c. 185-c. 253) shows evidence of having accepted the books commonly disputed (Hebrews, 2 Peter, 2 and 3 John, James, Jude). He held the Apocalypse to be among the accepted books (*homologoumena*).

Later growth of the canon in Egypt and Palestine

The Chester Beatty Papyri from the 3rd cen., edited in 1933-37 by Sir Frederic Kenyon, authenticate the four gospels, the Acts, the Pauline epistles and Hebrews (which comes after Romans), and the Revelation (only the portion 9:10-17:2 is preserved, however).

Artist's impression of two copper scrolls discovered among the many Dead Sea Scrolls from Qumran. The Dead Sea Scrolls, discovered since 1947, give us a Hebrew text a millennium earlier than we possessed before.

Dionysius of Alexandria (c. 200-265) authenticated Hebrews as Paul's epistle, as well as owning James and 2 and 3 John and the Revelation as inspired Scripture.

Athanasius of Alexandria (298-373) applied the term 'canonical' to the exact 27 books of our canonical NT.

Summary of the formation of the New Testament canon

The NT canon was formed spontaneously, not by the action of church councils. The inspiration and intrinsic authority of each individual book were the determining factors in their eventual recognition and canonization. By A.D. 200 the NT contained essentially the same books as we have today. These were regarded with the same authority and finality by Christians then as they are now.

In the 3rd cen. the *antilegomena* were debated. The book of Revelation was opposed in the East. Hebrews was controverted in the West. By the end of the 3rd cen. practically all the extracanonical books had been dropped from authoritative lists.

During the 4th cen., debate on questions of the canonical status of certain books practically ceased in the West, due to Jerome's and Augustine's influence and the clear distinctions made regarding the canon by Athanasius in Egypt. The Third Council of Carthage (397) sealed the decision reached, and from that time on no appreciable opposition to any of the NT books continued.

Debate in the East persisted, however, for some time longer. But the example of the West, of Athanasius in Alexandria, and the influence of the Cappadocian fathers, swept away all opposition. With the addition of 2 and 3 John, 2 Peter, Jude and the Revelation to the Peshitta (Syriac Bible), the question of the canon was settled for the East also. Thus the canonicity of the NT was settled, for all practical purposes, in the West around A.D. 400 and in the East by A.D. 500.

History of the canon till the present

Apart from a few very minor differences, the verdict of the first four centuries on the

NT canon has remained the verdict of the church down to the present. During the Reformation the reformers insisted on the authority of an infallible Bible over against the alleged authority of an infallible church.

However, concerning the OT canon, the Roman church at the Council of Trent in 1546, by the *Decree Sacrosancta,* declared 11 of the 14 apocryphal books canonical. These are Tobit, Judith, Wisdom of Solomon, Ecclesiasticus, Baruch, 1 and 2 Maccabees, the Song of the Three, Susanna, and Bel and the Dragon. They also accepted later additions to the book of Esther.

Text of the New Testament

No other document from antiquity has influenced the Western world as much as the NT. Nor is the text of any ancient document so well attested. It exists in almost 5,000 Greek manuscripts (handwritten copies) and in more than 10,000 manuscripts which are copies of the early versions, besides in thousands of quotations from the church Fathers. The problem of textual criticism is to use these copies in order to determine by study and comparison the pure original text.

Sources for New Testament textual criticism

The papyri. As a result of a century of archaeological research, more than 75 papyrus fragments of the NT text now exist, designated by the letter P, with index numbers, as P1, P2. These date from the 2nd to the 8th cen., covering parts of 25 books, about 40 percent of the NT text. P52 contains parts of John 18:31-34, 37-38 and dates around A.D. 135, being the oldest. P45, P46, P47 belong to the Chester Beatty Papyri I, II, III (c. A.D. 200). P66 is the famous Bodmer Papyrus II of John's gospel, dating c. A.D. 200. P75 is the newly acquired Bodmer Papyrus XIV -XV of John and Luke, dating c. A.D. 200.

Uncials. These are written on parchment in a semi-capital style letter, and were used in NT MSS. until c. 800. About 300 uncials exist.

Minuscules. Manuscripts of this class were executed in a cursive or running script and date from the 9th to the 18th cen. A total of 2,647 minuscules have been cataloged.

Versions. The most valuable are those executed from the original Greek prior to 1000. Of these, the most important are the Old Latin (2nd cen.), the Vulgate (Latin) of Jerome (382-84), the Syriac (4th, 5th cen.), Coptic (2nd-4th cen.), Armenian (early 5th cen.), Old Georgian (5th cen.), Ethiopic and Gothic (mid 4th cen.).

Lectionaries. These are church service books containing Scripture lessons to be read throughout the year. About 2,000 lectionaries exist, both uncials and cursives. They date from c. 280 to c. 1600.

Ostraca and Talismans. Twenty-five ostraca and nine talismans (amulets) are now known engraved with portions of the NT text. They date from about the 4th to the 13th cen.

Quotations from the church Fathers. More than 86,000 of these are known.

Oldest Old Testament manuscripts

The oldest Masoretic Hebrew MSS. date not earlier than the later 9th cen. These are the Cairo Codex of the Prophets (A.D. 895), the Aleppo Codex of

Artist's impression of a page from the Codex Sinaiticus, one of the oldest manuscripts of the New Testament.

the whole OT (c. 925) and the Leningrad Codex (completed A.D. 1108). This latter is used as the text of Kittel's *Biblia Hebraica*. The Dead Sea Scrolls, notably the two Isaiah MSS., discovered since 1947, however, give us a Hebrew text a millennium earlier, together with fragments of all but one of the OT books dating from the 2nd to the 1st cen. B.C.

Oldest New Testament manuscripts

Codex Sinaiticus (ℵ), 4th cen. The NT is complete on 148 leaves. It was discovered by Tischendorf in the monastery of St. Catherine at Mount Sinai in 1844 and 1859. Also it contains fragments of the OT in Greek.

Codex Alexandrinus (A), 5th cen. It contains most of the OT and NT. It was presented by the Patriarch of Constantinople to Charles I of England in 1627, and transferred to the British Museum in 1757.

Codex Vaticanus (B), 4th cen. This has been in the Vatican Library at Rome since 1481. It contains almost the complete OT and NT, except for Heb 9:14-13:25, the Pastoral Epistles, Philemon and the Revelation.

Codex Ephraemi (C), 5th cen. It contains 145 leaves of NT out of 238.

Codex Bezae (D), 5th cen. Not all the NT remains.

Chester Beatty Papyrus I (P45), early 3rd cen. It contains 30 leaves of the original papyrus codex of the gospels and Acts.

Chester Beatty Papyrus II (P46), early 3rd cen. Eighty-six of original 104 leaves of papyrus codex of Paul's epistles are in existence.

Chester Beatty Papyrus III (P47), late 3rd cen. Ten leaves of original 32 of papyrus codex of Revelation are extant.

Bodmer Papyrus II (P66), early 3rd cen. One hundred fifty pages of a papyrus codex of the gospel of John are in existence.

Bodmer Papyrus XIV-XV (P75), early 3rd cen. All 144 pages out of an original 144 pages of the gospels of Luke and John were found.

English versions of the Bible
Early Anglo-Saxon versions. Caedmon, by 680, had rendered Bible stories in common speech in poetic paraphrase, according to Bede. Bede (died 735) is credited with a translation of John's gospel. King Alfred (848-901) had portions of the Bible translated into the vernacular. But until the time of Wycliffe (14th cen.) and Tyndale (16th cen.), the Bible was translated into English only sporadically and piecemeal.

Wycliffe's version (1382). This was the first complete translation into English, revised c. 1400, condemned and burned in 1415. At least 170 MS. copies have survived. Its weakness was that it was based on the Latin Vulgate instead of the original Greek.

Tyndale's translation (1525-35). Translated from the original Hebrew and Greek, the significance of Tyndale's version lies in its being first in a line of translations, so creative and impressive in its style that it formed the backbone of the Authorized King James Version of 1611.

The Coverdale version (1535). Miles Coverdale leaned on Tyndale's scholarly work. He supplemented it, where it had not been finished, by his own translation from German and Latin. He presented the first

completed English Bible in print.

The Thomas Matthew Bible (1537). Largely a revision of Tyndale by Tyndale's friend John Rogers, it was nevertheless published under the name of Thomas Matthew.

Taverner's Bible (1539), a revision by Richard Taverner of the Matthew Bible minus most of the notes and polemic data.

The Great Bible (1539) was the first authorized Bible, called 'great' from its size. It was also styled the 'Cranmer Bible' because of Archbishop Cranmer's preface to the second edition (1540).

The Geneva Bible (1560) was a revision of the Great Bible. The Geneva Bible was the first English Bible in the U.S., being the most common version among the Puritans.

The Bishops' Bible (1568) was the second authorized English Bible and was intended to supersede the Geneva Bible, the Bible of the people, and the Great Bible, the pulpit Bible of the churches. The translation work was done mainly by scholarly bishops.

The Douay version (1609-10) was the first Roman Catholic Bible in English.

The King James Version (1611) was the culmination of these preceding early translations and revisions, and became the

Orsope you the
ophile first p mad
a sermoun or word
of alle þe þinges
þat iesus bigan
for to do & teche:
til in to þe day
in þe whiche he comaundede to þe
apostlis bi þe hooly goost: who
he chese was taken up. To whom
& he ȝaue hym self alyue or quyc
after his passioun in many ar
gumentis or preuyngis bi fourty
days: apperinge to hem & spekynge
of þe reume of god. And he eþge
to gydere comaundide to hem þat
þei schulden not departe fro ierusale:
but þei schulden þe abide þe biheeste
of þe fadir: þe ȝe herden bi
my mouþ. Soþely ioon baptizide in
water: but ȝee schuln be baptixd
in þe hooly goost: not after þes ma
ny days. Therfore þei camen to gi
dre: axeden hym seyinge: Lord ȝif
in þis þyme: schalt þou restore þe
ky ugedoue of israel. forsoþe he sei
de to hem. It is not ȝoure for to
haue knowe þe tymes or moneþ
tis: þe whiche þe fadir haþ putte
in his power. But ȝee schulu take
þe vertu of þe hooly goost cumynge
fro aboue in to ȝou & ȝee schuln be
witnessis to me in ierln in al iu
dee and samarie: & vnto þe vtmest
of þe erþe. And whanne he hadde
seide þese þinges hem seyinge: he
was lifup and a cloude receyued
hym fro þe eȝen of hem & whanne
þei byheelden hym goþinge in to
heuene: loo two men stooden niȝ
besides hem in whit cloþis þe
whiche also seyden aȝen of galilee:
what stondeu ȝee biholdinge in
to heuene: þis iesus þat is taken
up fro ȝou in to heuene: so schal
come as ȝee sawe hym goþinge in to

heuen. Than þei turneden aȝein
to ierln fro þe hill þat is clepid
of olyuete þe whiche is bisidis
ierusalem: hauynge þe iourneye
of a saboth. And whanne þei had
den entride in to þe scripture place
þei wenten up in to þe hiȝer þinges
Wher þei dwelten petir & ioon ia
mes & audrew philip & thomas.
bartholomewe & mathu iames of
alpheȝ and symon zelotes: & iudas
of iamys alle þes weren dwellinge
or lastynge to gidre in preier wiþ
wymmen and marie þe moder of ie
su and wiþ his breþeren. In þoo
dayes petir rishinge up in þe myd
dil of breþeren: seide. forsoþe þere
was a cumpanye of men to gider: al
mest an hundrip and twenty men
breþeren it byhoueþ þe scripture to
be fulfillid. whiche þe hooly goost
before seide by þe mouþ of dauiþ. of
iudas þat was leder of hem: þat
token iesu þe whiche was noumbrid
in vs: & gat þe lort of þis my
nystre. And forsoþe þis weldide a
feeld of þe hyur of wickidnesse and
he hangid to brast þe mydil: and
alle his entrailis ben sched abrod
& it was maad knowen to alle men
dwellinge in ierusalem: so þat þe
ilk feeld was clepid acheldemac in
þe laugage of hem: þat is þe feld
of bloode. forsoþe it is write in
þe booke of psalmys. The habita
cioun of hym be maad desert and
be þer not þat dwelle in it: and
an oþer take þe bischopriche of
hym: perfore it byhoueþ of þis men
þat maad ben gadrid to gider wiþ
vs in alle tyme in whiche þe lord
iesu entrede in & wente out amoug
vs bygynnynge fro þe baptyme
of ioon vnto þe day in whiche
he was taken up fro vs: oon of
þese for to be maad a witnesse

Above: Artist's impression of King James I of England examining pages from the new translation of the Bible which he commissioned.

Opposite: Title page of the first edition of the King James Version, often known as the Authorized Version.

from transient modernisms. It has enjoyed an enthusiastic reception in the U.S., but not without question by many evangelicals.

New American Standard New Testament (1963)

The Jerusalem Bible (1963)

New King James Version (1982)

New Jerusalem Bible (1985)

Revised English Bible (1989)**New Revised Standard Version** (1990)

Modern speech translations

The Twentieth Century New Testament (1898-1901, revised 1904), by an anonymous group of scholars.

The New Testament in Modern Speech (1903), by Richard F. Weymouth, which has been revised twice by others.

The New Testament: A New Translation (1913), by James Moffatt. His Old Testament appeared in 1924 and a final revision in 1935.

The New Testament: An American Translation (1923), by Edgar J. Goodspeed, in American colloquial language.

The Riverside New Testament (1923, revised 1934), by William G. Ballantine.

The New Testament: A Translation in the Language of the People (1937), by Charles B. Williams.

The New Testament: The Berkeley Version in Modern English (1945), by Gerrit Verkuyl. The Old Testament was completed in 1959 by a group of conservative scholars.

The New Testament in Plain English (1952), by Charles Kingsley Williams.

An Expanded Translation of the New Testament (1956-59), by Kenneth S. Wuest.

The New Testament in Modern English (1958), by J. B. Phillips. Four previously published translations, beginning with *Letters to Young Churches* (1947), were published as a single volume New Testament in 1958.

The Amplified Bible: New Testament (1958), Old Testament (1962-64). The complete Bible was published in one volume in 1965. An attempt to add clarifying shades of meaning to the single-word English equivalents of key Hebrew and Greek words.

third 'authorized' English Bible, sponsored by James I of England. It employed the chapter divisions of Stephen Langton, archbishop of Canterbury in the 13th cen., and the verse divisions of Robert Estienne (1551). This version reigned supreme from 1611 to 1881.

The Revised Version (1881-85). A revision of the King James Version based on a literal translation of the Greek and Hebrew texts by sixty-five English scholars.

The American Standard Version (1901). An American edition of the Revised Version of 1885, including preferred readings and format changes, by a group of American scholars under the direction of William H. Green of Princeton Seminary.

The Revised Standard Version of the Bible (1952); **New Testament** (1946). Authorized by the National Council of Churches of Christ in the U.S.A., widely used by denominations in that group and many not in its membership. Although this version has many excellencies, it is weak and obscure in its translation of certain key OT messianic passages.

The New English Bible: New Testament (1961). A completely new translation by English scholars under the direction of C. H. Dodd of Cambridge. It is aimed at rendering the original Greek into idiomatic English, free from archaisms and

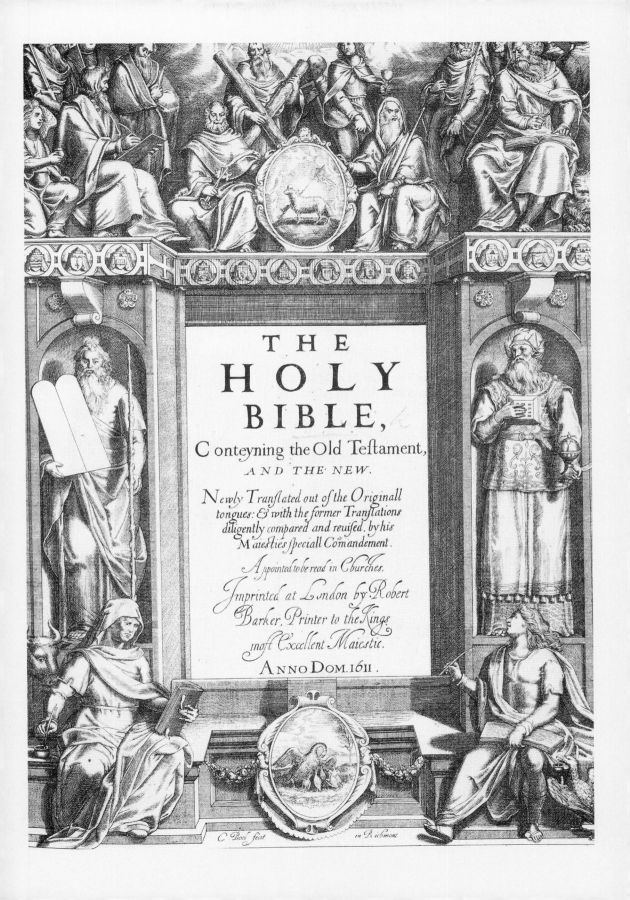

THE HOLY BIBLE,

C onteyning the Old Testament,
AND THE NEW.

Newly Translated out of the Originall
tongues: & with the former Translations
diligently compared and reuised, by his
Maiesties speciall Comandement.

Appointed to be read in Churches.

Imprinted at London by Robert
Barker, Printer to the Kings
most Excellent Maiestie.

ANNO DOM. 1611.

C Boel fecit   in Richmont

The New American Standard Bible: New Testament (1960-63), **Complete Bible** (1971). A revision of the *American Standard Version* (1901) by a group of conservative scholars.

The New International Version: New Testament (1973). Complete Bible (1978). New translation from Greek and Hebrew by an international team of conservative scholars.

The Living Bible: The Paraphrased Epistles (1962), **Living Prophecies:** *The Minor Prophets Paraphrased with Daniel and Revelation* (1965). **Complete Bible** (1971), by Kenneth N. Taylor.

The New Testament in the Language of Today (1963), by William F. Beck.

Today's English Version (Good News Bible) (1976)

Contemporary English Version (1995)

New Living Translation (1996)

English Standard Version (2001)

Bible statistics

Old Testament. Thirty-nine books, 929 chapters, 23,214 verses, 593,493 words. Middle book, Proverbs; middle chapter, Job 29; middle verses, 2 Chr 20:17-18; shortest book, Obadiah; about 30 extrabiblical books mentioned.

New Testament. Twenty-seven books, 260 chapters, 7,959 verses, 181,253 words. Middle book, 2 Thessalonians; middle chapter, Romans 13; middle verse, Acts 17:17; shortest book, 2 John; shortest verse, John 11:35. The name 'Jesus' occurs 700 times in the gospels and Acts, less than 70 times in the epistles. The name 'Christ' occurs 60 times in the gospels and Acts, some 240 times in the epistles and the Revelation.

The Bible. Middle book, Micah; largest book, Psalms; shortest book, 2 John. The name Jehovah (Yahweh, Lord) occurs 6,855 times. The human authors number about 50. Chapter and verse divisions are of comparatively later origin. Johann Gutenberg completed the first Bible printed from movable type in 1456. First American edition of the Bible was printed in Boston about 1752.

Outline of church history

The basis of church history

Definition. Church history is the chronological account and interpretation of the impact of Christ and His gospel upon mankind.

Preparation. (1) The Greek language, as a common language of the Graeco-Roman world, provided a suitable vehicle for the writing and preaching of the NT. (2) Roman law, and Roman political unity and granting of citizenship bound men together. The Roman peace (*pax Romana*) and road system facilitated 1st cen. evangelism. (3) Jewish monotheism provided the OT messianic hope and the basis for the NT revelation.

Periods of church history

Early Church Period A.D. 30-590.

30-100	Apostolic period
100-150	Sub-Apostolic Period
150-313	Conflict with Roman Empire and with Error
313-590	Growth of the Old Catholic Imperial Church

Medieval Church Period 590-1517

590-1054	Christianity in the West
1054-1305	Golden Age of Papal Power
1305-1517	Early Movement Toward Reformation

Modern Period 1517 to the Present

1517-1648	Protestant Reformation
1546-1648	Catholic Counter Reformation
1648-1789	Colonial Christianity and Revival
1789-1914	Christian Expansion in Britain and America
1914 to the present	The Church in the Twentieth Century

Early church period 30-590

Apostolic period (30-100)

Political	Religious
14-37 Tiberius	Founding of the church by the Holy Spirit. The gospel to Jerusalem, Judea and Samaria (Acts 1-12). Preaching of a crucified, risen Saviour in Jerusalem. Evangelization, persecution, Stephen's martyrdom. Samaria evangelized.
37-41 Caligula	Paul's conversion.
41-54 Claudius	Cornelius converted.
	The gospel to the ends of the earth (Acts 13-28). Missionary outreach from Antioch in Syria. Paul saved Christianity from legalism, evangelized cities of Roman Empire and wrote his great epistles.
54-68 Nero, first emperor to persecute Christians	
68-69 Galba **69** Otho and Vitellius	Peter's epistles, synoptics, Epistle to Hebrews.
69-79 Vespasian **79-81** Titus	Jerusalem destroyed (70).
81-96 Domitian persecutor	John banished to Patmos. Christians persecuted.
96-98 Nerva **98-117** Trajan, persecutor	NT books completed.

Sub-apostolic period (100-150)

Political	Religious
117-38 Hadrian	**Apostolic Fathers.** Among these were: Clement, bishop of Rome; Ignatius, bishop of Antioch, martyred; Papias, bishop of Hierapolis; Polycarp, bishop of Smyrna, martyred
138-61 Antoninus Pius also persecuted Christians	**Early writings.** Some of the more reliable: *Epistle to the Corinthians* by Clement *Epistle of Barnabas,* which presented Christ's death as alone sufficient for salvation apart from the Mosaic law. *Shepherd of Hermas* (apocalyptic literature) stressed responsibility and repentance. *The Didache* (catechetical) was written to instruct new converts.
Before 250, persecution was local and scattered, fomented by Jews, pagan intellectuals, and some of the emperors.	

Jewish coin of the Bar Kochba revolt depicting the Temple, which was destroyed in A.D. 70.

150-313
Conflict with Roman Empire and with error

Roman Emperors
Marcus Aurelius (161-80) persecuted Christians; Justin Martyr and Polycarp among those martyred.
Commodus (180-92)
Septimius Severus (193-211) Severe localized persecution, many being martyred in Alexandria, Egypt, N. Africa and Gaul. Christians were tortured, beheaded, burned and thrown to wild beasts.
Caracalla (211-17); Elagabalus (218-22); and Alexander Severus (222-35); all tolerated Christians.
Maximin (235-38) put to death many prominent Christian leaders; Origen barely escaped.
Gordian (238-44) and Philip (244-49) favored Christians.
Decius (249-51) inaugurated the period of violent and general persecution after 250; multitudes of Christians perished by cruel measures throughout the empire.
Valerian (253-60) fostered intense persecution; Cyprian was slain.
Diocletian (284-305), in an attempt to exterminate Christianity, inaugurated the most severe imperial persecution the church had yet faced.

Doctrinal errors
Gnosticism, positing dualism, taught that matter was inherently evil and thus Christ could not have a real body. *Neoplatonism* was a religious philosophy claiming that a divine substance pervaded and animated all objects worshiped in various religions, but denied this quality to Christianity. *Montanism* was an attempt by Montanus to counteract over-dependence upon human organization and formalism in the church. He claimed direct revelation of the Holy Spirit and stressed the immediacy of Christ's advent. *Monarchianism* stressed the unity of God, denying a trinity of Persons.

Apologists
Wrote to government officials seeking legal recognition of Christianity. Justin Martyr, the foremost apologist, defended the moral and spiritual value of Christianity and championed its being legalized in his *First Apology*. He also defended it against Judaism in his *Dialogue with Trypho*.

The Appian Way, approaching the city of Rome.

Extent of Christianity by A.D. 100

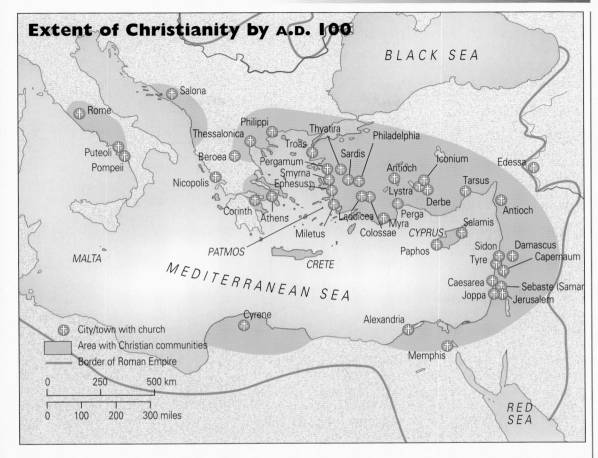

BLACK SEA

Salona

Rome

Philippi
Thessalonica
Thyatira
Philadelphia

Puteoli
Pompeii
Beroea
Troas
Sardis
Antioch
Iconium
Edessa
Pergamum
Smyrna
Tarsus
Nicopolis
Ephesus
Lystra
Derbe
Antioch

Corinth
Athens
Laodicea
Perga
Myra
Salamis
Miletus
Colossae
CYPRUS
Sidon
Damascus

MALTA
PATMOS
CRETE
Paphos
Tyre
Capernaum

Caesarea
Sebaste (Samar
Joppa
Jerusalem

MEDITERRANEAN SEA

Cyrene
Alexandria

Memphis

RED
SEA

- ✝ City/town with church
- ▭ Area with Christian communities
- ─ Border of Roman Empire

| 0 | 250 | 500 km |
| 0 | 100 | 200 | 300 miles |

Polemicists

Wrote against heresies. Irenaeus in *Against Heresies* upheld the deity and resurrection of Christ against Gnosticism. Origen, an allegorist, authored *De Principiis,* the first systematic theology, and the *Hexapla,* a monument of textual criticism. Tertullian formulated the doctrine of God's triunity in *Against Praxeas.* Cyprian formulated the doctrines of apostolic succession and Peter's primacy.

Church development

(1) Idea of the primacy of the bishop of Rome was born out of the need for leadership in time of persecution and in combating heresy. (2) The NT canon began to crystallize by A.D. 200. (3) Church calendar developed, with Christmas and Easter the principal festivals. (4) The early form of the Apostles' Creed became a symbol of orthodoxy.

Persecution

The basic reason for attack from the Roman state was the fear that separatist Christianity would jeopardize a pagan, religiously syncretistic state.

Archaeological light

The catacombs of Rome were caves of refuge for Christians. These great caverns contain thousands of inscriptions from this period.

Christianization of the Empire

The severe persecutions (250-311) not only failed to stamp out the faith but witnessed its phenomenal growth. Constantine established Sunday as a day of rest and worship (321); imperially favored Christianity; encouraged church building; moved his capital to Byzantium (Constantinople); ordered 50 Bibles on finest vellum to be prepared by Eusebius; reformed slavery and many pagan customs. This was a period when the

Division of the Empire
After A.D. 364

Valentinian I (364-75)	**Valens** (364-78)
Valentinian II (375-83)	**Theodosius** (378-95)
Theodosius the Great (383-95)	
Honarius (395-423)	**Arcadius** (395-408)
Valentinian III (423-55)	**Theodosius II** (408-50) etc.
Western Empire fell under inflow of barbarians (476).	**Anastasius** (491-50), etc. Justinian (527-65), etc.
Dark Ages Papal Empire emerges from the ruins of the Western Empire.	**Eastern Empire** lasted till the fall of Constantinople to the Turks (1453).

Majority Christian

Minority Christian

Few people Christian

AEGYPTUS   Province of Roman Empire

Boundary of Roman Empire

0	250	500 km

0	100	200	300 miles

church, no longer purified by persecution, was imperiled by the inrush of the world. The church's prosperity became her greatest peril. This era paved the way for the ecclesiastical corruption of the Dark Ages to follow. Instead of separation from paganism, the imperial church adapted itself to it.

Conversion of the barbarians
The Goths, Vandals, and Huns overthrew the empire. Some were Christianized but their conversion was nominal and helped introduce pagan practices into the church. Celtic Britons were evangelized by Roman Christians, the Irish by Patrick, the Goths by Ulfilas, the Scots by Columba, who established a monastery on the offshore island of Iona (563).

Creedal controversies (325-451).
Concerning Christ's person. Arius taught that Christ was a creature distinct in essence from God. Athanasius maintained He was coexistent and coeternal, of the same essence with the Father. The Council of Nicaea (325) condemned Arianism, deciding in favor of Athanasius' position.

Concerning Christ's two natures. Council of Constantinople (381) dealt with Apollinaris' heresy that Christ's human spirit was replaced by the Logos. Nestorius separated the two natures and over-emphasized the human, which was dealt with at the Council of Ephesus (431). The Council of Chalcedon (451) answered the Eutychian view that Christ's two natures were fused into one – the

Extent of Christianity by A.D. 300

GERMANIA
INFERIOR

Rhine R.

GERMANIA
SUPERIOR

RAETIA

NORICUM

PANNONIA

DACIA

ITALIA

DALMATIA

Danube R.

MOESIA

BLACK SEA

Rome

THRACIA

BITHYNIA
AND
PONTUS

GALATIA

Euphrates R.

CORSICA

Byzantium

MACEDONIA

ARMENIA

CAPPADOCIA

SARDINIA

EPIRUS

ASIA

MESOPOTAMIA

SICILIA

ACHAIA

LYCIA
AND
PAMPHYLIA

CILICIA

Antioch

SYRIA

CYPRUS

CRETA

MEDITERRANEAN SEA

JUDAEA

Alexandria

TRIPOLITANIA

CYRENAICA

AEGYPTUS

divine. The *Definition of Chalcedon* states the orthodox view of two natures united in one Person.

Concerning divine grace and human free will. Augustine of Hippo held to total depravity and the utter necessity for divine grace for salvation. Pelagius denied that view and insisted man was able to cooperate with divine grace.

Still other ecumenical councils dealt with doctrinal problems. Constantinople (553) dealt with the Monophysite controversy and Constantinople (680) with the two wills of Christ (Monothelitism). Nicaea (787) dealt with image worship.

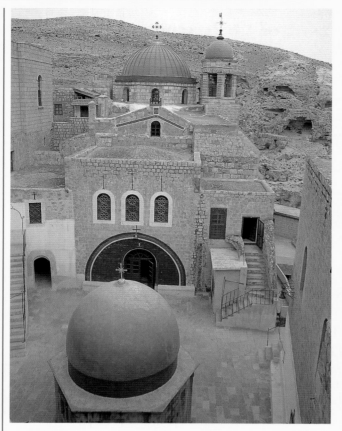

The wilderness monastery of Mar Saba, near Bethlehem. Christian monasticism began in Egypt with Paul of Thebes and Anthony about A.D. 250 and spread throughout the empire.

313–590

Growth of the Old Catholic imperial church

Political religious developments

Constantine (306-37) was converted to Christianity (312) and published the Edict of Milan (313).

Sylvester I became bishop of Rome. Constantine's three sons ruled the empire (337-61).

Julian 'the Apostate' (361-63) led a short-lived pagan reaction.

Jovian (363-64) restored the Christian faith.

Theodosius the Great (379-95) suppressed heathenism and made Christianity the legal state religion (380).

The imperial church of the 4th and 5th cen. became a different institution from the pilgrim church of the first three centuries.

Post-Nicene Fathers
Eastern Fathers

Chrysostom, the Golden Mouthed (345-407), was a great preacher and bishop of Constantinople. Theodore, bishop of Mopsuestia, championed sound grammatical-historical interpretation of the Bible. Eusebius of Caesarea (264-340), the Father of Church History, wrote an account of the fortunes of the church to his day (323).

Western Fathers.

Jerome (340-420) translated the Latin Vulgate, which became the Bible of Christendom for more than a thousand years. Augustine of Hippo (354-430) was an outstanding theologian. His *City of God* envisioned a universal Christian empire and his *Confessions* continue a classic in devotional literature.

Rise of the papacy

The title 'Pope' is Italian for 'Father.' Earlier it had been applied to all Western bishops, but by 500 it began to be restricted to the bishop of Rome, then gradually to 'universal bishop,' based on the Roman doctrine of apostolic succession and the primacy of Peter. Leo I (440-61) obtained recognition as primate of all bishops from Emperor Valentinian III (445). With his successor Hilarus (461-68), he advocated an exclusive universal papacy. The fall of the Western Empire (476) left the popes free to make advantageous alliances with the various new barbarian kingdoms that emerged. During the period from Simplicius (468-83) to Pelagius II (578-90), the authority of the popes increased greatly, preparing the way for the medieval and modern papacy.

Rise of monasticism

It began in Egypt with Paul of Thebes and Anthony about A.D. 250 and spread throughout the empire. Their aim was holiness by isolation from the world. In Europe monks lived in monasteries and in the Middle Ages developed education, learning, literature and farming.

Medieval church period 590-1517

590-1054

Christianity in the West

Growth of the papacy. Gregory I (590-604) was one of the most enlightened and finest of the popes. He laid the foundation of the medieval church about to be built on the ruins of the Roman Empire. As a theologian he synthesized Roman theology, emphasizing the concept of purgatory and the sacrificial character of the mass. He initiated the evangelization which won Britain to Roman Christianity through the efforts of Augustine of Canterbury.

Rise of Islam. Muhammad was born in 570. In 610 he declared himself a prophet. Though he was forced to flee Mecca in 622 (Hegira), he later conquered the city, making it his capital. He died in 632. In a short time western Asia and N Africa came under Islam, a religion of the sword and hate – Syria in 634, Jerusalem in 638, N Africa and Spain in 711. Charles Martel at the Battle of Tours (732) turned Islam back and saved Europe for Christianity.

Empire revived in the West. Pope Zacharias (741-52) helped Pepin the Short, Charlemagne's father, to become the king of the Germanic Franks. At the request of Stephen II (752-57), Pepin led his army into Italy, conquered the Lombards, and donated their lands to the Pope (754). This papal kingdom developed into the Papal States, which lasted till 1870. Charlemagne (742-814) built up a European empire and was crowned 'Emperor of the Romans' by Pope Leo III in 800. This event caused questions and problems regarding delegated authority in the church-state issue. In 962 Otto, a German ruler, was crowned Holy Roman Emperor over a kingdom that lasted till 1806.

Missionary expansion. Growing monasticism provided the bulk of the missionary force during this period, especially from Ireland and the island of Iona. Aidan carried the gospel to the Northumbrians in northeastern England (c. 634). At the Synod of Whitby (663) King Oswy decided in favor of Roman Christianity, prominent in the S as a result of Augustine of Canterbury's mission (596). Columbanus went to the Bergundians on the continent (589). Boniface (Winfrid) exerted the influence of the gospel on the Teutonic tribes (modern Germany) after 700. Willibrord, an Englishman, won Friesland for the papacy (692). Ansgar (801-65), the 'Apostle to the North,' reached Denmark and Sweden. Mid 9th cen. saw Cyril and Methodius, 'Apostles to the Slavs,' invent a Slavic alphabet, translate the Scriptures, convert the Bulgarians and Moravians to Christianity.

There was little missionary activity in the Eastern church, which was engaged in defending itself against Islam.

Papal degeneration (858-1054). Nicolas I (858-67), first pope to wear a crown, claimed papal supremacy by citing the Pseudo-Isidorian Decretals. Appearing in the mid 9th cen., the Decretals claimed to be letters and decrees of bishops, Constantine and church councils of the

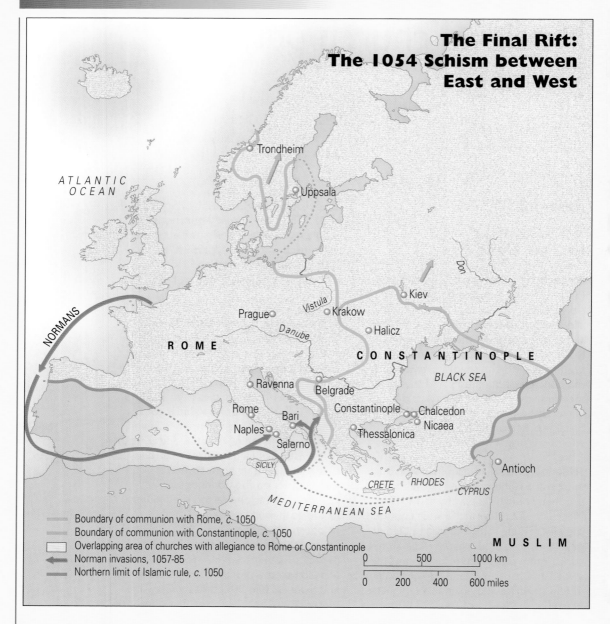

The Final Rift: The 1054 Schism between East and West

ATLANTIC OCEAN

Trondheim

Uppsala

NORMANS

Kiev

Don

Prague
Vistula
Krakow

Halicz

R O M E
Danube

C O N S T A N T I N O P L E

BLACK SEA

Ravenna

Belgrade

Rome
Bari

Constantinople
Chalcedon

Naples

Nicaea

Thessalonica

Salerno

SICILY

Antioch

CRETE   RHODES

CYPRUS

MEDITERRANEAN SEA

M U S L I M

Boundary of communion with Rome, c. 1050
Boundary of communion with Constantinople, c. 1050
Overlapping area of churches with allegiance to Rome or Constantinople
Norman invasions, 1057-85
Northern limit of Islamic rule, c. 1050

| 0 | 500 | 1000 km |
| 0 | 200 | 400 | 600 miles |

early centuries. They were later proved to be forged attempts to demonstrate the historicity and antiquity of the claims of the papacy. The corrupting influence of the concept of a papal kingdom and temporal power, in addition to weak, immoral successors, called for reform.

The Eastern Schism of Christendom.
Tension between the popes and the patriarch of Constantinople led to a split between the Eastern and Western churches. Disputes over the date of Easter, images in the churches, *filioque* (double procession of the Holy Spirit) and use of unleavened bread in the mass caused the Schism of 1054 and the formation of the Greek Orthodox church of the East.

1054-1305

Golden age of papal power

Summit of papal power. The popes of the 11th to the 14th cen. instituted reforms and humbled kings. Hildebrand (Gregory VII), whose concept of the papacy is outlined in the *Dictatus Papae,* reigned 1073-85. He put down clerical immorality, simony (sale of church offices), and humbled Henry IV of Germany (1077).

Innocent III (1198-1216) brought the medieval papacy to its greatest power by forcing the submission of the kings of France, England and the Holy Roman Empire. He assumed many titles, such as 'Vicar of Christ,' etc., and subordinated the state to the church. Through the Fourth Lateran Council (1215) he decreed the necessity of auricular confession and the doctrine of transubstantiation. He initiated papal inquisition, exterminated heretics (Albigenses), and sponsored the Fourth Crusade. The church countered the Albigenses and Waldenses with crusades, the Inquisition and a ban on the Scriptures.

Decline of the papacy. Weak popes succeeded Innocent. Boniface VIII (1294-1303) engaged in a power struggle with Philip the Fair of France during which he issued the papal bull *Unam Sanctum.* It stated that temporal authority was to be subject to the spiritual (the church, i.e., the pope); that there is 'one Holy Catholic and Apostolic Church and outside this church there is neither salvation nor remission of sins . . .'; that 'it is altogether necessary to salvation for every human creature to be subject to the Roman Pontiff.' Before he could be excommunicated, Philip had Boniface taken captive for a brief time, and he died shortly after his release. In 1309 Pope Clement V (1305-14), a Frenchman, moved the papacy to Avignon, beginning the 'Babylonian Captivity' of the papacy (1309-77).

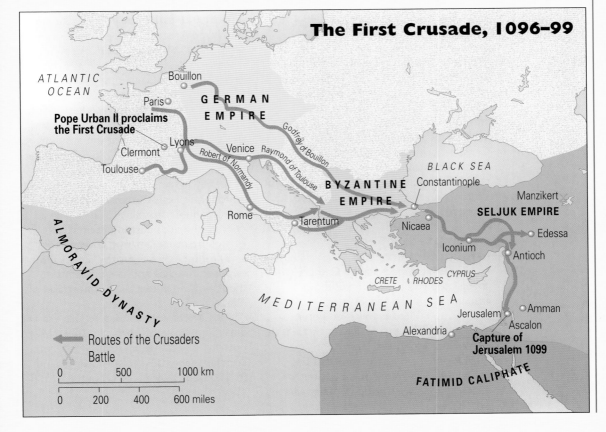

The First Crusade, 1096–99

ATLANTIC OCEAN

Bouillon

Paris

GERMAN EMPIRE

Pope Urban II proclaims the First Crusade

Clermont

Lyons

Godfrey of Bouillon

Venice

Raymond of Toulouse

Robert of Normandy

Toulouse

BLACK SEA

BYZANTINE EMPIRE

Constantinople

Manzikert

SELJUK EMPIRE

ALMORAVID DYNASTY

Rome

Tarentum

Nicaea

Iconium

Edessa

Antioch

CYPRUS

CRETE   RHODES

MEDITERRANEAN SEA

Jerusalem

Amman

Ascalon

Alexandria

Capture of Jerusalem 1099

FATIMID CALIPHATE

Routes of the Crusaders

Battle

0   500   1000 km

0   200   400   600 miles

The Cathedral at Albi, southern France, built as a fortress to withstand religious opponents.

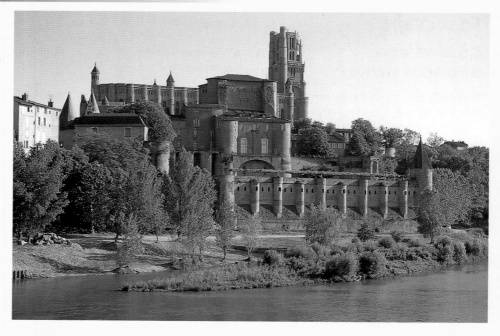

The crusades

Purpose: to recover Palestine from the Muslims, drive out the Moors in Spain, wipe out the Albigenses of France. The First Crusade, preached by Urban II, succeeded in setting up the Latin Kingdom of Jerusalem (1099-1187). The seven crusades in all did not accomplish the permanent freedom of the Holy Land but contributed to the weakening of feudalism, enhanced the power and prestige of the papacy, gave rise to the monastic military orders, stimulated East-West trade, and facilitated cultural exchange. The Fourth Crusade, diverted to Constantinople, set up the Latin Kingdom of Constantinople (1204-61), weakening the Eastern Empire and deepening the East-West church cleavage.

Attempted reform movements

(1) The Albigenses, called Cathari, around the city of Albi in southern France, resembled the Gnostics.

(2) The Waldenses followed Peter Waldo (c. 1150) in a simple back-to-Bible movement within the church.

(3) Monastic reforms were led by Bernard of Clairvaux, of the Cistercian order, and by the Knights Templars and Knights Hospitallers. The Mendicant orders, i.e., the Franciscans founded by Francis of Assisi (1182-1226) and the Dominicans founded by Dominic (1170-1221), also stressed reform.

Medieval theology

Scholasticism employed Aristotelian logic and philosophy to systematize Christian truth.

(1) Anselm of Canterbury (1033-1109), 'The Father of Systematic Theology,' was a realist, believing faith preceded reason. He wrote on the existence of God and the satisfaction theory of the atonement.

(2) Thomas Aquinas (1225-74) became the foremost Catholic theologian, especially in his *Summa Theologica*. He was a moderate realist, stressing the use of reason and Aristotelian logic to gain a degree of truth supplemented at a certain point by faith and revelation.

(3) John Duns Scotus (c. 1264-1308) opposed Aquinas and elaborated the theory of the immaculate conception of Mary.

(4) Others contributing to this era and development were Abelard (1079-1142), Bernard of Clairvaux (1091-1153), Peter Lombard (c. 1100-1160), Albert Magnus (c. 1206-80), William of Occam (c. 1300-49).

The church and learning in Medieval Europe

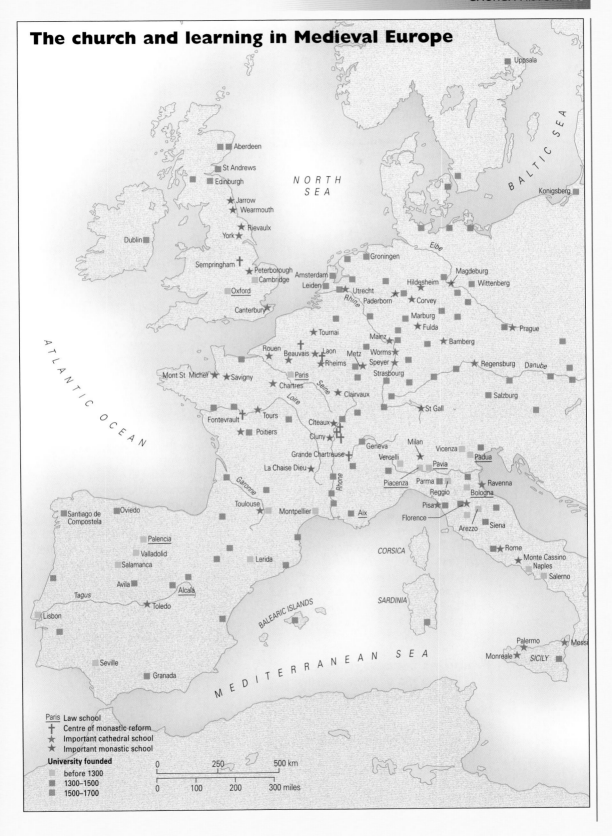

BALTIC SEA

Uppsala

Konigsberg

Aberdeen

St Andrews

Edinburgh

NORTH
SEA

Jarrow
Wearmouth

Rievaulx

York

Dublin

Elbe

Groningen

Magdeburg

Sempringham

Peterborough
Cambridge

Amsterdam
Leiden

Hildesheim

Wittenberg

Oxford

Utrecht
Paderborn

Corvey

Canterbury

Rhine

Marburg
Fulda

Prague

Tournai

Mainz

Bamberg

Rouen
Beauvais
Mont St Michel

Savigny

Laon
Rheims

Metz

Worms
Speyer

Regensburg

Danube

Paris

Strasbourg

Chartres

Seine

Clairvaux

St Gall

Salzburg

Loire

Fontevrault

Tours

Citeaux

Cluny

Milan

Vicenza

Padua

Poitiers

Grande Chartreuse

Geneva
Vercelli

Pavia

La Chaise Dieu

Rhone

Piacenza

Parma

Reggio

Ravenna

Bologna

ATLANTIC OCEAN

Garonne

Toulouse

Montpellier

Aix

Pisa
Florence

Arezzo

Siena

Santiago de
Compostela

Oviedo

CORSICA

Rome

Monte Cassino
Naples

Palencia

Valladolid

Lerida

Salerno

Salamanca

Tagus

Avila

Alcala

SARDINIA

Lisbon

Toledo

BALEARIC ISLANDS

Palermo

Messi

Seville

Monreale

SICILY

Granada

MEDITERRANEAN SEA

Paris — Law school

✝ Centre of monastic reform

★ Important cathedral school

★ Important monastic school

University founded

■ before 1300

■ 1300–1500

■ 1500–1700

0   250   500 km

0   100   200   300 miles

Statue of the Czech reformer John Huss, Prague.

1305-1517
Early movement toward reformation

Need for church reform (1305-1517). Immorality of the clergy, sale of indulgences and church offices; heavy papal taxes; papal interference in state affairs; the 'Babylonian Captivity' of the papacy at Avignon, France (1309-77); the Great Schism of 1378-1417, with rival popes at Rome and Avignon, all indicated the need for reform.

Pressures toward reform

(1) Groups more biblically oriented, like the mystics, the Friends of God, and the Brethren of the Common Life, exerted a wide influence.

(2) John Wycliffe (c. 1329-84), 'Morning Star of the Reformation,' translated the Bible into English and vigorously attacked papal authority and the mass (1378).

(3) John Huss (c. 1369-1415), Bohemian reformer, influenced by Wycliffe's ideas, condemned the sale of indulgences and proposed reform in the church.

(4) Savonarola (1452-98), a Florentine monk, preached against papal vice.

(5) Series of councils between 1409 and 1439 aimed at reform.

(6) The Renaissance of learning and the new interest in the Hebrew and Greek Scriptures exposed the unscriptural accretions of the medieval church.

(7) The rise of strong national states (especially England and France), and disenchantment with papal corruption, interference, taxation, and land ownership by the church, all favored reform.

Modern period
1517 to the present

1517-1648

Protestant Reformation era

Popes of the Reformation era

Pope Leo X (1513-21) dispatched John Tetzel to Germany to sell indulgences to raise funds to complete St. Peter's basilica in Rome. It was Leo's bull of excommunication which Luther burned on December 10, 1520. Pope Leo was followed by Pope Adrian V (1522-23) and Clement VII (1523-34). Pope Paul III (1534-49) authorized the formation of the Jesuits and instigated a war against German Protestants (1546-49), which was continued through the reign of Julius III (1550-55).

Luther and the break with Rome

Martin Luther (1483-1546), an Augustinian monk, became the greatest human emancipator since the apostle Paul.

Influences shaping his life

(1) Strict, superstitious peasant background. (2) Scholastic education in preparation for a career in law. (3) The sudden death of a friend, a narrow escape during a severe thunderstorm, and a deep consciousness of sin caused him to enter a monastery of the Augustinian order in 1505. He was ordained two years later. (4) While training for a professorship he received spiritual counsel and encouragement from Johann von Staupitz, the vicar-general of his order. (5) November 1510 to April 1511, he was shocked at corruption and practices in Rome, while there on business for his order. (6) Studied Scripture, St. Augustine, J. Tauler (mystic) and the *Theologica Germanica.* (7) Became convinced of the authority of the Bible and justification by faith *alone* as he lectured at the University of Wittenberg as doctor of theology and professor of Scripture. By close of 1516 Luther was assured of his own salvation, and the watchword became 'The righteous will live by faith' (Rom 1:17).

The growing break.

(1) October 31, 1517, Luther posted his Ninety-five Theses against the abuse of the indulgence system. This was prompted by extravagant preaching of John Tetzel (1470-1519), an agent of Albrecht of Brandenburg, archbishop of Mainz and archbishop of Magdeburg, who had been authorized by Pope Leo X to sell indulgences for construction of St.

Martin Luther (1483-1546).

Peter's in Rome. (2) Engaged in several debates, he was forced to the logical conclusions of his basic premises regarding faith and Scripture. (3) June 15, 1520, Pope Leo X gave Luther 60 days to submit in the papal bull *Exurge Domine*. (4) He wrote three treatises, *Address to the German Nobility, Babylonian Captivity* and *On the Freedom of Christian Men* (1520). (5) Famous 'Here I Stand' speech at Diet of Worms was made in April 1521. Put under imperial ban, he was kidnapped by friends.

Rise of Lutheranism (1) In 1522 Luther translated the NT into German while in hiding at Wartburg Castle. (2) On June 13, 1525, Luther married Katherine von Bora (1499-1552). (3) At Diet of Speier in 1529, Lutheran princes read their *Protestation,* hence the word protestant. (4) In 1529 at the Marburg Colloquy, Luther and Zwingli disagreed over the words 'this is my body' in the communion. The *Small Catechism* was published. (5) In 1530 the Augsburg Confession, the first Protestant confession, was drawn up stating the Lutheran position. Philip Melanchthon (1497-1560) was the chief author. He also wrote *Loci Communes,* the first Protestant theology, in 1521. (6) Lutherans began to ordain their own clergy (1535). (7) The Schmalkald wars in Germany began the year Luther died (1546). They were concluded at the Peace of Augsburg (1555), which extended legal rights to Lutherans as well as Roman Catholics. The principle of two religions in Germany, *cuius regio, ejus religio* ('In a prince's country, the prince's religion') was established. (8) After Luther's death controversies marred the unity of the Lutherans until they agreed on the Formula of Concord, completed in 1577 and published in 1580 as the *Book of Concord,* the definitive statement of Lutheran theology. (9) By the sixth decade of the 16th cen. Lutheranism had spread to all the Scandinavian countries and its reformational ideas to other countries.

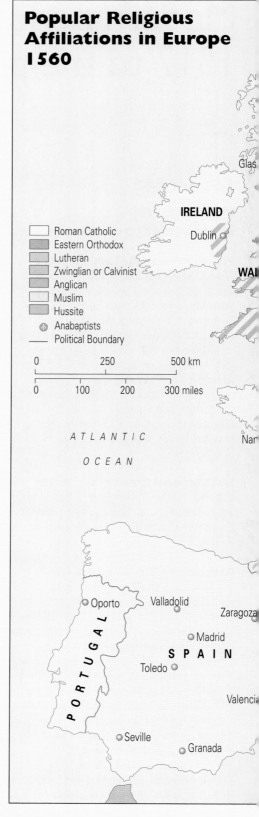

Popular Religious Affiliations in Europe 1560

- Roman Catholic
- Eastern Orthodox
- Lutheran
- Zwinglian or Calvinist
- Anglican
- Muslim
- Hussite
- Anabaptists
- Political Boundary

| 0 | 250 | 500 km |
| 0 | 100 | 200 | 300 miles |

IRELAND

Glas

Dublin

WAI

Nar

ATLANTIC

OCEAN

Oporto

Valladolid

Zaragoza

Madrid

SPAIN

Toledo

PORTUGAL

Valencia

Seville

Granada

NORWAY

SWEDEN

FINLAND

ESTONIA

RUSSIA

Stockholm

LIVONIA

COURLAND

NORTH SEA

DENMARK

BALTIC SEA

LITHUANIA

Copenhagen

Konigsberg

PRUSSIA

Danzig

COTLAND

nburgh

York

NGLAND

Warsaw

Groningen

Bremen Hamburg

P O L A N D

Amsterdam

Magdeburg

Munster

London

Antwerp

Wittenberg

anterbury

HOLY ROMAN

Zwickau

EMPIRE

Frankfurt

Prague

Rouen

Rheims

Edict of Worms, 1521,
condemns Lutheranism

BOHEMIA

MORAVIA

Brno

Paris

Regensburg

Worms

Augsburg

Vienna

Tours

Munich

Budapest

Zurich

Salzburg

Poitiers

Nevers

Peace of Augsburg, 1555,
recognizes existence of
Lutheranism

H U N G A R Y

F R A N C E

Lyons

Geneva

Milan

Venice

Bucharest

rdeaux

Modena

Ferrara

ADRIATIC SEA

Avignon

Florence

O T T O M A N
E M P I R E

Toulouse

Marseilles

PAPAL
STATES

Barcelona

Rome

KINGDOM
OF NAPLES

Naples

MEDITERRANEAN SEA

SICILY

The rise of the Reformed faith

In Switzerland Reformation came to Berne and Zurich through Ulrich Zwingli (1484-1531), who successfully opposed the Roman practices of indulgences, mass, celibacy, images and other unscriptural practices of his day in his *Commentary on True and False Religions* (1525). Geneva joined the Reformation under the preaching of Guillaume Farel (1489-1565), a French Protestant, and the teaching and organizing ability of John Calvin (1509-64), who after 1536 became the leader of the Reformed faith. Calvin's *Institutes of the Christian Religion* (1536) and his *Ecclesiastical Ordinances* (1541) remain classics today.

In France French Protestants created a Reformed Church in 1559 at a synod which adopted the Gallican Confession of Faith. After 1560 they were called Huguenots and became the target of persecution and religious wars, until the Edict of Nantes (1598) granted religious freedom. The terrible massacre of St. Bartholomew was begun in 1572 and in all, between 10,000 and 20,000 were killed. Admiral Coligny, leader of the Huguenots, was one of those murdered, apparently at the instigation of Catherine de Medici, a niece of Pope Clement VII.

In Scotland Patrick Hamilton (1504-28) preached reform and was consequently burned in 1528, and George Wishart (1513-46) was burned for his faith in 1546. John Knox (1513-72) between 1560 and 1567 secured the aid of Scottish nobility and merchants, defeating the attempt of Mary Stuart (Queen of Scots) to keep Scotland in Rome's fold. Knox established the Presbyterian church in Scotland in 1567.

In Holland Religious freedom from Rome was linked with the struggle for political freedom from Catholic Spain. The Reformed church was established in 1571, and political emancipation in 1581. William of Orange was the political liberator. James Arminius (1560-1609) rejected Calvinism, making divine grace resistable and the atonement unlimited. Although the Calvinistic Synod of Dort (1618) pronounced against Arminianism, it survives in some branches of Protestantism today.

In Northern Ireland James I of England (1566-1625), who sponsored the Authorized or King James Version of the Bible (1611), colonized Scottish Presbyterians in Northern Ireland after 1603 to reduce potential revolt. This resulted in the religious division of Ireland into Protestant North and Catholic South.

In the rest of Europe Calvinism and the Reformed faith also spread into Bohemia, Hungary and the German Palatinate.

The Anabaptist movement This group rejected a state church and infant baptism. Emerging from the Zwinglian movement in Zurich in 1525 under the leadership of Conrad Grebel (c.1490-1526), they required the rebaptism of all adult believers. They were called Anabaptists (baptize over again) as a term of derision. The movement spread to Germany and Moravia. Menno Simons (c. 1496-c. 1561) was converted to Anabaptist teachings from the Roman priesthood in 1536 to become the leader of the movement in Holland which bears his name (Mennonites). Basic beliefs of the Anabaptists include the authority of the Scriptures, believers' church, baptism of believers (no uniformity in mode among early movement), and separation of church and state.

England's break with Rome Henry VIII (reigned 1509-47) declared the church in England independent of the pope in the Act of Supremacy (1534), which made the king and his successors the only supreme head on earth of the church in England. He confiscated monastic properties, and gave the people the Scriptures in common English (the Great Bible). During the reign of Edward VI (1547-53) the ecclesiastical reform begun by Henry became essentially Protestant. Thomas Cranmer drew up the Forty-two Articles and the *Book of Common Prayer*. Mary Tudor (Bloody Mary, 1553-58) vainly sought to reinstate Catholicism. Large numbers of Protestants were martyred for their faith,

Cranmer, Ridley and Latimer among them.

The Elizabethan Settlement under Elizabeth I (1558-1603) re-established Protestantism as Anglicanism, the 'Middle Way.' *The Book of Common Prayer* was revised, and the Forty-two Articles were revised and reduced to Thirty-nine Articles, being then made the creed of the Church of England by Parliament in 1563. The papacy retaliated by excommunicating Elizabeth (1570), establishing a Jesuit training school at Douai in Flanders to train missionaries to recapture England, and enlisting the aid of Philip of Spain, who sent the great Spanish Armada against England. This effort was defeated in 1588, reducing the threat of the papacy.

The Puritan movement

Puritanism arose out of dissatisfaction with the Elizabethan Settlement. Advocating a more thorough break with Romanism, some wanted to purify the state Anglican Church further, change its polity to Congregationalism or Presbyterianism or separate entirely from it in the interest of doctrinal or ecclesiastical purity. Various Baptist

groups also emerged, such as General Baptists (affusionists and Arminians) and the Particular Baptists (immersionists and Calvinistic). In 1604 James I called the Hampton Court Conference to satisfy Puritan requests for further reform. The only result was authorization of the translation of the Scriptures, the celebrated King James Version (1611). Many Puritans migrated to America between 1629 and 1640. Others engaged in civil wars (1642-49) which left Puritans dominant. The Westminster Assembly met 1643-53 and formulated the Calvinistic Westminster Confession. Charles I was executed in 1649, and after the establishment of the Commonwealth Oliver Cromwell emerged as Lord Protector.

1546-1648

Catholic Counter Reformation

Within less than half a century the Protestant movement made tremendous gains in Europe. Most of the Continent, except Italy and Spain, appeared lost to the papacy. France was being threatened.

Replica of the 'Mayflower', one of the ships used by the Pilgrim Fathers.

To counteract the Protestant gains the Roman church sought to regain lost adherents, keep others from leaving the fold, and reform the church, thus removing some of the causes for the Reformation. Important to the movement are the following: (1) The impetus given to the reform movement by the Oratory of Divine Love. (2) The Jesuit order was founded by the Spaniard Ignatius of Loyola (1491-1556) and sanctioned by Pope Paul II in 1540. It required absolute, unquestioning obedience to the pope, thus providing the Roman Catholic church with one of its most effective weapons with which to stop defections, reclaim lost followers and deal with heresy. (3) The Council of Trent (1545-63), dominated by Italians, among other things dogmatized the medieval theology of the Scholastics. It made the Latin Vulgate, including 11 OT apocryphal books, the authorized Bible, and declared Scripture *and* tradition as ultimate authority. (4) The Inquisition, although of earlier origin, was employed as a means of dealing with heresy and defectors by papal bull in 1542. Ruthless tactics were employed to secure confessions and convictions of the accused. (5) The Index, a list of books not to be read by the faithful, was drawn up as early as 1543.

The Thirty Years' War (1618-1648). This was a struggle of Protestantism against Catholic intolerance in the Holy Roman Empire. The Bohemian and Danish phase (1618-29) was a victory for Rome. The Swedish phase (1630-34) saved Protestantism as the army of Gustavus Adolphus of Sweden defeated the Catholic armies. The final phase (1635-48) was a struggle of the House of Hapsburg against France, with the latter emerging as the strongest state in Europe. The Treaty of Westphalia (1648) gave legal status to Lutheranism and Calvinism, allowing lands which were Protestant prior to 1624 to legally remain so.

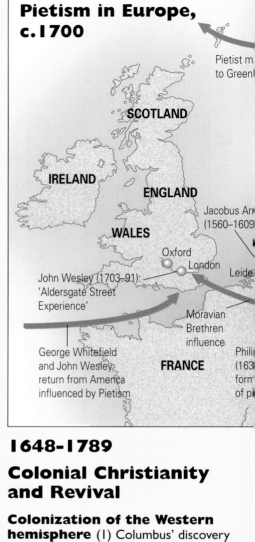

Pietism in Europe, c.1700

SCOTLAND

IRELAND

ENGLAND

WALES

Oxford

London

John Wesley (1703-91): 'Aldersgate Street Experience'

George Whitefield and John Wesley return from America influenced by Pietism

Pietist m to Green

Jacobus Ar (1560-1609

Leide

Moravian Brethren influence

FRANCE

Phili (163 form of pi

1648-1789

Colonial Christianity and Revival

Colonization of the Western hemisphere (1) Columbus' discovery of the New World (1492) had as one goal wider fields where the church might be planted. (2) English explorers took possession of the Atlantic seaboard. (3) Pilgrims settled at Plymouth in 1620. (4) John Endicott and the Puritans settled at Salem, New England (1628). (5) Connecticut was settled (1636-62). (6) Maryland was founded by Cecil Calvert in 1634, a Roman Catholic. (7) The Quakers under William Penn settled in Pennsylvania in 1681. (8) Georgia was settled by James Oglethorpe. (9) Protestantism was destined to predominate in North America, Catholicism in South America.

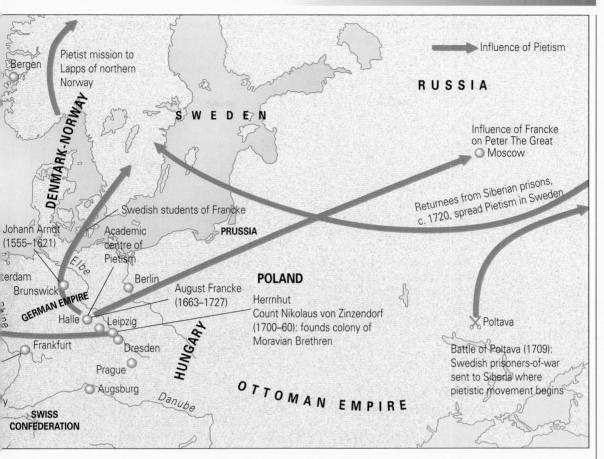

Bergen

Pietist mission to Lapps of northern Norway

RUSSIA

Influence of Pietism

DENMARK-NORWAY

S W E D E N

Influence of Francke on Peter The Great
Moscow

Swedish students of Francke

PRUSSIA

Returnees from Siberian prisons, c. 1720, spread Pietism in Sweden

Johann Arndt (1555–1621)

Academic centre of Pietism

Elbe

:erdam
Brunswick

GERMAN EMPIRE

Berlin

POLAND

August Francke (1663–1727)

Herrnhut
Count Nikolaus von Zinzendorf (1700–60): founds colony of Moravian Brethren

Poltava

Halle   Leipzig

HUNGARY

Battle of Poltava (1709): Swedish prisoners-of-war sent to Siberia where pietistic movement begins

Frankfurt

Dresden

Prague

Augsburg

Danube

O T T O M A N   E M P I R E

y

SWISS CONFEDERATION

Higher education in the colonies

A number of colleges were founded, such as Harvard (1636), William and Mary (1693), Yale (1701), Princeton (1746), Brown (1764), Rutgers (1766) and Haverford (1833). Most early schools were formed for the training of ministers.

Roman Catholic missions

Spanish conquest of Mexico (1520) was followed by 'conversion' of the natives to Roman ceremonies. French Jesuits (Joliet, Father Marquette and La Salle) planted mission stations in the Mississippi Valley taking possession for France, calling the territory Louisiana.

Religious revival in America

In New Jersey in 1726 under Theodore Frelinghuysen revival came among the Dutch Reformed people and spread to the Scotch-Irish Presbyterians under Gilbert Tennent and then through the Middle Colonies. George Whitefield furthered the revival in 1739. In New England Jonathan Edwards (1703-58) preached with power. The revival in the Southern Colonies was predominantly spread by the Baptists and Methodists. As a result, new life was infused into the churches and many were converted. This provided impetus to missions and education, created schisms, and demonstrated the possibility of intercolonial co-operation, thus aiding the War of Independence which was to follow.

Forms of revival in Europe

Pietism developed as a reaction to the cold orthodoxy of Lutheranism in Germany. Founded by Philip Spener (1635-1705), the University of Halle became the center of the movement, which turned out a number of missionaries. In addition to infusing new life into Lutheranism, it contributed also to the Moravian awakening under Count von Zinzendorf (1700-1760).

Spiritual awakening in England

The Wesleyan Revival under John Wesley (1703-91) and his hymn writer brother Charles influenced England after 1738. George Fox (1624-91) had founded Quakerism in 1648 and Robert Barclay, Quaker theologian, declared the inner light provided continuing direction and inspiration.

Rationalism and deism

Descartes (1596-1650) founded modern philosophy. Spinoza (1632-77) advocated pantheism. Deism taught a transcendent God and stressed man's goodness and perfectibility. This was a result of advance in science and the rationalistic philosophy of Locke, Leibnitz, Kant, Voltaire, Rousseau and Lessing. Deism developed in England and then spread to France and Germany. Deism and Unitarianism spread to America.

1789-1914

Protestantism and Romanism

American Christianity in the National Era

The War of Independence weakened the churches. Deism and infidelity became rampant (1775-1800). Thomas Paine's *Age of Reason* (1794) and the anti-religious aspects of the French Revolution had their negative effect. The expanding frontier had a great demoralizing influence, thus creating an extensive spiritual need.

The second Great Awakening

This began in several eastern colleges after 1786 and went up and down the seaboard. It spread to the western frontier beginning in Logan County, Kentucky, about 1800. Results were seen in new believers and churches, schisms and new denominations, a new sense of church freedom, moral reform, frontier camp meetings, new colleges, new seminaries such as Princeton and Andover, a spread of domestic and foreign missionary work (Adoniram Judson and others), and the formation of numerous Bible and tract societies.

Concerns for social reform

As a result of the spiritual awakening and a growing concern about existing conditions, the church became more actively involved in social activities. (1) Churches sponsored temperance and anti-slavery campaigns (the slavery question split Methodists, Presbyterians and Baptists). (2) YMCA and gospel mission work was projected. (3) Growth of the Sunday school was helped. This was a great boon to American Christianity. (4) Mormonism, Seventh-Day Adventism, Christian Science, and Spiritualism came on the scene, capitalizing on human and social concerns. (5) The 'social gospel' of Walter Rauschenbusch (1861-1918) advocated education and legislation rather than evangelism as the means of spiritual advance.

The papacy and the French Revolution

Rousseau, Montesquieu, and Voltaire attacked the Roman Church in France. Church lands were declared public property in France (1789). The church was ignominiously humiliated during the Revolution.

The papacy and Napoleon

The Concordat of 1801 recognized the Catholic religion as the religion of the majority but not as the established faith, nor did it return church property taken in 1790.

British Christianity

This became a vital force in the 19th cen. (1) Missionary work was projected in many lands, beginning in India with William Carey (1793) and in Africa with David Livingstone (1813-73). (2) Charles Haddon Spurgeon (1834-92) and others preached to multitudes in England. (3) Booth's Salvation Army (1865), John Darby's (1800-1882) Plymouth Brethren and other small nonconformist groups arose. (4) The Church of England had an influential segment represented by William Wilberforce (1759-1833) and John Newton (1725-1807), who were concerned with evangelism and social reform, especially the abolition of the slave trade (1807) and slavery itself

(1833), as well as social and economic reforms among laborers.

Foes of Christianity

(1) Rationalistic biblical criticism developed, based on the philosophy of Immanuel Kant (1724-1804), Georg Hegel (1770-1831), and Albrecht Ritschl (1822-89). Denial of Mosaic authorship and the authenticity of the Pentateuch were advanced by Johann Eichhorn (1752-1827), Hermann Hupfeld, Karl Graf and Julius Wellhausen. The Wellhausen theory makes the Pentateuch a compilation of late unreliable documents from about 800-500 B.C. Unity of Isaiah was attacked, as well as the historicity of Daniel. (2) Evolution was fostered by Darwin's *The Origin of Species* (1859) and *The Descent of Man* (1871).
(3) Communism was rooted in the materialistic philosophy of Karl Marx (1818-83) and of Friedrich Engels in the *Communist Manifesto* (1848).

Papal gains (1815-70). (1) The Jesuits (disbanded by papal action in 1773) were restored by Pius VII (1814). (2) This period of Romanticism was favorable to the colorful ritualism of the Roman Church. (3) Metternich, the powerful Austrian chancellor, favored Rome, and the Congress of Vienna, over which he presided, restored the papal states to the pope. (4) The Oxford Movement in the Anglican Church saw more than 600 prominent Anglicans and 250 Anglican clergymen return to the Roman faith between 1845 and 1862. (5) The reign of Pius IX (1846-78) resulted in two outstanding declarations: the doctrine of the Immaculate Conception of Mary (1854); and the decree of Papal Infallibility (1870) by the First Vatican Council. This doctrine claims that whenever the pope speaks *ex cathedra* (i.e., as the head of the church on earth), he is infallible in matters of faith and morals.

Papal losses (1870-1914). (1) Almost immediately after the declaration of papal infalliblity, anticlerical hostility developed. (2) When Italy was unified the pope lost his temporal power, retaining only the Vatican properties. (3) To build a strong unified Germany, Chancellor Bismarck stripped the church of much of her power in 1871. (4) In France a severe blow was administered in the Separation Law of 1905, which separated church and state. Even church property was confiscated by the state. The Roman Catholic church has not to this present time been able effectively to regain France for the papacy although her population is nominally Catholic.

1914 to the present

Protestantism and Romanism

Liberal-Fundamentalist controversy (1920-34). Liberalism was opposed by conservatism in theology. Evolution was attacked (Scopes Trial, 1925). J. Gresham Machen in 1929 withdrew from Princeton Seminary to champion orthodoxy. The Bible conference and Bible institute era was launched: Nyack Missionary College (1882) and Moody Bible Institute, Chicago (1886). Nearly 40 Bible institutes were founded between 1930 and 1940. Christian colleges come to the fore (Wheaton, Calvin, etc.).

Neo-orthodoxy Karl Barth and Emil Brunner adopted liberal biblical criticism, rejecting biblical inerrancy and full authority of the Scriptures. The movement, while unsound, did not produce the theological sterility of old-time liberalism. The Roman Church met liberalism by an attempt to adapt Aquinas' theology to the modern scientific era (neo-Thomism).

Advance of cults Christian Science, Mormonism and Jehovah's Witnesses are growing at a rapid rate throughout the world to further complicate the complex contemporary religious scene.

Present-day popes Pope Leo XIII (1878-1903) was an ardent claimer of papal infallibility. He denounced

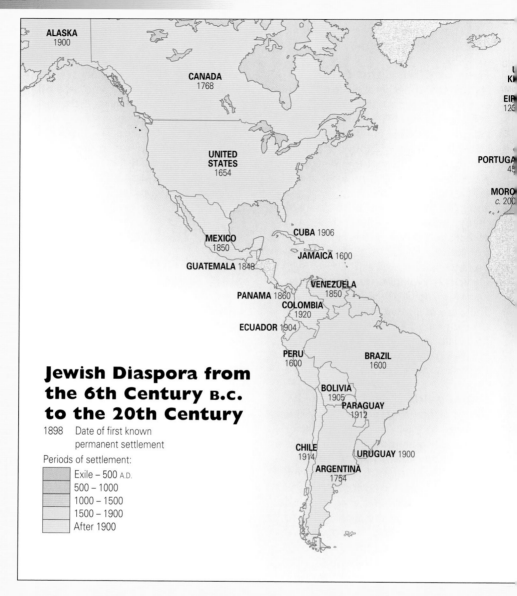

ALASKA
1900

CANADA
1768

UNITED
STATES
1654

MEXICO
1850

CUBA 1906

JAMAICA 1600

GUATEMALA 1848

VENEZUELA
1850

PANAMA 1860

COLOMBIA
1920

ECUADOR 1904

PERU
1600

BRAZIL
1600

BOLIVIA
1905

PARAGUAY
1912

CHILE
1914

URUGUAY 1900

ARGENTINA
1754

U
K
EIR
12

PORTUGA
4

MORO
c. 200

Jewish Diaspora from the 6th Century B.C. to the 20th Century

1898   Date of first known
permanent settlement

Periods of settlement:

- Exile – 500 A.D.
- 500 – 1000
- 1000 – 1500
- 1500 – 1900
- After 1900

Protestants as 'enemies of the Christian name.' Leo XIII was followed by Pius X (1903-14), Benedict XV (1914-22), and Pius XI (1922-39). During the reign of Pius XII (1939-58) the dogma of Mary's bodily Assumption was promulgated (1950). He with his immediate predecessor lacked the ecumenical emphasis exhibited by John XXIII (1958-63) and John's more conservative successor, Paul VI (1963-78). John Paul II (1978) has continued this conservative trend, reaffirming a hard line on birth control and urging Latin American clergy not to get involved in politics.

Vatican II An ecumenical council held from 1962 to 1965, Vatican II welcomed non-Catholics as 'separated brethren' and called for renewal within the Roman church. Popes John XXIII and Paul VI presided over a modernization that attempted to make the church better serve the world. Some results: worship services began to employ the language of the people; the Bible was considered more authoritative, and its use in worship services increased; and Catholics took a more active part in social concerns.

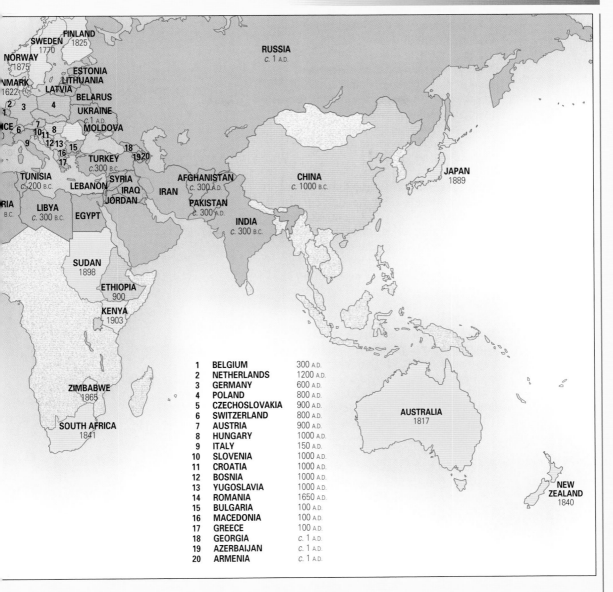

SWEDEN 1770
FINLAND 1825
NORWAY 1875
DENMARK 1622
ESTONIA
LITHUANIA
LATVIA
BELARUS
UKRAINE c.1 A.D.
MOLDOVA
RUSSIA c. 1 A.D.
JAPAN 1889
TUNISIA c.200 B.C.
LEBANON
SYRIA
IRAQ
JORDAN
IRAN
AFGHANISTAN c. 300 A.D.
PAKISTAN c. 300 A.D.
CHINA c. 1000 B.C.
TURKEY c.300 B.C.
LIBYA c. 300 B.C.
EGYPT
INDIA c. 300 B.C.
SUDAN 1898
ETHIOPIA 900
KENYA 1903
ZIMBABWE 1865
SOUTH AFRICA 1841
AUSTRALIA 1817
NEW ZEALAND 1840

1	BELGIUM	300 A.D.
2	NETHERLANDS	1200 A.D.
3	GERMANY	600 A.D.
4	POLAND	800 A.D.
5	CZECHOSLOVAKIA	900 A.D.
6	SWITZERLAND	800 A.D.
7	AUSTRIA	900 A.D.
8	HUNGARY	1000 A.D.
9	ITALY	150 A.D.
10	SLOVENIA	1000 A.D.
11	CROATIA	1000 A.D.
12	BOSNIA	1000 A.D.
13	YUGOSLAVIA	1000 A.D.
14	ROMANIA	1650 A.D.
15	BULGARIA	100 A.D.
16	MACEDONIA	100 A.D.
17	GREECE	100 A.D.
18	GEORGIA	c. 1 A.D.
19	AZERBAIJAN	c. 1 A.D.
20	ARMENIA	c. 1 A.D.

Ecumenicity This is a movement toward Christian unity. Within Catholicism, it seeks to attract 'non-Catholic Christians' back to the fold. Among Protestants, ecumenism is largely American inspired and led. Various groups have engaged in organic union or confederation in the quest of Christian unity. In some cases elements of the same denomination have united to form a united body (United Presbyterian Church in the U.S.A., etc.). Other groups have crossed denominational lines to create an entirely new denomination (United Church of Canada). Liberal and neo-orthodox leaders reason that all church members are believers, therefore all church members are one in Christ. The latter support the liberally orientated National Council of Churches of Christ in America and the World Council of Churches. Conservatives, realizing that true Christian unity is not predicated on organic unity, doctrinal relativity and uniformity, sponsor such organizations as the National Association of Evangelicals (1950) and its international organization, the World Evangelical Fellowship (1951), or the American Council of Churches (1941)

and its International Council of Christian
Churches (1948).

The Charismatic movement

One of the most important
developments in recent church history is
the phenomenal growth of the
charismatic movement, particularly
among mainline denominations, both
Protestant and Catholic.

The rise of Communism Not

even in existence until the 20th century,
this atheistic system now controls some
1.6 billion people, and threatens many
countries throughout the world.
Communist governments usually try to
destroy Christianity, and persecution in
communist countries is severe, although
small pockets of faith inevitably remain.

Advance and decline in
numbers worldwide At the

beginning of the twentieth century,
portions of the Bible had been translated
into 67 languages. By the early 21st
century, this number had increased to
2,167, potentially reaching 97 percent of
the world's population.

Use of the media by Christians has put
the gospel within the reach of many
millions, changing the nature of both
missionary work and the life of the
church. Close to 1,500 radio and TV
stations throughout the world were
Christian-oriented in 1980.

In Africa, Latin America and the Far
East, there has been a tremendous
growth of evangelical Christianity. In the
former communist world – and especially
in Eastern Europe – a clearly strong,
albeit hard to measure, evangelical
movement is taking hold. In the United
States, there has been church growth, but
not enough to keep up with the rise in
population. Western Europe has
experienced a dramatic decline in
Christian faith.

Principal Religions of the World

Jewish faith (Judaism) is the doctrines and rites of the descendants of Jacob as prescribed by the laws of Moses.

Islam (whose adherents are Muslims) is the sternly monotheistic religion founded by Muhammad (died 632). The Koran is its scripture.

Hinduism, the religion of India, is a constellation of many widely divergent beliefs and deities, with a general tendency towards Monism.

Buddhism views the world as both illusory and full of pain; and so presents a system of ascetic self-abnegation for leaving the material plane. The Buddha (6th c. B.C.) is sometimes worshipped.

Chinese Folk Religion is a combination of Buddhism, Taoism (a mystical philosophy which teaches conformity to nature), magic, and Animism (the belief that material objects are indwelt by spirits).

Tribal Religion is generally Animistic (see above), and reveres deities peculiar to a certain location and a certain group of people.

The Sikh religion is a combination of Hindu and Islamic elements. Founded about 1500 A.D., it is monotheistic.

Confucianism is the ethical, political, and philosophic system involving strong veneration of ancestors – living and dead – taught by Confucius of China (551-478 B.C.).

Bahaism is a 19th c. offshoot of Islam, teaching the spiritual unity of mankind and the truth of all religious beliefs.

Jainism is perhaps the oldest organized religion, restricted to India and teaching the liberation of the soul through ascetic practices.

Shintoism, a Japanese religion, is a mixture of the worship of nature, particularly the sun, and ancestor worship.

Communism is an atheistic philosophy of godless materialism which opposes religion. However, many who are under Communism's control are members of a religion nonetheless.

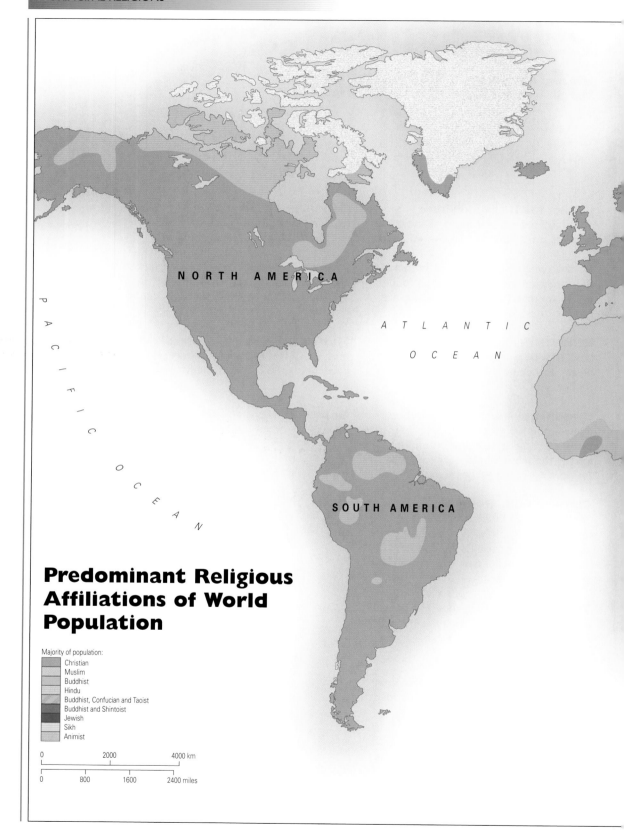

Predominant Religious Affiliations of World Population

Majority of population:
- Christian
- Muslim
- Buddhist
- Hindu
- Buddhist, Confucian and Taoist
- Buddhist and Shintoist
- Jewish
- Sikh
- Animist

NORTH AMERICA

SOUTH AMERICA

PACIFIC OCEAN

ATLANTIC OCEAN

0	2000	4000 km

0	800	1600	2400 miles

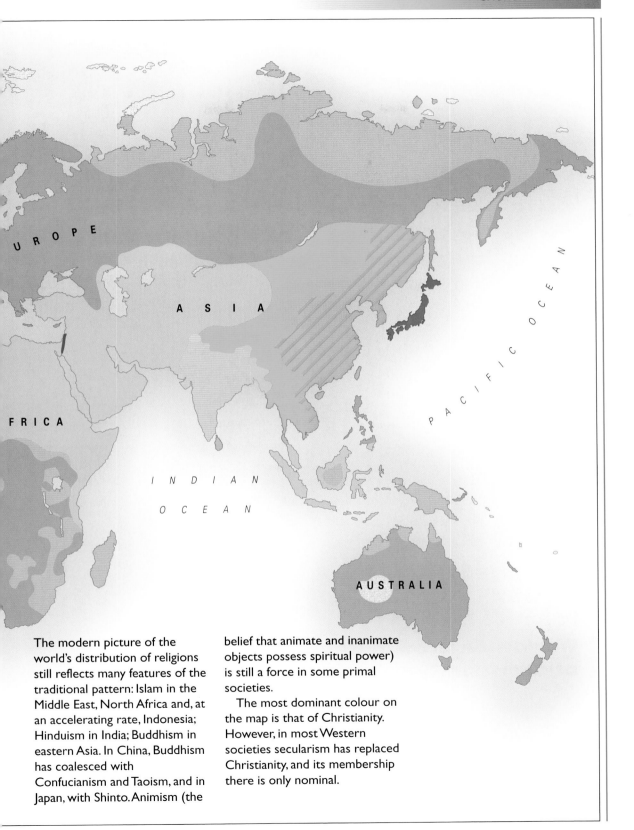

The modern picture of the world's distribution of religions still reflects many features of the traditional pattern: Islam in the Middle East, North Africa and, at an accelerating rate, Indonesia; Hinduism in India; Buddhism in eastern Asia. In China, Buddhism has coalesced with Confucianism and Taoism, and in Japan, with Shinto. Animism (the belief that animate and inanimate objects possess spiritual power) is still a force in some primal societies.

The most dominant colour on the map is that of Christianity. However, in most Western societies secularism has replaced Christianity, and its membership there is only nominal.

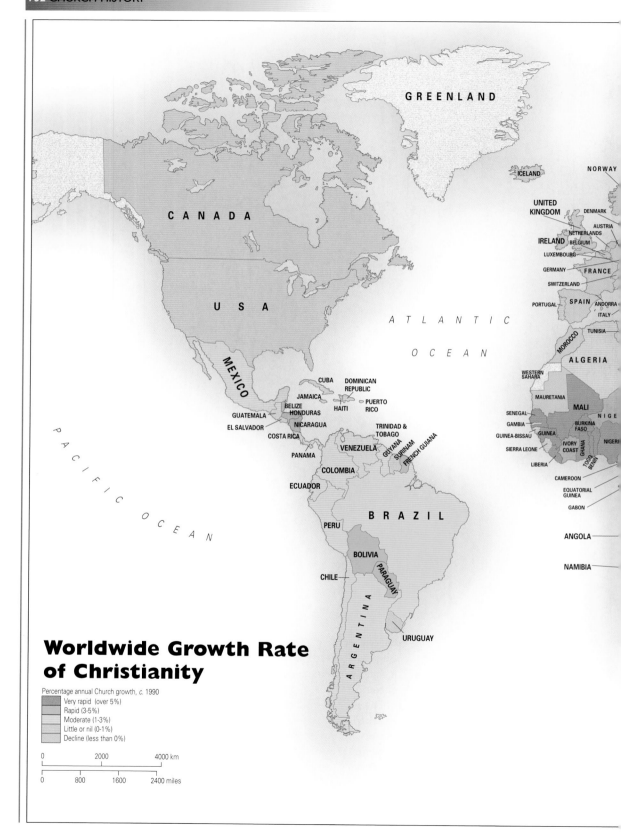

Worldwide Growth Rate of Christianity

Percentage annual Church growth, *c.* 1990

Very rapid (over 5%)
Rapid (3-5%)
Moderate (1-3%)
Little or nil (0-1%)
Decline (less than 0%)

0	2000	4000 km

0	800	1600	2400 miles

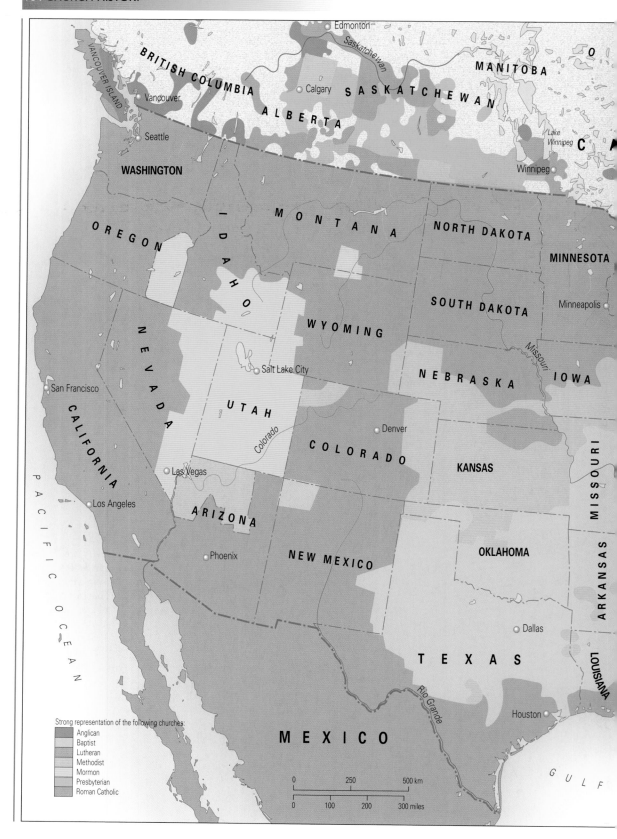

Strong representation of the following churches:
Anglican
Baptist
Lutheran
Methodist
Mormon
Presbyterian
Roman Catholic

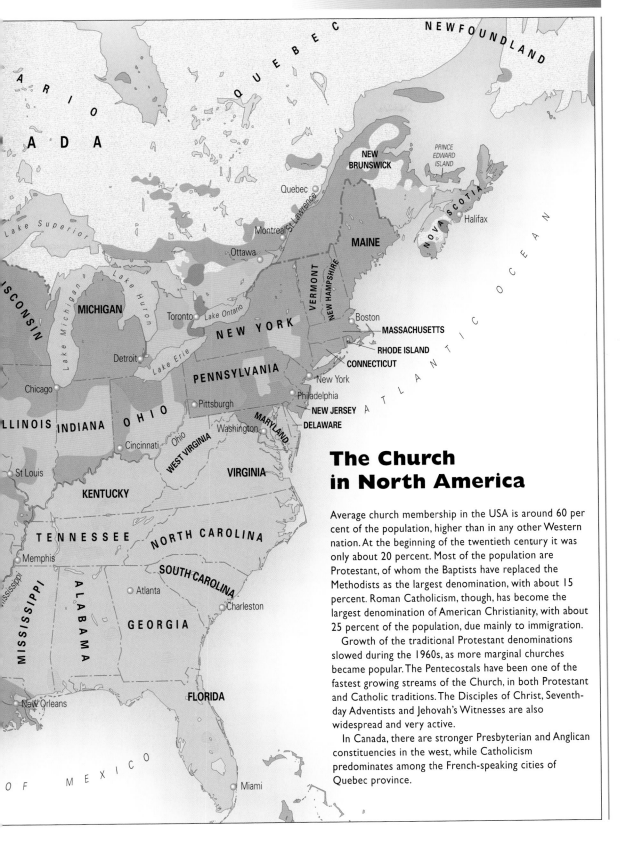

The Church in North America

Average church membership in the USA is around 60 per cent of the population, higher than in any other Western nation. At the beginning of the twentieth century it was only about 20 percent. Most of the population are Protestant, of whom the Baptists have replaced the Methodists as the largest denomination, with about 15 percent. Roman Catholicism, though, has become the largest denomination of American Christianity, with about 25 percent of the population, due mainly to immigration.

Growth of the traditional Protestant denominations slowed during the 1960s, as more marginal churches became popular. The Pentecostals have been one of the fastest growing streams of the Church, in both Protestant and Catholic traditions. The Disciples of Christ, Seventh-day Adventists and Jehovah's Witnesses are also widespread and very active.

In Canada, there are stronger Presbyterian and Anglican constituencies in the west, while Catholicism predominates among the French-speaking cities of Quebec province.

Index

A

Aaron 86, 94, 104, 106, 108
Aaron's rod 105, 106
Abel 42, 617
Abihu 94
Abijah 211
Abimelech 141
Abner 163–4
Abraham 24–6, 53–64, 504–6, 618
    covenant with 54, 58, 59, 63, 539–40, 613
Abram *see* Abraham
Absalom 168–9
Achan 128–9
Acts 464–99
Adadnirari III 198
Adam, covenant with 615
Adam and Eve 38, 40, 41–2
adultery 101–2
Agag 155
Agrippa 494
Ahab 179–81
Ahasuerus 225
Ahaz 192, 211
Ahaziah 185
Ahitophel 169
Ai 129
Albigenses 714
Alexander the Great 354, 365
    map 364
altars 87, 92, 129, 134, 361
Amaziah 191, 211
America 722–3, 724
    see also United States
Ammon 291, 345
Ammonites 141
Amnon 168
Amon 194, 213
Amos 327–31, 332

Anabaptism 720
Andrew 404
angels 602–4, 677
animism 729
Anna 425
Anselm 714
Antichrist 356
Antioch (Pisidia) 32, 476, 479
Antioch (Syria) 31, 471, 472, 476
Apocrypha 364, 368–9
Apollos 488
Apologists 706
apostasy 587–9
Arabia 265
Aram Naharaim 62
archaeology 23–32
    map 24–5
Arius 708
ark of the covenant 84, 105, 150, 151, 165, 202–3
Ark (Noah's) 44–5
Armageddon 268, 679–80, 681, 684
Arminius, James 720
Artaxerxes I Longimanus 221
Artemis 32
Asa 178, 211
Asaph 238–9
Ascension of Isaiah 370
asceticism 563
Ashurbanipal 198
Ashurnasipal II 198
Assumption of Moses 369
assurance 509–10, 651
Assyria 180, 192–3, 261–2, 282
    chart of kings 254
    judgment on 268, 270
    map of provinces 331
    see also Nineveh
Assyrian empire 194–5, 197–8
    map 198
Athaliah 188–9

Athanasius 696, 708
Athens 32, 483–5
atonement 96, 97
Augustine of Hippo 694, 709
authority 12, 642
Avignon 713, 716

B

Babel 24, 52–3, 55
Babylon 30, 263–5, 273–4 city 216
    exile in 286
    Jeremiah's prophecy against 292–3
    judgment on 263–4
    symbolic 678–9, 681–3
Babylonia 56
    exile in 195, 315
Babylonian empire, map 214
Bahaism 729
Balaam 108–10
baptism 445–8
    of Jesus 382, 402
Baptists 721
Barnabas 476, 478
    epistle 692
Bartholomew 404
Baruch 290
Basil the Great 695
Beatitudes 429
Bel and the Dragon 369
Belshazzar 30, 312–13
Berea 483
Bethel 65, 320
Bethlehem 31, 337, 423–5
    star of 381
Bible
    authority 642
    contents 11
    historical background 16–22
    name 8–9
    purpose 13
    statistics 703
    translations 698–702, 728
    transmission 690–702
blasphemy 97–8
Bodmer papyri 698
Body of Christ 546, 548–9
Boniface VIII (Pope) 713
Buddhism 729

C

Caesarea Palestine 31, 473–5
Caesarea Philippi 408
Cain 42
Caleb 131
calendar 118–19, 423
Calvary 459
Calvin, John 720
Cambyses 221
camp of Israelites in wilderness 102–3
Canaan 26, 613
    conquest 113, 125–34, 137
    maps 61, 127, 135, 139
    spied out 104
Canaanites 137
candlestick 85
canon
    New Testament 691–6
    Old Testament 690
Capernaum 31, 383, 405
Carmel 180
Carthage, Council of 694
censuses 31, 99, 100, 110, 171, 222, 423
centurions 432
Chalcedon, Definition of 709
Chaldean empire 214
Chaldeans 343
charismatic movement 728
Chester Beatty papyri 695, 698
childbirth 95
Chinese folk religion 729
Christ see Jesus Christ
Christian ministry 529–36
Christmas 423
Chronicles 200–16
Chrysostom, John 695
church 392–3
    councils 708–9
    growth rates 732–3
    history 704–35
    leaders 518, 520–2, 572–90, 592
        see also ministry
    map of early spread 469
    missionary expansion 711, 724
    unity 516, 549, 555, 557
circumcision 59, 127, 425
cities of refuge 113, 120, 132
    map 112
City of God 687–8
clean and unclean foods 94–5

Clement of Alexandria 695
Clement of Rome 694
    epistles 692
Codex Alexandrinus 697
Codex Bezae 698
Codex Ephraemi 698
Codex Sinaiticus 697
Colossae 32
Colossians 559–64
comfort 529, 572
Communism 728, 729
Confucianism 729
Constantinople, Councils of 708, 709
Corinth 32, 486–7
    plan 535
Corinthians, epistles to 515–36
Cornelius 471
Counter Reformation 721–2
covenant 9, 613
    with Abraham 54, 58, 59, 63, 539–40, 613
    with Adam 615
    broken 284
    concerning Canaan 613
    with David 165–6, 203, 613
    with Moses 80, 87–8, 611–12, 613
    new 542–3, 611, 612–15
    with Noah 613
    Palestinian 122–3
    renewal under Nehemiah 223
    and treaties 115
    under Joshua 134
creation 23, 37–8, 39–40
Crusades 713–14
Cyprus 472, 476, 494
Cyrus 30, 213, 218, 221, 273, 346

D

Damascus 181, 263, 291–2, 328, 469
Dan 144
Daniel 309–17
Darius I the Great 221, 313, 347
David 27, 155–71, 172–3, 202–3, 506
    campaign map 167
    covenant with 165–6, 203, 613
    and Psalms 232, 235–43
Day of the Lord 257–8, 266, 325–6, 329, 333, 345, 358, 568–9, 644–5
deacons 467, 579
Dead Sea Scrolls 31, 256, 372, 446

Deborah 138
Decalogue 82, 87–8, 116, 120
defilement 96
Deism 724
Demetrius 658
demonism 409, 434, 481
Derbe 476–8
Deuteronomy 114–24
devil see Satan
Didache 694, 962
Dinah 64
Dionysius of Alexandria 696
Diotrephes 658
disciples 403, 404, 429, 465
divination 120
divorce 121, 393
doctrinal error 561–2, 580, 642–4, 649, 651, 656, 660–1, 706
Duns Scotus 714

E

Ebal 129
Ecclesiastes 248–50
Ecclesiasticus 369
ecumenicity 726, 727–8
Eden 23, 38–42, 613
Edom 265, 291, 305, 333, 360
Egnatian Way 483
Egypt 56–8, 70–2, 263
    and Abraham 26, 54
    in Ezekiel's prophecy 304
    flight into 382
    Israelites in 27, 74
    and Jeremiah 290–1
    and Joseph 67–8
    judgment on 264
    map 75
    plagues 76–8
    warning against alliance with 268
Elam 292
elders 581, 592, 639, 670
election 547, 566
Elephantine 30
Eli 150
Elijah 180, 185
    map 187
Elisha 185–8
    map 187
Elizabeth I (Queen of England) 720–1
England 724–5

Reformation 720–1
Enoch 617
  Book of 370
Enuma elish 39
Ephesians 546–53
Ephesus 32, 486–92
  plan 577
Ephraim 68, 131, 267, 322, 323
Esarhaddon 198
Esau 66, 74, 360, 621
Esdras 364, 368
Essenes 372
Esther 30, 224–7, 368
eternal life 449, 450
eternity 686–7
Ethiopia 263, 264, 345
Evil-Merodach 214
Exodus from Egypt 27, 78–9
  map 79
Exodus (the book) 73–88
Ezekiel 30, 296–308
Ezra 217–20

F

faith 616–23, 652–3
  dead 627
  and works 627–8
Fall 23, 41–2
falling from grace 543
false teachers *see* doctrinal error
family life 552, 564, 636
Farel, Guillaume 720
fasts 353–4
feasts 97
Felix 494
fellowship 647–54
festivals 111, 119
Festus 494
  firstfruits 97, 122
Flood 24, 43–6
foreordination 547
France 720, 724, 725
free will 547
freedom *see* liberty
fruit of the Spirit 544–5
Fundamentalism 725

G

Gaius 658
Galatians 537–45
Galilee, Sea of 412
Gedaliah 290
genealogies 201
genealogies *see also under* Jesus Christ
Genesis 36–69
Geneva 720
Gentiles 277, 468, 471, 478, 673
Germany 717–18
Gethsemane 398, 418, 461–2
Gibeah 145
Gibeon 129, 173
Gibeonites 130, 170
Gideon 138–40
Gihon Spring 163
Gilgal 127
Gilgamesh 44
giving 533–4
Golgotha 398
Goliath 156
good Samaritan 434
Goshen 68
gospels 374–6
grace 543–4, 547–8
Great Awakening 724
Greek language 9, 32, 372
Gregory VII (Pope) 713

H

Habakkuk 342–3
Hagar 543
Haggai 30, 346–7
Ham 48
Haman 225–7
Hammurabi *227*
Haran 26, 62
harps *232*
Hazael 188
Hazor 130–1, 292
healing 186, 408, 411, 428, 450, 453
heaven 437
Hebrew language 690–1
Hebrews 599–623
hell 411–13, 437
Henry VIII (King of England) 720
heresy *see* doctrinal error

Hermas 692, 694
Herod 472
Herod Antipas 390
Hezekiah 194, 195, 211–13, 270
high places 284
high priest *93*
Hinduism 729
Hittites 49–52
holiness 96–7, 120–1, 341, 551–3,
  563–4, 568, 586, 634–5, 650
Holland 720
Holy Spirit 351, 451, 458–60, 465–6,
  472, 480, 516–17, 539, 544–5, 548,
  551
  fruit of 544–5
  gifts 522, 524
Horeb 180
Horites 66–7
Hosea 320–3
Hoshea 192, 197
humility 629–30
Huss, John 716

I

Ichabod 300
Iconium 476
idolatry 111–13, 116, 213, 271–3, 300,
  322, 488–9
Immanuel 262–3
incarnation 647
inheritance 110, 113
Innocent III (Pope) 713
Inquisition 722
inspiration 10–11
Ireland 720
Irenaeus 694
Isaac 63–4, 618
  map 65
Isaiah 30, 255–80
  and John's gospel 455
Ish-Bosheth 163–4
Ishmael 58, 63
Islam 711, 729
  see also Crusades
Israel
  chart of kings 254
  Ezekiel's prophecy of restoration 308
  God's purposes 510–12
  Hosea's prophecy of restoration 322,
    323

in Malachi's prophecy 360–1
maps 190, 193, 209, 210
remnant 672–3, 677
tribal allotments, map 133
in Zechariah's prophecy 356–7

J

Jacob 64, 66, 68, 69, 618
   map 66
Jainism 729
James (brother of Jesus) 406
James (brother of John) 404
James (epistle) 599, 624–31
James (son of Alphaeus) 404
Japheth 48
Jebusites 165
Jehoahaz 189
Jehoash 191
Jehoiachin 30, 194–5, 293
Jehoiakim 289
Jehoram 185–6, 211
Jehoshaphat 211
Jehovah 74
Jehu 188
Jephthah 141–2
Jeremiah 30, 281–93
   and Lamentations 294
Jericho 27, 31, 128, 180, 414
Jeroboam 176–8
Jeroboam II 189, 191
Jerome 694
Jerusalem *206–7*, 416–17
   church council 478, 480
   and David 163–5
   in Ezekiel's prophecy 299–303, 308
   falls to Babylon 195–6, 289–90
   judgment on 265, 267
   lamentations over 294–5
   plans 165, 223, 397
   prophecies concerning 275–6, 278,
      345, 356, 395
   walls rebuilt 222
   see also Temple
Jesuits 721, 722, 725
Jesus Christ 560–2
   as advocate 647–8
   ascension 442–3, 465
   baptism 382, 402, 426
   birth 421–5

burial 31, 399, 418, 441, 459, 462
childhood 383, 425–6
crucifixion 31, 398–9, 418–19, 441,
   462
future kingdom 676
genealogy 148, 381, 426
in Jerusalem 394–5, 413–18,
   439–41, 448–9, 455–8
millennial reign 266
miracles 392, 429, 432, 449, 450
predicted in OT 120, 234, 238, 242,
   259–63, 266, 287–8, 355–6
   see also Immanuel; Messiah
predicts his death and resurrection
   391, 411, 432, 460
resurrection 31, 399–400, 418–19,
   442–3, 461, 463, 525–6
sacrifice 614–15
second coming *see under* Messiah
and suffering 637–8
superiority 602–23
teaching 386–7, 393–4, 406, 413–15,
   433–9, 452–4
   see also parables
temptation 426–8
theme of Bible 12–13
transfiguration 392, 411, 433
trials 441, 462
   see also Body of Christ; Messiah
Jethro 80
Jewish diaspora 726–7
Joab 170
Joash 189, 211
Job 228–31
Joel 324–6
John 444
   epistles 646–58
   gospel 444–63
John the Baptist 382, 387–8, 390, 407,
   426, 445–8, 449
John (brother of Jesus) 646
John Chrysostom 695
Jonah 334–6
Jonathan 154
Jordan crossing 126
Jordan river 386
Joseph 67–9, 618–19
Josephus 10
Joshua 125–34, 619–20
Joshua (high priest) 349–50
Josiah 194, 213
Jotham 211

jubilee 98
Jubilees, Book of 370
Judah 131, 338
   and Chaldeans 343
   chart of kings 283
   fall 293
   map 210
   maps 190
Judaism 729
Judas Iscariot 45, 406
Jude
   epistle 659–61
   epistle of 599
Judges 27, 119, 136–45
judgment 523
   beginning eternity 686–7
   of Israel and the nations 396
Judith 368
justification 504–7, 538–42
Justin Martyr 695

K

Kadesh 104–5
Kadesh-Barnea 104
Kedar 292
Kidron Valley 298
kingdom, in Jesus' teaching 386–90
Kings (books of) 172–99
King's Highway 59, 66
Korah 106

L

Lamentations 294–5
lampstand 353
languages of the Bible 9
Laodicea 669–70
Last Supper 415
law of Moses 82, 87–8
   and Jesus' teaching 386
   purpose 540, 576
lawsuits 519
lawyers 434
Lazarus 455
legalism 562, 576
Leo X (Pope) 717
Leo XIII (Pope) 726
leprosy 95–6, 186
Levites 100, 102, 123–4, 132–4

Levitical cities 113
Leviticus 89–98
Liberalism 725
liberation theology 728
liberty 520, 521, 542, 543
longevity 23, 43
Lord's Supper 396–8, 521–2
Lot 64–5
love 652
Luke 420, 464
    gospel 420–43
Luther, Martin 717–18
Lutheranism 718
Lydia 480–1
Lystra 476–8

M

Macedonia 489
magi 382
Malachi 358–61
Malta 495
Manasseh 30, 68, 131, 194, 213
    Prayer of 369
manna 80, 103, 127
Marcion 694
Mark 401, 478
    gospel of 400–19
marriage 41, 42, 519–20, 552
Masoretes 690–1
Matthew 404
    gospel of 380–400
Matthias 465
Megiddo *172*
Melchizedek 58, 609–10
Melito 694–5
Mephibosheth 166–8
Mesopotamia 50–1, 56
Messiah 268, 272, 273–4, 276, 279,
    285–6, 305, 347, 348, 353, 360–1
    his kingdom 338–9
    reign of 357
    second coming 314, 330, 339, 350,
        354, 357, 395–6, 418, 458, 568,
        638–9, 644–5, 683–4, 688–9
metallurgy 23
Micah 144, 337–9
Michael (archangel) 677
Midianites 138–40
Midrash 371
Miletus 492

millennium 266, 308, 347
ministry 529–36, 566–7
miracles 429, 432
    of the disciples 466
    of Elisha 186, 188
    of Jesus 392, 407, 410, 449, 450
Miriam 104
Mitylene 492
Moab 186, 263, 264, 291, 345
monarchy 119–20, 152
    chart of kings 254
monasticism 710, 714
Mordecai 225–7
Moses 15, 74–6, 80, 104, 108, 110–11,
    115, 123–4, 619
    aided by elders 103
    compared with Christ 604
    covenant with 80, 87–8, 611–12, 613
    law *see* law of Moses
    law of, compared with Jesus' teaching
        386
Muratorian Canon 694
mysticism 562–3

N

Naaman 186
Nabonidus 216
Nabopolassar 214
Nadab 94
Nahor 62
Nahum 340–1
Nazareth 31, 427
Nazirites 102
Nebuchadnezzar I 290, 309–12
Nebuchadnezzar II 30, 214
Nehemiah 221–3
Neo-orthodoxy 725
Neriglissar 214–16
New Testament
    books 372
    canon 691–6
    manuscripts 32
    name 9
    political background 377
    textual transmission 696–702
    theme 372
Nicaea, Council of 708, 709
Nicodemus 449
Nicolas I (Pope) 711
Nimrod 109

Nimrud 55
Nineveh 197–9, 335–6, 340–1
Noah 43–6, 618
    covenant with 613
Numbers 99–113
Nuzi tablets 62

O

oaths 630–1
Obadiah 332–3
occult 120
Old Testament
    canon 690
    name 9
    order of books 9–10
    threefold division 10
Omri 179
Onesimus 597–8
Origen 692–3, 695
Orthodox churches 712

P

Paddan Aram 62
Palestine, maps 421
papacy 710, 711–13, 724, 725, 726
parables 388–90, 393–4, 396, 406, 433,
    435–8
passion week 440
Passover 78, 97, 102, 396–8, 415
pastors 584–7
    see also church, leaders
Patara 492–3
Patmos 665
patriarchs 26
    chronology 44
    family tree 67
    longevity 43
    map 34–5
Paul
    Acts of 692
    chronology 496
    epistles 501
        see also names of individual
            letters
    trials 494
    voyage to Rome 494–7
Paul III (Pope) 717
Paul of Tarsus

conversion 468, 470
  preaching 469, 476–83, 486–93
Paulus, Sergius 32
peace 558
Pekah 197
Pelagius 709
Pentateuch, authorship 15
Pentecost 97, 465–6, 472
Perga 476
Pergamum 32, 668, 673
persecution 566, 571, 630, 707
Persian empire 221
  chronology 351
  map 226–7
Peshitta 695
Peter 404, 463, 466, 469–71, 632
  Apocalypse of 692
  confession of Christ 391
  epistles of 599, 632–45
Petra 265
Pharisees 371, 390–1, 408, 415
Philadelphia 669
Philemon 596–8
Philip 404, 468
Philippi 32, 481–2
  plan 554
Philippians 554–8
Philistines 142–4, 151, 154, 160, 170,
  291, 345
Phinehas 111
Phrygia 539
Pietism 722–3
Pilate, Pontius 31
plagues of Egypt 76–8
poetry 228
Polemicists 707
polygamy 42
Pontius Pilate 31
Popes 710, 711–13, 724, 725, 726
potters 285
prayer 434, 548, 577, 653–4
Prayer of Manasseh 369
preaching 589–90
priesthood 86–7, 94, 106
  of Christ 606, 610–11
  high priest 93
prophets 253, 472
  false 301
  table of minor prophets 318–19
Proverbs 244–7
Psalms 232–43
Psalms of Solomon 370

Pseudepigrapha 369–70
Ptolemaic empire 366
Purim 227
Puritanism 721
purity 532
pyramids 56–7, 291

Q

quails 103–4
Quirinius 31, 423
Qumran 30, 371, 446–7, 647
Quo Vadis 633

R

Raamses 72
Rahab 126, 620, 1218
Ras Shamra texts 180
Rechabites 288
red heifer 106–8
Red Sea 79
redemption 547
Reed Sea 79
Reformation 717–21
Reformed faith 718–20
regeneration 635, 641, 654
Rehoboam 176–8, 208
religions of the world 729–31
Rephidim 80
resurrection 525–7, 568, 686
revelation 579
Revelation (book) 662–89
Roman citizenship 493
Roman empire 707–9
  map 378–9
Romans (epistle) 502–14
Rome 32
  Paul in 497–9
Ruth 146–8

S

sabbath 87, 106, 404
sabbatical year 98, 118
sacrifices 89–94, 612, 614–15
Sadducees 371
Samaria 181, 263, 302–3, 338
Samaria (Sebaste) 31

Samaritans 468
Samson 142–3, 145
Samuel 27, 149–71
sanctification 506–10, 544, 570
Sanhedrin 371, 398
Sarah 64, 543, 618
Sardis 32, 32, 668–9
Sargon II 197, 198
Satan 41, 266, 407, 426, 428, 435, 677,
  684–6
Saul (king) 27, 152–5, 157–60, 163, 202
Saul of Tarsus 468–9
  see also Paul
Savonarola 716
scholasticism 714
Scotland 720
scribes 372, 390–1
second coming of Christ see Messiah
Seleucid empire 366
Semites 52
Sennacherib 194, 195, 198, 271
  campaign map 212
separation 117–18
Septuagint 372
Sergius Paulus 32
serpent in the wilderness 108
Servant see Mark, gospel of
Servant prophecy 274, 276
service 527, 536
  Christian 512–14
sexual morality 519–20
Shalmaneser III 198
Shalmaneser V 197
Shamsi-Adad V 198
Sheba, Queen of 176, 208
Shechem 134
Shiloh 132, 151
Shintoism 729
Shishak 178
shofar 324
Shunammite woman 186, 188
Sibylline Oracles 370
Sikhism 729
Silas 480
Simeon 425
Simon the Zealot 406
sin 41–2, 503–4, 605, 627, 654,
  confession 647
  man of 572–3
Sinai 80, 81
slavery 564
slings 156

Smerdis 221
Smyrna 667, 671
social reform 724
Sodom and Gomorrah 26, 60, 660
Solomon 27–30, 173–7, 204–8, 251–2
    kingdom map 209
Song of Solomon 251–2
Song of the Three Children 369
sonship 542
Spener, Philip 723
sphinx *57*
spies 104–5, 126
Spirit *see* Holy Spirit
spiritism 159–60
spirituality 545
star of Bethlehem 381
statistics 703
Stephen 467–8
suffering 228, 534–6, 634–8
    see also persecution
Susa 226
    plan 225
Susanna 369
Switzerland 718–20
synagogues 31, 371, 430–1
synoptic gospels 420
Syria, chart of kings 254

Taberah 103
Tabernacle *82–6*, 88, *107*
    at Shiloh 132
    plan 83
Tabernacles, feast of 97, 111
table of shewbread 84, *109*
Talmud 370
Targums 370
Temple 31, 173, *174–5*, 205, 218–*20*,
    456–7, 600–1
    abandoned by God 300
    cleansed by Jesus 439, 448–9
    in Ezekiel's prophecy 306–8
    and Gentiles 492
    Jesus predicts its destruction 395
    millennial 347
temptation 626
Ten Commandments 82, 87–8, 116, 120
Terah 26
Tertullian 9
Testaments of the Twelve Patriarchs 370

Thaddeus 406
Thebes 72
Theodore of Mopsuestia 695
Theophilus 695
Thessalonians 565–74
Thessalonica 32, 482
Thirty Years' War 722
Thomas 404
Thomas Aquinas 714
Thyatira 668
Tiberias 451
Tiglath-Pileser III 198
    campaign map 192
Timna *176*
Timothy 478–80
    epistles to 575–90
Titus 591–5
Tobit 368
tongues 472, 524–5
transfiguration 392, 411, 433
translations 698–702, 728
Trent, Council of 722
tribal religion 729
Tribulation 395–6
Trinity 547
Troas 489, 492
trumpets 97, 103, 324
typology 13–14, 91, 273, 521, 605, 609,
    611–12
Tyre 265, 303–4

Ugaritic texts 180
uncleanness 94–5, 101–2
United States 734–5
    see also America
unleavened bread 97
Ur 24–6, 56
Uzziah 191, 211

Vatican II, Council 726–7
virgin birth 381
vows 98, 111

Waldenses 714
wealth 581–2
weights and measures 362–3
Wesley, John and Charles 724
widows 580
wilderness 275
    wanderings in 115
wisdom 516–17, 625–6, 629
Wisdom of Solomon 368–9
women 432, 514, 577–8
    in the church 521–2
Word 445
worldliness 517–18, 629, 649
writing 14–15
Wycliffe, John 716

Xerxes I 30, 221, 225
Xerxes II 221

Y

Yahweh 74

Z

Zacchaeus 438
Zechariah 30, 348–57
Zedekiah 195, 285, 288
Zephaniah 344–5
Zerubbabel 222
ziggurats *55*, 56
Zion 164–5
Zwingli, Ulrich 718–20

Some ways into your Bible

A Bible reading plan

If you would like to read the Bible systematically and carefully, the following reading order will be helpful. Although this plan does not include every book of the Bible, it will give you a good overview of Scripture if followed regularly.

New Testament
1. Mark
2. John
3. Luke–Acts
4. I Thessalonians
5. I Corinthians
6. Romans
7. Philemon
8. Philippians
9. Ephesians
10. 2 Timothy
11. I Peter
12. I John
13. Revelation (1–5 and 19:6–22:21)

Old Testament
14. Genesis
15. Exodus (1–24)
16. Numbers (10:11–21:35)
17. Deuteronomy (1–11)
18. Joshua (1–12 and 22–24)
19. Judges (sample)
20. 1–2 Samuel (sample)
21. 1–2 Kings (sample)
22. Nehemiah
23. Amos
24. Isaiah (1–12)
25. Jeremiah (1–25, 30–33)
26. Isaiah (40–55)
27. Ruth
28. Jonah
29. Psalms (some examples of the major types)
30. Job (perhaps 1–14 and 38–42)
31. Proverbs (1–9)
32. Daniel (1-6; sample chapters 7–12)

Some fascinating Bible statistics

	Old Testament	New Testament
Number of books	39	27
Number of chapters	929	260
Number of verses	23,214	7,959
Number of words	592,493	181,253
Longest book	Psalms	Matthew
Shortest book	Obadiah	2 John
Longest chapter	Psalm 119	Matthew 26
Shortest chapter	Psalm 117	Revelation 15
Longest verse	Esther 8:9	Revelation 20:4
Shortest verse	I Chronicles	John 11:35 ('Jesus wept.')
Middle book	Proverbs	2 Thessalonians
Middle chapter	Job 29	Romans 13–14
Middle verse	2 Chronicles 20:17-18	Acts 7:17

Total number of verses in both Testaments: 31,173.

Middle chapter of the Bible: Psalm 117

Middle verse: Psalm 118:5

Most mentioned character: David (1,118 times)

Longest word: Mahershalalhashbaz (*Isaiah 8:1*)

NB *These figures are based on English Bibles and may vary according to the translation.*

Bible translation facts
• More than 6,500 languages are spoken in the world.
• Of these, 2,167 languages have some or all of the Bible (355 complete Bibles, 850 New Testaments).
• About 4,333 languages are still without any part of the Bible.

The smallest Bible ever published was the Mite Bible published by Oxford University Press in 1896. Its pages were 28 x 41mm (1.62 x 1.12"), it was 900 pages long and 13mm (0.5") thick.

BIBLE VERSES FOR SPECIAL OCCASIONS

Birthdays

Joshua 1:1-9; Psalms 1; 23; 25; 37:3-7; 39:1-7; 90; 91; 139; Proverbs 3:5-8; 26:3-4; 41:10; 43:1-3; 46:4; Lamentations 3:22-26; Luke 1:46-55; John 6:35; 8:12; 10:1-30; Romans 8:28-39; 11:33-36; Ephesians 1:3-14; Philippians 4:4-7; Hebrews 10:23; 1 John 1:7-9

Baptism, dedication of children and confirmation

Joshua 1:5-9; 1 Samuel 1:27-28; Psalms 1; 23; 111; 121; Ecclesiastes 12:1; Matthew 3:11-17; 10:32-33; 28:18-20; Mark 10:13-16; John 3:1-21; 15:1-17; Acts 8:36-40; 16:30-33; 22:16; Romans 6:1-14; 1 Corinthians 12:12-13; Galatians 3:26-28; Ephesians 3:14-21; 4:1-6; Philippians 1:1-11; Colossians 2:6-14; 1 Timothy 6:11-16; Titus 3:4-7; 1 Peter 3:18-22; Jude 24

Thanksgiving

Deuteronomy 6:10-19; 8; Psalms 33; 65; 95; 100; 103; 104; 107; 111; 116; 126; 136; 145; 147; Isaiah 12; Luke 12:13-34; Acts 14:17; 1 Corinthians 3:5-9; Colossians 2:16-17; Hebrews 13:15-16; Revelation 5

Wedding day

Genesis 2:18-25; Ruth 1:16-17; Psalms 67; 84; 100; 118:24-29; 121; 127; 128; 139; Matthew 19:4-6; John 2:1-11; 1 Corinthians 7; 13; Ephesians 5:22-33; Colossians 3:12-21; 1 Peter 3:1-7

Retirement

Deuteronomy 33:27; Joshua 1:7-9; 1 Samuel 7:12; Psalms 23; 71:14-24; 93:12-15; Isaiah 26:3-4; 43:18-21; 46:4; John 14:27; 1 Corinthians 1:8; Philippians 3:7-16

CHRISTMAS AND NEW YEAR READING PLAN

December 20: *Luke 1:26-38*
Jesus' birth foretold

December 21: *Luke 1:39-56*
Mary and Elizabeth

December 22:
Luke 1:67-80
Zechariah's song

December 23:
Colossians 1:15-20
Who Jesus is

December 24:
John 1:1-18
The Word became flesh

Christmas Day: *Luke 2:1-7*
The Saviour is born

December 26:
Luke 2:8-20
The shepherds and the angels

December 27: *Matthew 2:1-12*
The Magi worship Jesus

December 28:
Luke 2:21-32
Jesus is presented in the Temple

December 29: *Luke 2:36-38*
The redemption of Jerusalem

December 30:
Matthew 2:13-18
Jesus is kept safe

December 31: *Psalm 90*
Teach us to number our days

New Year's Day:
Exodus 33:7-23
Show me your glory

January 2: *Philippians 3:7-14*
Pressing on to the goal

January 3: *Joshua 1:1-9*
Be strong and courageous

January 4: *Matthew 6:25-34*
Do not worry

January 5: *Romans 8:28-39*
More than conquerors

January 6: *Philippians 4:4-9*
Rejoice in the Lord

EASTER READING PLAN

Palm Sunday: *Luke 19:28-44*
The approach to Jerusalem

Monday: *Luke 19:45-48*
Jesus at the Temple

Tuesday: *Philippians 2:5-11*
Obedient to death

Wednesday: *1 Peter 2:21-25*
Christ suffered for you

Maundy Thursday:
Luke 22:7-71; John 17
The Last Supper; Jesus' arrest

Good Friday: *Luke 23; Isaiah 53*
The crucifixion

Saturday: *Matthew 27:62-66*
The guard at the tomb

Easter Day: *Matthew 28:1-15*
The resurrection

Easter Monday: *John 20:24-31*
My Lord and my God!

Tuesday:
1 Corinthians 15:12-58
Victory over death

Wednesday: *Acts 2:22-41*
Why Jesus died

Thursday: *Romans 1:1-7*
Jesus Christ our Lord

Friday: *Romans 6:5-14*
United with him

Saturday: *Colossians 3:1-4*
Raised with Christ

Sunday: *Revelation 1:4-18*
Alive for ever and ever

Ascension Day
Luke 24:50-53; Acts 1:1-11

Pentecost (Whitsun)
Acts 1:8; 2:1-2; 19:1-7; Ephesians 4:30

When you are in need . . .

Bible verses to look at when you need help

The Bible includes many promises that can help and encourage us in times of sadness, difficulty or stress. Here are some verses that show us God's help. Read and meditate over them:

• When you feel afraid
'I sought the LORD, and he answered me; he delivered me from all my fears' *Psalm 34:4.*
See also Psalms 27; 46; 56; 91; Matthew 8:23-27.

• When you feel alone
'So do not fear, for I am with you; do not be dismayed for I am your God' *Isaiah 41:10.*
See also Psalms 23; 73:23-24; Isaiah 49:14-16; John 14:15-21.

• When you are anxious or worried
'Cast all your anxiety on him, because he cares for you' *I Peter 5:7.*
See also Isaiah 43:1-13; Matthew 6:25-34; 11:28; Philippians 4:4-7.

• When you have been bereaved
'Blessed are those who mourn; for they will be comforted' *Matthew 5:4.*
See also Psalm 23; John 11:21-27; I Corinthians 15:51-57; I Thessalonians 4:13-18; Revelation 21:1-5.

• When you feel discouraged
'Why are you downcast, O my soul? Why so disturbed within me? Put your hope in God' *Psalm 42:5.*
See also Psalms 34:18; 40:1-3; Lamentations 3:20-23; Romans 8:28-39; 2 Corinthians 4:7-18.

• When you have doubts
'I do believe; help me overcome my unbelief!' *Mark 9:24.*
See also Isaiah 40:27-31; Matthew 11:1-6; John 20:19-29; Acts 17:22-28.

• When you feel you have done wrong
'But God demonstrates his own love for us in this: While we were still sinners, Christ died for us' *Romans 5:8.*
See also Psalm 51; Luke 15:11-24.

• When you feel distant from God
'Come near to God and he will come near to you' *James 4:8.*
See also Psalm 139:1-18; John 10:29; Acts 17:24-31.

• When you are ill or in pain
'My grace is sufficient for you, for my power is made perfect in weakness' *2 Corinthians 12:9.*
See also Psalm 103:1-4; Romans 8:18-25; 2 Corinthians 4:16-18.

• When you need peace
'You will keep in perfect peace him whose mind is steadfast, because he trusts in you' *Isaiah 26:3.*
See also John 14:27; Romans 5:1-5; Philippians 4:4-7.

• When you are tempted
'We have one [a High Priest] who has been tempted in every way, just as we are – yet was without sin' *Hebrews 4:15.*
See also Luke 4:1-13; Ephesians 6:10-20; James 1:2-6, 12-18; 4:7-8; I Peter 5:8-9.

• When you are tired or weak
'Come to me, all you who are weary and burdened, and I will give you rest. Take my yoke upon you and learn from me, for I am gentle and humble in heart, and you will find rest for your souls' *Matthew 11:28-29.*
See also Joshua 1:5-9; Isaiah 40:28-31; 2 Corinthians 4:16-18; 12:9-10; Philippians 4:12-13.

• When you need guidance
'In all your ways acknowledge him, and he will make your paths straight' *Proverbs 3:6.*
See also Psalm 48:14; John 14:16; 16:13.

Model prayers of the Bible

Complaint	*Numbers 14:13-19*
Confession	*Psalm 32; Psalm 51; Ezra 9:5-15*
Dedication	*2 Chronicles 6:14-42*
Dependence	*2 Chronicles 20:6-12*
Despair	*Psalm 73*
For believers	*Ephesians 1:16-23; Ephesians 3:15-21*
For blessing	*Psalm 90*
For deliverance	*Isaiah 37:14-20*
For healing	*Isaiah 38:3, 9-20*
For restoration	*Daniel 9:4-19*
For unity	*John 17*
In national crisis	*2 Kings 19:14-19*
Intercession	*Genesis 18:16-33; Exodus 32:11-13*
Petition	*Acts 4:24-30*
Praise	*Luke 1:46-55*
Recommitment	*John 2:2-9*
Thanksgiving	*I Samuel 2:1-10; Psalms 16; 65*
The Lord's Prayer	*Matthew 6:9-13; Luke 11:2-4*
Trust	*Psalm 23*

Some key Bible passages

The creation story	*Genesis 1:1–2:7*
The fall	*Genesis 3:1-24*
The flood	*Genesis 6:1–9:17*
The call of Abraham	*Genesis 12:1-9*
The Ten Commandments	*Exodus 20:1-17*
The shepherd's psalm	*Psalm 23*
The birth of Jesus	*Matthew 1:18–2:23; Luke 1:26–2:40*
The golden rule	*Luke 6:31*
The Sermon on the Mount	*Matthew 5–7*
The Beatitudes	*Matthew 5:3-11*
The Lord's Prayer	*Luke 11:2-4*
The prodigal son	*Luke 15:11-32*
The good Samaritan	*Luke 10:29-37*
The Last Supper	*Matthew 26:17-30; Mark 14:12-26*
The death of Christ	*Luke 23:26-56; John 19:16-42*
The resurrection of Christ	*Matthew 28; Luke 24; John 20*
The ascension of Christ	*Acts 1:1-12*
The coming of the Holy Spirit	*Acts 2:1-21*
The conversion of Paul	*Acts 9:1-31*
The love chapter	*1 Corinthians 13*
The faith chapter	*Hebrews 11*

Where to find help in the book of Psalms

Psalms to read when you're feeling:

Afraid *3, 13, 27, 46, 56, 59, 64, 91, 118, 121*
Alone *9, 12, 13, 27, 40, 43*
Angry *17, 28, 36, 37, 109*
Burned out *6, 63*
Cheated *41*
Confused *10, 12, 73*
Depressed *27, 34, 42, 43, 88, 143*
Disappointed *16, 92, 102, 130*
Distressed *13, 25, 31, 40, 107*
Guilty *19, 32, 38, 51*
Impatient *4, 13, 27, 37, 40, 89, 123*
Insecure *3, 5, 12, 91*
Insignificant *8, 23, 86, 90, 139*
Insulted *41, 70*
Jealous *37, 73*
Joyful *96, 149*
Like giving up *29, 43, 145*
Lost *23, 139*
Overwhelmed *25, 69, 142*
Proud *14, 30, 49*
Purposeless *25, 39, 90*
Self-confident *24*
Sorry/repentant *51, 66*
Stressed *12, 31, 34, 43, 56, 62, 84*
Thankful *30, 33, 66, 96, 103, 104, 113, 118, 136, 138*
Threatened *143, 144*
Trapped *7, 17, 42, 88, 142*
Vengeful *3, 109*
Weak *13, 18, 23, 28, 29, 62, 70, 86, 102*
Worried *37*
Worshipful *19, 29, 148, 150*

Psalms to read when you're facing:

Competition *113*
Criticism *35, 56, 120*
Danger *11*
Death *23*
Decisions *1, 25, 62, 119*
Discouragement *12, 42, 55, 86, 107, 142*
Discrimination *94*
Doubts *34, 37*
Enemies *3, 25, 35, 41, 56, 59*
Evil people *10, 36, 49, 52, 109*
Hypocrisy *26, 50*
Injustice *7, 9, 10, 17, 56, 94*
Insults *35, 43*
Lies *5, 12, 120*
Old age *71, 92*
Persecution *1, 3, 7*
Poverty *12, 34, 146*
Punishment *6, 38, 39*
Sickness *6, 22, 23, 41, 116, 139*
Slaughter *46, 83*
Sorrow/grief *6, 23, 31, 71, 77, 94, 123*
Success *18, 112, 126, 128*
Temptation *38, 141*
Troubles *34, 55, 86, 102, 142, 145*
Verbal cruelty *35, 120*

Psalms to read when you want:

Acceptance *139*
Answers *4, 17, 119*
Confidence *46, 71*
Courage *11, 27*
Fellowship with God *5, 16, 25, 37*
Forgiveness *32, 38, 40, 51, 86, 103*
Friendship *16*
Godliness *15, 25*
Guidance/direction *1, 19, 32, 37, 89, 146*
Healing *6, 41, 103*
Hope *16, 17, 18, 23, 27*
Humility *19, 131, 147*
Illumination *19*
Integrity *24, 25*
Joy *9, 16, 33, 47, 84, 96, 97, 98, 100*
Justice *2, 7, 14, 26, 37, 82*
Knowledge of God *18, 19, 29, 65, 89, 97, 103, 145, 147*
Leadership *72*
Miracles *60, 111*
Money *15, 16, 49*
Peace *3, 4, 85*
Perspective *2, 11, 73*
Prayer *5, 17, 27, 61*
Protection *7, 16, 18, 23, 27, 31, 91, 125*
Provision *34, 81*
Reassurance *15, 23, 26, 112, 121*
Rest *23, 27*
Salvation *103, 146*
Security *34, 84, 91*
Vindication *9, 35, 109*
Wisdom *1, 16, 19, 64, 111*

What does the Old Testament Apocrypha consist of?

The Apocrypha is a collection of books and additions to Old Testament books written between 300 BC and AD 100. These books were not accepted by the Jews as part of the Old Testament Scripture. The books of the Apocrypha are interesting, and valuable as historical documents, and range from narrative history to pious fiction. Most Protestants acknowledge the literary value and historical significance of the Apocrypha, but do not view it as possessing spiritual authority. Roman Catholics and some Eastern Orthodox churches recognise the Apocryphal writings as Scripture.

1 Esdras
An historical account, paralleling Chronicles, Ezra and Nehemiah, of the return of the Jews from Babylonian captivity.

2 Esdras (4 Ezra)
Visions and revelations of early Jewish rabbis.

Tobit
A didactic fiction about Tobit's trials living in eighth century B.C. Nineveh.

Judith
The fictional exploits of a Jewish heroine, Judith, who assassinated the Assyrian general Holofernes.

Additions to Esther (also known as The Rest of Esther)
Five additions which give a more religious emphasis to the book of Esther.

The Wisdom of Solomon
A first century B.C. exhortation to wisdom.

Ecclesiasticus also known as the Wisdom of Sirach/Ben Sira
A collection of the writings of Joshua ben-Sera (about 180 B.C.) giving his advice for a successful life – combining personal piety with practical wisdom.

Baruch
This book was allegedly written by Baruch, a friend of Jeremiah, and was meant as an encouragement to Jews in the Babylonian exile of 597 B.C..

The Letter of Jeremiah
An attack on idolatry in the form of a letter from Jeremiah, often added to the book of Baruch.

The Song of the Three Holy Children
A hymn of praise sung by Shadrach, Meshach and Abednego in the fiery furnace described in Daniel.

The Story of Susanna
The story of a virtuous woman who was falsely accused of adultery and defended by Daniel.

Bel and the Dragon
A folkloric story written to ridicule idolatry.

The Prayer of Mannaseh
The prayer of the idolatrous king Manasseh, begging for forgiveness, as referred to in 2 Chronicles 33:11-19.

1 Maccabees
The struggle of Jews against Hellenistic rulers (175-134 B.C), particularly the battle with Antiochus Epiphanes.

2 Maccabees
A narrative of the Maccabean revolt.

3 Maccabees
An account of Jewish life under Ptolemy IV (221-204 B.C).

4 Maccabees
A tract about the rule of reason over passion.

Psalm 151

What is the Septuagint?

Alexandria, the capital of Egypt under the Ptolemies, had a large community of Jews who could no longer speak Hebrew. They wanted a Greek translation of their Scriptures, and tradition has it that 72 scholars were sent from Jerusalem to complete the work. The translation became known as the Septuagint (= seventy), sometimes written as LXX (70 in Roman numerals). To begin with, only the first five books of the Old Testament were included, but other books were added later.

ΚΑΙ ΑΝΘΡѠΠΟϹ ΗΝ
ΙΟΥΔΑΙΟϹ ΕΝ ϹΟΥ
ϹΟΙϹ ΤΗ ΠΟΛΕΙ ΚΑΙ
ΟΝΟΜΑ ΑΥΤѠ ΜΑΡ
ΔΟΧΑΙΟϹ ΤΟΥ ΙΑΙ

Who wrote the New Testament?

Name	Nationality	Occupation	Writings	How he died
Matthew	Jewish	Tax-collector	Gospel of Matthew	By tradition martyred in Ethiopia
Mark	Jewish		Gospel of Mark	By tradition martyred
Luke	Greek	Physician	Gospel of Luke, Acts	By tradition martyred in Greece
John	Jewish	Fisherman	Gospel of John 1, 2 & 3 John, Revelation	Banished to Patmos; natural death
Paul	Jewish	Pharisee/ Tentmaker	Romans, 1 & 2 Corinthians Galatians, Ephesians, Philippians, Colossians, 1 & 2 Thessalonians, 1 & 2 Timothy, Titus, Philemon	By tradition martyred in Rome by Nero
James	Jewish		James	By tradition martyred
Peter	Jewish	Fisherman	1 & 2 Peter	By tradition crucified upside down in Rome by Nero
Jude	Jewish		Jude	By tradition martyred

Who are the different Marys of the New Testament?

Mary, mother of Jesus
The Jewish woman from Nazareth whom God chose to give birth to His son. Married to Joseph, she was a descendant of David. Mary stood at the foot of the cross when Jesus was killed.
Matthew 1:18-25;
Luke 1:27-45; John 19:25-27

Mary of Bethany
With her sister Martha and brother Lazarus, a close friend of Jesus, whose feet she anointed with perfume.
Luke 10:38-42; John 11:1-46; 12:1-3;
compare Matthew 26:7; Mark 14:3.

Mary, mother of James and Joseph (Joses)
A Galilean woman who, after being healed, followed Jesus and supported his ministry financially.
Matthew 27:56; 28:1;
Mark 15:40,41,47.

Mary Magdalene
Another Galilean woman whom Jesus healed, and who helped to support Jesus' ministry.
Matthew 27:56,61; 28:1; Mark 15:40,47; 16:1,9;
Luke 8:2; John 20:1,2,11-18.

Mary, mother of John Mark
A relative of Barnabas; her home was a gathering place for the Jerusalem church.
Acts 12:12,13;
Colossians 4:10.

Mary of Rome
A woman commended by Paul. *Romans 16:6.*

Which Bible people saw God?

- Jacob dreamt of 'a stairway resting on the earth, with its top reaching to heaven, and the angels of God . . . ascending and descending'. *Genesis 28:12-13*

- 'Moses and Aaron, Nadab and Abihu, and the seventy elders of Israel went up and saw the God of Israel.' *Exodus 24:9-10*

- Moses saw the back of God. *Exodus 33:23*

- Micaiah saw 'the LORD sitting on his throne with all the host of heaven standing on his right and on his left'. *2 Chronicles 18:18*

- Isaiah saw 'the Lord seated on a throne, high and exalted'. *Isaiah 6:1*

- Ezekiel saw 'what looked like a throne of sapphire, and high above on the throne . . . a figure like that of a man'. *Ezekiel 1:26*

- Daniel saw thrones 'set in place, and the Ancient of Days took his seat. His clothing was as white as snow; the hair of his head was white like wool. His throne was flaming with fire.' *Daniel 7:9*

- Stephen looked up to heaven 'and saw the glory of God, and Jesus standing at the right hand of God'. *Acts 7:55*

- Paul wrote, 'I know a man in Christ who . . . was caught up to the third heaven.' *2 Corinthians 12:2*

- John wrote, 'I was in the Spirit, and there before me was a throne in heaven with someone sitting on it.' *Revelation 4:2*

What are the names and titles of God in the Bible?

Ancient of Days (Aramaic *Attiq yomin*) *Daniel 7:9* The ultimate authority as judge of the world.

Creator *Isaiah 40:28*

Eternal God (Hebrew *El Olam*) *Genesis 21:33*

Father (Greek *Theos ho Pater*) *Malachi 2:10; Matthew 6:9; Ephesians 3:14*

Father of the heavenly lights *James 1:17*

God of Mountains (Hebrew *El Shaddai*) *Genesis 17:1; 49:25* God is all-powerful.

Most High (Hebrew *El Elyon*) *Genesis 14:18-20* God, the maker of heaven and earth.

God of all mankind *Jeremiah 32:27*

God of the covenant (Hebrew *El Berit*) *Judges 9:46* Maker and keeper of his covenants.

God of heaven *Nehemiah 2:4*

God of Israel (Hebrew *El Elohe-Yisra'el*) *Genesis 33:20*

Heavenly Father *Matthew 6:26*

Holy One *Job 6:10*

Holy One of Israel (Hebrew *Qedosh Yisra'el*) *Isaiah 1:4*

I AM *Exodus 3:14*

Judge (Hebrew *Shapat*) *Genesis 18:25*

King *Jeremiah 10:7*

King of kings *I Timothy 6:15*

Living God *Deuteronomy 5:26*

LORD (Hebrew *Yahweh*) *Exodus 3:13-16*

God of Armies (Hebrew *Yahweh-seba'ot, Sabaoth*) *I Samuel 1:11; 17:45* God is all-powerful.

LORD is my Banner (Hebrew *Yahweh-nissi*) *Exodus 17:15* God gives us victories.

LORD is Peace (Hebrew *Yahweh-shalom*) *Judges 6:24* God brings us inner harmony.

LORD is There (Hebrew *Yahweh-shammah*) *Ezekiel 48:35* God will be with his people at the end of history.

Lord of lords *I Timothy 6:15*

Lord, Master (Hebrew *Adonai*) *Psalm 2:4* God has authority.

LORD Provides (Hebrew *Yahweh-jireh*) *Genesis 22:14*

LORD Our Righteousness (Hebrew *Yahweh-tsidkenu*) *Jeremiah 23:6* By God's acts he declares and makes his people righteous.

Most High (Aramaic *Illaya*) *Daniel 7:18* God has final authority.

Saviour (Greek *Soter*) *John 4:42*

Word, The (Greek *Logos*) *John 1:1* Jesus communicates God to humanity.

Some Bible names and their meanings

Aaron enlightened
Abel breath, a meadow
Abigail father of joy, father's joy
Abraham father of a multitude
Absalom father of friendship, or of peace
Adam man
Agrippa causing pain at birth
Ahaz possessor
Amos burden, one with a burden
Andrew a man, manly
Anna grace, gracious
Apollos belonging to Apollo
Aquila an eagle

Balaam foreigner, Lord of the people
Barnabas son of consolation
Bartholomew son of Ptolemy
Bathsheba daughter of an oath, or of seven
Benjamin son of the right hand
Bernice bringer of victory
Boaz fleetness, strength

Cain acquisition, possession
Caleb a barker, dog
Cephas stone, rock
Cornelius of a horn
Cyrus sun, splendour

Dan judge
Daniel God is my judge
David dear, beloved
Deborah bee
Delilah weak, tender, unhappy

Ehud the only
Eleazar God my helper
Eli lifting up
Elijah Yahweh my God
Elisabeth oath of God
Elisha God as a Saviour
Enoch dedicated, consecrated
Esau hairy
Esther star
Eve life, living
Ezekiel God will strengthen

Ezra help

Felix happy
Festus joyful
Gabriel man of God
Gad good fortune, fortunate
Gaius of the earth
Gideon a hewer, tree-feller
Goliath expulsion, expeller

Habakkuk embrace
Haggai festive
Ham hot, black
Hannah grace, prayer
Herod heroic
Hezekiah might of Yahweh
Hosea deliverance, salvation

Immanuel God with us
Isaac laughter
Isaiah salvation of Yahweh
Ishmael whom God hears
Israel soldier of God

Jacob supplanter
James supplanter
Jason healer
Jehoiakim set up by Yahweh
Jehoshaphat Yahweh judges
Jehovah (= Yahweh) the eternally existing
Jehu Yahweh is he
Jeremiah exalted by God
Jesse wealth
Jesus healer, saviour
Jethro pre-eminent
Jezebel chaste
Joab Yahweh is father
Job afflicted
Joel whose God is Yahweh
John God's gift, grace
Jonah dove
Jonathan Yahweh is gracious
Joseph he shall add
Joshua Yahweh is salvation
Josiah God is healer
Jotham Yahweh is upright
Judah praised
Judas praised
Jude praised
Judith Jewess

Laban white, beautiful
Lazarus God my helper
Leah weary

Levi crowned
Lot covering, veil
Lucifer light-bringer
Luke light-giver
Lydia contention

Malachi messenger of Yahweh
Manasseh forgetting
Mark polite
Martha lady
Mary strong
Matthew gift of Yahweh
Melchizedek king of righteousness
Micah who is like God?
Miriam strong
Moab the desirable land
Mordecai consecrated to Merodach
Moses drawn out of the water

Nahum consolation, comforter
Naomi gracious, pleasant
Nathan gift (of God)
Nathanael gift of God
Nebuchadnezzar prince of the god Nebo
Nehemiah consolation from God
Nicodemus conqueror of the people
Noah rest

Obadiah servant of Yahweh

Paul little
Peter rock, stone
Philemon affectionate
Philip lover of horses
Priscilla ancient
Rachel ewe
Rahab gracious
Rebecca fetter
Reuben Yahweh has seen, God 's mercy
Ruth friend

Samson like the sun
Samuel name of God, placed by God, heard of God
Sarah princess
Saul asked for
Seth sprout
Simeon one heard
Simon one heard
Solomon peaceful
Stephen crown

Thaddaeus man of heart
Thomas twin

Timothy honoured by God
Titus honourable

Uriah light of Yahweh, Yahweh is my light
Uzziah power of Yahweh, strength of Yahweh

Zachariah remembered by Yahweh
Zedekiah justice of Yahweh
Zephaniah treasure of Yahweh